BRODART.   Cat. No. 23-221

HANDBOOK OF ANTISOCIAL BEHAVIOR

HANDBOOK OF ANTISOCIAL BEHAVIOR

Editors

DAVID M. STOFF

JAMES BREILING

AND

JACK D. MASER
National Institute of Mental Health

WILEY

John Wiley & Sons, Inc.
New York • Chichester • Weinheim • Brisbane • Singapore • Toronto

This text is printed on acid-free paper.

Library of Congress Cataloging-in-Publication Data:

Handbook of antisocial behavior / edited by David M. Stoff, James
    Breiling, Jack D. Maser
        p.   cm.
    Includes bibliographical references.
    ISBN 0-471-12452-4 (cloth : alk. paper)
    1. Antisocial personality disorders.   2. Violence.   I. Stoff,
David M.   II. Breiling, James.   III. Maser, Jack D.
    RC555.H35   1997
    616.85'82—dc21   96-53445
                                                            CIP

DEDICATION
TO SALEEM ALUM SHAH, Ph.D.

The tragic and untimely death of Saleem A. Shah in November 1992 deprived us of a friend, mentor, and colleague. Our field has lost leadership, energy, wisdom, knowledge, research direction, and a sense of the true public health significance of antisocial behavior. During his life, Saleem was recognized and honored with numerous awards. Near the end of his life, in recognition of his many contributions, the NIMH named him Senior Research Scholar for Law and Mental Health. Now, six years after his passing, we seek to honor him again. Our dedication of this book to Saleem is particularly poignant to us because he was the victim of the reprehensible and antisocial behavior of a drunken driver.

Thirty-one years ago at the National Institute of Mental Health, Saleem Shah organized a unique, highly productive, and high-quality extramural research program on aggressive, antisocial, and violent behavior and its consequences. This organizational entity, initially known as the Center for Studies of Crime and Delinquency, later became the Antisocial and Violent Behavior Research Branch and is presently the Violence and Traumatic Stress Research Branch. In each of its incarnations, this program has contributed notably to the development of an increasingly deep scientific knowledge base on topics related to its continuing mission.

The impressive accumulation of knowledge in this area since the inception of the Center for Studies of Crime and Delinquency made this volume both desirable and necessary. It was time to bring together, within a single volume, expert reviews of the state of knowledge in a field that Saleem had done so much to shape. For most people, that would be reason enough for this volume, but for Saleem, there would be two other reasons. One was accountability. What has the investment of considerable public monies produced? Are we moving toward an understanding of antisocial behavior that would ultimately work for the public good? Saleem would see the other reason for this volume as a means to facilitate the dissemination and utilization of the accumulated knowledge. The goal would be similar: to create policies, programs, and procedures that would be more humane and effective in reducing the "burden of suffering" caused by antisocial behaviors. In Saleem's perception, research was not an end in itself, but a means to an end.

In our initial plan for producing this book, we sought and

obtained Saleem's counsel. We believe that he would be pleased with the result, but we also know that he would gently, yet firmly, challenge all of us to do more. Saleem would see accomplishments but turn us back to the many important questions still left unanswered, to the research findings that still need to be obtained and then applied before the public good can be achieved. That we were able to come this far and recognize the challenges still before us is to acknowledge the profound influence that this remarkable man had on us and on nearly every contributor to this volume.

David M. Stoff
James Breiling
Jack D. Maser

Contributors

Mera M. Atlis, B.A.
University of Alaska at Anchorage
Anchorage, Alaska

Michael W. Arthur, Ph.D.
School of Social Work
University of Washington
Seattle, Washington

Beth Attar, M.A.
University of Illinois at Chicago
Chicago, Illinois

Howard E. Barbaree, Ph.D.
Clarke Institute of Psychiatry
Toronto, Ontario

Carmen Bayon, M.D.
Center for Psychobiology of Personality
Washington University School of Medicine
Washington University
St. Louis, Missouri

Mitchell E. Berman, Ph.D.
The University of Southern Mississippi
Hattiesburg, Mississippi

Paul F. Brain, Ph.D.
University of Wales at Swansea
Swansea, Wales

James Breiling, Ph.D.
National Institute of Mental Health Violence
  and Traumatic Stress Research Branch
Rockville, Maryland

Patricia A. Brennan, Ph.D.
Emory University
Atlanta, Georgia

Tom W. Cadwallader, Ph.D.
University of North Carolina at Chapel Hill
Chapel Hill, North Carolina

Robert B. Cairns, Ph.D.
University of North Carolina at Chapel Hill
Chapel Hill, North Carolina

Gregory Carey, Ph.D.
University of Colorado at Boulder
Boulder, Colorado

Stephen A. Cernkovich, Ph.D.
Bowling Green State University
Bowling Green, Ohio

Patricia Chamberlain, Ph.D.
Oregon Social Learning Center
University of Oregon
Eugene, Oregon

C. Robert Cloninger, M.D.
Center for Psychobiology of Personality
Washington University School of Medicine
Washington University
St. Louis, Missouri

J. Douglas Coatsworth, Ph.D.
University of Miami
Miami, Florida

Emil F. Coccaro, M.D.
Medical College of Pennsylvania ◆ Hahnmann University
   Medical School
Philadelphia, Pennsylvania

Elizabeth M. Corbitt, Ph.D.
Western Psychiatric Institute and Clinic
University of Pittsburgh School of Medicine
Pittsburgh, Pennsylvania

Geert J. De Vries, Ph.D.
University of Massachusetts at Amherst
Amherst, Massachusetts

Norman G. Dinges, Ph.D.
University of Alaska at Anchorage
Anchorage, Alaska

Thomas J. Dishion, Ph.D.
Oregon Social Learning Center
University of Oregon
Eugene, Oregon

Kenneth A. Dodge, Ph.D.
Vanderbilt University
Nashville, Tennessee

J. Mark Eddy, Ph.D.
Oregon Social Learning Center
University of Oregon
Eugene, Oregon

Leonard D. Eron, Ph.D.
Institute for Social Research
University of Michigan
Ann Arbor, Michigan

David Estell, Ph.D.
University of North Carolina at Chapel Hill
Chapel Hill, North Carolina

Jeffrey Fagan, Ph.D.
Columbia School of Public Health
New York, New York

David P. Farrington, Ph.D.
Institute of Criminology
University of Cambridge
Cambridge, England

Craig F. Ferris, Ph.D.
University of Massachusetts at Worcester
Worcester, Massachusetts

Patrick C. Friman, Ph.D.
Father Flanagan's Home
Boys Town, Pennsylvania

Peggy C. Giordano, Ph.D.
Bowling Green State University
Bowling Green, Ohio

David Goldman, Ph.D.
National Institute for Alcoholism and Alcohol Abuse
Bethesda, Maryland

Deborah Gorman-Smith, Ph.D.
University of Illinois at Chicago
Chicago, Illinois

Nancy G. Guerra, Ed.D.
University of Illinois at Chicago
Chicago, Illinois

John G. Gunderson, M.D.
McLean Hospital
Belmont, Massachusetts
Harvard Medical School
Cambridge, Massachusetts

W. Rodney Hammond, Ph.D.
National Center for Injury Prevention and Control
Center for Disease Control and Prevention
Atlanta, Georgia

Robert D. Hare, Ph.D.
University of British Columbia
Vancouver, British Columbia

Grant T. Harris, Ph.D.
Mental Health Centre
Penetanguishene, Ontario

Stephen D. Hart, Ph.D.
Simon Fraser University
Burnaby, British Columbia

J. David Hawkins, Ph.D.
School of Social Work
University of Washington
Seattle, Washington

Bill Henry, Ph.D.
Colby College
Waterville, Maine

Stephen P. Hinshaw, Ph.D.
University of California at Berkeley
Berkeley, California

L. Rowell Huesmann, Ph.D.
Institute for Social Research
University of Michigan
Ann Arbor, Michigan

Neil S. Jacobson, Ph.D.
Center for Clinical Research
University of Washington
Seattle, Washington

Jacqueline Jones-Alexander, Ph.D.
Emory University
Atlanta, Georgia

Laurence P. Karper, M.D.
Yale University School of Medicine
VA Connecticut Healthcare System
West Haven, Connecticut

Richard J. Kavoussi, M.D.
Medical College of Pennsylvania ◆ Hahnmann University
  Medical School
Philadelphia, Pennsylvania

Philip C. Kendall, Ph.D.
Temple University
Philadelphia, Pennsylvania

Karla R. Klein, Ph.D.
Western Psychiatric Institute and Clinic
University of Pittsburgh School of Medicine
Pittsburgh, Pennsylvania

Marvin D. Krohn, Ph.D.
State University of New York at Albany
Albany, New York

John H. Krystal, M.D.
Yale University School of Medicine
VA Connecticut Healthcare System
West Haven, Connecticut

William Kurtines, Ph.D.
Florida International University
Miami, Florida

Benjamin B. Lahey, Ph.D.
University of Chicago
Chicago, Illinois

Jaslean J. La Taillade, Ph.D.
Center for Clinical Research
University of Washington
Seattle, Washington

Scott O. Lilienfeld, Ph.D.
Emory University
Atlanta, Georgia

Markku Linnoila, M.D., Ph.D.
National Institute on Alcohol Abuse and Alcoholism
Bethesda, Maryland

Rolf Loeber, Ph.D.
Western Psychiatric Institute and Clinic
University of Pittsburgh School of Medicine
Pittsburgh, Pennsylvania

Jack D. Maser, Ph.D.
National Institute of Mental Health Mood, Anxiety,
  and Personality Disorders Research Branch
Rockville, Maryland

Sarnoff A. Mednick, Ph.D.
University of Southern California
Los Angeles, California

James A. Mercy, Ph.D.
National Center for Injury Prevention and Control
Atlanta, Georgia

Terrie E. Moffitt, Ph.D.
University of Wisconsin at Madison
Madison, Wisconsin

Jessica G. Moise, Ph.D.
Institute for Social Research
University of Michigan
Ann Arbor, Michigan

John Monahan, Ph.D.
University of Virginia
Charlottesville, Virginia

Edward P. Mulvey, Ph.D.
Western Psychiatric Institute and Clinic
University of Pittsburgh School of Medicine
Pittsburgh, Pennsylvania

Holly J. Neckerman, Ph.D.
Harborview Injury Prevention and Research
  Center
University of Washington
Seattle, Washington

Joseph P. Newman, Ph.D.
University of Wisconsin at Madison
Madison, Wisconsin

David R. Offord, M.D.
Chedoke-McMaster Hospitals
McMaster University
Hamilton, Ontario

Jeffrey J. Olson, M.S.W.
School of Social Work
University of Washington
Seattle, Washington

Gerald R. Patterson, Ph.D.
Oregon Social Learning Center
University of Oregon
Eugene, Oregon

Paul A. Pilkonis, Ph.D.
Western Psychiatric Institute and Clinic
University of Pittsburgh School of Medicine
Pittsburgh, Pennsylvania

Robert Plutchik, Ph.D.
Albert Einstein College of Medicine
Bronx, New York

Cheryl-Lynn Podolski, Ph.D.
Institute for Social Research
University of Michigan
Ann Arbor, Michigan

Lloyd B. Potter, Ph.D., M.P.H.
National Center for Injury Prevention and Control
Atlanta, Georgia

Herman M. van Praag, M.D.
University of Limburg
Maastricht, the Netherlands

Thomas R. Przybeck, Ph.D.
Center for Psychobiology of Personality
Washington University School of Medicine
Washington University
St. Louis, Missouri

Cynthia Purcell, M.A.
Emory University
Atlanta, Georgia

Adrian Raine, Ph.D.
University of Southern California
Los Angeles, California

John B. Reid, Ph.D.
Oregon Social Learning Center
University of Oregon
Eugene, Oregon

Marnie E. Rice, Ph.D.
Mental Health Centre
Penetanguishene, Ontario

Sir Michael Rutter, M.D., F.R.S.
Social, Genetic and Developmental Psychiatry
   Research Centre
Institute of Psychiatry
London, England

Daniel A. Santisteban, Ph.D.
University of Miami
Miami, Florida

David Schwartz, Ph.D.
Vanderbilt University
Nashville, Tennessee

Michael C. Seto, M.A.
Clarke Institute of Psychiatry
Toronto, Ontario

David M. Stoff, Ph.D.
National Institute of Mental Health Mood, Anxiety,
   and Personality Disorders Research Branch
Rockville, Maryland

Danile S. Shaw, Ph.D.
University of Pittsburgh
Pittsburg, Pennsylvania

Michael A. Southam-Gerow, Ph.D.
Temple University
Phildadelphia, Pennsylvania

Elizabeth J. Susman, Ph.D.
Pennsylvania State University
University Park, Pennsylvania

José Szapocznik, Ph.D.
University of Miami
Miami, Florida

Kenneth Tardiff, M.D., M.P.H.
The Payne Whitney Clinic
Cornell University Medical College
New York, New York

Terence P. Thornberry, Ph.D.
State University of New York at Albany
Albany, New York

Patrick H. Tolan, Ph.D.
University of Illinois at Chicago
Chicago, Illinois

Gina M. Vincent, B.A.
University of Alaska at Anchorage
Anchorage, Alaska

Roger P. Weissberg, Ph.D.
University of Illinois at Chicago
Chicago, Illinois

Helene Raskin White, Ph.D.
Center of Alcohol Studies
Rutgers University
Piscataway, New Jersey

Thomas A. Widiger, Ph.D.
University of Kentucky
Lexington, Kentucky

Cathy Spatz Widom, Ph.D.
State University of New York at Albany
Albany, New York

Deanna L. Wilkinson, Ph.D.
Columbia School of Public Health
New York, New York

Emily B. Winslow, Ph.D.
University of Pittsburgh
Pittsburg, Pennsylvania

Jennifer L. Woolard, M.A.
University of Virginia
Charlottesville, Virginia

Betty R. Yung, Ph.D.
Wright State University
Dayton, Ohio

Mary C. Zanarini, Ed.D.
McLean Hospital
Belmont, Massachusetts
Harvard Medical School
Cambridge, Massachusetts

Brian A. Zupan, Ph.D.
University of California at Berkeley
Berkeley, California

Antisocial Behavior Research: An Introduction

DAVID M. STOFF
JAMES BREILING
JACK D. MASER

The diverse forms of antisocial behavior expressed throughout the life span have represented a serious and perplexing problem since the beginning of Western civilization. Historically, the explanation for antisocial behavior has been based on folk and moral beliefs about bad behavior that has almost always been dealt with by punishment. In the early 1800s, the observations of Phillipe Pinel and Benjamin Rush provided the first clear presentations of the clinical features of antisocial individuals and served as the starting point for a clinical descriptive science to illuminate reasons and guide interventions for antisocial behavior. These psychiatrists noted that individuals who exhibited such behavior also evidenced moral ineptitude, characterized by impaired reasoning powers combined with socially deranged behaviors. The view that antisocial behaviors signify a reprehensible character defect without a corresponding feeling of shame laid the groundwork for recognizing these behaviors as a psychiatrically definable disorder.

In the latter part of this century, an increasingly vigorous and sophisticated scientific study of antisocial behavior has emerged. This major scientific activity is concerned with the measurement, course, antecedents and mediators, and development of precise intervention strategies that specifically target some of these factors. Just as other fields of inquiry have benefited from a scientific approach, this new science of antisocial behavior promises improved understanding about how these behaviors arise and how they might be prevented. Since the mid-1970s, a solid body of research knowledge on antisocial behavior has accumulated, as witnessed by this volume. This knowledge continues to grow into a database that will increasingly guide the implementation of effective intervention and prevention strategies and aid in the formulation of public policy.

The general term *antisocial behavior* refers to a spectrum of disruptive behaviors, most often aggressive, that have in common

transgressions against societal norms. When the term *antisocial behavior* is used, rather than specific terms (e.g., aggression, delinquency, conduct disorder, antisocial personality disorder), different expressions over the life course can be more easily taken into account. The subset of antisocial behaviors, those involving interpersonal aggression, constitutes the principal subject matter of this book. We focused on interpersonal aggression because it encompasses the most disturbing antisocial behaviors, representing a serious public health problem that impacts all segments of U.S. society. *Interpersonal aggression* may be defined as intentional threats, attempts or actual infliction of physical harm to other individuals. Specific forms of interpersonal aggression, such as homicides, assaults, spousal abuse and child abuse, are routinely reported in the mass media. They are of growing concern to the general public, to professionals, and to legislators. The higher homicide rate in the United States, relative to other Western industrialized countries, and the recognition that violence in adults is often preceded by aggression earlier in life (Robins, 1966), have called attention to the study of antisocial behavior over the life span. As a result of public awareness of violence, the scientific community has expressed an invigorated interest in studying the varied forms of antisocial behavior and their consequences. For most, the ultimate goal is the development and application of preventive intervention strategies.

Antisocial behavior can range from disruptive behaviors to the most heinous socially and criminally offensive acts. The numerous expressions of antisocial behavior include disobedience, aggressiveness, impulsivity, conduct problems, delinquency, criminality, assaults, homicide, media violence, sexual offenses, child abuse, spousal abuse, conduct disorder, and antisocial personality disorder. Interest has focused mostly on those types of antisocial behavior that are persistent and chronic, rather than intermittent and temporary, because of their poorer prognosis. Other forms of antisocial behavior also are of pressing concern but were excluded from this book. For example, antisocial behavior of large collective groups (e.g., riots, wars, state violence, and organized crime) was not included because it does not lend itself readily to the application of basic knowledge from the four domains that we

The authors thank Dr. Rex Cowdry for critically reading an early draft of this material. The opinions expressed are those of the authors only and do not necessarily reflect the official position of the National Institute of Mental Health or any part of the U.S. Department of Health and Human Services.

selected. Violence against oneself (suicide) was addressed only to the extent that it intersects with interpersonal aggression. This book covers a wide range of topics, but it is not exhaustive. For example, we did not cover adult criminal careers and the effects of justice system interventions.

The *Handbook of Antisocial Behavior* is a state-of-the-field compendium of contributions from distinguished · investigators who provide broad reviews of the forms and expressions of antisocial behavior from various research perspectives, including clinical, developmental, biological, and intervention approaches. The book presents research knowledge on our current level of understanding of the nature and course of antisocial behavior, its correlates, causes, consequences, and interventions. We attempted to capture the field's intellectual excitement and growth by the broad scope of this book. It may be unique in addressing the numerous and diverse expressions of antisocial behavior. Growth in the field has been so rapid that comprehensive reviews such as this one are needed to stay abreast of the information explosion.

Although a number of specialized monographs and books deal with specific forms of antisocial behavior or specific research approaches, there have been few attempts to consolidate related approaches into the same volume, with the notable exception of Reiss and Roth (1993). The *Handbook* continues in that spirit by updating knowledge and providing in-depth analyses of the research perspectives chosen. A single source, with complementary approaches, is essential in view of the multiple influences on antisocial behavior. We hope that this volume will help to increase dialogue and cross-fertilization among the different perspectives. Equally important, the *Handbook* challenges the field to integrate these perspectives and seeks to serve as a bridge over disciplinary barriers by promoting interdisciplinary communication.

The *Handbook* will serve as a reference in the field of antisocial behavior for scholars and practitioners in public health, behavioral and social sciences, psychiatry, neurosciences, and biomedical sciences. It will also provide a background of this growing research field for undergraduate and graduate courses. For the researcher, it is an opportunity to gain an overview of how related disciplines are investigating antisocial behavior. For the practicing clinician, the *Handbook* provides a wealth of useful information in the areas of assessment/diagnosis and intervention, as well as a theoretical grounding in the rationale behind intervention. For the general student, it provides the opportunity to gain an initial broad view.

This *Handbook* was designed to discuss four major research domains in separate sections: Part One: Clinical Issues (Chapters 1–11); Part Two: Development of Antisocial Behavior (Chapters 12–22); Part Three: Biology of Antisocial Behavior (Chapters 23–31); and Part Four: Prevention, Treatment, and Management (Chapters 32–43). Special Issues and Special Populations are covered in Part Five (Chapters 44–50). Most often, the different levels of analyses in Parts One to Four are considered singly because research is usually conducted according to the assumptions and boundaries of each major domain. Although these aspects have been presented separately for purposes of communication, in practice they overlap, are interdependent, and often complement one another. Because we attempted an understanding of the multiple influences on antisocial behavior, individual chapters reflect diverse disciplines, including psychology, sociology, criminology,

epidemiology and public health, psychiatry, neuroscience, biomedical science, and developmental sciences.

Part One deals with a broad range of clinical issues that illuminate the boundaries of antisocial behavior in antisocial personality disorder (ASPD), psychopathy, conduct disorder (CD), and the complex phenotypes, delinquency and criminality. The chapters include approaches from epidemiology, assessment, diagnosis, and comorbidity, forming the foundation for longitudinal, biological, and treatment investigations. Underlying a diagnostic emphasis, held by some but not all, is a medical model that generally describes a continuing pattern of antisocial behavior as a psychopathological disorder, in much the same way that depression or schizophrenia is currently recognized as a mental disorder. Its operational definitions are found in the *Diagnostic and Statistical Manual of Mental Disorders,* 4th ed. (*DSM-IV*; American Psychiatric Association, 1994). However, applying a clinical diagnosis to all antisocial behavior has been challenged. Some antisocial behaviors are thought to be frequently misrepresented as mental disorders when, in fact, they represent an exaggerated variant of normal personality variables or an adaptive response to environmental pressures (Richters & Cicchetti, 1993). Others in this book argue against any clinical diagnosis, advocating for a more dimensional approach for a better description of the nature and correlates of sustained antisocial behavior.

The opening chapter of Part One by Potter and Mercy presents descriptive epidemiological data demonstrating the importance of interpersonal violence as a significant public health problem. Such a public health perspective, with a multidisciplinary scientific approach, is explicitly directed toward identifying effective strategies for prevention. Cloninger, Bayon, and Przybeck (Chapter 2) extend the epidemiological approach to adult antisocial behavior, employing a sample similar to that of the National Institute of Mental Health Epidemiological Catchment Area project. They present clinical and epidemiological correlates of ASPD so that heterogeneity in course and comorbidity can be distinguished from other normal and abnormal personality variants and related to individual differences. Hart and Hare (Chapter 3) discuss the evolution of studies resulting in the development and validation of rating scales to tap key psychological variables of psychopathy. Their view suggests that the concept of psychopathy is an important causal factor in some criminal conduct. In the next two chapters (Chapters 4 and 5), we turn to the antisocial behavior of children and adolescents. Hinshaw and Zupan review its assessment, and Lahey and Loeber discuss relationships of antisocial behavior in adults. Both chapters focus on the importance of developmental issues and co-occurrence of different disruptive behavior disorders for evaluation, course, and outcome. The assessment of adult antisocial behavior is addressed by Lilienfeld, Purcell, and Jones-Alexander (Chapter 6), who concentrate on the conceptual and methodological problems in studying patients with ASPD. These authors review self-report, observer rating and laboratory measures of adult aggression in the context of a behavior-based approach that involves the direct assessment of antisocial behavior instead of underlying personality traits. The next series of chapters in this part (Chapters 7, 8, and 9) addresses the co-occurrence of psychiatric disorders with adult antisocial behavior. Widiger and Corbitt emphasize Axis II comorbidity and the impact of co-occurring personality disorder symptomatology on the manifestation of ASPD. Zanarini and Gunderson further evaluate the importance of Axis II comorbidity, especially borderline personality disorder; and Monahan addresses the issue of mental disorder as a significant risk factor for the occurrence of violence. Noting that some of the most important links to adult antisocial behavior are suicide and impulsivity, Plutchik and van Praag (Chapter 10) present some clinical and biological data on these interconnections and a theoretical model. Pilkonis and Klein conclude this section with an overview of the preceding chapters by identifying several themes such as conceptual distinctions, contextual factors, and the need for longitudinal investigation of developmental pathways and for reevaluation of categorical and dimensional approaches.

Part Two addresses the development of antisocial behavior. Development is considered a unifying concept in normal and dysfunctional behavior of children and adolescents (Eisenberg 1977). A developmental perspective involves the study of processes that constitute the crucial link between genetic and environmental variables, between social and psychological factors, and between biological and psychogenic causes. Developmental study provides important information about the sequences and pathways leading to antisocial behavior and about risk and protective factors that influence the course of normal and antisocial behavior development. The chapters in Part Two document the growing body of evidence that certain events occurring during critical developmental periods may influence the trajectory toward antisocial behavior. A major driving force in these studies is that basic research knowledge of precursors and developmental pathways informs the design of precise intervention strategies, the subject matter of Part Four.

The first series of chapters in Part Two (Chapters 12, 13, and 14) deals with important conceptual, methodological, and strategic issues in the developmental study of antisocial behavior. In the first chapter, Rutter presents a developmental psychopathology perspective focusing on the mechanisms and processes involved in both continuities and discontinuities over the life span. Many fundamental issues have yet to be resolved, among them questions about individual risk characteristics and the mechanisms by which antisocial behavior emerges, environmental risk processes, biological primacy, and the best models for conceptualizing psychopathology. In the next chapter, Loeber and Farrington consider the value of a longitudinal perspective and review the findings of important longitudinal studies together with key conceptual and methodological issues that these studies raise. Recommendations also are made for the direction of future longitudinal research to explain and ameliorate antisocial behavior in juveniles. In the following chapter, Eron draws on his pioneering studies of how aggression is learned in early life. He describes the utility of a behavioral-cognitive approach, other learning theory formulations, and the application of developmental psychological processes to treatment and prevention programs for antisocial behavior.

Chapters 15, 16, 17, and 18 deal with the early antecedents of antisocial behavior in young children. Shaw and Winslow see early externalizing problems in boys developing as a result of transactions between preschoolers and their environments over time. The rationale for this interest in early precursors is based on facilitating preventive interventions as early as possible. Widom focuses on the relationship between childhood victimization and witnessing vio-

lence and later antisocial behavior. The author calls for multifactorial models that incorporate more information on mechanisms, buffers, and mediators. Dodge and Schwartz offer a social information processing model that provides researchers with hypotheses regarding proximal predictors of aggressive behavior. The origins of aggressive response patterns are discussed in relation to the early developmental histories of children, histories of physical abuse, and deviant parenting. Huesmann, Moise, and Podolski review the large body of scientific literature that attempts to demonstrate that children's exposure to media violence relates to the development of violent behavior, especially for high-risk children. Their chapter considers observational learning of attitudes, beliefs, attributional biases, and scripts that promote aggressive behavior.

The last series of chapters in this part (Chapters 19, 20, and 21) attempts to bridge childhood and adolescent antisocial behavior problems. Cairns, Cadwallader, Estell, and Neckerman integrate developmental-criminological approaches to the study of peer groups of children and adolescent gangs and explore whether research on the development of social groups is useful in understanding gang formation, function, and prevention. Longitudinal studies identify the pathways from groups to gangs in different contexts and suggest possibilities for prevention or amelioration. Dishion and Patterson propose a unifying ecological framework to explain the timing and severity of child and adolescent antisocial behavior. They draw attention to the contribution of parenting practices and associating with deviant peers, and they point to an emerging intervention technology that suggests that developmental trajectories can be altered. Concentrating exclusively on adolescents, Thornberry and Krohn examine the role that peers play in drug use and delinquency. The hypothesis that association with deviant peers has a causal relation to antisocial behavior is systematically considered. Farrington's closing chapter in this part (Chapter 22) is a critical analysis of research on the development of antisocial behavior from childhood to adulthood. In addition to highlighting key findings in the preceding developmental chapters, Farrington discusses how the field has evolved, what has been learned, and future research directions to further elucidate developmental processes in antisocial behavior.

Part Three discusses the biology of antisocial behavior, a field of inquiry that recently has been drawn into renewed controversy because of sociopolitical questions about its study. The strategies used include behavioral and molecular genetics, neurochemistry, neuroendocrinology, neuroimaging, and neuropsychology. Investigators are beginning to use combinations of these strategies to take into account the panoply of neurobiological effects in antisocial behavior. When findings in neuroscience are related to specific forms of antisocial behavior, a host of interpretations has been offered. A prominent one involves the interaction of neurobiological and environmental variables. Other biological explanations have been causative, correlative, or predictive. Neurobiological research in antisocial behavior has been hindered by several misconceptions that have been discussed elsewhere (Stoff & Cairns, 1996). For example, some mistakenly believe in the primacy of biology even though evidence exists that biology and behavior have bidirectional influences on each other. Therefore, a complete understanding of the neurobiology of antisocial behavior must consider the complementary influences of biological and experiential variables.

The first two chapters (23, 24) in the biology section address general cross-cutting issues, genetics, and animal models. Carey and Goldman present an overview of genetic methods for examining antisocial behavior and then assess empirical data on epidemiological and molecular genetics. These data are seen as consistent with an important role for the environment and the relevance of genetic-environmental interactions to basic and applied science. Ferris and De Vries describe how animal models of aggressive behavior have evolved from laboratory techniques, such as brain lesion and electric shock, to ethological processes such as social behavior. These authors discuss the neurobiological mechanisms contributing to aggressive and affiliative behaviors and focus on how environmental/endocrine factors can affect neuronal plasticity. They attach special relevance to prosocial prevention strategies. Noting that biological risks for antisocial behavior may be related not only to central nervous system processes but also to health-related factors (e.g., nutrition, head injuries, prenatal and perinatal trauma, mineral imbalances), Brennan and Mednick (Chapter 25) review research examining the relationship between these physical health factors and antisocial behavior. The relevance of these biological variables to violent, early onset, or persistent antisocial behavior is discussed. Chapters 26, 27, 28, and 29 address more specific, methodologically driven, discipline-based issues. Modern neuroimaging methods, integrated with sensitive neuropsychological challenges, now afford unprecedented opportunities for the in vivo study of central nervous system function. Henry and Moffitt review the relations of language and executive neuropsychological deficits to juvenile antisocial behavior, adult criminal behavior, and the psychopathic personality as well as relatively scarce neuroimaging data in these samples. Raine updates the psychophysiology of antisocial behavior and offers a prefrontal dysfunction hypothesis that is consistent with some neuroimaging data. For decades, it has been suggested that the factors mediating mental states, including mental disorders, are neurochemical, but only recently has this knowledge been applied to antisocial behavior, as illustrated by Berman, Kavoussi, and Coccaro's chapter. They assess the available evidence for neurotransmitter correlates of human aggression using strategies for central neurochemical measures, challenge of neuroregulatory systems with pharmacological agents, and peripheral measures. The theme of reciprocal influences of biology and behavior is taken up by Brain and Susman. They review the state of the art of neuroendocrine findings and explore the hypothesis of hormones affecting human aggression and human aggression affecting hormones over the life course. Newman (Chapter 30) presents a conceptual model of the nervous system that integrates the array of factors that govern antisocial behavior, including physiological, neuroendocrine, psychophysiological, and psychological variables. Linnoila (Chapter 31) concludes the biology section with an overview, noting how key advances in the neurosciences have been applied toward a more comprehensive understanding of the causes and correlates of antisocial behavior.

In Part Four, the focus shifts from predicting and understanding to seeking change through prevention, treatment, and management strategies. A viable intervention research agenda rests on a knowledge base of basic and applied research in epidemiology, risk research, psychiatry, psychology, sociology, criminology, neurosciences, biomedical sciences, and the developmental sciences. Advances from these fields influence how we conceptualize intervention strategies and formulate public policy. The intervention efforts described in the chapters of Part Four encompass medical, educational, psychological, and pharmacological methods. These efforts have a history of great hope, problematic implementation, and shifts to other practices as new views emerge. Some major contributions of science in this area include the use of evaluation methodology and meta-analysis procedures (combining multiple studies) to statistically assess the effectiveness of interventions.

The first four chapters (32, 33, 34, and 35) are concerned with prevention, its viability and its implementation. Reid and Eddy argue for basing interventions on the growing body of developmental science and provide examples of successful interventions. They indicate that scientific success does not guarantee general utilization, because continued escalation in expenditures for corrections must be overcome if funds are to be available for effective prevention programs. Offord presents criteria for assessing experimental studies of several kinds of interventions. Dissemination and utilization are also addressed so that effective intervention programs are adopted for general use. Hawkins, Arthur, and Olson carry forward this concern for implementing effective interventions as established by research. They provide an overview of Communities That Care, which is their effort to help communities identify risk factors and generate effective programs. Guerra, Attar, and Weissberg highlight the unique challenges posed by the inner city: scarce economic resources, systemwide disorganization, family instability, and the "risky environment" created by the daily occurrence of serious violence. Their review points to the need for studies that build on knowledge of risk and protective factors and utilize multiple social and psychological components. Southam-Gerow and Kendall (Chapter 36) review the extensive and encouraging research on cognitive-behavioral interventions. Their discussion calls attention to diagnosis, co-occurring disorders, and methodological questions. The increasing minority population of the United States also requires research on culturally competent interventions. Coatsworth, Szapocznik, Kurtines, and Santisteban (Chapter 37) address cultural relevance for Hispanics. Of particular note is their cumulative program of research that shows how to significantly increase the proportion of Hispanic families who can be involved in a culturally compatible intervention. Tolan and Gorman-Smith (Chapter 38) summarize recent reviews of evaluations of interventions with delinquents that challenge the previous view that "nothing works." They also note the importance of researcher involvement. The other major focus of their chapter is the ways in which the juvenile court influences interventions and their impact. Chamberlain and Friman (Chapter 39) discuss four models of residential care and the need for research in this area that meets criteria for rigor. Such criteria are presented and illustrated. Rice and Harris (Chapter 40) review the long history of rehabilitation for adult offenders and the poor implementation and lack of research-based knowledge for treating this population. They describe interventions that offer the promise of some success with at least the nonpsychopathic criminal and present recommendations for intervening with psychopaths. Chapters 41 and 42 deal with medically based treatment approaches. Although most interventions are educational or psychotherapeutic, there is a growing body of research on pharmacological interventions for violence as discussed by Karper and Krystal, who present the pharmacological treatment of a range of violent patients based on studies of neurotransmitter mechanisms of action. A complementary discussion by Tardiff focuses on the violent psychiatric patient and provides recommendations for a comprehensive assessment and for both pharmacological and nonpharmacological management and treatment. Attention is paid to the safety of staff in health care settings. Mulvey and Woolard conclude this section in Chapter 43, noting the progress and needs in intervention research. They highlight the importance of risk factors and appropriate subgroups and discuss the transportability of intervention technologies to various settings.

This book closes with a final group of chapters in Part Five that deals with special issues and special populations, covering cross-cultural perspectives, minority group violence, gender differences, substance abuse, sexual aggression, domestic violence, and firearms. These topics are considered special only in the sense that they are not specifically covered in the preceding parts. Each is fundamental to the study of violence as we have come to appreciate it near the close of the 20th century.

In the first chapter of the final part, Dinges, Atlis, and Vincent (Chapter 44) provide a historical perspective on the evolution of antisocial personality disorder in the *Diagnostic and Statistical Manual*. This diagnosis began with an inferential, psychological substrate, moved to a definition that was more crime centered, and in *DSM-IV*, reverted back to include more psychological criteria. The emphasis of their chapter is on cross-cultural methodology in conceptualizing and defining antisocial personality disorder. Yung and Hammond (Chapter 45) identify challenges and methodological problems specific to ethnic minority groups. They analyze antisocial behavior patterns in Hispanics, Asian Americans, Native Americans, and African Americans for delinquency, gangs, substance abuse, violence, risk, and resiliency. Giordano and Cernkovich (Chapter 46) note the increased involvement and research interest in female antisocial behavior and consider the question of whether male-based theories can be correctly applied to criminal women. These authors evaluate causal factors, including biological and psychological variables, family and peer influences, and economic and community variables for their relative impact on female antisocial behavior. White (Chapter 47) discusses methodological issues involved in the connection between alcohol/drug use and violence and then examines the hypothesis that substance use and violence are both causally and spuriously related. Two types of individuals involved in alcohol-related violence are described, repetitive and situational offenders, for whom targeted interventions are appropriate. Seto and Barbaree (Chapter 48) review different approaches to understanding sexual aggression and some of the methodological issues that help to integrate research findings for this form of antisocial behavior. They propose a developmental model of sexual aggression that could have implications for offender disposition, treatment planning, and public policy. La Taillade and Jacobson (Chapter 49) review theory, methodology, and research on domestic or family violence. It is in this setting that a surprising amount of violence is reported. Special attention is given to studying the nature of marital interactions and psychological characteristics of violent couples. Fagan and Wilkinson (Chapter 50) examine the use

of firearms, the primary method for homicides among male youths. The authors compare the pattern of firearm use in the inner city across historical periods and identify contributory factors related to the recent escalation in violence.

The contributors to this volume have provided a tapestry of interacting frameworks for major areas of antisocial behavior research as well as conceptual underpinnings. Although additional areas could have been covered, the editors believe that the chapters presented will enhance knowledge and provide a research and clinical base to move the field forward. To the extent that the *Handbook* consolidates information and promotes understanding of clinical, developmental, biological, and treatment aspects of antisocial behavior, the editors will have achieved their goal. We hope that *The Handbook of Antisocial Behavior* will help guide the next generation of research and enable improved applications of the accumulated knowledge.

ACKNOWLEDGMENTS

We would like to acknowledge those individuals who have been most instrumental in bringing this book to fruition. First, we thank the contributors for sharing their findings and for their scholarly chapters. We appreciate the efforts they made to enhance the overall volume. From the inception of this book to its publication, past and present staff of the National Institute of Mental Health gave us their full support and belief in the importance of this project. In particular, we would like to thank Mary Blehar, Rex Cowdry, Ellen Gerrity, Frederick Goodwin, Samuel Keith, Alan Leshner, Darrel Regier, David Shore, Susan Solomon, and Jane Steinberg. Kelly Franklin at John Wiley & Sons has been generous with her excellent editorial direction and encouragement. We also thank Linda Pawelchak for improving the language of this book through expert copy-editing. Most of all, the editors would like to express some personal appreciations. For their love and support, David Stoff thanks his wife, Julie, and his children, Jeremy and Laura; Jim Breiling thanks his daughters, Bonnie, Robin, and Linda and his partner, Betty; Jack Maser thanks his wife, Irma.

REFERENCES

American Psychiatric Association. (1994). *Diagnostic and statistical manual of mental disorders* (4th ed.). Washington, DC: American Psychiatric Press.

Eisenberg, L. (1977). Development as a unifying concept in psychiatry. *British Journal of Psychiatry, 131,* 225-237.

Reiss, A. J., Jr., & Roth, J. A. (1993). *Understanding and preventing violence: Panel on the understanding and control of violent behavior.* Washington, DC: National Academy Press.

Richters, J. E., & Cicchetti, D. (1993). Mark Twain meets *DSM-III-R*: Conduct disorder, development and concept of harmful dysfunction. *Developmental Psychopathology, 5,* 5-29.

Robins, L. N. (1966). *Deviant children grown up.* Baltimore: Williams & Wilkins.

Stoff, D. M., & Cairns, R. M. (1996). *Aggression and violence: Genetic, neurobiological and biosocial perspectives.* Hillsdale, NJ: Erlbaum.

Contents

PART FOUR   PREVENTION, TREATMENT, AND MANAGEMENT

xxiiContents

PART ONE

Clinical Issues

CHAPTER 1

Public Health Perspective on Interpersonal Violence Among Youths in the United States

LLOYD B. POTTER and JAMES A. MERCY

Injury and death from interpersonal violence constitute a significant public health problem in the United States. *Interpersonal violence* refers to the threatened or actual use of physical force or power—against another person, a group, or a community—that either results in or has a high likelihood of resulting in injury, death, or deprivation. Public health provides us with a multidisciplinary, scientific approach that is explicitly directed toward identifying effective strategies for prevention. Clinical psychiatric populations and associated epidemiology are described elsewhere (Robins, Tipp, & Przybeck, 1991) and in this handbook (Cloninger, Bayon, & Przybeck, Chapter 2). Other chapters deal with the identification and description of risk factors (Farrington, Chapter 22; Hinshaw & Zupan, Chapter 4; Huesmann, Moise, & Podolski, Chapter 18; Lilienfeld, Purcell, & Jones-Alexander, Chapter 6; Shaw & Winslow, Chapter 15) and interventions for treating and preventing the development of antisocial behavior (Chamberlain & Friman, Chapter 39; Gurerra, Attar, & Weissberg, Chapter 35; Hawkins, Arthur, & Olson, Chapter 34; Reid & Eddy, Chapter 32; Tardiff, Chapter 42). In this chapter, our goal is to describe the problem of assaultive injuries from a public health perspective (Foege, Rosenberg, & Mercy, 1995; Mercy, Rosenberg, Powell, Broome, & Roper, 1993; Rosenberg, O'Carroll, & Powell, 1992). In doing so, we provide a framework for understanding the public health approach and describe the magnitude of the problems and trends in injury and death from interpersonal violence in the United States.

PUBLIC HEALTH APPROACH TO PREVENTING INTERPERSONAL VIOLENCE

We must use science to help prevent the problem of interpersonal violence. The public health approach (Figure 1.1) provides a multi-disciplinary, scientific method of identifying effective strategies for prevention. This approach starts with defining the problem and progresses to identifying associated risk factors and causes, developing

The opinions expressed are those of the authors only and do not necessarily reflect the official position of the Center for Disease Control and Prevention or any other part of the U.S. Department of Health and Human Services.

and evaluating interventions, and implementing interventions in programs. Although Figure 1.1 suggests a linear progression from the first step to the last, in reality many of these steps occur simultaneously; and the steps are often interdependent. For example, information systems used to define the problem may also be useful in evaluating programs. Similarly, information gained in program evaluation and implementation may lead to new and promising interventions.

Public health has always responded to epidemics of infectious disease with a focus on environmental modification and vaccination. During the past few decades, public health has incorporated efforts to modify high-risk behavior, with the goal of preventing chronic disease and injury. Because of the impact of homicide on premature mortality, the Centers for Disease Control and Prevention (CDC) initiated efforts to prevent injuries from violence by using a public health approach.

Defining the Problem

The first step includes delineating incidents of interpersonal violence and related mortality and morbidity, but it goes beyond simply counting cases. This step includes obtaining information on, for example, the demographic characteristics of the persons involved, the temporal and geographic characteristics of the incident, the victim-perpetrator relationship, and the severity and cost of the injury. The information collected should be useful for answering questions such as these: How often does interpersonal violence occur? When and under what circumstances does it occur? Who has been involved or witnessed the event? Were drugs or alcohol involved? These additional variables may be important in defining discrete subsets of interpersonal violence for which various interventions may be appropriate. Every community is unique, and we must collect information that will give an accurate picture of interpersonal violence and the related problems in specific communities. Information can be collected from focus groups, incident reports, and surveys. For homicide, information comes from the vital statistics system and from police reports. Because very little information about injury morbidity from interpersonal violence is available, we have a tremendous need to develop injury surveillance systems so that we can better understand the magnitude of the problem and any trends.

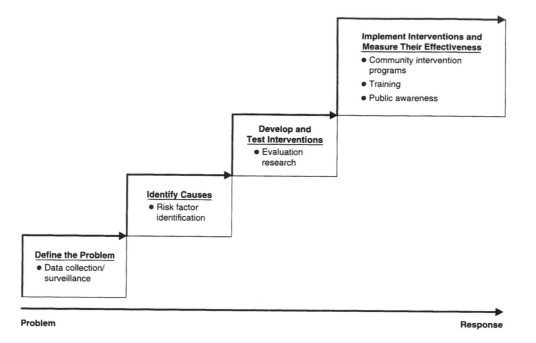

Figure 1.1   *Public health model of a scientific approach to prevention.*

Identifying Causes

Whereas the first step looks at who, when, where, what, and how, the second step looks at why. This step may also be used to define populations at high risk and to suggest specific interventions. Risk and protective factors can be identified by a variety of scientific research methodologies, including rate calculations and ethnographic, cohort, and case-control studies. Some research into the causes of violent behavior has been completed as demonstrated by other chapters in this volume (e.g., Farrington, Chapter 22; Huesmann et al., Chapter 18; Rutter, Chapter 12; Shaw & Winslow, Chapter 15; Thornberry & Krohn, Chapter 21). Whereas risk factors such as alcohol and drug use and misuse, media exposure to violence, and social and economic influences have been explored, many questions remain regarding the role that these and numerous other possible causes play in producing violent behavior and, more important, how these and other risk factors may be modified to prevent violent behavior.

Developing and Testing Interventions

The next step is to develop interventions based largely on information obtained from the previous steps and to test these interventions. This step includes evaluating the efficacy of programs, policies, or interventions already in place (Elliot, 1980). Methods for testing include prospective randomized controlled trials, comparisons of health outcomes in intervention and comparison populations, time series analyses of trends in multiple areas, and observational research studies, such as case-control studies.

Preventive interventions are usually efforts to break a causal chain between the potential for a negative outcome and achieving that outcome. Thus, the development of preventive interventions depends on the previous step in the public health model—identifying and understanding the causes of assaultive behavior. In practice, however, interventions are often implemented and occasionally evaluated with little or no specification of the causal chain or how the intervention will affect the chain.

Interventions can be thought of in terms of primary, secondary, and tertiary prevention. Additionally, we can target interventions at groups or at individuals. Violence prevention interventions may attempt to change high-risk behavior by targeting the attitudes and behavior of individuals or groups (e.g., peers, families, and communities). Clinical interventions are usually secondary and tertiary prevention efforts that target individuals after a problem has developed. Public health interventions usually employ primary prevention efforts that target groups. CDC has reviewed and summarized a range of strategies intended to prevent violence (National Center for Injury Prevention and Control, 1993).

Implementing Interventions and Measuring Prevention Effectiveness

The final step is to implement interventions that have demonstrated effectiveness in preventing interpersonal violence. Data collection to evaluate the program's implementation and effectiveness is essential because an intervention that has been found effective in a clinical trial or an academic study may perform differently in different settings. Another important component of this fourth step is determining the cost-effectiveness of such programs. Balancing the costs of a program against the cases prevented by the intervention can be helpful to policy makers in determining optimal public health practice.

At the implementation phase, public health professionals must develop guidelines and procedures for putting effective programs in place, and they must consider various factors. For example, how do they involve parents and students in programs designed to prevent interpersonal violence? How do they build effective coalitions across traditionally separate sectors such as criminal justice, education, and public health? How do they continually assess and improve the programs that are put into place? Assessing implementation and development of implementation guidelines is especially important because we have little information on the successful implementation of programs. We also have little information on how interventions can be adapted for particular community values, cultures, and standards and, at the same time, allow for and benefit from racially and culturally diverse participation from all segments of the community.

Applying the public health approach to preventing assaultive injury is a new endeavor. We are just beginning to implement more extensive surveillance efforts to understand the problem better. Little research has been completed that provides definitive answers regarding the causes of violent behavior. Many violence prevention programs are being implemented, and some of the first comprehensive evaluations of such programs are now being completed (Powell, Dahlberg, & Friday, 1996). Essentially, violence prevention, addressed from a scientific perspective, is a young science. However, we have made some significant progress in recent years in defining the magnitude of the problem and trends in interpersonal violence.

MAGNITUDE OF THE PROBLEM AND TRENDS IN INTERPERSONAL VIOLENCE

Understanding the magnitude of the problem and trends in interpersonal violence is an essential part of defining a public health problem. By using information from vital statistics, police reports, and various surveys, we can describe the magnitude of and trends in interpersonal violence.

Magnitude

As the magnitude of interpersonal violence has grown in the United States, so has the social resolve to address the problem. Yet the problem does not affect all Americans equally. In fact, the risk of homicide and violent victimization varies drastically by geography, age, and sex. To address this problem methodically, we must first understand who is most affected. This provides the ability both for individual risk assessment and for identifying population segments that should be targeted for prevention efforts.

Homicide rates among young men in the United States are vastly greater than those in other Western industrialized nations (Figure 1.2; Fingerhut & Kleinman, 1990; World Health Organization, 1995). In 1993, more than 26,000 people in the United States were killed, making homicide the 10th leading cause of death (National Center for Health Statistics, 1994). Adolescents and young adults face an extraordinarily high risk of death and injury

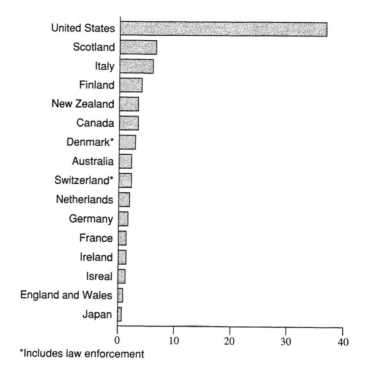

*Includes law enforcement

Figure 1.2 *International variations in homicide rates for males aged 15–24 years, 1991–1993. Source: World Health Organization, 1995.*

from violence. Among youth, however, the impact of homicide is even more significant. Homicide is the second leading cause of death among 15- to 24-year-olds in the United States and the leading cause of death for young African American males and females (Figure 1.3) (National Center for Injury Prevention and Control, 1996). Among persons aged 10 to 14 years, homicide is the third leading cause of death. In addition, 12- to 24-year-olds face the highest risk of nonfatal assault of any age group in our society (U.S. Department of Justice, 1992).

The impact of homicide on young people is further illustrated by years of potential life lost (YPPL), an indicator of the impact that specific causes of death have on the life expectancy of a population (Centers for Disease Control and Prevention, 1993). YPPL-65, for example, is the number of life-years that persons killed by a particular cause would have contributed to society had they all lived to age 65. YPPL emphasizes the causes of death that disproportionately affect younger persons and signifies societal loss in terms of lost productivity and quality of life. In 1991, homicide was the third leading cause of YPPL-65 for the general population, behind unintentional injury (motor vehicle crashes, falls, etc.) and cancer (Centers for Disease Control and Prevention, 1993). Among African Americans, homicide was the leading cause of YPPL-65. When we use YPPL to measure the impact of assaultive behavior on our nation's productivity and quality of life, we have little doubt that the cost is intolerable.

Homicide data also indicate that offenders tend to be demographically similar to their victims. Using data on victim-offender

Rank	\<1	1-4	5-9	10-14	15-24	25-34	35-44	45-54	55-64	65+	Total
					Age Groups						
1	Congenital Anomalies 7,129	Unintentional Injuries 2,590	Unintentional Injuries 1,599	Unintentional Injuries 1,867	Unintentional Injuries 13,966	Unintentional Injuries 14,022	Malignant Neoplasms 16,755	Malignant Neoplasms 42,372	Malignant Neoplasms 90,685	Heart Disease 619,755	Heart Disease 743,460
2	SIDS 4,669	Congenital Anomalies 804	Malignant Neoplasms 582	Malignant Neoplasms 507	Homicide 8,424	HIV 11,299	HIV 15,929	Heart Disease 32,679	Heart Disease 72,043	Malignant Neoplasms 371,549	Malignant Neoplasms 529,904
3	Short Gestation 4,310	Malignant Neoplasms 522	Congenital Anomalies 274	Homicide 462	Suicide 4,849	Homicide 7,278	Unintentional Injuries 13,255	Unintentional Injuries 8,029	Bronchitis Emphysema Asthma 10,671	Cerebro-vascular 131,551	Cerebro-vascular 150,108
4	Respiratory Distress Synd. 1,815	Homicide 464	Homicide 194	Suicide 315	Malignant Neoplasms 1,738	Suicide 6,307	Heart Disease 13,121	HIV 6,487	Cerebro-vascular 9,625	Bronchitis Emphysema Asthma 86,425	Bronchitis Emphysema Asthma 101,077
5	Maternal Complications 1,343	Heart Disease 296	Heart Disease 129	Congenital Anomalies 211	Heart Disease 981	Malignant Neoplasms 5,079	Suicide 6,170	Cerebro-vascular 5,057	Diabetes 7,478	Pneumonia & Influenza 73,853	Unintentional Injuries 90,523
6	Placenta Cord Membranes 994	HIV 204	HIV 100	Heart Disease 174	HIV 609	Heart Disease 3,539	Homicide 4,537	Liver Disease 4,703	Unintentional Injuries 6,405	Diabetes 40,502	Pneumonia & Influenza 82,820
7	Unintentional Injuries 898	Pneumonia & Influenza 182	Pneumonia & Influenza 72	Bronchitis Emphysema Asthma 95	Congenital Anomalies 472	Cerebro-vascular 797	Liver Disease 3,756	Suicide 4,168	Liver Disease 5,613	Unintentional Injuries 27,784	Diabetes 53,894
8	Perinatal Infections 772	Perinatal Period 100	Bronchitis Emphysema Asthma 43	Pneumonia & Influenza 63	Pneumonia & Influenza 251	Pneumonia & Influenza 724	Cerebro-vascular 2,519	Diabetes 3,449	Pneumonia & Influenza 3,704	Nephritis 19,743	HIV 37,267
9	Intrauterine Hypoxia 549	Septicemia 96	Benign Neoplasms 38	HIV 55	Cerebro-vascular 208	Liver Disease 721	Diabetes 1,697	Bronchitis Emphysema Asthma 2,494	Suicide 3,061	Septicemia 16,846	Suicide 31,102
10	Pneumonia & Influenza 530	Benign Neoplasms 77	Septicemia 36	Cerebro-vascular 46	Bronchitis Emphysema Asthma 206	Diabetes 602	Pneumonia & Influenza 1,551	Homicide 2,052	Nephritis 1,854	Athero-sclerosis 16,460	Homicide 26,009

Source: National Center for Injury Prevention and Control, Centers for Disease Control and Prevention, 1996

Figure 1.3 *Ten leading causes of death by age group—1993. Source: National Center for Injury Prevention and Control, Centers for Disease Control and Prevention, 1996.*

relationships from the Federal Bureau of Investigation–Supplemental Homicide Report (FBI–SHR), we have examined the age relationship between young homicide offenders and their victims (Figure 1.4; Federal Bureau of Investigation, 1995). In 1993, of the 205 victims whose offenders were aged 10 to 14 years, 26% were aged 15 to 19 years, and 17% were aged 10 to 14 years. Of the 3,181 victims whose offenders were aged 15 to 19 years, 30% were aged 15 to 19 years, and approximately 22% were aged 20 to 24 years; the percentage of victims tapers off with age. Few victims of 15- to 19-year-old offenders were of younger ages. Of the 3,298 homicide victims whose offenders were aged 20 to 24 years, 29% were 20 to 24 years old, 26% were 25 to 34 years old, and 15% were 15 to 19 years old. This information illustrates that homicide offenders tend to have victims who are of similar or proximate ages. Rarely are the victims of young homicide offenders much younger or much older than themselves. Additionally, homicide victims and offenders tend to be of similar sex and race (Centers for Disease Control, 1986).

Public health efforts to assess the magnitude of weapon carry-ing and fighting among youths are fairly recent and important as indicators of the potential for injury. Information from CDC's 1990 Youth Risk Behavior Survey asked high school students, "During the past 30 days, how many times have you carried a weapon, such as a gun, knife, or club, for self-protection or because you thought you might need it in a fight?" Results indicate that approximately 31.5% of males, 8.1% of females, and 19.6% of all surveyed students reported carrying a weapon (knife, razor, club, or firearm) at least once during the 30 days preceding the survey (Centers for Disease Control and Prevention, 1994b). Of the students who reported carrying weapons in the last 30 days, about 55% reported carrying a knife or razor, 24% reported carrying a club, and 21% reported carrying a firearm. Approximately 8.7% of the students interviewed reported carrying a weapon at least four times during the past 30 days, and these students accounted for about 71% of all reported weapon-carrying incidents. Thus, whereas almost one fifth of all students reported carrying a weapon in the past 30 days, less than one tenth of the students accounted for almost three fourths of the weapon-carrying

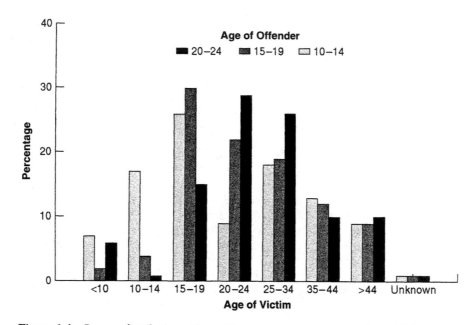

Figure 1.4 *Percent distribution of homicide offender ages by age of victim, United States, 1993. Source: Federal Bureau of Investigation, Supplemental Homicide Report, 1995.*

incidents reported. Although this smaller percentage of students is responsible for most of the weapon carrying, the magnitude of this behavior and the potential for injury is of great concern.

In addition to weapon carrying, fighting is common among youth. Fighting is obviously a precursor to assault-related injury. In the 1990 Youth Risk Behavior Survey (Centers for Disease Control and Prevention, 1992), students were asked, "During the past 30 days, how many times have you been in a physical fight in which you or the person you were fighting was injured and had to be treated by a doctor or a nurse?" Of all high school students answering, 7.9% reported they had been in such a fight, among males, 12.2%, and among females, 3.6%. An estimated 18 fights per 100 students occurred over the 30-day period. Among males, the incidence was 28 fights per 100 students, and among females, it was 7. Obviously, fighting incidence and prevalence are greater among males, and over the 30-day period, more than one fight occurred for every four students. These estimates are for high school students in the United States, and the rates and percentages vary between schools and specific subgroups. The magnitude of fighting and other indicators of interpersonal violence suggest that violence is a significant problem among youth in the United States.

Trends

Since 1933, rates of homicide victimization in the United States have varied more than twofold, ranging from a low of 4.5 homicides per 100,000 persons in 1955, 1957, and 1958 to a high of 10.7 homicides per 100,000 persons in 1980. The rate was 9.7 homicides per 100,000 persons in 1933, before declining during the 1950s, and then increasing substantially during the 1960s and early 1970s. Since the early 1970s, the rate has varied to some extent but has remained within 25% of its historical high in 1980.

Rates of nonfatal assaults have been tracked only since 1973, when data from the National Crime Victimization Survey first became available. Overall rates of nonfatal assaults, however, did not exhibit a discernible trend between 1973 and 1992 and ranged between 28 assaults per 1,000 persons to 35 assaults per 1,000 persons aged 12 years and older (U.S. Department of Justice, 1994).

These overall trends in rates of interpersonal violence, however, obscure some very important changes in the nature and patterns of interpersonal violence in the United States. First, over the past decade, rates of interpersonal violence have increased among young people, and the age of victims and perpetrators of interpersonal violence is getting younger and younger. Second, homicide rates among young males are increasing most rapidly. Third, the tendency is increasing for victims of young offenders to be either strangers or acquaintances. Finally, the lethality of interpersonal violence among young people has increased and appears to be associated with greater access to firearms, increases in caliber, increases in the number of automatic and semiautomatic weapons, or greater willingness to use firearms.

Rates of interpersonal violence among youths have increased. Young people are disproportionately represented among the perpetrators and victims of interpersonal violence. Arrest rates for homicide, rape, robbery, and aggravated assault in the United States peak among older adolescents and young adults (U.S. Department of Justice, 1993a). During the 1980s, more than 48,000 people were murdered by youths 12 to 24 years of age (Federal Bureau of Investigation, 1995). Interviews with assault victims indicate that offenders in this age range committed almost 50% of the estimated 6.4 million nonfatal crimes of violence in 1991 (U.S. Department of Justice, 1992).

The disproportionate involvement of youths in committing interpersonal violence has grown over the last few decades.

Between 1965 and 1993, arrest rates for murder and nonnegligent manslaughter increased by more than 100% for youths between the ages of 13 and 22 years, while arrest rates for those in every age group from 30 years and older declined (U.S. Department of Justice, 1993a). Arrest rates for the perpetration of nonfatal interpersonal violence increased among youths as well. Since 1965, arrest rates for violent offenses tripled among youths aged 13 to 18 years, more than doubled for those aged 19 to 39 years, while increasing more modestly among those 40 years of age and older (U.S. Department of Justice, 1993a).

As with the perpetration of interpersonal violence, the disproportionate involvement of youths as victims has increased as well. For example, between 1965 and 1985, homicide rates for 15- to 19-year-old males were one third to one half the rates of persons aged 20 to 34 years. Between 1985 and 1992, however, annual rates for 15- to 19-year-old males increased 154%, surpassing the rates for men 25 to 29 and 30 to 34 years old (Centers for Disease Control and Prevention, 1994a). Similarly, victimization rates for nonfatal interpersonal violence have increased among youths. Among teens 12 to 15 and 16 to 19 years old, nonfatal assault victimization rates increased by approximately 30% between 1973 and 1992, with most of this increase occurring since 1985 (U.S. Department of Justice, 1994). In comparison, nonfatal assault victimization rates increased only modestly or declined among persons aged 20 years and older. Because of the increasing involvement of youths in interpersonal violence, particularly during the last decade, the average age of both violent offenders and victims has been declining (U.S. Department of Justice, 1993a, 1994).

Rates of assault victimization are increasing more rapidly among young males than among young females. In 1994, the ratio of male-to-female homicide rates in the general population was about 28:1. Among children aged 5 to 9 years, the homicide rate sex ratio was .8:1; among those aged 10 to 14 years, the ratio was 2:1; and it was a dramatic 66:1 among persons aged 15 to 19 years. The increasing rate ratio of male-to-female homicides with age demonstrates that as males move into adolescence, the teenage years, and young adulthood, they are substantially more likely than females to be victims of homicide.

Homicide rates have also been increasing much more dramatically among young males than among young females. When we look at data for 1984, we see that the ratio of male-to-female homicides for the total population was 3.2:1. Among children aged 5 to 9 years, the homicide sex ratio was .8:1 in 1984; among those aged 10 to 14 years, the ratio was 1.1:1; and among those aged 15 to 19 years, it was 2.8:1. Thus, ratios for the general population changed slightly over the decade 1984 to 1994 while they almost doubled among children aged 10 to 14 and 15 to 19 years. The increasingly disparate ratio of male-to-female homicides among the young emphasizes that changes in the problem are largely due to changes in homicide among males.

Another disturbing trend is that young offenders are becoming more likely to kill strangers. FBI-SHR data also allow us to examine the social relationships between homicide victims and offenders (Federal Bureau of Investigation, 1995). Although many relationships are undetermined, by looking at trends over time, we observe some distinct patterns (Figure 1.5). In general, homicide

offenders aged 10 to 24 years are most likely to kill an acquaintance. Very few homicides are committed by children aged 10 to 14 years; however, of those children who did commit murder in 1993, almost 45% killed acquaintances, up from 36% in 1983. The percentage of 10- to 14-year-old homicide offenders who killed family members declined dramatically from 39% in 1983 to 18% in 1993, while the percentage of those who killed strangers increased from 11% in 1983 to 26% in 1993. Over this decade, very little change was observed in the percentage of 10- to 14-year-old homicide offenders for whom the relationship between the victim and offender was unknown.

The percentage of homicide offenders aged 15 to 19 years who killed family members also declined between 1983 and 1993, from 17% to 7%, while the percentage of acquaintance homicides increased from 48% to 52%, as did homicides involving strangers, from 22% to 29%. The percentage of undetermined relationships between 15- to 19-year-old offenders and their victims remained almost unchanged over the decade. This same pattern of declines and increases also was seen among homicide offenders aged 20 to 24 years, but the shifts were less dramatic. Perhaps the most striking shifts over the decade were among persons aged 15 to 19 years, with a substantial decline in the percentage of family homicides and an increase in homicides involving strangers.

The lethality of violence among adolescents and young adults also has increased substantially since the mid-1980s, as is suggested by trends in the number of homicides per 100,000 violent events by age from 1972 to 1992 (Figure 1.6; U.S. Department of Justice, 1993b, 1994). Data from the National Center for Health Statistics and the National Crime Victimization Survey indicate that although lethality over the 20-year period varied substantially,

Figure 1.5 *Percentage distribution of homicide offenders, by age and relation to victim, United States, 1983–1993. Source: Federal Bureau of Investigation, Supplemental Homicide Report, 1995.*

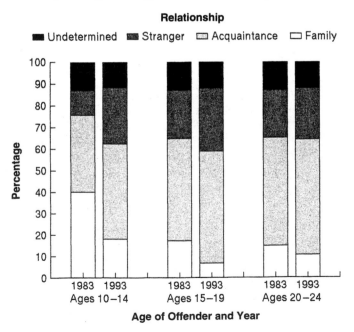

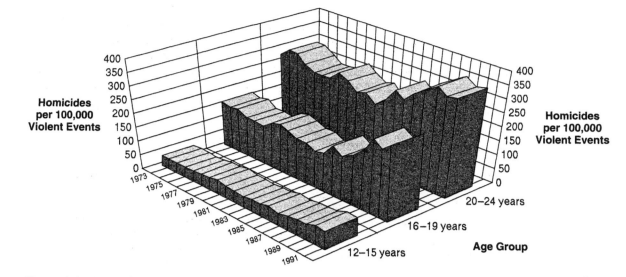

Figure 1.6 *Homicides per 100,000 violent events among persons aged 12–15, 16–19, and 20–24 years, United States, 1972–1992. Source: National Center for Health Statistics 1994; U.S. Department of Justice, 1992, 1993b, 1994.*

after the early 1980s, the lethality of assaults increased substantially among each age group between 12 and 24 years, particularly among teens 15 to 19 years old. No clear increase in the lethality of assaults was observed in other age groups, except the ≥65-year-old age group.

Trends in homicide victimization are strongly associated with firearm involvement. Since 1933, the proportion of homicides committed with a firearm have varied from a low of 51% in 1951 to a high of 69.8% in 1992. Overall trends in the rate of homicide victimization are strongly associated with trends in firearm homicide. That is to say, although rates of non-firearm-related homicide have remained fairly flat over time, rates of firearm-related homicide have closely tracked the overall U.S. homicide rate since 1933. Other evidence indicates quite clearly that recent increases in youth homicide are almost entirely attributable to increases in homicides involving firearms (Centers for Disease Control and Prevention, 1994a).

Implications

We have no definitive explanation for why rates of interpersonal violence among youths have increased, why this violence appears to be more lethal, and why the increased involvement of firearms has occurred over the last decade. However, three strands of scientific evidence may offer some clues. First, science-based research clearly indicates that the presence of a gun in a violent interaction dramatically increases the likelihood that one or more of the participants will be killed (Cook, 1991). Consequently, we could hypothesize that these trends are attributable to greater access to firearms or a greater willingness to use firearms on the part of young assailants. Second, and perhaps related to the previous point, firearms with greater firing power are increasingly available and may contribute to increasing lethality of interpersonal violence involving firearms. There is strong evidence that

handgun makers are increasingly manufacturing and distributing larger caliber handguns and handguns with larger ammunition capacities (now limited to 10 rounds by the 1994 crime bill; Wintemute, 1996). Finally, increases in the rate and lethality of interpersonal violence began with the widespread introduction of crack cocaine into inner cities; the recruitment of adolescents and young adults into the distribution of crack may have increased their access to guns and accelerated more widespread use of guns by a much larger group of young people (Blumstein, 1995).

Increases in homicides among young males over the past decade are almost completely driven by increases in homicides by firearms. Firearms are substantially more lethal than other weapons commonly used during assaultive confrontations. Youth may have increased access to firearms and consequently may be more likely to use them during conflicts. Although the overall number of violent incidents did not change, more incidents resulted in homicides because firearms were used. This same increase could have occurred even without an increase in the number of firearms accessible to youths simply by an increase in the number of youths using firearms in altercations. Murder by shooting can be achieved with minimal physical effort, whereas murder by knifing or bludgeoning involves intimate physical contact with the decedent and expenditure of more physical effort. Information on homicides by juvenile offenders indicates that firearm-related homicides increased substantially beginning in 1984 while the number of non-firearm-related homicides remained fairly constant (Snyder & Sickmund, 1995). This finding supports the possibility that physically violent behavior has changed little among juveniles and that less physical, perhaps more emotionally detached violent behavior is increasing because of greater accessibility of guns, greater willingness to use them, or a combination of these factors.

The trends we have observed among young homicide victims and offenders suggest that homicide may be becoming a more emotionally detached phenomenon. More and more homicides committed by youths involve firearms, which enable the killer to inflict fatal injuries on the victim from a distance, without the need for physical or even eye contact. Rather than struggling with the victim in a surge of violent anger, a perpetrator with a firearm may kill with the ease of pointing and pulling a trigger. The fact that the percentage of young homicide offenders that kill family is declining while the percentage that kill strangers is increasing also reinforces the notion that homicide completed by youth is becoming less emotive. If this is true—that youthful killers as a group are less emotive than in the past—it has some significant implications for improving our understanding of the problem of increasing homicides among youths and for our need to better understand and prevent antisocial behavior.

SUMMARY AND CONCLUSION

Assessments of the magnitude of and trends in homicide and injury from assaultive behavior among adolescents indicate that violent behavior is a significant public health problem. Homicide is a leading cause of death among young people and consequently accounts for a significant loss of years of potential life. Over the past decade, homicide and assault have increased markedly among young people, with an increased use of firearms and an increased tendency to assault strangers. The incidence and prevalence of assaultive behavior among youths make it appear to be less emotive. Whereas the drama of interpersonal violence is played out among individuals, the roles are defined by social and economic forces. To affect systematic change in the problem of interpersonal violence among youth, we must consider how social and economic processes and institutions influence the development of antisocial behavior.

The application of science-based public health principles for addressing the problem of interpersonal violence is a complementary approach to individual-level interventions and secondary and tertiary prevention efforts traditionally employed by criminal justice. By defining the problem, conducting research to understand the causes, developing and evaluating interventions for prevention, and implementing interventions in high-risk communities, public health provides a proven methodology for solving health-related problems.

Interpersonal violence and associated injuries pose a huge burden on our society. Examples of this burden can be seen in the numbers of deaths and injuries that occur each year. Yet these fairly concrete examples of the outcome of interpersonal violence highlight only the surface of the problem. Clearly, the economic and emotional costs associated with these deaths and injuries are quite significant, but our understanding of these costs is only rudimentary. Even with this limited understanding of the costs, society is beginning to recognize the burden of violence and is calling for solutions. Without question, the answers will be found in our social and economic institutions: families, schools, churches, police departments, community organizations, businesses, and others. The processes and information embodied in these institutions influence behavior of individuals. To effect positive change in recent trends of injury from interpersonal violence, we must each take personal responsibility for our young people. We are each challenged to do our part to move our society, and thus the individuals within it, toward nonviolent behavior, toward norms in which interpersonal violence is unacceptable, toward environments in which young people can grow and develop free of fear and free of violence.

REFERENCES

Blumstein, A. (1995). Youth violence, guns, and the illicit-drug industry. *The Journal of Criminal Law and Criminology, 86*(1), 10–36.

Centers for Disease Control and Prevention. (1986). *Homicide surveillance: High-risk racial and ethnic groups, 1970–1983.* Atlanta: Author.

Centers for Disease Control and Prevention. (1992). Physical fighting among high-school students, United States, 1990. *Morbidity and Mortality Weekly Report, 41*(6), 91–94.

Centers for Disease Control and Prevention. (1993). Years of potential life lost before age 65, United States, 1980–1991. *Morbidity and Mortality Weekly Report, 42*(13), 251–253.

Centers for Disease Control and Prevention. (1994a). Homicide among 15- to 19-year-old males. *Morbidity and Mortality Weekly Report, 43*(40), 725–727.

Centers for Disease Control and Prevention. (1994b). Weapon carrying among high-school students, United States, 1990. *Morbidity and Mortality Weekly Report, 40*(40), 681–684.

Cook, P. J. (1991). The technology of personal violence. In M. Tonry (Ed.), *Crime and justice: A review of research* (Vol. 14, pp. 1–72). Chicago: University of Chicago Press.

Elliot, D. S. (1980). Recurring issues in the evaluation of delinquency prevention and treatment programs. In D. Shichor & D. Kelly (Eds.), *Critical issues in juvenile delinquency* (pp. 237–261). Lexington, MA: Lexington Books (Heath).

Federal Bureau of Investigation. (1995). *Supplemental homicide report data tapes, 1980–1992.* Washington, DC: Author, U.S. Department of Justice.

Fingerhut, L. A., & Kleinman, J. C. (1990). International and interstate comparisons of homicide among young males. *Journal of the American Medical Association, 263,* 3292–3295.

Foege, W. H., Rosenberg, M. L., & Mercy, J. A. (1995). Public health and violence prevention. *Current Issues in Public Health, 1,* 2–9.

Mercy, J. A., Rosenberg, M. L., Powell, K. E., Broome, C. V., & Roper, W. L. (1993). Public health policy for preventing violence. *Health Affairs, 12*(4), 7–29.

National Center for Health Statistics. (1994). *Annual summary of births, marriages, divorces, and deaths: United States, 1993* (Monthly Vital Statistics Report 42:13). Hyattsville, MD: Public Health Service.

National Center for Injury Prevention and Control. (1993). *The prevention of youth violence: A framework for community action.* Atlanta, GA: Centers for Disease Control and Prevention.

National Center for Injury Prevention and Control. (1996). *1992—10 leading causes of death.* Atlanta, GA: Centers for Disease Control and Prevention.

Powell, K., Dahlberg, L., & Friday, J. (1996). Evaluation of specific youth violence prevention projects. *American Journal of Preventive Medicine, 12*(5)Suppl., Sept.–Oct.

Robins, L. N., Tipp, J., & Przybeck, T. (1991). Antisocial personality. In L. N. Robins & D. A. Regier (Eds.), *Psychiatric disorders in America* (pp. 258–290). New York: Free Press.

Rosenberg, M. L., O'Carroll, P. W., & Powell, K. E. (1992). Let's be clear: Violence is a public health problem. *Journal of the American Medical Association, 267*(22), 3071–3072.

Snyder, H. N., & Sickmund, M. (1995). *Juvenile offenders and victims: A national report.* Washington, DC: Office of Juvenile Justice and Delinquency Prevention.

U.S. Department of Justice. (1992). *Criminal victimization in the United States, 1991* (Report No. NCJ-139563). Washington, DC: Bureau of Justice Statistics, U.S. Department of Justice.

U.S. Department of Justice. (1993a). *Age-specific arrest rates and race-specific arrest rates for selected offenses, 1965–1992.* Washington, DC: Author.

U.S. Department of Justice. (1993b). *Criminal victimization in the United States, 1992* (Report No. NCJ-145125). Washington, DC: Bureau of Justice Statistics, U.S. Department of Justice.

U.S. Department of Justice. (1994). *Criminal victimization in the United States: 1973–92 trends* (Report No. NCJ-147006). Washington, DC: Bureau of Justice Statistics, U.S. Department of Justice.

Wintemute, G. J. (1996). The relationship between firearm design and firearm violence. *Journal of the American Medical Association, 275*(22), 1749–1753.

World Health Organization. (1995). *World health statistics annual, 1994.* Geneva: Author.

CHAPTER 2

Epidemiology and Axis I Comorbidity of Antisocial Personality

C. ROBERT CLONINGER, CARMEN BAYON, and THOMAS R. PRZYBECK

Antisocial personality is the only personality disorder that has been extensively studied in large-scale epidemiological surveys such as the Epidemiologic Catchment Area (ECA) project (Robins & Regier, 1991). It was included in the ECA because it could be reliably assessed using the Diagnostic Interview Schedule and ECA results could be compared with a substantial body of previous work (Robins, Tipp, & Przybeck, 1991). Persons with antisocial personality disorder (ASPD) are impulsive, aggressive, and aloof and are thought to have reduced capacities for work, love, guilt, and cooperation with authority figures. They have been studied in the general population (Robins et al., 1991), prospective longitudinal studies of child psychiatric patients (Robins, 1966) and adult felons (Goodwin & Guze, 1984), families of psychiatric patients and felons (Cloninger, Reich, & Guze, 1975a, 1975b), and adoptees (Crowe, 1972; Schulsinger, 1972).

Basic conclusions about the onset and course of ASPD have been inferred from prior longitudinal research. Antisocial personality disorder begins in childhood with behavior problems at home and school (Robins, 1966). It is five to seven times more common in males than females (Cloninger et al., 1975a; Sigvardsson, Cloninger, Bohman, & von Knorring, 1982). Consequently, data about ASPD are predominantly about men, but descriptive, longitudinal, and family studies have been carried out in women (Cloninger & Guze, 1970a, 1970b, 1973a, 1973b; Martin, Cloninger, Guze, & Clayton, 1985). Regardless of gender, the number and severity of indicators of antisocial conduct in childhood predict the probability of persistence into adulthood (Robins, 1978). Antisocial personality disorder continues throughout life in most cases but often becomes less problematic in middle or old age. More than a third of people with ASPD settle down and mature substantially by 50 years of age; they improve in their capacity for work and empathy, are better able to avoid serious legal problems, but usually remain impulsive, irritable, and aloof. Their maturation is most often delayed to their 30s but can occur at any age (Robins, 1966).

Major descriptive characteristics of ASPD, including its diagnostic features and other psychiatric syndromes that often co-occur in the same individual, have been based on clinical and family studies (Cloninger & Guze, 1970a, 1973a). The disorder is characterized by repeated antisocial behavior in a wide range of personal and social contexts. In childhood, impulsive-aggressive behavior is most prominent. This includes fighting, cruelty to animals and other people, fire setting, running away from home, and disrespect for rules at home and school leading to a wide variety of disciplinary problems and conflict with authority figures. In adulthood, the impulsive-aggressive features persist and are associated with impairment in work and empathic social relations. People with antisocial personality disorder usually change jobs repeatedly because they are fired or quit. When they marry or cohabit, they usually have frequent conflicts leading to abuse, infidelity, desertion, separation, or divorce. About half have felony convictions or multiple arrests for serious criminal activity other than traffic violations (Robins et al., 1991).

Individuals with ASPD also are frequently alcohol or drug abusers (Lewis, Helzer, Cloninger, Croughan, & Whitman, 1982; Robins et al., 1991). Women especially have an increased risk of somatization disorder (Cloninger & Guze, 1970a; Cloninger et al., 1975b). Such individuals have been reported to be at either increased (Robins et al., 1991b) or decreased (Cleckley, 1964) risk of mood and anxiety disorders, suggesting the possibility of psychosocial heterogeneity that is not well distinguished by current behavioral criteria.

Antisocial personality disorder, substance abuse, and somatization often are observed in genetic relatives of people with criminality or broadly defined ASPD, whether or not they are reared together (Cloninger et al., 1975b; Bohman, Cloninger, von Knorring, & Sigvardsson, 1984). The importance of biogenetic factors in the development of ASPD also is supported by the fact that it has been recognized in every era and type of society, regardless of political or economic system (Robins et al., 1991). However, low socioeconomic status and inconsistent discipline in the early rearing environment increase the risk of developing the disorder (Bohman et al., 1984; Cloninger, Sigvardsson, Bohman, & von Knorring, 1982).

Despite the wealth of available information, the most funda-

Supported in part by grants from the National Institutes of Health MH-31302, AA-07982, and AA-08028.

mental questions about ASPD remain unanswered. Is it a discrete category of illness, an extreme variant of one or more quantitative dimensions, or a pejorative label for nonconformists? What is its overlap with other personality disorders and psychiatric syndromes? What are the most promising ways for prevention and intervention with antisocial personality disorder? Is heterogeneity in course and comorbidity explained by individual differences in quantifiable components of personality? Here, we attempt to elucidate these basic questions by focusing on whether heterogeneity in the course and comorbidity of ASPD in the general population is explained by individual differences in quantifiable components of personality and psychopathology that have not been controlled for in earlier research.

THEORETICAL CONTEXT AND CONTROVERSIAL ISSUES

The limitations of prior work primarily are a consequence of problems in ascertainment and assessment of personality disorders. Current diagnostic criteria for personality disorders involve rather long checklists of many overlapping diagnostic features (American Psychiatric Association, 1994). Structured interviews for personality disorders are reliable but produce many overlapping diagnoses and take over 90 minutes to complete (Cloninger, Svrakic, & Przybeck, 1993; D. M. Svrakic, Whitehead, Przybeck, & Cloninger, 1993). Such interview methods are impractical for large-scale epidemiological research, which consequently has been limited to studies of one personality disorder (like the ECA) or to samples of treated cases. Treated cases may be unrepresentative for several reasons. In general, treatment samples overrepresent cases that are severely impaired, with multiple psychiatric syndromes, suggesting spurious associations (Berkson, 1946). In particular, treated cases may be unrepresentative of people with antisocial personalities, who seldom see themselves as the cause of their problems.

As a result of the limited assessment procedures available in the past, no data have compared antisocial personality disorder with other personality variants in the same sample of the general population. Recently, however, reliable and brief self-report questionnaires have been shown to distinguish subtypes of personality disorder (Cloninger et al., 1993; Livesley, 1987; D. M. Svrakic et al., 1993; Trull, 1992). Nearly all of this work has been conducted in nonclinical samples with few definite cases of personality disorder (Livesley, 1987; Trull, 1992). One instrument, however, the Temperament and Character Inventory (TCI), has been validated independently for differential diagnosis of personality disorders in both clinical and nonclinical samples (Cloninger, Przybeck, Svrakic, & Wetzel, 1994; Goldman, Skodal, McGrath, & Oldham, 1994; D. M. Svrakic et al., 1993). The validity of the TCI for differential diagnosis allows for efficient study of several controversial questions about ASPD.

The TCI distinguishes temperament traits, which are moderately heritable and stable throughout life, and character traits, which are weakly heritable, moderately influenced by social learning, and mature in a stagelike manner (Cloninger et al., 1993). *Temperament* refers to individual differences in basic emotional responses, such as anger, fear, and disgust. *Character* refers to individual differences in goals, values, and self-conscious emotions such as capacity for shame, guilt, and empathy. For example, ASPD is distinguished from other personality disorders by a unique profile of three temperament traits: high Novelty Seeking (i.e., impulsive, quick tempered), low Harm Avoidance (i.e., risk taking, fearless), and low Reward Dependence (i.e., aloof, independent). Other personality disorders can be distinguished by different profiles of high and low scores on these dimensions (Cloninger, 1987a; Goldman et al., 1994; D. M. Svrakic et al., 1993). In contrast, all types of personality disorder are characterized by immature character development. All cases of personality disorder are characterized by reduced ability to work and love. In other words, individuals who have a personality disorder are low in the TCI character dimension of Self-directedness: They are irresponsible, aimless, inept, low in self-esteem, and undisciplined. Many are also low in the TCI dimension of Cooperativeness: They are socially intolerant, lacking in empathy, selfish, revengeful, and unprincipled.

Consequently, the presence of any personality disorder can be detected by low scores on TCI character dimensions of Self-directedness and Cooperativeness. Different subtypes of personality disorder can be distinguished by their profile of temperament traits. Extreme temperament profiles, however, do not necessarily indicate a personality disorder, because they may be associated with mature character development. Thus, the combination of temperament and character defines the total personality, which may be either a mature personality or a personality disorder.

Substantial evidence supports the validity of diagnosing ASPD using the TCI. Discriminant validity has been demonstrated by its efficacy for differential diagnosis of personality disorders in several independent studies of psychiatric inpatients and outpatients (Cloninger et al., 1994; Goldman et al., 1994; D. M. Svrakic et al., 1993). Childhood and adolescent reports of the temperament profile of high Novelty Seeking, low Harm Avoidance, and low Reward Dependence are predictive of later antisocial conduct and substance abuse (Sigvardsson, Bohman, & Cloninger, 1987; Tremblay, Pihl, Vitaro, & Dobkin, 1994; Wills, Vaccaro, & McNamara, 1994). A sample of 223 criminals took Hare's Psychopathy Checklist and TCI temperament measures (Joseph Newman, personal communication, 1994, in Cloninger et al., 1994; see Newman, Chapter 30, this volume; Hart & Hare, Chapter 3, this volume). Factor 1 of the Psychopathy Checklist (PCL) measures core features of "primary" psychopathy, such as those described by Cleckley (1964), including superficial charm, habitual lying, and callous social detachment. This primary psychopathy factor of the PCL was correlated with the antisocial profile of high Novelty Seeking ($r = .26$), low Harm Avoidance ($r = -.10$), and low Reward Dependence ($r = -.24$). Factor 2 of the PCL measures "secondary" psychopathy or chronically unstable antisocial conduct. The unstable conduct factor corresponded to the explosive or borderline profile of high Novelty Seeking ($r = .45$), high Harm Avoidance ($r = .09$), and low Reward Dependence ($r = -.35$). In classifications antedating *DSM-III,* the first PCL factor corresponds to psychopaths who have a reduced ability to avoid punishment and to perform well on tasks mediated by fear and anxiety; in other words, primary psychopathy or PCL Factor 1 is associated with low TCI Harm Avoidance and high TCI Novelty Seeking. On the other hand, secondary psychopaths, who are neurotically unstable because of approach-avoidance conflicts about novelty, correspond to PCL Factor 2, which is associated with high TCI Harm Avoidance and high TCI Novelty Seeking. In more recent clinical work, secondary psychopaths usually would be diagnosed as having borderline personality disorder, which is characterized by the explosive temperament profile (Cloninger et al., 1994; also see Zanarini & Gunderson, Chapter 8, this volume). Secondary psychopathy overlaps extensively with chronic criminality and impulsive personality disorders in general.

Differential diagnosis of multiple personality disorders that share some features with antisocial personality disorder allows comparison of their course and clinical correlates. For example, cases with borderline and histrionic personality disorders according to *DSM-IV* are impulsive and aggressive, like those with ASPD, but differ in other traits, such as high Harm Avoidance (i.e., anxiety proneness, as in people with borderline personality disorder) or high Reward Dependence (i.e., social warmth, as in those with a histrionic personality). It is necessary to distinguish such subtypes of personality disorder to compare their epidemiology and comorbidity for such variables as differential risks for suicide attempts, alcoholism, and depression. Prior studies of antisocial psychiatric patients have reported a high risk of suicide and suicide attempts, whereas studies of antisocial personality disorder carried out in the criminal justice system report little suicidal behavior, even in studies by the same investigators (Goodwin & Guze, 1984; Martin et al., 1985). Resolution of these inconsistencies requires comprehensive assessments of personality and psychopathology in general population samples.

Furthermore, heterogeneity in the course of illness and comorbidity may depend on differences in overall severity or differences in specific components of personality. Consequently, it is crucial to have a reliable means of the quantifying severity of different components of personality. For example, people with ASPD show fewer social problems with advancing age but often remain impulsive and adventurous (Robins, 1966). This suggests that some components of antisocial personality disorder may improve more with age than others. In particular, Novelty Seeking decreases with age by approximately 18%, so that older individuals become noticeably less impulsive (more reflective), less rule breaking (more orderly), and less quick tempered (more stoical). Cooperativeness increases markedly in most children during school age and then increases slightly (by 12%, on average) after age 18; the development of Cooperativeness appears to be particularly impaired in those with antisocial and borderline personalities (D. M. Svrakic et al., 1993). Self-directedness increases markedly in most people during adolescence and young adulthood and then increases only slightly (on average, by 9%) after age 18. Of course, the practical significance of such changes depends on the extent of change in each case and the extent of the initial deviation.

In summary, to distinguish ASPD from other normal and abnormal personality variants, two kinds of data are needed that have not been available previously. First, the demographic and clinical correlates of antisocial personality disorder must be compared with those of other types of personality disorder in a general population. In addition, people with antisocial personality disorder should be compared with people who have extreme temperaments but are mature in character.

We attempted to do this by studying a stratified random sample of 1,000 noninstitutionalized adults, 18 years of age or older, who lived in the greater metropolitan area of St. Louis, Missouri. Potential participants initially were identified at random from standard telephone lists and asked if they were willing to participate in a questionnaire survey of personality and health sponsored by the National Institutes of Health and Washington University School of Medicine. Of 1,740 individuals solicited for possible participation, 243 declined (14% refusal). From the 1,497 volunteers, a final panel of 1,000 was accepted into demographic strata in numbers representative of the 1990 federal census according to age (18–34, 35–54, 55+), gender (male, female), ethnicity (White, Black, Hispanic, other), and geographical location of household (six counties). The 1,000 selected participants were mailed a questionnaire along with prepayment of $5 and paid another $20 on return of the completed questionnaire. Those who did not return the questionnaire after a few weeks were reminded with postcards and later phone calls. Altogether 866 subjects returned the questionnaire. Of these 804 were nearly complete and valid based on internal consistency checks built into the questionnaire to detect careless or inconsistent responding. Four additional cases are excluded because of some missing values.

The 800 complete and valid respondents included slightly more women than expected (56.9% observed vs. 52.0% expected) but were otherwise representative of the general population demographically. The respondents also were representative of the general population in terms of their personality and alcohol history, as assessed in a national area probability sample conducted as part of the 1987 General Social Survey for the National Science Foundation (Cloninger, Przybeck, & Svrakic, 1991). Data shown later indicate that the prevalences of psychiatric disorders and quantitative scale scores for other measures of psychopathology in this population are similar to those obtained in the ECA, a large multisite epidemiological survey using structured psychiatric interviews (Robins & Regier, 1991) and other community surveys using interviews and questionnaires (Myers & Weissman, 1980).

Assessment Questionnaires

Subjects completed a questionnaire booklet with separate sections for general demographic information, the TCI (Cloninger et al., 1994); the Inventory of Personal Characteristics (Waller & Zavala, 1993); the short Michigan Alcoholism Screening Test (SMAST; Selzer, Vinokur, & van Rooijen, 1975); the NIMH Center for Epidemiological Studies depression scale (CES-D; Radloff, 1977); the Medical Outcome Study (MOS) short-form General Health Survey (Stewart, Hays, & Ware, 1988), which includes the five-item Mental Health Inventory (MHI-5; Berwick et al., 1991); and additional questions described later about psychopathology and mental health treatment. The questionnaire was estimated to take about 75 minutes to complete on average. In a 12-month follow-up examination, the test-retest reliability of the personality ratings was high (i.e., correlations of .78 to .85 for each of the TCI dimensions), which supports the reliability and validity of the self-reports.

Measures of Psychopathology

The degree of character maturity was measured as the sum of TCI scores for Self-directedness and Cooperativeness, which measure the certainty and severity of personality disorder (D. M. Svrakic et al., 1993). A diagnosis of definite personality disorder was made in 141 individuals (17.6%), as shown in Table 2.1, which is about the bottom sixth of the population in character maturity. Subtypes of personality disorders and temperament types were specified as described in detail elsewhere (Cloninger, 1987a; D. M. Svrakic et al., 1993). Individuals were rated as high or low on a temperament dimension according to median splits. For example, people with antisocial personality disorder were those with definite personality disorder and an adventurous temperament profile (i.e., high Novelty Seeking, low Harm Avoidance, low Reward Dependence). Those with borderline personality disorder were those with definite personality disorder and an explosive temperament (i.e., high Novelty Seeking, high Harm Avoidance, and low Reward Dependence). Other erratic or impulsive personality disorders (Cluster B) were the others with high Novelty Seeking. Other definite personality disorders (nonimpulsive cases in Clusters A and C) were characterized by low Novelty Seeking. Other possible personality disorders were those in the second sextile of the population in maturity, as shown in Table 2.1. Mature types include those who were average or higher in maturity in Table 2.1 and were subdivided according to temperament type.

Measures of psychopathology from the SMAST, CES-D, and MHI-5 were based on other clinical validation studies in which both questionnaires and interview diagnoses were completed independently. The CES-D asks about 20 depressive symptoms, which are rated on a 4-point frequency scale for the past week. In a community sample, a CES-D score of 21 or higher had a sensitivity (i.e., proportion of true cases detected) of 54% and a specificity

(i.e., proportion of noncases correctly classified) of 96% for major depression diagnosed by structured interview; scores of 16 or higher had a sensitivity of 64% and a specificity of 94% (Myers & Weissman, 1980). The MHI-5 has five items about anxiety and depression rated on a 6-point frequency scale; scores of 17 or higher reliably indicate the presence of clinically significant anxiety or mood disorder (Berwick et al., 1991). In this sample, scores on the CES-D and MHI-5 were highly correlated ($r = .77$, $p < .001$). Therefore, these scales are useful for indicating the severity of anxiety and depression and screening for anxiety and depressive disorders, but not for distinguishing among specific categories of mood and anxiety disorders.

The use of self-report questionnaires has both strengths and limitations compared to interviews. Self-reports are inexpensive and practical for large-scale surveys. They eliminate observer bias and allow detailed analysis of psychometric properties of the instruments. Nevertheless, the CES-D and MHI-5 indicators do not distinguish well among different categories of mood and anxiety disorders. They do, however, reliably indicate the presence of any mood or anxiety disorder and the severity of anxiety and depression symptom levels (Berwick et al., 1991).

CURRENT FINDINGS ABOUT DEMOGRAPHIC PATTERNS

The relationship of temperament type to degree of character maturity was evaluated as a preliminary check on the prevalence of different types of personality disorder. Table 2.1 shows that 26 (27%) of the 98 individuals with adventurous temperaments had definite personality disorders using the TCI criterion calibrated to correspond to *DSM-IV* thresholds. The only temperament type with a

TABLE 2.1 Degree of Character Maturity for Each Type of Temperament, Rated Using the Temperament and Character Inventory in a General Adult Population (1994 St. Louis Health Survey)[a]

| Temperament Type | Number of Subjects | Personality Disorder | | No Personality Disorder | |
		Definite (row %)	Possible (row %)	Average (row %)	Mature (row %)
Adventurous (Nhr)	98	27	12	32	30
Explosive (NHr)	76	49	20	25	7
Dramatic (NhR)	134	4	10	39	47
Independent (nhr)	97	7	11	40	41
Sensitive (NHR)	100	27	19	38	16
Methodical (nHr)	147	22	30	33	15
Reliable (nhR)	79	1	6	30	62
Cautious (nHR)	69	7	16	36	41
Column total number	800	(n = 141)	(n = 131)	(n = 276)	(n = 252)
Row % of total		17.6%	16.4%	34.5%	31.5%

[a]Maturity of character was measured by the sum of TCI Self-directedness and Cooperativeness and divided into lowest sixth (definite PD), second lowest sixth (possible PD), middle third (average), and highest third (mature). Temperament type was measured by the configuration of three dimensions divided by median splits: Novelty Seeking high (N) or low (n), Harm Avoidance high (H) or low (h), and Reward Dependence high (R) or low (r).

TABLE 2.2   Prevalence Estimates of Antisocial Personality Disorder (ASPD) in the St. Louis Health Survey (SLHS) and the Epidemiologic Catchment Area (ECA) Study (all sites)

Population	Prevalence of ASPD		
	SLHS		ECA
	f/N	%	%
Total	26/800	3.3	2.6
Gender			
Males	22/345	6.4	4.5
Females	4/455	0.9	0.8
Race			
Whites	18/652	2.8	2.6
Blacks	6/125	4.8	2.3
Age			
18–29	15/178	8.4	3.8
30–44	7/274	2.6	3.7
45–64	3/216	1.4	1.4
65+	1/131	0.8	0.3

higher proportion (49%) of definite personality disorder was the explosive type associated with borderline personality disorder.

Gender, Race, and Age

Using this TCI classification procedure for definite personality disorder provided an estimate of the prevalence of antisocial personality disorder in the general population of the St. Louis Health Survey (SLHS), 3.3%, in approximate agreement with that obtained using the Diagnostic Interview Schedule in the ECA study, namely, 2.6% (Table 2.2). Likewise, young men were most likely to be diagnosed as having antisocial personality disorder in both studies. The slight excess of ASPD in Blacks was not statistically significant in the SLHS and was not observed in the ECA. In both studies gender and age had strong impacts.

A more complete account of the prevalence of antisocial personality disorder and other personality variants by gender and age

is shown in Table 2.3. Antisocial personality disorder shows a greater predominance of men and individuals under age 30 than any other personality disorder or temperament type. There is a sevenfold excess of men with ASPD, compared to a twofold excess of men with borderline personality disorder and a slight excess of women with other impulsive personalities (e.g., histrionic or narcissistic personality). Likewise, among mature temperament types, there is a twofold excess of men with adventurous temperaments in contrast to the excess of women with other types.

Because 22 of the 26 individuals with antisocial personality disorder were men, the prevalence of ASPD and other personality variants was examined by age in men only. With women excluded, it remains clear that all the impulsive personality disorders (antisocial, borderline, and other) are less prevalent in older age cohorts, whereas nonimpulsive personality disorders are slightly more frequent in older cohorts, increasing from 7% in those under 30 years to 10% in those over 65 years of age. This supports the suggestion in *DSM-IV* that impulsive (Cluster B) disorders are more likely than nonimpulsive (Clusters A and C) disorders to improve with age (APA, 1994). This prognostic difference may be explained partly by the decrease in Novelty Seeking with increasing age, as noted earlier, or partly by the possibility that individuals high in Novelty Seeking may have earlier mortality. In fact, the proportion of individuals who have any personality disorder is lower in older cohorts (under 40%) than in those under age 30 (over 60%). In positive terms, 39% of those under 30 years of age are mature (i.e., higher than the bottom third in Self-directedness and Cooperativeness) compared to 60% or more of those age 30 years or older. The association between character maturity and age occurs in both adventurous and other temperaments.

Education

Antisocial personality disorder has often been associated with low educational achievement, particularly failure to graduate from high school (Robins et al., 1991). This association is confounded partly by disciplinary problems in school being part of the diagnostic criteria. In the SLHS, it is possible to examine the association with educational level without this confound (Table 2.4). Borderline person-

TABLE 2.3   Prevalence of ASPD and Other Personality Variants by Gender and Age in the SLHS

Group	Gender (%)		Age (%)			
	Male (n = 345)	Female (n = 455)	18–29 (n = 178)	30–44 (n = 274)	45–64 (n = 216)	65+ (n = 131)
Personality Disorders						
Antisocial	6.4	0.9	8.4	2.6	1.4	0.8
Borderline	6.4	3.3	7.9	4.4	4.6	0.8
Other Impulsive	3.8	4.2	5.6	3.7	4.6	1.5
Not Impulsive	7.5	4.4	5.6	6.2	3.7	8.4
Any Possible	17.7	15.4	20.8	15.7	12.0	19.1
Mature Types						
Adventurous	10.7	5.1	6.7	8.4	8.3	5.3
Other	47.5	66.8	44.9	59.1	65.3	64.1
Total	100.0	100.0	100.0	100.0	100.0	100.0

TABLE 2.4   Education and Employment by Personality Type in SLHS

Personality Type	Number of Subjects	Years of Education[a]			Employment Status[b]		
		< 12 (row %)	12 (row %)	13+ (row %)	No Job (row %)	Part-Time (row %)	Full-Time (row %)
Personality Disorders							
Antisocial	26	8	38	54	0	12	65
Borderline	37	30	27	43	11	22	46
Other Impulsive	32	13	37	50	3	22	66
Not Impulsive	46	15	26	59	7	7	52
Any Possible	131	15	37	48	7	12	45
Mature Types							
Adventurous	60	3	10	87	7	13	55
Other	468	11	29	59	3	11	50
Total	800	12	30	58	5	12	51

[a]Not high school graduate (<12 yrs), high school graduate (12), 1–3 years of college (13–15 yrs), and 4 or more years college (16+).
[b]Employment status distinguished part-time paid employment, full-time paid employment, students/housemakers, retired, and no job (and none of preceding). The retired and student/homemakers not shown here.

ality disorder is associated with failure to graduate from high school (30% in people with borderline personality disorder vs. 12% in others), but antisocial personality disorder is not (8%). Furthermore, mature adventurous individuals are actually most likely to graduate from high school (97% vs. 88%) and continue with some college education (87% vs. 58%).

Employment

It is well established that antisocial personality disorder leads to occupational instability, such as frequently quitting or being fired (Robins, 1966; Robins et al., 1991). This association is confounded partly by occupational instability being part of the diagnostic criteria. Consequently, it is interesting to evaluate the association, if any, of ASPD with current employment status when ASPD is diagnosed on the basis of personality traits alone and not employment history. Table 2.4 shows that underemployment (i.e., part-time or no job) is associated with borderline and other impulsive personality disorders but not with antisocial personality disorder. Those with ASPD are usually employed full time, although not necessarily at the same job. This suggests that prior reports of chronic unemployment with ASPD may be confounded by criteria that do not adequately distinguish ASPD from borderline personality disorder. An alternative hypothesis is that a chronically unemployed person with an antisocial personality disorder becomes anxious or depressed, which could inflate his or her Harm Avoidance score and lead to a change in diagnosis from antisocial to borderline personality. This alternative hypothesis is unlikely in most cases, however, because older cohorts have fewer people with both antisocial and borderline personality, not more. Accordingly, underemployment appears to be attributable largely to a borderline, not an antisocial, personality. The rate of unemployment in this sample (5%) is similar to that officially reported for this region at the time, suggesting that unemployed people were accurately represented in the SLHS sample.

Marital Status

The association of antisocial personality disorder with marital instability is well known from prior studies. In the SLHS, antisocial personality was most strongly associated with having never been married (46% vs. 18%). Those with ASPD are less likely to have ever married than other types of definite personality disorders (46% vs. 20% to 32%) and much less likely than mature adventurous (20%) or other nonadventurous (13%) personalities. These differences may be partly a function of the lower mean age of those with antisocial personality disorder, but it is also seen when the comparison is limited to people younger than 30. Among the 178 people under age 30, 73% of the 15 having an antisocial personality were never married, compared with 55% of the 163 others. Furthermore, temperament substantially influences the rate of being single in people under 30 years of age: 67% of the 12 mature adventurous people under age 30 had remained single, which is similar to the single rate in those with antisocial personality disorder. With the recent decreased social pressure to marry early, people with ASPD appear to be more likely to remain single until they are older and more mature, rather than to enter into unstable early marriages.

Religious Activity

People with antisocial personality disorder were less likely than any other personality group to say they were affiliated with any religion (30% vs. 10% unaffiliated). They also indicated the lowest frequency of attending church of any group. Individuals with any type of personality disorder attended church less often than those without personality disorders. Two thirds of those with antisocial and borderline personalities reported that they rarely or never attended church, whereas two thirds of those without personality disorder reported attending church at least monthly and one third without personality disorders attended at least weekly.

CURRENT FINDINGS ABOUT HEALTH AND COMORBIDITY

In general, people with antisocial personality disorder report that their overall (mental and physical) health is very good (58%) but not excellent (12%). People with other types of personality disorders rate their overall health lower than very good more often than those with antisocial personality disorder (73% to 50% vs. 31%), whereas mature individuals more often rate their health excellent than those with antisocial personality disorder (26% vs. 12%). This confirms the general impression that people with antisocial personality disorder do not see themselves as ill.

Mental Health Treatment and Suicide Attempts

People with antisocial personality disorder do not report more mental health problems than others in general in the SLHS (Table 2.5). In contrast, people with borderline and nonimpulsive personality disorders are most likely to report problems, particularly psychiatric hospitalization and suicide attempts. Only 4% of those with antisocial personality disorder reported past suicide attempts compared to 30% of those with borderline personality disorder and 6% of the general population. Only 8% were ever hospitalized for their mental health compared with 22% of those with borderline personality disorder and 6% of the general population. Suicide attempts in men have often been associated with ASPD in psychiatric treatment samples; these data suggest that antisocial personality disorder is not well differentiated from borderline personality disorder when checklists of antisocial behavior are the basis for diagnosis. This hypothesis also is supported when comparisons are restricted to men.

Substance Abuse

Alcoholism often has been associated with antisocial personality disorder in past research (Cloninger, 1987b; Lewis et al., 1982; Robins et al., 1991), and this association is strongly confirmed in the SLHS (Table 2.6). The lifetime prevalence of definite alcoholism was estimated as 14.1% in the SLHS, which is similar to the prevalence of 13.8% in all ECA sites and 15.9% in St. Louis specifically (Robins

& Regier, 1991). In contrast to these overall rates, 39% of those with ASPD in the SLHS were definite alcoholics and another 12% were possible alcoholics. The only other group with a similarly elevated prevalence of alcoholism was borderline personality, with a 43% prevalence. The rates are slightly higher in other personality disorders (15% to 19%) than in mature people (9% to 13%).

The motivational mechanisms associated with substance abuse were examined further with another legal substance, cigarettes. Antisocial personalities, like those with all personality disorders, are more likely to have ever smoked than people who are not adventurous and mature (77% vs. 62%). They are also more likely to still smoke recently (65% vs. 46%). Consequently, they also are much less likely to stop smoking. Taking frequency of smoking into account, individuals with any impulsive personality disorder are less likely to quit than all other personality types; for example, among those who have smoked a pack per day, only 10% of those with antisocial personality disorder, 25% of those with borderline personality disorder, and 22% of those with other impulsive personalities have quit, which is lower than any other group (35% to 45%). Among light smokers, the rates of quitting are higher overall, but the difference between antisocial and borderline personality disorders (60%) versus nonimpulsive (82%) and mature types (67% to 77%) also holds.

Despite starting more and quitting less, however, antisocial personalities are *not* more likely than mature people to smoke a pack of cigarettes daily. They have the lowest rate of ever having smoked a pack of cigarettes daily (50%) compared to all other groups (58% to 83%). In other words, they have a high rate of lifelong light smoking (20%) compared to all other personality types (7% to 14%). This is consistent with other findings that individuals with impulsive personality disorders use substances such as alcohol and cigarettes for pleasant stimulation and do not want to quit using them (Cloninger, 1987b; Cloninger, Sigvardsson, Przybeck, & Svrakic, 1995).

Depression and Anxiety

Prior research indicates that most patients with personality disorders are likely to have comorbid anxiety and depressive disorders (D. M. Svrakic et al., 1993), but that antisocial personality disorder may be relatively resistant to anticipatory anxiety, depression, and guilt

TABLE 2.5 Indicators of Lifetime Mental Health Function by Personality Type in SLHS

Personality Type	Number of Subjects	Mental Health Treatment			
		Nerve Meds? (row %)	Psych Outpt? (row %)	Psych Inpt? (row %)	Attempt Suicide? (row %)
Personality Disorders					
Antisocial	26	15	15	8	4
Borderline	37	35	46	22	30
Other Impulsive	32	41	28	6	9
Not Impulsive	46	30	35	17	20
Any Possible	131	35	23	8	8
Mature Types					
Adventurous	60	13	15	7	5
Other	468	27	19	3	3
Total	800	28.2	21.5	6.4	6.4

TABLE 2.6 Prevalence of Definite Alcoholism, Definite Depression, and Multiple Somatic Complaints[a] by Personality Type in the SLHS

Personality Type	Number of Subjects	Definite Alcoholic (row %)	Definite Depressed (row %)	4+ Bodily Pains (row %)	2+ GI Symptoms (row %)	Both Pains + GI (row %)
Personality Disorders						
Antisocial	26	38	8	12	4	0
Borderline	37	43	46	32	32	14
Other Impulsive	32	19	50	6	25	3
Not Impulsive	46	15	54	15	28	9
Any Possible	131	17	30	10	21	5
Mature Types						
Adventurous	60	13	7	2	15	0
Other	468	9	6	7	14	3
Totals	800	14	17	9	17	4

Columns 4–8 grouped under "Multiple Somatic Complaints".

[a]Alcoholism based on SMAST; depression definite with CES-D score of 21 or more; four or more bodily pains and two or more GI complaints as seen in irritable bowel syndrome are characteristic of somatization disorder.

(Cleckley, 1964; Hare, 1978). Both of these observations were supported by findings about anxiety and depressive symptoms in the SLHS. The prevalence of definite depression according to the CES-D scale was about 8% in those with antisocial personality disorder, which is similar to that in mature personality types (6% to 7%) and much lower than in other personality disorders (46% to 54%). Likewise, using a more restrictive criterion for anxiety and depressive disorders based on the MHI-5, 4% of those with ASPD were ill, which is about the same as in mature individuals and much lower than in those with other personality disorders (31% to 46%). The rate of anxiety disorders in ASPD was lower than in all others both for cases with (0% vs. 4%) or without (4% vs. 8%) a history of panic attacks. The lifetime prevalence of either specific (23% vs. 25%) or social (19% vs. 18%) phobias was about the same in those with antisocial personality disorder as in mature people and about half that in those with other types of personality disorder (35% to 49% specific phobias and 25% to 57% social phobias).

Somatization

In contrast with the relative resistance to anticipatory worrying and anxiety in antisocial personality disorder, people with antisocial personality disorder are reportedly prone to multiple somatic complaints and, in some cases, somatization disorder (Cloninger & Guze, 1970a). Such somatization with little or no anticipatory anxiety may be associated with low tolerance for frustration and low endurance of pain in individuals with impulsive temperaments (Cloninger, 1988). Alternatively, somatization may be associated with immature character regardless of the temperament profile.

The diagnosis of somatization disorder in *DSM-IV* requires complaints of frequent pain in four or more body regions as well as two or more gastrointestinal symptoms, such as those reported in irritable bowel syndrome (Yutzy et al., 1995). Both the bodily pains and bowel complaints are necessary but not sufficient for the diagnosis of somatization disorder. Such complaints were evalu-

ated in the SLHS, as summarized in Table 2.6. Multiple somatic complaints were more frequent in cases of personality disorder than in mature individuals. In particular, the risk of four or more bodily pains was 18% in definite PD, 10% in possible PD, 6% in average individuals, and 5% in the most mature third of individuals. Multiple bodily pains occurred in 12% of those with antisocial personality disorder and only 2% of mature adventurous individuals. The combination of multiple bodily pains and irritable bowel complaints was common in those with borderline personalities (14%) but not in those with antisocial personalities (0%). This is explained by the additional observation that high Harm Avoidance was significantly correlated ($p < .001$) with the number ($r = .35$) and frequency ($r = .37$) of bodily pains as well as with the number ($r = .29$) and frequency ($r = .34$) of irritable bowel complaints. Furthermore, both high Harm Avoidance and low Self-directedness contributed significantly to the prediction of the number and frequency of bodily pains and irritable bowel complaints in multiple regression analyses. Similar associations with personality occurred regardless of gender, but women had higher rates of somatic complaints overall. In summary, somatization appears to covary with anxiety-proneness (i.e., high Harm Avoidance) and immature character in general (i.e., low Self-directedness) rather than a specific temperament profile or personality disorder subtype.

CONCLUSIONS

The SLHS is the first study of the clinical and epidemiological correlates of antisocial personality disorder in a general population in which all types of temperament and character variation were systematically assessed. The findings of this study allow resolution of several controversial issues about the epidemiology and Axis I comorbidity of ASPD. It also suggests conclusions about the basic concept of personality disorder.

First, personality disorders are not discrete diseases but clinically distinct and relatively stable configurations of multiple quantitative traits. No sharp natural boundary between disorder and maturity has ever been demonstrated for any personality disorder. Rather, there is quantitative variation in degree of character maturity, and about the bottom sixth of the population are sufficiently immature that they are distinguished as having a personality disorder. This distinction is not completely arbitrary or artificial, however. Studies of longitudinal development show that antisocial personality disorder is a moderately stable configuration in a complex adaptive network (N. M. Svrakic, D. M. Svrakic, & Cloninger, 1996). The dynamic interactions among multiple correlated dimensions make the antisocial personality syndrome more stable than intermediate or mixed configurations (Cloninger et al., 1994). Such stable multidimensional configurations make prevention and treatment difficult but not impossible.

Second, antisocial personality disorder is primarily a disorder of young men. With increasing age, Novelty Seeking decreases and the character traits of Self-directedness and Cooperativeness increase. These changes lead to improvement or remission of ASPD in many cases, as has been previously documented in longitudinal studies.

Third, antisocial personality disorder should be distinguished from borderline personality disorder, although both are partly characterized by impulsivity (i.e., high Novelty Seeking) and social detachment (i.e., low Reward Dependence). Borderline personality disorder is strongly associated with failure to graduate from high school, underemployment, anxiety, depression, somatization, and suicide attempts. In contrast, the associations of antisocial personality disorder with these psychosocial problems is weak at most, in contrast to the conclusions of prior studies that did not distinguish antisocial and borderline personality disorders. These two disorders can be distinguished by variation in a single dimension of temperament: Harm Avoidance scores are low in antisocial personality disorder and high in borderline personality disorder. Consequently, borderline personality disorder is more likely to be associated with more severe immature character development and with fearful responses to stress, including anxiety, depression, and somatization. The distinction between antisocial and borderline personalities appears to correspond to the distinction between primary and secondary psychopathy in the older literature (Cleckley, 1964).

Fourth, all the impulsive personality disorders (antisocial, borderline, histrionic, and narcissistic) are at increased risk for substance abuse, including alcoholism, cigarette smoking, and illegal drug use. The association between substance abuse and impulsive personality disorders is caused both by more frequent initiation and less frequent cessation of substance abuse for pleasant stimulation.

Finally, the current results are consistent with prior observations, if it is accepted that behavioral checklists for antisocial personality disorder, such as that in *DSM-IV*, allow overlap between antisocial and borderline personality disorders. More generally, the interpretation of the current findings is clearer than in prior work because of the availability of appropriate comparison groups, including both immature and mature personality types, within the same sample. Identification of all these subgroups within a sample of the general population provides assurance against the selection artifacts that confound interpretation of associations in treatment samples.

FUTURE WORK

The current findings demonstrate the ease and utility of recent improvements in case finding for all types of personality disorder. It no longer should be necessary to limit the diagnosis of personality disorders in large-scale epidemiological projects to antisocial personality disorder, as was necessary in the ECA study. The current findings show how important it is to assess personality comprehensively and quantitatively in order to understand the epidemiology and comorbidity of any particular syndrome.

A major limitation of the SLHS and most prior work on antisocial personality disorder is the small number of women with ASPD who have been studied. Although the public health problem involves primarily men, these women represent an extreme and highly informative risk group (see Giordano & Cernkovich, Chapter 46, this volume). This calls for much larger samples than the SLHS. Samples of 5,000 to 10,000 from the general population would be needed to ascertain 130 to 260 men and 20 to 40 women with antisocial personality disorder.

A developmental perspective is needed to understand the psychosocial problems associated with antisocial personality disorder (N. M. Svrakic et al., 1996). Large-scale longitudinal studies of individuals and family members are required to characterize the dynamic interactions of the many factors that influence the development of ASPD from childhood throughout adulthood.

Finally, public concern for violence and underemployment should lead to research on both antisocial and borderline personality disorders. Now that self-report measures are available that are quantitative and reliable for the differential diagnosis of all personality disorders, such studies do not require unusual expense for clinical assessment.

REFERENCES

American Psychiatric Association. (1994). *Diagnostic and statistical manual of mental disorders* (4th ed.). Washington, DC: Author.

Berkson, J. (1946). Limitations of the application of fourfold table analysis to hospital data. *Biometric Bulletin, 2*, 47–53.

Berwick, D. M., Murphy, J. M., Goldman, P. A., Ware, J. E., Jr., Barsky, A. J., & Weinstein, M. C. (1991). Performance of a five-item mental health screening test. *Medical Care, 29*, 169–176.

Bohman, M., Cloninger, C. R., von Knorring, A. L., & Sigvardsson, S. (1984). An adoption study of somatoform disorders: III. Cross-fostering analysis and genetic relationship to alcoholism and criminality. *Archives of General Psychiatry, 41*, 872–878.

Cleckley, H. (1964). *The mask of sanity* (4th ed.). St. Louis: Mosby.

Cloninger, C. R. (1987a). A systematic method for clinical description and classification of personality variants: A proposal. *Archives of General Psychiatry, 44*, 573–588.

Cloninger, C. R. (1987b). Neurogenetic adaptive mechanisms in alcoholism. *Science, 236*, 410–416.

Cloninger, C. R. (1988). A unified biosocial theory of personality and its role in the development of anxiety states: A reply to commentaries. *Psychiatric Development, 6*, 83–120.

Cloninger, C. R., & Guze, S. B. (1970a). Psychiatric illness and female criminality: The role of sociopathy and hysteria in the antisocial woman. *American Journal of Psychiatry, 127*, 303–311.

Cloninger, C. R., & Guze, S. B. (1970b). Female criminals: their personal, familial, and social backgrounds (the relations of these to the diagnoses of sociopathy and hysteria). *Archives of General Psychiatry, 23,* 554–558.

Cloninger, C. R., & Guze, S. B. (1973a). Psychiatric illness in the families of female criminals: A study of 288 first-degree relatives. *British Journal of Psychiatry, 122,* 697–703.

Cloninger, C. R., & Guze, S. B. (1973b). Psychiatric disorders and criminal recidivism: A follow-up study of female criminals. *Archives of General Psychiatry, 29,* 266–269.

Cloninger, C. R., Przybeck, T. R., & Svrakic, D. M. (1991). The tridimensional personality questionnaire: U.S. normative data. *Psychological Reports, 69,* 1047–1057.

Cloninger, C. R., Przybeck, T. R., Svrakic, D. M., & Wetzel, R. D. (1994). *The Temperament and Character Inventory (TCI): A guide to its development and use.* St. Louis: Washington University Center for Psychobiology of Personality.

Cloninger, C. R., Reich, T., & Guze, S. B. (1975a). The multifactorial model of disease transmission: I. Sex differences in the familial transmission of sociopathy (antisocial personality). *British Journal of Psychiatry, 127,* 11–22.

Cloninger, C. R., Reich, T., & Guze, S. B. (1975b). The multifactorial model of disease transmission: III. Familial relationship between sociopathy and hysteria (Briquet's syndrome). *British Journal of Psychiatry, 127,* 23–32.

Cloninger, C. R., Sigvardsson, S., Bohman, M., & von Knorring, A. L. (1982). Predisposition to petty criminality in Swedish adoptees: II. Cross-fostering analysis of gene-environment interaction. *Archives of General Psychiatry, 39,* 1242–1247.

Cloninger, C. R., Sigvardsson, S., Przybeck, T. R., & Svrakic, D. M. (1995). Personality antecedents of alcoholism in a national area probability sample. *European Archives of Psychiatry and Clinical Neuroscience, 245,* 239–244.

Cloninger, C. R., Svrakic, D. M., & Przybeck, T. R. (1993). A psychobiological model of temperament and character. *Archives of General Psychiatry, 50,* 975–990.

Crowe, R. R. (1972). The adopted offspring of women criminal offenders. *Archives of General Psychiatry, 27,* 600–603.

Goldman, R. G., Skodal, A. E., McGrath, P. J., & Oldham, J. M. (1994). Relationship between the Tridimensional Personality Questionnaire and *DSM-III-R* personality traits. *American Journal of Psychiatry, 151,* 274–276.

Goodwin, D. W., & Guze, S. B. (1984). *Psychiatric diagnosis* (3rd ed., pp. 209–225). New York: Oxford University Press.

Hare, R. D. (1978). Electrodermal and cardiovascular correlates of psychopathy. In R. D. Hare & D. Schalling (Eds.), *Psychopathic behavior: Approaches to research.* (pp. 107–144). New York: Wiley.

Lewis, C. E., Helzer, J., Cloninger, C. R., Croughan, J. L., & Whitman, B. (1982). Psychiatric diagnostic predispositions to alcoholism. *Comprehensive Psychiatry, 23,* 451–461.

Livesley, W. J. (1987). A systematic approach to the delineation of personality disorders. *American Journal of Psychiatry, 144,* 772–777.

Martin, R. L., Cloninger, C. R., & Guze, S. B. (1982). The natural history of somatization and substance abuse in women criminals: A six year follow-up. *Comprehensive Psychiatry, 23,* 528–537.

Martin, R. L., Cloninger, C. R., Guze, S. B., & Clayton, P. J. (1985). Mortality in a follow-up of 500 psychiatric outpatients: I. Total mortality. *Archives of General Psychiatry, 42,* 47–56.

Myers, J. L., & Weissman, M. M. (1980). Use of a self-report symptom scale to detect depression in a community sample. *American Journal of Psychiatry, 137,* 1081–1084.

Radloff, L. S. (1977). The CES-D Scale: A self-report depression scale for research in the general population. *Applied Psychological Measurement, 1,* 385–401.

Robins, L. N. (1966). *Deviant children grown up: A sociological and psychiatric study of sociopathic personality.* Baltimore: Williams & Wilkins.

Robins, L. N. (1978). Sturdy childhood predictors of adult outcomes: Replications from longitudinal studies. *Psychological Medicine, 8,* 611–622.

Robins, L. N., & Regier, D. A. (Eds.). (1991). *Psychiatric disorders in America: The Epidemiologic Catchment Area study.* New York: Free Press.

Robins, L. N., Tipp, J., & Przybeck, T. (1991). Antisocial personality. In L. N. Robins & D. A. Regier (Eds.), *Psychiatric disorders in America: The Epidemiologic Catchment Area study* (pp. 258–290). New York: Free Press.

Schulsinger, F. (1972). Psychopathy: Heredity and environment. In M. Roff, L. N. Robins, & M. Pollack (Eds.), *Life history research in psychopathology* (pp. 190–206). Minneapolis: University of Minnesota Press.

Selzer, M. L., Vinokur, A., & van Rooijen, L. (1975). A self-administered short Michigan Alcoholism Screening Test (SMAST). *Journal of Studies on Alcohol, 36,* 117–126.

Sigvardsson, S., Bohman, M., & Cloninger, C. R. (1987). Structure and stability of childhood personality: Prediction of later social adjustment. *Journal of Child Psychology and Psychiatry, 28,* 929–946.

Sigvardsson, S., Cloninger, C. R., Bohman, M., & von Knorring, A. L. (1982). Predisposition to petty criminality in Swedish adoptees: III. Sex differences and validation of the male typology. *Archives of General Psychiatry, 39,* 1248–1253.

Stewart, A. L., Hays, R. D., & Ware, J. E., Jr. (1988). The MOS Short-form General Health Survey: Reliability and validity in a patient population. *Medical Care, 26,* 724–735.

Svrakic, D. M., Whitehead, C., Przybeck T. R., & Cloninger, C. R. (1993). Differential diagnosis of personality disorders by the seven factor model of temperament and character. *Archives of General Psychiatry, 50,* 991–999.

Svrakic, N. M., Svrakic, D. M., & Cloninger, C. R. (1996). A general quantitative theory of personality development: Fundamentals of a self-organizing psychobiological complex. *Development and Psychopathology, 8,* 242–273.

Tremblay, R. E., Pihl, R. O., Vitaro, F., & Dobkin, P. L. (1994). Predicting early onset of male antisocial behavior from preschool behavior. *Archives of General Psychiatry, 51,* 732–739.

Trull, T. (1992). *DSM-III-R* personality disorders and the five factor model of personality: An empirical comparison. *Journal of Abnormal Psychology, 101,* 553–560.

Waller, N. G., & Zavala, J. (1993). Evaluating the Big Five. *Psychological Inquiry, 4,* 131–134.

Wills, T. A., Vaccaro, D., & McNamara, G. (1994). Novelty Seeking, risk taking, and related constructs as predictors of adolescent substance use: An application of Cloninger's theory. *Journal of Substance Abuse, 6,* 1–20.

Yutzy, S. H., Cloninger, C. R., Guze, S. B., Pribor, E. F., Martin, R. L., Kathol, R. G., Smith, G. R., & Strain, J. J. (1995). *DSM-IV* field trial: Testing a new proposal for somatization disorder. *American Journal of Psychiatry, 152,* 97–101.

CHAPTER 3

Psychopathy: Assessment and Association With Criminal Conduct

STEPHEN D. HART and ROBERT D. HARE

In this chapter, we discuss the assessment of psychopathy and the link between psychopathy and criminal conduct. Although the association between psychopathy and crime is strong and, in terms of social policy, important, we want to make it clear from the outset that they are distinct. *Psychopathy* is a personality disorder: a form of chronic mental disorder associated with a specific set of symptoms that impairs psychosocial functioning in a relatively small number of people in society. One important symptom of psychopathy is persistent, frequent, and varied asocial and antisocial behavior, starting at an early age (American Psychiatric Association, 1980, 1994; Hare, 1970, 1993). *Criminal conduct,* on the other hand, refers to behavior that causes significant (potential) harm to others and violates "deeply held and widely shared norms" (Andrews & Bonta, 1993, p. 1). Criminal conduct is much more common in society than psychopathy; indeed, it may even be normative for people to engage in isolated instances of less serious criminal conduct. For example, studies of teenage boys in North America and the United Kingdom have found that more than 50% admit to having committed one or more criminal offenses in the past (see Andrews & Bonta, 1993; Blackburn, 1993).

One aspect of the link between psychopathy and crime is clear: Many psychopaths engage in chronic criminal conduct and do so at a high rate, whereas only a small minority of those who engage in criminal conduct are psychopaths. This means that psychopaths are responsible for a disproportionate amount of crime in our society. There are other aspects to the link as well. Psychopaths are qualitatively different from others who routinely engage in criminal conduct, different even from those whose criminal conduct is extremely serious and persistent. They have distinctive "criminal careers" with respect to the number and type of antisocial behaviors they commit as well as the ages at which they commit them. Furthermore, it appears that the antisocial behavior of psychopaths is motivated by different factors than that of nonpsychopaths, with the result that the

behavioral topography of their criminal conduct (i.e., their victimology or modus operandi) also is different. The personality and social psychological factors that explain antisocial behavior in general (see Andrews & Bonta, 1993; Gottfredson & Hirschi, 1990; Wilson & Herrnstein, 1985) may not be applicable to psychopaths. Consequently, any comprehensive examination of crime must include a discussion of the distinctive role of psychopathy.

We begin with a discussion of issues surrounding the assessment of psychopathy, with special emphasis on the distinction between psychopathy, as defined by the criteria in the original and revised Psychopathy Checklist (PCL and PCL-R; Hare, 1980, 1991), and antisocial personality disorder (ASPD), as defined in the fourth edition of the *Diagnostic and Statistical Manual of Mental Disorders* (*DSM-IV;* American Psychiatric Association, 1994). The reasons for this are, first, psychopathy and ASPD are often treated as, but in fact are not, equivalent diagnoses; second, not all criminals are psychopaths or have ASPD, and not all those with ASPD are psychopaths; and, third, the association between psychopathy and criminal conduct becomes clear only when the disorder is assessed with reliable and valid procedures. We then turn to a review of research on the association between psychopathy and crime, most of it based on studies using the PCL and PCL-R.

THE ASSESSMENT OF PSYCHOPATHY: SOME IMPORTANT ISSUES

Clinical Features

Psychopathy—sometimes referred to as *antisocial, sociopathic,* or *dyssocial personality disorder*—is a specific form of personality disorder with a distinctive pattern of interpersonal, affective, and behavioral symptoms. Modern clinical descriptions of the psychopath have been consistent over time, beginning with Hervey Cleckley's *The Mask of Sanity* (1941), and continuing up to the present day; these clinical descriptions also are representative of the views of researchers and clinicians (see Cooke, Forth, & Hare, in press; Hare, 1970, 1993). We can summarize the descriptions as follows: Interpersonally, psychopaths are grandiose, arrogant, callous, superficial, and manipulative; affectively, they are short-tempered, unable to

Preparation of this chapter was supported by a BC Health Research Foundation Grant to Robert D. Hare and a SFU President's Research Award to Stephen D. Hart. The views expressed here are those of the authors and do not necessarily reflect those of the funding agencies.

form strong emotional bonds with others, and lacking in empathy, guilt, or remorse; and behaviorally, they are irresponsible, impulsive, and prone to violate social and legal norms and expectations.

Psychopathy Versus ASPD: Two Conceptual Traditions

Although little debate has centered on the key features of psychopathy, in recent years there has been disagreement concerning how best to diagnose the disorder. Two major approaches have influenced clinical practice and empirical research (Hare, Hart, & Harpur, 1991; Lilienfeld, 1994). One approach stems naturally from the rich European and North American clinical tradition associated with the construct of psychopathy—reflected in the criteria for dyssocial personality in the *International Classification of Diseases,* 10th edition (ICD-10; World Health Organization [WHO], 1992), and in the writings of, among others, Hervey Cleckley (1941, 1976)—and from the efforts of researchers to provide a sound psychometric basis for operationalizing the construct (Hare, 1970, 1980, 1991; Hart, Cox, & Hare, 1995). The other approach, part of the neo-Kraepelinian movement in psychodiagnosis, is closely associated with work emanating from Washington University in St. Louis, Missouri (e.g., Feighner et al., 1972; Robins, 1966).

Clinical Tradition and the PCL

An adequate diagnosis of psychopathy must be based on the full range of relevant symptomatology. A focus on behavioral symptoms (e.g., irresponsibility, delinquency) to the exclusion of inferred interpersonal and affective symptoms (e.g., grandiosity, callousness, deceitfulness, shallow affect, lack of remorse) may lead to the overdiagnosis of psychopathy in criminal populations and underdiagnosis in noncriminals (Hare, Hart, & Harpur, 1991; Lilienfeld, 1994; Widiger & Corbitt, 1995). We have spent considerable effort over the past 15 years developing and validating rating scales that tap the key features of psychopathy. To ensure accurate diagnosis, we believe that psychopathy should be assessed using expert observer (i.e., clinical) ratings, based on a review of case history materials—

such as interviews with family members and employers, criminal and psychiatric records, and so forth—and supplemented with interviews or behavioral observations whenever possible (Hare, 1991).

The original PCL (Hare, 1980) was a 22-item rating scale, later revised and shortened to 20 items (PCL-R; Hare, 1991). The PCL and PCL-R were designed for use in adult male forensic populations. Items are scored on a 3-point scale (0 = item does not apply, 1 = item applies somewhat, 2 = item definitely applies). As the two scales are highly correlated (Hare et al., 1990), we focus here on the PCL-R. Table 3.1 lists the PCL-R items, which are defined in detail in the test manual. Total scores can range from 0 to 40 and reflect the extent to which an individual matches the "prototypical" psychopath; scores of 30 or higher are considered diagnostic of psychopathy. The PCL and PCL-R have a reliable internal structure comprising two oblique factors, correlated about $r = .50$; Factor 1 reflects the interpersonal and affective features of psychopathy ("callous and remorseless use of others"), and Factor 2 reflects antisocial behavior ("chronically unstable and antisocial lifestyle"; Hare et al., 1990; Harpur, Hakstian, & Hare, 1988; Harpur, Hare, & Hakstian, 1989).

The PCL and PCL-R were designed for use with adult male prison inmates and forensic psychiatric patients in Canada and the United States, and much of the research validating the scales has been conducted in these populations (see reviews by Fulero, 1995; Stone, 1995). The scales also have been used successfully in other populations, including adult male European offenders (e.g., Cooke, 1995, 1996; Cooke & Michie, 1997; Haapasalo & Pulkkinen, 1992; Raine, 1985), young male offenders (e.g., Chandler & Moran, 1990; Forth, Hart, & Hare, 1990; Trevethan & Walker, 1989), adult female offenders (e.g., Loucks & Zamble, 1994; Strachan & Hare, 1997), and various groups of nonoffenders (e.g., Alterman, Cacciola, & Rutherford, 1993; Cooney, Kadden, & Litt, 1990; Forth, Brown, Hart, & Hare, 1996; af Klinteberg, Humble, & Schalling, 1992; Rutherford, Cacciola, Alterman, & McKay, 1996; Stanford, Ebner, Patton, & Williams, 1994). Recent work by Cooke and his colleagues (Cooke, 1995, 1996; Cooke & Michie, 1997), using Item Response Theory (IRT), indicates that the

TABLE 3.1   Items in the Hare Psychopathy Checklist–Revised (PCL-R)

Factor 1: Interpersonal or Affective	Factor 2: Social Deviance	Additional Items[a]
1. Glibness or superficial charm 2. Grandiose sense of self-worth 4. Pathological lying 5. Conning or manipulative 6. Lack of remorse or guilt 7. Shallow affect 8. Callous or lack of empathy 16. Failure to accept responsibility for own actions	3. Need for stimulation or proneness to boredom 9. Parasitic lifestyle 10. Poor behavioral controls 12. Early behavioral problems 13. Lack of realistic, long-term goals 14. Impulsivity 15. Irresponsibility 18. Juvenile delinquency 19. Revocation of conditional release	11. Promiscuous sexual behavior 17. Many short-term marital relationships 20. Criminal versatility

Note: The rater uses specific criteria, interview, and file information to score each item on a three-point scale (0, 1, 2).
[a]Items that do not load on either factor.
From Hare (1991).

PCL-R and the construct it purports to measure are generalizable across different populations and cultures. A new scale, the Screening Version of the PCL-R (PCL:SV; Hart, Cox, & Hare, 1995), has been developed for use with noncriminals and as a screen for psychopathy in criminal populations.

Normative data presented in the PCL-R manual (Hare, 1991) include ratings from seven samples of offenders ($N = 1,192$) and four samples of forensic patients ($N = 440$), all adult men (aged 16 or older) from institutions in Canada, the United States, and the United Kingdom. Analyses based on classical test theory indicate that the PCL-R has excellent psychometric properties. For example, the items have good validity (corrected item-total correlations), and total scores have high internal consistency (Cronbach's alpha) and item homogeneity (mean inter-item correlation). IRT analyses have yielded similarly positive results (Cooke & Michie, 1997). Furthermore, the interrater reliability of individual items is acceptable, and the interrater and test-retest reliabilities of total scores, as well as diagnoses based on those scores, range from good to excellent, particularly when based on average scores across two independent raters (see also Alterman et al., 1993). Finally, total scores on both scales have good dispersion across various settings, suggesting that they are capable of detecting variations in psychopathic traits even within populations in which serious antisocial behavior is very common (e.g., incarcerated offenders, forensic patients).

The Washington University Tradition: DSM Criteria for ASPD

The Washington University tradition is based on a number of influential works written by people who worked or trained at that institution. One of the fundamental assumptions of this approach is that assessment should focus on publicly observable behaviors, as clinicians are incapable of reliably assessing interpersonal and affective characteristics (Robins, 1978). Another assumption is that early-onset delinquency is a cardinal symptom of the disorder, one that helps to differentiate ASPD from adult antisocial behavior and from major mental illnesses. These assumptions account for the heavy emphasis on delinquent and antisocial behavior in criteria sets based on this tradition. We review the ASPD criteria only briefly here; for further discussion, see Lilienfeld, Purcell, and Jones-Alexander (Chapter 6, this volume).

The Washington University tradition is reflected primarily in the criteria for ASPD contained in the third and subsequent editions of the *DSM* (American Psychiatric Association, 1980, 1987, 1994). These criteria can be described as fixed and explicit. The *DSM-IV* lists four major criteria, two of which contain multiple subcriteria: (a) antisocial behavior since age 18; (b) current age at least 18; (c) conduct disorder before age 15; and (d) occurrence not limited to periods of schizophrenia or mania. The criteria are monothetic in nature: Each one is necessary and together they are jointly sufficient to diagnose ASPD.

The content of the *DSM-III* ASPD criteria was decided by a committee of the American Psychiatric Association's *DSM-III* Task Force and revised slightly by another committee for the *DSM-III-R* (Widiger, Frances, Pincus, Davis, & First, 1991). The *DSM-IV* criteria also were decided by committee, based only to a limited extent on the results of empirical research (Hare & Hart, 1994; Widiger & Corbitt, 1995).

The ASPD criteria do not constitute a scale or test. They have no response format per se, they do not yield a score, and they do not have norms. Rather, the assessor determines if each (sub)criterion is present/true or absent/false. The final decision is dichotomous: If the criteria are all present, then a lifetime diagnosis of ASPD is made; if one or more are absent, no such diagnosis is made. The *DSM* also does not specify a particular method for assessing ASPD. In the empirical literature, researchers have employed methods ranging from structured interview to semistructured interview plus a review of case history information to file review alone.

With respect to reliability, the *DSM-IV* criteria are too recent to have been the focus of published research. Even the *DSM-IV* ASPD field trial provided no useful information in this respect, because the ASPD criteria as they appear in *DSM-IV* were never actually tested in the field trial (Hare & Hart, 1995). As a consequence, we must infer the reliability of *DSM-IV* from research on the *DSM-III-R* criteria. In general, this research indicates that the interrater and test-retest reliability of ASPD diagnoses is good to excellent (Widiger & Corbitt, 1995).

Association Between PCL and DSM Criteria

Although here we emphasize the conceptual differences between criteria sets based on the two traditions, readers should keep in mind that the empirical associations between them are quite strong. The correlations between PCL-R scores and ASPD diagnoses or symptom counts typically are large in magnitude (about $r = .55$ to .65) and diagnostic agreement between the procedures typically is fair to good, even in forensic settings (e.g., Hare, 1980, 1985; Widiger et al., 1996). The disorders have different prevalence rates, however. According to DSM criteria, anywhere between 50% and 80% of offenders and forensic patients are diagnosed as ASPD, whereas only about 15% to 30% of the same people meet the PCL-R criteria for psychopathy (Hare, 1983, 1985; Hare et al., 1991; Robins, Tipp, & Przybeck, 1991). This has led many observers to criticize the *DSM* criteria for confounding ASPD with general criminality (see Hare, 1996a; Hare et al., 1991; Hare & Hart, 1995; Widiger et al., 1996). Indeed, *DSM-IV* itself explicitly acknowledges that a diagnosis of ASPD in forensic settings may need to be supplemented with inferences about the personality traits measured by the PCL-R (American Psychiatric Association, 1994, p. 647). Another important point is that the empirical link between psychopathy and ASPD is asymmetric: Most criminals (about 90%) diagnosed as psychopaths by PCL-R criteria meet the criteria for ASPD, whereas a minority (about 30%) of those with ASPD meet PCL-R criteria for psychopathy (e.g., Hart & Hare, 1989).

Construct-Related Validity of PCL and DSM Criteria

The PCL and PCL-R have a clear pattern of convergent and discriminant validities, the interpretation of which is greatly clarified by analysis of the two-factor structure of the scales. There is a significant association between psychopathy and substance use; however, this association is due primarily to the second (antisocial behavior) factor (Hemphill, Hart, & Hare, 1994; Smith & Newman, 1990). Similarly, the PCL scales correlate positively with *DSM-III-R* personality disorders from the "dramatic-erratic-emotional" cluster (Cluster B) and negatively with several personality disorders from the "anxious-fearful" cluster (Cluster C). The first factor of the PCL-R (interpersonal and affective symptoms) correlates positively with narcissistic and histrionic personality disorder and negatively with avoidant and dependent personality disorder; the second factor correlates positively with antisocial and borderline personality disorder (Hart & Hare, 1989). The factors also have distinct patterns of correlations with self-report measures of personality: Factor 1 correlates negatively with anxiety and empathy and positively with narcissism and dominance; Factor 2 correlates positively with sensation seeking and impulsivity and negatively with nurturance (Harpur et al., 1989; Harpur, Hart, & Hare, 1993; Hart, Forth, & Hare, 1991; Hart & Hare, 1994). Similar results have been found using projective measures (e.g., Gacono & Meloy, 1991; Gacono, Meloy, & Heaven, 1990). The PCL scales have good clinical specificity with respect to acute (i.e., *DSM-III-R* Axis I) mental disorders, both in absolute terms (Hart & Hare, 1989; Raine, 1986; Rice & Harris, 1995a) and relative to other measures (Howard, Bailey, & Newman, 1984).

As noted previously, numerous experimental investigations support the experimental validity of the PCL scales. Although no evidence has been found that psychopaths suffer from gross cerebral impairment (Hare, 1984; Hart, Forth, & Hare, 1990; Smith, Arnett, & Newman, 1992), they have impulsive and perhaps even impaired performance on cognitive tasks related to passive-avoidance learning (Howland, Kosson, Patterson, & Newman, 1993; LaPierre, Braun, & Hodgins, 1995; Newman & Kosson, 1986; Newman, Kosson, & Patterson, 1992; Newman, Patterson, Howland, & Nichols, 1991; Newman, Patterson, & Kosson, 1987). Jutai and Hare (1983) suggested that psychopaths are adept at focusing their attention but have difficulty with tasks that require divided attention, a view supported by more recent work (e.g., Harpur & Hare, 1990; Kosson & Newman, 1986). Hare and Craigen (1974) found that psychopaths also exhibit unusual patterns of physiological arousal, particularly in anticipation of noxious stimuli (also see Arnett, Howland, Smith, & Newman, 1993; Forth & Hare, 1989; Larbig, Veit, Rau, Schlottke, & Birbaumer, 1992; Ogloff & Wong, 1990; Raine & Venables, 1988a, 1988b). Hare (1978) interpreted this pattern of anticipatory physiological arousal as evidence of an adaptive coping response that helps psychopaths to ignore selectively cues of impending punishment but that also makes them susceptible to overfocusing on reward cues. Research also indicates that psychopaths have abnormal or weakly lateralized linguistic functions and that they give unusual behavioral and physiological responses to affective stimuli (Hare & Jutai, 1988; Hare & McPherson, 1984a; Hare, Williamson, & Harpur, 1988; Intrator et al., in press; Patrick, Bradley, & Lang, 1993; Patrick, Cuthbert, & Lang, 1994; Patrick & Erickson, 1994; Williamson, Harpur, & Hare, 1991). Finally, it is worth noting here that the construct validity of psychopathy does not seem to be unduly affected by race or culture (Cooke, 1995, 1996; Kosson, Smith, & Newman, 1990; Wong, 1985).

Relative to the PCL scales, the construct-related validity of the DSM criteria is weak. Once again, because the *DSM-IV* criteria are new and have not been the subject of published research, our comments are limited to research using the *DSM-III* and *-III-R* criteria. A rather large body of literature examines the association between ASPD and substance use. Probably the most common findings are that ASPD is significantly comorbid with substance use disorders and that substance use patients with ASPD are more socially deviant or have worse treatment outcomes than other patients (e.g., Woody & McLellan, 1985). Another common finding is that ASPD frequently is comorbid with other personality disorders, particularly borderline

personality disorder (e.g., Widiger, Frances, Harris et al., 1991; see also Zanarini & Gunderson, Chapter 8, this volume). These findings are not inconsistent with clinical views of psychopathy and thus can be considered evidence supporting the concurrent validity of ASPD, although the comorbidity with substance use may be great enough to impede differential diagnosis (Gerstley, Alterman, McLellan, & Woody, 1990). However, there also is evidence of unexpected or theoretically inconsistent comorbidity, such as overlap with obsessive-compulsive disorder, schizophrenia, and bipolar mood disorder (Boyd et al., 1984; Robins et al., 1991; Swanson, Bland, & Newman, 1995). There is little systematic experimental evidence to support the validity of the *DSM* criteria. Other reviewers (e.g., Widiger & Corbitt, 1995) have referred to a body of literature that includes biochemical, genetic, and adoption studies; however, because many (if not most) of these studies did not use *DSM* criteria and as the equivalence of *DSM-III(-R)* with the other criteria used in these studies is questionable (Widiger et al., 1996), their relevance is unclear.

Assessment via Self-Report

Although highly structured methods that rely on self-reports of behavior and attitudes may be useful for the assessment of many aspects of normal and pathological personality, such methods are less appropriate for the assessment of psychopathy (Hare, Forth, & Hart, 1989; Hart et al., 1991; Lilienfeld, 1994). First, most self-reports have limited applicability to forensic populations. For example, few of the major personality inventories have separate norms for correctional offenders or forensic psychiatric patients. Second, self-reports cannot adequately assess and control for the effects of deceitfulness, a key clinical feature of psychopathy. Third, self-report measures of psychopathy are strongly influenced by the respondent's emotional state at the time of assessment. Fourth, the content of self-report measures of psychopathy is problematic. Most tend to focus on overt delinquent and antisocial acts, to the exclusion of interpersonal and affective symptoms of psychopathy; others contain items that are theoretically unrelated to or even inconsistent with the disorder (e.g., sexual dysfunction, feelings of guilt).

Several studies that used popular psychological tests—such as the Minnesota Multiphasic Personality Inventory (MMPI; Hathaway & McKinley, 1940), the Millon Clinical Multiaxial Inventory (MCMI-II; Millon, 1987), and the California Psychological Inventory (CPI; Gough, 1957)—have found low to moderate correlations, typically between $r = .30$ and $r = .45$, between the various psychopathy-related scales in these inventories and clinical diagnoses based on PCL-R or *DSM* criteria (e.g., Cooney et al., 1990; Hare, 1985, 1991; Hart et al., 1991). These results are not simply the result of method variance, as the correlations among different psychopathy-related scales are as low as the correlations between these scales and clinical diagnoses (Hare, 1985). Further, most psychopathy-related self-report scales tend to be biased in their assessment of psychopathy, correlating more highly with the social deviance components—as measured by PCL-R Factor 2—than with the interpersonal/affective components of the disorder—as measured by PCL-R Factor 1 (e.g., Harpur et al., 1989; Hart et al., 1991). This may reflect a bias in the content of self-reports, as suggested earlier, but it also may reflect a tendency for psychopaths to be poor observers or reporters of their own interpersonal and emotional styles.

We do not mean to imply that self-report measures of psychopathy are without value. They can be useful in preparing clinical reports, uncovering research leads, and preliminary testing of various hypotheses about psychopathy (e.g., Blackburn, 1987, 1993; Widiger et al., 1996). They also can facilitate research with nonforensic (i.e., community, civil psychiatric) populations, for which the correlations between self-report and clinical methods tend to be somewhat higher than in clinical or forensic settings (Forth et al., 1996; Gustafson & Ritzer, 1995; Levenson, Kiehl, & Fitzpatrick, 1995). The Self-Report Psychopathy–II scale (SRP-II; Hare, 1991, 1996c), based on the PCL-R, has been used in numerous studies with noncriminals (e.g., Forth et al., 1996; Gustafson & Ritzer, 1995) and formed part of the *DSM-IV* field trial for ASPD (Widiger et al., 1996). However, scores on self-report scales for psychopathy should not be confused with clinical or behavioral assessments based on reliable and valid criteria for the disorder.

Dimensional Versus Categorical Construct

Is psychopathy a dimensional or a categorical construct? There is no clear answer to this question. If dimensional, then psychopathic traits exist in everyone to a greater or lesser degree; if categorical, then psychopaths are both quantitatively and qualitatively different from nonpsychopaths. Research using the PCL scales suggests that the association between dimensional scores and variables related to criminal behavior, for the most part, is near linear (i.e., positive and monotonic and reasonably linear according to statistical models; see later). This could be interpreted as support for a dimensional model. However, more recent and sophisticated analyses have discovered nonlinear aspects to the association, suggesting that underlying the PCL scales is a distinct clinical entity, or taxon (David Cooke, personal communication, July 1996; Harris, Rice, & Quinsey, 1994).

Taxonomic research has implications for the selection of cutoff scores for the diagnosis of psychopathy. Harris et al. (1994) scored the PCL-R from file information (no interview data) and used statistical procedures that allowed the emergence of only two groups or classes of patients, those in the psychopathy taxon and those not in the taxon. They concluded that the optimal PCL-R score for inclusion in the psychopathy taxon was about 25, somewhat lower than the cutoff score of 30 recommended for research purposes (Hare, 1991). In contrast, Cooke's analyses of very large samples of offenders from several countries (Cooke, personal communication, July 1996) were based on PCL-R scores derived from both semistructured interviews and file information and on taxonometric procedures that allowed for the emergence of more than two classes of offenders. Each of his samples yielded three classes, one clearly being a psychopathy taxon. The optimal PCL-R score for inclusion in this taxon was between 28 and 32, in line with the recommended cutoffs for the diagnosis of psychopathy.

Some laboratory research has found evidence of abnormal cognitive and cortical processing that seems reasonably specific to psychopaths and consistent with the view of the disorder as a taxon (e.g., Intrator et al., in press; Patrick, Bradley, & Lang, 1993; Patrick, Cuthbert, & Lang, 1994; Williamson et al., 1991).

Whether or not psychopathy is a discrete clinical construct, the PCL scales lend themselves to both categorical and dimensional analyses. By way of analogy, even those who view mental retardation as a categorical construct may diagnose it by applying carefully selected cutoffs scores to dimensional measures of intelligence and adaptive behavior. Both categorical and dimensional

measures of personality disorder may be useful in different contexts. For example, categorical models facilitate communication and decision making, whereas dimensional models yield measures that have greater precision and reliability. Even if research provides a definite answer concerning the "true" nature of psychopathy, there likely still will be a need for both kinds of measures.

PSYCHOPATHY AND CRIMINAL CONDUCT: A REVIEW OF RESEARCH

In this section, we review some of the major studies looking at the association between psychopathy and criminal conduct, focusing on the PCL and PCL-R. Although the PCL scales were designed to facilitate laboratory research on psychopathy, not to predict criminal conduct, they have emerged as potent predictors of such conduct (for reviews, see Hart & Hare, 1996; Salekin, Rogers, & Sewell, 1996). In fact, the predictive power of the PCL scales is significant even after controlling for past offenses (e.g., by removing variance accounted for by measures of criminality or by eliminating items related to criminal history) and equal or superior to that of actuarial instruments designed solely to predict recidivism.

Age at Onset of Criminal Conduct

Psychopathic offenders start their criminal careers at a young age. Hare (1981, Study 1) assessed a sample of 200 inmates using global clinical ratings of psychopathy (a procedure that predated the development of but is highly correlated with the PCL and PCL-R). The mean age at first adult arrest was 18.1 for psychopaths and 20.0 for nonpsychopaths. Wong (1985) conducted a file review study of a random sample of 315 adult male offenders and found the average age at first arrest in a high psychopathy group (PCL total scores ≥ 30) was 17.8 years, compared to 24.1 years for a low psychopathy group (total scores ≤ 20). Devita, Forth, and Hare (1990) examined the age at onset of criminality in two samples of offenders (total $N = 422$). They also examined whether the onset of criminality was affected by the quality of the family environment in which offenders were raised. Overall, psychopaths were no more likely than nonpsychopaths to have been raised in a poor family environment. However, psychopaths were arrested at an earlier age than nonpsychopaths and had a higher rate of offending prior to age 20. The quality of family environment had little impact on the age at onset of criminality in psychopaths: On average, those from a troubled family were first arrested about age 12, whereas those from less troubled families were first arrested at age 13. In contrast, family environment had a dramatic impact on nonpsychopaths. Nonpsychopaths from troubled families were first arrested, on average, at age 15, compared to age 22 for those from less troubled families. Four other studies examined the association between psychopathy and age at onset of antisocial behavior, with mixed results. Smith and Newman (1990) found a correlation of $r = -.47$ between PCL-R scores and age at first delinquency in a sample of 360 adult male offenders; Forth et al. (1990), using a slightly modified version of the PCL-R to assess 75 delinquents incarcerated in a maximum-security facility, found a correlation of $r = -.25$ with age of first reported delinquency. Haapasalo (1994) administered a modified version of the PCL-R to a sample of 94

Finnish nonviolent offenders. The mean age at first adult arrest in high-, medium-, and low-psychopathy groups was 19.6, 22.5, and 22.7 years, respectively; however, the differences between groups were not statistically significant. Similarly, Brown and Forth (1995) studied 60 adult male rapists and found that PCL-R scores did not correlate significantly with age at first sex offense ($r = .06$) or with age at first nonsexual offense ($r = -.17$).

Density and Versatility of Offending

Psychopaths can be considered "high-density" offenders: They commit offenses at a relatively high rate when they are at risk (i.e., residing in the community and thus able to commit new offenses); they also commit a wide variety of offenses. In Hare's (1981, Study 1) sample of 200 offenders, retrospective analyses indicated that psychopaths had more offenses per year at risk than nonpsychopaths (5.5 vs. 3.7); the psychopaths also had more offenses during the postassessment follow-up (4.6 vs. 4.1). Wong (1985) found that high-psychopathy offenders had an average offense rate more than twice that of low-psychopathy offenders (4.4 vs. 1.9 offenses per year free, respectively). The rate of institutional misbehavior also was greater in high-psychopathy than in low-psychopathy offenders (6.3 vs. 0.7 offenses per year, respectively); this pattern held true for both violent and nonviolent misbehaviors.

Kosson, Smith, and Newman (1990, Study 3) found a strong association between psychopathy and criminality in samples of 230 White and 70 Black adult male offenders, even after omitting Item 20 of the PCL-R (criminal versatility). They compared the violent and nonviolent offenses of psychopaths and nonpsychopaths. Psychopaths committed about 50% more offenses than nonpsychopaths, and this difference did not vary significantly as a function of race or offense type. Subsequent reanalyses of the data (Hare, 1991) indicated that in both racial groups PCL-R scores correlated significantly with the total number of offenses ($r = .40$ for Whites and .30 for Blacks) and with the number of different types of charges ($r = .46$ for Whites and .35 for Blacks).

Cooke (1995) examined the prevalence of several mental disorders, including psychopathy, in a representative sample of 247 adult male and 61 adult female offenders in Scottish prisons. He used the PCL-R to assess psychopathy and examined its correlates with past crimes and past institutional misbehavior. In men, a diagnosis of psychopathy correlated $r = .20$ with general offending. With respect to subtypes of crime, psychopathy correlated $r = .17$ with major offending (e.g., serious violence, drugs) and $r = .11$ with minor offending (e.g., property crimes, mischief, minor assaults); however, the correlation with sexual offending was not significant. Psychopathy diagnoses also correlated $r = .21$ with general institutional misbehavior and, more specifically, $r = .23$ with institutional violence (e.g., assaults against staff). The association between psychopathy and criminality was strongest in serious offenders (i.e., those serving long prison terms); for example, in a subsample of 31 men serving life sentences, a diagnosis of psychopathy was correlated $r = .62$ and .78 with general offending and general institutional misbehavior, respectively. Cooke also examined the correlation between PCL-R scores and correctional officers' ratings of prisoner adjustment made using the Prison Behavior Rating Scale (PBRS), an adaptation of the Adult Inmate Management System (Quay, 1983), in a sample of 92 offenders.

The PBRS ratings were made blind to PCL-R scores. PCL-R scores correlated $r = .35$ with the PBRS Anti-Authority scale, but not with the Dull-Confused or Anxious-Depressed scales ($r = .12$ and .13, respectively). In a subsample of 20 men serving life sentences, the correlation between the PCL-R and the PBRS Anti-Authority scale was extremely high ($r = .68$).

In Cooke's (1995) sample of 61 female offenders, a diagnosis of psychopathy correlated $r = .35$ with general offending and $r = .30$ with minor offending; it also correlated $r = .37$ with general institutional misbehavior and $r = .48$ with violent misbehavior. In a subsample of 31 women serving sentences of 7 months or longer, the association was even stronger: Here, psychopathy correlated $r = .56$ with general offending and $r = .80$ with general institutional misbehavior.

In Haapasalo's (1994) study of nonviolent offenders, men in the high-psychopathy group had been convicted of significantly more offenses, on average, than had those in the medium- and low-psychopathy groups (means = 14.0, 12.4, and 9.2, respectively).

The association between psychopathy and criminality also is observed in special subgroups of offenders. Hare (1991), in a reanalysis of data from a study of 80 adult men remanded for pretrial psychiatric evaluations (Hart & Hare, 1989), found the following correlations between PCL-R scores and offense variables: total number of offenses, $r = .35$; nonviolent offense rate, $r = .41$; violent offense rate, $r = .41$; rate of imprisonment, $r = .37$; and total time in prison, $r = .33$. All variables were corrected for age and time at risk. Quinsey, Rice, and Harris (1995) administered the PCL-R to a sample of 178 sex offenders. PCL-R scores correlated significantly with the number of previous nonsexual offenses ($r = .35$) and with the number of previous sex offenses against women ($r = .43$) but not with other sex offenses. Similarly, Brown and Forth (1995), in a study of 60 adult male rapists, found that PCL-R scores correlated $r = .51$ with the number of prior nonsexual offenses but did not correlate with prior sex offenses ($r = -.02$). Finally, in the Forth et al. (1990) study of delinquents, modified PCL-R scores correlated $r = .27$ with prior violent offenses but only $r = .12$ with number of prior nonviolent offenses.

Criminal Careers

Hare and his colleagues have studied changes in the criminality of psychopaths across the lifespan (Hare, 1981; Hare & Jutai, 1983; Hare, Forth, & Strachan, 1992; Hare, McPherson, & Forth, 1988). The participants were adult male offenders in federal prisons who volunteered for various research projects over a 20-year period. Some were assessed using the PCL and PCL-R, and others were assessed using a global rating procedure. Various indexes of criminality were calculated for 5-year periods of each participant's life (e.g., ages 16 to 20, 21 to 25). Because participants were different ages at the initial assessment and were followed up over different periods of time, the study has both retrospective (i.e., follow-back) and prospective (follow-up) components. The most recent paper in the series (Hare et al., 1992) presented criminal history data collected on 204 psychopaths and 317 nonpsychopaths; of these, 35 psychopaths and 47 nonpsychopaths were followed up to age 50. The study examined a number of variables for each 5-year period, including the percentage of each group imprisoned, the mean percentage of time in prison, and the mean rates for violent and nonviolent offenses. Psychopaths were more criminally active than nonpsychopaths across all the variables studied, with the largest between-group differences in the younger age periods. In fact, by ages 45 to 50, psychopaths and nonpsychopaths were about equal with respect to criminal activity, at least insofar as nonviolent offense rates are concerned. Subsequent longitudinal analyses, based on the small subsample followed from ages 16 to 50, yielded similar findings. It is interesting to note that decreases in the nonviolent criminality of psychopaths paralleled the decreases in PCL/PCL-R Factor 2 scores observed in a cross-sectional study of psychopathy and age (see Harpur & Hare, 1994). In contrast, Factor 1 scores were unrelated to age, suggesting that the interpersonal and affective features of psychopathy may be much more stable over time than the social deviance components.

Violence

The studies just reviewed suggest that psychopaths have relatively high rates of violent offending in the community and in institutions. Hare (1981, Study 2) examined past violent behavior in 243 adult male offenders, assessed using global ratings of psychopathy. Subjects were divided into high-, medium-, and low-psychopathy groups; 97% of the high-psychopathy group had at least one conviction for a violent offense, compared to 78% of the medium- and 74% of the low-psychopathy groups. The high-psychopathy group also had significantly higher rates of conviction for armed robbery, robbery, and assault; and the high psychopathy group was more likely to have engaged in fights and aggressive homosexuality in prison.

Hare and McPherson (1984b) looked at the association between the PCL and past violence in a sample of 227 adult male offenders. To reduce circularity, they omitted two items related to aggression (i.e., poor behavior controls) and criminality (i.e., criminal versatility). The offenders were divided into high-, medium-, and low-psychopathy groups. Global ratings of violence (1 = low, 5 = high) were significantly correlated with scores on the PCL ($r = .46$; see Hare, 1991); the mean rates of violent offenses per year free were 1.00, 0.36, and 0.27, respectively, in the high-, medium-, and low-psychopathy groups. In the high-psychopathy group, 85% of participants had at least one conviction for a violent offense between ages 16 and 30, compared to 64% in the medium-psychopathy group and 54% in the low-psychopathy group. With respect to specific offenses, psychopathy was significantly associated with a history of convictions for possession of weapons, robbery, assault, kidnapping, vandalism, and fighting. Psychopathy also was associated with institutional violence: 86% of the high-psychopathy group had at least one recorded incident of violent misbehavior in their files, compared to 80% of the medium-psychopathy group and 55% of the low-psychopathy group. Significant differences were observed with respect to incidents of verbal abuse, verbal threats, irritability, belligerence, and fighting.

In a study of 87 adult male offenders, Serin (1991) found that 100% of psychopaths assessed using the PCL-R had prior convictions for violence, compared with 68% of other offenders. Heilbrun et al. (in press) reported a correlation of $r = .30$ between PCL scores and number of aggressive incidents during the first 2 months after admission in a sample of 218 adult male forensic patients.

Psychopaths not only engage in more violence than nonpsychopaths, they also seem to engage in different types of violence. Williamson, Hare, and Wong (1987) examined police reports concerning the violent offenses of a random sample of adult male inmates who had been assessed using the PCL. About two thirds of the victims of psychopaths were male strangers, whereas two thirds of the victims of nonpsychopaths were female family members or acquaintances. Furthermore, the violence of psychopaths seemed to be motivated primarily by revenge or retribution, whereas nonpsychopaths committed acts of violence while in a state of extreme emotional arousal. Cornell et al. (1996) examined instrumental (i.e., predatory) versus reactive (i.e., hostile, impulsive) violence in a sample of adult male offenders. They found that almost all violent offenders had a history of reactive violence but that a minority also had a history of instrumental violence. Instrumentally violent offenders had significantly higher PCL-R scores than offenders who had committed only reactive violence. Similar results were obtained by Dempster, Lyon, Sullivan, and Hart (1996). In addition, Dempster et al. examined partial correlations between the PCL-R factor scores and ratings of instrumental versus reactive violence in a sample of mentally disordered offenders. PCL-R Factor 1 scores were correlated significantly with ratings of instrumental violence (after partialing Factor 2), whereas Factor 2 scores were correlated with ratings of reactive violence (after partialing Factor 1).

Sexual Violence

Child Molesters Versus Rapists

Psychopathy seems to be related to certain aspects of sexual offending. For example, Prentky and Knight (1991) reported that rapists, on average, are significantly more likely to be psychopaths than are those who offend against children or adolescents. Four studies have examined this issue in more detail. Forth and Kroner (1994) looked at the PCL-R scores of 456 incarcerated adult male sex offenders. They found that incest offenders were least likely to be psychopathic; their mean PCL-R score (SD in parentheses) was 14.9 (7.0), and only 5% were diagnosed as psychopaths. Rapists were the most psychopathic, with a mean PCL-R score of 23.0 (7.8) and a base rate of psychopathy of 26%. The mean score in "mixed" offenders (i.e., men who had offended against both children and adult women) was 20.3 (8.5), and the base rate of psychopathy was 18%. Quinsey et al. (1995) examined 178 sex offenders assessed or treated at a forensic psychiatric hospital and found a similar pattern of results: The mean PCL-R score was 12.9 (6.3) for child molesters, 18.4 (9.2) for rapists, and 16.7 (7.9) for mixed offenders. Miller, Geddings, Levenston, and Patrick (1994), in a study of 60 adult male sex offenders in a treatment facility, found that rapists had a mean PCL-R score of 31.0 (8.3), compared to 22.8 (10.4) for those who had assaulted adolescents and 21.1 (8.3) for those who had assaulted children. The base rate of psychopathy in these three groups was 77%, 25%, and 15%, respectively. Serin, Malcolm, Khanna, and Barbaree (1994), in a study of 65 incarcerated adult male sexual offenders, found that rapists had a mean PCL-R score of 17.1 (8.6), compared to 13.2 (7.8) for child molesters. The base rate of psychopathy was 12% in rapists and 8% in child molesters.

Offender Subtypes

Within broad categories of offenders, psychopathy is associated with specific motivational or behavioral offense characteristics. Two studies have examined the association between the PCL-R and the MTC:R3 classification system for rapists (see Prentky & Knight, 1991). The MTC:R3 system identifies four major types of rapists—Vindictive, Opportunistic, Sadistic, and Nonsadistic—that comprise nine subtypes. The primary motivation of the Sadistic and Nonsadistic types is sexual; and the primary motivation of the Vindictive and Opportunistic types is aggressive or hostile. Barbaree, Seto, Serin, Amos, and Preston (1994) examined 80 rapists, 60 of whom could be classified using the MTC:R3. The mean PCL-R score (*SD* in parentheses) for offenders in the four types was Vindictive, 17.5 (1.4); Opportunistic, 20.5 (6.1); Nonsadistic, 13.7 (6.5); and Sadistic, 19.6 (9.5). Because of the small sample size, the only statistically significant difference was that within the sexual group, Sadistic rapists had significantly higher PCL-R Factor 2 scores than Nonsadistic rapists.

Brown and Forth (1995) also used the MTC:R3 system in their study of 60 rapists. They found that 81% of the psychopaths were classified as nonsexual rapists (52% Opportunistic and 29% Vindictive). In contrast, 56% of nonpsychopaths were classified as nonsexual rapists (26% Opportunistic and 30% Vindictive).

Dixon, Hart, Gretton, McBride, and O'Shaugnessy (1995) examined the utility of the FBI's *Crime Classification Manual* (Douglas, J. E. Burgess, A. W. Burgess, & Ressler, 1992) in juvenile sex offenders. They found that those classified as Anger and Sadistic rapists had significantly higher mean PCL-R scores (28.7, *SD* = 4.0) than those who committed Domestic rape (e.g., incest, child abuse; 18.9, *SD* = 7.6), Entitlement rape (e.g., date rape, Power-Reassurance rape; 18.2, *SD* = 7.5), or Nuisance offenses (e.g., voyeurism, exhibitionism; 18.8, *SD* = 8.7).

Severity of Sexual Violence

Psychopathy is related to the type and degree of violence committed during sexual offenses. Miller et al. (1994) found, in their study of adult sex offenders, that those who used violence had significantly higher PCL-R scores than nonviolent offenders. Gretton, McBride, Lewis, O'Shaughnessy, and Hare (1994) found that during commission of a sexual offense, the violence of juvenile sex offenders diagnosed as psychopathic by the PCL-R was more frequent and more severe than was that of nonpsychopathic sex offenders.

Sexual Sadism

The studies on subtypes of sexual offenders hint that psychopathy may be associated with sexual sadism. Consistent with this view, two studies have found that PCL-R scores correlated with sexual arousal to violent stimuli as assessed by penile plethysmography in adult male sex offenders (*r* = .21 in Quinsey et al., 1995; *r* = .28 in Serin et al., 1994). Also, Dempster and Hart (1996), in a sample of 43 male juveniles charged with murder or attempted murder, found that those classified according to the *Crime Classification Manual* criteria as Sexual Homicide perpetrators had significantly higher PCL-R scores than Criminal Enterprise, Personal Cause, or Group Excitement perpetrators.

Predictive Studies: General Recidivism

Unlike actuarial scales designed specifically to predict recidivism, the PCL scales were developed to provide a reliable and valid operationalization of the construct of psychopathy. Yet, the PCL scales are at least as good as purpose-built actuarial scales in predicting general reoffending (see Hemphill, Templeman, & Wong, in press; Salekin et al., 1996; Serin, 1996).

Hart, Kropp, and Hare (1988) conducted the first predictive study of the PCL. They followed up 231 adult male offenders who had been assessed using the PCL for research purposes and who subsequently were granted conditional release. Release decisions were made independent of PCL scores. Inmates were divided into low-, medium-, and high-psychopathy groups. *Recidivism* was defined as revocation of conditional release or reconviction during the follow-up period; mean time at risk was approximately 20 months. A total of 107 releases (46.3%) ended in failure.

Psychopathy was a significant predictor of failure in this sample (*r* = .33). Hierarchical logistic regression analyses indicated that the PCL had significant incremental validity (*p* < .001) over a set of demographic and criminal history variables that included age at release, prior offenses, prior failures on conditional release, and type of release for index offense. The failure rates by group, unadjusted for time at risk, were as follows: for high PCL offenders, 42% failures on parole (i.e., discretionary release) and 70% failures on mandatory supervision (i.e., statutory release); for medium PCL offenders, 29% failures on parole and 55% failures on mandatory supervision; and for low PCL offenders, 19% failures on parole and 31% failures on mandatory supervision. When time at risk was controlled for using survival analysis, the estimated 1-year failure rates for any conditional release were as follows: high PCL, 62%; medium PCL, 47%; and low PCL, 20%. The estimated 3-year failure rates were 82%, 62%, and 29% for the high, medium, and low PCL groups, respectively.

Côté and Hodgins (1996) replicated these results in Quebec, using a French version of the PCL-R (see Hare, 1996d). They conducted a 1-year follow-up of 97 adult male offenders who received conditional releases. Of the 14 offenders in the high-psychopathy group, 50% recidivated; the recidivism rates in the medium- and low-psychopathy groups were 11% (5 of 44) and 8% (3 of 39), respectively. Survival analyses indicated that the high-psychopathy offenders recidivated faster and more often than the others.

Serin, Peters, and Barbaree (1990) found a strong association between psychopathy and failure on unescorted temporary absences in 93 adult male offenders. PCL scores correlated significantly with failure (*r* = .32); the failure rate in the high-psychopathy group (PCL scores > 31) was 38%, compared to 0% in the low-psychopathy group (scores < 17). Serin et al. (1990) subsequently followed up 72 of the original 93 offenders who were granted conditional releases. Once again, PCL scores correlated significantly (*r* = .27) with failure. Offenders in the high-psychopathy group had a failure rate of 33% and a mean time to failure of 8.0 months; in the low-psychopathy group, the failure rate was 7% and mean time to failure was 14.6 months. Although the PCL was not designed as a measure of recidivism, and even after dropping three items related to criminality, scores were moderately to highly correlated with actuarial scales of risk for recidivism and correlated more highly with failure on release than the actuarial measures.

Rice and Harris (1992) looked at recidivism rates in 96 male schizophrenics who had been found not guilty by reason of insanity and remanded to a forensic psychiatric facility. A control group consisted of 96 nonschizophrenic male forensic patients who had been remanded for brief pretrial psychiatric assessments and who were matched on a number of variables that included age, index offense, and criminal history. Even though schizophrenics had a significantly lower rate of general recidivism than nonschizophrenics (35% vs. 53%), the PCL-R correlated with general recidivism in the schizophrenics ($r = .33$) and in the combined sample ($r = .27$).

Predictive Studies: Violent Recidivism

Given their defining traits and behaviors, it is not surprising that the literature clearly indicates that psychopaths, as defined by the PCL scales, are at higher risk for violent recidivism than other offenders. Indeed, in their meta-analytic review of the PCL scales, Salekin et al. (1996) were able to conclude that "the PCL-R appears to be unparalleled as a measure for making risk assessments" (p. 211).

Two studies examined the association between the PCL-R and violent recidivism in adult male offenders. Serin and Amos (1995) followed up 300 offenders for an average of 5.5 years. Violent recidivism occurred more frequently and more quickly among psychopaths. Serin (1996) looked at violent recidivism among 81 offenders who were part of an earlier study (Serin et al., 1990). The correlation between PCL-R scores and violent recidivism was moderate ($r = .28$) and larger than the correlations between three actuarial risk scales and violence.

Several studies have examined the ability of the PCL-R to predict violence in forensic psychiatric patients. Webster, Harris, Rice, Cormier, and Quinsey (1994) summarized the results of a program of research that examined the predictive validity of various demographic, criminal history, and psychiatric variables in several cohorts of patients assessed or treated at a forensic hospital (Harris, Rice, & Cormier, 1991; Harris, Rice, & Quinsey, 1993; Rice & Harris, 1992, 1995a, 1995b; Rice, Harris, & Cormier, 1992). PCL-R scores were the best predictor of violent recidivism in this heterogeneous sample of 618 patients; the correlation between the PCL-R and violent recidivism was $r = .34$ over a follow-up period of 7 years.

Quinsey et al. (1995), extending an earlier study (Rice, Harris, & Quinsey, 1990), examined the prediction of violence in 178 sexual offenders assessed or treated at the same forensic hospital. They found that PCL-R scores correlated significantly with both violent recidivism ($r = .33$) and sexually violent recidivism ($r = .23$) in a follow-up period that averaged more than 78 months. Indeed, the PCL-R was the best predictor of general violence and the third best predictor of sexual violence (after prior convictions for sexual and nonsexual violence). Survival analyses indicated that recidivism was faster and more common in the high-psychopathy group. At 7 years postrelease, the estimated survival rate was less than 10% in this group, compared to more than 60% in the low-psychopathy group. This study recently was extended yet again to include a total of 288 sex offenders with an average follow-up period of 10 years (Rice & Harris, 1995b). It appears that the PCL-R total score was the best single predictor of general

and sexual violence; the combination of psychopathy and deviant sexual arousal (as assessed by penile plethysmography) was particularly predictive of sexual violence.

Wintrup, Coles, Hart, and Webster (1994) used health care and criminal records to follow up patients from the Hart and Hare (1989) study. A total of 72 patients were released and had complete records. Mean time at risk was 61 months. The correlation between PCL-R scores and violent recidivism was .33; the correlation between the PCL-R and number of charges and convictions for violent offenses was .38.

Heilbrun et al. (in press) followed up a sample of 191 forensic patients who were released into the community. PCL scores correlated significantly ($r = .16$) with the violent recidivism rate (charges and convictions per year at risk).

In the Forth et al. (1990) study, 71 delinquents were released after assessment and followed up via criminal records. The overall recidivism rate (new charges or convictions during the follow-up period) in this subsample was 79%; mean time at risk was approximately 27 months. Modified PCL-R scores were not correlated with time at risk ($r = .04$), any recidivism ($r = .14$), and number of nonviolent offenses ($r = .00$). However, the correlation between PCL-R scores and number of violent offenses during the follow-up period was significant ($r = .26$).

Response to Treatment

A number of reviews have examined response to treatment in recent years, all reaching the same conclusion: There is no good evidence that psychopathy is treatable, but neither is there conclusive evidence that it is untreatable (e.g., Dolan & Coid, 1993; Hare, 1992). Major methodological weaknesses in the relevant literature include inadequate assessment procedures, poorly defined treatments, lack of posttreatment follow-up, and lack of adequate control or comparison groups. To the best of our knowledge, only two treatment programs have been evaluated using the PCL or PCL-R; both were therapeutic community programs in Canada.

Ogloff, Wong, and Greenwood (1990) examined 80 adult male offenders who volunteered to attend a corrections-based therapeutic community program at the Regional Psychiatric Centre in Saskatoon, Saskatchewan. All offenders were assessed using the PCL-R and rated by treatment staff (blind to PCL-R scores) on degree of motivation and improvement in the program; 52 cases were examined retrospectively and 28 cases prospectively. Ogloff et al. also examined number of days in the program; offenders had agreed to stay at least 180 days. The results indicated that PCL-R scores correlated $r = -.29$ with time in treatment. On average, offenders in the high-psychopathy group spent 104 days in the program, compared to 207 days for those in the medium- and 242 days for the those in low-psychopathy groups. In the subsample of 28 cases examined prospectively, 10 patients left the program prematurely because of poor adjustment; 6 of the 10, including all 4 patients who were ejected for security reasons and the only patient ejected for lack of motivation, were from the high-psychopathy group. Patients in the high-psychopathy group also received significantly lower ratings for motivation or effort and improvement than those in the medium- and low-psychopathy groups. A follow-up of 106 adult male offenders who had attended this treatment program and subsequently were released from prison (Hemphill &

Wong, 1991) found that patients in the high-psychopathy group had a higher recidivism rate than those in the low-psychopathy group (73% versus 43%) and also tended to fail faster.

Rice et al. (1992; see also Harris et al., 1991) examined 176 men who had received at least 2 years (on average, more than 5 years) of intensive treatment in a complex and controversial therapeutic community program at a forensic hospital in Ontario. This group included mentally ill and personality disordered offenders, as well as forensic patients who had been found not guilty by reason of insanity or incompetent to stand trial. The treated offenders were compared to a group of 146 offenders who had been assessed at the hospital but, for a variety of reasons, not treated (no matches were found for 30 patients). Members of the untreated control group were matched to the treated patients on variables that included age, index offense, and offense history. Patients and control group members were assessed using the PCL-R and divided into high- and low-psychopathy groups.

Rice et al. (1992) coded progress in the treatment program from institutional files. Comparisons between the high- and low-psychopathy groups indicated that psychopaths had significantly more behavior problems while in the program, including more negative entries (concerning disruptive or countertherapeutic behavior) recorded by treatment staff in the files during the first and last years in treatment, more incidents of seclusion for disruptive behavior during the first and last years of treatment, more referrals to a disciplinary subprogram, and a higher rate of misbehavior. Psychopaths also had as many positive entries recorded by treatment staff in their files as nonpsychopaths.

Posttreatment general and violent recidivism (new charges, reincarceration, or rehospitalization due to criminal behavior) was examined in patients and controls over a follow-up period that averaged 10.5 years. The rate of general recidivism was 59% in the treated group and 68% in the control group; for violent recidivism, the rates were 40% and 46%, respectively. Thus, it appeared that treatment had little impact overall. However, when the patients and controls were subdivided into high- and low-psychopathy groups, a surprising finding emerged: Among psychopaths, the rates of general recidivism were equally high in the treated and untreated groups (87% vs. 90%, respectively); however, the rate of violent recidivism was significantly higher in the treated group than in the untreated group (77% vs. 55%). In contrast, the treated nonpsychopaths had significantly lower rates of general and violent recidivism (44% and 22%, respectively) than the untreated nonpsychopaths (58% and 39%). Therefore, although the therapeutic community appeared to be efficacious for nonpsychopaths, it actually may have been harmful for psychopaths, at least with respect to violent recidivism. The reason may be that group therapy and insight-oriented programs help psychopaths to develop better ways of manipulating, deceiving, and using people but do little to help them to understand themselves. In particular, such treatment does little to develop empathy or conscience.

This does not mean that a useful program for the control and management of psychopathic behavior is not feasible. Indeed, the broad outline of such a program recently was developed by a panel of international experts (see Hare, 1992). In brief, we proposed that relapse-prevention techniques be integrated with elements of the best available cognitive-behavioral correctional programs. The program would be concerned less with developing empathy and con-

science or effecting changes in personality than with convincing participants that they alone are responsible for their behavior and that they can learn more prosocial ways of using their strengths and abilities to satisfy their needs and wants. It would involve tight control and supervision, both in the institution and following release into the community, as well as comparisons with carefully selected groups of offenders treated in standard correctional programs. The experimental design would permit empirical evaluation of its treatment and intervention modules (what works and what does not work for particular individuals). That is, some modules or components might be effective with psychopaths but not with other offenders and vice versa. We recognized that correctional programs are constantly in danger of erosion because of changing institutional priorities, community concerns, and political pressures. To prevent this from happening, we proposed stringent safeguards for maintaining the integrity of the program.

CONCLUSIONS

The research reviewed here strongly indicates that psychopathy is an important factor in understanding and predicting criminal conduct. Indeed, several studies have found that psychopathy predicts crime as well as actuarial risk scales designed solely for predictive purposes (e.g., Rice et al., 1992; Serin et al., 1990). It is important to emphasize, however, that psychopathy is not merely a synonym for criminological constructs, such as *high-risk offender* (e.g., Rettinger & Andrews, 1992). A large body of research (some reviewed here) attests to the fact that psychopathy can be considered a "true" mental disorder, one that is reliably assessed; has important psychobiological correlates; and is not specific to any one race, culture, or socioeconomic level (see Cooke, 1995, 1996). As far as we are aware, no criminological theory or concept can account for these findings.

If psychopathy is a true mental disorder, does this mental disorder *cause* criminal conduct? Given our comments here, it is clear that most criminal conduct is not committed by psychopaths. Antisocial behavior in such cases may be related to a number of personality, social, and other factors, described elsewhere (see Andrews & Bonta, 1993; Gottfredson & Hirschi, 1990; Wilson & Herrnstein, 1985). In psychopaths, however, it seems that certain symptoms (e.g., impulsivity, grandiosity, lack of empathy) both increase the likelihood that affected individuals will consider engaging in criminal conduct and decrease the likelihood that the decision to act will be inhibited. Thus, the mental disorder does appear to play a strong causal role in the criminal conduct of psychopaths, although there is no reason to believe that it is the sole causal agent. This does not imply that psychopaths are legally insane. Consistent with Anglo-American law, our view is that psychopaths have sufficient cognitive ability to know that their antisocial behavior is morally reprehensible and sufficient volitional controls to inhibit their antisocial behavior; however, because they are relatively unaffected by punishment or by the suffering of others, they simply choose not to inhibit antisocial impulses (see Hare, 1993, 1996b).

Further research on psychopathy and crime is sorely needed. Although we have evidence of an empirical association between the two, our attention now should be focused on identifying the causal factors responsible for the link. This will be the first major step toward the development of crime prevention and management programs targeted specifically and systematically at psychopathic offenders.

REFERENCES

Alterman, A. I., Cacciola, J. S., & Rutherford, M. J. (1993). Reliability of the Revised Psychopathy Checklist in substance abuse patients. *Psychological Assessment: A Journal of Consulting and Clinical Psychology, 5,* 442–448.

American Psychiatric Association. (1980). *Diagnostic and statistical manual of mental disorders* (3rd ed.). Washington, DC: Author.

American Psychiatric Association. (1987). *Diagnostic and statistical manual of mental disorders* (3rd ed., revised). Washington, DC: Author.

American Psychiatric Association. (1994). *Diagnostic and statistical manual of mental disorders* (4th ed.). Washington, DC: Author.

Andrews, D. A., & Bonta, J. (1993). *The psychology of criminal conduct.* Cincinnati: Anderson.

Arnett, P. A., Howland, E. W., Smith, S. S., & Newman, J. P. (1993). Autonomic responsivity during passive avoidance in incarcerated psychopaths. *Personality and Individual Differences, 14,* 173–184.

Barbaree, H., Seto, M., Serin, R., Amos, N., & Preston, D. (1994). Comparisons between sexual and nonsexual rapist subtypes. *Criminal Justice and Behavior, 21,* 95–114.

Blackburn, R. (1987). Two scales for the assessment of personality disorder in antisocial populations. *Personality and Individual Differences, 8,* 81–93.

Blackburn, R. (1993). *The psychology of criminal conduct: Theory, research, and practice.* Chichester, England: Wiley.

Boyd, J. H., Burke, J. D., Gruenberg, E. M., Holzer, C. E., III, Rae, D. S., George, L. K., Karno, M., Stoltzman, R., McEvoy, L., & Nestadt, G. (1984). Exclusion criteria of *DSM-III*: A study of co-occurrence of hierarchy-free syndromes. *Archives of General Psychiatry, 41,* 983–989.

Brown, S. L., & Forth, A. E. (1995). Psychopathy and sexual aggression against adult females: Static and dynamic precursors [Abstract]. *Canadian Psychology, 36,* 19.

Chandler, M., & Moran, T. (1990). Psychopathy and moral development: A comparative study of delinquent and nondelinquent youth. *Development and Psychopathology, 2,* 227–246.

Cleckley, H. (1941). *The mask of sanity.* St. Louis: Mosby.

Cleckley, H. (1976). *The mask of sanity* (5th ed.). St. Louis: Mosby.

Cooke, D. J. (1995). Psychopathic disturbance in the Scottish prison population: Cross-cultural generalizability of the Hare Psychopathy Checklist. *Psychology, Crime, and Law, 2,* 101–118.

Cooke, D. J. (1996). Psychopathic personality in different cultures: What do we know? What do we need to find out? *Journal of Personality Disorders, 10,* 23–40.

Cooke, D. J., Forth, A. E., & Hare, R. D. (in press). *Psychopathy: Theory, research, and implications for society.* Dordrecht, The Netherlands: Kluwer.

Cooke, D., & Michie, C. (1997). An item response theory evaluation of Hare's Psychopathy Checklist-revised. *Psychological Assessment, 9,* 3–14.

Cooney, N. L., Kadden, R. M., & Litt, M. D. (1990). A comparison of methods for assessing sociopathy in male and female alcoholics. *Journal of Studies on Alcohol, 51,* 42–48.

Cornell, D., Warren, J., Hawk, G., Stafford, E., Oram, G., & Pine, D. (1996). Psychopathy in instrumental and reactive offenders. *Journal of Consulting and Clinical Psychology, 64,* 783–790.

Côté, G., & Hodgins, S. (1996). *L'Échelle De Psychopathie De Hare-Révisée: Éléments de la validation de la version française.* Toronto: Multi-Health Systems.

Dempster, R. J., & Hart, S.D. (1996, March). *Utility of the FBI's Crime Classification Manual: Coverage, reliability, and validity for adolescent murderers.* Paper presented at the biennial meeting of the American Psychology–Law Society (APA Div. 41), Hilton Head, South Carolina.

Dempster, R. J., Lyon, D. R., Sullivan, L. E., & Hart, S. D. (1996, August). *Psychopathy and instrumental aggression in violent offenders.* Paper presented at the annual meeting of the American Psychological Association, Toronto, Ontario.

Devita, E., Forth, A. E., & Hare, R. D. (1990). Family background of male criminal psychopaths [Abstract]. *Canadian Psychology, 31,* 346.

Dixon, M., Hart, S. D., Gretton, H., McBride, M., & O'Shaughnessy, R. (1995). Crime Classification Manual: Reliability and validity in juvenile sex offenders [Abstract]. *Canadian Psychology, 36,* 20.

Dolan, B., & Coid, J. (1993). *Psychopathic and antisocial personality disorders: Treatment and research issues.* London: Gaskell.

Douglas, J. E., Burgess, A. W., Burgess, A. G., & Ressler, R. K. (1992). *The Crime Classification Manual: A standard system for investigating and classifying violent crimes.* New York: Lexington.

Feighner, J. P., Robins, E., Guze, S. B., Woodruff, R. A., Winokur, G., & Munoz, R. (1972). Diagnostic criteria for use in psychiatric research. *Archives of General Psychiatry, 26,* 57–63.

Forth, A. E., Brown, S. L., Hart, S. D., & Hare, R. D. (1996). The assessment of psychopathy in male and female noncriminals: Reliability and validity. *Personality and Individual Differences, 20,* 531–543.

Forth, A. E., & Hare, R. D. (1989). Slow cortical potentials in psychopaths. *Psychophysiology, 26,* 676–682.

Forth, A. E., Hart, S. D., & Hare, R. D. (1990). Assessment of psychopathy in male young offenders. *Psychological Assessment: A Journal of Consulting and Clinical Psychology, 2,* 342–344.

Forth, A. E., & Kroner, D. (1994). *The factor structure of the Hare Psychopathy Checklist–Revised in sex offenders.* Unpublished manuscript.

Fulero, S. M. (1995). Review of the Hare Psychopathy Checklist–Revised. In J. C. Conoley & J. C. Impara (Eds.), *Twelfth mental measurements yearbook* (pp. 453–454). Lincoln, NE: Buros Institute

Gacono, C. B., & Meloy, J. R. (1991). A Rorschach investigation of attachment and anxiety in antisocial personality disorder. *Journal of Nervous and Mental Disease, 179,* 546–552.

Gacono, C., Meloy, J. R., & Heaven, T. (1990). A Rorschach investigation of narcissism and hysteria in antisocial personality disorder. *Journal of Personality Assessment, 55,* 270–279.

Gerstley, L. J., Alterman, A. I., McLellan, A. T., & Woody, G. E. (1990). Antisocial personality disorder in substance abusers: A problematic diagnosis? *American Journal of Psychiatry, 147,* 173–178.

Gillstrom, B., & Hare, R. D. (1988). Language-related hand gestures in psychopaths. *Journal of Personality Disorders, 2,* 21–27.

Gottfredson, M. R., & Hirschi, T. (1990). *A general theory of crime.* Stanford, CA: Stanford University Press.

Gough, H. (1957). *Manual for the California Psychological Inventory.* Palo Alto, CA: Consulting Psychologists Press.

Gretton, H., McBride, M., Lewis, K., O'Shaughnessy, R., & Hare, R. D. (1994, March). *Patterns of violence and victimization in adolescent sexual psychopaths.* Paper presented at the biennial meeting of the

American Psychology–Law Society (Div. 41 of the American Psychological Association), Santa Fe.

Gustafson, S. B., & Ritzer, D. R. (1995). The dark side of normal: A psychopathy-linked pattern called aberrant self-promotion. *European Journal of Personality, 9,* 1–37.

Haapasalo, J. (1994). Types of offense among the Cleckley psychopath. *International Journal of Offender Therapy and Comparative Criminology, 38,* 59–67.

Haapasalo, J., & Pulkkinen, L. (1992). The Psychopathy Checklist and nonviolent offender groups. *Criminal Behaviour and Mental Health, 2,* 315–328.

Hare, R. D. (1970). *Psychopathy: Theory and research.* New York: Wiley.

Hare, R. D. (1978). Electrodermal and cardiovascular correlates of psychopathy. In R. D. Hare & D. Schalling (Eds.), *Psychopathic behavior: Approaches to research* (pp. 107–144). Chichester, England: Wiley.

Hare, R. D. (1980). A research scale for the assessment of psychopathy in criminal populations. *Personality and Individual Differences, 1,* 111–119.

Hare, R. D. (1981). Psychopathy and violence. In J. R. Hays, T. K. Roberts, & K. S. Soloway (Eds.), *Violence and the violent individual* (pp. 53–74). Jamaica, NY: Spectrum.

Hare, R. D. (1983). Diagnosis of antisocial personality disorder in two prison populations. *American Journal of Psychiatry, 140,* 887–890.

Hare, R. D. (1984). Performance of psychopaths on cognitive tasks related to frontal lobe functions. *Journal of Abnormal Psychology, 93,* 133–140.

Hare, R. D. (1985). A comparison of procedures for the assessment of psychopathy. *Journal of Consulting and Clinical Psychology, 53,* 7–16.

Hare, R. D. (1991). *The Hare Psychopathy Checklist–Revised.* Toronto, Ontario: Multi-Health Systems.

Hare, R. D. (1992). *A model program for offenders at high risk for violence.* Ottawa, Canada: Correctional Service of Canada.

Hare, R. D. (1993). *Without conscience: The disturbing world of the psychopaths among us.* New York: Pocket Books.

Hare, R. D. (1996a). Psychopathy and antisocial personality disorder: A case of diagnostic confusion. *Psychiatric Times, 13,* 39–40.

Hare, R. D. (1996b). Psychopathy: A construct whose time has come. *Criminal Justice and Behavior, 23,* 25–54.

Hare, R. D. (1996c). *The Hare Self-Report Psychopathy Scale–II.* Toronto: Multi-Health Systems.

Hare, R. D. (1996d). *L'Échelle De Psychopathie De Hare-Révisée: Guide de cotation.* Toronto: Multi-Health Systems.

Hare, R. D., & Craigen, D. (1974). Psychopathy and physiological activity in a mixed-motive game situation. *Psychophysiology, 11,* 197–206.

Hare, R. D., Forth, A. E., & Hart, S. D. (1989). The psychopath as prototype for pathological lying and deception. In J. C. Yuille (Ed.), *Credibility assessment* (pp. 24–49). Dordrecht, The Netherlands: Kluwer.

Hare, R. D., Forth, A. E., & Strachan, K. (1992). Psychopathy and crime across the lifespan. In R. D. Peters, R. J. McMahon, & V. L. Quinsey (Eds.), *Aggression and violence throughout the life span* (pp. 285–300). Newbury Park, CA: Sage Publications.

Hare, R. D., Harpur, T. J., Hakstian, A. R., Forth, A. E., Hart, S. D., & Newman, J. P. (1990). The Revised Psychopathy Checklist: Reliability and factor structure. *Psychological Assessment: A Journal of Consulting and Clinical Psychology, 2,* 338–341.

Hare, R. D., & Hart, S. D. (1995). Commentary on antisocial personality disorder: The DSM-IV field trial. In W. J. Livesley (Ed.), *The DSM-IV personality disorders* (pp. 127–134). New York: Guilford.

Hare, R. D., Hart, S. D., & Harpur, T. J. (1991). Psychopathy and the *DSM-IV* criteria for antisocial personality disorder. *Journal of Abnormal Psychology, 100,* 391–398.

Hare, R. D., & Jutai, J. (1983). Criminal history of the male psychopath: Some preliminary data. In K. T. Van Dusen & S. A. Mednick (Eds.), *Prospective studies of crime and delinquency* (pp. 225–236). Boston: Kluwer-Nijhoff.

Hare, R. D., & Jutai, J. (1988). Psychopathy and cerebral asymmetry in semantic processing. *Personality and Individual Differences, 9,* 329–337.

Hare, R. D., & McPherson, L. M. (1984a). Psychopathy and perceptual asymmetry during verbal dichotic listening. *Journal of Abnormal Psychology, 93,* 140–149.

Hare, R. D., & McPherson, L. M. (1984b). Violent and aggressive behavior by criminal psychopaths. *International Journal of Law and Psychiatry, 7,* 35–50.

Hare, R. D., McPherson, L. E., & Forth, A. E. (1988). Male psychopaths and their criminal careers. *Journal of Consulting and Clinical Psychology, 56,* 710–714.

Hare, R. D., Williamson, S. E., & Harpur, T. J. (1988). Psychopathy and language. In T. E. Moffitt & S. A. Mednick (Eds.), *Biological contributions to crime causation* (pp. 68–92). Dordrecht, The Netherlands: Martinus Nijhoff.

Harpur, T. J., Hakstian, R. A., & Hare, R. D. (1988). Factor structure of the Psychopathy Checklist. *Journal of Consulting and Clinical Psychology, 56,* 741–747.

Harpur, T. J., & Hare, R. D. (1990). Psychopathy and attention. In J. Enns (Ed.), *The development of attention: Recent research and theory* (pp. 501–516). Amsterdam: North-Holland.

Harpur, T. J., & Hare, R. D. (1994). The assessment of psychopathy as a function of age. *Journal of Abnormal Psychology, 103,* 604–609.

Harpur, T. J., Hare, R. D., & Hakstian, R. A. (1989). A two-factor conceptualization of psychopathy: Construct validity and implications for assessment. *Psychological Assessment: A Journal of Consulting and Clinical Psychology, 1,* 6–17.

Harpur, T. J., Hart, S. D., & Hare, R. D. (1993). Personality of the psychopath. In P. T. Costa & T. A. Widiger (Eds.), *Personality disorders and the five-factor model of personality* (pp. 149–173). Washington, DC: American Psychological Association.

Harris, G. T., Rice, M. E., & Cormier, C. A. (1991). Psychopathy and violent recidivism. *Law and Human Behavior, 15,* 625–637.

Harris, G. T., Rice, M. E., & Quinsey, V. L. (1993). Violent recidivism of mentally disordered offenders: The development of a statistical prediction instrument. *Criminal Justice and Behavior, 20,* 315–335.

Harris, G. T., Rice, M. E., & Quinsey, V. L. (1994). Psychopathy as a taxon: Evidence that psychopaths are a discrete class. *Journal of Consulting and Clinical Psychology, 62,* 387–397.

Hart, S. D., Cox, D. N., & Hare, R. D. (1995). *Manual for the Hare Psychopathy Checklist–Revised: Screening Version (PCL:SV).* Toronto: Multi-Health Systems.

Hart, S. D., Forth, A. E., & Hare, R. D. (1990). Performance of criminal psychopaths on selected neuropsychological tests. *Journal of Abnormal Psychology, 99,* 374–379.

Hart, S. D., Forth, A. E., & Hare, R. D. (1991). The MCMI-II as a measure of psychopathy. *Journal of Personality Disorders, 5,* 318–327.

Hart, S. D., & Hare, R. D. (1989). Discriminant validity of the Psychopathy Checklist in a forensic psychiatric population. *Psychological Assessment: A Journal of Consulting and Clinical Psychology, 1,* 211–218.

Hart, S. D., & Hare, R. D. (1994). Psychopathy and the Big 5: Correlations between observers' ratings of normal and pathological personality. *Journal of Personality Disorders, 8,* 32–40.

Hart, S. D., & Hare, R. D. (1996). Psychopathy and risk assessment. *Current Opinion in Psychiatry, 9,* 380–383.

Hart, S. D., Kropp, P. R., & Hare, R. D. (1988). Performance of psychopaths following conditional release from prison. *Journal of Consulting and Clinical Psychology, 56,* 227–232.

Hathaway, S. R., & McKinley, J. C. (1940). A multiphasic personality schedule (Minnesota): I. Construction of the schedule. *Journal of Psychology, 10,* 249–254.

Heilbrun, K., Hart, S. D., Hare, R. D., Gustafson, D., Nunez, C., & White, A. (in press). Inpatient and post-discharge aggression in mentally disordered offenders: The role of psychopathy. *Journal of Interpersonal Violence.*

Hemphill, J., Hart, S. D., & Hare, R. D. (1994). Psychopathy and substance use. *Journal of Personality Disorders, 8,* 32–40.

Hemphill, J. F., & Wong, S. (1991). Efficacy of the therapeutic community for treating criminal psychopaths [Abstract]. *Canadian Psychology, 32,* 206.

Hemphill, J. F., Templeman, R., & Wong, S. W. (in press). Psychopathy and crime: Recidivism and criminal career profiles. In D. J. Cooke, A. E. Forth, & R. D. Hare (Eds.), *Psychopathy: Theory, research, and implications for society.* Dordrecht, The Netherlands: Kluwer.

Howard, R. C., Bailey, R., & Newman, F. (1984). A preliminary study of Hare's Research Scale for the Assessment of Psychopathy in mentally abnormal offenders. *Personality and Individual Differences, 5,* 389–396.

Howland, E. W., Kosson, D. S., Patterson, C. M., & Newman, J. P. (1993). Altering a dominant response: Performance of psychopaths and low-socialization college students on a cued reaction time task. *Journal of Abnormal Psychology, 102,* 379–387.

Intrator, J., Hare, R. D., Stritzke, P., Brichtswein, K., Dorfman, D., Harpur, T., Bernstein, D., Handelsman, L., Schaefer, C., Keilp, J., Rosen, J., & Machac, J. (in press). A brain-imaging (SPECT) study of semantic and affective processing in psychopaths. *Biological Psychiatry.*

Jutai, J., & Hare, R. D. (1983). Psychopathy and selective attention during performance of a complex perceptual-motor task. *Psychophysiology, 20,* 146–151.

af Klinterberg, B., Humble, K., & Schalling, D. (1992). Personality and psychopathy of males with a history of early criminal behavior. *European Journal of Personality, 6,* 245–266.

Kosson, D. S., & Newman, J. P. (1986). Psychopathy and allocation of attentional capacity in a divided-attention situation. *Journal of Abnormal Psychology, 95,* 257–263.

Kosson, D. S., Smith, S. S., & Newman, J. P. (1990). Evaluation of the construct validity of psychopathy in Black and White male inmates: Three preliminary studies. *Journal of Abnormal Psychology, 99,* 250–259.

Lapierre, D., Braun, C. M. J., & Hodgins, S. (1995). Ventral frontal deficits in psychopathy: Neuropsychological test findings. *Neuropsychologia, 11,* 139–151.

Larbig, W., Veit, R., Rau, H., Schlottke, P., & Birbaumer, N. (1992. October). *Cerebral and peripheral correlates in psychopaths during anticipation of aversive stimulation.* Paper presented at the annual meeting of the Society for Psychophysiological Research, San Diego.

Levenson, M. R., Kiehl, K. A., & Fitzpatrick, C. M. (1995). Assessing psychopathic attributes in a noninstitutionalized population. *Journal of Personality and Social Psychology, 68,* 151–158.

Lilienfeld, S. O. (1994). Conceptual problems in the assessment of psychopathy. *Clinical Psychology Review, 14,* 17–38.

Loucks, A. D., & Zamble, E. (1994). Criminal and violent behavior in incarcerated female federal offenders [Abstract]. *Canadian Psychology, 35,* 54.

Miller, M. W., Geddings, V. J., Levenston, G. K., & Patrick, C. J. (1994, March). *The personality characteristics of psychopathic and nonpsychopathic sex offenders.* Paper presented at the biennial meeting of the American Psychology–Law Society (Div. 41 of the American Psychological Association), Santa Fe.

Millon, T. (1987). *Manual for the Millon Clinical Multiaxial Inventory–II* (2nd ed.). Minneapolis: National Computer Systems.

Newman, J. P., & Kosson, D. S. (1986). Passive avoidance learning in psychopathic and nonpsychopathic offenders. *Journal of Abnormal Psychology, 95,* 252–256.

Newman, J. P., Kosson, D. S., & Patterson, C. M. (1992). Delay of gratification in psychopathic and nonpsychopathic offenders. *Journal of Abnormal Psychology, 101,* 630–636.

Newman, J. P., Patterson, C. M., Howland, E. W., & Nichols, S. L. (1991). Passive avoidance learning in psychopaths: The effects of reward. *Personality and Individual Differences, 11,* 1101–1114.

Newman, J. P., Patterson, C. M., & Kosson, D. S. (1987). Response perseveration in psychopaths. *Journal of Abnormal Psychology, 96,* 145–148.

Ogloff, J. R., & Wong, S. (1990). Electrodermal and cardiovascular evidence of a coping response in psychopaths. *Criminal Justice and Behavior, 17,* 231–245.

Ogloff, J. R. P., Wong, S., & Greenwood, A. (1990). Treating criminal psychopaths in a therapeutic community program. *Behavioral Sciences and the Law, 8,* 81–90.

Patrick, C. J., Bradley, M. M., & Lang, P. J. (1993). Emotion in the criminal psychopath: Startle reflex modulation. *Journal of Abnormal Psychology, 102,* 82–92.

Patrick, C. J., Cuthbert, B. N., & Lang, P. J. (1994). Emotion in the criminal psychopath: Fear image processing. *Journal of Abnormal Psychology, 103,* 523–534.

Patrick, C. J., & Erickson, L. M. (1994). Emotional imagery and startle reflex modulation in psychopathic and nonpsychopathic criminals [Abstract]. *Psychophysiology, 31,* S75.

Prentky, R. A., & Knight, R. A. (1991). Identifying critical dimensions for discriminating among rapists. *Journal of Consulting and Clinical Psychology, 59,* 643–661.

Quay, H. C. (1983). *Standards for adult correctional institutions.* Washington, DC: Federal Bureau of Prisons.

Quinsey, V. L., Rice, M. E., & Harris, G. T. (1995). Actuarial prediction of sexual recidivism. *Journal of Interpersonal Violence, 10,* 85–105.

Raine, A. (1985). A psychometric assessment of Hare's checklist for psychopathy in an English prison population. *British Journal of Clinical Psychology, 24,* 247–258.

Raine, A. (1986). Psychopathy, schizoid personality, and borderline/schizotypal personality disorders. *Personality and Individual Differences, 7,* 493–501.

Raine, A., & Venables, P. H. (1988a). Enhanced P3 evoked potentials and longer recovery times in psychopaths. *Psychophysiology, 25,* 30–38.

Raine, A., & Venables, P. H. (1988b). Skin conductance responsivity in psychopaths to orienting, defensive, and consonant-vowel stimuli. *Journal of Psychophysiology, 2,* 221–225.

Rettinger, L. J., & Andrews, D. (1992). Personality and attitudes correlates of the Psychopathy Checklist [Abstract]. *Canadian Psychology, 33,* 406.

Rice, M. E., & Harris, G. T. (1992). A comparison of criminal recidivism among schizophrenic and nonschizophrenic offenders. *International Journal of Law and Psychiatry, 15,* 397–408.

Rice, M. E., & Harris, G. T. (1995a). Psychopathy, schizophrenia, alcohol abuse, and violent recidivism. *International Journal of Law and Psychiatry, 18,* 333–342.

Rice, M. E., & Harris, G. T. (1995b). *Cross-validation and extension of an actuarial instrument for the prediction of recidivism among sex offenders* (Research Report, Vol. XII, no. 2). Penetanguishene, Ontario: Penetanguishene Mental Health Centre.

Rice, M. E., Harris, G. T., & Cormier, C. A. (1992). An evaluation of a maximum security therapeutic community for psychopaths and other mentally disordered offenders. *Law and Human Behavior, 16,* 399–412.

Rice, M. E., Harris, G. T., & Quinsey, V. L. (1990). A follow-up of rapists assessed in a maximum security psychiatric facility. *Journal of Interpersonal Violence, 4,* 435–448.

Robins, L. N. (1966). *Deviant children grown up: A sociological and psychiatric study of sociopathic personality.* Baltimore: Williams & Wilkins.

Robins, L. N. (1978). Aetiological implications in studies of childhood histories relating to antisocial personality. In R. D. Hare & D. Schalling (Eds.), *Psychopathic behavior: Approaches to research* (pp. 255–271). Chichester, England: Wiley.

Robins, L. N., Tipp, J., & Przybeck, T. (1991). Antisocial personality. In L. N. Robins & D. Regier (Eds.), *Psychiatric disorders in America: The Epidemiologic Catchment Area study* (pp. 258–290). New York: Free Press.

Rutherford, M. J., Cacciola, J. S., Alterman, A. I., & McKay, J. R. (1996). Reliability and validity of the Revised Psychopathy Checklist in women methadone patients. *Assessment, 3,* 43–54.

Salekin, R., Rogers, R., & Sewell, K. (1996). A review and meta-analysis of the Psychopathy Checklist and Psychopathy Checklist–Revised: Predictive validity of dangerousness. *Clinical Psychology: Science and Practice, 3,* 203–215.

Serin, R. C. (1991). Psychopathy and violence in criminals. *Journal of Interpersonal Violence, 6,* 423–431.

Serin, R. C. (1996). Violent recidivism in criminal psychopaths. *Law and Human Behavior, 20,* 207–217.

Serin, R. C., & Amos, N. L. (1995). The role of psychopathy in the assessment of dangerousness. *International Journal of Law and Psychiatry, 18,* 231–238.

Serin, R. C., Malcolm, P. B., Khanna, A., & Barbaree, H. E. (1994). Psychopathy and deviant sexual arousal in incarcerated sexual offenders. *Journal of Interpersonal Violence, 9,* 3–11.

Serin, R. C., Peters, R. D., & Barbaree, H. E. (1990). Predictors of psychopathy and release outcome in a criminal population. *Psychological Assessment: A Journal of Consulting and Clinical Psychology, 2,* 419–422.

Smith, S. S., Arnett, P. A., & Newman, J. P. (1992). Neuropsychological differentiation of psychopathic and nonpsychopathic criminal offenders. *Personality and Individual Differences, 13,* 1233–1243.

Smith, S. S., & Newman, J. P. (1990). Alcohol and drug abuse/dependence disorders in psychopathic and nonpsychopathic criminal offenders. *Journal of Abnormal Psychology, 99,* 430–439.

Stanford, M., Ebner, D., Patton, J., & Williams, J. (1994). Multi-impulsivity within an adolescent psychiatric population. *Personality and Individual Differences, 16,* 395–402.

Stone, G. L. (1995). Review of the Hare Psychopathy Checklist–Revised. In J. C. Conoley & J. C. Impara (Eds.), *Twelfth mental measurements yearbook* (pp. 454–455). Lincoln, NE: Buros Institute.

Strachan, K., & Hare, R. D. (1997). *Psychopathy in female offenders.* Manuscript under review.

Swanson, A. H., Bland, R. C., & Newman, S. C. (1995). Antisocial personality disorder. *Acta Psychiatrica Scandinavica, 89* (Suppl. 376), 63–70.

Trevethan, S. D., & Walker, L. J. (1989). Hypothetical versus real-life moral reasoning among psychopathic and delinquent youth. *Development and Psychopathology, 1,* 91–103.

Webster, C. D., Harris, G. T., Rice, M. E., Cormier, C. A., & Quinsey, V. L. (1994). *The Violence Prediction Scheme: Assessing dangerousness in high risk men.* Toronto: Centre of Criminology, University of Toronto.

Widiger, T. A., Cadoret, R., Hare, R. D., Robins, L., Rutherford, M., Zanarini, M., Alterman, A., Apple, M., Corbitt, E., Forth, A. E., Hart, S. D., Kultermann, J., & Woody, G. (1996). *DSM-IV* antisocial personality disorder field trial. *Journal of Abnormal Psychology, 105,* 3–16.

Widiger, T. A., & Corbitt, E. M. (1995). Antisocial personality disorder in *DSM–IV.* In J. Livesley (Ed.), DSM-IV *personality disorders* (pp. 127–134). New York: Guilford.

Widiger, T. A., Frances, A. J., Harris, M., Jacobsberg, L. B., Fyer, M., & Manning, D. (1991). Comorbidity among Axis II disorders. In J. M. Oldham (Ed.), *Personality disorders: New perspectives on diagnostic validity* (pp. 165–194). Washington, DC: American Psychiatric Press.

Widiger, T. A., Frances, A. J., Pincus, H. A., Davis, W. W., & First, M. (1991). Toward an empirical classification for *DSM-IV. Journal of Abnormal Psychology, 100,* 280–288.

Williamson, S. E., Hare, R. D., & Wong, S. (1987). Violence: Criminal psychopaths and their victims. *Canadian Journal of Behavioral Science, 19,* 454–462.

Williamson, S. E., Harpur, T. J., & Hare, R. D. (1991). Abnormal processing of affective words by psychopaths. *Psychophysiology, 28,* 260–273.

Wilson, J. Q., & Herrnstein, R. J. (1985). *Crime and human nature.* New York: Simon & Schuster.

Wintrup, A., Coles, M., Hart, S., & Webster, C. D. (1994). The predictive validity of the PCL-R in high-risk mentally disordered offenders [Abstract]. *Canadian Psychology, 35,* 47.

Wong, S. (1985). *Criminal and institutional behaviors of psychopaths.* Ottawa, Ontario: Programs Branch Users Report, Ministry of the Solicitor General of Canada.

Woody, G. E., & McLellan, A. T. (1985). Sociopathy and psychotherapy outcome. *Archives of General Psychiatry, 42,* 1081–1086.

World Health Organization. (1992). *The ICD-10 classification of mental and behavioral disorders: Clinical descriptions and diagnostic guidelines.* Geneva: Author.

CHAPTER 4

Assessment of Antisocial Behavior in Children and Adolescents

STEPHEN P. HINSHAW and BRIAN A. ZUPAN

One of the authors recalls taking a graduate seminar on assessment, more than 15 years ago, in which a student—apparently overwhelmed with the tasks that lay ahead of him in the class and, presumably, in his career—asked of the professor, "What can I learn that will help me to become a good assessor?" The immediate response made a lasting impression: "Learn all you can about psychopathology." In other words, the professor replied, a thorough understanding of manifestations, causal factors, and underlying mechanisms of disordered functioning, over and above knowledge of particular assessment tools per se, is essential for performing competent evaluations.

As we begin our review of assessment strategies, we reiterate such sage advice. Evaluation of antisocial behavior in children and adolescents requires knowledge of such diverse topics as developmental trajectories, biological and familial underpinnings, peer relationships, and the influences of wider systems in addition to such traditional "assessment" subject matter as measurement instruments, psychometrics, symptom patterns, and nosology. Indeed, the assessor who lacks grounding in (for example) current conceptions of subtyping, family psychopathology, behavior genetics, or neuropsychologic functioning runs the risk of using rating scales or structured interviews in a vacuum. Knowledge of this domain requires familiarity with the theoretical, environmental, and nosologic contexts in which it is embedded; assessment information will be decontextualized unless the assessor has a clear framework from which to interpret the findings. This entire handbook is thus fair game for those interested in learning about assessment and evaluation of antisocial behavior.[1]

TERMINOLOGY AND HISTORICAL OVERVIEW

An overlapping and potentially confusing array of terms and definitions is the first hurdle—and a daunting one—that the assessor of antisocial behavior must face. As detailed in Hinshaw and Anderson

(1996), the following terms convey distinct meanings: *Externalizing* behavior patterns include impulsive, overactive, inattentive, defiant, aggressive, or antisocial manifestations. Considerable evidence exists that aggression and antisocial actions show partial independence from the constituent behaviors of attention deficit/hyperactivity disorder (ADHD)—namely, inattention, impulsivity, and overactivity (Hinshaw, 1987). Although externalizing behavior patterns are typically distinguished from features termed *internalizing* (e.g., anxious, dysphoric, withdrawn, thought disordered, somaticizing; see Achenbach, 1991a), overlap between antisocial syndromes and disorders of anxiety and mood is clinically important.

Second, *antisocial behavior* (ASB) is the descriptive term commonly used to describe the subclass of externalizing actions in which the rights of others or society are violated. ASB includes but is not restricted to interpersonal aggression; indeed, the term incorporates both overt (aggressive, defiant, bullying) and covert (stealing, cheating, substance abuse, property destruction) manifestations (Loeber & Schmaling, 1985a), which have been shown to display diverging heritabilities, family interaction patterns, and outcomes (Hinshaw & Anderson, 1996). The heuristic meta-analysis of Frick et al. (1993) suggests that the domain of ASB comprises four quadrants demarcated by the orthogonal dimensions of overt versus covert and destructive versus nondestructive (see Figure 4.1). This figure conveys the topology of antisocial behavior and provides support for the diagnostic distinction between oppositional defiant disorder and conduct disorder (see later discussion).

From a legal perspective, child and adolescent manifestations of ASB are termed *delinquent*. Yet the usual necessity of official detection to invoke legal definitions, the virtual exclusion of young children, and the culturally relativistic nature of proscribed behavior defined by legal standards are all constraints. Current work on subtyping, in fact, reveals fundamental heterogeneity among delinquent youth (Moffitt, 1993).

Finally, in the psychiatric tradition of forming diagnostic categories, the diagnoses of *conduct disorder* (CD) and, more recently, *oppositional defiant disorder* (ODD) are the two mainstays of the *disruptive behavior disorders* (American Psychiatric Association [APA], 1994). ODD is denoted by the age-inappropriate and persistent display of angry, defiant, irritable, and oppositional behaviors; CD includes a far more severe list of aggressive and antiso-

Work on this chapter was supported by National Institute of Mental Health Grant R01 MH45064.

[1]We omit the vast domain of psychobiological and psychophysiological assessment related to antisocial behavior (see McBurnett & Lahey, 1994).

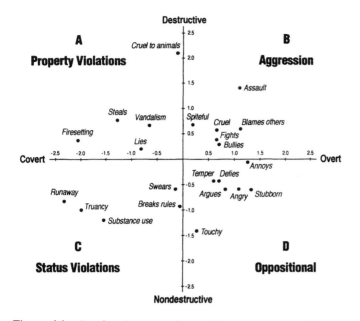

Figure 4.1 *Results of meta-analyses of factor analyses of disruptive child behaviors (see Frick et al., 1993). Copyright retained by Benjamin B. Lahey. Reprinted with permission.*

cial behaviors (e.g., initiating fights, breaking into others' homes, fire setting; APA, 1994). The constituent behaviors of CD are more destructive than the ODD symptom list (see Figure 4.1). The mean age of onset of ODD behavior patterns is in early childhood, whereas most CD behavior patterns tend to unfold in preadolescence; developmental progressions between ODD and CD have been elucidated, with high sensitivity but only modest predictive validity from the former to the latter (Hinshaw, Lahey, & Hart, 1993). The CD diagnosis includes persistent and impairing behavior patterns that are intended to signify underlying psychopathology; yet it is unknown whether lists of antisocial symptoms per se can automatically implicate underlying mental disorder or "pathology" (Richters & Ciccetti, 1993).[2]

We move next to a truncated history of assessment practices pertinent to ASB. For many years the predominant psychological assessment paradigm in the field was projective/intrapsychic, with attempts to uncover the intraindividual dynamics of delinquent or antisocial youth. Description and quantification of ASB per se were relatively neglected. Furthermore, with noteworthy exceptions (e.g., Glueck & Glueck, 1950), family assessment was left to caseworkers' home visits, and appraisal of neighborhood influences comprised the domain of sociology. Over the past 4 decades, however, several trends have greatly expanded the scope of assessment practices pertinent to ASB.

First, beginning with the seminal work of Jenkins and colleagues (e.g., Hewitt & Jenkins, 1946), quantified ratings have been increasingly used to appraise externalizing behavior (as well as the entire domain of child psychopathology). The work of Quay and Peterson (see Quay, 1979) and Achenbach (1991a) has been most influential in this regard. Relatedly, the behavioral revolution spurred interest in direct observation of both acting-out behavior and relevant family interaction patterns (e.g., Patterson, 1982). A second trend—toward recognition of discrete categories of deviant behavior—began with the publication of the first edition of the *Diagnostic and Statistical Manual of Mental Disorders (DSM-I)* in the early 1950s (APA, 1952) and gained empirical credibility with the publication of operational criteria in the groundbreaking *DSM-III* (APA, 1980). As highlighted later, a fruitful tension in the field regards the dimensional versus categorical approach to the classification of ASB patterns.

Third, as theoretical entrenchment has given way, in recent years, to integrated perspectives on ASB, assessors have incorporated such variegated strategies as family history interviews, evaluations of home climate and structure, peer sociometric appraisals, examination of neighborhoods, and key psychobiological indexes to their array of assessment methods. Although assessment of such domains may be beyond the scope and resources of most clinicians, the multiple risk and contextual factors related to ASB compel careful consideration of multivariate assessment strategies, driven by empirical validation and integration with key developmental themes (Mash & Terdal, 1988).

THEORETICAL CONTEXT AND CONTROVERSIAL ISSUES

Four key points are emphasized in our discussion of theoretical and empirical issues related to the assessment of ASB: (a) the necessity of adopting a developmental approach; (b) the relevance of identifying specific subtypes of antisocial individuals and behaviors; (c) the importance of reliably detecting and defining comorbid conditions; and (d) the challenges involved in amalgamating multi-informant data acquired across multiple settings. Two preliminary issues are salient. First, assessment per se (i.e., evaluating the cognitive, emotional, and behavioral functioning of an individual case) can be distinguished from classification (i.e., placing an individual into a discrete diagnostic category or empirically derived subgroup). Indeed, obtaining a diagnosis is typically just one of several goals of a sound assessment strategy, which may involve obtaining a thorough history, uncovering underlying mechanisms, setting treatment goals, and monitoring response to intervention, among other objectives. Yet because the central taxonomic issues currently under debate in the field are inextricably related to the assessment of ASB, the assessor must understand taxonomic and classification issues.

Second, as noted earlier, a key issue for the field involves categorical versus dimensional approaches to the assessment and classification of deviant behavior (e.g., Eysenck, 1986). Categorical approaches, by nature, rely on labeling the behavioral or emotional functioning of an individual as deviant when a certain threshold of symptom severity and impairment has been reached.

---

[2]We note in passing that the term for adults who display persistent antisocial behavior patterns is *antisocial personality disorder*, found on Axis II of *DSM-IV* (APA, 1994). This construct has recently been integrated, to some extent, with the older conception of *psychopathy* (Cleckley, 1976). For discussion of these categories, see Hinshaw and Anderson (1996) and Sutker (1994).

Disordered versus normal groups are assumed to differ qualitatively; individuals in the dysfunctional group would ideally share common family history, pathogenesis, long-term course, and response to treatment, differing from those of other taxa. In contrast, dimensional approaches quantify behavioral, cognitive, social, or emotional functioning, and level of severity is viewed in a continuous manner for each of the measured dimensions. Space limitations preclude full development of the issues surrounding dimensional versus categorical approaches, including instances of superiority for each (Robins & McEvoy, 1990; Rutter et al., 1990) and their possible compatibility and synthesis (Achenbach, 1993). The utility of categorizing ASB has been closely scrutinized in recent years, with criticism directed at (a) the potentially arbitrary nature of choosing symptom severity thresholds or cutoff points, possibly yielding dysfunctional versus normal groups that do *not* reflect true discontinuities (Hinshaw et al., 1993); (b) the limited ability of diagnostic criteria to take contextual and systemic information into consideration, resulting in an implied attribution to intraindividual causal factors (Hinshaw & Anderson, 1996); and (c) the potential failure of strict categorical diagnostic procedures to account for subthreshold comorbid disorders, with consequent neglect of potentially vital ancillary information (Richters & Cicchetti, 1993). The relatively small group of youngsters with early onset of ASB may well yield a distinct category, however (Moffitt, 1993); and adult psychopathy appears to form a viable taxon (Harris, Rice, & Quinsey, 1994). In short, assessors should use measurement tools that yield both dimensional *and* categorical data (e.g., Ollendick & King, 1994).

A Developmental Approach to the Assessment of Antisocial Behavior

For many individuals, high stability or continuity of ASB over time is evident (Hinshaw et al., 1993; Huesmann, Eron, Lefkowitz, & Walder, 1984). Yet the topography of ASB is more likely than not to change during the individual's life span (Moffitt, 1993). That is, individuals with early onset display diverse ASB across unfolding developmental stages—excessive hitting or biting may be apparent in toddlerhood, marked defiance during the preschool years, physical aggression toward peers (of a bullying or reactive nature) in elementary school, and covert features (truancy, shoplifting, and early drug use) during preadolescence. Subsequently, more serious property crimes may arise during the teenage years, followed by violent crimes and substance abuse in young adulthood with child or spousal abuse, fraud, or poor occupational adjustment evident in later adulthood. Such behavioral coherence of an inferred attribute or trait across developmental stages is called *heterotypic continuity* (Kagan, 1969; Moffitt, 1993). Thus, a developmental approach to assessment necessitates attention to *developmental trajectories* (Loeber, 1988), with differing evaluation strategies necessary at different ages.

A developmental approach to the assessment of ASB also implies sensitivity to systemic information. Indeed, severe ASB is intertwined with such contextual factors as coercive family interactions, deviant peer networks, and possibly subcultures as a whole (Patterson, DeBaryshe, & Ramsey, 1989; Quay, 1986), with the influences of these factors timed to the child's developmental level. For example, negative family interactions fuel the early display of defiant, aggressive behavior, which may be exacerbated by peer influences that promote subsequent intensification of ASB during preadolescence and adolescence (Patterson, Reid, & Dishion, 1992). Accurate assessment and appropriate weighting of such factors will aid in the formulation of a viable treatment plan and will force attention on the youth's developmental level.

Furthermore, in a developmental approach to evaluating ASB, the assessor must perform the difficult task of distinguishing accurately between developmentally appropriate versus nonnormative behaviors (e.g., occasional "rough and tumble" play vs. extreme and repetitive patterns of physical aggression in a preschool-aged boy). Instruments that are well normed across the age span are therefore essential. Additionally, it is important to measure individual strengths as well as deficits (e.g., academic skills that exceed grade level, prosocial behavior in specified situations) as the child's world expands to school and peer settings, in order to target important "building blocks" with respect to treatment recommendations. Indeed, although salient behavioral problems and prosocial functioning are correlated, they represent partially independent domains of child functioning (Kazdin, 1993). In all, assessors must search for instruments that capture distinct developmental pathways and processes that propel or maintain antisocial behavior patterns.

Distinguishing Subtypes of Antisocial Individuals and Behaviors

The diversity of the constituent behaviors subsumed by the ASB spectrum points to the importance of making theoretically and empirically meaningful distinctions related to specific subcategories of antisocial individuals and to subtypes of antisocial/aggressive behaviors. A brief overview of a number of dichotomized distinctions communicates the breadth of the domain; major reviews of the development of aggression provide more detailed descriptions (Feshbach, 1970; Parke & Slaby, 1983).

Subcategorization of Antisocial Individuals

Current classification systems (*DSM-IV;* APA, 1994) and proposed developmental taxonomies (Moffitt, 1993) feature two distinct subtypes or *developmental pathways* of conduct disorder (CD) or ASB: *child-onset* (also termed *early-starter* or *aggressive-versatile;* see review of McMahon, 1994) versus *adolescent-onset* (also called *late-onset* or *nonaggressive*). These subtypes differ with respect to characteristic presenting features, developmental history, course and severity, ratio of males to females, and prognosis. For example, compared to adolescent-onset individuals, child-onset youth (defined in *DSM-IV* by the presence of at least one criterion characteristic of CD prior to age 10) typically exhibit more serious physical aggression, have met diagnostic criteria for ODD earlier in childhood, experience severe peer and academic failures, display neuropsychological deficits, are prone to be male, and have a greater likelihood of persistent CD and the development of antisocial personality disorder as adults (Hinshaw et al., 1993; Moffitt, 1993).

Describing these two subtypes as *life-course-persistent* and *adolescence-limited,* Moffitt (1993) has presented a conceptual framework with disparate developmental pathways. For the former subtype, children's early neuropsychological deficits are held to interact with criminogenic environments in a cumulative fashion across the course of development, resulting in life-long pathology. Adolescence-limited ASB, which Moffitt (1993) views as a relatively transitory manifestation best understood in terms of social mimicry, underlies the high prevalence of ASB that is evident during teenage years.

Somewhat related, the classic work of Jenkins and colleagues yielded the distinction between *undersocialized* (or solitary type) versus *socialized* (or group type) ASB (Hewitt & Jenkins, 1946; Jenkins & Glickman, 1947), as evidenced by youths' differential patterns of antisocial activities and social bonds. The latter subtype is characterized by covert behavior within an established peer social network, often evident as gang membership. In contrast, undersocialized youths typically commit antisocial acts alone and the nature of their behavior is overtly aggressive and assaultive. Undersocialized, compared to socialized, youngsters typically exhibit more severe levels of psychopathology and have a poorer long-term outcome (Quay, 1987). Because of difficulties in operationalizing the socialization variable and because the age of onset and aggressive versus nonaggressive distinctions may, in fact, incorporate the socialized/undersocialized dichotomy, *DSM-IV* has dropped this distinction.

Subtyping of Antisocial/Aggressive Behavior Patterns

The assessor must also be aware that aggressive behavior has been subdivided in several ways that are theoretically important and empirically validated. For example, *physical* (bullying, fighting, assaulting) aggression often appears in rudimentary form early in development whereas *verbal* aggression has a somewhat later onset. Thus, persistence of physical aggression into grade school—and the early display of significant verbal aggression—may indicate the need for clinical attention. Similarly, certain levels of *instrumental* or goal-directed aggression (Feshbach, 1970) are normative for toddlers (e.g., pushing others away to obtain a favored toy or object), in contrast to *hostile* aggression (the infliction of pain on others), which is clinically important at any developmental stage if performed at high rates. Relatedly, Dodge (1991) has made the distinction between *proactive* (bullying, threatening) versus *reactive* (retaliatory) aggression, with specific social cognitive information processing deficits and distortions unique to each subtype. Specifically, biases in interpreting peers' cues and tendencies to attribute hostile intentions to others characterize reactive aggression (Dodge & Coie, 1987), whereas proactive aggression is marked by a propensity toward favorable evaluation of outcomes involving aggressive behavior (Dodge, 1991). Reactivity may be linked, as well, to concepts of impulsive aggression (see Vitiello, Behar, Hunt, Stoff, & Ricciuti, 1990); the latter construct has been important in investigations of both self-inflicted and other-directed destructive behavior, with emphasis on serotonergic systems (Kruesi et al., 1992).

Aggression can also be classified as *direct* versus *indirect*. Whereas direct aggression includes the types of openly verbal and physical acts cited earlier, indirect aggression includes spreading rumors, encouraging a peer group to ostracize or shun a targeted individual, or using a third party to "get even" via physical means.

Indirect aggression may pertain to girls more than boys (Bjorkqvist, Osterman, & Kaukianinen, 1992), and its recognition may mitigate the oft-cited gender differences in rates of aggression and ASB (Goodman & Kohlsdorf, 1994; see also the similar construct of *relational aggression* posited by Crick & Grotpeter, 1995).

Finally, regarding the differentiation of overt and covert ASB (see earlier discussion), we point out that current *DSM-IV* criteria for CD include both sets of actions, yet not in a manner sensitive to the distinction. Thus, *DSM-IV* confounds overt and covert behavior patterns, resulting in heterogeneity of the CD diagnostic category (Achenbach, 1993).

In short, far too many clinical assessments and research reports discuss "aggression" or "antisocial behavior" as if these were unidimensional constructs, when considerable evidence supports the distinctions noted earlier in this section. Knowledge of the precise kinds of aggressive and antisocial behavior patterns exhibited by clinical cases or research samples is necessary for greater precision in both clinical assessments and research reports.

Issues of Comorbidity

Interest in comorbidity related to child psychopathology has surged in recent years (Caron & Rutter, 1991). True comorbidity can be defined as the overlap or co-occurrence of independent disorders at levels exceeding chance overlap. Although comorbidity has long been neglected in both clinical case reports and descriptions of research samples, evidence is beginning to mount that disparate developmental histories, associated features, developmental trajectories, and response to treatment pertain to CD when associated with different comorbidities (e.g., Capaldi, 1991; Hinshaw et al., 1993). Thus, assessment tools (rating scales or interviews) that focus solely on ASB are insufficient; viable assessment batteries must include measures sensitive to ADHD, internalizing disorders, and academic underachievement, to name three critical areas of comorbidity. For more extensive coverage see Hinshaw and Anderson (1996), Caron and Rutter (1991), and Lahey and Loeber (Chapter 5, this volume).

For one thing, almost all boys with child-onset CD meet diagnostic criteria for oppositional defiant disorder (ODD), defined by significant levels of defiant, argumentative, angry, and irritable behavior. The reverse pattern, however, is not true; only a minority of youngsters meeting criteria for ODD progress to CD (Hinshaw et al., 1993). ODD can thus be viewed as both developmentally related to CD and quite likely to co-occur with (and serve as a precursor to) child-onset ASB, but it does *not* appear to be a part of the developmental pathway of adolescent-onset ASB. Such developmental staging implies that ODD and CD are likely to be age-related manifestations of underlying antisocial tendencies in the relatively small group of early-onset youth.

Second, although ASB and ADHD are partially independent dimensions of externalizing behavior (Hinshaw, 1987; Loney, 1987), the comorbidity of these two disorders is high (Biederman, Newcorn, & Sprich, 1991). Marked severity of dysfunction is specific to this comorbidity (Walker, Lahey, Hynd, & Frame, 1987), including an early-onset, persistent course of ASB and a pernicious set of associated features (Hinshaw et al., 1993). The comorbid ASB–ADHD subgroup represents more than a simple cumulation of the individual behavioral, cognitive, and academic deficits separately associated with pure CD versus pure ADHD; the unique pattern of underachievement, severe peer rejection, extremely poor prognosis, and resistance to treatment in the CD + ADHD subgroup suggests a true hybrid (see review in Hinshaw, 1994a), with the possibility of separate means of genetic transmission (Biederman et al., 1992; Faraone, Biederman, Keenan, & Tsuang, 1991).

Evidence also exists that children and adolescents with CD are much more likely than non-CD youths to display anxiety and depressive disorders (Zoccolillo, 1992). Whereas the co-existence of anxiety disorder is associated with *less* severe overt aggression during childhood (Walker et al., 1991), the presence of comorbid anxiety disorder in preadolescence may be linked with *increased* levels of aggressive behavior (Lahey & McBurnett, 1992). Furthermore, (a) CD and depression co-occur at greater-than-chance levels in clinical samples; (b) child-onset CD may place individuals (particularly girls) at risk for adolescent and adult depression; (c) depressive episodes in some adolescents lead to antisocial behaviors; and (d) comorbid CD and depression may be linked to increased risk for suicidal behavior (see coverage in Hinshaw et al., 1993).

Finally, with growing significance for etiological models and for identification of early risk markers, *academic underachievement* within a constellation of early aggression and ADHD appears linked to greater persistence of severe ASB later in life (Hinshaw, 1992; Moffitt, 1990). Thus, as a prevalent correlate of ASB (particularly in adolescence), a risk factor for poor outcome, and a separate target for intervention, academic performance is most deserving of assessment in individuals suspected of ASB patterns.

Formulating Assessment Strategies and Combining Disparate Sources of Information

Current etiological models feature the role of several complex and interactive causal pathways leading to the development of ASB (Moffitt, 1993; Patterson et al., 1992). Factors thought to play either a causal role or to be influential in maintaining or exacerbating deviant behavior encompass a diverse array, spanning hereditary components, early temperament, family psychopathology (especially antisocial-spectrum disorders), family composition and status (e.g., family size, single vs. two parent, socioeconomic status, evidence of family violence), parenting styles in the context of the reciprocal nature of child–parent interactions, peer relations, academic performance, and early signs of neuropsychological deficits (see the summary table of Hinshaw & Anderson, 1996). This partial list conveys the rather daunting task facing the assessor.

Several guiding principles should prove useful when choosing and implementing assessment strategies to capture such disparate factors. First, as posited by Skinner (1981), assessors must pay attention not only to the reliability but also to the convergent, divergent, predictive, and construct validity of instruments they use. An overview of the specific psychometric properties of measures commonly utilized in the assessment of ASB appears in the section "Assessment Methods and Findings." Second, because of the diversity and pervasiveness of ASB, because of its changing behavioral manifestations with development, and because of the extremely modest correspondence of data from different informants (Achenbach, McConaughy, & Howell, 1987), it is necessary to employ assessment procedures that tap multiple behaviors and symptoms across multiple settings as measured by multiple informants (McMahon, 1994). Indeed, although interinformant agreement is stronger for externalizing than for internalizing symptomatology, amounts of shared variance between, for example, parents and teachers are distressingly low.[3] Furthermore, the high prevalence of antisocial *symptoms* (in contrast to a full CD *syndrome* or *diagnosis*) in the general population (e.g., Offord, Boyle, & Racine, 1991) means that relying on a single method of measurement (e.g., rating scales) or a single source of information (e.g., parental report) presents a danger for biased assessment and overstating of prevalence. Within the externalizing areas of oppositional and hyperactive behaviors, evidence is clear that children greatly underreport symptomatology in comparison to adult informants (e.g., Loeber, Green, Lahey, & Stouthamer-Loeber, 1989, 1991). Thus, particularly for preadolescents, self-report of behavior patterns pertinent to ODD or ADHD appears to have little, if any, utility. Yet youths themselves may be uniquely situated to report on more severe conduct problems, particularly covert antisocial symptoms, and on internalizing patterns (see Herjanic & Reich, 1982; Loeber et al., 1991). Additionally, Offord, Boyle, and Racine (1991) offer evidence suggesting that adolescents report antisocial symptoms more openly in self-report than in interview format, suggesting that computer-driven diagnostic interviews may yield greater candor and validity. A continuing research agenda pertains to the viability of different informants and assessment methods for ASB and its common comorbidities.

We reiterate that disparity across informants and measurement sources does not imply the unilateral exclusion of certain individuals from assessment procedures nor the exclusion of certain formats or techniques from specific informants. Potentially valuable background, diagnostic, and treatment-relevant information would be lost. Yet amalgamating disparate information from multiple informants presents conceptual and statistical issues, with one important dichotomy pertaining to simple versus complex solutions. In simple information-combining strategies, information from all sources is equally weighted or a symptom's presence is counted if any informant has endorsed it (note the ascendancy of the latter strategy for ASB; Loeber & Farrington, 1994). Complex strategies, on the other hand, provide differential weights for different sources, involving algorithms or multivariate combinations. If all sources of diagnostic information are valid, current evidence favors the use of simple rather than complex solutions (Piacentini, Cohen, & Cohen, 1992). In addition, greater uniformity across individual assessors, clinics, and measures can be achieved as the potential idiosyncrasies involved with complex algorithms are eliminated (Piacen-

---

[3]Achenbach et al. (1987) highlight that modest levels of association across informants do not imply unreliability; indeed, each source often shows impressive stability or internal consistency. Rather, children's behavior may differ in distinct contexts and settings, and each assessment source may contribute important information. Also, related to a different externalizing disorder (ADHD), Biederman, Keenan, and Faraone (1990) have shown that parental accounts of their children's behavior patterns yield a 90% positive predictive power with respect to teacher-based diagnoses. Thus, assessment based on one adult informant may be predictive of important criterion measures from another.

tini et al., 1992). For additional discussion of this important topic, see Bird, Gould, and Staghezza (1992), who discuss the use of "optimal" informants for various domains of functioning.

Summary

In this section we have discussed several conceptual and theoretical issues pertinent to the assessment of ASB, including the distinction between categorical/taxonomic and dimensional/quantitative strategies, the importance of developmental considerations (and appropriate age norms) in the evaluation process, the necessity of recognizing subcategories of individuals with ASB patterns and subtypes of aggressive behavior, the need to assess comorbid conditions and associated impairments, and the complexities of amalgamating assessment information from disparate (and weakly correlated) sources of data. Bearing these issues in mind, we turn to specific strategies.

ASSESSMENT METHODS AND FINDINGS

Our review of assessment methods and tools is limited by space constraints, precluding any kind of thorough measure-by-measure coverage. More detailed accounts are found in such sources as Kazdin (1987), Mash and Terdal (1988), and Shaffer and Richters (in press). Our attempt here is to capture the essence of particular assessment tools, with emphasis on conceptual, practical, and psychometric issues as well as on strengths and weaknesses.

Reports From Adult Informants

Rating Scales

Rating scales, also termed behavioral checklists, provide a quantitative index of adult informants' global impressions of children's behavior and have long served as a cornerstone of measurement in child psychopathology. Such instruments often initiate the referral and assessment process in clinical settings. Offering many attractive conceptual, empirical, and practical advantages over alternative assessment devices, a plethora of rating scales have been developed. Such checklists are best regarded as a necessary yet insufficient measurement tool in the assessment of ASB.

Rating scales require parents or teachers to judge a child's behavioral patterns in terms of the presence/absence (i.e., binary judgments) or severity (i.e., Likert-type ratings) of specific behavioral complaints. The relative ease and speed of administration as well as the quantified nature of the significant adults' perceptions compose the major advantages of rating scales. Furthermore, based upon overall breadth and depth of item coverage, a rating scale can assess dimensions ranging from molecular to molar levels. Checklists that are broad in scope include items descriptive of antisocial/conduct-disordered actions along with symptoms of other childhood disorders. Two prominent examples of such checklists are the widely used Child Behavior Checklist and Revised Child Behavior Profile (CBCL and RCBP; Achenbach 1991a) and the Revised Behavior Problem Checklist (RBPC; Quay & Peterson, 1983). Other rating scales with narrower item coverage have been

devised specifically for the assessment of disruptive behavior disorders in children; these are suitable for such purposes as assessing the presence and severity of overtly aggressive behaviors (Eyberg Child Behavior Inventory; Eyberg & Robinson, 1983), identifying co-existing conduct disorder and hyperactive symptomatology (Conners Abbreviated Symptom Questionnaire; Conners, 1990), or discriminating inattention/overactivity from aggression/defiance (IOWA Conners Teacher Rating Scale; Loney & Milich, 1982). For a review, see Hinshaw and Nigg (in press).

Although the majority of rating scales yield respectable to excellent psychometric properties, broad scales are, on average, psychometrically superior, given the larger and more diverse normative bases from which they have been derived (Hinshaw & Nigg, in press). The CBCL is exemplary in this regard, providing the assessor with global indexes of total, externalizing, and internalizing problems as well as useful clinical profiles comprising empirically derived combinations of several narrowband scales. It is important to note that the psychometric properties of the CBCL narrowband externalizing scales (Aggression, measuring overt manifestations, and Delinquency, tapping covert behavior patterns) are at least as good as those of many narrower scales derived specifically for disruptive behavior disorders (Achenbach, 1991a). The CBCL also includes a Social Competence index, unlike most other checklists that tend to exclude positive behaviors. The CBCL's large normative base yields clinical cutpoints across various age subgroups (ages 2 to 3, 4 to 5, 6 to 11, and 12 to 17) for each gender, exemplifying sensitivity to developmental context. Parallel parent and teacher forms (Teacher Report Form; Achenbach, 1991b), as well as a Youth Self-Report form for adolescents (Achenbach, 1991c), provide reliable and valid multiagent information, with evidence supporting the differential predictive value of parent versus teacher reports (Verhulst, Koot, & Van der Ende, 1994).

Rating scales are not, however, immune to methodological and practical shortcomings. First, because their items and format do not precisely parallel formal diagnostic criteria, and because checklists lack precision regarding onset and duration of symptom patterns, rating scales are neither appropriate nor sufficient for making a diagnosis. Far more children may surpass cutoff scores on a given rating scale than the number truly exhibiting "disorders." Second, reliance on only one adult informant introduces the danger of obtaining a potentially skewed clinical picture, with the risk of misidentifying important cross-situational behavioral patterns. Third, as described in detail by Hinshaw and Nigg (in press), ratings of disruptive behavior may be biased because of (a) adult informants' differential subjective interpretations of the content or definition of specific items; (b) the possibility that ratings are more reflective of the informant's high level of distress rather than of actual child behavior; (c) the informant's implicit personality theories about disruptive behaviors; and (d) halo effects (i.e., systematic over- or underinflation of ratings). The latter two biases can lead to exceedingly high intercorrelations among subdomains on a global checklist; furthermore, teacher ratings of ASB tend to "spill over" and lead to spurious inference of ADHD-related behavior patterns (Abikoff, Courtney, Pelham, & Koplewicz, 1993). Such potential biases underscore the necessity of multiinformant/multimethod strategies.

Fourth, although even the longest global checklists may take only 15 to 20 minutes of the informant's time, certain circumstances (e.g., repeated use of the measure to monitor treatment progress) may limit their feasibility and utility. Finally, if the goal is to monitor the effects of psychosocial intervention for children with ASB, parents and teachers (who are the primary agents of intervention) cannot provide "blind" appraisal of outcome on rating scales. More objective tools are required.

The choice of rating scale(s) should be guided by the overall needs of the particular assessment situation. Well-normed and validated broad scales may be used as a primary means of assessment, despite the limitations discussed earlier. As a first step in the assessment process, they may afford an initial overview of externalizing and internalizing symptomatology, with subsequent assessment procedures necessary to facilitate a formal diagnosis and treatment plan. In some instances, however, the advantages of using narrower scales may outweigh the benefits of obtaining a more global clinical picture. For example, narrow scales are most appropriately used if relevant global information has been reliably acquired via alternative modalities or when ease of repeated measurement is a practical consideration. Furthermore, in large-scale research investigations, narrow scales may serve as a low-cost, easily gathered initial inclusion criterion or "gate," to be followed up with broader scales and more thorough assessment strategies if preliminary cutoff scores are surpassed. Such multiple-gating assessment procedures are important for large clinical trials (e.g., Patterson, 1982). In all, the assessor needs a well-formulated assessment plan when weighing the trade-offs between broad and narrow scales.

Interviews

Interviews with adult informants have long been a mainstay of clinical assessments pertaining to children and adolescents. Most interviews have traditionally been unstructured (or at most semistructured), with the interviewee largely directing the flow of the interchange. In the semistructured domain, a thorough developmental history (although limited by retrospective recall) may be an extremely helpful tool for uncovering temperamental origins and family reactions to a long history of externalizing behavior (e.g., Hinshaw, 1994a). Yet the heightened interest in formal diagnosis in recent years, requiring precise information on symptom patterns and timing, has propelled structured interviews to the fore. Indeed, for research investigations, diagnostic information based on structured interviews is virtually a necessity (Hodges, 1994). Our brief coverage focuses on several issues relevant to the optimal use of such interviews with respect to ASB.

First, to a greater extent than rating scales, structured interviews specify a precise time frame within which parents (or teachers) describe behavioral patterns. These are necessary for purposes of localizing symptom onset, offset, or both and therefore for specifying diagnoses. Second, directives from the interviewer or from the instruction set can aid in clarifying the meaning of the behaviors under discussion, an important consideration given the ambiguity or misinterpretations that may accrue from the reading of an item from a rating scale. Third, although structured interviews are geared toward diagnosis, counts of the number of symptoms can be retained, consistent with dimensional approaches to

evaluation. Fourth, crucial information on internalizing diagnoses that may be comorbid with ASB patterns mandates the use of sensitive structured interview strategies. In short, the far greater time and effort required to obtain structured interviews (as opposed to collecting rating scale information) has the potential for yielding more precise information consistent with making categorical diagnostic decisions.

Reviews of specific interviews are outside the scope of this chapter, but several additional points regarding their use are in order.[4] For one thing, as with rating scales, correspondence across different informants is not high. Although such agreement appears to be stronger for externalizing than for internalizing behavior patterns (Hodges, 1993, 1994), we reiterate that on self-report versions of structured interviews, children greatly underreport symptom patterns pertinent to ADHD and ODD (see Loeber et al., 1989; Loeber et al., 1991). For another, the use of structured interviews requires careful attention to the training of interviewers and to the need for monitoring of cross-interviewer agreement in the asking of questions and the recording of responses. Whereas all structured interviews are manual-driven, some protocols are quite structured, with little or no variation in the presentation of questions (cf. the DISC), whereas others require trained clinicians who have more leeway in questioning. In either case, appraisal of reliability is crucial. Furthermore, assessment of the validity of structured interviews requires careful attention to the base rates of disorders in question, mandating caution in comparing psychometric properties across varying populations (e.g., clinic vs. community samples). Finally, unless functional level or impairment is assessed, strict symptom counts from structured interviews will tend to overdiagnose child populations (Hodges, 1993). Supplemental information on the impairment that accrues to problem behavior may be necessary (e.g., Bird et al., 1993).

In short, investigators or clinicians desiring more complete information about structured interviews will need to invest time in researching the alternative formats and psychometric properties of the growing number of interviews in the field. Although structured interviews are increasingly important when clinical or research diagnoses are desired, they cannot be considered sufficient, as information about functioning in psychological, academic, peer-related, and familial domains is also needed.

Self-Report Measures

Driven by recognition of the value of children's self-reported feelings in the assessment and diagnosis of internalizing disorders (e.g., Herjanic & Reich, 1982) and the prominent role of children's cognitions, self-perceptions, and self-monitoring capabili-

---

[4]Structured interviews with algorithm-generated diagnoses include the Diagnostic Interview Schedule for Children (DISC), designed for epidemiological research and revised several times over the past decade (e.g., Fisher et al., 1993); the Child and Adolescent Psychiatric Assessment (CAPA), also intended for lay interviewers (e.g., Angold, Cox, Prendergast, Rutter, & Simonoff, 1987); and the Child Assessment Schedule, which features a format more like that of traditional clinical interviews (e.g., Hodges, Cools, & McKnew, 1989).

ties in emergent models of child psychopathology (e.g., Kendall & Hammen, 1995), procedures that directly assess children's emotions, cognitions, and behavior patterns have expanded rapidly in recent decades.[5] Despite the construction of parallel child and parent versions of structured diagnostic interviews and the development of numerous semistructured interviews and rating scales tailored for use with children, issues concerning the reliability and validity of such devices persist—particularly as a function of the child's age and the type of symptomatology under consideration (Edelbrock, Costello, Dulcan, Kalas, & Conover, 1985; Loeber et al., 1991). Within a cautious interpretative framework, however, the self-report of antisocial youths may be essential to the measurement of covert or infrequently occurring ASB and to the uncovering of concomitant internalizing features.

Structured Interviews

The format of structured diagnostic interviews for children is nearly identical to that of parent versions, as described in the previous section; modifications in the phrasing/language of certain questions are intended to produce age-appropriate child versions without jeopardizing item content or diagnostic validity. Although the most widely used diagnostic interviews encourage administration to children ages 6 to 18, structured interviews are typically not appropriate for youngsters under age 10 because of extremely unreliable reporting of symptoms (Edelbrock et al., 1985). As noted earlier, this caveat pertains especially to reports of oppositional/defiant or attention-disordered symptomatology. Devoting a few minutes to an informal interview (i.e., abbreviated play session, going for a brief walk) or mental status examination, however, can be productive with younger children in terms of establishing rapport, obtaining an initial (albeit cursory) assessment of prominent characteristics (e.g., verbal and social skills, potential thought disorder), and ascertaining the child's understanding of the referral.

With children aged 10 and above, administration of a structured interview may serve as a useful diagnostic aid. For example, Edelbrock et al. (1985) reported increasing reliability with age for children's report of psychiatric symptoms on the initial version of the DISC. This pattern of reliability is especially relevant with regard to internalizing symptoms and severe antisocial acts, as such behavior is reported less frequently by mothers than by their children (Herjanic & Reich, 1982). Thus, age and content considerations are salient in the decision to perform diagnostic interviews with children.

Semistructured Interviews and Rating Scales

Overall, relatively few self-report measures of ASB for children are in widespread use. Although some investigators have indicated that conduct-disordered children often underpresent levels of *overt* aggressive behavior compared to their mothers and teachers

(Kazdin, Esveldt-Dawson, Unis, & Rancurello, 1983; Ledingham, Younger, Schwartzman, & Bergeron, 1982), other findings point to reliable, valid, and independent contributions of child-based reports of *covert* ASB (Loeber & Schmaling, 1985b; Loeber, Green et al., 1989). As stated earlier, parents are typically less aware of covert behaviors, especially as youths move into adolescence and spend more time away from home and direct parental supervision. Furthermore, most delinquent acts (an estimated 90%; Empey, 1982) go undetected or are not acted upon officially. Thus, similar to parent reports, official records are likely to underestimate the actual incidence of covert ASB, necessitating the acquisition of self-report data to detect, for example, vandalism, theft, and drug use.[6]

Examples of potentially useful self-report devices aimed at assessing ASB include the Interview for Antisocial Behavior (IAB; Kazdin & Esveldt-Dawson, 1986), a semistructured interview appropriate for children aged 6 to 13 that yields scores for severity, duration, and total ASB (including separate factors of overt and covert behaviors); the Self-Report of Delinquency questionnaire (SRD; Elliott, Huizinga, & Ageton, 1985), a semistructured interview, based on the National Youth Survey, intended for youths aged 11 to 17 and measuring the frequency with which an individual has engaged in delinquent behavior, alcohol and drug use, and related offenses; the Self-Report of Antisocial Behavior (SRA), a modified version of the SRD appropriate for children aged 7 to 10 that taps overt and covert ASB (Loeber, Stouthamer-Loeber, Van Kammen, & Farrington, 1989); and the Youth Self-Report (YSR) of the CBCL (Achenbach, 1991c), appropriate for youths 12 to 17 years of age, which yields indexes of behavior problems and social competence similar to the adult CBCL scales. Although the YSR and the SRD have been evaluated somewhat more extensively than the SRA and IAB, all of these measures have acceptable psychometric properties and allow the assessor to obtain crucial information directly from children or adolescents.

Direct Observations

Compared to rating scales that appraise ASB, direct observational strategies yield several key methodological advantages: greater objectivity, less potential for bias, and the power to sharpen distinctions between constructs of interest (e.g., Hinshaw, Simmel, & Heller, 1995). Indeed, in the classic work of Kent, O'Leary, Diament, and Dietz (1974), global raters were markedly influenced by expectations of treatment-related benefits for the children under consideration, but observational methods did not yield biased data. As discussed earlier, intervention studies involving psychosocial intervention with parents and teachers produce non-treatment-

---

[5]Although *indirect* "self-report" assessment methods (e.g., projective devices) have a long tradition, these instruments have been plagued historically by weak psychometric properties. Improvements in standardized scoring have recently been achieved on some fronts (see Exner, 1990, regarding the Rorschach), and projective assessment techniques have received advocacy from cognitive as well as psychodynamic investigators. We view such devices as having limited incremental utility, however, and deemphasize their role in the assessment of ASB.

[6]Whenever possible, however, institutional and societal records should be included in assessment databases. The potential utility of such measures has been noted by Kazdin (1987). Particularly with preadolescents and teens, information pertaining to police contacts, arrest records, school attendance, grades, suspensions, and expulsions should be collected by the assessor if readily available. Furthermore, such indexes have long played a vital role as outcome variables in longitudinal research and intervention studies.

blind adults whose appraisal of gains via ratings or questionnaires is suspect. For many reasons, then, direct observational methods appear advantageous for appraising externalizing behavior. Indeed, objective observations have been important means of ascertaining diagnostic status and treatment response in children with ADHD (Abikoff & Gittelman, 1985; Hinshaw, Henker, Whalen, Erhardt, & Dunnington, 1989).

The key drawbacks of observational data collection involve expense and logistic constraints. Quite simply, training observers for live or videotaped coding of discrete behavioral events is time consuming and costly, and maintaining interobserver agreement is an ongoing process requiring ample supervision. Furthermore, for most applications, sending observers into home or classroom settings requires permission for access that may not be easily obtainable. Coding from videotapes, moreover, mandates either placement of cameras and microphones in the natural environment or the recording of clinic analogue procedures. Whereas direct observational methods are prohibitive for most clinical applications, observations of externalizing, aggressive, and ASB patterns have produced essential data with regard to family interaction patterns (e.g., C. Anderson, Hinshaw, & Simmel, 1994; K. Anderson, Lytton, & Romney, 1986; Patterson et al., 1992), linkages with peer status (Erhardt & Hinshaw, 1994), and response to intervention (see Patterson, 1982). We therefore advocate their use when feasible, particularly in research endeavors. In addition, even informal observations can be quite revealing in clinical applications. Two key issues in the observation of ASB are salient.

First, ASB typically occurs with rather low base rates (lower, for example, than the inattentive or impulsive behaviors of youngsters with ADHD). Thus, repeated sampling is usually necessary, adding to the burden that accrues to observational methodology. One methodological advance regarding the recording of infrequent but important ASB patterns involves the daily telephone report procedures of Patterson, Dishion, and colleagues (Patterson et al., 1992), in which brief calls to family members, the youths themselves, or both probe the occurrence, that day, of a number of important antisocial actions. With repeated calls, density of recording may be optimized with minimal respondent burden. When coupled with live home observations of coercive family interchange, such methodologies (which are actually a cross between ratings and observations per se) have proven central to advancing the field's understanding of familial underpinnings of the development of ASB.

Second, by definition, covert ASB occurs surreptitiously, constraining the utility of direct observational methods. In an attempt to yield objective counts of the covert actions of stealing, property destruction, and cheating, Hinshaw, Heller, and McHale (1992) and Hinshaw et al. (1995) devised a laboratory temptation paradigm in which individual children were tempted to take money and small objects, misuse materials in a room, or use an answer key for a worksheet. Counts of these covert actions were reliably made and showed correspondence with naturalistic indexes of parallel behaviors. Furthermore, youngsters with ADHD were far more likely than comparison children to commit such acts, and stimulant medication significantly influenced their rates (Hinshaw et al., 1992). It is important to note that the laboratory indexes of stealing and property destruction formed an empirical dimension distinct from naturalistically observed overt aggression (Hinshaw et al., 1995).[7]

Parent-Child Interactions and Family Processes

Current etiological models of aggression and ASB center on the intergenerational nature of antisocial behavior patterns and the importance of family-level variables for the genesis and maintenance of the salient behavior patterns (Patterson et al., 1992). Although parental and child behaviors are likely to be reciprocally determined, ASB is clearly familial, implicating examination of such variables as family history, home climate, marital conflict, parental child-rearing attitudes and practices, and specific parent-child interaction patterns, to name several of the most salient constructs. Whereas illumination of this vast area is beyond the scope of this chapter, we highlight the need for assessors to appraise such specific variables as family history of psychopathology, the structure of the home, quality of parental interactions with each other, reward and punishment practices, history of abusive interactions, and quality of parent-child interactions, to name only a few (see Cairns, Cadwallader, Estell, & Neckerman, Chapter 19, this volume; Dishion & Patterson, Chapter 20, this volume; Widom, Chapter 16, this volume). Just as with the evaluation of ASB patterns per se, assessment of familial factors requires input from multiple assessors through multiple methods. Key measures might include structured interviews with parents about current and past psychopathology, Q-sorts or interviews regarding child-rearing attitudes, and direct observations of marital interaction and parent-child interchange.

Space permits only a smattering of discussion about such assessment strategies. First, structured interviews and pertinent questionnaires with parents have uncovered the antisocial-spectrum family psychopathology in which severe antisocial activity (particularly of the early-onset type) is embedded (Hetherington & Martin, 1986). Second, despite general consensus that marital conflict predicts acting-out behavior patterns (Emery, 1982), global questionnaires of marital satisfaction are less helpful than interactional appraisal of specific types of couple conflict. Indeed, recent research has uncovered specificity between couple interactional style and child problem behavior (Katz & Gottman, 1993). Third, analysis of sequential patterns of parent-child interaction gleaned from objective, in-home observation has guided major contributions to the field (Patterson, 1982), in which theoretical and empirical models of coercive interchange have been tested. In short, hostile, inconsistent parenting provides modeling, positive reinforcement, and negative reinforcement for overt ASB; and

---

[7]This "covert" paradigm is an example of experimental laboratory methods for directly observing ASB. Other examples in recent years include the paradigms of Atkins and Stoff (1993), Murphy, Pelham, and Lang (1992), and Pelham et al. (1991), in which alleged provocations are intended to elicit analogues of reactive (hostile) or instrumental aggression. Whereas the ecological validity of laboratory methods is always a key question and ethical issues are important considerations (Hinshaw et al., 1992), the control afforded by such controlled conditions may afford fine-grained analysis of specific components of ASB and of environmental parameters.

poor monitoring appears related to covert manifestations (Patterson, 1982). Fourth, such variables as parental stress cannot be overlooked as both contributors to and consequences of ASB in offspring. For thorough coverage of the role of family-level variables in the genesis and maintenance of ASB patterns, see Hetherington and Martin (1986), Hinshaw and Anderson (1996), and Frick (1993).

Cognitive Deficits, Academic Underachievement, and Neuropsychological Processing

Recent accounts of the development of ASB implicate cognitive deficits and academic underachievement in early-onset forms of CD (Hinshaw, 1992; Moffitt & Lynam, 1994; Patterson et al., 1992). Although thorough discussion of the neuropsychological and cognitive contributions to aggression and ASB far transcends this chapter (see Henry & Moffitt, Chapter 26, this volume), several summary points are salient. First, in childhood, the more specific linkage is between attention deficits (rather than aggression per se) and early cognitive problems or underachievement (Hinshaw, 1992). Thus, as highlighted earlier, viable assessment strategies for aggression must ascertain the presence of comorbid ADHD. Second, a history of neuropsychological deficits may interact with poor family relationships and family distress to solidify impulsive, aggressive behavior patterns (Moffitt, 1990), mandating evaluation of pertinent familial factors. Third, by adolescence, ASB is linked with underachievement and early school termination (Moffitt, 1993), requiring continued monitoring of academic progress throughout development.

In all, individual assessment of intellectual functioning, academic achievement, and more fine-grained neuropsychological processing is often of crucial importance for both clinical and research purposes. Obtaining releases to gather school records should be a preliminary step for all evaluations pertinent to ASB. If resources allow, formal intelligence and achievement testing is strongly recommended (Sattler, 1992). More time-consuming and costly neuropsychological assessment will be indicated if referral questions are pertinent or if research hypotheses focus on underlying processing skills.

Peer Sociometrics

A large body of research using peer sociometric assessment has consistently demonstrated the strong relationship between aggression and peer rejection in childhood (Coie, Dodge, & Kupersmidt, 1990; Erhardt & Hinshaw, 1994) and the prognostic power of negative social status regarding such outcomes as school dropout, criminality, and adult psychopathology (Parker & Asher, 1987). Furthermore, measurement of peer social status may lend incremental utility and validity in the specification of various subgroups of externalizing youngsters (Milich & Landau, 1989). Unfortunately, logistical constraints and potential ethical considerations typically curtail the routine use of peer-based appraisals in clinical sociometric assessments. If peer-based appraisals can be obtained, Asher and Coie (1990) and Newcomb, Bukowski, and Pattee (1993) provide useful reviews of current sociometric procedures for children. Although teacher estimates of a child's peer status are only partially valid, they are worthy of consideration in the absence of peer-based information.[8]

From a developmental perspective, although early-starter or life-course-persistent antisocial individuals are likely to suffer from peer rejection in childhood and evince continued relationship difficulties throughout development (Hinshaw, 1994b; Moffitt, 1993), youths with "pure" aggression are likely to display controversial sociometric status, involving high rates of liking *and* disliking from peers (Milich & Landau, 1989). The subgroup of youngsters with comorbid ADHD and aggression is nearly uniformly rejected by agemates (Hinshaw & Melnick, 1995). Furthermore, early-onset youngsters may enjoy some time-limited popularity during adolescence as they take on the role of modeling deviant behavior to "less accomplished" late-starters (Moffitt, 1993). Adolescent-onset youths, as a group, will probably show no remarkable history in terms of negative peer appraisal throughout their course of development. We highlight, at a broader level, the influence of deviant peer groups on the emergence of ASB in adolescence. In short, information on peer relationships and peer status is likely to be important theoretically and clinically.

Neighborhood and Sociocultural Factors

Numerous contextual factors have been implicated as risk factors in the development of ASB (for a seminal review, see Capaldi & Patterson, 1994). Often included are parental variables (parental criminality, ASB, or depression), family status variables (divorce or parental transitions), large family size, overall intrafamilial stress (e.g., unemployment of one or both parents), and such broader neighborhood and sociocultural variables as disorganized, high-crime locations; low socioeconomic status (SES); and extrafamilial stress. Indeed, the high rates of crime and delinquency in urban areas (Rutter, 1981), the marked variation in delinquency rates across neighborhoods within the same urban setting (Rutter & Giller, 1983), and the elevated delinquency rates in specific socially fragmented, highly disorganized, and adult crime-ridden areas (Sampson, 1985) are all well established in the literature. Furthermore, low SES has consistently predicted early-onset (but not adolescent-onset) CD above and beyond the effects of other correlates and disorders (Offord et al., 1991; Rutter, 1981).

Neighborhood and SES variables are best viewed as macrocontextual conditions, the effects of which are mediated by their relationship with and impact on the microcontextual factors of parental functioning and family management practices (Capaldi &

---

[8]If teacher-based sociometric data are pursued, procedures that evaluate "whether the child is liked" rather than "what the child is like" should be obtained (Parker & Asher, 1987). The former type of evaluation would potentially provide unique information to the assessor, whereas the latter approximates behavior checklist data supplied by the same informant (i.e., the teacher). Hinshaw and Melnick (1995) present data indicating the positive (albeit modest) associations between teacher- and peer-appraised sociometric status of children with externalizing disorders.

Patterson, 1994). Such contextual factors are relevant to our discussion in two ways. First, researchers assessing contextual and systems factors in the development of ASB must pay heed to the complex interrelationships among these dimensions by adopting multivariate approaches to circumvent the limited perspective that would result from examining any single factor (Capaldi & Patterson, 1994). Second, in clinical settings, the specification of contextual factors will no doubt yield a more thoroughly elucidated portrait of the clinical picture. Specific contextual factors may become focal points for certain treatment goals and recommendations; for example, lower SES and parental psychiatric status (especially antisocial-spectrum disorders in the father and affective and somaticizing disorders in the mother) place the parents at risk for inadequate parenting skills, which are in turn related to poor child adjustment and the early onset of CD (Capaldi & Patterson, 1994; Offord et al., 1991). Multimodal intervention at a broader, familial level should drive treatment efforts in such cases. Recommendations following a thorough assessment might include treatment of parental psychopathology (e.g., maternal depression), coping with intrafamilial stress (e.g., unemployment, parental transitions), and training in parent management skills.

For late-onset CD, adolescence marks an increased risk period for contact with deviant peer groups (Dishion & Patterson, 1992; Moffitt, 1993), and neighborhoods with higher densities of deviant peers present greater risks for negative peer associations. Such associations can be costly in terms of the commission and maintenance of antisocial acts for adolescence-limited youth. Indeed, for this subgroup, such peer contact comprises a direct path leading to delinquency that is not mediated by family-level variables (Capaldi & Patterson, 1994). Following the delineation of such factors during the assessment process, attempting to diminish contact with such deviant peer groups would quite possibly serve as a salient treatment goal.

CONCLUSIONS AND FUTURE DIRECTIONS

We have summarized the use of a variety of assessment tools and strategies for evaluating ASB and common comorbid conditions, including rating scale and interview measures from adult informants and from youths themselves, direct observations and experimental laboratory paradigms, parent- and family-level variables, indexes of academic achievement, direct assessment of peer status, and evaluation of wider contextual factors. We framed the task for the clinician or investigator in terms of such issues as multi-agent/multimethod evaluation, dimensional versus categorical assessment, the importance of subcategorization and subtyping, and the need for developmental relevance in the assessment process. We emphasized several issues above all others: (a) the importance for assessors to appraise the specific psychometric characteristics and normative database of the particular measures they are considering; (b) the necessity of gearing measurement strategies that are keyed to the child's developmental level; and (c) the need to transcend assessment of ASB per se and include evaluation of comorbid conditions, associated features, competencies, and relevant processes.

In closing, we highlight two key issues. First, we advocate greater attention to coverage of the affective and interpersonal styles of youngsters referred for ASB. Salient variables could include, for example, level of empathy, evidence of grandiose ideation, fear of punishment (or lack thereof), or the extent of emotional bonds with peers. Note that such evaluation will, of necessity, extend beyond assessment of behavior patterns through ratings and interviews, requiring expansion into coverage of psychological, interpersonal, and emotional processes and mandating expert interviewers. In recent years, the assessment and classification of adult antisocial personality disorder have been criticized for an overly behavioral, descriptive focus to the neglect of psychological and affective processes underlying the construct of psychopathy (see Hinshaw, 1994b; Sutker, 1994). Such a critique also could apply to ASB and CD among youths. Assessment of key psychological and affective variables in children and adolescents should lead to a richer database that can help to pinpoint the developmental precursors of psychopathic as well as strictly antisocial functioning in later life. We note that the best-validated measure of psychopathy in adults recently has been reconfigured and renormed for adolescents, with the extant 2-factor structure (separable dimensions of interpersonal and affective style vs. chronic antisocial behavior) almost perfectly replicated (Forth, Cox, & Hare, in press). Whether important interpersonal and affective characteristics of psychopathy can be reliably and validly captured in preadolescents awaits future research.

Second, the rising prevalence, salience, and cost of ASB and criminal activity in our society have intensified the field's call to arms for the utilization of assessment as a screening procedure to identify high-risk individuals and to initiate early preventive intervention strategies (e.g., Reid, 1993). Indeed, extensive efforts abound in which the implementation and evaluation of large-scale family-, school-, and community-based screening and prevention programs are delivered to children identified as at-risk for the development of antisocial trajectories (McCord & Tremblay, 1992; see also this volume's chapters by Guerra, Attar, & Weissberg, Chapter 35; Hawkins, Arthur, & Olson, Chapter 34; and Reid & Eddy, Chapter 32). Assessment in this context raises important sociopolitical concerns related to the potential negative consequences of imprecise screening procedures. For example, if the screening protocol lacks acceptable levels of specificity (i.e., identifies exceedingly high levels of false positive cases), the overselection of youths from disadvantaged backgrounds may occur. Moreover, the danger of possible iatrogenic effects associated with labeling pertains to universal (e.g., targeting all schoolchildren in a high-risk neighborhood) as well as selected (e.g., specific targeting of certain at-risk children) prevention strategies. On the other hand, the long-term effectiveness of preventive approaches with at-risk children may rely on the intervention's timely implementation during specific critical periods of development and in certain situational contexts (Loeber & Farrington, 1994; Reid, 1993), requiring the types of developmentally relevant assessments discussed here. Such complex issues mandate advances in assessment screening techniques. In all, assessment of ASB involves both psychometric and social policy–related issues; clinicians and investigators must become well versed in each.

REFERENCES

Abikoff, H., Courtney, M., Pelham, W. E., & Koplewicz, H. S. (1993). Teachers' ratings of disruptive behaviors: The influence of halo effects. *Journal of Abnormal Child Psychology, 21,* 519–533.

Abikoff, H., & Gittelman, R. (1985). Hyperactive children treated with stimulants: Is cognitive therapy a useful adjunct? *Archives of General Psychiatry, 42,* 953–961.

Achenbach, T. M. (1991a). *Manual for the Child Behavior Checklist/4-18 and 1991 Profile.* Burlington: University of Vermont Department of Psychiatry.

Achenbach, T. M. (1991b). *Manual for the Teacher's Report Form and 1991 Profile.* Burlington: University of Vermont Department of Psychiatry.

Achenbach, T. M. (1991c). *Manual for the Youth Self-Report and 1991 Profile.* Burlington: University of Vermont Department of Psychiatry.

Achenbach, T. M. (1993). Taxonomy and comorbidity of conduct problems: Evidence from empirically based approaches. *Development and Psychopathology, 5,* 51–64.

Achenbach, T. M., McConaughy, S. H., & Howell, C. T. (1987). Child/adolescent behavioral and emotional problems: Implications of cross-informant correlations for situational specificity. *Psychological Bulletin, 101,* 213–232.

American Psychiatric Association. (1952). *Diagnostic and statistical manual of mental disorders* (1st ed.). Washington, DC: Author.

American Psychiatric Association. (1980). *Diagnostic and statistical manual of mental disorders* (3rd ed.). Washington, DC: Author.

American Psychiatric Association. (1994). *Diagnostic and statistical manual of mental disorders* (4th ed.). Washington, DC: Author.

Anderson, C. A., Hinshaw, S. P., & Simmel, C. (1994). Mother-child interactions in ADHD and comparison boys: Relationships to overt and covert externalizing behavior. *Journal of Abnormal Child Psychology, 22,* 247–265.

Anderson, K. E., Lytton, H., & Romney, D. M. (1986). Mothers' interactions with normal and conduct-disordered boys: Who affects whom? *Developmental Psychology, 22,* 604–609.

Angold, A., Cox, A., Prendergast, M., Rutter, M., & Simonoff, E. (1987). *The Child and Adolescent Psychiatric Assessment (CAPA).* Unpublished manuscript, Duke University Medical Center, Durham.

Asher, S. R., & Coie, J. D. (1990). *Peer rejection in childhood.* New York: Cambridge University Press.

Atkins, M. S., & Stoff, D. M. (1993). Instrumental and hostile aggression in childhood disruptive behavior disorders. *Journal of Abnormal Child Psychology, 21,* 165–178.

Biederman, J., Faraone, S. V., Keenan, K., Benjamin, J., Krifcher, B., Moore, C., Sprich-Buckminster, S., Ugaglia, K., Jellinek, M. S., Steingard, R., Spencer, T., Norman, D., Kolodny, R., Kraus, I., Perrin, J., Keller, M. B., & Tsuang, M. T. (1992). Further evidence for family-genetic risk factors in attention deficit hyperactivity disorder: Patterns of comorbidity in probands and relatives in psychiatrically and pediatrically referred samples. *Archives of General Psychiatry, 49,* 728–738.

Biederman, J., Keenan, K., & Faraone, S. V. (1990). Parent-based diagnosis of attention deficit disorder predicts a diagnosis based on teacher report. *Journal of the American Academy of Child and Adolescent Psychiatry, 29,* 698–701.

Biederman, J., Newcorn, J., & Sprich, S. E. (1991). Comorbidity of attention deficit hyperactivity disorder with conduct, depressive, anxiety, and other disorders. *American Journal of Psychiatry, 148,* 564–577.

Bird, H. R., Gould, M. S., & Staghezza, B. (1992). Aggregating data from multiple informants in child psychiatry epidemiological research. *Journal of the American Academy of Child and Adolescent Psychiatry, 31,* 78–85.

Bird, H. R., Shaffer, D., Fisher, P., Gould, M., Staghezza, B., Chen, J. Y., & Hoven, C. (1993). The Columbia Impairment Scale (CIS): Pilot findings on a measure of global impairment for children and adolescents. *International Journal of Methods in Psychiatric Research, 3,* 167–176.

Bjorkqvist, K., Osterman, K., & Kaukianinen, A. (1992). The development of direct and indirect aggressive strategies in males and females. In K. Bjorkqvist & P. Niemala (Eds.), *Of mice and women: Aspects of female aggression* (pp. 51–64). New York: Academic Press.

Capaldi, D. M. (1991). Co-occurrence of conduct problems and depressive symptoms in early adolescent boys: I. Familial factors and general adjustment and Grade 6. *Development and Psychopathology, 3,* 277–300.

Capaldi, D. M., & Patterson, G. R. (1994). Interrelated influences of contextual factors on antisocial behavior in childhood and adolescence for males. In D. C. Fowles, P. Sutker, & S. H. Goodman (Eds.), *Progress in experimental personality and psychopathology research* (pp. 165–198). New York: Springer.

Caron, C., & Rutter, M. (1991). Comorbidity in child psychopathology: Concepts, issues, and research strategies. *Journal of Child Psychology and Psychiatry, 32,* 1063–1080.

Cleckley, H. (1976). *The mask of sanity* (5th. ed.). St. Louis: Mosby.

Coie, J. D., Dodge, K. A., & Kupersmidt, J. (1990). Peer group behavior and social status. In S. R. Asher & J. D. Coie (Eds.), *Peer rejection in childhood* (pp. 17–59). New York: Cambridge University Press.

Conners, C. K. (1990). *Manual for Conners' Rating Scales.* Toronto, Canada: Multi-Health Systems.

Crick, N. R., & Grotpeter, J. K. (1995). Relational aggression, gender, and social-psychological adjustment. *Child Development, 66,* 710–722.

Dishion, T. J., & Patterson, G. R. (1992). Age effects in parent training outcome. *Behavior Therapy, 23,* 719–729.

Dodge, K. A. (1991). The structure and function of reactive and proactive aggression. In D. J. Pepler & K. H. Rubin (Eds.), *The development and treatment of childhood aggression* (pp. 201–218). Hillsdale, NJ: Erlbaum.

Dodge, K. A., & Coie, J. D. (1987). Social-information-processing factors in reactive and proactive aggression in children's peer groups. *Journal of Personality and Social Psychology, 53,* 1146–1158.

Edelbrock, C., Costello, A. J., Dulcan, M. K., Kalas, R., & Conover, N. C. (1985). Age differences in the reliability of the psychiatric interview of the child. *Child Development, 56,* 265–275.

Elliott, D. S., Huizinga, D., & Ageton, S. S. (1985). *Explaining delinquency and drug use.* Thousand Oaks, CA: Sage Publications.

Emery, R. E. (1982). Interparental conflict and the children of discord and divorce. *Psychological Bulletin, 92,* 310–330.

Empey, L. T. (1982). *American delinquency: Its meaning and construction.* Homewood, IL: Dorsey.

Erhardt, D., & Hinshaw, S. P. (1994). Initial sociometric impressions of hyperactive and comparison boys: Predictions from social behaviors and from nonbehavioral variables. *Journal of Consulting and Clinical Psychology, 62,* 833–842.

Exner, J. (1990). *A Rorschach Workbook for the Comprehensive System.* Ashville, NC: Rorschach Workshops.

Eyberg, S. M., & Robinson, E. A. (1983). Conduct problem behavior: Standardization of a behavioral rating scale with adolescents. *Journal of Clinical Child Psychology, 12,* 347–354.

Eysenck, H. J. (1986). A critique of classification and diagnosis. In T. Millon & G. L. Klerman (Eds.), *Contemporary directions in psychopathology* (pp. 73–98). New York: Guilford.

Faraone, S. V., Biederman, J., Keenan, K., & Tsuang, M. T. (1991). Separation of *DSM-III* attention deficit disorder and conduct disorder: Evidence from a family genetic study of American child psychiatry patients. *Psychological Medicine, 21,* 109–121.

Feshbach, S. (1970). Aggression. In P. H. Mussen (Ed.), *Carmichael's manual of child psychology* (pp. 159–259). New York: Wiley.

Fisher, P. W., Shaffer, D., Piacentini, J. C., Lapkin, J., Kafantaris, V., Leonard, H., & Herzog, D. B. (1993). Sensitivity of the Diagnostic Interview Schedule for Children 2nd Ed. (DISC-2.1) for specific diagnoses of children and adolescents. *Journal of the American Academy of Child and Adolescent Psychiatry, 32,* 666–673.

Forth, A. E., Cox, S., & Hare, R. D. (in press). *Psychopathy Checklist–Revised: Youth Version.* Toronto, Canada: Multi-Health Systems, Inc.

Frick, P. J. (1993). Childhood conduct problems in a family context. *School Psychology Review, 22,* 376–385.

Frick, P. J., Lahey, B. B., Loeber, R., Tannenbaum, L., Van Horn, Y., Christ, M. A. G., Hart, E. L., & Hanson, K. (1993). Oppositional defiant disorder and conduct disorder: A meta-analytic review of factor analyses and cross-validation in a clinic sample. *Clinical Psychology Review, 13,* 319–340.

Glueck, S., & Glueck, E. (1950). *Unravelling juvenile delinquency.* Cambridge, MA: Harvard University Press.

Goodman, S. H., & Kohlsdorf, B. (1994). The developmental psychopathology of conduct problems: Gender issues. In D. C. Fowles, P. Sutker, & S. H. Goodman (Eds.), *Progress in experimental personality and psychopathology research* (pp. 121–161). New York: Springer.

Harris, G. T., Rice, M. E., & Quinsey, V. L. (1994). Psychopathy as a taxon: Evidence that psychopaths are a discrete class. *Journal of Consulting and Clinical Psychology, 62,* 387–397.

Herjanic, B., & Reich, W. (1982). Development of a structured psychiatric interview for children: Agreement between child and parent on individual symptoms. *Journal of Abnormal Child Psychology, 10,* 307–324.

Hetherington, E. M., & Martin, B. (1986). Family interaction patterns. In H. C. Quay & J. S. Werry (Eds.), *Psychopathological disorders of childhood* (3rd ed., pp. 332–390). New York: Wiley.

Hewitt, L. E., & Jenkins, R. L. (1946). *Fundamental patterns of maladjustment: The dynamics of their origin.* Springfield: State of Illinois.

Hinshaw, S. P. (1987). On the distinction between attentional deficits/hyperactivity and conduct problems/aggression in child psychopathology. *Psychological Bulletin, 101,* 443–463.

Hinshaw, S. P. (1992). Externalizing behavior problems and academic underachievement in childhood and adolescence: Causal relationships and underlying mechanisms. *Psychological Bulletin, 111,* 127–155.

Hinshaw, S. P. (1994a). *Attention deficits and hyperactivity in children.* Thousand Oaks, CA: Sage Publications.

Hinshaw, S. P. (1994b). Conduct disorder in childhood: Conceptualization, diagnosis, comorbidity, and risk status for antisocial functioning in adulthood. In D. C. Fowles, P. Sutker, & S. H. Goodman (Eds.), *Progress in experimental personality and psychopathology research* (pp. 3–44). New York: Springer.

Hinshaw, S. P., & Anderson, C. A. (1996). Conduct and oppositional defiant disorders. In E. J. Mash & R. A. Barkley (Eds.), *Child psychopathology* (pp. 108–149). New York: Guilford.

Hinshaw, S. P., Heller, T., & McHale, J. P. (1992). Covert antisocial behavior in boys with attention-deficit hyperactivity disorder: External validation and effects of methylphenidate. *Journal of Consulting and Clinical Psychology, 60,* 274–281.

Hinshaw, S. P., Henker, B., Whalen, C. K., Erhardt, D., & Dunnington, R. E. (1989). Aggressive, prosocial, and nonsocial behavior in hyperactive boys: Dose effects of methylphenidate in naturalistic settings. *Journal of Consulting and Clinical Psychology, 57,* 636–643.

Hinshaw, S. P., Lahey, B. B., & Hart, E. L. (1993). Issues of taxonomy and comorbidity in the development of conduct disorder. *Development and Psychopathology, 5,* 31–49.

Hinshaw, S. P., & Melnick, S. M. (1995). Peer relationships in boys with attention-deficit hyperactivity disorder with and without comorbid aggression. *Development and Psychopathology, 7,* 627–647.

Hinshaw, S. P., & Nigg, J. (in press). Behavioral rating scales in the assessment of disruptive behavior disorders in childhood. In D. Shaffer & J. E. Richters (Eds.), *Assessment in child psychopathology.* New York: Guilford.

Hinshaw, S. P., Simmel, C., & Heller, T. (1995). Multimethod assessment of covert antisocial behavior in children: Laboratory observations, adult ratings, and child self-report. *Psychological Assessment, 7,* 209–219.

Hodges, K. (1993). Structured interviews for assessing children. *Journal of Child Psychology and Psychiatry, 34,* 49–68.

Hodges, K. (1994). Debate and argument: Reply to David Shaffer: Structured interviews for assessing children. *Journal of Child Psychology and Psychiatry, 35,* 785–787.

Hodges, K., Cools, J., & McKnew, D. (1989). Test-retest reliability of a clinical research interview for children: The Child Assessment Schedule. *Psychological Assessment, 1,* 317–322.

Huesmann, L. R., Eron, L. D., Lefkowitz, M. M., & Walder, L. O. (1984). Stability of aggression over time and generations. *Developmental Psychology, 20,* 1120–1134.

Jenkins, R. L., & Glickman, S. (1947). Patterns of personality organization among delinquents. *Nervous Children, 6,* 329–339.

Kagan, J. (1969). The three faces of continuity in human development. In D. A. Goslin (Ed.), *Handbook of socialization theory and research* (pp. 983–1002). Chicago: Rand McNally.

Katz, L. F., & Gottman, J. M. (1993). Patterns of marital conflict predict children's internalizing and externalizing behaviors. *Developmental Psychology, 29,* 940–950.

Kazdin, A. E. (1987). *Conduct disorders in childhood and adolescence.* Thousand Oaks, CA: Sage Publications.

Kazdin, A. E. (1993). Changes in behavioral problems and prosocial functioning in child treatment. *Journal of Child and Family Studies, 2,* 5–22.

Kazdin, A. E., & Esveldt-Dawson, K. (1986). The Interview for Antisocial Behavior: Psychometric characteristics and concurrent validity with child psychiatric inpatients. *Journal of Psychopathology and Behavioral Assessment, 8,* 289–303.

Kazdin, A. E., Esveldt-Dawson, K., Unis, A. S., & Rancurello, M. D. (1983). Child and parent evaluations of depression and aggression in psychiatric inpatient children. *Journal of Abnormal Child Psychology, 11,* 401–413.

Kendall, P. C., & Hammen, C. (1995). *Abnormal psychology.* Boston: Houghton Mifflin.

Kent, R. N., O'Leary, K. D., Diament, C., & Dietz, A. (1974). Expectation biases in observational evaluation of therapeutic change. *Journal of Consulting and Clinical Psychology, 42,* 774–780.

Kruesi, M. J. P., Hibbs, E. D., Zahn, T. P., Keysor, C. S., Hamburger, S. D., Bartko, J. J., & Rapoport, J. D. (1992). A 2-year prospective follow-up study of children and adolescents with disruptive behavior disorders. *Archives of General Psychiatry, 49,* 429–435.

Lahey, B. B., & McBurnett, K. (1992, February). Behavioral and biological correlates of aggressive conduct disorder: Temporal stability. In D. Routh (Chair), *The psychobiology of disruptive behavior disorders in children: In tribute to Herbert Quay.* Symposium conducted at the annual meeting of the Society for Research in Child and Adolescent Psychopathology, Sarasota, FL.

Ledingham, J. E., Younger, A., Schwartzman, A., & Bergeron, G. (1982). Agreement among teacher, peer, and self-ratings of children's aggression, withdrawal, and likeability. *Journal of Abnormal Child Psychology, 10,* 363–372.

Loeber, R. (1988). Natural histories of conduct problems, delinquency, and associated substance use: Evidence for developmental progressions. In B. B. Lahey & A. E. Kazdin (Eds.), *Advances in clinical child psychology* (pp. 73–124). New York: Plenum.

Loeber, R., & Farrington, D. P. (1994). Problems and solutions in longitudinal and experimental treatment studies of child psychopathology and delinquency. *Journal of Consulting and Clinical Psychology, 62,* 887–900.

Loeber, R., Green, S. M., Lahey, B. B., & Stouthamer-Loeber, M. (1989). Optimal informants on childhood disruptive behaviors. *Development and Psychopathology, 1,* 317–337.

Loeber, R., Green, S. M., Lahey, B. B., & Stouthamer-Loeber, M. (1991). Differences and similarities between children, mothers, and teachers as informants on disruptive behavior disorders. *Journal of Abnormal Child Psychology, 19,* 75–95.

Loeber, R., & Schmaling, K. B. (1985a). Empirical evidence for overt and covert patterns of antisocial conduct problems: A meta-analysis. *Journal of Abnormal Child Psychology, 13,* 337–352.

Loeber, R., & Schmaling, K. B. (1985b). The utility of differentiating between mixed and pure forms of antisocial child behavior. *Journal of Abnormal Child Psychology, 13,* 315–335.

Loeber, R., Stouthamer-Loeber, M., Van Kammen, W. B., & Farrington, D. P. (1989). Development of a new measure of self-reported antisocial behavior for young children: Prevalence and reliability. In M. W. Klein (Ed.), *Self-report methodology in criminal research* (pp. 203–225). Boston: Kluwer-Nijhoff.

Loney, J. (1987). Hyperactivity and aggression in the diagnosis of attention deficit disorder. In B. B. Lahey & A. E. Kazdin (Eds.), *Advances in clinical child psychology* (Vol. 10, pp. 99–135). New York: Plenum.

Loney, J., & Milich, R. (1982). Hyperactivity, inattention, and aggression in clinical practice. In M. Wolraich & D. K. Routh (Eds.), *Advances in developmental and behavioral pediatrics* (Vol. 2, pp. 113–147). Greenwich, CT: JAI.

Mash, E. J., & Terdal, L. G. (1988). Behavioral assessment of child and family disturbance. In E. J. Mash & L. G. Terdal (Eds.), *Behavioral assessment of childhood disorders* (2nd ed., pp. 3–69). New York: Guilford.

McBurnett, K., & Lahey, B. B. (1994). Neuropsychological and neuroendocrine correlates of conduct disorder and antisocial behavior in children and adolescents. In D. C. Fowles, P. Sutker, & S. H. Goodman (Eds.), *Progress in experimental personality and psychopathology research* (pp. 199–231). New York: Springer.

McCord, J., & Tremblay, R. E. (1992). *Preventing antisocial behavior: Interventions from birth through adolescence.* New York: Guilford.

McMahon, R. J. (1994). Diagnosis, assessment, and treatment of externalizing problems in children: The role of longitudinal data. *Journal of Consulting and Clinical Psychology, 62,* 901–917.

Milich, R., & Landau, S. (1989). The role of social status variables in differentiating subgroups of hyperactive children. In L. M. Bloomingdale & J. M. Swanson (Eds.), *Attention deficit disorder* (Vol. 4, pp. 1–16). Oxford, England: Pergamon.

Moffitt, T. E. (1990). Juvenile delinquency and attention deficit disorder: Boys' developmental trajectories from age 3 to age 15. *Child Development, 61,* 893–910.

Moffitt, T. E. (1993). "Life-course persistent" vs. "adolescence-limited" antisocial behavior: A developmental taxonomy. *Psychological Review, 100,* 674–701.

Moffitt, T. E., & Lynam, D. (1994). The neuropsychology of conduct disorder and delinquency: Implications for understanding antisocial behavior. In D. C. Fowles, P. Sutker, & S. H. Goodman (Eds.), *Progress in experimental personality and psychopathology research* (pp. 233–262). New York: Springer.

Murphy, D. A., Pelham, W. E., & Lang, A. R. (1992). Aggression in boys with attention deficit hyperactivity disorder: Methylphenidate effects on naturalistically observed aggression, response to provocation, and social information processing. *Journal of Abnormal Child Psychology, 20,* 451–466.

Newcomb, A. F., Bukowski, W. M., & Pattee, L. (1993). Children's peer relations: A meta-analytic review of popular, rejected, neglected, controversial, and average sociometric status. *Psychological Bulletin, 113,* 99–128.

Offord, D. R., Boyle, M. H., & Racine, Y. A. (1991). The epidemiology of antisocial behavior in childhood and adolescence. In D. J. Pepler & K. H. Rubin (Eds.), *The development and treatment of childhood aggression* (pp. 31–54). Hillsdale, NJ: Erlbaum.

Ollendick, T. H., & King, N. J. (1994). Diagnosis, assessment, and treatment of internalizing problems in children: The role of longitudinal data. *Journal of Consulting and Clinical Psychology, 62,* 918–927.

Parke, R. D., & Slaby, R. G. (1983). The development of aggression. In E. M. Hetherington (Ed.), *Socialization, personality, and development* (pp. 547–641). Vol. 4 of P. Mussen (Ed.), *Handbook of developmental psychology.* New York: Wiley.

Parker, J. G., & Asher, S. R. (1987). Peer relations and later personal adjustment: Are low accepted children at risk? *Psychological Bulletin, 102,* 357–389.

Patterson, G. R. (1982). *Coercive family process.* Eugene, OR: Castalia.

Patterson, G. R., DeBaryshe, B. D., & Ramsey, E. (1989). A developmental perspective on antisocial behavior. *American Psychologist, 44,* 329–335.

Patterson, G. R., Reid, J. B., & Dishion, T. J. (1992). *Antisocial boys.* Eugene, OR: Castalia.

Pelham, W. E., Milich, R., Cummings, E. M., Murphy, D. A., Schaughency, E. A., & Greiner, A. R. (1991). Effects of background anger, provocation, and methylphenidate on emotional arousal and aggressive responding in attention-deficit hyperactivity disordered boys with and without concurrent aggression. *Journal of Abnormal Child Psychology, 19,* 407–426.

Piacentini, J. C., Cohen, P., & Cohen, J. (1992). Combining discrepant information from multiple sources: Are complex algorithms better than simple ones? *Journal of Abnormal Child Psychology, 20,* 51–63.

Quay, H. C. (1979). Classification. In H. C. Quay & J. S. Werry (Eds.), *Psychopathological disorders of childhood* (2nd ed., pp. 1–42). New York: Wiley.

Quay, H. C. (1986). Conduct disorders. In H. C. Quay & J. S. Werry (Eds.), *Psychopathological disorders of childhood* (3rd ed., pp. 35–72). New York: Wiley.

Quay, H. C. (1987). Patterns of delinquent behavior. In H. C. Quay (Ed.), *Handbook of juvenile delinquency* (pp. 118–138). New York: Wiley.

Quay, H. C., & Peterson, D. R. (1983). *Interim manual for the Revised Behavior Problem Checklist.* Unpublished manuscript, University of Miami.

Reid, J. B. (1993). Prevention of conduct disorder before and after school entry: Relating interventions to developmental findings. *Development and Psychopathology, 5,* 243–262.

Richters, J. E., & Cicchetti, D. (1993). Mark Twain meets *DSM-III-R:* Conduct disorder, development, and the concept of harmful dysfunction. *Development and Psychopathology, 5,* 5–29.

Robins, L. N., & McEvoy, L. (1990). Conduct problems as predictors of substance abuse. In L. N. Robins & M. Rutter (Eds.), *Straight and devious pathways from childhood to adulthood* (pp. 182–204). Cambridge, England: Cambridge University Press.

Rutter, M. (1981). The city and the child. *American Journal of Orthopsychiatry, 51,* 610–625.

Rutter, M., Bolton, P., Harrington, R., Le Couteur, A., Macdonald, H., & Simonoff, E. (1990). Genetic factors in child psychiatric disorders: I. A review of research strategies. *Journal of Child Psychology and Psychiatry, 31,* 3–37.

Rutter, M., & Giller, H. (1983). *Juvenile delinquency: Trends and perspectives.* New York: Guilford.

Sampson, R. (1985). Neighborhood and crime: The structural determinants of personal victimization. *Journal of Research on Crime and Delinquency, 22,* 7–40.

Sattler, J. M. (1992). *Assessment of children* (3rd ed.). San Diego, CA: Author.

Shaffer, D., & Richters, J. E. (in press). *Assessment in child psychopathology.* New York: Guilford.

Skinner, H. A. (1981). Toward the integration of classification theory and methods. *Journal of Abnormal Psychology, 90,* 68–87.

Sutker, P. B. (1994). Psychopathy: Traditional and clinical antisocial concepts. In D. C. Fowles, P. Sutker, & S. H. Goodman (Eds.), *Progress in experimental personality and psychopathology research* (pp. 73–120). New York: Springer.

Verhulst, F. C., Koot, H. M., & Van der Ende, J. (1994). Differential predictive value of parents' and teachers' reports of children's problem behaviors: A longitudinal study. *Journal of Abnormal Child Psychology, 22,* 531–546.

Vitiello, B., Behar, D., Hunt, J., Stoff, D., & Ricciuti, A. (1990). Subtyping aggression in children and adolescents. *Journal of Neuropsychiatry and Clinical Neurosciences, 2,* 189–192.

Walker, J. L., Lahey, B. B., Hynd, G. W., & Frame, C. L. (1987). Comparison of specific patterns of antisocial behavior in children with conduct disorder with or without coexisting hyperactivity. *Journal of Consulting and Clinical Psychology, 55,* 910–913.

Walker, J. L., Lahey, B. B., Russo, M. F., Christ, M. A. G., McBurnett, K., Loeber, R., Stouthamer-Loeber, M., & Green, S. M. (1991). Anxiety, inhibition, and conduct disorder in children: I. Relation to social impairment. *Journal of the American Academy of Child and Adolescent Psychiatry, 30,* 187–191.

Zoccolillo, M. (1992). Co-occurrence of conduct disorder and its adult outcomes with depressive and anxiety disorders: A review. *Journal of the American Academy of Child and Adolescent Psychiatry, 31,* 547–556.

CHAPTER 5

Attention-Deficit/Hyperactivity Disorder, Oppositional Defiant Disorder, Conduct Disorder, and Adult Antisocial Behavior: A Life Span Perspective

BENJAMIN B. LAHEY and ROLF LOEBER

The goal of this chapter is to describe the developmental relationship among the three disruptive behavior disorders (attention deficit/hyperactivity disorder, ADHD; oppositional defiant disorder, ODD; and conduct disorder, CD) during childhood and adolescence and their joint relationship to antisocial behavior in adulthood. ADHD refers to developmentally inappropriate levels of attention problems, motor hyperactivity, and impulsive behavior. Although some youths who are classified as ADHD exhibit high levels of inattention or hyperactivity-impulsivity only, most exhibit high levels of both types of problems. ODD refers to developmentally inappropriate levels of irritable, argumentative, and defiant interactions with others. CD is defined as persistently high levels of fighting, lying, bullying, vandalism, and other antisocial behaviors during childhood or adolescence.

Childhood ADHD has long been linked to antisocial behavior in two ways. First, it is clear that children with ADHD are more likely than children without ADHD to exhibit antisocial behavior during adolescence and adulthood (Hechtman, Weiss, & Perlman, 1984; Loney, Kramer, & Milich, 1981; Satterfield, Hoppe, & Schell, 1982). Second, it appears that the prognosis for persistence in CD over time is worse for youths who also exhibit concurrent ADHD. Indeed, the poor developmental outcome of concurrent ADHD and CD has been cited as a prime example of why it is important to study the co-occurrence of disorders (Caron & Rutter, 1991). Much less is known about the developmental relationship of ODD to CD and adult antisocial behavior, but some evidence suggests that ODD is more strongly linked to CD than is ADHD (Lahey & Loeber, 1994; Lahey, Loeber, Quay, Frick, & Grimm, 1992).

The existing literature was accessed through searches of electronic databases and personal reprint files. In addition, our strategy has been to attempt to replicate and extend key findings in the published literature by conducting new analyses of two existing data sets. The Developmental Trends Study (Lahey et al., 1995) is an ongoing longitudinal study of clinic-referred boys who were 7 to 12 years of age at the start of the study. The *DSM-IV* Field

Trials for the Disruptive Behavior Disorders (Lahey et al., 1994) was also a study of clinic-referred youth, but in this case, cross-sectional data are available on a sample of males and females ages 4 to 17 years. These studies both used versions of the same structured diagnostic interview of multiple informants. Descriptions of the specific methods of these studies can be found in their cited published reports. Unfortunately, few data are currently available on the association of ADHD and ODD to antisocial behavior before elementary school ages and after early adulthood. Therefore, our review of developmental relationships is most relevant to the period from about 6 years of age through the first decade of adulthood.

THEORETICAL CONTEXT AND CONTROVERSIAL ISSUES

Research on the relationships among ADHD, ODD, CD, and adult antisocial behavior has been largely atheoretical in nature. Although a sizable body of evidence exists, little effort has been made to explain the relationships among these three topographically distinct patterns of maladaptive behavior. This does not mean, however, that there are no controversies regarding the interpretation of empirical findings. Rather, the controversies that are discussed in this chapter are at the descriptive level. At the close of this review, however, we suggest some plausible directions for future explanatory theories.

METHODOLOGY

Although a considerable number of studies have provided evidence on the developmental relationships among ADHD, ODD, and CD, it is important to recognize several important limitations of that evidence. First, these studies have been conducted over many years, during which time the diagnostic definitions of

ADHD, ODD, and CD have changed across editions of the *Diagnostic and Statistical Manual of Mental Disorders (DSM)*. Although these evolving diagnostic definitions have included the same core characteristics in each version, they have changed considerably at their boundaries, sometimes resulting in sizable changes in the prevalence of the disorders (Lahey et al., 1990).

In addition, some investigators chose to use diagnostic conceptualizations of ADHD, ODD, and CD, whereas others have used dimensional constructs such as *aggression, delinquency,* and *hyperactivity*. Furthermore, a wide range of measurement strategies has been used in these studies to quantify ADHD, ODD, CD, and related constructs, including rating scales (completed by parents, teachers, or both), structured diagnostic interviews, and other measurement strategies. In this chapter, we use the terms *ADHD, ODD,* and *CD* to refer to these varying constructs and definitions for the sake of simplicity, but the possibility that this practice could obscure important differences must be kept in mind. Given the broad variation in definitions and measures, it is remarkable that a number of reasonably consistent findings have emerged in the existing literature.

It is also important to note that the studies reviewed either excluded girls or did not include enough girls with ADHD, ODD, or CD to analyze their data separately. Therefore, it is entirely possible that the conclusions of this review are applicable only to boys. It is also important to note that existing samples did not always include representative numbers of youths from the major ethnic groups in the United States. These are important deficits that must be remedied by future research.

Another potential source of variation in findings among the studies reviewed in this chapter is sample constitution. Most studies have used clinic-referred samples, whereas others drew population-based samples. Although clinic samples are rich sources of youths with uncommon disorders, they are biased by a multitude of factors. In particular, cross-sectional age comparisons using clinic samples are potentially biased by factors that result in youths with different problems (and concurrent combinations of problems) being referred at different ages. These referral biases may render younger children systematically different from older youths in ways that do not represent true developmental differences. Data from population-based samples are not biased in these ways, but they typically have not been large enough to contain enough youths with any particular disorder to allow stable cross-sectional age comparisons. Thus, there is a need for population-based studies that are large enough to contain adequate numbers of youths with disorders, particularly studies that employ prospective longitudinal methods (Goodman et al., in press).

CURRENT FINDINGS

In spite of the limitations of the existing database, it is possible to sketch out the likely relationships among ADHD, ODD, CD, and adult antisocial behavior over the life span. This description of relationships among variables yields strong hypotheses that deserve close attention in future research, but no firm conclusions. We first examine the changing concurrent relationships among ADHD, ODD, and CD during childhood and adolescence (i.e.,

their pattern of co-occurrence across childhood and adolescence). As part of this discussion, we focus on the persistence of concurrent CD and ADHD in childhood into adolescence and adulthood. Finally, we summarize and evaluate evidence that suggests that uncomplicated childhood ADHD (i.e., childhood ADHD without concurrent ODD or CD) may be a precursor to adolescent and adult antisocial behavior.

Co-Occurrence of ADHD, ODD, and CD During Childhood and Adolescence: Opposing Development Trends

ADHD, ODD, and CD co-occur at greater-than-chance levels during childhood and adolescence, but the degree of co-occurrence varies markedly with the youth's age (Loeber & Keenan, 1994). Two studies of population-based samples of youths suggest that the degree of co-occurrence of ADHD and CD is greater in prepubertal children than in adolescents. Offord, Adler, and Boyle (1986) reported a decline in the degree of association between ADHD and CD with increasing age in a cross-sectional sample of 4- to 17-year-old Ontario youths. Similarly, the longitudinal Dunedin study of a community birth cohort from New Zealand also found a decline in the degree of co-occurrence with ADHD from age 11 to age 15 years. Unfortunately, that study combined diagnoses of CD with ODD, making the results ambiguous. Even more problematic is the fact that different informants were used at younger ages than at older ages in both studies, confounding age with type of informant.

The declining associations among ADHD, ODD, and CD with increasing age appear to reflect three distinct developmental trends, one of which largely offsets the other two. We first describe two developmental trends that have the effect of *increasing* the degree of associations between ADHD and ODD with CD over increasing age, then describe the third trend that *decreases* the degree of associations of ADHD and ODD with CD over increasing age. The next two sections describe these opposing developmental trends.

Proportion of Youths With ADHD, ODD, or Both Who Also Exhibit CD Increases With Age

The period of highest risk for the onset of CD is later and more prolonged than for ADHD and ODD. The age of greatest risk for the onset of ADHD and ODD is during the preschool years, whereas the risk period for the onset of CD extends through adolescence (Green, Loeber, & Lahey, 1991; Loeber & Keenan, 1994). This means that the proportion of youths with ADHD, ODD, or both in childhood who meet criteria for CD will increase with age as the youths pass through the lengthy period of risk for the onset of CD. New cross-sectional analyses of the *DSM-IV* Field Trials data presented in Figure 5.1 show the increasing percentage of youths with ADHD, ODD, or both who also meet criteria for CD with increasing age. Among these clinic-referred youths, the rate of CD among those with ADHD increases from less than 20% among 4- to 6-year-olds, who are not yet in the peak risk period for CD, to almost 50% for 11- to 17-year-olds. Similar age trends can be seen for youths with ODD and for

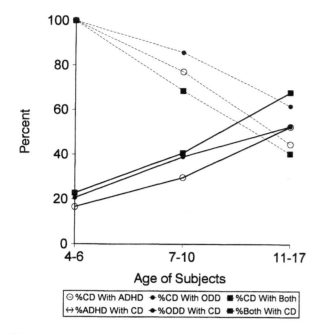

Figure 5.1 *The percentage of 4- to 17-year-old youths who meet criteria for ADHD, ODD, or both ADHD and ODD who also meet criteria for CD as a function of age (ascending lines) and the percentage of youths who meet criteria for CD who also meet criteria for ADHD, ODD, or both ADHD and ODD as a function of age (descending lines) in the* DSM-IV *Field Trials data.*

youths with both ADHD and ODD (all of which are statistically significant, $p < .05$). Thus, one developmental trend appears to increase the co-occurrence of ADHD, ODD, or both with CD over age by leading to increased rates of CD among youths with ADHD, ODD, or both at older ages as they pass through the risk period for the onset of CD.

Co-Occurrence of ADHD and CD During Childhood Is Associated With Greater Persistence of Both Disorders

Although some children with ADHD or CD cease to meet criteria for the disorder by adolescence (Barkley, Fisher, & Edelbrock, 1990; Graham & Rutter, 1973; Hart et al., 1995; Lahey et al., 1995; Mannuzza, Klein, Bessler, Malloy, & LaPadula, 1993), several studies suggest that youths with *concurrent* ADHD and CD in childhood are more likely to continue to meet criteria for *both* ADHD and CD over time than are youths with either ADHD or CD during childhood.

ADHD Is More Persistent When It Co-Occurs With CD in Childhood. Evidence suggesting that ADHD is more persistent when it co-occurs with CD in childhood comes from a variety of studies. In the prospective Developmental Trends Study, Hart et al. (1995) showed that the co-occurrence of ADHD and CD before puberty is associated with greater persistence of ADHD into adolescence than is ADHD in boys without CD. This study replicated findings of previous prospective studies that showed that higher levels of aggression and conduct problems in childhood among children with ADHD predicted both short- and long-term persistence of ADHD (August, Stewart, & Holmes, 1983; Loney et al., 1981; Taylor, Sandberg, Thorley, & Giles, 1991). It should be noted, however, that a longer term follow-up of one of these samples reported by Taylor, Chadwick, Hepinstall, and Danckaerts (1994) did not find a lower rate of persistence among children with ADHD alone than among children with concurrent ADHD and CD.

CD Is More Persistent When It Co-Occurs With ADHD in Childhood. Schachar, Rutter, and Smith (1981) provided an important reanalysis of data from the longitudinal population-based Isle of Wight study. A previous report from this study had shown that CD in 10- to 11-year-old children was found to be rather persistent when reassessed 4 years later (Graham & Rutter, 1973). Schachar et al. (1981) reported that the degree of persistence of antisocial disorder depended on the presence or absence of concurrent hyperactivity, however. Youths given the diagnosis of CD at age 10 to 11 years were much more likely to be given the same diagnosis again at age 14 to 15 years if they also received high ratings from parents or teachers on motor hyperactivity at age 10 to 11 years.

A number of other studies have supported the conclusions of Schachar et al. (1981). Loeber (1988a) conducted a follow-up study of boys who were ages 10, 13, or 16 at the start of the study. The boys were divided into four groups on the basis of parent and teacher ratings at the start of the study: (a) high ratings on aggression only, (b) high ratings on ADHD (hyperactivity, impulsivity, and attention problems) only, (c) high ratings on both dimensions, and (d) high ratings on neither dimension. Over the next 5 years, boys with high ratings on both aggression and ADHD exhibited significantly higher rates of criminal offending (two to three times as high) than boys rated high on aggression only. In a similar analysis of a different sample, Farrington, Loeber, and van Kammen (1990) found that boys rated high on both childhood conduct problems and ADHD in childhood were more likely to engage in delinquent or criminal behavior in both adolescence and adulthood than boys rated high on conduct problems only during childhood. Similarly, Magnusson and Bergman (1990) found that boys who were rated high on both aggression and ADHD at age 13 years had markedly higher rates of registered criminality and alcohol abuse at ages 18 to 23 than boys rated high on aggression only at age 13.

The results of a prospective study of a school sample by Lambert (1988) were only partially consistent with other studies, however. The outcome of youths rated as exhibiting both hyperactivity and aggression during elementary school was uniformly poor, with this group differing significantly from controls on numbers of symptoms of aggressive CD, nonaggressive CD, and the rate of court-adjudicated delinquency. The outcome of youths with high ratings of aggression only during elementary school was almost as poor, however. These youths were more likely than controls to have symptoms of both aggressive and nonaggressive CD during adolescence, but not to be adjudicated as delinquent or to use hard drugs.

The association between ADHD and CD appears to increase with increasing age for two reasons: (a) Children with ADHD increasingly meet criteria for CD as they pass through the long risk period for the onset of CD, and (b) children with ADHD or CD alone are more likely than children with concurrent ADHD and CD to cease meeting criteria for their disorder by adolescence. Thus, an increasing proportion of youths with either ADHD or CD during childhood have *both* disorders by the time they reach adolescence. New evidence presented earlier from the *DSM-IV* Field Trials suggests that the former statement may also be correct for ODD, but no evidence is currently available on the persistence of CD among youths who do or do not also meet criteria for ODD.

Proportion of Youths With CD Who Also Exhibit ADHD, ODD, or Both Decreases With Age

On the other hand, a second developmental trend has the opposite effect of *decreasing* the association of ADHD and ODD with CD over increasing age. This second trend probably does not represent a declining relationship over increasing age among children with ADHD, ODD, or both since childhood but apparently reflects the emergence of a new group of youths with CD during adolescence. As discussed in detail in the next section, Moffitt (1990) and others have suggested that youths whose antisocial behavior emerges for the first time after puberty are unlikely to have met criteria for ADHD in childhood. Thus, it appears that *an increase in CD during adolescence among youths who never met criteria for ADHD reduces the degree of co-occurrence of ADHD with CD during adolescence* by increasing the percentage of adolescents with CD but not ADHD.

Using the cross-sectional clinic-referred sample of the *DSM-IV* Field Trials, the tendency for the proportion of youths with CD who also meet criteria for ADHD, ODD, or both to decrease with increasing age can be seen by referring again to Figure 5.1. All of the 4- to 6-year-old children with CD also have ADHD and ODD, indicating a very strong association among these three disorders at this age. By 11 to 17 years of age, however, the proportion of youths with CD who also have ODD has fallen to less than 60%, and the proportion of youths with CD who also meet criteria for ADHD (or both ADHD and ODD) has fallen to about 40%.

Some of this decline is no doubt due to some children with concurrent CD and ADHD, ODD, or both in childhood ceasing to meet criteria for ADHD, ODD, or both in adolescence but continuing to meet criteria for CD. This does not appear to be a major component of this trend, however. For example, among boys with both CD and ADHD in Year 1 in the Developmental Trends Study, 87% continued to meet criteria for ADHD in Year 4; and 94% continued to meet criteria for ODD in Year 4 if they also continued to meet criteria for CD in Year 4. This suggests that most of the decline in the rate of co-occurrence of ADHD and ODD with CD with increasing age found in previous studies is due to an influx of new youths meeting criteria for CD during adolescence.

It is interesting to note that the associations of ADHD and ODD to CD in all of the new analyses presented in this chapter have been quite similar. It is also potentially important that a high proportion of youths with ADHD or ODD at all ages met criteria for both disorders. Thus, the associations of ADHD and ODD with CD do not appear to be independent.

ADHD, ODD, and the Age of Onset of CD

Using age at the time of assessment as an index of development is a weak strategy, however, as it confounds the youth's current age with age of onset of his or her disorder(s). It is important for our inquiry into developmental trends to shift our attention to the age of onset of CD. The most consistent finding in the existing literature is that ADHD is associated with the *early onset* of antisocial behavior. Offord, Sullivan, Allen, and Abrams (1979) found in their study of delinquent youths that the age of onset of serious delinquent behavior was significantly earlier for delinquents with ADHD. Walker, Lahey, Hynd, and Frame (1987) similarly found that children with both *DSM-III* CD and ADHD were significantly younger at the time of referral than children with CD without ADHD.

Data from the Developmental Trends Study on ADHD and the age of onset of CD are consistent with these earlier findings. We conducted new analyses for this chapter that show that 72% of clinic-referred boys who met criteria for CD in Year 1 (when they were 7 to 12 years of age) also met criteria for ADHD in Year 1. In contrast, only 44% of boys who met criteria for CD for the first time during Years 2 to 4 (when they were 1 to 3 years older) met criteria for ADHD in Year 1. Thus, boys who met criteria for CD at earlier ages were more likely to exhibit ADHD than boys who met criteria for CD at somewhat later ages.

Similarly, Loeber, Green, Keenan, and Lahey (1994) found that boys who first met criteria for CD in Years 2 to 6 of the Developmental Trends Study who also exhibited ADHD were significantly younger at the time of first meeting criteria for CD than boys without ADHD. This latter finding is particularly important because, unlike previous studies, it did not rely on retrospective reports of the age of onset of CD. Rather, the differences in the age of onset of CD associated with ADHD were found using prospective data.

Moffitt (1990) also used prospective longitudinal data to examine differences in the age of onset of antisocial behavior associated with ADHD. Using extensive data gathered on a New Zealand birth cohort, she found that delinquent youths with ADHD at age 13 had exhibited highly deviant levels of antisocial behavior during every assessment since 3 years of age, whereas 13-year-old delinquents without ADHD exhibited *normal* levels of antisocial behavior during every assessment from 3 to 11 years. Thus, Moffitt (1990) provided strong evidence that the onset of antisocial behavior was markedly later in delinquents without a history of ADHD.

We have used data from the *DSM-IV* Field Trials for the Disruptive Behavior Disorders (Lahey et al., 1994) to illustrate the consistency and strength of the relationship between ADHD and ODD and the age of onset of antisocial behavior. In new analyses for this chapter, we limited the sample to 380 clinic-referred youths ages 4 to 17 years for whom a parent informant was available for structured diagnostic interviews so that the parent could answer questions regarding the age of onset of ADHD and antisocial behavior. The relationships between age of onset of the first symptom of CD and ADHD and ODD are presented in Figure 5.2. Over 80% of the 51 youths in whom the first symptom of CD emerged between 1 and 3 years of age met *DSM-III-R* criteria for both ADHD and ODD, but the percentage with ADHD, ODD, or both declined steadily with increasing ages of onset of the first symptom of CD. The function shown in Figure 5.2 could be an artifact of age, however. Because only older youths in this sample could have later ages of onset of CD symptoms, and because older

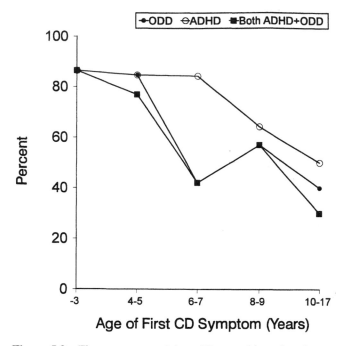

Figure 5.2 *The percentage of 4- to 17-year-old youths who meet criteria for CD who also meet criteria for ADHD, ODD, or both ADHD and ODD as a function of the age of onset of the first CD symptom to emerge in the* DSM-IV *Field Trials data.*

youths who previously exhibited ADHD in childhood may have "outgrown" enough symptoms to no longer meet criteria for ADHD (Hart et al., 1995), it may incorrectly appear that youths with older ages of onset of CD behaviors are less likely to exhibit ADHD. To examine this possibility, we split the sample at the median age of 9 and repeated the analyses with only the older half of the sample. The same relationship between ADHD, ODD, or both to the age of onset of CD was found, however, suggesting that this finding was not artifactual.

When these several studies are considered together, there is little doubt that ADHD is associated with an earlier age of onset of antisocial behavior. Indeed, ADHD is more closely associated with the age of onset of antisocial behavior than with exhibiting antisocial behavior per se. Thus, it appears that childhood-onset CD frequently co-occurs with ADHD, but CD that emerges for the first time during adolescence does not. Emerging evidence suggests that a relationship also may exist between ODD and the age of onset of CD.

Patterns of Antisocial Behavior Among Youths With Conduct Disorder and Concurrent ADHD

Several studies suggest that youths who exhibit both antisocial behavior and ADHD manifest more severe antisocial behavior, particularly greater physical aggression. Offord et al. (1979) conducted a study of adjudicated delinquent youths who were on probation to determine if delinquent youths with hyperactivity differ from those without hyperactivity. They found that the hyperactive

delinquents were significantly more likely to engage in fighting, drug abuse, and reckless and irresponsible behavior than the non-hyperactive delinquents.

Walker et al. (1987) similarly compared children who met *DSM-III* criteria for both CD and ADHD with children who met criteria for CD but not ADHD. The group with both CD and ADHD also was found to be more likely to engage in physical fighting, to exhibit a higher total number of CD symptoms (mean of 5.3 vs. 3.1 symptoms), and to receive higher peer ratings of aggression and social rejection. All differences were still found when the group with CD but not ADHD was limited to those with at least one concurrent diagnosis, which suggests that the greater aggressiveness and severity was specific to concurrent ADHD and not simply to the presence of any concurrent disorder. On the other hand, Moffitt (1990) found that 13-year-old delinquents with and without ADHD at age 11 did not differ in overall ratings of antisocial behavior at age 13. Consistent with the previous literature, however, the delinquents with concurrent ADHD did exhibit significantly higher numbers of aggressive acts when they were reassessed at age 15.

We attempted to replicate the previously reported difference between antisocial youths with and without concurrent ADHD in terms of aggression by conducting new analyses of the *DSM-IV* Field Trials data set and the Developmental Trends Study. In both sets of analyses, youths with CD and ADHD did not differ from those with CD without ADHD on the number of aggressive symptoms, nonaggressive symptoms, or total number of symptoms of CD.

There are many possible reasons for these failures to replicate, including differences in samples and instruments. We examined the possibility that the failure to replicate may have been due to the use of more stringent *DSM-III-R* criteria, but we found no differences in severity of CD associated when *DSM-III* criteria were used. However, we did find evidence that the effect may be dependent on the age of the subjects. Although there was not a significant difference in the number of aggressive symptoms associated with ADHD during Year 1 of the Developmental Trends Study (when the boys were prepubertal), boys with CD and concurrent ADHD did exhibit significantly more aggressive behaviors than boys with only CD in Year 4 (when they were 10 to 15 years of age). Thus, it is possible that there are no differences in the severity of CD associated with ADHD until adolescent-onset CD enters the developmental picture. Additional research on this hypothesis is clearly needed.

Is Childhood ADHD a Precursor to the Onset of New Antisocial Behavior in Adolescence and Adulthood?

Some theorists have suggested that children with ADHD who do not exhibit CD in childhood are nonetheless at increased risk for antisocial behavior during adolescence and adulthood (Gittelman, Mannuzza, Shenker, & Bonagura, 1985; Mannuzza et al., 1991; Mannuzza et al., 1993). A number of prospective longitudinal studies have shown that children with ADHD exhibit increased levels of antisocial behavior during adolescence and adulthood (Hechtman et al., 1984; Loney et al., 1981; Satterfield et al., 1982). It is not possible to conclude on the basis of these studies, however, that childhood ADHD predicts the emergence of *new* antisocial behavior after childhood. No attempt was made to exclude from these studies children with concurrent CD during childhood, as the intent was to examine the adolescent and adult outcomes of the full range of youths with ADHD. Thus, as noted by Lilienfeld and Waldman (1990), it is possible that most of the elevated rates of antisocial behavior in adulthood in the children with ADHD in these studies were due to concurrent ADHD and CD during childhood rather than to ADHD that occurred in the absence of concurrent CD. Indeed, the insightful analyses of Loney et al. (1981) of their longitudinal sample suggest that this may be the case. They found that the level of aggression in childhood predicted the level of aggression in adolescence, but the level of childhood hyperactivity did not.

Since that time, a number of studies have directly investigated the possibility that childhood ADHD may be a precursor to later antisocial behavior even in the absence of concurrent CD during childhood. These studies have failed to provide an unambiguous answer to this question, however. Magnusson and Bergman (1990) examined the possible role played by ADHD as a precursor to new adult antisocial behavior in a prospective study conducted in Sweden. At age 13, 530 boys were rated on aggression and ADHD by teachers who had known them for 3 years. Boys with high ratings only on ADHD had adult outcomes that did not differ significantly from boys who were rated low on both dimensions.

As noted earlier, Loeber (1988a) conducted a 5-year follow-up of 210 boys from the Oregon Youth Study who were 10 to 16 years of age at the start of the study. The group that was rated high only on ADHD had the lowest absolute rates of offending of any group at follow-up and did not differ significantly from the group that was rated as low on both ADHD and aggression. Farrington et al. (1990) attempted to replicate the findings of the Loeber (1988a) study using the 411 boys of the Cambridge Study in Delinquent Development, but their results were mixed. Compared to boys with low ratings on both childhood conduct problems and ADHD, boys who were rated high only on ADHD had significantly higher numbers of convictions for delinquency during adolescence but did not have higher levels of adolescent delinquency when a self-report measure was used. Furthermore, the boys rated high on only ADHD did not exhibit higher levels of antisocial behavior during adulthood than the normal controls. Indeed, boys with high levels of only ADHD had the lowest absolute levels of criminal behavior during adulthood of any group.

Taylor et al. (1994) conducted a longitudinal study of children selected from a larger community survey in England. The children were 6 to 7 years old at the time of the initial assessment and 16 to 18 years when reassessed. Their study also yielded mixed findings regarding the adolescent outcome of children with ADHD. Youths with ADHD but not CD at the time of the initial assessment ($N = 30$) did not exhibit significantly higher rates of CD in adolescence than did youths without any childhood diagnosis ($N = 29$). The youths with ADHD did receive somewhat higher parent ratings of conduct problems during adolescence than did the control youths, however.

Stronger support for the hypothesis that ADHD is a precursor to later antisocial behavior comes from two separate longitudinal studies of clinic-referred boys conducted by Klein and her colleagues (Gittelman et al., 1985; Mannuzza et al., 1991; Mannuzza

et al., 1993). The first sample consisted of 104 boys ages 6 to 12 years with strict *DSM-II* diagnoses of hyperkinetic reaction who were reassessed at an average age of 18.5 years (Gittelman et al., 1985) and again at an average age of 25.5 years (Mannuzza et al., 1993). The boys were accepted into the study only if they were not referred primarily because of aggression and had a primary diagnosis of hyperkinetic reaction. It is possible, however, that at least some boys with secondary diagnoses of CD were included in this sample. The second sample of 103 boys ages 5 to 12 years was selected in the same way, except that more control was exercised over secondary diagnoses. Only one subject in the second sample received a secondary clinical diagnosis of CD. The second sample was reassessed at an average age of 18.6 years. Control subjects were selected for both samples from patients of other departments of the same medical center.

At 18 years of age, 27% of the first of Klein's samples and 32% of the second sample met criteria for either CD or antisocial personality disorder. These rates were significantly higher than the 8% found in both of the control groups. When the first sample was reevaluated at age 23, significantly more of the formerly hyperkinetic youths than the control subjects (2%) met criteria for antisocial personality (16%). Thus, in two samples in which an effort was made to exclude youths with CD, Klein and her colleagues found that a significantly higher proportion of youths with the *DSM-II* version of ADHD exhibited antisocial behavior in adolescence and early adulthood. This outcome suggests that ADHD alone may be a developmental precursor to serious antisocial behavior.

Similar results were reported by Lambert (1988). She followed 240 youths considered to be hyperactive during elementary school and 127 same-age controls until age 17 or 18 years. Youths with high ratings by parents and teachers on hyperactivity only during elementary school were more likely to exhibit symptoms of both aggressive and nonaggressive CD and to be frequent users of hard drugs in late adolescence than youths with ratings on both hyperactivity and aggression in the normal range during childhood.

Thus, two studies provided no support for the hypothesis that children with ADHD in the absence of CD are at increased risk for later antisocial behavior (Loeber, 1988a; Magnusson & Bergman, 1990); two studies found support for this hypothesis on some but not other dependent variables (Farrington et al., 1990; Taylor et al., 1994); and three studies have reported consistent evidence of increased risk for later antisocial behavior (Gittelman et al., 1985; Mannuzza et al., 1991; Mannuzza et al., 1993; Lambert, 1988).

Loeber et al. (1994) recently conducted analyses of data from the Developmental Trends Study that stand in contrast to the studies of Gittelman, Mannuzza, and Lambert. Although most boys in the Developmental Trends Study who met criteria for CD during any year of the 6-year study already did so during Year 1, 32 boys met criteria for CD for the first time during Years 2 to 6. Loeber et al. (1994) found that ADHD in Year 1 was not a significant predictor of CD in Years 2 to 6. In contrast, ODD in Year 1 was a strong and significant predictor of CD, as 80% of the new cases of CD in Years 2 to 6 met criteria for ODD in Year 1. This suggests that ODD is the developmental precursor to CD rather than ADHD. If confirmed in future research, these analyses suggest that children with ADHD are not at increased risk for later CD unless they also exhibit significant oppositional behavior in childhood. This finding would be of great importance for both theory construction and clinical prognosis if it is replicated in future research.

In some ways, the most interesting finding reported by Loeber et al. (1994) was the association between ADHD and early ages of onset of CD reported earlier in this chapter. Among the 32 boys with new onsets of CD in Years 2 to 6, the boys with ADHD in Year 1 were significantly more likely to be less than 12 years of age at the time that criteria for CD were first met. This suggests that the youths in the Klein and Mannuzza studies who did not meet criteria for CD at the time of referral may have met criteria for ODD and progressed to CD shortly after the first assessment. Unfortunately, ODD was not assessed in these studies, and the follow-up assessments were widely spaced making it impossible to directly assess these assertions.

CONCLUSIONS

The existing literature on associations among ADHD, ODD, CD, and adult antisocial behavior is limited by methodological shortcomings. As such, it can support no firm conclusions but can provide the basis for a number of strong, descriptive hypotheses. Because a number of longitudinal studies designed to test these hypotheses are currently ongoing, clear answers may not be long in coming to these basic questions regarding ADHD, ODD, and antisocial behavior.

It appears likely that ADHD and CD co-occur during childhood at much higher-than-chance levels. Over time, the prevalence of co-occurring CD among youths with ADHD, ODD, or both increases for two reasons: (a) The risk period for the onset of CD extends through adolescence (although most cases of CD may emerge before puberty among children with ADHD, ODD, or both, and (b) both ADHD and CD are more persistent when they co-occur in childhood than when they occur alone. On the other hand, the prevalence of ADHD, ODD, or both among youths with CD appears to decline with increasing age, probably because most youths who develop CD for the first time in adolescence do not have a history of ADHD, ODD, or both.

In contrast to several well-supported hypotheses regarding the relationship between ADHD and CD, the available evidence regarding uncomplicated ADHD as a predictor to adolescent-onset CD is quite conflictual. Although most studies suggest that CD tends to emerge prior to puberty in youths with CD, some studies suggest that children with ADHD in the absence of childhood CD may still be at risk for later onsets of CD. If this is found to be true in future studies, we hypothesize that these new onsets of CD emerge mostly among youths with concurrent ADHD and ODD during childhood. That is, we hypothesize that children with ADHD who do not meet criteria for ODD in childhood are not at elevated risk for CD in adolescence or antisocial behavior during adulthood.

Relationship of CD to Adult Antisocial Behavior

It is clear that CD in childhood and adolescence is a strong predictor of antisocial behavior in adulthood. Studies using official court records have shown that 50% to 70% of youths who meet criteria for CD or are arrested for delinquent acts during childhood or adolescence are arrested in adulthood (Loeber, 1982, 1990, 1991; Harrington, Fudge, Rutter, Pickles, & Hill, 1991; McCord, 1979; Osborn & West, 1978). Robins (1966) similarly found that children with high numbers of antisocial behaviors had a 42% chance of meeting criteria for antisocial personality disorder during adulthood; and Zoccolillo, Pickles, Quinton, and Rutter (1992) found that 40% of institutionally reared boys and 35% of institutionally reared girls who met relaxed *DSM-III* criteria for CD in childhood later met criteria for antisocial personality disorder in adulthood. Harrington et al. (1991) followed a sample of boys and girls who had attended a large psychiatric clinic in London into adulthood. They found that 43% of the youths who had CD during childhood met criteria for antisocial personality disorder during adulthood, compared with 13% among youths who had not had CD in childhood.

These results also make it clear, however, that not all youths with CD engage in serious antisocial behavior in adulthood. What predicts whether a child with CD in childhood will be antisocial in adulthood? Relatively few predictive factors have been identified to date, but Robins found in two samples that children with CD with a biological parent with antisocial personality disorder were more likely to meet criteria for antisocial personality disorder themselves than children with CD without a biological parent with antisocial personality disorder (Robins, 1966; Robins & Ratcliff, 1979). Several other studies suggest that lower intelligence is associated with the persistence of delinquency and CD into late adolescence and adulthood (Farrington, 1991; Schonfeld, Shaffer, O'Connor, & Portnoy, 1988; Stattin & Magnusson, 1989). A recent longitudinal study similarly has found that a history of antisocial personality disorder in a biological parent is the strongest predictor of persistence of CD from childhood into early adolescence but that this predictive relationship is modified by a statistical interaction with verbal intelligence (Lahey et al., 1995). This interaction indicated that youths with verbal intelligence scores above 100 who did not have a biological parent with antisocial personality disorder had a lower risk of persistence than all other youths with CD. The ongoing follow-up into adulthood in this study (Lahey et al., 1995) is not yet completed, however.

FUTURE WORK

As stated earlier, firm conclusions cannot be reached about relationships among ADHD, ODD, CD, and antisocial behavior in adulthood for a variety of methodological reasons. Future research must include adequate numbers of female subjects and must cover more of the life span, particularly the preschool period. Because the descriptive hypotheses concerning ADHD, ODD, and CD focus on developmental sequences, prospective longitudinal studies should be the primary method for future studies. Because of the important advantages inherent in studying the co-occurrence of disorders in general population samples rather than clinic samples, the focus should be on longitudinal studies of population-based samples that are large enough to contain substantial numbers of children and adolescents with ADHD and CD.

When the descriptive hypotheses stated in this chapter and others like them have been confirmed or revised, explanatory theories will be in order. If, for example, the assertion that CD that co-occurs with ADHD during childhood is more persistent than CD that occurs alone is confirmed, it will be necessary to explain this fact. It may turn out that CD that co-occurs with ADHD is a fundamentally different disorder from CD that occurs alone (Loeber, 1988b; Moffitt, 1993). If so, the childhood-onset form of CD may have a different etiology than adolescent-onset CD. On the other hand, there may be only one type of CD, but ADHD in childhood might contribute to its early onset and persistence by interfering with parent-child, teacher-child, and peer relationships in early childhood. When such explanatory models have been proposed and tested, strong hypotheses concerning new methods of treatment and prevention should not be far behind.

REFERENCES

August, G. J., Stewart, M. A., & Holmes, C. S. (1983). A four-year follow-up of hyperactive boys with and without conduct disorder. *British Journal of Psychiatry, 143,* 192–198.

Barkley, R. A., Fisher, M., Edelbrock, C., & Smallish, L. (1990). The adolescent outcome of hyperactive children diagnosed by research criteria: I. An 8-year prospective follow-up study. *Journal of the American Academy of Child and Adolescent Psychiatry, 29,* 546–557.

Caron, C., & Rutter, M. (1991). Comorbidity in child psychopathology: Concepts, issues and research strategies. *Journal of Child Psychology and Psychiatry, 32,* 1063–1080.

Farrington, D. P. (1991). Childhood aggression and adult violence: Early precursors and later-life outcomes. In D. J. Pepler & K. H. Rubin (Eds.), *The development and treatment of childhood aggression* (pp. 5–29). Hillsdale, NJ: Erlbaum.

Farrington, D. P., Loeber, R., & van Kammen, W. B. (1990). Long term criminal outcomes of hyperactivity—impulsivity—attention deficit and conduct problems in childhood. In L. N. Robins & M. R. Rutter (Eds.), *Straight and devious pathways to adulthood* (pp. 62–81). New York: Cambridge University Press.

Gittelman, R., Mannuzza, S., Shenker, R., Bonagura, N., et al. (1985). Hyperactive boys almost grown up: I. Psychiatric status. *Archives of General Psychiatry, 42,* 937–947.

Goodman, S. H., Lahey, B. B., Fielding, B., Dulcan, M., Narrow, W., & Regier, D. (in press). Representativeness of clinical samples of youth with mental disorders: A preliminary population-based study. *Journal of Abnormal Psychology.*

Graham, P., & Rutter, M. (1973). Psychiatric disorder in the young adolescent: A follow-up study. *Proceedings of the Royal Society of Medicine, 66,* 58–61.

Green, S. M., Loeber, R., & Lahey, B. B. (1991). Stability of mothers' recall of the age of onset of their child's attention and hyperactivity problems. *Journal of the American Academy of Child and Adolescent Psychiatry, 30,* 135–137.

Harrington, R., Fudge, H., Rutter, M., Pickles, A., & Hill, J. (1991). Adult outcome of childhood and adolescent depression: I. Links with antisocial disorder. *Journal of the American Academy of Child and Adolescent Psychiatry, 30,* 434–439.

Hart, E. L., Lahey, B. B., Loeber, R., Applegate, B., Green, S. M., & Frick, P. J. (1995). Developmental change in the attention-deficit hyperactivity disorder in boys: A four-year longitudinal study. *Journal of Abnormal Child Psychology, 23,* 729–749.

Hechtman, L., Weiss, G., & Perlman, T. (1984). Hyperactives as young adults: Past and current substance abuse and antisocial behavior. *American Journal of Orthopsychiatry, 54,* 415–425.

Lahey, B. B., Applegate, B., Barkley, R. A., Garfinkel, B., McBurnett, K., Kerdyk, L., Greenhill, L., Hynd, G. W., Frick, P. J., Newcorn, J., Biederman, J., Ollendick, T., Hart, E. L., Perez, D., Waldman, I., & Shaffer, D. (1994). *DSM-IV* field trials for oppositional defiant disorder and conduct disorder in children and adolescents. *American Journal of Psychiatry, 151,* 1163–1171.

Lahey, B. B., & Loeber, R. (1994). Framework for a developmental model of oppositional defiant disorder and conduct disorder. In D. K. Routh (Ed.), *Disruptive behavior disorders in childhood* (pp. 139–180). New York: Plenum.

Lahey, B. B., Loeber, R., Hart, E. L., Frick, P. J., Applegate, B., Zhang, Q., Green, S. M., & Russo, M. F. (1995). Four-year longitudinal study of conduct disorder in boys: Patterns and predictors of persistence. *Journal of Abnormal Psychology, 104,* 83–93.

Lahey, B. B., Loeber, R., Quay, H. C., Frick, P. J., & Grimm, J. (1992). Oppositional defiant and conduct disorders: Issues to be resolved for *DSM-IV. Journal of the American Academy of Child and Adolescent Psychiatry, 31,* 539–546.

Lahey, B. B., Loeber, R., Stouthamer-Loeber, M., Christ, M. A. G., Green, S., Russo, M. F., Frick, P. J., & Dulcan, M. (1990). Comparison of *DSM-III* and *DSM III-R* diagnoses for prepubertal children: Changes in prevalence and validity. *Journal of the American Academy of Child and Adolescent Psychiatry, 29,* 620–626.

Lambert, N. M. (1988). Adolescent outcomes for hyperactive children: Perspectives on general and specific patterns of childhood risk for adolescent educational, social, and mental health problems. *American Psychologist, 43,* 786–799.

Lilienfeld, B., & Waldman, I. (1990). The relationship between childhood attention-deficit hyperactivity disorder and adult antisocial behavior reexamined: The problem of heterogeneity. *Clinical Psychology Review, 10,* 699–725.

Loeber, R. (1982). The stability of antisocial and delinquent child behavior: A review. *Child Development, 53,* 1431–1446.

Loeber, R. (1988a). Behavioral precursors and accelerators of delinquency. In W. Buikhuisen & S. A. Mednick (Eds.), *Explaining criminal behavior* (pp. 51–67). Leiden, Holland: Brill.

Loeber, R. (1988b). Natural histories of conduct problems, delinquency, and associated substance use: Evidence for developmental progressions. In B. B. Lahey & A. E. Kazdin (Eds.), *Advances in clinical child psychology* (pp. 73–124). New York: Plenum.

Loeber, R. (1990). Development and risk factors of juvenile antisocial behavior and delinquency. *Clinical Psychology Review, 10,* 1–41.

Loeber, R. (1991). Antisocial behavior: More enduring than changeable? *Journal of the American Academy of Child and Adolescent Psychiatry, 30,* 393–397.

Loeber, R., Green, S. M., Keenan, K., & Lahey, B. B. (1994). Which boys will fare worse? Early predictors of the onset of conduct disorder in a six-year longitudinal study. *Journal of the American Academy of Child and Adolescent Psychiatry, 34,* 499–509.

Loeber, R., & Keenan, K. (1994). The interaction between conduct disorder and its comorbid conditions: Effects of age and gender. *Clinical Psychology Review, 14,* 497–523.

Loney, J., Kramer, J., & Milich, R. S. (1981). The hyperactive child grows up: Predictors of symptoms, delinquency, and achievement at follow-up. In K. D. Gadow & J. Loney (Eds.), *Psychosocial aspects of drug treatment for hyperactivity* (pp. 381–415). Boulder, CO: Westview Press.

Magnusson, D., & Bergman, L. R. (1990). A pattern approach to the study of pathways from childhood to adulthood. In L. Robins & M. Rutter (Eds.), *Straight and devious pathways from childhood to adulthood* (pp. 101–115). Cambridge, England: Cambridge University Press.

Mannuzza, S., Klein, R. G., Bessler, A., Malloy, P., & LaPadula, M. (1993). Adult outcome of hyperactive boys: Educational achievement, occupational rank, and psychiatric status. *Archives of General Psychiatry, 50,* 565–576.

Mannuzza, S., Klein, R. G., Bonagura, N., Malloy, P., Giampino, T. L., & Addalli, K. A. (1991). Hyperactive boys almost grown up: Replication of psychiatric status. *Archives of General Psychiatry, 48,* 77–83.

McCord, J. (1979). Some child-rearing antecedents of criminal behavior in adult men. *Journal of Personality and Social Psychology, 9,* 1477–1486.

Moffitt, T. E. (1990). Juvenile delinquency and attention deficit disorder: Boys' developmental trajectories from age 3 to 15. *Child Development, 61,* 893–910.

Moffitt, T. E. (1993). Adolescence-limited and life course persistent antisocial behavior: A developmental typology. *Psychological Review, 100,* 674–701.

Offord, D. R., Adler, R. J., & Boyle, M. H. (1986). Prevalence and sociodemographic correlates of conduct disorder. *American Journal of Social Psychiatry, 4,* 272–278.

Offord, D. R., Sullivan, K., Allen, N., & Abrams, N. (1979). Delinquency and hyperactivity. *Journal of Nervous and Mental Disease, 167,* 734–741.

Osborn, S. G., & West, D. J. (1978). The effectiveness of various predictors of criminal careers. *Journal of Adolescence, 1,* 101–117.

Robins, L. N. (1966). *Deviant children grown up: A sociological and psychiatric study of sociopathic personality.* Baltimore: Williams & Wilkins.

Robins, L. N., & Ratcliff, K. S. (1979). Risk factors in the continuation of childhood antisocial behavior into adulthood. *International Journal of Mental Health, 7,* 96–115.

Satterfield, J. H., Hoppe, C. M., & Schell, A. M. (1982). A prospective study of delinquency in 110 adolescent boys with attention deficit disorder and 88 normal adolescent boys. *American Journal of Psychiatry, 139,* 795–798.

Schachar, R., Rutter, M., & Smith, A. (1981). The characteristics of situationally and pervasively hyperactive children: Implications for syndrome definition. *Journal of Child Psychology and Psychiatry, 22,* 375–392.

Schonfeld, I. S., Shaffer, D., O'Connor, P., & Portnoy, S. (1988). Conduct disorder and cognitive functioning: Testing three causal hypotheses. *Child Development, 59,* 993–1007.

Stattin, H., & Magnusson, D. (1989). The role of early aggressive behavior in the frequency, seriousness, and types of later crime. *Journal of Consulting and Clinical Psychology, 57,* 710–718.

Taylor, E., Chadwick, O., Hepinstall, E., & Danckaerts, M. (1994). *Hyperactivity and conduct disorder as risk factors for adolescent development.* Manuscript under editorial review.

Taylor, E., Sandberg, S., Thorley, G., & Giles, S. (1991). *The epidemiology of childhood hyperactivity.* London: Institute of Psychiatry.

Walker, J. L., Lahey, B. B., Hynd, G. W., & Frame, C. L. (1987). Comparison of specific patterns of antisocial behavior in children with conduct disorder with or without coexisting hyperactivity. *Journal of Consulting and Clinical Psychology, 55,* 910–913.

Zoccolillo, M., Pickles, A., Quinton, D., & Rutter, M. (1992). The outcome of childhood conduct disorder: Implications for defining antisocial personality disorder and conduct disorder. *Psychological Medicine, 22,* 971–986.

CHAPTER 6

Assessment of Antisocial Behavior in Adults

SCOTT O. LILIENFELD, CYNTHIA PURCELL, and JACQUELINE JONES-ALEXANDER

The assessment of adult antisocial behavior has been beset by a variety of conceptual and methodological difficulties. In this chapter, we discuss the major theoretical and practical issues involved in the measurement of antisocial behavior in adults and review the psychometric evidence concerning the most frequently used measures in this domain. We place particular emphasis on measures of the *DSM-III* (American Psychiatric Association [APA], 1980), *DSM-III-R* (APA, 1987), and *DSM-IV* (APA, 1994) diagnoses of antisocial personality disorder (ASPD), as ASPD has become the primary focus of mental health research on adult antisocial behavior. In addition, we review self-report, observer rating, and laboratory measures of aggression, as these indexes may provide additional information in the assessment of adult antisocial behavior over and above measures of ASPD. Aggregate measures of criminality used in epidemiological research, such as official crime incidence reports and citizen-defined victimizations, have been reviewed elsewhere (e.g., P. G. Jackson, 1990) and are not discussed here.

HISTORICAL REVIEW

The *DSM-IV* field trial for ASPD examined proposals to provide (a) increased coverage of the personality traits relevant to psychopathy[1] and (b) a more "user-friendly" criteria set (Hare & Hart, 1996; Hare, Hart, & Harpur, 1991). This field trial involved five major sites consisting of samples with high base rates of ASPD, including prisoners, psychiatric inpatients, psychiatric outpatients with substance use disorders, and persons in homeless shelters. The *DSM-III-R* criteria were tested along with three other criteria sets: a simplified version of the *DSM-III-R* criteria, a simplified version of Hare's (1990) Psychopathy Checklist–Revised (PCL-R) containing several major personality features of psychopathy, and the International Classification of Diseases (ICD)–10 (World

Health Organization, 1993) criteria for dyssocial personality disorder, which also consist largely of personality traits. External validating variables for these criteria sets included self-report measures of empathy and Machiavellianism, interviewer and clinician ratings of ASPD, family history of antisocial behavior, and impairment indexes (e.g., number of arrests, number of divorces).

Two major findings emerged from the field trial analyses. First, the simplified *DSM-III-R* criteria set identified essentially the same individuals as the original criteria set. Consequently, the *DSM-IV* criteria were modified to incorporate these simplified criteria. It should be noted, however, that the seven adult ASPD criteria in *DSM-IV* were never actually tested in the field trial; the items tested were the *DSM-III-R* precursors to the *DSM-IV* items (Hare & Hart, 1996). Second, with the exception of the prison setting, the *DSM-III-R* criteria correlated about as highly with the external validating variables as did the Hare (1990) psychopathy items and the ICD-10 criteria. Subsidiary analyses indicated that the two latter measures did not contribute to the prediction of external validating variables over and above the *DSM-III-R* criteria (Widiger et al., 1996). Consequently, the ASPD diagnosis was not modified to incorporate additional personality features of psychopathy.

The *DSM-III*, *DSM-III-R*, and *DSM-IV* criteria for ASPD reflect a polythetic approach to categorization. In this approach, the criteria for each disorder are neither necessary nor sufficient for their respective diagnosis (Widiger & Frances, 1985).[2] As a result, the diagnosis of ASPD can be fulfilled in an enormous number of ways. Rogers and Dion (1991) calculated that 29 trillion different combinations could be used to satisfy the *DSM-III-R* criteria for ASPD. They arrived at this figure by computing all possible permutations of criteria and subcriteria. Although Rogers and Dion used this figure to argue that the ASPD diagnosis is extremely heterogeneous, heterogeneity at the level of manifest indicators (i.e., diagnostic criteria) does not necessarily imply het-

---

[1]Unless otherwise noted, we use the term *psychopathy* to refer to a constellation of personality traits (e.g., guiltlessness, dishonesty, absence of anticipatory anxiety) that sometimes underlies antisocial behavior and the term *antisocial personality disorder* to refer to a syndrome characterized by a chronic history of antisocial and criminal behaviors.

[2]Technically, however, the diagnosis of ASPD itself (as opposed to the adult and child antisocial behaviors of ASPD) is monothetic, because the four overarching criteria (presence of childhood antisocial symptoms, presence of adult antisocial symptoms, age 18 or older, and absence of the two exclusion criteria) are both necessary and sufficient for this diagnosis.

erogeneity at the level of the latent construct (i.e., the entity presumably underlying the ASPD diagnosis). It is conceivable, for example, that ASPD is underpinned by a latent taxon that is manifested in a multitude of forms depending on such factors as learning history, intelligence, and modifying personality traits. By a *taxon,* we mean a category existing in nature (presumably produced by a dichotomous causal agent), rather than a category produced solely by an arbitrary cutting point on a dimension (Meehl & Golden, 1982). Although the possibility that ASPD is taxonic is not discussed further here (see Hart & Hare, Chapter 3, this volume), preliminary evidence suggests that childhood, but not adult, antisocial behaviors are produced by an underlying categorical entity (Harris, Rice, & Quinsey, 1994).

THEORETICAL CONTEXT AND CONTROVERSIAL ISSUES

Personality-Based and Behavior-Based Approaches

Two approaches to the assessment of adult antisocial behavior can be distinguished: personality-based and behavior-based (Lilienfeld, 1994). In this chapter, we emphasize the behavior-based approach, as this approach involves the direct assessment of antisocial behavior. Although the personality- and behavior-based approaches overlap to some extent empirically (Harpur, Hare, & Hakstian, 1989), they differ in their theoretical underpinnings and assessment implications. Advocates of the personality-based approach (e.g., Cleckley, 1941/1982; Hare, 1990; Lykken, 1995) emphasize the underlying personality traits constituting psychopathy, such as guiltlessness, dishonesty, callousness, and egocentricity. Proponents of this approach regard antisocial behavior as neither necessary nor sufficient for the diagnosis of this syndrome. Advocates of the behavior-based approach, in contrast, place primary emphasis on overt antisocial behaviors, which fit well with the readily observable criteria of *DSM-III, DSM-III-R,* and *DSM-IV.* Much of the impetus behind the behavior-based approach reflects the increased emphasis on reliability characteristic of the post-*DSM-II* era (Faust & Miner, 1986; Spitzer & Fleiss, 1974).

Because many of the traits constituting psychopathy require a considerable degree of inference, the interrater reliability of the personality-based approach has been presumed by many authors (e.g., Cloninger, 1978) to be lower than that of the behavior-based approach. Indeed, ASPD is the only *DSM* personality disorder to consistently achieve high levels of interrater reliability in clinical practice (Mellsop, Varghese, Joshua, & Hicks, 1982). Moreover, the chance-corrected indexes of agreement (kappas) for ASPD using standardized interviews have typically been high. Across 15 studies, the mean kappa coefficient for ASPD using standardized interviews with independent raters is .77 (Zimmerman, 1994), which is the highest reliability figure of all *DSM* personality disorders. It should be noted, however, that personality-based criteria for psychopathy can achieve levels of interrater reliability comparable to those of behavior-based criteria. Hare (1990), for example, reported that a composite of items assessing criteria for psychopathy similar to those of Cleckley (1941/1982) achieved interrater reliabilities ranging from .66 to .83 across six samples of prison inmates.

Criticisms of the Behavior-Based Approach

Some authors (e.g., Lykken, 1995) have charged that the behavior-based approach sacrifices construct validity for the sake of increased reliability. This criticism appears to reflect a deeper concern that *DSM-III* and its progeny have embraced a blindly empirical approach that encourages the premature reification of diagnostic entities (Faust & Miner, 1986). Specifically, a number of authors have suggested that the ASPD diagnosis suffers from both overinclusiveness (i.e., heterogeneity) and underinclusiveness (Lilienfeld, 1994; Widiger & Corbitt, 1993).

Overinclusiveness

Critics of the behavior-based approach argue that chronic antisocial behavior in adulthood is etiologically heterogeneous, and that *DSM-III* and similar criteria have rendered ASPD virtually synonymous with chronic criminality (Wulach, 1983). These critics have further suggested that ASPD encompasses a variety of conditions in addition to psychopathy (see Lykken, 1995, for a review). Such putative conditions include (a) *neurotic psychopathy* (i.e., antisocial behavior that is an expression of anxiety and neurotic conflict), (b) *dyssocial psychotherapy* (i.e., antisocial behavior resulting from allegiance to a culturally deviant subgroup), and (c) *schizoid psychopathy* (i.e., a schizophrenia spectrum disorder in which antisocial behavior results from poor judgment and impulsivity; Heston, 1970). Nonetheless, the research evidence for the existence of these subtypes is relatively scant. Few investigators have attempted to isolate these proposed subtypes within samples of ASPD patients, nor has it been demonstrated that these subtypes differ on external validating criteria. Perhaps the strongest evidence for the heterogeneity of ASPD derives from a study of 80 forensic patients by Hart and Hare (1989), who found that most individuals with ASPD appeared not to possess the personality features of psychopathy (as assessed by the PCL, an earlier version of the PCL-R). Because Hart and Hare apparently did not utilize the *DSM-III* exclusion criteria for ASPD (1989, p. 213), however, their diagnoses of ASPD may have included a number of false positives. This possibility seems likely given that the rates of schizophrenia and bipolar disorder in their sample were high (33.8% and 10%, respectively). Moreover, a study by Hare (1983) did not provide compelling evidence for the heterogeneity of ASPD. Of 64 inmates diagnosed with ASPD, 63 had high or medium PCL scores and only 1 had a low score.

Several authors have argued that the assessment of adult antisocial behavior may be complicated by substance abuse and dependence (Alterman & Cacciola, 1991; Gerstley, Alterman, McLellan, & Woody, 1990; see White, Chapter 47, this volume). For example, in the Epidemiological Catchment Area (ECA) study, alcohol abuse and dependence co-occurred with ASPD 15.5 times more often than expected by chance (Boyd et al., 1984). Moreover, some symptoms of ASPD, such as arrests, may result from the abuse of alcohol and other substances (Schuckit, 1973). These problems have been handled differently by different criteria sets. The Research Diagnostic Criteria (RDC) required that adult ASPD symptoms not be a consequence of substance use. In contrast, *DSM-III* and its two revisions allow antisocial behaviors to count toward the ASPD diagnosis regardless of their presumed causal relation to substance use. Not surprisingly, among substance abusers the prevalence of RDC diagnoses of ASPD is lower than the prevalence of *DSM-III* diagnoses of ASPD (Gerstley et al., 1990).

Although it is unclear which of these two approaches yields greater construct validity, the results of one study suggest that the *DSM*'s inclusion of antisocial behaviors that are secondary to substance use may result in a heterogeneous group of individuals. Hasin, Grant, and Endicott (1988) found that alcoholics whose antisocial behavior was judged to be independent of their drinking reported a higher prevalence of ASPD among family members than alcoholics whose antisocial behavior was judged to be secondary to drinking. Thus, the antisocial behaviors of the latter group may be etiologically unrelated to ASPD.

Others have suggested that the ASPD diagnosis is biased against the homeless. Because homelessness was a criterion for ASPD in *DSM-III* and *DSM-III-R* and because homelessness may lead to several adult symptoms of ASPD (e.g., failure to sustain consistent work behavior), this possibility is a cause for concern. In a study examining this issue, North, Smith, and Spitznagel (1993) administered the Diagnostic Interview Schedule (DIS) to 900 homeless individuals. North et al. found that even among this sample, most adult ASPD symptoms were significantly correlated with childhood ASPD (i.e., conduct disorder, CD) symptoms, suggesting that the former did not typically arise de novo as a result of homelessness. Moreover, they reported that the onset of homelessness tended to follow, rather than precede, ASPD symptoms. North et al.'s (1993) data do not indicate that the ASPD diagnosis is biased against the homeless, although this conclusion would be strengthened by the inclusion of additional external validating variables (e.g., family history).

As noted earlier, some authors have contended that ASPD, as operationalized by *DSM-III* and its two revisions, is essentially synonymous with chronic criminality. Although there may be some truth to this criticism, approximately 50% of incarcerated criminals do not satisfy criteria for ASPD (Hare, 1990). Moreover, results from the ECA study indicate that only 37% of individuals with repeated arrests fulfilled criteria for ASPD and that only 47% of individuals with ASPD had a history of repeated arrests (Robins, Tipp, & Przybeck, 1991). Although ASPD overlaps considerably with chronic criminality, the two concepts are not isomorphic.

Underinclusiveness

It is often not appreciated that an increase in the reliability of a diagnosis can result in decreased construct validity. This state of affairs can arise if the revised diagnosis provides an overly narrow operationalization of the construct (Meehl, 1986). In this context, some critics argue that the behavior-based approach, although highly reliable, is underinclusive in that it fails to detect "subclinical" or "successful" psychopaths, that is, psychopaths who have managed to avoid repeated contact with the legal system (Widom, 1977). Indeed, the results of two studies indicate that individuals recruited from the community via newspaper advertisements containing many of the personality features of psychopathy described by Cleckley (1941/1982) resemble incarcerated psychopaths on personality and family history measures (Widom, 1977; Widom & Newman, 1985). Nonetheless, because between 70% and 80% of subjects in both studies fulfilled Robins's (1966) criteria for sociopathy, these studies do not demonstrate that a large proportion of adult psychopaths lack histories of antisocial behavior.

Further research using external validating variables (e.g., biological and laboratory correlates of psychopathy) will be necessary to determine whether the behavior-based approach fails to detect a sizable number of psychopaths.

Rutherford, Alterman, Caccioa, and Snider (1995) argued that *DSM-III-R*'s emphasis on aggressive CD symptoms (e.g., cruelty to animals, rape) may lead to an underdiagnosis of ASPD in females. In a study of methadone patients, they reported that many CD items in *DSM-III-R*, particularly those assessing physical violence, exhibited very low base rates in females. More important, these aggressive CD items tended to have low or even negative item-total correlations in females, but not in males, suggesting the presence of gender bias. This gender disparity in validity was not found for the CD items in *DSM-III*, buttressing the authors' claim that *DSM-III-R*'s focus on aggressive CD symptoms has decreased the validity of the ASPD diagnosis among females. The extent to which Rutherford et al.'s findings can be generalized to patients without substance use problems requires investigation.

The Two-Factor Model

Based on factor analyses of the PCL-R, Harpur et al. (1989) formulated a "two-factor model" of psychopathy. Factor 1 consists of such personality traits as grandiosity, lack of empathy, and shallow affect and seems to correspond to the personality-based conception of psychopathy. Factor 2, which correlates moderately ($r = .5$) with Factor 1, consists of such characteristics as a parasitic lifestyle, irresponsibility, and early behavior problems and seems to correspond to the *DSM-III* conception of ASPD. Factor 2, unlike Factor 1, is moderately correlated with *DSM-III* ASPD (Harpur et al., 1989). PCL-R Factors 1 and 2 appear to provide reasonable operationalizations of the personality- and behavior-based conceptions, respectively. The two-factor model promises to facilitate research on adult antisocial behavior by providing a vehicle for comparing the construct validity of the personality- and behavior-based approaches. Harpur et al. (1989) found, for example, that the two PCL-R factors possess different correlates. Whereas Factor 1 is weakly related to measures of verbal intelligence, social class, and education, Factor 2 is moderately to highly related to these indexes. One interpretation of this finding is that the personality factors underlying psychopathy are relatively independent of cognitive and shared environmental factors but that these variables play a major role in determining which psychopaths develop antisocial behavior.

METHODOLOGY

In addition to the conceptual issues already discussed, several methodological problems confront researchers who assess adult antisocial behavior. In particular, three factors may attenuate the validity of adult antisocial behavior measures: response styles, state-trait effects, and correlated error.

Response Styles

A particular concern in the assessment of adult antisocial behavior is the presence of response styles, which are systematic ways of responding to items that are essentially irrelevant to item content. Response styles are hypothesized to reduce validity and produce correlations among measures that are attributable to respondents' test-taking approaches, rather than to the substantive constructs of interest. The response style of greatest concern in the assessment of antisocial behaviors is impression management, because (a) such behaviors tend to be socially devalued and (b) many of the individuals with high rates of such behaviors, such as psychopaths, are known for dishonesty. Relatively few data are available concerning the impact of response styles on the assessment of adult antisocial behavior. Note that self-report measures of psychopathy, as well as PCL-R Factor 2, have been found to be weakly negatively correlated with validity indexes of impression management (Harpur et al., 1989), perhaps because these indexes in part reflect a propensity to deny socially undesirable attributes. If so, this finding suggests that psychopaths and perhaps individuals with antisocial behavior in general are willing to admit to at least some negative characteristics. Nevertheless, this finding does not exclude the possibility that a nontrivial number of individuals underreport their antisocial behaviors.

Consistent with this possibility is a study by Clark and Tifft (1966), in which the anonymous responses of college students to antisocial behavior items were compared with their responses to these items during (a) an interview during which they were informed that their responses would later be verified by a polygraph test and (b) an actual polygraph test. The investigators assumed that the threat of the polygraph test, as well as the social pressure of the test itself, would result in more honest responses. Clark and Tifft found that three fourths of responses altered following the initial questionnaire were in the direction of increased deviance, suggesting that subjects had tended to underreport the frequency of their antisocial behaviors on the questionnaire. Because Clark and Tifft's conditions were not counterbalanced, however, their results are potentially attributable to the tendency of subjects to exhibit superior recall of their behaviors following repeated questioning.

Moreover, there is evidence that when official arrest records are used as criteria, a substantial amount of underreporting of crimes is evident on questionnaires assessing antisocial behavior. In one large-scale New York study using self-report measures, approximately 20% of subjects appear to have either hidden or forgotten some antisocial behaviors, and approximately 20% of antisocial behaviors appear to have gone unreported (Huizinga & Elliott, 1986). There are indications that the amount of underreporting is somewhat greater among African Americans than among Whites (Huizinga & Elliott, 1986), although the reason for this finding is unclear. In addition, the amount of underreporting may be greater for more serious than for less serious crimes (Elliott & Voss, 1974).

Nevertheless, it should be noted that nontrivial amounts of overreporting (e.g., 36% in the New York study cited earlier; Huizinga & Elliott, 1986) may occur on self-report measures of antisocial behavior, although such "overreporting" may sometimes be a consequence of incomplete arrest records. Overreporting may be especially likely in response to items inquiring about trivial offenses. For example, some respondents may regard pilfering a pen from work as an example of "theft" (Gold & Reimer, 1975).

Although it is often assumed that self-report measures are particularly vulnerable to impression management (Hare, 1985), interviews typically involve a greater degree of contact with subjects and may be even more susceptible than self-report measures to demand characteristics and social pressures. Moreover, self-report measures, unlike interviews, can assess response styles systematically (Widiger & Frances, 1987). Despite this potential advantage, few self-report measures of adult antisocial behavior contain validity indexes designed to detect impression management and related response styles.

State-Trait Effects

The state-trait effect refers to the tendency for transient mood changes (i.e., states) to influence the reporting of enduring dispositions (i.e., traits). This effect is a potentially serious methodological artifact (Loranger et al., 1991), because states may color the reporting of long-lasting behavior patterns and thereby attenuate the validity of personality disorder indexes. It is generally assumed that depression, anxiety, and other negative mood states will produce an overreporting of undesirable personality characteristics (Zimmerman, 1994).

Several investigators have examined the influence of state factors on the reporting of ASPD symptoms. Although most studies (e.g., Loranger et al., 1991; Mavissakalian & Hamann, 1987) have demonstrated few or no changes in ASPD diagnoses or symptoms following treatment for depression, anxiety, and other mood states, the results of three studies (Joffe & Regan, 1988; Kennedy, McVey, & Katz, 1990; Libb et al., 1990) reveal significant increases in reported ASPD or ASPD symptoms following treatment of Axis I disorders. All three of these studies utilized the Millon Clinical Multiaxial Inventory, a self-report measure discussed in the following section. If these results can be replicated, they would suggest that transient mood disturbances can produce an underreporting of antisocial behaviors. It is not clear why this should be the case, although the inhibition and withdrawal produced by depression and anxiety may render more difficult the recall of risk taking and impulsive behaviors.

Trull and Goodwin (1993), in contrast, reported opposite findings from those above using one of two self-report measures of ASPD (the Personality Diagnostic Questionnaire–Revised, discussed in the following section); scores on this measure decreased significantly among outpatients over a 6-month interval. The reasons for the discrepancy between Trull and Goodwin's findings and those of previous researchers are unclear. It is worth noting that the four studies demonstrating a state-trait effect for ASPD all utilized self-report measures. Self-report measures may be more susceptible than interviews to state-trait effects, because questionnaires do not permit probing with follow-up questions (Loranger et al., 1991). Wherever possible, researchers and clinicians assessing ASPD symptoms via self-report should consider assessing these symptoms following recovery from acute mood disturbances.

Correlated Error

A fundamental assumption of correlational techniques (as well as statistical methods based on these techniques, such as multiple regression) is the absence of a correlation between error scores and the "true score," that is, the underlying construct of interest.

In the case of certain self-report and interview indexes of adult antisocial behavior, however, such an assumption may be untenable. There is evidence that compared with individuals with low levels of antisocial behavior, individuals with high levels of antisocial behavior have greater difficulty recalling correctly the number of antisocial acts they have performed (Huizinga & Elliott, 1986), presumably because it becomes increasingly difficult to estimate accurately the number of antisocial acts one has engaged in as the total number of these acts increases. Such a tendency would result in heteroscedasticity (i.e., unequal variance at different levels of a bivariate distribution), which violates a fundamental assumption of correlational methods (Berry, 1993). This problem poses difficulties for measures that rely on frequency counts of antisocial acts. In contrast, this problem may pose less of a difficulty for assessments of the *DSM-IV* criteria for ASPD, which place more emphasis on global judgments of frequency (e.g., "irritability and aggressiveness, as indicated by repeated physical fights and assaults"; APA, 1994, p. 650) than on specific frequency counts.

CURRENT FINDINGS ON THE ASPD DIAGNOSIS

In this section, we restrict our attention to self-report and interview measures of ASPD. Indexes of psychopathy, such as the MMPI Psychopathic Deviate Scale (McKinley & Hathaway, 1944) and CPI Socialization Scale (Gough, 1960), are not reviewed here, as they do not explicitly assess adult antisocial behaviors.

Self-Report Measures

Although a large number of self-report measures of ASPD have been developed (e.g., Coolidge & Merwin, 1992; Klein et al., 1993), an adequate body of psychometric data is available for only three: the Personality Diagnostic Questionnaire–Revised (PDQ-R; Hyler & Rieder, 1987), the Millon Clinical Multiaxial Inventory–Revised (MCMI-R; Millon, 1987), and the MMPI *DSM-III* Personality Disorders Scales (Morey, Waugh, & Blashfield, 1985), all of which utilize a true-false response format. The PDQ-R was developed by constructing items to directly assess each *DSM-III-R* criterion. Virtually all of the ASPD criteria are assessed by a single item. Thirty percent of the items on the ASPD scale are reversed in scoring to minimize the possibility of an acquiescence response style. The PDQ-R contains two validity scales, TG ("too good") and SQ ("suspect questionnaire"), which assess impression management and careless responding/malingering, respectively. Because all of these validity items are grouped together, however, many subjects may be able to identify their intent. The internal consistency of the PDQ-R ASPD scale in a college sample has been reported to be .78 (Lilienfeld, 1990). Its 3-month test-retest reliability in a psychiatric sample was .75 (Trull, 1993).

The MMPI *DSM-III* Personality Disorder (PD) scales were developed by asking psychologists to select items from the MMPI that appeared to assess each *DSM-III* personality disorder. These preliminary scales were refined by eliminating items with low item-total correlations. Unlike the PDQ-R scales, the MMPI *DSM-III* PD scales do not directly assess the *DSM* criteria for each per-

sonality disorder. The internal consistency of the MMPI *DSM-III* ASPD scale in a psychiatric sample has been reported to be .78 (Morey et al., 1985). Its 3-month test-retest reliability in a psychiatric sample was .82 (Trull, 1993).

The MCMI-II was designed to assess the principal dimensions of Millon's (1981) biosocial theory of personality. Partly in response to criticisms that the MCMI was insufficiently tied to the *DSM-III* taxonomy of personality disorders (e.g., Widiger, Williams, Spitzer, & Frances, 1985), Millon revised the MCMI to bring it into closer alignment with the *DSM-III-R* personality disorders. The MCMI-II, like the MMPI PD scales, does not directly assess *DSM* criteria. The test-retest reliability of the MCMI-II ASPD scale among a sample of inpatients has been reported to be .84 (Piersma, 1989).

Two consistent findings have emerged from studies examining self-report measures of adult antisocial behavior. First, when questionnaire measures of ASPD are scored dimensionally (i.e., in terms of the number of criteria endorsed), they generally exhibit poor convergent validity (i.e., low intercorrelations) and poor discriminant validity (i.e., higher intercorrelations with personality disorders other than ASPD than with each other). Morey and LeVine (1988), for example, reported a nonsignificant correlation of $r = .25$ between the MMPI *DSM-III* and MCMI ASPD scales. Moreover, for these two measures, 0/10 and 1/10 monomethod (i.e., same test) discriminant validity comparisons, respectively, were statistically significant. In other words, in only 1 case out of 20 did the correlation between the two ASPD measures significantly exceed the correlation between each measure of ASPD and the measures of other personality disorders assessed by the same instrument. In addition, only 3 of 20 heteromethod (i.e., different test) comparisons were significant, meaning that in only 3 cases did the correlation between the two ASPD measures significantly exceed the correlation between each measure of ASPD and measures of other personality disorders assessed by the other instrument. These findings paint a picture of poor discriminant validity.

Streiner and Miller (1988) similarly reported that the MMPI *DSM-III* ASPD scale correlated only .30 with the MCMI ASPD scale. This correlation, although significant, was lower than that between the MMPI *DSM-III* ASPD scale and the MCMI compulsive and passive-aggressive personality disorder scales, and lower than that between the MCMI ASPD scale and the *DSM-III* narcissistic personality disorder scale. The relatively high correlation of the MMPI *DSM-III* ASPD scale with the MCMI compulsive scale is inconsistent with diagnostic descriptions of individuals with ASPD as impulsive and reckless (e.g., APA, 1994). The significance of the monomethod and heteromethod comparisons for the two ASPD scales was not reported.

McCann (1991), in contrast, reported a correlation of .57 between the MMPI *DSM-III* and MCMI-II ASPD scales. This relatively high correlation may be attributable to the greater similarity of the MCMI-II ASPD scale than the MCMI ASPD scale to the *DSM-III-R* operationalization of ASPD. In 18 of 20 cases, this correlation exceeded the monomethod correlations and in 21 of 22 cases exceeded the heteromethod correlations. Again, the statistical significance of these comparisons was not reported.

Trull (1993) examined the correlations between the PDQ-R

and MMPI *DSM-III* personality disorder scales in 51 outpatients. The two ASPD scales correlated at *r* = .51, indicating modest convergent validity. The evidence for discriminant validity was inconsistent. Although all 20 heteromethod correlations were lower than the correlation between the two ASPD scales, 4 of 20 monomethod correlations exceeded the correlation between the two ASPD scales.

Hills (1995) administered the MMPI-2 and MCMI-II to 125 subjects who were either outpatients or participants in either residential or day hospital programs. The kappa coefficient of agreement for diagnoses of ASPD was .37. Indexes of dimensional agreement were not reported.

A second consistent finding is that the PDQ-R yields high rates of ASPD and ASPD symptoms in nonclinical samples. Johnson and Bornstein (1992) reported that 30% of a sample of 258 college students (152 females, 106 males) met *DSM-III-R* criteria for ASPD using the PDQ-R; this percentage dropped to 17% when subjects with elevations on the SQ scale were excluded (see Coolidge, Merwin, Wooley, & Hyman, 1990, for similar findings). Given that the estimated population prevalences of ASPD in *DSM-IV* are 3% among males and 1% among females, these figures suggest that the PDQ-R overestimates the base rate of ASPD in nonclinical samples. This finding may be due to the fact that many of the PDQ-R items appear to assess ASPD symptoms below the threshold of severity specified by *DSM-III-R*. For example, the item "I have no trouble keeping jobs or staying in school" is intended to assess the *DSM-III-R* criterion of "is unable to sustain consistent work behavior." But many individuals who experience difficulty keeping jobs or staying in school can sustain consistent work behavior. Similar problems are present for several other PDQ-R ASPD items. With the exception of Reich and Troughton (1988), who did not find a high rate (2.5%) of MCMI-defined ASPD among normals, few researchers have examined the extent to which other self-report measures overdiagnose ASPD in nonclinical samples.

In summary, self-report indexes of ASPD tend to exhibit relatively weak intercorrelations and sometimes exhibit higher correlations with measures of other personality disorders than they do with one another. Consumers of the ASPD literature should not assume that findings based on one self-report ASPD measure will generalize to findings based on others. Although the PDQ-R tends to yield high prevalences of ASPD and ASPD symptoms in nonclinical samples, the degree to which this finding extends to other self-report measures is unclear.

Structured and Semistructured Psychiatric Interviews

A number of structured and semistructured interviews are available for the assessment of personality disorders, including ASPD. The interviews we focus on here are the Structured Clinical Interview for *DSM-III-R,* Axis II (SCID-II; First et al., 1995; Spitzer, Williams, Gibbon, & First, 1990); the Structured Interview for *DSM-III-R* Personality (SIDP-R; Pfohl, Blum, Zimmerman, & Stangl, 1989); the Personality Disorder Examination (PDE; Loranger, 1988); the Diagnostic Interview for Personality Disorders

(DIPD; Zanarini, Frankenburg, Chauncey, & Gunderson, 1987); and the DIS (Robins, Helzer, Croughan, & Ratcliff, 1981), the last of which does not assess personality disorders other than ASPD. The format and content of these measures have been reviewed elsewhere (Perry, 1992; Widiger & Frances, 1987) and are not discussed here. In this section, we review studies examining the interrater reliabilities of these measures, as well as studies examining diagnostic agreement among these measures.

As noted earlier, the interrater reliability of ASPD using standardized interviews is high. This finding holds regardless of whether the design involves a joint interview or a short (i.e., less than 1 week) or long (i.e., greater than 1 week) test-retest interval. The mean kappa coefficients across these three designs for ASPD are .77, .77, and .84, respectively (Zimmerman, 1994). The interviews used in these investigations included the SIDP, PDE, SCID-II, and DIPD. In contrast to the high levels of interrater agreement for ASPD when the same interview is administered on different occasions, the levels of agreement for ASPD across different interviews are less impressive. For example, Perry, Lavori, Cooper, Hoke, and O'Connell (1987) administered the DIS and a clinical interview to 82 patients. Both interviews utilized *DSM-III* criteria, although the format of the clinical interview was not described. The kappa coefficient for the ASPD diagnosis was .54. Dimensional analyses were not reported.

Hyler, Skodol, Kellman, Oldham, and Rosnick (1990) administered the SCID-II and PDE to 87 inpatients. These measures were administered in a balanced fashion in which interviewer and interview were alternated. The kappa coefficient between these two interviews for ASPD was .64, and the intraclass correlation for dimensional scores was .46. Skodol, Oldham, Rosnick, Kellman, and Hyler (1991) compared the rates of diagnostic agreement between the SCID-II and the PDE among 100 inpatients. The two interviews were administered in counterbalanced order, generally within the same day. The kappa coefficient for *DSM-III-R* ASPD was .59, and the correlation between dimensional scores was .87.

Only two groups of investigators have compared the validity of different interviews for ASPD against an external criterion. Perry et al. (1987) obtained follow-up data on antisocial behavior across several 3-month intervals using the Antisocial Symptom Scale of the Psychiatric Status Schedule (Spitzer, Endicott, & Fleiss, 1970). This scale consists of structured interview questions primarily assessing concrete antisocial behaviors such as stealing and prostitution. The authors reported that the clinical interview predicted future antisocial behavior better than the DIS and that the DIS significantly predicted antisocial behavior only when in agreement with the clinical interview. Perry et al. conjectured that the highly structured nature of the DIS requires interviewers to accept subjects' reports of antisocial behaviors and prohibits interviewers from probing for nonconfirmatory information. As a result, the DIS may overdiagnose ASPD among individuals with mild or transient antisocial symptoms. The extent to which Perry et al.'s findings apply to less structured interviews requires further investigation.

Skodol et al. (1991) compared the SCID-II and PDE against Longitudinal Expert Evaluations Using All Data (LEAD; Spitzer, 1983) diagnoses following 6 weeks of observation. When ASPD diagnoses based on the SCID-II were compared with LEAD diagnoses, positive predictive power (PPP) was good (.75), and negative predictive power (NPP) was excellent (1.00).[3] PPP is the probability of a diagnosis given a positive test result, whereas NPP is the probability of the absence of a diagnosis given a negative test result. PPP and NPP for ASPD diagnoses from the PDE were similar to those above (.67 and .97, respectively).

Taken together, the studies reviewed in this section indicate that the interrater reliability of the ASPD diagnosis as assessed by standardized interviews tends to be good to excellent. Agreement rates across different interviews appear to be less impressive, although this conclusion is based on only three studies. Few data are available concerning the comparative validity of different ASPD interviews, although the results of one study (Perry et al., 1987) suggest that the predictive validity of the DIS may be inferior to that of interviews permitting greater interviewer judgment. At the present time, there is little empirical justification for preferring one interview for ASPD over others.

Relations Between Self-Report Measures and Interviews

In contrast to the paucity of studies comparing different interviews for ASPD, a large number of studies have compared self-report and interview measures of ASPD. Hyler et al. (1989) compared PDQ diagnoses of ASPD with clinical diagnoses of ASPD among 552 outpatients. The kappa coefficient between the PDQ and clinical diagnoses of ASPD was only .07, although the correlation between these two measures treated dimensionally was .48. Using the clinical interview as a "criterion," the PDQ-R was found to have a sensitivity (true positive rate) of only .27 and a specificity (true negative rate) of .94. In addition, the PDQ produced substantially higher rates of ASPD than the clinical interview. Thirty-two patients received PDQ-R diagnoses of ASPD, whereas only 11 received diagnoses of ASPD based on the clinical interview. Hyler et al. (1989) also reported a tendency for the PDQ-R to yield more co-occurring diagnoses than the clinical interview. For example, 84% of patients diagnosed with ASPD by the PDQ-R, compared with 33% of patients diagnosed with ASPD by the clinical interview, met criteria for borderline personality disorder.

Hyler et al. (1990) administered the PDQ-R, SCID-II, and PDE to 87 inpatients. Kappa coefficients between the PDQ-R, on the one hand, and the SCID-II and PDE, on the other, were .42 and .36, respectively. Intraclass correlations for comparisons using dimensional scores were .46 and .46, respectively. For diagnoses of definite ASPD (i.e., ASPD diagnoses present according to both interviews), the sensitivity and specificity of the PDQ-R were high (.75 and .89, respectively). The PPP of the PDQ-R was only .25, whereas its NPP was .98.

Zimmerman and Coryell (1990) compared the PDQ and SIDP in a sample of 697 first-degree relatives of depressed patients, patients with psychotic disorders, and normals. The kappa coefficient between the PDQ and SIDP for ASPD was only .14, although the correlation between dimensional ASPD scores was .55. ASPD was the only personality disorder for which the mean SIDP score exceeded the mean PDQ score. Zimmerman and Coryell suggested that the PDQ may yield low rates of certain adult antisocial behaviors, such as employment history and recklessness, because of its use of single items to assess a number of ASPD symptoms.

Trull and Larson (1994) compared diagnoses from the PDQ-R and MMPI *DSM-III* Personality Disorders scales with those from the SIDP in a sample of 57 outpatients. Using the SIDP ASPD scale as a criterion, the kappa coefficients for the PDQ-R and MMPI ASPD scales were .46 and .20, respectively. Because the base rate of SIDP-diagnosed ASPD was only 5%, however, these figures may be unstable. Kappa tends to be unreliable when base rates are low (Grove, 1987). Correlations between dimensional scores for the SIDP, on the one hand, and the PDQ-R and MMPI ASPD, on the other, were .44 and .53, respectively. Analysis of conditional probabilities revealed slightly higher sensitivities and specificities for the PDQ-R than for the MMPI ASPD scale (1.0 and .89 vs. .67 and .80, respectively). NPPs were comparable (1.0 and .98), but PPP was somewhat higher for the PDQ-R than for the MMPI ASPD scale (.33 versus .15).

Several researchers have compared the MCMI with standardized interviews in the assessment of ASPD. Soldz, Budman, Demby, and Merry (1993) administered the MCMI-II and PDE to 97 outpatients. When a definite PDE diagnosis of ASPD was used as the criterion, agreement between the two measures was no better than chance (kappa = .00); when the criterion was extended to include both definite and probable diagnoses, agreement between the two measures improved somewhat (kappa = .38). This latter figure, however, was based on only two cases diagnosed positive by the PDE. For combined definite and probable ASPD diagnoses, the MCMI had low PPP (.25) and perfect NPP (1.00). Dimensional scores based on the two measures correlated moderately (r = .37). Hogg, Jackson, Rudd, and Edwards (1990) examined the relation between the MCMI and the SIDP among 40 recent-onset schizophrenics. Because of the low base rate of ASPD, kappa coefficients were not computed. The correlation between dimensional scores was low and nonsignificant (r = .23). H. J. Jackson, Gazis, Rudd, and Edwards (1991) administered the MCMI and SIDP to 82 inpatients. Kappa for the ASPD diagnosis was low (.06), as were correlations between dimensional scores (r = .14). Using the SIDP as a criterion, PPP for the MCMI was low (.20), but NPP was high (.92). In a study described earlier, Hills (1995) administered the MMPI-2, MCMI-II, and SCID-II to 125 patients. The kappa coefficient of agreement between the MMPI-2 personality disorder scales (Morey & LeVine, 1988) and the SCID-II for the diagnosis of ASPD was only .19; the corresponding kappa between the MCMI-II and the SCID-II was .37.

In summary, diagnostic concordance between self-report and interview measures of ASPD tends to be relatively poor, although this state of affairs may be improved slightly by the use of dimensional scores. Because the validity of self-report and interview measures of ASPD has yet to be systematically compared, no clear basis exists for justifying the use of one such measure over another.

---

[3]Although we use the terms *sensitivity, specificity, positive predictive power, negative predictive power, false positive,* and *false negative* in the remainder of the chapter, we should note that these terms technically presume that ASPD is a taxon with a known base rate.

CURRENT FINDINGS ON SELF-REPORT, OBSERVER RATING, AND LABORATORY MEASURES OF AGGRESSION

Although the primary focus of this chapter is on indexes of ASPD, a large literature also exists on the assessment of aggression via self-report, observer rating, and laboratory measures. Such measures may complement dimensional indexes of ASPD in their emphasis on subclinical levels of adult antisocial behavior and may supplement these indexes by providing an assessment of personality domains (e.g., hostility, irritability) that are associated with increased risk for such behavior. Moreover, these measures may be especially useful for examining mild manifestations of antisocial behavior in nonclinical (e.g., student, community) samples.

Self-Report Measures of Aggression

Although self-report indexes of trait aggression have often been treated almost interchangeably, the correlations among many of these indexes tend to be weak or at best moderate (Edmunds & Kendrick, 1980). Much of the reason for these low correlations probably stems from the fact that different self-report aggression measures assess different superordinate dimensions of personality. Measures that assess subjective anger and hostility tend to load on the higher order factor of negative affectivity or neuroticism, which represents a predisposition to experience negative affects (e.g., stress reactivity, irritability, mistrust) of many kinds. In contrast, measures that assess behavioral aggression tend to load (negatively) on the higher order factor of agreeableness (Watson, Clark, & Harkness, 1994).

Perhaps the best known self-report measure of aggression is the Buss Durkee Hostility Inventory (BDHI; Buss & Durkee, 1957). The BDHI was constructed by writing items to assess seven domains, each of which is measured by a separate subscale: Assault, Indirect Aggression, Irritability, Negativism, Resentment, Suspicion, and Verbal Aggression. Factor analyses of the BDHI have generally revealed a two-factor structure, with one factor representing overt or behavioral aggression and the other representing covert aggression or aggressive attitudes (Bushman, Cooper, & Lemke, 1991). In the construction of the BDHI, efforts were made to minimize the social undesirability of the item pool by providing justifications for the use of aggression (e.g., "If I have to resort to physical violence to protect my rights, I will") and by using idiomatic and informal language (e.g., "Other people always seem to get the breaks"). Some evidence suggests that these efforts were successful. Govia and Velicer (1985), for example, reported low and nonsignificant correlations between all seven BDHI scales and a self-report measure of social desirability. In addition, the developers of the BDHI attempted to minimize the impact of an acquiescence response set by including a substantial number of both true and false keyed items (Buss & Durkee, 1957).

The BDHI has been found to relate to life history indexes of adult antisocial behavior (Brown et al., 1982) and to psychopathological syndromes characterized by high levels of antisocial behavior. For example, the BDHI has been reported to be associated with *DSM-III* diagnoses of ASPD (Haertzen, Hickey, Rose, &

Jaffe, 1990; Muntaner et al., 1990) and to differentiate patients with borderline personality disorder from normals (Gardner, Leibenluft, O'Leary, & Cowdry, 1991) and from patients with schizotypal personality disorder (Serper et al., 1993). In addition, the BDHI has been reported to correlate with biological variables hypothesized by some authors to be related to impulsive aggression. Coccaro, Silverman, Klar, Horvath, and Siever (1994), for example, reported that elevated BDHI scores are associated with reduced serotonergic functioning in males with personality disorders (see also Brown et al., 1982).

A large number of other self-report indexes of aggression are available, including the Manifest Hostility Scale (Siegal, 1956), Cook and Medley's (1954) Hostility Scale, and Green and Stacey's (1967) Aggression and Hostility Questionnaire. Most of these measures appear primarily to assess subjective anger and hostility, rather than behavioral aggression, and there is only limited evidence that they are associated with indexes of antisocial behavior (Edmunds & Kendrick, 1980).

Another self-report measure that has received substantial research attention is the MMPI Aggression Index (Huesmann, Lefkowitz, & Eron, 1978), which is obtained by summing the T scores on the MMPI F (Frequency), Pd (Psychopathic Deviate), and Ma (Hypomania) scores. This index has been found to distinguish delinquents from normals even after controlling statistically for intelligence and social class (Huessman et al., 1978), to discriminate parents who abuse their children from those who do not (Plotkin, Twentyman, & Perri, 1982), and to correlate with the number of lifetime violent convictions among male offenders (Holland, Beckett, & Levi, 1981). There are few data, however, on the discriminant validity of the MMPI Aggression Index. Given that F, Pd, and Ma are associated with a broad spectrum of impulsive psychopathology, the possibility that this index is a nonspecific measure of disinhibition needs to be ruled out.

A recently developed self-report aggression measure that may hold promise in the assessment of adult antisocial behavior is the Aggression scale of the Multidimensional Personality Questionnaire (MPQ; Tellegen, 1978/1982). This scale, like the other lower order MPQ scales, was developed iteratively by a process of successive construct reformulation, item rewriting, and factor analysis and was designed to be relatively independent of other MPQ lower order scales. The MPQ Aggression scale has been reported to distinguish patients with ASPD from those with other personality disorders (DiLalla, 1989) and to exhibit convergent validity with peer ratings of aggression (Harkness, Tellegen, & Waller, 1995). This scale has also been found to load on an Irritability/(Low) Agreeableness factor defined primarily by high loadings on several other MPQ scales, such as Alienation and (Low) Harmavoidance, and several MMPI scales, such as Masculinity and (Low) Hysteria (DiLalla, Gottesman, Carey, & Vogler, 1993).

Observer Rating Measures of Aggression and Antisocial Behavior

Among the better known observer rating indexes of aggression and antisocial behavior are the Hostile Belligerence subscale of the Psychotic Inpatient Profile (Lorr & Vestre, 1968), the Belligerence subscale of the Katz Adjustment Scales (Katz & Lyerly, 1963), the Irritability subscale of the Nurses' Observation Scale for Inpatient Observation (NOSIE; Honigfeld, Gillis, & Klett, 1966), the Paranoid Hostility subscale of the Symptom Rating Scale (Jenkins, Stauffacher, & Hester, 1959), and the Belligerence subscale of the Discharge Readiness Inventory (Hogarty, 1966). In addition, the commonly used Brief Psychiatric Rating Scale (Overall & Gorham, 1962) contains one item each assessing hostility and uncooperativeness.

Most of these measures assess behavioral expressions of anger and physical assaultiveness and are designed for inpatient units in which staff have had the opportunity to observe patients for prolonged time periods. These measures generally appear to possess reasonable psychometric properties; the reader is referred to Lyerly (1981) for a comprehensive review of their reliability and construct validity. Nevertheless, the assessment of antisocial behaviors provided by these measures tends to be narrow in scope and is limited to a small number of acts (e.g., assaults, verbal aggression toward staff) that are problematic on psychiatric units. In addition, most of these measures cannot differentiate mild from severe aggressive behaviors or provide detailed information concerning specific types of aggressive behavior (Yudofsky, Silver, Jackson, Endicott, & Williams, 1986).

In an effort to redress these limitations, Yudofsky et al. (1986) developed the Overt Aggression Scale (OAS). The OAS, although also designed to measure antisocial behavior among patients in psychiatric units, assesses a broad spectrum of behaviors in four categories: verbal aggression, physical aggression against objects, physical aggression against self, and physical aggression against others. In two samples of adult inpatients, the OAS demonstrated good interrater reliability; intraclass correlations between nurse ratings for the four subscales ranged from .72 to 1.00 (Yudofsy et al., 1986). The OAS has been reported to discriminate aggressive from nonaggressive psychiatric inpatients (Kay, Wolkenfeld, & Murrill, 1988), to be sensitive to the treatment effects of sertraline (a serotonin reuptake inhibitor) among patients with personality disorders (Kavoussi, Liu, & Coccaro, 1994), and to be sensitive to the treatment effects of nadolol (a beta-blocker) among psychiatric inpatients (Ratey et al., 1992). In addition, decreases in OAS scores following treatment of aggression have been found to exhibit high levels of agreement with global staff ratings of improvement (Malone, Luebbert, Pena-Ariet, Biesecker, & Delany, 1994).

A promising rating measure of adult antisocial behavior that can be used outside of psychiatric settings is the Brown-Goodwin Assessment for Life History of Aggression (Brown, Goodwin, Ballenger, Goyer, & Major, 1979). This measure consists of nine items, each scored on a 0 to 4 scale, that assess the frequency of lifetime antisocial behaviors, such as physical assaults, school disciplinary problems, police contacts, temper tantrums, and fighting in childhood and adolescence. These items are scored on the basis of written psychiatric or medical chart information. The average interrater reliability of the Brown-Goodwin measure as scored by three psychiatrists has been reported to be extremely high (r > .98; Brown et al., 1979). In addition, the Brown-Goodwin measure has been found to correlate negatively with levels of the serotonin metabolite 5-HIAA (Brown et al., 1979; Brown et al., 1982) and with other indexes of serotonergic functioning (Coccaro et al., 1989). The Brown-Goodwin scale has also been reported to correlate positively with scores on the BDHI and MMPI Pd scale (Brown et al., 1982), to be associated with personality disorder diagnoses characterized by high levels of antisocial behavior and impulsivity (e.g., antisocial, explosive, hysterical), and to distinguish subjects involuntarily discharged from military duty from subjects who were not involuntarily discharged (Brown et al., 1979).

Laboratory Measures of Aggression

The use of laboratory measures of aggression as analogues of real-world antisocial behavior has a lengthy tradition in social psychological research. A number of classic studies in social psychology have demonstrated that the presence of powerful situational factors, such as authority figures (Milgram, 1974), can induce a large proportion of nonclinical subjects to engage in aggressive behavior (i.e., administration of electric shocks to a fictitious "subject"). In addition, such studies sometimes revealed systematic individual differences in such behavior. Milgram (1974), for example, found that subjects with low levels on Kohlberg's scale of moral development and those with high scores on a measure of authoritarianism were more likely than other subjects to administer shocks to a fictitious confederate.

Several laboratory tasks have since been used to examine individual differences in antisocial behavior. One of the best known of these paradigms involves the use of the "aggression machine" pioneered by Buss (1961). In this paradigm, subjects are cast in the role of a "teacher" and are told to administer shocks to a "learner" (actually an accomplice of the experimenter who receives no shocks) in the context of a study examining the facilitation of learning by punishment. Subjects can select any of 10 shock intensities when delivering punishment. Studies of the aggression machine typically examine three dependent variables: shock intensity, shock duration, and total aversive stimulation, which is the product of shock intensity and shock duration (Baron & Richardson, 1994). Shock intensity is often used as a measure of direct aggression, whereas shock duration is often used as a measure of indirect aggression.

A number of studies attest to the construct validity of the aggression machine (Baron & Richardson, 1994). Individuals rated by others as highly aggressive, for example, have been found to deliver more intense shocks than other individuals (e.g., Shemberg, Leventhal, & Allman, 1968). Wolfe and Baron (1971) reported that male prisoners incarcerated for violent acts administered more intense shocks compared with a group of age-matched college students, although it should be noted that this difference may have been due to variables other than aggressiveness (e.g., frustration arising from imprisonment). Caprara et al. (1987) found that shock levels on the Buss aggression task were positively correlated with self-report indexes of emotional vulnerability and dissipation-rumination (with more ruminative subjects selecting higher shock levels).

Despite these generally positive findings, the results of several other studies suggest that some subjects who deliver high shock intensities on the Buss aggression machine do so for prosocial, rather than antisocial, reasons. Specifically, some subjects appear to administer intense shocks in an attempt to facilitate the learner's mastery of the task and to help the learner avert future punishment

(Baron & Richardson, 1994). In response to this interpretive problem, some investigators (e.g., Baron & Eggleston, 1972) have modified the traditional instructions to the Buss aggression paradigm by informing subjects that the purpose of the study is to examine the relation between shock and the learner's physiological reactivity. There is some evidence that shock intensities delivered under these neutral instructional conditions are negatively correlated with subjects' reported desire to help the learner (Baron & Eggleston, 1972). Researchers using the Buss aggression paradigm would be well advised to use both the traditional and modified instructions to examine the differential correlates of this paradigm under these different instructional conditions.

A second widely used laboratory paradigm for investigating aggression is the Taylor (1967) competitive reaction-time (RT) task, in which subjects receive electric shocks from, and administer electric shocks to, an imaginary "opponent" in the context of a competitive task. The Taylor RT paradigm differs from the Buss aggression paradigm in that the subject receives shocks and is given the opportunity to retaliate. Unlike the Buss aggression paradigm, which appears primarily to assess proactive aggression, the Taylor RT paradigm appears primarily to assess reactive aggression (see Dodge & Coie, 1987, for a discussion of these two types of aggression). The Taylor RT paradigm also differs from the Buss aggression paradigm in that scores on the former are potentially confounded by individual differences in competitiveness (Baron & Richardson, 1994), although manipulations designed to alter the competitive nature of the task do not appear to influence subjects' choice of shock intensities (Gaebelein & Taylor, 1971).

Several studies provide evidence for the construct validity of the Taylor RT paradigm. Bernstein, Richardson, and Hammock (1987) found that shock intensities delivered during the Taylor RT task were moderately positively correlated with shock intensities delivered during the Buss aggression task (rs ranged from .26 to .57 across several blocks of trials). Moreover, these correlations were higher during earlier trials. This finding accords with prediction, because the earlier trials of the Taylor RT task involve less provocation of the subject and are more similar to the Buss paradigm in its emphasis on proactive aggression. Dengerink (1971) found that subjects with low scores on the Activity Preference Questionnaire (Lykken, Tellegen, & Katzenmeyer, 1973), a measure of fearfulness that is correlated (negatively) with indexes of antisocial behavior, selected higher shock intensities than subjects with high scores. Giancola and Zeichner (1994) used the Taylor RT task to examine the relation between frontal lobe functioning and laboratory aggression in a sample of nonclinical subjects. They reported that subjects with low scores on the Conditional Association Task (CAT), a measure of frontal lobe functioning that requires subjects to associate a series of pieces of paper with a series of lights, chose more intense and longer shocks compared with subjects with high CAT scores. This difference did not emerge for another measure of frontal lobe functioning (the Self-Ordered Pointing Task), however, raising questions concerning the replicability of Giancola and Zeichner's findings.

The Taylor RT task has also been used extensively to examine the effects of substance use on aggression (Taylor, 1993). Subjects who consume alcohol have been found to select higher shock intensities compared with subjects who consume either a placebo or no beverage (Shuntich & Taylor, 1972). Similar findings have been reported for benzodiazepines (e.g., Bond & Lader, 1988). Moreover, the amount of shock selected is dose dependent, with higher quantities of alcohol associated with higher shock intensities (Taylor & Gammon, 1975).

Several investigators have modified the Taylor RT task by requiring subjects to press a button that ostensibly results in the loss of points (later exchangeable for money) to another (fictitious) subject. At prearranged intervals, this subject subtracts points from the actual subject. Kelly, Cherek, Steinberg, and Robinson (1988) found that high doses of alcohol facilitated aggressive responding in this modified Taylor RT paradigm. Cherek, Steinberg, Kelly, and Robinson (1987) reported that d-amphetamine decreased aggressive responding in this paradigm; similar results have been reported for caffeine (Cherek, Steinberg, & Brauchi, 1983).

FUTURE WORK

Despite a large body of evidence on the psychometric properties of measures of adult antisocial behavior, a number of important conceptual and methodological issues in this domain remain unresolved. In this concluding section, we focus on five that appear especially pressing and outline several recommendations for investigators in this domain.

1. Although the personality- and behavior-based approaches to antisocial behavior differ both conceptually and empirically, few investigators have directly compared the construct validity of these approaches. As Hare et al. (1991) pointed out, the PCL-R (which appears to assess most of the major personality traits of psychopathy) has generally been reported to be a superior predictor of outcome (e.g., recidivism, postrelease violent offending) compared with measures of *DSM-III* ASPD. Harpur et al.'s (1989) two-factor model represents an important advance that promises to facilitate research on the comparative validity of these two approaches.

Recommendations. We suggest that researchers assess both the personality features of psychopathy and antisocial behaviors so that the construct validity of these alternative operationalizations, as well as their incremental validity relative to each other, can be compared. Because the two factors of the PCL-R represent satisfactory operationalizations of the personality- and behavior-based approaches, comparisons of the capacity of these factors to predict external criteria should become a major priority among investigators.

2. Although a number of authors (e.g., Lykken, 1995) have argued that the diagnosis of ASPD is etiologically heterogeneous, there are few data bearing directly on this issue. Few investigators have attempted to determine whether the subtypes that have been proposed to be nested within the ASPD diagnosis (e.g., psychopathy, neurotic psychopathy, dyssocial psychopathy) are characterized by different external correlates. Consequently, it is unclear whether ASPD is etiologically heterogeneous, as implied by critics of this diagnosis, or whether it is etiologically unitary, as implied by *DSM-IV.*

Recommendations. We recommend that, whenever feasible, researchers who utilize categorical indexes of ASPD examine the differential correlates of the principal subtypes that have been proposed to be nested within this diagnosis. For example, researchers may want to administer measures of negative affectivity or neuroticism (Watson & Clark, 1984) in conjunction with indexes of ASPD to examine potential differences between neurotic psychopaths with ASPD and other subjects with ASPD. At the very least, we suggest that researchers subdivide subjects with ASPD into high versus low psychopathy subgroups (e.g., using the PCL-R) to ascertain whether more psychopathic individuals with ASPD differ from less psychopathic individuals with ASPD with respect to external validating variables.

3. Little evidence exists concerning either (a) the comparative construct validity or (b) the incremental validity of different ASPD measures relative to others. We identified no studies comparing the validity of different self-report measures of ASPD for external validating criteria, nor studies examining the incremental contribution of different self-report measures of ASPD above and beyond other self-report measures for such criteria. The same holds for comparisons of the construct validity and incremental validity of self-report indexes with interviews. Moreover, only two groups of researchers (Perry et al., 1987; Skodol et al., 1991) have compared the validity of different ASPD interviews, both of which used longitudinal data as a criterion. Although it has sometimes been assumed that standardized interviews are generally superior to self-report measures in the assessment of ASPD (Zimmerman, 1994), no research has been conducted to investigate this assumption.

Recommendations. Because of the lack of either comparative construct validity or incremental validity data, we suggest that researchers utilize multiple operationalizations of ASPD wherever possible. These multiple operationalizations could be used in three different, although not mutually exclusive, ways. Specifically, they could be (a) analyzed separately, so that their overall construct validity and incremental validity relative to other ASPD measures could be assessed, (b) used to estimate a latent construct of ASPD by means of structural modeling techniques (Loehlin, 1992), and (c) aggregated by clinical judgment or a predetermined algorithm to arrive at "best estimate" diagnoses (Leckman, Sholomskas, Thompson, Belanger, & Weissman, 1982) of ASPD. Although we do not regard any one of these approaches as inherently superior to the others, we recommend that, whenever possible, investigators utilizing multiple measures of ASPD examine the construct and incremental validity of these measures for external validating criteria.

4. Little attention has been paid to the issue of self versus informant report in the assessment of adult antisocial behavior. Given that some *DSM-IV* symptoms of ASPD, such as lack of remorse (APA, 1994), may require at least a modicum of insight for accurate self-reporting, outside observers may better be able to contribute valid information regarding such characteristics. In a study comparing self and observer reports, Zimmerman, Pfohl, Coryell, Stangl, and Corenthal (1988) found that self and informant reports of *DSM-III* ASPD yielded virtually identical mean values when scored dimensionally. Although Zimmerman et al. found that the two measures correlated moderately ($r = .61$), they did not report whether informant data possessed incremental validity above and beyond self-reports for external criteria. Although few standardized measures are available to assess ASPD via informant reports, the recent development of family history measures of personality disorders (e.g., Reich, 1988) should facilitate research on the self versus informant report issue.

Recommendations. Whenever possible, we recommend that researchers obtain both self and informant reports of adult antisocial behavior so that the construct and incremental validity of these reports for external validating criteria can be compared. Although it may be useful to aggregate self and informant reports for diagnostic purposes, for research purposes it may be useful to keep these reports separate to examine the possibility that they possess different correlates (Grove & Tellegen, 1991).

5. Although a variety of different methods, including self-report, observer rating, and laboratory indexes, have been used to study aggression in adults, there are few data bearing on either the interrelations among measures utilizing different methods of assessment or the incremental validity of one method of assessment above and beyond others in the prediction of relevant criteria. For example, there is little information regarding the relation between self-report and laboratory measures of aggression. Moreover, in many cases, there are few data concerning the relation of aggression indexes, particularly laboratory measures, to antisocial behavior in the real world. Because laboratory measures of personality have often been criticized for their situational specificity (Block, 1977; Epstein, 1979), further investigation of the construct validity of laboratory measures of aggression appears warranted. In addition, as noted earlier, there is some evidence that different measures of aggression assess different superordinate personality dimensions. For example, self-report indexes of behavioral aggression primarily assess negative affectivity or neuroticism, whereas self-report indexes of subjective hostility or anger primarily assess (low) agreeableness (Watson et al., 1994). Nevertheless, the relation between many rating and laboratory measures of aggression and higher order personality constructs requires clarification. This issue is of theoretical and practical importance, because many aggression measures heretofore treated as largely interchangeable may turn out to assess different components of personality.

Recommendations. We recommend that investigators who examine trait aggression in adults use measures from multiple methods of assessment (viz., self-report, rating, laboratory) so that their differential correlates can be examined. Moreover, it will be important to determine the extent to which any of these modes of assessment tends to possess incremental validity above and beyond others in the prediction of real-world antisocial behavior and other pertinent criteria. Finally, we suggest that investigators who utilize these measures administer them in conjunction with omnibus measures of personality so that their relations to higher order trait dimensions can be ascertained.

REFERENCES

Alterman, A. I., & Cacciola, J. S. (1991). The antisocial personality disorder diagnosis in substance abusers: Problems and issues. *Journal of Nervous and Mental Disease, 179,* 401–409.

American Psychiatric Association. (1980). *Diagnostic and statistical manual of mental disorders* (3rd ed.). Washington, DC: Author.

American Psychiatric Association. (1987). *Diagnostic and statistical manual of mental disorders* (3rd ed., rev.). Washington, DC: Author.

American Psychiatric Association. (1994). *Diagnostic and statistical manual of mental disorders* (4th ed.). Washington, DC: Author.

Baron, R. A., & Eggleston, R. J. (1972). Performance on the "aggression machine": Motivation to help or harm? *Psychonomic Science, 26,* 321–322.

Baron, R. A., & Richardson, D. R. (1994). *Human aggression* (2nd ed.). New York: Plenum.

Bernstein, I. S., Richardson, D., & Hammock, G. (1987). Convergent and discriminant validity of the Taylor and Buss measures of physical aggression. *Aggressive Behavior, 13,* 15–24.

Berry, W. D. (1993). *Understanding regression assumptions.* Newbury Park, CA: Sage Publications.

Block, J. (1977). Advancing the psychology of personality: Paradigm shift or improving the quality of research? In D. Magnusson & N. S. Endler (Eds.), *Personality at the crossroads* (pp. 37–63). Hillsdale, NJ: Erlbaum.

Bond, A., & Lader, M. (1988). Differential effects of oxazepam and lorazepam on aggressive responding. *Psychopharmacology, 95,* 369–373.

Boyd, J. H., Burke, J. D., Gruenberg, E., Holzer, C. E., Rae, D., George, L. K., Karno, M., Stoltzman, R., McEvoy, L., & Nestadt, G. (1984). Exclusion criteria of *DSM-III:* A study of co-occurrence of hierarchy-free syndromes. *Archives of General Psychiatry, 41,* 983–989.

Brown, G. L., Ebert, M. H., Goyer, P. F., Jimerson, D. C., Klein W. J., Bunney, W. E., & Goodwin, F. K. (1982). Aggression, suicide, and serotonin: Relationships to CSF amine metabolites. *American Journal of Psychiatry, 139,* 741–746.

Brown, G. L., Goodwin, F. K., Ballenger, J. C., Goyer, P. F., & Major, L. F. (1979). Aggression in humans correlates with cerebrospinal fluid metabolites. *Psychiatry Research, 1,* 131–139.

Bushman, B. J., Cooper, H. M., & Lemke, K. M. (1991). Meta-analysis of factor analyses: An illustration using the Buss-Durkee Hostility Inventory. Special Issue: Meta-analysis in personality and social psychology. *Personality and Social Psychology Bulletin, 17,* 344–349.

Buss, A. H. (1961). *The psychology of aggression.* New York: Wiley.

Buss, A. H., & Durkee, A. (1957). An inventory for assessing different kinds of hostility. *Journal of Consulting Psychology, 21,* 343–349.

Caprara, G. V., Gargaro, T., Pastorelli, C., Prezza, M., Renzi, P., & Zelli, A. (1987). Individual differences and measures of aggression in laboratory studies. *Personality and Individual Differences, 8,* 885–893.

Cherek, D. R., Steinberg, J. L., & Brauchi, J. T. (1983). Consumption of regular and decaffeinated coffee and subsequent human aggressive behavior. *Psychiatry Research, 8,* 137–145.

Cherek, D. R., Steinberg, J. L., Kelly, T. H., & Robinson, D. (1987). Effects of d-amphetamine on aggressive responding of normal male subjects. *Psychiatry Research, 21,* 257–265.

Clark, J. P., & Tifft, L. L. (1966). Polygraph and interview validation of self-reported deviant behavior. *American Sociological Review, 31,* 516–523.

Cleckley, H. (1941/1982). *The mask of sanity.* St. Louis: Mosby.

Cloninger, C. R. (1978). The antisocial personality. *Hospital Practice, 13,* 97–106.

Coccaro, E. F., Siever, L. J., Klar, H. M., Maurer, G., Cochrane, K., Cooper, T. B., Mohs, R. C., & Davis, K. L. (1989). Serotonergic studies in patients with affective and personality disorders. Correlates with suicidal and impulsive aggressive behavior. *Archives of General Psychiatry, 46,* 587–599.

Coccaro, E. F., Silverman, J. M., Klar, H. M., Horvath, T. B., & Siever, L. J. (1994). Familial correlates of reduced central serotonergic system function in patients with personality disorders. *Archives of General Psychiatry, 51,* 318–324.

Cook, W. W., & Medley, D. M. (1954). Proposed hostility and pharisaic virtue scales for the MMPI. *Journal of Applied Psychology, 38,* 414–418.

Coolidge, F. L., & Merwin, M. M. (1992). Reliability and validity of the Coolidge Axis II Inventory: A new inventory for the assessment of personality disorders. *Journal of Personality Assessment, 59,* 223–238.

Coolidge, F. L., Merwin, M. M., Wooley, M. J., & Hyman, J. N. (1990). Some problems with the diagnostic criteria of the antisocial personality disorder in *DSM-III-R:* A preliminary study. *Journal of Personality Disorders, 4,* 407–413.

Dengerink, H. A. (1971). Anxiety, aggression, and physiological arousal. *Journal of Experimental Research in Personality, 5,* 223–232.

DiLalla, D. L. (1989). *Dimensions of personality and their relationship to psychopathology: An analysis of the Multidimensional Personality Questionnaire.* Unpublished doctoral dissertation, University of Virginia.

DiLalla, D. L., Gottesman, I. I., Carey, G., & Vogler, G. P. (1993). Joint factor structure of the Multidimensional Personality Questionnaire and the MMPI in a psychiatric and high risk sample. *Psychological Assessment, 5,* 207–215.

Dodge, K. A., & Coie, J. D. (1987). Social information-processing factors in reactive and proactive aggression in children's peer groups. *Journal of Personality and Social Psychology, 53,* 1146–1158.

Edmunds, G., & Kendrick, D. C. (1980). *The measurement of human aggressiveness.* Chichester, England: Ellis Horwood Limited.

Elliott, D. S., & Voss, H. L. (1974). *Delinquency and dropout.* Lexington, MA: D. C. Heath.

Epstein, S. (1979). The stability of behavior: I. On predicting more of the people more of the time. *Journal of Personality and Social Psychology, 37,* 1097–1126.

Faust, D., & Miner, R.A. (1986). The empiricist and his new clothes: *DSM-III* in perspective. *American Journal of Psychiatry, 143,* 962–967.

First, M. B., Spitzer, R. L., Gibbon, M., Williams, J. B. W., Davies, M., Borus, J., Howes, M. J., Kane, J., Pope, H. G., & Rounsaville, B. (1995). The Structured Clinical Interview for *DSM-III-R* Personality Disorders (SCID-II). Part II: Multisite Test-Retest Reliability Study. *Journal of Personality Disorders, 9,* 2–104.

Gaebelin, J. W., & Taylor, S. P. (1971). The effects of competition and attack on physical aggression. *Psychonomic Science, 24,* 65–67.

Gardner, D. L., Leibenluft, E., O'Leary, K. M., & Cowdry, R. W. (1991). Self-ratings of anger and hostility in borderline personality disorder. *Journal of Nervous and Mental Disease, 179,* 157–161.

Gerstley, L. J., Alterman, A. I., McLellan, A. T., & Woody, G. E. (1990). Antisocial personality disorder in substance abusers: A problematic diagnosis? *American Journal of Psychiatry, 147,* 173–178.

Giancola, P. R., & Zeichner, A. (1994). Neuropsychological performance on tests of frontal-lobe functioning and aggressive behavior in men. *Journal of Abnormal Psychology, 103,* 832–835.

Gold, M., & Reimer, D. J. (1975). Changing patterns of delinquent behavior among Americans 13 through 16 years old: 1967–1972. *Crime Delinquency Literature, 7,* 483–517.

Gough, H. G. (1960). Theory and measurement of socialization. *Journal of Consulting and Clinical Psychology, 24,* 23–30.

Gouia, J. M., & Velicer, W. F. (1985). Comparison of multidimensional measures of aggression. *Psychological Reports, 57,* 207–215.

Green, R. T., & Stacey, B. G. (1967). The development of a questionnaire measure of hostility and aggression. *Acta Psychologica, 26,* 265–285.

Grove, W. M. (1987). The reliability of psychiatric diagnosis. In C. G. Last & M. Hersen (Eds.), *Issues in diagnostic research* (pp. 99–119). New York: Plenum.

Grove, W. M., & Tellegen, A. (1991). Problems in the classification of personality disorders. *Journal of Personality Disorders, 5,* 31–41.

Haertzen, C. A., Hickey, J. E., Rose, M. R., & Jaffe, J. H. (1990). The relationship between a diagnosis of antisocial personality and hostility: Development of an antisocial hostility scale. *Journal of Clinical Psychology, 46,* 679–686.

Hare, R. D. (1983). Diagnosis of antisocial personality disorder in two prison populations. *American Journal of Psychiatry, 140,* 887–890.

Hare, R. D. (1985). Comparison of procedures for the assessment of psychopathy. *Journal of Consulting and Clinical Psychology, 53,* 7–16.

Hare, R. D. (1990). *Manual for the Revised Psychopathy Checklist.* Toronto: Multi-Health Systems.

Hare, R. D., & Hart, S. D. (1996). A comment on the *DSM-IV* antisocial personality disorder field trial. In W. J. Livesley (Ed.), DSM-IV *personality disorders* (pp. 127–134). New York: Guilford.

Hare, R. D., Hart, S. D., & Harpur, T. J. (1991). Psychopathy and the *DSM-IV* criteria for antisocial personality disorder. *Journal of Abnormal Psychology, 100,* 391–398.

Harkness, A. R., Tellegen, A., & Waller, N. (1995). Differential convergence of self-report and informant data for Multidimensional Personality Questionnaire traits: Implications for the construct of negative emotionality. *Journal of Personality Assessment, 64,* 185–204.

Harpur, T. J., Hare, R. D., & Hakstian, A. R. (1989). Two-factor conceptualization of psychopathy: Construct validity and assessment implications. *Psychological Assessment: A Journal of Consulting and Clinical Psychology, 1,* 6–17.

Harris, G. T., Rice, M. E., & Quinsey, V. L. (1994). Psychopathy as a taxon: Evidence that psychopaths are a discrete class. *Journal of Consulting and Clinical Psychology, 62,* 387–397.

Hart, S. D., & Hare, R. D. (1989). Discriminant validity of the psychopathy checklist in a forensic population. *Psychological Assessment: A Journal of Consulting and Clinical Psychology, 1,* 211–218.

Hasin, D. S., Grant, B. F., & Endicott, J. (1988). Lifetime psychiatric comorbidity in hospitalized alcoholics: Subject and familial correlates. *International Journal of the Addictions, 23,* 827–850.

Heston, L. L. (1970). The genetics of schizophrenia and schizoid disease. *Science, 167,* 249–256.

Hills, H. A. (1995). Diagnosing personality disorders: An examination of the MMPI-2 and MCMI-II. *Journal of Personality Assessment, 65,* 21–34.

Hogarty, G. E. (1966). Discharge readiness: The components of casework judgment. *Social Casework, 47,* 165–171.

Hogg, B., Jackson, H. J., Rudd, R. P., & Edwards, J. (1990). Diagnosing personality disorders in recent-onset schizophrenia. *Journal of Nervous and Mental Disease, 178,* 194–199.

Holland, T. R., Beckett, G. E., & Levi, M. (1981). Intelligence, personality, and criminal violence: A multivariate analysis. *Journal of Consulting and Clinical Psychology, 49,* 106–111.

Honigfeld, G., Gillis, R. D., & Klett, J. C. (1966). NOSIE-30: A treatment-sensitive word behavior scale. *Psychological Reports, 19,* 180–182.

Huesmann, L. R., Lefkowitz, M. M., & Eron, L. D. (1978). Sum of MMPI scales F, 4, and 9 as a measure of aggression. *Journal of Consulting and Clinical Psychology, 46,* 1071–1078.

Huizinga, D., & Elliott, D. S. (1986). Reassessing the reliability and validity of self-report delinquency measures. *Journal of Quantitative Criminology, 2,* 293–327.

Hyler, S. E., & Rieder, R. O. (1987). *PDQ-R personality questionnaire.* New York: New York State Psychiatric Institute.

Hyler, S. E., Rieder, R. O., Williams, J. B. W., Spitzer, R. L., Lyons, M., & Hendler, J. (1989). A comparison of clinical and self-report diagnoses of *DSM-III* personality disorders in 552 patients. *Comprehensive Psychiatry, 30,* 170–178.

Hyler, S., Skodol, A., Kellman, D., Oldham, J., & Rosnick, L. (1990). Validity of the Personality Diagnostic Questionnaire–Revised: Comparison with two structured interviews. *American Journal of Psychiatry, 147,* 1043–1048.

Jackson, H. J., Gazis, J., Rudd, R. R., & Edwards, J. (1991). Concordance between two personality disorder instruments with psychiatric inpatients. *Comprehensive Psychiatry, 32,* 252–260.

Jackson, P. G. (1990). Sources of data. In K. Kempf (Ed.), *Measurement issues in criminology* (pp. 21–50). New York: Springer-Verlag.

Jenkins, R. L., Stauffacher, J., & Hester, R. A. (1959). A symptom rating scale for use with psychotic patients. *Archives of General Psychiatry, 1,* 197–204.

Joffe, R. T., & Regan, J. J. (1988). Personality and depression. *Journal of Psychiatric Research, 22,* 279–286.

Johnson, J. G., & Bornstein, R. F. (1992). Utility of the Personality Diagnostic Questionnaire–Revised in a nonclinical population. *Journal of Personality Disorders, 6* 450–457.

Katz, M. M., & Lyerly, S. B. (1963). Methods for measuring adjustment and social behavior in the community: I. Rationale, description, discriminative validity, and scale development. *Psychological Reports Monograph, 13,* 503–535.

Kavoussi, R. J., Liu, J., & Coccaro, E. F. (1994). An open trial of sertraline in personality disordered patients with impulsive aggression. *Journal of Clinical Psychiatry, 55* 137–141.

Kay, S. R., Wolkenfeld, F., & Murrill, L. M. (1988). Profiles of aggression among psychiatric patients: I. Nature and prevalence. *Journal of Nervous and Mental Disease, 176,* 539–546.

Kelly, T. H., Cherek, D. R., Steinberg, J. L., & Robinson, D. (1988). Effects of provocation and alcohol on human aggressive behavior. *Drug and Alcohol Dependence, 21,* 105–112.

Kennedy, S. H., McVey, G., & Katz, R. (1990). Personality disorders in anorexia nervosa and bulimia nervosa. *Journal of Psychiatric Research, 24,* 259–269.

Klein, M. H., Benjamin, L. S., Rosenfeld, R., Treece, C., Husted, J., & Greist, J. (1993). The Wisconsin Personality Disorders Inventory: Development, reliability, and validity. *Journal of Personality Disorders, 7,* 285–303.

Leckman, J. F., Sholomskas, D., Thompson, D., Belanger, A., & Weissman, M. (1982). Best estimate of lifetime psychiatric diagnoses: A methodological study. *Archives of General Psychiatry, 39,* 879–883.

Libb, J. W., Stankovic, S., Freeman, A., Sokol, R., Switzer, P., & Houck, C. (1990). Personality disorders among depressed outpatients as identified by the MCMI. *Journal of Clinical Psychology, 46,* 277–284.

Lilienfeld, S. O. (1990). *Development and preliminary validation of a self-report measure of psychopathic personality.* Doctoral dissertation, University of Minnesota.

Lilienfeld, S. O. (1994). Conceptual problems in the assessment of psychopathy. *Clinical Psychology Review, 14,* 17–38.

Loehlin, J. C. (1992). *Latent variable models: An introduction to factor, path, and structural analysis.* Hillsdale, NJ: Erlbaum.

Loranger, A. W. (1988). *Personality Disorder Examination (PDE) Manual.* Yonkers, NY: DV Communications.

Loranger, A. W., Lenzenweger, M. F., Gartner, A. F., Susman, V. L., Herzig, J., Zammit, G. K., Gartner, J. D., Abrams, R. C., & Young, R. C. (1991). Trait-state artifacts and the diagnosis of personality disorders. *Archives of General Psychiatry, 48*, 720–728.

Lorr, M., & Vestre, N. D. (1968). *Psychotic Inpatient Profile Manual.* Los Angeles: Western Psychological Services.

Lyerly, S. B. (Ed.). (1981). *Handbook of psychiatric rating scales.* New York: Research and Education Association.

Lykken, D. T. (1995). *The antisocial personalities.* New York: Wiley.

Lykken, D. T., Tellegen, A., & Katzenmeyer, C. (1973). *Manual for the Activity Preference Questionnaire.* Minneapolis: University of Minnesota.

Malone, R. P., Luebbert, J., Pena-Ariet, M., Biesecker, K., & Delaney, M. A. (1994). The Overt Aggression Scale in a study of lithium in aggressive conduct disorder. *Psychopharmacology Bulletin, 30*, 215–218.

Mavissakalian, M., & Hamann, M. S. (1987). *DSM-III* personality disorder in agoraphobia: II. Changes with treatment. *Comprehensive Psychiatry, 28*, 356–361.

McCann, J. T. (1991). Convergent and discriminant validity of the MCMI-II and MMPI personality disorder scales. *Psychological Assessment: A Journal of Consulting and Clinical Psychology, 3*, 9–18.

McKinley, J., & Hathaway, S. R. (1944). The MMPI: Hysteria, hypomania, and psychopathic deviate. *Journal of Applied Psychology, 28*, 153–174.

Meehl, P. E. (1986). Diagnostic taxa as open concepts: Metatheoretical and statistical questions about reliability and construct validity in the grand strategy of nosological revision. In T. Millon & G. L. Klerman (Eds.), *Contemporary directions in psychopathology: Toward the DSM-IV* (pp. 215–231). New York: Guilford.

Meehl, P. E., & Golden, R. R. (1982). Taxometric methods. In P. C. Kendall & J. N. Butcher (Eds.), *Handbook of research methods in clinical psychology* (pp. 127–181). New York: Wiley.

Mellsop, G., Varghese, F. T. N., Joshua, S., & Hicks, A. (1982). Reliability of Axis II of *DSM-III. American Journal of Psychiatry, 139*, 1360–1361.

Milgram, S. (1974). *Obedience to authority: An experimental view.* New York: Harper & Row.

Millon, T. (1981). *Disorders of personality, DSM-III: Axis II.* New York: Wiley.

Millon, T. (1987). *Manual for the MCMI-II* (2nd ed.). Minneapolis: National Computer Systems.

Morey, L. C., & LeVine, D. J. (1988). A multitrait-multimethod examination of Minnesota Multiphasic Personality Inventory (MMPI) and Millon Clinical Multiaxial Inventory (MCMI). *Journal of Psychopathology and Behavioral Assessment, 10*, 333–344.

Morey, L. C., Waugh, M., & Blashfield, R. (1985). MMPI scales for *DSM-III* personality disorders: Their derivation and correlates. *Journal of Personality Assessment, 49*, 245–251.

Muntaner, C., Walter, D., Nagoshi, C., Fishbein, D., Haertzen, C. A., & Jaffe, J. H. (1990). Self-report vs. laboratory measures of aggression as predictors of substance abuse. *Drug and Alcohol Dependence, 25*, 1–11.

North, C. S., Smith, E. M., & Spitznagel, E. L. (1993). Is antisocial personality a valid diagnosis among the homeless? *American Journal of Psychiatry, 150*, 578–583.

Overall, J. E., & Gorham, D. R. (1962). The brief psychiatric rating scale. *Psychological Reports, 10*, 799–812.

Perry, J. C. (1992). Problems and considerations in the valid assessment of personality disorders. *American Journal of Psychiatry, 149*, 1645–1653.

Perry, J. C., Lavori, P. W., Cooper, S. H., Hoke, L., & O'Connell, M. E. (1987). The Diagnostic Interview Schedule and *DSM-III* antisocial personality disorder. *Journal of Personality Disorders, 1*, 121–131.

Pfohl, B., Blum, N., Zimmerman, M., & Stangl, D. (1989). *Structured interview for DSM-III-R personality: SIDP-R.* Iowa City, IA: Author.

Piersma, H. L. (1989). The stability of the MCMI-II for psychiatric inpatients. *Journal of Clinical Psychology, 45*, 781–785.

Plotkin, R. C., Twentyman, C. T., & Perri, M. G. (1982). The utility of a measure of aggression in differentiating abusing parents from other parents who are experiencing familial disturbance. *Journal of Clinical Psychology, 38*, 607–610.

Ratey, J. J., Sorgi, P., O'Driscoll, G. A., Sands, S., Daehler, M. L., Fletcher, J. R., Kadish, W., Spruiell, G., Polakoff, S., Linden, K. J., Bemporad, J. R., Richardson, L., & Rosenfeld, B. (1992). Nadolol to treat aggression and psychiatric symptomatology in chronic psychiatric inpatients: A double-blind, placebo-controlled study. *Journal of Clinical Psychiatry, 53*, 41–46.

Reich, J. H. (1988). A family history method for *DSM-III* anxiety and personality disorders. *Psychiatry Research, 26*, 131–139.

Reich, J. H., & Troughton, E. (1988). Frequency of *DSM-III* personality disorders in patients with panic disorder: Comparison with psychiatric and normal control subjects. *Psychiatry Research, 26*, 131–139.

Robins, L. N. (1966). *Deviant children grown up.* Baltimore: Williams & Wilkins.

Robins, L. N., Helzer, J. E., Croughan, J., & Ratcliff, K. S. (1981). National Institute of Mental Health Diagnostic Interview Schedule: Its history, characteristics, and validity. *Archives of General Psychiatry, 38*, 381–389.

Robins, L. N., Tipp, J., & Przybeck, T. (1991). Antisocial personality. In L. N. Robins & D. A. Regier (Eds.), *Psychiatric disorders in America* (pp. 258–290). New York: Free Press.

Rogers, R., & Dion, K. (1991). Rethinking the *DSM-III-R* diagnosis of antisocial personality disorder. *Bulletin of the American Academy of Psychiatry and Law, 19*, 21–31.

Rutherford, M. J., Alterman, A. I., Cacciola, J. S., & Snider, E. C. (1995). Gender differences in diagnosing antisocial personality disorder in methadone patients. *American Journal of Psychiatry, 152*, 1309–1316.

Schuckit, M. (1973). Alcoholism and sociopathy: Diagnostic confusion. *Quarterly Journal of Studies in Alcohol, 34*, 157–164.

Serper, M. R., Bernstein, D. P., Maurer, G., Harvey, P. D., Horvath, T., Klar, H., Coccaro, E. F., & Siever, L. J. (1993). Psychological test profiles of patients with borderline and schizotypal personality disorders: Implications for *DSM-IV. Journal of Personality Disorders, 7*, 144–154.

Shemberg, K. M., Leventhal, D. B., & Allman, L. (1968). Aggression machine performance and rated aggression. *Journal of Experimental Research in Personality, 3*, 117–119.

Shuntich, R. J., & Taylor, S. P. (1972). The effects of alcohol on human physical aggression. *Journal of Experimental Research in Personality, 6*, 34–38.

Siegal, S. M. (1956). The relationship of hostility to authoritarianism. *Journal of Abnormal and Social Psychology, 52*, 368–373.

Skodol, A., Oldham, J., Rosnick, L., Kellman, H. D., & Hyler, S. (1991). Diagnosis of *DSM-III-R* personality disorders: A comparison of two structured interviews. *International Journal of Methods in Psychiatric Research, 1*, 13–26.

Soldz, S., Budman, S., Denby, A., & Merry, J. (1993). Diagnostic agreement between the Personality Disorder Examination and the MCMI-II. *Journal of Personality Assessment, 60*, 486–499.

Spitzer, R. L. (1983). Psychiatric diagnosis: Are clinicians still necessary? *Comprehensive Psychiatry, 24,* 399–411.

Spitzer, R. L., Endicott, J., & Fleiss, J. L. (1970). The Psychiatric Status Schedule: A technique of evaluating psychopathology and impairment in social role functioning. *Archives of General Psychiatry, 23,* 41–55.

Spitzer, R. L., & Fleiss, J. L. (1974). A re-analysis of the reliability of psychiatric diagnosis. *British Journal of Psychiatry, 125,* 341–347.

Spitzer, R. L., Williams, J. B. W., Gibbon, M., & First, M. (1990). *User's guide for the Structured Clinical Interview for DSM-III-R.* Washington, DC: American Psychiatric Association Press.

Streiner, D. L., & Miller, H. R. (1988). Validity of MMPI scales for *DSM-III* personality disorders: What are they measuring? *Journal of Personality Disorders, 2,* 238–242.

Taylor, S. P. (1967). Aggressive behavior and physiological arousal as a function of provocation and the tendency to inhibit aggression. *Journal of Personality, 35,* 197–210.

Taylor, S. P. (1993). Experimental investigation of alcohol-induced aggression in humans. *Alcohol Health & Research World, 17,* 108–112.

Taylor, S. P., & Gammon, C. B. (1975). Effects of type of dose of alcohol on human physical aggression. *Journal of Personality and Social Psychology, 32,* 169–175.

Tellegen, A. (1978/1982). *Manual for the Multidimensional Personality Questionnaire.* Unpublished manuscript, University of Minnesota, Minneapolis.

Trull, T. J. (1993). Temporal stability and validity of two personality disorder inventories. *Psychological Assessment: A Journal of Consulting and Clinical Psychology, 5,* 11–18.

Trull, T. J., & Goodwin, A. H. (1993). Relationship between mood changes and the report of personality disorder symptoms. *Journal of Personality Assessment, 61,* 99–111.

Trull, T. J., & Larson, S. L. (1994). External validity of two personality disorder inventories. *Journal of Personality Disorders, 8,* 96–103.

Watson, D., & Clark, L. A. (1984). Negative affectivity: The disposition to experience negative emotional states. *Psychological Bulletin, 98,* 219–235.

Watson, D., Clark, L. A., & Harkness, A. R. (1994). Structures of personality and their relevance to psychopathology. *Journal of Abnormal Psychology, 103,* 18–31.

Widiger, T. A., Cadoret, R., Hare, R., Robins, L., Rutherford, M., Zanarini, M., Alterman, A., Apple, M., Corbitt, E., Forth, A., Hart, S., Kultermann, J., Woody, G., & Frances, A. (1996). *DSM-IV* antisocial personality disorder field trial. *Journal of Abnormal Psychology, 105,* 3–16.

Widiger, T. A., & Corbitt, E. M. (1993). Antisocial personality disorder. Proposals for *DSM-IV. Journal of Personality Disorders, 7,* 63–77.

Widiger, T. A., & Frances, A. (1985). The *DSM-III* personality disorders: Perspectives from psychology. *Archives of General Psychiatry, 42,* 615–623.

Widiger, T. A., & Frances, A. (1987). Interviews and inventories for the measurement of personality disorders. *Clinical Psychology Review, 7,* 49–75.

Widiger, T. A., Williams, J. B. W., Spitzer, R. L., & Frances, A. (1985). The MCMI as a measure of *DSM-III. Journal of Personality Assessment, 4,* 366–378.

Widom, C. S. (1977). A methodology for studying noninstitutionalized psychopaths. *Journal of Consulting and Clinical Psychology, 45,* 674–683.

Widom, C. S., & Newman, J. P. (1985). Characteristics of noninstitutionalized psychopaths. In J. Gunn & D. Farrington (Eds.), *Current research in forensic psychiatry and psychology* (Vol. 2, pp. 57–80). New York: Wiley.

Wolfe, B. M., & Baron, R. A. (1971). Laboratory aggression related to aggression in naturalistic social situations: Effects of an aggressive model on the behavior of college student and prisoner observers. *Psychonomic Science, 24,* 193–194.

World Health Organization. (1993). *International classification of diseases and related health problems* (10th rev.). Geneva, Switzerland: Author.

Wulach, J. S. (1983). Diagnosing the *DSM-III* antisocial personality disorder. *Professional Psychology: Research and Practice, 14,* 330–340.

Yudofsky, S. C., Silver, J. M., Jackson, W., Endicott, J., & Williams, D. (1986). The Overt Aggression Scale for the objective rating of verbal and physical aggression. *American Journal of Psychiatry, 143,* 35–39.

Zanarini, M. C., Frankenburg, F. R., Chauncey, D. L., & Gunderson, J. G. (1987). The Diagnostic Interview for Personality Disorders: Interrater and test-retest reliability. *Comprehensive Psychiatry, 28,* 467–480.

Zimmerman, M. (1994). Diagnosing personality disorders: A review of issues and research methods. *Archives of General Psychiatry, 51,* 225–245.

Zimmerman, M., & Coryell, W. H. (1990). Diagnosing personality disorders: A comparison of self-report and interview measures. *Archives of General Psychiatry, 47,* 527–531.

Zimmerman, M., Pfohl, B., Coryell, W. H., Stangl, D., & Corenthal, C. (1988). Diagnosing personality disorder in depressed patients: A comparison of patient and informant interviews. *Archives of General Psychiatry, 45,* 733–737.

CHAPTER 7

Comorbidity of Antisocial Personality Disorder With Other Personality Disorders

THOMAS A. WIDIGER and ELIZABETH M. CORBITT

This chapter discusses the comorbidity of the antisocial personality disorder (ASPD) with other personality disorders (PDs) (the comorbidity of childhood conduct disorder with other mental disorders is discussed in Lahey & Loeber, Chapter 5, this volume). We begin with a brief historical background, followed by a discussion of theoretical issues, methodological issues, current findings, conclusions, and suggestions for future research.

HISTORICAL BACKGROUND

The *Diagnostic and Statistical Manual of Mental Disorders* (*DSM-IV*) includes 10 personality disorders, each considered to be a distinct clinical condition with its own etiology and pathology (American Psychiatric Association [APA], 1994). If a person met the *DSM-IV* diagnostic criteria for the antisocial, borderline, and narcissistic personality disorders, this person would be said to have three comorbid PDs that co-exist and interact in a manner comparable to the presence of three comorbid physical disorders.

The initial discussion of comorbidity is credited to Feinstein (1970). The comorbidity of mental disorders is now of considerable theoretical and clinical interest, as systematic co-occurrence "raises many fundamental questions about psychopathology and emerges as a test of our classification systems" (Maser & Cloninger, 1990, p. 4), particularly in the context of the substantial prevalence of comorbidity within clinical settings (Boyd et al., 1984; Clark, Watson, & Reynolds, 1995). Texts on ASPD often concern a prototypic case occurring in isolation from any other PD, but ASPD in the presence of narcissistic, paranoid, histrionic, or borderline traits will have a much different course, presentation, etiology, and pathology than ASPD by itself (e.g., Stone, 1993).

The co-occurrence of ASPD with another PD may not in fact suggest a comorbidity of ASPD with the other PD. It may suggest instead a lack of validity of one or both of the two diagnoses. These issues have been discussed in a number of prior reviews, including papers by Clark et al. (1995), Frances, Widiger, and Fyer (1990), Klein and Riso (1993), Lilienfeld, Waldman, and Israel (1994), and Livesley, Schroeder, Jackson, and Jang (1994).

THEORETICAL ISSUES

The extent and complexity of the co-occurrence among PDs have led to a variety of recommendations. Lilienfeld et al. (1994) found the difficulties so daunting that they suggested abandoning altogether the term and concept of *comorbidity*: "Application of the term comorbidity to psychopathological syndromes encourages the premature reification of diagnostic entities and arguably has led to more confusion than clarification. . . . We thus recommend that, with the possible exception of certain organic mental disorders, the term comorbidity be avoided in psychopathology research" (pp. 71–80).

Another approach is to abandon one of the offending diagnoses. An early PD co-occurrence study was provided by Pfohl, Coryell, Zimmerman, and Stangl (1986). Rather than suggest that there is substantial comorbidity of *DSM-III* ASPD with passive-aggressive PD (PAPD), they concluded that "the best solution may be to eliminate passive-aggressive PD altogether" (Pfohl et al., 1986, p. 30), an approach to the problem that was in fact implemented in *DSM-IV* (Gunderson, 1996).

Another approach is to collapse co-occurring diagnoses into a single disorder. Lilienfield, VanValkenburg, Larntz, and Akiskal (1986) reported that 63% of 70 patients with ASPD met the *DSM-III* criteria for histrionic PD, and 63% of 70 histrionic patients likewise met the *DSM-III* criteria for ASPD. They proposed that these two disorders represent gender variants of a common underlying disposition, perhaps impulsivity or sensation seeking. From this perspective, the co-occurrence of ASPD and histrionic PD would not represent the comorbidity of two distinct disorders; it would represent instead the confusion of a single, common disposition that is expressed (or diagnosed) somewhat differently in males and females.

A similar argument has been made for the co-occurrence of ASPD with narcissistic PD. Hart and Hare (1989) suggest that *DSM-IV* narcissistic PD provides a more valid representation of Cleckley's (1941) description of psychopathy than *DSM-IV* ASPD with such traits as lack of empathy, arrogant self-appraisal, exploitation, and glib charm. From this perspective, the co-occurrence of ASPD with narcissistic PD does not represent the comorbidity of two distinct disorders; it represents instead illusory distinctions within a common disorder of psychopathy.

An even more extreme approach to the co-occurrence among the PDs is to abandon all of the categorical distinctions (e.g., Widiger et al., 1991). The *DSM-IV* PD diagnoses may represent arbitrary distinctions along various dimensions of personality. It may be more accurate to say that a person has one personality disorder characterized by an array of maladaptive personality traits than to suggest that the person has two or more distinct, comorbid personality disorders (Widiger & Sanderson, 1995).

A more conservative approach to excessive co-occurrence is to revise the diagnostic criteria sets to improve the differentiation among the presumably distinct PDs. This has been the approach taken in *DSM-III* (Frances, 1980), *DSM-III-R* (Widiger, Frances, Spitzer, & Williams, 1988), and *DSM-IV* (Gunderson, 1996).

METHODOLOGICAL ISSUES

The co-occurrence of ASPD with other PDs can also reflect a variety of methodological artifacts. Two issues that are particularly important for ASPD are (a) the populations from which the data were sampled and (b) the instruments with which the disorders were assessed.

Populations

Studies that are confined to clinical populations can exaggerate the true comorbidity of ASPD with other PDs. Clinical populations will favor the most dysfunctional variants of each PD that will then have more multiple PD symptomatology. Less co-occurrence among PDs might be obtained in persons with PDs who are not sufficiently dysfunctional to desire or seek clinical treatment. An illustration was provided by Boyd et al. (1984), who reported that the presence of any *DSM-III* disorder increased the odds for the presence of almost any other disorder within clinical populations.

Any particular clinical population might also have its own particular bias. For example, the emphasis within prison populations on criminal behavior not only results in a substantial rate of ASPD, it may also alter the specificity of the ASPD diagnostic criteria. Failure to conform to social norms with respect to lawful behavior is the first item within the *DSM-IV* diagnostic criteria for ASPD because such behavior is relatively specific to ASPD within most clinical settings (Widiger & Corbitt, 1995). However, such behavior will be relatively nonspecific within a prison setting. In this setting, such traits of psychopathy as lack of empathy, glib charm, and arrogant self-appraisal may then be more diagnostic of ASPD. As a result, the co-occurrence of ASPD with narcissistic PD may be higher within a prison setting than within a general clinical setting.

ASPD is also a disorder that is seen more often in males than in females (APA, 1994), whereas histrionic PD is a disorder that is seen more often in females (APA, 1987). The comorbidity of ASPD with histrionic PD may then be affected by the extent to which the population favors male or female subjects. For example, the comorbidity of ASPD with histrionic PD that is observed within a veterans' hospital (predominated by male subjects) may not be replicated in a more general clinical population.

The best estimate of a true rate of comorbidity of ASPD with other PDs might be obtained only through a representative sample of the entire adult population, but no such study has yet been attempted. ASPD was included within the NIMH Epidemiologic Catchment Area (ECA) study (Robins, Tipp, & Przybeck, 1991) and the National Comorbidity Survey (Kessler et al., 1994), whose purpose was in part to provide a comprehensive and systematic assessment of the prevalence of mental disorders within the U.S. population. However, none of the other personality disorders were included in these studies, and no data were then obtained on the comorbidity of ASPD with other PDs. Samuels, Nestadt, Romanoski, Folstein, and McHugh (1994) used data from the Baltimore site of the ECA study to provide an estimate of the comorbidity among the *DSM-III* PDs (reported later), but this study was constrained somewhat by substantial limitations of the assessment procedure.

Assessment Instruments

The preferred method of assessment in PD research is to use a semistructured interview (Loranger, 1992; Zimmerman, 1994), although semistructured interviews can contain their own limitations in the assessment of comorbidity. This was demonstrated in the very informative comorbidity study by Oldham et al. (1992). Oldham et al. administered both the Personality Disorder Examination (PDE; Loranger, 1988) and the Structured Clinical Interview for *DSM-III-R* PDs (SCID-II; Spitzer, Williams, Gibbon, & First, 1990) to 100 applicants for long-term, inpatient treatment of severe PDs. They found a significant co-occurrence of ASPD with histrionic PD using the PDE, but not when they used the SCID-II. Overall, "the SCID-II diagnosed a greater number of disorders . . . than did the PDE, but the SCID-II demonstrated considerably fewer patterns of significant co-occurrence" (Oldham et al., 1992, p. 216).

The PDE and SCID-II discrepancies were attributed in part to their different formats. The PDE reorganizes the diagnostic criteria according to similar thematic contents, whereas the SCID-II retains the organization of the PD criteria sets. As a result, the SCID-II format may encourage more diagnoses to be given (e.g., interviewers probe for more information to confirm an impression of an emerging positive diagnosis) while at the same time discouraging multiple diagnoses (e.g., once a diagnostic impression is made, the interviewer may reject overlapping symptomatology). SCID-II interviewers might also be better able to make distinctions among the PDs because they are more aware of the PD that is being assessed by a respective criterion. Interviewers using the thematic-content format may lose sight of the particular expression or understanding of a symptom in the context of the disorder in which it occurs. For example, physical fights are evident in both the antisocial and borderline PDs (APA, 1987, 1994), but the manner or expression of such fights may vary across these PDs. Interviewers who are unaware of which PD is being assessed when subjects report the presence of physical fights will not be able to make any distinction.

It is in any case ironic that semistructured interviews are considered to be advantageous over self-report inventories because they allow the interviewer to use his or her professional expertise to assess each diagnostic criterion (resulting in less co-occurrence among the PDs than is obtained by self-report inventories) when at the same time semistructured interviews are considered to be advantageous over unstructured clinical interviews because they curtail these same judgments (resulting in more co-occurrence among the PDs than is obtained by unstructured clinical interviews). The optimal degree of structure is at times unclear. Robins (1994) argues that only with a strict adherence to the diagnostic criteria will informative, replicable, and objective findings be obtained:

> These interviews do not create the multiplicity of diagnoses; they try to be true to what the diagnostic manual says, even when its authors may have meant something a bit different. When standardized interviews demonstrate that a single patient qualifies for an unreasonable number of diagnoses, that should motivate the field to rethink this proliferation of categories. (Robins, 1994, p. 94)

Such findings, however, are then best understood as providing the co-occurrence of inadequate and flawed diagnostic criteria sets rather than the actual comorbidity of the disorders. The PD diagnostic criteria were revised for *DSM-III-R* (Widiger et al., 1988) and *DSM-IV* (Gunderson, 1996) because the co-occurrence rates that were provided by semistructured interview studies were thought to be excessive (e.g., Pfohl et al., 1986). If a rigid adherence to the *DSM-III-R* diagnostic criteria produced an accurate estimate of the comorbidity among the PDs, there would not have been any need to revise these criteria sets to increase their specificity for *DSM-IV.*

The purpose of a semistructured interview is not necessarily to adhere rigidly to *DSM-IV* but to provide more specific instructions for the interpretation of each *DSM-IV* criterion (Widiger, Mangine, Corbitt, Ellis, & Thomas, 1995). To the extent that the assessment of a criterion is unambiguous, a semistructured interview would not be necessary. A semistructured interview attempts to resolve this ambiguity by providing more specific instructions on how to interpret and assess each criterion, and these instructions could include how to make better differentiations among PD diagnostic criteria, thereby reducing the co-occurrence of the disorders.

For example, semistructured interviews vary in the manner and extent to which they distinguish between antisocial "irritability and aggressiveness" (APA, 1994, p. 650) and borderline "inappropriate, intense anger or difficulty controlling anger" (APA, 1994, p. 654). A distinction is suggested in *DSM-IV,* in that borderline anger includes frequent displays of temper or constant anger, whereas antisocial irritability is "indicated by repeated physical fights or assaults" (APA, 1994, p. 650). However, borderline anger can also include "recurrent physical fights" (APA, 1994, p. 654). The Personality Disorder Interview-IV (PDI-IV; Widiger et al., 1995) suggests that the repeated physical fights of ASPD will often involve an explicit effort to subjugate, control, intimidate, humiliate, or harm someone (e.g., an assault), whereas the fights of borderline PD will tend to be more impulsive, explosive, and dyscontrolled. It would be more indicative of the borderline person to initiate a fight that he or she would clearly lose (in *DSM-III,* physical fights were presented as an example of borderline physically self-damaging acts; APA, 1980).

Semistructured interviews improve the reliability of PD assessments by providing more explicit and specific instructions for each PD criterion than does the *DSM-IV.* The reliability of a PD assessment reported by Pfohl et al. (1986) when using the Structured Interview for *DSM-III* Personality Disorders (SIDP) was not the reliability of the *DSM-III* PD diagnosis—it was the reliability of the SIDP assessment of that PD. Some instruments are more reliable than others because they provide more structure. Likewise, the co-occurrence rates among the *DSM-III* PDs reported by Pfohl et al. did not provide the comorbidity among the PDs; they provided the co-occurrence rates of the *DSM-III* PD diagnoses as operationalized by the SIDP (Oldham et al., 1992).

EMPIRICAL FINDINGS

Table 7.1 presents the co-occurrence of ASPD with other PDs as indicated in 12 studies that were based on clinical or semistructured interviews. It is apparent from Table 7.1 that one cannot rely on the findings from any particular study, as the results vary substantially. The percentage of persons with ASPD who also met the criteria for paranoid PD varied from 0% (Dahl, 1986; Samuels et al., 1994) to 62% (Oldham et al., 1992), and for borderline PD from 0% (Samuels et al., 1994) to 100% (Oldham et al., 1992).

The variability is due in part to the methodological factors discussed earlier. For example, the low rate of co-occurrence in Brooner, Herbst, Schmidt, Bigelow, and Costa (1993) may reflect an atypical population. Their 203 opioid-dependent outpatients had a substantial rate of ASPD (23%) and very few other PDs (the next highest rate was 8% for the borderline PD). Very low co-occurrence rates were obtained within the two nonclinical samples (i.e., Samuels et al., 1994; Zimmerman & Coryell, 1989). However, their low co-occurrence rates were not due simply to the low prevalence of ASPD within a nonclinical sample. One could still obtain substantial co-occurrence when there are few cases. For example, 80% of the 5 ASPD cases in Pfohl et al. (1986) also met the *DSM-III* criteria for borderline PD, whereas 15 of the 20 cases of ASPD in the community study by Samuels et al. (1994) failed to meet the criteria for any other *DSM-III* PD. The low co-occurrence within nonclinical samples may be due primarily to their higher functioning (Boyd et al., 1984). More comorbidity is observed within clinical cases because these persons have additional motivation or need for treatment that is provided by the presence of additional PD symptomatology.

According to Robins et al. (1991, p. 286), "Persons with antisocial personality rarely seek medical care for treatment of its symptoms." Only 14.5% of all of the ECA ASPD cases had ever discussed their ASPD symptoms with a doctor. Only 4% of ASPD cases that lacked a comorbid mental disorder had made a contact with a mental health clinician within the past 6 months, a rate that was no greater than that of persons without any disorder. With a concurrent disorder, the rate rose to 21%, indicating that it was the presence of the comorbid disorder that impelled treatment, not ASPD itself. In other words, the vast majority of ASPD cases are not within treatment, and those within treatment are there for a disorder other than ASPD. Therefore, findings on ASPD within clinical populations may concern a very atypical variant of ASPD and are likely to be confounded substantially with the effects of the comorbid disorder(s).

TABLE 7.1 Percentage of Persons Diagnosed With ASPD Also Diagnosed With Each Other PD

Study	N	ASPD	DSM	Method	Pop.	PAR	SZD	SZT	BDL	HST	NAR	AVD	DEP	OBC	PAG	None
Brooner et al. (1993)	203	46	DSM-3-R	SCID-II	Opioid	4	0	0	20	7	0	11	4	0	13	61
Corbitt (1993	50	16	DSM-3-R	PIQ-III	Inpts	31	25	12	56	19	12	12	12	6	44	0
Dahl (1986)	103	34	DSM-3	"SADS"	Pts	0	6	38	76	38	6	15	0	0	0	24
Freiman & Widiger (1989)	50	14	DSM-3-R	PIQ-II	Inpts	36	14	36	71	29	36	36	43	0	36	8
Millon & Tringone (1989)	584	14	DSM-3-R	Guided	Pts	14	0	0	7	14	7	7	0	0	0	7
Morey (1988)	291	17	DSM-3-R	Guided	Pts	28	6	6	44	33	56	17	11	0	50	—
Oldham et al. (1992)[a]	100	8	DSM-3-R	PDE	Inpts	25	0	38	75	62	50	25	62	12	0	—
Oldham et al. (1992)[b]	100	8	DSM-3-R	SCID-II	Inpts	62	0	12	100	50	50	25	12	25	38	—
Pfohl et al. (1986)	131	5	DSM-3	SIDP	Pts	0	0	20	80	60	0	20	0	0	60	20
Pfohl & Blum (1990)	112	4	DSM-3-R	SIDP-R	Pts	25	25	25	75	75	25	50	25	25	25	0
Samuels et al. (1994)	95	20	DSM-3	SPE	Cmnty	0	0	0	0	33	0	0	0	0	0	75
Zanarini et al. (1987)	253	102	DSM-3	DIPD	Pts	2	1	29	80	56	28	6	21	0	29	14
Zimmerman & Coryell (1989)	797	26	DSM-3	SIDP	Reltvs	8	4	23	15	15	0	4	0	4	8	50

Notes. N = total number of subjects; ASPD = number with ASPD; *DSM* = edition of *DSM*; Method = method of interview; Pop = population; Inpts = inpatients; Pts = patients; Opioid = opioid-dependent outpatients; Cmnty = community; Reltvs = relatives; PAR = paranoid; SZD = schizoid; SZT = schizotypal; BDL = borderline; HST = histrionic; NAR = narcissistic; AVD = avoidant; DEP = dependent; OBC = obsessive-compulsive; PAG = passive-aggressive.
[a]Based on the PDE; [b]Based on the SCID-II.

Comparably low rates of co-occurrence, however, also are provided by some clinical studies, particularly those that failed to use a semistructured interview. The co-occurrence rates reported by Millon and Tringone (1989) and Morey (1988) within clinical populations were almost as low as the co-occurrence rates reported by Samuels et al. (1994) and Zimmerman and Coryell (1989). The assessments of the clinicians surveyed by Millon, Morey, and Tringone, however, were based on a memory of a prior, unstructured interview, rather than on a systematic assessment of each criterion. Semistructured interviews identify more co-occurrence among the PDs than less structured interviews not only because they curtail clinical judgment but also because they are more thorough, comprehensive, and systematic in their assessments of the PD symptomatology.

In any case, it is apparent from the data provided in Table 7.1 that the co-occurrence of ASPD with other PDs is extensive within clinical populations, particularly with respect to the borderline and histrionic PDs, but also with respect to the narcissistic, passive-aggressive, and paranoid PDs. If one confines the methodology to the studies within general clinical populations that used a semistructured interview (i.e., Corbitt, 1993; Freiman & Widiger, 1989; Oldham et al., 1992; Pfohl & Blum, 1990; Pfohl et al., 1986; Zanarini, Frankenburg, Chauncey, & Gunderson, 1987), the median rate of comorbidity of ASPD with borderline PD was 75%, for histrionic PD it was 56%, for passive-aggressive PD 36%, for paranoid PD 31%, and for narcissistic PD 28%. The extent of co-occurrence of ASPD with other PDs might be less than is found for other PDs, such as the borderline, dependent, and avoidant, but it is nevertheless substantial. It appears that most persons with ASPD within clinical settings will meet the criteria for at least one other PD. Very few, and often none, will fail to have other clinically significant maladaptive personality traits.

CONCLUSIONS

The majority of persons with ASPD within clinical settings meet the criteria for another PD. Therefore, ASPD pathology being studied within clinical settings will usually be confounded with the pathology of another PD. Co-occurrence is particularly evident with the borderline and histrionic PDs, and to a lesser but still substantial extent, with the passive-aggressive, paranoid, and narcissistic PDs.

The predominant approach to this problem has been to revise the diagnostic criteria to reduce co-occurrence (Gunderson, 1996; Widiger et al., 1988) or to implement further distinctions within respective semistructured interviews (e.g., Loranger, 1988; Widiger et al., 1995). It is our expectation, however, that these efforts either will fail or will simply increase the number of cases of personality disorder, not otherwise specified (PDNOS). PDNOS is a residual diagnosis that covers cases of PD that do not meet the diagnostic criteria for any one of the 10 officially recognized PDs (APA, 1994). PDNOS is a rarely researched diagnosis, yet it has been the most prevalent PD diagnosis in almost every study in which it has been included (Widiger & Costa, 1994). The prevalence of PDNOS will likely increase as other PDs become more narrowly defined. Clark et al. (1995) document well the reliance across the entire *DSM-III-R* on the residual diagnosis of NOS.

Oldham et al. (1992) suggest including a diagnosis that recognizes the heterogeneity and complexity of the symptomatology: "Given the rates of multiple diagnoses and percents of co-occurrence found . . . we believe that a persuasive case can be made for a two-level diagnostic system" (p. 219). If a single PD does appear to describe a patient's pathology adequately, then the respective PD diagnosis could be provided. For patients with more complex symptom patterns, however, "a single diagnosis of 'extensive personality disorder' might be made, with a dimensional description of the predominant characteristics of the disorder" (p. 219). Oldham et al. (1992) recommended that the existing *DSM* constructs be used to provide the dimensions to describe a patient's PD symptomatology (e.g., extensive PD, with antisocial, borderline, and passive-aggressive features). A comparable proposal was in fact considered for *DSM-IV* (Widiger & Sanderson, 1995).

We would suggest, however, that the existing PD constructs might fail to provide the optimal set of dimensions with which to describe PD pathology. The 10 PDs contained within *DSM-IV* (plus the two within the appendix) were obtained from a variety of sources, they overlap substantially, and they may fail to fully capture all the important variations in personality dysfunction.

A number of alternative dimensional models are currently being researched. One model that will garner interest is the seven-factor model of Cloninger and his colleagues, consisting of the dimensions of reward dependence, harm avoidance, novelty seeking, persistence, self-directedness, cooperativeness, and self-transcendence (Cloninger, Svrakic, & Przybeck, 1993). ASPD is said in this model to represent excessively high novelty seeking, coupled with excessively low harm avoidance and low reward dependence (Cloninger, 1987), along with low self-directedness and low cooperativeness (Cloninger et al., 1993; Svrakic, Whitehead, Przybeck, & Cloninger, 1993). An attraction of this model is its effort to assess neurotransmitter and learning mechanisms that are predicted to have a relevance to ASPD (e.g., Tremblay, Pihl, Vitaro, & Dobkin, 1994). Its reliance upon and commitment to a particular neurochemical model, however, may eventually prove to be a limitation. In addition, its empirical support with respect to ASPD is confined to just one study (Svrakic et al., 1993), which in fact failed to confirm the presence of low harm avoidance.

ASPD researchers may find the empirically derived models of Clark and Livesley to be more useful. Clark and her colleagues have identified dimensions of PD symptomatology (Clark, 1990; Clark, McEwen, Collard, & Hickok, 1993) that underlie the *DSM-III-R* PD diagnostic categories, including such dimensions as disinhibition, aggression, impulsivity, mistrust, and entitlement. These dimensions are often the focus of consideration in discussions of the etiology and pathology of ASPD. Similar dimensions were identified by Livesley and his colleagues (e.g., conduct problems, suspiciousness, passive oppositionality, stimulus seeking, and interpersonal disesteem; Livesley, Jackson, & Schroeder, 1989). Rather than infer the extent of disinhibition, impulsivity, and aggression within heterogeneous samples of persons diagnosed with ASPD, it may be more useful to provide a more direct assessment of these personality dimensions.

An additional advantage of the dimensions of Clark and Livesley is that they can be understood within the broader dimensions of normal personality functioning, thereby integrating theory and research concerning ASPD within the more general context of personality theory and research. For example, Clark and Livesley (1994) have indicated how their dimensions of personality dysfunction relate closely to the five-factor model of personality. The broad dimensions of personality within the five-factor model are neuroticism (or negative affectivity), extraversion (or positive affectivity), openness (or unconventionality), antagonism, and conscientiousness (or constraint) (Digman, 1990; McCrae & Costa, 1990). Costa and McCrae (1995) differentiate each of these broad domains into underlying facets. Antagonism (vs. agreeableness) would be particularly relevant to the description of persons with ASPD, as it includes such facets as deception and manipulativeness (vs. straightforwardness), exploitation (vs. altruism), tough-mindedness (vs. tender-mindedness), oppositionalism and aggression (vs. compliance), arrogance (vs. modesty), and suspiciousness (vs. trust). ASPD may represent in large part extreme variants of the facets of exploitation, aggression, tough-mindedness (low empathy), arrogance, and deception (or manipulation); traits that are also present within the narcissistic, passive-aggressive, histrionic, and borderline PDs (Widiger, Trull, Clarkin, Sanderson, & Costa, 1994). Relevant facets from other five-factor domains include excitement seeking from the domain of extraversion (shared with the histrionic PD), irresponsibility from the domain of conscientiousness (shared with the passive-aggressive PD), and impulsivity and angry hostility from the domain of neuroticism (shared with the borderline PD). The apparent comorbidity of ASPD with other PDs may depend largely on which facets are particularly evident in each individual case, as persons diagnosed with ASPD will not share the same facets to the same degree (Widiger et al., 1994). Some may be characterized by their impulsivity, angry hostility, oppositionalism, and manipulation (i.e., those with comorbid diagnoses of borderline PD), whereas others may be characterized in particular by their low empathy, arrogance, and exploitation (i.e., those with a comorbid diagnosis of narcissistic PD).

Initial research on the relationship of ASPD or psychopathy to the five-factor model has been provided by Brooner et al. (1993), Harpur, Hart, and Hare (1994), and Hart and Hare (1994), as well as by studies that have involved all of the PDs (Widiger & Costa, 1994). These studies have emphasized the role of antagonism and its facets in understanding ASPD. However, the domain of neuroticism or negative affectivity may also be pivotal. For example, Patrick (1994) has proposed that the apparent absence of a startle response potentiation in psychopathic persons reflects a temperamental deficit in the capacity for negative affect. Subjects high in negative affectivity (or neuroticism) show dramatic startle potentiation, whereas those low in negative affectivity do not. This research, however, has rarely involved clinical populations. Most persons within clinical settings will be characterized by moderate to high levels of neuroticism (negative affectivity) and, as we noted earlier, substantial PD comorbidity. The comorbidity will in fact be due in large part to this high neuroticism that is present in most of the other *DSM-IV* PDs (Widiger et al., 1994).

FUTURE RESEARCH

Future research on ASPD should consider the potential impact of the variable and co-occurring PD symptomatology. Persons who meet the *DSM-IV* criteria for ASPD will vary substantially in the extent to which they are elevated on such underlying dimensions of personality as excitement seeking, impulsivity, tough-mindedness, irresponsibility, aggression, manipulativeness, and negative affectivity. Yet current ASPD research is often confined to simply the presence versus the absence of an ASPD diagnosis. This can provide a substantial and unnecessary hindrance to the validation of hypotheses concerning antisocial personality traits (Widiger & Sanderson, 1995). We would recommend that future researchers consider the inclusion of those additional measures of personality dimensions that may underlie the ASPD diagnosis and provide a more differentiated and exact description of each subject's PD pathology (Widiger & Costa, 1994).

Less confusion also might be obtained with nonclinical, community samples. Most ASPD cases within clinical samples will be characterized by symptoms of additional PD diagnoses. Clinical populations are often preferred because they provide the cases most relevant to clinical practice. However, their severity of dysfunction may also provide an atypical and distorted view of antisocial pathology that is contaminated by comorbid personality traits, such as negative affectivity.

A similar point can, of course, be made for any particular setting or population. Cases of ASPD sampled from prison populations may be characterized by higher levels of impulsivity, lower intelligence, lower socioeconomic background, and other factors that contributed to the likelihood of being convicted for a criminal act. Psychopathic traits such as deception, manipulation, low empathy, and exploitation are likely to result in the commission of illegal acts, but not necessarily in the arrest and conviction for these acts.

A final recommendation is to consider the effect of the assessment instrument(s). Semistructured interviews vary in the extent and manner in which they differentiate among the *DSM-IV* PD diagnostic criteria. Clarification of findings across studies will not likely be obtained without the inclusion of multiple methods of measurement that allow at least some degree of confirmation and comparison across instruments and sites. Studies that directly compare alternative semistructured interviews will be particularly informative, especially if they include multiple methods of assessment, such as self or peer reports.

REFERENCES

American Psychiatric Association. (1980). *Diagnostic and statistical manual of mental disorders* (3rd ed.). Washington, DC: Author.

American Psychiatric Association. (1987). *Diagnostic and statistical manual of mental disorders* (3rd ed., rev.). Washington, DC: Author.

American Psychiatric Association. (1994). *Diagnostic and statistical manual of mental disorders* (4th ed.). Washington, DC: Author.

Boyd, J. H., Burke, J. D., Gruenberg, E., Holzer, C. E., Rae, D. S., George, L. K., Karno, M., Stoltzman, R., McEvoy, L., & Nestadt, G. (1984).

Exclusion criteria of *DSM-III*. A study of co-occurrence of hierarchy-free syndromes. *Archives of General Psychiatry, 41,* 983–989.

Brooner, R. K., Herbst, J. H., Schmidt, C. W., Bigelow, G. E., & Costa, P. T. (1993). Antisocial personality disorder among drug abusers. Relations to other personality diagnoses and the five-factor model of personality. *Journal of Nervous and Mental Disease, 181,* 313–319.

Clark, L. A. (1990). Toward a consensual set of symptom clusters for assessment of personality disorder. In J. N. Butcher & C. D. Spielberger (Eds.), *Advances in personality assessment* (Vol. 8, pp. 243–266). Hillsdale, NJ: Erlbaum.

Clark, L. A., & Livesley, W. J. (1994). Two approaches to identifying the dimensions of personality disorder: Convergence on the five-factor model. In P. T. Costa & T. A. Widiger (Eds.), *Personality disorders and the five-factor model of personality* (pp. 261–277). Washington, DC: American Psychological Association.

Clark, L. A., McEwen, J., Collard, L. M., & Hickock, L. G. (1993). Symptoms and traits of personality disorder: Two new methods for their assessment. *Psychological Assessment, 5,* 81–91.

Clark, L. A., Watson, D., & Reynolds, S. (1995). Diagnosis and classification of psychopathology: Challenges to the current system and future directions. *Annual Review of Psychology, 46,* 121–153.

Cleckley, H. (1941). *The mask of sanity.* St. Louis: C. V. Mosby.

Cloninger, C. R. (1987). A systematic method for clinical description and classification of personality variants. *Archives of General Psychiatry, 44,* 573–588.

Cloninger, C. R., Svrakic, D. M., & Przybeck, T. R. (1993). A psychobiological model of temperament and character. *Archives of General Psychiatry, 50,* 975–990.

Corbitt, E. M. (1993). *Sex bias and the personality disorders: A reinterpretation from the five-factor model.* Unpublished doctoral dissertation, University of Kentucky, Lexington.

Costa, P. T., & McCrae, R. R. (1995). Domains and facets: Hierarchical personality assessment using the Revised Neo Personality Inventory. *Journal of Personality Assessment, 64,* 21–50.

Dahl, A. A. (1986). Some aspects of the *DSM-III* personality disorders illustrated by a consecutive sample of hospitalized patients. *Acta Psychiatrica Scandinavica, 73* (328), 61–66.

Digman, J. M. (1990). Personality structure: Emergence of the five-factor model. *Annual Review of Psychology, 41,* 417–440.

Feinstein, A. R. (1970). The pre-therapeutic classification of co-morbidity in chronic disease. *Journal of Chronic Diseases, 23,* 455–468.

Frances, A. J. (1980). The *DSM-III* personality disorders: A commentary. *American Journal of Psychiatry, 137,* 1050–1054.

Frances, A. J., Widiger, T. A., & Fyer, M. R. (1990). The influence of classification methods on comorbidity. In J. D. Maser & C. R. Cloninger (Eds.), *Comorbidity of mood and anxiety disorders* (pp. 41–59). Washington, DC: American Psychiatric Press.

Freiman, K., & Widiger, T. A. (1989). [Co-occurrence and diagnostic efficiency statistics]. Unpublished raw data.

Gunderson, J. G. (1996). Personality disorders. In T. A. Widiger, A. J. Frances, H. A. Pincus, R. Ross, M. First, & W. Davis (Eds.), DSM-IV sourcebook (Vol. 2, pp. 647–664). Washington, DC: American Psychiatric Association.

Harpur, T. J., Hart, S. D., & Hare, R. D. (1994). Personality of the psychopath. In P. T. Costa & T. A. Widiger (Eds.), *Personality disorders and the five-factor model of personality* (pp. 149–173). Washington, DC: American Psychological Association.

Hart, S. D., & Hare, R. D. (1989). Discriminant validity of the Psychopathy Checklist in a forensic psychiatric population. *Psychological Assessment, 1,* 211–218.

Hart, S. D., & Hare, R. D. (1994). Psychopathy and the Big 5: Correlations between observers' ratings of normal and pathological personality. *Journal of Personality Disorders, 8,* 32–40.

Kessler, R. C., McGonagle, K. A., Zhao, S., Nelson, C. B., Hughes, M., Eshleman, S., Wittchen, H., & Kendler, K. (1994). Lifetime and 12-month prevalence of *DSM-III-R* psychiatric disorders in the United States. Results from the National Comorbidity Survey. *Archives of General Psychiatry, 51,* 8–19.

Klein, D. N., & Riso, L. P. (1993). Psychiatric disorders: Problems of boundaries and comorbidity. In C. G. Costello (Ed.), *Basic issues in psychopathology* (pp. 19–66). New York: Guilford.

Lilienfeld, S. O., VanValkenburg, C., Larntz, K., & Akiskal, H. S. (1986). The relationship of histrionic personality disorder to antisocial personality and somatization disorders. *American Journal of Psychiatry, 143,* 718–722.

Lilienfeld, S. O., Waldman, I. D., & Israel, A. C. (1994). A critical examination of the use of the term and concept of comorbidity in psychopathology research. *Clinical Psychology: Science and Practice, 1,* 71–83.

Livesley, W. J., Jackson, D., & Schroeder, M. L. (1989). A study of the factorial structure of personality pathology. *Journal of Personality Disorders, 3,* 292–306.

Livesley, W. J., Schroeder, M. L., Jackson, D. N., & Jang, K. L. (1994). Categorical distinctions in the study of personality disorders: Implications for classification. *Journal of Abnormal Psychology, 103,* 6–17.

Loranger, A. W. (1988). *Personality Disorder Examination (PDE) manual.* Yonkers, NY: DV Communications.

Loranger, A. W. (1992). Are current self-report and interview measures adequate for epidemiological studies of personality disorders? *Journal of Personality Disorders, 6,* 313–325.

Maser, J. D., & Cloninger, C. R. (1990). Comorbidity of mood and anxiety disorders: Introduction and overview. In J. D. Maser & C. R. Cloninger (Eds.), *Comorbidity of mood and anxiety disorders* (pp. 3–12). Washington, DC: American Psychiatric Press.

McCrae, R. R., & Costa, P. T. (1990). *Personality in adulthood.* New York: Guilford.

Millon, T., & Tringone, R. (1989). [Co-occurrence and diagnostic efficiency statistics]. Unpublished raw data.

Morey, L. C. (1988). Personality disorders under *DSM-III* and *DSM-III-R:* An examination of convergence, coverage, and internal consistency. *American Journal of Psychiatry, 145,* 573–577.

Oldham, J. M., Skodol, A. E., Kellman, H. D., Hyler, S. E., Rosnick, L., & Davies, M. (1992). Diagnosis of *DSM-III-R* personality disorders by two structured interviews: Patterns of comorbidity. *American Journal of Psychiatry, 149,* 213–220.

Patrick, C. J. (1994). Emotion and psychopathy: Startling new insights. *Psychophysiology, 31,* 319–330.

Pfohl, B., & Blum, N. (1990). [Co-occurrence and diagnostic efficiency statistics]. Unpublished raw data.

Pfohl, B., Coryell, W., Zimmerman, M., & Stangl, D. (1986). *DSM-III* personality disorders: Diagnostic overlap and internal consistency of individual *DSM-III* criteria. *Comprehensive Psychiatry, 27,* 21–34.

Robins, L. N. (1994). How recognizing "comorbidities" in psychopathology may lead to an improved research nosology. *Clinical Psychology: Science and Practice, 1,* 93–95.

Robins, L. N., Tipp, J., & Przybeck, T. (1991). Antisocial personality. In L. N. Robins & D. A. Regier (Eds.), *Psychiatric disorders in America* (pp. 258–290). New York: Free Press.

Samuels, J. F., Nestadt, G., Romanoski, A. J., Folstein, M. F., & McHugh, P. R. (1994). *DSM-III* personality disorders in the community. *American Journal of Psychiatry, 151,* 1055–1062.

Spitzer, R. L., Williams, J. B. W., Gibbon, M., & First, M. (1990). *User's guide for the Structured Clinical Interview for* DSM-III-R *(SCID-II)*. Washington, DC: American Psychiatric Press.

Stone, M. H. (1993). *Abnormalities of personality within and beyond the realm of treatment.* New York: W. W. Norton.

Svrakic, D. M., Whitehead, C., Przybeck, T. R., & Cloninger, C. R. (1993). Differential diagnosis of personality disorders by the seven-factor model of temperament and character. *Archives of General Psychiatry, 50,* 991–999.

Tremblay, R. E., Pihl, R. O., Vitaro, F., & Dobkin, P. L. (1994). Predicting early onset of male antisocial behavior from preschool behavior. *Archives of General Psychiatry, 51,* 732–739.

Widiger, T. A., & Corbitt, E. M. (1995). Antisocial personality disorder in *DSM-IV.* In W. J. Livesley (Ed.), DSM-IV *personality disorders* (pp. 103–126). New York: Guilford.

Widiger, T. A., & Costa, P. T. (1994). Personality and personality disorders. *Journal of Abnormal Psychology, 103,* 78–91.

Widiger, T. A., Frances, A. J., Harris, M., Jacobsberg, L. B., Fyer, M., & Manning, D. (1991). Comorbidity among Axis II disorders. In J. Oldham (Ed.), *Axis II: New perspectives on diagnostic validity* (pp. 163–194). Washington, DC: American Psychiatric Press.

Widiger, T. A., Frances, A. J., Spitzer, R. L., & Williams, J. B. W. (1988). The *DSM-III-R* personality disorders: An overview. *American Journal of Psychiatry, 145,* 786–795.

Widiger, T. A., Mangine, S., Corbitt, E. M., Ellis, C. G., & Thomas, G. V. (1995). *Personality Disorder Interview-IV: A semistructured interview for the assessment of personality disorders.* Odessa, FL: Psychological Assessment Resources.

Widiger, T. A., & Sanderson, C. J. (1995). Towards a dimensional model of personality disorder in *DSM-IV* and *DSM-V.* In W. J. Livesley (Ed.), DSM-IV *personality disorders* (pp. 433–458). New York: Guilford.

Widiger, T. A., Trull, T. J., Clarkin, J. F., Sanderson, C. J., & Costa, P. T. (1994). A description of the *DSM-III-R* and *DSM-IV* personality disorders with the five-factor model of personality. In P. T. Costa & T. A. Widiger (Eds.), *Personality disorders and the five-factor model of personality* (pp. 41–56). Washington, DC: American Psychological Association.

Zanarini, M. C., Frankenburg, F. R., Chauncey, D. L., & Gunderson, J. G. (1987). The Diagnostic Interview for Personality Disorders: Interrater rater and test-retest reliability. *Comprehensive Psychiatry, 28,* 467–480.

Zimmerman, M. (1994). Diagnosing personality disorders. A review of issues and research methods. *Archives of General Psychiatry, 51,* 225–245.

Zimmerman, M., & Coryell, W. (1989). *DSM-III* personality disorder diagnoses in a nonpatient sample. Demographic correlates and comorbidity. *Archives of General Psychiatry, 46,* 682–689.

CHAPTER 8

Differential Diagnosis of Antisocial and Borderline Personality Disorders

MARY C. ZANARINI and JOHN G. GUNDERSON

Kernberg (1975) considered both antisocial personality disorder (ASPD) and borderline personality disorder (BPD) to share a common "borderline" level of personality organization. As such, both had psychologies characterized by generally intact reality testing (seeing the world as others do), poorly developed identities (having little idea of who they are), and reliance on primitive defenses (handling painful feelings in a maladaptive manner). When the definition of these disorders became operationalized in *DSM-III* (American Psychiatric Association, 1980), *DSM-III-R* (American Psychiatric Association, 1987), and *DSM-IV* (American Psychiatric Association, 1994), they remained linked as components of the "dramatic" cluster (i.e., ASPD, BPD, histrionic personality disorder, and narcissistic personality disorder). The criteria sets for both of these diagnoses identify their impulsivity and unstable interpersonal relationships. But the diagnoses were now distinguished descriptively insofar as identity problems, lapses of reality testing, and intense affects are now cited as criteria for BPD, not as features of ASPD.

Remarkably, despite the reasons to believe these disorders are psychopathological cousins, BPD and ASPD are conceptualized quite differently. Whereas most clinicians recognize that patients with BPD are difficult to treat successfully, ample documentation suggests that multiple modalities can be useful (Gunderson & Links, 1995). In contrast, the prevailing wisdom about ASPD is that those with the disorder are untreatable by standard psychotherapies. Indeed, the primary importance of this diagnosis to clinicians is that if they have failed to recognize it, they will have been exploited, misspent their time, or will have inadvertently endangered the welfare of others.

Even though borderline personality disorder and antisocial personality disorder often are thought to be comorbid in clinical settings, relatively little research has investigated their relationship. We review the relevant literature, following the paradigm for validating a psychiatric disorder outlined by Robins and Guze (1970). The first area that we review is Axis II comorbidity. Next we review the family history of psychiatric disorder, childhood antecedents, course and outcome, temperament, and subsyndromal phenomenology.

AXIS II COMORBIDITY

To date, nine studies assessing criteria-defined borderline patients for rates of comorbid ASPD have been published. Four other studies have assessed the comorbidity of all Axis II disorders in samples of nonpsychotic patients. The rates of comorbid ASPD in these methodologically varied samples are reported here. (See Widiger & Corbitt, Chapter 7, this volume, for a different perspective on this issue.)

In the first of these studies, Akiskal (1981) studied 100 consecutively admitted outpatients at two urban mental health centers in Tennessee who met at least five of the six Gunderson and Singer (1975) criteria for borderline personality disorder. Each of these patients also met the *DSM-III* criteria for BPD. After an extensive clinical interview, Akiskal found that 13% of his BPD sample met *DSM-III* criteria for antisocial personality disorder.

As part of McGlashan's (1983) larger study of the comorbidity of BPD, McGlashan and Heinssen (1989) studied the antisocial features of a retrospectively diagnosed subsample of 58 inpatients meeting Diagnostic Interview for Borderlines (DIB; Gunderson, Kolb, & Austin, 1981) or *DSM-III* criteria for borderline personality disorder. A research team reviewed the charts of all patients 16 to 55 years of age on admission who were discharged from the Chestnut Lodge between 1950 and 1975, had a hospitalization of at least 90 days, and were not suffering from an organic brain syndrome. After careful chart review, they found that none of the 58 patients meeting DIB or *DSM-III* criteria for borderline personality disorder met the *DSM-III* criteria for antisocial personality disorder but that 31% had significant antisocial traits.

Pope, Jonas, Hudson, Cohen, and Gunderson (1983) studied the comorbidity of a group of 33 inpatients at McLean Hospital who met the *DSM-III* criteria for BPD. This sample was culled by review of the charts of 39 patients who had previously been given a clinical or DIB diagnosis of BPD. Pope et al. found that 9% of their borderline sample met *DSM-III* criteria for antisocial personality disorder.

This work was supported in part by NIMH grant MH47588.

Andrulonis and Vogel (1984) studied the phenomenology of three groups of inpatients at the Institute of Living who met *DSM-III* criteria for the following disorders: 106 nonschizotypal borderlines, 55 schizophrenics, and 55 patients with some form of (mostly unipolar) affective disorder. These diagnoses were made by a research psychiatrist on the basis of a clinical interview and chart review. None of those with a borderline diagnosis currently was suffering from a major affective disorder and none of the control patients had a concurrent Axis II diagnosis. In addition, no patient had an IQ of less than 80 or a primary diagnosis other than BPD, schizophrenia, or an affective disorder. Phenomenological data, which were collected through a chart review, had to be well documented by past psychiatric or legal records. Andrulonis and Vogel found that 69% of their borderline cohort had engaged in antisocial acting out (violence toward property or others, criminal acts, promiscuity, and running away). Andrulonis and Vogel also found that borderline patients were significantly more likely than those in either control group to have engaged in antisocial acts.

Frances, Clarkin, Gilmore, Hurt, and Brown (1984) studied 76 outpatients between the ages of 18 and 45 at the Payne Whitney Evaluation Service who were thought to meet criteria for an Axis II disorder but not to be suffering from a psychotic or organic disorder. After a 1-hour clinical interview performed conjointly by one to three raters, all appropriate Axis II diagnoses were made. Twenty-six patients met the *DSM-III* criteria for BPD, whereas 46 of the 50 patients in the control group met *DSM-III* criteria for at least one nonborderline form of personality disorder. Frances et al. found that none of their borderline patients met *DSM-III* criteria for antisocial personality disorder.

Perry and Cooper (1985) studied the syndromal phenomenology of a group of 82 outpatients, symptomatic volunteers, and probationers from the metropolitan Boston area. After a lengthy semistructured diagnostic interview, the sample was divided into the following five groups: definite BPD = 23, BPD trait = 14, ASPD = 14, BPD/ASPD = 12, and bipolar II disorder = 19. After the initial interview, trained research assistants administered the Diagnostic Interview Schedule (DIS; Robins, Helzer, Croughan, & Ratcliff, 1981), a structured interview designed to assess the lifetime prevalence of various psychiatric disorders. Perry and Cooper found that 25% of their 49 BPD patients met *DSM-III* criteria for antisocial personality disorder.

Links, Steiner, Offord, and Eppel (1988) screened consecutive inpatients who met three or more of the seven best indicators for BPD (Gunderson & Kolb, 1978). Patients were excluded if they met any of the following criteria: (a) a primary diagnosis of alcoholism or drug dependence, (b) organicity based on clinical evidence of a CNS abnormality of any etiology, (c) any physical disorders of known psychiatric significance, (d) borderline mental retardation, (e) a history of hospitalization for more than 2 years cumulatively of the previous 5, and (f) inability to understand English. The remaining 130 patients were interviewed with the DIB and the Schedule for Affective Disorders and Schizophrenia (SADS; Endicott & Spitzer, 1978), which assesses disorders according to Research Diagnostic Criteria (RDC; Spitzer, Endicott, & Robins, 1978). Of these patients, 88 met DIB criteria for BPD, whereas 42 in a borderline trait control group did not. In terms of lifetime diagnoses, 13% met RDC criteria for antisocial personality disorder.

Zanarini, Gunderson, and Frankenburg (1989) studied the lifetime Axis I and II phenomenology of 50 borderline patients meeting both Revised Diagnostic Interview for Borderlines (DIB-R; Zanarini, Gunderson, Frankenburg, & Chauncey, 1989) and *DSM-III* criteria for BPD using the Structured Clinical Interview for *DSM-III* Axis I Disorders (SCID I; Spitzer & Williams, 1984) and the Diagnostic Interview for Personality Disorders (DIPD; Zanarini, Frankenburg, Chauncey, & Gunderson, 1987). They also studied the lifetime syndromal phenomenology of 29 individuals in an antisocial control group and 26 in a control group who met the *DSM-III* criteria for dysthymic disorder and the *DSM-III* criteria for a nonborderline and nonantisocial form of personality disorder. All patients met the following inclusion criteria: (a) age between 18 and 40, (b) average or better intelligence, and (c) no history or current symptomatology of a clear-cut organic condition or major psychotic disorder (i.e., schizophrenia or bipolar disorder). Zanarini et al. found that 60% of their BPD cohort met *DSM-III* criteria for ASPD. When compared with the control group, those diagnosed as borderlines, as expected, were significantly more likely than those in the dysthymic OPD control group and significantly less likely than those in the antisocial control group to have met the *DSM-III* criteria for ASPD. In terms of Axis I disorders, both unipolar affective disorders and substance use disorders were common among patients with borderline and antisocial diagnoses. However, dysthymic disorder was significantly more common among patients with a borderline than an antisocial diagnosis. In contrast, both alcohol abuse/dependence and drug abuse/dependence were significantly more common among those with antisocial rather than borderline diagnoses. (See Cloninger, Bayon, & Przybeck, Chapter 2, this volume, for further discussion of the Axis I comorbidity of ASPD.)

Coid (1993) studied the Axis II phenomenology of 72 female inpatients in England who met *DSM-III* criteria for BPD using the Structured Clinical Interview for *DSM-III* Axis II Disorders (SCID II; Spitzer & Williams, 1983). He found that 49% of his sample met *DSM* criteria for antisocial personality disorder.

As previously mentioned, four other studies have assessed the comorbidity of all Axis II disorders in samples of nonpsychotic patients. In the first of these studies, Dahl (1986) assessed the Axis II psychopathology of 103 inpatients, many of whom had drug problems and had been transferred from prison, using two semistructured interviews and relevant clinical information. He found that 20% of these patients met *DSM-III* criteria for BPD and 18% met the *DSM-III* criteria for ASPD. He also found that 68% of his patients diagnosed as borderline met *DSM-III* criteria for ASPD but that 77% of his patients diagnosed as antisocial met *DSM-III* criteria for BPD.

Pfohl, Coryell, Zimmerman, and Strangl (1986) assessed the Axis II status of 131 patients using a semistructured interview. Of the 67 patients who met criteria for at least one personality disorder, 43% met *DSM-III* criteria for BPD and 8% met *DSM-III* criteria for ASPD. These authors also found that 14% of their patients diagnosed as borderline met criteria for ASPD and 80% of their patients diagnosed as antisocial met criteria for BPD.

Morey (1988) asked a group of clinicians to fill out a questionnaire rating the presence of the *DSM-III-R* criteria for 11 Axis II disorders in 291 of their personality-disordered patients. He found that 33% of these patients met the *DSM-III-R* criteria for BPD and 6% met the *DSM-III-R* criteria for ASPD. He also found that 8% of his patients diagnosed as borderline met *DSM-III-R* criteria for ASPD but that 44% of his patients diagnosed as antisocial met *DSM-III-R* criteria for BPD.

Oldham and his associates (1992) assessed the Axis II status of 100 applicants for long-term inpatient treatment of severe personality pathology using two semistructured interviews. They found that 62% to 64% of the patients met *DSM-III-R* criteria for BPD and 7% to 9% met *DSM-III-R* criteria for ASPD. They also found no co-occurrence between these two disorders.

Taken together, the results of these studies suggest varying degrees of comorbidity between BPD and ASPD. In studies focusing on criteria-defined BPD samples, rates of ASPD comorbidity ranged from 0% to 60%, with most studies reporting rates of co-occurrence between about 10% and 25%. In studies focusing solely on rates of Axis II comorbidity in samples of nonpsychotic patients, a substantially smaller percentage of patients meeting criteria for BPD also met criteria for ASPD than those meeting criteria for ASPD showed co-occurring BPD.

Some of the differences noted seem to be due to socioeconomic status (SES) factors. More specifically, Zanarini et al., Coid, and Dahl all found very high rates of comorbidity and each was studying lower SES samples. In contrast, no comorbidity was found by Frances et al. and Oldham et al., both of whom were studying subjects attempting to gain admission to highly selective clinical services specializing in psychodynamically oriented treatment.

Some of the differences noted also seem to be due to the overall nature of the sample involved and how it was gathered. More specifically, the high rates of co-occurrence found in samples that were not designed with mutually exclusive (or hierarchically ordered) patient groups may have been a result of the research finding that the *DSM-III* and *DSM-III-R* criteria sets for BPD may be too inclusive (Zanarini, Gunderson, Frankenburg, Chauncey, & Glutting, 1991). Put another way, the many patients diagnosed as antisocial who met criteria for BPD in the studies of Dahl, Pfohl et al., and Morey may not have been core borderline patients but patients with borderline features.

FAMILY HISTORY OF PSYCHIATRIC DISORDER

To date, six studies have been published that assessed a range of psychiatric disorders in the first-degree relatives of patients diagnosed as borderline meeting modern research criteria for BPD. In the first of these studies, Loranger, Oldham, and Tulis (1982) studied the family history of 83 female patients diagnosed as borderline, 100 female patients diagnosed as bipolar, and 100 female patients diagnosed as schizophrenic who had been hospitalized at the Westchester division of New York Hospital between 1976 and 1980. Two raters reviewed the charts of all appropriate female patients and selected those who unequivocally met *DSM-III* criteria for their respective disorders. Two other raters, who were blind to proband diagnosis, then reviewed the chart information on the 188 parents, siblings, and children of these patients who had been treated for some type of emotional disorder and assigned diagnoses of borderline personality disorder, bipolar disorder, schizo-

phrenia, and major depression. It should be noted that whereas the criteria sets for the Axis I disorders were somewhat less stringent than those found in *DSM-III*, the criteria set used to diagnose BPD in treated relatives was far more encompassing than that found in *DSM-III* (i.e., only two of the following criteria were required: emotional, dramatic, demanding, problem with anger, sexual acting out, antisocial behavior, physically self-damaging acts, substance abuse, physical violence). Loranger et al. found that the first-degree relatives of these borderline probands had a morbid risk of 11.7% of being treated for borderline personality disorder. They also found that the morbid risk of being treated for BPD among the first-degree relatives of borderline probands was significantly higher than that found for the relatives of those in either control group. It is unclear from the criteria set used to define BPD, however, whether BPD "breeds true" in these families or is an admixture of BPD and ASPD, as four of the nine criteria used to define familial BPD are more commonly associated with ASPD (sexual acting out, antisocial behavior, substance abuse, and physical violence).

Pope and his McLean associates (1983) also studied the family histories of their borderline sample. A research psychiatrist, blind to all information about the proband, reviewed the chart of each BPD patient and assigned *DSM-III* diagnoses, where appropriate, to all first-degree relatives. The charts of 34 members of a bipolar control group and 39 members of a schizophrenic control group were reviewed in a similar manner. Pope et al. found that 6.2% of the 130 first-degree relatives of the borderline patients met criteria for antisocial personality disorder.

Soloff and Millward (1983) studied the family histories of 48 patients with a borderline diagnosis, 42 with schizophrenia, and 32 patients with unipolar depression who were between the ages of 16 and 36. Family histories were obtained by social workers. Of the data, 43% were gathered through interviews of the patient and family members; 57% were obtained through retrospective chart review. Soloff and Millward found that 7% of the first-degree relatives of the patients with borderline personality disorder had a history of antisocial behavior.

Links, Steiner, and Huxley (1988) also collected family history data on 69 of their borderline cohort of 88 (78%) using RDC criteria. Information was obtained on 320 family members: 36% were interviewed directly and 64% were diagnosed based on indirect data. Links et al. found that 15.3% of the first-degree relatives of their patients diagnosed as borderline were at risk for BPD, and 9.6% were at risk for ASPD.

Zanarini, Gunderson, Marino, Schwartz, and Frankenburg (1988) also collected family history data on their cohort of 50 patients diagnosed as borderline, 29 in an antisocial control group, and 26 in a dysthymic OPD control group by interviewing the proband using a semistructured interview based on *DSM-III* criteria. All told, information was collected on 488 first-degree relatives. Zanarini et al. found that 24.9% of the first-degree relatives of the 48 BPD patients (2 of the sample of 50 were adopted and had no knowledge about their biological relatives) were at risk for BPD and 13.6% were at risk for ASPD. Zanarini et al. also found that a significantly higher percentage of the first-degree relatives of borderline probands were at risk for BPD than the relatives of those in either control group. In addition, the first-degree relatives of BPD patients were at greater risk than the first-degree relatives of antisocial patients of developing both major depression and dysthymic disorder. However, there were no significant differences in the risk of developing either alcohol abuse/dependence or drug abuse/dependence. In contrast, the risk of developing ASPD was substantially greater in the first-degree relatives of ASPD (21.4%) than BPD patients (13.6%).

Schulz and her colleagues (1989) studied the family histories of 26 inpatients diagnosed as borderline who met both DIB and *DSM-III* criteria for BPD (but did not meet criteria for ASPD) and compared them with the family histories of 59 controls diagnosed as schizophrenic. All borderline and schizophrenic probands were interviewed about their families using the family history version of the RDC criteria. In addition, at least one relative of each schizophrenic patient and at least one relative of 42% of the borderline probands were interviewed using the same criteria. Schulz et al. found that 7.5% of the first-degree relatives of the BPD patients met criteria for ASPD. Schulz et al. also found that relatives of those with borderline personality disorder had significantly higher prevalence rates of antisocial personality disorder than the relatives of the controls with schizophrenia.

Taken together, the results of these studies suggest a strong familial link between BPD and ASPD. More specifically, these studies indicate that about 1 out of every 11 first-degree relatives of borderline probands meets the research criteria for antisocial personality disorder, even in Schulz et al.'s study, which specifically excluded borderline probands who met criteria for ASPD. The rate of antisocial personality disorder found among the relatives of borderline probands also was higher than that found in the relatives of those in all control groups other than antisocial patients themselves. Additionally, Loranger et al. found that BPD is significantly more common among the first-degree relatives of borderlines than controls. However, many of Loranger et al.'s group of relatives fitting the BPD criteria may well have had antisocial personality disorder rather than borderline personality disorder, given the strong antisocial trend in their criteria set for familial BPD.

CHILDHOOD ANTECEDENTS

Over time, a number of childhood factors have been associated with the development of borderline personality disorder (see Zanarini, 1996, for a review of this topic). Initially, researchers focused on early separations and losses. Then they focused on difficulties in parental bonding, often finding that borderline patients reported that their parents were emotionally uninvolved with them. More recently, numerous studies have found that a high percentage of borderline patients report a childhood history of physical or sexual abuse. Typically the prevalence of physical abuse is not discriminating from that reported by controls but the history of sexual abuse is. Similar patterns of neglect and abuse have also been found in the childhoods of ASPD patients (Robins, 1966). (See Widom, Chapter 16, this volume, for a further discussion of the childhood experiences of individuals with ASPD.)

Only Zanarini, Gunderson, Marino, Schwartz, and Frankenburg (1989) have studied a full range of the childhood experiences of both borderline and antisocial patients. In this study, BPD

patients reported the following rates of parental abuse and neglect: 72% verbal abuse, 46% physical abuse, 26% sexual abuse, 24% physical neglect, 56% emotional withdrawal, and 48% inconsistent treatment. ASPD patients also reported substantial rates of neglect and abuse: 31% verbal abuse, 28% physical abuse, 7% sexual abuse, 17% physical neglect, 28% emotional withdrawal, and 35% inconsistent treatment. Only verbal abuse and emotional withdrawal significantly distinguished BPD patients from ASPD patients. However, overall rates of both abuse and neglect were reported by a significantly higher percentage of BPD than ASPD patients, suggesting that BPD patients may have experienced more cumulative pathological experiences than ASPD patients.

COURSE AND OUTCOME

Although borderline personality disorder is a topic of intense clinical interest and empirical research, relatively little is known about its course and outcome. To date, the results of nine small-scale, prospective studies of the short-term course and outcome of BPD and the results of four large-scale, follow-back studies of the long-term course and outcome of BPD have been published (see Zanarini, Chauncey, Grady, & Gunderson, 1991, for a review of these studies). In general, these short-term studies have found that most borderline patients continue to have substantial difficulty functioning both socially and vocationally 2 to 7 years after their initial evaluation. In addition, they tend to remain highly symptomatic and to need continuing psychiatric care.

In contrast, the results of these long-term studies have usually been interpreted to mean that the average patient with borderline personality disorder is functioning reasonably well a mean of 14 to 16 years after his or her index admission. However, a closer look at the results of these studies reveals that only one half to three quarters of these patients were functioning well and as many as 9% to 10% of those traced had committed suicide.

Longitudinal studies of the course of ASPD have also yielded optimistic views of the course of this disorder. Robins (1966), for example, has found that 2% of patients with antisocial personality disorder remit each year after the age of 30.

Only one short-term, prospective study and none of the long-term, follow-back studies, however, have concurrently assessed the course of BPD and ASPD. Perry and Cooper (1985) reported that both patients with borderline and antisocial disorder function in the fair range when assessed several years after their baseline assessment. In terms of BPD/ASPD comorbidity, Stone (1990) reported that patients diagnosed as borderline with a concomitant antisocial diagnosis have a worse long-term course than those without antisocial features. In contrast, McGlashan and Heinssen (1989) found that antisocial features do not worsen the long-term course of BPD.

UNDERLYING TEMPERAMENT
AND PERSONALITY DIMENSIONS

If Hippocrates were alive today, he would surely suggest that persons with both borderline and antisocial disorder suffer a choleric (i.e., irritable, impulsive) temperament. Modern psychiatrists have resumed the search for underlying biological dispositions to personality. Siever and Davis (1991) are among those who see both disorders as linked by a personality dimension of anger or impulsivity. This dimension of personality is tied to disturbed neurophysiological regulation of serotonin, a disturbance validated by Cocarro and his associates (1989). Cloninger has made another and quite original effort to define basic temperaments (Cloninger, 1987). He predicted that the impulsivity characteristic of those with antisocial and borderline disorders would make them high on his Novelty Seeking temperament. Recent research has now confirmed that both those with borderline and those with antisocial disorders score high on Novelty Seeking (Svrakic, Cloninger, Przybeck, & Whitehead, 1993). This work has also shown that those with ASPD are low on the temperament of Harm Avoidance whereas those with BPD are high. Moreover, those with ASPD also are very low (much lower than normal persons and those with BPD) on the temperament of Reward Dependence. Both diagnostic groups score notably and similarly low on the character variables of being Self-directed and being Cooperative.

Other approaches to defining how underlying dimensions of personality relate to its disorders have approached the issue from a descriptive view that is tied to neither clinical observations nor biological theory. An example is Livesley's (1987; Livesley, Jackson, & Schroeder, 1989) factor analytic search of the *DSM-III-R* personality disorder criteria for their underlying dimensions, a process he refers to as *construct validation*. He concludes that the underlying dimension of personality pathology that ASPD and BPD share is interpersonal exploitation. In contrast, the ASPD patients did not have the instability dimension (of self-concept, moods, and relationships) that typified BPD patients. Livesley's work, unfortunately, largely has been on nonclinical samples. There is clearly a need for much more research of this type. Such work might identify features that clarify the distinctions between these disorders or identify more basic underlying personality dimensions that are shared by both categories.

Studies that deploy factor-analytically derived typologies of the dimensions in normal personality that depart from the *DSM* criteria sets have been used to examine similarities and distinctions between personality disorders. The most widely commented on is the five-factor model popularized by Costa and McCrae (1990, 1992). These five dimensions are Neuroticism, Extraversion, Openness, Agreeableness, and Conscientiousness. Neuroticism, originating in the early seminal work by Eysenck (1947), refers to being anxious, self-conscious, temperamental, moody, and impulsive. Studies of personality disorder samples have demonstrated such high Neuroticism scores for BPD (Costa & McCrae, 1990; Trull, Widiger, & Guthrie, 1990) that Trull and his colleagues have suggested that BPD be reconceptualized as an extreme variant of this normally occurring set of traits. These studies have also shown that ASPD and BPD share a particularly low score on the dimension of Agreeableness.

Yet another perspective derives from the so-called circumplex models of personality and psychopathology. These models derive from an emphasis on dysfunctional interpersonal patterns as the defining or at least highly significant basis for categorizing personality psychopathology. Developed by Sullivan (1953), these models have been adapted and applied to personality by others such as Leary (1957), Kiesler (1983), Millon (1981), Wiggins (1982), and Benjamin (1993). Typically such models classify personality types on dimensions with pathological extremes (e.g., very dominant vs. very submissive or very intrusive vs. very reclusive). Of importance is that studies have generally failed to locate the interpersonal styles of BPD and ASPD patients in closely related sectors (see Pincus & Wiggins, 1990; Strack, Lorr, & Campbell, 1990). The person with an antisocial personality is generally seen as distant, distrustful, and dominant, whereas those with a borderline personality are seen as intensely involved, dependent, and volatile.

SUBSYNDROMAL PHENOMENOLOGY

Until recently little research was conducted that dealt with the specific clinical features that distinguished borderline personality disorder patients from antisocial personality disorder patients. Zanarini, Gunderson, Frankenburg, and Chauncey (1990) compared 120 criteria-defined BPD patients with 103 Axis II control group members on the 22 summary statements of the DIB-R. These authors found that 4 of the 22 features were common in but nondiscriminating for borderline disorder, 11 were discriminating for but nonspecific to borderline disorder, and 7 were more specific to borderline disorder. These seven features are quasipsychotic thought (transient, circumscribed delusions or hallucinations); self-mutilation; manipulative suicide efforts; concerns with abandonment, engulfment, or annihilation (fears of being left, smothered, or destroyed by interpersonal contact); demandingness or entitlement; treatment regression (feeling substantially worse or behaving in a substantially more maladaptive manner as a result of psychiatric treatment); and countertransference difficulties (arousing intense loving or rejecting feelings in the psychiatric staff). These authors conclude that many clinical features thought to be indicative of borderline disorder are better viewed as personality-disordered traits and that the seven more specific features, alone or in conjunction with one another, may be particularly useful markers for borderline personality disorder.

More recently, Zanarini, Dubo, Zornberg, Majcher, and Haynes (1992) reported on a closer examination of this sample of 223 personality-disordered patients. Of the 103 members of a control group, 53 met *DSM-III* criteria for antisocial personality disorder and 50 met *DSM-III* criteria for another form of personality disorder. (The results that follow pertain only to those patients who met criteria for BPD or ASPD.) As expected, a significantly higher percentage of the BPD group than the ASPD group was female (73% vs. 19%).

BPD and ASPD patients were compared on the prevalence of the 22 symptomatic areas assessed by the DIB-R. A significantly higher percentage of borderline personality than antisocial personality patients reported being symptomatic in 19 of the 22 areas of psychopathology associated with BPD. The only areas of symptomatology that were found equally commonly in borderline personality and antisocial personality patients were sexual deviance (usually promiscuity), other impulsive patterns (not including sexuality, substance abuse, self-mutilation, and suicidality), and interpersonal problems with devaluation, manipulation, or sadism.

BPD and ASPD patients also were compared on the prevalence of the 21 *DSM-III* criteria for antisocial personality disorder. Nine of the 12 juvenile criteria for ASPD and 6 of the 9 adult criteria for ASPD were significantly more common among patients with an antisocial personality than a borderline personality. Only the juvenile criteria of academic underachievement, running away from home, and persistent lying as well as the adult criteria of poor work record, failure to plan ahead, and irresponsible parenting failed to significantly discriminate between the two groups.

Because these results indicated relatively high rates of many antisocial behaviors among BPD patients, it was decided to assess the differences between those with borderline personalities who did and those who did not meet *DSM-III* criteria for ASPD. Of the BPD patients 59% did not meet these criteria, but 41% did meet them.

Patients with pure borderline personalities were significantly more likely to be female (86%) than those in either the BPD/ASPD (55%) or the ASPD group (19%). Patients with an antisocial and borderline personality also were significantly more likely to be female than those with a pure antisocial personality.

The three groups were then compared on the 22 summary statements of the DIB-R and the 21 *DSM-III* criteria for antisocial personality disorder. Those with pure ASPD were significantly less likely than those with pure BPD or BPD/ASPD to be symptomatic in 18 of the 22 areas of borderline psychopathology measured by the DIB-R. In contrast, only substance abuse/dependence; stormy relationships; and devaluation, manipulation, or sadism significantly distinguished between pure BPD and BPD/ASPD.

Those with a pure borderline personality were significantly less likely to meet each of the 12 juvenile criteria for ASPD than those with an antisocial and borderline personality or a pure antisocial personality. They were also significantly less likely to meet eight of nine adult criteria than those with BPD/ASPD and those with pure ASPD. In contrast, only one juvenile criterion (initiation of fistfights) significantly distinguished between those with BPD/ASPD and those with pure ASPD.

The data comparing the samples of those with borderline and those with antisocial personalities on the criteria for either of these disorders dramatically demonstrate their distinctiveness. Indeed, it was the exceptional criterion for either of these disorders that failed to demonstrate the expected difference in a highly significant way. Two of the three DIB-R borderline criteria that failed to distinguish them involved the dimension of impulsivity common to both disorders, that is, sexual promiscuity and "other impulsive patterns" (e.g., eating binges, spending sprees, verbal outbursts). Similarly, the only antisocial criteria that failed to differentiate those with antisocial from those with borderline personalities involved some finer tuned discrimination of types of impulsive action. Specifically, as adults, both patients with ASPD and those with BPD were characterized equally by a poor work record, failure to plan ahead, and being abusive or neglectful toward their children. In other respects, however, the impulsive pattern of the antisocial patients could be distinguished quite easily.

The juvenile criteria for ASPD distinguished the ASPD sample from the BPD sample on some specific antisocial actions such as thefts, fistfights, and trouble with the law that might relate to impulsivity. As was noted during the *DSM-IV* development

process, some of these juvenile criteria include gender-biased issues that may not do justice to the types of antisocial behaviors more common in females. In this respect, the childhoods of those with BPD were frequented equally by the juvenile criteria related to underachievement, running away from home, and lying. We believe these areas of phenomenological overlap during development reflect the similarities in unstable and abusive families within which both disorders have been shown to develop. In general, the areas of overlap were congruent with expectations and the prevailing areas of distinction suggested that these criteria sets identified two very different populations.

Because of the overwhelmingly high levels of distinction between the antisocial personality and borderline personality populations on their own criteria sets, the more interesting observations from this study may relate to the very high frequency with which patients meet criteria for both. This high level of overlap indicates that despite the high levels of discrimination found by deploying the criteria sets, these disorders have areas of commonality not represented by their criteria.

Examination of the demographics suggests that, as expected, these diagnostic categories are highly gender related; that is, the BPD group was 73% female whereas the ASPD group was 81% male. The pure BPD group was 86% female, whereas the pure antisocial group was only 19% female. The mixed group was 55% female and 45% male. Insofar as both disorders arise from dysfunctional, unstable families with frequent exposure to abuse and substance abuse, the source of these marked gender differences will probably be found in gender-based genetic or social influences. (For a further discussion of the gender issues involved in the antisocial diagnosis, see Giordano & Cernkovich, Chapter 46, this volume.)

The common observation that infant boys are more instrumental and infant girls are more affiliative may reflect dispositions that, other things being equal, incline the males toward later psychopathology being evidenced in outward-directed aggression, whereas for females the equivalent psychopathology is evidenced in inward-directed aggression and interpersonal struggles. In this regard, we have previously documented the high frequency with which pre-BPD patients report childhood reliance on transitional objects and how this contrasts with their relative absence in the developmental histories of ASPD patients (Morris, Gunderson, & Zanarini, 1986).

DIFFERENTIAL DIAGNOSIS

Differential diagnosis of this mixed group poses a significant problem because the two diagnoses carry different clinical implications. It is easy for clinicians to ignore the self-mutilation in males who meet criteria for an antisocial personality, and it is equally easy for them to ignore dishonesty in the woman who meets criteria for a borderline personality. Yet the presence of the mutilation often indicates that the male patient might better be conceptualized and treated as having borderline psychopathology, whereas the presence of the dishonesty might suggest that the female patient is better conceptualized and treated as having an antisocial personality disorder. We have observed that from a public health point of view, the failure to recognize antisocial personality characteristics in BPD patients often results in prolonged, unproductive, and even destructive treatment. On the other hand, the failure to recognize the borderline personality qualities in persons with ASPD who are placed in forensic institutions provides the background for some of their most recurrent and vexing management problems (e.g., rageful jealousies, hypochondriasis, and suicide attempts).

Three vignettes may best express the differences among these three groups. The first vignette deals with a pure BPD patient, the second vignette with a pure ASPD patient, and the third with a patient with mixed BPD/ASPD.

Vignette 1

Ms. A is a 28-year-old single woman. She has experienced feelings of dysphoria and anger as well as stormy relationships since childhood. As she grew older, she began to experience people as being mean to her and giving her an unnecessarily hard time. She often experienced feelings of depersonalization (feeling unreal) and derealization (feeling the world is unreal) as well. In addition, she was chronically concerned that people she was dependent on would abandon her. She also began to threaten suicide when things seemed like they would never get better and she could no longer bear her emotional pain. Although she was very hard working and achievement oriented, she sometimes hid what was actually going on with her or embellished the truth of her life.

Vignette 2

Mr. B is a 24-year-old single man. He began stealing, vandalizing property, and assaulting other children when he was only 8. These behaviors continued in adolescence. In adulthood, he was unable to hold a steady job, sold drugs and ran an insurance scam, repeatedly was arrested for driving under the influence, and showed little remorse for his actions, justifying them as "what a guy has to do to survive in a world of fools."

Vignette 3

Mr. C is a 49-year-old married man. As a boy, he frequently skipped school, stole from his family and neighbors, and started fistfights. As an adolescent, he began to feel very unhappy and worthless and dealt with these feelings by cutting himself and overdosing. These self-destructive behaviors continued into adult life and were joined by intense fears that his wife would abandon him. Although he worked steadily at a responsible job, he also worked as a bookmaker to bolster his self-esteem, as he felt it was the only thing at which he had ever excelled.

Perhaps an even better way to make the distinction between BPD and ASPD, particularly in patients with features of both disorders, is their style of presentation. More specifically, Zanarini and Frankenburg (1994) have suggested that a pattern of emotional hypochondriasis underlies the urgent presentation common to BPD patients. ASPD patients, in contrast, are not insistent on

their pain being recognized and tend to deny that they are in any type of pain or discomfort.

THERAPY IMPLICATIONS

We believe that patients who meet criteria for both of these disorders are better understood and treated as if the borderline diagnosis were the dominant (i.e., hierarchically more significant) designation. In the first place, this honors the basic principle that patients deserve to have a trial of treatment that may be helpful. Having stated this, it is important to recognize that the assessment of treatability involves a complex process that the descriptive features address only partly. Of great importance is whether the patient evidences (not primarily in words) a hunger for getting attached to others. It is also critical to evaluate whether the person has a capacity to bare unpleasant feelings, especially sadness, shame, guilt, or envy. Third are the ASPD/BPD patient's social supports. Are there allies who support the need for the patient to change or are there only neglectful or indifferent family members? Do the patients profess or adhere to socially important values such as work or charity? Affirmative responses in these nondescriptive characteristics of a patient fulfilling criteria for both ASPD and BPD will go a long way toward indicating whether an individual is likely to respond to treatment.

Once an attachment has been initiated for ASPD/BPD patients, clinicians need to remain careful about monitoring their progress. It is important but difficult for the clinician to be able to comfortably identify such patients' failure to get emotionally involved, interpersonally attached, or show evidence of learning. It sometimes is difficult to predict without treatment trials. Many clinicians have a biased view because the cases that do not work are the most evident, whereas those that succeed disappear from view. (For a discussion of the treatment of antisocial offenders, see Rice & Harris, Chapter 40, this volume.)

CONCLUSIONS

Patients with BPD often meet criteria for comorbid ASPD or exhibit strong antisocial personality trends. There is also overlap in their family patterns of psychopathology. In addition, there are similarities in their pathological childhood experiences, the course of their disorder, and their basic underlying temperaments. Recent research has found that a third group seems to meet the full criteria for both BPD and ASPD. Whether this represents a third disorder or only a variation on the borderline personality theme is not yet known. However, it may be that BPD and ASPD (along with substance use disorders and eating disorders) are both part of the impulse disorder spectrum (Zanarini, 1993).

DIRECTIONS FOR FUTURE RESEARCH

The research reviewed here suggests that BPD and ASPD are separate and distinct disorders. It also suggests, however, that a significant subgroup meets the criteria for both disorders. Further research needs to be conducted into the similarities and differences among those with pure ASPD, those with pure BPD, and those meeting criteria for both disorders. Particularly important are studies of the longitudinal course and treatment response of these three subgroups of patients. Further research focusing on core ASPD patients and their degree of overlap with BPD patients in all of the areas reviewed also is necessary.

REFERENCES

Akiskal, H. S. (1981). Subaffective disorders: Dysthymic, cyclothymic and bipolar II disorders in the "borderline" realm. *Psychiatric Clinics of North America, 4*, 25–46.

American Psychiatric Association. (1980). *Diagnostic and statistical manual of mental disorders* (3rd ed.). Washington, DC: Author.

American Psychiatric Association. (1987). *Diagnostic and statistical manual of mental disorders* (3rd ed., rev.). Washington, DC: Author.

American Psychiatric Association. (1994). *Diagnostic and statistical manual of mental disorders* (4th ed.). Washington, DC: Author.

Andrulonis, P. A., & Vogel, N. G. (1984). Comparison of borderline personality subcategories to schizophrenic and affective disorders. *British Journal of Psychiatry, 44*, 358–363.

Benjamin, L. S. (1993). *Interpersonal diagnosis and treatment of personality disorders.* New York: Guilford.

Cloninger, C. R. (1987). A systematic method for clinical description and classification of personality variants. *Archives of General Psychiatry, 44*, 573–588.

Cloninger, C. R., Przybeck, T. R., & Svrakic, D. M. (1993). A psychobiological model of temperament and character. *Archives of General Psychiatry, 50*, 975–990.

Coccaro, E. F., Siever, L. J., Klar, H. M., Maurer, G., Cochrane, K. I., Cooper, T. B., Mohs, R. C., & Davis, K. L. (1989). Serotonergic studies in patients with affective and personality disorders: Correlations with suicidal and impulsive aggressive behavior. *Archives of General Psychiatry, 35*, 837–862.

Coid, J. W. (1993). An affective syndrome in psychopaths with borderline personality disorder. *British Journal of Psychiatry, 216*, 641–650.

Costa, P. T., & McCrae, R. R. (1990). Personality disorders and the five-factor model of personality. *Journal of Personality Disorders, 4*, 362–371.

Costa, P. T., & McCrae, R. R. (1992). The five-factor model of personality and its relevance to personality disorders. *Journal of Personality Disorders, 6*, 343–359.

Dahl, A. A. (1986). Some aspects of the *DSM-III* personality disorders illustrated by a consecutive sample of hospitalized patients. *Acta Psychiatrica Scandinavica Suppl., 328*, 61–67.

Endicott, J., & Spitzer, R. L. (1978). A diagnostic interview: The schedule for affective disorders and schizophrenia. *Archives of General Psychiatry, 35*, 837–862.

Eysenck, H. J. (1947). *The dimensions of personality.* London: Kegan Paul, Trench & Trubner.

Frances, A., Clarkin, J. F., Gilmore, M., Hurt, S. W., & Brown, R. (1984). Reliability of criteria for borderline personality disorder: A comparison of *DSM-III* and the Diagnostic Interview for Borderline Patients. *American Journal of Psychiatry, 141*, 1080–1084.

Gunderson, J. G., & Kolb, J. E. (1978). Discriminating features of borderline patients. *American Journal of Psychiatry, 135*, 792–796.

Gunderson, J. G., Kolb, J. E., & Austin, V. (1981). The diagnostic interview for borderlines. *American Journal of Psychiatry, 138*, 896–903.

Gunderson, J. G., & Links, P. (1995). Treatment of borderline personality disorder. In G. Gabbard (Ed.), *Treatments of psychiatric disorders: The DSM-IV edition* (pp. 2291–2309). Washington, DC: American Psychiatric Press.

Gunderson, J. G., & Singer, M. T. (1975). Defining borderline patients: An overview. *American Journal of Psychiatry, 132*, 1–10.

Kernberg, O. (1975). *Borderline conditions and pathological narcissism.* New York: Jason Aronson.

Kiesler, D. J. (1983). The 1982 interpersonal circle: A taxonomy for complementarity in human transactions. *Psychological Review, 90*, 185–214.

Leary, T. (1957). *Interpersonal diagnosis of personality.* New York: Guilford.

Links, P. S., Steiner, M., & Huxley, G. (1988). The occurrence of borderline personality disorder in the families of borderline patients. *Journal of Personality Disorders, 2*, 14–20.

Links, P. S., Steiner, M., Offord, D. R., & Eppel, A. (1988). Characteristics of borderline personality disorder: A Canadian study. *Canadian Journal of Psychiatry, 33*, 336–340.

Livesley, W. J. (1987). A systematic approach to the delineation of personality disorders. *American Journal of Psychiatry, 44*, 772–777.

Livesley, W. J., Jackson, D. N., & Schroeder, M. L. (1989). A study of the factorial structure of personality pathology. *Journal of Personality Disorders, 3*, 292–306.

Loranger, A. W., Oldham, J. M., & Tulis, E. H. (1982). Familial transmission of *DSM-III* borderline personality disorder. *Archives of General Psychiatry, 39*, 795–799.

McGlashan, T. H. (1983). The borderline syndrome: II. Is it a variant of schizophrenia or affective disorder? *Archives of General Psychiatry, 40*, 1319–1323.

McGlashan, T. H., & Heinssen, R. K. (1989). Narcissistic, antisocial, and noncomorbid subgroups of borderline disorder: Are they distinct entities by long-term clinical profile? *Psychiatric Clinics of North America, 12*, 653–670.

Millon, T. (1981). *Disorders of personality.* New York: Wiley.

Morey, L. C. (1988). Personality disorders in *DSM-III* and *DSM-III-R*: Convergence, coverage, and internal consistency. *American Journal of Psychiatry, 145*, 573–577.

Morris, H., Gunderson, J. G., & Zanarini, M. C. (1986). Transitional object use and borderline psychopathology. *American Journal of Psychiatry, 143*, 1534–1538.

Oldham, J. M., Skodol, A. E., Kellman, H. D., Hyler, S. E., Rosnick, L., & Davies, M. (1992). Diagnosis of *DSM-III-R* personality disorders by two structured interviews: Patterns of comorbidity. *American Journal of Psychiatry, 149*, 213–220.

Perry, J. C., & Cooper, S. H. (1985). Psychodynamics, symptoms, and outcome in borderline and antisocial personality disorders and bipolar type II affective disorder. In T. H. McGlashan (Ed.), *The borderline: Current empirical research* (pp. 21–41). Washington, DC: American Psychiatric Press.

Pfohl, B., Coryell, W., Zimmerman, M., & Stangl, D. (1986). *DSM-III* personality disorders: Diagnostic overlap and internal consistency of individual *DSM-III* criteria. *Comprehensive Psychiatry, 27*, 21–34.

Pincus, A. L., & Wiggins, J. S. (1990). Interpersonal problems and conceptions of personality disorders. *Journal of Personality Disorders, 4*, 342–352.

Pope, H. G., Jonas, J. M., Hudson, J. I., Cohen, B. M., & Gunderson, J. G. (1983). The validity of *DSM-III* borderline personality disorder. A phenomenologic, family history, treatment response, and long-term follow-up study. *Archives of General Psychiatry, 40,* 23–30.

Robins, E., & Guze, S. B. (1970). Establishment of diagnostic validity in psychiatric illness: Its application to schizophrenia. *American Journal of Psychiatry, 126,* 983–987.

Robins, L. N. (1966). *Deviant children grown up.* Baltimore: Williams & Wilkins.

Robins, L. N., Helzer, J. E., Croughan, J., & Ratcliff, K. S. (1981). National Institute of Mental Health Diagnostic Interview Schedule: Its history, characteristics, and validity. *Archives of General Psychiatry, 38,* 381–389.

Schulz, P. M., Soloff, P. H., Kelly, T., Morgenstern, M., Di Franco, R., & Schulz, S. C. (1989). A family history of borderline subtypes. *Journal of Personality Disorders, 3,* 217–229.

Siever, L. J., & Davis, K. L. (1991). A psychobiological perspective on the personality disorders. *American Journal of Psychiatry, 148,* 1647–1658.

Soloff, P. H., & Millward, J. W. (1983). Psychiatric disorders in the families of borderline patients. *Archives of General Psychiatry, 40,* 37–44.

Spitzer, R. L., Endicott, J., & Robins, E. (1978). Research diagnostic criteria: Rationale and reliability. *Archives of General Psychiatry, 35,* 773–779.

Spitzer, R. L., & Williams, J. B. W. (1983). *Structured clinical interview for* DSM-III *Axis II disorders.* New York: New York State Psychiatric Institute.

Spitzer, R. L., & Williams, J. B. W. (1984). *Structured clinical interview for* DSM-III *Axis I disorders.* New York: New York State Psychiatric Institute.

Stone, M. H. (1990). *The fate of borderline patients.* New York: Guilford.

Strack, S., Lorr, M., & Campbell, L. (1990). An evaluation of Millon's circular model of personality disorders. *Journal of Personality Disorders, 4,* 353–361.

Sullivan, H. S. (1953). *The interpersonal theory of psychiatry.* New York: Norton.

Svrakic, D. M., Cloninger, C. R., Przybeck, T. R., & Whitehead, C. (1993). Differential diagnosis of personality disorders by the seven-factor model of temperament and character. *Archives of General Psychiatry, 40,* 991–999.

Trull, T. J., Widiger, T. A., & Guthrie, P. (1990). The categorical versus dimensional status of borderline personality disorder. *Journal of Abnormal Psychology, 99,* 40–48.

Wiggins, J. S. (1982). Circumplex models of interpersonal behavior in clinical psychology. In P. S. Kendall & J. N. Butcher (Eds.), *Handbook of research methods in clinical psychology* (pp. 183–221). New York: Wiley.

Zanarini, M. C. (1993). BPD as an impulse spectrum disorder. In J. Paris (Ed.), *Borderline personality disorder: Etiology and treatment* (pp. 67–85). Washington, DC: American Psychiatric Press.

Zanarini, M. C. (1996). Evolving perspectives on the etiology of borderline personality disorder. In M. C. Zanarini (Ed.), *Role of sexual abuse in the etiology of borderline personality disorder* (pp. 1–16). Washington, DC: American Psychiatric Press.

Zanarini, M. C., Chauncey, D. L., Grady, T. A., & Gunderson, J. G. (1991). Outcome studies of borderline personality disorder. In S. Mirin, J. Gossett, & M. C. Grob (Eds.), *Psychiatric treatment: Recent advances in outcome research* (pp. 181–194). Washington, DC: American Psychiatric Press.

Zanarini, M. C., Dubo, E. D., Zornberg, G., Majcher, D., & Haynes, K. (1992, May). *Who is antisocial: The effect of criteria change* [Abstract 76E]. Proceedings of the 145th annual meeting of the American Psychiatric Association, Washington, DC.

Zanarini, M. C., & Frankenburg, F. R. (1994). Emotional hypochondriasis, hyperbole, and the borderline patient. *Journal of Psychotherapy Practice and Research, 3,* 25–36.

Zanarini, M. C., Frankenburg, F. R., Chauncey, D. L., & Gunderson, J. G. (1987). The diagnostic interview for personality disorders: Interrater and test-retest reliability. *Comprehensive Psychiatry, 28,* 467–480.

Zanarini, M. C., Gunderson, J. G., & Frankenburg, F. R. (1989). Axis I phenomenology of borderline personality disorder. *Comprehensive Psychiatry, 30,* 149–156.

Zanarini, M. C., Gunderson, J. G., Frankenburg, F. R., & Chauncey, D. L. (1989). The revised diagnostic interview for borderlines: Discriminating BPD from other Axis II disorders. *Journal of Personality Disorders, 3,* 10–18.

Zanarini, M. C., Gunderson, J. G., Frankenburg, F. R., & Chauncey, D. L. (1990). Discriminating borderline personality disorder from other Axis II disorders. *American Journal of Psychiatry, 147,* 161–167.

Zanarini, M. C., Gunderson, J. G., Frankenburg, F. R., Chauncey, D. L., & Glutting, J. H. (1991). The validity of the *DSM-III* and *DSM-III-R* criteria sets for borderline personality disorder. *American Journal of Psychiatry, 148,* 870–874.

Zanarini, M. C., Gunderson, J. G., Marino, M. F., Schwartz, E. O., & Frankenburg, F. R. (1988). *DSM-III* disorders in the families of borderline outpatients. *Journal of Personality Disorders, 2,* 292–302.

Zanarini, M. C., Gunderson, J. G., Marino, M. F., Schwartz, E. O., & Frankenburg, F. R. (1989). Childhood experiences of borderline patients. *Comprehensive Psychiatry, 30,* 18–25.

CHAPTER 9

Major Mental Disorders and Violence to Others

JOHN MONAHAN

"Here's a madman will murder me," wrote Shakespeare in *The Taming of the Shrew*. Likewise, in *Henry the Sixth, Part Two*, a character is admonished for failing to impose "knife control" on a person with mental disorder: "You put sharp weapons in a madman's hands." The association between mental disorder and violence in the public consciousness did not begin with Shakespeare, however. The belief was ancient even in his day. References in Greek and Roman literature to the violence potential of people with mental disorder date from the fifth century before the Christian era began. As the historian George Rosen (1968) noted, in the ancient world "two forms of behaviour were considered particularly characteristic of the mentally disordered, their habit of wandering about and their proneness to violence" (p. 98). Plato, for example, in *Alcibiades II,* records a dialogue between Socrates and a friend. The friend claimed that many citizens of Athens were "mad." Socrates refuted this claim by arguing that the rate of mental disorder in Athens could not possibly be very high, since the rate of violence in Athens was very low: "How could we live in safety with so many crazy people? Should we not long ago have paid the penalty at their hands, and have been struck and beaten and endured every other form of ill usage which madmen are wont to inflict?" (quoted in Rosen, 1968, p. 100).

It is important to emphasize that even in ancient times, the public perception was not that all or most or even many of the mentally disordered were violent, just that a disproportionate number were. The Roman philosopher Philo Judaeus, for example, divided the mentally disordered into two groups. The larger one was made up of disordered people "of the easy-going gentle style," and the other, smaller one consisted of those "whose madness was . . . of the fierce and savage kind, which is dangerous both to the madmen themselves and those who approach them" (quoted in Rosen, 1968, p. 89).

The perception of a link between major mental disorder and violence endures. A poll conducted by the Field Institute (1984) for the California Department of Mental Health asked 1,500 representative California adults whether they agreed with the statement, "A person who is diagnosed as schizophrenic is more likely to commit a violent crime than a normal person." Almost two thirds of the sample (61%) said that they definitely or probably agreed. Similarly, in a survey of 1,000 adults from all parts of the

United States conducted by the DYG Corporation (1990) for the Robert Wood Johnson Foundation Program on Chronic Mental Illness, 24% of the respondents agreed that "people with chronic mental illness are, by far, more dangerous than the general population." In the most recent national poll on this topic, conducted by Mark Clements Research (1993), 57% of American adults surveyed answered yes to the question, "Do you think the mentally ill are more likely to commit acts of violence?"

These figures no doubt reflect the impact of the media in projecting a sensational image of people with mental disorder (Steadman & Cocozza, 1978). One content analysis found that 17% of all prime-time American television programs that could charitably be classified as "dramas" depicted a character as mentally ill (Gerbner, Gross, Morgan, & Signorielli, 1981). Seventy-three percent of these mentally ill characters were portrayed as violent, compared with 40% of the "normal" characters, and 23% of the mentally ill characters were shown to be homicidal, compared with 10% of the "normal" characters. Nor are such caricatures limited to television. A content analysis of stories from the United Press International database (Shain & Phillips, 1991) found that in 86% of all print stories dealing with former mental patients, a violent crime—"usually murder or mass murder" (p. 64)—was the focus of the article.

THEORETICAL CONTEXT AND CONTROVERSIAL ISSUES

Public perception that mental disorder is strongly linked to violent behavior is important for two reasons. The first is that such a belief drives the formal laws and policies by which society attempts to control the behavior of disordered people and to regulate the provision of mental health care. The assumption of a connection between violence and mental disorder has played an animating role in the prominence of "dangerous to others" as a criterion for civil commitment and the commitment of persons acquitted of crime by reason of insanity, in the creation of special statutes for the extended detention of mentally disordered prisoners, and in the imposition of tort liability on psychologists and psychiatrists who fail to anticipate the violence of their patients (Appelbaum, 1988;

Grisso, 1991). Most recently, the assumed link between disorder and violence has resulted in a "direct threat" exception to the employment protections afforded by the Americans with Disabilities Act (Campbell & Kaufman, 1997) and to the Brady Handgun Violence Prevention Act's ban on handgun sales to persons who have been "adjudicated as a mental defective or committed to a mental institution" (Appelbaum & Monahan, 1994).

The second and perhaps even more important reason why a belief in the violence potential of people with mental disorder is important is that it also determines our informal responses and modes of interacting with individuals who are perceived to be mentally ill. An ingenious study by Link, Cullen, Frank, and Wozniak (1987) vividly makes this point. These researchers investigated the extent to which a person's status as a former mental patient fostered social distance on the part of others. *Social distance* was measured by questions tapping the willingness of the respondent to have as a coworker or neighbor someone described in a vignette as having once been a patient in a mental hospital. Consistent with much prior research (e.g., Gove, 1980), Link et al. found no main effect of the former patient label. But when they disaggregated their subjects (drawn from the open community) into those who believed that mental disorder was linked to violence and those who did not, strong labeling effects emerged. Remarkably, people who believed that there was no connection between mental disorder and violence exhibited what might be called an "affirmative action" effect; they responded as if they were *more* willing to have as a coworker or neighbor someone who had been a mental patient than someone never hospitalized. People who believed that the mentally disordered were prone to violence, however, strongly rejected and wished to distance themselves from the former patient. More recent data by Penn et al. (1994) are consistent with these findings: The more people associate mental disorder with "dangerousness," the less contact they have with people who have mental disorders, and the less contact they want to have.

The public perception that persons with mental disorder constitute an especially violence-prone class of people is therefore a significant obstacle in the path of those who would advocate for patients' legal rights and for their social acceptance in the community. It should perhaps not be surprising that advocates in the past have often responded to the taunt of "dangerousness" with an unconditional denial that there existed any relationship whatsoever between mental disorder and violence. For example, a pamphlet published by the National Mental Health Association (1987) states that "people with mental illnesses pose no more of a crime threat than do other members of the general population." Likewise, a volume produced by a leading ex-patient advocacy group for the California Department of Mental Health (Well-Being Project, 1989) states that "studies show that while, like all groups, some members are violent, mental health clients are no more violent than the general population" (p. 88). In making such statements, patient advocates are clearly and commendably motivated by the desire to dispel vivid "homicidal maniac" images pandered by the media and to counter the stigma and social distancing that are bred by public fear. Given the findings of Link et al. (1987), they surely are right to be concerned. And the research evidence that existed at the time these claims were made tended to support the "no relationship" position (Monahan & Steadman, 1983).

The data necessary for adequately answering the empirical question of the relationship between mental disorder and violence, however, did not exist until recently. In the past several years, a remarkable amount of epidemiological and clinical research on violence among people with mental disorder and on mental disorder among people who are violent has become available. This newer and much more sophisticated research has recast the terms of the empirical and policy debate.

METHODOLOGY

There are two ways to determine whether a relationship exists between mental disorder and violent behavior and, if it does, to estimate the strength of that relationship. If being mentally disordered raises the likelihood that a person will commit a violent act—that is, if mental disorder is a "risk factor" for the occurrence of violent behavior—then the actual (or "true") prevalence rate for violence should be higher among disordered than among nondisordered populations. And to the extent that mental disorder is a contributing cause to the occurrence of violence, the true prevalence rate of mental disorder should be higher among people who commit violent acts than among people who do not.

Within each generic category, two types of research exist. The first seeks to estimate the relationship between mental disorder and violence by studying people who are being *treated* either for mental disorder (in hospitals) or for violent behavior (in jails and prisons). The second seeks to estimate the relationship between mental disorder and violence by studying people *unselected* for treatment status in the open community. Both types of studies are valuable in themselves, but both have limitations taken in isolation.

Several kinds of studies provide data from institutionalized mental patients that can be used to estimate the relationship between mental disorder and violence. One type looks at the prevalence of violent acts committed by patients *before* they entered the hospital. A second type looks at the prevalence of violent incidents committed by mental patients *during* their hospital stay. A final type of study addresses the prevalence of violent behavior among mental patients *after* they have been released from the hospital.

Each of these three types of research has important policy and practice implications. Studies of violence before hospitalization supply data on the workings of civil commitment laws and the interaction between the mental health and criminal justice systems (Monahan & Steadman, 1994). Studies of violence during hospitalization have significance for the level of security required in mental health facilities and the need for staff training in managing aggressive incidents (see Tardiff, Chapter 42, this volume). Studies of violence after hospitalization provide essential base-rate information for use in the risk assessments involved in release decision making and in after-care planning.

For the purpose of determining whether there is a fundamental relationship between mental disorder and violent behavior, however, each of these three types of research is unavailing. Only rarely did the studies provide any comparative data on the prevalence of similarly defined violence among nonhospitalized groups. Although the rates of violence by mental patients before, during, or after hospitalization reported in the studies certainly appear much higher than would be expected by chance, the general lack of data from nonpatients makes comparison speculative. But even if such data were available, several sources of systematic bias would make their use for epidemiological purposes highly suspect. Since these studies dealt with persons who were subsequently, simultaneously, or previously institutionalized as mental patients, none of them can distinguish between the *participation* of the mentally disordered in violence—the topic of interest here—and the *selection* of that subset of mentally disordered persons who are violent in the community for treatment in the public sector inpatient settings in which the research was carried out. Further, studies of violence after hospitalization suffer from the additional selection bias that only those patients clinically predicted to be nonviolent were released. Nor can the studies of violence during and after hospitalization distinguish the effect of the *treatment* of potentially violent patients in the hospital from the existence of a prior relationship between mental disorder and violence.

For example, to use the prevalence of violence before hospitalization as an index of the fundamental relationship between mental disorder and violence would be to thoroughly confound rates of violence with the legal criteria for hospitalization. Given the rise of the "dangerousness standard" for civil commitment in the United States and throughout the world (Monahan & Shah, 1989; United Nations, 1991), it would be surprising if many patients were not violent before they were hospitalized; violent behavior is one of the *reasons* that these disordered people were selected out of the total disordered population for hospitalization. Likewise, the level of violent behavior exhibited on the ward during hospitalization is determined not only by the differential selection of violent people for hospitalization (or, within the hospital, the further selection of violence-prone patients for placement in the locked wards that were often the sites of the research) but by the skill of ward staff in defusing potentially violent incidents and by the efficacy of treatment in mitigating disorder (or by the effect of medication in sedating patients).

Because the prevalence of violence after hospitalization may be a function of the type of patients selected for hospitalization, of the nature and duration of the treatment administered during hospitalization, and of the risk assessment cutoffs used in determining eligibility for discharge, these data, too, tell us little about whether a basic relationship between mental disorder and violence exists.

Only by augmenting studies of the prevalence of violence among *treated* (i.e., hospitalized) samples of the mentally disordered with studies of the prevalence of violence among samples of disordered people *unselected* for treatment status in the community can population estimates free of selection and treatment biases be offered. This is precisely what was done in the community epidemiological studies, to be described in the next section.

CURRENT FINDINGS

Violence Among the Disordered

As mentioned, three types of studies provide data from hospitalized mental patients that can be used to estimate the relationship between mental disorder and violence. One type looks at the prevalence of violent acts committed by patients *before* they entered the hospital. A second type looks at the prevalence of violent incidents committed by mental patients *during* their hospital stay. A final type of study addresses the prevalence of violent behavior among mental patients *after* they have been released from the hospital.[1]

Research of each type has been reviewed elsewhere (Beck, 1994; Hodgins, 1995; Monahan, 1992; Mullen, 1997; Mulvey, 1994; Torrey, 1994; Wessely & Taylor, 1991). Eleven studies published since 1975 provided data on the prevalence of violent behavior among persons who eventually became mental patients. The time period investigated was typically the 2 weeks prior to hospital admission. The findings across the various studies vary considerably: Between approximately 10% and 40% of the patient samples (with a median rate of 15%) committed a physically assaultive act against another person shortly before they were hospitalized. Twelve studies with data on the prevalence of violence by patients on mental hospital wards are also available. The periods studied varied from a few days to a year. The findings here also range from about 10% to 40% (with a median rate of 25%).

There is a very large literature, going back to the 1920s, on violent behavior by mental patients after they have been discharged from civil hospitals (Rabkin, 1979). Klassen and O'Connor (1988, 1990) found that approximately 25% to 30% of male patients with at least one violent incident in their past—a very relevant but highly selective sample of patients—are violent within a year of release from the hospital. In the ongoing MacArthur Risk Assessment Study (Steadman et al., 1994), 27% of released male and female patients report at least one violent act within a mean of 4 months after discharge.

As discussed in the previous section, these studies of institutionalized populations of mental patients, although valuable for many purposes, have serious biases when used to draw inferences about the fundamental relationship between violence and mental disorder. For that purpose, data on unselected samples of people from the open community are needed to augment the findings based on the behavior of identified mental patients. Fortunately, a seminal study by Swanson, Holzer, Ganju, and Jono (1990) provides this essential epidemiological information. Swanson and his colleagues drew their data from the National Institute of Mental Health's Epidemiological Catchment Area (ECA) study. Representative weighted samples of adult household residents of Baltimore, Durham, and Los Angeles were pooled to form a database of approximately 10,000 people. The NIMH–Diagnostic Interview Schedule (DIS), a structured interview designed for use by trained laypersons, was used to establish mental disorder according to the criteria established in the American Psychiatric Association's

---

[1]This discussion is restricted to findings on violent behavior toward others and excludes violence toward self, verbal threats of violence, and property damage. *Mental disorder* refers, unless otherwise noted, to those "major" disorders of thought or mood—principally schizophrenia and affective disorder—that form a subset of Axis I of the American Psychiatric Association's (1994) *Diagnostic and Statistical Manual* (4th ed.) (*DSM-IV*).

(1980) *Diagnostic and Statistical Manual* (3rd ed.) (*DSM-III*). Five items on the DIS[2]—four embedded among the criteria for antisocial personality disorder and one that formed part of the diagnosis of alcohol abuse/dependence—were used to indicate violent behavior. A respondent was counted as positive for violence if he or she endorsed at least one of these items and reported that the act occurred during the year preceding the interview. This index of violent behavior, as Swanson et al. (1990) note, is a "blunt measure": It is based on self-report without corroboration, the questions overlap considerably, and it does not differentiate in terms of the frequency or the severity of violence. Yet there is little doubt that each of the target behaviors is indeed violent, and the measure is a reasonable estimate of the prevalence of violent behavior.

Confidence in the Swanson et al. (1990) findings is increased by their conformity to the demographic correlates of violence known from the criminological literature. Violence in the ECA study was seven times as prevalent among the young as among the old, twice as prevalent among males as among females, and three times as prevalent among persons of the lowest social class as among persons of the highest social class.

But it is three clinical findings that are of direct interest here: (a) the prevalence of violence is over 5 times higher among people who meet criteria for a *DSM-III* Axis I diagnosis (11% to 13%) than among people who are not diagnosable (2%); (b) the prevalence of violence among persons who meet criteria for a diagnosis of schizophrenia, major depression, or mania/bipolar disorder is remarkably similar (between 11% and 13%); and (c) the prevalence of violence among persons who meet criteria for a diagnosis of alcoholism (25%) is 12 times that of persons who receive no diagnosis, and the prevalence of violence among persons who meet criteria for being diagnosed as abusing drugs (35%) is 16 times that of persons who receive no diagnosis.

When both demographic and clinical factors were combined in a regression equation to predict the occurrence of violence, several significant predictors emerged. Violence was most likely to occur among young, lower-class males, among those with a substance abuse diagnosis, and among those with a diagnosis of major mental disorder (Swanson & Holzer, 1991).

Another equally notable study not only confirms the ECA data but takes them a large step further. Link, Andrews, and Cullen (1992) analyzed data from a larger study conducted using the Psychiatric Epidemiology Research Interview (PERI; Shrout et al., 1988) to measure symptoms and life events. Link et al. (1992) studied rates of arrest and self-reported violence (including hitting, fighting, weapon use, and "hurting someone badly") in a sample of approximately 400 adults from the Washington Heights area of New York City who had never been in a mental hospital or sought help from a mental health professional. The rates of this group were compared with rates of arrest and self-reported violence in several samples of former mental patients from the same area. To eliminate alternative explanations of their data, the researchers controlled, in various analyses, for an extraordinary number of factors: age, gender, educational level, ethnicity (African American, White, and Hispanic), socioeconomic status, family composition (e.g., married with children), homicide rate of the census tract in which a subject lived, and the subject's "need for approval." This last variable was included to control for the possibility that patients might be more willing than nonpatients to report socially undesirable behavior (such as violence).

The patient groups were almost always more violent than the never-treated community sample, often two to three times as violent. As in the ECA study, demographic factors clearly related to violence (e.g., males, the less educated, and those from high-crime neighborhoods were more likely to be violent). But even when all the demographic and personal factors, such as social desirability, were taken into account, significant differences between the patients and the never-treated community residents remained. The association between mental patient status and violent behavior, as the authors noted, was "remarkably robust" to attempts to explain it away as artifact.

Most important, Link et al. (1992) then controlled for recent symptomatology by using the psychotic symptoms scale of the PERI (e.g., "During the past year, how often have you heard things that other people say they can't hear?"). Remarkably, not a single difference in rates of recent violent behavior between patients and never-treated community residents remained significant when current psychotic symptoms were controlled. The psychotic symptomatology scale, on the other hand, was significantly and strongly related to most indexes of recent violent behavior, even when additional factors, such as alcohol and drug use, were taken into account (cf. Modestin & Ammann, 1995). Thus, almost all of the difference in rates of violence between patients and nonpatients could be accounted for by the level of active psychotic symptoms that the patients were experiencing. In other words, when mental patients were actively experiencing psychotic symptoms such as delusions and hallucinations, their risk of violence was significantly elevated compared to that of nonpatients; and when patients were not actively experiencing psychotic symptoms, their risk of violence was not appreciably higher than demographically similar members of their home community who had never been treated. Finally, Link et al. (1992) also found that the psychotic symptomatology scale significantly predicted violent behavior among the never-treated community residents. Even among people who had never been formally treated for mental disorder, actively experiencing psychotic symptoms was associated with the commission of violent acts.

Link and Stueve (1994) have recently reanalyzed the data used in Link et al. (1992) to allow for a much more precise specification of *what kind* of psychotic symptoms are most related to violence. Three symptoms on the psychotic symptoms scale largely

---

[2]The items were, "(1) Did you ever hit or throw things at your wife/husband/partner? [If so] Were you ever the one who threw things first, regardless of who started the argument? Did you hit or throw things first on more than one occasion? (2) Have you ever spanked or hit a child (yours or anyone else's) hard enough so that he or she had bruises or had to stay in bed or see a doctor? (3) Since age 18, have you been in more than one fight that came to swapping blows, other than fights with your husband/wife/partner? (4) Have you ever used a weapon like a stick, knife, or gun in a fight since you were 18? (5) Have you ever gotten into physical fights while drinking?"

explained the relationship between mental disorder and violence.[3] The authors refer to these as "threat/control-override symptoms," because they either involve the overriding of internal self-controls by external factors (items 1 and 2) or imply a specific threat of harm from others (item c). Link and Stueve (1994) explain their results by invoking a principle of "rationality-within-irrationality":

> The principle of rationality-within-irrationality posits that once one suspends concern about the irrationality of psychotic symptoms and accepts that they are experienced as real, violence unfolds in a "rational" fashion. By rational we do not mean reasonable or justified but rather understandable. Specifically, we suggest that when a person fears personal harm or feels threatened by others interpersonal violence becomes more likely. In addition we argue that violence is more likely when internal controls that might otherwise block the expression of violence break down. From this perspective the nature and content of the psychotic experience become important. If the psychotic experience involves the removal of self-control through, for example, thought insertion or having one's mind dominated by outside forces, routine, self-imposed constraints on behavior are more likely to be overridden, and violence becomes a greater possibility. Further, if the afflicted person believes that he or she is gravely threatened by someone who intends to cause harm, violence is again more likely. In contrast, if the psychotic episode involves odd experiences such as hearing voices, seeing visions, or having one's thoughts taken away, without the intrusion of external, uncontrollable, and threatening forces, violence is less likely. (p. 143)

Swanson, Borum, Swartz, and Monahan (1996) have replicated Link and Stueve's (1994) central finding with data from the Epidemiological Catchment Area (ECA) study. Respondents who reported threat/control-override symptoms were twice as likely as those with other psychotic symptoms to report violence and about 6 times as likely as those with no mental disorder. People with threat/control-override symptoms combined with alcohol or other drug use disorders were 8 to 10 times more likely to report violence than those without mental disorder.

Finally, the first longitudinal prospective study of an unselected birth cohort, including data on both mental disorder and violence, has recently been published. Using this powerful design, Hodgins (1992) performed a 30-year follow-up of all 15,117 persons born in Stockholm, Sweden, in 1953 and still residing there in 1963. Mental hospitalization records (for estimating mental disorder) and police records (for estimating violence) were compared. Men with a major mental disorder—schizophrenia or major affective disorder—were 4 times more likely to be convicted of a violent crime than men without a major mental disorder (or intellectual handicap). Women with a major mental disorder were 27 times more likely to be convicted of a violent crime than women without a major disorder (or intellectual handicap).

These data have only recently become available. They provide the crucial missing element that begins to fill out the epidemiological picture of mental disorder and violence. Together, these studies suggest that the currently mentally disordered—those actively experiencing certain serious psychotic symptoms—are involved in violent behavior at rates several times those of nondisordered members of the general population and that this difference persists even when a wide array of demographic and social factors are taken into consideration. Because the studies were conducted using representative samples of the open community, selection biases are not a plausible alternative explanation for their findings.

Disorder Among the Violent

Recall that there is a second empirical tack that might be taken to determine whether a fundamental relationship between mental disorder and violence exists and to estimate the magnitude of that relationship. If mental disorder is in fact a contributing cause to the occurrence of violence, then the prevalence of mental disorder should be higher among people who commit violent acts than among people who do not. As before, there are two ways to ascertain the existence of such a relationship: (a) by studying treated cases—in this instance, people "treated" for violence by being institutionalized in local jails and state prisons—and determining their rates of mental disorder, and (b) by studying untreated cases—people in the open community who are violent but not institutionalized for it—and determining their rates of mental disorder.

A large number of studies exist that estimate the prevalence of mental disorder among jail and prison inmates. Of course, not all jail and prison inmates have been convicted of a violent crime. Yet 66% of state prisoners have a current or past conviction for violence (Bureau of Justice Statistics, 1991), and there is no evidence that the rates of disorder of jail inmates charged with violent offenses differ from those of jail inmates charged with nonviolent offenses. So data on the prevalence of disorder among inmates in general also apply reasonably well to violent inmates in particular.

Teplin (1990) reviewed 18 studies of mental disorder among jail samples performed since 1975. Most of the studies were conducted on inmates referred for a mental health evaluation and thus present obviously inflated rates of disorder. Among those few studies that randomly sampled jail inmates, rates of mental disorder varied widely, from 5% to 16% psychotic. Roth (1980), in reviewing the literature on the prevalence of mental disorder among prison inmates, concluded that the rate of psychosis was "on the order of 5% or less of the total prison population" (p. 688), and the rate of any form of disorder was in the 15% to 20% range. More recent studies have reported somewhat higher rates of serious mental disorder. Steadman, Fabisiak, Dvoskin, and Holohean (1987), in a "level of care" survey of over 3,000 prisoners in New York State, concluded that 8% had "severe mental disabilities" and another 16% had "significant mental disabilities."

Although the rates of mental disorder among jail and prison inmates appear high, comparison data for similarly defined mental disorder among the general noninstitutionalized population were typically not available. As well, the methods of diagnosing mental disorder in the jail and prison studies often consisted of unstandardized clinical interviews or the use of proxy variables such as prior mental hospitalization (Steadman et al., 1985).

---

[3]These items were, During the past year . . . (1) "How often have you felt that your mind was dominated by forces beyond your control?" (2) "How often have you felt that thoughts were put into your head that were not your own?" and (3) "How often have you felt that there were people who wished to do you harm?"

More recently, however, several studies have become available that use jail inmates and prisoners as subjects and the Diagnostic Interview Schedule (DIS) as their diagnostic instrument. The DIS not only allows for a standardized method of assessing disorder independent of previous hospitalization but also permits comparison across the studies and between these institutionalized populations and the random community samples of the ECA research.

In the first study, Teplin (1990) administered the DIS to a stratified random sample—half misdemeanants and half felons—of 728 males from the Cook County (Chicago) jail. In the most comparable of the prison studies, the California Department of Corrections (1989) commissioned a consortium of research organizations to administer the DIS to a stratified random sample of 362 male inmates in California prisons. Comparative data from the ECA study for gender, race, and age-matched respondents were provided by Teplin.

These studies reveal that the prevalence of schizophrenia (3%) is approximately three times higher in the jail and prison samples than in the general population samples (1%), and the prevalence of major depression (4%) is four times higher than in the general population (1%). Overall, the prevalence of any severe disorder (6% to 8%) was three to four times higher than in the general population (2%). Although there were no controls for demographic factors in the prison study, Teplin (1990) controlled for race and age in the jail study, and the jail–general population differences persisted. Although these studies all relied on male inmates, comparable data for female prisoners recently have been reported by Teplin, Abram, and McClelland (1996; see also Daniel, Robins, Reid, & Wilfley, 1988). Holding age and race constant, Teplin and her colleagues found the prevalence of all disorders to be significantly higher among women in jail than among women in the general urban ECA population (with the exception of schizophrenia, where the difference in rates did not reach significance).

These findings on the comparatively high prevalence of mental disorder among jail and prison inmates have enormous policy implications for mental health screening of admissions to these facilities and for the need for mental health treatment in correctional institutions (Steadman, McCarty, & Morrissey, 1989). But given the systematic bias inherent in the use of identified criminal offenders, these findings cannot fully address the issue of whether there is a fundamental relationship between mental disorder and violence. Mentally disordered offenders may be more or less likely than nondisordered offenders to be arrested and imprisoned. On the one hand, Robertson (1988) found that offenders who were schizophrenic were much more likely than nondisordered offenders to be arrested at the scene of the crime or to give themselves up to the police. Teplin (1985), in the only actual field study in this area, found the police more likely to arrest disordered than nondisordered suspects. On the other hand, Klassen and O'Connor (1988) found that released mental patients whose violence in the community evoked an official response were twice as likely to be rehospitalized—and thereby to avoid going to jail—than they were to be arrested. An individual's status as a jail or prison inmate, in short, is not independent of the presence of mental disorder. As before, complementary data on the prevalence of mental disorder among unselected samples of people in the open community who commit violent acts are necessary to fully address this

issue. And as before, the analysis of the ECA data by Swanson et al. (1990) provides the required information.

The prevalence of schizophrenia among respondents who endorsed at least one of the five questions indicating violent behavior in the past year (4%) was approximately four times higher than among respondents who did not report violence (1%); the prevalence of affective disorder (9%) was three times higher (3%); and the prevalence of substance abuse (either alcohol or other drugs; 42%) was eight times higher (5%) among persons who reported violence than among persons who did not report violence.

CONCLUSIONS

The data reviewed here, which have become available only since 1990, fairly read, suggest that whether the measure is the prevalence of violence among the disordered or the prevalence of disorder among the violent, whether the sample is made up of people who are selected for treatment as inmates or patients in institutions or people randomly chosen from the open community, and no matter how many social and demographic factors are statistically taken into account, there appears to be a greater-than-chance relationship between mental disorder and violent behavior. Mental disorder may be a statistically significant risk factor for the occurrence of violence.

Demonstrating the existence of a statistically significant relationship between mental disorder and violence is one thing, however; demonstrating the legal and policy significance of the magnitude of that relationship is another. By all indications, the great majority of people who are currently disordered—approximately 90% from the Swanson et al. (1990) study—are not violent. None of the data give any support to the sensationalized caricature of the mentally disordered served up by the media, the shunning of former patients by employers and neighbors in the community, or "lock 'em all up" laws proposed by politicians pandering to public fears. The policy implications of mental disorder as a risk factor for violent behavior can be understood only in relative terms. Compared to the magnitude of risk associated with the combination of male gender, young age, and lower socioeconomic status, for example, the risk of violence presented by mental disorder is modest. Compared to the magnitude of risk associated with alcoholism and other drug abuse, the risk associated with "major" mental disorders such as schizophrenia and affective disorder is modest indeed. Clearly, mental illness status makes at best a trivial contribution to the overall level of violence in society.[4]

This judgment is in accord with that of Mulvey (1994). He

---

[4]But see Note (1974) on the legal justification—"because [the mentally disordered] are . . . unable to make autonomous decisions" (p. 1233)—for preventively intervening in the lives of disordered people in situations where we do not intervene with nondisordered people, even when the nondisordered people present a higher risk of violence. On the issue of the decision-making competence of people with mental disorder, see Grisso and Appelbaum (1995).

concluded that on the basis of the available literature, six statements could be made about the relationship between violence and mental disorder:

1. Mental illness appears to be a risk factor for violence in the community. A body of research, taken as a whole, supports the idea that an association exists between mental illness and violence in the general population.

2. The size of the association between mental illness and violence, while statistically significant, does not appear to be very large. Also, the absolute risk for violence posed by mental illness is small.

3. The combination of a serious mental illness and a substance abuse disorder probably significantly increases the risk of involvement in a violent act.

4. The association between mental illness and violence is probably significant even when demographic characteristics are taken into account. However, no sizable body of evidence clearly indicates the relative strength of mental illness as a risk factor for violence compared with other characteristics such as socioeconomic status or history of violence.

5. Active symptoms are probably more important as a risk factor than is simply the presence of an identifiable disorder.

6. No clear information about the causal paths that produce the association between mental illness and violence is available. (pp. 663–665)

Not all in the field are in agreement on these points. Torrey (1994), for example, appears to see the relationship between violence and mental disorder as at least somewhat stronger than other reviewers. In general, however, the sober conclusion that major mental disorder is a "modest" risk factor for violence appears to be becoming the consensus view. As Wessely, Castle, Douglas, and Taylor (1994) have stated:

Viewed in terms of attributable risk, the contribution made by those with schizophrenia to the level of recorded crime in the community is slender. The strongest predictors of crime in those with schizophrenia are the same as those in subjects without psychosis. Nevertheless, serious mental illness also exerts a small, but significant independent effect on recorded crime. Low risk is not the same as no risk, and these findings must be taken seriously. (p. 500)

In this regard, the MacArthur Research Network on Mental Health and the Law collaborated with the National Stigma Clearinghouse, a family and consumer-oriented advocacy group, to produce a "Consensus Statement" that has been endorsed by a large number of researchers and advocates and may serve as a point of agreement in an area that lends itself to political controversy (Monahan & Arnold, 1996):

"Mental disorder" and violence are closely linked in the public mind. A combination of factors promotes this perception: sensationalized reporting by the media whenever a violent act is committed by "a former mental patient," popular misuse of psychiatric terms (such as "psychotic" and "psychopathic"), and exploitation of stock formulas and narrow stereotypes by the entertainment industry. The public justifies its fear and rejection of people labeled "mentally ill," and attempts to segregate them in the community, by this assumption of "dangerousness."

The experience of people with psychiatric conditions and of their family members paints a picture dramatically different from the stereotype. The results of several recent large-scale research projects conclude that only a weak association between mental disorders and violence exists in the community. Serious violence by people with major mental disorders appears concentrated in a small fraction of the total number, and especially in those who use alcohol and other drugs. Mental disorders—in sharp contrast to alcohol and drug abuse—account for a minuscule portion of the violence that afflicts American society.

The conclusions of those who use mental health services and of their family members, and the observations of researchers, suggest that the way to reduce whatever relationship exists between violence and mental disorder is to make accessible a range of quality treatments including peer-based programs, and to eliminate the stigma and discrimination that discourage, sometimes provoke, and penalize those who seek and receive help for disabling conditions. (pp. 69–70)

FUTURE DIRECTIONS

Future research on the relationship between violence and mental disorder is likely to focus not on whether such a relationship exists but on the precise form that the relationship takes. Relationships between given *symptom patterns* (such as the "threat/control-override" symptoms identified by Link et al., 1994, and replicated by Swanson et al., 1996) and violence, rather than correlations based on diagnosis alone, are likely to be reported more often in future studies. As the National Institute of Mental Health's *Caring for People with Severe Mental Disorders: A National Plan of Research to Improve Services* (1991) stated:

The practices of criminal and civil commitment rest on untested assumptions about violent behavior. . . . Particularly informative would be investigations of the relationship between violence and specific aspects of mental illness—for example, the nature, extent, and effect of delusions. (p. 44)

In this regard, the MacArthur Risk Assessment Study (Steadman et al., 1994) is currently assessing a large sample (more than 1,000) of male and female acute civil patients at several facilities on a wide variety of variables believed to be related actuarially to the occurrence of violence. The risk factors fall into four domains. One domain consists of *dispositional* variables, which refer, for example, to the demographic factors of age, race, gender, and social class, as well as to personality variables (e.g., impulsivity and anger control) and neurological factors (e.g., head injury). A second domain consists of *historical* variables. This domain includes significant events experienced by subjects in the past (e.g., family history, work history, mental hospitalization history, history of violence, and criminal and juvenile justice history). A third domain consists of *contextual* variables, referring to indexes of current social supports, social networks, and stress, as well as to physical aspects of the environment, such as the presence of weapons. The final domain consists of *clinical* variables. This includes types and symptoms of mental disorder, personality disorder, drug and alcohol abuse, and level of functioning. Measures of several variables in each of these domains are being actuarially associated with violence occurring in the community, measured during interviews with the patients and a collateral[5] that occur five times over the course of a 1-year, postrelease follow-up, as well as official arrest and mental hospitalization records. Along with further analyses of the database from which the Lidz, Mulvey, and Gardner (1993) NIMH-supported research on clinical violence prediction derives, the MacArthur Risk Assessment Study has the potential to provide the field with significant new knowledge over the next several years.

REFERENCES

American Psychiatric Association. (1980). *Diagnostic and statistical manual of mental disorders* (3rd ed.). Washington, DC: Author.

American Psychiatric Association. (1994). *Diagnostic and statistical manual of mental disorders* (4th ed.). Washington, DC: Author.

Appelbaum, P. (1988). The new preventive detention: Psychiatry's problematic responsibility for the control of violence. *American Journal of Psychiatry, 145,* 779–785.

Appelbaum, P., & Monahan, J. (1994, July 29). Brady bill's false step. *The Boston Globe,* p. 19.

Beck, J. (1994). Epidemiology of mental disorder and violence: Beliefs and research findings. *Harvard Review of Psychiatry, 2,* 1–6.

Bureau of Justice Statistics. (1991). *Violent crime in the United States* (Report No. NCJ-127855). Washington, DC: Author.

California Department of Corrections, Office of Health Care Services. (1989). *Current description, evaluation, and recommendations for treatment of mentally disordered criminal offenders.* Sacramento: Author.

Campbell, J., & Kaufman, C. (1997). Equality and difference in the ADA: Unintended consequences for employment of people with mental health disabilities. In R. Bonnie & J. Monahan (Eds.), *Mental disorder, work disability, and the law* (pp. 221–239). Chicago: University of Chicago Press.

Daniel, A., Robins, A., Reid, J., & Wilfley, D. (1988). Lifetime and six-month prevalence of psychiatric disorders among sentenced female offenders. *Bulletin of the American Academy of Psychiatry and the Law, 16,* 333–342.

DYG Corporation. (1990). *Public attitudes toward people with chronic mental illness.* Elmsford, NY: Author.

Field Institute. (1984). *In pursuit of wellness: A survey of California adults* (Vol. 4). Sacramento: California Department of Mental Health.

Gerbner, G., Gross, L., Morgan, M., & Signorielli, N. (1981). Health and medicine on television. *New England Journal of Medicine, 305,* 901–904.

Gove, W. (1980). Labeling and mental illness: A critique. In W. Gove (Ed.), *The labeling of deviance: Evaluating a perspective* (2nd ed., pp. 264–270). Beverly Hills: Sage Publications.

Grisso, T. (1991). Clinical assessments for legal decisionmaking: Research recommendations. In B. Sales & S. Shah (Eds.), *Law and mental health: Major developments and research needs* (pp. 49–80). Washington, DC: Government Printing Office.

Grisso, T., & Appelbaum, P. (1995). The MacArthur Treatment Competence Study: III. Abilities of patients to consent to psychiatric and medical treatment. *Law and Human Behavior, 19,* 149–174.

Hodgins, S. (1992). Mental disorder, intellectual deficiency, and crime: Evidence from a birth cohort. *Archives of General Psychiatry, 49,* 476–483.

Hodgins, S. (1995). Major mental disorder and crime: An overview. *Psychology, Crime, and the Law, 2,* 5–17.

Klassen, D., & O'Connor, W. (1988). Crime, inpatient admissions, and violence among male mental patients. *International Journal of Law and Psychiatry, 11,* 305–312.

Klassen, D., & O'Connor, W. (1990). Assessing the risk of violence in released mental patients: A cross-validation study. *Psychological Assessment: A Journal of Consulting and Clinical Psychology, 1,* 75–81.

Lidz, C., Mulvey, E., & Gardner, W. (1993). The accuracy of predictions of violence to others. *Journal of the American Medical Association, 269,* 1007–1011.

Link, B., Andrews, A., & Cullen, F. (1992). The violent and illegal behavior of mental patients reconsidered. *American Sociological Review, 57,* 275–292.

Link, B., Cullen, F., Frank, J., & Wozniak, J. (1987). The social rejection of former mental patients: Understanding why labels matter. *American Journal of Sociology, 92,* 1461–1500.

Link, B., & Stueve, A. (1994). Psychotic symptoms and the violent/illegal behavior of mental patients compared to community controls. In J. Monahan & H. Steadman (Eds.), *Violence and mental disorder: Developments in risk assessment* (pp. 137–159). Chicago: University of Chicago Press.

Mark Clements Research. (1993). *Mental illness: A Parade Magazine survey.* Unpublished manuscript.

Modestin, J., & Ammann, R. (1995). Mental disorders and criminal behaviour. *British Journal of Psychiatry, 166,* 667–675.

Monahan, J. (1992). Mental disorder and violent behavior: Perceptions and evidence. *American Psychologist, 47,* 511–521.

Monahan, J., & Arnold, J. (1996). Violence by people with mental disorder: A consensus statement by advocates and researchers. *Psychiatric Rehabilitation Journal, 19,* 67–70.

Monahan, J., & Shah, S. (1989). Dangerousness and commitment of the mentally disordered in the United States. *Schizophrenia Bulletin, 15,* 541–553.

Monahan, J., & Steadman, H. (1983). Crime and mental disorder: An epidemiological approach. In M. Tonry & N. Morris (Eds.), *Crime and justice: An annual review of research* (Vol. 4, pp. 145–189). Chicago: University of Chicago Press.

Monahan, J., & Steadman, H. (1994). Toward the rejuvenation of risk research. In J. Monahan & H. Steadman (Eds.), *Violence and mental disorder: Developments in risk assessment* (pp. 1–17). Chicago: University of Chicago Press.

Mullen, P. (1997). A reassessment of the link between mental disorder and violent behaviour and its implications for clinical practice. *Australian and New Zealand Journal of Psychiatry, 31,* 23–31.

Mulvey, E. (1994). Assessing the evidence of a link between mental illness and violence. *Hospital and Community Psychiatry, 45,* 663–668.

National Institute of Mental Health. (1991). *Caring for people with severe mental disorders: A national plan of research to improve services.* Washington, DC: Government Printing Office.

National Mental Health Association. (1987). *Stigma: A lack of awareness and understanding.* Alexandria, VA: Author.

Note. (1974). Developments in the law: Civil commitment of the mentally ill. *Harvard Law Review, 87,* 1190–1406.

---

[5]Funding for the addition of collaterals was provided by NIMH.

Penn, D., Guynan, K., Daily, T., Spaulding, W., Garbin, C., & Sullivan, M. (1994). Dispelling the stigma of schizophrenia: What sort of information is best? *Schizophrenia Bulletin, 20,* 567–574.

Rabkin, J. (1979). Criminal behavior of discharged mental patients: A critical appraisal of the research. *Psychological Bulletin, 86,* 1–27.

Robertson, G. (1988). Arrest patterns among mentally disordered offenders. *British Journal of Psychiatry, 153,* 313–316.

Rosen, G. (1968). *Madness in society: Chapters in the historical sociology of mental illness.* Chicago: University of Chicago Press.

Roth, L. (1980). Correctional psychiatry. In W. Curran, A. McGarry, & C. Petty (Eds.), *Modern legal medicine, psychiatry and forensic science* (pp. 677–719). Philadelphia: Davis.

Shain, R., & Phillips, J. (1991). The stigma of mental illness: Labeling and stereotyping in the news. In L. Wilkins & P. Patterson (Eds.), *Risky business: Communicating issues of science, risk, and public policy* (pp. 61–74). Westport, CT: Greenwood Press.

Shrout, P., Lyons, M., Dohrenwend, B., Skodol, A., Solomon, M., & Kass, F. (1988). Changing time frames on symptom inventories: Effects on the Psychiatric Epidemiology Research Interview. *Journal of Consulting and Clinical Psychology, 56,* 567–572.

Steadman, H., & Cocozza, J. (1978). Selective reporting and the public's misconceptions of the criminally insane. *The Public Opinion Quarterly, 41,* 523–533.

Steadman, H., Fabisiak, S., Dvoskin, J., & Holohean, E. (1987). A survey of mental disability among state prison inmates. *Hospital and Community Psychiatry, 38,* 1086–1090.

Steadman, H., McCarty, D., & Morrissey, J. (1989). *The mentally ill in jail: Planning for essential services.* New York: Guilford.

Steadman, H., Monahan, J., Appelbaum, P., Grisso, T., Mulvey, E., Roth, L., Robbins, P., & Klassen, D. (1994). Designing a new generation of risk assessment research. In J. Monahan & H. Steadman (Eds.), *Violence and mental disorder: Developments in risk assessment* (pp. 297–318). Chicago: University of Chicago Press.

Steadman, H., Monahan, J., Duffee, B., Hartstone, E., & Robbins, P. (1985). The impact of state mental hospital deinstitutionalization on United States prison populations, 1968–1978. *Journal of Criminal Law and Criminology, 75,* 474–490.

Swanson, J., Borum, R., Swartz, M. & Monahan, J. (1996). Psychotic symptoms and disorders and the risk of violent behavior in the community. *Criminal Behaviour and Mental Health, 6,* 309–329.

Swanson, J., & Holzer, C. (1991). Violence and the ECA data. *Hospital and Community Psychiatry, 42,* 79–80.

Swanson, J., Holzer, C., Ganju, V., & Jono, R. (1990). Violence and psychiatric disorder in the community: Evidence from the Epidemiologic Catchment Area Surveys. *Hospital and Community Psychiatry, 41,* 761–770.

Teplin, L. (1985). The criminality of the mentally ill: A dangerous misconception. *American Journal of Psychiatry, 142,* 676–677.

Teplin, L. (1990). The prevalence of severe mental disorder among male urban jail detainees: Comparison with the Epidemiologic Catchment Area Program. *American Journal of Public Health, 80,* 663–669.

Teplin, L., Abram, K., & McClelland, G. (1996). The prevalence of psychiatric disorder among incarcerated women: I. Pretrial jail detainees. *Archives of General Psychiatry, 53,* 505–512.

Torrey, E. (1994). Violent behavior by individuals with serious mental illness. *Hospital and Community Psychiatry, 45,* 653–662.

United Nations. (1991, December 17). Principles for the protection of persons with mental illness and for the improvement of mental health care. UN General Assembly Resolution 119, 46th Session.

Well-Being Project. (1989). *The Well-Being Project: Mental health clients speak for themselves.* Sacramento, CA: California Department of Mental Health.

Wessely, S., Castle, D., Douglas, A., & Taylor, P. (1994). The criminal careers of incident cases of schizophrenia. *Psychological Medicine, 24,* 483–502.

Wessely, S., & Taylor, P. (1991). Madness and crime: Criminology versus psychiatry. *Criminal Behaviour and Mental Health, 1,* 193–228.

CHAPTER 10

Suicide, Impulsivity, and Antisocial Behavior

ROBERT PLUTCHIK and HERMAN M. VAN PRAAG

The published literature on suicide has been largely concerned with the identification of risk factors for suicide or suicide attempts. The literature on antisocial behavior covers a wider range; it includes sociological, ethological, and sociobiological analyses and relates to the concepts of violence, homicide, and aggression. Surprisingly, relatively little research has been directed toward understanding the systematic connections between suicidal behavior and antisocial (or other-directed violent) behavior. The focus of the present chapter is on the relations between these domains. In addition, we present a theoretical model of their interconnections.

EMPIRICAL STUDIES OF THE RELATION
BETWEEN SUICIDE AND VIOLENCE

Psychoanalytic theory has long assumed a connection between suicide or self-directed aggressive behavior and violence directed toward other people. Menninger (1956), for example, has said that suicide involves both a wish to die as well as a wish to kill, implying that there should be some degree of similarity in the impulses underlying these wishes. Consistent with this idea, various statistical studies have revealed a positive relation between violence directed to oneself and violence directed toward others. Using homicide rates in the United States as a measure of violence, Holinger, Offer, Barter, and Bell (1994) reported that homicide and suicide rates in adolescents and young adults have tended to rise and fall in parallel ways from 1930 to 1985, but from about 1985 to the present, homicide rates have risen precipitously while suicide rates have remained stable. Other studies have shown that regions within state may vary widely in such indexes. For example, in North Carolina, there are wide variations in homicide and suicide rates depending on the regions of the state (Humphrey & Kupferer, 1977). Marked variations in such rates also exist as a function of race, age, and sex (Holinger, 1987).

Using data from the National Center for Health Statistics for the period from 1900 to 1979, Holinger (1987) reported a correlation of +.33 between homicide rates and suicide rates, and a correlation of +.59 between suicide rates and unemployment rates. He also reports a correlation of +.37 between homicide rates and unemployment rates. These findings are inconsistent with the early report by Henry and Short (1954) of a generally inverse relation between homicide and suicide. They indicate that suicides, homicides, and motor vehicle accidents have epidemiological patterns that are similar over time, but that changes in the economy, war, and population shifts influence the absolute magnitude of these rates.

Clinical studies with psychiatric populations have generally confirmed the positive correlation between suicide or suicidal behavior and violence toward others. Plutchik and colleagues have published a number of studies that revealed a moderate positive correlation (of the order of magnitude of +.5 ± .1) between self-report measures of suicide risk and violence (Apter et al., 1989; Apter et al., 1990; Apter et al., 1991; Botsis, Plutchik, Kotler, & van Praag, 1995; Greenwald, Reznikoff, & Plutchik, 1994; Plutchik, van Praag, & Conte, 1989). Garrison, McKeown, Valois, and Vincent (1993) report similar findings in 3,764 South Carolina high school students; those who reported severe suicidal behaviors also had the highest levels of aggressive behavior toward others. This has also been reported for psychiatric inpatients as well (Convit, Jaeger, Lin, Meisner, & Volavka, 1988). Cairns, Patterson, and Neckerman (1988) evaluated 1,120 assaultive and violent juveniles and found that suicidal adolescents were most likely to be diagnosed as having a conduct disorder. Inamdar, Lewis, Siomopoulos, Shanok, and Lamela (1982) found that among 51 hospitalized adolescent psychotic patients, 67% had been violent, 43% suicidal, and 27% *both* violent and suicidal. Similarly, Pfeffer, Newcorn, Kaplan, Mizruchi, and Plutchik (1989) found four subgroups among 129 adolescent psychiatric inpatients: suicidal only patients, assaultive only patients, both suicidal and assaultive patients, and neither suicidal nor assaultive patients. Hillbrand (1992) found that of 50 habitually aggressive men in a psychiatric forensic facility, 15 men (30%) made suicide attempts.

In a study of over 4,156 patients in Missouri mental hospitals, Altman, Sletten, Eaton, and Ulett (1971) found that suicidal thoughts were the highest single predictor of homicidal ideas and vice versa. (It is interesting that depression was a significant predictor of suicidal thoughts but not of homicidal ideas.) Based on a study of 5,128 incident reports in a mental hospital, it was found that for all diagnostic groups, a positive correlation existed between assaultive and suicidal behaviors (Evenson, Sletten, Altman, & Brown, 1974).

The implication of these studies is that suicidal and assaultive behaviors are often found in the same individual. This implication is further supported by a study that compared assaultive (violent) psychiatric patients with suicidal patients and nonviolent individuals. Both suicide-attempting and assaultive patients were characterized by high levels of hostility and depression in contrast to the control group (Marrero, O'Sullivan, Michael, & Vitaliano, 1989). A clinical investigation of manifest dream content in psychiatric patients also supports the overlap of aggressive characteristics in suicidal and violent patients. This study found that both suicidal and violent patients had more death content and destructive violence in their dreams than did a patient control group (Firth, Blovin, Natarajan, & Blovin, 1986).

A number of studies have reported that about 30% of violent individuals have a history of self-destructive behavior, whereas 10% to 20% of suicidal persons have a history of violent behavior (Bach-Y-Rita & Veno, 1974; Skodal & Karasu, 1978). Both male and female assaultive patients were three to four times more likely than nonassaultive patients to have attempted suicide (Tardiff & Sweillan, 1982). Evidence of antisocial behavior toward others has been found to be a risk factor for suicide (Burk, Kurz, & Moller, 1985; Shafii, Carrigan, Whillinghil, & Derrick, 1985), just as a history of suicide attempts has frequently been identified among particularly violent prisoners (Climent, Raynes, Rollins & Plutchik, 1974; Climent, Rollins, Ervin & Plutchik, 1973; Plutchik & van Praag, 1990). Data on the effects of crowding in prisons (Cox, Paulus, & McCain, 1984) indicate that population increases in prisons are associated with increased rates of suicide, disciplinary infractions (violence), psychiatric commitment, and death. Decreases in prison populations are associated with decreases in assaults, suicide attempts, and death rates. Among one sample of violent juvenile delinquents, 6 out of 10 had made suicide attempts in the past (Alessi, McManus, Brickman, & Grapentine, 1984). There is thus abundant clinical evidence that suicide and aggression are positively correlated and tend to occur together in many individuals (see Monahan, Chapter 9, this volume).

BIOLOGICAL STUDIES OF SUICIDE AND VIOLENCE

A large number of studies have attempted to identify biochemical markers in suicidal patients. The most consistently reported finding is a low level of 5-hydroxyindoleacetic acid (5-HIAA) in the cerebrospinal fluid (CSF) of suicidal patients who used "violent" methods to try to kill themselves or who succeeded in self-destruction. These findings are not universal, and there is debate over the definition of a "violent" suicide attempt (Golden et al., 1991; Pickar et al., 1986). In addition, low CSF 5-HIAA can be found in some normal individuals as well as in those with other psychiatric diagnoses, such as schizophrenia (van Praag, 1983). Brown and Goodwin (1986) cite six studies in which aggressive/impulsive behaviors, as well as suicidal behaviors, are associated with decreases in CSF 5-HIAA. Roy, Virkkunen, Guthrie, and Linnoila (1986) showed that antisocial and explosive personality types had significantly lower CSF 5-HIAA levels than a paranoid group. They also reported that a group of 17 violent

offenders who had attempted suicide had lower 5-HIAA levels than a group of 19 violent offenders who had not. Arsonists and violent offenders had lower 5-HIAA levels than normal controls. These authors postulated that a functional serotonergic deficit may be related to poor impulse control, which, in turn, may be correlated with violent outbursts, suicide attempts, and alcohol abuse. These observations suggest a low specificity for 5-HIAA as a predictor variable for suicide, but another interpretation is that decreased serotonin metabolism is related to aggressive impulses only, which in the presence of other variables may be expressed in suicide, schizophrenia, depression, or antisocial characteristics.

Linnoila and Virkkunen (1992) have cited a number of studies showing that low CSF 5-HIAA tends to be associated with violent suicide attempts by patients with unipolar depression and personality disorders. Without these correlated factors, the low CSF 5-HIAA may not result in suicide attempts. These authors also report a similar inverse correlation between impulsive, externally directed aggressive behavior and CSF 5-HIAA in a subgroup of violent offenders. They propose the hypothesis of a "low serotonin syndrome" for such violent individuals characterized by low CSF 5-HIAA, mild hypoglycemia, a history of early-onset alcohol and substance abuse, a family history of type II alcoholism, and disturbances in diurnal activities.

Further support for the role of serotonin dysfunction in aggression is provided by Siever and Trestman (1993). Their review of the preclinical literature implies that serotonin dysfunction leads to increased violent behavior in animal models and that such violence is related to the impulsive, aggressive behavior seen in antisocial personalities.

The general idea that serotonin abnormality is related to both violence and suicide also is supported by a study by Marazziti, Rotondo, Presta, and Pancioli-Guadagnucci (1993) of three groups of adults: (a) severely aggressive, (b) suicide attempters, and (c) normal controls. They conclude that an abnormality of the serotonin system exists in connection with aggressive behaviors of any type regardless of whether it is directed outwardly or inwardly. Basically the same conclusion was reached by Coccaro, Kavoussi, and Lesser (1992) after a review of the serotonin literature (see also Berman, Kavoussi, & Coccaro, Chapter 28, this volume. Brown et al. (1982) also reported that in a group of patients with borderline personality disorder there was a significant association between a history of aggressive behaviors and a history of suicide attempts. They also found that both aggression and suicidal actions were associated with lower 5-HIAA levels. And a study of violent offenders and fire setters revealed that many had made serious suicide attempts (Virkkunen, DeJong, Bartko, & Linnoila, 1989).

A DIMENSIONAL VIEW OF SUICIDE AND VIOLENCE

The preceding sections demonstrated a positive relation between violent behavior directed toward oneself and violent behavior directed toward others. In other words, people who make suicide attempts have a higher than average risk of being violent toward others; conversely, people who are violent toward others have a higher than average risk of being violent toward themselves.

These observations suggest the presence of an underlying aggressive impulse that can be directed toward self or others depending on the presence of other factors or variables. They also suggest that the biological variables thus far studied have only a limited connection with overt suicide or violence. Just as the presence of high depression or hopelessness does not necessarily mean that an individual will attempt suicide, a low CSF 5-HIAA does not necessarily mean that a person will attempt suicide or become a criminal. All variables—biological, social, environmental, and personal—are conditional and exert their effects only through the effects of a combination of positive and negative forces at any one point in time. The hope of finding biological markers of psychiatric conditions has not been fulfilled. Low CSF 5-HIAA concentrations are of low specificity and occur cross diagnostically:

> To fancy that there exists such a thing as the biology of, for instance, antisocial personality disorder, taking into account the overlap with other personality disorders, the impossibility of defining its borders with normality, the heterogeneity of the concept, and the ambiguity of many of its features, is stretching the imagination beyond the limits of credibility. (van Praag, 1993, p. 212)

Consistent with this conclusion is the statement made by Berman et al. (see Chapter 28, this volume) that

> No biologic factor has yet been shown to be either a necessary or sufficient cause of aggressive behavior ... Although studies of neurotransmitter functioning provide one avenue to understanding human aggression, economic, political, and cultural factors are clearly important in the development and expression of violent behavior, perhaps more so than individual differences in biology.

An alternative approach for studying the relations between biological (or social) variables and suicide or violence has been called the *functional* or *dimensional* approach. In this strategy, the elementary units of classification in psychopathology are discrete dimensions rather than nosologic entities or syndromes. Rather than attempt to relate suicide or antisocial personality disorder to diagnostic labels, connections are sought between such variables as impulsivity, depression, or ego strength and specific types of violent behavior. The same type of violent behavior may be found as part of many diagnostic syndromes such as depression, schizophrenia, panic states, anxiety states, and personality disorders. The high levels of comorbidity that are frequently found among diagnostic syndromes are a direct reflection of this fact.

COMMON RISK FACTORS FOR SUICIDE AND VIOLENCE

The previous sections have demonstrated that impulses to act violently toward others and violently toward oneself are often found within the same individuals. In this section, evidence is presented to show that many of the same variables are correlated with violent and suicidal behaviors.

In one demonstration of this fact, Plutchik et al. (1989) found that over 14 variables were significantly correlated with self-report measures of both suicide risk and violence risk. These variables included depression, number of life problems, hopelessness, recent psychiatric symptoms, impulsivity, family problems, and menstrual problems. Similarly Apter, Plutchik, and van Praag (1993) found anger and impulsivity correlated with both suicide and violence risk as did depression, impulsivity, and disturbed reality testing (Plutchik, Botsis, & van Praag, 1995). Alcohol dependence, drug dependence, and displacement as an ego defense all correlated significantly with both suicide and violence risk (Greenwald et al., 1994). A study of psychiatric patients found that the number of behavioral problems in oneself and in one's first degree relatives was significantly correlated with both suicide and violence risk (Botsis et al., 1995). Ego defenses of regression and displacement correlated with both suicide and violence risk (Apter et al., 1989). In a review of the literature on inward- and outward-directed aggressiveness, Plutchik (1995) identified 37 risk factors for violent behavior. Of great interest is the fact that more than half of them have also been identified as risk factors for suicide or suicidal behavior, as shown in Table 10.1.

These investigators reveal that a number of variables correlate positively with both suicidality and violence. This implies that suicide and violence have something in common, and two hypotheses suggest themselves. One is that the common element underlying suicide and violence is a generalized behavioral dyscontrol; the other is that the common element is aggression. It is also possible that both hypotheses are true.

Behavioral Dyscontrol or Impulsivity

The concept of *impulsivity* plays a major role in clinical psychiatry. It is considered to be part of the defining characteristics of such diagnoses as borderline and antisocial personality disorders, as well as several neurological disorders, the hyperactive syndrome in children, alcohol and substance abuse, delinquency, and suicide (Plutchik & van Praag, 1995). Although impulsivity has sometimes been confused with aggression, the differences from both a theoretical and practical standpoint are important.

Impulsivity or *dyscontrol* is generally recognized as a deficit phenomenon. It appears when "normal" regulation is not functioning. It often appears when brain function is impaired, as in cases of brain damage and attention deficit disorder. Impulsivity is a multidimensional concept that is related to difficulty in restraining one's behavior, difficulty showing emotions in socially appropriate ways, particularly sexual and aggressive ones, concern with novelty seeking, and inability to delay gratification. Although impulsivity may become a trait as a consequence of certain family experiences, social stresses, or drug use, several large-scale studies of twins and adopted children have revealed genetic components that underlie impulse expression. In humans, there are wide individual differences in impulsivity (or self-control).

A theory of impulsivity has been proposed by Soubrie and Bizot (1990) on the basis of animal research. They assume that impulsivity can be measured in lower animals in terms of waiting capacity or in terms of the tolerance to delay acceptance of rewards. In rat studies, they found that serotonin (5-hydroxytryptamine or 5-HT) uptake blockers and beta stimulants, which enhance nonadrenergic transmission, decreased impulsivity. Drugs that reduced serotonin

TABLE 10.1   Risk Factors for Violent Behaviors, Suicidal Behaviors, or Both[a]

Psychiatric Variables	Violence Risk	Suicide Risk
Schizophrenia	X	X
Episodic dyscontrol	X	
Alcohol abuse	X	X
Drug abuse	X	X
Borderline personality disorder	X	
Antisocial personality disorder	X	
Previous suicidal behavior	X	X
History of previous psychiatric hospitalization	X	X
Biological Variables		
Many soft neurological signs	X	X
Medical and neurological problems in one's immediate family	X	X
History of menstrual problems	X	
High testosterone levels	X	
Neurological abnormalities	X	X
Low CSF 5-HIAA	X	X
Strong sex drive	X	X
Homosexuality	X	X
Personality Variables		
Poor impulse control	X	X
Sadistic behavior toward animals or people	X	
Impulsivity	X	X
Instability	X	
Suspiciousness	X	X
Resentfulness	X	X
Defense mechanism of regression	X	X
Defense mechanism of displacement	X	X
Social Variables		
Previous trouble with the law	X	
Fire setting	X	
Previous arrests and convictions for violent crimes	X	
Recent stresses	X	
Social conflicts over resources	X	
Easy access to weapons	X	X
Troubled early school experiences	X	
Total number of life problems	X	X
Family Variables		
Violence in one's own family	X	X
Loss of mother at an early age	X	X
Loss of father at an early age	X	X
Deviant family environment	X	X

[a]These findings are based on studies by Plutchik and his colleagues (see references).

transmission, such as 5-HT$_{1A}$ agonists and benzodiazepines, increased impulsivity. In general, it was found that all antidepressant drugs studied enhanced waiting capacity (or reduced impulsivity). These observations may account for the beneficial effects of antidepressants on impulse-control disorders such as bulimia and

anorexia. The evidence implies that both serotonergic and nonadrenergic systems interact to influence waiting capacity.

Another way of conceptualizing impulsivity was proposed by Gray, Owen, Davis, and Tsaltas (1983), discussed in more detail by Newman (Chapter 30, this volume). They suggest that a behavioral inhibition system (BIS) acts to inhibit behavior or functions as a "stop" system. In constant interaction with the BIS is a behavioral activation system (BAS) or a "go" system. Impulsive individuals are assumed to have an excessive functioning of the BAS that results in a tendency to respond in atypical ways to reward and punishment situations. One implication of this view is that individuals whose BAS strongly overrides their BIS may be predisposed to antisocial behavior.

These ideas are consistent with the views developed by Moffitt (1993); (see Henry & Moffitt, Chapter 26, this volume). She cites extensive evidence indicating that it is only a very small group of individuals that engages in antisocial behavior at every stage of their lives, whereas a much larger group shows antisocial behavior only during adolescence. For the small lifetime antisocial group, stealing, alcohol abuse, sexual promiscuity, dangerous driving, violent assaults, multiple and unstable relationships, minor physical anomalies, neuropsychological deficits, and psychiatric illness tend to occur during most of the individual's life. Impulsivity is another characteristic often found in lifelong antisocial and delinquent individuals (White et al., 1994).

Aggression

In contrast to impulsivity, which is generally thought of as problematic and undesirable, aggression has been frequently described in the ethological and clinical literature as adaptive behavior directed at dealing with barriers to the satisfaction of needs. We distinguish here between aggression, as a theoretical concept implying a genetically based tendency to overcome obstacles, and violence, which refers to destructive behavior as the overt expression of the aggressive impulse.

Aggressive impulses appear to be present in all species and are connected with the overt behavior of fight and defense. Ethologists have pointed out that aggressive behavior serves to increase the probability of access to resources, helps deal with conflicts among individuals, and increases the chances of successful courtship and mating. The overall function of aggression is that it increases the chance of individual survival as well as inclusive fitness, that is, the likelihood of gene representation in future generations.

Neurophysiological research has established the existence of brain structures that organize patterns of aggressive behavior (e.g., lateral hypothalamus, ventral tegmental areas, midbrain central gray area, and the central and anterior portions of the septum). Various neurotransmitter systems are now known to be involved in the expression of aggression. For example, animals fed a tryptophan-free diet became increasingly aggressive, implying that low serotonin levels are associated with a risk of violent behavior (Gibbons, Barr, Bridger, & Leibowitz, 1979).

The recent literature on behavioral genetics has revealed that many, if not most, emotional characteristics are heritable. Aggressivity has been shown to be heritable in mice and dogs (Fuller, 1986), and human studies of personality and temperament have also indicated significant genetic components in assertiveness, extraversion, and dominance (Loehlin, Horn, & Willerman, 1981; Loehlin & Nichols, 1976; Wimer & Wimer, 1985). The behavior and molecular genetics of aggression have been reviewed by Carey and Goldman (Chapter 23, this volume).

A review of the literature on predation within species (i.e., cannibalism) has demonstrated that the killing and eating of an individual of one's own species are widespread. It has been observed in about 1,300 species, including humans (Polis, 1981). It appears to have a strong genetic component, although its frequency can be affected by the availability of food supplies. In some species, cannibalism has a major influence on population size. It has been observed in at least 14 species of carnivorous mammals. In most of these cases, adults preyed on immature conspecifics and cubs. Cannibalism has also been reported in 60 human cultures (Schankman, 1969).

This brief overview of the function of aggression from the point of view of evolutionary biology suggests that aggressive behavior has fundamental importance both for survival and for the regulation of populations in humans and lower animals. The evidence indicates that there are neurological structures and biochemical processes that are intimately connected with aggressive behavior and that there are genetic contributions to the individual differences seen in aggressive traits. Based on these and other considerations (Plutchik & van Praag, 1990), the authors of this chapter have developed a theory of the relation between violence and suicide, which we call a two-stage model of countervailing forces.

THE TWO-STAGE MODEL OF COUNTERVAILING FORCES

The theory is based on the following ideas:

1. Aggressive impulses are defined as impulses (inner states, tendencies, dispositions, or motivations) to injure or destroy an object or person. An individual may have aggressive impulses without showing violent behavior. In our terminology, aggression refers to a theoretical inner state and violence refers to an overt act.

2. Various kinds of life events tend to increase aggressive impulses. These include threats, challenges, changes in hierarchical status, and loss of social attachments (Blanchard & Blanchard, 1984), as well as physical pain, loss of power or respect, insults, and disappointments (Shaver, Schwartz, Kirson, & O'Connor, 1987).

3. Whether or not the aggressive impulse is expressed in overt behavior depends on the presence of a large number of variables, some of which act as amplifiers of the aggressive impulse and some as attenuators of the aggressive impulse. The balance and vectorial interaction of these factors or forces at any given moment determines whether the aggressive impulse exceeds a threshold and is then expressed in overt behavior. We refer to these amplifiers and attenuators as Stage I countervailing forces.

4. Overt action, however, requires a goal object toward which it is directed. The model assumes that the variables that determine whether the violent behavior will be directed at oneself in a suicidal act or toward other people are different.

5. One of the model's important ideas is that the overt behavior

of violence toward others or violence toward oneself serves a negative feedback function in terms of interpersonal interactions. For example, the violent behavior toward others may act as an intimidation that reduces threat or violence from others. The suicidal act may function as a call for help, or as a desire to create guilt, both of which may help the suicidal person deal with a crisis or with an unsatisfactory relationship by attempting to reduce the level of stress. The violent behavior thus functions as a feedback system designed to keep social interactions within certain limits. This process is exactly the same as occurs in emotional reactions (Plutchik, 1980, 1993, 1994). The study of violence and suicide may thus be thought of as an aspect of the general study of emotion.

Two implications of the theory should be mentioned. At the present time 32 amplifiers of the aggressive impulse have been identified. So far only 17 attenuators have been identified (Table 10.2). Future research should be concerned to an increasing degree with the positive side of life. We assume that large numbers of attenuators must exist given the comparatively low frequency of violence and suicide in most societies.

6. The model, which is fundamentally a vectorial one, helps us understand why both suicidal and violent acts are so difficult to predict. It is evident that many of the interacting variables may change from day to day or even from moment to moment, so that the dynamic equilibrium between countervailing forces is generally unstable. This is why an apparently trivial event to an outside observer may sometimes appear to trigger a suicide attempt or a violent outburst. This is also why it is impossible to describe the relative importance of each variable as if its effects were forever fixed and why precise prediction will always be impossible. This notion is similar to some basic concepts of chaos theory in which

TABLE 10.2 Protective Factors That Decrease the Risk of Violent Behavior or Suicide

Family Variables

Father's sociability
Mother's sociability
Father's acceptance
Mother's acceptance
Marriage
Religiosity
Large social network
Social supports

Personality Variables

High ego strength
High self-esteem (for suicide risk only)
Trait anxiety (for violence risk only)
Calm mood states
Happy mood states
"Replacement" as a coping style
"Overcoming shortcomings" as a coping style
Denial as a defense mechanism (for suicide risk only)
Repression as a defense mechanism (for violence risk only)

two important principles operate: (a) Trivial events can have major consequences; and (b) variables that are important in a large population may be of little or no importance for an individual case. This last point implies that it is impossible to unequivocally determine the relative importance of any single variable in determining a violent or suicidal act.

SUMMARY

Empirical research on the relations between aggression directed toward oneself (or suicidal behavior) and aggression directed toward other people reveals a moderate positive correlation in almost all studies. Variations from this positive correlation are due to the influence of a large number of other variables, some of which act to increase suicidal behavior while others act to increase violent behavior directed toward others. Of great interest is the existence of attenuators of aggression (or so-called protective factors) that may decrease the likelihood of violent expressions of aggression.

Biological studies of violence and suicide have revealed a tendency for low levels of 5-HIAA to be correlated with high levels of aggressive behavior. Such behavior, however, may be directed inwardly or outwardly. It is evident that variations in serotonin metabolism are relatively nonspecific correlates of a variety of psychiatric states and are not specific to suicide per se. This fact suggests that the goal of finding unique biological markers for diagnostic states may be an impossible one. An alternative approach is to consider the elementary units of classification in psychopathology to be those dimensions such as impulsivity, depression, and ego strength that are found to some degree in all individuals.

Additional studies have shown that many of the same variables correlate with both suicide and violence and in the same direction. The dimension of impulsivity or dyscontrol is of particular interest because of its presence in many diagnostic states. Our view is that impulsivity is a generalized trait influenced by family experiences, social stressors, drug use, and genetics. It is generally found as a socially dysfunctional trait. In contrast, aggression has been shown by many ethological studies to be highly adaptive in a wide variety of settings and is the basis of survival related to fight and defense. The chapter concluded with a brief description of a two-stage model of countervailing forces that attempts to systematically relate violence and suicide.

FUTURE DIRECTIONS

It is now evident that a potentially large number of variables influence both violent behavior and suicidal behavior. Future research should begin to measure and study these many variables and not limit itself to traditional sociological, demographic, and diagnostic variables. To illustrate the potential value of expanding the range of variables studied, note that a number of variables have been identified that correlate with suicide risk as high as or higher than does depression. These variables are number of life problems, MMPI schizophrenia scale scores, dyscontrol scores, recent psychiatric symptoms, passivity, total number of family problems,

impulsivity, and poor reality testing. Such observations suggest that our research may have placed too much attention on too few variables.

At the present time, we believe that there are at least 37 amplifiers of the aggressive impulse, whereas only 17 attenuators have been identified. Future research should be concerned to an increasing degree with the positive side of life. We assume that large numbers of attenuators must exist in view of the comparatively low frequency of violence and suicide in most societies.

Although much contemporary research on suicide focuses exclusively on suicide and some of its correlates, the present view emphasizes the idea that suicide is part of a suicide-aggression system. All studies of suicide are therefore as much about aggression and violence as they are about suicide. Many of the studies carried out by this author and his colleagues have demonstrated the important insights gained by incorporating measures of violence risk along with measures of suicide risk.

Many drug studies have looked at antidepressants as a method of treatment, partly because depression is known to be a common correlate of suicide. However, if the theory is correct that suicide is primarily an aspect of the study of aggression, then medications designed to inhibit aggression should work as well as do antidepressants. It seems likely that the new class of drugs called "serenics" should be at least as effective as antidepressants in reducing suicidal behavior.

Finally, the theory sensitizes clinicians to the multiple variables that interact to produce violent acts. This fact should lead to clinical interventions on the part of the clinician that attempt to decrease the amplifiers of aggression and to increase the strength and number of its attenuators.

REFERENCES

Alessi, N. E., McManus, M., Brickman, A., & Grapentine, L. (1984). Suicide behavior among serious juvenile offenders. *American Journal of Psychiatry, 141,* 286–287.

Altman, H., Sletten, I. W., Eaton, M. E., & Ulett, G. A. (1971). Demographic and mental status profiles. Patients with homicidal, assaultive, suicidal, persecutory and homosexual ideation. The Missouri Automated Standard System of Psychiatry. *Psychiatric Quarterly, 45,* 57–64.

Apter, A., Kotler, M., Sevy, S, Plutchik, R., Brown, S., Foster, H., Hillbrand, M., Korn, M. L., & van Praag, H. M. (1991). Correlates of risk of suicide in violent and nonviolent psychiatric patients. *American Journal of Psychiatry, 148,* 853–887.

Apter, A., Plutchik, R., Sevy, S., Korn, M., Brown, S., & van Praag, H. M. (1989). Defense mechanisms in risk of suicide and risk of violence. *American Journal of Psychiatry, 146,* 1027–1031.

Apter, A., Plutchik, R., & van Praag, H. M. (1993). Anxiety, impulsivity and depressed mood in relation to suicidal and violent behavior. *Acta Psychiatrica Scandinavica, 78,* 1–5.

Apter A., van Praag, H. M., Plutchik, R., Sevy, S., Korn, M., & Brown, S. (1990). Interrelationships among anxiety, aggression, impulsivity and mood: A serotonergically linked cluster? *Psychiatry Research, 148,* 191–199.

Bach-Y-Rita, G., & Veno, A. (1974). Habitual violence: A profile of 82 men. *American Journal of.Psychiatry, 131,* 1015–1017.

Blanchard, D. C., & Blanchard, R. J. (1984). Affect and aggression: An animal model applied to human behavior. In R. J. Blanchard & D. C. Blanchard (Eds.), *Advances in the study of aggression* (pp. 2–63). New York: Academic Press.

Botsis, A. J., Plutchik, R., Kotler, M., & van Praag, H. M. (1995). Parental loss and family violence as correlates of suicide and violence risk. *Suicide and Life-Threatening Behavior, 25*, 263–270.

Brown, G. L., Ebert, M. H., Goyer, T. F., Jimmerson, D. C., Klein, W. J., Bunny, W. E., & Goodwin, F. K. (1982). Aggression, suicide and serotonin: Relationships of CSF amine metabolites. *American Journal of Psychiatry, 139*, 741–746.

Brown, G. L., & Goodwin, F. K. (1986). Human aggression and suicide. *Suicide and Life Threatening Behavior, 16*, 223–243.

Burk, R., Kurz, A., & Moller, H. J. (1985). Suicide risk scales: Do they help to predict suicidal behavior? *European Archives of Psychiatry and Neurological Sciences, 235*, 153–157.

Cairns, R. B., Patterson, G., & Neckerman, H. J. (1988). Suicidal behavior in aggressive adolescents. *Journal of Clinical Child Psychology, 17*, 298–309.

Climent, C. E., Raynes, A., Rollins, A. & Plutchik, R. (1974). Epidemiological studies of female prisoners: II. Biological, psychological and social correlates of drug addiction. *International Journal of the Addictions, 9*, 345–350.

Coccaro, E. F., Kavoussi, R. J., & Lesser, J. C. (1992). Self-and-other-directed human aggression: The role of the central serotonergic system. *International Journal of Clinical Psychopharmacology, 6*, 70–83.

Convit, A. J., Jaeger, S. P., Lin, M., Meisner, J., & Volanka, J. (1988). Predicting assaultiveness in psychiatric inpatients: A pilot study. *Hospital & Community Psychiatry, 39*, 429–434.

Cox, V. C., Paulus, A., & McCain, G. (1984). Prison crowding research: The relevance for prison housing standards and a general approach regarding crowding phenomena. *American Psychologist, 39*, 1148–1160.

Evenson, R. C., Sletten, I. W., Altman, H., & Brown, M. L. (1974). Disturbing behavior: A study of incident reports. *Psychiatric Quarterly, 48*, 266–275.

Firth, S. T., Blovin, J., Natarajan, C., & Blovin, A. (1986). A comparison of the manifest content in dreams of suicidal, depressed and violent patients. *Canadian Journal of Psychiatry, 31*, 48–53.

Fuller, J. L. (1986). Genetics and emotions. In R. Plutchik & H. Kellerman (Eds.), *The biological foundations of emotions* (pp. 199–218). New York: Academic Press.

Garrison, C. Z., McKeown, R. E., Valois, R. F., & Vincent, M. L. (1993). Aggression, substance use and suicidal behaviors in high school students. *American Journal of Public Health, 83*, 179–184.

Gibbons, J. L., Barr, G. A., Bridger, W. H., & Leibowitz, S. F. (1979). Manipulation of dietary tryptophan: Effects on mouse killing and brain serotonin in the rat. *Brain Research, 169*, 139–153.

Golden, R. N., Gilmore, J. H., Corrigan, M. H., Ekstrom, R. D., Knight, B. T., & Garbutt, J. C. (1991). Serotonin, suicide, and aggression: Clinical studies. *Journal of Clinical Psychiatry, 52* (Suppl.), 61–69.

Gray, J. A., Owen, S., Davis, N., & Tsaltas, E. (1983). Psychological and physiological relations between anxiety and impulsivity. In M. Zuckerman (Ed.), *The biological bases of sensation seeking, impulsivity, and anxiety* (pp. 181–227). Hillsdale, NJ: Erlbaum.

Greenwald, D. J., Reznikoff, M., & Plutchik, R. (1994). Suicide risk and violence in alcoholics: Predictions of aggressive risk. *The Journal of Nervous and Mental Disease, 182*, 3–8.

Henry, A. F., & Short, J. (1954). *Suicide and homicide*. Glencoe, IL: Free Press.

Hillbrand, M. (1992). Self-directed and other-directed aggressive behavior in a forensic service. *Suicide and Life Threatening Behavior, 22*, 333–340.

Holinger, P. C. (1987). *Violent deaths in the United States*. New York: Guilford.

Holinger, P. C., Offer, D., Barter, J. T., & Bell, C. C. (1994). *Suicide and homicide among adolescents*. New York: Guilford.

Humphrey, F. A., & Kupferer, M. H. J. (1977). Pockets of violence: An exploration of homicide and suicide. *Diseases of the Nervous System, 38*, 833–837.

Inamdar, S. C., Lewis, D. O., Siomopoulis, G., Shanok, S. S., & Lamela, M. (1982). Violent and suicidal behavior in psychotic adolescents. *American Journal of Psychiatry, 139*, 932–935.

Linnoila, V. M., & Virkkunen, M. (1992). Aggression, suicidality and serotonin. *Journal of Clinical Psychiatry, 53* (Suppl.), 46–51.

Loehlin, J. C., Horn, J. M., & Willerman, L. (1981). Personality resemblance in adoptive families. *Behavior Genetics, 11*, 309–330.

Loehlin, J. C., & Nichols, B. C. (1976). *Heredity, environment and personality: A study of 850 twins*. Austin, TX: University of Texas at Austin Press.

Marazziti, D., Rotondo, A., Presta, S., & Pancioli-Guadagnucci, M. L. (1993). Role of serotonin in human aggressive behavior. *Aggressive Behavior, 19*, 347–353.

Marrero, R. D., O'Sullivan, M. J., Michael, M. C., & Vitaliano, P. P. (1989). Anger, hostility, and depression in assaultive vs. suicide-attempting males. *Journal of Clinical Psychology, 45*, 531–541.

Menninger, K. A. (1956). *Man against himself*. New York: Harcourt Brace & Co.

Moffitt, T. E. (1993). Adolescence-limited and life-course-persistent antisocial behavior: A developmental taxonomy. *Psychological Review, 100*, 674–701.

Pfeffer, C. R., Newcorn, J., Kaplan, G., Mizruchi, M. S., & Plutchik, R. (1989). Subtypes of suicidal and assaultive behaviors in adolescent psychiatric inpatients: A research note. *Journal of Child Psychology and Psychiatry, 30*, 151–163.

Pickar, D., Roy, A., Breier, A., Doran, A., Wolkowitz, O., Colison, J., & Agren, H. (1986). Suicide and aggression in schizophrenics: Neurobiologic correlates. *Annals of the New York Academy of Sciences, 487*, 189–196.

Plutchik, R. (1980). *Emotion: A psychoevolutionary synthesis*. New York: Harper & Row.

Plutchik, R. (1993). Emotions and their vicissitudes: Emotions and psychopathology. In M. Lewis & I. M. Haviland (Eds.), *Handbook of emotions* (pp. 53–66). New York: Guilford.

Plutchik, R. (1994). *The psychology and biology of emotion*. New York: HarperCollins.

Plutchik, R. (1995). Outward and inward directed aggressiveness: The interaction between violence and suicidality. *Pharmacopsychiatry, 28* (Suppl.), 47–57.

Plutchik, R., Botsis, A. J., & van Praag, H. M. (1995). Psychopathology, self-esteem, sexual and ego functions as correlates of suicide and violence risk. *Archives of Suicide Research, 1*, 27–38.

Plutchik, R., & van Praag, H. M. (1990). Psychosocial correlates of suicide and violence risk. In H. M. van Praag, R. Plutchik, & A. Apter (Eds.), *Violence and suicidality: Perspectives in clinical and psychobiological research* (pp. 37–65). New York: Brunner/Mazel.

Plutchik, R., & van Praag, H. M. (1995). The nature of impulsivity: Definitions, ontology, genetics, and relations to aggression. In F. Hollander & D. J. Stein (Eds.), *Impulsivity and aggression* (pp. 7–24). New York: Wiley.

Plutchik, R., van Praag, H. M., & Conte, H. R. (1989). Correlates of suicide and violence risk: III. A two stage model of countervailing forces. *Psychiatry Research, 28,* 215–225.

Polis, G. A. (1981). The evolution and dynamics of intraspecific predation. *Review of Ecological Systematics, 12,* 225–252.

Roy, A., Virkkunen, M., Guthrie, S., & Linnoila, M. (1986). Indices of serotonin and glucose metabolism in violent offenders, arsonists, and alcoholics. *Annals of the New York Academy of Sciences, 487,* 202–220.

Schankman, P. L. (1969). Le roti et le bouilli: Levi-Strauss' theory of cannibalism. *American Anthropology, 71,* 54–69.

Shafii, M., Carrigan, S., Whillinghil, L., & Derrick, A. (1985). Psychological autopsy of completed suicide in children and adolescents. *American Journal of Psychiatry, 142,* 1061–1064.

Shaver, P., Schwartz, J., Kirson, D., & O'Connor, C. (1987). Emotion knowledge: Further explorations of a prototype approach. *Journal of Personality and Social Psychology, 52,* 1061–1086.

Siever, L., & Trestman, R. L. (1993). The serotonin system and aggressive personality disorders. *International Clinical Psychopharmacology, 8* (Suppl. 2), 33–39.

Skodal, A. E., & Karasu, T. B. (1978). Emergency psychiatry and the assaultive patient. *American Journal of Psychiatry, 135,* 202–205.

Soubrie, P., & Bizot, J. C. (1990). Monoaminergic control of waiting capacity (impulsivity) in animals. In H. M. van Praag, R. Plutchik, & A. Apter (Eds.), *Violence and suicidality: Perspectives in clinical and psychobiological research* (pp. 257–274). New York: Brunner/Mazel.

Tardiff, K., & Sweillan, A. (1982). Assaultive behavior among chronic inpatients. *American Journal of Psychiatry, 159,* 212–215.

van Praag, H. M. (1983). CSF 5-HIAA and suicide in nondepressed schizophrenics. *Lancet, 2,* 977–978.

van Praag, H. M. (1993). *"Make-believes" in psychiatry, or the perils of progress.* New York: Brunner/Mazel.

Virkkunen, M., DeJong, J., Bartko, J., & Linnoila, M. (1989). Psychobiological concomitants of a history of suicide attempts among violent offenders and impulsive fire setters. *Archives of General Psychiatry, 46,* 604–606.

White, J. L., Moffitt, T. E., Caspi, A., Bartusch, D. J., Needles, D. J., & Stouthamer-Loeber, M. (1994). Measuring impulsivity and examining its relationship to delinquency. *Journal of Abnormal Psychology, 103,* 192–205.

Wimer, R. E., & Wimer, C. C. (1985). Animal behavior genetics: A search for the biological foundations of behavior. *Annual Review of Psychology, 36,* 171–218.

CHAPTER 11

Commentary on the Assessment and Diagnosis
of Antisocial Behavior and Personality

PAUL A. PILKONIS and KARLA R. KLEIN

The previous chapters have described the cost of antisocial behavior to individuals and society (see Monahan, Chapter 9; Plutchik & van Praag, Chapter 10, both this volume); demonstrated the value of descriptive epidemiology for grasping the scope of the phenomenon in the United States (see Potter & Mercy, Chapter 1, this volume); and characterized the issues and debates concerning the conceptualization, assessment, and diagnosis of antisocial behavior and personality. The integration of these issues leads to the emergence of several themes as central in the study of antisocial behavior and personality traits and disorders. These themes include (a) conceptual distinctions between antisocial behavior and antisocial personality, (b) contextual factors associated with antisocial behavior and personality, and (c) future directions for methodology of research on antisocial behavior and personality, including the need for longitudinal investigation of developmental pathways and for rapprochement between dimensional and categorical approaches to assessment of personality.

CONCEPTUAL ISSUES

The major debate in the conceptualization of antisocial behavior and personality concerns the primacy of and relationship between two constructs that are consistently distinguished in the literature. The first construct, labeled *primary psychopathy* by Cleckley (1941), *Factor 1* (affective and interpersonal markers) by Hart and Hare (Chapter 3, this volume), and *intrapersonal and interpersonal characteristics* by Dinges, Atlis, and Vincent (Chapter 44, this volume), refers to cognitive, affective, and interpersonal traits (e.g., dishonesty, callousness, egocentricity, lack of remorse, lack of capacity for emotional bonds). This construct is emphasized in the Cleckley tradition reviewed by Hart and Hare, also described as the *personality-based approach* by Lilienfeld, Purcell, and Jones-Alexander (Chapter 6, this volume). The second construct, labeled *secondary psychopathy* by Cleckley (1941), *Factor 2* (behavioral markers) by Hart and Hare, and *interpersonal/criminal behavior* by Dinges et al., refers to chronic unstable social conduct and conflicts with legal norms. This construct is the focus of the Washington University tradition described by Hart and Hare and the *behavior-based approach* discussed by Lilienfeld et al.

Critics of the personality-based approach question the accuracy with which clinicians can make assessments of intrapsychic processes, particularly in individuals with antisocial characteristics (i.e., manipulativeness, dishonesty). Likewise, critics of the behavior-based approach stress that an overemphasis on antisocial behavior, to the exclusion of intrapsychic and interpersonal characteristics, may lead to the confusion of psychopathy and chronic criminality. Factor 2 (focusing on behavioral indicators) has become more identified with categorical approaches, largely through its influence on the *DSM* definitions of antisocial personality disorder (ASPD), whereas Factor 1 (affective and interpersonal features) has become more identified with dimensional approaches and variants of normal personality. There is no necessary reason why this should be so, but the two factors have been confounded with these different approaches to classification. Although Hart and Hare point out that correlations between the two criteria sets (assessed continuously) are high, it is also true that prevalence rates (assessed categorically) can differ rather dramatically, particularly in criminal samples. In such samples, the prevalence of ASPD tends to be much larger than the prevalence of psychopathy. Thus, although empirical associations are strong between the two constructs, the clinical and practical implications of each may be different.

CONTEXTUAL ISSUES IN CONCEPTUALIZATION
AND ASSESSMENT

In the effort to establish a maximally useful way of conceptualizing and assessing antisocial behavior and personality, a variety of factors related to dimensions of the individual's functioning and interaction with the environment must be taken into account. These factors may be described as "contextual" factors, referring to variables that are both internal and external to the individual and that influence behavior as well as personality. The clarification of internal and external contextual factors associated with antisocial behavior and personality is crucial if effective modes of intervention are to be developed.

The spectrum of external (i.e., environmental) contextual factors includes elements that are both proximal and distal. Proximal external factors include aspects of the individual's direct interaction with the social environment or the history of such experiences, for example, characteristics of the family, peer group, neighborhood, and community. Distal external factors include more global aspects of the environment in which the individual functions, such as cultural and ethnic influences and socioeconomic conditions. Internal contextual factors include personal attributes such as temperament, physiology, cognitive functioning, psychological functioning, internalized ethnic identity, and level of socioemotional development.

The roles of contextual factors in the etiology of antisocial behavior and personality are receiving increased attention in the research literature. As Dinges et al. point out, a fundamental question is whether the diagnostic criteria for ASPD should be based on a theory of social deviance or a theory of personality. They distinguish between antisocial and criminal behavior and psychopathic personality, asserting that the influence of sociocultural (external contextual) factors is quite different for these two constructs. Given that antisocial behavior is strongly associated with multiple sociocultural factors, it must be conceptualized and assessed within the social context in which it occurs. In contrast, they suggest that psychopathic personality is more universal in nature (i.e., observed in all cultures), so that this pattern of cognitive, affective, and interpersonal traits may be more independent of sociocultural influences. Thus, it could be argued that a "culture-free" conceptualization of ASPD should weight internal contextual factors more heavily, whereas antisocial behavior should be examined in a more qualified way that emphasizes external contextual factors.

Although it is clearly important to consider contextual factors associated with antisocial behavior and personality across the life span, it is crucial for these issues to receive adequate attention in the conceptualization and assessment of children's functioning. The process of development itself is the most powerful internal contextual factor for children. Thus, a child's behavior is influenced by not only the internal flux associated with development but also the match between internal stages of development and the demands of the external context. When a child's ability to cope with either internal or external developmental challenges falters, behavioral manifestations of this inability are likely to occur. Thus, it is common for children to exhibit externalizing behavior (i.e., acting out) as well as internalizing responses (i.e., withdrawal, negative affect) to a variety of internal states, such as depression, separation anxiety, obsessive-compulsive disorder, or attention deficit/hyperactivity disorder (ADHD).

External contextual factors may also exert a powerful influence on children's antisocial behavior. Children exist within environments molded by adults and over which they possess little control. Therefore, they are at risk for suffering negative consequences from a host of external factors, such as chaotic living situations, maladaptive community norms, or poor functioning of adult caretakers. Children may manifest antisocial behaviors in the process of adapting to environmental conditions that fail to appropriately discourage such behavior or that actually promote it as a strategy for adaptation to external contextual demands.

In light of the complexity of contextual issues unique to children, it is clear that care must be taken not to misinterpret childhood externalizing behavior as a stable antisocial trait when it may be reflective of an adjustment problem, adaptation to a chaotic family environment, inadequate parenting, developmental difficulties, other Axis I disorders, learning disabilities, or an unfortunate but rational effort at adaptation to social norms in less than optimal environmental situations (e.g., some inner-city neighborhoods). Complex interactions between developmental and environmental factors may be responsible for antisocial behavior observed cross-sectionally during childhood or adolescence. Therefore, as Hinshaw and Zupan (Chapter 4, this volume) point out, it is crucial to conduct thorough assessments of children's functioning in order to make accurate differential diagnoses and to intervene appropriately with children manifesting antisocial characteristics.

FUTURE DIRECTIONS FOR METHODOLOGY

Longitudinal Investigations of Developmental Pathways

A common call has been made in the previous chapters for longitudinal research that examines clearly articulated developmental pathways leading to antisocial behavior and personality. Although associations between numerous internal and external contextual factors (i.e., temperament; cognitive, affective, and neuropsychological functioning; familial, sociocultural, and community characteristics) and antisocial behavior and personality have been demonstrated, their causal, mediating, or moderating roles are far from clear. Theory-driven models of development, hypothesizing relationships among risk factors, moderators of risk, and both antisocial behavior and antisocial personality structure should be developed and tested. Such models should serve the dual goals of improving the construct validity of measures of both antisocial behavior and personality and identifying useful targets of clinical intervention. In order to develop prevention and intervention programs aimed at predictors and antecedents of antisocial behavior, it is imperative that the roles of these contextual factors be better understood.

For example, as Lahey and Loeber (Chapter 5, this volume) point out, research has failed thus far to clarify the relationships between ADHD, oppositional defiant disorder (ODD), and conduct disorder (CD). Contextual variables from both internal and external domains have been associated with these childhood disorders. However, the mechanisms by which these factors compromise the functioning of children over time are not clear. Lahey and Loeber suggest that ADHD may pose a risk for CD principally through its combination with ODD. These two disorders may interact specifically to pose a high risk for CD, or it may simply be the additive effects of multiple compromises to children's functioning that pose the risk. Factors that predict, mediate, or moderate this developmental trajectory toward adolescent and adult antisocial behavior must be identified in order for effective intervention to take place.

It is plausible, of course, that multiple developmental pathways lead to adult antisocial behavior and personality. One possible developmental model is a cumulative risk pathway, such that more childhood adversity in all its forms leads to poorer outcome. Such a general model, however, requires that the risk factors distinctive for antisocial behavior and personality be clearly identified.

A second possible developmental model stems primarily from internal factors. In such a model, underlying biological predispositions are assumed to drive the system. For instance, internal child factors (e.g., ADHD, temperament, neuropsychological and cognitive functioning) may elicit external familial patterns (e.g., parenting practices) that increase the risk for oppositional behavior, which escalates to CD in adolescence and may result in criminal behavior.

A third plausible model focuses more exhaustively on external contextual factors, such that the developmental trajectory toward antisocial behavior and personality is motivated principally by characteristics of the social environment. In this model, it may be proposed that family, community, or social norms are the "active ingredients" in promoting the development of antisocial behavior.

Clearly, longitudinal research is the most effective method of investigating models of developmental pathways. Although the feasibility of longitudinal research is frequently debated, given the current era of serious constraints on research support, the efficiency of longitudinal studies can be improved through creative efforts, especially those that foster collaboration across investigators. One possibility, for example, may be to use follow-back designs (with previously identified patients) that also include a shorter term, prospective component (Ronald Kessler, personal communication). Another efficient model is one in which multiple investigators utilize a common sample to explore a variety of domains of functioning and outcomes (cf. the Pittsburgh Youth Study).

Conceptually, it is important that tests of hypotheses about developmental pathways be more distinctive than simple description and analysis of repeated measurements. For this purpose, there are increasingly sophisticated quantitative tools available (i.e., hierarchical regression models, growth curve analysis), but they require large sample sizes to be used effectively. Thus, to make these longitudinal explorations practical and cost efficient, some mechanisms for aggregating data across investigators may be necessary. Clearly, standards in conceptualization, assessment, and diagnosis must be firmly established in order for collaborative efforts such as these to be useful.

Integrating Dimensional and Categorical Approaches to Measurement

Consistent with the conceptual issues discussed earlier regarding the distinction between antisocial behavior and antisocial personality, an active discussion exists in the literature concerning the diagnosis of ASPD. Problems in formulating reliable and valid diagnoses of any personality disorder are well documented, and the diagnosis and assessment of ASPD are no exception, a fact reflected in the conceptual and methodological problems cited in several of the chapters in this section. A number of issues in the identification of cases of PDs have been thoughtfully discussed both here and elsewhere: the advantages and disadvantages of different sources of information (self-report vs. informants vs. clinical diagnosis vs. structured research diagnosis; Hart & Hare, Chapter 3, this volume; Hinshaw & Zupan, Chapter 4, this volume; Lilienfeld et al., Chapter 6, this volume; Zimmerman, 1994); discrepancies between instruments, even when using the same kind of data (Lilienfeld et al.; Perry, 1992); the relative lack

of attention paid to alternative ways in which caseness can be operationalized (Kraemer, 1992; Pilkonis et al., 1995; Zarin & Earls, 1993); and the absence of gold standards for validity (Faraone & Tsuang, 1994), which has resulted in a greater emphasis on reliability and fewer efforts to ensure external validity.

With the *DSM* nosology, there are serious concerns about the discriminant validity of individual PD diagnoses. The typical finding is that patients meet criteria for multiple diagnoses (Oldham et al., 1992), and the evidence is mixed about whether such diagnoses aggregate within the a priori clusters proposed: cluster A, odd, eccentric, schizotypal disorders; cluster B, dramatic, expressive, externalizing disorders; and cluster C, fearful, anxious, internalizing disorders (Bell & Jackson, 1992; Dowson & Berrios, 1991; Hyler et al., 1990; Kass, Skodol, Charles, Spitzer, & Williams, 1985; Livesley, Jackson, & Schroeder, 1992). Widiger and Corbitt (Chapter 7, this volume) focus on the issue of comorbidity between ASPD and the other Axis II disorders and summarize five potential strategies for decreasing comorbidity: abandon the concept of comorbidity altogether; abandon certain "offending" diagnoses; collapse frequently co-occurring diagnoses into a single category; abandon categorical distinctions in general and adopt dimensional models of personality; and revise criteria sets to improve differentiation. With regard to these issues, the liveliest debate occurs around the usefulness of categorical versus dimensional approaches to assessment (Livesley, Schroeder, Jackson, & Jang, 1994; Widiger & Sanderson, 1995).

Finally, there are problems regarding the use of different instruments in different settings in which base rates of Axis II disorders may vary widely (e.g., community samples with low base rates vs. clinical or forensic settings in which base rates may be quite high). The goal is to develop instruments whose diagnostic efficiency is maintained even when base rates vary, but this is a difficult outcome to achieve. Several authors here advocate increased attention to nonclinical, community samples as one way to develop more robust conclusions about ASPD (e.g., Cloninger, Bayon, & Przybeck, Chapter 2; Lahey & Loeber, Chapter 5; Widiger & Corbitt, Chapter 7, all this volume).

For the present discussion, the important message is not that the two approaches be polarized but rather that we find ways to use them in complementary fashion. Dimensions are attractive psychometrically; categories are attractive clinically—neither approach is going to disappear, so we need to find ways to integrate them profitably. One model for doing so is provided by Cloninger et al., who comment that PDs are not "discrete diseases but are clinically distinct and relatively stable configurations of multiple quantitative traits." That is, we may define multidimensional trait models, and we can examine such models to try to identify clusterings of features that define groups that appear to be relatively homogeneous within themselves and different from other groups. One task for future research is to provide evidence regarding the construct validity of such groups. Thus, the best categories are likely to grow out of the best profiling that we can do across the relevant traits. Such an effort presumes that we have assessed all the relevant traits and all the relevant samples. Again, one theme across several of the chapters is the different outcomes that one sees in clinical versus nonclinical samples.

Another strategy for blending dimensional and categorical

approaches is the use of signal detection analyses with continuous data to identify thresholds regarding significant markers and categorical outcomes. One can allow for different thresholds for different problems and utilities, for example, acute treatment response, longer term functional impairment, specific life attainments, or whatever other outcomes are of interest. Not all thresholds need to be the same, but it is essential that they be cross-validated in different settings and samples.

In terms of cross-validation, several authors note the relative absence of research with young girls and women and call for the inclusion of gender issues in research on antisocial behavior and personality (see also Giordano & Cernkovich, Chapter 46, this volume). This focus should be a priority in the exploration of developmental pathways to antisocial behavior as well as comorbidity of symptomatology between personality disorders. Zanarini and Gunderson (Chapter 8, this volume), in discussing the specific comorbidity of borderline personality disorder (BPD) and ASPD, make an argument for the existence of three groups: pure BPD patients, who are women; pure ASPD patients, who are men; and a mixed group, with an approximately equal breakdown by sex. They point out that persons with BPD appear to have suffered more cumulative pathological experiences and are at greater risk for psychosocial impairment, a statement consistent with the findings of Cloninger et al. on the greater vulnerability of persons with a borderline/explosive profile (high Novelty Seeking, high Harm Avoidance, and low Reward Dependence) on the Temperament and Character Inventory compared with persons with an antisocial profile (high Novelty Seeking, low Harm Avoidance, and low Reward Dependence). Zanarini and Gunderson suggest that the clear sex difference in their three-group typology provides an important starting point for any model of etiology.

REFERENCES

Bell, R. C., & Jackson, H. J. (1992). The structure of personality disorders in *DSM-III*. *Acta Psychiatrica Scandinavica, 85,* 279–287.

Cleckley, H. (1941). *The mask of sanity.* St. Louis: Mosby.

Dowson, J. H., & Berrios, G. E. (1991). Factor structure of *DSM-III-R* personality disorders shown by self-report questionnaire: Implication for classifying and assessing personality disorders. *Acta Psychiatrica Scandinavica, 84,* 555–560.

Faraone, S. V., & Tsuang, M. T. (1994). Measuring diagnostic accuracy in the absence of a "gold standard." *American Journal of Psychiatry, 151,* 650–657.

Hyler, S. E., Lyons, M., Rieder, R. O., Young, L., Williams, J. B. W., & Spitzer, R. L. (1990). The factor structure of self-report *DSM-III* Axis II symptoms and their relationship to clinicians' ratings. *American Journal of Psychiatry, 147,* 751–757.

Kass, F., Skodol, A. E., Charles, E., Spitzer, R. L., & Williams, J. B. W. (1985). Scaled ratings of *DSM-III* personality disorders. *American Journal of Psychiatry, 142,* 627–630.

Kraemer, H. C. (1992). *Evaluating medical tests: Objective and quantitative guidelines.* Newbury Park, CA: Sage Publications.

Livesley, W. J., Jackson, D. N., & Schroeder, M. L. (1992). Factorial structure of traits delineating personality disorders in clinical and general population samples. *Journal of Abnormal Psychology, 101,* 432–440.

Livesley, W. J., Schroeder, M. L., Jackson, D. N., & Jang, K. L. (1994). Categorical distinctions in the study of personality disorder: Implications for classification. *Journal of Abnormal Psychology, 103,* 6–17.

Oldham, J. M., Skodol, A. E., Kellman, H. D., Hyler, S. E., Rosnick, L., & Davies, M. (1992). Diagnosis of *DSM-III-R* personality disorders by two structured interviews: Patterns of comorbidity. *American Journal of Psychiatry, 149,* 213–220.

Perry, J. C. (1992). Problems and considerations in the valid assessment of personality disorders. *American Journal of Psychiatry, 149,* 1645–1653.

Pilkonis, P. A., Heape, C. L., Proietti, J. M., Clark, S. W., McDavid, J. D., & Pitts, T. E. (1995). The reliability and validity of two structured diagnostic interviews for personality disorders. *Archives of General Psychiatry, 52,* 1025–1033.

Widiger, T. A., & Sanderson, C. J. (1995). Toward a dimensional model of personality disorders. In W. J. Livesley (Ed.), *The* DSM-IV *personality disorders* (pp. 433–458). New York: Guilford.

Zarin, D. A., & Earls, F. (1993). Diagnostic decision making in psychiatry. *American Journal of Psychiatry, 150,* 197–206.

Zimmerman, M. (1994). Diagnosing personality disorders: A review of issues and research methods. *Archives of General Psychiatry, 51,* 225–245.

PART TWO

Development of Antisocial Behavior

CHAPTER 12

Antisocial Behavior: Developmental Psychopathology Perspectives

MICHAEL RUTTER

The concept of *antisocial behavior* is unusual in the field of psychopathology in being largely defined in terms not of abnormal psychological features but rather of behavior that contravenes the norms of society. Because societies vary in their conventions and expectations, because countries differ in their laws, and because even within countries laws change over time, it would seem to follow that antisocial behavior must be a slippery, value-laden concept incapable of unambiguous definition. Years ago, Wootton (1959) drew attention to the severe dangers of defining psychopathology in terms of social criteria. If a change in the law can, at a stroke, rule out major classes of behavior from that deemed antisocial (e.g., decriminalizing of suicidal behavior) or bring in new behaviors (e.g., raising the drinking age, recognizing violence to spouses as assault, or making the corporal punishment of children illegal), how can any definition have any enduring meaning? If the concept cannot be defined, how can it be studied?

It might be supposed, therefore, that attempts to investigate possible biological bases for this socially defined construct would be particularly inappropriate. However, strong claims are being made in books by academics that are aimed at the popular market (e.g., Moir & Jessel, 1995). It is no wonder, one might think, that other scientists are scathing in their attack on what they view as dangerous biological determinism (S. Rose, 1995). Similar problems would seem to arise with respect to the inclusion of *conduct disorder* in psychiatric classifications (Richters & Cicchetti, 1993).

Nevertheless, despite these problems, numerous studies have shown that, of all forms of childhood psychopathology, antisocial behavior shows an unusually strong degree of persistence over time (Maughan & Rutter, in press). Moreover, childhood conduct disorders show a very marked tendency to lead on to serious social impairments, including handicapping personality disorders, in adult life (Robins, 1978; Zoccolillo, Pickles, Quinton, & Rutter,

1992). On the face of it, this would seem enough to justify the conceptualization of antisocial behavior in *trait* or *disorder* terms. That is perhaps especially so in view of the fact that there is quite a high degree of consistency in empirical research findings on the correlates of antisocial behavior (Earls, 1994; Farrington, 1995a; Robins, 1991; Rutter & Giller, 1983).

HETEROGENEITY OF ANTISOCIAL BEHAVIOR

How may this dilemma be resolved? How can antisocial behavior be both a value-laden concept and a reflection of a disorder leading to social impairment? The starting point has to be a recognition of the heterogeneity of antisocial behavior (Rutter, 1996b). To begin with, it is clearly unacceptable to equate breaking the law with individual disorder or psychopathology. At least some forms of civil disobedience represent highly principled, carefully considered acts designed to change the law or prevailing practice. The suffragette movement in the early part of the 20th century and the civil protest against racial segregation in the United States both represent examples of this kind. The struggle against apartheid in South Africa is yet another. In other cases, breaking the law is a matter of conscience. Pacifists' refusal to enter the armed forces and their subsequent imprisonment in the United Kingdom during World War I provide an illustration.

There are also behaviors (such as the occasional recreational taking of cannabis) that are outside the law but that are nevertheless acceptable within subgroups of society. In addition, there are behaviors that are illegal only because they occur below a legally defined age limit (e.g., underage drinking of alcohol) or because certain activities such as school attendance are compulsory (e.g., truancy). On the one hand, these behaviors are shown, at least occasionally, by many otherwise law-abiding young people without any other evidence of either antisocial behavior or psychopathology. On the other hand, drug taking, truancy, and underage drinking also show substantial associations with conduct problems as manifest in other ways—such as theft, violence, or burglary (Farrington, 1995a; Jessor, Donovan, & Costa, 1991; Kaplan, 1995; Rönkä & Pulkkinen, 1995).

I am much indebted, for both research findings and ideas, to the many colleagues with whom I have had the pleasure of working over the years. Particular thanks are due to Henri Giller, Ann Hagell, Barbara Maughan, Joanne Meyer, Andrew Pickles, Judy Silberg, Emily Simonoff, and Eric Taylor.

Much the same difficulty, with respect to the viewing of antisocial behavior as psychopathology, arises even with behaviors such as stealing or interpersonal violence or destruction of personal property, each of which would be viewed as unacceptable in almost all societies regardless of age or legal constraints. The point is that antisocial behavior constitutes a behavioral tendency shown by almost all human beings to some degree. Many surveys have shown that, at some time, the majority of boys commit occasional acts that are outside the law and that could have led to prosecution if they had been caught (Graham & Bowling, 1995; Rutter & Giller, 1983). Indeed, in inner cities, over one quarter of males actually acquire an official crime record. Also, the U.S. National Youth Survey showed that over one quarter of males admitted committing at least one serious violent offense, such as aggravated assault, robbery, or rape (Elliott, 1994). On the other hand, although many young people engage in antisocial behavior at some time, they account for a relatively low proportion of total crime. A small minority of chronic offenders are responsible for the bulk of serious crime (Thornberry, Huizinga, & Loeber, 1995).

At the other extreme, a few instances of antisocial behavior are strongly associated with either overt mental disorder or a medical condition. Some of the violent crimes committed by people with schizophrenia (P. J. Taylor, 1993; Wessely, Castle, Douglas, & Taylor, 1994) or Asperger syndrome (Tantam, 1988; Wolff, 1995) would fall in the first category, as would many cases of infanticide (D'Orban, 1979; Kumar & Marks, 1992) or family killings deriving from a severe depressive disorder (Häfner & Böker, 1982; West, 1965). The causal role of the mental illness is indicated both by the temporal relationship (in which the illness precedes the violence) and by the pattern of correlates, which differ from those ordinarily associated with antisocial behavior (see Monahan, Chapter 9, this volume). The association between monoamine oxidase A deficiency (a single gene medical condition) and increased antisocial impulsive behavior (such as aggression, arson, and predatory sexuality) perhaps represents the second category (Brunner, 1996).

In between these extremes of normality and manifest illness lies a wide spectrum of behavior. As already noted, persistent and varied antisocial behavior, or recidivist delinquency, is associated with a greatly increased risk of severe and widespread social malfunction in adult life, severe illnesses and accidents, and even early death (Earls, 1994). By any reckoning, this provides a major source of concern, whatever the arguments about its conceptualization as a form of psychiatric disorder (Richters & Cicchetti, 1993). In addition, there are important associations with individual psychological characteristics such as relatively low cognitive skills, hyperactivity, sensation seeking, and impulsivity (Farrington, 1995a; Moffitt, 1993b; Raine & Venables, 1992); with physiological features such as reduced autonomic reactivity (Lahey, McBurnett, Loeber, & Hart, 1995); and with biological risk factors such as low brain serotonin turnover (Virkkunen, Goldman, & Linnoila, 1996) or the chromosomal anomaly XYY (Ratcliffe, 1994). Of course, these associations refer to group differences, and at an individual level, there is much variation. The question is whether these individual differences could serve to define subcategories of antisocial behavior.

DEVELOPMENTAL PSYCHOPATHOLOGY PERSPECTIVES

The perspectives of developmental psychopathology provide one useful way forward. Their essence lies in a set of research approaches and concepts that capitalize on just those features that seem to provide a problem for traditional psychiatry and psychology. That is, they focus on continuities and discontinuities over the span of behavioral variation extending from normality to overt handicapping disorder or disease states (Rutter, 1993, 1996a; Sroufe & Rutter, 1984). Neither continuity nor discontinuity is assumed; rather, their examination is a way of understanding the nature of particular behaviors and of investigating sources of heterogeneity. Similarly, developmental psychopathology focuses on continuities and discontinuities over the course of development from infancy to adult life. The key question is not about the strength of correlations over time but rather about the mechanisms and processes involved in both continuity and discontinuity—the possible heterogeneity indexed by variations in age of onset and the possible heterogeneity reflected in individual differences in persistence over the life span.

A third perspective associated with developmental psychopathology (although by no means confined to it) is a recognition that causation represents a range of rather different questions and not just one. Thus, causes ordinarily tend to be thought of in relation to individual differences—why X is antisocial whereas Y is not. Even if the causation of antisocial behavior is seen in individual liability terms, however, a distinction needs to be drawn between the factors that lead to the initiation of such behavior and those that underlie its perpetuation or its desistance over time (Farrington, 1995a). The last point is an important one if only because the falloff of antisocial behavior in early adult life is such a striking and consistent phenomenon. But the cause of individual differences is only one type of causal question and not necessarily the most important one from the point of view of public policy. Thus, in addition, there is the need to consider the causes of group differences in *level*. Such differences may apply over time; for example, there has been a massive rise over the last 50 years in rates of delinquency in virtually all Western countries (Smith, 1995). Differences in level may also concern variations among countries, for example, the fact that the murder rate is over a dozen times higher in the United States than in Europe. Both of these differences in level are important, not only because the differences are so extremely large, but also because it is quite implausible that they derive from biological differences between populations, however influential biological factors are with respect to individual differences (Rutter, 1996b).

In addition, there are well-established situational effects (Clarke, 1985; Tonry & Farrington, 1995), with their reminder that an individual propensity to engage in antisocial behavior is one thing but the translation of that propensity into the commission of antisocial acts is another (Rutter & Giller, 1983; Rutter et al., in press). Such situational effects may be ones that influence individual inhibitions (such as the effects of alcohol on violence—see Kaplan, 1995; Royal College of Physicians, 1979, 1995), or they may concern the disincentives provided by effective surveillance and supervision of either individuals or places (e.g., as provided by neighbors, the opportunities for observation being affected by housing estate design, TV cameras, or guards on trains of football supporters), or they may derive from "target-hardening" measures (e.g., car locks or a changed design of telephone booths), or they may stem from steps to alter the "attractiveness" of targets (e.g., vandalism of buildings is more likely when broken windows or graffiti are already visible). Sometimes interventions designed to influence situational factors are dismissed on the grounds that they merely affect *where* delinquent acts are committed and not *whether* they take place. Of course, displacement of delinquent activities may take place (and often does), but to assume that is *all* that happens has to be based on a prior assumption that individual liability is a fixed quantity and that it translates directly and inevitably into antisocial behavior regardless of context. It is most unlikely that is the case. The issue of the translation of propensities into behavior is a general one. Thus, a suicidal predisposition is much influenced by the presence of both major depression and impulsive personality qualities. But whether predisposed people actually commit suicide is influenced by the availability of means and by their lethality (e.g., the drop in suicide rates in the United Kingdom following the detoxification of domestic gas—Clarke & Mayhew, 1988). Similarly, there are individual differences in propensity to alcoholism, but rates of alcoholism are also influenced by the cost and availability of alcohol (Royal College of Physicians, 1979, 1995). Comparable issues are likely to apply to the commission of antisocial acts.

The final causal consideration is the need to differentiate between risk *indicators* and risk mechanisms (Rutter, 1994b). Far too many researchers rest content with the demonstration of some statistical association and do not move on to the crucial next step of testing whether the postulated risk factor actually contributes to the causal process. As a consequence, the research literature is cluttered with a mass of somewhat misleading findings. In some cases, what are thought to be environmental effects prove to be at least partially genetically mediated (Plomin & Bergeman, 1991); in other cases, what seem to be parental influences on children actually represent in part the effects of children on parents (Lytton, 1990); in yet other instances, the effect reflects an association with some third variable that is much closer to the causal process. For example, broken homes and family change (as represented by divorce, separation, etc.) are associated with delinquency, but the evidence suggests that this association is largely a function of the association with family discord (Fergusson, Horwood, & Lynskey, 1992). Discord unassociated with family breakup predisposes to antisocial behavior, but family change not associated with discord does not do so. Similarly, it has commonly been supposed that low social class or status constitutes a major risk factor for both antisocial behavior and other forms of psychopathology (see review by Rutter & Giller, 1983). Multivariate analyses, however, make clear that the risk derives from lower scores on intelligence tests and not from lower social class (e.g., Goodman, Simonoff, & Stevenson, 1995; Rutter, Tizard, & Whitmore, 1970; Schonfeld, Shaffer, O'Connor, & Portnoy, 1988). Of course, this finding necessarily leads to the further question of the mechanisms by which lower intelligence scores are involved in

risk processes. It is necessary to find the means by which to test causal hypotheses, such as through the study of intra-individual change, natural experiments, dose-response relationships, and planned interventions (Rutter, 1994a).

THE FALLACIES OF BIOLOGICAL PRIMACY AND BIOLOGICAL DETERMINISM

With respect to causal inferences, a word of caution is needed on the danger of assuming biological primacy or biological determinism simply because research shows that some biological factor is statistically associated with antisocial behavior (see Eisenberg, 1995, for a reasoned discussion of the interconnection between brain and mind). For example, both blood and cerebrospinal fluid testosterone levels have been found to be associated with aggression (Olweus, Mattson, Schalling, & Löw, 1980; Virkkunen et al., 1994). But is the increase in sex hormone levels a *cause* of the aggression or does the causal arrow run in the opposite direction? The causal process could work either way. Thus, winners in a closely matched chess (Mazur, Booth, & Dabbs, 1992) or tennis (Mazur & Lamb, 1980) game show a rise in testosterone whereas losers show a drop. Similarly, in animals, changes in social status lead to changes in hormone level (Raleigh & McGuire, 1991; R. M. Rose, Holaday, & Bernstein, 1971). Even more surprisingly, people pretending to behave in a mentally ill fashion have been found to show some of the biochemical changes associated with the illness they were copying (Post & Goodwin, 1973). Of course, that is not at all to argue that biochemical abnormalities cannot have behavioral consequences; obviously, they can and do. Rather, the point is that there is a complex two-way interplay between soma and psyche, and it cannot be assumed that the biological feature is primary (see Brain & Susman, Chapter 29, this volume). This applies to all manner of biological investigations. For example, Raine et al. (1994) found brain imaging differences between mentally ill murderers and controls and argued that a brain abnormality may have played a contributory role in the causation of the antisocial behavior. That is certainly possible, but, putting aside problems of sampling and controls, it cannot be inferred that a *difference* in brain activity means an *abnormality* in brain structure, and even less can it be concluded that either *caused* the antisocial behavior. Changes in thinking patterns lead to changes in brain activity; indeed, that constitutes the rationale for using cognitive task performance as a stimulus for functional imaging studies. Learning leads to brain changes (e.g., Horn, 1990), and stress experiences have effects on neuroendocrine structure and function (Hennessey & Levine, 1979).

Nevertheless, even taking full account of these necessary caveats and cautions about causal inferences, it is crucial to recognize the importance of biological factors in individual differences in liability to antisocial behavior (Bock & Goode, 1996; A. J. Reiss, Miezek, & Roth, 1994; see also Linnoila, Chapter 31, this volume). Thus, it is clear that genetic factors play a major role in the origins of early-onset antisocial behavior associated with hyperactivity (Silberg et al., 1996a, 1996b). Also, it is highly likely that the huge male preponderance among delinquents, and especially among violent offenders, involves some form of biological propensity, as well as a reflection of sociocultural influences (Maccoby & Jacklin, 1980). Animal studies implicate the serotonin system in impulsivity, and human studies provide parallels (e.g., Virkkunen et al., 1996), although there are serious inconsistencies yet to be explained (e.g., Brunner, 1996). There can be no doubt that biological research will have much to contribute to an understanding of the genesis of antisocial behavior. Even so, it is essential that we do not slide into unwarranted assumptions of biological determinism. Any suggestion that there could be, for example, a "gene for crime" is patently preposterous and biologically naive (Rutter, 1997).

Four main points need to be made regarding causal mechanisms. First, it is exceedingly unlikely that genes could code for a socially defined behavior such as "crime"; it is equally implausible that a biochemical abnormality or a brain disorder could cause antisocial behavior directly. Rather, the effects are likely to apply to indirect risk factors such as impulsivity, hyperactivity, sensation seeking, low autonomic responsivity, cognitive impairment, or aggressivity (e.g., Moffitt, 1993b; Raine & Venables, 1992). Second, it may well be that the biological risk process requires (at least for its full effect) some interplay with adverse experiences. This possibility has been strongly suggested by adoptee findings (e.g., Bohman, 1996; Cadoret, Yates, Troughton, Woodworth, & Stewart, 1995; Crowe, 1974), case-control investigations (e.g., Biederman et al., 1995), and longitudinal studies (E. Taylor, Chadwick, Heptinstall, & Danckaerts, 1996).

Third, indirect chain effects are likely to be operative in many instances. For example, delinquent activities lead to incarceration, but the experience of incarceration in turn predisposes (via effects on employment) to the continuation of criminal behavior into adult life (Sampson & Laub, 1993). Marital discord and marital breakdown are predictable to an important extent by antisocial behavior in childhood (e.g., Quinton, Pickles, Maughan, & Rutter, 1993; Robins, 1966), but, despite this, the experience of marital harmony or dysharmony has an independent effect on people's behavior in adult life (Quinton et al., 1993; Sampson & Laub, 1993). Similarly, conduct disturbance in childhood predisposes to later alcohol and drug abuse, but, equally, drug taking and alcoholism independently serve to foster the continuation of criminal behavior and, more directly (probably through disinhibition), predispose to violent acts (Ito, Miller, & Pollack, 1996; Kaplan, 1995; Robins & McEvoy, 1990; Sampson & Laub, 1993). Or, again, childhood aggression and oppositional defiant behavior influence parental behavior (Lytton, 1990), but parenting practices, in turn, have an effect on the children's later antisocial behavior (Patterson, 1995, 1996; Snyder & Patterson, 1995). Events and experiences that people bring about through their own actions can nevertheless have effects on their subsequent behavior. The strong implication is that longitudinal studies are essential if these bidirectional effects and indirect chain reactions are to be identified and understood.

Fourth, as already noted, biological factors are unlikely to play a major role in certain sorts of causal processes, such as the large rise in crime over the last 50 years. The implication is that causal research needs to investigate secular trends, national differences, and situational effects as well as individual differences.

CATEGORIES OF ANTISOCIAL BEHAVIOR

Although it is obvious that antisocial behavior is heterogeneous (see earlier section), attempts to derive discrete categories have been rather disappointing until the early 1980s (Rutter & Giller, 1983). Numerous studies have shown that most delinquents commit a wide variety of antisocial acts, and there is little future in attempts to classify according to the type of crime committed (with a few possible exceptions). Similarly, although it seemed apparent that socialized delinquency (i.e., that committed in groups by individuals with good peer relationships) and unsocialized aggression (i.e., solitary acts associated with social maladjustment and disturbed interpersonal relationships) must be different (Hewitt & Jenkins, 1946), the dichotomy has proved troublesome to apply in practice. Equally, the presence or absence of associated emotional disturbance has not proved to be a particularly useful differentiator (Rutter & Giller, 1983).

Instead, recent research, using a range of different strategies, has emphasized several other key distinctions. First, there is the importance of an association with hyperactivity/inattention (see Hinshaw & Zupan, Chapter 4, Lahey & Loeber, Chapter 5, both this volume), perhaps particularly when it has an onset in the preschool years and is pervasive across situations. Twin studies show that this pattern involves a strong genetic component, whereas antisocial behavior without hyperactivity/inattention is mainly environmentally determined (Silberg et al., 1996a, 1996b). Longitudinal study findings, too, indicate a worse long-term prognosis for antisocial behavior when it is associated with hyperactivity/inattention (Farrington, Loeber, & Van Kammen, 1990; E. Taylor et al., 1996). It might be thought that the presence of hyperactivity is merely a marker of severity, but that seems not to be the case. The correlates and course of hyperactivity are rather different from those of conduct disturbance. Hyperactivity predicts later conduct problems, but the reverse does not apply; and the presence of hyperactivity is predictive of later functioning independent of initial overall symptom level (Fergusson & Horwood, 1995a; E. Taylor et al., 1996). Second, research findings indicate that the genetic component in violent crime is less than that in petty crime (e.g., stealing; Brennan, Mednick, & Jacobsen, 1996). There may be some value in this differentiation despite the difficulties in deciding what to include in the violent category. Nevertheless, longitudinal data show huge overlap among predictors of violent and nonviolent crime (Farrington, 1995b). Third, Bohman's (1996) adoptee data suggest that crime associated with alcoholism may differ from that not so associated. Mention has already been made of the extent to which violent crime committed by schizophrenic individuals is a rather separate category.

Fourth, increasing attention has come to be paid to the age of onset of antisocial behavior and to its persistence into adult life (Lahey & Loeber, 1994; Moffitt, 1993a; Patterson, 1995). Two somewhat different distinctions have been discussed. First, twin studies show that adult crime involves a stronger genetic component than juvenile delinquency (DiLalla & Gottesman, 1989; Lyons et al., 1995; Rutter et al., in press). Second, longitudinal data indicate the greater seriousness and persistence of unusually early-onset antisocial behavior (Farrington et al., 1990; Patterson, 1995; Tolan & Thomas, 1995). It might be thought that these two sets of findings are inconsistent with one another, but probably they are not. The likely implication is that adolescent-onset antisocial behavior is largely environmentally determined, is unassociated with hyperactivity, and tends not to persist into adult life or be associated with widespread social malfunction. By contrast, early-onset antisocial behavior involves a strong genetic component; is often accompanied by hyperactivity, inattention, or both; and shows a strong tendency to persist into adult life with associated and widespread social problems. If correct (and further research is needed to test the possibility), the implication is that early age of onset and presence of hyperactivity are both reflecting the same feature. It is necessary, therefore, to ask whether age of onset has an effect on persistence that is independent of its correlates (such as hyperactivity). If it does, this would suggest the value of delaying onset in preventive programs, whereas if it were merely an index of a different sort of psychopathology, this would not be expected to be of value. Data from the U.S. National Youth Survey (Tolan & Thomas, 1995) suggest that the effect of onset is both a marker of an underlying antisocial propensity and also a (probably minor) independent influence in its own right.

Further research into the age of onset will need to pay attention to what the onset refers to. Does the effect apply only to overt delinquent acts or does it apply to oppositional/defiant behavior? It is important to pose the question because the latter is characteristically a feature of early childhood (Loeber & Hay, 1994) and is even evident in infancy (Shaw, Keenan, & Vondra, 1994). It may well be that the precursors of later antisocial behavior can be found early in life (Tremblay, Pihl, Vitaro, & Dobkin, 1994; White, Moffitt, Earls, Robins, & Silva, 1990), but that does not necessarily mean that age differences in the onset of these early precursors carry predictive power. After all, much early oppositional behavior does *not* lead to later conduct disorder.

DIMENSIONS AND CATEGORIES

Much heat, and rather little light, has been generated in disputes (often between psychologists and psychiatrists) over whether antisocial behavior (or other forms of psychopathology) should be conceptualized in dimensional or categorical terms (e.g., Fergusson & Horwood, 1995b; Jensen, 1995). Researchers supporting a dimensional approach point to its greater statistical power (Fergusson & Horwood, 1995b) and to the finding that subclinical levels of antisocial behavior have patterns of correlates and consequences that are much the same as those shown by severe clinical categories of conduct disorder (Robins & McEvoy, 1990; Robins, Tipp, & Przybeck, 1991). Proponents of a categorical approach point to the crucial differences associated with some distinctions but emphasize that meaningful categories are rarely defined in terms of severity. Thus, hyperkinetic disorder differs from conduct disorder in a host of features, but the differentiation between the two diagnoses lies in the *pattern* of psychopathology and not in the severity of antisocial behavior (E. Taylor, 1994).

Both dimensional and categorical models have advantages and disadvantages; the two are not mutually exclusive (Cantwell & Rutter, 1994; Klein & Riso, 1993). Perhaps, five main points deriving from medical research are most important. First, a behav-

ior may function dimensionally for some purposes but categorically for others. Thus, intelligence test scores function as a dimension predictively (with respect to educational attainment, social functioning, and psychopathological risk). Nevertheless, the causes of severe mental retardation (such as chromosomal anomalies and single gene disorders) are quite different from the causes of individual variations in intelligence within the normal range. Second, a condition that obviously constitutes a category with respect to pathology and mortality may nevertheless involve a causal process based on dimensional risk factors. For example, myocardial infarction (heart attack) clearly represents a qualitative break from normality, but, even so, its origins lie in dimensional variables such as cholesterol levels, by which the risk increases in parallel with rises even within the normal range. Third, there are usually clinically important dimensions operating even within qualitatively distinct disease categories. Fourth, identification of qualitatively distinct categories is heavily reliant on the recognition of key differentiating features; almost never do they derive from statistical analyses focusing on distributions, severity cutoffs, and the like. The crucial distinction between insulin-dependent and non-insulin-dependent diabetes is not based on blood glucose levels or even just age of onset (despite the fact that the former characteristically begins in childhood and the latter in later life); rather, it is based on metabolic pattern differences and a quite different etiology. The need for careful clinical distinctions in the field of antisocial behavior is emphasized by Kerr, Tremblay, Pagani-Kurtz, and Vitaro's (in press) demonstration that the contradictory findings on the implications of a co-occurrence of social withdrawal and disruptive behavior are a function of a failure to differentiate between social anxiety (which decreases the risk of later delinquency) and social isolation (which increases it). Fifth, categorical distinctions must be validated by means of criteria (such as etiology) that are independent from those defining the category. The diabetes example illustrates this point.

ENVIRONMENTAL RISK PROCESSES

Despite a vast literature full of empirical research findings, our understanding of the environmental risk processes involved in antisocial behavior remains decidedly limited. Five key unresolved issues stand out. First, as already noted, very few studies have used designs that can differentiate genetic and environmental mediation. Numerous studies have shown the strength of parental criminality as a predictor of antisocial behavior in the offspring (e.g., Farrington, 1995b), but we lack good data on the extent to which the risk is genetically or environmentally mediated. Circumstantial evidence certainly suggests that some family risk factors operate environmentally, at least in part (Rutter, 1994b), but a clear differentiation between genetic and environmental mediation has still to be obtained.

Second, most risk factors are expressed in terms that are too general to indicate their likely mode of operation. For example, there is good evidence that family discord is associated with an increased risk of antisocial behavior (Rutter, 1994b). But to what extent does this have to be focused on an individual child to create a risk? The findings of D. Reiss et al. (1995) suggest that the focus is crucial and that negativity aimed at a sibling involves *no* increase in risk. Does the same lack of risk apply to marital conflict? If it does not, does the risk stem from conflict as such or rather from a failure to resolve conflict (Davies & Cummings, 1994)? But, also, what is it about discord that creates the risk? Patterson (1982, 1995) and his colleagues have argued that the explanation lies in faulty contingencies in coercive parental responses to the children's negative behavior. But the possible roles of modeling and of supervision and monitoring also need to be taken into account.

Third, what do environmental risk factors do to the organism? They must do something because there are sequelae many years after the risk occurred. Are the effects a function of an alteration in social information processing, as findings by Dodge, Pettit, Bates, and Valente (1995) suggest they may be in part? Or are they a consequence of an impaired attachment security, as Greenberg and colleagues suggest (Greenberg, Speltz, & DeKlyen, 1993; Speltz, DeKlyen, Greenberg, & Dryden, 1995)? Or do they reflect altered patterns of learned behavior, as Patterson (1995) argues? Or may serious early psychosocial deprivation lead to alterations in neuronal organization, as Goodman (1994) tentatively proposed?

Fourth, what are the effects of extrafamilial or broader social variables such as schools, peer groups, community characteristics, or poverty? Some evidence suggests that much of their influence lies in their impact on family functioning; that is, the effects on the children are indirect, being mediated through an interference with parenting or family relationships (R. D. Conger, K. J. Conger, Elder, & Lorenz, 1993; R. D. Conger et al., 1992; Dodge, Pettit, & Bates, 1994; Patterson, 1995). We might also inquire whether individual risk pathways to antisocial behavior vary according to type of neighborhood, ethnicity, or sociocultural circumstances (Kaplan, 1995; Loeber & Wikström, 1993). It seems unlikely that schools (Rutter, Maughan, Mortimore, Ouston, & Smith, 1979) and peer groups (Quinton et al., 1993; Rowe, Woulbron, & Gulley, 1994) operate only through the family, but their strength of effect in varying circumstances remains unclear.

Fifth, to what extent are major environmental effects restricted to children who are genetically at risk? Finally, are these factors that serve to protect children from high-risk backgrounds (genetic or environmental) but that have little positive impact in other circumstances (Farrington, 1995b; Rutter, 1990)?

INDIVIDUAL RISK CHARACTERISTICS

Although there are extensive data on individual features associated with a higher risk of antisocial behavior, surprisingly little is known about how such features operate. Clearly, the best established risk factor is being male, but does that reflect temperamental features, prenatal or postnatal hormones, or sociocultural expectations? Hyperactivity/impulsivity/inattention is also a well-established risk factor, but is this because it reflects a discrete diagnostic category or because it constitutes a dimensional risk factor irrespective of diagnosis? Which aspect of this constellation of behaviors constitutes the key risk feature—the overactivity, the impulsivity, or the inattention? What is the crucial aspect of impulsivity—sensation seeking, an impaired ability to delay action or

inhibit responses, or acting without thought (Schachar, 1991; Schachar, Tannock, Marriott, & Logan, 1995; Sonuga-Barke, Taylor, & Heptinstall, 1992a; Sonuga-Barke, Taylor, Sembi, & Smith, 1992b)? Does it represent a deficit in higher cognitive functioning or a motivational problem? Does it cause a direct risk for antisocial behavior, or is the risk (at least partially) dependent on adverse patterns of rearing or on negative effects of parents?

Somewhat comparable questions arise with respect to the risks associated with lower intelligence (Hinshaw, 1992; Moffitt, 1993b). At one time lower intelligence test scores were thought to reflect the negative effects of educational failure (Rutter & Giller, 1983). Indeed, that may well constitute an aspect of the risk mechanism in childhood, but it does not account for the relative increase in risk associated with lower intelligence across the entire range of scores (Goodman et al., 1995). More recently, the pendulum has swung to a view of the risk being mainly mediated through the association with hyperactivity (Hinshaw, 1992) and operating through an impairment in executive planning (Moffitt, 1993b). But, if that is the case, why did the association between reading difficulties and antisocial behavior in the Maughan, Pickles, Rutter, Hagell, and Yule (1996) longitudinal study disappear by adulthood? After all, the risks associated with hyperactivity particularly apply to antisocial behavior extending into adult life (Farrington et al., 1990). Similar questions arise with respect to other individual risk characteristics. Little is known about the extent to which they operate independently of one another, little is known about the extent to which they involve risk when *not* part of a broader constellation of adverse attributes (Magnusson & Bergman, 1990), and even less is known about their mode of operation.

CONCLUSION

The last decade has brought important advances in both the conceptualization of antisocial behavior and the study of causal processes. As a result, we are in a much better position for framing the questions to be addressed and in planning research strategies in order to test their hypotheses. But, as this brief overview has indicated, most of the fundamental issues have yet to be resolved. Perhaps most crucially, it remains unclear whether the main focus should be on antisocial deeds (in the sense of acts, such as stealing, that are contrary to the law—Rutter & Giller, 1983); on conduct disorder associated with substantial social impairment on a broad syndrome of multiple social problems (Earls, 1994; Jessor et al., 1991); on lifestyle features involving irresponsible, but not necessarily criminal, behaviors (Farrington, 1995b); or on an antisocial personality syndrome that begins in childhood but which shows its most distinctive characteristics in adult life (Robins, 1966). Epidemiological studies have also highlighted the extent of comorbidity among childhood disorders—with conduct disorders co-occurring with hyperactivity, with reading difficulties, and with depression (Caron & Rutter, 1991). Does this represent a comorbidity between essentially separate conditions, the coming together of dimensional risk factors, or does it reflect the varied manifestations of a single syndrome? It is important to test competing hypotheses on these associations (Schachar

& Tannock, 1995), if only because the answers will shape the research strategies most likely to be successful in determining the crucial risk processes for antisocial behavior.

REFERENCES

Biederman, J., Milberger, S., Faraone, S. V., Kiely, K., Guite, J., Mick, E., Ablon, J. S., Warburton, R., Reed, E., & Davis, S. G. (1995). Impact of adversity on functioning and comorbidity in children with attention-deficit hyperactivity disorder. *Journal of the American Academy of Child & Adolescent Psychiatry, 34,* 1495–1503.

Bock, G. R., & Goode, J. A. (Eds.). (1996). *Genetics of criminal and antisocial behaviour. Ciba Foundation Vol. 194.* Chichester, England and New York: Wiley.

Bohman, M. (1996). Predisposition to criminality: Swedish adoption studies in retrospect. In G. R. Bock & J. A. Goode (Eds.), *Genetics of criminal and antisocial behaviour. Ciba Foundation Vol. 194* (pp. 99–114). Chichester, England and New York: Wiley.

Brennan, P. A., Mednick, S. A., & Jacobsen, B. (1996). Assessing the role of genetics in crime using adoption cohorts. In G. R. Bock & J. A. Goode (Eds.), *Genetics of criminal and antisocial behaviour. Ciba Foundation Vol. 194* (pp. 115–128). Chichester, England and New York: Wiley.

Brunner, H. G. (1996). MAOA deficiency and abnormal behaviour: Perspectives on an association. In G. R. Bock & J. A. Goode (Eds.), *Genetics of criminal and antisocial behaviour. Ciba Foundation Vol. 194* (pp. 155–167). Chichester, England and New York: Wiley.

Cadoret, R. J., Yates, W. R., Troughton, E., Woodworth, G., & Stewart, M. A. (1995). Genetic-environmental interaction in the genesis of aggressivity and conduct disorders. *Archives of General Psychiatry, 52,* 916–924.

Cantwell, D. P., & Rutter, M. (1994). Classification: Conceptual issues and substantive findings. In M. Rutter, E. Taylor, & L. Hersov (Eds.), *Child and adolescent psychiatry: Modern approaches* (3rd ed., pp. 3–21). Oxford, England: Blackwell Scientific Publications.

Caron, C., & Rutter, M. (1991). Comorbidity in child psychopathology: Concepts, issues and research strategies. *Journal of Child Psychology and Psychiatry, 32,* 1063–1080.

Clarke, R. V. G. (1985). Jack Tizard memorial lecture. Delinquency, environment, and intervention. *Journal of Child Psychology and Psychiatry, 26,* 505–523.

Clarke, R. V., & Mayhew, P. (1988). The British gas suicide story and its criminological implications. In M. Tonry & N. Morris (Eds.), *Crime and justice* (Vol. 10, pp. 79–116). Chicago: University of Chicago Press.

Conger, R. D., Conger, K. J., Elder, G. H., & Lorenz, F. O. (1993). Family economic stress and adjustment of early adolescent girls. *Developmental Psychology, 29,* 206–219.

Conger, R. D., Conger, K. J., Elder, G. H., Lorenz, F. O., Simons, R. L., & Whitbeck, L. B. (1992). A family process model of economic hardship and adjustment of early adolescent boys. *Child Development, 63,* 526–541.

Crowe, R. R. (1974). An adoption study of antisocial personality. *Archives of General Psychiatry, 31,* 785–791.

Davies, P. T., & Cummings, E. M. (1994). Marital conflict and child adjustment: An emotional security hypothesis. *Psychological Bulletin, 116,* 387–411.

DiLalla, L. F., & Gottesman, I. I. (1989). Heterogeneity of causes for delinquency and criminality: Lifespan perspectives. *Development and Psychopathology, 1,* 339–349.

Dodge, K. A., Pettit, G. S., & Bates, J. E. (1994). Socialization mediators of the relation between socioeconomic status and child conduct problems. *Child Development, 65,* 649–665.

Dodge, K. A., Pettit, G. S., Bates, J. E., & Valente, E. (1995). Social information-processing patterns partially mediate the effects of early physical abuse on later conduct problems. *Journal of Abnormal Psychology, 104,* 632–643.

D'Orban, P. T. (1979). Women who kill their children. *British Journal of Psychiatry, 134,* 560–571.

Earls, F. (1994). Oppositional-defiant and conduct disorders. In M. Rutter, E. Taylor, & L. Hersov (Eds.), *Child and adolescent psychiatry: Modern approaches* (3rd ed., pp. 308–329). Oxford, England: Blackwell Scientific Publications.

Eisenberg, L. (1995). The social construction of the human brain. *American Journal of Psychiatry, 152,* 1563–1575.

Elliott, D. S. (1994). Serious violent offenders: Onset, developmental course, and termination—The American Society of Criminology 1993 Presidential Address. *Criminology, 32,* 1–21.

Farrington, D. P. (1995a). The challenge of teenage antisocial behavior. In M. Rutter (Ed.), *Psychosocial disturbances in young people: Challenges for prevention* (pp. 83–130). New York: Cambridge University Press.

Farrington, D. P. (1995b). The Twelfth Jack Tizard Memorial Lecture. The development of offending and antisocial behaviour in childhood: Key findings from the Cambridge Study of Delinquent Development. *Journal of Child Psychology and Psychiatry, 36,* 929–964.

Farrington, D., Loeber, R., & Van Kammen, W. B. (1990). Long-term criminal outcomes of hyperactivity-impulsivity-attention deficit and conduct problems in childhood. In L. Robins & M. Rutter (Eds.), *Straight and devious pathways from childhood to adulthood* (pp. 62–81). Cambridge, England: Cambridge University Press.

Fergusson, D. M., & Horwood, L. J. (1995a). Early disruptive behavior, IQ, and later school achievement and delinquent behavior. *Journal of Abnormal Child Psychology, 23,* 183–199.

Fergusson, D. M., & Horwood, L. J. (1995b). Predictive validity of categorically and dimensionally scored measures of disruptive childhood behaviors. *Journal of the American Academy of Child and Adolescent Psychiatry, 34,* 477–485.

Fergusson, D. M., Horwood, L. J., & Lynskey, M. T. (1992). Family change, parental discord, and early offending. *Journal of Child Psychology and Psychiatry, 33,* 1059–1075.

Goodman, R. (1994). Brain development. In M. Rutter & D. F. Hay (Eds.), *Development through life: A handbook for clinicians* (pp. 49–78). Oxford, England: Blackwell Scientific Publications.

Goodman, R., Simonoff, E., & Stevenson, J. (1995). The impact of child IQ, parent IQ, and sibling IQ on child behavioural deviance scores. *Journal of Child Psychology and Psychiatry, 36,* 409–426.

Graham, J., & Bowling, B. (1995). *Young people and crime.* Home Office Research Study 145. London, England: Home Office.

Greenberg, M. T., Speltz, M. L., & DeKlyen, M. (1993). The role of attachment in the early development of disruptive behavior problems. *Development and Psychopathology, 5,* 191–213.

Häfner, H., & Böker, W. (1982). *Crimes of violence of mentally abnormal offenders* (H. Marshall, Trans.). Cambridge, England: Cambridge University Press. (Original work published 1973)

Hennessey, J. W., & Levine, S. (1979). Stress, arousal and the pituitary-adrenal system: A psychoendocrine hypothesis. In J. M. Sprague & A. N. Epstein (Eds.), *Progress in psychobiology and physiological psychology* (pp. 133–178). New York: Academic Press.

Hewitt, L. E., & Jenkins, R. L. (1946). *Fundamental patterns of maladjustment: The dynamics of their origin.* Urbana: University of Illinois Press.

Hinshaw, S. P. (1992). Externalizing behavior problems and academic underachievement in childhood and adolescence: Causal relationships and underlying mechanisms. *Psychological Bulletin, 111,* 127–155.

Horn, G. (1990). Neural bases of recognition memory investigated through an analysis of imprinting. *Philosophical Transactions of the Royal Society, 329,* 133–142.

Ito, T. A., Miller, N., & Pollock, V. E. (1996). Alcohol and aggression: A meta-analysis on the moderating effects of inhibitory cues, triggering evetns, and self-focused attention. *Psychological Bulletin, 120,* 60–82.

Jensen, P. S. (1995). "Predictive validity of categorically and dimensionally scored measures of disruptive childhood behaviors": Comment. *Journal of the American Academy of Child and Adolescent Psychiatry, 34,* 485–487.

Jessor, R., Donovan, J. E., & Costa, F. M. (1991). *Beyond adolescence: Problem behavior and young adult development.* Cambridge, England: Cambridge University Press.

Kaplan, H. B. (Ed.). (1995). *Drugs, crime, and other deviant adaptations: Longitudinal studies.* New York: Plenum.

Kerr, M., Tremblay, R. E., Pagani-Kurtz, L., & Vitaro, F. (in press). Boys' behavioral inhibition and the risks of later delinquency. *Archives of General Psychiatry.*

Klein, D. N., & Riso, L. P. (1993). Psychiatric disorders: Problems of boundaries and comorbidity. In C. G. Costello (Ed.), *Basic issues in psychopathology* (pp. 19–66). New York: Guilford.

Kumar, R., & Marks, M. (1992). Infanticide and the law in England and Wales. In J. A. Hamilton & P. N. Harberger (Eds.), *Postpartum psychiatric illness: A picture puzzle* (pp. 256–273). Philadelphia: University of Pennsylvania Press.

Lahey, B. B., & Loeber, R. (1994). Framework for a developmental model of oppositional defiant disorder and conduct disorder. In D. Routh (Ed.), *Disruptive behavior disorders in childhood: Essays in honor of Herbert C. Quay* (pp. 139–180). New York: Plenum.

Lahey, B. B., McBurnett, K., Loeber, R., & Hart, E. L. (1995). Psychobiology of conduct disorder. In G. P. Scholevar (Ed.), *Conduct disorders in children and adolescents: Assessments and interventions* (pp. 27–44). Washington, DC: American Psychiatric Press.

Loeber, R., & Hay, D. F. (1994). Developmental approaches to aggression and conduct problems. In M. Rutter & D. F. Hay (Eds.), *Development through life: A handbook for clinicians* (pp. 488–516). Oxford, England: Blackwell Scientific Publications.

Loeber, R., & Wikström, P.-O. H. (1993). Individual pathways to crime in different types of neighbourhood. In D. P. Farrington, R. J. Sampson, & P.-O. H. Wikström (Eds.), *Integrating individual and ecological aspects of crime* (pp. 169–204). Stockholm: National Council for Crime Prevention/Fritzes.

Lyons, M. J., True, W. R., Eisen, S. A., Goldberg, J., Meyer, J. M., Faraone, S. V., Eaves, L. J., & Tsuang, M. T. (1995). Differential heritability of adult and juvenile antisocial traits. *Archives of General Psychiatry, 52,* 906–915.

Lytton, H. (1990). Child and parent effects in boys' conduct disorder: A reinterpretation. *Developmental Psychology, 26,* 683–697.

Maccoby, E. E., & Jacklin, C. N. (1980). Sex differences in aggression: A rejoinder and reprise. *Child Development, 51,* 964–980.

Magnusson, D., & Bergman, L. R. (1990). A pattern approach to the study of pathways from childhood to adulthood. In L. Robins & M. Rutter (Eds.), *Straight and devious pathways from childhood to adulthood* (pp. 101–115). Cambridge, England: Cambridge University Press.

Maughan, B., Pickles, A., Hagell, A., Rutter, M., & Yule, W. (1996). Reading problems and antisocial behaviour: Developmental trends in comorbidity. *Journal of Child Psychology and Psychiatry, 37,* 405–418.

Maughan, B., & Rutter, M. (in press). Continuities and discontinuities in antisocial behavior from childhood to adult life. In T. H. Ollendick & R. J. Prinz (Eds.), *Advances in clinical child psychology* (Vol. 20). New York: Plenum.

Mazur, A., Booth, A., & Dabbs, J. M. (1992). Testosterone and chess competition. *Social Psychology Quarterly, 55,* 70–77.

Mazur, A., & Lamb, T. A. (1980). Testosterone, status, and mood in human males. *Hormones and Behavior, 14,* 236–246.

Moffitt, T. E. (1993a). Adolescence-limited and life course-persistent antisocial behavior: A developmental taxonomy. *Psychological Review, 4,* 674–701.

Moffitt, T. E. (1993b). The neuropsychology of conduct disorder. *Developmental Psychopathology, 5,* 135–151.

Moir, A., & Jessel, D. (1995). *A mind to crime: The controversial link between the mind and criminal behaviour.* London: Michael Joseph.

Olweus, D. (1979). Stability of aggressive reaction patterns in males: A review. *Psychological Bulletin, 86,* 852–875.

Olweus, D., Mattson, A., Schalling, D., & Löw, H. (1980). Testosterone, aggression, physical, and personality dimensions in normal adolescent males. *Psychosomatic Medicine, 42,* 253–269.

Patterson, G. R. (1982). *Coercive family processes.* Eugene, OR: Castalia.

Patterson, G. R. (1995). Coercion as a basis for early age of onset for arrest. In J. McCord (Ed.), *Coercion and punishment in long-term perspectives* (pp. 81–105). New York: Cambridge University Press.

Patterson, G. R. (1996). Some characteristics of a developmental theory for early onset delinquency. In M. F. Lenzenweger & J. Haugaard (Eds.), *Frontiers of developmental psychopathology* (pp. 81–124). New York: Oxford University Press.

Plomin, R., & Bergeman, C. S. (1991). The nature of nurture: Genetic influence on "environmental" measures. *Behavioral and Brain Sciences, 14,* 373–427.

Post, R. M., & Goodwin, F. K. (1973). Simulated behaviour states: An approach to specificity in psychobiological research. *British Journal of Psychiatry, 7,* 237–254.

Quinton, D., Pickles, A., Maughan, B., & Rutter, M. (1993). Partners, peers, and pathways: Assortative pairing and continuities in conduct disorder. *Development and Psychopathology, 5,* 763–783.

Raine, A., Buchsbaum, M. S., Stanley, J., Lottenberg, S., Abel, L., & Stoddard, J. (1994). Selective reductions in prefrontal glucose metabolism in murderers. *Biological Psychiatry, 36,* 365–373.

Raine, A., & Venables, P. H. (1992). Antisocial behavior: Evolution, genetics, neuropsychology, and psychophysiology. In A. Gale & M. Eysenck (Eds.), *Handbook of individual differences: Biological perspectives* (pp. 287–321). London: Wiley.

Raleigh, M., & McGuire, M. T. (1991). Bidirectional relationships between tryptophan and social behavior in vervet monkeys. *Advances in Experimental Medicine and Biology, 294,* 289–298.

Ratcliffe, S. G. (1994). The psychological and psychiatric consequences of sex chromosome abnormalities in children based on population studies. In F. Poutska (Ed.), *Basic approaches to genetic and molecular bio-*

logical developmental psychiatry (pp. 99–122). Berlin: Quintessatz Verlags.

Reiss, A. J., Miezek, K. A., & Roth, J. A. (Eds.). (1994). *Understanding and preventing violence. Vol. 2. Biobehavioral influences.* Washington, DC: National Academy Press.

Reiss, D., Hetherington, M., Plomin, R., Howe, G. W., Simmens, S. J., Henderson, S. H., O'Connor, T. J., Bussell, D. A., Anderson, E. R., & Law, T. (1995). Genetic questions for environmental studies: Differential parenting and psychopathology in adolescence. *Archives of General Psychiatry, 52,* 925–936.

Richters, J. E., & Cicchetti, D. (1993). Mark Twain meets *DSM-III-R:* Conduct disorder, development, and concept of harmful dysfunction. *Developmental Psychopathology, 5,* 5–29.

Robins, L. (1966). *Deviant children grown up.* Baltimore: Williams & Wilkins.

Robins, L. (1978). Sturdy childhood predictors of adult antisocial behaviour: Replications from longitudinal studies. *Psychological Medicine, 8,* 611–622.

Robins, L. N. (1991). Conduct disorder. *Journal of Child Psychology and Psychiatry, 32,* 193–212.

Robins, L. N., & McEvoy, L. (1990). Conduct problems as predictors of substance abuse. In L. Robins & M. Rutter (Eds.), *Straight and devious pathways from childhood to adulthood* (pp. 182–204). Cambridge, England: Cambridge University Press.

Robins, L. N., Tipp, J., & Przybeck, T. (1991). Antisocial personality. In L. N. Robins & D. A. Regier (Eds.), *Psychiatric disorders in America: The Epidemiologic Catchment Area study* (pp. 258–290). New York: Free Press.

Rönkä, A., & Pulkkinen, L. (1995). Accumulation of problems in social functioning in young adulthood: A developmental approach. *Journal of Personality and Social Psychology, 69,* 381–391.

Rose, R. M., Holaday, J. W., & Bernstein, I. S. (1971). Plasma testosterone, dominance risk, and aggressive behaviour in male rhesus monkeys. *Nature, 231,* 366–368.

Rose, S. (1995). The rise of neurogenetic determinism. *Nature, 373,* 380–382.

Rowe, D. C., Woulbron, E. J., & Gulley, B. L. (1994). Peers and friends as nonshared environmental influences. In E. M. Hetherington, D. Reiss, & R. Plomin (Eds.), *Separate social worlds of siblings: The impact of nonshared environment on development* (pp. 159–173). Hillsdale, NJ: Erlbaum.

Royal College of Physicians. (1979). *Alcohol and alcoholism.* London: Tavistock.

Royal College of Physicians. (1995). *Alcohol and the young: Report of a joint working party of the Royal College of Physicians and the British Paediatric Association.* London: Author.

Rutter, M. (1990). Psychosocial resilience and protective mechanisms. In J. Rolf, A. Masten, D. Cicchetti, K. Nuechterlein, & S. Weintraub (Eds.), *Risk and protective factors in the development of psychopathology* (pp. 181–214). New York: Cambridge University Press.

Rutter, M. (1993). Developmental psychopathology as a research perspective. In D. Magnusson & P. Casaer (Eds.), *Longitudinal research on individual development: Present status and future perspectives* (pp. 127–152). Cambridge, England: Cambridge University Press.

Rutter, M. (1994a). Beyond longitudinal data: Causes, consequences, changes, and continuity. *Journal of Consulting and Clinical Psychology, 62,* 928–940.

Rutter, M. (1994b). Family discord and conduct disorder: Cause, consequence, or correlate? *Journal of Family Psychology, 8,* 170–186.

Rutter, M. (1996a). Developmental psychopathology: Concepts and prospects. In M. F. Lenzenweger & J. Haugaard (Eds.), *Frontiers of developmental psychopathology* (pp. 209–237). New York: Oxford University Press.

Rutter, M. (1996b). Introduction: Concepts of antisocial behaviour, of cause, and of genetic influences. In G. R. Bock & J. A. Goode (Eds.), *Genetics of criminal and antisocial behaviour. Ciba Foundation Vol. 194* (pp. 1–20). Chichester, England and New York: Wiley.

Rutter, M. (1997). Integrating nature and nurture: The example of antisocial behavior. *American Psychologist, 52*(4), 1–7.

Rutter, M., & Giller, H. (1983). *Juvenile delinquency: Trends and perspectives.* Harmondsworth, Middlesex, England: Penguin Books.

Rutter, M., Maughan, B., Meyer, J., Pickles, A., Silberg, J., Simonoff, E., & Taylor, E. (in press). Heterogeneity of antisocial behavior: Causes, continuities, and consequences. In R. Dienstbier (Series Ed.) & D. W. Osgood (Vol. Ed.), *Nebraska symposium on motivation: Vol. 44. Motivation and delinquency.* Lincoln: University of Nebraska Press.

Rutter, M., Maughan, B., Mortimore, P., & Ouston, J. (with Smith, A.). (1979). *Fifteen thousand hours: Secondary schools and their effects on children.* London: Open Books; Cambridge, MA: Harvard University Press. (Reprinted, 1994, London: Paul Chapman Publishers)

Rutter, M., Tizard, J., & Whitmore, K. (Eds.). (1970). *Education, health, and behaviour.* London: Longman. (Reprinted, 1981, Melbourne, FL: Krieger)

Sampson R. J., & Laub, J. H. (1993). *Crime in the making: Pathways and turning points through life.* Cambridge, MA: Harvard University Press.

Schachar, R. (1991). Childhood hyperactivity. *Journal of Child Psychology and Psychiatry, 32,* 155–191.

Schachar, R., & Tannock, R. (1995). Test of four hypotheses for the comorbidity of attention-deficit hyperactivity disorder and conduct disorder. *Journal of the American Academy of Child and Adolescent Psychiatry, 34,* 639–648.

Schachar, R., Tannock, R., Marriott, M., & Logan, G. (1995). Deficient inhibitory control in attention deficit hyperactivity disorder. *Journal of Abnormal Child Psychology, 23,* 411–437.

Schonfeld, I. S., Shaffer, D., O'Connor, P., & Portnoy, S. (1988). Conduct disorder and cognitive functioning: Testing three causal hypotheses. *Child Development, 59,* 993–1007.

Shaw, D. S., Keenan, K., & Vondra, J. I. (1994). Developmental precursors of externalizing behavior: Ages 1 to 3. *Developmental Psychology, 30,* 355–364.

Silberg, J., Rutter, M., Meyer, J., Maes, H., Hewitt, J., Simonoff, E., Pickles, A., Loeber, R., & Eaves, L. (1996a). Genetic and environmental influences on the covariation between hyperactivity and conduct disturbance in juvenile twins. *Journal of Child Psychology and Psychiatry, 37,* 803–816.

Silberg, J., Meyer, J., Pickles, A., Simonoff, E., Eaves, L., Hewitt, J., Maes, H., & Rutter, M. (1996b). Heterogeneity among juvenile antisocial behaviours: Findings from the Virginia Twin Study of Adolescent Behavioural Development. In G. R. Bock & J. A. Goode (Eds.), *Genetics of criminal and antisocial behaviour. Ciba Foundation Vol. 194* (pp. 76–92). Chichester, England and New York: Wiley.

Smith, D. J. (1995). Youth crime and conduct disorders: Trends, patterns, and causal explanations. In M. Rutter & D. J. Smith (Eds.), *Psychosocial disorders in young people: Time trends and their causes* (pp. 389–489). Chichester, England: Wiley.

Snyder, J. J., & Patterson, G. R. (1995). Individual differences in social aggression: A test of a reinforcement model of socialization in the natural environment. *Behavior Therapy, 26,* 371–391.

Sonuga-Barke, E. J. S., Taylor, E., & Heptinstall, E. (1992a). Hyperactivity and delay aversion: II. The effects of self versus externally imposed stimulus presentation periods on memory. *Journal of Child Psychology and Psychiatry, 33,* 399–410.

Sonuga-Barke, E. J. S., Taylor, E., Sembi, S., & Smith, J. (1992b). Hyperactivity and delay aversion: I. The effect of delay on choice. *Journal of Child Psychology and Psychiatry, 33,* 387–398.

Speltz, M. L., DeKlyen, M., Greenberg, M. T., & Dryden, M. (1995). Clinic referral for oppositional defiant disorder: Relative significance of attachment and behavioral variables. *Journal of Abnormal Child Psychology, 23,* 487–507.

Sroufe, L. A., & Rutter, M. (1984). The domain of developmental psychopathology. *Child Development, 55,* 17–29.

Tantam, D. (1988). Lifelong eccentricity and social isolation: I. Psychiatric, social, and forensic aspects. *British Journal of Psychiatry, 153,* 777–782.

Taylor, E. (1994). Syndromes of attention deficit and overactivity. In M. Rutter, E. Taylor, & L. Hersov (Eds.), *Child and adolescent psychiatry: Modern approaches* (3rd ed., pp. 285–308). Oxford, England: Blackwell Scientific Publications.

Taylor, E., Chadwick, O., Heptinstall, H., & Danckaerts, M. (1996). Hyperactivity and conduct problems as risk factors for adolescent development. *Journal of the American Academy of Child & Adolescent Psychiatry, 35,* 1213–1226.

Taylor, P. J. (1993). Schizophrenia and crime: Distinctive patterns in association. In S. Hodgins (Ed.), *Crime and mental disorder* (pp. 63–85). Beverly Hills, CA: Sage Publications.

Thornberry, T. P., Huizinga, D., & Loeber, R. (1995). The prevention of serious delinquency and violence: Implications from the program of research on the causes and correlates of delinquency. In J. C. Howell, B. Krisberg, J. D. Hawkins, & J. J. Wilson (Eds.), *Sourcebook on serious, violent, and chronic juvenile offenders* (pp. 213–237). Thousand Oaks, CA: Sage Publications.

Tolan, P. H., & Thomas, P. (1995). The implications of age of onset for delinquency risk: II. Longitudinal data. *Journal of Abnormal Child Psychology, 23,* 157–181.

Tonry, M., & Farrington, D. P. (Eds.). (1995). *Building a safer society: Strategic approaches to crime prevention.* Chicago & London: University of Chicago Press.

Tremblay, R. E., Pihl, R. O., Vitaro, F., & Dobkin, P. L. (1994). Predicting early onset of male antisocial behavior from preschool behavior. *Archives of General Psychiatry, 51,* 732–739.

Virkkunen, M., Goldman, D., & Linnoila, M. (1996). Serotonin in alcoholic violent offenders. In G. R. Bock & J. A. Goode (Eds.), *Genetics of criminal and antisocial behaviour. Ciba Foundation Vol. 194* (pp. 168–182). Chichester, England and New York: Wiley.

Virkkunen, M., Rawlings, R., Tokola, R., Poland, R. E., Guidotti, A., Nemeroff, C., Bissette, G., Kalogeras, K., Karonen, S-L., & Linnoila, M. (1994). CSF biochemistries, glucose metabolism, and diurnal activity rhythms in alcoholic, violent offenders, fire setters, and healthy volunteers. *Archives of General Psychiatry, 51,* 20–27.

Wessely, S. C., Castle, D., Douglas, A. J., & Taylor, P. J. (1994). The criminal careers of incident cases of schizophrenia. *Psychological Medicine, 24,* 483–502.

West, D. J. (1965). *Murder followed by suicide.* London: Heinemann.

White, J. L., Moffitt, T. E., Earls, F., Robins, L., & Silva, P. A. (1990). How early can we tell? Predictors of childhood conduct disorder and adolescent delinquency. *Criminology, 28,* 507–533.

Wolff, S. (1995). *Loners: The life path of unusual children.* London: Routledge.

Wootton, B. (1959). *Social science and social pathology.* London: George Allen & Unwin.

Zoccolillo, M., Pickles, A., Quinton, D., & Rutter, M. (1992). The outcome of childhood conduct disorder: Implications for defining adult personality disorder and conduct disorder. *Psychological Medicine, 22,* 971–986.

CHAPTER 13

Strategies and Yields of Longitudinal Studies on Antisocial Behavior

ROLF LOEBER and DAVID P. FARRINGTON

Part Two of this volume deals with the development of antisocial behavior. Most of what we know about the development of antisocial behavior derives from an array of longitudinal studies that have been conducted during the past four decades (see Table 13.1 for examples). The generic term *antisocial behavior* is used here to include disruptive behaviors, such as serious oppositional behavior, conduct problems, and delinquent behavior. Where appropriate, we discuss the psychiatric disorders of oppositional defiant disorder and conduct disorder.

Longitudinal studies have improved our understanding of important aspects of antisocial behavior, such as their frequency, variety (including co-occurrence), seriousness, and ages of onset and offset (i.e., the age at which an individual commits a particular antisocial act for the first or last time, respectively). Two major contributions have been made by longitudinal studies. Such studies have provided us with information about developmental sequences and pathways leading to serious antisocial behavior, including differences between the development of antisocial and normal behavior. They also have provided information about risk and protective factors that influence the course of normal and antisocial development in individuals. Knowledge of these two points is important, not only for explaining antisocial behavior, but also for planning and evaluating intervention techniques.

This chapter addresses the following topics. First, we review the findings of the most important longitudinal studies on antisocial behavior. Second, we highlight major theoretical and controversial questions raised by these studies. Third, we address methodological issues arising in the studies, particularly their design and the need to introduce experimental interventions. We close with a set of recommendations and an outline for what we

see as promising future work needed to explain and ameliorate antisocial behavior in juveniles.

Before starting our review, we should point out that not all social scientists are convinced about the need for longitudinal studies on antisocial behavior. Particularly Hirschi and Gottfredson (1983) indicated that, because the relation between age and crime is much the same from study to study, the relationship between risk factors and offending was the same at all ages; hence longitudinal studies were not needed. However, Blumstein, Cohen, and Farrington (1988) argued that the relationship between risk factors varied between different ages. For example, truancy was a risk factor only during the school years, and divorce was a risk factor only after the school years. Moreover, the relationship between the risk factors and onset of offending often is different from risk factors for desistance in offending (Farrington & Hawkins, 1991; Loeber, Stouthamer-Loeber, Van Kammen, & Farrington, 1991).

KEY LONGITUDINAL STUDIES ON ANTISOCIAL BEHAVIOR

Table 13.1 summarizes the key longitudinal studies on juvenile antisocial behavior. We used the following criteria for inclusion in this list: a sample size of at least several hundred subjects; a large number of different types of variables measured; a longitudinal design spanning at least 5 years (as evident from publications); a prospectively chosen general population sample; personal contact with the subjects (as opposed to data from records); and the use of measures of antisocial behavior, including delinquency and general externalizing problem behaviors. Because the prevalence of these behaviors changes dramatically between childhood and adulthood, cumulative curves help document when prevalence accelerates or slows down. In addition, the surveys provide key information about ages of onset, duration of problems, ages of offset, and periods of escalation or de-escalation.

The key longitudinal surveys show relative stability in antisocial behavior over time, in the sense that the rank ordering of individuals tends to stay constant (even though the absolute prevalence, frequency, or seriousness may change over time).

This chapter is based partly on an earlier paper, "Problems and Solutions in Longitudinal and Experimental Treatment Studies of Child Psychopathology and Delinquency" (*Journal of Consulting and Clinical Psychology, 62,* 887–900). The paper was written with financial support of Grant MH 48890 of the National Institute of Mental Health, and Grant No. 86-JN-CX-0009 of the Office of Juvenile Justice and Delinquency Prevention. Points of view or opinions in this document are those of the authors and do not necessarily represent the official position of either agency. We are very grateful to JoAnn Fraser for her valuable assistance in producing this paper.

**TABLE 13.1   Classic Longitudinal Studies on Juvenile Antisocial Behavior
(principal investigators, sample, and a typical recent publication)**

Cairns & Cairns (U.S.): Follow-up of 695 boys and girls in fourth and seventh grade, started in 1981. Assessments included the children, parents, grandparents, and other caretakers. Since then, follow-up at yearly intervals with a high degree of subject cooperation. Focus on aggression, school dropout, gender differences (Cairns & Cairns, 1994).

Cohen (U.S.): Random sample of 975 children living in upper New York State, aged 1 to 10 in 1975. Psychiatric evaluations included each child and mother. Follow-up interviews of children in 1983 and 1985–1986 (Cohen et al., 1993).

Douglas & Wadsworth (UK): 5,362 children selected from all legitimate single births in England, Scotland, and Wales during one week of March 1946. Followed up in criminal records to age 21. Mainly medical and school data collected, but samples were interviewed at ages 26, 36, and 43 (Wadsworth, 1991).

Elliott & Huizinga (U.S.): Nationally representative sample of 1,725 adolescents aged 11 to 17 years old in 1976. Interviewed in 5 successive years (1977–1981) and again in 1984, 1987, 1990, and 1993. Arrest records collected (Elliott, 1994).

Eron & Huesmann (U.S.): 875 8-year-old children in a semirural setting of New York State first assessed in 1960. Focus was on aggressive problem behavior. Follow-up interviews 10 and 22 years later (Eron & Huesmann, 1990).

Fergusson (New Zealand): 1,265 children born in Christchurch in 1977. Studied at birth, age 4 months, 1 year, and annually up to age 15. Data taken from mother, child, and teacher, including self-reported delinquency and substance use (Fergusson, Hopwood, & Lynskey, 1994).

S. Glueck & E. Glueck (U.S.): 500 male delinquents in Massachusetts correctional schools in 1939–1944, and 500 matched nondelinquents. Contacted at average ages of 14, 25, and 31. Nondelinquents were followed up to age 47 by Vaillant. Original data reanalyzed by Sampson and Laub (Glueck & Glueck, 1968; Sampson & Laub, 1993).

Hawkins & Catalano (U.S.): All 919 fifth-grade students in 18 elementary schools in Seattle in fall 1985. Some of sample had been studied since first grade and exposed to an experimental school intervention. Annual follow-up interviews until 1993 (Peterson, Hawkins, Abbott, & Catalano, 1994).

Huizinga, Elliott, & Weiher (U.S.): Probability sample of households in high-risk neighborhoods of Denver, of boys and girls aged 7, 9, 11, 13, and 15 years old in 1988. Follow-up at almost yearly intervals and still ongoing (Huizinga, 1995).

Janson & Wikström (Sweden): All 15,117 children born in Stockholm in 1953 and living in Stockholm in 1963. Tested in schools in 1966. Subsample of mothers interviewed in 1968. Follow-up in police records until 1983 (Wikström, 1990).

Jessor (U.S.): A sample of 1,126 high school students (grades 7 to 9) first assessed in 1969 (average age 14), and a sample of 497 freshman college students first assessed in 1970 (average age 19). Self-reports of problem behavior and substance use. Follow-up until 1981 (Jessor, Donovan, & Costa, 1991).

Kellam & Ensminger (U.S.): Sample of 1,242 first graders in an African American Chicago neighborhood (Woodlawn) first assessed in 1966 to 1967. Focus was on shy and aggressive behaviors and substance use. Reassessed in 1975 to 1976. Follow-up by Ensminger and McCord in 1993 (Ensminger et al., 1983).

Le Blanc & Fréchette (Canada): (1) Representative sample of 3,070 French-speaking Montreal adolescents. Completed self-report questionnaires in 1974 at ages 12 to 16 and again in 1976; (2) 470 male delinquents seen at age 15 in 1974 and again at ages 17 and 22. All were followed up in criminal records to age 25. Male samples interviewed at age 32 (Le Blanc, 1994).

Loeber & Lahey (U.S.): Sample of 177 clinic-referred boys, 7 to 12 years old at the beginning of the study (1987–1988). Yearly follow-up with diag-nostic assessments and many other measurements. Currently in the ninth year of follow-up (Loeber, Green, Keenan, & Lahey, 1995a).

Loeber, Stouthamer-Loeber, & Farrington (U.S.): Sample of 1,517 boys initially enrolled in the first, fourth, and seventh grades of Pittsburgh public schools (called *youngest, middle,* and *oldest samples*). Follow-up since 1987–1988. Assessments made of the boys, their parents, and teachers. Information gathered on delinquency, substance use, and mental health problems. Currently, the youngest and oldest samples are in the ninth year of follow-up (Loeber, Russo, Stouthamer-Loeber & Lahey, 1994).

Magnusson & Stattin (Sweden): 1,027 children (age 10) in Orebro in 1965. Follow-up at ages 13 and 15. Follow-up in criminal records to age 30. Two other cohorts born in 1950 and 1952 also followed up (Klinteberg, Anderson, Magnusson, & Stattin, 1993).

J. McCord & W. McCord (U.S.): 650 boys (average age 10) nominated as difficult or average by Cambridge and Somerville (Massachusetts) schools in 1937–1939. Experimental group visited by counselors for an average of 5 years. Follow-up in 1975–1980 by mail questionnaires and interviews and in criminal records (McCord, 1991).

Miller & Kolvin (UK): All 1,142 children born in Newcastle in May and June 1947. Children and families contacted at least once a year up to age 15 and finally at age 22. Children followed up in criminal records to ages 32 to 33. Subsample (N = 266) interviewed at ages 32–33. Original sample, their spouses, and their children now being followed up in criminal records to 1994 (Kolvin, Miller, Scott, Gatzanis, & Fleeting, 1990).

Patterson (U.S.): Follow-up of 206 fourth-grade boys in Eugene, Oregon, at yearly intervals with intensive assessments every other year (latest published at eighth grade). Also follow-up in juvenile court records (Capaldi & Patterson, 1994; Stoolmiller, 1994).

Pulkkinen (Finland): 369 children ages 8–9 in Jyvaskyla in 1968 completing peer, teacher, and self-ratings. Follow-up at ages 14, 20, and 26 with questionnaires and to age 26 in criminal records (Pulkkinen & Pitkanen, 1993).

Robins (U.S.): (1) 524 children treated in St. Louis child guidance clinic in 1924–1929 and 100 public school children. Interviewed more than 30 years later; (2) 235 Black males born in St. Louis in 1930–1934 and located in elementary school records. Interviewed in 1965–1966 (Robins, 1979).

Rutter & Quinton (UK): (1) All 1,689 10-year-old children in an inner London borough attending state schools in 1970; (2) all 1,279 10-year-old children on the Isle of Wight attending state schools in 1964. Both samples retested at age 14. Inner London children follow-up to age 25 in criminal records (Rutter, 1981).

Schwartzmann (Canada): 324 French-Canadian first graders (age 7) in Montreal assessed by peers and self-reports in 1978. Follow-up at ages 10 and 14 when self-reported delinquency was measured (Tremblay, Massé et al., 1992).

Silva & Moffitt (New Zealand): 1,037 children born in 1972–1973 in Dunedin, first assessed at age 3 and follow-up to age 18. Biannual evaluations on health, psychological, educational, and family factors. Self-reported delinquency measured at ages 13, 15, and 18. Police records collected up to the 18th birthday (Krueger, Caspi, Moffitt, White, & Stouthamer-Loeber, 1996).

Thornberry, Lizotte, & Krohn (U.S.): 1,000 seventh and eighth graders first assessed in 1988, disproportionally sampled from high-crime neighborhoods. Three quarters are male, the remainder are female. Initial assessments done at half-yearly intervals, and subsequent assessments done yearly with one interval and are ongoing (Thornberry, Lizotte, Krohn, Farnworth, & Jang, 1994).

Tremblay (Canada): 1,161 kindergarten boys in Montreal assessed by teachers and follow-up to age 12. Subsamples of disruptive boys part of prevention experiment (Tremblay et al., 1992).

TABLE 13.1   (Continued)

Verhulst (The Netherlands): 2,600 children ages 4 to 16 from Zuid-Holland, first assessed in 1983, followed up at 2-year intervals over 8 years. Assessment of mental health functioning by mothers and self-reports (Ferdinand & Verhulst, 1994).

Werner (U.S.): 698 children in Hawaii tracked from birth in Kauai in 1955. Interviewed at ages 10, 18, and 32. Health, education, and police records collected (Werner & Smith, 1992).

West & Farrington (UK): 411 boys ages 8 to 9 in 1961–1962; all those of that age in six London schools. Boys contacted about every 2 to 3 years up to age 32. Families contacted every year while boys at school. Boys and all biological relatives searched in criminal records up to 1994 (Farrington & West, 1990; West & Farrington, 1973, 1977).

Persistence has been highlighted in many studies, showing, for example, that male aggressive and delinquent behavior often is highly stable over several decades (Huesmann, Eron, Lefkowitz, & Walder, 1984; Loeber & Stouthamer-Loeber, 1987; Olweus, 1979). A study of clinic-referred boys showed that 87.7% of the boys with a diagnosis of conduct disorder continued to qualify for a diagnosis of conduct disorder in the next 3 years (Lahey et al., 1995). Similarly, Farrington (1992) found that 76% of males convicted between ages 10 and 16 were reconvicted between ages 17 and 24. Although such stability is in evidence within the same category of behavior over time, it is essential to broaden the inquiry about continuity by including a wider range of behaviors within a specific child problem behavior domain. For example, in the domain of disruptive behavior, Farrington (1991) analyzed the continuity of behavior from ages 8 to 10 to age 32 in the Cambridge Study in Delinquent Development. More than twice as many of the most disruptive boys at ages 8 to 10 were convicted of a violent offense by age 32 than were the less disruptive boys in the 8 to 10 group.

Generally, the studies show that individual factors are the best predictors of antisocial behaviors, followed by parental factors, such as supervision and discipline (Loeber & Dishion, 1983). The measurement of peer factors is somewhat more problematic. Peer delinquency correlates highly with the target child's delinquency (Elliott, Huizinga, & Ageton, 1985), but this may merely reflect that most antisocial acts are committed with peers. When temporally distinguished, however, peer delinquency is associated with the onset of delinquency in boys (Keenan, Loeber, Zhang, Stouthamer-Loeber, & Van Kammen, 1995). Neighborhood factors generally influence a child's antisocial behavior only indirectly, through the impact they have on families (Farrington, 1993; Rutter, 1981). More longitudinal studies of antisocial behavior are needed that investigate *all* of the biological, individual, family, peer, school, and neighborhood factors. Few studies have attempted to investigate interaction effects, for example, whether individual development is different in different types of neighborhoods (e.g., Loeber & Wikström, 1993).

The studies listed in Table 13.1 vary enormously in their inclusion and exclusion of the various domains of problem behavior. Many concentrated on delinquency and substance use, but relatively few focused on child mental health problems (e.g., Elliott, Huizinga, & Menard, 1989; Fergusson et al., 1994; Krueger, Caspi, Moffitt, White, & Stouthamer-Loeber, 1996). Others concentrated only on mental health problems (e.g., Cohen & Brook, 1987).

For several reasons, an extended rather than a narrow range of domains of problem behavior is fruitful in longitudinal studies. First, at one time or another in development, children are likely to experience problems in several domains of functioning. Therefore, it is not uncommon for youths with conduct problems to start to abuse substances or to become depressed or for depressed youngsters to become delinquent. The second reason is that the evaluation of adjustment in adulthood, when restricted to a single domain, often misses individuals who are not functioning well in other domains. Although some seriously deprived youths may not eventually become antisocial in adulthood, they often are isolated and impaired socially (Farrington, Gallagher, Morley, St. Ledger, & West, 1988). Also, it is important to document co-occurring conditions and identify multiply deviant individuals, who may be responsible for many of the findings in each domain. Therefore, the best longitudinal studies focus on multiple domains of functioning so that the interactions between different domains can be traced and adjustment across domains can be evaluated.

The studies listed in Table 13.1 vary enormously as to the age, type, and representativeness of the subjects included. The sample size listed in Table 13.1 is the original sample size. Most concerned adolescent populations, with few starting in elementary school (e.g., Eron, Huesmann, Dubow, Romanoff, & Yarmel, 1987) and even fewer in first grade (e.g., Kellam, Ensminger, & Simon, 1980). For most studies, it is difficult to discern whether the optimal age period was selected. Under the best of circumstances, this critical choice should be based on knowledge of the risk period for pathology, with a sufficiently wide window to cover the typical period of onset, worsening, and improvement in problem behavior. Many of the problems of concern here—serious delinquency, oppositional behavior, and substance use—take years and sometimes decades to emerge. However, studies that covered childhood, adolescence, *and* early adulthood were in the minority. Some studies did not allow the examination of factors affecting different ethnic groups (e.g., Capaldi & Patterson, 1994), but others did (e.g., Elliott, 1994; Sampson & Laub, 1993).

Because of space limitations, we cannot describe each study in detail, but several themes are worth emphasizing. An important issue is to what extent different types of longitudinal studies yield data relevant to antisocial behavior.

RETROSPECTIVE AND PROSPECTIVE LONGITUDINAL STUDIES

Most longitudinal studies fall into one of three types: retrospective, prospective, or combined retrospective and prospective. Retrospective longitudinal studies, as the term implies, cover only the past and reconstructed circumstances of past psychopathology. Retrospectively collected data may be biased (e.g., because of faulty memory or destruction of old records) or they may be incomplete because of a lack of access to past events or behaviors. Among the retrospective studies, Robins (1978) distinguished "follow-back" retrospective studies, in which a sample was defined using information collected sometime in the past, from "catch-up" retrospective studies, in which samples are defined prospectively using old records. An example of a catch-up study occurs when the sample is defined as "all juveniles who attended a clinic for antisocial behavior." In general, catch-up studies are superior to follow-back studies because the catch-up studies allow estimation of prospective probabilities (such as the probability of children from certain backgrounds becoming delinquent). However, because of old and inadequate records, catch-up studies usually are not informative about the onset of delinquent behaviors. In contrast, follow-back studies can be extremely useful when they use a case-control design to investigate a rare phenomenon such as juvenile homicide that cannot be easily studied prospectively. In this example, juvenile homicide offenders would be the "cases" and would be compared to some control group retrospectively on their early development.

The second type of longitudinal study is prospective, following samples forward into the future. An example is the Cambridge Study in Delinquent Development (Farrington & West, 1990), in which London inner-city boys were assessed for the first time at age 8, then reassessed at ages 10, 14, 16, 18, 21, 25, and, most recently, at age 32. The principal advantage of the prospective longitudinal study is that investigators can choose what measures to use in testing specific hypotheses for particular age periods. To the extent that these measures are chosen for theoretical reasons, they may become dated (i.e., outdated) quickly. Also retrospective bias is not as central an issue. A disadvantage of some prospective longitudinal designs is that many start several years after birth, rather than at birth. Consequently, many of the existing prospective longitudinal studies lack good data about early behavioral development prior to the first longitudinal assessment (but, for exceptions, see Fergusson et al., 1994; Krueger et al., 1996; Wadsworth, 1991; Werner & Smith, 1992).

The third type of longitudinal study combines retrospective and prospective designs to obtain the most comprehensive scope of development. For example, the Pittsburgh Youth Study (Loeber, Stouthamer-Loeber, Van Kammen et al., 1991) first assessed children in the youngest of three samples at age 7, when retrospective information was obtained from the mother about the boy's behavior over his first 7 years of life. Subsequently, the boys, their mothers, and their teachers were reassessed every 6 months to obtain prospective data about behavioral changes over time. In this design, retrospective information (from the mother) and prospective information were merged to study the children's complete life course of behavioral development. Reliability checks showed that informants' recall of the age ordering of the development of disruptive child behaviors was quite good (Loeber et al., 1993). However, the combined retrospective-prospective design is of limited use in studying risk factors that occurred prior to the first assessment. Although some constant risk factors may be taken into account by means of retrospectively collected information, most risk factors may vary over time and, therefore, need to be assessed prospectively.

MULTIPLE COHORT STUDIES AND THE ACCELERATED LONGITUDINAL DESIGN

The main disadvantage of prospective longitudinal studies on antisocial behavior is the long time it takes to obtain key results. For example, the risk window for the onset of antisocial behavior is relatively long, from the preschool years to about age 16 (although the risk window for life-course persistence may range from birth to early adolescence, but precise data are wanting). As a result, a prospective follow-up focusing on onset takes years to complete, while researchers age along with the subjects.

To remedy this general problem of longitudinal studies, Bell (1953, 1954) suggested the use of an "accelerated" longitudinal design to speed up the longitudinal assessments. In such a design, several age cohorts of subjects are followed up for the same number of years, so that the age of one cohort at the end of the assessments coincides with the beginning age of the next oldest cohort. In this design, a risk period of, for example, 9 years can be split into three sections of 3 years each, thereby reducing the duration of the study to 3 years. More specifically, one cohort could be followed up from ages 6 to 9, another from ages 9 to 12, and a third from ages 12 to 15.

Despite its advantages, this type of design has the drawback that the first assessment may generate higher prevalence rates of problem behaviors than subsequent assessments because of testing effects (i.e., resulting from the repeated assessments of participants; see, e.g., Thornberry, 1989). In addition, cohorts may have different rates of antisocial behavior because of differing circumstances under which each cohort has been raised. For these reasons, the last assessment of one cohort may not necessarily be equivalent to the first assessment of the next oldest cohort. The accelerated longitudinal design raises challenging questions about statistical analyses, since breaks in segments also constitute breaks in the within-subject change in problem behavior over time (Farrington, 1988b). Stanger, Achenbach, and Verhulst (1994) suggested matching subjects from different age cohorts within the design as a way of overcoming this handicap, but it remains to be seen whether this technique can be used when there are marked testing effects. Finally, we need to determine if the accelerated longitudinal design is useful for the evaluation of interventions, because interventions for one age group often are not identical to those for another age group.

MAIN ADVANTAGES AND PURPOSES OF LONGITUDINAL STUDIES ON ANTISOCIAL BEHAVIOR

Longitudinal studies, in contrast to cross-sectional studies, have many advantages for the study of antisocial behavior (see Farrington, 1979, 1988a; Verhulst & Koot, 1991, for reviews). Briefly, longitudinal studies can measure the onset, offset, and duration of antisocial behavior as they naturally emerge. Second, longitudinal studies allow the study of continuity and discontinuity, frequency and seriousness, specialization (i.e., a concentration into a narrow range of types of offenses), and escalation of antisocial behavior (i.e., an increase in the severity of offending). This is particularly important because the manifestations of antisocial behavior dramatically change from childhood through adolescence. Third, longitudinal studies allow the prediction of later outcomes from earlier factors. When frequent measurements are taken, such studies can quantify the impact of risk exposure and duration of exposure on later outcomes.

A fourth advantage is that longitudinal studies can help establish developmental sequences in problem behaviors and identify pathways shared by different individuals leading to common outcomes (see later). Fifth, longitudinal studies can examine the effect of critical periods of life and help establish to what extent turning points in juveniles' lives (e.g., the transition from elementary to middle or high school or the transition to leaving school) influence the frequency, seriousness, and variety of antisocial acts. The sixth advantage is that longitudinal studies can help establish which factors are relevant for preventive interventions and at what stage of development such interventions are likely to be most effective. Seventh, such studies can better help establish the degree of intergenerational transmission of antisocial behavior and also establish factors that are related to discontinuity in intergenerational transmission. A final advantage arises from a combination of a longitudinal study and an experimental intervention. We briefly address each of these points.

The Natural History of the Development of Antisocial Behavior

Repeated measurements in prospective longitudinal studies allow examination of the development of antisocial behavior. These measurements are superior to data collected in several cross-sectional studies with different age cohorts, because longitudinal studies can show not only aggregated age trends but also within-subject age trends over time (Farrington, 1988b). This is particularly relevant for antisocial acts because their behavioral manifestations change dramatically over time. For example, at an early age we may see a high degree of verbal aggression and minor pilfering, whereas at a later age more serious forms of physical fighting and property violations become more prominent.

It is unclear to what extent these different manifestations of problem behaviors reflect a developmental shift in which one behavior is a stimulus for the emergence of a different behavior or whether the different behavioral manifestations essentially are symptoms of a general underlying antisocial propensity. Developmental changes in antisocial behavior can be studied as a function of some maturational process, for example, menarche or hormonal and neurological processes (Magnusson, Stattin, & Allen, 1986).

The natural history of the development of antisocial behavior may be different for different types of people. For example, Moffitt (1993) suggested that offenders should be divided into two types, the "adolescent limited," who started late and had relatively short criminal careers, and the "life-course persistent," who started early and had relatively long criminal careers. Several researchers have shown that a small minority of "chronic" offenders account for a large proportion of all offenses (Farrington & West, 1993; Huizinga, Loeber, & Thornberry, 1995; Wolfgang, Figlio, &

Sellin, 1972). It is important to investigate how far these chronic offenders can be predicted at an early age, so that early intervention can be implemented to reduce their offending.

Onset and Offset

Longitudinal data are needed to provide information about age of onset, age of offset, and duration of the antisocial behavior pattern. The study of onset is crucial because it is the first step in a process that may or may not lead to serious antisocial acts and often is the first realistic opportunity for intervention. Cumulative prevalence curves for different kinds of antisocial behavior may give a first hint of the sequential ordering of these behaviors as they unfold over time (Loeber et al., 1993), thus revealing the developmental ordering of behaviors. Longitudinal designs also have the potential to reveal the developmental ordering between external (possibly causal) events and behaviors.

Several difficulties need to be taken into account in the study of the onset. First, some behaviors may have an insidious or gradual onset, such as chronic disobedience. Second, the best informant on onset is not always clear. Should this informant be the parent, the child, or someone else who has relevant information? And how much bias is there in reporting age at onset?

Irrespective of measurement problems, studies uniformly have shown that for males the onset of serious disruptive problem behaviors at an early, age-atypical time is of particular developmental relevance. The earlier the onset of such behavior, the higher is the degree of continuity and the higher is the likelihood of escalation to chronic forms of offending (Loeber, 1982; Tolan, 1987). Age at onset also is important for understanding developmental sequences in antisocial behavior and developmental pathways toward serious problem behaviors (see later). In contrast, the age of offset has been studied less often (but see Farrington, 1992; Le Blanc & Fréchette, 1989).

A critical issue in the study of children's behavior is our inability to discriminate *prospectively* between those youngsters who will outgrow their early problem behaviors and those who will not. We need to be able to discriminate prospectively between youth who will become, because of their problem behaviors, impaired in functioning and those who will not and to differentiate between those youth whose infliction of harm is transitory and those who are on the road to persistence in these behaviors.

Developmental Pathways

Knowledge of different ages of onset of various problem behaviors is suggestive but does not prove that the majority of antisocial individuals experience the onset of one problem behavior in a regular sequence prior to the onset of other specified problem behaviors. The concept of a developmental pathway has been proposed to capture this putative trend. A developmental pathway occurs when a group of individuals shows a deviant behavioral development that is distinct from the behavioral development of another group of individuals. Two issues are important for our understanding of developmental pathways. The first is how many individuals go through each particular sequence of onsets of different behaviors; the second is how best to classify individuals over time. As to the first issue, if we find that the onset of minor theft happens prior to the onset of burglary, we have to ask how many individuals actually have an onset of both minor theft and burglary in the specified order. (This is a shift from the *variable paradigm,* based on the relationship between variables, to the *within-subject change paradigm,* based on changes of characteristics, e.g., variables, within each subject over time.) The second issue is one of classification. We have long known that individuals can be classified cross-sectionally as property or violent offenders, but the question posed here is how to classify individuals on the basis of their antisocial behavior over time. Is it possible to classify juveniles on the basis of their behavioral development in terms of the age of onset, frequency, and variety of the behavior? And, what is the utility of such a dynamic classification?

To advance the concept of pathways in disruptive and antisocial behavior, Loeber et al. (1993) and Loeber, Keenan, Zhang, and Sieck (1995) studied the two oldest samples of the Pittsburgh Youth Study. Retrospective and prospective data on the onset of antisocial behavior were obtained from the parents and the boys. After testing several models, the best fit to the data was achieved by assuming three pathways. These pathways can be thought of as lines of development, in which individuals may progress on more than one pathway at the time. The first was an *overt pathway,* which represented an escalation from minor aggression (annoying others, bullying) to physical fighting (including gang fighting) and eventually to violence (robbery, rape). A second pathway, called the *covert pathway,* had minor covert acts (shoplifting and frequent lying) as a first step, property damage (fire setting, vandalism) as a second step, and more serious forms of theft (e.g., breaking and entering) as a third step. The third pathway, called the *authority conflict pathway,* had as its first step stubborn behavior, followed by serious disobedience and defiance, and last by authority avoidance before the age of 12 (staying out late at night, truancy, and running away). Some juveniles progressed on a single pathway; others advanced on multiple pathways. For some boys, problem behaviors were short lived and not a reliable indication of following in these pathways.

The three pathways are behavioral manifestations that presumably unfold alongside impairments in moral development. Kohlberg (1976) has shown that moral development takes place according to stages that are orderly and predictable.

To return to the behavioral manifestations, because the onset of a disruptive behavior is different from the frequency or recurrence of such behavior, Loeber, Keenan et al. (1995) made a distinction between those boys who experimented with antisocial behavior and those who persisted in it. Taking this distinction into account, the authors showed that most of the persisters entered a pathway at the first step measured in the study rather than at a later step. Also, the rate of offending increased with persisting boys' penetration in a pathway and was particularly high for those boys who were developing in multiple pathways.

In summary, developmental pathways in antisocial behavior help quantify and specify different manifestations of problem behaviors as they unfold over time within individuals. In that sense, knowledge of individual youths' positions on developmental pathways is much more specific than information gleaned from a *DSM-IV* diagnosis of disruptive behavior disorder (oppositional or conduct disorder; American Psychiatric Association, 1994). Knowledge of pathways can help early identification of those juveniles who are at high risk for later deviancy. At the same time, pathways can help to specify which problems are likely to emerge next in those youths who have gone through the early steps of disruptive pathways. Last, another advantage of pathways is that factors can be investigated to explain why some youths are only experimenters, why some youths penetrate into a pathway and then desist, and why others become highly involved in crime.

Life Events and Critical Periods

The study of significant life events can improve our understanding of the etiology of antisocial behavior and can be investigated best in prospective longitudinal studies. Longitudinal data allow comparison of the subject's antisocial behavioral development prior to a life event and subsequent to it. Even if a behavioral change is observed, it is essential to investigate whether the change is due to third variables occurring around the time of the life event (see Farrington, 1977). It should be kept in mind, however, that the study of life events can easily lead to oversimplification. In the case of marital breakup, for example, life events often are not sharply demarcated at a particular point in time, and the divorce may have long-lasting acrimonious consequences that can further affect a child's behavior.

Life events of the same type usually occur at different ages. A principal advantage of longitudinal data is that they allow identification of all subjects who experience the life event, although such life events may have been experienced at different points in time. By means of data manipulation, these life events can be aligned. Analyses may examine the impact of risk factors on subsequent behavior change to tease out which life events have had an impact on the development of antisocial behavior of different categories of juveniles. (Age or some maturational factor may be included as a covariate in such analyses.)

An issue that warrants more attention is the possibility that life events may not affect children in the same way at every developmental period. It is likely that there are critical periods in which growth and stabilization of specific types of behaviors take place. When development of those types does not occur or is disturbed, some individuals may be less likely to subsequently "catch up," and these individuals may be more likely to show symptomatic behaviors at a later age period. Increasing evidence suggests that the first few years of life are crucial for the acquisition of prosocial skills, and frequent disruptions and changes in caretakers at that age may impair socialization for years to come (MacDonald, 1985; Rothe, 1985; Shaw & Bell, 1993). This period also is crucial for the outgrowing of "normal" oppositional behavior, aggressive acts, and lying (Loeber & Hay, 1994). Delays in the emergence of such behaviors may constitute the first steps toward entry into disruptive pathways.

Longitudinal data also are able to illuminate periods in which stabilization of deviant behaviors occurs. For instance, several longitudinal studies have shown that the stability coefficients (i.e., the time-to-time correlations) for aggression in males tend to increase from middle childhood to adolescence (Loeber, 1982). Shifts in such stability coefficients may indicate that there is a group of boys who become more persistent in fighting. The importance of discovering such shifts in stability coefficients is that it may indicate that there is a period prior to early stabilization that is critical for the crystallization of behaviors. Ideally, remedial intervention should take place during the period prior to stabilization of behaviors.

Important Methodological Issues in Longitudinal Studies on Child Antisocial Behavior

Sources of Data

It is recognized more and more that the best longitudinal studies have multiple informants (see Hinshaw & Zupan, Chapter 4, this volume). The reasons are simple: Reliability can be established, and the validity of reporting usually is higher when multiple, rather than single, informants are available. It should be understood, though, that not all sources of information are equally useful. The careful choice of sources can enhance the results of longitudinal studies. For example, young children before the age of 7 or 8 are not thought to be good informants on their own behavior. Even after that age, it is clear that children are not the best informants on their own attention problems, hyperactivity, and oppositional behaviors (Loeber, Green, & Lahey, 1990; Loeber, Green, Lahey, & Stouthamer-Loeber, 1989). Also, parents may not be able to observe covert behaviors of their children, and for that reason, children's self-reports are more important, as are peer reports. Peer nominations are often used (e.g., Eron et al., 1987). Although very valuable, peer nominations in longitudinal studies often are complicated by movement from one classroom to another, and new consent forms may be needed from each new group of peers and their parents.

The best longitudinal studies on antisocial behavior collect information from different informants on behavioral development, risk factors, and psychophysiological and neuropsychological event measures (e.g., Moffitt, 1990). Because of practical limitations in the execution of such studies, however, direct observations and biological measures usually apply to relatively narrow segments of time, which are much smaller than the regular intervals between longitudinal assessments. Nevertheless, the integration of survey data, behavioral observations, and biological measures is an informative combination to be pursued in longitudinal analyses. Particularly necessary are studies demonstrating the extent to which youths with demonstrable biological vulnerabilities for antisocial behavior *do not* develop that behavior. Such studies make it possible to investigate what the protective factors are in these youths' social environment that appear to inhibit the manifestation of the biological vulnerability for antisocial behavior in this group.

Types of Samples

Three types of samples are relevant in longitudinal studies: general population, high-risk, and case-control samples. The main advantage of a general population sample is representativeness. Also, because antisocial behavior emerges naturally, this sample avoids the problem of selecting a non-antisocial control group. The principal advantage of population samples is that they allow the study of onset, escalation, and offset of problem behaviors in the general population. A disadvantage of population samples is that they may not necessarily contain enough subjects with antisocial personalities. Therefore, some longitudinal studies have used a screening procedure to enhance the number of high-risk individuals in a sample (e.g., Loeber, Stouthamer-Loeber, Van Kammen, & Farrington, 1989).

It may be advantageous to start a study of high-risk individuals alongside a population study (e.g., Le Blanc, 1994; Loeber, Stouthamer-Loeber, & Green 1991). A high-risk sample may be derived from clinic-referred youths or delinquents referred to the juvenile court. The principal advantage of the follow-up of a sample of high-risk, referred individuals is that it allows the study of escalation toward serious antisocial acts, the emergence of coexisting conditions, and offset.

Duration of Studies

There are no hard and fast rules as to the ideal interval between follow-ups in longitudinal studies, but the following points are worth considering. Foremost is to what extent one wants to cover the window of risk in which antisocial behaviors emerge or persist. If the focus is to study the onset of problem behaviors, then depending on the definition of onset, the period from preschool to about 16 years may be the most appropriate. However, if offset is the main focus, two periods are relevant. Offset of conduct problems and delinquency can be studied best in the period from late childhood through early adulthood. If co-occurrence is an issue, then the period should be targeted to co-occur with the emergence of co-occurring conditions. In general, decisions about the interval between follow-ups within a longitudinal study should be based on the duration and course of the problem behaviors of interest and the duration and course of the co-occurring conditions.

Another major consideration for longitudinal studies is their cost, most of which lies in personnel (Stouthamer-Loeber, Van Kammen, & Loeber, 1992) and is amplified by the number of occasions on which subjects are recontacted and reassessed. A serious consideration in the execution of longitudinal studies is attrition (loss of subjects for a variety of reasons, principally refusal or difficulty in locating them). Individuals with antisocial personalities are most likely not to cooperate and to be elusive. However, careful data collection and tracking procedures can overcome many attrition problems. For example, Farrington et al. (1990) in the Cambridge Study and Stouthamer-Loeber et al. (1992) in the Pittsburgh Youth Study showed that high rates of cooperation can be achieved. Generally, investigators will have more success obtaining cooperation if they leave sufficient time to locate and recontact the subjects. High-risk subjects may not show up for appointments and may be elusive in other respects, making the availability of human resources to stay with these individuals and eventually interview them of crucial importance.

Frequency of Assessments and Intervals Between Them

There is no clear prescription as to the ideal number of assessments and intervals between them. Fixed-interval follow-ups have several advantages, such as the ability to express rates of change over equivalent periods of time and the study of the onset of new problem behaviors. However, the fixed-interval design works best when the interval is not too long, because of the problem of retrospective recall. It is particularly difficult to measure potentially causal factors that have taken place in the distant past, and ideally causal factors should be measured at the time they exert their influence (Cohen, 1991). In the Pittsburgh Youth Study, we found it advantageous to begin with 6-month assessments to maximize retrospective recall. However, after six to eight assessments, it became clear that we could not continue this frequency of assessments because of decreased subject cooperation and the cost of intensive staff effort. For those reasons, we switched to yearly assessments. As a result, we have been able to study antisocial behavior over a period of 7 years now in the Pittsburgh Youth Study, with more years to follow. Thirteen assessments have been completed thus far, and the average cooperation rate is still 94% of the original sample.

Not all factors need to be assessed at the same intervals. Variables that change quite quickly, such as friendship patterns, need to be measured relatively frequently. In contrast, more stable features, such as intelligence, may be measured less often.

Age, Period, and Cohort Effects

Another advantage of longitudinal studies is the ability to achieve some separation of age, period, and cohort effects (e.g., Baltes, Reese, & Lipsitt, 1980; Glenn, 1977). *Age* effects are those that change as a function of subjects' aging; *period* effects reflect societal changes (e.g., in types of substances used in populations); and *cohort* effects are those due to one age cohort developing in a different way than another age cohort. Cohort and period effects may be particularly important in the area of antisocial behavior, because the manifestation of antisocial behavior may be different from one age cohort to the next. For example, the increasing use of crack cocaine in the 1980s dramatically changed the nature of the associated violence. This affected the problem behavior of successive age cohorts compared to age cohorts in earlier periods in which both crack and the associated violence were less important. Cohort and period effects need to be distinguished from changes that occur with age. For example, aging eventually leads to physical deterioration for all birth cohorts.

Data Analyses

The availability of information about the age of onset of problem behaviors opens up a new arena of data analyses. Techniques such as survival analyses (onset analyses adjusted for the proportion of subjects who did not have an onset) or event history analyses (e.g., comparison of offending prior to and after an event such as marital breakup; see Allison, 1984) often require information about the exact times at which specific events occur. Similarly, growth curve analyses (Goldstein, 1995; Rasbash & Woodhouse, 1995; Woodhouse, 1995) can be used when a single dependent variable is being studied with a number of explanatory variables accounting for the time it takes for the phenomenon to emerge.

Complex longitudinal studies can pose major problems of data reduction. Factor analyses can be used to reduce variables to smaller numbers that reflect underlying theoretical dimensions.

Multiple factor analyses at different waves of data collection usually are not practical, however; each factor analysis is prone to produce idiosyncratic results that are difficult to link longitudinally. Also, low base-rate events, such as serious types of antisocial acts, cannot be accommodated easily within this statistical technique; researchers often delete low base-rate behaviors before undertaking factor analyses. For that reason, more a priori data reduction methods, soundly embedded in some theoretical conceptualization, have to be used.

Generally, clustering techniques to categorize individuals have not been used in the study of antisocial behavior (but see Magnusson & Bergman, 1988). However, such techniques are sensitive to the number and type of variables on which the clustering is based, with minor changes in input often leading to very different clusters. What we mentioned about factor analyses at different waves of data collection also applies to cluster analyses. The clustering of individuals at each wave produces data that are difficult to link across waves, especially when different measures are used in the different assessments. An alternative clustering of individuals over time is captured by the concept of developmental pathways reviewed earlier.

One of the strengths of longitudinal analyses is the analysis of the different manifestations of antisocial behavior as they unfold over time, because manifestations at an early age may be very different from manifestations at another age. For example, Farrington (1986), in a "stepping-stone" analysis, used successive regressions to predict successive outcome variables at different ages. The strength of these analyses is that they help to determine to what extent similar or different explanatory variables account for successive manifestations of problem behavior. Another strength is that earlier problem behavior can be taken into account as a predictor for later problem behavior in a stepwise fashion (see Collins & Horn, 1991; Tonry, Ohlin, & Farrington, 1991, Chapter 11).

Future analyses should address the extent to which one or many manifestations of antisocial behavior and successive manifestations represent a single underlying phenomenon. Different approaches to this problem have been advocated by different researchers. For example, Patterson, Reid, and Dishion (1992), by means of structural equation modeling, indicated that different manifestations of antisocial behavior could be best represented by a single antisocial trait.[1] Although attractive in some respects, the explanatory power of representing antisocial behavior by a single antisocial trait may not be very great. It may be more useful to understand links between different manifestations of antisocial behavior using several "underlying" constructs, particularly those that are different in content from the antisocial acts and that can better help explain differences among individuals. Examples of such underlying constructs are impulsivity, lack of moral development, sensation seeking, and physiological underarousal.

---

[1]These analyses did not take into account strong method effects, as shown by high intercorrelations between different constructs reported by the same informants. It remains to be seen whether the results also apply when the method effects are incorporated in the structural modeling.

Causality

The study of antisocial behavior, like any social phenomenon, is fraught with difficulties in demonstrating causality, both within and between individuals. Cross-sectional studies, in contrast to longitudinal studies, are particularly disadvantaged in establishing causality.

What can be achieved in longitudinal studies? One of the first steps is to determine not only whether one variable is correlated with a second variable, but also whether it precedes the second in time and predicts the second independent of other variables (Le Blanc & Loeber, 1993). For instance, consider the relationship between oppositional symptoms and symptoms of conduct disorder, which constitute distinctly different patterns of behavior. Oppositional symptoms can be measured at Time 1 and conduct symptoms at successive times, and then the extent that oppositional symptoms predict conduct symptoms can be investigated. However, several caveats need to be taken into account. First, it needs to be established that oppositional behavior (with its criteria that are very distinct from the criteria of conduct disorder) predicts conduct problems at Time 2, even when conduct problems at Time 1 are taken into account. Otherwise, the results may merely reflect the fact that conduct problems predict themselves over time. Second, one may want to establish that oppositional behavior predicts the onset of conduct problems, which practically ensures their independence in measurement. For example, Loeber, Green et al. (1995) found that the onset of conduct disorder was best predicted by the earlier presence of oppositional defiant disorder.

Several other techniques narrow down risk factors to plausible causal factors (Le Blanc & Loeber, 1993). In longitudinal studies, it is possible to examine causation in terms of explaining both between-group differences in antisocial behavior and within-subject changes in antisocial behavior over time. Much needs to be learned about the extent to which these two sets of analyses lead to similar or different conclusions.

The psychological explanation of antisocial behavior traditionally has focused on the psychosocial spheres, such as family functioning, peer factors, and neighborhood factors. However, an increasing body of literature (e.g., Raine, 1993) has substantiated that antisocial individuals differ from non-antisocial individuals in terms of such biological factors as the galvanic skin response (GSR) and heart rate. We know much less about the extent to which these biological factors indicating neurotransmitters are related and perhaps influence psychosocial processes, and conversely, the extent to which psychosocial processes influence the biological processes. Biological factors may often interact with psychosocial processes; for example, Brennan and Mednick (1994) showed that pregnancy complications predicted violence only among deprived children.

Researchers should aim for a multilayered explanation of antisocial behavior over time. Biological, psychosocial, and situational factors should be included as interlinked and integrated variables across the different levels of analysis. This will help to explain why some individuals, even though they are biologically prone to violence, do not become violent, despite exposure to certain environments or as a result of experience. Likewise, it will help us understand why others who have a biological predisposition become violent. Third, we need to understand much better

about what psychological and other factors influence individuals with no biological predisposition to become antisocial over time.

Use of Experimental Treatment Interventions in Longitudinal Studies

The major way to narrow down causal factors is by experimental interventions in which variables are carefully manipulated and resulting behavioral change is carefully measured. We advocate the use of a combined longitudinal and experimental design. In this design, subjects are followed over time, but some subjects are randomly assigned to receive a treatment or intervention, whereas others serve as a nontreated control group. A third, placebo intervention group sometimes may be necessary. It should be understood that it is not necessary for all subjects in a longitudinal study to be participating in an intervention experiment. Some could be designated as a "natural history" group to be followed, that is, not allocated to either an intervention or a control group.

The principal advantage of the longitudinal-experimental design is that it allows for the study of the naturalistic "normal" course of development without intervention, at least any deliberately initiated by the investigators. Otherwise, the effects of naturally occurring factors that influence children's behavior may not be distinguishable from the effects of factors that are modified as part of the experiment. The experimental part of the longitudinal-experimental research will help to identify more factors that can be changed and might have causal effects.

Generally, experimental treatment interventions can be of two types (Schwartz, Flamant, & Lelouch, 1980). The first type is a *pragmatic clinical trial* that serves to show that a particular intervention or preventive strategy is effective. The second type is an *explanatory trial* that demonstrates that a change in one factor (or theoretical construct) causes a change in another. The results of explanatory trials shed light on the causal status of a specific risk factor. In a pragmatic trial, treatment usually consists of the manipulation of several variables and, therefore, provides less information about the causal status of each. We still need a programmatic way of approaching explanatory trials, preferably with a series of promising specific interventions that later can be integrated into more broad-base, pragmatic clinical trials.

The crucial link between the two types of interventions is the formulation of causal hypotheses. Causal hypotheses can be derived not only from pragmatic intervention studies, but also from nonexperimental longitudinal studies. Experiments using controlled observation are the best method for testing the effects of variation between individuals, whereas longitudinal studies investigate the effect of naturally occurring changes within individuals. A combined longitudinal-treatment design compares the impact of variations in risk and protective factors with the impact of change as a result of an intervention. This comparison allows the investigator to see if the same results are obtained with the same individuals. In that sense, a combined longitudinal-treatment design can link findings on antisocial behavior, which essentially concern variations between individuals, with findings on within-individual change, which are the hallmark of intervention studies.

When interventions are undertaken in longitudinal studies, it often is advantageous to have longitudinal measurements beforehand to establish a baseline and to understand pre-existing trends or developmental sequences that may take place prior to the first intervention (Blumstein, Cohen, & Farrington, 1988). Baseline information helps verify that comparison groups are equivalent and helps investigate interactions between types of persons (i.e., types of individuals classified from details of their prior histories) and types of treatments. Moreover, the effects of interventions need to be ascertained with repeated follow-up data. This is particularly important with antisocial behavior as an outcome, because antisocial behavior tends to fluctuate over time. For that reason, a single measurement at outcome may not be sufficient (e.g., Lahey et al., 1995).

The long-term impact of interventions needs to be assessed by repeated follow-ups after termination of the intervention. Wolf, Braukmann, and Ramp (1987) point out that antisocial behavior is often intractable in a proportion of juveniles. For that reason, booster treatments often are indicated rather than single treatments over short periods. Again, this reinforces the notion that repeated follow-ups are needed to monitor antisocial behavior over long time periods.

Problems of Longitudinal-Experimental Research

When undertaking longitudinal-experimental designs, it is desirable to check that the treatment experiment does not interfere with the goals of the longitudinal study. Some of the longitudinal sample probably will be excluded altogether from the experiment; some will be allocated to the treatment group; others will be allocated to the control group. Careful thought needs to be given to the proportions in each group. After the experimental treatment intervention is completed, it would probably be inadvisable to draw conclusions about the natural history of antisocial behavior from the experimental group, because this would have been treated in an unusual way. Even if there is no difference between the experimental and control groups on some measured outcomes, some other differences may make it risky to amalgamate the groups. Can these subjects be merged with the others? Moreover, the experimental intervention may increase or decrease attrition from the longitudinal study.

It is less clear that experimental subjects would have to be eliminated in investigations that use quasi-experimental analyses. If the experimental treatment intervention could be viewed as just another independent variable impinging on the subjects, then the investigation of the effect of nonmanipulated independent variables might be based on the whole sample. This decision may depend on how unusual the treatment is in its impact on children's lives. Certainly, it would be important to investigate whether the impact of an independent variable differed between the treatment and control groups.

It could be argued that each person should receive only one experimental treatment and the treatment may make the person different from a control subject. However, there may be good reasons to investigate the interactive effects of two consecutive treatments. For example, it may be desirable to begin the treatment of hyperactive children with stimulant medication and then continue with parent training and child management procedures. If the "controls" received a special treatment (e.g., being denied something that is usually available in the community), then it might even be argued that they also had been changed and should not be

included in a subsequent experiment. It seems unlikely that more than one or two treatment experiments could be conducted in any longitudinal study before the number of "naturalistic" subjects dropped below some critical level.

Limitations of Experiments

Methodological and practical problems arise in treatment experiments. For example, it is hard to ensure that all subjects in the treatment group actually received the treatment, and that all those in the control group did not. Resistance among subjects or their caretakers to being denied treatment is common, and they may try to obtain it anyway (e.g., stimulant medication for hyperactivity and attention problems). It is well known that differential attrition can affect the interpretation of treatment effects and that differential attrition is more likely with antisocial subjects.

We need to come back to how to investigate causality. Typically, it is possible to study the effect of only one or two independent variables at two or three different levels (different experimental conditions) in a randomized treatment experiment. For example, few of the possible causes of antisocial behavior, in practice, could be studied experimentally, because few of the important variables can be experimentally manipulated. Some variables are inherently nonmanipulable (e.g., age and sex), and others cannot be manipulated because of ethical, legal, and practical limitations (e.g., single-parent families). It is extremely difficult to create a dose-response curve using randomized experiments. Hence, a theory of antisocial behavior that was limited to results obtained only in experiments would be inadequate. A crucial question that can be addressed in longitudinal experimental designs is the extent to which experimental and nonexperimental results agree on the importance of explanatory variables. We should be cautious about the possibility that poor control in nonexperimental research may lead to an overestimation of the importance of certain variables. Although epidemiologists use an index of attributable risk (Schlesselman, 1982), this does not necessarily mean that variables actually can be manipulated in the community to the extent suggested by the magnitude of the attributable risk index.

Another limitation of experiments should be considered: They are usually designed to investigate only immediate or short-term causal effects. It is rare to find subjects followed up for more than 1 year. However, some experimental interventions may have long-term rather than short-term effects, and in some cases the long-term effects may differ from the short-term ones (e.g., Waldo & Griswold, 1979). More fundamentally, researchers rarely know the time delay between cause and effect, suggesting that measurements at several different intervals are desirable. If a delayed effect occurs, it is desirable to investigate the intervening factors that best explain the delay and how such factors are important for future intervention studies. Also, as mentioned before, the effect of the treatment may wear off, and it may be necessary to include booster sessions. How can such wearing off and the need for booster designs best be conceptualized in terms of causal factors? These and other problems of experiments probably can be addressed best through combined longitudinal-experimental study.

The passage of time itself is a problem. A treatment experiment that was desirable and feasible at one time (e.g., the start of a longitudinal study) may be less desirable and feasible later because of changes in theory, policy concerns, methodology, or practical constraints (e.g., a change in a gatekeeper, such as a school superintendent). Many youngsters, and particularly antisocial youngsters and their families, often move their households. It may be that an experiment can be conducted only in a specific location. For that reason, the mobility of antisocial individuals may pose certain restraints on the type of experimental intervention that can be conducted.

Although the impact of intervention with antisocial children is intended to have desirable effects, it also can have unexpected undesirable effects. The follow-up by McCord (1978) of the Cambridge-Somerville Study is a case in point. This showed that more of the participants in the experimental treatment group, compared to controls, became alcoholic, developed mental illness, suffered from stress-related diseases, or died early. Obviously, such negative treatment effects are of great concern and pose major questions about causality.

On the more positive side, experimental treatment interventions can have positive benefits, often extending over many years. The important experiment of the Perry Project (Berrueta-Clement, Schweinhart, Barnett, Epstein, & Weikart, 1984) consisted of a preschool intellectual enrichment program targeted on disadvantaged African American children. The experimental children attended a daily preschool program, backed up by a weekly home visit, usually for 2 years, covering ages 3 and 4. The principal aim of the program was to provide intellectual stimulation, to increase cognitive abilities, and to increase later school achievement. The experimental group had an increase in intelligence, but this soon wore off. The true significance of the program became apparent only after a long-term follow-up to age 15 (Schweinhart & Weikart, 1980) and showed beneficial effects, including increased school achievement, reduced self-reported offending, and improved classroom behavior. At ages 19 and 27, participants in the experimental group were less likely than the controls to have been arrested, more likely to be employed, more likely to have graduated from high school, and more likely to have received college or vocational training (Schweinhart & Wallgren, 1993).

A new generation of pioneering longitudinal-experimental studies in antisocial child behavior is now emerging. Examples are those directed by Hawkins in Seattle (Hawkins, Von Cleve, & Catalano, 1991; Hawkins et al., 1992), Tremblay in Montreal (e.g., Tremblay et al., 1991; Tremblay et al., 1992), the Fast Track program on the treatment of conduct problems (Coie et al., 1993), and the multidisciplinary collaborative treatment program for attention deficit/hyperactivity disorder (ADHD; Richters et al., in press). In addition, the National Institute of Justice, in collaboration with the MacArthur Foundation, has set in motion the Project on Human Development in Chicago Neighborhoods (Visher, 1994). This project, although it currently has no experimental intervention component, is the largest longitudinal study on delinquency that is presently underway.

CONCLUSIONS AND RECOMMENDATIONS

Compared with cross-sectional research, the major advantages of longitudinal studies on antisocial behavior are in establishing the natural history of development, continuity and stability over time,

developmental sequences and pathways, and the effects of life events on the course of antisocial development. Causal inferences can be drawn more convincingly in longitudinal studies because they permit the establishment of time ordering and prediction of later maladjustment, permit the analysis of within-individual changes and between-individual variations, and avoid problems of retrospective bias.

The major problems of longitudinal studies are attrition; testing effects; distinguishing among age, period, and cohort effects; and establishing causes with high internal validity. Longitudinal studies can lead to problems of long-delayed results and outdated instrumentation, methods, theories, and policy concerns. We have suggested ways of overcoming these problems, including the use of the accelerated longitudinal design and the inclusion of experimental treatment interventions in longitudinal studies.

The design of much past research on antisocial behavior has been cross-sectional or correlational. The use of longitudinal and experimental treatment methods represented a great step forward in methodology. The time is now ripe to combine these strong designs to capitalize on the advantages of both. More multiple-cohort longitudinal-experimental studies should now be mounted in different regions of the country. Such studies should have several years of personal contacts with the subjects before and after an intervention and repeated, frequent data collection from a variety of sources.

The main advantages of these studies are that they yield information about long-term development within a relatively short time period, permit better causal conclusions, and measure both short-term and long-term effects of interventions. Another advantage is that such multisite studies can establish the extent that interventions can be accomplished in different cultural settings.

The major problems of the longitudinal-experimental studies are how to link up cohorts in the accelerated design and the extent to which the experimental intervention may interfere with the aims of the longitudinal study (but see Stanger et al., 1994). Such longitudinal-experimental studies would be costly, although one way of minimizing the cost may be to add an experimental intervention to an existing longitudinal study.

It is desirable to mount new multiple-cohort accelerated longitudinal studies. One might begin with a sample of pregnant women with childhood cohorts (e.g., ages 3, 6, and 9 years) and with adolescent cohorts (e.g., ages 12, 15, and 18 years). A comprehensive research program should investigate a wide range of possible influences on antisocial behavior, including biological, individual, family, peer, school, and community factors (Tonry et al., 1991). Such studies would have to be collaborative and multidisciplinary. Previous longitudinal studies rarely have investigated all of these different types of factors, each of which may have different effects at different ages.

More needs to be known about developmental sequences and progressions in problem behavior from childhood to adulthood. In the case of delinquency, it may be hypothesized that children with poor temperament and low empathy at age 2 tend to show cruelty to animals and other symptoms of conduct disorder at age 8; minor delinquency, such as shoplifting at age 12; more serious delinquency such as burglary at age 15; robbery and violence at age 20; and eventually spouse abuse, child abuse, and alcoholism in their 20s and 30s. It is important to investigate what types of behaviors act as precursors to other types, why some children at risk do not progress into adult antisocial behavior, what protective factors are most important, what intervention strategies to prevent this progression are most promising, and at what developmental stages these interventions are most effective.

A few studies relate factors measured prenatally or soon after birth, or in early childhood, to later adult antisocial behavior (cf. White, Moffitt, Earls, Robins, & Silva, 1990; see also Brennan & Mednick, Chapter 25, this volume). In childhood, individual factors such as high impulsivity and low intelligence should be measured, as well as peer rejection, adverse family experiences, school underachievement, and physical health and growth. Biological measures should be taken, including birth weight, resting pulse rate, and neurotransmitter and hormone levels. The focus should be on risk factors for antisocial behavior and its precursors, on critical periods of development, and on the effect of life transitions.

Experimental treatment interventions should be included in longitudinal studies to investigate the effectiveness of methods of interrupting the course of development of antisocial behavior. However, in general, these interventions should be preceded and followed by several years of naturalistic data collection, because the impact of treatment can be better understood in the context of pre-existing developmental trends. Information should be collected at least yearly, directly from the subjects themselves and from other informants. The most important interventions that should be tested in childhood and adolescent cohorts are a preschool intellectual enrichment program including good health care and nutrition, parent training in child-rearing methods, moral education, and social skills training in peer interaction.

To summarize, funding agencies should mount several accelerated longitudinal studies in culturally diverse settings. These would include treatment interventions to lay the foundation for securing the knowledge about antisocial behavior that will be needed to alleviate troubling social problems in the next century. The time to begin is now!

REFERENCES

Allison, P. D. (1984). *Event history analysis: Regression for longitudinal event data.* Beverly Hills, CA: Sage Publications.

American Psychiatric Association. (1994). *Diagnostic and statistical manual of mental disorders* (4th ed.). Washington, DC: Author.

Baltes, P. B., Reese, H. W., & Lipsitt, L. P. (1980). Life-span developmental psychology. *Annual Review of Psychology, 31,* 65–110.

Bell, R. Q. (1953). Convergence: An accelerated longitudinal approach. *Child Development, 24,* 145–152.

Bell, R. Q. (1954). An experimental test of the accelerated longitudinal approach. *Child Development, 25,* 281–286.

Berrueta-Clement, J. R., Schweinhart, L. J., Barnett, W. S., Epstein, A. S., & Weikart, D. P. (1984). *Changed lives.* Ypsilanti, MI: High/Scope.

Blumstein, A., Cohen, J., & Farrington, D. P. (1988). Longitudinal and criminal career research: Further clarifications. *Criminology, 26,* 57–74.

Brennan, P. A., & Mednick, S. A. (1994). Evidence for the adoption of a learning theory approach to criminal deterrence: A preliminary study.

In E. G. M. Weitekamp & H. Kerner (Eds.), *Cross-national longitudinal research on human development and criminal behavior* (pp. 371–379). Dordrecht, The Netherlands: Kluwer.

Cairns, R. B., & Cairns, B. D. (1994). *Lifelines and risks, pathways of youth in our time.* Cambridge, England: University of Cambridge Press.

Capaldi, D. M., & Patterson, G. R. (1994). Interrelated influences of contextual factors on antisocial behavior in childhood and adolescence for males. In D. C. Fowles, P. Sutker, & S. H. Goodman (Eds.), *Progress in experimental personality and psychopathology research 1994: Special focus on psychopathy and antisocial personality, a developmental perspective* (pp. 165–198). New York: Springer.

Cohen, P. (1991). A source of bias in longitudinal investigations of change. In L. M. Collins & J. L. Horn (Eds.), *Best methods for the analysis of change* (pp. 18–25). Washington, DC: American Psychological Association.

Cohen, P., & Brook, J. (1987). Family factors related to the persistence of psychopathology in childhood and adolescence. *Psychiatry, 50,* 332–345.

Cohen, P., Cohen, J., Kasen, S., Velez, C. N., Johnson, J. et al. (1993). An epidemiological study of disorders in late childhood and adolescence: I. Age and gender specific prevalence. *Journal of Child Psychology and Psychiatry, 34,* 851–867.

Coie, J. D., Watt, N. F., West, S., Hawkins, J. D., Asarnow, J., Markman, H., Ramsey, S. L., Shure, M., & Long, B. (1993). The science of prevention: A conceptual framework and some directions for a national research program. *American Psychologist, 48,* 1013–1033.

Collins, L. M., & Horn, J. L. (Eds.). (1991). *Best methods for the analysis of change.* Washington, DC: American Psychological Association.

Elliott, D. S. (1994). Serious violent offenders: Onset, developmental course, and termination—The American Society of Criminology 1993 presidential address. *Criminology, 32,* 1–21.

Elliott, D. S., Huizinga, D., & Menard, S. (1989). *Multiple problem youth.* New York: Springer-Verlag.

Elliott, D. S., Huizinga, D., & Ageton, S. S. (1985). *Explaining delinquency and drug use.* Beverly Hills, CA: Sage Publications.

Ensminger, M. E., Kellam, S. G., & Rubin, B. R. (1983). School and family origins of delinquency: Comparisons by sex. In K. T. Van Dusen & S. A. Mednick (Eds.), *Antecedents of aggression and antisocial behavior* (pp. 73–98). Boston: Kluwer-Nijhoff.

Eron, L. D., & Huesmann, L. R. (1990). The stability of aggressive behavior—even unto the third generation. In M. Lewis & S. M. Miller (Eds.), *Handbook of developmental psychopathology* (pp. 147–156). New York: Plenum.

Eron, L. D., Huesmann, L. R., Dubow, E., Romanoff, R., & Yarmel, P. W. (1987). Aggression and its correlates over 22 years. In D. H. Crowell, I. M. Evans, & C. R. O'Donnell (Eds.), *Childhood aggression and violence* (pp. 249–262). New York: Plenum.

Farrington, D. P. (1977). The effects of public labelling. *British Journal of Criminology, 17,* 112–125.

Farrington, D. P. (1979). Longitudinal research on crime and delinquency. In N. Morris & M. Tonry (Eds.), *Crime and justice* (Vol. 1, pp. 289–348). Chicago: University of Chicago Press.

Farrington, D. P. (1986). Stepping stones to adult criminal careers. In D. Olweus, J. Block, & M. R. Yarrow (Eds.), *Development of antisocial and prosocial behavior* (pp. 359–383). New York: Academic Press.

Farrington, D. P. (1988a). Advancing knowledge about delinquency and crime: The need for a coordinated program of longitudinal research. *Behavioral Sciences and the Law, 6,* 307–331.

Farrington, D. P. (1988b). Studying changes within individuals: The causes of offending. In M. Rutter (Ed.), *Studies of psychosocial risk: The power of longitudinal data* (pp. 158–183). Cambridge, England: Cambridge University Press.

Farrington, D. P. (1991). Childhood aggression and adult violence: Early precursors and later life outcomes. In D. J. Peppler & K. H. Rubin (Eds.), *The development and treatment of childhood aggression* (pp. 5–29). Hillsdale, NJ: Erlbaum.

Farrington, D. P. (1992). Criminal career research: Implications for crime prevention. *Studies on Crime and Crime Prevention, 1,* 7–29.

Farrington, D. P. (1993). Have any individual, family or neighborhood influences on offending been demonstrated conclusively? In D. P. Farrington, R. J. Sampson, & P.-O. Wikström (Eds.), *Integrating individual and ecological aspects of crime* (pp. 7–38). Stockholm: National Council for Crime Prevention.

Farrington, D. P., Gallagher, B., Morley, L., St. Ledger, R. J., & West, D. J. (1988). Are there any successful men from criminogenic backgrounds? *Psychiatry, 51,* 116–130.

Farrington, D. P., Gallagher, B., Morley, L., St. Ledger, R., & West, D. J. (1990). Minimizing attrition in longitudinal research. In D. Magnusson & L. Bergman (Eds.), *Data quality in longitudinal research* (pp. 122–147). Cambridge, England: Cambridge University Press.

Farrington, D. P., & Hawkins, J. D. (1991). Predicting participation, early onset, and later persistence in officially recorded offending. *Criminal Behaviour and Mental Health, 1,* 1–33.

Farrington, D. P., & West, D. J. (1990). The Cambridge study in delinquent development: A long-term follow-up of 411 London males. In H. J. Kerner & G. Kaiser (Eds.), *Kriminalitat: Personlichkeit, Lebensgeschichte und Verhalten* [Criminality: Personality, behavior and life history] (pp. 115–138). Berlin: Springer-Verlag.

Farrington, D. P., & West, D. J. (1993). Criminal, penal and life histories of chronic offenders: Risk and protective factors and early identification. *Criminal Behaviour and Mental Health, 3,* 492–523.

Ferdinand, R. F., & Verhulst, F. C. (1994). The prediction of poor outcome in young adults: Comparison of the Young Adult Self-Report, the General Health Questionnaire and the Symptom Checklist. *Acta Psychiatrica Scandinavica, 89,* 405–410.

Fergusson, D. M., Hopwood, L. J., & Lynskey, M. (1994). The childhoods of multiple problem adolescents: A 15 year longitudinal study. *Journal of Child Psychology and Psychiatry, 35,* 1123–1140.

Glenn, N. D. (1977). *Cohort analysis.* Beverly Hills, CA: Sage Publications.

Glueck, S., & Glueck, E. (1968). *Delinquents and non-delinquents in perspective.* Cambridge, MA: Harvard University Press.

Goldstein, H. (1995). *Multilevel statistical models.* New York: Halstead.

Hawkins, J. D., Catalano, R. F., Morrison, D. M., O'Donnell, J., Abbott, R. D., & Day, L. E. (1992). The Seattle Social Development Project: Effects of the first four years on protective factors and problem behaviors. In J. McCord & R. E. Tremblay (Eds.), *Preventing antisocial behavior: Interventions from birth through adolescence* (pp. 139–161). New York: Guilford.

Hawkins, J. D., Von Cleve, E., & Catalano, R. F. (1991). Reducing early childhood aggression: Results of a primary prevention program. *Journal of the American Academy of Child and Adolescent Psychiatry, 30,* 208–217.

Hirschi, T., & Gottfredson, M. (1983). Age and the explanation of crime. *American Journal of Sociology, 89,* 552–584.

Huesmann, L. R., Eron, L. D., Lefkowitz, M. M., & Walder, L. O. (1984). Stability of aggression over time and generations. *Developmental Psychology, 20,* 1120–1134.

Huizinga, D. (1995). Developmental sequences in delinquency: Dynamic typologies. In L. J. Crockett & A. C. Crouter (Eds.), *Pathways through adolescence* (pp. 15–34). Hillsdale, NJ: Erlbaum.

Huizinga, D., Esbensen, F., & Weiher, A. (1991). Are there multiple paths to delinquency? *Journal of Criminal Law & Criminology, 82,* 83–118.

Huizinga, D., Loeber, R., & Thornberry, T. (1995). *Recent findings from the Program on the Causes and Correlates of Delinquency.* Report to the Office of Juvenile Justice and Delinquency Prevention.

Jessor, R., Donovan, J. E., & Costa, F. M. (1991). *Beyond adolescence: Problem behavior and young adult development.* New York: Cambridge University Press.

Jessor, R., & Jessor, S. L. (1977). *Problem behavior and psychosocial development.* New York: Academic.

Keenan, K., Loeber, R., Zhang, Q., Stouthamer-Loeber, M., & Van Kammen, W. B. (1995), The influence of deviant peers on the development of disruptive and delinquent behavior: A temporal analysis. *Development and Psychopathology, 7,* 715–726.

Kellam, S. G., Ensminger, M. E., & Simon, M. B. (1980). Mental health in first grade and teenage drug, alcohol and cigarette use. *Drug and Alcohol Dependency, 5,* 273–304.

Klinteberg, B. A., Andersson, T., Magnusson, D., & Stattin, H. (1993). Hyperactive behavior in childhood as related to subsequent alcohol problems and violent offending: A longitudinal study of male subjects. *Personality and Individual Differences, 15,* 381–388.

Kohlberg, L. (1976). Moral stages and moralization: The cognitive development approach. In T. Lickona (Ed.), *Moral development and behavior.* New York: Holt, Reinhart and Winston.

Kolvin, I., Miller, F. J. W., Scott, D., McI., Gatzanis, S. R. M., & Fleeting, M. (1990). *Continuities of deprivation? The New Castle 1000 Family Study.* Brookfield, USA: Avebury.

Krueger, R. F., Caspi, A., Moffitt, T. E., White, J., & Stouthamer-Loeber, M. (1996). Delay of gratification, personality and psychopathology: Is low self-control specific to externalizing problems? *Journal of Personality, 64,* 107–129.

Lahey, B. B., Loeber, R., Hart., E. L., Frick, P. J., Appelgate, B., Zhang, Q., Green, S. M., & Russo, M. F. (1995). Four-year longitudinal study of conduct disorder in boys: Patterns and predictors of persistence. *Journal of Abnormal Psychology, 104,* 83–93.

Le Blanc, M. (1994). Family, school, delinquency and criminality: The predictive power of an elaborated social control theory for males. *Criminal Behaviour and Mental Health, 4,* 101–117.

Le Blanc, M., & Fréchette, M. (1989). *Male criminal activity from childhood through youth: Multilevel and developmental perspectives.* New York: Springer-Verlag.

Le Blanc, M., & Loeber, R. (1993). Precursors, causes and the development of offending. In D. F. Hale & A. Angold (Eds.), *Precursors, causes and psychopathology* (pp. 233–264). Chichester, England: Wiley.

Loeber, R. (1982). The stability of antisocial and delinquent child behavior: A review. *Child Development, 53,* 1431–1446.

Loeber, R., & Dishion, T. J. (1983). Early predictors of male delinquency: A review. *Psychological Bulletin, 94,* 68–99.

Loeber, R., Green, S. M., Keenan, K., & Lahey, B. B. (1995). Which boys will fare worse? Early predictors of the onset of conduct disorder in a six-year longitudinal study. *Journal of the American Academy of Child and Adolescent Psychiatry, 34,* 499–509.

Loeber, R., Green, S. M., & Lahey, B. B. (1990). Mental health professionals' perception of the utility of children, mothers, and teachers as informants on childhood psychopathology. *Journal of Clinical Child Psychology, 19,* 136–143.

Loeber, R., Green, S. M., Lahey, B. B., & Stouthamer-Loeber, M. (1989). Optimal informants on childhood disruptive behaviors. *Development and Psychopathology, 1,* 317–337.

Loeber, R., & Hay, D. H. (1994). Developmental approaches to aggression and conduct problems. In M. Rutter & D. H. Hay (Eds.), *Development through life: A handbook for clinicians* (pp. 488–515). Oxford: Blackwell.

Loeber, R., Keenan, K., Zhang, Q., & Sieck, W. (1995). *Persisters and experimenters in developmental pathways toward serious antisocial behavior.* Unpublished manuscript.

Loeber, R., Russo, M. F., Stouthamer-Loeber, M., & Lahey, B. B. (1994). Internalizing problems and their relation to the development of disruptive behaviors in adolescence. *Journal of Research on Adolescence, 4,* 615–637.

Loeber, R., & Stouthamer-Loeber, M. (1987). Prediction. In H. C. Quay (Ed.), *Handbook of juvenile delinquency* (pp. 325–382). New York: Wiley.

Loeber, R., Stouthamer-Loeber, M., & Green, S. M. (1991). Age at onset of problem behavior in boys, and later disruptive and delinquent behavior. *Criminal Behaviour and Mental Health, 1,* 229–246.

Loeber, R., Stouthamer-Loeber, M., Van Kammen, W. B., & Farrington, D. P. (1989). Development of a new measure of self-reported antisocial behavior for young children: Prevalence and reliability. In M. Klein (Ed.), *Cross-national research in self-reported crime and delinquency* (pp. 203–225). Dordrecht, The Netherlands: Kluwer.

Loeber, R., Stouthamer-Loeber, M., Van Kammen, W. B., & Farrington, D. P. (1991). Initiation, escalation and desistance in juvenile offending and their correlates. *Journal of Criminal Law and Criminology, 82,* 36–82.

Loeber, R., & Wikström, P.-O. (1993). Individual pathways to crime in different types of neighborhood. In D. P. Farrington, R. J. Sampson, & P.-O. Wikström (Eds.), *Integrating individual and ecological aspects of crime* (pp. 169–204). Stockholm: Liber Forlag.

Loeber, R., Wung, P., Keenan, K., Giroux, B., Stouthamer-Loeber, M., Van Kammen, W. B., & Maughan, B. (1993). Developmental pathways in disruptive child behavior. *Development and Psychopathology, 5,* 101–131.

McCord, J. (1978). A thirty-year follow-up of treatment effects. *American Psychologist, 33,* 284–289.

McCord, J. (1991). Family relationships, juvenile delinquency, and adult criminality. *Criminology, 29,* 397–417.

MacDonald, K. (1985). Early experience, relative plasticity, and social development. *Developmental Review, 5,* 99–121.

Magnusson, D., & Bergman, L. (1988). Individual and variable-based approaches to longitudinal research in early risk factors. In M. Rutter (Ed.), *Studies of psychosocial risk: The power of longitudinal data* (pp. 45–51). Cambridge, England: Cambridge University Press.

Magnusson, D., Stattin, H., & Allen, V. (1986). Differential maturation among girls and its relation to social adjustment: A longitudinal perspective. In P. B. Baltes, D. L. Featherman, & R. M. Lerner (Eds.), *Life-span development and behavior* (Vol. 7, pp. 135–172). Hillsdale, NJ: Erlbaum.

Moffitt, T. E. (1990). The neuropsychology of juvenile delinquency: A critical review. In M. Tonry & N. Morris (Eds.), *Crime and justice* (Vol. 12, pp. 99–169). Chicago: University of Chicago Press.

Moffitt, T. E. (1993). Adolescence-limited and life-cycle persistent antisocial behavior: A developmental taxonomy. *Psychological Review, 100,* 674–701.

Olweus, D. (1979). Stability of aggressive reaction patterns in males: A review. *Psychological Bulletin, 86,* 852–857.

Patterson, G. R., Reid, J. B., & Dishion, T. J. (1992). *Antisocial boys: A social interaction approach* (Vol. 4). Eugene, OR: Castalia.

Peterson, P. L., Hawkins, J. D., Abbott, R. D., & Catalano, R. F. (1994). Disentangling the effects of parental drinking, family management and parental alcohol norms on current drinking by Black and White adolescents. *Journal of Research on Adolescence, 4,* 203–227.

Pulkkinen, L., & Pitkanen, T. (1993). Continuities in aggressive behavior from childhood to adulthood. *Aggressive Behavior, 19,* 249–263.

Raine, A. (1993). *The psychopathology of crime.* San Diego: Academic Press.

Rasbash, J., & Woodhouse, G. (1995). *MLn command reference.* London: Institute of Education, University of London.

Richters, J. E., Arnold, L. E., Jensen, P. S., Abikoff, H., Conners, C. K., Greenhill, L. L., Hechtman, L. T., Hinshaw, S. P., Pelham, W. E., & Swanson, J. M. (in press). The National Institute of Mental Health Collaborative Multisite Multimodal Treatment Study of Children with Attention Deficit/Hyperactivity Disorder: I. Background and rationale. *Journal of the American Academy of Child and Adolescent Psychiatry.*

Robins, L. N. (1978). Longitudinal methods in the study of normal and pathological development. In K. P. Kisker, J. E. Meyer, C. Muller, & E. Stromgren (Eds.), *Psychiatrie der Gegenwart* (Vol. 1, 2nd ed., pp. 672–684). Heidelberg, Germany: Springer-Verlag.

Robins, L. N. (1979). Sturdy childhood predictors of adult outcomes: Replications from longitudinal studies. In J. E. Barrett, R. M. Rose, & A. L. Kleman (Eds.), *Stress and mental disorder* (pp. 219–235). New York: Raven.

Rothe, W. (1985). Some consequences of frequent changes of environment in early childhood. *International Journal of Rehabilitation Research, 8,* 196–199.

Rutter, M. (1981). Epidemiological-longitudinal strategies and causal research in child psychiatry. *Journal of the American Academy of Child Psychiatry, 20,* 513–544.

Sampson, R. J., & Laub, J. H. (1993). *Crime in the making. Pathways and turning points through life.* Cambridge, MA: Harvard University Press.

Schlesselman, J. J. (1982). *Case-control studies: Design, conduct, analysis.* New York: Oxford University Press.

Schwartz, D., Flamant, R., & Lelouch, J. (1980). *Clinical trials.* London: Academic Press.

Schweinhart, L. J., & Weikart, D. P. (1980) *Young children grow up: The effects of the Perry Pre-school Program on youths through age 15.* Ypsilanti, MI: High/Scope.

Schweinhart, L. J., & Wallgren, C. R. (1993). Effects of a follow through program on school achievement. *Journal of Research in Childhood Education, 8,* 43–56.

Shaw, D. S., & Bell, R. Q. (1993). Developmental theories of parental contributors to antisocial behavior. *Journal of Abnormal Psychology, 21,* 493–518.

Stanger, C., Achenbach, T. M., & Verhulst, F. C. (1994), Accelerating longitudinal research in child psychopathology. *Psychological Assessment, 6,* 102–107.

Stoolmiller, M. (1994). Antisocial behavior, delinquent peer association and unsupervised wandering for boys: Growth and change from childhood to early adolescence. *Multivariate Behavioral Research, 29,* 263–288.

Stouthamer-Loeber, M., Van Kammen, W. B., & Loeber, R. (1992). The nuts and bolts of implementing large-scale longitudinal studies. *Violence and Victims, 7,* 63–78.

Thornberry, T. P. (1989), Panel effects and the use of self-reported measures of delinquency in longitudinal studies. In M. Klein (Ed.), *Cross-national research in self-reported crime and delinquency* (pp. 347–369). Dordrecht, The Netherlands: Kluwer.

Thornberry, T. P., Lizotte, A. J., Krohn, M. D., Farnworth, M., & Jang, S. J. (1994). Delinquent peers, beliefs, and delinquent behavior: A longitudinal test of interaction theory. *Criminology, 32,* 601–637.

Tolan, P. H. (1987). Implications of age of onset for delinquency. *Journal of Abnormal Child Psychology, 15,* 47–65.

Tonry, M., Ohlin, L. E., & Farrington, D. P. (1991). *Human development and criminal behavior.* New York: Springer-Verlag.

Tremblay, R. E., McCord, J., Boileau, H., Charlebois, P., Gagnon, C., Le Blanc, M., & Larivée, S. (1991). Can disruptive boys be helped to become competent? *Psychiatry, 54,* 148–161.

Tremblay, R. E., Masse, B., Perron, D., Le Blanc, M., Schwartzman, A. E., & Ledingham, J. E. (1992). Early disruptive behavior, poor school achievement, delinquent behavior. *Journal of Consulting and Clinical Psychology, 60,* 64–72.

Tremblay, R. E., Vitaro, F., Bertrand, L., Le Blanc, M., Beauchesne, H., Boileau, H., & David, L. (1992). Parent and child training to prevent early onset of delinquency: The Montreal longitudinal-experimental study. In J. McCord & R. E. Tremblay (Eds.), *Preventing antisocial behavior: Interventions from birth through adolescence* (pp. 117–138). New York: Guilford.

Verhulst, F. C., & Koot, H. M. (1991). Longitudinal research in child and adolescent psychiatry. *Journal of the American Academy of Child and Adolescent Psychiatry, 30,* 361–368.

Visher, C. A. (1994, November). Understanding the roots of crime: The Project on Human Development in Chicago Neighborhoods. *National Institute of Justice Journal,* no. 228, 9–15.

Wadsworth, M. E. J. (1991). *The imprint of time.* Oxford: Oxford University Press.

Waldo, G. P., & Griswold, D. (1979). Issues in the measurement of recidivism. In L. Sechrest, S. O. White, & E. D. Brown (Eds.), *The rehabilitation of criminal offenders: Problems and prospects* (pp. 225–250). Washington, DC: National Academy of Sciences.

Werner, E. E., & Smith, R. S. (1992). *Overcoming the odds.* Ithaca, NY: Cornell University Press.

West, D. J., & Farrington, D. P. (1973). *Who becomes delinquent?* London: Heinemann.

West, D. J., & Farrington, D. P. (1977). *The delinquent way of life.* London: Heinemann.

White, J. L., Moffitt, T. E., Earls, F., Robins, L., & Silva, P. A. (1990). How early can we tell? Predictors of childhood conduct disorder and adolescent delinquency. *Criminology, 28,* 507–528.

Wikström, P. O. (Ed.). (1990). *Crime and measures against crime in the city.* Stockholm: National Council for Crime Prevention.

Wolf, M. M., Braukmann, C. J., & Ramp, K. A. (1987). Serious delinquent behavior may be part of a significantly handicapping condition: Cures and supportive environments. *Journal of Applied Behavior Analysis, 20,* 347–359.

Wolfgang, M. E., Figlio, R. M., & Sellin, T. (1972). *Delinquency in a birth cohort.* Chicago: University of Chicago Press.

Woodhouse, G. (1995). *A guide to MLn for new users.* London: Institute of Education, University of London.

CHAPTER 14

The Development of Antisocial Behavior
From a Learning Perspective

LEONARD D. ERON

Aggression is a learned behavior and it is usually learned very early in a child's development. This is the conclusion reached by the Commission on Violence and Youth of the American Psychological Association, which recently issued its final report, Reason to Hope (Eron, Gentry, & Schlegel, 1994). The title for this report was selected because members of the commission believed, on the basis of their extensive review of the findings by psychologists and others over the past 50 years, that violence in our society is not an intractable problem. If aggression is learned, then it can be unlearned; and it should be possible to implement prevention and treatment programs based on sound, theoretically driven psychological principles. Such programs should have an impact on the prevention and amelioration of aggression and violence in our society.

TERMS AND DEFINITIONS

In this chapter, the terms *aggression* and *violence,* which are used interchangeably, are considered the epitome of antisocial behavior. According to the definition adopted by the American Psychological Association (APA) commission, *interpersonal violence* is "behavior by persons against persons that threatens, attempts, or completes intentional infliction of physical or psychological harm." Much of the research on violence has dealt with physical violence, probably because psychological harm is more difficult to observe and measure. The definition of *aggression* used in this chapter is "a behavior that is intended to injure another person." This, too, is the definition of *antisocial behavior* that this author uses in research on the learning of aggression (Eron, 1987), to be described later.

This commonly accepted definition includes both behavior motivated primarily by a desire for tangible rewards and behavior motivated primarily by hostility. However, it does not include many commonplace meanings of *aggression,* including assertive behaviors, for example, an aggressive salesperson. As with many definitions in psychology, there are numerous gray areas in which the classification of behaviors as aggressive or nonaggressive is problematic. For some of these areas, such as contact sports and war, the key distinction may be whether the behavior is restricted to the game, played under specific rules, and sanctioned by soci-

ety. In war, for example, one might argue that most individual acts of killing derive from prosocial rather than antisocial motives.

Nowhere in the APA report can the word *psychopathology* or the classification term *conduct disorder* be found. That is because the panel, after a review of the research evidence, came to the conclusion that it would be an error to apply a categorical disease model to a phenomenon, aggressive behavior, that essentially is noncategorical and is not an illness. However, aggressive behavior may be one of a number of symptoms of an illness or a co-occurrence with that illness; for example, in affective disorders (Roy, 1994), suicide attempts occur in a minority of cases: "Suicide is probably best conceptualized as a multi-determined behavior. Social, psychiatric, psychodynamic, genetic, personality and biological factors all play a part . . . and . . . it is largely state dependent" (Roy, 1994, p. 233).

Aggressive behavior in children and adults falls on a continuum, not into discrete categories. Children do not suddenly "come down" with aggression or "catch aggression." Aggression is not something one either has or does not have. Everyone's behavior can be evaluated on its aggressiveness. Such evaluations inevitably produce a continuum on which all individuals can be placed. This continuum most often, if not always, is positively skewed with a few persons scoring zero, many persons scoring toward the low end, some scoring toward the high end, and a few persons scoring very high. Regardless of the measure used, this distribution of scores is obtained and it can be divided into categories that may fit the conceptual framework medical practitioners and epidemiologists are accustomed to using. But the division is a distortion. Defining people as pathological who are in the upper 5% or over some other arbitrary score gives a meaning to the results that they do not deserve. It is possible, of course, to define categories and create consensus across research groups by adopting similar definitions, but unless the underlying phenomena are categorical, the result is arbitrary and a distortion of reality.

Violent human behavior is multiply determined. The factors involved range from genetics, neuroanatomy, endocrinology, and physiology through exogenous substances and firearms to peer, gang, family, and community influences. A plethora of research has been done on each of these factors and some of them are discussed in various chapters of this book. However, none by itself can explain much of the variance in the extent or intensity of violent behavior in the population, much less predict who will engage in such behavior. Only when there is a convergence of a number of variables does aggressive or violent behavior occur (Eron, 1982; Huesmann & Eron, 1984).

Aggressive or violent behavior does not routinely occur even when these factors converge, however; and all children are not similarly affected. The individual most likely to behave aggressively and violently is one who has been programmed to respond in this way through previous experience and learning (Eron, 1982). Individuals with given genetic, neurological, and physical endowments and living under circumstances, such as inadequate parenting, that put them at risk for violence still vary in their likelihood of behaving violently. Aggressive behavior must somehow have been learned in the past and incorporated into the individual's repertoire of responses before it can be elicited by some external situation or stimulation from within the individual and receive a response from the environment that encourages or discourages future expression of the specific or similar behavior. In addition, alternative prosocial behaviors must not have been learned or, at least, not learned as well as aggressive behavior.

Violence is not a behavior that springs forth spontaneously when a child reaches adolescence. The groundwork has been prepared long before this. Somewhere in the youngster's background, bombarded by all the genetic, physiological, social, and economic conditions mentioned previously, he or she must have somehow, somewhere learned to solve interpersonal problems, relieve frustration, and acquire material possessions by the use of violence. As a youngster, the violent adolescent must have seen this type of behavior at home, in the neighborhood, in school, or on the TV screen; must also have seen it rewarded and approved; might subsequently have fantasized about it; and perhaps engaged in it and been rewarded for it. Although aggression is caused by many factors, ultimately it is a learned behavior. This is the one hopeful note in the depressing concatenation of causal factors. As mentioned previously, if aggression is learned, then it can be unlearned or conditions arranged so it is not learned in the first place.

THE LEARNING OF AGGRESSION

How is aggression learned? A number of different learning theories of aggression were proposed in the 1970s by Bandura (1973); Berkowitz (1974); Eron, Walder, and Lefkowitz (1971); Patterson (1986b); and others. More recently, researchers have introduced learning models based on current thinking in cognitive psychology (Berkowitz, 1990; Dodge, 1980; Guerra & Slaby, 1990; Huesmann, 1988; Huesmann & Eron, 1984). The various learning theories have differed in terms of exactly what is learned—whether specific behaviors, cue-behavior connections, response biases, beliefs, or scripts. In all cases, though, learning is hypothesized to occur both as a result of one's own behaviors (enactive learning) and as a result of viewing others behave (observational learning).

The specific conditions that have been shown empirically to be most conducive to the learning and maintenance of aggression are those in which the child is rewarded for his or her own aggression (e.g., Patterson, 1986a, 1986b), is provided many opportunities to observe aggression (e.g., Bandura, 1977; Eron, Huesmann, Lefkowitz, & Walder, 1972), is given few opportunities to develop positive affective social bonds with others (e.g., Hawkins & Weis, 1985), and is the target of aggression (e.g., Dodge, Bates, & Petit, 1990). Although these conditions can exist in all social classes, they are more likely in the inner-city environment with its extreme economic and social deprivation (McLoyd, 1990). Thus, this environment increases the general level of risk for all children growing up there. Classical conditioning also has been invoked as an explanation for aggressive (especially delinquent and criminal) behavior. It is hypothesized, largely on the basis of skin conductance studies (Eysenck, 1977), that repeat offenders have a deficit in classical conditioning, specifically of the fear response. This predisposes them to deficient development of a conscience and poorly socialized behavior. For a review of these studies, not all uniformly positive, see Raine, Chapter 27, this volume.

THE FRUSTRATION-AGGRESSION HYPOTHESIS

The first major attempt by psychologists to account for the development of aggression on the basis of learning principles and observable behavior appeared in the monograph *Frustration and Aggression* by Dollard, Doob, Miller, Mowrer, and Sears (1939), a group of psychologists at Yale University from 1930 to 1940. Heretofore, aggression had been considered by most investigators to be both instinctual and inherent in humans as well as animals. Although they did not deny that there was a biological basis to aggressive behavior, the Yale group insisted that there was a large learning component in the development of aggression. The centrality of frustration in this process had been suggested to them by the psychoanalytic thinking of that time. According to Freudian theory, pleasure seeking and pain avoidance were the basic mechanisms of mental functioning, and frustration occurred when these activities were blocked. The Yale researchers, who were basically behaviorists, proposed, however, to translate the Freudian propositions into more objective behavioral terms that could be put to empirical test. For example, the Yale group's hypothesis about instigation to injure the frustrator finds a close parallel in Freud's (1957/1915) statement that "if the object is a source of unpleasant feelings . . ." this can eventually lead to "an aggressive inclination against the object . . . an instigation to destroy it" (p. 137).

Following on these psychological suppositions, it was the Yale researchers' premise that when people become frustrated, they respond aggressively. On the very first page of their monograph, the authors state their thesis that "the occurrence of aggressive behavior always presupposes the existence of frustration and, contrariwise, that the existence of frustration always leads to some form of aggression." *Aggression* was defined by them as "an act whose goal-response is injury to an organism (or organism-surrogate)" (Dollard et al., 1939, p. 11). This definition implied an intent to injure.

It was the authors' premise that when individuals become frustrated, they respond with aggression. What was unusual about their position was their assumption of the inevitability and inexorability of the relation. Frustration always leads to some form of aggression, and when aggression occurs it can be presumed that frustration was an antecedent event. This position quickly was seen by researchers as too extreme. One of the authors, Neal Miller, just two years later (1941) denied the inevitability of the relation stating, "Frustration produces instigation to a number of different types of responses, one of which is an instigation to some form of aggression" (p. 338). The frustration-aggression premise was further called into question by a number of researchers (Berkowitz, 1969; Buss, 1966; Cohen, 1955; Pastore, 1952) and the theory itself lost its explanatory power, but not before stimulating many other researchers to investigate the validity of the factors specified by its authors as those that lead to aggression and determine how and when it can be expressed. Thus, the frustration-aggression hypothesis probably has stimulated more research than any other proposition in psychology over the last 50 years and, in modified form, has been influential in the theorizing of psychologists (see Bandura, 1973; Feshbach, 1970; Parke & Slaby, 1983, for reviews). Berkowitz (1989), for example, differentiates emotional aggression, a behavior motivated primarily by a desire to hurt someone, from instrumental aggression "carried out deliberately and to achieve a purpose other than injuring the victim" (p. 62). For the former type of aggression, he finds great explanatory power in the frustration-aggression hypothesis; that is, frustrations generate aggressive tendencies only to the degree that they are unpleasant, and aversive experiences activate the desire to hurt others. Buss (1961), on the other hand, discounted the importance of frustration as an emotional instigator and stressed the instrumental value of aggression.

HULL-SPENCE LEARNING THEORY

The authors of the frustration-aggression hypothesis, all students or colleagues of Clark Hull at Yale, applied the tenets of his learning theory formulations to understanding how aggression is learned and maintained as a response to stimulation from the environment. Most of the early research had been done with animals, including the extensions and refinements to the theory made by another of Hull's students, Kenneth Spence (1957). Later, Dollard and Miller (1950) brought the learning theory formulations, based primarily on animal behavior, to bear on complex human behavior. For them the important elements of the learning situation were "drive, cue, response and reward." In the instance of aggression, it was supposed that frustration was the drive that activates the aggressive behavior. The cue is the situation precipitating the response, which often had characteristics resembling the original learning situations. The reward is the subsequent positive or negative consequences accruing to the individual making the response. It was assumed that the aggressive response itself reduced the drive and, therefore, was experienced as reinforcing. If punishment followed on the aggressive response, that response would tend not to be repeated and, with successive occurrences of the aggressive behavior not being reinforced, the behavior ultimately would be extinguished.

Data my colleagues and I collected in 1960 on the aggressive behavior of over 850 8-year-old children, as observed in the school setting, and the child-rearing practices reported by their parents tended to substantiate this model with a few exceptions

and elaborations (Eron et al., 1971). Generally, we found that punishment for aggression by parents was related to increased aggression in school. However, for a small subsample of boys, those who closely identified with their fathers, punishment by their father for aggression was indeed related to decreased aggression in school. Also important were indications on the part of the child that there was a beginning of the incorporation of parental standards and a semblance of a guilty conscience for having engaged in prohibited behavior: "One of the major instigators of aggression in children seemed to be a general lack of favorable support from both parents, which, in turn, tended to reduce the effectiveness of any punishment administered as a deterrent to aggressive behavior" (Eron, 1987, p. 437).

OPERANT BEHAVIORISM

From the perspective of operant psychology, the concept of frustration as an instigator to aggression was more or less ignored. What was important was the reaction of the environment to any specific aggressive response displayed by the individual. Aggressive responses that are rewarded over time would be repeated; those that are not reinforced would tend to be extinguished. Very important to operant behaviorists is the availability of an alternative unpunished response, preferably one that could be rewarded, to replace the punished response (Azrin & Holz, 1966).

Such operant principles have been employed successfully by Gerald Patterson and his colleagues, who have proposed a theory of the development of antisocial behavior based almost exclusively on operant principles. Their coercion theory places the genesis of aggressive behavior in the parent-child relationship and the disciplinary practices used by the parent; that is, inept discipline and poor monitoring lead to antisocial behavior in the child. The correlational data that they have gathered in the observation of parent-child interactions have been supported by manipulative experiments (Patterson, Dishion, & Chamberlain, 1993).

Patterson and his colleagues invoke the concept of mutual reinforcement, both negative and positive, between parent and child to explain the development and amelioration of aggressive behavior. They also recognize that other processes, such as modeling, social attribution, and affective expression, also can influence the development of aggressive behavior. However, neither cognitive nor social skills training is believed "necessary or sufficient for the treatment of antisocial children" (Patterson et al., 1993, p. 55), and behavioral training of both parent and child is an essential component of any treatment package.

SOCIAL LEARNING THEORY

Quite a different direction away from frustration-aggression theory was taken by researchers who placed a greater emphasis on external environmental cues as elicitors of aggression than on inherent or drive factors (see Bandura, 1973; Eron, 1987). With this push toward an environmental learning model, a number of researchers began to understand aggression in terms of stimuli, reinforcements, and punishments. Bandura (1973), for example, proposed that aggressive behavior is *learned* and *maintained* through environmental experiences, either directly or vicariously, and that the learning of aggression is controlled by reinforcement contingencies and punishment, just like the learning of any other new behaviors. For instance, these new behaviors may be acquired when an individual attempts a new behavior and is rewarded with a positive outcome. However, new behaviors will be avoided in the future if these behaviors are punished. Social learning theory, as Bandura terms his theory, holds that new behaviors also may be acquired vicariously by watching an influential role model engage in an action that has positive consequences. More than 35 years ago, the current author demonstrated that vicarious learning occurs in natural settings as well as in the laboratory; that is, aggressive behaviors are learned by "training" from "various socializing agents, specifically parents, teachers, and peers" (Eron, 1961, p. 296) and also from watching violent models on television. Inherent in all of these accounts is that external, environmental consequences control the acquisition of aggression.

Finally, the maintenance of aggressive behavior almost always is subject to the principles of reinforcement by the environment. As a rule, behaviors that are reinforced will be repeated; behaviors that are not reinforced will be extinguished. Bandura (1973) points out that according to a social learning model, aggression usually is seen as being controlled by *positive* reinforcement; in contrast, from a drive model perspective, aggression usually is mediated by *negative* reinforcement or the escape from an internally motivated aversive state.

The study mentioned previously, concerned with the child-rearing practices of parents and aggressive behavior of their children in school (Eron et al., 1971), was the first phase of a longitudinal study conducted over 22 years. My colleagues and I found that, although some of the results supported social learning theory, other results were contradictory to this model (Eron, Huesmann, Dubow, Romanoff, & Yarmel, 1987). On the support side, we acquired data showing that when children are exposed to aggressive role models, their aggression will increase. We initially found that physical punishment by parents often serves as a model for future aggression on the part of the child (Eron et al., 1971; Eron, 1987). Also, we found that aggressive models on television "teach" children future aggression (Lefkowitz, Eron, Walder, & Huesmann, 1977).[1] This finding, as mentioned previously, offered even more support for the social learning model.

Although these findings support a social learning position, other elements of the theory, as mentioned previously, were not fully corroborated by this study. For example, we originally hypothesized that aggressive children who were punished for their aggressive actions at home would behave less aggressively, but we found instead that these children behaved more aggressively at school (Eron et al., 1971). Additionally, we found that closeness of identification with the parent was an important mediating variable and that a simple, direct relation between physical punishment and aggression had to be challenged. The relation held up only for boys who closely identified with their fathers. For these boys, the punishment worked the way the fathers intended—if they were punished for aggression they tended not to be aggressive. If they did not closely identify with their fathers, however, the instigating quality of the punishment appeared to be more influential and these youngsters became more aggressive when they were punished. It occurred to us (at long last it might be said, but remember, we were committed behaviorists) that what might be important is not that the punishment itself occurred with some intensity, perhaps, but the interpretation the youngster put on that punishment—about its justification and appropriateness. The child who was so identified might interpret the punishment as justified because of his misbehavior and administered because his father wanted him to be a good person, just like the father. A youngster who lacked this close identification might interpret the punishment as unjustified and a demonstration of the way adults solve interpersonal problems; therefore, that youngster would model the punitive behavior.

More significantly, at the 10-year follow-up, we found that punishment of aggressive acts at the earlier age no longer was related to current aggression; instead, other variables such as parental nurturance and children's identification with their parents were more important in predicting later aggression. Because this finding could not be explained by a straight social learning model, we began to reinterpret our results from a different theoretical standpoint—namely, from a cognitive-behavioral perspective. I and my colleague Rowell Huesmann (Eron, 1987; Huesmann, 1977; Huesmann & Eron, 1984), as well as a number of other investigators such as Dodge and Coie (1987); Perry, Perry, and Rasmussen (1986); and Berkowitz (1984), have advocated cognitive models, which build on the merits of both the frustration-aggression drive theory and the social learning model. The theories have differed in terms of exactly what is learned: specific behaviors, cue-behavior connections, attitudes, perceptual biases, response biases, or scripts or programs for behavior. They all agree, however, that the way in which the individual perceives and interprets environmental events determines whether he or she will respond with aggression or some other behavior. Additionally, Bandura (1986) introduced the concept of *self-efficacy,* which emphasizes how competent the youngster feels in responding either aggressively or nonaggressively.

COGNITIVE MODELS

To understand the development and reduction of aggressive behavior, it is necessary to consider the learned cognitions associated with aggressive behavior, either as antecedents or consequents. For example, Bandura (1986) expanded his social learning theory of aggression, which earlier had emphasized observation of such behavior and its subsequent reinforcement as essential ingredients. He found it necessary to include internal, cognitive factors to account for aggressive behavior and its stability in children. According to Bandura, the cognitive evaluation of events taking place in the child's environment and how competent he or she feels (self-efficacy) in responding in different ways are important

---

[1]For an extensive review of the effects of viewing violence on television on the aggressive behavior of young persons and the mediating psychological processes, see Huesmann, Moise, and Podolski, Chapter 18, this volume.

in determining the child's behavior at that time and also in the future. Berkowitz (1988), on the other hand, emphasizes the importance of enduring associations. Aggression is a behavior stimulated by aversive events, which produce negative affect. In most people this negative affect is associated with "expressive-motor reactions, feelings, thoughts and memories that are associated with both fight and flight tendencies" (p. 8). The strength of these tendencies is affected by genetic, situational, and learned factors. The stronger tendency is the one acted on, and if fight is stronger than flight, the emotional experience is interpreted as anger. The generation of the behavior and the associated anger are relatively automatic. Attributions about the behavior may occur later as a controlled cognitive process.

Dodge (1980) emphasizes the importance of attributional biases. Aggressive children are viewed as possessing defective cognitive processes for the interpretation of others' behavior and the selection of their own behavior from a previously learned repertoire. Huesmann (1988; Huesmann & Eron, 1984) views the child as a processor of information who develops programs or scripts to guide social behavior. The aggressive child is one who has developed many aggressive scripts and few prosocial ones. The concept of scripts was introduced by Abelson (1981). A script suggests what events are to happen in the environment, how the person should behave in response to these events, and what the likely outcome of that behavior would be. Scripts may be used to guide behavior in a controlled manner, producing seemingly reflective behavior, or after they are well learned, in an automatic manner generating seemingly impulsive behavior (Schneider & Shiffrin, 1977).

In the late 1970s and early 1980s, Huesmann (1977, 1980, 1982, 1988) proposed a comprehensive theory to explain the development of aggression based on the models of human cognition elaborated in the 1960s and 1970s by information processing theorists. Huesmann hypothesized that social behavior, to a great extent, is controlled by programs for behavior that have been learned during an individual's early development. These programs are described as cognitive scripts stored in memory and used as guides for behavior and social problem solving. Scripts are learned through observation, reinforcement, and the personal experiences of situations in which aggression is a salient behavior. As we have pointed out (Huesmann & Eron, 1984), these strategies or scripts become "encoded, rehearsed, stored, and retrieved in much the same way as are other strategies for intellectual behaviors" (p. 244). Once a script has been encoded, it is more or less likely to be retrieved in situations that bear some resemblance or relation to the original situation in which the script was encoded. However, not all scripts that are retrieved are translated to overt behavior. Once a script is retrieved, the child evaluates its appropriateness in light of existing internalized norms and also evaluates the likely consequences. Huesmann (1988) maintains that the most important feature of a script's evaluation is the extent to which the sequence is perceived as congruent with the child's self-regulating internal standards for behavior. A child with weak or nonexistent internalized prohibitions against aggression or one who believes it is normative to behave in this way is much more likely to use aggressive scripts.

The failure of a child to incorporate appropriate standards will affect the way in which the child evaluates scripts and subsequently the way in which the child interacts with others. Previously, this author (Eron, 1987) had suggested that the internalization of appropriate standards is a critical variable that distinguishes between aggressive and nonaggressive children. A child's failure to store such a script during critical periods of socialization easily could lead to the expression of aggression with the persistence and stability that a number of studies have revealed. Indeed, we have demonstrated that aggressive behavior at age 8 predicts criminal behavior, arrests and convictions, traffic offenses (especially driving while intoxicated), spousal abuse, punitiveness toward the subjects' own children, and self-ratings of the subjects' own behavior and attitudes at age 30. We can predict consistency of aggression for over 22 years. This consistency supports our contention that aggression is a personality trait that characterizes the individual over time and across many situations.

These recent theoretical approaches have the common theme that the child's cognitions play a key role in maintaining the stability or in changing the developmental trajectory of aggressive behavior over time and across situations. However, the cognitions the child forms are not unaffected by what goes on around her or him. Contextual variables both within the family (socioeconomic status, parent child-rearing practices, stressful life events, parental substance abuse) and outside the family (neighborhood violence and poverty level, association with deviant peers, exposure to violent media) help mold the cognitions, which then exert a more direct influence on aggressive behavior. Although cognitive schemata are critical to understanding social behavior, they do not operate in a vacuum. Environmental conditions continuously interact with previously learned attributions, scripts, and beliefs to exert a strong influence on aggressive behavior. A recent study by Guerra, Huesmann, Tolan, Van Acker, and Eron (1995) has shown how the combination of neighborhood stress, life-event stress, and a child's normative beliefs about the appropriateness of aggression predicted individual differences among urban, high-risk youths living in poverty. The child's peers are an important part of the context.[2] Deviant peers and gangs provide immediate social acceptance for many aggressive behaviors as well as support for the development of normative beliefs approving of aggression (Cairns, 1979; Dishion, Patterson, & Greisler, 1994; Goldstein, 1994).

STABILITY OF AGGRESSIVE BEHAVIOR

Aggression, as a way of interacting with others and solving problems, is learned very early in life and usually is learned very well. The payoff often is high, so that despite occasional or even more frequent punishment, it is difficult to unlearn; and so the behavior persists. This probably is why most interventions and rehabilitation programs instituted in adolescence and young adulthood largely have been unsuccessful.

Individual differences in social behavior related to aggression (e.g., early temperament) have been detected before age 2 (Kagan, 1988), and it has been shown that at least by age 6, many children

---

[2]See Thornberry and Krohn (Chapter 21, this volume) for effect of associating with antisocial peers on increasing the seriousness of antisocial behavior.

have adopted characteristic aggressive patterns of behavior that are apparent across many interpersonal situations (Parke & Slaby, 1983). The extent of aggressive behavior in children tends to increase into adolescence. By the time a youngster is in middle childhood, however, characteristic ways of behaving aggressively or nonaggressively in interpersonal and other problem-solving situations have become so well practiced that they are highly resistant to change. Further, these early aggressive behaviors, which may appear to some to reflect no more perhaps than "boisterousness and incivility" (e.g., boys being boys), are predictive of future serious antisocial behavior of the type that brings the individual into contact with the law (Farrington, 1994; Huesmann, Eron, Lefkowitz, & Walder, 1984; Magnusson, Stattin, & Duner, 1983; McCord, 1994; Olweus, 1979).

One of the clearest findings concerning adolescent and adult aggressive and antisocial behavior is that such behavior is predictable statistically from early antisocial, aggressive, and hyperactive behavior. The more aggressive child is likely to become both the more aggressive adult and the more antisocial and criminal adult. No other factor measured in childhood, whether physiological, cognitive, environmental, or familial, has been shown to predict more of the variation in adult antisocial behavior than early aggression. For example, in data on 875 youngsters, collected in 1960, we found that peer nominations of a child's aggression measured at age 8 predicted a variety of aggressive and antisocial behaviors displayed 22 years later, at age 30, including officially tallied criminal convictions (Huesmann et al., 1984).

Does that mean, as some have suggested, that we believe that all criminal behavior is aggressive behavior? Or, all aggressive behavior is criminal behavior? No, of course not. It does suggest, however, that the developmental psychological processes underlying aggressive behavior also underlie other forms of antisocial and criminal behavior. Furthermore, aggression is a behavior that occurs frequently among even very young children and, therefore, is amenable to study as part of a developmental process and also amenable to change.

If aggression—which, as we have defined it, includes intent to harm—already is apparent with wide individual differences by age 6 and becomes a stable characteristic of the individual by age 8, that leaves just a brief period of developmental years during which preventive action must begin by parents, teachers, and other socializing agents. How these agents respond to the first indications of aggression is important in determining subsequent development or inhibition of such behaviors. The models of behavior presented by the parent or other socializing agents also are of prime importance. Because of the malleability of behavior in young children and the relative intractability of aggressive and violent dispositions once developed, it is important that we focus on learning in preadolescent children.

PREVENTIVE INTERVENTIONS

Patterson (1982, 1986a, 1986b) offers compelling evidence that aggression and violence are learned within the home in a child's interaction with his or her parents and siblings. Violence is seen as a coercive act on the part of the child either to get the parent to pay

attention to him or her or to turn off some frustration or irritation. Patterson has described an intervention program with families of delinquent and predelinquent youngsters, in which family members are taught the necessary social skills to interact in positive ways; parents are encouraged to monitor their children's behavior more closely; and the child is taught that coercive behavior will not be tolerated, by the parent's refusing to comply with coercive behavior on the part of the child and instituting time-out procedures (rather than physical punishment) when aggression does occur.

A number of other intervention programs with antisocial children are based on established principles of learning and recent thinking in cognitive psychology. The assumption underlying these interventions is that aggressive children engage in deficient or deviant cognitive processes (i.e., beliefs, perceptions, attributions, expectations, or problem-solving skills) that contribute to the learning and maintenance of aggressive or violent behavior. The problems that aggressive youngsters have and these programs attempt to correct are (a) with the interpretation of social cues—for example, they are more likely than nonaggressive youngsters to attribute hostile intent to their peers; (b) with response access—that is, they are less able to generate many response alternatives; and (c) with evaluation of the generated response—that is, what outcome might be expected to accompany the given response. In each of the intervention programs, methods have been devised that alter the youngster's cognitions and ultimately, it is hoped, his or her behavior.

Members of these research teams have devoted much effort to designing and implementing intervention programs to decrease aggressive behavior by applying these cognitive principles. However, to date, none has proven an unqualified success. At least three reviews (Lahey & Strauss, 1982; Lochman, 1990; and Kazdin, 1987) have outlined problems with the research studies, including failure to replicate, limited maintenance of treatment effects, and no consistent evidence showing generalization of treatment effects across situations.[3]

The problem is that the research has examined mostly unidimensional treatment programs within limited time frames. These programs may have been theoretically sound, but they were not nearly comprehensive or extensive enough to affect the subjects' lives or their behavior. The utility of short-term unidimensional interventions for the prevention of serious antisocial behavior in high-risk populations is dubious. According to Kazdin, Bass, Siegel, and Thomas (1989), it is highly unlikely that focusing on a particular set of processes within the child, or home, or school by itself can provide the breadth and magnitude of changes required to alleviate the problem, and they recommend a more comprehensive treatment focus that addresses multiple domains. This is a challenge to funding agencies as much as to individual researchers. They must set aside their preference for theoretically

---

[3]See Guerra, Attar, and Weissberg (Chapter 35, this volume) on preventive interventions, for a more extensive discussion of the problems and possibilities of intervention research with inner-city children and youth. Also see the unpublished paper by M. Lipsey, referred to by Tolan and Gorman-Smith (Chapter 38, this volume), which describes a meta-analysis of over 400 research studies dealing with outcomes of intervention programs with juvenile delinquents.

tight, circumscribed studies testing one or two hypotheses and completed in 1 to 3 years and give more support to large-scale studies over a long period of time. The payoff for such studies may be a long time in coming, but its magnitude may be well worth the patience of the investigators and the funding agencies.

CONCLUSION

The concepts currently being used by most psychologists to understand the causes, prevention, and amelioration of aggressive and violent behavior can be best described as behavioral-cognitive. There is an emphasis on the initial and subsequent responses of the environment to the appearance of the behavior—whether it is rewarded, punished, or ignored. The cognitive spin—that it is appropriate, normative, and effective—the individual places on the behavior to justify its use also is learned. These cognitions are important in maintaining the stability of aggressive behavior over time and across situations. The various predisposing and precipitating factors can influence behavior over time by affecting these cognitions. Similarly, the direct effect of any predisposing factor can be moderated by the cognitions the child already has developed.

REFERENCES

Abelson, R. P. (1981). The psychological status of the subject concept. *American Psychologist, 36,* 715–729.

Azrin, N. H., & Holtz, W. C. (1966). Punishment. In W. K. Honig (Ed.), *Operant behavior: Areas of research and application* (pp. 380–447). New York: Appleton-Century-Crofts.

Bandura, A. (1973). *Aggression: A social learning analysis.* Englewood Cliffs, NJ: Prentice Hall.

Bandura A. (1986). *Social foundations of thought and action: A social-cognitive theory.* Englewood Cliffs, NJ: Prentice Hall.

Berkowitz, L. (1969). The frustration-aggression hypothesis revisited. In L. Berkowitz (Ed.), *Roots of aggression: A reincarnation of the frustration-aggression hypothesis* (pp. 1–28). New York: Atherton.

Berkowitz, L. (1974). Some determinants of impulsive aggression. The role of mediated associations with reinforcements for aggression. *Psychological Review, 81,* 165–176.

Berkowitz, L. (1984). Some effects of thoughts on anti and prosocial influences of media events: A cognitive-neoassociation analysis. *Psychological Bulletin, 95,* 410–427.

Berkowitz, L. (1988). Frustrations, appraisals, and aversively stimulated aggression. *Aggressive Behavior, 14,* 3–12.

Berkowitz, L. (1989). Frustration-aggression hypothesis: Examination and reformulation. *Psychological Bulletin, 106,* 59–73.

Berkowitz, L. (1990). On the formation and regulation of anger and aggression: A neo-associationistic analysis. *American Psychologist, 45,* 497–503.

Buss, A. H. (1961). *The psychology of aggression.* New York: Wiley.

Buss, A. H. (1966). Instrumentality of aggression, feedback, and frustration as determinants of physical aggression. *Journal of Personality and Social Psychology, 3,* 153–162.

Cairns, R. B. (1979). *Social development: The origins and plasticity of interchanges.* San Francisco: Freeman.

Cohen, A. (1955). Social norms, arbitrariness of frustration and status of the agent of frustrations in the frustration-aggression hypotheses. *Journal of Abnormal and Social Psychology, 81,* 165–176.

Dishion, T. J., Patterson G. R., & Greisler, P. C. (1994). Peer adaptations in the development of antisocial behavior: A confluence model. In L. R. Huesmann (Ed.), *Aggressive behavior: Current perspectives* (pp. 61–96). New York: Plenum.

Dodge, K. A. (1980). Social cognition and children's aggressive behavior. *Child Development, 53,* 620–635.

Dodge, K. A., Bates, J. E., & Pettit, G. S. (1990). Mechanisms in the cycle of violence. *Science, 250,* 1678–1683.

Dodge, K. A., & Coie, J. D. (1987). Social-information-processing factors in reactive and proactive aggression in children's peer groups. *Journal of Personality and Social Psychology, 53,* 1146–1158.

Dollard, J., Doob, L. W., Miller, N. E., Mowrer, O. H., & Sears, R. R. (1939). *Frustration and aggression.* New Haven, CT: Yale University Press.

Dollard, J., & Miller, N. E. (1950). *Personality and psychotherapy.* New York: McGraw-Hill.

Eron, L. D. (1961). Use of theory in developing a design. In L. D. Eron (Ed.), Application of role and learning theories to the study of the development of aggression in children. *Psychology Reports, 9,* 292–334.

Eron, L. D. (1982). Parent-child interaction, television violence and aggression of children. *American Psychologist, 37,* 71–77.

Eron, L. D. (1987). The development of aggressive behavior from the perspective of a developing behaviorism. *American Psychologist, 42,* 435–442.

Eron, L. D., Gentry, J. H., & Schlegel, P. (1994). *Reason to hope: A psychosocial perspective on violence and youth.* Washington, DC: American Psychological Association.

Eron, L. D., Huesmann, L. R., Dubow, E., Romanoff, R., & Yarmel, P. W. (1987). Aggression and its correlates over 22 years. In D. Cowell, I. M. Evans, & C. R. O'Donnell (Eds.), *Childhood aggression and violence* (pp. 249–262). New York: Plenum.

Eron, L. D., Huesmann, L. R., Lefkowitz, M. M., & Walder, L. O. (1972). Does television violence cause aggression? *American Psychologist, 27,* 253–263.

Eron, L. D., Walder, L. O., & Lefkowitz, M. M. (1971). *The learning of aggression in children.* Boston: Little Brown.

Eysenck, H. J. (1977). *Crime and personality* (3rd ed.). St. Albans: Paladin.

Farrington, D. (1994). Childhood, adolescent and adult factors of violent males. In L. R. Huesmann (Ed.), *Aggressive behavior: Current perspectives* (pp. 225–240). New York: Plenum.

Feshbach, S. (1970). Aggression. In P. Mussen (Ed.), *Carmichael's manual of child psychology* (Vol. 2, pp. 159–259). New York: Wiley.

Freud, S. (1957). Instincts and other vicissitudes. *Standard edition* (Vol. 4, pp. 109–140). London: Hogarth. (Original work published 1915)

Goldstein, A. P. (1994). Delinquent gangs. In L. R. Huesmann (Ed.), *Aggressive behavior: Current perspectives* (pp. 255–274). New York: Plenum.

Guerra, N. G., Huesmann, L. R., Tolan, P. H., Van Acker, R., & Eron, L. D. (1995). Stressful events and individual beliefs as correlates of economic disadvantage and aggression among urban children. *Journal of Consulting and Clinical Psychology, 63,* 518–528.

Guerra, N. G., & Slaby, R. G. (1990). Evaluative factors in social problem solving by aggressive boys. *Journal of Abnormal Child Psychology, 17,* 277–289.

Hawkins, D., & Weis, X. (1985). The social development model: An integrated approach to delinquency prevention. *Journal of Primary Pediatrics, 6,* 73–97.

Huesmann, L. R. (1977, June). *Formal models of social behavior.* Meeting of the Society for Experimental Social Psychology, Austin, TX.

Huesmann, L. R. (1981). *Encoding specificity in observational learning.* Colloquium at Institute of Psychology, University of Warsaw, Poland.

Huesmann, L. R. (1982). Television violence and aggressive behavior. In D. Pearl, L. Bouthilet, & J. Lazar (Eds.), *Television and behavior: Ten years of scientific programs and implications for the 80's.* Washington, DC: U.S. Government Printing Office.

Huesmann, L. R. (1988). An information model for the development of aggression. *Aggressive Behavior, 14,* 13–24.

Huesmann, L. R., & Eron, L. D. (1984). Cognitive processes and the persistence of aggressive behavior. *Aggressive Behavior, 10,* 243–251.

Huesmann, L. R., Eron, L. D., Lefkowitz, M. A., & Walder, L. O. (1984). The stability of aggression over time and generations. *Developmental Psychology, 20,* 1120–1134.

Kagan, J. (1988). Temperamental contributions to social behavior. *American Psychologist, 44,* 668–674.

Kazdin, A. E. (1987). Treatment of antisocial behaviors in children: Current status and future directions. *Psychological Bulletin, 102,* 187–201.

Kazdin, A. E., Bass, D., Siegel, T., & Thomas, C. (1989). Cognitive-behavioral therapy and relationship therapy in the treatment of children referred for antisocial behavior. *Journal of Consulting and Clinical Psychology, 57,* 522–535.

Lahey, B. B., & Straus, C. C. (1982). Some considerations in evaluating the clinical utility of cognitive behavior therapy with children. *School Psychology Review, 11,* 67–74.

Lefkowitz, M. M., Eron, L. D., Walder, L. O., & Huesmann, L. R. (1977). *Growing up to be violent: A longitudinal study of the development of aggression.* Elmsford, NY: Pergamon.

Lipsey, M. (1992, October 31–November 3). *Effects of treatment on juvenile delinquents: Results from meta-analyses.* Paper presented at NIMH meeting, Bethesda, MD.

Lochman, J. E. (1990). Modification of childhood aggression. In A. M. Hersen, R. Ersler, & P. Miller (Eds.), *Progress in behavior modification* (p. 23). New York: Academic Press.

Magnusson, D., Stattin, H., & Duner, A. (1983). Aggression and criminality in a longitudinal perspective. In K. T. Van Dusen & S. A. Mednick (Eds.), *Prospective studies of crime and delinquency* (pp. 277–302). Boston: Kluwer-Nijhoff.

McCord, J. (1994). Aggression in two generations. In L. R. Huesmann (Ed.), *Aggressive behavior: Current perspectives* (pp. 241–254). New York: Plenum.

McLoyd, V. C. (1990). The impact of economic hardship on Black families and children: Psychological distress, parenting, and socioemotional development. *Child Development, 61,* 311–346.

Miller, N. E. (1941). The frustration-aggression hypothesis. *Psychological Review, 48,* 337–342.

Olweus, D. (1979). The stability of aggressive reaction patterns in males: A review. *Psychological Bulletin, 86,* 852–875.

Parke, R. D., & Slaby, R. G. (1983). The development of aggression. In P. Mussen (Ed.), *Handbook of child psychology* (pp. 547–642). New York: Wiley.

Pastore, N. (1952). The role of arbitrariness in the frustration-aggression hypothesis. *Journal of Abnormal and Social Psychology, 47,* 728–731.

Patterson, G. R. (1982). *A social learning approach: Coercive family process.* Eugene, OR: Castilia.

Patterson, G. R. (1986a). The contribution of siblings to training for fighting: A microsocial analysis. In D. Olweus, J. Block, & M. Radke Yarrow (Eds.), *Development of antisocial and prosocial behavior* (pp. 235–261). Orlando, FL: Academic Press.

Patterson, G. R. (1986b). Performance models for antisocial boys. *American Psychologist, 41,* 432–444.

Patterson, G. R., Dishion, T. J., & Chamberlain, P. (1993). Outcomes and methodological issues relating to the treatment of antisocial children. In T. R. Giles (Ed.), *Effective psychotherapy: A handbook of comparative research* (pp. 43–88). New York: Plenum.

Perry, D. G., Perry, L. C., & Rasmussen, P. (1986). Cognitive social learning mediators of aggression. *Child Development, 57,* 700–711.

Roy, A. (1994). Affective disorders. In M. Hersen, R. T. Ammerman, & L. A. Sisson (Eds.), *Handbook of aggressive and destructive behavior in psychotic patients* (pp. 221–236). New York: Plenum.

Schneider, W., & Shiffrin, R. (1977). Controlled and automatic human information processing: Detection, search and attention. *Psychological Review, 84,* 1–66.

Spence, K. (1957). The empirical basis and theoretical structure of psychology. *Philosophy of Science, 24,* 97–108.

CHAPTER 15

Precursors and Correlates of Antisocial Behavior From Infancy to Preschool

DANIEL S. SHAW and EMILY B. WINSLOW

Recently, interest has been growing in identifying the early antecedents of antisocial behavior. The rationale for this interest is clear. First, antisocial behavior is extremely costly to society in terms of damaged property and disruption of normal patterns of living. Second, both epidemiological and developmental studies have found aggressive behavior to be highly stable beginning as early as age 2, particularly among males (Cummings, Iannotti, & Zahn-Waxler, 1989; Olweus, 1979). Third, serious forms of antisocial behavior have been found to be highly resistant to change in school-age children and adolescents—few interventions consistently have proven to be reliably effective (see Kazdin, 1987; Tolan & Gorman-Smith, Chapter 38, this volume). Fourth, the period from infancy to preschool is one of the most critical in development. During these years, developmental trajectories leading to adaptive or maladaptive outcomes begin (Campbell, 1995). Moreover, rapid cognitive and physical development occurs during this time, requiring concomitant changes in parenting. For these reasons it is important to examine precursors of antisocial behavior in young children. Delineating developmental trajectories leading to later antisocial behavior may suggest important targets and the appropriate timing for intervention. Parent and child factors associated with later antisocial behavior may be more responsive to treatment prior to school age.

Although early retrospective studies documented the emergence of parent-child difficulties and disruptive behavior problems prior to school age (e.g., S. Glueck & E. Glueck, 1950), only recently have prospective studies been initiated to examine the stability and predictive validity of specific risk factors. As these have emerged, a number of substantive and methodological techniques have been borrowed from other areas (e.g., developmental psychology). Earlier studies were concerned primarily with providing information about the types of disruptive behavior experienced by young children (Crowther, Bond, & Rolf, 1981) and their stability during early childhood (Richman, Stevenson, & Graham, 1982). However, in the 1980s researchers began to examine risk factors

associated with later antisocial behavior and to incorporate an interactionist perspective, which takes into account both child *and* parent contributors (Campbell, Breaux, Ewing, & Szumowski, 1986). For instance, rather than attributing the development of antisocial behavior solely to parenting practices, researchers also began to examine the child's previous behavioral adjustment. In addition, with the emergence of the field of developmental psychopathology, researchers have begun to incorporate knowledge about the developmental status of the child, the concomitant challenges faced by parents, and the theoretical perspectives and methods by which developmentalists have conceptualized and measured normal socialization processes (Dumas & Wahler, 1985). Theoretically, this has involved integrating findings from research on children's normative development (e.g., attachment, parenting practices). As a result, more researchers have conceptualized the development of antisocial behavior using a reciprocal and transactional perspective, exploring concurrent and longitudinal effects of parents on children and children on parents.

Along with greater theoretical sophistication, advances have been made in the measurement of both risk factors and child disruptive behavior, including use of multiple informants and methods to measure independent and dependent variables (Fagot & Kavanagh, 1990; Renken, Egeland, Marvinney, Mangelsdorf, & Sroufe, 1989). Previously, many investigators relied solely on maternal reports to measure risk factors and externalizing behavior. The validity of relying on one informant to assess both risk factors and child behavior has been shown to inflate relations artificially (Fergusson, Lynskey, & Horwood, 1993).

In this chapter, investigations that have taken advantage of advances in theory and methods are stressed more than others. Our aim is to highlight progress, rather than to conduct an exhaustive review of the literature. We emphasize prospective studies beginning with pre-school-age children or younger, focusing primarily on investigations using multiple informants and methods. Most of these studies have paid greater attention to family factors than those outside of the home because of young children's greater dependence on parents early in life. However, because of the increase in use of alternative child care resources with young children, studies noting influences external to the nuclear family are reviewed as well. Finally, in most cases we use the term *external-*

Preparation of this paper was supported in part by the National Institute of Mental Health, U.S. PHS grants MH46925 and MH50907.

izing behavior rather than *antisocial behavior* to discuss the less severe disruptive and destructive behavior of children age 5 and younger. It is clear from the literature on school-age children and adolescents, particularly regarding the stability of aggression, that externalizing problems is highly associated with serious forms of antisocial behavior. A major goal of this chapter is to examine the strength of the association between earlier forms of externalizing problems with those found during the school-age period.

THEORETICAL CONTEXT
AND CONTROVERSIAL ISSUES

To provide a contextual framework, we examine four interdependent theoretical issues: (a) the benefits and costs of beginning research prior to the onset of true serious antisocial behavior; (b) the influence of environmental and biological factors in the development of antisocial behavior; (c) the developmental status of the child; and (d) the selection of appropriate risk factors.

As with other types of prevention research, costs and benefits are associated with studying precursors (see Reid & Eddy, Chapter 32, this volume). Given the stability of antisocial behavior and the lack of treatment efficacy in working with older children and adults who show high rates of it, researchers need to explore antecedents of such behavior. Even if specific factors are found to consistently predict later antisocial behavior, most likely some of these would be more amenable than others to intervention. For instance, child behavior or parent-child interaction patterns that have been in existence for only 1 to 5 years might be more malleable to change than longstanding personality characteristics of parents. Moreover, unless researchers can show an extremely high probability of specific risk factors being associated with later antisocial behavior, there exists the danger of intervening with many children who would not develop these problems. One possible solution may lie in developing early preventative interventions that are effective in modeling appropriate ways of caring for children before parent-child interaction patterns and subsequent child externalizing behavior become less malleable to change. Such programs have been instituted in the first year of life among high-risk families in Hawaii, with the result being a significant decrease in infant abuse patterns (Breakey & Pratt, 1991).

A second issue concerns the nature-nurture debate and the relative contribution of genetic versus environmental influences. In a series of articles by Lytton (1990), Dodge (1990), and others, the merits of both viewpoints are discussed. Even though we believe that Lytton is correct in pointing out that child effects have been understudied in this area, particularly in parent-child interaction studies, we also concur with Dodge that the debate itself is moot. Studies of *both* environmental and biological influences need to be undertaken. Within the study of young children's development of antisocial behavior, the issue of biological versus environmental influences is just beginning to unfold. In a recent study by Raine, Brennan, and Mednick (1994), however, evidence was found for an interaction between biological risk and early caregiving in predicting later antisocial behavior. Raine and colleagues discovered that birth complications (e.g., umbilical cord prolapse and breech delivery) and an early maternal rejection factor (i.e., placement of

infant in institutionalized care, attempts to abort the fetus, and unwanted pregnancy) interacted to predict violent offending at ages 17 and 19. Neither variable predicted later violence in isolation. For a more thorough discussion of the nature-nurture issue with respect to antisocial behavior, the reader is referred to Carey and Goldman (Chapter 23, this volume).

In addition to taking into account both biological and environmental influences, it is important to consider the developmental status of the child. Social behavior tolerated by parents during a child's second year (e.g., noncompliance, undirected aggression) is viewed as disruptive during the preschool period. Similarly, parenting strategies that may be seen as appropriate during the preschool period (e.g., reprimanding a child for crying uncontrollably) may be considered inappropriate for infants. As children grow, researchers need to consider influences external to the nuclear family. Because the recent trend has been for both parents to work, extrafamilial influences, such as day care, have become important at earlier ages. Thus, factors both within and outside the nuclear family need to be addressed to account for the social ecology of young children.

Several types of risk factors have been examined with respect to early externalizing behavior problems and later antisocial behavior. First, researchers have studied child factors, such as infant temperament (Bates, Maslin, & Frankel, 1985), early disruptive behavior (Campbell, 1990; Richman et al., 1982), and infant attachment security (Erickson, Sroufe, & Egeland, 1985; Lyons-Ruth, Alpern, & Repacholi, 1993). Because most theorists posit attachment security to be primarily a function of the quality of parental caregiving, it is reviewed within the context of parenting. Second, investigators have identified parent characteristics and parenting behavior such as depression (Zahn-Waxler et al., 1988), personality characteristics (Shaw, Vondra, Dowdell Hommerding, Keenan, & Dunn, 1994), and parental conflict (Dadds & Powell, 1991) as risk factors leading to externalizing behavior problems. Most studies of parenting have focused on parental responsiveness and involvement (Gardner, 1989; Shaw, Keenan, & Vondra, 1994) or discipline practices (Campbell, 1994). Third, influences external to the family have included day care (Crowther et al., 1981; Goosens, Ottenhoff, & Koops, 1991) and peer relations (Olson, 1991). Finally, investigators have explored the effects of social adversity on the development of early externalizing problems, interactively and cumulatively (Sanson, Oberklaid, Pedlow, & Prior, 1991; Shaw, Vondra et al., 1994).

METHODOLOGICAL ISSUES

Several methodological issues of importance have emerged in the past few years as researchers have gradually become more sophisticated in both their data collection and data analytic procedures. These include (a) sample selection, (b) design issues, (c) selection of measures, and (d) the developmental appropriateness of assessment techniques.

The issue of sample selection is complex because, in contrast to school-age children, no diagnostic criteria are available for identifying young children with externalizing behavior problems. At this juncture, we can only identify children "at-risk" for later problems. It should not be surprising that investigators have used various methods from which to select at-risk samples. These include use of both representative (Sanson et al., 1991) and low socioeconomic (SES) community samples (Fagot & Kavanaugh, 1990; Renken et al., 1989; Shaw, Keenan, & Vondra, 1994), as well as samples in which children have been identified based on early disruptive behavior (Campbell, Pierce, March, Ewing, & Szumowski, 1994), parental risk status (Cummings et al., 1989), or previous child maltreatment (Lyons-Ruth et al., 1993).

Given the state of our knowledge, the heterogeneity in sample selection seems appropriate, although it warrants caution when comparing findings across studies. In addition, selecting at-risk samples based solely on early disruptive behavior at one time point may be problematic due to the amount of change young children undergo. As Campbell (1990) notes, many externalizing-type behaviors are related to transitions in child development and parenting during this period. Toddlerhood is one such phase in which child defiant behavior and parenting discipline problems appear normative, as children are "suddenly" informed that some behaviors in certain contexts will not be tolerated (e.g., hitting a toy vs. hitting a sibling). In developing criteria for young children's externalizing disorders, researchers will need to differentiate noncompliant and aggressive behavior that is the result of such transitions in development from more stable, pervasive patterns. A disorder should involve a pervasive and severe pattern of symptoms showing at least short-term stability that goes beyond a transient adjustment to stress or change (Campbell, 1995).

The design of studies also appears to be a critical issue, in large part due to the paucity of research in the area. The few longitudinal studies have been conducted within the context of normal development. Among the scant epidemiological studies beginning during infancy and prospective studies with samples based on previous child disruptive behavior, very few have been able to provide microanalytic observations using large and diversified samples (Campbell et al., 1994; Renken et al., 1989). Thus, the depth and sophistication of measurement in the epidemiological studies, and the homogeneity and small sample size in the child-identified studies, have limited our ability to understand the *pathways* by which early antisocial behavior begins. Many of the procedures employed in studying developmental processes of middle-class children and their families have not been applied with young children at-risk for later antisocial behavior.

More longitudinal studies of high-risk families need to be conducted beginning during infancy to trace the pathways of child and parent behavior leading to antisocial behavior. However, these approaches should be supplemented with designs that incorporate both experimental and naturalistic quasi-experimental approaches to parcel out the relative impact of parent and child effects. As Bell and Harper (1977) pointed out, 17 design strategies are available for use, most of which are appropriate for the study of antisocial behavior. Researchers continue to rely on one, two, or three of these methods, however. For instance, an experimental approach has been used to study the interaction patterns of families with school-age children with attention deficit/hyperactivity disorder (ADHD). Tarver-Behring, Barkley, and Karlsson (1985) observed parents interacting with children with ADHD and their nonhyperactive brothers, allowing them to examine the impact of ADHD on parenting.

In addition, few researchers have incorporated reciprocal or transactional processes into their methods of data collection (Shaw & Bell, 1993). Despite research by developmentalists demonstrating independent effects of parent and child behavior in this age period, relatively few investigators have examined these influences simultaneously or interactively, as a reciprocal model would demand. Similarly, from a transactional perspective (Sameroff, 1990), it is important to examine the contributions of earlier child and parent behavior before interpreting the effects of current child or parent behavior to the other. Again, few studies in the area meet this criterion (Campbell, 1994; Shaw, Keenan, & Vondra, 1994).

The rapidity of change during this period also dictates that special attention be given to the selection of developmentally appropriate measures. Our work on maternal responsiveness has shown that the context of responsiveness changes from the first to the second years of life. Using a measure of responsiveness based on the mother's ability to match the intensity of her behavior to the infant's cues for attention, we replicated a result found by Martin (1981) in which low maternal responsiveness at 12 months was related to aggression at 24 months and a broad factor of externalizing problems at 36 months (Shaw, Keenan, & Vondra, 1994). In both studies, the finding was valid only for boys and when assessments of responsiveness were conducted at the end of the child's first year. In an attempt to replicate the finding, we used the same procedure at 12 *and* 18 months with a different sample to predict externalizing problems at 42 months. We were able to replicate the relation between 12-month low responsiveness and later externalizing problems, but no such relation was found between 18-month responsiveness and later externalizing behavior (Shaw et al., 1995). We believe the measure's lack of relation to later externalizing problems, when used at 18 versus 12 months, reflects the changing nature of maternal responsiveness during this time period. At 12 months most parents are continuing to serve the infant's needs on demand, but as the infant's mobility, cognitive capacities, and ability to function independently increase in the second year, parents begin to use more discretion in responding to the infant's attention-seeking behavior. In situations when harm to the child is unlikely, such as the Martin high-chair task, the parent may be making a maturity demand by intentionally not responding to an 18-month-old's fussing. Investigators using observational or interview methods prior to school age should pay special attention to the rapidly changing context of child and parenting behavior to ensure the validity of the continued appropriateness of their measures.

CURRENT FINDINGS

Our review of the current literature focuses on four broad domains: (a) child contributors, (b) sex differences, (c) parent contributors, and (d) extrafamilial influences. For additional information on pathways leading to antisocial behavior during school age and adolescence, the reader is referred to Loeber and Farrington (Chapter 13, this volume).

Child Effects

One set of studies exploring the child's contribution to the development of antisocial behavior has focused on the role of infant temperament. Several investigators have examined the relation between early temperamental difficulty and later behavioral adaptation, beginning with Thomas, Chess, and Birch's (1968) groundbreaking study and continuing with the study of behavioral inhibition by Kagan, Reznick, and Snidman (1987). Although the conceptualization of temperament remains controversial, there is some consensus about what constitutes difficult temperament during infancy (i.e., fussiness, irritability). Difficult temperament is believed to possibly influence the course of later externalizing problems, directly through its relation to later oppositional and aggressive behavior (Graham, Rutter, & George, 1973) or indirectly through its effects on attitudes and behaviors of caregivers (Bates, 1980). Studies examining the direct effects of difficult temperament on later externalizing behavior problems have shown modest to moderate relations (Maziade, Cote, Bernier, Boutin, & Thivierge, 1989; Sanson et al., 1991). Unfortunately, these studies relied solely on mothers' reports of infant difficulty *and* later behavior problems. In the few studies using different informants (e.g., teachers, observers) to report on later externalizing problems, relations between maternal reports of infant difficulty and later externalizing problems have been modest or insignificant (Bates et al., 1985; Thomas et al., 1968).

These findings raise the possibility that the magnitude of the relation between temperament and externalizing problems has been overestimated due to observer bias. A similar bias has been documented in the relation between maternal reports of depression and behavior problems (Fergusson et al., 1993; Richters, 1992). This also calls for research to be conducted in which maternal reports of infant temperament are supplemented with observational systems or teacher reports. In our own research, we have found nonsignificant associations between maternal reports and observations of infant difficulty at 12 and 18 months for girls and 12 months for boys, with modest convergence for boys at 18 months (i.e., $r = .25$, $p < .001$, $n = 293$; Owens, Shaw, & McGuire, 1993). In terms of predicting maternal perception of behavior problems at ages 2 and 3½, we have found only maternal reports of infant difficulty to be associated with later externalizing problems, not observations of infant difficulty (Shaw, Keenan, Vondra et al., 1994). This indicates that the relation between infant temperament and later externalizing problems may be the result of the parent's stable perception of the child, rather than the child's behavior. However, this bias may still be important to a child's outcome by influencing the relationship between the parent and child and ultimately increasing the use of parenting techniques that may promote externalizing behavior problems (e.g., harsh discipline, uninvolvement, permissiveness).

Fortunately, research on the continuity of early disruptive behaviors has been conducted using a wider array of sources. Parental reports appear to be the most commonly employed method, but teacher reports and laboratory and classroom observations have been used as well. Most of these studies begin in the preschool period either by identifying children who show persistent externalizing problems or by using larger epidemiological sampling strategies. In one of the first studies of the latter type, Richman et al. (1982) identified the top 14% of 3-year-olds from a parental questionnaire of behavior problems and followed them in comparison with a control group of children from similar backgrounds. According to maternal report, problems persisted in 63% of these children at age 4 compared to 11% of the control group, and 62% at age 8 compared to 22% of the control group. Although continuity was lower according to teacher report at age 8, group differences were found in comparison to children not previously identified (39% of problem group vs. 24% in the control group, $p < .05$).

Campbell and colleagues followed two cohorts of hard-to-manage children from preschool through school age (Campbell, 1990; Campbell et al., 1986). In the first cohort, children first identified at age 3 according to parental reports showed a strong continuity of behavior problems at ages 6, 9, and 13. According to maternal reports, 50% and 48% showed clinically significant problems at ages 6 and 9, respectively, with teacher ratings also distinguishing between identified children and controls. A second cohort of overactive and inattentive boys was recruited during the preschool period based on teacher and parental reports of attention deficit disorder (ADD) in the preschool period. Compared to a demographically matched comparison group at ages 5 and 6, a strong continuity of externalizing problems emerged from both parent and teacher ratings of target children's behavior problems (Campbell, 1994; Campbell et al., 1994).

Several other studies beginning in early childhood corroborate the results of Richman and Campbell. A moderate to strong continuity of early externalizing problems has been found as early as infancy to school age (Keenan & Shaw, 1994; McGee, Feehan, & Williams, in press; Rose, Rose, & Feldman, 1989). In a study conducted by Cummings and colleagues (1989), the stability of physical aggression from ages 2 to 5 was .76 for boys. This study is notable because it is one of the few in which observational data were obtained at both assessment points to evaluate aggression.

Similarly, using a large sample of boys attending French public schools in Quebec, Tremblay, Pihl, Vitaro, and Dobkin (1994) discovered that hyperactivity rated by teachers in kindergarten (i.e., restless, overactive, and fidgety behaviors) predicted boys' self-reported delinquency at ages 10 and 13 better than early anxiety and reward dependence. However, boys who were high on hyperactivity, low on anxiety, and high on reward dependence in kindergarten were *not* at greater risk for subsequent delinquent behavior compared to nonhyperactive boys, suggesting a buffering effect for boys characterized by the "histrionic" personality profile.

In our own work, we have found moderate support for the continuity of disruptive behavior beginning during infancy using a transformational model (Shaw et al., 1995). This involves taking into account the changing meaning of aggression from ages 1 to 3 and including other forms of less destructive, but nonetheless aversive child behaviors, which may have an impact on parenting and subsequent child behavior. Using only observational methods, persistent attention-seeking behavior at 12 months was found to be the child variable most highly related to 18-month noncompliance, which, in turn, was related to 24-month aggression. Aggression at 24 months was then related to 36-month externalizing problems, reported by mothers. It is interesting that noncompliance at 18 months was more strongly associated with 24-month aggression than 18-month aggression, a finding we have now replicated with two cohorts (Shaw et al., 1995). It should be noted that this transformational pattern appears to be more valid for boys. For girls, a more direct link between observed noncompliance and later maternal report of behavior problems was evident.

Sex Differences

The issue of sex differences in disruptive behavior recently has been of greater interest as more is known about the prevalence rates and stability of antisocial behavior during the school-age period. The reader is referred to Giordano and Cernkovich (Chapter 46, this volume) and to a series of articles in *Development and Psychopathology* (Vol. 5, 1993) for more information concerning the merits of using different diagnostic criteria to establish conduct disorder for boys and girls (e.g., Achenbach, 1993). The emergence of boys' higher rates of externalizing behavior seems to occur during the latter part of the preschool period. Although several investigators have documented the absence of sex differences in externalizing behaviors from ages 1 to 3 (Achenbach, 1993; Keenan & Shaw, 1994; Richman et al., 1982; Rose et al., 1989), this pattern appears to shift beginning at ages 4 and 5 (Rose et al., 1989). These differences become more dramatic during the school-age period and persist into adulthood (Kazdin, 1987).

In a review of studies examining sex differences in the prevalence and correlates of behavior problems among young children, Keenan and Shaw (1997) propose two explanations for the emergence of sex differences beginning at ages 4 to 5. The first explanation involves differential socialization practices of parents. As a result of being reinforced for sex-stereotyped behavior, girls' problems may be channeled more in the direction of internalizing difficulties. The socialization hypothesis is supported by data that during the preschool period, parents are more likely to use physical punishment with sons and more inductive techniques and reasoning with daughters (Block, 1978). Similarly, research indicates that relative to boys, mothers encourage girls to have more concern for others, to share or even relinquish toys to peers, and to behave prosocially (Ross, Tesla, Kenyon, & Lollis, 1990). Dodge and Frame (1982) have found that deficits in these affective perspective-taking skills are highly related to antisocial behavior among school-age children. It is unclear whether these differences in parental behavior initially emerge in the preschool period or become evident at younger ages.

The second explanation attributes the greater decline in girls' externalizing problems to their more advanced adaptive skills, which, in turn, facilitate prosocial behavior. From infancy to the preschool period, girls are found to have more rapid biological, cognitive, and social and emotional development than boys. Boys appear more vulnerable than girls to several neurodevelopmental disorders such as mental retardation, autism, learning disabilities, and ADHD (American Psychiatric Association, 1987). Cognitively, girls appear to have greater skills in language development (Huttenlocher, Haight, Bryk, Seltzer, & Lyons, 1991) and greater ability to retain attention in the face of disruption (Gold, Crombie, & Noble, 1987). In the area of social and emotional development, Hay, Zahn-Waxler, Cummings, and Iannotti (1992) have shown that pre-school-age girls are more likely than boys to recommend prosocial rather than aggressive strategies for resolving conflict.

Taken together, these findings provide tentative support for the validity of both the socialization and advanced maturity hypotheses in explaining the greater prevalence of boys' externalizing behavior problems. However, more work is needed in this area before firm conclusions can be drawn. For instance, it will be important to identify specific ages and specific practices at which parents begin treating girls and boys differently.

Parental Attributes and Support

Several researchers have attempted to identify parental characteristics related to the development of children's antisocial behavior. For example, the occurrence of conduct disorder and delinquency in school-age and adolescent children is associated with antisocial personality characteristics in both mothers and fathers (Robins, West, & Herjanic, 1975). In a younger sample, Keenan and Shaw (1994) found that familial criminality was related to boys' aggression at age 2, after controlling for aggression at 18 months and maternal age. Although relations between parental antisocial personality and behavior problems in younger children rarely have been examined, parents' antisocial behavior has been shown to precede older children's behavior problems (Robins et al., 1975).

In addition to an antisocial personality, associations between child behavior problems and other forms of parental psychopathology, such as unipolar and bipolar depression, have been explored. Zahn-Waxler et al. (1988) followed a small group of children from families in which one parent had been hospitalized for bipolar disorder prior to the children's birth. Compared to a matched control group, target children were more likely to have a variety of psychiatric problems, particularly conduct disorder, at age 6. Investigators comparing young children with disruptive behavior problems to normal controls have found that mothers of children with behavior problems report more depressive symptomatology (Mash & Johnston, 1983), and these differences in externalizing problems persist at follow-up (Campbell, March, Pierce, Ewing, & Szumowski, 1991; Webster-Stratton, 1990a). However, some researchers have found that depressive symptoms are related to a parental perception of behavior problems but not with teacher or observer ratings of child behavior (Zahn-Waxler, Iannotti, Cummings, & Denham, 1990). Parents reporting a depressed mood may overestimate their children's behavior problems, thereby confounding the observed association.

In addition to examining parental personality and adjustment, investigators have identified sources of stress and support within and outside the family system that are related to the occurrence of child behavior problems. For example, marital conflict has emerged across studies as a strong correlate and predictor of child behavior problems, particularly when disagreements over child-rearing practices have been examined (Dadds & Powell, 1991; Jouriles, Murphy, & O'Leary, 1989; Shaw, Emery, & Tuer, 1993). In a sample of low-income families, Shaw, Vondra et al. (1994) found that parental disagreements over child rearing when boys and girls were 2 years old predicted externalizing problems at age 3. Katz and Gottman (1993) were able to predict children's externalizing problems at age 8 from observations of parents' interaction patterns when the children were 5 years old. High levels of hostility expressed between parents during a marital interaction task predicted boys' and girls' externalizing problems 3 years later.

Although overt marital conflict was related to later behavior problems in Katz and Gottman's (1993) study, marital *satisfaction* was not significantly correlated with child behavior. Other researchers have documented weak associations between marital satisfaction and externalizing problems (Webster-Stratton, 1990a). Moreover, in some studies other contextual factors, such as SES, life stress, and social support, do not make independent contributions to the prediction of behavior problems (Mash & Johnston, 1983; Renken et al., 1989). Rutter and colleagues have suggested that the presence of multiple familial stressors may be a better predictor of child behavior problems than any specific factor alone (Rutter, Cox, Tupling, Berger, & Yule, 1975). Consistent with this hypothesis, several investigators have found that the likelihood of behavior problems increases with the number of stressors present (Sanson et al., 1991; Shaw, Vondra et al., 1994).

Although the cumulative stressor model is plausible, another possibility is that some factors are related indirectly to children's adjustment. For example, in a study of low-income families, Renken et al. (1989) reported significant zero-order correlations between children's aggression and SES, stressful life events, and social support. However, these relations were nonsignificant after controlling for the effects of children's earlier attachment security and negative affect, as well as the amount of hostility expressed by mothers in interactions with the children. In our own sample, hostile, rejecting parenting mediated relations between externalizing problems in Caucasian boys 42 months of age and earlier maternal depressive symptoms, marital satisfaction, and parenting hassles (Winslow, Shaw, Bruns, & Kiebler, 1995). Due to multicolinearity among risk factors, such as SES, stress, marital relations, and social support, researchers need to examine these factors simultaneously to form models that best characterize their associations with child behavior problems (Shaw & Emery, 1988).

Parenting Factors

During infancy, much of the research on parenting factors associated with externalizing behavior problems has focused on maternal unresponsiveness (Shaw & Bell, 1993). Parental unresponsiveness has been conceptualized by attachment theorists as being most critical to the development of self-regulation skills. Accordingly, differences in caregiver sensitivity, and the resultant bond between parent and infant, should be important factors in later patterns of the child's behavior (Bowlby, 1969; Sroufe, 1983). Theoretically, a child who has received less contingent caregiving might act more disruptively to obtain parental attention (Greenberg & Speltz, 1988) and have less to lose by disobeying parental requests (i.e., loss of love; Shaw & Bell, 1993). Such interaction patterns could promote the beginning of coercive interaction patterns, a style found in some families with school-age conduct-disordered children (Patterson, 1982).

Research examining infant attachment security and direct observations of maternal responsiveness during infancy have found support for their relation with later externalizing problems, particularly among samples of high-risk boys. The measurement of infant attachment security has been operationalized and studied using the Strange Situation (Ainsworth & Wittig, 1969). Whereas research with well-educated middle-class families has produced inconsistent results (Bates et al., 1985; Fagot & Kavanaugh, 1990), in samples of high-risk families, insecure attachments during infancy have been associated with an increased risk of later externalizing problems during the toddler (Shaw & Vondra, 1995), pre-school-age (Erickson et al., 1985; Lyons-Ruth et al., 1993), and school-age (Renken et al., 1989) periods. Buffers of the middle-class child's ecosystem, such as economic and social support and the quality of alternative care facilities, may prevent the insecurely attached infant from becoming dysfunctional. These same factors that make insecure attachment a more likely outcome among low-SES families may increase an insecure infant's vulnerability for developing psychopathology by continuing to affect the quality of parenting during the toddler and pre-school-age periods and beyond (Shaw & Vondra, 1995). Because of their greater vulnerability for externalizing problems, insecurely attached boy infants may be at greater risk for these problems than girls (Erickson et al., 1985; Renken et al., 1989).

Direct observations of maternal responsiveness also have shown cross-sectional and longitudinal associations with externalizing problems, again particularly for boys (Gardner, 1987). Using a model of mother-infant interaction based on the mother's ability to match the intensity of the infant's attention-seeking behavior, Martin (1981) found that for boys only low maternal responsiveness at 10 months was associated with lower rates of compliance at 22 months and higher rates of coercive child behavior at 42 months. Martin also found that infant demandingness at 10 months and its interaction with maternal responsiveness contributed unique variance to the prediction of compliance at 22 months.

We have found general support for Martin's (1981) model, using the same procedures with two cohorts of low-income infants, in contrast to Martin's middle-class subjects. As noted earlier, this association has been found more consistently with assessments of maternal behavior at 12 versus 18 months and more consistently for boys than girls (Shaw, Keenan, & Vondra, 1994; Shaw et al., 1995). In the first sample, maternal *un*responsiveness was associated with observed aggression at 24 months and maternal report of externalizing behavior problems at 36 months. In the second ongoing investigation, unresponsiveness at 12 months was strongly associated with maternal reports of externalizing problems at 24 months.

Among toddlers and pre-school-age children, researchers studying the relations between caregiving and externalizing behavior problems have identified several characteristics of parenting related to children's behavior, such as parental involvement, hostility, consistency, and harsh discipline (Gardner, 1987; Zahn-Waxler et al., 1990). For example, Pettit and Bates (1989) discovered that low rates of maternal positive involvement during infancy and toddlerhood strongly predicted children's deviant behavior at age 4. Renken et al. (1989) showed that maternal hostility and abuse when children were 42 months old predicted children's aggression during elementary school. On the other hand, reviews of the literature indicate that parenting practices have not been consistently related to child behavior across studies (Grusec & Lytton, 1988; Maccoby & Martin, 1983). In a meta-analysis of 47 studies, Rothbaum and Weisz (1994) discovered that investigators obtained stronger relations with child behavior when they measured multiple characteristics of parenting, such as use of parental approval, guidance, and coercive control. Intuitively, it makes sense that parenting *styles,* rather than individual dimensions, would be better predictors of children's adjustment because "good parenting" brings to mind a combination of characteristics (i.e., high warmth, involvement, and consistency of discipline).

Alternative Caregiving

Some investigators have found that children enrolled in day care are more irritable, aggressive, and less compliant in preschool and early elementary school than peers without day care experience (Haskins, 1985). Belsky (1988) has pointed out that this pattern is most characteristic of children involved in day care for more than 20 hours a week beginning in their first year of life. Factors related to the quality of care, such as availability of caregivers and curriculum objectives, have been associated with children's behavior. Haskins found that children enrolled in a day care center that focused on promoting intellectual development were 13 times *more* aggressive than home-reared children.

Despite the elevated rates of aggression and noncompliance in children exposed to early day care, it is unclear whether these children have a greater risk of developing behavior problems. For example, although Rubenstein, Howes, and Boyle (1981) reported higher levels of aggression and noncompliance for preschoolers with previous day care experience, they did not find that these children had more behavior problems than home-reared peers. Moreover, longitudinal studies have not shown that children enrolled in day care remain more aggressive throughout their schooling. Instead, these children seem to show elevated levels of aggression only during the early elementary years (Goossens et al., 1991; Hegland & Rix, 1990). In addition, most studies have not randomly assigned children to day care and home-reared conditions, leaving open the possibility that relations between day care experience and higher rates of disruptive behavior are the result of other factors, such as selection bias.

Peer Rejection

A plethora of studies have documented that children who are rejected by peers are more likely to be disruptive in the classroom and aggressive in social interactions (see Coie, Dodge, & Kupersmidt, 1990, for a review). However, cross-sectional studies do not address whether children's peer relations are causally related to the development of behavior problems. Several longitudinal investigations have provided evidence suggestive of such an association. For example, in a follow-up of parent-referred preschoolers with externalizing problems, Campbell (1987) discovered that children who continued to experience moderate to severe behavior problems at age 6 initially differed from normal controls on symptoms of peer problems, whereas those who had improved by age 6 did not differ from controls as preschoolers. However, because initial problem severity was not controlled, this finding may not reflect the contribution of poor peer relations.

After controlling for initial levels of problem behavior, some researchers have found that the quality of children's peer relations is associated with later behavior. For example, using sociometric ratings, Vitaro, Tremblay, Gagnon, and Boivin (1992) reported that children who were classified as rejected by their peers in kindergarten and grade 1 were more aggressive and hyperactive in second grade than nonrejected classmates. Although children who initially were rejected had higher rates of behavior problems in kindergarten, peer status contributed uniquely to the prediction of grade 2 externalizing behavior after controlling for initial problems.

Even though children who are rejected by peers early in their school experiences already have higher rates of externalizing behavior compared to nonrejected peers, peer rejection may heighten the children's risk for continued problems. Olson (1992) attempted to delineate the relation between early peer interaction and the development of behavior problems in a sample of 4- and 5-year-old boys from low-income families. Behavioral observations of peer interaction, sociometric nominations, and teacher ratings of problem behavior were collected at the beginning and end of the preschool year. Olson discovered that children who were described by peers and teachers as behaviorally maladjusted (i.e., fights a lot, gets mad easily, is mean to others) demonstrated relatively high rates of aggressive behavior toward peers at the beginning of the year. At the same time, peers' aggressive behavior toward maladjusted children was *not* related to maladjustment scores. By the end of the school year, however, nonrejected peers tended to initiate verbally and physically aggressive interactions with children initially rated as maladjusted. Likewise, maladjusted children tended to respond aggressively. Olson's results support a transactional model in that, as the year progressed, initially aggressive children tended to elicit more unprovoked aggressive exchanges with peers, followed by counteraggresssion by the target children.

CONCLUSIONS AND FUTURE DIRECTIONS

Recently, investigators have begun to place greater emphasis on identifying early precursors of antisocial behavior. A few well-designed studies have been conducted using multiple informants and measurement methods. Findings that have been replicated across samples using different designs provide the most reliable bases from which to begin delineating developmental trajectories. Because risk factors do not remain stable over different developmental periods, transactions and transformations that occur between children and their environments must be plotted across development to identify specific pathways. We have chosen to summarize current findings within a developmental context, beginning with risk factors during infancy and ending with those relevant when children first enter school.

Figures 15.1 and 15.2 used a transactional model to conceptualize the development of early externalizing problems in boys. (Because of the paucity of available research, we have not attempted to specify a model for girls.) Solid lines represent well-

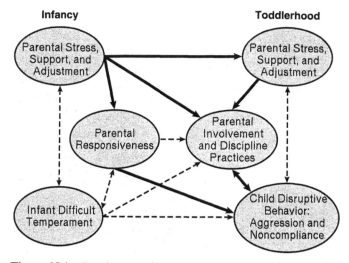

Figure 15.1   *Developmental precursors of antisocial behavior for boys: Infancy to toddlerhood.*

documented associations; dashed lines indicate relations with less empirical support, due to inconsistencies among studies or methodological limitations. Risk factors are presented as ellipses rather than rectangles to indicate latent variables that we hope would be measured repeatedly using multiple informants and methods. Because of space limitations, factors are presented in abridged form. For example, "parental stress, support, and adjustment" includes parental support within and outside the nuclear family as well as parental psychological well-being.

According to our model, antisocial behavior develops as a result of transactions between children and their environments over time. The model takes into account transformations that occur in both child and parent behavior as children mature. For example, temperamentally difficult infants might be more noncompliant as toddlers, compared to easy infants. Moreover, par-

ents who are not responsive during infancy might be less involved and more permissive with their toddlers. At the same time, transactions between parent and child might help maintain continuity: Persistently noncompliant behavior makes enforcing rules more difficult, and permissive parenting reinforces noncompliance.

In addition to child and parent behavior, the model considers the potential effects of stressors within and outside the family. Whether or not contextual factors and parental characteristics, such as depression and antisocial personality, are independent or cumulatively related to child behavior problems, they may affect child behavior indirectly by disrupting parenting. Although such a mediating model has not been tested with younger children, it has received support from research with school-age children (Patterson, 1982). One exception might be overt marital conflict, which could have a direct effect on child behavior through exposure to aggressive resolution strategies. Finally, factors that become salient later in development, such as peer rejection, may exacerbate existing externalizing problems, helping to maintain the continuity of disruptive behavior.

Although we have outlined a model that might apply to the development of antisocial behavior, other models are plausible as well. To test models such as the one presented, researchers must supplement cross-sectional research with more longitudinal, experimental, and quasi-experimental studies of high-risk populations that employ developmentally appropriate, multimethod assessment techniques. Risk factors need to be measured simultaneously to identify the nature of relations among these factors. Multicolinearity among risk factors obscures our ability to interpret findings from studies that include only a few of these factors. Of course, expanding the scope of individual investigations might require collaboration among researchers to find sufficient resources to conduct multiple assessments with large samples. By permitting the delineation of developmental trajectories leading to antisocial behavior, such large-scale projects have the potential to form the basis of *effective* preventive programs.

Figure 15.2   *Developmental precursors of antisocial behavior for boys: Toddlerhood to preschool.*

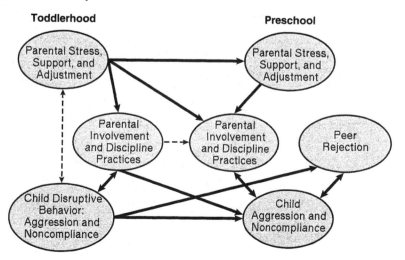

REFERENCES

Achenbach, T. M. (1993). Taxonomy and comorbidity of conduct problems: Evidence from empirically-based approaches. *Development and Psychopathology, 5,* 51–64.

Ainsworth, M. D. S., & Wittig, B. A. (1969). Attachment and the exploratory behavior of 1-year-olds in a strange situation. In B. M. Foss (Ed.), *Determinants of infant behavior* (Vol. 4, pp. 113–136). London: Methuen.

American Psychiatric Association. (1987). *Diagnostic and statistical manual* (3rd ed., rev.). Washington, DC: Author.

Bates, J. E. (1980). The concept of difficult temperament. *Merrill-Palmer Quarterly, 26,* 299–319.

Bates, J. E., Maslin, C. A., & Frankel, K. A. (1985). Attachment security, mother-child interaction, and temperament as predictors of behavior-problem ratings at age three years. In I. Bretherton & E. Waters (Eds.), *Monographs of the Society for Research in Child Development, 50*(1–2), 167–193.

Bell, R. Q., & Harper, L. V. (1977). *The effects of children on parents.* Hillsdale, NJ: Erlbaum.

Belsky, J. (1988). The "effects" of infant day care reconsidered. *Early Childhood Research Quarterly, 3,* 235–272.

Block, J. H. (1978). Another look at sex differentiation in the socialization behavior of mothers and fathers. In J. Sherman & F. L. Denmark (Eds.), *The psychology of women: Future directions of research* (pp. 29–87). New York: Psychological Dimensions.

Bowlby, J. (1969). *Attachment.* New York: Basic Books.

Breakey, G., & Pratt, B. (1991). Healthy growth for Hawaii's "healthy start": Toward a systematic statewide approach to the prevention of child abuse and neglect. *Zero to Three, 11,* 16–22.

Campbell, S. B. (1987). Parent-referred problem three-year-olds: Developmental changes in symptoms. *Journal of Child Psychology and Psychiatry, 28,* 835–845.

Campbell, S. B. (1990). *Behavior problems in preschool children: Clinical and developmental issues.* New York: Guilford.

Campbell, S. B. (1994). Hard-to-manage preschool boys: Externalizing behavior, social competence, and family context at two-year follow-up. *Journal of Abnormal Child Psychology, 22,* 147–166.

Campbell, S. B. (1995). Behavior problems in preschool children: A review of recent research. *Journal of Child Psychology and Psychiatry, 36,* 113–149.

Campbell, S. B., Breaux, A. M., Ewing, L. J., & Szumowski, E. K. (1986). Correlates and predictors of hyperactivity and aggression: A longitudinal study of parent-referred problem preschoolers. *Journal of Abnormal Child Psychology, 14,* 425–440.

Campbell, S., March, C., Pierce, E., Ewing, L., & Szumowski, E. (1991). Hard-to-manage preschool boys: Family context and the stability of externalizing behavior. *Journal of Abnormal Child Psychology, 19,* 301–310.

Campbell, S. B., Pierce, E., March, C., Ewing, L. J., & Szumowski, E. K. (1994). Hard-to-manage preschool boys: Symptomatic behavior across contexts and time. *Child Development, 65,* 836–851.

Coie, J., Dodge, K., & Kupersmidt, J. (1990). Peer group behavior and social status. In S. R. Asher & J. D. Coie (Eds.), *Peer rejection in childhood* (pp. 17–59). New York: Cambridge University Press.

Crowther, J. K., Bond, L. A., & Rolf, J. E. (1981). The incidence, prevalence, and severity of behavior disorders among preschool-age children in day care. *Journal of Abnormal Child Psychology, 9,* 23–42.

Cummings, E. M., Iannotti, R. J., & Zahn-Waxler, C. (1989). Aggression between peers in early childhood: Individual continuity and developmental change. *Child Development, 72,* 887–895.

Dadds, M. R., & Powell, M. B. (1991). The relationship of interparental conflict and global marital adjustment to aggression and immaturity in aggressive and nonclinic children. *Journal of Abnormal Child Psychology, 19,* 553–567.

Dodge, K. A. (1990). Nature versus nurture in childhood conduct disorder: It is time to ask a different question. *Developmental Psychology, 26,* 698–701.

Dodge, K. A., & Frame, C. M. (1982). Social cognitive biases and deficits in aggressive boys. *Child Development, 53,* 620–635.

Dumas, J., & Wahler, R. G. (1985). Indiscriminate mothering as a contextual factor in aggressive-oppositional child behavior: "Damned if you do and damned if you don't." *Journal of Abnormal Child Psychology, 13,* 1–18.

Erickson, M. F., Sroufe, L. A., & Egeland, B. (1985). The relationship between quality of attachment and behavior problems in preschool in a high-risk sample. In I. Bretherton & E. Waters (Eds.), Growing points of attachment theory and research. *Monographs of the Society for Research in Child Development, 50*(1–2), 147–167.

Fagot, B. I., & Kavanagh, K. (1990). The prediction of antisocial behavior from avoidant attachment classifications. *Child Development, 62,* 864–873.

Fergusson, D. M., Lynskey, M. T., & Horwood, L. J. (1993). The effect of maternal depression on maternal ratings of child behavior. *Journal of Abnormal Child Psychology, 21,* 245–270.

Gardner, F. E. (1987). Positive interaction between mothers and conduct-problem children: Is there training for harmony as well as fighting? *Journal of Abnormal Child Psychology, 15,* 283–293.

Gardner, F. (1989). Inconsistent parenting: Is there evidence for a link with children's conduct problems? *Journal of Abnormal Child Psychology, 17,* 223–233.

Glueck, S., & Glueck, E. (1950). *Unraveling juvenile delinquency.* Cambridge, MA: Harvard University Press.

Gold, D., Crombie, G., & Noble, S. (1987). Relations between teachers' judgements of girls' and boys' compliance and intellectual competence. *Sex Roles, 16,* 351–358.

Goosens, F., Ottenhoff, G., & Koops, W. (1991). Day care and social outcomes in middle childhood: A retrospective study. Special issue: International perspective on day care for young children. *Journal of Reproductive and Infant Psychology, 9,* 137–150.

Graham, P., Rutter, M., & George, S. (1973). Temperamental characteristics as predictors of behavior disorders in children. *American Journal of Orthopsychiatry, 43,* 328–339.

Greenberg, M. T., & Speltz, M. (1988). Attachment and the ontogeny of conduct problems. In J. Belsky & T. Nezworski (Eds.), *Clinical implications of attachment* (pp. 177–218). Hillsdale, NJ: Erlbaum.

Grusec, J., & Lytton, H. (1988). *Social development: History, theory, and research.* New York: Springer-Verlag.

Haskins, R. (1985). Public school aggression among children with varying day care experience. *Child Development, 56,* 689–703.

Hay, D. F., Zahn-Waxler, C., Cummings, E. M., & Iannotti, R. J. (1992). Young children's views about conflict with peers: A comparison of the daughters and sons of depressed and well women. *Journal of Child Psychology and Psychiatry, 33,* 669–683.

Hegland, S., & Rix, M. (1990). Aggression and assertiveness in kindergarten children differing in day care experiences. *Early Childhood Research Quarterly, 5,* 105–116.

Huttenlocher, J., Haight, W., Bryk, A. Seltzer, M., & Lyons, T. (1991). Early vocabulary growth: Relation to language input and gender. *Developmental Psychology, 27,* 236–248.

Jouriles, E., Murphy, C., & O'Leary, K. D. (1989). Interspousal aggression, marital discord, and child problems. *Journal of Consulting and Clinical Psychology, 57,* 453–455.

Kagan, J., Reznick, S. J., & Snidman, N. (1987). The physiology of behavioral inhibition in children. *Child Development, 58,* 1459–1473.

Katz, L. F., & Gottman, J. (1993). Patterns of marital conflict predict children's internalizing and externalizing behaviors. *Developmental Psychology, 29,* 940–950.

Kazdin, A. E. (1987). *Conduct disorders in childhood and adolescence.* Newbury Park, CA: Sage Publications.

Keenan, K., & Shaw, D. S. (1994). The development of aggression in toddlers: A study of low income families. *Journal of Abnormal Child Psychology, 22,* 53–77.

Keenan, K., & Shaw, D. S. (1997). Developmental influences on young girls' behavioral and emotional problems. *Psychological Bulletin, 121,* 95–113.

Lyons-Ruth, K., Alpern, L., & Repacholi, B. (1993). Disorganized infant attachment classification and maternal psychosocial problems as predictors of hostile-aggressive behavior in the preschool classroom. *Child Development, 64,* 572–585.

Lytton, H. (1990). Child and parent effects in boys' conduct disorder: A reinterpretation. *Developmental Psychology, 26,* 683–697.

Maccoby, E., & Martin, J. (1983). Socialization in the context of the family: Parent-child interaction. In E. M. Hetherington (Ed.), *Handbook of child psychology: Vol. 4. Socialization, personality, and social development* (pp. 1–101). New York: Plenum.

Martin, J. (1981). A longitudinal study of the consequences of early mother-infant interaction: A microanalytic approach. *Monographs of the Society for Research in Child Development, 46.*

Mash, E., & Johnston, C. (1983). Parental perceptions of child behavior problems, parenting self-esteem, and mothers' reported stress in younger and older hyperactive and normal children. *Journal of Consulting and Clinical Psychology, 51,* 86–99.

Maziade, M., Cote, R., Bernier, H., Boutin, P., & Thivierge, J. (1989). Significance of extreme temperament in infancy for clinical status in preschool years. *British Journal of Psychiatry, 154,* 544–551.

McGee, R., Feehan, M., & Williams, S. (in press). Long-term follow-up of a birth cohort. In F. C. Verhulst & H. M. Koot (Eds.), *The epidemiology of child and adolescent psychopathology.*

Olson, S. L. (1991). Assessment of peer rejection and externalizing behavior problems in preschool boys: A short-term longitudinal study. *Journal of Abnormal Child Psychology, 20,* 327–350.

Olson, S. L. (1992). Development of conduct problems and peer rejection in preschool children: A social systems analysis. *Journal of Abnormal Child Psychology, 20,* 327–350.

Olweus, D. (1979). Stability of aggressive reaction patterns in males: A review. *Psychological Bulletin, 86,* 852–875.

Owens, E., Shaw, D. S., & McGuire, M. (1993). *Infant temperament and maternal responsiveness in a low SES sample: Reciprocal influences during the second year of life.* Paper presented at the convention of the Society for Research in Child Development, New Orleans.

Patterson, G. (1982). *Coercive family processes* (Vol. 3). Eugene, OR: Castalia.

Pettit, G., & Bates, J. (1989). Family interaction patterns and children's behavior problems from infancy to 4 years. *Developmental Psychology, 25,* 413–420.

Raine, A., Brennan, P., & Mednick, S. A. (1994). Birth complications combined with maternal rejection at age 1 year predispose to violent crime at age 18 years. *Archives of General Psychiatry, 51,* 984–988.

Renken, B., Egeland, B., Marvinney, D., Mangelsdorf, S., & Sroufe, A. (1989). Early childhood antecedents of aggression and passive-withdrawal in early elementary school. *Journal of Personality, 57,* 257–281.

Richman, M., Stevenson, J., & Graham, P. J. (1982). *Preschool to school: A behavioral study.* London: Academic Press.

Richters, J. E. (1992). Depressed mothers as informants about their children: A critical review of the evidence for distortion. *Psychological Bulletin, 112,* 485–499.

Robins, L., West, P., & Herjanic, B. (1975). Arrests and delinquency in two generations: A study of Black urban families and their children. *Journal of Child Psychology and Psychiatry, 16,* 125–140.

Rose, S. L., Rose, S. A., & Feldman, J. F. (1989). Stability of behavior problems in very young children. *Development and Psychopathology, 1,* 5–19.

Ross, H., Tesla, C., Kenyon, B., & Lollis, S. (1990). Maternal intervention in toddler peer conflict: The socialization of principles of justice. *Developmental Psychology, 26,* 994–1003.

Rothbaum, F., & Weisz, J. (1994). Parental caregiving and child externalizing behavior in nonclinical samples: A meta-analysis. *Psychological Bulletin, 116,* 55–74.

Rubenstein, J., Howes, C., & Boyle, P. (1981). A two-year follow-up of infants in community-based care. *Journal of Child Psychology and Psychiatry and Allied Disciplines, 22,* 209–218.

Rutter, M., Cox, A., Tupling, C., Berger, M., & Yule, W. (1975). Attainment and adjustment in two geographical areas: I. The prevalence of psychiatric disorder. *British Journal of Psychiatry, 126,* 493–509.

Sameroff, A. J. (1990). *Prevention of developmental psychopathology using the transactional model: Perspectives on host, risk agent, and environment interactions.* Paper presented at the conference on the Present Status and Future Needs of Research on Prevention of Mental Disorders.

Sanson, A., Oberklaid, F., Pedlow, R., & Prior, M. (1991). Risk indicators: Assessment of infancy predictors of preschool behavioural adjustment. *Journal of Child Psychology and Psychiatry, 32,* 609–626.

Shaw, D. S., & Bell, R. Q. (1993). Developmental theories of parental contributors to antisocial behavior. *Journal of Abnormal Child Psychology, 21,* 493–518.

Shaw, D. S., & Emery, R. E. (1988). Chronic family adversity and school-age children's adjustment. *Journal of the American Academy of Child and Adolescent Psychiatry, 27,* 200–206.

Shaw, D. S., Emery, R. E., & Tuer, M. D. (1993). Parental functioning and children's adjustment in families of divorce: A prospective study. *Journal of Abnormal Child Psychology, 21,* 119–134.

Shaw, D. S., Keenan, K., Owens, E., Winslow, E. B., Hood, N., & Garcia, M. (1995, April). *Developmental precursors of externalizing behavior among two samples of low-income families: Ages 1 to 5.* Paper presented at the biennial meeting of the Society for Research in Child Development, Indianapolis, IN.

Shaw, D. S., Keenan, K., & Vondra, J. I. (1994). The developmental precursors of antisocial behavior: Ages 1–3. *Developmental Psychology, 30,* 355–364.

Shaw, D. S., Keenan, K., Vondra, J., Winslow, E. B., Owens, E., & Hood, N. (1994, June). *Developmental precursors of antisocial behavior: Exploration and replication.* Paper presented at the Society for Research in Child and Adolescent Psychopathology, London.

Shaw, D. S., & Vondra, J. I. (1995). Attachment security and maternal predictors of early behavior problems: A longitudinal study of low-income families. *Journal of Abnormal Child Psychology, 23,* 335–357.

Shaw, D. S., Vondra, J. I., Dowdell Hommerding, K., Keenan, K., & Dunn, M. (1994). Chronic family adversity and early child behavior problems: A longitudinal study of low income families. *Journal of Child Psychology and Psychiatry, 35,* 1109–1122.

Sroufe, L. A. (1983). Infant-caregiver-attachment and patterns of adaptation in preschool: The roots of maladaption and competence. In M. Perlmutter (Ed.), *Minnesota symposium in child psychology* (Vol. 16, pp. 41–81). Hillsdale, NJ: Erlbaum.

Tarver-Behring, S., Barkley, R. A., & Karlsson, J. (1985). The mother-child interactions of hyperactive boys and their normal siblings. *American Journal of Orthopsychiatry, 55,* 202–208.

Thomas, A., Chess, S., & Birch, H. (1968). *Temperament and behavior disorders in children.* New York: New York University Press.

Tremblay, R. E., Pihl, R. O., Vitaro, F., & Dobkin, P. L. (1994). Predicting early onset of male antisocial behavior from preschool behavior. A test of two personality theories. *Archives of General Psychiatry, 51,* 732–738.

Vitaro, F., Tremblay, R., Gagnon, C., & Boivin, M. (1992). Peer rejection from kindergarten to grade 2: Outcomes, correlates, and prediction. *Merrill-Palmer Quarterly, 38,* 382–400.

Webster-Stratton, C. (1990a). Long-term follow-up of families with young conduct problem children: From preschool to grade school. *Journal of Clinical Child Psychology, 19,* 144–149.

Webster-Stratton, C. (1990b). Stress: A potential disrupter of parent perceptions and family interactions. *Journal of Child Clinical Psychology, 4,* 302–312.

Winslow, E. B., Shaw, D. S., Bruns, H., & Kiebler, K. (1995, April). *Parenting as a mediator of child behavior problems and maternal stress, support, and adjustment.* Paper presented at the biennial meeting of the Society for Research in Child Development, Indianapolis, IN.

Zahn-Waxler, C., Iannotti, R. J., Cummings, E. M., & Denham, S. (1990). Antecedents of problem behaviors in children of depressed mothers. *Development and Psychopathology, 2,* 271–292.

Zahn-Waxler, C., Mayfield, A., Radke-Yarrow, M., McKnew, D., Cytryn, L., & Davenport, Y. (1988). A follow-up investigation of offspring of bipolar parents. *American Journal of Psychiatry, 145,* 506–509.

Zahn-Waxler, C., Radke-Yarrow, M., & King, R. A. (1979). Child-rearing and children's pro-social initiations toward victims of distress. *Child Development, 50,* 319–330.

CHAPTER 16

Child Abuse, Neglect, and Witnessing Violence

CATHY SPATZ WIDOM

This chapter focuses on the relationship between childhood victimization and witnessing violence and antisocial behavior. A broad range of behaviors is included, from aggression, to such illegal behaviors as delinquency, adult criminality, and violence, to psychiatric diagnoses of conduct disorder (CD) and antisocial personality disorder (ASPD). Most studies of abused and neglected children do not extend into adulthood. Thus, this chapter devotes considerable attention to research on child and adolescent behavior problems and symptoms thought to be precursors of later antisocial behavior. The terms *antisocial personality disorder* and *psychopathy* are used interchangeably here, although the practice does not imply that the two are synonymous. Recent research on the effects of witnessing violence on children's development is also reviewed, and the potential relationships to antisocial behavior considered.

The federal Child Abuse Prevention and Treatment Act of 1988 defines child abuse and neglect as

> the physical or mental injury, sexual abuse or exploitation, negligent treatment, or maltreatment of a child by a person who is responsible for the child's welfare, under circumstances which indicate that the child's health or welfare is harmed or threatened.

Although the literature on childhood victimization deals with several distinct phenomena, including physical abuse, sexual abuse, neglect, severe physical punishment, and psychological maltreatment, this chapter focuses primarily on the first four forms of childhood maltreatment. A new area of concern—the effects of witnessing violence—is also addressed here. A few definitions may be helpful. *Physical abuse* generally refers to incidents of striking, punching, kicking, biting, throwing, or burning a child. *Sexual abuse* covers a wide variety of behaviors from relatively nonspecific charges of "assault and battery with intent to gratify sexual desires" to more specific incidents involving fondling and touching, sodomy, and incest. *Neglect* refers to behavior that represents serious omission by parents or caretakers, for example, a failure to provide children with needed food, clothing, shelter, medical attention, and protection from hazardous conditions. *Witnessing violence* refers to the child's indirect exposure to violence, through witnessing family violence (as occurs when children witness a parent being battered) or through witnessing violence in the community (such as in shootings or other acts of extreme aggression).

There are essentially three streams of research and theory that contribute to an understanding of these relationships. The first, more historical, is drawn from two decades of British and American writings and describes a fairly consistent picture of the childhood of the psychopath as involving some form of early disturbance in family relationships. During this period, in the search for the causes of psychopathy, a number of writers called attention to the importance of the child's early social relationships, emphasizing parental inadequacies such as physical abuse or neglect.

Second, in the early 1970s, research on psychopathy left the clinic and entered the experimental laboratory where carefully selected samples of psychopaths, primarily incarcerated males, were studied. The field grew and our knowledge base was expanded with information about physiological responsivity and autonomic functioning of psychopaths (Hare, 1970) as well as passive avoidance learning (Lykken, 1955) or anticipation of punishment (Lippert & Senter, 1966). Beginning in the 1980s, the development and reports of the psychometric qualities of the Psychopathy Checklist (PCL, Hare, 1980; see Hart & Hare, Chapter 3, this volume) provided an important assessment instrument to advance knowledge in the field.

Third, while research on psychopathy was progressing steadily, a new field of research on child abuse and neglect was beginning to emerge, initially from the field of medicine. In the early 1960s, an important paper on the "battered child syndrome" appeared, defining a clinical condition experienced by children who had been injured deliberately by physical assault by a parent or caretaker (Kempe, Silverman, Steele, Droegemueller, & Silver, 1962). Gradually, the terms *child abuse, child abuse and neglect, child maltreatment,* and *childhood victimization* were used in place of the less encompassing term *battered child syndrome.*

This research was supported in part by grants from the National Institute of Mental Health (RO1-MH49467), National Institute on Alcoholism and Alcohol Abuse (RO3-AA09238), and the National Institute of Justice (86-IJ-CX-0033 and 89-IJ-CX-0007). Points of view are those of the author and do not necessarily represent the position of the U.S. Department of Justice.

At about the same time, Curtis (1963, p. 368) expressed the concern that children maltreated by parental brutality and neglect would "become tomorrow's murderers and perpetrators of other crimes of violence, if they survive." The notion of an intergenerational transmission of violence, or the cycle of violence, became the primary developmental hypothesis in the field of child abuse and neglect, despite the fact that the relationship had "not really passed scientific muster" (Garbarino & Gilliam, 1980, p. 111). Beginning with a series of insightful clinical reports, more systematic work on the relationship between child abuse, neglect, and delinquency, adult criminality, and violence began to emerge. Research with abused and neglected young children was also conducted to document evidence of problem behaviors at an early age.

Research and writing in the field of child abuse and neglect followed a separate and distinct path from the work on antisocial personality disorder or psychopathy. However, in its 1994 edition, the American Psychiatric Association's *Diagnostic and Statistical Manual of Mental Disorders* (*DSM-IV;* American Psychiatric Association [APA], 1994) indicated that child abuse or neglect may increase the likelihood that CD in childhood will evolve into ASPD.

THEORETICAL CONTEXT

A variety of theories have been put forth to explain the linkage between childhood victimization, witnessing violence, and antisocial behavior. These range from more traditional explanations, such as those from psychoanalytic theory, to more recent models drawing on social information processing theories and extrapolations from the literature on children's responses to stressful life events. A general critique of these theories follows in the section on Methodological Issues.

From a psychoanalytical perspective, one popular early theory about antisocial behavior, ASPD, and psychopathy related these behaviors to some form of early disturbance in family relationships, whether it be parental loss, parental rejection or emotional deprivation, excessively punitive behavior, or inconsistent disciplinary techniques. The psychopath's inability to maintain close relationships with others was attributed to this early rejection, little opportunity to identify with parents, and lack of experiences with normal relationships. Furthermore, because psychopaths did not develop an adequate conscience, they showed little evidence of behavioral control.

From a social learning perspective, physical aggression between family members provided a model for the learning of aggressive behavior as well as for the appropriateness of such behavior within the family (Bandura, 1973; Feshbach, 1980). Children learn behavior, at least in part, by imitating someone else's behavior. Thus, children learn to be aggressive through observing aggression in their families and the surrounding society (Feshbach, 1980). White and Straus (1981, p. 265) suggested that physical punishment "lays the groundwork for the normative legitimacy of all types of violence." According to this view, "each generation learns to be violent by being a participant in a violent family" (Straus, Gelles, & Steinmetz, 1980, p. 121). Aggressive parents tend to produce aggressive children (e.g., Bandura & Walters, 1959; Egeland & Sroufe, 1981; Eron, Walder, & Lefkowitz,

1971). More recently, Huesmann, Moise, and Podolski (see Chapter 18, this volume) suggested that children learn "scripts" that guide their actions, perceptions, and interpretations of the world.

Attachment theory has also provided an explanation for some of the developmental outcomes of abused and neglected children (see Shaw & Winslow, Chapter 15, this volume). The assumption is that inconsistent, haphazard care or rejection of an infant can create an insecure-avoidant child, who is likely to interpret neutral or even friendly behavior as hostile and may show inappropriate aggressive behavior. Along these lines, Dodge, Bates, and Pettit (1990) have suggested that physical abuse leads to chronic aggressive behavior by having an impact on the development of hostile social information processing patterns, or the "acquisition of a set of biased and deficient patterns of processing social provocative information" (p. 1679). In their own work, physically harmed 4-year-old children showed deviant patterns of processing social information at age 5, and these patterns were related to aggressive behavior (Dodge et al., 1990).

Widom (1994; Luntz & Widom, 1995) has suggested other possible mechanisms to explain the linkage between childhood victimization and subsequent antisocial behavior. For example, abuse or neglect may encourage the development of certain styles of coping that might be less than adaptive. Characteristics such as a lack of realistic long-term goals, being conning or manipulative, pathological lying, or glibness and superficial charm might begin in the child as a means of coping with an abusive home environment. Childhood victimization might lead to the development of early behavior problems including impulsive behavioral styles that, in turn, translate into inadequate school performance, or less than adequate functioning in occupational spheres. Adaptations that may be functional at one point in development (avoiding an abusive parent or desensitizing oneself against feelings) may later compromise the person's ability to draw upon the environment in a more adaptive and flexible way.

The experiences of early abuse and neglect may lead to bodily changes that, in turn, relate to the development of antisocial behavior. As a result of being beaten continually, a child might become desensitized to future painful or anxiety-provoking experiences. Thus, this desensitization might influence the child's later behavior, making him or her less emotionally and physiologically responsive to the needs of others, callous and nonempathic, and without remorse or guilt. This desensitization may lead to the child's nonresponsiveness to conditioning by punishment (such as found in the psychopath) and ultimately to be associated with the person's need for external stimulation and inability to tolerate boredom. Under these conditions, successful socialization experiences would be unlikely.

Early childhood victimization might also be related to later antisocial behavior through stress mechanisms. Theoretically, if stress associated with abuse or neglect occurs during critical periods of development, then it may give rise to abnormal brain chemistry that may, in turn, lead to aggressive behavior (Eichelman, 1990). Childhood victimization and antisocial behavior may also be in part related through brain neurotransmitters (Lewis, 1992).

Another approach might take the position that the relationship between childhood abuse, neglect, and antisocial behavior is spurious, masking a rather different etiology. For example, Quay

(1977) has argued that the psychopath is born with a biological predisposition to seek external stimulation. Theoretically, parents may react negatively to such a predisposition in their child,[1] with excessively harsh or inconsistent discipline, rejection, or retreat. In turn, the child may react by developing antisocial behavior and personality characteristics associated with psychopathy. Although some evidence exists that infants and young children with different temperaments may elicit different parental behaviors (Bates, 1989) and that children with difficult temperaments may be singled out for abuse (e.g., Friedrich & Boriskin, 1976; Herrenkohl & Herrenkohl, 1981), other researchers have not found this to be the case (e.g., Dodge et al., 1990; Silver, Dublin, & Lourie, 1969).

A final possibility is that antisocial behavior may be an indirect by-product of early childhood victimization. Abuse and neglect may lead to changed environments or family conditions that, in turn, may predispose a person to later antisocial behavior. Thus, antisocial behavior may result not so much directly from these childhood experiences but rather as a result of a subsequent chain of events.

Although a broad range of theories has been offered to explain the potential linkage between childhood victimization and antisocial outcomes, research in the field of child maltreatment is in the early stages of development. Scholars are beginning to identify and empirically validate these fundamental relationships. As part of this development, researchers have called attention to methodological problems that have limited the scientific credibility of past research. These are described briefly next.

METHODOLOGICAL ISSUES

Over the last several years, scholarly reviews of the child maltreatment literature have criticized existing research as methodologically flawed and limited in its generalizability and scientific validity (Aber & Cicchetti, 1984; Berger, 1980; Newberger, Newberger, & Hampton, 1983; Widom, 1989b; Wolfe & Mosk, 1983). Many of these limitations are relevant here.

Definitional Issues

The first problem concerns the lack of specificity in defining predictor and outcome variables. Criteria for child abuse or neglect are often questionable, vary widely, and include unsubstantiated cases. There is also a reliance on second-hand information (e.g., parental reports) rather than on directly observed or validated behaviors. Basic differences in the definitions of, or criteria for, abuse or neglect affect the replicability of the assessment and comparability of research findings.

In some cases, child abuse is limited to a clinical condition

(broken bones or severe physical trauma). In other cases, criteria might refer to a wider range of activities, milder forms of physical punishment, or neglect (the failure to provide adequate food, clothing, shelter, medical attention, or proper care for the child). Few studies use systematic assessment instruments to assess a history of childhood victimization. Indeed, there is no consensus about the way to define or measure child abuse and neglect, concurrently or retrospectively. Despite the fact that numerous instruments are available and are being used, there is relatively little research on their reliability and validity.

Most studies restrict their subjects to victims of excessive physical force by parents, usually in the home environment. Abuse outside the home is rarely addressed, and sexual abuse is typically treated as a separate topic. In some studies, sexual abuse cases are included; in others they are excluded. Age boundaries for definitions of childhood abuse or neglect also vary tremendously.

There is wide variation in the definitions of antisocial and violent behaviors and means of assessment. Few studies have used standardized measurement or assessment techniques to assess antisocial behavior, although there has been greater utilization of standardized measures in the assessment of children and adolescents. For example, many studies use the Child Behavior Checklist (Achenbach & Edelbrock, 1983) as an index of internalizing and externalizing problem behaviors. More recent studies (Luntz & Widom, 1994) have turned to structured interview schedules to assess psychiatric disorders according to the various editions and revisions of the *DSM*.

Delinquency is usually defined as a legal phenomenon and often refers to contact with the police or a court official for unlawful behaviors. However, assessments of antisocial behavior and violence have been based on parental reports or surveys (standardized and nonstandardized), self-reports of violent behaviors, evidence of assaultive and aggressive behaviors, and arrests or convictions for violent offenses. For example, Steinmetz (1986, p. 52) defined violence as "an act carried out with the intention of, or perceived as having the intention of, physically hurting another person." This was operationalized as self-reports of actions ranging from a slap (slight pain) to murder. On the other hand, Strasburg (1978, p. 6) defined violent behavior as arrests for "illegal use or threat of force [against a person]" and this included assault, aggressive assault, robbery, aggressive robbery, gross sexual impositions, rape, arson, threatening behavior, menacing, kidnapping, injury to the person, aggressive burglary, burglary and entering an inhabited building, and murder.

Design Limitations

There is a widespread reliance on correlational studies, with information collected at one point in time. Although a reasonable place to begin inquiries into new areas of investigation, research based on nonexperimental and correlational designs rarely addresses issues of causality, thus introducing ambiguity into understanding the temporal nature of the relationships. Whereas the majority of research is based on the assumption that childhood victimization leads to subsequent antisocial behavior or characteristics, it is possible that some of these characteristics or behaviors precede the abuse or neglect (see earlier discussion of Quay).

---

[1]Patterson and his colleagues (Patterson, DeBaryshe, & Ramsey, 1989; see also Dishion & Patterson, Chapter 20, this volume) have described a model that begins with a troublesome child or parents who lack firmness and skills in discipline, and this leads to coercive cycles of interaction during early childhood. Thus, problems in the home or hyperactivity in the child has an effect on the development of antisocial behavior.

Research on childhood victimization is often limited because of designs that lack appropriate comparison or control groups. Much childhood victimization occurs in the context of multiproblem homes, and child abuse or neglect may be only one of many family problems. The general effects of other family variables, such as poverty, unemployment, parental alcoholism or drug problems, or other inadequate social and family functioning, need to be disentangled from the specific effects of childhood abuse or neglect, particularly in studies of how antisocial behavior develops. For example, in her classic work, Robins (1966) described the adult social and psychiatric status of people who had been referred to a child guidance clinic some 30 years earlier. Robins found that more of the sociopaths had a father who was sociopathic or alcoholic and came from impoverished homes in comparison to other patients. She suggested that the apparent connection between sociopathy and dysfunctional parent-child relationships may be spurious, "occurring only because having an antisocial father simultaneously produces adult antisocial behavior in the children and marital discord between the parents" (p. 179).

Control groups matched on socioeconomic status and other relevant variables become necessary and vital components of this research in order to determine the effect of childhood victimization on later behavior, *independent* of family and demographic characteristics that are frequently found to correlate with problem behaviors (Widom, 1989b). Beitchman, Zucker, Hood, DaCosta, and Akman (1991, p. 538) also concluded that the child sexual abuse literature "has been vague in separating effects directly attributable to sexual abuse from effects that may be due to preexisting psychopathology in the child, family dysfunction, or to the stress associated with disclosure."

Research designs are often weakened by questionable accuracy of information because of the retrospective nature of the data, with information based on remembered accounts of earlier victimization experiences. A significant risk of distortion and loss of information is associated with the recollection of events from a prior time period (Rizley & Cicchetti, 1981; Widom, 1989b; Yarrow, Campbell, & Burton, 1970).

Studies based on retrospective accounts of abuse or neglect are open to a number of potential biases. For example, if asked to recall early childhood events, it is possible that respondents forget or redefine their behaviors in accordance with later life circumstances and their current situation. It is also possible that a person might redefine someone else's behavior in light of current knowledge. Unconscious denial (or repression of traumatic events in childhood) may be at work in preventing the recollection of severe cases of childhood abuse. Thus, despite one's best intentions, there is considerable slippage in accuracy in retrospective reporting (Williams, 1992).

Social desirability is another issue that warrants attention. Given society's disapproval of various forms of family violence, adults who are asked to provide retrospective accounts of their own childhood experiences might reconstruct these histories to be consistent with or to explain their present behavior. This is of concern because, in many of the developmental studies, abusive mothers are often the major source of information about their children. Frequently, this research is based on self-reports by parents (often mothers) who are typically participants, either voluntarily or involuntarily, in groups for abusing parents.

Some researchers have suggested that stress can influence mothers' reports of their children's behavior (Brody & Forehand, 1986; Hughes, 1988). Hughes and Barad (1983) found a pervasive tendency for mothers of abused children to rate their children more negatively than did other observers. A more recent report concluded that the effects of domestic violence cannot be considered without considering the source of information—because levels of agreement among informants are low: "When parents or their partners are abusive, they may consciously or unconsciously prefer not to recognize signs of the damage wrought, whereas children's self-reports may be biased defensively" (Sternberg et al., 1993, p. 50).

These methodological problems pose significant challenges to researchers in the field. Notwithstanding the real difficulties involved, there is an urgent need to develop reliable and valid ways to assess histories of childhood victimization and witnessing violence. There is also a need for prospective, longitudinal studies that extend beyond childhood and adolescence and into adulthood. As Fantuzzo and Lindquist (1989) lamented, it is difficult to distinguish between reactive and more long-term negative sequelae of direct victimization or witnessing violence.

CURRENT FINDINGS

Reflecting the broad scope of this chapter, findings from five general areas of research are summarized: (a) childhood victimization and antisocial behavior (delinquency and adult criminality); (b) childhood victimization and violent behavior; (c) childhood victimization (or specific forms of childhood abuse and neglect) and antisocial personality disorder (psychopathy); (d) problem behaviors in abused and neglected children; and (e) the effects of witnessing violence in the family and in the community.

Childhood Victimization and Antisocial Behavior (Delinquency and Adult Criminality)

An extensive body of research has examined the relationship between childhood victimization and later delinquency (see Garbarino & Plantz, 1986; Widom, 1989b, 1991). Less research has traced the consequences of childhood abuse and neglect into adulthood. In prospective studies that follow adolescents who have been abused or neglected as children, the incidence of delinquency is estimated to be about 20% to 30%. In retrospective studies in which delinquents were asked about their earlier childhood backgrounds, estimates of abuse ranged from approximately 8% to 26% (Widom, 1989b). In general, this body of research suggests that the majority of abused and neglected children did not become delinquent and that the majority of delinquents were not abused or neglected as children. In at least one study (McCord, 1983), rejected male children had higher rates of delinquency than abused, neglected, or loved children.

In an attempt to overcome a number of the methodological limitations in past research, Widom (1989c) used a prospective cohorts design study (Leventhal, 1982; Schulsinger, Mednick, & Knop, 1981) to examine the long-term consequences of early childhood victimization. In this study, substantiated cases of child abuse and neglect from the years 1967 to 1971 in a midwestern metropolitan county area were matched on the basis of age, race, sex, and approximate family social class with a group of children with no official records of abuse or neglect and both groups were followed prospectively into young adulthood.

The prospective nature of this study and the inclusion of a matched control group help to disentangle the effects of childhood victimization from other potentially confounding factors. Because of the matching procedure, the subjects are assumed to differ in the risk factor (i.e., having experienced childhood sexual or physical abuse and neglect). However, it is not possible to randomly assign subjects to groups (and obviously this could not be done); therefore, the assumption of equivalency for the groups is an approximation. (For complete details of the study design and subject selection criteria, see Widom, 1989a.)

Early childhood victimization significantly increased a person's risk for arrest during adolescence by more than 50% (26% vs. 17%). Abused and neglected children also began their official criminal activity approximately 1 year earlier than the control subjects (16.5 years vs. 17.3 years) and had approximately two times the number of arrests. The same pattern emerged for adult criminality. Abused and neglected children were at increased risk of arrest as an adult, in comparison to the control children (29% vs. 21%). In this research, the majority of abused and neglected children did not become delinquents or adult criminals. To what extent do victims of abuse and neglect become violent victimizers when they grow up?

Childhood Victimization and Violent Behavior

Clinical reports and case histories often have reported abuse in the backgrounds of violent or homicidal offenders. Larger and more systematic studies also described relationships between child abuse, neglect, and violent behavior in delinquents and patient groups. After reviewing this literature, however, Widom (1989b) concluded that there was limited support for the "cycle of violence." Some studies did not support the linkage (Alfaro, 1981; Kratcoski, 1982), and at least one study found that abused delinquents were less likely to engage in aggressive crimes (Gutierres & Reich, 1981).

In her own cohorts design study, Widom (1989c) found that abused and neglected children in general were at significantly increased risk for being arrested for a violent crime compared with controls (11% vs. 8%). However, the majority of these individuals did not become violent offenders, suggesting that the "victim-to-victimizer" hypothesis may not be as deterministic as commonly believed.

In sum, research findings provide some support for a connection between child abuse, neglect, and violent behavior, although the findings are not consistent. Discrepancies may be attributed to a variety of factors, including differences in study designs, reliance on self-reports of maltreatment, and different measures to assess antisocial and violent behavior.

Childhood Victimization and Antisocial Personality Disorder (Psychopathy)

Early studies called attention to disturbed family relationships in the childhood backgrounds of psychopaths, and Gregory (1958) concluded that some form of parental loss was fairly common in

persons who later became psychopaths or antisocial. Based on findings from their longitudinal study, McCord and McCord (1964) concluded that emotional deprivation or severe parental rejection was one of the main causes of psychopathy. They also noted that mild rejection, in combination with brain damage or a psychopathic parent, erratic and punitive discipline, or absence of adult supervision, can lead to psychopathy.

It is interesting that a study by Oltman and Friedman (1967) indicated that psychopaths and drug addicts had higher rates of parental loss due to separation (mostly from father) than individuals with other forms of psychiatric disorder. However, they suggested that parental deprivation per se was of less importance in producing psychopathy than the emotional and physical disturbances that most likely preceded the separation: "The parent (usually the father) who deserts his family is presumptively unstable, irresponsible, and heedless of the children. He may be alcoholic, physically abusive, promiscuous, shiftless" (p. 303).

Despite the fairly consistent implication of disturbed family relationships in the backgrounds of psychopaths, not everyone in the field agreed with this notion. In an early version of his classic work on psychopaths, Cleckley (1959) commented that he had not regularly observed any specific type of error in parent-child relationships in the early history of his cases. Cleckley (1964, p. 452) commented: "During all my years of experience with hundreds of psychopaths . . . no type of parent or of parental influence, overt or subtle, has been regularly demonstrable." Likewise, in the fifth edition of his book, Cleckley (1976, p. 24) reiterated his position that he did not believe "obvious mistreatment or any simple egregious parental errors can justifiably be held as the regular cause of a child's developing this complex disorder."

Acknowledging this atypical position adopted by Cleckley, Hare (1970, p. 97) suggested that this may be due to the fact that Cleckley's "patients were largely from middle-class backgrounds where disturbed parent-child relationships may be more subtle and less likely to come to the attention of social agencies and investigators than are similar disturbances that occur in the lower-class family environments."

Others (Hare, 1970; McCord & McCord, 1959) also cautioned against accepting uncritically the parental rejection and inconsistent socialization interpretations of psychopathy because most people who experience these childhoods do *not* become psychopaths. They noted that these childhood experiences may be risk factors for the development of psychopathy, but they are neither necessary nor sufficient conditions.

More recently, Luntz and Widom (1994) reported a significant increase in the risk of subsequent antisocial personality disorder in abused and neglected children when grown up. The data were from Widom's prospective cohorts design study in which abused and neglected children were matched with nonvictimized children and followed prospectively into young adulthood. In 1989 through 1991, 699 subjects were located and administered a 2-hour interview that included a psychiatric assessment using the NIMH Diagnostic Interview Schedule. At the time of the interview, participants ranged in age from 18 to 35 years, with an average age of 27.53 years.

Overall, significantly more of the abused and neglected subjects met the criteria for lifetime ASPD (current or remitted) than the controls (13.5% vs. 7.1%, respectively). Although childhood victims of both sexes were more likely than controls to have ASPD diagnoses, the difference between abused and neglected and control males (20.3% vs. 10.1%, respectively) was statistically significant, whereas the difference between abused and neglected and control females (5.3% vs. 2.6%, respectively) was not. Being abused or neglected as a child was also a significant predictor of the number of ASPD symptoms and the likelihood of being diagnosed with ASPD, despite controls for demographic characteristics of age, sex, race, and socioeconomic status and criminal history.

These findings provide fairly strong empirical support for childhood victimization as an antecedent to ASPD. However, the vast majority of the abused and neglected group did not meet ASPD criteria, and slightly more than 7% of the controls did meet these criteria, suggesting that factors other than childhood victimization play a role in its etiology. For childhood victims of abuse and neglect, protective factors (personal attributes, environmental conditions, biological predispositions, or positive life events) may have acted to mitigate potential negative consequences of their earlier childhood experiences. Some of the control group children may also have experienced punitive or inconsistent parenting, which may not have been severe enough to come to the attention of the authorities at the time but nonetheless was important in the development and maintenance of ASPD.

In a further examination, Luntz and Widom (1995) investigated whether abused and neglected children were also more likely than a matched control group to grow up to become psychopaths as young adults. In this analysis, Luntz and Widom used the PCL-R (Hare et al., 1990) as an index of psychopathy. Victims of childhood abuse and neglect had higher PCL-R scores than nonabused and nonneglected individuals, again, despite controls for demographic characteristics and criminal history. Thus, these new findings support the earlier work and indicate that not only are victimized children at risk for being diagnosed as ASPD, but they are at increased risk for becoming psychopaths. However, these findings also make clear that child abuse and neglect are only one set of factors placing children at risk for developing these disorders.

Problem Behaviors in Abused and Neglected Children

A number of experimental and laboratory studies addressing the relationship between abuse, neglect, and aggressive behavior in young children indicate that abused children manifest aggressive, problematic behavior and conduct disorder, even at early ages (Friedrich & Luecke, 1988; Kolko, Moser, & Weldy, 1990; Rogeness, Amrung, Macedo, Harris, & Fisher, 1986). Abused infants ignored or refused maternal distractions (Wasserman, Green, & Allen, 1983); abused toddlers physically assaulted peers and harassed caregivers (George & Main, 1979); abused children (ages 6 to 7) were more aggressive in fantasy and free play and in school settings (Reidy, 1977); and abused 5- to 12-years-olds were deficient in emotional development, particularly self-concept and aggression (Kinard, 1980). However, there were also the contradictory findings that abused and neglected children did not show differences from comparison group children (Friedrich, Einben-

der, & Luecke, 1987; Rohrbeck & Twentyman, 1986). Some studies reported that physically abused children show higher levels of aggressive behavior than other maltreated children (Hoffman-Plotkin & Twentyman, 1984; Kaufman & Cicchetti, 1989), whereas others suggest that neglected children may be more dysfunctional (Bousha & Twentyman, 1984).

Generally, these studies do not suffer from the same methodological problems as the studies reviewed earlier. In these studies, age groups vary, as do definitions of abuse and neglect. However, abuse and neglect are carefully defined, cases of abuse and neglect are substantiated and validated, and there is less reliance on retrospective data. Assessment strategies range from those that depend exclusively on a mother's report of the child's behavior to those that involve multimodal assessment of behavior, based on teacher and parent ratings and direct observations or assessments of the child's behavior.

Two methodological limitations are of concern in this set of studies. First, a number of the studies were conducted while the child's parent was in treatment or in training programs specifically related to the abuse or neglect incident. Given the earlier discussion and empirically demonstrated role played by social desirability (Herrenkohl, Herrenkohl, & Toedter, 1983), it is possible that abusive parents may redefine their behavior or their description of their child's behavior in line with their current situation. This is particularly problematic when the mother's report is the only source of information about the child. Second, with some exceptions (Egeland & Sroufe, 1981; Martin & Beezley, 1977; Morse, Sahler, & Friedman, 1970), these studies are cross-sectional and the time between the abuse or neglect incident and the laboratory testing or assessment was rather short.

Effects of Witnessing Violence in the Home or Community

Although some studies have reported that the effect of a child's witnessing violence toward parents may be as harmful as the experience of direct victimization (Rosenbaum & O'Leary, 1981), findings from other research have not produced similar results (Christopoulos et al., 1987; Hughes, 1988; Wolfe, Zak, Wilson, & Jaffe, 1986). In some studies children from violent homes showed more externalizing behavior problems than did comparison group children (Jaffe, Wolfe, Wilson, & Zak, 1986; Wolfe et al., 1986). One study found that exposure to marital violence was associated with increased levels of aggression in females only (Forsstrom-Cohen & Rosenbaum, 1985), whereas another study found increased risk of aggressive behavior in school-age boys from violent homes (Hughes & Barad, 1983). Hershorn and Rosenbaum (1985) found no differences between violent and nonviolent groups if the families displayed about the same amount of marital discord. And Wolfe, Jaffe, Wilson, and Zak (1985) found that if concurrent maternal psychological adjustment and family stress and crises were factored in, the differences in the magnitude of externalizing problems between children from violent and nonviolent homes were eliminated.

Fantuzzo et al. (1991) reported that witnessing verbal hostility and physical violence between parents is associated with higher levels of internalizing and externalizing behavior by the child (as measured by parent rating scales) and lower levels of child competence based on direct interviews, compared to witnessing verbal hostility alone. However, Sternberg et al. (1993) found that witnessing spouse abuse did not affect children's evaluations of their adjustment as much as did being a victim of physical abuse or being a victim and witness of spousal abuse.

A new area of research focuses on the effects of witnessing community violence. Clinical descriptive studies have been done following traumatic events, such as sniper attacks (Pynoos & Nader, 1989) or following the experiences of the 26 children kidnapped from their school bus and buried alive (Terr, 1990). Frederick (1985) characterized children traumatized by catastrophic situations as having fears of recurrence, continuing concerns about security, anger, and preoccupations about revenge, among other problems. In play, children have been found to repeat the traumatic themes they have witnessed, particularly those of fear or aggression (Terr, 1990).

Based on their study of young children living in situations of chronic violence, Osofsky and her colleagues (Osofsky, Wewers, Hann, & Fick, 1993, p. 37) described symptoms of "reduced involvement with the external world resulting in constricted affect, fewer interests, and feelings of estrangement." Some of these children developed post-traumatic stress disorder (PTSD), whereas others became angry and violent. These children became more aggressive in their play in imitating behaviors they had seen, showed a desperate effort to protect themselves and to "act tough" to deal with their fear, developed a counterphobic reaction, and acted uncaring because of having to deal with so much hurt and loss. Similarly, in a study of low-income African American youth (ages 7 to 18), Fitzpatrick (1993, p. 530) found that "youths chronically exposed to violence experienced a desensitization process such that these types of daily stressors had little or no impact on their well-being," in contrast to victimization that was positively related to reporting depression symptoms.

It is too early to draw firm conclusions from this new research on the effects of witnessing violence, especially about the relationship between these childhood experiences and adult antisocial behavior. None of these studies has traced these children into adulthood. However, this review has raised a number of provocative issues that warrant further discussion.

CONTROVERSIAL ISSUES AND QUESTIONS

Are Abused and Neglected Children At-Risk for the Development of Multiple Problem Behaviors, Not Exclusively Antisocial Personality Disorder?

Research in the area of childhood victimization has generally not been undertaken to examine the interrelationships among problem behaviors. To what extent are victims of childhood abuse and neglect at-risk for the development of multiple problem behaviors, not just antisocial behavior? For example, the co-occurrence of alcoholism, ASPD, and substance use has been noted among male jail detainees (Abram, 1990). Alcoholics often attempt suicide (Schuckit, 1986), and diagnoses of alcoholism are complicated by

the presence of ASPD, which, in turn, includes components of criminal behavior and sexual promiscuity. Engaging in any one of these behaviors, then, might increase the likelihood of involvement in other at-risk behaviors, and ultimately, the diagnosis of ASPD.

Research has shown an increased risk for abused and neglected children to engage in antisocial behaviors as children and adolescents and to be diagnosed with ASPD in young adulthood (Luntz & Widom, 1994). Because recent work suggests that childhood victims and children who witness extreme violence develop PTSD, what is the relationship between PTSD and ASPD? What causes some children to develop ASPD and others to develop PTSD? Hodge (1992), for example, has proposed that psychopathy has its origins in PTSD, caused by childhood sexual and physical abuse. When do the effects of witnessing violence lead to PTSD and when to ASPD?

Early childhood victimization may increase a person's risk of exhibiting a syndrome of problem behaviors. To what extent are victims of early child abuse or neglect at-risk for the development of problem behaviors in general or specific antisocial outcomes? Some researchers believe that various manifestations of problem behaviors should be considered in terms of a single underlying tendency, often referred to as a *problem behavior syndrome* (Jessor, 1987; Kaplan, 1980; Robins, 1978; Robins & Wish, 1977). Others believe that different sets of problem behaviors represent fundamentally different etiologies (Elliott, Huizinga, & Menard, 1989; Kandel & Andrews, 1987; Kandel, Kessler, & Margulies, 1978; McCord, 1990). These contrasting models have different implications for intervention strategies. Researchers who emphasize syndromes believe that reducing problem behaviors depends on prevention or intervention to influence a common underlying trait. If specific problem behaviors represent specific etiologies, then a single general strategy might fail to reduce the problems of most individuals.

To What Extent Does the Co-Occurrence of Other Problems Influence the Consequences of Victimization and Witnessing Violence?

One of the difficulties in assessing risk for abused and neglected children is the co-occurrence of other problems in the children and their parents. Although certain forms of childhood victimization may represent acute events, child abuse and neglect often occur against a background of more chronic adversity. There is a need to disentangle the effects of childhood abuse and neglect from the impact of other stressors. Children living in abusive and neglectful families may also experience parental separations, the poor physical and emotional health of their caretakers, and the need to cope with financial and social problems, in addition to their own maltreatment or witnessing assaultive behavior. Although shelters provide physical protection for women and children, residential transitions and the separations from fathers, friends, and neighborhoods can also be stressful. To what extent does the presence or absence of other characteristics or adverse events influence a child's response to childhood victimization? Adverse effects may interact with one another, so that the combined effects may be greater than the sum of the effects considered separately (Rutter, 1979).

Are There Gender Differences in the Consequences of Childhood Victimization and Witnessing Violence?

Sex differences in coping responses (Pearlin & Schooler, 1978; Zaslow & Hayes, 1986), in children's responses to marital discord (Emery, 1982), and in manifestations of distress (Dohrenwend & Dohrenwend, 1976; Horwitz & White, 1987; Widom, 1984) have been documented. However, gender differences in the consequences of abuse and neglect have not received much attention, despite the fact that the response of males and females to childhood victimization may be substantively different.

Few studies have directly compared the consequences of child abuse and neglect in males and females, although there may be a number of reasons for this omission. Because males and females may experience different types of abuse, any differences in their responses to maltreatment may be a function of the type of maltreatment rather than gender differences. Early clinical reports of violence primarily describe violent male adolescents. Studies of sexual promiscuity and teenage pregnancy use samples of females and primarily females who were sexually abused. For each of these sex-linked outcomes (violence:male and sexuality:female), studying the nonstereotypic sex may yield important insights.

If sex differences in response to childhood victimization exist, do they parallel gender differences in expressions of psychopathology? Are abused and neglected males more likely than females to be diagnosed ASPD? Are abused and neglected females more likely than males to have diagnoses for substance abuse, depression, or borderline personality disorder?

Recent findings from Widom's cohort study suggest differential long-term consequences of childhood victimization for males and females for at least two diagnoses. In two papers, abused and neglected females were at-risk for subsequent alcohol problems. Widom, Ireland, and Glynn (1995) found a significant relationship between childhood abuse and neglect and subsequent alcohol problems (as measured by a *DSM-III-R* diagnosis for alcohol abuse and/or dependence) for females, but not for males. And this sex difference was also apparent in an analysis of arrests for alcohol and drug offenses (Ireland & Widom, 1994). In contrast, Luntz and Widom (1994) found that abused and neglected males were at increased risk for ASPD, but females were not.

To what extent does the internalization/externalization dimension follow gender lines? In some studies of children who witnessed violence, differences were reported, with externalizing behavior problems more common in males and internalizing behavior problems in females (e.g., Fantuzzo & Lindquist, 1989; Forsstrom-Cohen & Rosenbaum, 1985; Jaffe et al., 1986). However, other researchers have reported little gender variation in symptomatology (Christopoulos et al., 1987; Jouriles, Barling, & O'Leary, 1987; Pynoos et al., 1987; Richters & Martinez, 1992; Sternberg et al., 1993).

In their study of African American youth in the Chicago area, Bell and Jenkins (1993) found that girls were as likely as boys to report having been assaulted or to have seen a stabbing or shooting, although boys reported more frequent involvement in fights than did girls. However, girls were more likely to know of others being victimized across all categories of molestation, rape, rob-

bery, assault, and murder and were more than twice as likely as boys to report that a close other had been murdered: "While we cannot rule out the explanation that these young males, for some reason, are less likely to know about others' victimizations, the findings, nonetheless, raise questions about young black males' perceptions and recall of threatening events" (p. 51).

What Is the Role of Violent Behavior in the Context of a Relationship Between Childhood Victimization and Antisocial Personality Disorder?

Studies have linked child abuse and neglect to violence and child abuse and neglect to psychopathy and ASPD. What is the role of violent behavior in the context of a relationship between childhood victimization and ASPD? Research with male forensic samples has found that psychopathic offenders are more violent than nonpsychopathic offenders (see Hart & Hare, Chapter 3, this volume). In the study by Luntz and Widom (1995), the relationship between childhood victimization and violence was mediated through antisocial personality disorder. On the other hand, violence has not traditionally been identified as a characteristic of psychopathy. Of Cleckley's (1976) 16 defining characteristics, the one closest to suggesting violence is "inadequately motivated antisocial behavior":

> Only a small proportion of typical psychopaths are likely to be found in penal institutions, since the typical patient ... is not likely to commit major crimes that result in long prison terms. ... Though he regularly makes trouble for society, as well as for himself, and frequently is handled by the police, his characteristic behavior does not usually include committing felonies which would bring about permanent or adequate restriction of his activities. (p. 19)

To What Extent Does the Age of the Child at the Time of Victimization or Witnessing Violence Influence Outcomes?

If the child is viewed as a developing organism and not simply a static one, then we can ask how outcomes differ depending on the age of the child when the abuse occurs. The form of children's response to childhood victimization may be influenced by their age and level of development at the time. However, relatively little is known about age-related effects of child abuse and neglect.

If victims are assessed as children, the full extent of the effects of their abuse or neglect may not be manifest. As children grow and develop, new symptoms associated with their earlier abuse or neglect may emerge. It is also possible that age of onset is related to the duration and type of abuse experienced, and this might be confounded with outcomes. Young children may not have suffered the abuse for a long period of time or may not have experienced the use of force and threats that may be more common among some types of abuse in older children and adolescents (Beitchman et al., 1991; Gomes-Schwartz, Horowitz, & Sauzier, 1985; Peters, 1976). Unfortunately, the dimension of time makes discussion of risk factors for subsequent problem behaviors complicated.

Has Neglect Been Neglected?

What is the role of childhood neglect in the development of antisocial behavior? Most of the theories of psychopathy and ASPD have focused on the experiences of physical abuse or extreme physical punishment. Most past research has focused on physical and sexual abuse, with relatively little attention paid to neglect. Some findings suggest that neglect by itself may have serious long-term negative consequences (Bousha & Twentyman, 1984; McCord, 1983; Widom, 1989b, 1989c). Furthermore, indicators of ASPD include "neglect of one's children" (*DSM-IV*). To what extent is there an intergenerational transmission of neglect? The common practice of treating abused and neglected children together, or eliminating one type of maltreatment from study, may reveal only a partial portrait of childhood victims' risk for subsequent problem behaviors. The neglect of neglect is a serious concern because the number of cases of child neglect far outweigh those for physical or sexual abuse in national statistics (Westat, 1988).

CONCLUSIONS AND SUGGESTIONS FOR FUTURE WORK

The study of childhood victimization has been developing rapidly, with increased sensitivity to the limitations of designs based exclusively on retrospective self-reports and increased recognition of the need for more sophisticated research designs with large sample sizes, carefully defined abuse and neglect cases, and incorporation of matched control groups. Increasingly, there is a need for more complicated models of developmental outcomes associated with childhood victimization, as well as a recognition that multiple factors determine outcomes. Ultimately, research in the field needs to move away from its almost exclusive concentration on descriptive studies to more complicated ones of mechanisms, buffers, and mediating factors.

Few studies of abused and neglected children have used methods of assessment and diagnostic criteria that permit simultaneous examination of multiple characteristics and consequences. Studies are needed with sample sizes large enough to examine multiple outcomes while simultaneously controlling for relevant demographic characteristics. In studies of the effects of witnessing violence, whether in the home or in the community, the collection of behavior ratings from multiple sources (e.g., family members, teachers, neighbors, or peers) should be essential elements of research. However, researchers also need to pay attention to what abused and neglected children and child witnesses say about their own adjustment (Sternberg et al., 1993). Researchers must address the challenge of contradictory findings associated with different sources of information. At a minimum, researchers should publish their rules or methods used to resolve such differences.

Very little is known about the role of parents (particularly fathers) in this field. Some abusive parents have been characterized as having low levels of empathy (Friedrich & Wheeler, 1982; Miller & Eisenberg, 1988), poor self-esteem and high impulsivity (Friedrich & Wheeler, 1982), and general behavioral problems and psychological dysfunction (Wolfe, 1985). Although fathers are often not present, the potential contribution of *both* parents' characteristics or psychiatric disorder on the developing child should not be ignored.

In addition, the possibility of a genetic contribution to ASPD should not be left out of this discussion (see relevant chapters in this volume). Because people with ASPD often display behavior characterized by repeated physical fights and assaults, including spouse and child abuse (*DSM-III-R*), the intergenerational transmission of antisocial behavior may overlap substantially with the cycle of violence (Widom, 1989c). Future research needs to consider familial contributions to these relationships.

Two new avenues of research—the effects of witnessing family violence and witnessing community violence—represent important developments in the field. It is hoped that researchers will build on knowledge gained from studies of the consequences of direct exposure to childhood abuse and neglect. An early focus on the link between exposure to violence and PTSD is understandable. However, future researchers should recognize the potential for antisocial behavior among the same children and the potential knowledge to be gained from studying both developmental outcomes.

REFERENCES

Aber, J. L., & Cicchetti, D. (1984). The socio-emotional development of maltreated children: An empirical and theoretical analysis. In H. Fitzgerald, B. Lester, & M. Yogman (Eds.), *Theory and research in behavioral pediatrics* (Vol. 2, pp. 147–199). New York: Plenum.

Abram, K. (1990). The problem of co-occurring disorders among jail detainees: Antisocial personality disorder, alcoholism, drug abuse, and depression. *Law and Human Behavior, 14*, 333–345.

Achenbach, T. M., & Edelbrock, C. S. (1983). *Manual for the Child Behavior Checklist and Revised Child Behavior Profile.* Burlington: University of Vermont.

Alfaro, J. D. (1981). Report on the relationship between child abuse and neglect and later socially deviant behavior. In R. J. Hunner & Y. B. Walker (Eds.), *Exploring the relationship between child abuse and delinquency* (pp. 175–219). Montclair, NJ: Allanheld, Osmun.

American Psychiatric Association. (1994). *Diagnostic and statistical manual of mental disorders* (4th ed. rev.). Washington, DC: Author.

Bandura, A. (1973). *Aggression: A social learning analysis.* Englewood Cliffs, NJ: Prentice Hall.

Bandura, A., & Walters, R. H. (1959). *Adolescent aggression.* New York: Ronald Press.

Bates, J. E. (1989). Applications of temperament concepts. In G. A. Kohnstamm, J. E. Bates, & M. K. Rothbart (Eds.), *Temperament in childhood* (pp. 321–355). Chichester, England: Wiley.

Beitchman, J., Zucker, K., Hood, J. E., DaCosta, G. A., & Akman, D. (1991). A review of the short-term effects of child sexual abuse. *Child Abuse and Neglect, 15*, 537–556.

Bell, C. C., & Jenkins, E. J. (1993). Community violence and children on Chicago's southside. *Psychiatry: Interpersonal and Biological Processes, 56*(1), 46–54.

Berger, A. M. (1980). The child abusing family: I. Methodological issues and parent-related characteristics of abusing families. *American Journal of Family Therapy, 8*, 53–66.

Bousha, D. M., & Twentyman, C. T. (1984). Mother-child interactional style in abuse, neglect, and control groups: Naturalistic observations in the home. *Journal of Abnormal Psychology, 93*, 106–114.

Brody, G. H., & Forehand, R. (1986). Maternal perceptions of child maladjustment as a function of the combined influence of child behavior and maternal depression. *Journal of Consulting and Clinical Psychology, 54,* 237–240.

Christopoulos, C., Cohn, D. A., Shaw, D. S., Joyce, S., Sullivan-Hanson, J., Kraft, S. P., & Emery, R. E. (1987). Children of abused women: I. Adjustment at time of shelter residence. *Journal of Marriage and the Family, 49,* 611–619.

Cleckley, H. (1959). Psychopathic states. In S. Arieti (Ed.), *American handbook of psychiatry.* New York: Basic Books.

Cleckley, H. (1964). *The mask of sanity* (4th ed.). St Louis: Mosby.

Cleckley, H. (1976). *The mask of sanity* (5th ed.). St Louis: Mosby.

Curtis, G. C. (1963). Violence breeds violence—perhaps? *American Journal of Psychiatry, 120,* 386–387.

Dodge, K. A., Bates, J. E., & Pettit, G. S. (1990). Mechanisms in the cycle of violence. *Science, 250,* 1678–1683.

Dohrenwend, B. P., & Dohrenwend, B. S. (1976). Sex differences in psychiatric disorders. *American Journal of Sociology, 81,* 1147–1154.

Egeland, B. E., & Sroufe, L. A. (1981). Developmental sequelae of maltreatment in infancy. In R. Rizley & D. Cicchetti (Eds.), *Developmental perspectives in child maltreatment* (pp. 77–92). San Francisco: Jossey-Bass.

Eichelman, B. (1990). Neurochemical and psychopharmacologic aspects of aggressive behavior. *Annual Review of Medicine, 41,* 149–158.

Elliott, D. S., Huizinga, D., & Menard, S. (1989). *Multiple-problem youth: Delinquency, substance use, and mental health problems.* New York: Springer-Verlag.

Emery, R. E. (1982). Interparental conflict and the children of discord and divorce. *Psychological Bulletin, 92,* 310–330.

Eron, L., Walder, L. O., & Lefkowitz, M. M. (1971). *Learning aggression in children.* Boston: Little Brown.

Fantuzzo, J. W., DePaola, L. M., Lambert, L., Martino, T., Anderson, G., & Sutton, S. (1991). Effects of interparental violence on the psychological adjustment and competencies of young children. *Journal of Consulting and Clinical Psychology, 59,* 258–265.

Fantuzzo, J. W., & Lindquist, C. U. (1989). The effects of observing conjugal violence on children: A review and analysis of research methodology. *Journal of Family Violence, 4*(1), 77–94.

Feshbach, S. (1980). Child abuse and the dynamics of human aggression and violence. In J. Gerbner, C. J. Ross, & E. Zigler (Eds.), *Child abuse: An agenda for action.* New York: Oxford University Press.

Fitzpatrick, K. M. (1993). Exposure to violence and presence of depression among low-income, African-American youth. *Journal of Consulting and Clinical Psychology, 61*(3), 528–531.

Forsstrom-Cohen, B., & Rosenbaum, A. (1985). The effects of parental marital violence on young adults: An exploratory investigation. *Journal of Marriage and the Family, 47,* 467–472.

Frederick, C. (1985). Children traumatized by catastrophic situations. In J. Laube & S. A. Murphy (Eds.), *Perspectives on disaster recovery* (pp. 10–30). New York: Appleton-Century-Crofts.

Friedrich, W., & Boriskin, J. A. (1976). The role of the child in abuse: A review of the literature. *American Journal of Orthopsychiatry, 46,* 580–590.

Friedrich, W., Einbender, A. J., & Luecke, W. J. (1987). Cognitive and behavioral characteristics of physically abused children. *Journal of Consulting and Clinical Psychology, 51,* 313–314.

Friedrich, W., & Wheeler, K. K. (1982). The abusing parent revisited: A decade of psychological research. *Journal of Nervous and Mental Disease, 170*(10), 577–587.

Garbarino, J., & Gilliam, G. (1980). *Understanding abusive families.* Lexington, MA: Lexington Books.

Garbarino, J., & Plantz, M. (1986). Part I: Review of the literature. In E. Gray, *Child abuse: Prelude to delinquency?* (pp. 5–18). Findings of a research conference conducted by the National Committee for Prevention of Child Abuse, 7–10 April 1984. Washington, DC: U.S. Department of Justice, Office of Juvenile Justice and Delinquency Prevention.

George, C., & Main, M. (1979). Social interactions of young abused children: Approach, avoidance, and aggression. *Child Development, 50,* 306–318.

Gomes-Schwartz, B., Horowitz, J. M., & Sauzier, M. (1985). Severity of emotional distress among sexually abused preschool, school-age, and adolescent children. *Hospital and Community Psychiatry, 36,* 503–508.

Gregory, I. (1958). Studies of parental deprivation in psychiatric patients. *American Journal of Psychiatry, 115,* 432–442.

Gutierres, S., & Reich, J. A. (1981). A developmental perspective on runaway behavior: Its relationship to child abuse. *Child Welfare, 60,* 89–94.

Hare, R. D. (1970). *Psychopathy: Theory and research.* New York: Wiley.

Hare, R. D. (1980). A research scale for the assessment of psychopathy in criminal populations. *Personality and Individual Differences, 1,* 111–119.

Hare, R. D., Harpur, T. J., Hakstian, A. R., Forth, A. E., Hart, S. D., & Newman, J. P. (1990). The Revised Psychopathy Checklist: Descriptive statistics, reliability, and factor structure. *Psychological Assessment: A Journal of Consulting and Clinical Psychology, 2,* 338–341.

Herrenkohl, E. L., Herrenkohl, R. C., & Toedter, L. J. (1983). Perspectives on the intergenerational transmission of abuse. In D. Finkelhor, R. J. Gelles, G. T. Hotaling, & M. A. Straus (Eds.), *The dark side of families* (pp. 305–316). Beverly Hills, CA: Sage Publications.

Herrenkohl, R. C., & Herrenkohl, E. C. (1981). Some antecedents and developmental consequences of child maltreatment. In R. Rizley & D. Cicchetti (Eds.), *New directions for child development: Developmental perspectives on child maltreatment* (Vol. 11, pp. 57–76). San Francisco: Jossey-Bass.

Hershorn, M., & Rosenbaum, A. (1985). Children of marital violence: A closer look at the unintended victims. *American Journal of Orthopsychiatry, 55,* 260–266.

Hodge, J. E. (1992). Addiction to violence: A new model of psychopathy. *Criminal Behaviour and Mental Health, 2,* 212–223.

Hoffman-Plotkin, D., & Twentyman, C. (1984). A multimodal assessment of behavioral and cognitive defects in abused and neglected preschoolers. *Child Development, 55,* 794–802.

Horwitz, A. V., & White, H. R. (1987). Gender role orientations and styles of pathology among adolescents. *Journal of Health and Social Behavior, 28,* 158–170.

Hughes, H. M. (1988). Psychological and behavioral correlates of family violence in child witnesses and victims. *American Journal of Orthopsychiatry, 58,* 77–90.

Hughes, H. M., & Barad, S. J. (1983). Psychological functioning of children in a battered women's shelter: A preliminary investigation. *American Journal of Orthopsychiatry, 53,* 525–531.

Ireland, T., & Widom, C. S. (1994). Childhood victimization and risk for alcohol and drug arrests. *International Journal of the Addictions, 29,* 235–275.

Jaffe, P., Wolfe, D., Wilson, S., & Zak, L. (1986). Similarities in behavioral and social maladjustment among child victims and witnesses to family violence. *American Journal of Orthopsychiatry, 56,* 142–146.

Jessor, R. (1987). Problem-behavior theory, psychosocial development, and adolescent problem drinking. *British Journal of Addictions, 82,* 331–342.

Jouriles, E. N., Barling, J., & O'Leary, K. D. (1987). Predicting child behavior problems in maritally violent families. *Journal of Abnormal Child Psychology, 15*(2), 165–173.

Kandel, D. B., & Andrews, K. (1987). Process of adolescent socialization by parents and peers. *International Journal of the Addictions, 22,* 319–342.

Kandel, D. B., Kessler, R. C., & Margulies, R. Z. (1978). Antecedents of adolescent initiation into stages of drug use: A developmental analysis. In D. B. Kandel (Ed.), *Longitudinal research on drug use* (pp. 73–99). New York: Wiley.

Kaplan, H. B. (1980). *Deviant behavior in defense of self.* New York: Academic Press.

Kaufman, J., & Cicchetti, D. (1989). Effects of maltreatment on children's socioemotional development: Assessments in a day-camp setting. *Developmental Psychology, 25,* 516–524.

Kempe, C. H., Silverman, F. N., Steele, B. F., Droegemueller, W., & Silver, H. K. (1962). The battered-child syndrome. *Journal of the American Medical Association, 181,* 17–24.

Kinard, E. M. (1980). Emotional development in physically abused children. *American Journal of Orthopsychiatry, 50,* 686–696.

Kolko, D., Moser, J., & Weldy, S. (1990). Medical/health histories and physical evaluation of physically and sexually abused child psychiatric patients: A controlled study. *Journal of Family Violence, 5,* 249–266.

Kratcoski, P. C. (1982). Child abuse and violence against the family. *Child Welfare, 61,* 435–444.

Leventhal, J. M. (1982). Research strategies and methodologic standards in studies of risk factors for child abuse. *Child Abuse and Neglect, 6,* 113–123.

Lewis, D. O. (1992). From abuse to violence: Psychophysiological consequences of maltreatment. *Journal of the American Academy of Child and Adolescent Psychiatry, 31,* 383–391.

Lippert, W. W., & Senter, R. J. (1966). Electrodermal responses in the sociopath. *Psychonomic Science, 4,* 25–26.

Luntz, B. K., & Widom, C. S. (1994). Antisocial personality disorder in abused and neglected children grown up. *American Journal of Psychiatry, 151,* 670–674.

Lykken, D. T. (1955). A study of anxiety in the sociopathic personality. *Dissertation Abstracts International, 16*(01), 795. (University Microfilms No. 15944)

Martin, H. P., & Beezley, P. (1977). Behavioral observations of abused children. *Developmental Medicine and Child Neurology, 19,* 373–387.

McCord, J. (1983). A forty-year perspective on effects of child abuse and neglect. *Child Abuse and Neglect, 7,* 265–270.

McCord, J. (1990). Problem behaviors. In S. S. Feldman & G. R. Elliott (Eds.), *At the threshold: The developing adolescent* (pp. 414–430, 602–614). Cambridge, MA: Harvard University Press.

McCord, W., & McCord, J. (1959). A follow-up report on the Cambridge-Sommerville Youth Study. *Annals of the American Academy of Political and Social Science, 322,* 89–96.

McCord, W., & McCord, J. (1964). *The psychopath: An essay on the criminal mind.* New York: D. Van Nostrand.

Miller, P. A., & Eisenberg, N. (1988). The relation of empathy to aggressive and externalizing/antisocial behavior. *Psychological Bulletin, 103*(3), 324–344.

Morse, C. W., Sahler, O. J., & Friedman, S. B. (1970). A 3-year follow-up study of abused and neglected children. *American Journal of Diseases of Children, 120,* 439–446.

Newberger, E. H., Newberger, C. M., & Hampton, R. L. (1983). Child abuse: The current theory base and future research needs. *Journal of the American Academy of Child Psychiatry, 22,* 262–268.

Oltman, J., & Friedman, S. (1967). Parental deprivation in psychiatric conditions, III. *Diseases of the Nervous System, 28,* 298–303.

Osofsky, J. D., Wewers, S., Hann, D. M., & Fick, A. C. (1993). Chronic community violence: What is happening to our children? *Psychiatry: Interpersonal and Biological Processes, 56*(1), 36–45.

Patterson, G. R., DeBaryshe, B. D., & Ramsey, E. (1989). A developmental perspective on antisocial behavior. *American Psychologist, 44,* 329–335.

Pearlin, L. T., & Schooler, C. (1978). The structure of coping. *Journal of Health and Social Behavior, 19,* 2–21.

Peters, J. J. (1976). Children who are victims of sexual assault and the psychology of offenders. *American Journal of Psychotherapy, 30,* 398–421.

Pynoos, R. S., Frederick, C., Nader, K., Arroyo, W., Steinberg, A., Eth, E., Nunez, F., & Fairbanks, L. (1987). Life threat and posttraumatic stress in school-age children. *Archives of General Psychiatry, 44,* 1057–1063.

Pynoos, R. S., & Nader, K. (1989). Case study: Children's memory and proximity to violence. *Journal of American Academy of Child and Adolescent Psychiatry, 28,* 236–241.

Quay, H. C. (1977). Psychopathic behavior: Reflections on its nature, origins, and treatment. In I. Uzgiris & F. Weizmann (Eds.), *The structuring of experience* (pp. 371–383). New York: Plenum.

Reidy, T. J. (1977). The aggressive characteristics of abused and neglected children. *Journal of Clinical Psychology, 33,* 1140–1145.

Richters, J. E., & Martinez, P. (1993). The NIMH community violence Project: I. Children as victims of and witnesses to violence. *Psychiatry: Interpersonal and Biological Processes, 56*(1), 7–21.

Rizley, R., & Cicchetti, D. (Eds.). (1981). *Developmental perspectives on child maltreatment.* San Francisco: Jossey-Bass.

Robins, L. N. (1966). *Deviant children grown up.* Baltimore: Williams & Wilkins.

Robins, L. N. (1978). Sturdy childhood predictors of adult antisocial behavior: Replications from longitudinal studies. *Psychological Medicine, 8,* 611–622.

Robins, L. N., & Wish, E. (1977). Childhood deviance as a developmental process: A study of 223 urban black men from birth to 18. *Social Forces, 56,* 448–473.

Rogeness, G., Amrung, S., Macedo, C., Harris, W., & Fisher, C. (1986). Psychopathology in abused and neglected children. *Journal of the American Academy of Child Psychiatry, 25,* 659–665.

Rohrbeck, C., & Twentyman, C. (1986). Multimodal assessment of impulsiveness in abusing, neglecting, and nonmaltreating mothers and their preschool children. *Journal of Consulting and Clinical Psychology, 54,* 231–236.

Rosenbaum, A., & O'Leary, K. D. (1981). Marital violence: Characteristics of abusive couples. *Journal of Consulting and Clinical Psychology, 49,* 63–71.

Rutter, M. (1979). Protective factors in children's response to stress and disadvantage. In M. W. Kent & J. E. Rolf (Eds.), *Primary prevention of psychopathology: Vol. 3. Social competence in children* (pp. 49–74). Hanover, NH: New England Press.

Schuckit, M. A. (1986). Primary men alcoholics with a history of suicide attempts. *Journal of Studies on Alcohol, 47,* 78–81.

Schulsinger, F., Mednick, S. A., & Knop, J. (1981). *Longitudinal research: Methods and uses in behavioral sciences.* Boston: Martinus Nijhoff.

Silver, L. R., Dublin, C. C., & Lourie, R. S. (1969). Does violence breed violence? Contributions from a study of the child abuse syndrome. *American Journal of Psychiatry, 126,* 152–155.

Steinmetz, S. K. (1986). The violent family. In M. Lystad (Ed.), *Violence in the home: Interdisciplinary perspectives* (pp. 51–70). New York: Brunner/Mazel.

Sternberg, K. J., Lamb, M. E., Greenbaum, C., Cicchetti, D., Dawud, S., Cortes, R. M., Krispin, O., & Lorey, F. (1993). Effects of domestic violence on children's behavior problems and depression. *Developmental Psychology, 29*(1), 44–52.

Strasburg, P. A. (1978). *Violent delinquents: A report to the Ford Foundation.* New York: Monarch.

Straus, M. A., Gelles, R. J., & Steinmetz, S. K. (1980). *Behind closed doors: Violence in the American family.* Garden City, NY: Anchor.

Terr, L. (1990). *Too scared to cry: Psychic trauma in childhood.* Grand Rapids, MI: Harper & Row.

Wasserman, G. A., Green, A., & Allen, R. (1983). Going beyond abuse: Maladaptive patterns of interaction in abusing mother-infant pairs. *Journal of the American Academy of Child Psychiatry, 22,* 245–252.

Weiler, B. L., & Widom, C. S. (1996). Psychopathy and violent behaviour in abused and neglected young adults. *Criminal Behaviour and Mental Health, 6,* 253–271.

Westat, Inc. (1988). *Study findings: Study of national incidence and prevalence of child abuse and neglect: 1988.* Washington, DC: U.S. Department of Health and Human Services.

White, S. O., & Straus, M. A. (1981). The implications of family violence for rehabilitation strategies. In S. E. Martin, L. B. Sechrest, & R. Redner (Eds.), *New directions in the rehabilitation of criminal offenders* (pp. 255–288). Washington, DC: National Academy Press.

Widom, C. S. (1984). Sex roles, criminality, and psychopathology. In C. S. Widom (Ed.), *Sex roles and psychopathology* (pp. 187–213). New York: Plenum.

Widom, C. S. (1989a). Child abuse, neglect and adult behavior: Research design and findings on criminality, violence, and child abuse. *American Journal of Orthopsychiatry, 59,* 355–367.

Widom, C. S. (1989b). Does violence beget violence? A critical examination of the literature. *Psychological Bulletin, 106,* 3–28.

Widom, C. S. (1989c). The cycle of violence. *Science, 244,* 160–166.

Widom, C. S. (1991). Childhood victimization: Risk factor for delinquency. In M. E. Colten & S. Gore (Eds.), *Adolescent stress: Causes and consequences* (pp. 201–222). New York: Aldine de Gruyter.

Widom, C. S. (1994). Childhood victimization and risk for adolescent problem behaviors. In M. E. Lamb & R. Ketterlinus (Eds.), *Adolescent problem behaviors* (pp. 127–164). Hillsdale, NJ: Erlbaum.

Widom, C. S., Ireland, T., & Glynn, P. J. (1995). Alcohol abuse in abused and neglected children followed-up: Are they at increased risk? *Journal of Studies on Alcohol, 56,* 207–217.

Williams, L. M. (1992). Adult memories of childhood abuse: Preliminary findings from a longitudinal study. *The Advisor,* Summer, 19–21.

Wolfe, D. A. (1985). Child-abusive parents: An empirical review and analysis. *Psychological Bulletin, 97*(3), 462–482.

Wolfe, D. A., Jaffe, P., Wilson, S. K., & Zak, L. (1985). Children of battered women: The relation of child behavior to family violence and maternal stress. *Journal of Consulting and Clinical Psychology, 53,* 657–665.

Wolfe, D. A., & Mosk, M. D. (1983). Behavioral comparisons of children from abusive and distressed families. *Journal of Consulting and Clinical Psychology, 51,* 702–708.

Wolfe, D. A., Zak, L., Wilson, S., & Jaffe, P. (1986). Child witnesses to violence between parents: Critical issues in behavioral and social adjustment. *Journal of Abnormal Child Psychology, 14,* 95–104.

Yarrow, M. R., Campbell, J. D., & Burton, R. V. (1970). Recollections of childhood: A study of the retrospective method. *Monographs for the Society for Research in Child Development* (Serial No. 138, Vol. 135, no. 5).

Zaslow, M., & Hayes, C. (1986). Sex differences in children's responses to psychosocial stress: Toward a cross-cultural context analysis. In M. E. Lamb, A. L. Brown, & B. Rogoff (Eds.), *Advances in developmental psychology* (Vol. 4, pp. 285–338). Hillsdale, NJ: Erlbaum.

CHAPTER 17

Social Information Processing Mechanisms in Aggressive Behavior

KENNETH A. DODGE and DAVID SCHWARTZ

Analyses of interpersonally aggressive events almost inevitably point to a critical mental process that serves to ignite the aggressive action. For example, during a social exchange, one participant might infer that another person has "dissed" him, thereby justifying retaliatory action. Another participant might evaluate that a potential victim is unlikely to defend herself, thereby leading her to bully the victim. Anecdotal interviews with incarcerated prisoners indicate that such mental processes are crucial parts of the genesis of criminal violence (Toch, 1969). Likewise, experimental studies indicate that the intention of a provocateur as hostile or benign dramatically alters the probability of reactive aggression by the provoked person (Dodge, Murphy, & Buchsbaum, 1984). Even our legal system recognizes the importance of the aggressor's mental processes during criminally violent acts (Dodge, 1991). Highly passionate mental states can constitute a legal excuse for violence, and various attributions of intent, beliefs, and attitudes are associated with different punishments for violent acts.

The theoretical origins of the mental mechanisms of social behaviors are rooted in cognitive structuralist theory (Piaget, 1965), personal construct theory (Kelly, 1955), and attribution theory (Jones & Davis, 1965). Both Bandura (1973) and Berkowitz (1963) feature mental processes as crucial mechanisms in aggressive acts (although they focus on different processes). More recently, social information processing theorists (e.g., Dodge, 1986; Huesmann, 1988) have integrated these concepts into a comprehensive model of the sequential mental actions that mediate the relation between a social cue (such as a provocation) and an aggressive behavioral response. Social information processing models are a subset of the more general cognitive information processing models that have their basis in research on symbol-manipulating processing (Estes, 1991), memory (Underwood, 1969), and problem solving (Newell & Simon, 1972). An important contribution of this model is that it offers a theoretical account of how socialization effects on later aggressive behavior might operate.

The goals of this chapter are to (a) describe a social information processing model of aggressive behavior; (b) review empirical research that demonstrates that individual differences in processing patterns are related to individual differences in aggressive

behavior; (c) examine the origins of aggressogenic processing patterns in children's early developmental histories (especially histories of physical abuse and deviant parenting); and (d) discuss current issues in research on social information processing mechanisms in aggression. These issues include distinctions between reactive and proactive aggression, the role of intelligence in processing, and the relation between biological mechanisms and mental mechanisms. The chapter ends with a call for experimental studies of the relations among socializing experiences, processing patterns, and aggressive behavior, through interventions.

SOCIAL INFORMATION PROCESSING MODELS

Social information processing (SIP) perspectives on aggressive behavior posit that a child's decision to respond aggressively to a particular social stimulus emerges from a systematized series of sequential mental operations. Through these operations, social situations are represented internally and interpreted, and behavioral responses are generated. This cognitive and emotional processing occurs in real time and may reflect both conscious and unconscious operations (see Rabiner, Lenhart, & Lochman, 1990). In either case, processing occurs on an ongoing basis. Individuals continually internalize and respond to new information in their social environment.

A child's behavior in a particular social situation will occur as a direct reflection of his or her mental processing of that situation. Competent SIP will usually result in adaptive social behavior, whereas biased, inaccurate, or ineffective processing will usually lead to more problematic behavior (e.g., antisocial/aggressive behavior). Stable propensities to engage in maladaptive behavior are hypothesized to occur as a function of underlying distortions or deficits in the SIP system.

Much of the recent research on the SIP mechanisms underlying aggressive behavior has been guided by a model initially proposed by Dodge (1986) and later reformulated by Crick and Dodge (1994). This model proposes that there are six processing stages, each of which is characterized by a specific mental operation or set of operations. In this model, processing is presumed to be sequential, but feedback between stages is acknowledged.

Processing Steps

The first stage of processing involves *encoding of social cues* into short-term memory. Encoding is primarily a sensory task that is dependent on the child's perceptual abilities. However, encoding is guided by selective attention. Social situations offer complex arrays of stimuli, and efficiency demands prohibit the encoding of all available information. Thus, children learn to attend selectively to certain cues in their social environment that are of particular relevance or importance. Hypervigilance to threatening cues might lead a child to be perceptually ready to respond with retaliatory aggression.

At the second stage of processing, following encoding of the situation, the child generates an *interpretation of the social cues*. A mental representation of the previously encoded information is formed and stored in long-term memory. This representation is a meaningful abstraction of the situation rather than untransformed sensory input. Attempts to assign meaning to the encoded cues may involve a number of independent processes including causal analysis of the represented events, inferences on the motives and intents of the involved actors, and inferences on the meaning of the event for the self and others. Advances in perspective taking, which accrue with development (Piaget, 1965), should facilitate competent processing at this stage. A child who displays a hostile attributional bias (i.e., a tendency to attribute hostile intent to others under circumstances of ambiguous cues) may be especially likely to respond with aggressive retaliatory behavior.

Once the child has made a meaningful interpretation of the social cues, he or she may assess whether past desired goals have been successfully reached. *Clarification of goals* for the current situation will be the primary mental task of the third stage of processing. Goals may be instrumental (e.g., obtaining an object or position) or interpersonal (e.g., friendship, peer group regard) in nature (Renshaw & Asher, 1983). Goal selection may be influenced by the child's enduring orientation (e.g., an angry child may be more likely to select goals that involve hostile themes), but goals are also influenced by transient circumstances (e.g., fatigue and salience of resources, such as a desired object that a peer possesses) and emotional states (such as frustration or anger). Thus, the likelihood of aggressive action partially depends on the child's goal construction.

Following selection of a goal (or goals) for the situation, the fourth stage of processing focuses on *response access or construction*. This process will typically involve a search of long-term memory for previously learned social behaviors (i.e., scripts; see Huesmann, 1988). A new response may also be constructed. In either case, the generated response might represent a strategy for reaching the previously identified goals or may reflect other aspects of the social situation. A child who has a large repertoire of highly accessible aggressive responses in memory may be likely to engage in aggressive actions.

At the fifth stage of processing, the *response evaluation and decision* stage, children may consider the generated response(s) with regard to a number of criteria. The response will be evaluated with respect to salient dimensions of the child's belief systems, such as beliefs regarding morality (e.g., an aggressive response may be viewed as "bad" or "wrong" if it is inconsistent with a child's moral beliefs). The child will also consider the expected outcomes for the situations. Behavioral responses that are expected to lead to desirable interpersonal, instrumental, or intrapersonal outcomes will be positively evaluated and selected (Crick & Ladd, 1990; Quiggle, Garber, Panak, & Dodge, 1992). The child will also consider efficacy beliefs regarding the behavior (i.e., beliefs about the probability that the generated response can be successfully performed; see Bandura, 1982) and will tend to select responses for which he or she has positive efficacy beliefs (Perry, Perry, & Rasmussen, 1986). Thus, a child who evaluates an aggressive response as morally acceptable, leading to desired outcomes, and easily performed will be likely to select and enact that response. In addition, a child might not engage in active evaluation of a response at all if behavioral inhibition or delay of gratification systems are not well developed biologically or are suspended temporarily (due to fatigue, alcohol, or other causes). In that case, if an aggressive response is the first one accessed from one's repertoire, it will be enacted without regard to its consequences.

At the sixth and final stage of processing, the *behavioral enactment* of the selected response strategy occurs. Enactment often requires sophisticated motor and verbal skills. Children who lack these skills will be unable to perform socially competent behaviors successfully and, as a result, will be negatively evaluated by the peer group (see Dodge, Pettit, McClaskey, & Brown, 1986). A child might resort to aggressive enactments if his or her skills for enacting nonaggressive responses are weak.

Consider the case of a young boy who has just had paint spilled on his art project by a peer. In order to respond to this event, the child must first encode the situation, attending to the relevant social cues and internalizing as much information as possible. The child might, for example, attend to cues about his peer (e.g., facial expression, body posture) as well as other elements of the social context (e.g., position of the teacher in the classroom). A meaningful mental representation of the situation must then be generated (e.g., "The other kid did it on purpose! He is being mean!"), followed by selection of a desired goal for the event (e.g., "I want to get even!"). An appropriate behavioral response will then be generated (e.g., "I'll spill paint on the other kid's art project."). If the child evaluates this response positively (e.g., "Spilling paint is a good thing to do; I know how to do it; it will help me reach my goal of getting even."), he will then attempt to enact the behavior. Processing does not stop with behavior, however. The child continually processes the reactions to his or her behavior, and the pattern is continually repeated in ongoing social interaction.

Latent Knowledge Structures

The described mental processes are presumed to be the proximal mechanisms underlying children's social behavior. Influencing behavior on a more distal level are latent knowledge structures that guide SIP at each stage. Latent knowledge structures (e.g., "scripts," "schemas," "beliefs," and "prototypes") are "abstract representations of information, representations that presumably preserve important and ignore unimportant detail" (Schneider, 1991, p. 532). These structures represent meaningful generalizations of past experiences that are stored in long-term memory. Because human cognition is biased toward the preservation of such structures, children may encode, store, and interpret social stimuli in a manner consistent with their existing schemata (Crick & Dodge, 1994). Knowledge structures also provide children with cognitive heuristics that simplify processing of complex social situations (Schneider, 1991).

A number of theorists have hypothesized that well-crystallized latent knowledge structures are the primary mechanisms underlying the stability of particular patterns of maladaptive behavior. Huesmann (1988), for example, has argued that aggressive behavior becomes highly stable over time because some children "acquire aggressive scripts that tend to be resistant to change" (p. 13). Knowledge structures of this nature may bias or distort SIP at multiple levels.

Because latent knowledge structures incorporate generalizations of past experience, early socialization history presumably plays a central role in the development of aggressogenic cognitive schemata. Experiences that are strongly associated with development of such structures (e.g., early exposure to harsh physical discipline; see Weiss, Dodge, Bates, & Pettit, 1992) are predictive of stable individual differences in aggressive behavior. Early experience is hypothesized to lead to antisocial behavior through the mediating influence of well-crystallized maladaptive patterns of SIP.

SOCIAL INFORMATION PROCESSING CORRELATES OF AGGRESSION

Relatively little work has been done to falsify the entire SIP model. Rather, empirical attention has been placed on using this model to generate falsifiable hypotheses on the processing styles that could be predictive of aggressive behavior. Research efforts to evaluate linkages between biases or deficits in SIP and aggressive behavior have used a number of different methodological approaches. One frequently used approach involves hypothetical social situations that are presented to children in the form of illustrated vignettes or videotaped stimuli with confederate actors. Following presentation of the stimuli, children are asked a series of questions designed to assess their SIP about the hypothetical situation. An advantage is that the stimuli can be structured to assess social cognition about types of situations having particular relevance for social adaptation with peers (see Dodge, McClaskey, & Feldman, 1985; Guerra & Slaby, 1989).

A less common methodology focuses on children's SIP about actual events. This approach incorporates experimental simulation of problematic social situations (e.g., Dodge & Somberg, 1987; Steinberg & Dodge, 1983). Following exposure to such manipulations, children are typically interviewed to ascertain their interpretation of the situation.

Both approaches suffer from potential limitations. The data are often correlational and, as a result, only limited conclusions can be drawn on causal associations between cognition and aggressive behavior. The described methodologies also focus primarily on conscious cognitive processes. However, aggressive behavior is often subconscious or occurs as "automatic processing" (see Dodge, 1986). There may be important differences in children's competency for automatic and conscious processing (Rabiner et al., 1990).

Despite these difficulties, much has been learned from investi-

gation of the social cognitive correlates of aggression. We now briefly summarize the findings of the research in this area. The focus of this discussion is on linkages between aggression and specific deficits or biases in processing at each stage of children's SIP.

Encoding

Competent performance at this stage of SIP involves unbiased encoding of a sufficient number of relevant cues. Aggressive children encode a relatively small number of cues (Dodge & Newman, 1981; Dodge et al., 1986; Finch & Montgomery, 1973; Milich & Dodge, 1984). They attend to fewer cues than do their less aggressive peers, even when the absolute number of available cues is experimentally controlled (Dodge & Tomlin, 1987). Moreover, when confronted with ambiguous social situations, aggressive children seek additional information less frequently than do other children (Slaby & Guerra, 1988). Encoding by these children also appears to be biased toward provocative stimuli. Gouze (1987) found that they selectively attend to hostile cues. Dodge and Frame (1982) reported that aggressive children selectively attend to and recall threatening social cues.

Interpretation of Social Cues

Numerous researchers have found that aggressive children display a marked tendency toward interpreting ambiguous social cues as provocative (this tendency has been labeled a "hostile attributional bias" by Nasby, Hayden, & DePaulo, 1979). Investigators have described linkages between such biases and aggressive behavior in school-age children (Aydin & Markova, 1979; Dodge, 1980; Feldman & Dodge, 1987; Quiggle et al., 1992; Waas, 1988), adolescents (e.g., Guerra & Slaby, 1989), clinical samples (Milich & Dodge, 1984; Nasby et al., 1979), and incarcerated juvenile offenders (Dodge, Price, Bachorowski, & Newman, 1990; Slaby & Guerra, 1988). Hostile attributional biases increase the probability of aggressive responding for both ambiguous and benign stimuli (Dodge et al., 1984). Moreover, aggressive children demonstrate these biases in response to both hypothetical stories (Dodge, 1980) and actual situations (Steinberg & Dodge, 1983).

Goal Selection

Children's goal selection in social situations has been the subject of a number of recent investigations (for a review, see Dodge, Asher, & Parkhurst, 1989). Nonetheless, the focus of much of this research has been on sociometrically rejected children rather than on aggressive children (e.g., Renshaw & Asher, 1983). Although there is a strong association between aggressiveness and peer rejection (Coie, Dodge, & Coppotelli, 1982), not all aggressive children are rejected nor are all rejected children aggressive (Perry, Kusel, & Perry, 1988). Accordingly, only limited conclusions on the types of social goals associated with aggressiveness can be drawn at this point and further investigation on this issue will be needed. Based on the research available, however, it is reasonable to hypothesize that aggressive children might evaluate goals such as dominance and control more positively than more relational goals (as suggested by Renshaw & Asher, 1982). Consistent with this hypothesis, Slaby and Guerra (1988) found that aggressive and antisocial adolescents select hostile goals during interpersonal encounters. Thus, an aggressive adolescent, who is confronted by a peer cheating at a board game, is likely to formulate a goal of retaliation. In contrast, a nonaggressive adolescent would be more likely to formulate a goal of preservation of the social relationship.

Response Access and Construction

When faced with a problematic social situation, aggressive children generate fewer potential responses than do other children (Spivak, Platt, & Shure, 1976). There is also a negative correlation between the number of responses that a child generates and that child's rate of aggression (Spivak & Shure, 1980). It is interesting that the strength of this association appears to decline after the early elementary school years.

For older children, response quality may be a more central issue than response quantity. Investigators have found that aggressive children tend to produce responses that are either hostile in nature (e.g., Deluty, 1981; Dodge et al., 1986; Quiggle et al., 1992; Richard & Dodge, 1982) or ineffective and irrelevant (Dodge et al., 1986). Aggressive children may be particularly prone toward producing maladaptive responses after the first response they generate proves to be ineffective (Richard & Dodge, 1982).

Response Decision

Researchers have consistently found that aggressive children and adolescents evaluate the potential outcomes of aggressive behavior more positively than do their nonaggressive peers. Aggressive children believe that aggression will result in tangible rewards, peer group approval, reduction of aversive consequences, enhancement of self-esteem, and positive feelings (Crick & Dodge, 1989; Guerra & Slaby, 1989; Perry et al., 1986; Slaby & Guerra, 1988). These children also expect that their hostile behaviors will not lead to suffering in their victims (Slaby & Guerra, 1988). Moreover, there is some evidence that aggressive children hold negative outcome expectations for more prosocial behaviors (Crick & Dodge, 1989).

Boldizar, Perry, and Perry (1989) found that aggressive children also value the outcomes of aggression more highly than do nonaggressive children. That is, aggressive children not only evaluate aggressive behavior more positively than do their peers, but also attach greater importance to the potential outcomes of such behavior. In the Boldizar et al. study, aggressive children were found to value control of victims more than nonaggressive children and to attach less importance to the possibility that their behavior would lead to negative interpersonal relationship outcomes.

There is also strong evidence that aggressive children evaluate their ability to engage in hostile behavior more positively than do their nonaggressive peers. Several researchers have reported that aggressive children are characterized by positive efficacy beliefs for aggression (Crick & Dodge, 1989; Perry et al., 1986; Quiggle et al., 1992). Aggressive children also believe that they will have difficulty

enacting behavioral strategies that minimize conflict (e.g., withdrawing from provocative situations; Crick & Dodge, 1989).

Knowledge Structures

As discussed earlier, latent knowledge structures are presumed to influence operations at each of the discussed stages of SIP. Investigators have recently attempted to examine these structures (e.g., Huesmann, Guerra, Miller, & Zelli, 1992). Stromquist and Strauman (1991), for example, asked children to describe peers in their own words and found that aggressive children have richer schema and social constructs in memory on aggression than do other children. Still, further research will be needed before strong conclusions can be drawn about the higher order cognitive structures underlying aggressive behavior.

PROCESSING PATTERNS AS A MEDIATOR OF SOCIALIZATION EFFECTS

Studies have determined that SIP patterns by children within specific types of social situations (e.g., in response to provocations by peers and in response to directives by authority figures) become relatively stable across time during the early elementary school years (Dodge, Pettit, Bates, & Valente, 1995). These patterns begin to act as acquired personality-like characteristics that guide behavior propensities in different situations. The various aspects of processing are not redundant. Instead, they operate relatively independently on a child's behavior, so that processing patterns at each stage provide unique increments in the prediction of aggressive behavior. Thus, profiles of processing patterns have been found to be remarkable predictors of individual differences in aggressive behavior, both concurrently (Dodge et al., 1986; Slaby & Guerra, 1988) and predictively (Dodge et al., 1995; Weiss et al., 1992). Slaby and Guerra (1988) reported that an adolescent's profile of processing patterns accounted for over 80% of the variance in aggressive behavior among incarcerated youth. Dodge and Price (1994) reported a more modest level of association, but nonetheless found that processing patterns do appear to provide unique increments in the prediction of social behavior.

Given that a child's processing patterns appear to represent a proximal path to aggressive behaviors, the origin of these patterns has been given more attention recently (see Widom, Chapter 16, this volume). Crittendon and Ainsworth (1989) hypothesized that chronic child maltreatment may lead a child to develop working models of the social world (identified within the processing model as latent knowledge structures) as a hostile place, which, in turn, might lead a child to be perceptually ready to attribute hostility to others in ambiguous situations. Following these hypotheses, Dodge, Bates, and Pettit (1990) found that an early history of physical abuse of a child by adults is likely to lead a child to become hypervigilant to hostile social cues, to interpret ambiguous cues as hostile, and to generate aggressive responses from memory with great ease.

The experience of social prejudice and discrimination is also predictive of unique patterns of processing social cues. Dodge et al. (1995) found that African American children are relatively likely to display hostile attributional biases and to evaluate the outcomes of aggression as favorable. African American boys are known to be at high risk for mortality in Caucasian-dominated American society. It may be that the experience of discrimination and the presence of danger conspire to lead some children to become hypervigilant. Part of this effect could be explained by socioeconomic status; that is, children from lower socioeconomic backgrounds also demonstrate a hostile attributional bias, and ethnicity correlates with socioeconomic status in this sample. However, even controlling for socioeconomic status, an effect was still found that African American children show a hostile attributional bias.

Events in socialization that lead to aggressogenic processing patterns are also hypothesized to lead to aggressive behaviors. Indeed, early physical maltreatment has long been associated with aggressive behavior outcomes in children (although it has been associated with other outcomes as well; National Research Council, 1993a, 1993b). Recently, Dodge et al. (1995) found that physical abuse in the first 5 years of life is predictive of later externalizing problems in elementary school. Over 28% of the abused group came to display clinically deviant conduct problems (defined as receiving a teacher-rated conduct problem score that was more than two standard deviations greater than the national mean in grade 3 or 4). In contrast, just 6% of the nonabused group developed behavior problems of clinical significance. This predictive relation held, even when other ecological and child factors were controlled statistically, including socioeconomic status, family stressors, and child temperament.

It also has been hypothesized that the mechanism through which early socialization experiences exert an impact on later conduct problems is the mediating impact of acquired processing patterns. That is, early socialization experiences lead a child to process the social world in stylistic ways, which, in turn, lead to behaviors that follow from the processing patterns. Dodge et al. (1995) found that acquired processing patterns involving encoding errors, hostile attributional biases, aggressive response generation, and positive evaluations of the outcomes of aggressing account for a full third of the total effect of early physical abuse on later conduct problems.

ISSUES IN PROCESSING PERSPECTIVES ON AGGRESSION

Subtypes of Aggression

Research on the characteristic SIP styles of aggressive children has provided considerable insight into the proximal mechanisms underlying aggressive behavior. However, theoretical perspectives on aggression and antisocial behavior suggest that topographically and functionally distinct subtypes of aggression exist (e.g., Dodge, 1991; Hartup, 1974; Rule, 1974; see Hinshaw & Zupan, Chapter 4, this volume, for a discussion). The multidimensional nature of aggression is important to consider because different mental processes may underlie each of the distinct forms.

One general subtype of aggression has theoretical roots in the frustration-aggression model (Berkowitz, 1963; Dollard, Doob,

Miller, Mowerer, & Sears, 1939). This subtype, labeled *reactive aggression* by Dodge and Coie (1987), is an angry retaliatory response to a perceived provocation. Reactive aggression is a "hot-blooded" behavior that is motivated by underlying states of anger and frustration (Price & Dodge, 1989). Because reactively aggressive behavior is contingent on perception of a threat, the primary social cognitive mechanisms underlying it are hypothesized to involve encoding and interpretation of cues. Inappropriate displays of reactive aggression are, therefore, presumed to be associated with difficulties in intention-cue interpretation (as suggested by Dodge, 1991).

Theorists also have described a second form of aggression that is goal directed and unprovoked and does not involve underlying states of anger (e.g., Dodge, 1991). The theoretical roots of this subtype, labeled *proactive aggression* by Dodge and Coie (1987), are in social learning theory (e.g., Bandura, 1973). Proactive aggression is acquired and maintained through positive environmental contingencies. Accordingly, the underlying mental mechanisms are presumed to involve positive evaluation of aggressive strategies (see Perry et al., 1986). Children who frequently display proactive aggression behavior are, therefore, hypothesized to have positive efficacy and outcome beliefs for such behaviors.

Evidence supporting these hypotheses has been generated by research on the social cognitive attributes of children whose aggressive behavior is characterized more predominately by one subtype of aggression than the other. Dodge and Coie (1987), for example, found that reactively aggressive children are more prone toward hostile attributional biases than are proactively aggressive children. This finding was later replicated by Crick and Dodge (1996). Crick and Dodge also found that, compared to other children, proactively aggressive children hold more positive outcome expectancies for aggressive behavior and more often identify instrumental goals for social situations, in contrast with social relationship goals. For example, a proactively aggressive child is more likely to endorse a goal of winning a game than maintaining a positive relationship with a peer competitor.

Studies examining dimensional relations between individual differences in social cognition and aggressive behavior also have provided supporting data. In an investigation of the social behavior of elementary school boys in a contrived play group setting, Dodge and Coie (1987) found a positive correlation between hostility of attributional bias and observed rates of reactively aggressive behavior. Rates of proactive aggression were, in contrast, not correlated with attributional bias. Using a similar design, Schwartz and colleagues (Schwartz et al., 1995) later found that rates of reactive aggression are positively correlated with hostility of attributional bias but not correlated with outcome expectancies for aggression. In contrast, Schwartz et al. reported that rates of proactive aggression are positively correlated with outcome expectancies of aggression but not correlated with attributional bias. Taken together, the results of these studies support the hypothesis that different mental processes underlie each of the two general subtypes of aggression. The SIP mechanisms underlying reactively aggressive behavior appear to involve encoding and interpretation of social situations. Proactive aggression appears to be more closely associated with positive evaluations of aggressive behavior at the response decision stage of SIP (see Crick &

Dodge, 1994). Distortions or deficits in processing at these specific stages might, therefore, be associated with maladaptive displays of the relevant subtype of aggression.

Although the SIP mechanisms for each subtype of aggression may predominately involve specific classes of cognitive operations, it should be emphasized that aggressive behavior is determined by processing at multiple stages. For example, high rates of reactively aggressive behavior are presumed to be associated with hostile attributional biases (Dodge, 1991). However, such biases may lead to a more submissive-victimized behavioral profile when accompanied by unusually negative outcome expectancies for aggressive and assertive behavior (Schwartz et al., 1995). Hostile attributional biases also may be associated with depression when accompanied by internal, stable, and global attributions for negative peer group outcomes (Quiggle et al., 1992).

Independent converging evidence about the importance of this subtyping comes from work by Atkins and Stoff. In a laboratory study (Atkins & Stoff, 1993), they found that attention deficits were related to the display of hostile aggression (angry reactions to experimenter-induced frustration) but not instrumental aggression (proactively using aggressive acts to impede the progress of a competitor). A second study (Atkins, Stoff, Osborne, & Brown, 1993) showed that hostile (reactive) aggression is correlated more specifically with poor impulse control (in contrast with instrumental aggression, which is not related to impulse control).

Remaining to be identified are the early socialization experiences and biological markers that lead to individual differences in reactive and proactive aggression (through the mediating influence of social cognitive mechanisms). There may be distinct socialization pathways to each subtype. Dodge (1991) has hypothesized that the hostile attributional biases displayed by reactively aggressive children are associated with early histories of physical abuse and harsh discipline, whereas the positive evaluation of aggressive behaviors displayed by proactively aggressive children are linked to early histories of exposure to aggressive role models. Although further research on these hypothesized pathways is needed, recent studies have provided support for this formulation (Dodge, Lochman, Harnish, Bates, & Pettit, 1997).

Discriminant Validity of Processing From Intelligence

The mental actions depicted in models of social information processing are similar in some respects to actions involved in intelligent behavior. Indeed, it can be postulated that social information processing models describe social intelligence. Theoretically, it is important to determine whether the processes captured in assessments of SIP provide incremental prediction of aggressive behavior beyond the prediction afforded by intelligence itself. Two studies have shown that SIP assessments do provide this unique incremental prediction.

Dodge, Murphy, and Buchsbaum (1984) assessed children's skills in interpreting peers' intentions (called intention-cue detection skill) using a procedure that required children to discriminate among various intentions depicted through videorecorded social vignettes. They speculated that this skill should predict social behavior above and beyond any prediction afforded by children's generic skills at discrimination (specifically, their skills at dis-

criminating among geometric shapes). After controlling for generic discrimination skill, intention-cue detection skill did predict social behavior.

Waldman (1988) used a similar measure of children's intention-cue detection skill. He found that even after controlling for a general measure of intelligence, this measure significantly predicted children's aggressive behavior. Thus, it appears that although the processes being measured in assessments of social information processing are conceptually consistent with formulations of general intelligence, they are distinct from general intelligence and provide unique information in predicting children's aggressive behavior.

On the Relation Between Biological Mechanisms and Mental Mechanisms

One of the misinterpretations of models of social information processing is that they represent a nonbiological alternative to biological models of aggressive behavior. No such inference is warranted. In fact, SIP models, like biological models, posit brain mechanisms for aggressive actions. We hypothesize that genetic, constitutional, and acquired biological predictors of antisocial behavior operate through the mediating mechanism of social information processing. It is doubtful that genetic influences operate directly on aggressive behavior; rather, they operate through impulsivity, delay of gratification, or other tendencies (Raine, 1994). Impulsivity and delay of gratification are operationalized in SIP models as the tendency to select for enactment the first behavioral response accessed from memory, without regard to an evaluation of its likely consequences. We would predict that a genetic predictor of aggressive behavior may be mediated, at least in part, by a measure of this response decision heuristic. Likewise, a constitutional predictor of antisocial behavior has been hypothesized as a difficult, fussy temperament (Bates, Freeland, & Lounsbury, 1979). This characteristic might well be operationalized within an SIP model as a tendency to interpret situations as negative. Therefore, it is hypothesized that fussy temperament may lead to aggressive behavior through a tendency to interpret social stimuli as negative, threatening, or hostile. An acquired biological risk for antisocial behavior (such as through a lack of oxygen at birth or toxic poisoning) might lead to attention deficits that are associated with aggressive behaviors. Attention deficits are operationalized in an SIP model as deficits in encoding skill. Thus, biological risk factors may operate on antisocial outcomes through mechanisms of social information processing.

Finally, we note that mental operations leading to aggressive behavior may also have biological effects. An attribution that another person is being hostile or that one is under threat might well lead to heart rate and hormonal changes as the individual's biological stress response is initiated. In the long term, repeated appraisals of the world as a hostile place might have lasting effects on blood pressure, heart disease, and even survival (Barefoot, Dodge, Peterson, Dahlstrom, & Williams, 1989).

Empirical research has begun to emerge on the relation between mental and biological mechanisms for aggressive behavior (see Raine, Chapter 27, this volume). Perhaps the rhetoric of antagonism between these models at a theoretical level has contributed to the lack of empirical inquiry. We can only work toward a synthesis in future years that depicts the interactive relations between these variables.

IMPLICATIONS FOR INTERVENTION

The general hypothesis that social cognitive factors play a role in aggressive behavior problems has led to numerous attempts at intervention (see Reid and Eddy, Chapter 32; Southam-Gerow & Kendall, Chapter 36; Guerra, Attar, & Weissberg, Chapter 35; and Tolan & Gorman-Smith, Chapter 38, all in this volume). Chandler (1973) was one of the first to try to teach juvenile delinquents skills of perspective taking and understanding social cues, and Spivack et al. (1976) were pioneers in the teaching of social problem-solving skills to young behavior-problem children. More recently, Hudley and Graham (1993) developed an intervention for aggressive African American boys to reduce their tendency to make hostile attributions. The intervention included three components: (a) role play and discussion designed to help boys learn how to detect others' intentions accurately (e.g., some sessions focused on reading facial expression); (b) brainstorming and discussion designed to help boys generate nonhostile interpretations to negative events; and (c) teaching boys decision rules that lead to nonaggressive behaviors (e.g., "When I don't have the information to tell what he meant, I should act as if it were an accident."). Randomly assigned aggressive boys who received this intervention became less likely than were control group boys to attribute hostile intent in both hypothetical and laboratory-simulation settings and were rated as less aggressive by their teachers following treatment.

The meta-analysis by Lipsey (1992) suggests that structured treatments such as skills training lead to an average of a 24% reduction from the 50% recidivism rate of control groups (i.e., expected change from 50% to 38% recidivism). Even though Kazdin (1995) concluded that problem-solving skills training represents "an extremely promising approach" (p. 81) to treatment with reliable changes being demonstrated, he also notes that many treated youths improve but remain outside the range of normative functioning (Kazdin, Siegel, & Bass, 1992). A major reason for this problem may be that most treatments focus on only one component of social information processing (e.g., attributions *or* problem solving but not both). Because aggressive behavior occurs as a function of a cascade of processes, a multicomponent intervention may be required to achieve lasting change. Guerra and Slaby (1990) used an SIP model of multiple cognitive steps in aggression to develop a multifaceted treatment program for incarcerated violent adolescents. Randomly assigned recipients of this treatment, administered in small group sessions, demonstrated significant reductions in aggressive behavior, with no change in the control group. Furthermore, changes in aggressive behavior were directly related to intervening changes in social cognitive variables in the treated group.

Another promising approach has been initiated by Hammond (1991; Hammond & Yung, 1991), who has developed the Positive Adolescent Choices Training (PACT) program for African American youth to reduce their risk for becoming perpetrators or victims of violence. His program involves cognitive-behavioral training to improve multiple skills, including problem identification, anger reduction, problem solving, and negotiation. The treatment is administered in small groups using specially prepared videotapes about common but provocative social situations. The group of randomly assigned middle school students who received 20 hours of training demonstrated an 18% juvenile court referral rate in the 3 years following training, in contrast with a 49% juvenile court referral rate for the control group (Hammond & Yung, 1993).

Because the forces that act on children's social information processing are many, we suggest that the most long-lasting effects will come from interventions that are prevention oriented and include components that focus on parenting, peer relations, and academic achievement, in addition to direct focus on social information processing. One example is the FAST Track intervention directed toward aggressive first graders at high risk for conduct disorder (Conduct Problems Prevention Research Group, 1992). Yet another implication of the discriminant validity of reactive (hostile) aggression and proactive (instrumental) aggression is that different interventions might be appropriate for each type of problem. Interventions directed at reactive aggression should focus on impulsivity, attention, and perceptions of stimuli, whereas interventions directed at proactive aggression should focus on problem solving and outcome expectancies.

CONCLUSIONS AND IMPLICATIONS

Social information processing models have provided researchers with hypotheses on proximal predictors of aggressive behavior. Measures of social information processing have been developed and found to correlate with antisocial behavior both at the level of the single aggressive act as well as at the level of enduring individual differences. The magnitude of relation between a processing variable and aggressive behavior has typically been modest and context specific; however, profiles of processing patterns across situations have been strongly predictive of aggressive behavior patterns. Moreover, measures of processing have been found to mediate the effects of socialization experiences (such as early physical abuse) on later conduct problems, thus supporting their hypothesized role as proximal mechanisms of aggressive actions.

Future theory and research in this area must be devoted to at least four thorny dilemmas. First is the need for integration between mental mechanisms and biological mechanisms in aggressive behaviors (Newman, Chapter 30, this volume; Raine, Chapter 27, this volume). These mechanisms may have reciprocal effects as well as operate simultaneously, but the empirical research is lacking. Studies of psychophysiological, hormonal, and brain wave correlates of SIP actions are needed.

Second, the origins of SIP patterns are not well understood. Studies of the outcomes of early physical abuse offer insight into how SIP patterns develop, but studies of other socializing and biological experiences are needed. As examples, early out-of-home day care has been found to be a predictor of antisocial behavior in children (Belsky & Eggebeen, 1991), but the mechanisms of this effect are not understood and might well lie in the way that children learn to process social information; likewise, genetic influences on aggression have been posited (e.g., Lytton, 1990), but the mechanisms of this influence are not known (Carey & Goldman, Chapter 23, this volume). Processing patterns offer a theoretical link between genes and aggression, but this path awaits empirical inquiry.

Third, little research has examined the role of SIP patterns in understanding age- and gender-related effects on rates of aggressive behavior. It is hypothesized that much of the gender difference in aggressive behavior will be linked to gender differences in social information processing patterns. Likewise, it is hypothesized that decreases in the commission of violent acts during adult development are associated with changes in the way that persons process social information. These hypotheses, and this level of analysis, have received little attention to date.

Finally, a major problem in this area is the lack of experimental studies of the relation between social information processing and aggressive behavior. One of the few studies performed manipulated children's expectancies about an upcoming social interaction and found significant effects on children's subsequent behavioral outcomes (Rabiner & Coie, 1989). More research is needed at the level of specific, transient, processing-behavior linkages and at the level of enduring individual differences in processing and aggressive behavior. The latter type of study is an intervention experiment, in which clinical efforts to change the way that children process social information (through social skills training, cognitive-behavioral therapy, or other efforts) are evaluated by their effects on children's aggressive behavior. When these studies are conducted, empirical analyses of the effects of the experimental intervention must be coupled with analyses of the impact of the intervention through mediating influences, such as changes in SIP patterns across time.

REFERENCES

Atkins, M. S., & Stoff, D. M. (1993). Instrumental and hostile aggression in childhood disruptive behavior disorders. *Journal of Abnormal Child Psychology, 21,* 165–178.

Atkins, M. S., Stoff, D. M., Osborne, M., & Brown, K. (1993). Distinguishing instrumental and hostile aggression: Does it make a difference? *Journal of Abnormal Child Psychology, 21,* 355–365.

Aydin, O., & Markova, I. (1979). Attribution tendencies of popular and unpopular children. *British Journal of Social and Clinical Psychology, 18,* 291–298.

Bandura, A. (1973). *Aggression: A social learning analysis.* Englewood Cliffs, NJ: Prentice Hall.

Bandura, A. (1982). Self-efficacy mechanism in human agency. *American Psychologist, 37,* 122–147.

Barefoot, J. C., Dodge, K. A., Peterson, B. L., Dahlstrom, W. G., & Williams, R. B., Jr. (1989). The Cook-Medley hostility scale: Item content and ability to predict survival. *Psychosomatic Medicine, 51,* 46–57.

Bates, J. E., Freeland, C. B., & Lounsbury, M. L. (1979). Measurement of infant difficultness. *Child Development, 50,* 794–803.

Belsky, J., & Eggebeen, D. (1991). Early and extensive maternal employment/child care and 4–6 year olds' socioemotional development: Children of the National Longitudinal Study of Youth. *Journal of Marriage and the Family, 53,* 1083–1098.

Berkowitz, L. (1963). *Aggression: A social learning analysis.* Englewood Cliffs, NJ: Prentice Hall.

Boldizar, J. P., Perry, D. G., & Perry, L. C. (1989). Outcome values and aggression. *Child Development, 60,* 571–579.

Chandler, M. J. (1973). Egocentrism and antisocial behavior: The assessment and training of social perspective taking skills. *Developmental Psychology, 9,* 326–332.

Coie, J. D., Dodge, K. A., & Coppotelli, J. (1982). Dimensions of types of social status: A cross-age perspective. *Developmental Psychology, 18,* 557–560.

Conduct Problems Prevention Research Group. (1992). A developmental and clinical model for the prevention of conduct disorder: The FAST Track Program. *Development and Psychopathology, 4,* 509–527.

Crick, N. R., & Dodge, K. A. (1989). Children's evaluations of peer entry and conflict situations: Social strategies, goals, and outcome expectations. In B. Schneider, J. Nadel, G. Attili, & R. Weissberg (Eds.), *Social competence in developmental perspective* (pp. 396–399). Dordrecht, The Netherlands: Kluwer.

Crick, N. R., & Dodge, K. A. (1994). A review and reformulation of social information-processing mechanisms in children's social adjustment. *Psychological Bulletin, 1,* 74–101.

Crick, N. R., & Dodge, K. A. (1996). Social information-processing mechanisms in reactive and proactive aggression. *Child Development, 67,* 993–1002.

Crick, N. R., & Ladd, G. W. (1990). Children's perception of the outcomes of aggressive strategies: Do the ends justify being mean? *Developmental Psychology, 26,* 612–620.

Crittendon, P. M., & Ainsworth, M. D. S. (1989). Child maltreatment and attachment theory. In D. Cicchetti & V. Carlson (Eds.), *Child maltreatment: Theory and research on the causes and consequences of child abuse and neglect* (pp. 432–463). New York: Cambridge University Press.

Deluty, R. H. (1981). Alternate-thinking ability of aggressive, assertive, and submissive children. *Cognitive Therapy and Research, 5,* 309–312.

Dodge, K. A. (1980). Social cognition and children's aggressive behavior. *Child Development, 51,* 162–170.

Dodge, K. A. (1986). A social information processing model of social competence in children. In M. Perlmutter (Ed.), *The Minnesota symposium on child psychology* (Vol. 18, pp. 77–125). Hillsdale, NJ: Erlbaum.

Dodge, K. A. (1991). The structure and function of reactive and proactive aggression. In D. Pepler & K. Rubin (Eds.), *The development and treatment of childhood aggression* (pp. 201–218). Hillsdale, NJ: Erlbaum.

Dodge, K. A., Asher, S. R., & Parkhurst, J. T. (1989). Social life as a goal coordination task. In C. Ames & R. Ames (Eds.), *Research on motivation in education* (Vol. 3, pp. 107–135). San Diego, CA: Academic Press.

Dodge, K. A., Bates, J. E., & Pettit, G. S. (1990). Mechanisms in the cycle of violence. *Science, 250,* 1678–1683.

Dodge, K. A., & Coie, J. D. (1987). Social information-processing factors in reactive and proactive aggression in children's playgroups. *Journal of Personality and Social Psychology, 53,* 1146–1158.

Dodge, K. A., & Frame, C. L. (1982). Social-cognitive biases and deficits in aggressive boys. *Child Development, 53,* 620–635.

Dodge, K. A., Lochman, J. E., Harnish, J. D., Bates, J. E., & Pettit, G. S. (1997). Reactive and proactive aggression in school children and psychiatrically impaired chronically assaultive youth. *Journal of Abnormal Psychology, 106*(1), 37–51.

Dodge, K. A., McClaskey, C. L., & Feldman, E. (1985). A situational approach to the assessment of social competence in children. *Journal of Consulting and Clinical Psychology, 53,* 344–353.

Dodge, K. A., Murphy, R. R., & Buchsbaum, K. (1984). The assessment of intention-cue detection skills in children: Implications for developmental psychopathology. *Child Development, 55,* 163–173.

Dodge, K. A., & Newman, J. P. (1981). Biased decision making processes in aggressive boys. *Journal of Abnormal Psychology, 90,* 375–379.

Dodge, K. A., Pettit, G. S., Bates, J. E., & Valente, E. (1995). Social-information-processing patterns partially mediate the effect of early physical abuse on later conduct problems. *Journal of Abnormal Psychology, 104,* 632–643.

Dodge, K. A., Pettit, G. S., McClaskey, C. L., & Brown, M. M. (1986). Social competence in children. *Monographs of the Society for Research in Child Development, 51* (2, Serial No. 213).

Dodge, K. A., & Price, J. M. (1994). On the relation between social information processing and socially competent behavior in early school-aged children. *Child Development, 65,* 1385–1397.

Dodge, K. A., Price, J. M., Bachorowski, J. A., & Newman, J. P. (1990). Hostile attributional biases in severely aggressive adolescents. *Journal of Abnormal Psychology, 99,* 385–392.

Dodge, K. A., & Somberg, D. R. (1987). Hostile attributional biases among aggressive boys are exacerbated under conditions of threats to the self. *Child Development, 58,* 213–224.

Dodge, K. A., & Tomlin, A. M. (1987). Utilization of self-schemas as a mechanism of interpretational bias in aggressive children. *Social Cognition, 5,* 280–300.

Dollard, J., Doob, C. W., Miller, N. E., Mowrer, O. H., & Sears, R. R. (1939). *Frustration and aggression.* New Haven, CT: Yale University Press.

Estes, W. K. (1991). Cognitive architectures from the standpoint of an experimental psychologist. *Annual Review of Psychology, 42,* 1–28.

Feldman, E., & Dodge, K. A. (1987). Social information processing and sociometric status: Sex, age, and situational effects. *Journal of Abnormal Child Psychology, 15,* 211–227.

Finch, A. J., & Montgomery, L. E. (1973). Reflection-impulsivity and information seeking in emotionally disturbed children. *Journal of Abnormal Child Psychology, 1,* 358–362.

Gouze, K. R. (1987). Attention and social problem solving as correlates of aggression in preschool males. *Journal of Abnormal Child Psychology, 15,* 181–197.

Guerra, N. G., & Slaby, R. C. (1989). Evaluative factors in social problem solving by aggressive boys. *Journal of Abnormal Child Psychology, 17,* 277–289.

Guerra, N. G., & Slaby, R. C. (1990). Cognitive mediators of aggression in adolescent offenders: 2. Intervention. *Developmental Psychology, 26,* 269–277.

Hammond, R. (1991). *Dealing with anger: Givin' it, takin' it, workin' it out.* Champaign, IL: Research Press.

Hammond, R., & Yung, B. (1991). Preventing violence in at-risk African-American youth. *Journal of Health Care for the Poor and Underserved, 2,* 359–373.

Hammond, R., & Yung, B. (1993). *Evaluation and activity report: Positive adolescent choices training.* Unpublished grant report, U.S. Maternal and Child Health Bureau.

Hartup, W. W. (1974). Aggression in childhood: Developmental perspectives. *American Psychologist, 29,* 336–341.

Hudley, C., & Graham, S. (1993). An attributional intervention to reduce peer-directed aggression among African-American boys. *Child Development, 64,* 124–138.

Huesmann, L. R. (1988). An information processing model for the development of aggression. *Aggressive Behavior, 14,* 13–24.

Huesmann, L. R., Guerra, N. G., Miller, L., & Zelli, A. (1992). The role of social norms in the development of aggression. In H. Zumkley & A. Ffraczek (Eds.), *Socialization and aggression* (pp. 139–151). New York: Springer-Verlag.

Jones, E. E., & Davis, K. E. (1965). From acts to dispositions: The attribution process in person perception. In L. Berkowitz (Ed.), *Advances in experimental social psychology* (Vol. 2, pp. 220–266). New York: Academic Press.

Kazdin, A. E. (1995). *Conduct disorders in childhood and adolescence.* Thousand Oaks, CA: Sage Publications.

Kazdin, A. E., Siegel, T., & Bass, D. (1992). Cognitive problem-solving skills training and parent management training in the treatment of antisocial behavior in children. *Journal of Consulting and Clinical Psychology, 60,* 733–747.

Kelly, G. A. (1955). *The psychology of personal constructs.* New York: Norton.

Lipsey, M. W. (1992). *The effects of treatment on juvenile delinquents: Results from meta-analysis.* Presentation to the NIMH Meeting for Potential Applicants for Research to Prevent Youth Violence, Bethesda, MD.

Lytton, H. (1990). Child and parent effects in boys' conduct disorder: A reinterpretation. *Developmental Psychology, 26,* 683–697.

Milich, R., & Dodge, K. A. (1984). Social information processing in child psychiatric populations. *Journal of Abnormal Child Psychology, 12,* 471–490.

Nasby, W., Hayden, B., & DePaulo, B. M. (1979). Attributional biases among aggressive boys to interpret unambiguous social stimuli as displays of hostility. *Journal of Abnormal Psychology, 89,* 459–468.

National Research Council. (1993a). *Understanding child abuse and neglect.* Washington, DC: National Academy Press.

National Research Council. (1993b). *Understanding and preventing violence.* Washington, DC: National Academy Press.

Newell, A., & Simon, H. A. (1972). *Human problem solving.* Englewood Cliffs, NJ: Prentice Hall.

Perry, D. G., Kusel, S. J., & Perry, L. C. (1988). Victims of peer aggression. *Developmental Psychology, 24,* 807–814.

Perry, D. G., Perry, L. C., & Rasmussen, P. (1986). Cognitive social learning mediators of aggression. *Child Development, 57,* 700–711.

Piaget, J. (1965). *The moral judgment of the child.* London: Kegan Paul.

Price, J. M., & Dodge, K. A. (1989). Reactive and proactive aggression in childhood: Relations to peer status and social context dimensions. *Journal of Abnormal Child Psychology, 4,* 455–471.

Quiggle, N., Garber, J., Panak, W. F., & Dodge, K. A. (1992). Social-information processing in aggressive and depressed children. *Child Development, 63,* 1305–1320.

Rabiner, D. L., & Coie, J. D. (1989). Effect of expectancy inductions on rejected children's acceptance by unfamiliar peers. *Developmental Psychology, 25,* 450–457.

Rabiner, D. L., Lenhart, L., & Lochman, J. E. (1990). Automatic versus reflective social problem solving in relation to children's sociometric status. *Developmental Psychology, 26,* 1010–1016.

Raine, A. (1994). *The psychopathology of crime.* San Diego: Academic Press.

Renshaw, P. D., & Asher, S. R. (1982). Social competence and peer status: The distinction between goals and strategies. In K. Rubin & H. Ross (Eds.), *Peer relationships and social skills in children* (pp. 375–396). New York: Springer-Verlag.

Renshaw, P. D., & Asher, S. R. (1983). Children's goals and strategies for social interaction. *Merrill-Palmer Quarterly, 29,* 353–374.

Richard, B. A., & Dodge, K. A. (1982). Social maladjustment and problem solving in school-aged children. *Journal of Consulting and Clinical Psychology, 50,* 226–233.

Rule, B. G. (1974). The hostile and instrumental functions of human aggression. In J. deWit & W. W. Hartup (Eds.), *Determinants and origins of aggressive behavior.* The Hague: Mouton.

Schneider, D. J. (1991). Social cognition. *Annual Review of Psychology, 42,* 527–561.

Schwartz, D., Dodge, K. A., Coie, J. D., Hubbard, J. A., Cillessen, A. H. N., Lemerise, E., & Bateman, H. (1995). *Social-cognitive and behavioral correlates of subtypes of aggression and victimization in boys' play groups.* Manuscript submitted for publication.

Slaby, R. C., & Guerra, N. G. (1988). Cognitive mediators of aggression in adolescent offenders: I. Assessment. *Developmental Psychology, 24,* 580–588.

Spivak, G., Platt, J. J., & Shure, M. B. (1976). *The problem solving approach to adjustment: A guide to research and intervention.* San Francisco: Jossey-Bass.

Spivak, G., & Shure, M. B. (1980). Interpersonal problem-solving as a mediator of behavioral adjustment in preschool and kindergarten children. *Journal of Developmental Psychology, 1,* 29–44.

Steinberg, M. D., & Dodge, K. A. (1983). Attributional bias in aggressive adolescent boys and girls. *Journal of Social and Clinical Psychology, 1,* 312–321.

Stromquist, V. J., & Strauman, T. J. (1991). Children's social constructs: Nature, assessment, and association with adaptive versus maladaptive behavior. *Social Cognition, 9,* 330–358.

Toch, H. (1969). *Violent men.* Chicago: Aldine.

Underwood, B. J. (1969). Attributes of memory. *Psychological Review, 76,* 559–573.

Waas, G. A. (1988). Social attributional biases of peer-rejected and aggressive children. *Child Development, 59,* 969–992.

Waldman, I. D. (1988). *Relationships between non-social information processing, social perception, and social status in 7- to 12-year-old boys.* Unpublished doctoral dissertation, University of Waterloo, Ontario, Canada.

Weiss, B., Dodge, K. A., Bates, J. E., & Pettit, G. S. (1992). Some consequences of early harsh discipline: Child aggression and a maladaptive social information processing style. *Child Development, 63,* 1321–1335.

CHAPTER 18

The Effects of Media Violence on the Development of Antisocial Behavior

L. ROWELL HUESMANN, JESSICA F. MOISE, and CHERYL-LYNN PODOLSKI

CAUSES FOR CONCERN

Central to an understanding of the research on media violence and aggressive behavior and to the public concern that has surrounded the issue are two demographic trends from the second half of this century: (a) the very large increase in youth violence since the late 1940s and (b) the dramatic increase in the exposure of our youths to the mass visual media during the same period. The co-occurrence of these two trends has focused scientific, policy, and public attention on the relation between youth violence and violence in the mass media.

Of course, the co-occurrence of increases in violent behavior and increases in violence in the media might be suggestive of a relation between them, but, by itself, it would hardly qualify as evidence. Over the past four decades, however, a large body of scientific literature on the relation between media violence and violent behavior that overwhelmingly demonstrates that exposure to media violence does indeed relate to the development of violent behavior has emerged (Huesmann, 1982; Huesmann & Miller, 1994). The relations are not statistically large, but they are robust, replicable, and large enough to generate social concern (Rosenthal, 1986). The more interesting issues have now become the microscopic questions about the psychological processes that produce this relation. What are the processes? What do these processes suggest about the effects of the emerging new visual media, about who is most at risk for learning aggression from the media, and about media's role in specific forms of aggression? What do these processes suggest about how to mitigate the effects of media violence on the viewing audience?

In this chapter we review most of the empirical research relevant to understanding how violence on television, in film, in music videos, in video games, and on the news can engender violent behavior in the audience. First, though, we must set the stage by reviewing the demographic trends in violent behavior and youth exposure to media violence by summarizing the psychological theory that appears most relevant for understanding the development of individual differences in aggressive behavior, and by describing the roles that the observation of media violence might play in that development.

Increases in Violent Behavior

Crime prevention and protection from victimization have clearly become of paramount concern to the U.S. public during the last decade. According to the U.S. Department of Justice (1990), by 1990, 56% of the adult population of the United States personally feared becoming a victim of a violent crime. In late 1994, Congress passed a bill introduced by President Clinton with one of the largest increases in funding for anticrime measures in history. This most recent concern of the public and government with violent crime is the culmination of constantly growing anxiety paralleling the dramatic increase in violent crime that has occurred since the end of World War II (described in Part One of this volume). Though few other highly developed Western societies (except those beset by terrorism, drug wars, and revolutionary social upheaval, e.g., Columbia, Russia, South Africa) have violent crime rates similar to those in the United States, most such countries (excluding Japan) have also seen violent crime increases since World War II, particularly among youths (World Health Organization [WHO], 1965, 1982, 1993).

Corresponding Introduction of Mass Visual Media

The large increase in interpersonal violence in the past half-century has occurred at the same time as have the other dramatic changes in lifestyles produced by the great technological revolutions of the late 20th century. For child development, among the most notable has been the introduction of mass visual media into the everyday lives of children. When two highly salient events co-occur, it is common to hypothesize a causal relation between them; so it is not surprising that speculation about the role of media violence in stimulating violent behavior has been prevalent ever since motion pictures depicting violent acts first were distributed. With the advent in the early 1950s of television, the speculation advanced to the point of theorizing, and the first studies were initiated.

When television was introduced to the United States in the 1930s, few Americans could afford a television set and programming was limited. It was not until 1950 that television began to expand dramatically. Between 1950 and 1960, television ownership rose from less than 5% to more than 60% (Liebert, Sprafkin, & Davidson, 1982, p. 3). Since the 1950s, the television industry has grown tremendously and programming is now extremely pervasive in U.S. society. By 1992, 98.3% of U.S. households contained at least one television, and the average number of television sets in homes was 2.1 (U.S. Bureau of the Census, 1993, p. 561). It is estimated that children between the ages of 10 to 11 watch approximately 28 hours of television a week and teenagers watch about 23.5 hours a week (Comstock & Paik, 1991, p. 57). African Americans and Hispanics are reported to spend more time viewing television regardless of their social economic status (Tangney & Feshbach, 1988), and those persons of a low social economic status are often the heaviest viewers (Kubey & Csikszentmihalyi, 1990). Furthermore, the increase in single parent homes and dual-working parents during the past decade has changed the environment in which the U.S. child views television. More and more often, children view television without supervision.

What is the content of the programming to which our children and youths are exposed during those 28 plus hours of weekly television viewing? Huesmann and Eron (1986) reported that in the late 1970s, about 15% of all programs in the United States could be classified as very violent. Contrary to popular belief, the percentage is about the same in most other Western countries. The absolute frequency of media violence, however, is much lower in most of these countries because far fewer programming hours are presented each week (Huesmann & Eron, 1986). More recently, Gerbner and Signorelli (1990) reported that there were five to six violent acts per hour on prime time television and 20 to 25 acts on Saturday morning children's programs. The most recent and most detailed surveys (Mediascope, 1996) show little change in these figures. For example, 57% of all programs are reported to contain violence and 33% of those violent programs were categorized as very violent, yielding an overall rate of 19% for very violent programs.

Recent Changes and Advances in Mass Visual Media

Not only has television become more widely distributed, but a number of other significant changes in mass visual media have occurred in the last two decades that have heightened concern over the potential role of the media to stimulate antisocial behavior.

During the 1970s and 1980s, cable television grew to become a part of U.S. life. With its advent, the viewing selection changed drastically. In 1980, the continental United States had 17.7 million subscribers to cable television. By 1992, that number had grown to 57.2 million. In 1992, of the 92 million households with television, 60.2% subscribed to cable television (U.S. Bureau of Census, 1993, p. 561). Cable television brought increased programming selection to U.S. households. In addition to regularly broadcast network programs, viewers could watch recycled old films and movie box office hits during all hours of the day and night. Many of these shows had greater violent content than the normal network dramas.

The spread of the videocassette recorder (VCR) has also increased the availability of violent films for viewing. Home VCR equipment boomed during the late 1980s, bringing box office entertainment into the home. In 1980, 1.1% of households with television had VCR equipment. By 1990, that number had increased to 72.5% of households with television (U.S. Bureau of Census, 1993, p. 561). It is predicted that ownership of video equipment will rise to between 75% and 85% before leveling off (Dorr & Kunkel, 1990). These increases in the United States are paralleled by increases in other Western countries (Greenberg, Linsangan, & Soderman, 1987). Not only does VCR equipment provide a mechanism through which children can view the most violent films, it erodes the ability of society to control their exposure as well.

Another new form of entertainment that has raised concern among child advocates is the music video. Music videos entered the family home during the 1970s and became pervasive in 1981 with the introduction of MTV—an all-music video channel. Music videos are viewed primarily by 12- to 34-year-olds (Hansen & Hansen, 1990a). Viewing time has been reported at about 1 hour each weekday and about an hour and a half on Saturdays and Sundays (Hansen & Hansen, 1990a). Music videos have been frequently criticized for portraying violence, and according to a report by Huston et al. (1992), 50% of music videos contain at least one occurrence of violence. However, it remains to be studied whether the amount of graphically portrayed violence that most children observe in music videos compares with the amount they observe in dramatic films and television shows.

Advances in technology also brought an interactive form of visual entertainment—the video game—into widespread use by the end of the 1970s. By the end of the 1980s, the home video game was a regular part of almost every child's life (Provenzo, 1991). By 1985, annual industry sales were at $100 million, and by 1990 they reached a high of $4 billion. A *CBS News* report projected that 1992 sales would reach $6 billion (Provenzo, 1991). As video games have proliferated, violent video games have become a regular part of U.S. life, particularly for boys. In a survey of 357 seventh- and eighth-grade middle-class Americans, about 67% of girls played video games at least 1 to 2 hours per week at home and about 20% played in arcades. However, 90% of boys played at home and 50% in arcades. For boys, approximately half of the preferred games were violent and only 2% were educational (Funk, 1993). In the United States, video game revenues total $5.3 billion, about $400 million more than is spent at the movies (Elmer-Dewitt, 1993).

These technological advances have increased concerns about the extent to which extensive presentations of violence in the visual mass media increase violence in society. Music videos couple violent acts with repetitive lyrics; cable television and video equipment allow for unlimited access to unrated violent films; video games provide graphic visual displays of violence created at the control of the player; and interactive television is on the verge of explosion into U.S. society. Given these technological advances, the potential for the mass media to influence behavior—for better or for worse—would seem to be greater than ever. But before we can explore the empirical links between violent media and violent behavior in detail, we need to review the current state of theorizing about violent behavior.

THEORIES OF VIOLENT AND AGGRESSIVE BEHAVIOR

There are two clear conclusions that one can draw from the research to date on the development of human aggressive behavior. First, severe aggressive behavior is most often the product of multiple causes. Second, the best predictor of aggressive or violent behavior is previous aggressive or violent behavior.

Multiple Causes

The existing research suggests that childhood aggression is most often a product of a number of interacting factors: genetic, perinatal, physiological, familial, and learning. In fact, it seems most likely that severe antisocial aggressive behavior occurs only when there is a convergence of several of these factors. The evidence linking these factors to the development of aggressive behavior is covered in other chapters in this volume (Part Two) and is not reiterated here. What is important for the investigation of the role of media violence is that no one should expect the learning of aggression from exposure to media violence to explain more than a small percentage of the individual variation in aggressive behavior.

Continuity Over Time

Equally strong is the evidence that habitual aggressive behavior emerges in the early years and predicts later aggressive behavior. Individual differences in social behavior related to aggression (e.g., early temperament) are apparent before age 2 (Kagan, 1988). By age 6, a number of children have adopted aggressive patterns of behavior in their interactions with others (Parke & Slaby, 1983). From that point on, the extent of aggressive behavior in children tends to increase into adolescence. By age 8, children are characteristically more or less aggressive over a variety of situations, and aggression becomes a relatively stable characteristic of the individual youngster predicting adult aggression (Ensminger, Kellam, & Rubin, 1983; Farrington, 1982, 1990; Huesmann, Eron, Lefkowitz, & Walder, 1984; Loeber & Dishion, 1983; Magnusson, Duner, & Zetterblom, 1975; Moffitt, 1990; Olweus, 1979; Robins & Ratcliff, 1980; Spivack, 1983). The more aggressive child becomes the more aggressive adult.

The Learning of Aggression

Within this framework of multiple causes and early emergence, is there any one process that seems most important in accounting for individual differences in aggression? Yes, taken as a whole, the past 50 years of research on human aggression suggest that habitual aggressive behavior in young humans is to a great extent learned from the child's early interactions with the environment (Bandura, 1973; Berkowitz, 1974; Eron, Walder, & Lefkowitz, 1971; Huesmann et al., 1984). Although genetic and physiological factors clearly predispose some children more than others toward aggression, it is mostly children's early learning experiences that mold them into youths who behave more or less aggressively.

What are the key elements of the child's environment that mold the development of aggressive behavior? One must distinguish between instigators that may motivate or cue aggressive responses and affect behavior immediately and those components of the child's environment that mold the child's long-term responses to these stimuli and socialize the child. An environment full of deprivations, frustrations, and provocations is one in which aggression is frequently stimulated, as the high level of aggression in our urban ghettos attests. However, the environmental elements that are most important theoretically in determining individual differences in habitual responses to deprivation, frustration, and provocation are the child's family, peers, and cultural surroundings, *including the mass media*. Predisposing differences in arousal level, impulsivity, and irritability may be moderated or exacerbated by the child's early learning experiences; but once habitual patterns of behavior are well learned, they become very hard to change.

Because of the malleability of behavior in young children and the relative intractability of aggressive and violent dispositions once they have been developed, it is important that theories concerning the development of habitual aggressive behavior focus on behavior in *young* children. What are the dimensions and parameters of the socialization processes that lead to individual differences in habitual aggressive behavior? Through what psychological processes does the influence of this early socialization process extend into adulthood? These are key issues for understanding of the long-term effects of exposure to media violence.

Cognitions as Mediators of Socialization

In recent years, a number of researchers have offered theories that implicate the child's cognitions in the learning and maintenance of aggressive habits. These models put the stress primarily on cognitive processes and the steps through which a child must proceed to react appropriately, competently, and nonaggressively to a social situation. Among the most influential of these have been the revised formulation of Bandura (1986), the neo-associationist perspective of Berkowitz (1984, 1988), and the information processing theories put forth by Huesmann (1982, 1988; Huesmann & Eron, 1984) and Dodge (1982; Crick & Dodge, 1994). All of these theorists recognize the importance of predisposing factors and emotional abnormalities in stimulating anger and impulsiveness, but they stress the role that learned cognitions can play in moderating these effects. The common theme among these dominant, current theories of aggression is that the processes through which media violence exerts its effect must involve the child's cognitions and that it is through such cognitions that early sustained exposure to media violence influences behavior throughout the life course.

DIFFERENT METHODOLOGICAL APPROACHES TO RESEARCH ON MEDIA VIOLENCE

Before proceeding to review the empirical evidence concerning the relation between media violence and aggression, a few methodological comments are required. Four distinctly different types of studies have been undertaken to test the relation between exposure to media violence and aggressive behavior by the viewer: true-experiments performed in well-controlled but artificial settings; quasi-experiments performed in poorly controlled real-life settings; one-shot observational studies in real-life settings; and longitudinal observational studies in real-life settings. One common fatal error that many critics of the field have made (e.g., Freedman, 1984; Howitt & Cumberbatch, 1975) is to ignore one or more of these approaches and focus attacks narrowly on one or two approaches. Thus, Freedman (1984) completely ignores true-experiments, in which cause and effect are easily teased apart, and criticizes the field studies for not demonstrating a causal relation. Others have attacked the true-experiments for being "artificial" and ignore the real-life field studies. A second common error of critics has been to ignore age differences in aggregating results. The dominant cognitive theories all suggest that media violence should have an effect on children who are developing their habitual styles of social behavior, but these theories make many fewer clear-cut predictions about the effects of media violence on adults. The lack of a relation among a sample of adults or even teenagers should not be taken as evidence falsifying a theory about children, yet it often has.

THE EMPIRICAL RELATION BETWEEN DIFFERENT TYPES OF MEDIA VIOLENCE AND AGGRESSIVE BEHAVIOR

Dramatic Violence

The majority of research on the relation between exposure to violence in the media and violent behavior has focused on the effects of watching dramatic violence on television and film. Experimental studies, static observational studies, longitudinal studies, and meta-analyses all indicate that exposure to dramatic violence on television and in the movies is related to violent behavior (Huesmann & Miller, 1994).

In contrived experimental studies, children exposed to violent behavior on film or television behave more aggressively immediately afterward. Large numbers of laboratory and field experiments have demonstrated this fact over the past quarter-century (see reviews by Comstock, 1980; Geen, 1983, 1990; Geen & Thomas, 1986). The typical paradigm is that randomly selected children who are shown either a violent or a nonviolent short film are observed as they play with each other or with objects such as *Bobo* dolls (Bandura, Ross, & Ross, 1961, 1963a, 1963b). The consistent finding is that children who see the violent film clip behave more aggressively immediately afterward. Just as children learn cognitive and social skills from watching people act out these skills, they learn violent behaviors from watching other people behave violently. Such results have been obtained both for aggression directed at inanimate objects (e.g., *Bobo* dolls) and for aggression directed at peers (Bjorkqvist, 1985; Josephson, 1987). In one very typical study Bjorkqvist (1985) in Finland exposed 5- to 6-year-old children to either violent or nonviolent films. These children were then observed playing together in a room by two observers who did not know which type of film each child had seen. Children who had just seen the violent film ended up being rated higher on physical aggression (hitting other children, wrestling, etc.), verbal aggression (screaming at others, threatening others), and aggression at objects (intentional destruction of toys, etc.).

The effects of violent television or films on the affective responses that mediate aggression have also been clearly demonstrated with valid experiments. For example, Bushman and Geen (1990) demonstrated that violent videotapes elicit both aggressive cognitions and higher systolic blood pressure in college students.

It is also true that in the laboratory, children can be taught to be less aggressive by being shown films with prosocial models (Eron & Huesmann, 1986; Pitkannen-Pulkkinen, 1979). These short-term effects are not limited to children but have been observed in teenagers and adults, particularly when the dependent measures reflect attitudes or opinions rather than behaviors (Malamuth & Donnerstein, 1982). In these well-controlled laboratory studies, there can be no doubt that it is the children's observation of the scenes of violence that *causes* the changes in behavior. Some critics would dismiss these studies completely as "artificial" approximations of life (Freedman, 1984) and focus only on field studies. But such a position is not defensible in light of the complementary nature of experimental and nonexperimental research in this area (Huesmann, Eron, Berkowitz, & Chaffee, 1991).

The demonstration of a relation between the observation of dramatic television and film violence and the commission of aggressive behavior has not been limited to the laboratory. Evidence from field studies over the past 20 years has led most reviewers to conclude that a child's current aggressiveness and the amount of television and film violence the child is regularly watching are positively related to some degree. Children who watch more violence on television and in the movies behave more violently and express beliefs more accepting of aggressive behavior (see reviews by Andison, 1977; Chaffee, 1972; Comstock, 1980; Eysenck & Nias, 1978; Hearold, 1979; Huesmann, 1982; Huesmann & Miller, 1994; Paik & Comstock, 1994; Wood, Wong, & Chachere, 1991). Clearly, this relation is robust though the effect size is not large by standards used in the measurement of intellectual abilities and varies as a function of environmental, familial, cognitive, and television programming variables. However, the relation is usually statistically significant and is substantial by the standards of personality measurements with children. Correlations of the magnitude usually obtained in the field can have real social significance (Rosenthal, 1986). Moreover, the relation is highly replicable even across researchers who disagree about the reasons (e.g., Huesmann, Lagerspetz, & Eron, 1984; Milavsky, Kessler, Stipp, & Rubens, 1982) and across countries (Huesmann & Eron, 1986). In contrast to the childhood data, significant correlations between adults' aggression and adults' concurrent violence viewing have been observed only rarely in the field.

Whereas these one-shot field studies showing a correlation between media violence viewing and aggression suggest that the causal conclusions of the experimental studies may well generalize to the real world, longitudinal studies can test the plausibility of causal hypotheses more directly. The data available from the few existing longitudinal studies do, in fact, provide additional support for the hypothesis that television violence viewing leads to the development of aggressive behavior. These longitudinal studies have employed a wide range of samples and methodologies, but all of the studies done with *children* seem to reveal long-term effects of exposure to television violence.

In a study initiated in 1960 on 870 youth in Columbia County, New York, Eron and his colleagues found that a boy's early childhood aggression in elementary school was statistically related to his aggressive and antisocial behavior 10 years later (after graduating from high school), even controlling for initial aggressiveness, social class, education, and other relevant variables (Eron,

Huesmann, Lefkowitz, & Walder, 1972; Lefkowitz, Eron, Walder, & Huesmann, 1977). A 22-year follow-up of these same subjects revealed that their early violence viewing also related to their adult criminality at age 30 (Huesmann, 1986).

A 3-year longitudinal study of children in five countries conducted by Huesmann and his colleagues in the late 1970s (Huesmann & Eron, 1986; Huesmann, Lagerspetz, & Eron, 1984) revealed that the television habits of children as young as first-graders also predicted subsequent childhood aggression. This was true for both boys and girls even in countries without large amounts of violent programming, such as Israel, Finland, and Poland (Huesmann & Eron, 1986). In most countries, the more aggressive children also watched more television, preferred more violent programs, identified more with aggressive characters, and perceived television violence as more like real life than did the less aggressive children. The combination of extensive exposure to violence coupled with identification with aggressive characters was a particularly potent predictor of subsequent aggression for many children. A field experiment conducted as part of this study also provided evidence that what is being learned from the observation of violence may be attitudes about aggression as much as specific behaviors. In this field experiment, aggression in a randomly selected experimental group of third-graders was reduced relative to a control group by changing their attitudes about the acceptability of the violence shown on television (Huesmann, Eron, Klein, Brice, & Fischer, 1983).

A few longitudinal studies seemed to produce results at variance with the thesis that media violence causes aggression, but closer inspection of most of these studies reveals that their results are not discrepant, but simply not strongly supportive of the thesis. (For a review, see Huesmann & Miller, 1994.) For example, NBC's longitudinal study conducted in the 1970s (Milavsky et al., 1982) actually reports regression coefficients that, although not significant, are in the predicted direction in 22 of 30 critical tests for the causal theory.

More recently, Centerwall (1989, 1992) has used aggregated population crime and media viewing data to argue that media violence is one of the major causes of increased crime rates in Western society. Using time series analyses of data from the United States, Canada, and South Africa, where television has been introduced only recently, he concludes that the introduction of television, with its associated frequent portrayal of violent acts, significantly increases interpersonal violence in a society. As discussed later in the section on news coverage, however, such conclusions must be treated judiciously because of the many threats to the validity of conclusions from quasi-experiments using aggregated population data.

Finally, one cannot complete a review of major studies on this topic without mentioning two meta-analyses that summarize findings from studies conducted over the past 30 years on media violence and aggression. Paik and Comstock (1994) calculated the obtained effect sizes for over 1,000 comparisons derived from 217 different experiments, static field studies, and longitudinal studies. After extensive analyses, they concluded that the association between exposure to television violence and antisocial and aggressive behavior is extremely robust. Furthermore, they conclude, "The data of the past decade and a half strengthens rather than

weakens the case that television violence increases aggressive and antisocial behavior" (p. 54). Wood et al. (1991) analyzed 30 comparisons in 23 studies in which the outcome variable was aggression measured in unstructured social interaction, such as a nursery school playground. They concluded that exposure to media violence significantly enhanced viewers' aggressive behavior when the findings were aggregated across studies, though the effect was not uniform across investigations.

Music Videos

The increasing popularity of several new forms of media that contain high levels of violence, such as music videos and video games, adds a new dimension to this relation between exposure to media violence and violent behavior. Content analyses of music videos have documented very high levels of violence (Baxter, Di Riemer, Landini, Leslie, & Singletary, 1985; Brown & Campbell, 1986; Caplan, 1985; Hansen & Hansen, 1989; Sherman & Dominick, 1986) and show that videos often portray antisocial behavior in a positive light (Hansen & Hansen, 1989). Although very few experimental or static observational studies have been conducted on the behavioral effects of watching violent music videos, several studies have been done on the effects they have on viewers' attitudes, finding that watching violent music videos increases viewers' acceptance and endorsement of violent behavior and attitudes (Greeson & Williams, 1986; Hansen & Hansen, 1989, 1990a). For example, Hansen and Hansen (1990a) found that after neutral music videos, subjects' evaluations of a target were more negative when the target made an obscene gesture toward the experimenter than when he did not. However, after viewing videos containing antisocial behavior, the obscene gesture did not decrease the subjects' rating of the target. Whereas these types of studies do not directly test the link between viewing and behavior, they do seem to indicate that exposure to antisocial rock music videos alters the viewers' judgments of antisocial behavior.

One genre that has garnered particular attention is that of rap music videos. As with music videos in general, little research has been done on the effects of rap music on aggressive behavior. However, two recent studies have looked at the effects of exposure to rap music videos on the attitudes of African American adolescents. One study found that exposure to nonviolent rap music videos that depict women in sexually subordinate roles increased females' acceptance of teen dating violence but had no effect on males' acceptance (Johnson, Adams, Ashburn, & Reed, 1995). A second study found that subjects exposed to violent rap music videos reported greater acceptance of the use of violence and increased probability that they would engage in violent behavior. In addition, when compared to those subjects who did not see rap music videos, in a hypothetical situation given to them after viewing the video, subjects exposed to either violent or nonviolent videos expressed a greater desire to be like the materialistic young man who uses illegal means to get what he wants than the young man in college who is aspiring to be a lawyer (Johnson, Jackson, & Gatto, 1994). These results indicate that rap music videos may, in fact, affect both male and female adolescents' attitudes toward aggressive behavior.

Video Games

Video games also have become a focus of concern due to the high levels of violence they contain and the fact that children are active participants in the violence, rather than passive observers, as they are with television. As with music videos, video games are a fairly recent medium and as such their impact on the aggressive behavior of the players has not yet been studied extensively. However, the results of the studies that have been conducted, most of which are experimental studies done in the laboratory, seem to support the notion that observing and engaging with a medium that has violent content is related to violent behavior in the observer/player. Several studies have shown that children's aggressive play increases after playing a violent video game (Cooper & Mackie, 1986; Schutte, Malouff, & Post-Gorden, 1988; Silvern & Williamson, 1987). For example, one study looked at the differences in 28 four- to six-year-old children's play before and after viewing a violent cartoon and after playing a violent video game (Silvern & Williamson, 1987). They found that children exhibited double the aggressive behavior and less prosocial behavior after playing the video game or watching the cartoon than at the baseline.

News Violence

Little research has been conducted specifically on the effects of watching violence in news coverage on behavior. From a theoretical perspective, however, there is little reason to believe that the effects on the audience of news violence should be much different from the effects of dramatic violence. True, the audience knows that the news violence is real, which might heighten its effects, but children, who are most likely to be affected by video violence, often also perceive dramatic violence (not to mention "reenactment" dramas) as "telling about life just like it is" (Huesmann & Eron, 1986). Furthermore, graphic portrayals of actual acts of violence are seldom shown in the news; rather, the story usually is reported after the fact.

Most of the investigations that have examined the effects of violent news on the audience have been time-series field studies that used aggregated population data to relate population trends to specific news events. They have yielded mixed results. On the whole, these studies support the theory of imitative suicide but provide only weak evidence for the occurrence of imitative violent crime after well-publicized violent events (Phillips, 1979, 1982; Simon, 1979; Stack, 1989). One study using monthly data from 1968 to 1980 found that publicized mass murders or suicides correlated with subsequent suicide rates, but not with subsequent homicide rates (Stack, 1989). Phillips's (1983) frequently cited finding of increases in violent crimes following televised prize fights has not been widely accepted by researchers because of methodological challenges raised by others (Baron & Reiss, 1985; see Phillips & Bollen, 1985, for a response). However, another study by Berkowitz and Macaulay (1971) reported that there was an increase in violent crimes, but not property crimes, after several high-profile murder cases in the early and mid-1960s, including the assassination of President Kennedy. The threats to the validity of the conclusions of all such time-series studies using aggregated population data are numerous. Thus, the relation between news coverage of violent crime and violent behavior must still be considered unclear and needs to be investigated more rigorously in the future with prospective studies examining the longitudinal effects on individuals. Such research seems particularly vital as the nature of news coverage changes and the distinction between news and entertainment blurs with the increase in reality-based police shows that overrepresent the prevalence of violent crime (Oliver, 1994).

WHY IS EXPOSURE TO VIOLENCE RELATED TO VIOLENT BEHAVIOR?

The previous review, although brief, revealed a preponderance of evidence indicating that exposure to dramatic media violence is predictive of increased aggressive behavior in young children. The evidence that video games and music videos have the same effect is much weaker, but it is hard to understand how television and films could have an effect and video games and music videos would not have an effect. Let us now turn to the question of what processes produce these relations. In line with our previous discussion of the current state of theorizing about aggression, we need to focus on mechanisms through which media violence directly stimulates aggressive behavior, influences the cognitions controlling aggressive behavior, and influences the emotional and arousal processes underlying aggressive behavior.

Before exploring these processes, however, let us dispense with one old theory that has plagued discussions of the role of media violence for decades, the catharsis theory developed by Freud (1933). This theory posits that watching aggression on television acts as a purging of aggressive tendencies or drive. Certainly, physically aggressive actions can reduce tension in subjects who have been frustrated (Hokanson & Burgess, 1962), but so can physical exertion that is nonaggressive. The more important fact is that there are no convincing data to indicate that watching violent acts reduces tension or the propensity of one to act aggressively (Doob & Wood, 1972). The one field study often cited as demonstrating a catharsis process (Feshbach & Singer, 1971) has methodological flaws (Huesmann et al., 1991) that the authors have recognized. As shown earlier, the majority of evidence demonstrates that violence viewing and aggression are *positively* related, which contradicts the catharsis hypothesis. Furthermore, studies that have examined the relation between fantasizing about aggression and aggressive behavior have shown that children who fantasize more behave more aggressively (Huesmann & Eron, 1986; Viemero & Paajanen, 1992). As an explanation of the relation between aggressive behavior and viewing violence, catharsis theory can be put to rest.

Observational Learning of Behaviors

On the basis of the accumulated evidence, it seems clear that children learn both specific aggressive behaviors and cognitions supporting more complex aggressive behaviors through observational learning. It has become an accepted tenet of developmental theory that through observational learning and vicarious reinforcements (Bandura, 1977, 1986), children develop habitual modes of behavior that are resistant to extinction. The application of observational learning to explain the acquisition of specific aggressive behaviors that children observe in others (in person or in the media) is straightforward (Bandura, Ross, & Ross, 1963a). But there are additional predictions of vicarious learning theories that also have been confirmed. For instance, it has been shown that the extent to which a child imitates an actor is greatly influenced by the reinforcements received by the actor. If the actor is seen being rewarded for aggressive behavior, the child is more likely to imitate that behavior (Bandura, 1965; Bandura et al., 1963a, 1963b; Walters, Leat, & Mezei, 1963). If the actor is punished for a behavior, that behavior is less likely to be modeled (Bandura, 1965; Walters & Parke, 1964). Other studies have indicated that the persistence of such learned behavior seems to depend on the direct reinforcements that the child receives (Bandura, 1965; Hayes, Rincover, & Volosin, 1980). Finally, whether the child identifies with the model (Huesmann & Eron, 1986; Huesmann, Lagerspetz, & Eron, 1984) and whether the model is perceived as possessing valued characteristics also appear to influence whether a child will imitate the model (Bandura, 1977; Hicks, 1965; Neely, Heckel, & Leichtman, 1973; Nicholas, McCarter, & Heckel, 1971).

Observational Learning of Cognitions

In more recent years, a number of other theorists, drawing both on Bandura's social learning theory and cognitive psychology, have extended the concept of observational learning to argue that children also learn cognitions supporting aggressive behavior that generalize across time and situations (Huesmann, 1982, 1988; Huesmann & Eron, 1984; Huesmann & Miller, 1994). Huesmann has argued that children learn, from observing violent dramas in the media, scripts for complex aggressive behaviors, normative beliefs, attributional biases, and attitudes supporting aggression. *Scripts* are programs for behaviors and *normative beliefs* are internal self-regulating standards that filter out unacceptable behaviors (Huesmann & Guerra, 1997). Huesmann argues that both scripts and normative beliefs are learned through a process in which observational learning interacts with cognitive rehearsal of the observed material and instrumental enactive learning. The observed correlations between violence viewing, aggressive fantasizing, and aggression reflect the role of fantasizing as rehearsal (Huesmann & Eron, 1986; Viemero & Paajanen, 1992). According to this theory, a child's observation of dramatic or real violence in childhood contributes to the construction of lasting cognitive structures that affect the child's aggressive attitudes and behavior into adulthood. These cognitive structures contribute to the perpetuation of aggressive behavior even in the face of negative consequences by providing false evaluation of the outcome of the behavior, limiting the ability to generate any alternative scripts, causing an alteration of evaluative schema to make aggression more palatable, and arranging the environment so aggression is more acceptable (Huesmann, 1988).

A substantial body of data has accumulated indicating that media violence does, in fact, change beliefs and attitudes about violence. The more televised violence a child watches, the more accepting is the child's attitude toward aggressive behavior (Dominick & Greenberg, 1972). Equally important, the more a person watches television, the more suspicious a person is, and the greater is the person's expectancy of being involved in real violence (Gerbner & Gross, 1974, 1980). Why is this? From an infor-

mation processing standpoint, attitudes are attributions, rules, and explanations induced from observations of behavior. They serve as heuristics for future behavior. If a child's, or even an adult's, major exposure to social interaction occurs through television, the conception of social reality would quite naturally be based on such observations. Heavy television viewers would have more positive attitudes toward aggression because they perceive aggressive behavior to be the norm. Perhaps even the perception of what is an aggressive act changes.

Cognitive Justification Processes

The justification hypothesis posits that people who are aggressive like to watch violent television because they can then justify their own behavior as being normal (Huesmann, 1982). It involves the observational learning of attitudes, but it operates in the opposite direction from the process described earlier. According to this theory, television violence viewing does not stimulate the child's aggressiveness; it results from it. A child's own aggressive behaviors normally should elicit guilt in the child, but this guilt could be relieved if the child who has behaved aggressively watches violent television, which justifies his or her own aggressiveness.

Unfortunately, little research has been conducted to test this model. A number of psychologists have suggested that aggressiveness might be a precursor of violence viewing (e.g., Kaplan & Singer, 1976), but most of them have operated in a theoretical vacuum without any process model to explain such an effect. Unfortunately, the one experiment aimed at assaying whether aggressive behavior might be a precursor of violence viewing demonstrated only that subjects who are told to think about aggressive words choose to watch aggressive films afterward (Fenigstein, 1979). More research clearly needs to be conducted to test this theory.

Cognitive Cueing/Priming

Whereas the observational learning process explains how exposure to media violence can teach lasting aggressive habits, priming theory can account for how aggressive habits learned in other venues may be triggered by violent media displays. Berkowitz (1984) has proposed that "the aggressive idea suggested by a violent movie can 'prime' other semantically related thoughts, heightening the chances that viewers will have other aggressive ideas in this period" (p. 411). In this way, viewing an aggressive act on television activates thoughts, emotions, and even behaviors that are cognitively associated with the act. This idea of cognitive priming is useful in explaining why the observation of aggression in the media is often followed by aggressive acts that differ from the observed behavior. Many studies have demonstrated this phenomenon using television violence (Berkowitz, 1970; Berkowitz & Rogers, 1986; Worchel, 1972; Wyer & Hartwick, 1980; Wyer & Srull, 1981) and violence in music videos (Hansen & Hansen, 1990a). For example, in one study it was found that subjects who viewed slides of weapons were more willing to severely punish a target than were the subjects who viewed neutral slides (Leyens & Parke, 1975). Presumably, viewing the weapons stimulated other aggressive ideas and emotions that then affected the viewers' subsequent attitudes and behaviors.

A related view focuses on the importance of cues in the retrieval process of aggression learned through observation. The idea of cueing is that at the time of observation the viewer encodes both the aggressiveness of the act and any relevant pieces of information in the surrounding environment (such as a particular object) that later can serve as retrieval cues. One study that demonstrated this effect was Josephson's (1987) study of schoolboy hockey players. Josephson deliberately frustrated the boys who were then shown either a violent or nonviolent television program. A walkie-talkie was used by the aggressive actor in the program and thus was predicted to act as a retrieval cue. In fact, this seemed to be the case because during a subsequent hockey game, boys were most aggressive if they had previously seen the aggressive film and the referee carried a walkie-talkie. This idea of cueing seems particularly important in reference to the effects of music videos because the audio portion of the video may serve as a cue for the aggression observed in the video, causing these aggressive acts to be retrieved when the music is heard in the future.

Emotional and Cognitive Desensitization

Cognitive desensitization refers to the idea that the more an individual is exposed to violence, the more violence will come to be seen as a normal and acceptable form of behavior. This process, in turn, will increase the person's acceptance of violent behavior, decrease the individual's emotional reaction to violence, and make it more likely that the individual will model the aggressive acts. Many studies have demonstrated this effect in both children (Drabman & Thomas, 1974; Thomas & Drabman, 1975) and adults (Linz, Donnerstein, & Penrod, 1988; Malamuth & Check, 1981).

One designates the changes in attitudes brought about by frequent violence viewing as a cognitive desensitization to violence. Similarly, there is some evidence that a real physiological desensitization can occur. In a quasi-experimental field study (Cline, Croft, & Courrier, 1973), boys who regularly watched a heavy diet of television displayed less physiological arousal in response to new scenes of violence than did control subjects. Although these results have apparently been difficult to replicate in the field, Thomas, Horton, Lippincott, and Drabman (1977) discovered similar short-term effects in laboratory studies of changes in skin conductance in response to violence. It should not be surprising that emotional and physiological responses to scenes of violence habituate as do responses to other stimuli. It is more difficult to make the case that such habituation would influence the future probability of aggressive behavior. One needs to argue that the arousal that is naturally stimulated by viewing violent behavior is unpleasant and therefore is a negative reinforcer of one's own violent behavior. Several studies do seem to support this hypothesis (Halpern, 1975; Winn, 1977).

Arousal and Excitation Transfer

On the other hand, some theorists have argued that arousal heightens the propensity of the person to behave aggressively, and television violence increases or perpetuates arousal. Studies by Geen and O'Neal (1969) and Zillmann (1971) demonstrate that increasing a subject's general arousal increases the probability of aggressive behavior. In the typical study, a subject engages in physical activity that raises his or her heart rate and then is tested on the tendency to respond aggressively in response to provocation (Zillmann, Katcher, & Milavsky, 1972). Although there is some tendency of subjects to respond more "aggressively," for example, select stronger punishments for someone else, in this situation it is difficult to separate the arousal from the physical exertion as the cause.

This excitation transfer theory has also been used to explain how nonviolent pornography could stimulate aggressive behavior. Zillmann (1978, 1983, 1984) posited that physiological arousal produced by a sexual or other stimulus in one situation may influence aggressive behavior in another situation that is close in time. It is argued that when excitation is produced by more than one source of stimulation, the individual is unable to distinguish between the excitation produced by each source. Excitation from multiple sources is thought to be additive, so that the arousing sexual stimulus can have the effect of intensifying anger, for example. Presumably, people at higher levels of arousal are more likely to respond strongly and impulsively to provoking stimuli and therefore are more likely to behave aggressively due to this "transferred" excitation. The duration of such excitation is relatively short term (i.e., undetectable after a few hours); thus, this theory cannot be invoked to explain long-term effects of media violence.

This process of excitation transfer could also explain how the viewing of violent music videos could increase aggression. Although this idea is plausible, the results with music videos have been mixed. One study did find that the level of arousal caused by the music was strongly related to the subjects' rating of the appeal of the music video and to the strength of the emotions generated by the video (Hansen & Hansen, 1990b). These emotions were mostly positive, however, which might not affect aggressive behaviors. Nevertheless, these findings could have profound implications as music videos and video games (which have three sources of stimulation: visual, audio, and kinetic) become more prominent forms of entertainment. However, more research needs to be done to confirm an excitation effect on aggressive behavior.

WHO IS MOST AT RISK?

Whereas the research reviewed in this article provides support for the hypothesis that viewing television violence leads to the development of aggressive behavior, clearly it is not the only cause of aggressive behavior. Many other factors, both individual and societal, also contribute to its development. Of particular interest are those factors that put an individual most at risk. Research on this topic is quite scarce; however, there has been some theorizing and a small amount of empirical data that have tried to identify the societal- and individual-level factors that put some people more at risk for being affected by viewing violence in the media.

Societal-Level Risks

Much has been written about the "culture" of violence that has developed over the years in the United States (Anderson, 1990). It has been speculated that living in a culture that rewards violence puts a child at a higher risk for being affected by the violence viewed on television, and some studies have shown this to be true. For example, our cross-national study found that kibbutz-raised children in Israel were significantly less affected by viewing television violence than were city-raised Israeli children and children in Poland, Finland, and the United States (Huesmann & Bachrach, 1988). This result may be due to the powerful group norms against aggression prevalent in the kibbutz society. Thus, television has a greater effect on the development of aggression when the aggressive behaviors learned by observing television are not countered by a norm against aggression. Similarly, the same cross-national study found that the longitudinal effects for boys are very similar in the United States and Finland, but the results for girls were not. In Finland, girls do not seem to be affected by the amount of violence they view on television (Huesmann, Lagerspetz, & Eron, 1984). This result was explained in terms of differing cultural norms in the two countries. Finnish girls may be more encouraged than Finnish boys to inhibit whatever aggressive behaviors are stimulated by television violence, whereas girls in the United States in the 1980s and 1990s are being encouraged to behave as aggressively as boys. The power of cultural norms to influence aggression has been documented in a number of other countries and cultures as well (Landau, 1984).

It also appears as if the family environment can increase or decrease an individual's propensity to be affected by viewing violence. Tangney and Feshbach (1988) found that certain family television behaviors were correlated with lower levels of aggressiveness and restlessness. These family characteristics include (a) establishment of television rules, (b) parents who engage in active discussions with children, (c) regulation/mediation of television use, and (d) lower frequency of television viewing.

Putting together these findings concerning society and family with our earlier discussion of the importance of attitudes, beliefs, attributional biases, and cognitive scripts in controlling social behavior, one can readily see how children in neighborhoods and countries beset by violence could be most at risk for being influenced by media violence. The more realistic and appropriate the depicted violent behaviors may seem, the more likely they are to have a lasting influence. The more violence and retribution are sanctioned by the family and the culture, the less possibility there is for societal and family forces to counteract the pernicious influence of media violence.

Individual-Level Risks

In addition to varying societal-level factors, some risk factors for susceptibility to media violence lie at the individual level. Many factors have been suggested as risk factors, such as neurological deficits, age, cognitive ability, ethnicity, social class, sex, personality characteristics, and mental health differences, but little empirical work has been done to test these hypotheses; and the studies that have been conducted have provided mixed results (Dorr & Kovaric, 1980).

Many of the theories used to explain why exposure to violence in the media is related to aggressive behavior posit that young children are at a higher risk for being affected by what they view on television due to their impressionability and less mature cognitive structures. However, research on age difference appears to be mixed, indicating that whereas younger children may be more susceptible to influence from television, no age is immune from influence (Dorr & Kovaric, 1980). A related factor is the differences in cognitive ability between children of the same age. It is theorized that children with greater cognitive ability are less susceptible to the effects of viewing violence on television because they realize that the images on television do not represent reality, and, in fact, children who perceive television violence as less realistic do tend to be less aggressive (Huesmann & Eron, 1986). Research on general cognitive ability has provided mixed results, however, indicating that although low intelligence scores are sometimes correlated with higher television viewing and aggression (Huesmann & Eron, 1986; Huesmann, Eron, & Yarmel, 1987), children of all cognitive abilities can be affected by exposure to violence on television (Dorr & Kovaric, 1980).

Ethnicity and social class have been of some concern in the past due to the data showing that there are differences in the amount and type of television watched by people from different social classes and of different races. Many studies have demonstrated that Blacks tend to watch more television in general than do Whites (Huston et al., 1992; Tangney & Feshbach, 1988) and more violent television in particular (Greenberg, 1974–1975). Similarly, several studies looking at differences in viewing habits by class found lower SES youths watch more television in general (Huesmann & Eron, 1986; Huston et al., 1992; Tangney & Feshbach, 1988) and more televised violence specifically (Chaffee & McLeod, 1972) than do middle and upper SES youths. Thus, whereas certain racial and economic populations may be at a higher risk because they watch more violence, there has not been much research investigating whether these populations are differentially affected by the same amount of exposure.

One factor that has been studied more extensively than others is gender. Many surveys report that boys watch more television and also more violent programs than girls. Boys also report playing more video games in general and more violent video games specifically than do girls (Funk, 1993). Finally, boys are generally more aggressive than girls (Huesmann et al., 1984). All of these initial findings have led to the hypothesis that boys may be more at risk for being affected by television violence. Earlier studies showed that boys were more affected by exposure to television violence than were girls (Eron et al., 1972); however, more recent studies seem to indicate that the development of aggression for both boys and girls is equally affected by exposure to televised violence (Bjorkqvist, 1985; Huesmann & Eron, 1986).

Finally, there has been some speculation as to whether personality differences and mental health affect one's susceptibility to violence in the media. Two early experiments found that emotionally disturbed and nondisturbed boys generally did not differ in their reactions to exposure to aggression on television (Heller & Polsky, 1976; Walters & Willows, 1968). Similarly, a study on personality, psychopathology, and video game use found no differences in personality or psychopathology for frequent versus infrequent video game players (Kestenbaum & Weinstein, 1985). Although several studies have found that "more aggressive youth were more likely than were less aggressive youth to be impacted by exposure to televised or film violence" (Dorr & Kovaric, 1980, p. 192), other studies (Huesmann, Lagerspetz, & Eron, 1984) have found that the strength of the longitudinal relation varied little as a function of the child's pre-existing level of aggression.

SUMMARY

The co-occurrence since World War II of increases in interpersonal violence in the United States and increases in the exposure of youths to the mass visual media has focused scientists', policy makers', and the public's attention on the possible effects of media violence on youth violence. Over the past four decades, a large body of scientific literature has emerged that overwhelmingly demonstrates that exposure to media violence does indeed relate to the development of violent behavior. The emerging theories and data suggest that multiple processes are involved, but that the most important seem to involve the observational learning of attitudes, beliefs, attributional biases, and scripts that promote aggressive behavior. Desensitization of emotional processes may also play a role in long-term effects as may a cognitive justification process in which the more aggressive children use media violence to justify their acts. At the same time, powerful shorter term effects of media violence may be engendered by excitation transfer from media violence to real life and by the tendency of media violence to cue well-learned aggressive habits. These processes would seem to place children most at-risk who already live in "a culture of violence," in which there are few norms against aggressive behavior, in which there are ethnic or nationalistic forces that support violence against dehumanized targets, and in which there is little family or educational intervention to moderate the effects of media violence. Given the robust body of literature that leads to the inevitable conclusion that viewing media violence stimulates aggressive behavior in children, future research should move beyond the simple causal issue and focus on a better understanding of the psychological processes involved and on how to inoculate children against the insidious effects of exposure to media violence.

REFERENCES

Anderson, E. J. (1990). *Streetwise: Race, class, and change in an urban community.* Chicago: University of Chicago Press.

Andison, F. S. (1977). TV violence and viewer aggression: A cumulation of study results 1956–1976. *Public Opinion Quarterly, 41,* 314–331.

Bandura, A. (1965). Influence of models' reinforcement contingencies on the acquisition of imitative responses. *Journal of Abnormal and Social Psychology, 66,* 575–582.

Bandura, A. (1973). *Aggression: A social learning analysis.* Englewood Cliffs, NJ: Prentice Hall.

Bandura, A. (1977). *Social learning theory.* Englewood Cliffs, NJ: Prentice Hall.

Bandura, A. (1986). *Social foundations of thought and action: A social cognitive theory.* Englewood Cliffs, NJ: Prentice Hall.

Bandura, A., Ross, D., & Ross, S. A. (1961). Transmission of aggression through imitation of aggressive models. *Journal of Abnormal Social Psychology, 63,* 575–582.

Bandura, A., Ross, D., & Ross, S. A. (1963a). Imitation of film-mediated aggressive models. *Journal of Abnormal and Social Psychology, 66,* 3–11.

Bandura, A., Ross, D., & Ross, S. A. (1963b). Vicarious reinforcement and imitative learning. *Journal of Abnormal and Social Psychology, 67,* 601–607.

Baron, J. N., & Reiss, P. C. (1985). Same time next year: Aggregate analyses of the mass media and violent behavior. *American Sociological Review, 50,* 347–376.

Baxter, R. L., DeRiemer, C., Landini, A., Leslie, L., & Singletary, M. W. (1985). A content analysis of music videos. *Journal of Broadcasting and Electronic Media, 29,* 333–340.

Berkowitz, L. (1970). Aggressive humor as a stimulus to aggressive responses. *Journal of Personality and Social Psychology, 2,* 359–369.

Berkowitz, L. (1974). Some determinants of impulsive aggression: The role of mediated associations with reinforcements for aggression. *Psychological Review, 81,* 165–176.

Berkowitz, L. (1984). Some effects of thoughts on anti- and prosocial influences of media events: A cognitive-neoassociation analysis. *Psychological Bulletin, 95,* 3, 410–427.

Berkowitz, L. (1988). Frustrations, appraisals, and aversively stimulated aggression. *Aggressive Behavior, 14,* 3–12.

Berkowitz, L., & Macaulay, J. (1971). The contagion of criminal violence. *Sociometry, 34,* 238–260.

Berkowitz, L., & Rogers, K. H. (1986). A priming effect analysis of media influences. In J. Bryant & D. Zillman (Eds.), *Perspectives on media effects* (pp. 57–82). Hillsdale, NJ: Erlbaum.

Bjorkqvist, K. (1985). *Violent films, anxiety and aggression.* Helsinki: Finnish Society of Sciences and Letters.

Brown, D., & Campbell, K. (1986). Race and gender in music videos: The same beat but a different drummer. *Journal of Communications, 36,* 94–106.

Bushman, B. J., & Geen, R. G. (1990). Role of cognitive-emotional mediators and individual differences in the effects of media violence on aggression. *Journal of Personality and Social Psychology, 58*(1), 156–163.

Caplan, R. E. (1985). Violent program content in music video. *Journalism Quarterly, 62,* 144–147.

Centerwall, B. S. (1989). Exposure to television as a risk factor for violence. *American Journal of Epidemiology, 129,* 643–652.

Centerwall, B. S. (1992). Television and violence: The scale of the problem and where to go from here. *Journal of the American Medical Association, 267,* 3059–3063.

Chaffee, S. H. (1972). Television and adolescent aggressiveness (overview). In G. A. Comstock & E. A. Rubinstein (Eds.), *Television and social behavior: Vol. 3. Television and adolescent aggressiveness* (pp. 1–34). Washington, DC: Government Printing Office.

Chaffee, S. H., & McLeod, J. M. (1972). Adolescent television use in the family context. In G.A. Comstock & E. A. Rubinstein (Eds.), *Television and social behavior: Vol. 3. Television and adolescent aggressiveness* (pp. 149–172). Washington, DC: Government Printing Office.

Cline, V. B., Croft, R. G., & Courrier, S. (1973). Desensitization of children to television violence. *Journal of Personality and Social Psychology, 27,* 360–365.

Comstock, G. A. (1980). New emphases in research on the effects of television and film violence. In E. L. Paler & A. Dorr (Eds.), *Children and the faces of television: Teaching, violence, selling* (pp. 129–148). New York: Academic Press.

Comstock, G. A., & Paik, H. (1991). *Television and the American child.* San Diego, CA: Academic Press.

Cooper, J., & Mackie, D. (1986). Video games and aggression in children. *Journal of Applied Social Psychology, 16,* 726–744.

Crick, N. R., & Dodge, K. A. (1994). A review and reformulation of social information processing mechanisms in children's adjustment. *Psychological Bulletin, 115,* 74–101.

Dodge, K. A. (1982). Social cognitive biases and deficits in aggressive boys. *Child Development, 51*(1), 162–170.

Dominick, J. R., & Greenberg, B. S. (1972). Attitudes toward violence: The interaction of television exposure, family attitudes, and social class. In G. A. Comstock & E. A. Rubinstein (Eds.), *Television and social behavior: Vol. 3. Television and adolescent aggressiveness* (pp. 314–335). Washington, DC: Government Printing Office.

Doob, A. N., & Wood, L. (1972). Catharsis and aggression: The effects of annoyance and retaliation on aggressive behavior. *Journal of Personality and Social Psychology, 22,* 156–162.

Dorr, A., & Kovaric, P. (1980). Some of the people some of the time—but which people? Televised violence and its effects. In E. L. Palmer & A. Dorr (Eds.), *Children and the faces of television* (pp. 183–199). New York: Academic Press.

Dorr, A., & Kunkel, D. (1990). Children and the media environment: Change and constancy amid change. *Communication Research, 17,* 5–25.

Drabman, R. S., & Thomas, M. H. (1974). Does media violence increase children's toleration of real-life aggression? *Developmental Psychology, 10,* 418–421.

Elmer-Dewitt, P. (1993, September 27). The amazing video game. *Time,* p. 68.

Ensminger, M. E., Kellam, S. G., & Rubin, B. R. (1983). School and family origins of delinquency: Comparisons by sex. In K. T. Van Dusen & S. A. Mednick (Eds.), *Prospective studies of crime and delinquency* (pp. 73–97). Boston: Kluwer-Nijhoff.

Eron, L. D., & Huesmann, L. R. (1986). The role of television in the development of prosocial and antisocial behavior. In D. Olweus, J. Block, & M. Radke-Yarrow (Eds.), *Development of antisocial and prosocial behavior* (pp. 285–314). New York: Academic Press.

Eron, L. D., Huesmann, L. R., Lefkowitz, M. M., & Walder, O. (1972). Does television violence cause aggression? *American Psychologist, 27,* 253–263.

Eron, L. D., Walder, L. O., & Lefkowitz, M. M. (1971). *The learning of aggression in children.* Boston: Little Brown.

Eysenck, H. J., & Nias, D. K. (1978). *Sex, violence, and the media.* London: Maurice Temple Smith.

Farrington, D. P. (1982). Longitudinal analyses of criminal violence. In M. E. Wolfgang & N. A. Weiner (Eds.), *Criminal violence* (pp. 171–200). Beverly Hills, CA: Sage Publications.

Farrington, D. P. (1990). Childhood aggression and adult violence: Early precursors and later-life outcomes. In D. J. Pepler & K. H. Rubin (Eds.), *The development of childhood aggression* (pp. 5–29). Hillsdale, NJ: Erlbaum.

Fenigstein, A. (1979). Does aggression cause a preference for viewing media violence? *Journal of Personality and Social Psychology, 37,* 2307–2317.

Feshbach, S., & Singer, R. D. (1971). *Television and aggression: An experimental field study.* San Francisco: Jossey-Bass.

Freedman, J. (1984). Effect of television violence on aggressiveness. *Psychological Bulletin, 96,* 227–246.

Freud, S. (1933). *New introductory lectures on psychoanalysis.* (W. J. H. Sproutt, Trans.). New York: Norton.

Funk, J. A. (1993). Reevaluating the impact of video games. *Clinical Pediatrics, 32,* 86–90.

Geen, R. G. (1983). Aggression and television violence. In R. G. Geen & E. I. Donnerstein (Eds.), *Aggression: Theoretical and empirical reviews: Vol. 2. Issues and research* (pp. 103–125). New York: Academic Press.

Geen, R. G. (1990). *Human aggression.* Pacific Grove, CA: Brooks/Cole.

Geen, R. G., & O'Neal, E. C. (1969). Activation of cue-elicited aggression by general arousal. *Journal of Personality and Social Psychology, 11,* 289–292.

Geen, R. G., & Thomas, S. L. (1986). The immediate effects of media violence on behavior. *Journal of Social Issues, 42,* 7–28.

Gerbner, G., & Gross, L. P. (1974). *Violence profile no. 6: Trends in network television drama and viewer conceptions of social reality: 1967–1973.* Unpublished manuscript, Annenberg School of Communications, University of Pennsylvania.

Gerbner, G., & Gross, L. P. (1980). The violent face of television and its lessons. In E. L. Palmer & A. Dorr (Eds.), *Children and the faces of television: Teaching, violence, selling* (pp. 149–162). New York: Academic Press.

Gerbner, G., & Signorelli, N. (1990). *Violence profile, 1967 through 1988–1989: Enduring patterns.* Unpublished manuscript, Annenberg School of Communication, University of Pennsylvania.

Greenberg, B. S., Linsangan, R. L., & Soderman, A. (1987). *Adolescents and their exposure to television and movie sex.* (Project CAST Rep. No. 4). East Lansing: Michigan State University, Department of Telecommunication.

Greenberg, D. F. (1974–1975). British children and televised violence. *Public Opinion Quarterly, 38,* 531–547.

Greeson, L. E., & Williams, R. A. (1986). Social implications of music videos for youth. *Youth and Society, 188,* 177–189.

Halpern, W. I. (1975). Turned-on toddlers. *Journal of Communication, 25,* 66–70.

Hansen, C. H., & Hansen, R. D. (1989). *The content of MTS's daily countdown: "Dial MTV" for sex, violence, and antisocial behavior.* Unpublished manuscript.

Hansen, C. H., & Hansen, R. D. (1990a). Rock music videos and antisocial behavior. *Basic and Applied Social Psychology, 11,* 357–369.

Hansen, C. H., & Hansen, R. D. (1990b). The influence of sex and violence on the appeal of rock music videos. *Communication Research, 17,* 212–234.

Hayes, S. C., Rincover, A., & Volosin, D. (1980). Variables influencing the acquisition and maintenance of aggressive behavior: Modeling versus summary reinforcement. *Journal of Abnormal Psychology, 89,* 254–262.

Hearold, S. L. (1979). *Meta-analysis of the effects of television on social behavior.* Unpublished doctoral dissertation, University of Colorado.

Heller, M. S., & Polsky, S. (1976). *Studies in violence and television.* New York: American Broadcasting Company.

Hicks, D. J. (1965). Imitation and retention of film-mediated aggressive peer and adult models. *Journal of Personality and Social Psychology, 2,* 97–100.

Hokanson, J., & Burgess, M. (1962). The effects of status, type of frustration and aggression on vascular processors. *Journal of Abnormal and Social Psychology, 65,* 232–237.

Howitt, D., & Cumberbatch, G. (1975). *Mass media, violence, and society.* New York: Wiley.

Huesmann, L. R. (1982). Television violence and aggressive behavior. In D. Pearl, L. Bouthilet, & J. Lazar (Eds.), *Television and behavior: Ten years of programs and implications for the 80's* (pp. 126–137). Washington, DC: Government Printing Office.

Huesmann, L. R. (1986). Psychological processes promoting the relation between exposure to media violence and aggressive behavior by the viewer. *Journal of Social Issues, 42,* 3, 125–139.

Huesmann, L. R. (1988). An information processing model for the development of aggression. *Aggressive Behavior, 14,* 13–24.

Huesmann, L. R., & Bachrach, R. S. (1988). Differential effects of television violence in kibbutz and city children. In R. Patterson & P. Drummond (Eds.), *Television and its audience: International research perspectives* (pp. 154–176). London: BFI Publishing.

Huesmann, L. R., & Eron, L. D. (1984). Cognitive processes and the persistence of aggressive behavior. *Aggressive Behavior, 10,* 243–251.

Huesmann, L. R., & Eron, L. D. (1986). *Television and the aggressive child: A cross-national comparison.* Hillsdale: NJ: Erlbaum.

Huesmann, L. R., Eron, L. D., Berkowitz, L., & Chaffee, S. (1991). The effects of television violence on aggression: A reply to a skeptic. In P. Suedfeld & P. Tetlock (Eds.), *Psychology and social policy* (pp. 191–200). New York: Hemisphere.

Huesmann, L. R., Eron, L. D., Klein, R., Brice, P., & Fischer, P. (1983). Mitigating the imitation of aggressive behaviors by children's attitudes about media violence. *Journal of Personality and Social Psychology, 44,* 899–910.

Huesmann, L. R., Eron, L. D., Lefkowitz, M. M., & Walder, L. O. (1984). Stability of aggression over time and generations. *Developmental Psychology, 20,* 1120–1134.

Huesmann, L. R., Eron, L. D., & Yarmel, P. W. (1987). Intellectual functioning and aggression. *Journal of Personality and Social Psychology, 52,* 232–240.

Huesmann, L. R., & Guerra, N. G. (1997). Children's normative beliefs about aggression and aggressive behavior. *Journal of Personality and Social Psychology, 72*(2), 408–419.

Huesmann, L. R., Lagerspetz, K., & Eron, L. D. (1984). Intervening variables in the TV violence-aggression relation: Evidence from two countries. *Developmental Psychology, 20,* 746–775.

Huesmann, L. R., & Miller, L. S. (1994). Long-term effects of repeated exposure to media violence in childhood. In L. R. Huesmann (Ed.), *Aggressive behavior: Current perspectives* (pp. 153–186). New York: Plenum.

Huston, A. C., Donnerstein, E., Fairchild, H., Feshbach, N. D., Katz, P. A., Murray, J. P., Rubinstein, E. A., Wilcoz, B. L., & Zuckerman, D. (1992). *Big world, small screen: The role of television in American society.* Lincoln: University of Nebraska Press.

Johnson, J. D., Adams, M. S., Ashburn, L., & Reed, W. (1995). Differential gender effects of exposure to rap music on African American adolescents' acceptance of teen dating violence. *Sex Roles, 33*(7/8), 597–605.

Johnson, J. D., Jackson, L. A., & Gatto, L. (1994). Violent attitudes and deferred academic aspirations: Deleterious effects of exposure to rap music. *Basic and Applied Social Psychology, 16*(1&2), 27–41.

Josephson, W. L. (1987). Television violence and children's aggression: Testing the priming, social script, and disinhibition predictions. *Journal of Personality and Social Psychology, 53*(5), 882–890.

Kagan, J. (1988). Temperamental contributions to social behavior. *American Psychologist, 44,* 668–674.

Kaplan, R. M., & Singer, R. D. (1976). Television violence and viewer aggression: A reexamination of the evidence. *Journal of Social Issues, 32,* 35–70.

Kestenbaum, G. I., & Weinstein, L. (1985). Personality, psychopathology, and developmental issues in male adolescent video game use. *Journal of American Academic Child Psychiatry, 24,* 329–337.

Kubey, R., & Csikszentmihalyi, M. (1990). *Television and the quality of life: How viewing shapes everyday experience.* Hillsdale, NJ: Erlbaum.

Landau, S. F. (1984). Trends in violence and aggression: A cross-cultural analysis. *International Journal of Comparative Sociology, 25,* 133–158.

Lefkowitz, M. M., Eron, L. D., Walder, L. O., & Huesmann, L. R. (1977). *Growing up to be violent: A longitudinal study of the development of aggression.* Elmsford, NY: Pergamon.

Leyens, J. P., & Parke, R. D. (1975). Aggressive slides can induce a weapons effect. *European Journal of Social Psychology, 5*(2), 229–236.

Liebert, R. M., Sprafkin, J. N., & Davidson, E. S. (1982). *The early window: Effects of television on children and youth.* Elmsford, NY: Pergamon.

Linz, D. G., Donnerstein, E., & Penrod, S. (1988). Effects of long-term exposure to violent and sexually degrading depictions of women. *Journal of Personality and Social Psychology, 55,* 758–768.

Loeber, R., & Dishion, T. J. (1983). Early predictors of male delinquency: A review. *Psychological Bulletin, 94,* 68–94.

Magnusson, D., Duner, A., & Zetterblom, G. (1975). *Adjustment: A longitudinal study.* Stockholm: Almqvist & Wiksell.

Malamuth, N. M., & Check, J. V. P. (1981). The effects of mass media exposure on acceptance of violence against women: A field experiment. *Journal of Research in Personality, 15,* 436–446.

Malamuth, N. M., & Donnerstein, E. (1982). The effects of aggressive and pornographic mass media stimuli. In L. Berkowitz (Ed.), *Advances in experimental social psychology* (Vol. 15, pp. 103–136). New York: Academic Press.

Mediascope. (1996). *National television violence study: Executive summary 1994–1995.* Studio City, CA: Author.

Milavsky, J. R., Kessler, R., Stipp, H., & Rubens, W. S. (1982). Television and aggression: Results of a panel study. In D. Pearl, L. Bouthilet, & J. Lazar (Eds.), *Television and behavior: Ten years of scientific progress and implications for the 80's: Vol. 2. Technical reviews* (pp. 138–157). Washington, DC: Government Printing Office.

Moffitt, T. E. (1990). Juvenile delinquency and attention deficit disorder: Boys developmental trajectories from age 3 to age 15. *Child Development, 61,* 893–910.

Neely, J. J., Heckel, R. V., & Leichtman, H. M. (1973). The effect of race of model and response consequences to the model on imitation in children. *Journal of Social Psychology, 89,* 225–231.

Nicholas, K. B., McCarter, R. E., & Heckel, R. V. (1971). Imitation of adult and peer television models by White and Negro children. *Journal of Social Psychology, 85,* 317–318.

Oliver, M. B. (1994). Portrayals of crime, race, and aggression in "reality-based" police shows: A content analysis. *Journal of Broadcasting & Electronic Media, 38,* 179–192.

Olweus, D. (1979). Stability of aggressive reaction patterns in human males: A review. *Psychological Bulletin, 85,* 852–875.

Paik, H., & Comstock, G. A. (1994). The effects of television violence on antisocial behavior: A meta-analysis. *Communication Research, 21,* 516–546.

Parke, R. D., & Slaby, R. G. (1983). The development of aggression. In P. Mussen (Ed.), *Handbook of child psychology* (Vol. 4, pp. 547–642). New York: Wiley.

Phillips, D. P. (1979). Suicide, motor vehicle fatalities, and the mass media: Evidence toward a theory of suggestion. *American Journal of Sociology, 84,* 1150–1174.

Phillips, D. P. (1982). The impact of fictional television stories on U.S. adult fatalities: New evidence on the effect of the mass media on violence. *American Journal of Sociology, 87,* 1340–1359.

Phillips, D. P. (1983). The impact of mass media violence on U.S. homicides. *American Sociological Review, 48,* 560–568.

Phillips, D. P., & Bolen, K. A. (1985). Same time last year: Selective data dredging for negative findings. *American Sociological Review, 50,* 364–371.

Pitkannen-Pulkkinen, L. (1979). Self-control as a prerequisite for constructive behavior. In S. Feshbach & A. Fraczek (Eds.), *Aggression and behavior change* (pp. 250–270). New York: Praeger.

Provenzo, E. F. (1991). *Video kids: Making sense of Nintendo.* Cambridge, MA: Harvard University Press.

Robins, L. N., & Ratcliff, K. S. (1980). Childhood conduct disorders and later arrest. In L. N. Robins, P. J. Clayton, & J. K. Wing (Eds.), *The social consequences of psychiatric illness* (pp. 248–263). New York: Brunner/Mazel.

Rosenthal, R. (1986). Media violence, antisocial behavior, and the social consequences of small effects. *Journal of Social Issues, 42,* 141–154.

Schutte, N. S., Malouff, J. M., & Post-Gorden, J. C. (1988). Effects of playing videogames on children's aggressive and other behaviors. *Journal of Applied Social Psychology, 18,* 454–460.

Sherman, B. L., & Dominick, J. R. (1986). Violence and sex in music videos: TV and rock 'n' roll. *Journal of Communication, 36,* 79–93.

Silvern, S. B., & Williamson, P. A. (1987). The effects of video game play on young children's aggression, fantasy, and prosocial behavior. *Journal of Applied Developmental Psychology, 8,* 453–462.

Simon, A. (1979). Violence in the mass media: A case of modeling. *Perceptual and Motor Skills, 48,* 1081–1082.

Spivack, G. (1983). *High-risk early behaviors indicating vulnerability to delinquency in the community and school.* Washington, DC: NIMH.

Stack, S. (1989). The effect of publicized mass murders and murder-suicide on lethal violence. *Social Psychiatry and Psychiatric Epidemiology, 24,* 202–208.

Tangney, J. P., & Feshbach, S. (1988). Children's television-viewing frequency: Individual differences and demographic correlates. *Personality and Social Psychology Bulletin, 14*(1), 145–158.

Thomas, M. H., & Drabman, R. S. (1975). Toleration of real life aggression as a function of exposure to televised violence and age of subject. *Merrill-Palmer Quarterly, 21,* 227–232.

Thomas, M. H., Horton, R. W., Lippincott, E. C., & Drabman, R. S. (1977). Desensitization to portrayals of real life aggression as a function of television violence. *Journal of Personality and Social Psychology, 35,* 450–458.

U.S. Bureau of Census. (1993). *Statistical abstract of the United States* (p. 561). Washington, DC: Government Printing Office.

U.S. Department of Justice. (1990). *Sourcebook of criminal justice statistics-1990.* Washington, DC: Government Printing Office.

Viemero, V., & Paajanen, S. (1992). The role of fantasies and dreams in the TV viewing-aggression relationship. *Aggressive Behavior, 18*(2), 109–116.

Walters, R. H., Leat, M., & Mezei, L. (1963). Inhibition and disinhibition of responses through empathic learning. *Canadian Journal of Psychology, 17,* 235–243.

Walters, R. H., & Parke, R. D. (1964). Influence of response consequences to a social model on resistance to deviation. *Journal of Experimental Child Psychology, 1,* 269–280.

Walters, R. H., & Willows, D. C. (1968). Imitative behavior of disturbed and nondisturbed children following exposure to aggressive and nonaggressive models. *Child Development, 39,* 79–89.

Winn, M. (1977). *The plug-in-drug.* New York: Viking.

Wood, W., Wong, F. Y., & Chachere, G. (1991). Effects of media violence on viewers' aggression in unconstrained social interaction. *Psychological Bulletin, 109*(3), 371–383.

Worchel, S. (1972). The effect of films on the importance of behavioral freedom. *Journal of Personality, 40,* 417–435.

World Health Organization. (1965). *1962 world health statistics annual.* Geneva, Switzerland: Author.

World Health Organization. (1982). *1982 world health statistics annual.* Geneva, Switzerland: Author.

World Health Organization. (1993). *1992 world health statistics annual.* Geneva, Switzerland: Author.

Wyer, R. S., Jr., & Hartwick, J. (1980). The role of information retrieval and conditional inference processes in belief formation and change. In L. Berkowitz (Ed.), *Advances in experimental social psychology* (Vol. 13, pp. 241–284). New York: Academic Press.

Wyer, R. S., Jr., & Srull, T. (1981). Category accessibility: Some theoretical and empirical issues concerning the processing of information. In E. Higgins, C. Herman, & M. Zanna (Eds.), *Social cognition: The Ontario Symposium on Personality and Social Psychology* (Vol. 1, pp. 161–197). Hillsdale, NJ: Erlbaum.

Zillmann, D. (1971). Excitation transfer in communication-mediated aggressive behavior. *Journal of Experimental Social Psychology, 7,* 419–434.

Zillmann, D. (1978). Attribution and misattribution of excitatory reactions. In J. H. Harvey, W. J. Ickes, & R. F. Kidd (Eds.), *New directions in attribution research* (Vol. 2, pp. 335–368). Hillsdale, NJ: Erlbaum.

Zillmann, D. (1983). Transfer of excitation in emotional behavior. In J. T. Cacioppo & R. E. Petty (Eds.), *Social psychophysiology: A sourcebook* (pp. 215–240). New York: Guilford.

Zillmann, D. (1984). *Connections between sex and aggression.* Hillsdale, NJ: Erlbaum.

Zillmann, D., Katcher, A. H., & Milavsky, B. (1972). Excitation transfer from physical exercise to subsequent aggressive behavior. *Journal of Experimental Social Psychology, 8,* 247–259.

CHAPTER 19

Groups to Gangs: Developmental and Criminological Perspectives and Relevance for Prevention

ROBERT B. CAIRNS, TOM W. CADWALLADER, DAVID ESTELL, and HOLLY J. NECKERMAN

Requests have been made in recent years for greater cooperation across disciplines in order to understand and prevent antisocial and violent behavior (e.g., *Healthy People 2000;* Reiss & Roth, 1993). One of the more important design advances has been the use of interdisciplinary longitudinal studies to investigate the influence of families and individual factors on antisocial behavior and crime. This information has extended our knowledge of the trajectories of antisocial behavior in individual development (e.g., Moffitt, 1993; Sampson & Laub, 1993). In addition, the use of development-informed models has expanded our understanding of the contributions of biological and genetic factors to prevention (e.g., Earls, Cairns, & Mercy, 1993; Stoff & Cairns, 1996).

There remain, however, significant areas in which seemingly linked disciplines behave as if they live in different worlds. One of these has been the investigation of social and group influences in developmental psychology and criminology. The study of gangs and gang activities by criminologists historically has had only modest overlap with the investigation of friendships, social organization, and social networks by developmental psychologists. Save for some important exceptions (e.g., Huizinga, Esbensen, & Weiher, 1991; Thornberry, Krohn, Lizotte, & Chard-Wierschem, 1993), work on gangs rarely cites advances in understanding the ontogeny of normal peer group relations. Conversely, developmental studies of social group formation and friendships among children show little awareness of the rapidly expanding findings on gangs and gang activities.

In the light of the different foci of the two areas, the lack of overlap is regrettable but understandable. Criminological investigations of gangs are primarily concerned with the dark side of synchrony, whereas developmental studies are concerned with productive and adaptive products of friendships and social groups. But are the processes that give rise to these different social out-

comes related? To adumbrate one of the conclusions of this chapter, key issues in both disciplines may be clarified by looking across areas at groups and gangs in terms of methods, issues, and findings.

DEFINITIONS AND DISTINCTIONS

Disciplinary separation has been associated with increasing distance in the evolution of concepts of social behavior that, on commonsense grounds, seem to have considerable overlap.[1] The definitions of group and gang provide a case in point. In criminology, the concept of *gang* is wedded to legal and illegal considerations. According to Miller (1975):

> A gang is a group of recurrently associating individuals with identifiable membership and internal organization, identifying with or claiming control over territory in the community, and engaging either individually or collectively in violent or other forms of illegal behavior. (p. 22)

Accordingly, violence, community coercion, and illegal behavior have been salient and defining features of gangs. The other criteria—including identifiable internal organization and the claim of control over territory in the community—may be less general across conceptual and international boundaries. This definition speaks to U.S. street gangs rather than, say, family gang organiza-

---

[1]Conversely, use of the same term with different definitions can provide the illusion of similarity when different concepts are involved. The differential uses and meanings of the term *attachment* in psychology and criminology illustrate the point. The neopsychoanalytic term popularized by Bowlby (1969) and Ainsworth (1972) in psychology and psychiatry referred to the mother-infant bond and had precise meaning in the context of object relations theory and measurement. In criminology, however, *attachment* refers to a key feature of control theory (Hirschi, 1969) and peer group analysis (Elliott, Huizinga, & Menard, 1989). In this context, it refers to the quality and intensity of the individual's commitment to the conventional institutions of society, including school, home, and family.

This research was supported in part by funds from the National Institute of Mental Health (P50 MH52429 and RO1 MH45532). Beverly D. Cairns was co-principal investigator of the Carolina Longitudinal Study, and we thank her for her several contributions to this chapter.

tions in the United States or gangs of homeless urban street children common in the cities of Meso America and South America.[2]

By contrast, developmental investigators employ the constructs of social group, cluster, and clique to refer to informal sets of recurrently associated individuals. Moreover, developmentalists typically emphasize the happy side of such associations: Friendships, popularity, and being accepted by a peer group are presumed to promote self-identity, social integration, and social competence (e.g., Ladd, 1990; Youniss, 1980). Less attention has been given to the shadows of synchrony and the factors that give rise to coercion, deviance, and violence in groups. To the extent that this fundamental difference characterizes the two orientations, it is small wonder that the research programs and interpretations of criminology and developmental psychology have evolved in different directions.

Is a rapprochement possible? Perhaps, given that the developmental conception of social groups, unlike the criminological definition of gangs, is theoretically open with respect to the functions, structures, and behavioral qualities associated with groups. In the developmental framework, groups can be associated with either productive or destructive consequences. They can have a fluid, penetrable structure or a tight, hierarchical organization. In this regard, Cairns, Leung, Buchanan, and Cairns (1995) indicate that

> Peer social network is an inclusive concept, referring to the social relations among all students and groups of students in a specific context (classroom, grade, school). Social group refers to subsets of persons (cliques or clusters) within the network. Not all persons in the network necessarily belong to a social group, and some persons may belong to two or more groups. (p. 1332)

More generally, the stability, ontogeny, structure, membership, and functions of social groups are posed as issues that are open to systematic investigation rather than closed by initial definition.

Is a rapprochement worth the effort? There is much to argue for the view that there are large areas in criminology for which developmental considerations are only marginally relevant and vice versa (e.g., Hirschi & Gottfriedson, 1983).[3] Moreover, in some domains, the two disciplines have been at loggerheads for nearly the entire century (Schlossman & Cairns, 1993). The differences lie not merely in specific methods, theories, or professional rivalries. The more general difficulty is that some of the core concepts of the two disciplines are not readily transplanted because of different orientations to human behavior. Delinquency and crime speak to legal concepts; developmental considerations speak to the causes of prosocial and adaptive behaviors. The defi-

nitions of gangs and groups provide a case in point. Within each discipline, precise definition is achieved by embedding constructs within a network of relations specific to its application and use in that domain of inquiry.

Despite these hazards, we believe that developmental analyses potentially can be informative with respect to some issues central to criminology. Moreover, the study of the concrete realities of adolescent deviance may provide a new dimension to the work and thinking of developmentalists. Accordingly, this chapter explores whether the findings, concepts, and perspectives of research on the development of social groups can be useful in understanding gang formation, function, and prevention.[4] In the light of recent empirical research, we critically evaluate seven issues, namely:

- Social rejection in childhood groups and adolescent gangs
- Developmental transitions from groups and gangs
- Pathways to gang involvement
- Stability and fluidity in groups and gangs
- Gender similarities and differences in groups and gangs
- Strategies of intervention and prevention
- Advances in methodology and assessment

SOCIAL REJECTION IN CHILDHOOD GROUPS AND ADOLESCENT GANGS

The proposition that deviant groups and gangs are composed of youths who, as children, were rejected by peers has a lengthy history in criminology and developmental psychology. It continues to be the dominant theme in both disciplines, despite conflicting evidence.

The Proposal

The childhood-rejection-to-adolescent-deviance idea has been influential in both criminology and developmental psychology. Hirschi's (1969) control theory of delinquency, Yablonsky's (1962) descriptions of gangs, and the sociometric status analyses of "rejected" children (Asher & Coie, 1990) can be integrated to present a compelling story. In this regard, Yablonsky (1962) writes,

> Today's violent delinquent is a displaced person—suspicious, fearful, and not willing or able to establish a concrete human relationship. . . . Violent gang organization is ideally suited to the defective personality and limited social ability of these disturbed youths. . . . they join gangs because they lack the social ability to relate to others, not because the gang gives them a "feeling of belonging." (pp. 3–4)

Following this line of reasoning, delinquent and aggressive youth are socially marginal or incompetent. Rejected by conventional

---

[2]In the recent literature in ethology and developmental psychology, the term *gang* has been used loosely to refer to tightly knit groups of adolescents but without reference to the essential element of deviance. In this regard, Suomi (1996) refers to gangs of juvenile rhesus monkeys (i.e., preadult males who associate in closely knit groups during the transition from infancy to adulthood).

[3]These include, for example, descriptions of structural-demographic factors in crime, the processes of the legal system and how it functions, and the sociopolitical factors involved in penal policies.

[4]Whereas this discussion inevitably reflects our concern with developmental issues, it should be noted that one of the authors (RBC) was employed in the psychological clinic of a juvenile residential facility and the second (TWC) was a supervising criminal investigator.

society and peers, delinquent youth are forced to join with other social deviants. Hirschi (1969) writes, "The idea that delinquents have comparatively warm, intimate social relations with each other (or with anyone) is a romantic myth" (p. 159).

A similar theme characterizes contemporary cognitive–social learning views, albeit with a shift toward the primacy in deficiencies in social cognition rather than social affiliations. This shift follows an emphasis on the role of cognitive factors in some basic processes of social learning, including modeling, social reinforcement, and social motivation (Bandura & Walters, 1963; Cairns, 1961). In this model, distortions in information processing predispose problems of social interchange. These distortions lead in turn to aggressive behaviors by the child and subsequent social rejection, isolation, or both. Once rejected by peers, the individual becomes the target for further aggression. So the cycle goes. The upshot is that the aggressive adolescent is seen as being rejected or controversial in his or her social status, unpopular with peers, and marginally competent in social settings (see also Asher & Dodge, 1986; Coie & Dodge, 1983; Roff & Wirt, 1984).

Two Unresolved Issues

Two theoretical issues can be raised. One has to do with the abrupt shift in the rejected child's ability to be a member of a social group, deviant or otherwise, when the individual becomes an adolescent. How can a person who is isolated or rejected from social groups in childhood become incorporated into a social group or gang in adolescence? One answer, proposed by Moffitt (1993), is that the social context and social roles of children shift when they reach puberty. Hence, the antisocial and aggressive behavior that is rejected in childhood becomes more acceptable in adolescence, and the once-rejected antisocial child becomes a prototype for admiration and acceptance in adolescence. Another answer is that adolescent gains in affiliative capabilities are only illusions. Deviant groups and gangs of adolescence are composed of social rejects, and they have modest or nonexistent social ties to each other.

These two propositions—role transformation and affiliation by exclusion—are open to empirical evaluation. They can be assessed directly by examining the nature and quality of intimate social relationships and friendships formed by aggressive and antisocial individuals in childhood and adolescence.

This brings up a second issue of theory, namely, the basic problem of why there should be a link between social rejection, social cognitive deficits, and deviant behaviors in adolescence. Social rejection and social deficit propositions explain deviant behaviors by a focus on what is absent rather than what is present. Alternative proposals point to the social context and the productive support of antisocial behavior provided by dynamic events in the immediate environment (see Clarke-McLean, 1996, for a succinct review).

Relevant Developmental Data

Three classes of developmental data seem relevant to these theoretical issues, namely information on (a) the formation of friendships among aggressive children prior to adolescence, (b) the kinds of social groups formed by individuals in childhood and adolescence, and (c) the quality of social relationships established by aggressive children in both age frames.

First, do highly aggressive children have friends and form groups in childhood, or are they isolated and rejected? The empirical answer depends on the method employed. On the one hand, *social network and friendship* analyses indicate that highly aggressive children have as many reciprocated friendships as children as do nonaggressive children. Developmental studies show that peer groups among aggressive children are established in elementary school as early as the third and fourth grades (Cairns, Cairns, Neckerman, Gest, & Gariépy, 1988; Farmer & Hollowell, 1994). Furthermore, the groups to which they belong are as likely to be central in the school social networks as are nonaggressive groups (Cairns et al., 1988), and highly aggressive children are as likely to be nuclear in social status as nonaggressive children (Cairns et al, 1988; Farmer & Rodkin, 1996).

On the other hand, *sociometric status* analyses consistently show that aggressive children are (a) less likely to be named in classroom nominations as persons who are liked and (b) more likely by all other classmates to be named as persons who are hostile and disliked. In computing sociometric status categories, the combination of positive and negative classroom votes that many highly aggressive children receive qualify them for the "rejected" sociometric status category (Bukowski, Pizzamiglio, Newcomb, & Hoza, 1996). The sociometric designation "rejected" thus includes many children who are dominant or bullies and otherwise control the peer social network in addition to those who may be isolated and ostracized by peers.

The paradox is that sociometrically "rejected" children have been shown to have as many reciprocated friendships as children in "nonrejected" sociometric categories. Although such "rejected" children may be feared and disliked by many of their classmates, they are no more likely than other children to be isolated or on the periphery of the social group (Farmer & Rodkin, 1996). In brief, this appears to be a case in which the operational meaning of the sociometric construct "rejection" differs from its common language meaning. *In the sociometric status framework, "rejection" captures one common language feature of the term (i.e., being disliked by many) but misses the mark with respect to other equally critical aspects (i.e., being friendless, ostracized, or socially ineffective).*

Second, the children with whom aggressive children form friendships and social groups tend to be aggressive themselves. That is, there is a selective affiliation and selective choice on the basis of behavior, particularly acting-out, assertive behaviors. This dual selection appears in both childhood and adolescence (e.g., Cairns & Cairns, 1994; Dishion, 1990; Leung, 1996). Even with the restricted range of antisocial behaviors of adolescents who live in a maximum security reform center, persons within the same social groups "had similar levels of behavioral adjustment and perceptions of intimacy with peers" (Clarke-McLean, 1996, p. 203).

Such groups can become dominant in a social network, whether in the school or the reform institution. Once established, they can undermine the authority of classroom teachers and school principals and challenge the integrity of conventional institutions. In the face of such challenges, groups of aggressive children or adolescents may paradoxically be consolidated by the efforts of authorities to disengage, disband, or diminish their power.

A third question follows directly from the preceding findings. Even if the aggressive children form friendships and establish groups, are these relationships not inherently more fragile and less intimate than those formed by nonaggressive children? The answer to this question is provided by investigations that have assessed intimacy directly. Giordano, Cernkovich, and Pugh (1986) reported the self-reports of friendships from youths representing the full range of delinquency involvement. Deviant youths have friends who are of a similar deviant status. Moreover, the more seriously delinquent girls report the same levels of intimacy and trust in their relationships as do the less delinquent girls. These findings on similar levels of intimacy were replicated and expanded by Clarke-McLean (1996) in her investigation of the social networks of incarcerated youths (see also Elliott, Huizinga, & Menard, 1989). How then is the question on childhood rejection and adolescent gangs to be answered? Given the present evidence, it looks as if the problem lies in discrepant uses of terms and constructs rather than discrepant empirical findings. The available data now support the conclusion that aggressive and deviant youths have close friends and are members of social groups in both childhood and adolescence. The evidence indicates that these relationships are as numerous and intimate as those of nondeviant youths. But there is a difference in the kinds of persons with whom they affiliate: Deviant children tend to affiliate with others like themselves, and the same holds for nondeviant children. Group formation, among both deviant and nondeviant children, is not an invention of adolescence. Hence, there is no need to postulate a newfound social competence for deviant youths at puberty.

Although aggressive youths tend to have friends and form social groups, such friends and affiliations are hardly protective. To the contrary, groups of aggressive and deviant children tend to be disfavored and rejected by conventional institutions (e.g., school administrators and teachers). Hence, the term *school dropout* may be a euphemism for the active rejection of youths by the school authorities, including suspension and expulsion. Negative feelings generated in teachers and administrators by disruptive behavior can be transmitted to classmates and become incorporated into peer attitudinal structures. Insofar as preference contests are influenced by these conventional attitudes, aggressive and deviant youths taken as groups may be seen as being feared or disliked by classmates and teachers alike. Over time, aggressive children who are not committed to schools become as adolescents increasingly disenfranchised from conventional institutions and vulnerable to multiple problems of living (i.e., early school dropout, teenage parenthood, arrests for violence). If these youths live in neighborhoods or communities where gangs are prevalent, they are also at high risk for gang involvement.

DEVELOPMENTAL TRANSITIONS FROM GROUPS AND GANGS

Developmental analyses indicate that peer social networks and deviant subgroups do not emerge de novo in adolescence. They are alive and well by 10 years of age and before. Some of the primary findings on development of social clusters concern their emergence in childhood, behavioral and nonbehavioral dimensions critical for biselection, continuity of roles and groups over time, and developmental changes in group composition and dynamics. As it turns out, it does not seem necessary to invent special principles for the negative outcomes of peer groups; the same processes appear to operate for the positive ones.

Four Propositions

In a recent analysis of the tracking of social groups over time, Cairns and Cairns (1994) point to some general propositions whereby the friendships and groups of childhood become translated, under special circumstances, into the gangs of adolescence.

The first proposition is that a strong bias exists toward social synchrony at all developmental stages, in that actions and attitudes of other persons are readily enmeshed with the behavioral organization of the individual. One by-product of this reciprocal integration is mutual similarity. Beginning in late childhood and early adolescence, there is a sharp developmental increase in the ability to reciprocate behaviors beyond the dyad in unstructured relationships with peers. The resultant peer clusters develop norms and behavioral similarities that can support—or compete with—those of other social units, including the family and the school.

A second proposition is that social clusters not only provide for intimacy and personal identity but are tools to express individual aggression and control. There are norms for initial acceptance into the cluster that serve to promote internal synchrony. Such "gate-keeping" criteria help to heighten the likelihood of initial similarity of cluster members with regard to key characteristics. These criteria shift as a function of age, context, and the goals and needs of the members. In childhood, gender membership is universally important, and most childhood clusters are unisex. What is valued (or devalued) reflects parental standards and expectations, as well as the age-gender status of the individual. With the onset of adolescence, cluster boundaries become increasingly rigid, and the conditions for selection and entry become more clearly delineated in terms of behaviors and values.

A third proposition is that strong reciprocal forces operate on all members toward conformity with respect to salient attitudes and behaviors. An extension of influence across persons within the cluster leads to the establishment of generalized patterns of deviance, beyond the index behavior that may have been required for initial group entry. But a common standard for deviance is only one of the outcomes of the reciprocal exchanges within groups. Once in a social group, there is conformity with respect to a broad spectrum of behaviors and attitudes, including shared linguistic and communication patterns, areas of worry and concern, and "lifestyle" characteristics. For many youths, the problem is to escape from synchrony with deviant or escalating values. Hence, social isolation is often a buffer from delinquency.

The fourth proposition is that there are powerful effects of reciprocal influence within groups, leading to high levels of behavioral and attitudinal similarity, regardless of the initial status of the persons involved. The evidence on adolescent group dynamics strongly points to the operation of both differential selection factors and reciprocal influences. At every stage, individuals are changed by their associations, and they carry to the next set of relationships the behavioral residue of the recent past. These changes provide the basis for new alliances and a fresh network of supporting relationships.

In sum, social relations over the life course do not depict static structures. Over time, specific social relationships among persons and groups may fade into the background or be thrust into the foreground, depending on time and context. Over the life span, persons tend to affiliate with, to influence, and to be influenced by others who share common interests, behaviors, and beliefs. At each developmental stage, this web of social relations provides boundaries, opportunities, and a frame of reference for actions and attitudes. According to Cairns (1996),

> Social groups . . . are themselves embedded within larger social units which cohere on the basis of similarities in gender, age, race, time, and space. . . . The individual is enmeshed throughout development in a fabric of influence that includes the immediate dyads and groups with which she/he affiliates and the social network of which these groups are a part. (p. 113)

But why are gangs a special concern for adolescents and young adults and not, say, for children and persons in middle age? Gang formation at this stage of development seems to reflect the developmental convergence of three factors, namely, (a) dissociation from the constraints of conventional community and parental authority that many youth enjoy at adolescence, (b) the persistence of patterns of direct aggressive confrontation from childhood to adolescence, and (c) the special role that aggression and coercive behavior play in the organization and direction of groups when external constraints are absent.[5] Whenever these three factors are present, the probability of aggressive and violent group formation—gangs—is heightened, regardless of gender. Accordingly, the greater the abdication of authority by the communities and their natural representatives (parents, schools, police), the more likely that gangs of youths will form to create their own rules and impose them on others in the community.

Age and Gangs

Many criminologists view the proliferation of gangs as the product of social forces, driven by a deepening urban underclass (Hagedorn & Macon, 1988; Jackson, 1995). Gangs are seen as held together by forces external to the group, such as out-group aggression (Klein & Crawford, 1967; Strodtbeck & Short, 1983). Gang membership as a group process is believed to serve the function of facilitating delinquent behavior (Thornberry et al., 1993).

The issue of age in gang membership has a long background in the criminology literature. In his classic work on gangs, Thrasher (1927) found in his survey of 1,313 gangs in the Chicago area that most of the gangs were made up of "earlier adolescents" from the ages of 11 to 17 (455 gangs, or 37.51% of the total) and "later adolescents" from the ages of 16 to 25 (305 gangs, or 25.15% of the total). He identified only 18 gangs (1.48% of the total) that fell into

the "childhood" category, with age ranges of 6 to 12 years. These childhood gangs were described as more "mischievous" than violent. Adult gangs (21 to 50 years of age) made up 3.13% of the total sample, with 38 cases. There are some large problems with Thrasher's work, however. He used an inclusive definition of gangs, and it was so broad as to encompass athletic clubs (though these were treated separately from the data just given). However, later researchers found that the age ranges of gangs in Chicago in the 1960s were of similar overall composition but that any given single gang had a wide range of ages (Cartwright, Thompson, & Schwartz, 1975). The difference in overall gang patterns of age and individual gang patterns may simply be due to the fact that Thrasher considered age-graded divisions of gangs to be separate gangs (e.g., the Little Murderers and Big Murderers), thus by definition reducing the age range for a particular gang. Later researchers tend to consider such divisions to be auxiliaries of the same gang.

In a commentary on factors important to gang behavior, Rojek and Jensen (1982) suggest age as an important but little-studied variable and call for a closer look at it. Despite a lack of an abundance of age studies, some evidence does exist for a change in age trends. It has been suggested that the age range for some gangs has expanded to 9 to 30 years, with the younger children being utilized largely as lookouts for illegal activity (Goldstein, 1991) and the older members remaining because of increasingly few legitimate employment opportunities. Some theorists echo this view, speculating that gangs are getting older (Horowitz, 1990; Huff, 1989, 1990; Klein, 1995; Klein & Maxson, 1989, 1990; Short, 1990); a prevailing interpretation is that a lack of economic opportunities in poorer sectors of society, where gangs usually form (Covey, Menard, & Franzese, 1992; Klein, 1995). This leads to a prolonged adolescence because of the limited opportunities for adult employment (Covey et al., 1992). Part of this prolonged adolescence is prolonged involvement in gang activity.

Even these contentions about gangs getting older have been refuted by some. Lasley (1992) concludes that gangs are not in fact getting older, based on his study of Los Angeles gang members, whose age peaked at around 16 to 17 years and declined thereafter. In the gangs from low socioeconomic status backgrounds, he found that 6.5% of the members were under the age of 13, and 14.8% were over the age of 20. Compared with Thrasher's data of 1.48% for the 6 to 12 age group and 3.13% for the 21 to 50 age group, a possible trend emerges: The peak is still at around 16 to 17, but it appears as though the extremes are increasing in numbers. Further evidence for a possible lowering in age comes indirectly from several sources. In 1984, the average age of gang members in Chicago was 15 but dropped to 13.5 by 1987 (Covey et al., 1992). Miller, Geertz, and Cutter (1968) indicate that 2.5% of all crimes are committed by 8- to 12-year-olds, and the National Research Council report on prevention and understanding of violence indicates a continuity of aggression after 7 to 8 years of age (Reiss & Roth, 1993), making gang involvement a possibility at these early ages. With the enactment of laws in many states that lower the age at which juvenile offenders can be tried as adults (in major offenses, the minimum age in California is down to 12 years), a logical result may be recruitment by gangs of increasingly young members who face less harsh treatment at the hands of the juvenile authorities, a role for which anyone under the age of 14 or 15 was suited a few years ago.

---

[5]All things equal, the activities of individuals in groups are organized around highly salient coercive and aggressive acts (Cairns, 1979; Hall & Cairns, 1984; Patterson, 1982; Raush, 1965).

Pathways to Gang Involvement

Who gets recruited or otherwise attracted to adolescent gang involvement? If not rejected children, who are the prime candidates? It is unfortunate that there have been virtually no prospective studies of the processes by which individual children are drawn into gangs. Nonetheless, the information available suggests that there are at least two distinct routes and possibly three. The routes differ with respect to the background of the individual and the supporting community context.

One pathway involves the direct escalation in the intensity of aggressive actions and the level of deviant, illegal behavior. Given the continuity in aggressive behavior and aggressive groups over time, it seems reasonable to expect that aggressive groups of children are drawn, in some circumstances, to deviant gangs of adolescents. In this regard, Cairns and Cairns (1994) report that there is high awareness of gang activity and gang presence among children in the inner city, from the 4th grade through high school. In the same inner-city community, Gaines (1993) found that the most central and salient group in a large middle city consisted of six males in the 7th grade who were also named as members of a recognized street gang. Rather than being on the periphery of the social networks in the school, the gang was central and dominant. Further prospective research is required to determine how such groups develop over time and the consequences for individuals of belonging to emergent gangs (see also Xie, 1995).

The other pathway to gang involvement appears to reflect, in part, the circumstances described by Yablonsky (1962). Again, the data on the matter are fragmentary but suggestive. In their 16-year longitudinal study, Cairns and Cairns (1994) found that the members of their representative cohorts who become involved in gang activity tend to be otherwise disaffiliated and ostracized, including runaways and homeless youths. In one of the cases they cite, Heidi was an above-average seventh grader living in a middle-class home in a small midsouthern town near the Atlantic coast. She hung around with a group of three other girls who had a lot in common: worries about home, fantasies about boys, and a concern about school grades. After the seventh grade, things fell apart in Heidi's relationships at home, particularly with her stepmother. She ran away and at 15 years of age became "homeless" on the streets of a community in southern California. The next year, she recalled:

> It was an awful place, but you know I found a few friends on one street—it was called Broadway. It was kinda like Main Street around here you know. It's awful. It was the slums. There were a few good people there. It was all right. They wouldn't let nothing happen to me 'cause I was the baby on the street. (p. 137)

She then became, at 16 years of age, the "old lady" for the head of a well-known motorcycle gang. In response to the interview's query about current concerns and worries, Heidi said:

> The things I worry about—my Old Man getting busted—going to jail or anyone—you know, the guys that live here. You know we're all one family there. I'm afraid something'll happen to them. (p. 130)

In concluding their discussion, Cairns and Cairns (1994) write:

For Heidi, the progression from an average middle school adolescent to a homeless street person to a "family" member is not merely a story of social alienation—her rejection of society and conventional norms as much as vice-versa—it also has elements of acceptance. The bonds formed by Heidi at these stages were perceived by her to be strong and protective. They were also critical for survival. (pp. 137–138)

With age, both pathways may give way to a more enduring economic structure. Illicit drug activity—where gangs and gang members are given responsibility for local sales and regional distribution—is a volatile but potentially extremely profitable business. The semi-organized crime associated with drug sales carries serious hazards, yet it can yield large returns. Members do not have to be users to be dealers. For related persons, crime can be a family business. This kind of family enterprise is not limited to the mafioso; such family organizations have been found in virtually all cities, suburbs, or rural areas where longitudinal studies have been conducted. When the returns of sporadic and semi-organized crime graduates to the more organized sort, economic inducements can provide powerful support for continued involvement in gang activity.

In brief, different pathways underscore the diversity of persons and circumstances that give rise to and support gang activity. In the first instance, the deterioration of the social community in which youths develop invites gang involvement at some stage. This is the pathway that has been highlighted in recent developmental models and earlier theories of differential association in criminology (e.g., A. K. Cohen, 1955). In the second instance, the young person may become involved in an alienation cycle in which one of the only remaining options is the insecurity of homelessness and the partial security of gang affiliation. This is the pathway that has been focused on by control theory (e.g., Brennan, Huizinga, & Elliott, 1978; Hirschi, 1969). The third pathway of economic inducement and family enterprise may be seen as a separate route but, more realistically, as a complement to the other routes in early adolescence. In any case, it seems of great importance to continue to explore in prospective longitudinal analyses these and other potential pathways to social adaptation and social security.

STABILITY AND FLUIDITY IN GROUPS AND GANGS

There is an abiding assumption in both developmental psychology and criminology that stability and predictability in social relations are good, whereas instability and change are suspect. For instance, it has been assumed that children who have been classified as "popular" will have more stable friendships and will show higher levels of adjustment than those who have been classified as "rejected" (Ladd, 1990). The data on the stability of social groups are mixed. For instance, Hallinan (1980) reported that 18% of the naturally formed peer groups in middle school classes remained stable over the school year. J. M. Cohen (1977), on the other hand, reported that 76% of the peer groups in high school remained stable from the fall to the spring semesters. Because the two investigations differed on several factors relevant to stability—age of subjects, criteria for identifying groups, methods for assessing stability—the reason for the difference in findings was unclear.

This discrepancy illustrates the general failure of published investigations of peer social groups to specify linkages between different methods, analyses, and constructs. The methods of collecting data have ranged from self-reports (e.g., Giordano et al., 1986) and parental nominations of a child's social networks (Feiring & Lewis, 1987), to direct observations (e.g., Cairns, Gariépy, & Kindermann, 1990; Ladd, Price, & Hart, 1988; Strayer & Santos, 1996) and ethnographic reports (Dunphy, 1963; Eder, 1985; Savin-Williams, 1979). It seems reasonable to expect that these data collection procedures differ not only in economy and accessibility but also in the extent they reflect biases in reporting.

In attempting to resolve these discrepancies, Cairns et al. (1995) recently explored the effects of different criteria and methods of assessment. They found that regardless of the method employed, social relationships among peers in schools endure over the short-term, but even close relationships and coherent social groups are likely to wax and wane in strength.

Their data may help explain the difference between the 76% group stability estimate of J. M. Cohen (1977) and the 18% stability estimate of Hallinan (1980). Beyond the difference in age of subjects in the two studies, there was a major difference between the Cohen and Hallinan investigations in the criterion adopted for stability. In Cohen's investigation, at least 50% of the fall group's members had to be members of the same group in the spring (or vice versa), and there was a single reassessment. For Hallinan, a "stable clique was defined as one that retains at least three of its members for an entire year" (p. 335). In addition, at least three members had to be represented in all successive assessments over the school year (there were a minimum of six assessments for each classroom). In recognition of the severity of this criterion, Hallinan concluded, "This phenomenon [low stability] may be an artifact of the definition of clique employed in the analysis: a weaker definition is likely to result in more stable cliques" (p. 337). A strict criterion in the Cairns et al. (1995) work yielded an estimate consistent with the low stability reported by Hallinan (1980); a relaxed criterion was consistent with the high stability estimate reported by J. M. Cohen (1977).

More generally, there is little support for the belief that same-sex peer groups are relatively stable and constant over time (Berndt & Hoyle, 1985; Cairns et al., 1995; Neckerman, 1996). Neckerman (1996) describes the peer group as a fluid, ongoing process, but one that is significantly constrained by opportunity and proximity. The social groups of 220 fourth graders and 475 seventh graders were tracked longitudinally over 1 year. The overall results indicated that approximately 30% of the social groups were identified as stable (i.e., they maintained at least 50% of their membership over the year). Moreover, the stability in group affiliations was a function of the stability of the composition of the classroom. When schools did not promote classrooms as a unit, 7% of social groups were stable, compared to 55% group stability when the school promoted classrooms as a unit. There was high correlation (r_s = .97) between classroom stability and group stability when the classroom was taken as the unit of analysis. Neckerman (1996) concludes, "In unstable classrooms, individuals were more likely to maintain affiliations when group members

were assigned to the same classroom" (p. 139). This work suggests that stable environments promote stable relationships, which, in turn, may promote greater continuity in the organization of behavioral patterns, for good or for ill. Other reports find few differences in the stability of social groups (Neckerman, 1992) and friendships (Buchanan, 1995) among highly aggressive and matched-nonaggressive subjects over a period of 6 years.

These findings indicate that the fluidity and change in gangs and gang membership may be part of a broader picture of the fickleness of social relationships in adolescence. Indeed, the previous theoretical analysis suggests that there may be even greater stability among deviant groups and gangs than among nondeviant groups. The stability could be promoted by forces within the group (i.e., distinctive similarities in common activities) and forces without (i.e., greater hazards for leaving a gang than remaining in it). Even in moderately deviant aggressive groups of childhood and adolescence, there is a tendency toward social inertia—for stability to be maintained in group influences despite changes in group composition. Although there are changes in group membership or friendships, children and adolescents reconstitute the same type of group with which they have been previously affiliated. Therefore, youths who have been in a deviant group in the prior year tend to become members of a similarly deviant group during the current and upcoming year. In brief "there is consistency in influence, despite changing faces" (Cairns & Cairns, 1994, p. 259).

GENDER SIMILARITIES AND DIFFERENCES IN GROUPS AND GANGS

Investigations of girls and gangs have lagged relative to the study of parallel phenomena in boys. This difference in scientific investment is consistent with the pervasive gender bias that exists in developmental research on aggressive and criminological studies of antisocial and violent behavior. However, the literature indicates that (a) girls have become increasingly likely during the 20th century to be arrested for crimes of violence and assault (Schlossman & Cairns, 1993); (b) girls show high levels of homophily for aggressive behavior in the groups that they form in adolescence (Cairns & Cairns, 1994); and (c) female gangs do exist, and they have similar structure and initiation rites as male gangs and can be very violent (Campbell, 1984).

Cernkovich and Giordano (1979) make the point that the difference between male and female delinquents is the number of their delinquent acts, not the type of acts in which they might engage. Though arrest rates are lower for females, delinquency rates of female gang members exceed those of both male and female nongang members (Fagan, 1990; Miller, 1975, 1977; Spergel, 1986). The criminology literature indicates that although female participation in gangs was primarily in auxiliaries to male gangs (Miller, 1975, 1977; Short 1968), such auxiliary-only roles may decline as more female gangs form (Bowker, 1978; Bowker & Klein, 1983).

One of the more interesting recent findings concerns what is required to gain status among peer groups. Specifically, in inner-city samples of children and adolescents, the cohesive groups that girls form tend to be supportive of conventional values, and girls who are central in the social network tend to be viewed by teachers as being popular. Conversely, boys who have high centrality and status in the inner-city schools are characterized by high levels of aggressive behavior (Xie, 1995). These findings are consistent with the proposition that there are greater restrictions on the formation of antisocial female gangs than on antisocial male gangs in inner-city populations. These restrictions may come from school authorities, and they may also reflect attitudes that prevail among the children and adolescents themselves.

STRATEGIES OF INTERVENTION AND PREVENTION

Can normative groups prevent deviant gang involvement? Some of the criminological theory leans in this direction, especially the social ecology theories that identify the failure of family, school, and job opportunities as key factors in the formation of gangs (Covey et al., 1992; Shaw & McKay, 1942; Thrasher, 1927). However, the empirical findings tend to contradict this view. Boston's Mid-City Project of 1954–1957 sought to involve gang members in normative activities such as sports and involved churches, schools, and other such normative institutions as a way of intervening and ameliorating deviant behaviors. It failed, and court appearances actually increased for the kids involved (Covey et al., 1992). Further, Group Guidance and Detached Workers, another intervention program, organized gangs into social groups and directed them toward prosocial activities. It also failed; gang cohesiveness increased because of the focal point the program provided, and delinquency followed suit (Klein, 1969). All these programs were intervention in nature, not prevention oriented, however. The question thus changes to, "Can *prior* membership in a normative group prevent gang membership?"

It has been widely reported that intervention programs are less than effective in reducing gang violence (see Chapter 10 of Covey et al., 1992, for a review of many failed attempts over the years). Prevention programs, on the other hand, seem more effective (Reiss & Roth, 1993), as summed up by Cairns and Cairns (1994): "Problem behaviors are more readily prevented than ameliorated, once established" (p. 269). This all leads to the conclusion that prevention of gang activity is the preferred method of reducing gang activity and that this prevention must obviously occur prior to the beginning of gang behavior or it becomes intervention. If, in fact, gang membership is expanding in range to include younger members, prevention might come too late to dissuade some from the path to gang activity and all the risks to future prospects (i.e., imprisonment, death) that come with it. Knowledge of the youngest ages at which preadolescent youths are joining gangs, if indeed they are, could help to shape policy as to when such programs should be implemented.

ADVANCES IN METHODOLOGY AND ASSESSMENT

Investigations of gangs and delinquency have historically focused on events that occur in adolescence and beyond (Huff, 1990; Klein, Maxson, & Miller, 1995). Recently, however, serious efforts have been made to employ longitudinal research designs to explore gang involvement and intervention success (Covey et al., 1992; Thornberry et al., 1993). In addition, there have been serious shortcomings in the assessment of gang presence and gang activities. On this score, Hagedorn (1990) complains about the "notoriously unreliable" survey data used by some researchers and calls for more field studies to go beyond what he describes as "courthouse criminology [and] surrogate sociology" (p. 245).

Parallel shortcomings have been identified in the developmental study of social relationships beyond the dyad and preestablished social units (i.e., families). In this regard, the journal *Social Development* recently devoted a special issue to these matters (i.e., *Development Approaches to Social Networks: Methods, Issues, and Findings*, 1996, No. 2). This special issue documents the shortcomings of procedures of group analysis that have been employed, including respondent enhancement and the projective properties of ego reports (Leung, 1996), the apparent instability of peer structures (Neckerman, 1996), the problems of tracking groups over time (Strayer & Santos, 1996), and the failure to identify specific relationships (Kindermann, 1996). In addition, the special issue describes innovative assessment solutions that have been successfully employed to plot the formation, stability, and functions of social groups. These procedures have proved to be effective in investigating group formation, stability, and processes over diverse natural settings—schools (Kindermann, 1996), maximum security facilities for delinquent youths (Clarke-McLean, 1996), preschool programs (Strayer & Santos, 1996), cross-cultural comparisons (Leung, 1996), and residential settings for emotionally disturbed children (Farmer & Rodkin, 1996). These procedures have been combined with traditional assessments to describe the transition from groups to gangs (Gaines, 1993).

CONCLUDING COMMENTS

The integration of developmental-criminological approaches to the study of groups and gangs has hardly begun. Nevertheless, even the limited amount of empirical information available is sufficient to reject enduring myths and resolve long-standing controversies. The results indicate that social group formation is inevitable in development, for good or for ill. Given the primacy of deviant and aggressive actions in group processes, it does not appear that a special model needs to be formulated to account for the evolution from groups to gangs. Social groups of childhood and adolescence wax and wane, and the fluidity of group membership and friendships should be expected as conditions and contexts shift. Curiously, gangs may be distinctive among other social groups in that they have higher—rather than lower—relationship stability and membership continuity. Even though the composition of adolescent groups changes over time, individuals tend to develop new friendships and join groups similar to the ones they left. It seems likely that the same principle holds for gang affiliations.

One of the most important proposals to emerge from studies of ontogeny concerns the multiple pathways to deviant group and gang membership. In U.S. inner cities where street gangs are prevalent, there is only modest support for the hypothesis that gang membership is restricted to youths with serious social cognitive and relationship deficits. To the contrary, the most highly aggressive youths in childhood often become dominant in the social networks of their schools and communities. As adolescents, they are highly vulnerable—in some disorganized communities— to become members and leaders of street gangs. However, there are other pathways to gang membership, not unlike those described in control theory (Hirschi, 1969). One such pathway occurs when the individual is homeless, alienated, and no conventional social institutions are open, regardless of his or her personal characteristics and qualities.

An increase in deviant group and gang activity seems inevitable in the immediate future of the United States (Klein, 1995). To be sure, the track record of social sciences in the 20th century indicates they are suspect as guides for diminishing or redirecting problems of antisocial and criminal behavior. Nonetheless, their capability to understand—if not redirect—the ontogeny, stability, and functions of groups and gangs has been enhanced by recent advances in method and design. At the least, further longitudinal analyses will be useful to illuminate the pathways from groups to gangs in different contexts and, possibly, how they can be prevented or ameliorated. The sheer magnitude of the problem for modern societies—both industrialized and emerging—should be a powerful stimulus to explore fresh interdisciplinary approaches.

REFERENCES

Ainsworth, M. D. S. (1972). Attachment and dependency: A comparison. In J. L. Gewirtz (Ed.), *Attachment and dependency* (pp. 97–137). New York: Wiley.

Asher, S. R., & Coie, J. D. (Eds.). (1990). *Peer rejection in childhood*. New York: Cambridge University Press.

Asher, S. R., & Dodge, K. A. (1986). Identifying children who are rejected by their peers. *Developmental Psychology, 22*, 444–449.

Bandura, A., & Walters, R. H. (1963). *Social learning and personality development*. New York: Holt, Rinehart and Winston.

Berndt, T. J., & Hoyle, S. G. (1985). Stability and change in childhood and adolescent friendships. *Developmental Psychology, 21*, 1007–1015.

Bowker, L. (1978). *Women, crime, and the criminal justice system*. Lexington, MA: D. C. Heath.

Bowker, L., & Klein, M. W. (1983). The etiology of female juvenile delinquency and gang membership: A test of psychological and social structure explanations. *Adolescence, 18*, 739–751.

Bowlby, J. (1969). *Attachment and loss. Vol. 1: Attachment*. New York: Basic Books.

Brennan, T., Huizinga, D., & Elliott, D. S. (1978). *The social psychology of runaways*. Lexington: MA: D. C. Heath.

Buchanan, L. G. (1995). *Friendships across adolescence: Developmental patterns and young adult outcomes*. Unpublished master's thesis, Pennsylvania State University, University Park.

Bukowski, W. M., Pizzamiglio, M. T., Newcomb, A. F., & Hoza, B. (1996). Popularity as an affordance for friendship: The link between group and dyadic experience. *Social Development, 5*, 189–202.

Cairns, R. B. (1961). The influence of dependency inhibition on the effectiveness of social approval. *Journal of Personality, 29*, 466–488.

Cairns, R. B. (1979). *Social development: The origins and plasticity of social interchanges*. San Francisco: Freeman.

Cairns, R. B. (1996). Editorial. *Social Development, 5*, 113–166.

Cairns, R. B., & Cairns, B. D. (1994). *Lifelines and risks: Pathways of youth in our time*. Cambridge, England: Cambridge University Press.

Cairns, R. B., Cairns, B. D., Neckerman, J. J., Gest, S., & Gariépy, J.-L. (1988). Social networks and aggressive behavior: Peer support or peer rejection? *Developmental Psychology, 24*, 815–823.

Cairns, R. B., Gariépy, J.-L., & Kindermann, T. (1990). *Identifying social clusters in natural settings*. Chapel Hill: University of North Carolina, Social Development Laboratory.

Cairns, R. B., Leung, M.-C., Buchanan, L., & Cairns, B. D. (1995). Friendships and social networks in childhood and adolescence: Fluidity, reliability, and interrelations. *Child Development, 66*, 1330–1345.

Campbell, A. (1984). *The girls in the gang: A report from New York City*. Oxford, England: Basil Blackwell.

Cartwright, D. S., Thompson, B., & Schwartz, H. (1975). *Gang delinquency*. Belmont, CA: Wadsworth Publishing Company.

Cernkovich, S. A., & Giordano, P. C. (1979). A comparative analysis of male and female delinquency. *Sociological Quarterly, 20*, 131–145.

Clarke-McLean, J. G. (1996). Social networks among incarcerated juvenile offenders. *Social Development, 5*, 203–217.

Cohen, A. K. (1955). *Delinquent boys: The culture of the gang*. Glencoe, IL: Free Press.

Cohen, J. M. (1977). Sources of peer group homogeneity. *Sociology of Education, 50*, 227–241.

Coie, J. D., & Dodge, K. A. (1983). Continuities and changes in children's social status: A five year longitudinal study. *Merrill-Palmer Quarterly, 29*, 261–282.

Covey, H. C., Menard, S., & Franzese, R. J. (1992). *Juvenile gangs*. Springfield, IL: Charles C Thomas.

Dishion, T. J. (1990). The peer context of troublesome behavior in children and adolescents. In P. Leone (Ed.), *Understanding troubled and troublesome youth* (pp. 128–153). Beverly Hills, CA: Sage Publications.

Dunphy, D. C. (1963). The social structure of urban adolescent peer groups. *Sociometry, 26*, 230–246.

Earls, F., Cairns, R. B., & Mercy, J. (1993). The control of violence and the promotion of non-violence in adolescence. In S. G. Millstein, A. C. Petersen, & E. O. Nightingale (Eds.), *Promoting the health of adolescents: New directions for the twenty-first century* (pp. 285–304). New York: Oxford University Press.

Eder, D. (1985). The cycle of popularity: Interpersonal relations among female adolescents. *Sociology of Education, 58*, 154–165.

Elliott, D. S., Huizinga, D., & Menard, S. (1989). *Multiple problem youth: Delinquency, substance use, and mental health problems*. New York: Springer-Verlag.

Fagan, J. (1990). Social processes of delinquency and drug use among urban gangs. In C. R. Huff (Ed.), *Gangs in America* (pp. 183–219). Newbury Park, CA: Sage Publications.

Farmer, T. W., & Hollowell, J. H. (1994). Social networks in mainstream classrooms: Social affiliations and behavioral characteristics of students with emotional and behavioral disorders. *Journal of Emotional and Behavioral Disorders, 2*, 143–155, 163.

Farmer, T. W., & Rodkin, P. (1996). Antisocial and prosocial correlates of classroom social positions: The social network centrality perspective. *Social Development, 5*, 174–188.

Feiring, C., & Lewis, M. (1987). The child's social network: Sex differences from three to six years. *Sex Roles: A Journal of Research, 17*, 621–636.

Gaines, K. R. E. (1993). *Social networks, attitudes toward school, and vulnerability for school dropout in an inner city middle school.* Unpublished master's thesis, University of Alabama, Birmingham.

Giordano, P. C., Cernkovich, S. A., & Pugh, M. D. (1986). Friendships and delinquency. *American Journal of Sociology, 91*(5), 1170–1202.

Goldstein, A. P. (1991). *Delinquent gangs: A psychological perspective.* Champaign, IL: Research Press.

Hagedorn, J. M. (1990). Back in the field again: Gang research in the nineties. In C. R. Huff (Ed.), *Gangs in America* (pp. 240–259). Newbury Park, CA: Sage Publications.

Hagedorn, J., & Macon, P. (1988). *People and folks: Gangs, crime, and the underclass in a rustbelt city.* Chicago: Lake View Press.

Hall, W. M., & Cairns, R. B. (1984). Aggressive behavior in children: An outcome of modeling or reciprocity? *Developmental Psychology, 20,* 739–745.

Hallinan, M. T. (1980). Patterns of cliquing among youth. In H. C. Foot, A. J. Chapman, & J. R. Smith (Eds.), *Friendship and social relations in children* (pp. 321–342). New York: Wiley.

Healthy people 2000: National health promotion and disease prevention objectives. (1990). Washington, DC: Government Printing Office.

Hirschi, T. (1969). *Causes of delinquency.* Berkeley: University of California Press.

Hirschi, T., & Gottfriedson, M. (1983). Age and explanation of crime. *American Journal of Sociology, 89,* 552–584.

Horowitz, R. (1990). Sociological perspectives on gangs: Conflicting definitions and concepts. In C. R. Huff (Ed.), *Gangs in America* (pp. 37–54). Newbury Park, CA: Sage Publications.

Huff, C. R. (1989). Youth gangs and public policy. *Crime and Delinquency, 35*(4), 524–537.

Huff, C. R. (Ed.). (1990). *Gangs in America.* Newbury Park, CA: Sage Publications.

Huizinga, D., Esbensen, F., & Weiher, A. (1991). Are there multiple paths to delinquency? *Journal of Criminal Law and Criminology, 82*(1), 83–118.

Jackson, P. I. (1995). Crime, youth gangs, and urban transition: The social dislocations of the postindustrial economic development. In M. Klein, C. L. Maxson, & J. Miller (Eds.), *The modern gang reader* (pp. 139–146). Los Angeles: Roxbury.

Kindermann, T. A. (1996). Strategies for the study of individual development within naturally existing peer groups. *Social Development, 5,* 158–173.

Klein, M. W. (1969). Gang cohesiveness, delinquency, and a street worker program. *Journal of Research in Crime and Delinquency, 6,* 135–166.

Klein, M. W. (1995). *The American street gang: Its nature, prevalence, and control.* New York: Oxford University Press.

Klein, M. W., & Crawford, L. Y. (1967). Groups, gangs, and cohesiveness. *Journal of Research in Crime and Delinquency, 30*(1), 75–85.

Klein, M. W., & Maxson, C. (1989). Street gang violence. In N. A. Weiner & M. E. Wolfgang (Eds.), *Violent crime, violent criminals* (pp. 198–234). Newbury Park, CA: Sage Publications.

Klein, M. W., & Maxson, C. (1990). Street gang violence: Twice as great, or half as great? In C. R. Huff (Ed.), *Gangs in America* (pp. 71–100). Newbury Park, CA: Sage Publications.

Klein, M. W., Maxson, C. L., & Miller, J. (Eds.). (1995). *The modern gang reader.* Los Angeles: Roxbury.

Ladd, G. W. (1990). Having friends, keeping friends, making friends, and being liked by peers in the classroom: Predictors of children's early school adjustment? *Child Development, 61,* 1081–1100.

Ladd, G. W., Price, J. M., & Hart, C. H. (1988). Predicting preschoolers' peer status from their playground behaviors. *Child Development, 59,* 986–992.

Lasley, J. R. (1992). Age, social context, and street gang membership: Are "youth" gangs becoming "adult" gangs? *Youth and Society, 23,* 434–451.

Leung, M.-C. (1996). Social networks and self enhancement in Chinese children: A comparison of self reports and peer reports of group membership. *Social Development, 5,* 146–157.

Miller, W. B. (1975). *Violence by youth gangs and youth groups as a crime problem in major American cities.* Report submitted to the National Institute for Juvenile Justice and Delinquency Prevention, Washington, DC.

Miller, W. B. (1977). Rumble this time. *Psychology Today, 10*(2), 52–88.

Miller, W. B., Geertz, H., & Cutter, H. S. G. (1968). Aggression in a boys' street-corner group. In J. F. Short (Ed.), *Gang delinquency and delinquent subcultures* (pp. 52–78). New York: Harper & Row.

Moffitt, T. E. (1993). Life course persistent and adolescent limited aggression. *Psychological Review, 100,* 674–701.

Neckerman, H. J. (1992). *A longitudinal investigation of the stability and fluidity of social networks and peer relationships of children and adolescents.* Unpublished doctoral dissertation, University of North Carolina, Chapel Hill.

Neckerman, H. J. (1996). The stability of social groups in childhood and adolescence: The role of the classroom social environment. *Social Development, 5,* 131–145.

Patterson, G. R. (1982). *Coercive family systems.* Eugene, OR: Castalia.

Raush, H. L. (1965). Interaction sequences. *Journal of Personality and Social Psychology, 2,* 487–499.

Reiss, A. J., & Roth, J. A. (Eds.). (1993). *Understanding and preventing violence.* Washington, DC: National Academy Press.

Roff, J. D., & Wirt, R. D. (1984). Childhood aggression and social adjustment as antecedents of delinquency. *Journal of Applied Social Psychology, 12,* 111–126.

Rojek, D. G., & Jensen, G. F. (1982). *Readings in juvenile delinquency.* Lexington, MA: D. C. Heath.

Sampson, R. J., & Laud, J. H. (1993). *Crime in the making: Pathways and turning points through life.* Cambridge, MA: Harvard University Press.

Savin-Williams, R. C. (1979). Dominance hierarchies in groups of early adolescents. *Child Development, 50,* 923–935.

Schlossman, S., & Cairns, R. B. (1993). Problem girls: Some observations on past and present. In J. Modell, R. Parke, & G. H. Elder Jr. (Eds.), *Children in time and place: Intersecting historical and developmental insights* (pp. 110–130). New York: Cambridge University Press.

Shaw, C. R., & McKay, H. D. (1942). *Juvenile delinquency and urban areas.* Chicago: University of Chicago Press.

Short, J. F. (1968). *Gang delinquency and delinquent subcultures.* New York: Harper & Row.

Short, J. F. (1990). New wine in old bottles: Change and continuity in American gangs. In C. R. Huff (Ed.), *Gangs in America* (pp. 223–239). Newbury Park, CA: Sage Publications.

Spergel, I. (1986). The violent gang problem in Chicago: A local community approach. *Social Service Review, 60,* 94–131.

Stoff, D. M., & Cairns, R. B. (Eds.). (1996). *Aggression and violence: Genetic, neurobiological, and biosocial perspectives.* Hillsdale, NJ: Erlbaum.

Strayer, F. F., & Santos, A. J. (1996). Affiliative structures in preschool peer groups. *Social Development, 5,* 117–130.

Strodtbeck, F. L., & Short, J. F., Jr. (1983). The response of gang leaders to status threats. *American Journal of Sociology, 68,* 571–578.

Suomi, S. J. (1996, March). *Monkey adolescence.* Invited paper read at the Biennial Meeting of the Society for Research in Adolescence, Boston, MA.

Thornberry, T. P., Krohn, M. D., Lizotte, A. J., & Chard-Wierschem, D. (1993). The role of juvenile gangs in facilitating delinquent behavior. *Journal of Research in Crime and Delinquency, 30*(1), 55–87.

Thrasher, F. M. (1927). *The gang: A study of 1,313 gangs in Chicago.* Chicago: University of Chicago Press.

Xie, H. (1995). *Social networks of children and adolescents in inner-city schools.* Unpublished master's thesis, University of North Carolina, Chapel Hill.

Yablonsky, L. (1962). *The violent gang.* New York: Macmillan.

Yablonsky, L., & Haskell, M. R. (Eds.). (1988). *Juvenile delinquency* (4th ed.). New York: Harper & Row.

Youniss, J. (1980). *Parents and peers in social development.* Chicago: University of Chicago Press.

CHAPTER 20

The Timing and Severity of Antisocial Behavior: Three Hypotheses Within an Ecological Framework

THOMAS J. DISHION and GERALD R. PATTERSON

A useful theory of delinquent behavior should account for both the timing and the severity of antisocial behavior in the course of development. It is well known that boys who start antisocial behavior early are at greater risk for chronic offending and adult criminal careers (Blumstein, Cohen, Roth, & Visher, 1986; Glueck & Glueck, 1950). It is also understood that childhood onset is one of the major factors accounting for violent behavior in adolescence (Capaldi, Crosby, & Stoolmiller, 1996; Farrington, 1991). There are a number of theoretical positions one could take in considering these facts. First, antisocial behavior in childhood and adolescence is an outcome of a flawed internal reaction mechanism in the individual. Second, environmental factors (e.g., reinforcement contingencies) are responsible for the learning and maintenance of antisocial behavior over time. Third, flawed internal reaction mechanisms interact with learning effects to account for the timing and severity of antisocial behavior throughout the life span.

An ecological model of development endorses the latter position: The simultaneous consideration of the context of the child's life, the function of the child's behavior within relationships, and the child's characteristics interact to determine onset and severity of antisocial behavior (Bronfenbrenner, 1989; Hinde, 1989; Magnusson, 1992). This is not to say, however, that all three factors are causally equivalent. The majority of the data supports a strong emphasis on environmental causes of the development of serious antisocial behavior. At a theoretical level, review of the evidence overwhelmingly documents contextual and social interactional processes that are concurrently and predictively associated with onset and severity of antisocial behavior (Dishion, French, & Patterson, 1995). Pragmatically, the data are compelling that changing social interaction processes are associated with changes in some form of children's antisocial

behavior (Patterson, Dishion, & Chamberlain, 1993; Reid, 1993). The goal of this chapter is to render an environmental explanation of the timing and severity of child and adolescent antisocial behavior that can be reorganized into three basic hypotheses:

1. The social interaction hypothesis: Antisocial behavior has a function within the individual's immediate social environment.
2. The individual variation hypothesis: The influence of characteristics of the child on antisocial behavior is mediated by social interactional processes.
3. The contextual sensitivity hypothesis: Contexts largely define the form and function of antisocial behavior in relationships and potentially amplify characteristics of the individual that interplay with social interactional processes.

These propositions are referred to as hypotheses to encourage empirical examination. The first hypothesis is the cornerstone of the social interactional model of antisocial behavior. We have spent years of research to understand the function of antisocial behavior within family, sibling, and peer relationships. The individual variation hypothesis addresses a recurring theme in the developmental and criminological literature that attributes antisocial behavior to some characteristic of the individual. Underscoring the need to continually consider the impact of context on basic social interactional processes and reaction patterns of the individual is the contextual sensitivity hypothesis. These three hypotheses are the basic underpinnings of an ecological approach to understanding antisocial behavior.

It is important to clarify from the outset that the ecological perspective is heuristic. One of the major problems in developing a "model" of antisocial behavior is misspecification. This is a technical issue understood by statisticians but rarely discussed by developmentalists. Gollob and Reichardt (1987) discussed the problem of not specifying the autoregressive effect in longitudinal panel models. Many causal models were emerging that did not incorporate estimates of the individual's prior behavior in models predicting future behavior. These models, according to Gollob and Reichartd (1987), were misspecified, meaning the multivariate estimates of the effects in the models were biased in the liberal direction: a tendency to reject the null hypothesis when, in fact, it is true.

This research was supported by grant R01 DA07031 from the National Institute on Drug Abuse at the National Institutes of Health to the first author; by grant R37940 from the Center for Studies of Violent Behavior and Traumatic Stress, NIMH, U.S. PHS to the second author; and by grant P50 MH46690 from the Prevention Research Branch, NIMH, U.S. PHS to John B. Reid. Jan Mustoe is gratefully acknowledged for her assistance in preparing this manuscript.

There has been some controversy about this specific issue (Stoolmiller, 1994); however, the principle remains an important one. If a developmental model neglects a key theoretical construct (or causal influence), it remains misspecified and is, therefore, of only limited utility. For example, it is currently understood that neglecting the influence of peers in a model of antisocial behavior results in a misspecified model. The influence of poor self-esteem would drop to zero if deviant peer associations were entered into the equation.

When researching antisocial behavior, how do we know when we have explored all the key theoretical constructs? The ecological framework provides a logical grid for organizing studies and simplifies the problem of specification. We know that children and adolescents spend a good portion of their time at home, school, or in the community and that their relationships are primarily with friends and family. We also know that there is variation among children with respect to gender, age, competence, and emotional adjustment. In the effort to develop a model of antisocial behavior, knowing the relationship ecology of a developmental stage suggests what kinds of relationships and contexts need to be considered.

THE SOCIAL INTERACTIONAL HYPOTHESIS

Antisocial behavior refers to a broad class of behaviors that are similar regarding their effects on the interactants. Social interactional analysis emphasizes the *functional quality* of antisocial behavior within close relationships. These behaviors occur because they "work" (Dishion, French et al., 1995; Patterson, 1982; Patterson, Reid, & Dishion, 1992). It is the similarity in function, not the topography, that provides a clue as to why some of these behaviors tend to be intercorrelated.

Social interactional research has focused on two functional processes to date: coercion in close relationships (Gardner, 1992; Hops et al., 1987; Patterson, 1982; Snyder & Patterson, 1995) and confluence processes (Figure 20.1; Dishion, Capaldi, Spracklen, & Li, 1995; Dishion, Patterson, & Griesler, 1994; Dishion, Spracklen, Andrews, & Patterson, 1996).

To study the function of a behavior, it is necessary to capture social interaction as it unfolds over time. Three steps (i.e., lags) in the sequence are optimal, but many studies have established the functional utility of a behavior using only two events within a social interaction. Nevertheless, Figure 20.1 depicts the function of behavior from the perspective of a child. In the coercive process, the child's aversive behavior functions to terminate the aversive behavior of the parent. The parent's behavior at Time 1 is mildly aversive and then becomes neutral at Time 3. The confluence process, on the other hand, is more typical of friendships (and some sibling relationships): A positive behavior by the child is responded to in kind by the peer. If one were to extend the analysis of a confluence interaction, it would become apparent that the interactants tend to reward behaviors (verbal and otherwise) that are similar to their own. Over time, the confluence process has a dynamic impact on the child's developmental trajectory.

Coercive Family Process

The functional utility of a behavior is likely to vary as a function of the developmental status of the child and the relationship context. In early childhood, children may learn to use relatively

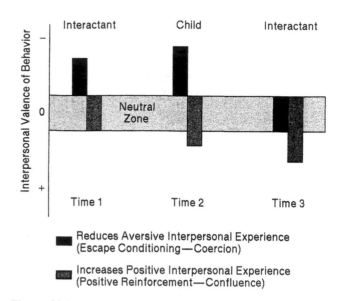

Figure 20.1   *Functional events within dyadic social interactions (Social Interaction Hypothesis).*

innocuous aversive tactics (e.g., whine, argue, cry, tease) to successfully terminate conflicts involving other family members (Patterson, 1982; Snyder, 1995). In this sense, *coercion* (noncompliance, whining, tantrums, etc.) may serve a similar function to terminate parental intrusions. Studies of these families show a second extremely important characteristic: The parents do not actively promote prosocial skills. One might say that these parents are relatively *noncontingent* in their interactions with the child. Because of the noncontingent environment, it is not functional for young children to develop prosocial skills. It may be that aversive tactics are a better way to organize their familial world.

In the family, it is the reaction of family members during conflict episodes that determines the relative rates of prosocial and coercive reactions (Patterson et al., 1992; Snyder & Patterson, 1995). The parents most at-risk tend to be irritable and nonsupportive of prosocial behaviors during nonconflict situations. In such families, the siblings simply follow suit (Patterson, 1984, 1986). The effect is to produce a preschool child who tends to be highly coercive and socially unskilled.

Past research at Oregon Social Learning Center (OSLC) has focused on examining whether coercive acts that serve similar functions cluster together (Patterson, Cobb, & Ray, 1972). In the family setting, child tease and hit are controlled by an overlapping network of antecedent events such as sibling tease (Patterson, 1982). Observational data showed that given sibling tease, the conditional likelihood of target child hit was .060, and the conditional for target child tease was .149. Both of these conditionals were at least 5 times greater than their base rate values. Sibling tease may be said to be functionally related to target child hit and tease. Both responses produced a similar pattern of consequences (e.g., laugh, hit, yell).

Family management skills are a child's protection against involvement in a myriad of family coercive exchanges. Longitudinal studies that measured parenting practices in toddlerhood and followed through to middle childhood suggested that harsh and punitive discipline practices in toddlerhood correlated with externalizing behaviors in elementary school (Fagot & Leve, in press). Other longitudinal research has documented the predictive validity of parenting practices in middle childhood to more severe delinquent behavior in adolescence (Loeber & Dishion, 1983).

Our initial efforts to measure parenting constructs (i.e., Discipline, Monitoring, Positive Reinforcement, Problem Solving) resulted in multimethod, multiagent (MMA) indicators of parenting concepts and child adjustment. The details of the psychometric studies are presented in Capaldi and Patterson (1989). Presumably, MMA-defined models will be more likely to replicate across samples and sites. An adequate performance model, we believe, must

be replicable and account for a minimum of 30% of the variance of the compositive MMA score measuring child outcome. A study of Forgatch (1991) examined structural equation models (SEM) from three at-risk samples to demonstrate that the parenting model was indeed robust. In each case, both Monitoring and Discipline made significant contributions to the measures of antisocial behavior. The variance accounted for ranged from 30% to 50%.

An important feature of the models shown in Figure 20.2 is that coercive family exchanges can also undermine family management practices, parent monitoring in particular. Repeated failures to influence a child can lead to "rejection" and "giving up." Such an affective

Model A. Parenting model for at-risk boys aged 9 - 10 years (*N* = 201)

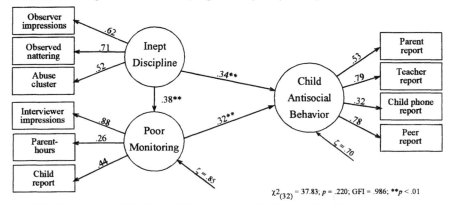

$\chi^2_{(32)} = 37.83; p = .220;$ GFI = .986; **$p < .01$

Model B. Parenting model for boys of divorced parents 9 - 12 years (*N* = 96)

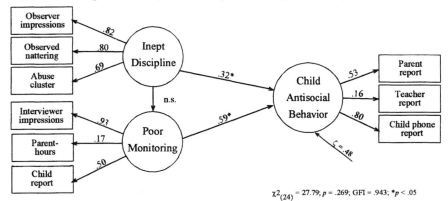

$\chi^2_{(24)} = 27.79; p = .269;$ GFI = .943; *$p < .05$

Model C. Parenting for clinical sample of boys and girls aged 5 - 12 (*N* = 71)

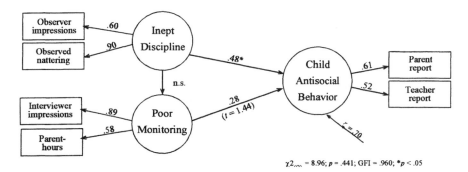

$\chi^2_{(9)} = 8.96; p = .441;$ GFI = .960; *$p < .05$

Figure 20.2 *Replication across three different risk samples: Similar measurement models.*

state reduces the likelihood that parents will track and monitor their child as the child matures and becomes more involved with peers.

Confluence in Friendships

In middle childhood, coercive behaviors may begin to be systematically reinforced by the peer group. By adolescence, antisocial behavior can be the membership card for entry in some adolescent peer groups; it certainly forms the basis for many adolescent friendships (Dishion, Capaldi et al., 1995; Dishion et al., 1994).

Until recently, very few empirical studies were concerned with the means by which peers actually trained for deviant behavior. Given the theorizing by Burgess and Akers (1966) and Akers (1977) regarding the role of peer reinforcement processes and delinquent behavior, this is a surprising omission indeed. We undertook an in-depth analysis of the friendship characteristics and socialization processes that began when the boys participating in the Oregon Youth Study (OYS) were approximately 15 years old. Perusal of the videotaped interactions led us to consider how positive affective reactions organized the boys' endorsement of deviant values and norms. We developed the Topic Code (Poe, Dishion, Griesler, & Andrews, 1990) for rule-breaking and normative topics and positive and negative interpersonal reactions. Using a reinforcement model as a guide, we hypothesized that contingent, positive reactions to rule-breaking talk would relate to escalations in problem behavior. We were partially right about this but omitted an important corollary: Deviant dyads also tend *not to react positively* to normative talk. According to matching law, it is not the overall rate of reinforcement that influences behavior but the relative rate of reinforcement (Conger & Simons, in press; McDowell, 1988; Snyder & Patterson, 1995). Individuals in ecologies with low levels of reinforcement for prosocial behavior are particularly vulnerable to reinforcement for deviancy.

Figure 20.3 reveals the relationship between the rate of rule-breaking talk and reinforcement for rule-breaking talk (Dishion et al., 1996). We also found that contingent laughter in response to rule-breaking talk resulted in longer discussions of deviancy (Dishion & Spracklen, 1996). It is this *deviancy training process* that predicts adolescent initiation and escalation of problem behavior.

Inspection of the longitudinal data from the OYS shows dramatic increases in delinquent lifestyle behaviors (e.g., alcohol or drug use, lying or cheating, arguing, and hanging out with troublemakers) in boys involved early on with a deviant peer group. We hypothesized that changes in the form of deviant behavior represented a metamorphosis of childhood forms of antisocial acts. The longitudinal growth model (LGM) uniquely integrates the issues of onset, continuity, and growth in antisocial behavior. Early disruption of family management accounts for childhood onset, and increasingly unsupervised time with deviant peers accounts for growth in severity during adolescence (Patterson, 1993).

THE INDIVIDUAL VARIATION HYPOTHESIS

A recurrent theme in criminology and psychology is that a flawed internal control mechanism accounts for either the timing (early onset) or the severity of children's behavior. From this perspective, environmental influences might be seen as reactive to the antisocial

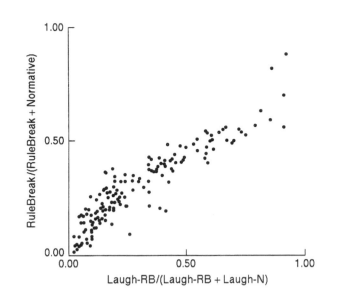

Figure 20.3 *A matching law analysis of rule-breaking discourse in boys' friendship dyads (N = 181).*

child (Rowe, 1989). The individual variation hypothesis states that genotypic characteristics of the child have an indirect effect on the development of antisocial behavior, *mediated* by social interactional patterns in the family and the peer group. These individual variations in the child's emotional character, cognitive functioning, and physical characteristics that can affect social interactional patterns among families and peers that are pathogenic to the development of antisocial behavior. Extreme constitutional handicaps, however, may actually prevent the child from exposure to these social interactional processes.

Review of the literature indicates that the child's genotype is a modest predictor of antisocial behavior and delinquency (Cadoret, 1978; Cloninger & Gottesman, 1987; Loeber & Dishion, 1983; Plomin, Nitz, & Rowe, 1990). The strongest genetic link is to antisocial personality, defined post hoc in adulthood. DiLalla and Gottesman (1989), Pulkkinen (1983), and Robins (1966) have proposed that studies of adolescent delinquents really include three groups of children: continuous antisocials, transitory delinquents, and late bloomers. This argument has been pursued and expanded by Moffitt (1993). The idea is that life-course antisocial behavior is more biologically based than adolescent-limited delinquency. Specifying the nature of the biological basis for this particular developmental trajectory has been problematic.

Loeber and Dishion (1983) found that the characteristics of a child were relatively modest predictors of later delinquency. When determining the importance of a variable in explaining a future behavior, *more than* the density of the characteristics within the risk group should be considered (Loeber & Dishion, 1983; Meehl, 1954; Wiggins, 1973). For example, consider the relationship between intelligence and delinquency. There is evidence to support a correlation between childhood onset of antisocial behavior and compromised intellectual functioning (Moffitt, 1990). It is a fallacy, however, to think that this is a *cause* of delinquency. The vast majority of children with low intellectual functioning are well socialized (Loeber & Dishion, 1983).

Emotional Regulation

Investigators have become interested in how the child's emotional predisposition might influence the development of antisocial behavior (Thomas & Chess, 1977). Katz and Gottman (1991) stated:

> We define emotional regulation as consisting of children's ability to (1) inhibit inappropriate behavior related to strong negative or positive affect, (2) self-soothe any physiological arousal that strong affect has induced, (3) focus attention, and (4) organize themselves for coordinated action in the service of an external goal. (p. 130)

This definition is an improvement over previous psychological constructs. It allows for (a) testable predictions regarding the relation between specific emotional responding and real-world social behavior that is developmentally significant, (b) solid measurement in emotional responding via facial expression (Ekman, 1992; Gottman & Levenson, 1986) or physiological responding (e.g., measures reflecting vagal tone; Dipietro, Greenspan, & Porges, 1991; Katz & Gottman, 1991), (c) variation in emotional responding that has predictable developmental progressions (Izard & Harris, 1995) and provides (d) a direct link to known physiological mechanisms and, therefore, unifies developmental science with basic research in emotional

and cognitive psychology (Dishion, French, et al., 1995; Fowles, 1984, 1987; Gray, 1982; Rothbart, Posner, & Hershey, 1995).

It is hypothesized that patterns of emotional responding are mediated through social interactions with parents and peers in the prediction and explanation of antisocial behavior. In this respect, emotional regulation is seen as an individual variation factor that is useful in understanding the process (Figure 20.4).

The focus in Figure 20.4 is on the child. However, emotional regulation patterns in parents would similarly influence the course of an interaction sequence. The same studies by Cadoret (1978) showed that the biological contributions were significant for both genders. One might assume that an irritable, uninvolved approach to child rearing may reflect in part biological determinants. Modeling studies using the OSLC data-set consistently showed that antisocial fathers and mothers were at greater risk for disrupted discipline practices (Capaldi & Patterson, 1991; Patterson & Dishion, 1988). These results were replicated in structural equation modeling (SEM) of data from separated and divorced families (Bank, Forgatch, Patterson, & Fetrow, 1993). After reanalyzing the social interaction data with the Family Process Code (Dishion, Gardner, Patterson, Reid, & Thibodeaux, 1983), Snyder (1995) showed that hostile affective valence by either interactant significantly increased the intensity and duration of the conflict. Thus,

Figure 20.4 *Child characteristics as input into developmental processes (Marginal Deviation Hypothesis).*

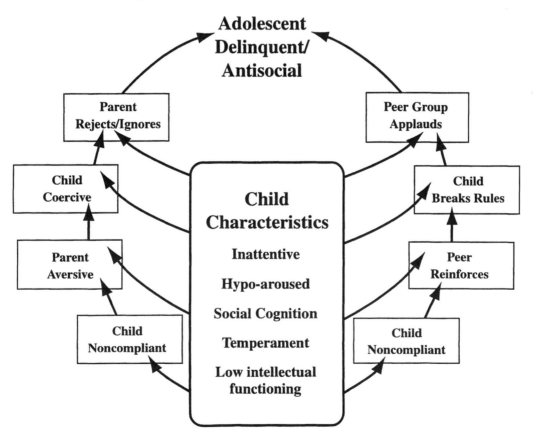

emotional reactivity in the child or parent is a risk factor for coercion. Consistent with the individual variation hypothesis, however, we expect that most individuals with this genetically determined trait do not engage in coercive family processes.

The extent to which the child's emotional disposition could exacerbate deviancy training within friendships is more speculative. We linked responsivity-sensitivity to positive reinforcement as the underlying risk predisposition (Dishion, Eddy et al., 1995). Children who are prone to perseverate under conditions of positive reinforcement would be more at-risk for peer influences (Quay, 1993). We expected that peer reinforcement for rule breaking would have differential effects, depending on the emotional regulation patterning of the young adolescent (Dishion et al., 1996). This hypothesis remains to be explored.

Burgeoning possibilities for making important connections between the experimental psychopathology tradition and the field study tradition typical of research on antisocial behavior and delinquency are developing. Difficult temperament, measured in infancy, is associated with early development of antisocial behavior (Bates, Bayles, Bennett, Ridge, & Brown, 1991). Ratings of difficult temperament as seen in middle childhood are indirectly related to the etiology of adolescent outcomes and aggression (Lerner, Hertzog, Hooker, Hassibi, & Thomas, 1988; Olweus, 1980). We are arriving at a point where we can better specify which patterns of emotional responding are relevant and how they might feed into the social interaction processes that seem to underlie the development of serious outcomes (Rothbart et al., 1995).

Attention Deficit With Hyperactivity

The attention deficit/hyperactivity disorder (ADHD) phenomenon could be considered another individual variation factor. Attention is a multifaceted process involving unique selection, orientation, and vigilance abilities. The deficits of ADHD within these attentional processes are not entirely clear. The diagnostic label unfortunately combines several aspects of what might generally be described as a difficult child, including activity levels, cognitive deficits, and patterns of emotional responding. Rothbart et al. (1995) discuss the linkage between attentional processes and emotional regulation. For example, children diagnosed as ADHD perform quite well on attentional tasks when incentives are provided for "appropriate responding." We identified ADHD symptoms as a disruptor of family management practices and peer socialization processes and, therefore, a factor to be considered when understanding individual variation.

Social Cognition

Finally, the connection between emotional regulation and cognition was made by Dodge (1991). Cicchetti and Toth (1995) emphasized social cognition as a mediating factor between environmental input and behavioral responding. Hostile attribution bias is a construct that demonstrates how patterns of emotional reactance might affect how one sees the world. Dodge (1993) confirmed that abusive parenting in early childhood predicted children's tendency to attribute hostile intent in hypothetical scenarios of peer interaction. Negative affect is certainly related to one's attention to and interpretation of a social stimuli (Rothbart et al., 1995). Understanding these processes will enhance comprehension of individual differences in reaction to social events. Thus, hostile attribution bias can be seen as an individual variation factor whose impact is mediated through extended chains of social interactions with parents and peers.

THE CONTEXTUAL SENSITIVITY HYPOTHESIS

Human behavior is highly sensitive to social contexts. From a behavioral perspective, sensitivity to contexts is thought to be a critical feature of the ability to use language. Linguistic associations can affect the emotional valence of the behavior setting within which social interactions unfold (Hayes, 1988). For example, raising one's hand to speak at a dinner party would be considered immature at best; however, the same behavior is demanded in most public school settings. Similarly, the presence of contextual cues (e.g., slogans on one's T-shirt) and unfair distribution of resources in an aggregate unit (family, peer group, and community) can radically affect the nature of interactions within those settings. Humans are symbolically oriented, and context can have a dramatic impact on the nature of developmentally significant social exchanges.

Developmental psychology has evolved to incorporate the impact of social contexts on children's development (Bronfenbrenner, 1979). Much of the work on context has explored the indirect effects on childhood outcomes. The idea is relatively simple: Context has an immediate effect on the individual exchanges by amplifying existing patterns. This effect is exemplified very clearly in the dynamic research of Elder and colleagues in studying the impact of the Great Depression on parenting practices and childhood outcomes (Elder, Caspi, & Van Nguyen, 1986; Elder, Van Nguyen, & Caspi, 1985). Similarly, the social disorganization theory emphasizes the role of the communities in disrupting basic socialization processes in families and peer groups. Analyses by Sampson and Laub (1994) suggested that all cultural groups are vulnerable to the undermining influence of "toxic" environments. McLoyd (1990) has illustrated the processes of disruption by poverty of African American single parents.

Patterson and Bank (1989) discussed the amplification process in the antisocial behavior of the parents. Stress on the family was a disrupter of the mother's discipline practices directly and indirectly via amplification of her antisocial behavior. Of course, it stands to reason that if stress can amplify parents' antisocial traits, a similar effect is conceivable for children. The hypothesis that stress experienced by the child directly affects the child's level of antisocial behavior and exacerbates underlying emotional regulation patterns has drawn some support (Cummings & Cummings, 1988).

To focus our discussion on antisocial behavior, we defined three features of a toxic social context (Figure 20.5): poverty (level of resources), stigmatization and isolation (level of social support), and deviancy (cultural-community norms). These features can be used to describe communities in general or specific behavior settings in which social interactions transpire (e.g., families, schools, and neighborhoods). We focused our discussion on families.

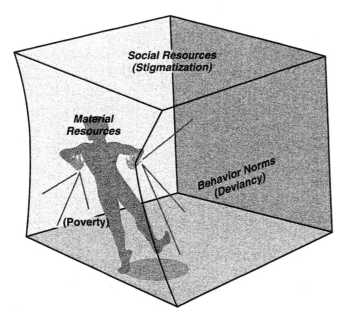

Figure 20.5 *Dimensions of the environmental context with impact on antisocial behavior (Contextual Sensitivity Hypothesis).*

Family Disruption

Previous research indicates that the context in which the family lives has a significant impact on both micro and macro processes (Radke-Yarrow, 1990). We used extended studies of mother-child interactions to demonstrate that on days when the mother was most highly stressed, she also tended to be the most irritable when interacting with her preschool child (Patterson, 1983). Snyder (1991) replicated this effect with a larger sample. He also extended the model by including daily measures of stress, maternal mood, discipline, and child adjustment. The resulting model showed that variations in stress influenced the mother's mood, which in turn was related to ineffective discipline and negative child outcomes. This general model was tested and found to replicate in two longitudinal samples. Both studies used similar assessment batteries and an MMA strategy in building the same model for families of young adolescent boys (Conger, Patterson, & Ge, 1995). The fact that the two sites used the same indicator for only 1 out of 10 indicators attests to the robustness of building models based on MMA assessments.

Our studies have also included other contextual variables such as social disadvantage (Larzelere & Patterson, 1990), divorce (Patterson, Forgatch, & Stoolmiller, under review), antisocial parent (Bank et al., 1993), stress (Forgatch, 1989), and frequency of family restructuring transitions (marriage, moving to a new neighborhood, change in employment; Capaldi & Patterson, 1991). Although remarriage is often considered a positive event, it can lead to a deterioration in family functioning. Along with stepparenting comes ambiguity in parental roles, conflict in blended families, and general stress from change. Moreover, the possibility of antisocial behavior among potential partners increases with each successive divorce and remarriage. Confluence on antisocial and substance use patterns can lead to deterioration in family func-

tioning. Even when relationships are positive, parenting is often lost in the process of nurturing a romantic love.

In every instance, the finding has been that the impact of context on child adjustment is mediated through parenting practices. The parents can be subjected to severe stress, but if they manage to keep their parenting practices relatively intact, the negative context will not have a significant impact on child adjustment. Effective discipline, monitoring, and family problem-solving practices are the strongest protective factors that we have seen in the literature.

Schooling

The school ecology (rules, policies, and procedures for monitoring playground violence) is of interest in the etiology of childhood-onset antisocial behavior (Walker, Stieber, Ramsey, & O'Neill, 1993). When entering the school system, there is a strong tendency for cross-setting consistency in the behavior patterns of extremely antisocial children (Loeber & Dishion, 1984; Ramsey, Patterson, & Walker, 1990). For the general population, however, children's interactions with parents and with peers on the playground are only modestly correlated (Dishion et al., 1994). The modest correlation confirms the hypothesis that variation in school contexts can significantly affect children's social trajectories (Rutter, 1978).

For the antisocial child, it is easy to see how behavior might produce a cascade of experiences leading to increased severity of antisocial behavior. Such behavior, coupled with academic failure, elicits peer rejection (Coie & Kupersmidt, 1983; Dishion, 1990; Dodge, 1983). Antisocial children appear to be mutually attracted to one another (Cairns, Cairns, Neckerman, Gest, & Gariépy, 1988), and association with troubled children can begin as early as preschool (Snyder, 1995). Peer rejection and academic failure appear to accentuate the deviant peer group as an appealing social context (Dishion, Patterson, Stoolmiller, & Skinner, 1991).

Transitions

Social transitions are, in part, defined by developmental transitions in the child. Children go through two school transitions in early adolescence; they move from elementary school to middle school and from middle school to high school. There has been very little research of how these transitions affect basic social interaction processes. It is clear, however, that shifts in the peer group are especially relevant to progressions in antisocial behavior.

When children shift into middle school settings and begin experiencing more unsupervised time, they acquire opportunities to increase their connection to a like-minded peer group. The large-scale survey by Elliott and Menard (1988) showed that starting at age 12, there were dramatic increases in contacts with deviant peers. The availability peaked at age 16 for groups in which most of the members were active delinquents and peaked at age 18 for groups with moderate densities of deviant members. Hirschi and Gottfredson (1983) suggested that the age-crime distribution shows a ubiquitous trend across cultures, peaking at age 16, just as the exposure to deviant peers peaks. Thus, contact with deviant peers and antisocial behavior may be confounded. Analyses by Warr (1993), however, suggested that age effects disappear in the context of multivariate analyses that model the role of differential association with deviant peers.

Our studies of boys and their friends indicated that after controlling for the boys' antisocial behavior in childhood and the families' harsh discipline practices, the boys' involvement in deviant friendships accounted for individual differences in violence in adolescence (Dishion, Eddy et al., 1995). Because violence, even among antisocial boys, is a relatively low base-rate event, we aggregated the boys' reports of violent acts across ages 14, 16, and 18. We also aggregated the scores derived from the boys' and their best friends' 25-min interaction tasks.

We found that for the videotaped discussions, very few of the boys brought in the same friend across assessment waves. Despite the transitory nature of adolescent friendships, the stability in the deviancy training was quite high from one wave to the next ($r = -.40$). Thus, the faces change, but the process remains the same; socialization processes within the peer group underlie escalations in the severity of problem behavior.

Aggregating randomly assigned high-risk youths to cognitive-behavior interventions revealed unintended escalations in both delinquent behavior and drug use (Dishion & Andrews, 1995). These findings indicated that peer affiliations are causally elated. Social transitions (including those intended to mediate the antisocial behavior) can produce social contexts that influence the social interactional processes that exacerbate the severity of antisocial behavior.

THE ECOLOGICAL FRAMEWORK

We have reviewed the evidence supporting two basic social interactional processes that contribute to the development of antisocial behavior: coercive family process and deviancy training in the peer group. Further, we introduced the individual variation hypothesis, that characteristics of the child may exacerbate coercion and deviancy training and, therefore, are indirectly related to antisocial behavior. Finally, we presented data addressing the hypothesis that toxic environments for families included poverty, stress, and divorce. On the other hand, contextual shifts that affect peer processes focused on transitions in peer groups. Note that when considering the impact of context, the model specifies that individuals are actively selecting contexts to maximize payoffs. The antisocial person focuses on the short-term payoffs. In the aftermath of divorce, the antisocial mother may select an antisocial stepfather; the antisocial child moves directly into a deviant peer group when the school context shifts.

We used the ecological framework (social interactional patterns, characteristics of the child, and context) to explain the developmental patterns of childhood- and adolescent-onset antisocial behavior.

Childhood Onset

There are individual difference factors that account for vulnerability to the influence of deviant peers. Dishion et al. (1991) found that a history of academic failure, peer rejection, and poor family

management accounted for early adolescent association with antisocial peers.

Childhood and adolescent onset may represent two very different trajectories leading to juvenile offending (Moffitt, 1993; Patterson, DeBaryshe, & Ramsey, 1989; Patterson & Yoerger, 1993). In the Oregon model, early police arrest is thought to be the joint outcome of disruptions in the parenting process and very early involvement with a deviant peer group, accompanied by unsupervised wandering. Presumably, disrupted parenting practices produce antisocial children; the more antisocial the child, the earlier the involvement with deviant peers.

Blumstein et al. (1986) have noted that boys arrested early in life tend to be at-risk for chronic offending, violence, and adult arrest. Boys who are arrested before the age of 14 are significantly different from those who are arrested after that age (Patterson et al., 1989). Our findings demonstrated that childhood-onset boys can be differentiated from adolescent-onset boys in terms of their association with higher risk contexts (poverty, divorce, antisocial parent) and significantly less effective parenting practices, which increase the potential for progression from childhood antisocial behavior to early arrest to chronic and violent offending.

Notice that it is *when* the child comes into unsupervised contact with deviant peers that is of critical importance. On the one hand, it means that the child will be performing juvenile offenses at an early age and is thus at-risk for early arrest. On the other hand, those young children who are extremely antisocial are also at-risk to be socially unskilled. Early arrest means, among other things, less socially skilled. When this group reaches late adolescence and the early adult years, the relative positive payoffs for prosocial behaviors will be low, compared with the positive payoffs for remaining in the crime process (Conger & Simons, in press). The relative payoffs for childhood-onset youths are such that they are likely to remain in the criminal process during their young adult years.

We hypothesized that the mechanism that predicts skill deficits, early involvement with deviant peers, and the risk of early arrest is simply the overall frequency of antisocial acts. Early timing for deviant peer involvement is thought to be determined by high frequencies of antisocial acts. Although the vast bulk of childhood antisocial acts are relatively trivial (e.g., whining and noncompliance), the higher the rate of such acts, the greater the risk of serious problem behavior. We presume that for unsupervised youths, the frequency of performance of new forms of antisocial behavior will roughly match the rates for childhood forms of antisocial acts. It is the high rate of delinquent-type behaviors that also place the youth at-risk for an early first arrest.

Severity Progressions

The primary hypothesis behind the design of the OYS longitudinal study was that the severity of antisocial behavior during childhood would predict childhood onset for juvenile and chronic offending (Patterson, 1995; Patterson et al., 1989). The idea was that a single model might account for the description of the progression reported in Figure 20.6.

The likelihood of moving from above the median antisocial behavior (assessed at Grade 4) to early arrest by age 14 was .46.

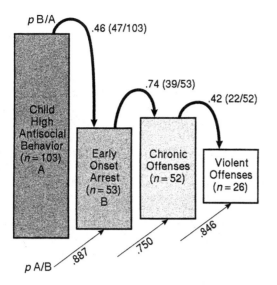

Figure 20.6 *Descriptors for a progression to violence.*

Not all antisocial children are arrested early, but by age 18, 72% will have been arrested at some time. Almost all of the boys (89%) who had been arrested early had also been antisocial as children (Patterson et al., under review). From the childhood-onset group, 75% were chronic offenders, and 86% of the violent boys were from the chronic group. The findings implied that arrival at any given stage of juvenile offending carried with it the information that the youth had also been involved in the immediate prior stage. This is a rather weak description of transitivity. What is required is a more formal study of the relationship between one stage and another. Logistic regression analyses showed that each of the stages in the sequence was linked to the one that immediately followed.

The odds of an early arrest were more than 13 times greater for children scoring above the median on childhood antisocial behavior than for children scoring below the median. Similarly, given that the child was arrested at an early age, the odds were 16 times greater that the child was a chronic offender. Given chronic offending, the odds of being a violent offender were 24 times greater than if the youth were nonchronic (Patterson & Chamberlain, 1994). This analysis was replicated by Forgatch and Stoolmiller (1994) for a follow-up study of divorced families.

Adolescent Onset

Patterson and Yoerger (1993) hypothesized that boys arrested after the age of 14 represented a very different path to juvenile offending than was the case for those with childhood onset. In keeping with the findings by DiLalla and Gottesman (1989), we presumed that the adolescent-onset boys would not be as deviant or as socially unskilled as the childhood-onset boys but would constitute a point midway between the extreme scores for the childhood-onset group

and the point defining nondelinquents as a group. By this definition, the adolescent-onset boys may be said to be marginally adjusted.

Within the ecological framework, the individual variation hypothesis can be used to explain adolescent onset of antisocial behavior. Studies by French (1990) indicated that many factors are associated with peer rejection. In fact, 50% of the peer-rejected boys were nonaggressive (French, 1988). Marginal deviations such as early maturation can catapult a child into a deviant peer group (Magnusson, Stattin, & Allen, 1985).

Capaldi and Patterson (1994) carried out an extensive analysis of one child disposition, two family management, and seven contextual variables that differentiated childhood-onset from adolescent-onset boys. Five of the context variables showed significant differences among the early-, late-, and no-arrest groups. Paired comparison for early arrest versus late arrest and the configuration of the mean values for late arrest versus no arrest showed that the general pattern of results was consistent with the marginality hypothesis. The families of adolescent-onset boys tended to be intermediate in terms of income, social disadvantage, antisocial parent, parent employed, and frequency of transition (from intact to single, or remarriage). As predicted, adolescent onset showed better parental discipline and monitoring practices than did childhood onset, but the findings were significant only for discipline practices. There were no significant differences in parenting practices between the late-arrest and the no-arrest group. Inspection of the distribution for the monitor score suggested highly restricted variance (i.e., the measure might be an inappropriate measure for most 10-year-olds).

We hypothesize that future analyses will demonstrate that for adolescent-onset youths, the vast bulk of training in delinquency occurs under the aegis of the deviant peer group. We examined the peer interactional processes associated with (a) childhood onset and persistence into adolescence, (b) childhood onset and desistance, and (c) adolescent onset (Dishion et al. 1994). Peer contexts and social interactional processes were completely concordant with these developmental patterns. The key then becomes that of understanding which variables in early and middle adolescence determine involvement with deviant peers. Elder (1980) has suggested a "flight to deviant peers" (p. 380) hypothesis as a developmental process to account for adolescent onset. He stressed the importance of family conflict as cause for flight. Montemayor and Flannery (1989), as well as Paikoff and Brooks-Gunn (1990), emphasized increased time spent with peers during early adolescence, frequently accompanied by conflict.

There is an interesting scenario that fits these findings. One might imagine that it is the conflict generated in the "great autonomy wars" that leads to increasing payoffs for child antisocial behaviors such as arguing, truancy, clothing, hairstyle, and street time. As these behaviors escalate, it becomes increasingly difficult to supervise youths who now are physically the same size as their parents. Given modern parental uncertainty about their responsibilities for supervision and child rights, one can imagine their sense of relief when they finally step aside and permit unsupervised wandering.

As noted earlier, the family is thought to play a key role in initiating the adolescent-onset process. To test this idea, Patterson and Yoerger (1993) used the data from Cohort I of the OYS. In the SEM, only data from those boys who scored below the median on the antisocial construct were used.

IMPLICATIONS

After all of the empirical studies are reviewed, it is interesting to note that the division between childhood onset and adolescent onset seems strangely reminiscent of the early factor analytic work by Jenkins and Hewitt (1944). Their differentiation of the unsocialized delinquent is almost a paraphrase for our childhood-onset group. As noted by Quay (1987), the lack of social skills combined with chronic offending identifies this type as someone who makes a career out of antisocial behavior. Quay also speculated that it was the unsocialized delinquent who most likely reflected some heritable characteristics, similar to the childhood-onset boys (Patterson et al., 1992).

Jenkins and Hewitt's (1944) socialized delinquent also sounds like a prototypic adolescent-onset boy: more socially skilled than the unsocialized delinquent, with a short-lived career in crime.

What we have added to these distinguished beginnings are the functional emphasis for understanding timing and severity, the contribution of parenting practices as determinants, the contribution of deviant peers as socializing agents, and an emerging intervention technology that suggests that the trajectories may be altered.

A Unifying Framework

Although we have discussed the childhood- and adolescent-onset models of antisocial behavior, an ecological framework unifies these into one set of variables. At the hub of this causal wheel is understanding the function of antisocial behavior for a particular child, the child's nature, and how the context of family and peer environments are organized as secondary concerns.

Actually, unification and parsimony can be pushed to another level. Conger and Simons (in press) introduced the matching law as an integrated paradigm for understanding life-course patterns in antisocial behavior. This is quite consistent with the ecological framework. The task is to study the action-reaction matrix of the child's total ecology. Computations of the functional utility of all of the behaviors in the child's "action repertoire" will provide an accurate prediction of the child's level of antisocial behavior at that point in time. As we have seen, moving through time, the matrix will change form. Antisocial children are selected and tracked into increasingly deviant environments.

We can expect increased levels (frequency and variety) of antisocial behavior, along with more severe forms. It is not surprising that in some urban settings we see alarmingly high levels of extreme problem behavior. Recent studies by Sampson and Laub (1994) suggested that these high levels are not attributed to ethnicity but are best understood as social processes.

Plasticity and Continuity

Antisocial behavior is a highly stable behavior pattern. Caspi and Herbener (1990) stated that the mechanism is cumulative continu-

ity: In the absence of countervailing forces, the child's behavior continues to select and elicit environments that contribute to the intransigence of behavior patterns.

Interventions that support parents' monitoring and constructive management of their child's behavior have shown reductions in problem behavior in childhood and adolescence (Patterson et al., 1993). We propose that family-based interventions are the key, as only parents can simultaneously change the functional utility of the child's behavior at home and access to peers that support deviancy. Interventions aimed at children may at times have an iatrogenic effect: Aggregating high-risk youths inadvertently promotes contact with deviancy-training peers and possibly undermines the influence of parents.

The question arises of the timing of intervention. We suggest a view of prevention and intervention that emphasizes harm reduction and moves away from disease-model conceptualizations of antisocial behavior. There are several points in development that involve significant contextual changes (e.g., pregnancy, infancy, toddlerhood, school entry, middle school entry, high school entry). These are risk points and opportunities for intervention.

Figure 20.7 suggests the life-cycle view of preventive interventions. From this perspective, interventions for adolescents can be seen as prevention strategies that potentially affect the transmission of risk for the following generation. The lines between "early" and "late" intervention, therefore, fade, and one becomes concerned with all developmental phases of the antisocial process.

If one "gives up" on troubled adolescents because their behavior has "crystallized," the opportunity to support change during transition into adulthood (as well as the possibility of the prevention of problem behavior in the next generation) is lost. Research by Olds (1989), for example, implied that prenatal care with *first time* teenage mothers has significant effects on reducing the problem behavior of their offspring in childhood and adolescence. The key is intervening with high-risk individuals at major developmental transition points. The ecological model indicates that for

Figure 20.7 *A life-cycle view of preventive interventions.*

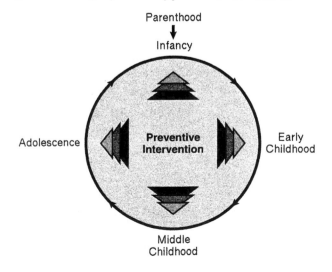

these interventions to be effective in promoting prosocial over antisocial adaptations, consideration of community contexts as well as social interactional processes is requisite.

REFERENCES

Akers, R. L. (1977). *Deviant behavior: A social learning approach* (2nd ed.). Belmont, CA: Wadsworth.

Bank, L. M., Forgatch, M. S., Patterson, G. R., & Fetrow, R. A. (1993). Parenting practices of single mothers: Mediators of negative contextual factors. *Journal of Marriage and the Family, 55,* 371–384.

Bates, J. E., Bayles, K., Bennett, D. S., Ridge, B., & Brown, N. M. (1991). Origins of externalizing behavior problems at eight years of age. In D. J. Pepler & K. H. Rugin (Eds.), *The development and treatment of childhood aggression* (pp. 93–120). Hillsdale, NJ: Erlbaum.

Blumstein, A., Cohen, J., Roth, J. A., & Visher, C. A. (1986). Participation in criminal careers. In A. Blumstein, J. Cohen, J. A. Roth, & C. A. Visher (Eds.), *Criminal careers and career criminals* (Vol. 1, pp. 31–54). Washington, DC: National Academy Press.

Bronfenbrenner, U. (1979). *The ecology of human development: Experiments by nature and by design.* Cambridge, MA: Harvard University Press.

Bronfenbrenner, U. (1989). Ecological systems theory. In R. Vasta (Ed.), *Annals of child development: Vol. 6. Six theories of child development: Revised formulations and current issues* (pp. 187–249). London: JAI Press.

Burgess, R. L., & Akers, R. L. (1966). A differential association-reinforcement theory of criminal behavior. *Social Problems, 14,* 128–147.

Cadoret, R. J. (1978). Psychopathology in adopted-away offspring of biological parents with antisocial behavior. *Archives of General Psychiatry, 35,* 176–184.

Cairns, R. B., Cairns, B. D., Neckerman, H. J., Gest, S. D., & Gariépy, J. (1988). Social networks and aggressive behavior: Peer support or peer rejection. *Developmental Psychology, 24,* 815–823.

Capaldi, D. M., Crosby, L., & Stoolmiller, M. (1996). Predicting the timing of first sexual intercourse for adolescent males. *Child Development, 67,* 344–359.

Capaldi, D., & Patterson, G. R. (1989). *Psychometric properties of fourteen latent constructs from the Oregon Youth Study.* New York: Springer-Verlag.

Capaldi, D., & Patterson, G. R. (1991). The relation of parental transitions to boys' adjustment problems: I. A test of linear hypothesis. II. Mothers at risk for transitions and unskilled parenting. *Development and Psychopathology, 3,* 277–300.

Capaldi, D. M., & Patterson, G. R. (1994). Interrelated influences of contextual factors on antisocial behavior in childhood and adolescence for males. In D. Fowles, P. Sutker, & S. Goodman (Eds.), *Psychopathy and social personality: A developmental perspective* (pp. 165–198). New York: Springer.

Caspi, A., & Herbener, D. S. (1990). Continuity and change: Assorted marriages and the consistency of personality in adulthood. *Journal of Personality and Social Psychology, 58,* 250–258.

Cicchetti, D., & Toth, S. L. (1995). Developmental psychopathology and disorders of affect. In D. Cicchetti & D. J. Cohen (Eds.), *Developmental psychopathology: Vol. 2. Risk, disorder, and adaptation* (pp. 369–420). New York: Wiley.

Cloninger, C. R., & Gottesman, I. I. (1987). Genetic and environmental factors in antisocial behavior disorders. In S. A. Mednick, T. E. Moffitt, & S. A. Stack (Eds.), *The causes of crime: New biological approaches* (pp. 92–109). New York: Cambridge University Press.

Coie, J. D., & Kupersmidt, J. B. (1983). A behavioral analysis of emerging social status in boys' groups. *Child Development, 54,* 1400–1416.

Conger, R. D., Patterson, G. R., & Ge, X. (1995). A mediational model for the impact of parents' stress on adolescent adjustment. *Child Development, 66,* 80–97.

Conger, R. D., & Simons, R. L. (in press). Life-course contingencies in the development of adolescent antisocial behavior: A matching law approach. In T. P. Thornberry (Ed.), *Developmental theories of crime and delinquency.* New Brunswick, NJ: Transaction Books.

Cummings, E. M., & Cummings, J. L. (1988). A process-oriented approach to children's coping with adults' angry behavior. *Developmental Review, 8,* 296–321.

DiLalla, L. F., & Gottesman, I. I. (1989). Heterogeneity of causes of delinquency and criminality: Life span perspectives. *Development and Psychopathology, 1,* 339–349.

Dipietro, J. A., Greenspan, S. I., & Porges, S. W. (1991). Psychophysiological characteristics of the regulatory disordered infant. *Infant Behaviors and Development, 14,* 37–50.

Dishion, T. J. (1990). Peer context of troublesome behavior in children and adolescents. In. P. Leone (Ed.), *Understanding troubled and troublesome youth* (pp. 128–153). Beverly Hills, CA: Sage Publications.

Dishion, T. J., & Andrews, D. W. (1995). Preventing escalation in problem behaviors with high-risk young adolescents: Immediate and 1-year outcomes. *Journal of Consulting and Clinical Psychology, 63,* 538–548.

Dishion, T. J., Capaldi, D., Spracklen, K. M., & Li, F. (1995). Peer ecology of male adolescent drug use. *Development and Psychopathology, 7,* 803–824.

Dishion, T. J., Eddy, M., Li, F., Haas, E., & Spracklen, K. (1995, November). *Adolescent friendships and later violent behavior.* Paper presented at the annual meeting of the Association for the Advancement of Behavior Therapy, Washington, DC.

Dishion, T. J., French, D. C., & Patterson, G. R. (1995). The development and ecology of antisocial behavior. In D. Cicchetti & D. Cohen (Eds.), *Manual of developmental psychopathology: Vol. 2. Risk, disorder, and adaptation* (pp. 421–471). New York: Wiley.

Dishion, T. J., Gardner, K., Patterson, G. R., Reid, J. B., & Thibodeaux, S. (1983). *The Family Process Code: A multidimensional system for observing family interaction.* Unpublished technical report. (Available from Oregon Social Learning Center, 207 E. 5th Ave., Suite 202, Eugene, OR 97401.)

Dishion, T. J., Patterson, G. R., & Griesler, P. C. (1994). Peer adaptation in the development of antisocial behavior: A confluence model. In L. R. Huesmann (Ed.), *Aggressive behavior: Current perspectives* (pp. 61–95). New York: Plenum.

Dishion, T. J., Patterson, G. R., Stoolmiller, M., & Skinner, M. S. (1991). Family, school, and behavioral antecedents to early adolescent involvement with antisocial peers. *Developmental Psychology, 27,* 172–180.

Dishion, T. J., & Spracklen, K. M. (1996, May). *A matching law account of deviancy training within adolescent boys' friendships: An emphasis on duration.* Paper presented at the annual meeting of the Association for Behavior Analysis, San Francisco, CA.

Dishion, T. J., Spracklen, K. M., Andrews, D. W., & Patterson, G. R. (1996). Deviancy training in male adolescent friendships. *Behavior Therapy, 27,* 373–390.

Dodge, K. A. (1983). Behavioral antecedents: A peer social status. *Child Development, 54,* 1386–1399.

Dodge, K. A. (1991). The structure and function of proactive and reactive aggression. In D. J. Pepler & K. H. Rubin (Eds.), *The development and treatment of childhood aggression* (pp. 201–218). Hillsdale, NJ: Erlbaum.

Dodge, K. A. (1993). The future of research and the treatment of conduct disorder. *Development and Psychopathology, 5,* 311–319.

Ekman, P. (1992). Facial expressions of emotions: New findings, new questions. *Psychological Science, 3,* 34–37.

Elder, G. H. (1980). *Family structure and socialization.* New York: Arno Press.

Elder, G. H., Caspi, A., & Van Nguyen, T. (1986). Resourceful and vulnerable children: Family influences in hard times. In R. K. Silbereisen, K. Eyferth, & G. Rudinger (Eds.), *Development as action in context: Problem behavior and normal youth development* (pp. 167–186). New York: Springer-Verlag.

Elder, G. H., Van Nguyen, T., & Caspi, A. (1985). Linking family hardship to children's lives. *Child Development, 56,* 361–375.

Elliott, D. S., & Menard, S. (1988). *Delinquent behavior and delinquent peers: Temporal and developmental patterns.* Unpublished manuscript. (Available from Behavioral Research Institute, Boulder, CO.)

Fagot, B. I., & Leve, L. D. (in press). Gender identity and play. In D. P. Fromberg & D. Bergen (Eds.), *Play from birth to twelve: Contexts, perspectives, and meanings.* New York: Garland.

Farrington, D. P. (1991). Childhood aggression and adult violence: Early precursors and later life outcomes. In D. J. Pepler & K. H. Rubin (Eds.), *The development and treatment of childhood aggression* (pp. 5–29). Hillsdale, NJ: Erlbaum.

Forgatch, M. S. (1989). Patterns and outcome in family problem-solving: The disrupting effect of negative emotion. *Journal of Marriage and the Family, 51,* 115–124.

Forgatch, M. S. (1991). The clinical science vortex: Developing a theory for antisocial behavior. In D. J. Pepler & K. H. Rubin (Eds.), *The development and treatment of childhood aggression* (pp. 291–315). Hillsdale, NJ: Erlbaum.

Forgatch, M. S., & Stoolmiller, M. (1994). Emotions as contexts for adolescent delinquency: A mediational model. *Journal of Research on Adolescence, 4,* 601–614.

Fowles, D. C. (1984). Biological variables in psychopathology: A psychobiological perspective. In H. E. Adams & J. B. Sutker (Eds.), *Comprehensive handbook of psychopathology* (pp. 77–106). New York: Plenum.

Fowles, D. C. (1987). Application of a behavioral theory of motivation to the concepts of anxiety and impulsivity. *Journal of Research in Personality, 21,* 417–435.

French, D. C. (1988). Heterogeneity of peer-rejected boys: Aggressive and nonaggressive subtypes. *Child Development, 59,* 882–886.

French, D. C. (1990). Heterogeneity of peer-rejected girls. *Child Development, 61,* 2028–2031.

Gardner, F. E. M. (1992). Parent-child interaction and conduct disorders. *Educational Psychology Review, 4,* 135–163.

Glueck, S., & Glueck, E. (1950). *Unraveling juvenile delinquency.* Cambridge, MA: Harvard University Press.

Gollob, H. F., & Reichardt, C. S. (1987). Taking account of time lags in causal models. *Child Development, 58,* 80–92.

Gottman, J. M., & Levenson, R. W. (1986). Assessing the role of emotion in marriage. *Behavioral Assessment, 8,* 31–48.

Gray, J. A. (1982). *The neuropsychology of anxiety: An inquiry into the function of the septo-hypocampal system.* New York: Clarendon.

Hayes, S. C. (1988). Contextualism and the next wave of behavioral psychology. *Behavior Analyses, 23,* 7–22.

Hinde, Robert, A. (1989). Ethological and relationships approaches. In R. Vasta (Ed.), *Annals of child development; Vol. 6. Six theories of child development: Revised formulations and current issues* (pp. 251–285). London: JAI Press.

Hirschi, T., & Gottfredson, M. (1983). Age and the explanation of crime. *American Journal of Sociology, 89,* 552–583.

Hops, H., Biglan, A., Sherman, L., Arthur, J., Friedman, L., & Osteen, V. (1987). Home observations of family interactions of depressed women. *Journal of Consulting and Clinical Psychology, 55,* 341–346.

Izard, C. E., & Harris, P. (1995). Emotional development and developmental psychopathology. In D. Cicchetti & D. J. Cohen (Eds.), *Developmental psychopathology: Vol. 2. Risk, disorder, and adaptation* (pp. 467–503). New York: Wiley.

Jenkins, R. L., & Hewitt, L. (1944). Types of personality structure encountered in child guidance clinics. *American Journal of Orthopsychiatry, 14,* 84–94.

Katz, L. F., & Gottman, J. M. (1991). Marital discord and child outcomes: A social psychophysiological approach. In J. Garber & K. A. Dodge (Eds.), *The development of emotion regulation and dysregulation: Cambridge studies in social and emotional development* (pp. 129–155). New York: Cambridge University Press.

Larzelere, R. E., & Patterson, G. R. (1990). Parental management: Mediators of the effect of socioeconomic status on early delinquency. *Criminology, 28,* 301–323.

Lerner, J. V., Hertzog, C., Hooker, K. A., Hassibi, M., & Thomas, A. (1988). A longitudinal study of negative emotional states and adjustment from early childhood through adolescence. *Child Development, 59,* 356–366.

Loeber, R., & Dishion, T. J. (1983). Early predictors of male delinquency: A review. *Psychological Bulletin, 94,* 68–99.

Loeber, R., & Dishion, T. J. (1984). Boys who fight at home and school: Family conditions influencing cross-setting consistency. *Journal of Consulting and Clinical Psychology, 52,* 759–768.

Magnusson, D. (1992). Individual development: A longitudinal perspective. *European Journal of Personality, 6,* 119–138.

Magnusson, D., Stattin, H., & Allen, D. L. (1985). Biological maturation and social development: A longitudinal study of some adjustment processes from mid-adolescence to adulthood. *Journal of Youth and Adolescence, 14,* 267–283.

McDowell, J. J. (1988). Matching theory in natural human environments. *Behavior Analyst, II,* 95–109.

McLoyd, V. C. (1990). The impact of economic hardship on Black families and children: Psychological distress, parenting, and socioemotional development. *Child Development, 61,* 311–346.

Meehl, P. E. (1954). *Clinical versus statistical prediction: A theoretical analysis and a review of evidence.* Minneapolis: University of Minnesota Press.

Moffitt, T. E. (1990). The neuropsychology of juvenile delinquency: A critical review. In M. Tonry & N. Morris (Eds.), *Crime and justice: A review of research* (Vol. 12, pp. 99–169). Chicago: University of Chicago Press.

Moffitt, T. E. (1993). Adolescence-limited and life course persistent antisocial behavior: Developmental taxonomy. *Psychological Review, 100,* 674–701.

Montemayor, R., & Flannery, D. (1989). A naturalistic study of the involvement of children and adolescents with their mothers and friends: Developmental differences in expressive behavior. *Journal of Adolescent Research, 4,* 3–14.

Olds, D. (1989). The Prenatal/Early Infancy Project: A strategy for responding to the needs of high-risk mothers and their children. *Prevention in Human Services, 7,* 59–87.

Olweus, D. (1980). Familial and temperamental determinants of aggressive behavior in adolescent boys: A causal analysis. *Developmental Psychology, 16,* 644–660.

Paikoff, R. L., & Brooks-Gunn, J. (1990). Physiological processes: What role do they play during the transition to adolescence? In R. Montemayor, G. R. Adams, & T. P. Gullotta (Eds.), *From childhood to adolescence: A transitional period* (pp. 310–348). Newbury Park, CA: Sage Publications.

Patterson, G. R. (1982). *Coercive family process.* Eugene, OR: Castalia.

Patterson, G. R. (1983). Stress: A change agent for family process. In N. Garrezy & M. Rutter (Eds.), *Stress, coping, and development in children* (pp. 235–264). New York: McGraw-Hill.

Patterson, G. R. (1984). Microsocial process: A view from the boundary. In J. Masters & K. Yorkin-Levin (Eds.), *Boundary areas in social psychology* (pp. 43–67). New York: Academic Press.

Patterson, G. R. (1986). Performance models for antisocial boys. *American Psychologist, 41,* 432–444.

Patterson, G. R. (1992). Developmental changes in antisocial behavior. In R. D. Peters, R. J. McMahon, & V. L. Quinsey (Eds.), *Aggression and violence throughout the life span* (pp. 52–82). Newbury Park, CA: Sage Publications.

Patterson, G. R. (1993). Orderly change in a stable world: The antisocial trait as a chimera. *Journal of Consulting and Clinical Psychology, 61,* 911–919.

Patterson, G. R. (1995). Coercion as a basis for early age of onset for arrest. In J. McCord (Ed.), *Coercion and punishment in long-term perspective* (pp. 81–105). New York: Cambridge University Press.

Patterson, G. R., & Bank, L. (1989). Some amplifying mechanisms for pathologic processes in families. In M. R. Gunnar & E. Thalen (Eds.), *Systems and development: The Minnesota Symposia on Child Psychology* (Vol. 22, pp. 167–209). Hillsdale, NJ: Erlbaum.

Patterson, G. R., & Chamberlain, P. (1994). A functional analysis of resistance during parent training therapy. *Clinical Psychology: Science and Practice, 1,* 53–70.

Patterson, G. R., Cobb, J. A., & Ray, R. S. (1972). Direct intervention in the classroom: A set of procedures for the aggressive child. In F. W. Clark, D. R. Evans, & L. A. Hamerlynck (Eds.), *Implementing behavioral programs for schools and clinics* (pp. 151–201). Champaign, IL: Research Press.

Patterson, G. R., DeBaryshe, B. D., & Ramsey, E. (1989). A developmental perspective on antisocial behavior. *American Psychologist, 44,* 329–335.

Patterson, G. R., & Dishion, T. J. (1988). Multilevel family process models: Traits, interactions, and relationships. In R. Hinde & J. Stevenson-Hinde (Eds.), *Relationships and families: Mutual influences* (pp. 283–310). Oxford: Clarendon.

Patterson, G. R., Dishion, T. J., & Chamberlain, P. (1993). Outcomes and methodological issues relating to treatment of antisocial children. In T. R. Giles (Ed.), *Effective psychotherapy: A handbook of comparative research* (pp. 43–88). New York: Plenum.

Patterson, G. R., Forgatch, M. S., & Stoolmiller, M. (under review). A stage-sequence model for childhood antisocial behavior, early arrest, and chronic offending juveniles. *Criminology.*

Patterson, G. R., Reid, J. B., & Dishion, T. J. (1992). *Antisocial boys.* Eugene, OR: Castalia.

Patterson, G. R., & Yoerger, K. (1993). Developmental models for delinquent behavior. In S. Hodgins (Ed.), *Crime and mental disorders* (pp. 140–172). Newbury Park, CA: Sage Publications.

Plomin, R., Nitz, K., & Rowe, D. C. (1990). Behavior genetics and aggressive behavior in childhood. In M. Lewis & S. Miller (Eds.), *Handbook of developmental psychology* (pp. 119–133). New York: Plenum.

Poe, J., Dishion, T. J., Griesler, P., & Andrews, D. W. (1990). *Topic code.* Unpublished coding manual. (Available from Oregon Social Learning Center, 207 E. 5th Ave., Suite 202, Eugene, OR 97401.)

Pulkkinen, L. (1983). Youthful smoking and drinking in a longitudinal perspective. *Journal of Youth and Adolescence, 12,* 253–283.

Quay, H. C. (1987). Patterns of delinquent behavior. In H. C. Quay (Ed.), *Handbook of juvenile delinquency* (pp. 118–138). New York: Wiley.

Quay, H. C. (1993). The psychobiology of undersocialized aggressive conduct disorder: A theoretical perspective. *Development and Psychopathology, 5,* 165–180.

Radke-Yarrow, M. (1990). Family environments of depressed and well parents and their children: Issues of research and methods. In G. R. Patterson (Ed.), *Depression and aggression in family interaction* (pp. 169–184). Hillsdale, NJ: Erlbaum.

Ramsey, E., Patterson, G. R., & Walker, H. M. (1990). Generalization of the antisocial trait from home to school settings. *Journal of Applied Developmental Psychology, 11,* 209–233.

Reid, J. B. (1993). Prevention of conduct disorder before and after school entry: Relating interventions to development findings. *Development and Psychopathology, 5,* 243–262.

Robins, L. N. (1966). *Deviant children grow up: A sociological and psychiatric study of sociopathic personality.* Baltimore: Williams & Wilkins.

Rothbart, M. K., Posner, M., & Hershey, K. L. (1995). Temperament, attention, and developmental psychopathology. In D. Cicchetti & D. J. Cohen (Eds.), *Developmental psychopathology: Vol. 1. Theory and methods* (pp. 315–340). New York: Wiley.

Rowe, D. (1989). Families and peers: Another look at the nature-nurture question. In T. J. Berndt & G. W. Ladd (Eds.), *Peer relationships in child development* (pp. 274–299). New York: Wiley.

Rutter, M. (1978). Family, area, and school influences in the genesis of conduct disorders. In L. A. Herson, M. Berger, & D. Schaffer (Eds.), *Childhood and adolescence* (pp. 95–111). London: Blackwell.

Sampson, R. J., & Laub, J. H. (1994). Urban poverty and the family context of delinquency: A new look at structure and process in a classic study. *Child Development, 65,* 523–540.

Snyder, J. J. (1991). Discipline as a mediator of the impact of maternal stress and mood on child conduct problems. *Development and Psychopathology, 3,* 263–276.

Snyder, J. J. (1995, June). *Testing the peer group selectivity hypothesis.* Seminar presented at the Oregon Social Learning Center, Eugene, OR.

Snyder, J. J., & Patterson, G. R. (1995). Individual differences in social aggression: A test of a reinforcement model of socialization in the natural environment. *Behavior Therapy, 26,* 371–391.

Stoolmiller, M. (1994). Antisocial behavior, delinquent peer association, and unsupervised wandering for boys: Growth and change from childhood to early adolescence. *Multivariate Behavioral Research, 29,* 263–288.

Thomas, A., & Chess, S. (1977). *Temperament and development.* New York: Brunner/Mazel.

Walker, H. M., Stieber, S., Ramsey, E., & O'Neill, R. (1993). Fifth grade school adjustment and later arrest rate: A longitudinal study of middle school antisocial boys. *Journal of Child and Family Studies, 2,* 295–315.

Warr, M. (1993). Age, peers, & delinquency. *Criminology, 31,* 17–40.

Wiggins, J. S. (Ed.). (1973). *Personality and prediction: Principles of personality assessment.* Reading, MA: Addison-Wesley.

CHAPTER 21

Peers, Drug Use, and Delinquency

TERENCE P. THORNBERRY and MARVIN D. KROHN

This chapter is about the role that peers play in explaining drug use and delinquency, especially among adolescents. There is strong empirical evidence that adolescents who associate with peers who use drugs are likely to use drugs and that adolescents who associate with delinquent peers are likely to engage in delinquency. Indeed, the peer-behavior interconnection is one of the oldest in the research literature on delinquency and drug use. As far back as the 1920s and 1930s, scholars using observational and official data demonstrated the strong correlation between delinquent peers and delinquency (Shaw & McKay, 1931; Thrasher, 1927). Early self-report studies of delinquency also demonstrated a strong correlation between having delinquent friends and delinquent behavior (Short, 1957, 1958, 1960).

The study of drug use is somewhat more recent, but here too early empirical studies demonstrated a strong relationship between peer associations and behavior. Among others, Vaillant (1966), Kandel (1975), and Jessor and Jessor (1977) showed that associating with peers who use drugs is linked to an elevated level of use. This relationship was observed for alcohol, marijuana, and narcotic drugs.

Not only is peer influence empirically linked to deviant behavior,[1] but it has played a prominent role in theories of deviance. One of the earliest theories incorporating peer influences as a cause of delinquency and drug use is Sutherland's (1939) theory of differential association. First fully stated in 1939, it argues that delinquent behavior is learned through a process of differential associations, especially associations with delinquent peers. Both social disorganization (e.g., Shaw & McKay, 1942) and strain theories (e.g., Cloward & Ohlin, 1960; Cohen, 1955), discussed later, also emphasize the importance of peers.

Theories of drug use have also granted a prominent place to peer influence. Early work by Tec (1972) and Krohn (1974) used differential association theory to predict marijuana use, and Akers first applied his social learning theory to the explanation of alcohol and marijuana use (Akers, Krohn, Lanza-Kaduce, & Radosevich, 1979). Jessor and Jessor's (1977) problem behavior theory

also views peers as having a major impact on drug use (see also Jessor, Donovan, & Costa, 1991).

Although peer influence has a prominent place in the history of thought on delinquency and drug use, its place is not without controversy. Early empirical and theoretical work stimulated another school of thought that argued that the impact of peers was trivial. Epitomized by Glueck and Glueck's (1950) pithy comment—"birds of a feather flock together" (p. 164)—this perspective argues that prior factors cause delinquency and then already delinquent youth band together as friends. Although not denying the empirical association between peers and behavior, this perspective robs the relationship of any theoretical or causal importance.

The debate initiated by Sutherland and Glueck and Glueck remains a lively and important one because a fundamental understanding of the causes of delinquency and drug use is at stake. In this chapter, we explore the ramifications of this debate and examine the theoretical and empirical relationships between peers and behavior.

THE ROLE OF PEERS IN THEORIES OF DEVIANCE

Virtually all theoretical models of delinquent behavior and drug use acknowledge the observed relationship between these behaviors and association with others who engage in similar behaviors. The position of the peer variable in the causal structure, however, differentiates among theoretical perspectives. Three general perspectives can be identified. Theories based on a subcultural tradition view delinquency as an outcome of a learning process and argue that association with delinquent peers is a key causal variable. Theories that fall within the social control perspective view association with peers as a consequence of participating in delinquent behavior or as caused by a third variable that also causes delinquency. Theories that adopt an interactional or life-course perspective view these variables as being reciprocally interrelated over time.

Cultural Deviance Theories

Early explanations for crime were greatly influenced by the heterogeneity and diversity that increasingly characterized U.S. cities at the

---

[1]Because this chapter is concerned with both drug use and delinquency, we use the term *deviant behavior* or *deviance* in statements that apply equally to both of these behaviors.

218

beginning of the 20th century. Sellin (1938), for example, suggested that the distinctive behaviors of subcultural groups often become criminalized because they conflict with the interests of more powerful groups. This cultural conflict results in some people committing crime because they adhere to the norms of their own subculture. Thus, criminal behavior was seen as an outgrowth of being socialized to values and behavior that had been defined as criminal.

Sociologists of the Chicago School, most notably represented by Shaw and McKay (1942), viewed inner-city areas of large cities as socially disorganized and unable to control the behavior of their residents, particularly their youthful residents. Shaw and McKay also suggested that delinquent subcultures form in these disorganized neighborhoods. Youths who are exposed to these subcultures are recruited into them and are socialized to criminalistic values by them.

Although the emphasis in both culture conflict and social disorganization theories is on aggregate-level concepts, peers play a crucial role in the cultural transmission processes. Although important to these aggregate-level theories, it was not until the more individual-level theory of Sutherland (1939), however, that attention clearly focused on the role of peers in the delinquency-generating process.

Sutherland based his differential association theory on the assumption that criminal behavior is learned through interacting and communicating with other people (Sutherland & Cressey, 1978). Sutherland did not view all associations as having equal influence on the learning process, however. He recognized that learning takes place best within intimate primary groups such as peer networks. Hence, Sutherland accorded peers a key role in the learning process. From these intimate personal groups, people learn definitions that are favorable or unfavorable to the violation of the law. Criminal behavior is more likely if there is an excess of definitions favorable to, versus those unfavorable to, the violation of the law. Thus, the effect of peer associations on delinquent behavior is indirect, operating through the learning of definitions (Figure 21.1a). Sutherland recognized that one could learn definitions favorable to the violation of the law from noncriminal companions and unfavorable definitions from criminal companions. In other words, the theory suggests that it is more than merely associations with "bad companions" that increases the probability of criminal behavior. The actor must interpret what is being conveyed as a definition favorable to law violation in order for it to have a delinquency-inducing effect.

Empirical examinations of differential association have been hindered by the difficulty of measuring the ratio of definitions favorable and unfavorable to the violation of the law over the life course. Indeed, many studies simply omit definitions from the analysis and focus on delinquent companions only. The theory also has been criticized for not identifying the process by which behavior is learned. This failure led to the development of social learning theory by Burgess and Akers (1966) and Akers (1973).

Burgess and Akers (1966) modified Sutherland's (1939) theory to make it more testable and to ground it in research from experimental psychology. To do this, they incorporated principles from operant conditioning, stating that the probability of a behavior occurring is contingent on the consequences of that behavior. If delinquent behavior has been reinforced more than nondelinquent behavior in similar past situations, then delinquent behavior is more likely to occur in future similar situations. Differential peer

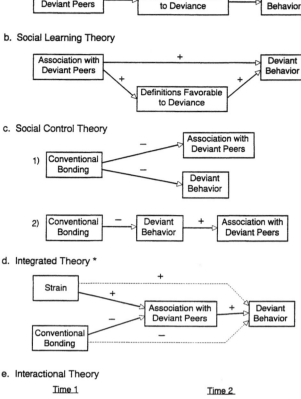

Figure 21.1 *Causal models specifying the relationship between association with deviant peers and deviant behavior.*

association is a critical feature of social learning theory because primary groups provide the context in which behavior is reinforced, imitation takes place, and definitions that serve as discriminative stimuli are learned.

Whereas Sutherland (1939) saw the effect of peers on delinquency as being indirect, operating through the learning of definitions favorable to the violation of the law, Akers (1973) posited two causal paths. One, as in Sutherland's model, is an indirect effect through definitions; the second is a direct effect generated by vicarious learning (imitation) and the reinforcements provided by peers. This causal structure is illustrated in Figure 21.1b (see also Liska, 1987).

Jessor and Jessor (1977) employed a somewhat different social learning theory to account for drug use. Based on Rotter's (1954) social learning model, problem behavior theory categorizes variables into three major psychosocial systems: the personality system, the perceived environment system, and the behavior system. These variables, differentiated in terms of their proximity to the problem behavior in the causal chain, generate a dynamic state called *proneness,* or the likelihood of occurrence of a problem behavior. Peer approval and peer models are part of the perceived environment system and, as proximal to problem behavior, should have a strong impact on drug use and other problem behaviors (Jessor et al., 1991; Jessor & Jessor, 1977).

Control Theory

Control theory adopts a very different perspective on the relationship between peers and behavior. The difference lies in two major areas: the causal order of the relationship and the quality of friendship patterns for delinquents as compared to nondelinquents.

In a pure control theory, "companionship with delinquents is an incidental by-product of the real causes of delinquency" (Hirschi, 1969, p. 137). There are two somewhat different versions of this perspective represented in Figure 21.1.c. In the first, the relationship between association with deviant peers and deviant behavior is spurious; both variables are caused by weak conventional bonds. In the second, weak bonds cause deviant behavior; and that, in turn, leads to association with deviant peers.

As indicated earlier, Glueck and Glueck (1950) dismissed the strong empirical relationship between association with delinquent peers and engaging in delinquency by arguing that it represented nothing more than birds of a feather flocking together. They posited that other variables, especially family process variables, cause adolescent delinquency. Once delinquency is exhibited, delinquents tend to seek each other out for companionship, but the peer group exerts no real causal influence on behavior. As a result, associating with delinquent peers is seen as a consequence, not a cause, of delinquency.

Although this position originated with Glueck and Glueck (1950), it was presented most forcefully by Hirschi (1969), who argued that the relationship between delinquent companions and delinquency is, at best, spurious. Delinquency is caused by a weak bond to society. The bond to conventional society is represented by four elements—attachment to others (especially parents), commitment to conventional institutions, involvement in conventional activities, and belief in conventional values. As these elements of the bond become weakened, control over the individual's behavior is reduced, and deviant behavior becomes more likely. Weak bonds also cause association with delinquent companions, but there is no causal connection between association with delinquent peers and delinquency—both are caused by a weakening of the social bond (Hirschi, 1969, pp. 152–154). This is often referred to as a selection, as opposed to a socialization, model.

Hirschi's (1969) version of control theory also differs from cultural deviance theories in the prediction it makes concerning the quality of peer attachments for delinquents as compared to nondelinquents. Cultural deviance models generally predict that delinquents not only associate with but are attached to their delinquent friends. Cohen (1955), in describing delinquent gangs, articulated this position clearly: "Relations with gang members tend to be intensely solidary and imperious" (p. 31). Hirschi's (1969) position is diametrically opposed: Delinquents may associate with

one another, but they are relatively unattached to one another. Hirschi characterized social relations among delinquents as "cold and brittle" and claimed that their "social skills are severely limited [and that they] are incapable of influencing each other in a manner suggested by those who see the peer group as a decisive factor in delinquency" (p. 141).

Integrated Theories

Unlike control theory, peer associations have a prominent causal position in integrated models of delinquency and drug use such as those presented by Conger (1976), Elliott, Huizinga, and Ageton (1985), Hawkins and Weis (1985), R. E. Johnson (1979), and Simons, Conger, and Whitbeck (1988). These models attempt to combine the propositions of such theories as strain, control, and differential association/social learning theories to better explain delinquency and drug use.

Integrated theories argue that each traditional theory—such as cultural deviance theory or control theory—offers something of value to the explanation of drug use and delinquency but that none offers a complete explanation. A more comprehensive explanation, they argue, can be accomplished by combining the better aspects of these traditional models. For example, integrated theories criticize the amotivational stance of control theory and the resulting absence of a causal role for deviant companions. As R. E. Johnson (1979) said, "It is unsatisfactory to answer the question of motivation by simply stating 'we would if we dared' [as Hirschi did]" (p. 60). Seeking a fuller explanation of deviant behavior, integrated models look to deviant companions as the primary source of motivation for delinquency and drug use.

Similarly, integrated models criticize differential association and social learning theories for failing to provide a coherent explanation for why some adolescents associate with deviant peers in the first place. Adopting a control theory perspective, integrated theories typically hypothesize that weak social bonds increase the odds that adolescents will have delinquent friends: "Those who are less attached to their parents, and *especially* those who are less attached to school . . . will tend to find one another in the process of seeking and sorting companionships" (R. E. Johnson, 1979, pp. 60–61; emphasis in original).

Thus, integrated models pose a two-step causal process that leads to drug use and delinquency (Figure 21.1d). First, as the level of strain increases or as a person's bond to society is weakened, control over behavior diminishes, thereby increasing the *possibility* of drug use and delinquency. Second, actual involvement in these behaviors requires reinforcements and social support, and these are provided most directly by deviant peers. Elliott et al. (1985), for example, hypothesized that absent peer associations, the causal effects of strain and low stakes in conformity "will be quite small" precisely because "there are no social supports for delinquency" (p. 68).

Interactional Theory

We have described two approaches to incorporating peer effects into causal models of drug use and delinquency. Control theory argues either that deviant behavior leads to peer association or that these variables are causally unrelated. Differential association, social learning, and integrated theories argue that association with deviant peers is a major cause of deviance. A third approach is possible. Interactional or developmental perspectives hold that *both* causal influences operate to produce behavior over the life course. This perspective is most clearly seen in the interactional theory developed by Thornberry (1987).

Interactional theory argues that because deviant peers model and reinforce deviant behavior and because they provide a social context rich in normative support for deviance, associating with deviant peers is likely to cause both the initiation and the maintenance of deviance. This causal influence is viewed as part of a process that plays out over time. For example, the longer one associates with deviant peers and the more deviant the group becomes, the greater will be the impact on the actor's behavior.

Deviant behavior is also seen as exerting a strong causal impact on other variables, including association with deviant peers. Interactional theory posits a balance or consistency model between behavior and associations; people prefer to associate with and have as their friends people who are similar to them. Because of that the more heavily engrossed in drug use and delinquency individuals become, the more likely they are to seek deviant friends. Deviant behavior can also cause increased association with deviant peers through exclusionary processes. Prosocial peer groups can become close to people who engage in deviance because the deviance violates the normative structure of the group (see Becker, 1963). The impact of behavior on associations is also part of a process that plays out over time. For example, the longer one's deviant career lasts and the more serious it becomes, the greater will be the impact on associational patterns.

Thus, interactional theory posits a bidirectional causal relationship for association with deviant peers and deviant behavior that develops over the life course (Figure 21.1e). The model includes stability effects for both association with deviant peers and deviant behavior. It also includes reciprocal causal influences, represented by cross-lagged effects from peers at one time to behavior at the next and from behavior at one time to peers at the next.

Other theories also have discussed a bidirectional relationship for peers and behavior. Whereas Elliott et al. (1985) included only a causal effect from peers to behavior, they recognized that the relationship is probably bidirectional: "Bonding to delinquent peer groups and delinquent behavior are mutually reinforcing variables with approximately equal influence on each other" (p. 88). In his initial development and testing of social learning theory, Akers (1973; Akers et al., 1979) adopted a unidirectional causal structure. More recently, however, he has discussed the learning process as a complex one, involving reciprocal and feedback effects. He suggested that differential association typically precedes the committing of delinquent acts. However, he also hypothesized that once associations are established and reinforcement has taken place, "both the continuation of old and the seeking of new associations (over which one has any choice) will themselves be affected" (Akers, 1994, p. 100).

In brief, five different types of theoretical models have been proposed to account for the observed empirical relationship between peers and behavior (Figure 21.1). After discussing a number of methodological issues in this area of inquiry, we return

to these theoretical issues and review the level of empirical support for these different approaches.

METHODOLOGICAL ISSUES

Several methodological issues confront the study of the relationship between association with deviant peers and involvement in drug use and delinquency. Three of them are discussed in this section: research design, source of data on peer deviance, and the independence of the measurements of peer deviance and self deviance.

Research Design

The first issue concerns the use of cross-sectional versus longitudinal research designs. Most studies of the relationship between deviant peers and deviant behavior have used cross-sectional designs in which all the variables are measured simultaneously. Although the correlation between variables can be estimated with cross-sectional designs, it is difficult, if not impossible, to ensure proper temporal order and to examine causal relationships among the variables.

Fortunately, an increasing number of longitudinal data sets are available to examine the issue of causal relationships between association with deviant peers and deviant behavior. Longitudinal designs with repeated measures of the same individuals can ensure that the measure of the independent variables precedes the measure of the dependent variable in examining either specification of the causal order between peer associations and deviant behavior. They also allow for the assessment of the impact of one variable on the other controlling for stability effects. Finally, they allow for an assessment of how change in one variable produces change in the other variable.

Given the methodological advantages of longitudinal designs, it is important to base inferences about causal relationships between association with deviant peers and involvement in deviant behavior on analyses of longitudinal data that maintain proper temporal sequence. Because of that, our review, although including cross-sectional studies, focuses on results from longitudinal studies.

Source of Data

Perhaps the most serious methodological problem in this research area is the measurement of the peer variable. Overwhelmingly, peer deviance is measured through the perception of the target subject; rarely are peers interviewed directly and asked to report on their own behavior. Thus, both variables—peer deviance and self deviance—share common measurement variance. This measurement strategy may be problematic for several reasons.

On the one hand, whereas people often know a great deal about the behavior of their friends, they obviously do not know everything their friends do. This may be particularly true of drug use and delinquency in as much as people may conceal deviant behavior from their friends. If so, reports from target subjects about their friends' involvement in deviance would underestimate the level of peer drug use and delinquency.

On the other hand, because the information to measure these

two variables comes from target subjects, their level of deviance may influence the measurement of peer deviance. People heavily involved in drug use and delinquency may overestimate the extent of involvement by their friends; nonusers and nondelinquents may underestimate the extent of involvement by their friends. If this in fact happens, then studies that rely on target subjects for information on both peer deviance and self deviance will overestimate the magnitude of the relationship between these two concepts.

We have identified few studies that used peer reports of their own behavior in assessing the relationship between association with deviant peers and deviant behavior. Kandel's (1978a) study of high school students was based on a sample of best school friend dyads; thus, the measure of deviance was based on each friend's own self-reports. For marijuana use, the correlations across different types of friendship dyads are reasonably large, ranging from .22 for dyads that dissolved during the course of one academic year to .58 for reciprocated, stable dyads. For minor delinquency, the correlations range from .16 for unstable pairs to .31 for reciprocated, stable pairs. The magnitude of the correlations, especially for drug use, are generally in the same range as those reported in studies that relied on target respondents to report on peer deviance.

Elliott and Voss (1974) used two measures of peer delinquency, one based on focal respondents' perceptions of delinquency among their immediate friends and the other based on self-reports "on the part of persons listed as friends in a sociometric question" (p. 158). They concluded that measures based on the target respondents' reports of friends' delinquency tend to overestimate the magnitude, but not the direction or significance, of this relationship.

Fisher and Bauman (1988) used a similar strategy to study peer influences on the use of beer and hard liquor among a sample of middle school students. Peer alcohol use was measured through both focal respondents' reports and reports collected directly from the respondents' best school friends. In assessing the bivariate relationship between peer alcohol use and respondent alcohol use, the researchers found that the "use of subject report for friend behavior consistently yields a larger coefficient than when friend report is used" (Fisher & Bauman, 1988, p. 296).

Huizinga, Weiher, and Esbensen (1992) examined this issue as part of the Denver Youth Survey. They collected information on peer involvement in drug use and delinquency from the focal respondents and then directly from two best friends nominated by each focal respondent. Unfortunately, the measures are not exactly comparable because the focal respondents reported on the deviant behavior of their friends in general, not just their two best friends. The correlation between the focal respondents' reports of peer deviance and peer self-reports of deviance, across types of delinquency, range from .14 to .19; for alcohol and drug use, they range from .30 to .32. Clearly, there is a substantial degree of slippage between these two measures of peer deviance. Huizinga et al. (1992) also reported that the correlation between association with deviant peers and respondents' deviant behavior varies with the source of data on peer deviance. For delinquency, the correlations between associations and behavior range from .43 to .51 when focal respondents' reports of peer delinquency are used but drop to approximately .10 when peer self-reports are used. For drug use, the correlation is .50 when focal respondents' reports of peer drug

use are used but drops to about .20 when peer self-reports are used (Huizinga et al., 1992, pp. 12–14).

Finally, Aseltine (1995) reported on a panel study of delinquency and marijuana use in three Boston area high schools. By asking respondents to identify their best school friends, Aseltine was able to create best friend dyads for 67% of his sample (pp. 106–107). He did not measure peer deviance through the target respondents' perceptions, however.

The bivariate correlation between respondent delinquency and peer delinquency at Time 1 is .23 and at Time 2 is .29; the correlation between respondent marijuana use and peer marijuana use is .49 at Time 1 and .61 at Time 2 (Aseltine, 1995, p. 110). These correlations, especially those for delinquency, appear to be slightly smaller than those reported in studies based on respondent reports of peer deviance. Nevertheless, the correlations between deviance and peer deviance reported by Aseltine (1995) are sizable and significant.

Aseltine (1995) claimed that prior studies based on respondents' perceptions of peer deviance "grossly overstate" the impact of peer deviance on respondent deviance. His claim is based primarily on the fact that the standardized path coefficients he found are smaller than those typically reported in the literature. It is difficult to evaluate this claim, however, because he simultaneously changed the measure *and* estimated bidirectional effects for these variables, either or both of which could attenuate the magnitude of the relationship. Indeed, when Aseltine (1995) imposes a unidirectional causal structure—from peer marijuana use to respondent marijuana use only—the coefficient increases from .28 to .44, a coefficient similar to that typically found in the literature (p. 116). Thus, it is not clear whether the change observed by Aseltine is due to a change in measurement, causal structure, or both.

In sum, studies that measure peer deviance directly through self-reports provided by the peer suggest that the relationship between association with deviant peers and deviant behavior may be somewhat smaller than when the measure of peer deviance is based on the target subject's perception of peer deviance. This attenuation appears to be somewhat larger for delinquency than for drug use. The smaller impact of measurement source on drug use may be because adolescent drug use is more likely than delinquency to be a public, group activity. Although use of peer self-reports of deviance reduces the magnitude of the relationship between association with deviant peers and involvement in deviant behavior, the association variable remains a strong and significant predictor of respondent behavior, stronger than other variables included in multivariate models (Aseltine, 1995; Huizinga et al., 1992).

Independence of Measures

Gottfredson and Hirschi (1990) challenged the basic validity of measures based on respondents' perceptions of peer deviant behavior, arguing that "the variable—self-reported peer delinquency— may merely be another measure of self-reported delinquency. . . . The delinquent activities reported for friends are *the same delinquent activities* previously reported by the respondent for himself" (p. 157; emphasis added). If this view is correct, virtually the entire body of research assessing the relationship between association with deviant peers and self-reported deviance would be useless because the measures are not independent. Although Gottfredson and Hirschi (1990) presented no empirical evidence to substantiate their claim, a number of research findings address this issue.

First, if correct, the Gottfredson/Hirschi position implies that the typical relationship between peer behavior and self behavior is entirely an artifact of the measures and would disappear when appropriately independent measures of peer behavior are used. The studies reviewed in the previous section indicate, however, that association with deviant peers and deviant behavior are significantly and often substantially correlated even when self-reports of deviance by the peer are used. The relationship may be attenuated under these conditions, but it is not eliminated.

Second, if the peer measure of deviance is really nothing more than "another measure of self-reported delinquency," one would expect items measuring respondent perceptions of peer deviance and self-reports of deviance to load highly on a single factor in a factor analysis. Thornberry, Lizotte, Krohn, Farnworth, and Jang (1994), however, found that although the peer delinquency items loaded on a single factor, self-reported delinquency items loaded on a different factor or did not load on any factor (p. 62). Other researchers report similar results (Agnew, 1991b; Reed & Rose, 1991).

Elliott and Menard (1992) used a somewhat different approach to examine this issue by analyzing the temporal sequence of the onset of association with delinquent peers and the onset of offending. If Gottfredson and Hirschi (1990) are correct, and these measures really refer to the same behaviors, their onset should be simultaneous. Elliott and Menard (1992) found very little, if any, support for this prediction, even though they only have annual data—a measurement strategy that favors the Gottfredson/Hirschi approach.

Third, Gottfredson and Hirschi's (1990) argument that the strong relationship between associations and behavior is simply a function of both peer and self measures referring to "the same delinquent activities" can be tested by ensuring that they do not. Thornberry et al. (1994) examined reciprocal relationships between associating with delinquent peers and self-reported delinquency, using as a measure of peer delinquency the focal respondents' reports of how many of their friends engaged in delinquency. They then replicated the analysis using a measure of peer *drug use* and retained the measure of self-reported *delinquency*. In this case, the peer and self measures cannot refer to the "same delinquent activities" because they cover different domains of deviant behavior. The substantive results are virtually identical, however, to those found when both variables referred to delinquency (Thornberry et al., 1994, p. 70).

In brief, there is little, if any, empirical support for Gottfredson and Hirschi's (1990) argument. Although relying on the focal respondents' perceptions of peer deviance is not ideal, these measures of association with deviant peers and self-reported deviance are hardly identical.

THE EMPIRICAL RELATIONSHIP BETWEEN PEERS AND BEHAVIOR

The contemporaneous relationship between adolescents having friends who commit deviant acts and their own delinquency or use of drugs is well established. Kornhauser (1979, p. 236) states that this relationship has been found in "all inquiries" that have inves-

tigated it, and Kandel (1978b) characterized peer use of drugs as the strongest and most consistently related correlate of drug use.

Although early research recognized the group nature of delinquent behavior (Shaw & McKay, 1942; Thrasher, 1927), it was not until researchers began to use the self-report method that the relationship between peers and delinquent behavior began to be systematically researched. It is not surprising, therefore, that the seminal work on this relationship was conducted by a pioneer in the self-report methodology, James Short.

In a series of studies, Short (1957, 1958, 1960) explored the implications of Sutherland's (1939) differential association theory, focusing in particular on the modalities of differential association—frequency, priority, duration, and intensity—and correlating them with self-reported delinquent behavior. Short correlated self-reported delinquent behavior with both the individual measures of these modalities and a global scale combining them. For both institutionalized and noninstitutionalized youth, he found the individual measures of differential association and the global differential association scale to be significantly related to general delinquency. This relationship held for both boys and girls.

Since the publication of Short's research, many studies have examined the cross-sectional relationship between measures of differential association and self-reported delinquent behavior. All of these studies (Agnew, 1991b; Conger, 1976; Elliott et al., 1985; Erikson & Empey, 1965; Jensen, 1972; Jessor & Jessor, 1977; R. E. Johnson, 1979; R. E. Johnson, Marcos, & Bahr, 1987; Krohn, Lanza-Kaduce, & Akers, 1984; LaGrange & White, 1983; Marcos, Bahr, & Johnson, 1986; Matsueda, 1982; Poole & Regoli, 1979; Reiss & Rhodes, 1964; Voss, 1964) have replicated Short's basic findings in different study populations and using different measures of association with delinquent peers.

Adolescent drug use, especially the use of marijuana, is also strongly related to peer drug use (Akers et al., 1979; Brook, Nomura, & Cohen, 1989; Ginsberg & Greenley, 1978; Huba, Wingard, & Bentler, 1979; Jessor & Jessor, 1977; Kandel, 1978a, 1978b; Krohn, 1974; Pruitt, Kingery, Mirzaee, Heuberger, & Hurley, 1991). Tec (1972) provided one of the early studies of this relationship. He surveyed adolescents aged 15 to 18 and asked how many of their friends used marijuana and how often they themselves used it. The findings indicate that of those who had many friends who used marijuana, 50% are regular marijuana users and 11% are abstainers. Among those who indicate that none of their friends used marijuana, only 0.3% are regular users whereas 91% are abstainers.

A strong relationship between peer deviance and self-reported deviant behavior is found in longitudinal studies as well. For example, Elliott et al. (1985), using three waves of data from the National Youth Survey (NYS), found that involvement with deviant peers is the only variable, other than Time 1 deviant behavior, that is directly related to various forms of delinquency and drug use. Other longitudinal studies have found association with deviant peers to be either the strongest correlate or one of the strongest correlates of both delinquent behavior and drug use (Brook et al., 1989; Burkett & Warren, 1987; Ginsberg & Greenley, 1978; Jessor & Jessor, 1977; Kandel & Andrews, 1987; Kaplan, Johnson, & Bailey, 1987; Reed & Rose, 1991; Thornberry et al., 1994; White, Pandina, & LaGrange, 1987).

Overwhelmingly, the empirical literature indicates a strong, positive relationship between association with deviant peers and involvement in deviance. Although this relationship is well established, there are a number of issues regarding the nature of this relationship that continue to be explored. These issues vary in their complexity, and our discussion proceeds from simpler to methodologically more complex issues.

Comparing Peer Deviance With Other Potential Predictors

A question that is often addressed concerns the predictive power of delinquent peer associations relative to other theoretical variables, especially family variables. Because the family is the primary institution for socialization it may well be more important than peers in determining adolescent behavior. In particular, the quality of the child-parent relationship, the degree of supervision or monitoring that parents exert over the child, and the type of disciplinary practices parents use are hypothesized to be related to delinquency and drug use.

In most studies that compare the relative effects of parental relationships and deviant peers, the peer variable has been found to explain significantly more of the variance in deviant behavior than any of the parental relationship variables (Akers & Cochran, 1985; Brook et al., 1989; Brook, Whiteman, & Scovell Gordon, 1983; Coombs, Paulson, & Richardson, 1991; Dishion & Loeber, 1985; Elliott et al., 1985; Elliott, Huizinga, & Menard, 1989; Jensen, 1972; Jessor & Jessor, 1977; R. E. Johnson, 1979; Kandel, 1985; Krohn, 1974; LaGrange & White, 1983; Linden, 1978; Marcos et al., 1986; Smith & Brame, 1994; Swadi, 1988, 1992). For example, Dishion and Loeber (1985) provided a comparison of the effects of parental monitoring and peer deviance on the use of alcohol and marijuana. They found that both parental monitoring and peer deviance are significantly related to marijuana use but that peer deviance is the stronger predictor. Only peer deviance is related to alcohol use.

A rare exception in this line of research is the Brook, Lukoff, and Whiteman (1980) study of the initiation of marijuana use. They found that once personality and family factors are controlled, peer use does not have a significant effect on subjects' initiation of marijuana use. They argued that peer determinants relate to later marijuana use because both are heavily influenced by prior factors. Later work by Brook and associates (Brook et al., 1989; Brook et al., 1983; Brook, Whiteman, Scovell Gordon, Nomura, & Brook, 1986), however, found a strong and independent effect of peer use on initiation and continued use of alcohol and drugs.[2]

Comparisons that have been made between other predictor variables and peer deviance are consistent with the findings regarding the relative effects of family versus peers on deviant behavior. For example, R. E. Johnson's (1979) path model incorporated other social control dimensions (e.g., commitment to school), as well as several strain theory variables (e.g., blocked

opportunities) along with association with deviant peers. His results confirm that peer deviance is a stronger predictor of delinquency than school-related, family, strain, and belief variables (see also, Elliott et al., 1985).

Indirect and Interactive Effects

Differential association theory states that association with deviant peers is related to deviant behavior because it brings actors into an environment in which they learn definitions favorable to the violation of the law. It is assumed that people are in a continual process of acquiring definitions, and, according to Sutherland (1939), it is the ratio of definitions favorable to the violation of the law to those unfavorable that determines the probability of deviant behavior.

This argument has two implications for how association with peers affects the probability of deviant behavior. First, differential association theory sees the relationship between deviant peers and deviant behavior as indirect, operating through the acquisition of definitions. Second, association with deviant peers should interact with definitions to predict the probability of deviant behavior (Orcutt, 1983, 1987). That is, the effect of deviant peers on deviant behavior should vary by the nature of the definitions held by actors. Extending this argument, the effect of deviant peers should also vary by the level of prosocial forces such as parental influences (Elliott et al., 1985).

Indirect Effects

The research evidence does not support Sutherland's argument that association with deviant peers has only an indirect effect on deviant behavior through deviant beliefs. Research using both cross-sectional and longitudinal analyses has found that delinquent peers have an effect on delinquency regardless of definitions favorable or unfavorable to law violation (Elliott et al., 1985; Jensen, 1972; R. E. Johnson, 1979; R. E. Johnson et al., 1987; V. Johnson, 1988; Kandel, 1985; Menard & Elliott, 1994; Warr & Stafford, 1991). Most of this research indicates that association with deviant friends is related both directly and indirectly through beliefs to deviance. For example, Warr and Stafford (1991) explored the interrelationships of peer behavior, peer attitudes, respondent attitude, and respondent behavior using the NYS data. In both cross-sectional and longitudinal analyses for three different types of deviance (cheating, larceny, and marijuana use), they found not only that peer behavior has direct effects on deviance but also that the effect of peer behavior is larger than that for either attitudinal measure.

Sellers and Winfree (1990) found that the relative effect of peer use and personal approval of alcohol use on drinking varies by age. For middle school students, peer use is the stronger predictor; for senior high school students, personal approval is the stronger predictor. Sellers and Winfree (1990) suggest that these results support a social learning theory explanation. At young ages, adolescents use alcohol because their friends do, but as they gain more experience with alcohol use, their opinions become crystallized and more important in their decisions concerning further use.

A prominent study that failed to find a direct effect of association with deviant peers on delinquency was conducted by Matsueda (1982). He examined causal models derived from differen-

---

[2]Differences in the relative predictive power of delinquent associations and parental relationship variables have been observed for different developmental stages. These variations will be discussed later.

tial association theory, control theory, and multiple factor theories. Matsueda (1982) found that his measure of definitions "mediates all but a trivial and statistically nonsignificant portion" of the effect of peer association on delinquency (p. 500). However, he may not have found a direct effect of peer association on delinquency because of the limited way in which the association variable was measured. A single item, asking respondents to indicate whether any of their friends had been picked up by the police, was used, rather than a more general scale indicating whether friends had committed delinquent behavior. The constrained variance on Matsueda's measure may explain its relatively weak effect on self-reported delinquency.

In any event, the evidence consistently supports a direct effect of association with deviant peers on deviant behavior. These findings suggest that mechanisms other than the transmission of values are necessary to explain why association with deviant peers has an effect on deviance. Warr and Stafford (1991) have suggested that social learning mechanisms such as imitation or the effects of group pressure on deviant behavior may be particularly important.

Interactive Effects

Orcutt (1983, 1987) made a strong argument against studies that focus exclusively on additive effects, ignoring interactive effects among peers, beliefs, and behavior. He suggested that association with marijuana users will have different effects on marijuana use depending on the respondents' definitions about marijuana use; that is, he predicted that the relationship between peers and behavior will be conditioned by the level of positive and negative definitions about the behavior. Orcutt offered very precise predictions concerning the expected proportions of marijuana users based on knowledge of the number of friends who use marijuana and the respondents' definitions about use. For the most part, his predictions are borne out by the data. When both associations and definitions are high, marijuana use is high; when both are low, marijuana use is low. More important, though, Orcutt found a significant interaction effect of these variables on marijuana use. Of particular interest are the findings for respondents who hold neutral definitions and have a mixed peer group; the proportion of users under these conditions is .50 and, according to Orcutt, exactly what would be predicted given the balance of prodrug and antidrug influences.

Warr and Stafford (1991) examined a related issue: whether the effect of peer behavior on delinquent behavior is contingent on peer attitudes. Congruence between the attitudes and behaviors of friends does have an effect over and above the main effects of these two variables. When the attitudes and behaviors of peers are inconsistent, however, peer behavior is more important in predicting delinquency.

Agnew (1991a), using data from the NYS, examined the interaction between having delinquent friends and three indicators of the quality of peer relationships: (a) attachment to peers, (b) time spent with peers, and (c) the extent to which peers present delinquent patterns. For minor delinquency, the impact of having delinquent friends is not conditioned by, that is, does not interact with, the other variables. For serious delinquency, however, he found that when the peer relationship variables are at or below the mean, association with delinquent peers has no impact on delinquency; when these variables are greater than the mean, though, peer delinquency has a strong impact on the subject's delinquency.

Researchers have also been interested in the interaction between relationships with parents and association with deviant peers. Parents may serve to condition the effect of having friends who engage in deviant behavior; adolescents with friends who use drugs but who have good relations with their parents may be less likely to use drugs than those who have poor relations with their parents.

Early studies found that the effect of deviant peer association is conditioned by the relationship between adolescents and parents (Elliott & Voss, 1974; Linden & Hackler, 1973; Poole & Regoli, 1979). More recent studies have also found this to be the case. For example, Brook et al. (1986) examined the effect of personality, parent, school, and peer variables on alcohol use among 9th and 10th grade high school students. Examining a series of two-way interactions, they found that family factors did condition the effect of peer risk conditions; peer effects are weaker when there are strong mother-child relationships. Brook et al. (1989) also found that school factors condition the relationship between peer use of drugs and alcohol and drug use.

Elliott et al. (1985) examined the conditioning effect of a more global measure of conventional bonding that incorporates both school and parent bonding variables. They found that when association with delinquent peers is high and conventional bonds are weak, delinquent behavior and marijuana use are at their highest levels. When deviant associations are high but conventional bonds are strong, delinquency and drug use are moderately high. When deviant associations are low, delinquency and drug use are also low, and conventional bonds exert a relatively modest effect on behavior under these conditions (see also, Elliott & Menard, 1992).

Warr (1993), also using the NYS data, measured both attachment to parents and the quantity of time spent with parents and examined the interaction effect of these parental variables with peer delinquency on six different types of drug use and delinquency. He found that time spent with parents does diminish the impact of having delinquent friends but getting along with parents does not. Warr (1993) stated that his findings suggest that "small amounts of quality time may not be sufficient to offset the criminogenic aspects of peer culture to which adolescents are commonly exposed" (p. 262).

Summary

The examination of the research literature on the form of the relationship between association with deviant peers and deviant behavior leads to two rather firm conclusions. First, the evidence clearly indicates that association with deviant peers has a direct effect on delinquency and drug use. This is contrary to Sutherland's (1939) differential association argument but consistent with a social learning theory approach. Peer association also appears to have an indirect effect on deviant behavior through definitions or beliefs.

Second, the effect of association with deviant peers is conditioned by definitions or beliefs about deviance and by parental and school variables. Hence, attitudes supportive of deviance can enhance or retard the effect of having friends who engage in this behavior. The quality of the relationship between parent and child can have the same effect, although there is some disagreement over whether the effect is due to the affectional tie between parent and child or to the monitoring that comes with substantial time with one's children.

CAUSAL ORDER

The most contentious issue in this research area is that of causal order. As noted in the theoretical section, virtually all conceivable causal orders have been proposed for these two concepts. Some models argue that the relationship is spurious, others that behavior causes associations, others that associations cause behaviors, and still others that they are bidirectionally related.

Spurious or Real

Glueck and Glueck (1950), Hirschi (1969), Gottfredson and Hirschi (1990), and some other control theorists have claimed that the relationship between association with deviant peers and involvement in deviance is spurious; both concepts are thought to be caused by weak conventional bonds. Is there any empirical support for this position?

If the peer/behavior relationship is spurious, one would expect the correlation between peers and behavior to become nonsignificant once bonding variables are held constant (see Hirschi & Selvin, 1967). That does not happen, however, in either multivariate additive models or in path analytic models. Indeed, as reported earlier, it is the effect of the bonding variables, not the peer variables, that tends to vanish in multivariate analyses.

Virtually all multivariate, additive models report that association with deviant peers remains a strong and significant predictor of deviant behavior even when the effects of bonding variables are controlled. Akers and Cochran's (1985) study of marijuana use is a good illustration. Similarly, studies that rely on path analytic strategies consistently find that association with deviant peers remains one of the strongest and most proximal influences on deviance even when controlling for prior bonding variables. See, for example, the results reported by R. E. Johnson (1979) and Elliott et al. (1985).

Not only does social control theory argue that association with deviant peers is not a cause of deviance, but it also argues that deviants are not even strongly attached to peers. Hirschi (1969) characterized the belief that delinquents have warm, intimate relationships as "a romantic myth" (p. 159), asserting instead that relationships among deviants are "cold and brittle" (p. 141). In contrast, Sutherland assumed that there would be no difference in the quality of the relationships among deviant friends as compared to conventional friends. Friends who are more intimate should have the greatest influence on one another, whether that influence is in the direction of deviant or conventional behavior.

Cairns, Cairns, Neckerman, Gest, and Gariépy (1988) examined this issue in a survey of fourth and seventh grade students. They found that aggressive youngsters are less attractive friendship choices for their classmates but that they are no less likely to have friends. Moreover, the relationships they establish are equally as strong as those for less aggressive students. Gillmore, Rogers, Hawkins, Day, and Catalano (1992) reported very similar results for fifth grade students, using as a measure of deviance whether the respondent had gotten into trouble with the teacher. They, too, found that more conventional youths are more attractive friendship choices. However, deviants are no less attached to their friends than are their conventional classmates. Gillmore et al. (1992) concluded that deviant adolescents may have difficulty attracting friends, but once they do, they form close relationships with them.

Giordano, Cernkovich, and Pugh (1986) provided the most extensive comparison of the dimensions of friendships among delinquents and nondelinquents based on a sample of 12- to 19-year-olds. Overall, they found little to differentiate the characteristics of friendships among delinquents and nondelinquents. There are no differences in the stability or frequency of contact among friends when adolescents who engage in delinquency are compared to those who do not; however, delinquents are more willing to confide in friends, although they also have more conflict with them: "Contrary to the central assertion of the cold and brittle relationships argument, delinquents were no less likely than others to believe that they have the trust of friends and that these friends 'really care about them and what happens to them'" (Giordano et al., 1986, p. 1191).

Hawkins and Fraser (1985) examined the network characteristics of adult drug users who were residents in drug treatment centers. Drug users have close-knit attachments to their friends, but they do not think of their friends as role models. Hawkins and Fraser (1985) suggested that drug users perceive friends as being close and trusted, but those friends who use drugs are viewed as less desirable associates, an outcome consistent with what Cairns et al. (1988) and Gillmore et al. (1992) found for young adolescents. Whereas Hawkins and Fraser (1985) did not compare the friendship networks of adult drug users with those of non–drug users, Kandel and Davies (1991) did. Few differences were found in the level of intimacy of friends for those who use drugs and those who do not, although drug users are more likely to confide in their friends and to interact with them more often.

Krohn and Thornberry (1993) also compared several characteristics of the social networks of drug users and non–drug users. Consistent with much of the research on the structure of friendship networks, they found that drug users have more intimate social networks than non–drug users when intimacy is measured in terms of the willingness to confide in one's friends. However, they also found that the networks of users are more likely to change over time.

In sum, the research literature supports differential association theory's view of close ties among friends who engage in deviant behavior rather than the cold and brittle ties suggested by some proponents of control theory. There are also indications, however, that although those who engage in deviance are close to their friends, their friendships may not be as stable as those among people who are less likely to engage in deviance. The nature of friendship relationships is complex and, at this point, not fully understood.

Integrated Theories

Unlike control theory that views association with deviant peers as either unrelated to or a consequence of deviance, integrated theories view association with deviant peers as a proximal cause of deviant behavior, mediating the causal impact of antecedent variables. These antecedent variables are drawn from a variety of theories but most commonly include the bonding variables of attachment, commitment, involvement, and belief. The basic argument is as follows: Weak bonding increases the chances that youths will associate with deviant peers, and, in turn, those associations provide the social environment in which deviance is learned, reinforced, and maintained. In these models, association with deviant peers has an immediate and powerful impact on deviant behavior; bonding and other antecedent variables are thought of as having weaker direct effects, indirect effects, or both on behavior (see Figure 21.1d). Many studies have used path analytic techniques to test integrated models of this sort.

Perhaps the best known is Elliott et al.'s (1985) test of their integrated model using data from the NYS. This model incorporates variables from strain, control, and learning theories. The empirical results indicate the following:

> The only direct paths leading to self-reported delinquency are from the Involvement with Delinquent Peers Index and prior SRD [self-reported delinquency] measure. The strain variables affect the conventional bonding variables that, in turn, affect involvement with delinquent peers, but neither strain nor conventional bonding variables have a direct influence on delinquency. (Elliott et al., 1985, p. 109)

Elliott et al. (1985) tested the model for males and females separately and for a variety of deviant behaviors, including general delinquency, index offenses, minor offenses, marijuana use, and hard drug use. The pattern of results is identical across all of these models: Strain and bonding variables have only indirect effects on behavior, whereas delinquent peer bonding has direct and rather sizable effects.

R. E. Johnson (1979) developed a similar integrated model and tested it in a cross-sectional study of high school students. The results are quite close to those reported by Elliott et al. (1985). When the frequency of delinquency is used as the dependent variable, both strain and bonding variables have only indirect effects on behavior. These effects are mediated by delinquent associations and delinquent values that, in turn, have direct effects on behavior.

Kaplan et al. (1987) examined a somewhat different set of antecedent variables than those based on a social control perspective. Specifically, they looked at self-rejection, disposition to deviance, and prior deviance, as well as deviant peer associations. Their longitudinal study was based on a sample of junior high school students; deviance was defined as a latent construct including both delinquency and drug use. Deviant peer associations have the largest direct effect on behavior and partially mediate the direct effects of self-rejection, prior deviance, and disposition to deviance. The other three variables continue to have direct, albeit somewhat smaller, effects on deviant behavior.

Simons, Wu, Conger, and Lorenz (1994) examined family, personality, and peer effects on self-reports of official delinquency, using a multimethod measurement strategy including family observation measures. They estimated the model for early- and late-onset offenders to test Patterson, Capaldi, and Bank's (1991) "early-starter" model (see later section). For both early and late starters, deviant peers were the most proximal cause of delinquency, mediating the impact of effective parenting and oppositional/defiant orientation on delinquent behavior.

In addition to the studies just summarized, a number of others have tested models consistent with an integrated theoretical perspective. In general, these studies reported results that are quite consistent with this perspective. See, for example, the work by Brook et al. (1989), Elliott et al. (1989), Elliott and Menard (1990), R. E. Johnson et al. (1987), LaGrange and White (1983), and Patterson and Dishion (1985). In all of these studies, association with deviant peers has a strong direct effect on deviant behavior, mediating all or part of the impact of antecedent variables.

Interactional Theory

An interactional perspective concurs, in part, with the logic and findings of integrated theories. It too argues that association with deviant peers causes deviant behavior. In addition, it argues that deviant behavior also exerts a causal impact on association with deviant peers. Using a life-course perspective, these variables are bidirectionally related; there are both socialization effects (i.e., peers influence behavior) and selection effects (i.e., behavior influences peer selection).

Kandel (1978a) was one of the first researchers to address this issue, using longitudinal data containing information on 959 friendship pairs. Some of these friendship pairs changed over time; thus, data on friends to be, former friends, and current friends are available. This unique data set allowed for an analysis of the role of similarity in the formation and change of friendships. Kandel found that adolescents who share common behaviors and characteristics are more likely to become friends, supporting a selection argument. She also found that friends, especially in reciprocated dyads, become more similar over time in terms of their behavior patterns, supporting a socialization argument. Kandel concluded that selection and socialization effects contributed about equally to intrafriendship similarity.

Fisher and Bauman (1988) used a similar data set and research design to investigate selection and socialization effects on adolescent smoking and drinking. They found that behavioral similarity is important in the acquisition of friends but not in the "deselection" process. They also found support for the influence of friends on behavior but concluded that selection effects are stronger.

Elliott and Menard (1992) used a different strategy to investigate the relative effects of selection and socialization. Based on data from the NYS, they found that association with delinquent others generally precedes one's own initiation into delinquent behavior. After one initiates delinquent behavior, the probability of increased association with delinquent others becomes higher. This, in turn, results in an increased probability of more serious forms of delinquency. They concluded that both selection and socialization effects are important with the effect from peers to delinquency predominating, especially at onset.

Recently, Menard and Elliott (1994) used NYS data to estimate three-wave lagged and contemporaneous models incorporating measures of delinquent peers and delinquent behavior. For minor delinquency, these variables are reciprocally related in the lagged model. However, in the contemporaneous model, only the effect from peers to delinquency is significant. When index offending is used as the measure of delinquency, there are significant reciprocal effects for both the lagged and contemporaneous models.

Meier, Burkett, and Hickman (1984) and Burkett and Warren (1987) studied a sample of 10th graders to examine different aspects of marijuana use. Among other issues, Meier et al. (1984) investigated the relationship between marijuana use and peer use of marijuana over three waves of data. They found that there are contemporaneous effects from peers to marijuana and 1-year lagged effects from marijuana use to peers.

Burkett and Warren's (1987) investigation included bonding variables, belief in the sinfulness of marijuana use, and peer associations. Peer associations have contemporaneous, but not lagged, effects on use. Marijuana use, on the other hand, has lagged effects on peer associations but does not have significant contemporaneous effects. It would appear that marijuana use leads to peer associations, and, in turn, associations with others who use marijuana increase the respondents' level of use.

Aseltine (1995) examined reciprocal effects among parental attachment, parental monitoring, peer deviance, and both delinquency and drug use. Aseltine's (1995) study is important because he obtained reports directly from the target respondents' friends about their own drug use and delinquent behavior. He found that peer delinquency is significantly related to respondent delinquency but that respondent delinquency is not contemporaneously related to peer delinquency. There is, however, an indirect lagged effect of respondent delinquency on peer delinquency through the parental monitoring variable. Turning to drug use, respondent drug use had a tendency to affect peer use but did not meet the usual criterion for statistical significance; peer drug use does have a significant effect on respondent drug use. Aseltine (1995) concluded that there is a need to emphasize social interaction, instead of social influence, in as much as he sees both selection and socialization forces at work.

Thornberry et al. (1994) explored the selection/socialization issue in a three-wave panel model using data from the Rochester Youth Development Study. Associating with delinquent peers increases delinquency, and, in turn, engaging in delinquency exerts a positive effect on associating with delinquent peers. Krohn, Lizotte, Thornberry, Smith, and McDowall (1996) extended this line of research by using five waves of data and estimating both lagged and contemporaneous models in an examination of drug use. In both the lagged and contemporaneous models, they found strong support for bidirectional relationships between association with drug-using peers and the use of drugs. These studies suggest that neither a selection model nor a socialization model is correct. Rather, they argued that the results support an interactional model incorporating bidirectional relationships between peers and behavior.

Overwhelmingly, the studies that have formally tested bidirectional models have found support for bidirectional effects. Although a few of the estimated paths are not statistically significant (e.g., Aseltine, 1995), the weight of the evidence reviewed here suggests that, over time, association with deviant peers leads to deviant behavior and that deviant behavior leads to association with deviant peers. A number of other studies that estimate bidirectional influences, for both drug use and delinquency, arrived at similar conclusions (e.g., Agnew, 1991b; Elliott et al., 1985; Ginsberg & Greenley, 1978; Paternoster, 1988; Reed & Rose, 1991). These results suggest that differential association, social learning, and integrated theories all offer a correct but too limited view of these causal influences; they also suggest that control theory offers a correct but too limited view. It appears that both selection and socialization effects are present, a theoretical specification presented in interactional theory.

LIFE-COURSE ISSUES

A number of developmental or life-course issues have been examined with respect to the relationship between deviant peers and deviant behavior. In this section, we review three of them: life-course changes in types of peers, the impact of peers on the relationship between age and deviant behavior, and developmental changes in the role of peers in accounting for deviant behavior.

Types of Peers

Many youth associate with deviant peers, and, as we have seen, those associations have a large impact on behavior. Recently, researchers have begun to investigate associational patterns from a developmental perspective. Elliott and Menard (1992) and Warr (1993) have both used the NYS dataset to describe continuities in friendship patterns during adolescence.

On the one hand, there appears to be substantial change in the types of peer groups youths associate with over the adolescent years. Using data from the first six waves of the National Youth Survey, Elliott and Menard (1992) created peer group types, ranging from prosocial, through mixed groups, to highly delinquent groups. In general, prosocial groups are the most common type up to middle adolescence, become somewhat less common during late adolescence, and increase again in the early adult years. Mixed and delinquent peer groups show a countervailing trend. They are somewhat less common during early adolescence and early adulthood, reaching their highest frequency during middle adolescence: "That period in the lifespan with the highest levels of exposure to delinquency in the peer groups . . . is the period from 15 to 18" (Elliott & Menard, 1992, pp. 17–18).

Warr (1993), using NYS data from the first five waves, extended the analysis to include drug use as well as delinquency. Results for association with delinquent peers were quite similar to those reported by Elliott and Menard (1992). Age curves for delinquent friends have an inverted U-shape during adolescence, reaching a peak during the middle adolescent years. The age curves for drug-using friends are quite different, however. Very few 11- or 12-year-olds have friends who use drugs, but that proportion increases in a steep linear fashion over the adolescent years (Warr, 1993, pp. 21–24).

On the other hand, both studies found substantial stability in friendship patterns. Elliott and Menard (1992) examined transition matrices for friendship types from ages 11 to 12 through ages 19 to 20. When respondents shifted from one type of peer group to another, the shifts tended to be to adjacent types. For example, shifts from peer groups characterized as "saints" were more likely to be to prosocial groups rather than to delinquent groups; shifts from delinquent peer groups were more likely to be to mixed groups rather than to "saints." There appears to be considerable inertia in the system, and changes that do occur are gradual movements toward or away from delinquent peers rather than sharp jumps in peer types.

Warr (1993), using NYS data to age 17, also examined transitions over time. His analysis indicated that delinquent friendships tended to be, in his term, "sticky." That is, once acquired, friendships with delinquent and drug-using peers were more apt to continue than to change back to prosocial friendships. This pattern could help explain the maintenance of delinquent behavior and drug use. Unfortunately, Warr's analysis covers only the middle adolescent period when deviance and association with deviant peers are at their peak. It is not clear if deviant friendships become less sticky as respondents move toward adulthood. Elliott and Menard's (1992) analysis suggests they do.

In sum, these analyses of the NYS data suggest that there are noticeable, albeit gradual, shifts in association with deviant peers over the adolescent/young adult period. Association with delinquent peers peaks during middle adolescence, and association with drug-using peers appears to peak during the early adult years. Given this pattern, the next logical question concerns the ability of these changing peer associations to explain the age-crime curve.

Age, Deviance, and Deviant Peers

Both delinquency and drug use are rather specifically located in the life course. The age-crime curve suggests that delinquency has an earlier age of onset than drug use, peaks in the mid-teens, and drops rather precipitously after that (Blumstein, Cohen, Roth, & Visher, 1986; Elliott et al., 1989; Farrington, Ohlin, & Wilson, 1986; Wolfgang, Thornberry, & Figlio, 1987). Drug use, especially "hard drug" and polydrug use, usually starts somewhat later, increases sharply during the late teenage years, and continues to increase through the mid-20s (Akers, 1992; Bachman, O'Malley, & Johnston, 1984; Elliott et al., 1989; National Institute on Drug Abuse, 1990). Can the changing patterns of association with deviant peers just observed help account for these age patterns in behavior?

Warr (1993) has investigated this issue in depth using data from the first five waves of the NYS, covering ages 11 through 21. He first regressed measures of delinquency and drug use on age and then added a measure of deviant peers to the equations and reestimated them. As expected, age has a pronounced effect on deviant behavior. When peer variables, especially the number of delinquent friends, are added to the equation, however, almost all the age coefficients become nonsignificant, whereas the peer coefficients are significant. Warr (1993) concluded that "when measures of peer influence are held constant, the association between age and crime is substantially weakened and, for some offenses, disappears entirely" (p. 35). Menard (1992) also examined this issue using data from the NYS. He estimated age, cohort, and period effects on both the prevalence and frequency of general delinquency, index delinquency, alcohol use, marijuana use, and polydrug use. As expected, there are substantial age effects on delinquency and drug use. Adding delinquent bonding to the equations, however, "resulted in the elimination of age from the combined equation" in 9 of the 10 instances (Menard, 1992, p. 186).

Developmental Patterns of Peer Influence

Most developmental theories expect peer influences to be relatively weak during childhood and early adolescence and then increase in potency during the adolescent years. For example, Brown, Clasen, and Eicher (1986) argued that the impact of peers on behavior over the course of adolescence should exhibit an inverted U-shape: "Peer conformity dispositions and conformity behavior increase from childhood through early or middle adolescence, then decline in later adolescence" (p. 521). Thornberry (1987) argued that peer influences would increase in magnitude as the respondent moves from childhood to adolescence and would remain strong well into the early adult years. Patterson and his colleagues (Patterson et al., 1991; Patterson, Crosby, & Vuchinich, 1992) presented a model that also argued for enhanced peer effects during adolescence. For offenders with an early age of onset, their model posits that parental deficits during childhood lead to a noncompliant orientation. That, in turn, leads to association with delinquent peers during adolescence, which tends to maintain delinquent behavior. For offenders who begin their delinquent careers during adolescence, the model posits that parental deficits are less salient and that peer influences are much larger. In general, therefore, developmental theories expect peer influences to peak during adolescence.

Brown et al. (1986) estimated developmental changes in a cross-sectional, trend design using a sample of students from Grade 6 to Grade 12. They examined developmental changes in three areas: (a) the level of peer conformity dispositions, (b) perceptions of peer pressure to engage in antisocial behavior, and (c) the impact of both peer conformity dispositions and perceptions of peer pressure on self-reported behavior. With respect to peer conformity dispositions, Brown et al. (1986) found "a significant, inverted U-shaped age trend . . . for anti-social conformity disposition scores" (p. 524). For perceived peer pressure, however, the expected U-shaped distribution was not evident; perceptions of peer pressure to engage in antisocial behavior exhibited a significant linear increase with age. Finally, the analyses offered little support for the hypotheses that the relationship between peer conformity dispositions and self-reported antisocial behavior, or between peer pressure to engage in antisocial behavior and self-reported antisocial behavior, would peak at ages 15 to 16.

A more common way in which these developmental changes have been analyzed is to examine the relative impact of parents and peers on behavior at different ages. Consistent with most developmental perspectives, Kandel (1985) reported that parental influences on drug use are stronger at early stages of drug involvement, centering on issues of initiation. After initiation, however, parental influences weaken, and peer influences become much more potent. Jessor and Jessor (1977) reported similar results for alcohol use: Throughout high school, peer influences become more and more influential, whereas parental influences remain stable.

Huba and Bentler (1980) examined developmental issues within a very narrow age range—from seventh to ninth grades—using a cross-sectional, trend design. Over these 3 years, respondents report an increased perception of the number of peer and adult models for drug use. Also, the correlation between perceived peer use and self use increases with age, whereas the correlation for perceived adult use and self use remains flat. These findings, although limited by the age range and the cross-sectional design, suggest that peer influence on drug use does increase at the transition from early to middle adolescence.

Simons et al. (1994) tested Patterson et al.'s (1991) early starter model using longitudinal data from a rural Iowa sample. Their results are generally consistent with theoretical expectations. Family and noncompliant orientation have stronger effects for the early versus late starters, and peer effects during adolescence are stronger for the late versus early starters.

Although there have not been many explicitly developmental studies of peer effects on deviant behavior, the ones that have been conducted are generally consistent with theoretical predictions. Peer influences are important at all ages, from childhood on, but these effects tend to be particularly strong during adolescence.

CONCLUSION

Having friends who engage in illegal or disapproved activities has been and continues to be a key factor in many explanations of adolescent drug use and delinquency. Research exploring the relationship between association with deviant peers and deviant behavior overwhelmingly finds a strong correlation between these variables. In spite of the widespread recognition of the importance that deviant friends have in the deviance-producing process, the issue has generated a number of controversies that we have explored in this review.

Methodologically, the most troubling aspect of examining the relationship between deviant peers and deviant behavior is how to measure whether a respondent's friends have committed deviant acts. On the surface, this would seem like a fairly straightforward process: Simply ask respondents whether their friends have engaged in deviance. Indeed, most of the research in this area has used a variant of this design. When respondents are asked to provide information on their own deviance and that of their friends, however, there is a clear potential for problems associated with common method variance. The few studies that have obtained data on deviant activities directly from the friends of respondents have demonstrated that reliance on respondent reports of peer behavior has resulted in an overestimation of the relationship between deviant peers and deviant behavior. Although the problem is a serious one, it must be recognized that even in those studies that obtained data directly from respondents' friends, association with deviant peers is still one of the most, if not the most, important predictors of deviant behavior. However, the overestimation that results from common method variance does have implications for how we design our studies and, perhaps most troubling, the cost involved in doing studies that avoid this problem.

Theoretically, the key question that has been raised concerns the appropriate causal order among deviant peers, deviant behavior, and other related variables. Is the relationship between deviant peers and deviant behavior spurious? Do deviant peers affect behavior only through other mechanisms such as definitions favorable to deviance? Do peers socialize adolescents in a way that leads to deviance, or do adolescents who commit deviant behavior seek out others who also engage in those activities?

Our review of the literature leads to the conclusion that association with deviant peers does have a causal relationship with deviant behavior that has yet to be accounted for by any antecedent variable. This relationship is both direct and indirect, operating through definitions that are favorable to deviant behavior. Moreover, longitudinal research has shown that association with deviant peers and deviant behavior are reciprocally related. Adolescents who engage in deviant behavior do seek out friends who engage in these behaviors, and that, in turn, leads to greater involvement in deviance. This spiraling loop is difficult to break and may help explain why it is so difficult to intervene effectively to interrupt the development of deviance during adolescence.

This general conclusion has implications for prevention and treatment policy and programs. Interventions that bring groups of delinquents or drug users together may have the unintended effect of enhancing the spiraling loop created by the reciprocal relationship between association with deviant peers and deviant behavior. Interventions that foster associations with prosocial peers have greater potential for success. For example, Henggeler, Melton, and Smith (1992) have developed a Multisystemic Treatment Approach in which the emphasis is placed on encouraging parents to work with their children to establish more prosocial friendship networks. The goal of the approach is to empower parents with the necessary skills to address difficulties their children are having, including their choice of friends. This approach has proven to be effective in reducing long-term delinquency (over a $2^1/_2$-year period) and improving intrafamilial relationships. The approach suggested by Chamberlain and Friman (Chapter 39, this volume) is also consistent with the goal of building prosocial peer relationships.

Association with deviant peers is clearly not the only variable that is important in explaining deviant behavior. Bonding, strain, disorganization, and learning variables also have major impacts. But it is also clear that future work exploring the reasons why adolescents engage in delinquent behavior and use drugs must continue to attend to the role that association with deviant peers plays. From the review conducted here, it appears that the research literature has established a good base on which to stand as we endeavor to learn more about how peers influence and are influenced by deviant behavior.

REFERENCES

Agnew, R. S. (1991a). The interactive effect of peer variables on delinquency. *Criminology, 29,* 47–72.

Agnew, R. S. (1991b). A longitudinal test of social control theory and delinquency. *Journal of Research in Crime and Delinquency, 28,* 126–156.

Akers, R. L. (1973). *Deviant behavior: A social learning perspective.* Belmont, CA: Wadsworth.

Akers, R. L. (1992). *Drugs, alcohol, and society.* Belmont, CA: Wadsworth.

Akers, R. L. (1994). *Criminological theories: Introduction and evaluation.* Los Angeles: Roxbury.

Akers, R. L., & Cochran, J. K. (1985). Adolescent marijuana use: A test of three theories of deviant behavior. *Deviant Behavior, 6,* 323–346.

Akers, R. L., Krohn, M. D., Lanza-Kaduce, L., & Radosevich, M. (1979). Social learning and deviant behavior: A specific test of a general theory. *American Sociological Review, 44,* 636–655.

Aseltine, R. H. (1995). A reconsideration of parental and peer influences on adolescent deviance. *Journal of Health and Social Behavior, 36,* 103–121.

Bachman, J., O'Malley, P., & Johnston, L. (1984). Drug use among young adults: The impacts of role status and social environment. *Journal of Personality and Social Psychology, 47,* 629–645.

Becker, H. S. (1963). *The outsiders.* New York: Free Press.

Blumstein, A., Cohen, J., Roth, J. A., & Visher, C. A. (1986). *Criminal careers and career criminals.* Washington: National Academy Press.

Brook, J. S., Lukoff, I. F., & Whiteman, M. (1980). Initiation into adolescent marijuana use. *Journal of Genetic Psychology, 137,* 133–142.

Brook, J. S., Nomura, C., & Cohen, P. (1989). A network of influences on adolescent drug involvement, neighborhood, school, peer, and family. *Genetic, Social, and General Psychology Monographs, 115,* 123–145.

Brook, J. S., Whiteman, M., & Scovell Gordon, A. (1983). Stages of drug use in adolescence: Personality, peer, and family correlates. *Developmental Psychology, 19,* 269–277.

Brook, J. S., Whiteman, M., Scovell Gordon, A., Nomura, C., & Brook, D. (1986). Onset of adolescent drinking: A longitudinal study of intrapersonal and interpersonal antecedents. *Advances in Alcohol and Substance Abuse, 5,* 91–110.

Brown, B. B., Clasen, D. R., & Eicher, S. A. (1986). Perceptions of peer pressure, peer conformity dispositions, and self-reported behavior among adolescents. *Developmental Psychology, 22,* 521–530.

Burgess, R., & Akers, R. L. (1966). A differential association-reinforcement theory of criminal behavior. *Social Problems, 14,* 128–147.

Burkett, S. R., & Warren, B. O. (1987). Religiosity, peer influence, and adolescent marijuana use: A panel study of underlying causal structures. *Criminology, 25,* 109–131.

Cairns, R. B., Cairns, B. D., Neckerman, H. J., Gest, S. D., & Gariépy, J.-L. (1988). Social networks and aggressive behavior: Peer support or peer rejection? *Developmental Psychology, 24,* 815–823.

Cloward, R. A., & Ohlin, L. E. (1960). *Delinquency and opportunity.* Glencoe, IL: Free Press.

Cohen, A. K. (1955). *Delinquent boys.* Glencoe, IL: Free Press.

Conger, R. (1976). Social control and social learning models of delinquent behavior: A synthesis. *Criminology, 14,* 17–40.

Coombs, R. H., Paulson, M. J., & Richardson, M. A. (1991). Peer vs. parental influence in substance use among Hispanic and Anglo children and adolescents. *Journal of Youth and Adolescence, 20,* 73–88.

Dishion, T. J., & Loeber, R. (1985). Adolescent marijuana and alcohol use: The role of parents and peers revisited. *American Journal of Drug and Alcohol Abuse, 11,* 11–25.

Elliott, D. S., Huizinga, D., Ageton, S. S. (1985). *Explaining delinquency and drug use.* Beverly Hills, CA: Sage Publications.

Elliott, D. S., Huizinga, D., & Menard, S. (1989). *Multiple problem youth: Delinquency, substance use, and mental health problems.* New York: Springer-Verlag.

Elliott, D. S., & Menard, S. (1990, August). Conventional bonding, delinquent peers, and delinquent behavior. Paper presented at the annual meeting of the American Sociological Association, Washington, DC.

Elliott, D. S., & Menard, S. (1992). *Delinquent friends and delinquent behavior: Temporal and developmental patterns.* Unpublished manuscript.

Elliott, D. S., & Voss, H. (1974). *Delinquency and dropout.* Lexington, MA: Heath.

Erikson, M. L., & Empey, L. T. (1965). Class position, peers, and delinquency. *Sociology and Social Research, 49,* 268–282.

Farrington, D. P., Ohlin, L. E., & Wilson, J. Q. (1986). *Understanding and controlling crime: Toward a new research strategy.* New York: Springer-Verlag.

Fisher, L. A., & Bauman, K. E. (1988). Influence and selection in the friend-adolescent relationship: Findings from studies of adolescent smoking and drinking. *Journal of Applied Social Psychology, 18,* 289–314.

Gillmore, M. R., Hawkins, J. D., Day, L. E., & Catalano, R. F. (1992). Friendship and deviance: New evidence on an old controversy. *Journal of Early Adolescence, 12,* 80–95.

Ginsberg, I. J., & Greenley, J. R. (1978). Competing theories of marijuana use: A longitudinal study. *Journal of Health and Social Behavior, 19,* 22–34.

Giordano, P. G., Cernkovich, S. A., & Pugh, M. D. (1986). Friendships and delinquency. *American Journal of Sociology, 91,* 1170–1202.

Glueck, S., & Glueck, E. T. (1950). *Unraveling juvenile delinquency.* New York: Commonwealth Fund.

Gottfredson, M. R., & Hirschi, T. (1990). *A general theory of crime.* Stanford, CA: Stanford University Press.

Hawkins, J. D., & Fraser, M. W. (1985). The social networks of street drug users: A comparison of two theories. *Social Work Research Abstracts, 21,* 3–12.

Hawkins, J. D., & Weis, J. G. (1985). The social development model: An integrated approach to delinquency prevention. *Journal of Primary Prevention, 6,* 73–97.

Henggeler, S. W., Melton, G. B., & Smith, L. (1992). Family preservation using multisystemic therapy: An effective alternative to incarcerating serious juvenile offenders. *Journal of Consulting and Clinical Psychology, 60,* 953–961.

Hirschi, T. (1969). *Causes of delinquency.* Berkeley: University of California Press.

Hirschi, T., & Selvin, H. C. (1967). *Delinquency research: An appraisal of analytic methods.* New York: Free Press.

Huba, G. J., & Bentler, P. M. (1980). The role of peer and adult models for drug taking at different stages in adolescence. *Journal of Youth and Adolescence, 9,* 449–465.

Huba, G. J., Wingard, J. A., & Bentler, P. M. (1979). Beginning adolescent drug use and peer and adult interaction patterns. *Journal of Consulting and Clinical Psychology, 47,* 265–276.

Huizinga, D., Weiher, A., & Esbensen, F.-A. (1992, March). Intergenerational transmission of delinquency and drug use. Prepared for the meeting of the Society for Research on Adolescence, Washington, DC.

Jensen, G. F. (1972). Parents, peers, and delinquent action: A test of the differential association perspective. *American Journal of Sociology, 78,* 562–575.

Jessor, R., Donovan, J. E., & Costa, F. M. (1991). *Beyond adolescence: Problem behavior and young adult development.* New York: Cambridge University Press.

Jessor, R., & Jessor, S. L. (1977). *Problem behavior and psychosocial development: A longitudinal study of youth.* New York: Academic Press.

Johnson, R. E. (1979). *Juvenile delinquency and its origins.* Cambridge: University of Cambridge Press.

Johnson, R. E., Marcos, A. C., & Bahr, S. J. (1987). The role of peers in the complex etiology of adolescent drug use. *Criminology, 25,* 323–340.

Johnson, V. (1988). Adolescent alcohol and marijuana use: A longitudinal assessment of a social learning perspective. *American Journal of Drug and Alcohol Abuse, 14,* 419–439.

Kandel, D. B. (1975). Some comments on the relationships of selected criteria variables to adolescent drug use. In D. J. Lettieri (Ed.), *Predicting adolescent drug abuse: A review of issues, methods, and correlates* (pp. 345–361). Rockville, MD: National Institute of Drug Abuse.

Kandel, D. B. (1978a). Homophily, selection, and socialization in adolescent friendships. *American Journal of Sociology, 84,* 427–436.

Kandel, D. B. (Ed.). (1978b). *Longitudinal research on drug use: Empirical findings and methodological issues.* Washington, DC: Hemisphere Publishing Corporation.

Kandel, D. (1985). On processes of peer influence in adolescent drug use: A developmental perspective. *Alcohol and Substance Abuse in Adolescence, 4,* 139–163.

Kandel, D., & Andrews, K. (1987). Processes of adolescent socialization by parents and peers. *The International Journal of the Addictions, 22,* 319–342.

Kandel, D. B., & Davies, M. (1991). Friendship networks, intimacy, and elicit drug use in young adulthood: A comparison of two competing theories. *Criminology, 29,* 441–470.

Kaplan, H. B., Johnson, R. J., & Bailey, C. A. (1987). Deviant peers and deviant behavior: Further elaboration of a model. *Social Psychology Quarterly, 50,* 277–284.

Kornhauser, R. (1979). *Social sources of delinquency: An appraisal of analytical models.* Chicago: University of Chicago Press.

Krohn, M. D. (1974). An investigation of the effect of parental and peer associations on marijuana use: An empirical test of differential association theory. In M. Riedel & T. P. Thornberry (Eds.), *Crime and delinquency: Dimensions of deviance* (pp. 75–87). New York: Praeger.

Krohn, M. D., Lanza-Kaduce, L., & Akers, R. L. (1984). Community context and theories of deviant behavior: An examination of social learning and social bonding theories. *Sociological Quarterly, 25,* 353–372.

Krohn, M. D., Lizotte, A. J., Thornberry, T. P., Smith, C., & McDowall, D. (1996). Reciprocal causal relationships among drug use, peers, and beliefs: A five-wave panel model. *Journal of Drug Issues, 26,* 405–428.

Krohn, M. D., & Thornbery, T. P. (1993). Network theory: A model for understanding drug abuse among African-American and Hispanic youth. In M. De La Rosa & J.-L. Recio Adrados (Eds.), *Drug abuse among minority youth: Advances in research methodology* (pp. 102–128). NIDA Research Monograph 130, U.S. Department of Health and Human Services.

LaGrange, R. L., & White, H. Raskin (1983). Age differences in delinquency: A test of theory. *Criminology, 23,* 19–46.

Linden, E. (1978). Myths of middle class delinquency: A test of generalizability of social control theory. *Youth and Society, 9,* 407–432.

Linden, E., & Hackler, J. C. (1973). Affective ties and delinquency. *Pacific Sociological Review, 16,* 27–46.

Liska, A. E. (1987). *Perspectives on deviance.* Englewood Cliffs, NJ: Prentice Hall.

Marcos, A. C., Bahr, S. J., & Johnson, R. E. (1986). Test of a bonding/association theory of adolescent drug use. *Social Forces, 65,* 135–161.

Matsueda, R. (1982). Testing control theory and differential association: A causal modeling approach. *American Sociological Review, 47,* 489–504.

Meier, R. F., Burkett, S. R., & Hickman, C. A. (1984). Sanctions, peers, and deviance: Preliminary models of a social control process. *Sociological Quarterly, 25,* 67–82.

Menard, S. (1992). Demographic and theoretical variables in the age-period-cohort analysis of illegal behavior. *Journal of Research in Crime and Delinquency, 29,* 178–199.

Menard, S., & Elliott, D. S. (1994). Delinquent bonding, moral beliefs, and illegal behavior: A three-wave panel model. *Justice Quarterly, 11,* 173–188.

National Institute on Drug Abuse. (1990). *National Household Survey on Drug Abuse: Main findings 1988.* Rockville, MD: U.S. Department of Health and Human Services.

Orcutt, J. D. (1983). *Analyzing deviance.* Homewood, IL: The Dorsey Press.

Orcutt, J. D. (1987). Differential association and marijuana use: A closer look at Sutherland (with a little help from Becker). *Criminology, 25,* 341–358.

Paternoster, R. (1988). Examining three-wave deterrence models: A question of temporal order and specification. *Journal of Criminal Law and Criminology, 79,* 135–179.

Patterson, G. R., Capaldi, D., & Bank, L. (1991). An early starter model for predicting delinquency. In D. J. Pepler & K. H. Rubin (eds.), *The development and treatment of childhood aggression* (pp. 139–168). Hillsdale, NJ: Erlbaum.

Patterson, G. R., Crosby, L., & Vuchinich, S. (1992). Predicting risk of early police arrest. *Journal of Quantitative Criminology, 8,* 335–355.

Patterson, G. R., & Dishion, T. J. (1985). Contributions of families and peers to delinquency. *Criminology, 23,* 63–79.

Poole, E. D., & Regoli, R. M. (1979). Parental support, delinquent friends, and delinquency: A test of interaction effects. *Journal of Criminal Law and Criminology, 70,* 188–193.

Pruitt, B. E., Kingery, P. M., Mirzaee, E., Heuberger, G., & Hurley, R. S. (1991). Peer influence and drug use among adolescents in rural areas. *Journal of Drug Education, 21,* 1–11.

Reed, M. D., & Rose, D. R. (1991). *Modeling the reciprocal relations of delinquent beliefs, delinquent attitudes, and serious delinquency: A covariance structure analysis.* Unpublished manuscript.

Reiss, A. J., & Rhodes, A. L. (1964). An empirical test of differential association theory. *Journal of Research in Crime and Delinquency, 1,* 13–17.

Rotter, J. B. (1954). *Social learning and clinical psychology.* Englewood Cliffs, NJ: Prentice Hall.

Sellers, C. S., & Winfree, L. T., Jr. (1990). Differential associations and definitions: A panel study of youthful drinking behavior. *The International Journal of the Addictions, 25,* 755–771.

Sellin, T. (1938). *Culture, conflict, and crime.* New York: Social Science Research Council (Bulletin 41).

Shaw, C. R., & McKay, H. D. (1931). *Report on the causes of crime: Volume II. Social factors in juvenile delinquency.* Washington, DC: National Commission on Law Observance and Enforcement.

Shaw, C. R., & McKay, H. D. (1942). *Juvenile delinquency and urban areas.* Chicago: University of Chicago Press.

Short, J. F., Jr. (1957, January). Differential association and delinquency. *Social Problems,* pp. 233–239.

Short, J. F., Jr. (1958, Spring). Differential association with delinquent friends and delinquent behavior. *Pacific Sociological Review,* pp. 20–25.

Short, J. F., Jr. (1960). Differential association as a hypothesis: A panel study of youthful drinking behavior. *The International Journal of the Addictions, 25,* 755–771.

Simons, R. L., Conger, R. D., & Whitbeck, L. (1988). A multistage social learning model of the influences of family and peers upon adolescent substance abuse. *The Journal of Drug Issues, 18,* 293–315.

Simons, R. L., Wu, C., Conger, R. D., & Lorenz, F. O. (1994). Two routes to delinquency: Differences between early and late starters in the impact of parenting and deviant peers. *Criminology, 32,* 247–276.

Smith, D. A., & Brame, R. (1994). On the initiation and continuation of delinquency. *Criminology, 32,* 607–630.

Sutherland, E. H. (1939). *Principles of criminology* (3rd ed.). Philadelphia: Lippincott.

Sutherland, E. H., & Cressey, D. R. (1978). *Criminology* (10th ed.). Philadelphia: Lippincott.

Swadi, H. (1988). Adolescent drug taking: Role of family and peers. *Drug and Alcohol Dependence, 21,* 157–160.

Swadi, H. (1992). Relative risk factors in detecting adolescent drug abuse. *Drug and Alcohol Dependence, 29,* 253–254.

Tarde, G. (1912). *Penal philosophy* (R. Howell, Trans.). Boston: Little, Brown. (Original work published 1890)

Tec, N. (1972). The peer group and marijuana use. *Crime and Delinquency, 18,* 298–309.

Thornberry, T. P. (1987). Toward an interactional theory of delinquency. *Criminology, 25,* 863–891.

Thornberry, T. P., Lizotte, A. J., Krohn, M. D., Farnworth, M., & Jang, S. J. (1994). Delinquent peers, beliefs, and delinquent behavior: A longitudinal test of interactional theory. *Criminology, 32,* 601–637.

Thrasher, F. M. (1927). *The gang.* Chicago: University of Chicago Press.

Vaillant, G. E. (1966). A twelve-year follow-up of New York narcotic addicts: Some social and psychiatric characteristics. *Archives of General Psychiatry, 15,* 599–609.

Voss, H. L. (1964). Differential association and reported delinquent behavior: A replication. *Social Problems, 12,* 78–85.

Warr, M. (1993). Parents, peers, and delinquency. *Social Forces, 72,* 247–264.

Warr, M., & Stafford, M. (1991). The influence of delinquent peers: What they think or what they do. *Criminology, 29,* 851–865.

White, H., Pandina, R. J., & LaGrange, R. L. (1987). Longitudinal predictors of serious substance use and delinquency. *Criminology, 25,* 715–740.

Wolfgang, M. E., Thornberry, T. P., & Figlio, R. M. (1987). *From boy to man, from delinquency to crime.* Chicago: University of Chicago Press.

CHAPTER 22

A Critical Analysis of Research on the Development of Antisocial Behavior From Birth to Adulthood

DAVID P. FARRINGTON

This chapter first discusses the key developmental issues raised throughout this volume, then the key theoretical issues, and finally some current focal concerns. Throughout, I refer to results obtained in the Cambridge Study in Delinquent Development, which is a prospective longitudinal survey of more than 400 London boys and their families, studied from age 8 to age 40 (Farrington, 1995b).

KEY DEVELOPMENTAL ISSUES

Continuity

An emphasis on the continuity and stability of antisocial behavior over time pervades most of the chapters in this volume. For example, Shaw and Winslow (Chapter 15) note that developmental trajectories leading to antisocial behavior begin in the infancy to preschool period and that there is moderate to strong continuity of externalizing behavior from infancy to school age; they cite a .76 correlation between aggression at ages 2 and 5. From the consistency over time, Eron (Chapter 14) argues that aggression is a personality trait that characterizes the individual over time and across situations and that aggressive children tend to become antisocial and criminal adults.

Despite the impressive unanimity of authors about the continuity of antisocial behavior, many questions remain unanswered. First of all, despite a great deal of continuity, there is also a great deal of change. Several years ago, Lee Robins (1986, p. 228) concluded that, looking forward, only about half of the children with conduct disorder became antisocial adults, but looking backward, virtually all antisocial adults had previously shown at least one symptom of conduct disorder. Obviously, the precise prospective and retrospective proportions depend on such factors as the time interval and the cutoff points for antisocial behavior (Farrington, 1991), but a substantial number of antisocial children do not become antisocial adults. To some extent, questions about the stability of antisocial behavior are similar to questions about whether a glass is half full or half empty. Establishing reasons for early desistance potentially could have important implications for interventions, which are unlikely to be successful to the extent that there is stability in antisocial behavior.

Problems arise because of the use of the words *continuity* and *stability* as equivalent, when they have somewhat different connotations. It is plausible to assume that the same underlying theoretical construct (e.g., antisocial personality) can have different behavioral manifestations at different ages (see, e.g., Rutter, Chapter 12). For example, Loeber and Farrington (Chapter 13) hypothesize that children showing a difficult temperament at age 2 tend to show cruelty to animals and other symptoms of conduct disorder at age 8, minor delinquency such as shoplifting at age 12, more serious delinquency such as burglary at age 15, robbery and violence at age 20, and eventually spousal abuse, child abuse, and alcoholism in their 20s and 30s. This is an example of continuity but not stability in behavior. However, there may be stability in the relative rankings of individuals on an underlying construct such as antisocial tendency.

The recognition that there are changing manifestations of theoretical constructs at different ages implies that different operational definitions are needed to measure them. Some measures are applicable only at certain ages; for example, truancy from school could not be measured at age 30, just as absenteeism from work could not be measured at age 10. The age at which a behavior occurs may influence its definition; for example, an attack by one child on another child may not be defined as violence. There also is the complication that behavioral manifestations of antisocial tendency may be different at different time periods, for example, as fashionable drugs come and go.

A further problem is that the same indicator may reflect different underlying constructs at different ages. For example, having sexual intercourse at age 13 is statistically deviant, but having sexual intercourse at age 23 is statistically abnormal. Only the developmental course or precocity of the behavior is statistically normal, not the behavior itself. Statistically normal behavior tends not to be associated with other indicators of antisocial behavior. For example, Farrington (1991) found that conflict with parents was related to other antisocial indicators at age 32 but not at age 18, when it was common; and drunk driving was related to other antisocial indicators at age 18 but not at age 32 (when the majority of drivers, in the previous 5 years, had driven after consuming excess alcohol).

In investigating the continuity and stability of antisocial behavior, it is desirable to have multiple measures from multiple sources of multiple constructs, as Dishion and Patterson (Chapter 20) advocate. In some cases, low continuity and stability may be a function of inadequate measurement. For example, at older ages such age-specific behaviors as spousal assault, child abuse, and cheating on income tax may not be measured. It also is desirable to measure opportunities for antisocial behaviors; those without spouses cannot commit spousal assault, those who do not drive cannot drive drunk, and those without jobs cannot cheat on their income tax. Also, it is important to record death, emigration, hospitalization, physical impairment, long-term incarceration, and other events that might account for low measured continuity and stability.

Farrington (1990a) gave many examples of how absolute change in the prevalence of different types of antisocial behavior coincided with relative stability; in other words, the most deviant individuals at one age still tended to be the most deviant at a later age, even though absolute levels of manifest behavioral deviance could change quite dramatically over time. For example, the prevalence of marijuana use declined significantly, from 29% at age 18 to 19% at age 32. However, there was a significant tendency for the users at age 18 also to be users at age 32 (44% of users at age 18 were users at age 32, whereas only 8% of nonusers at age 18 were users at age 32). In contrast, the prevalence of binge drinking and drunk driving increased significantly between ages 18 and 32, and there again was significant consistency over time. The prevalence of heavy smoking did not change significantly between ages 18 and 32, and there again was significant consistency over time. Therefore, relative consistency could coexist with absolute increases, decreases, or constancy.

Onset and Types of Offenders

Several of the chapters (e.g., Dishion & Patterson, Chapter 20; Loeber & Farrington, Chapter 13) emphasize the importance of the age of onset of antisocial behavior, stressing that a relatively early age of onset predicts a long and serious antisocial career and chronic offending. As Rutter (Chapter 12) points out, a key issue is whether early onset is a marker or symptom of an underlying antisocial personality, which then persists over time (with increasingly serious behavioral manifestations), or whether an early onset has some additional causal effect on the later career, perhaps because antisocial habits established early tend to be more persistent or because the earlier experience of the reinforcing effects of antisocial behavior increases the probability of escalation. Nagin and Farrington (1992a, 1992b) compared these two hypotheses and concluded that the Cambridge Study data were more consistent with the assumption of time-stable individual differences than with any causal effect of early onset.

One problem with research on onset is that "early" onset means different things to different researchers and, of course, differs according to the type of antisocial behavior. It is useful to study developmental sequences of onsets of different types of antisocial behavior. Loeber and Farrington (Chapter 13) and Cairns, Cadwallader, Estell, and Neckerman (Chapter 19) review evidence for different developmental pathways, and Rutter (Chapter 12) points out that the frequency and versatility of antisocial behavior tend to predict subsequent escalation. However, it would be useful to incorporate the idea of desistance into these kinds of models and to predict desistance. The importance of studying

desistance tends to have been overlooked in the excitement of studying onset, but knowledge about desistance can have equally important implications for intervention.

Several chapters mention the influential theory of Moffitt (1993), linking age of onset with types of offenders ("adolescence limited" vs. "life-course persistent"). In a test of this theory, Nagin, Farrington, and Moffitt (1995) concluded that it was only partially supported in the Cambridge Study. By age 32, the work records of the adolescence-limited offenders were indistinguishable from unconvicted men and substantially better than those of the chronic (life-course persistent) offenders. The adolescence-limited offenders also had established better relationships with their spouses than the chronic offenders. However, the seeming reformation of adolescence-limited offenders was less than complete. Even though they no longer were getting convicted by age 32, they continued to use drugs, drink heavily, get into fights, and commit criminal acts (according to self-reports).

In Chapter 12, Rutter suggests that adolescence-onset antisocial behavior is largely environmentally determined, is not associated with hyperactivity, and tends not to persist into adult life or be associated with widespread social malfunction. In contrast, early-onset antisocial behavior involves a strong genetic component, is often accompanied by hyperactivity or inattention, and shows a strong tendency to persist into adult life with associated widespread social problems.

An important issue is whether early- and later-onset offenders differ in degree or in kind. Most researchers in the past have assumed that people are essentially homogeneous and that causal factors have essentially the same effects on everyone. This assumption may be unrealistic, however, and future researchers should investigate what are the most useful typologies of individuals. Typologies, of course, are implied in diagnoses such as conduct disorder and antisocial personality disorder, but Eron (Chapter 14) argues that aggressive behavior falls on a continuum, not into discrete categories, and hence that a dimensional approach to antisocial behavior is preferable. It is interesting that Rutter (Chapter 12) points out that dimensional and categorical models are not mutually exclusive and that the causes of deviant conditions (e.g., mental retardation) are quite different from the causes of individual variations in intelligence within the normal range. Ideas of onset and desistance imply sharp discontinuities in development.

Comorbidity

Several of the chapters (e.g., Loeber & Farrington, Chapter 13; Rutter, Chapter 12; Widom, Chapter 16) identify the crucial importance of comorbidity in antisocial behavior. There seems little doubt that people who show one type of antisocial behavior also tend to show other types and, hence, that antisocial behavior tends to be versatile rather than specialized. Many years ago, Lee Robins (1979) suggested that there was an "antisocial personality" that arose in childhood and persisted into adulthood, with numerous different behavioral manifestations, including offending; and this idea is embodied in the *DSM-IV* diagnosis of antisocial personality disorder (American Psychiatric Association, 1994). According to Robins, the antisocial adult male generally failed to maintain close personal relationships with anyone else, tended to perform poorly in his jobs, tended to be involved in crime, failed to support himself and his dependents without outside aid, and tended to change his plans impulsively and lose his temper in response to minor frustrations. As a child, he tended to be restless, impulsive, and lacking in guilt, performed badly in school, was truant, ran away from home, was cruel to animals or people, and committed delinquent acts.

The Cambridge Study also shows that delinquency is only one element of a much larger syndrome of antisocial behavior that tends to persist over time. For example, the boys who were convicted up to age 18 (most commonly for offenses of dishonesty, such as burglary and theft) were significantly more deviant than the nondelinquents on almost every factor that was investigated at that age (West & Farrington, 1977). The convicted delinquents drank more beer, they got drunk more often, and they were more likely to say that drink made them violent. They smoked more cigarettes, they had started smoking at an earlier age, and they were more likely to be heavy gamblers. They were more likely to have been convicted for minor motoring offenses, to have driven after drinking at least 10 units of alcohol (e.g., 5 pints of beer), and to have been injured in road accidents. The delinquents were more likely to have taken prohibited drugs such as marijuana or LSD, although few of them had convictions for drug offenses. Also, they were more likely to have had sexual intercourse, especially with a variety of different partners and beginning at an early age, but they were less likely to use contraceptives.

At age 18, the convicted delinquents tended to hold relatively well paid but low status (unskilled manual) jobs, and they were more likely to have erratic work histories, including periods of unemployment. They were more likely to be living away from home, and they tended not to get on well with their parents. They were more likely to be tattooed, possible reflecting their "machismo" orientation. The delinquents were more likely to go out in the evenings and were especially likely to spend time hanging about on the street. They tended to go around in groups of four or more and were more likely to be involved in group violence or vandalism. They were much more likely to have been involved in fights, to have started fights, to have carried weapons, and to have used weapons in fights. They also were more likely to express aggressive and antiestablishment attitudes on a questionnaire (negative to police, school, rich people, and civil servants).

In spite of the general agreement about comorbidity, many key issues remain to be resolved. One obvious problem is whether all types of antisocial behavior are essentially symptoms of the same underlying syndrome or whether one type of antisocial behavior tends to act as a stepping stone to or facilitate another type. To throw more light on comorbidity, detailed information is required about the prevalence and frequency of different types of antisocial behavior at different ages. The best current information on this has been provided by Verhulst and Van der Ende (1995). Future researchers need to investigate the concurrent or consecutive development of different types of antisocial behavior, and the development of individuals with multiple problems (see, e.g., Elliott, Huizinga, & Menard, 1989). Also, theories need to acknowledge comorbidity and be less compartmentalized in focusing primarily on specific types of antisocial behavior. It is important to establish whether developmental processes are similar or different for all types of problems.

The optimistic side of comorbidity is its implications for intervention. Successful prevention and treatment techniques are likely to be cost effective because, if they reduce one type of antisocial behavior, they are likely to reduce a whole range of associated social problems, including accidents, injuries, smoking, drinking, drug use, and problems associated with promiscuous sexual activity. Hence, it is important to measure a wide variety of outcomes in intervention research, and such research should help in advancing knowledge about causal or developmental sequences in antisocial behavior.

KEY THEORETICAL ISSUES

Risk Factors in General

Many of the chapters focus on risk factors for antisocial behavior rather than, for example, explanatory variables. The idea of risk factors implies discontinuous or dichotomous variables rather than continuous ones, because typically a risk factor is considered to be either present or absent. Also, the idea of risk factors tends to sidestep the issue of which factors have direct causal effects on antisocial behavior. Rutter (Chapter 12) outlines a number of ways of establishing causality, and I want to highlight especially the study of within-individual change, which (surprisingly) has been sorely neglected by developmental researchers.

Farrington (1988) articulated arguments in favor of studying within-individual change to establish causality. As an example, Farrington and West (1995) investigated the effects of getting married, becoming separated from a spouse, and having a child on the course of development of offending, by following up individuals before and after these life events. In general, risk factors and variables are studied far more than discrete life events, although Loeber and Farrington (Chapter 13) recommend research on the effects of life events at different ages, and Dishion and Patterson (Chapter 20) highlight the importance of school transitions.

Several chapters (e.g., Loeber & Farrington, Chapter 13; Thornberry & Krohn, Chapter 21; Widom, Chapter 16) point out that it is important to investigate whether risk factors have different effects at different ages or on different aspects of antisocial careers, such as onset and persistence. For example, Loeber, Stouthamer-Loeber, Van Kammen, and Farrington (1991) in the Pittsburgh Youth Study found that the risk factors influencing onset were different from those influencing escalation. It might be expected that parental influences would be more important at the time of onset, whereas peer influences might be more important for persistence. For example, in the developmental progression theory of Patterson, De Baryshe, and Ramsey (1989), poor parental discipline and monitoring in early childhood lead to conduct problems, which in turn lead to peer rejection and school failure in middle childhood, which in turn lead to commitment to deviant peers and delinquency in adolescence.

Few studies have examined risk factors for persistence versus desistance. However, in the Cambridge Study, Farrington and Hawkins (1991) investigated factors that predicted whether convicted offenders before age 21 would persist or desist between ages 21 and 32. The best independent predictors of persistence included rarely spending leisure time with the father at ages 11 to

12, low intelligence at ages 8 to 10, employment instability at age 16, and heavy drinking at age 18. Indeed, nearly 90% of the convicted males who were frequently unemployed and heavy drinkers as teenagers went on to be reconvicted after age 21.

Several chapters (e.g., Rutter, Chapter 12; Shaw & Winslow, Chapter 15; Thornberry & Krohn, Chapter 21) emphasize that there could be reciprocal effects; for example, children could influence parents, and parents could influence children. Similarly, it is important to investigate sequences of causal effects. Several chapters (e.g., Dishion & Patterson, Chapter 20; Loeber & Farrington, Chapter 13; Rutter, Chapter 12) point out that neighborhood and socioeconomic factors seem to have indirect effects on antisocial behavior via their effects on family and child-rearing factors. The duration of risk factors such as parental discord may be important (Thornberry & Krohn, Chapter 21), and another key problem is the causal lag between risk factors and outcomes (Loeber & Farrington, Chapter 13).

An important issue (raised by Huesmann, Moise, & Podolski, Chapter 18; and by Shaw & Winslow, Chapter 15) is whether specific risk factors predict specific types of antisocial behavior, or whether the number of risk factors is what matters, irrespective of which ones. A related issue is whether each specific risk factor predicts a large number of different types of antisocial behavior or, relatedly, whether it predicts individuals with multiple problems. In the past, Robins and Ratcliff (1978) argued against specific predictability, stating that an accumulation of risk factors predicted an accumulation of problem behaviors, but more research is clearly needed on this topic. Eron (Chapter 14) contends that violence is unpredictable except when there is an accumulation of adversities. As Loeber and Farrington (Chapter 13) point out, it is important to investigate the extent to which chronic offenders can be identified at an early age.

Another important issue is whether risk factors have different effects alone, in combination with other specified risk factors, or as part of a wider constellation of adversities (see, e.g., Rutter, Chapter 12; Widom, Chapter 16). In general, insufficient attention has been paid by developmental researchers to interaction effects, although several chapters (e.g. Cairns et al., Chapter 19; Dodge & Schwartz, Chapter 17; Huesmann et al., Chapter 18; Shaw & Winslow, Chapter 15) pay attention to male-female differences, and Rutter (Chapter 12) discusses whether individual development varies in different neighborhood contexts. Perhaps the most important interaction effects are those concerning protective factors (Rutter, 1985). Despite their importance for theory and intervention, protective factors have been neglected compared with risk factors, although Dishion and Patterson (Chapter 20) argue that an adverse neighborhood context would not have a significant impact on child adjustment if parents used effective discipline and monitoring. They contend that these child-rearing practices are strong protective factors.

Specific Risk Factors

To investigate interactive and sequential effects of different risk factors, it is essential to measure a wide range of different variables, including biological, individual, family, peer, school, and neighborhood factors (Loeber & Farrington, Chapter 13). Numerous important risk factors are reviewed in the chapters, including difficult temperament (Shaw & Winslow, Chapter 15), hyperactivity-impulsivity-inattention (HIA) problems (Rutter, Chapter 12), parental conflict (Shaw & Winslow, Chapter 15), child abuse and neglect (Widom, Chapter 16) and school failure (Dishion & Patterson, Chapter 20). Several chapters (e.g. Cairns et al., Chapter 19; Dishion & Patterson, Chapter 20; Thornberry & Krohn, Chapter 21) focus particularly on peer influence, and Cairns and his colleagues should be particularly commended for their brave attempt to bring together developmental research on peer influence and criminological research on gangs.

As is often the case, Rutter's (Chapter 12) discussion of mechanisms and processes are especially thought provoking. For example, in regard to HIA problems, he first asks which aspect of this constellation of behaviors constitutes the key risk feature: overactivity, impulsivity, or inattention? Then he focuses on impulsivity and enquires what is the crucial mechanism in this: sensation seeking, an impaired ability to delay action or inhibit responses, or acting without thought? Next he enquires whether this represents a deficit in higher cognitive functioning or a motivational problem. Finally, he wonders whether HIA causes a direct risk for antisocial behavior or whether the risk depends on other factors such as adverse child-rearing practices. This kind of thoughtful analysis needs to be repeated by all researchers for all risk factors to guide future research and foster the development of cumulative knowledge.

Whereas most researchers focus on risk factors one by one, a combination of specific risk factors may be important. For example, Shaw and Winslow (Chapter 15) recommend the use of "parenting style" rather than individual dimensions of parenting. They contend that what matters is a combination of characteristics, such as high parental warmth, high involvement with the child, and consistent discipline, that together constitute "good parenting." An alternative problem is how to disentangle one factor (e.g., child abuse, Widom, Chapter 16) from the usual constellation of adversities.

It is also difficult to decide if any given risk factor is an indicator (symptom) or possible cause of antisocial tendency. For example, do heavy drinking, truancy, unemployment, and divorce measure antisocial tendency or do they cause (an increase in) it? It is important not to include a measure of the dependent variable as an independent variable in causal analyses, because this will lead to false conclusions and an overestimation of explanatory or predictive power (see, e.g., Amdur, 1989).

It is not unreasonable to argue that the preceding examples may be both indicative and causal. For example, long-term variations *between* individuals in antisocial tendency may be mirrored by variations in alcohol consumption, just as short-term variations *within* individuals in alcohol consumption may cause more antisocial behavior during the heavier drinking periods. The interpretation of other factors may be more clear-cut. For example, being exposed as a child to poor parental child-rearing techniques might cause an antisocial tendency but would not be an indicator of it; and burgling a house might be an indicator of antisocial tendency but would be unlikely to cause it (although it might be argued that when an antisocial act is successful in leading to positive reinforcement, this reinforcement causes an increase in the underlying antisocial tendency).

Theories

It is important, of course, to incorporate risk factors, interactions, and causal sequences within larger theories of antisocial behavior. Numerous theories are described in these chapters. For example, Eron (Chapter 14) and Huesmann et al. (Chapter 18) describe learning or reinforcement and observational learning theories of violence, with Huesmann et al. focusing particularly on the link between media violence and violent behavior. Thornberry and Krohn (Chapter 21) provide a particularly extensive review of criminological theories, in discussing the link between the association with delinquent peers and the commission of delinquent acts. Their chapter is an excellent example of the complexities that arise when researchers carefully articulate and test alternative explanations of even one apparently simple link. However, admitting a personal interest, I would have liked them to pay more attention to research on co-offending (e.g., Reiss & Farrington, 1991).

Several chapters (Dodge & Schwartz, Chapter 17; Eron, Chapter 14; Huesmann et al., Chapter 18) focus on the cognitive processes intervening between risk factors and antisocial behavior. Dodge and Schwartz argue that aggressive children are different in their social information processing, which is a relatively stable, personality-like feature. They link social information processing to child maltreatment, difficult temperament, and impulsivity as well as to the important concepts of proactive and reactive aggression. Eron and Huesmann et al. emphasize the importance of cognitive scripts stored in memory.

The focus on cognitive processes more easily explains the behavioral manifestation of antisocial acts than the development on an underlying antisocial potential (or antisocial personality). Most past theories of antisocial behavior have been concerned with the development of this potential rather than with how the potential becomes the actuality in specific situations. Rutter (Chapter 12) raises the issue of whether the focus should be on syndromes or acts and points out the importance of situational factors in influencing the occurrence of antisocial acts.

Farrington (1995a) proposed a theory that attempted to integrate explanations of the long-term development of criminal potential with explanations of the short-term occurrence of criminal acts. Long-term influences included well-known biological, individual, family, peer, school, and community factors, whereas short-term influences included boredom, frustration, anger, and drunkenness. The criminal potential arising from these short-term and long-term influences interacted with criminal opportunities, and individuals decided whether to offend, taking account of the perceived costs, benefits, and probabilities of different possible outcomes. The consequences of offending (e.g., rewards, punishments, labeling) then fed back into the decision-making process and into long-term criminal potential. More efforts should be made to integrate explanations of the development of antisocial persons with explanations of the occurrence of antisocial acts.

CURRENT FOCAL CONCERNS

Traditionally, criminologists have focused on offending in the teenage years, when it is in full flow, and have neglected the continuity between early child development and teenage antisocial behavior and between teenage antisocial behavior and adult life adjustment problems. Some of the chapters (especially Shaw & Winslow, Chapter 15) show an increasing concern with very early development and with prediction from the first few years of life to antisocial behavior in the teenage years. Several chapters (e.g., Eron, Chapter 14; Huesmann et al., Chapter 18) mention Kagan's discovery of temperamental differences before age 2 that are relevant to later antisocial behavior. There is far less concern with development after the teenage years, however, which is arguably just as important theoretically and for intervention implications, or with adult social dysfunction (Zoccolillo, Pickles, Quinton, & Rutter, 1992).

The authors disagree somewhat on the predictability of antisocial behavior, despite the widespread acceptance of continuity. As already mentioned, Eron (Chapter 14) argues that no single factor explains much of the variance in antisocial behavior, and Dishion and Patterson (Chapter 20) deny that low intelligence is a cause of delinquency, apparently on the ground that the vast majority of children with low intellectual functioning are well socialized. Against this, Widom (Chapter 16) notes that, although only about 20% to 30% of abused children later become criminals, child abuse doubles the risk of later criminality. To a large extent, conclusions about predictability depend on the statistical methods used. For example, a doubling of the risk of antisocial behavior from 10% to 20% typically would correspond (in a 2 x 2 table) to a correlation of .10 or to only 1% of the variance explained (Farrington & Loeber, 1989).

In research by Farrington (1991) on the Cambridge Study, antisocial personality scales at ages 8 to 10 and 18 correlated .38 (with 14% of the variance explained), but 43% of the most antisocial boys at ages 8 to 10 were still among the most antisocial at 18, compared with 16% of the remainder (odds ratio = 3.8). Relative stability increased with age. Antisocial personality scales at ages 18 and 32 correlated .55 (with 28% of the variance explained), but 60% of the most antisocial boys at 18 were still among the most antisocial at 32, compared with 14% of the remainder (odds ratio = 9.3). Is antisocial behavior predictable over 8 to 12 years? Arguably, the use of risk factors and the odds ratio provides a more realistic indication of predictability than the use of continuous variables and correlations.

Apart from Chapter 16 by Widom, there is little concern with the intergenerational transmission of antisocial behavior, despite the importance of antisocial parents as predictors of antisocial children. For example, Farrington (1993b) found that boys who were bullies at ages 14 or 18 tended in their 30s to have children who were bullies. More research is needed on the genetic and environmental mechanisms underlying these kinds of links. Environmental mechanisms have been investigated in the Cambridge Study.

In this research, the concentration of offending in a small number of families was remarkable. Fewer than 6% of the families were responsible for half of the criminal convictions of all members (fathers, mothers, sons, and daughters) of all 400 families (Farrington, Barnes, & Lambert, 1996). Having a convicted mother, father, brother, or sister significantly predicted a boy's own convictions. Furthermore, convicted parents and delinquent siblings were related to self-reported as well as official offending (Farrington, 1979).

Unlike most early precursors, a convicted parent was related less to early-onset (ages 10 to 13) offending than to later offending (Farrington, 1986). Also, a convicted parent predicted which juvenile offenders went on to become adult criminals and which recidivists at age 19 continued offending rather than desisted (West & Farrington, 1977) and predicted convictions up to age 32 independent of all other factors (Farrington, 1990b, 1993a). As many as 59% of boys with a convicted parent were themselves convicted up to age 32.

In investigating why criminal parents tended to have delinquent children, no evidence was found that they directly encouraged their children to commit crimes or taught them criminal techniques. On the contrary, criminal parents were highly critical of their children's offending; for example, 89% of convicted men at age 32 disagreed with the statement, "I would not mind if my son/daughter committed a criminal offense." Also, it was extremely rare for a parent and a child to be convicted for an offense committed together (Reiss & Farrington, 1991).

Some evidence was found that having a convicted parent increased a boy's likelihood of being convicted, over and above his actual level of antisocial behavior (West & Farrington, 1977). However, the fact that a convicted parent predicted self-reported offending as well as convictions shows that the labeling of children from known criminal families was not the only reason for the intergenerational transmission of criminality. The main link in the chain between criminal parents and delinquent children that was discovered in the Cambridge Study was the markedly poor supervision by criminal parents. More research is needed on the links between antisocial parents and antisocial children.

Apart from Chapter 12 by Rutter, little concern focuses on the importance of secular trends over time; and apart from Chapter 13 by Loeber and Farrington, little concern focuses on disentangling aging, period, and cohort effects. Age clearly is a key variable in developmental research, which makes this disentangling all the more important.

Several researchers recommend prospective longitudinal studies, and the advantages and problems of these are articulated in detail by Loeber and Farrington (Chapter 13). They also discuss the multiple-cohort accelerated longitudinal design (see also Tonry, Ohlin, & Farrington, 1991) and the desirability of including experimental interventions in prospective longitudinal studies (see also Farrington, Ohlin, & Wilson, 1986). A large-scale multiple cohort longitudinal study is currently underway in Chicago (Earls & Reiss, 1994). Loeber and Farrington also point out the need for multisite comparative studies (e.g., Huizinga, Loeber, & Thornberry, 1993) and long-term studies that span the whole period of onset, persistence, and desistance of offending. Comparative studies can be particularly useful in throwing light on the mechanisms by which risk factors operate in different contexts.

An important issue is how to draw conclusions about interventions from knowledge gained in naturalistic longitudinal studies containing no interventions. It is difficult to know how and when it is best to intervene, because of the lack of knowledge about developmental sequences, ages at which causal factors are most salient, and different influences on onset, persistence, and desistance. For example, if truancy leads to delinquency in a developmental sequence, intervening successfully to decrease truancy should lead to a decrease in delinquency. On the other hand, if truancy and delinquency are merely different behavioral manifestations of the same underlying construct, tackling one symptom would not necessarily change the underlying construct.

Causal factors may be more salient at some ages than others. For example, assuming that child-rearing factors are likely to be most influential before the teenage years, the same intervention technique targeted on parents may be more effective for children aged 8 than for those aged 16. Similarly, causal factors may have different effects on different stages of the antisocial career. As an example, if delinquent peers affect persistence but not onset, an intervention technique targeted on peers should be applied after an antisocial career has begun (as treatment) rather than before (as prevention). It seems important to intervene at developmental stages when there is moderate predictability to antisocial outcomes. If predictability is low, a successful intervention may not prevent a later outcome, and if predictability is high the underlying antisocial personality may be so stable that it is difficult to change.

CONCLUSIONS

As these chapters show, a great deal has been learned about the development of antisocial behavior in the past 20 years, especially from the increasing number of prospective longitudinal surveys. The continuity of antisocial behavior is a key issue, and relative stability can coincide with absolute change. A great deal of emphasis is placed on studying the age of onset of antisocial behavior and comparing early- and later-onset offenders. Additional research is needed on more complex typologies of individuals that are theoretically and empirically useful. It is impressive that studies of the development of antisocial behavior are now being pushed back to birth, but more research is needed on development after the teenage years and on desistance. The comorbidity of antisocial behavior is marked, but more research is needed on developmental sequences and pathways.

A great deal is known about risk factors for antisocial behavior, but less is known about its causes. More analyses of within-individual changes and more experiments are required to throw light on these causes. More research is needed on interaction effects and especially on protective factors. No current theory is sufficiently wide ranging to explain all the discoveries about the development of antisocial behavior made in the last 20 years. In particular, theories of the development of antisocial individuals need to be integrated with theories of the occurrence of antisocial acts.

To advance knowledge further, new prospective longitudinal studies need to be mounted, and existing studies need to be continued in the adult years. New studies should aim to measure a wide range of risk factors from different sources at frequent intervals, including biological, individual, family, peer, school, and neighborhood influences. More efforts should be made to design longitudinal studies so that implications can be drawn from them about interventions, and more efforts should be made to draw implications about interventions from existing and past longitudinal studies. With more of these kinds of efforts, future longitudinal studies could make an even greater contribution to the reduction of many different types of antisocial behavior.

REFERENCES

Amdur, R. L. (1989). Testing causal models of delinquency: A methodological critique. *Criminal Justice and Behavior, 16,* 35–62.

American Psychiatric Association. (1994) *Diagnostic and statistical manual of mental disorders* (4th ed.). Washington, DC: Author.

Earls, F. J., & Reiss, A. J. (1994). *Breaking the cycle: Predicting and preventing crime.* Washington, DC: National Institute of Justice.

Elliott, D. S., Huizinga, D., & Menard, S. (1989) *Multiple problem youth.* New York: Springer-Verlag.

Farrington, D. P. (1979). Environmental stress, delinquent behavior, and convictions. In I. G. Sarason & C. D. Spielberger (Eds.), *Stress and anxiety* (Vol. 6, pp. 93–107). Washington, DC: Hemisphere.

Farrington, D. P. (1986). Stepping stones to adult criminal careers. In D. Olweus, J. Block, & M. R. Yarrow (Eds.), *Development of antisocial and prosocial behavior* (pp. 359–384). New York: Academic Press.

Farrington, D. P. (1988). Studying changes within individuals: The causes of offending. In M. Rutter (Ed.), *Studies of psychosocial risk* (pp. 158–183). Cambridge: Cambridge University Press.

Farrington, D. P. (1990a). Age, period, cohort, and offending. In D. M. Gottfredson & R. V. Clarke (Eds.) *Policy and theory in criminal justice: Contributions in honor of Leslie T. Wilkins* (pp. 51–75). Aldershot: Avebury.

Farrington, D. P. (1990b). Implications of criminal career research for the prevention of offending. *Journal of Adolescence, 13,* 93–113.

Farrington, D. P. (1991). Antisocial personality from childhood to adulthood. *The Psychologist, 4,* 389–394.

Farrington, D. P. (1993a). Childhood origins of teenage antisocial behavior and adult social dysfunction. *Journal of the Royal Society of Medicine, 86,* 13–17.

Farrington, D. P. (1993b). Understanding and preventing bullying. In M. Tonry (Ed.), *Crime and justice* (Vol. 17, pp. 381–458). Chicago: University of Chicago Press.

Farrington, D. P. (1995a). Key issues in the integration of motivational and opportunity-reducing crime prevention strategies. In P.-O. H. Wikström, R. V. Clarke, & J. McCord (Eds.), *Integrating crime prevention strategies: Propensity and opportunity* (pp. 333–357). Stockholm: National Council for Crime Prevention.

Farrington, D. P. (1995b). The development of offending and antisocial behavior from childhood: Key findings from the Cambridge study in delinquent development. *Journal of Child Psychology and Psychiatry, 36,* 929–964.

Farrington, D. P., Barnes, G., & Lambert, S. (1996). The concentration of offending in families. *Legal and Criminological Psychology, 1,* 47–63.

Farrington, D. P., & Hawkins, J. D. (1991). Predicting participation, early onset, and later persistence in officially recorded offending. *Criminal Behavior and Mental Health, 1,* 1–33.

Farrington, D. P., & Loeber, R. (1989). Relative improvement over chance (RIOC) and Phi as measures of predictive efficiency and strength of association in 2 x 2 tables. *Journal of Quantitative Criminology, 5,* 201–213.

Farrington, D. P., Ohlin, L. E., & Wilson, J. Q. (1986). *Understanding and controlling crime.* New York: Springer-Verlag.

Farrington, D. P., & West, D. J. (1995). Effects of marriage, separation and children on offending by adult males. In J. Hagan (Ed.), *Current perspectives on aging and the life cycle: Vol. 4. Delinquency and disrepute in the life course* (pp. 249–281). Greenwich, CT: JAI Press.

Huizinga, D., Loeber, R., & Thornberry, T. P. (1993). Longitudinal study of delinquency, drug use, sexual activity, and pregnancy among children and youth in three cities. *Public Health Reports, 108,* 90–96.

Kagan, J. (1988) Temperamental contributions to social behavior. *American Psychologist, 44,* 668–674.

Loeber, R., Stouthamer-Loeber, M., Van Kammen, W. B., & Farrington, D. P. (1991). Initiation, escalation and desistance in juvenile offending and their correlates. *Journal of Criminal Law and Criminology, 82,* 36–82.

Moffitt, T. E. (1993). Adolescence-limited and life-course-persistent antisocial behavior: A developmental taxonomy. *Psychological Review, 100,* 674–701.

Nagin, D. S., & Farrington, D. P. (1992a). The onset and persistence of offending. *Criminology, 30,* 501–523.

Nagin, D. S., & Farrington, D. P. (1992b) The stability of criminal potential from childhood to adulthood. *Criminology, 30,* 235–260.

Nagin, D. S., Farrington, D. P., & Moffitt, T. E. (1995) Life-course trajectories of different types of offenders. *Criminology, 33,* 111–139.

Patterson, G. R., De Baryshe, B. D., & Ramsey, E. (1989). A developmental perspective on antisocial behavior. *American Psychologist, 44,* 329–335.

Reiss, A. J., & Farrington, D. P. (1991). Advancing knowledge about co-offending: Results from a prospective longitudinal survey of London males. *Journal of Criminal Law and Criminology, 82,* 360–395.

Robins, L. N. (1979) Sturdy childhood predictors of adult outcomes: Replications from longitudinal studies. In J. E. Barrett, R. M. Rose, & G. L. Klerman (Eds.), *Stress and mental disorder* (pp. 219–235). New York: Raven Press.

Robins, L. N. (1986). Changes in conduct disorder over time. In D. C. Farran & J. D. McKinney (Eds.), *Risk in intellectual and social development* (pp. 227–259). New York: Academic Press.

Robins, L. N., & Ratcliff, K. S. (1978). Risk factors in the continuation of childhood antisocial behavior into adulthood. *International Journal of Mental Health, 7,* 96–116.

Rutter, M. (1985). Resilience in the face of adversity: Protective factors and resistance to psychiatric disorder. *British Journal of Psychiatry, 147,* 598–611.

Tonry, M., Ohlin, L. E., & Farrington, D. P. (1991). *Human development and criminal behavior: New ways of advancing knowledge.* New York: Springer-Verlag.

Vehulst, F. C., & Van der Ende, J. (1995). The eight-year stability of problem behavior in an epidemiologic sample. *Paediatric Research, 38,* 612–617.

West, D. J., & Farrington, D. P. (1977). *The delinquent way of life.* London: Heinemann.

Zoccolillo, M., Pickles, A., Quinton, D., & Rutter, M. (1992). The outcome of childhood conduct disorder: Implications for defining adult personality disorder and conduct disorder. *Psychological Medicine, 22,* 971–986.

PART THREE

Biology of Antisocial Behavior

CHAPTER 23

The Genetics of Antisocial Behavior

GREGORY CAREY and DAVID GOLDMAN

In this chapter, we discuss the important contributions from genetic epidemiology and molecular genetics to the understanding of antisocial behavior. The chapter is divided into four parts. The first part is an overview of the methods for examining the genetics of antisocial behavior. The second part examines the empirical data on the genetic epidemiology of antisocial behavior. The third part is an overview of the current molecular genetic data on the topic; and the fourth examines future directions for research in the area of genetic epidemiology.

METHODS IN GENETIC EPIDEMIOLOGY

Background

The fact that some trait runs in families is often used to implicate genetics. However, family studies cannot be used with antisocial behavior to justify the role of genetics (or lack of it). First, many potential family environmental factors can make siblings or other relatives similar for antisocial behavior; for example, single-parent households, poverty, housing density, and other neighborhood characteristics. Second, short-term changes in aggression can be induced in the laboratory through social learning mechanisms (Bandura & Walters, 1959), raising the possibility that modeling the aggression of other family members induces familial similarity. Hence, it is imperative that studies of twins, separated relatives, and adoptive relatives be used to distinguish the influence of family environment from genes.

Twin Method

The twin method is intuitive. Monozygotic (MZ), or identical, twins are effectively genetic clones, sharing all of their genes. Dizygotic (DZ), or fraternal, twins share only half of their genes on average. Hence, if genes play an important role, then MZ twin

pairs will tend to have more similar behavior than DZ twin pairs. Let γ denote the actual correlation for the genotypes of twins, $\gamma = 1.0$ for MZ pairs and around .50 for DZ pairs. The exact value of the correlation for DZ twins depends on the relative strengths of assortative mating, which will increase the correlation, and nonadditive genetic variance, which will decrease it.

For the environmental, let η denote the correlation between the environments of the twins. For twins raised apart, η will be close to 0. For twins raised together, the value of η will depend on the extent to which the similar environments of the twins produce similar antisocial behavior. Note that these environments are *trait relevant*. Twins may be perfectly correlated for many environments such as astrological sign, but unless those environments influence individual differences in antisocial behavior, they will not enter into this mathematical model. If h is the correlation between the genotype and the phenotype (i.e., the observed trait) and e is the correlation between the environment and the phenotype, then the correlation for a specific type of twin will equal $\gamma h^2 + \eta e^2$. By letting $\gamma = 1$ for MZ twins but $\gamma = .50$ for DZ pairs, one can then solve for the quantities h^2, e^2, and η to arrive at the heritability (the proportion of observed variance attributable to genetic variance) and environmentability (the proportion of variance attributable to the environment).

The central assumption of the twin method is that the η for MZ twins equals (or at least is very close to) the η for DZ twins. For several reasons, this assumption may be questioned for antisocial behavior. First, MZ twins tend to spend more time together and share more similar peer groups than DZ twins (Loehlin & Nichols, 1976). Spending more time together permits MZ twins to imitate each other more than DZ twins, and indeed, there is some evidence suggesting that this is the case for antisocial behavior (Carey, 1992). Sharing peer groups could increase MZ similarity relative to DZ similarity, depending on such factors as the extent to which peers influence antisocial behavior in the twins and the mechanisms that get twins into similar peer groups in the first place. The empirical evidence on this assumption as it influences antisocial behavior is reviewed later in this chapter. The bottom line is that the assumption is probably violated, but the violations are not so extreme as to seriously compromise the validity of the twin method.

This research was supported in part by a NIDA grant DA-05131 and by an IMPART grant from the University of Colorado.

The Adoption Method

The study of fostered and separated relatives most often has used the formal adoption design. Here, antisocial behavior in adoptees is correlated with that of their biological relatives (who share genes but not environment) and that of adoptive relatives (who share environments but not genes). Correlations with biological relatives suggest genetic influences whereas those with adoptive relatives suggest important family environmental influences.

Critics of genetic research often point out that selective placement is a critical assumption in this design (e.g., Lewontin, Rose, & Kamin, 1984). In selective placement, adoptees whose biological parents have certain attributes are placed with adoptive parents who have similar attributes. Actually, the extent to which this process may compromise the design depends on the relative strengths of genetic versus family environmental transmission. If family environmental effects are much larger than genetic effects, selective placement will result in (a) a large correlation with adoptive relatives, (b) a more modest correlation with biological relatives, and (c) overestimation of any genetic effects. On the other hand, if genetic transmission is much stronger than family environmental transmission, then (a) correlations with biological parents will be large, (b) correlations with adoptive relatives will be modest, and (c) the magnitude of family environment will be overestimated.

With respect to antisocial behavior, a more critical assumption of the adoption design is the representativeness of adoptive families. Many negative parental attributes associated with an offspring's antisocial behavior—for example, parental alcoholism, drug abuse, felony convictions, extreme poverty, child abuse—disqualify couples from becoming adoptive parents in the first place. Consequently, the adoption design may not adequately assess the influence of family environment, particularly if the effect is nonlinear, with its major impact at the antisocial tail of the distribution of family environments.

Empirical Literature in Genetic Epidemiology

The literature on twins and adoption has been extensively reviewed elsewhere in recent publications (Carey, 1994b, 1996; Gottesman & Goldsmith, 1994; Goldsmith & Gottesman, 1996). Tables 23.1 and 23.2, taken from Carey (1996) present the references to the primary literature on, respectively, twins and adoptees. Here, we highlight the results and refer the reader to the original reviews and the primary sources for details about sampling, measures, analyses, and the like. The major results of the literature are as follows:

1. As evidenced in Tables 23.1 and 23.2, the literature is very consistent in showing that identical twins are more similar than fraternal twins and that adoptees correlate with their biological relatives. This happens for multiple definitions of antisocial behavior. The phenotype may be defined narrowly as a conviction for a felony or more broadly as symptom counts for antisocial personality disorder, self-reported delinquency, or personality scales of hostility or aggression.

2. Violations of the assumptions of the twin method and the adoption strategy are not sufficiently large to account for the pattern in Table 23.1. Twin imitation may occur for deviant, antisocial behavior. Accounting for this imitation effect lowers estimates of heritability but does not make them disappear (Carey, 1992). Twins raised apart (Grove et al., 1990, in Table 23.1) still show significant similarity for symptoms counts of antisocial personality disorder (ASPD) despite the lack of opportunity for personal interaction. Strong selective placement would predict a very large correlation between adoptive relatives and offspring with a weaker correlation between adoptee and biological relatives. Exactly the opposite pattern is found in the observed correlations (see Baker, 1986; Baker et al., 1989; Mednick et al., 1984). A telling analysis (Miles & Carey, 1997) was performed for the Socialization scale of the California Psychological Inventory (CPI), a strong predictor of involvement in delinquency. Sufficient data were available on this scale for twins

TABLE 23.1 Synopsis of Modern Twin Studies of Antisocial Behavior

Twin Population	Phenotype	References	Evidence for a Genetic Effect?
Norwegian adults	Registered and self-reported criminal acts	Dalgard & Kringlen, 1976	No
U.S. teenagers	Self-reported delinquent acts	Rowe, 1983, 1985, 1986	Yes
Danish adults	Registered criminal acts or convictions	Christiansen, 1968, 1970, 1974; Cloninger et al., 1978; Gottesman, Carey, & Hansen, 1983; Cloninger & Gottesman, 1987; Carey, 1992	Yes
Largely U.S. and UK adults raised apart	Count of DIS[a] antisocial personality disorder symptoms	Grove et al., 1990	Yes
Children/teenagers	Symptoms of conduct disorder	Eaves et al., 1993	Yes
Adult veterans	Count of DIS[a] antisocial personality disorder symptoms	Lyons et al., 1993, 1995, 1996	Yes
Adult psychiatric patients	Count of DIS[a] antisocial personality symptoms	Carey, 1993	Yes

[a]DIS = Diagnostic Interview Schedule.

TABLE 23.2   Modern Adoption Studies of Antisocial Behavior

Twin Population	Phenotype	References	Genetic Effect?
Offspring of U.S. female felons	Records and self-reports of arrests and convictions	Crowe, 1972, 1974	Yes
Danish adults	Police and court registrations	Hutchings, 1972; Hutchings & Mednick, 1971, 1975	Yes
U.S. children	Conduct disorder symptoms	Cadoret, 1978; Cadoret, Cunningham, Loftus, & Edwards, 1975	Yes
U.S. teenagers & young	Symptoms of antisocial personality	Cadoret & Cain, 1980; Cadoret et al., 1983, 1985, 1986, 1995	Yes
Swedish adults	Arrest and court records	Bohman, 1978, 1983; Bohman, Cloninger, Sigvardsson, & von Knorring, 1982; Bohman et al., 1984; Cloninger, Sigvardsson, Bohman, & von Knorring, 1982; Sigvardsson et al. (1982)	Partly
Danish adults[a]	Court convictions	Mednick & Finello, 1983; Mednick, Brennan, & Kandel, 1988; Mednick, Gabrielli, & Hutchings, 1984; Mednick et al., 1983, 1987; Gabrielli & Mednick, 1983, 1984; Mednick, 1987; Baker, 1986; Moffitt, 1987; Baker, Mack, Moffitt, & Mednick, 1989	Yes

[a]Partly overlaps with the sample of Danish adults given previously.

raised apart, twins raised together, and adoptive families to permit rigorous tests of the violation of these assumptions. The effect of allowing the selective placement correlation to take the unrealistically high value of 1.0 and allowing the environments of twins raised apart to be as similar as those of siblings raised in the same household was to lower the heritability estimate from about .42 to .40. Consequently, the consistent pattern found in Tables 23.1 and 23.2 implicates some genetic involvement in antisocial behavior.

3. All the data implicate the environment. The best evidence for this is that correlations and concordance for identical twins are lower than unity even when measurement error is taken into account. Unfortunately, most of the "clinical" measures of antisocial behavior have not assessed reliability; however, the personality measures have. The internal consistency and repeatability reliabilities for the Aggression scale of Tellegen's Multidimensional Personality Questionnaire (Tellegen, 1985) would place an upper limit for the identical twin correlation at about .80. The observed correlations for identical twins are .46 (raised apart) and .43 (raised together; Tellegen et al., 1988). Similar patterns occur for both the CPI and the Minnesota Multiphasic Personality Inventory (MMPI). Hence, somewhere around 40% to 50% of the valid variance in these measures must be environmental. This highlights the sterility of the nature versus nurture debate and shifts the research perspective into examining the interplay of nature and nurture in the development of individual differences (Gottesman & Goldsmith, 1994; Plomin, Owen, & McGuffin, 1994).

4. A consistent pattern for common environment is stronger among adolescents than among adults. This suggests that some social causal factors may assist the initiation of antisocial behavior but not its persistence. The nature of such factors must await the appropriate longitudinal study of genetically informative individuals.

5. The existing evidence suggests genetic involvement in the comorbidity between antisocial behavior, alcohol abuse/dependence, and other substance abuse/dependence (Carey, 1993). Few studies have looked simultaneously at these phenotypes, but those that did report positive correlations among the genetic liabilities. At the present time, it is premature to speculate about the magnitude of these influences. Indeed, one of the major areas for future research should be multivariate analyses of these phenotypes.

6. Evidence for the heritability of violent behavior (assault, robbery, rape, homicide) is much less consistent than the evidence for heritability of general deviant and antisocial behavior. Only three studies (the Danish twins, Danish adoptees, and Swedish adoptees) report on violent crime per se. One (Mednick et al., 1984, 1988) reports no resemblance between adoptees and biological relatives. The second (Cloninger & Gottesman, 1987) reports a nonsignificant trend for identical twins to be more similar than fraternal twins. And the third (Bohman et al., 1982) does not apparently find a significant effect for violence but does report a significant genetic correlation between violent offenses in a biological father and alcohol abuse in his adopted-away offspring. The reason for this lack of clarity is unknown but may involve two factors. The first is simply the low base rate for violent offending among Scandinavian populations, making it difficult to fill cells and achieve satisfactory statistical power. The second is the substantive possibility that heritability for violence, in fact, is low in these populations. Criminals who specialize in violence are actually very rare (Blumstein, Cohen, Roth, & Visher, 1986). The general pattern is for violence to occur sporadically and unpredictably within a career of more general deviant behavior. If the major impact of the genetic contribution is toward generalized deviant behavior, then the heritability of violence will equal the heritability of this generalized tendency multiplied by the square of the correlation between this general tendency and violence. If the former statistic is .50 and the latter is .60, then

the heritability of violence will be .50 x .36 = .18. Whatever the reason, future multivariate genetic research is required to unravel the possible causal connections among the various aspects of deviant behavior, especially violence.

7. Although the existing data provide strong evidence implicating DNA, they must be interpreted cautiously with respect to a common family environment. The twin studies produce indirect estimates of a common environment. However, if there is any nonadditive genetic action—and there probably is some—then the twin method can underestimate the influence of a common environment. The adoption strategy can provide direct estimates of a common environment but may not generate accurate ones in the case of antisocial behavior. The litany of familial correlates of deviant behavior—single-parent households, school dropout, strong poverty, parental criminality, parental alcohol and drug abuse—will exclude these families from becoming adoptive parents. Hence, the adoptive families are "missing" the lower tail of the distribution. The effect of this censoring is unknown, but it may be large, especially when there is a nonlinear relationship between family environment and deviancy.

8. Strong caution must be exercised in extrapolating from the existing literature to other populations. The large, epidemiological populations of Tables 23.1 and 23.2 are all Scandinavian, one of them (the Danish twins) being a cohort born between 1880 and 1910. The literature in the United States, although generally consistent with that in Scandinavia, has much smaller sample sizes or more specialized populations. A large, representative sample from the United States that includes the entire range of environments, from urban to suburban to rural, may arrive at different estimates of heritability and common environment than the Scandinavian studies. A further cause for caution is the well-established secular trends that occur over time for crime. Wilson and Herrnstein (1985) have argued that these occur much too abruptly and much too strongly to be attributed to genetic mechanisms such as natural selection. The interplay between these social trends and genes has never been studied. The most egregious error of extrapolation occurs when the data on within-group heritability is applied to mean differences among ethnic groups. Some of the existing studies may have included minorities, but simply no data have been published on the heritability of antisocial behavior among any ethnic group other than Whites. Furthermore, a basic precept of genetics is that heritability *within* groups does not imply that mean differences *between* groups are heritable. Hence, even if there were heritability within both White and non-White populations in America, then it could not be concluded that mean differences between white and non-White groups are heritable.

MOLECULAR GENETIC METHODS

The heritability of antisocial and aggressive traits, in both humans and other animals, implies that naturally occurring variants (alleles) of genes contribute to differences in brain physiology, development, or whatever. Recent, dramatic advances in molecular genetics now offer the possibility that individual genes contributing to antisocial behavior may be identified. The two major strategies used with molecular genetics are the linkage design and the association design.

The Linkage Strategy

The purpose of linkage is to *locate* the gene(s) for a trait somewhere among the 22 autosomal chromosomes and the two sex chromosomes. Loci that are close together on a chromosome segregate together. That is, they are almost always inherited as a single unit. Linkage analysis capitalizes on this by starting with a marker locus with a known location on the chromosomes and then tracing the cosegregation of the trait locus with this marker locus throughout pedigrees. If the marker is inherited independent of the trait, then the trait is not located near that marker. In this case, there will be no regularity between the marker genotype and the trait genotype in a pedigree. On the other hand, if the trait locus is physically linked to the marker, then both marker and trait locus will be "coinherited." That is, those individuals within the pedigree who show the trait should also tend to have the same marker allele.

The main advantage of this approach is that, at present, it is the only comprehensive approach for sieving the *entire* genome. Genetic linkage does not depend on the previous identification of a gene or knowledge of the physiology affecting the trait, so highly informative panels of genetic markers spanning all of the chromosomes can be typed. If a hint of linkage is found within an area, then the panel of genetic markers within that area is examined until, ideally, the gene is found.

The major complication for linkage strategies lies less in genetics per se than in the problems generated from phenotypes such as antisocial behavior. The major successes of linkage have been for cleanly diagnosed disorders in two areas: where the epidemiology and mode of transmission were well established before linkage analysis was conducted, and for complex disorders in which only loaded pedigrees were analyzed. Antisocial behavior differs from these phenotypes in several important ways. First, although conventions such as *DSM-IV* treat antisocial behavior in a dichotomous way, it is uncertain that diagnoses of antisocial personality disorder can be characterized as a "cleanly diagnosed disorder" or as the tail end of a continuous distribution.

Second, even if it turns out to be a dichotomous entity, it is uncertain whether the current criteria select the optimal cutoff point for diagnosing it. False negative diagnostic errors can be accommodated in linkage analysis by reducing penetrance (the probability that an individual with the susceptible genotype[s] actually develops the disorder). False positive errors, on the other hand, can greatly compromise linkage analysis, particularly if they are made on key members of a pedigree.

Third, if the phenotype is indeed continuous, then linkage must focus on detecting a quantitative trait locus (QTL); general programs for this type of analysis in humans have been available for some time (e.g., the Pedigree Analysis Package, PAP; LINKAGE; and Fastlink). The difficulty with these algorithms, however, is that it is still uncertain exactly how the family environment operates in antisocial behavior. For example, the effects of family environmental heterogeneity have not been explored. Finally, and most important, the number of loci that contribute to antisocial behavior is unknown. Current estimates of power for QTL linkage suggest that the probability of detecting a major locus that contributes to less than 10% of the phenotypic variance is remote (Carey & Williamson, 1991; Risch

& Zhang, 1995). Hence, there may be insufficient power in the linkage strategy to detect loci of small effect.

The Association Design

For these reasons, there has been increasing enthusiasm for a second approach in molecular genetics, the association study. In the association study, one begins with a gene that has a theoretical possibility of causing individual differences in the central nervous system (e.g., a gene for a serotonin receptor). If there is a polymorphism very close to this gene (or preferably a polymorphism in the gene itself), then one genotypes individuals on that polymorphism and tests whether differences in genotype are associated with differences in phenotype. For example, are there differences in aggression or antisocial behavior among genotypes *AA, Aa,* and *aa?*

A special and important type of association study is *direct gene analysis.* This strategy identifies DNA variations (alleles) responsible for the alteration in function or level of expression of the gene product that ultimately may be correlated with phenotypic differences. This task involves either sequencing the gene or using some other method, most often denaturing gradient gel electrophoresis (DGGE) or single-strand conformational polymorphism (SSCP) analysis, which efficiently detect variants of the DNA sequence. Direct gene analysis may be performed subsequent to the discovery of a genetic linkage. More often, it is used to evaluate genes thought to be involved in the biochemical physiology of a trait. The advantage of the direct gene analysis approach is its power to identify variant alleles even when these are very rare—even in only one individual—and it is a necessary last step in relating an inherited effect on behavior to a difference in the sequence of the DNA.

There are two advantages of the general strategy. The first is statistical power. Under favorable circumstances, an association design can detect loci that contribute to only 1% or 2% of the phenotypic variance. The second advantage is that a positive association gives some insight into the nature of the neurobiological mechanisms contributing to the behavior.

The two major disadvantages for the association design have been discussed by Crowe (1993) and Kidd (1993). The first problem is that population stratification can produce true statistical associations that are not causal. In the United States, there is a true association between sickle cell anemia and genes for skin pigmentation, but the pigmentation genes play no causal role in the disorder. Darker skin pigmentation simply occurs in high frequencies among those Old World populations in which malaria had high frequency and the sickling allele increased in frequency because it conferred resistance to that disease.

Within-family strategies (Falk & Rubinstein, 1987) can overcome the problem of population strategy, although they require additional effort to gather the informative families. This strategy generally uses a sibling as a control. For example, consider a large number of families in which the parental genotypes are *Aa* and *aa.* If the *Aa* offspring of these families are more antisocial than the *aa* offspring, then allele *A* (or another locus very close to that gene) contributes to the antisocial behavior.

The second disadvantage of the association design is simply the number of potential loci that might be analyzed. The number of genes expressed in the mammalian central nervous system is enormous, numbering in the tens of thousands. Testing large numbers of candidate genes will result in many false positive results. Although sometimes statistical techniques can remedy this (Carey, 1994a), the trade-off is that loci must have larger and larger effect sizes to be detected.

Empirical Data on the Molecular Genetics of Aggression and Antisocial Behavior

Because of the many behavioral contexts in which aggressive and antisocial behaviors arise and the diversity of neuromolecular mechanisms in these behaviors, we anticipate that numerous alleles will be identified to influence aggressive behaviors. The implication is that the level of genetic heterogeneity may be high and the predictive power of a single gene that eventually will be identified generally may be low. Therefore, the main values of molecular genetic research in aggression are (a) understanding the diversity of human behavioral variation, which is part of our human individuality; (b) improving knowledge of mechanisms in normal and pathological behavior; (c) developing better interventions for pathological behavior; (d) refining diagnostic precision so that therapy can be individualized or, where useless, avoided; and (e) identifying environmental influences that currently are masked by the genetic variation.

Several alleles associated with aggressive behavior have been identified at the level of the DNA sequence. These gene variants differ by large margins in their frequencies in populations, in the extent to which their presence is predictive of behavior, and in the mechanisms of their effects. Aggression is a complex and difficult to define phenotype. Therefore, it should not be surprising that the behaviors perturbed by the different alleles discussed next are diverse. The reader may choose to view any or all of the alleles described as only secondarily relating to aggression. Aggression alleles per se (in other words, influencing aggression but nothing else) may not exist. In the discussion that follows, some attempt is made to distinguish findings that are tentative from ones that are secure and to describe some of the main techniques being used in this area.

Aldehyde Dehydrogenase

A strong correlation has been found between antisocial behavior and alcohol problems. One half or more of violent acts, including domestic violence and vehicular homicide, are carried out under the influence of alcohol (Miczek, Haney, Tidey, Vivian, & Weerts, 1994). Hence, a gene that influences alcohol abuse or dependence is a ripe candidate for antisocial behavior. One allele known to influence alcoholism is the aldehyde dehydrogenase 2 (ALDH2[2]) allele.

The ALDH enzyme is involved in the second step in the metabolism of alcohol, namely, the conversion of acetaldehyde to acetate. The ALDH2[2] allele is a glutamate487lysine substitution found at high frequency in East Asian populations, for example, in approximately one half of Japanese (Tu & Israel, 1995; Yoshida, Huang, & Ikawa, 1984). ALDH2[2] is rare in other racial groups including Whites, Blacks, and the Native Americans tested to date. As a result of the deficiency, following ingestion of alcohol there is a buildup of acetaldehyde followed by an uncomfortable flushing response. ALDH2[2] acts dominantly so that individuals who carry one copy of this allele are deficient in the enzyme activity and show a 4- to 10-fold reduction in vulnerability to alcoholism. No data have yet been reported on the antisocial behavior of individuals with the ALDH2² allele, so its association with aggression and antisocial behavior remains undemonstrated.

Thyroid Hormone Receptor

Children with attention deficit/hyperactivity disorder (ADHD) are at increased risk for a variety of future difficulties, including criminal behavior and diagnoses of conduct disorder (CD) and antisocial personality disorder (ASPD). Hauser et al. (1993) observed that approximately one third of children with inherited deficiency of thyroid hormone receptor function had ADHD. A large number of thyroid hormone receptor mutations have been detected; each is uncommon, and the majority so far have been observed only in one family. Once again, the thyroid hormone receptor is a viable candidate for an association study, but the relevant empirical data for CD and ASPD have not been reported.

Monoamine Oxidase A

Monoamine oxidases (MAO) A and B metabolize monoamine neurotransmitters such as serotonin, norepinephrine, and dopamine. Although the action of these neurotransmitters in the synaptic cleft is terminated by their reuptake by specific transporters, MAO still plays an important role in neurotransmission as witnessed by the fact that several MAO inhibitors are potent antidepressant drugs. Further, the administration of monoamine neurotransmitters or the stimulation of their release in the face of MAO inhibition can be fatal.

Brunner and colleagues studied a Dutch family in which six males were identified as having a behavioral syndrome marked by impulsive and aggressive tendencies. Psychiatric interviews were not performed; however, behaviors that were recorded included arson and indecent exposure, although apparently only one of the males had actually been arrested. Using the genetic linkage approach, Brunner and colleagues (Brunner, Nelen, Breakfield, Ropers, & Van Oost, 1993; Brunner, Nelen, van Zandvoort et al., 1993) mapped a locus for this syndrome to the region of the X chromosome, which contains MAOA and MAOB. Identification of a locus on the X chromosome explained the preponderance of affected males in this family. Levels of MAOB, the monoamine oxidase found in both brain and platelets, were normal in platelets. However, a stop codon mutation (which prematurely truncates the amino acid sequence and renders inactive the MAOA enzyme) was discovered. MAOA is found in brain serotonin neurons. Abnormalities of monoamine metabolite levels both in the urine and in the cerebrospinal fluid were observed in several of these males so that, in a sense, the loop of causation—from variant gene to inactive enzyme to altered neurotransmitter metabolism to altered behavior—was closed. However, it is unclear why slowing the metabolism of serotonin or dopamine could lead to impulsive behavior. In addition, another pedigree with Brunner's syndrome has yet to be reported.

Hypoxanthine Guanine Ribosyl Transferase (HPRT)

Purines are required for a variety of purposes, including DNA and RNA synthesis, the regulation of signaling proteins, neurotrans-

mission, cellular energy transfer, and as cofactors for many enzymes and in phosphorylation. HPRT ordinarily salvages hypoxanthine and guanine so that the need for de novo purine synthesis is reduced. A series of rare HPRT variants produce the Lesch-Nyhan syndrome, which is characterized by self-mutilation, mental retardation, spasticity, and hyperuricemia. All of the variants that cause the syndrome nearly inactivate HPRT. The exact mechanism by which the self-mutilation is produced is unknown.

Proposed Genetic Linkages and Associations

As a result of its role in reinforcement and activation, the neurotransmitter dopamine could be subject to genetic variation influencing impulsivity and aggression. At the DRD4 dopamine receptor gene are at least four structural polymorphisms that could have functional relevance and therefore could directly affect the phenotype. Thus far, none is known to do so. A 16 amino acid domain within the third exon is repeated from 2 to 10 times (Lichter et al., 1993) and an amino acid substitution has also been observed in this exon (Seeman et al., 1994). The seven repeat allele of the 16 amino acid domain may have a modest effect on ligand affinity (Asghari et al., 1994; Van Tol et al., 1992). The first exon contains two deletion polymorphisms, 1 of 12 base pain (bp) (Catalano, Nobile, Novelli, Nothen, & Smeraldi, 1993) and the other of 13 bp (Nothen et al., 1994).

The personality construct of sensation seeking or thrill seeking often has been associated with sociopathy (Lykken, 1995). One study (Ebstein et al., 1996) detected an association of the DRD4 seven repeat allele to the Novelty Seeking scale of the Tridimensional Personality Questionnaire (TPQ), and a second group (Benjamin, Patterson, Greenberg, Murphy, & Hamer, 1996) reported on a population association and sib-pair linkage to similar scales of the NEO Personality Inventory (Costa & McCrae, 1985). Although these are promising leads, it is puzzling that a population of alcoholic Finnish offenders, many of whom were highly impulsive, showed no increase in frequency of the allele as compared to psychiatrically interviewed Finnish controls. Another recent study (Pogue-Geile, Ferrell, Deka, Debeski, & Masnuck, 1996) has failed to find an association. A study that raises serious questions about the subtle phenotypic effects of DRD4 repeat alleles on the phenotype is the description of a male who is homozygous for a 3′ deletion, which disrupts the reading frame of the mRNA leading to a truncated, nonfunctional receptor. The subject is moderately obese but not psychiatrically ill (Nothen et al., 1994).

The DRD2 dopamine receptor contains three uncommon or relatively rare polymorphisms, which involve amino acid substitutions. The Cys311 substitution, which has an allele frequency of 3% in Whites, may be deficient in signal transduction. Cys311 and the DRD2 amino acid substitutions are unassociated with schizophrenia or alcoholism and otherwise their possible effect on the behavioral phenotype has scarcely been investigated. However, a great deal of attention has been focused on the Taq1A RFLP, whose site is approximately 10 kilobases downstream from the DRD2 gene. That RFLP has been associated, but not linked in families, to a variety of conditions: alcoholism, smoking, obesity. Six years subsequent to the original association of the Taq1A polymorphism to alcoholism, there have been numerous substantial failures to replicate it, large population differences that could mask or create the association have been identified, and the abundant functional variant with which the Taq1A marker would have to be in strong disequilibrium remains undetected (Goldman et al., 1993, and elsewhere).

Serotonin is a neurotransmitter widely thought to be involved in impulse control and aggression. Lower concentrations of the serotonin metabolite 5-HIAA have been observed in the brain and cerebrospinal fluid of impulsive individuals, particularly suicide attempters (Asberg, Traskman, & Thoren, 1976) but also impulsive violent individuals (Linnoila, Verkonnen, & Scheinin, 1983), and these findings have been replicated extensively (as reviewed, Roy & Linnoila, 1990). Lower 5-HIAA concentrations are thought to reflect lower turnover and release of serotonin. In primates, variation in 5-HIAA concentration can be environmentally induced, for example, by changes in social status. The variation also is in part genetically determined. One heritability study carried out in Rhesus macaque monkeys detected a heritability of >50% for CSF 5-HIAA levels (Higley et al., 1993). Tryptophan hydroxylase is rate limiting for serotonin synthesis and thus is one candidate gene for inherited influences on serotonin function. A polymorphism within intron seven was found to be associated with history of suicide attempts and low cerebrospinal fluid 5-HIAA (Nielsen et al., 1993). A more recent study on TPH and suicide found no association (Abbar et al., 1995), but a different marker was used and the subjects were apparently much less impulsive (Nielsen et al., 1993). The salient observation is that no functionally significant TPH polymorphisms are known.

Upward of 16 serotonin receptors have been identified and the serotonin transporter has been cloned. Naturally occurring structural variants of several serotonin receptors and the transporter have been identified (reviewed by Goldman, Lappalainen, & Ozaki, in press), and it is likely that certain variants eventually will be identified that influence irritable aggression. For example, increased platelet 5HT2A receptor binding has been observed in suicide attempters (Marazziti, 1989; Simonsson et al., 1991); the prolactin response to fenfluramine challenge was seen to be diminished in suicide attempters (Coccaro et al., 1989); reduced 5HT uptake sites in postmortem brain was reported in some studies (Stanley et al., 1982); and increased 5-HT2 density was reported among violent suicides (Arora & Meltzer, 1989), although results were inconsistent (Lowther et al., 1994).

Activation of the 5HT1A receptor is effective in reversing aggression in serotonin-depleted rats. Two uncommon amino acid substitutions of the 5HT1A receptor have been identified (Nakhai et al., 1995), and one of these appears to affect the ability of the receptor to be down regulated by the ligand 8-OHDPAT (Rotondo et al., unpublished). Both 5HT1B (5HT1Db) and 5HT2C knockout mice are aggressive. For 5HT2C, a rather common cys23ser variant is known (Lappalaien et al., 1995). Because 5HT2C is encoded by a gene on the X chromosome and the frequency of 23Ser is 0.13, 13% of males are homozygous for the 23Ser, which may alter the affinity of the receptor for larger ligands such as MCPP. Thus far, none of these variants has been found to have any definite role in human behavior.

In conclusion, it can be seen that the combination of genetic linkage and association, especially direct gene analysis, is still in its infancy. Twin studies of antisocial behavior were initiated early in this century, and it took decades before a clear picture of the genetic epidemiology emerged. Many excellent candidate genes are available for study, but as with genetic epidemiology, it may take many years of data collection before the results can be written into textbooks.

DIRECTIONS FOR FUTURE RESEARCH

The current state of genetic-epidemiological research on deviant behavior parallels that for behavioral genetic research in general and points to two major conclusions. First, almost all behavior is influenced in some way by genes; the magnitude of this influence may vary from one trait to another, but generally it is in the moderate range, explaining about 40% of variance (Loehlin & Nichols, 1976; Plomin et al., 1994). Second, *all* human behavior has an important environmental component. Consequently, future research will be uninformative if it persists in asking, "Is there a genetic influence on antisocial behavior?" Instead, research will be more focused on identifying mechanisms for the genetic effect. In this section, we demonstrate how genetic epidemiology and molecular genetics may be unified in a single approach to examine those mechanisms.

It defies credulity to imagine that millions of years of primate and then hominid evolution produced a sequence of DNA whose sole raison d'être is to forge checks or cheat on income taxes. Instead, speculation about the genetic role in antisocial behavior views the phenotype as an end product with more primary psychological mechanisms generating this phenotype. So the identical twin of the contemporary forger, were he or she born and raised in a preliterate agricultural society, might be more likely than the average person in that society to steal a neighbor's crop. Hence, evolutionary psychologists have speculated quite intensely about dimensions such as selfishness versus altruism or simply cheating as being important mediators for antisocial behavior (MacMillan & Kofoed, 1984; Raine, 1993).

Recent methodological advances in genetic epidemiology, termed *direction-of-causation models,* are aimed at detecting these types of mediators, whether they be personality traits or serotonin receptors. This literature is quite technical and the reader is referred to the original publications of Heath et al. (1993), Duffy and Martin (1994), Neale et al. (1994), and Carey and DiLalla (1994) for a detailed description. Here, the flavor of this technology is explained using intelligence as an example.

A correlation between criminal offending and cognitive ability has been documented since the beginning of this century both in England (Goring, 1913) and America (Goddard, 1914). With few exceptions, the literature consistently points to a lower IQ as a correlate of both officially adjudicated perpetrators and self-reported delinquency (Wilson & Herrnstein, 1985). The mean difference between offenders and the general population in IQ is estimated at approximately one half of a standard deviation. Several lines of evidence suggest—but do not unequivocally prove—a direct causal role for intelligence. Prospective studies show the IQ differential begins before the onset of overt juvenile offending (White & Moffitt, 1989), and the association is independent of social status and education (Lynam, Moffitt, & Stouthamer-Loeber, 1993). Also, the correlation is not due to the fact that lower intelligence merely increases the probability of getting caught (Moffitt & Silva, 1988).

The association is so robust that, in discussing the reasons for the known continuity through life of antisocial behavior, Caspi and Moffit (1995, p. 477) state, "Perhaps the best choice for our study of continuity is compromised cognitive ability." Many theorists assume that low cognitive ability is a direct but partial cause of antisocial behavior, although they disagree on the mechanism (Eysenck, 1977; Lynam et al., 1993; Wilson & Herrnstein, 1985). If cognitive ability has such strong theoretical and empirical support, then it is a legitimate question to ask whether the familial transmission of intelligence can explain a large part of the familial transmission for antisocial behavior.

A model for the relationship between intelligence and antisocial behavior is depicted in Figure 23.1. Here, two siblings are denoted by the subscripts 1 and 2. Siblings are correlated for in antisocial behavior for two reasons (ASB in Figure 23.1). First, they are similar for cognitive ability (IQ in Figure 23.1) and cognitive ability is a causal risk factor for antisocial behavior. Second, factors other than cognitive ability influence ASB (denoted by the residuals or u in Figure 23.1) and the siblings are correlated on those factors. The advantage of the new methods is that the correlation between IQ in one sibling and ASB in the other sibling gives information about a putative causal role for IQ and permits the quantification of this effect.

Given the recency of this approach, no body of published data has evaluated the technique. However, we illustrate it here using data from a pilot study of the families of adolescent substance abusers along with control families selected from the general community. Because there is no way to separate the influence of shared genes from shared environment in these data, the effects are termed *familial* instead of genetic. All of the substance-abusing probands had received a *DSM-III-R* diagnosis of conduct disorder, so it is clear that the results apply to antisocial behavior as well as substance abuse.

Both probands and family members were administered structured psychiatric interviews and the vocabulary and block design scales of either the Weschler Adult Intelligence Scale–Revised (WAIS) or Weschler Intelligence Scale for Children–Revised (WISC), depending on the individual's age. As in previous studies, mean IQ for the substance-abusing probands was significantly lower than that for their controls (99.7 vs. 105.2). Similarly, the mean IQ for the first-degree relatives of substance-abusing probands also was lower than that for the first-degree relatives of controls (95.3 vs. 103.1).

Given the well-established familiality for IQ (Bouchard & McGue, 1981), it is now a natural question to ask whether the familiality of antisocial behavior may be due to the transmission of IQ, which then influences deviance. To test this, we analyzed the two IQ variables along with symptom counts, corrected for the age and sex of the individual and for three disorders—conduct disorder/antisocial personality disorder, alcohol abuse/dependence, and other drug abuse/dependence. The model assumes that IQ is a risk factor for psychopathology. Once again, the advantage of using family data is that the correlation between one person's IQ and a relative's psychopathology provides additional information about the impact of intelligence on psychopathology.

Statistically, it was not possible to set the coefficients from IQ to psychopathology to zero, suggesting that IQ acts as a risk factor for psychopathology. However, the magnitude of these path coefficients was quite small. Even more sobering are the results given in Table 23.3, which presents the extent to which the familial transmission of the three psychopathologies may be attributable to the familial transmission of IQ. For example, the 9.4% figure for drug abuse means that of all those reasons why drug abuse runs in families, only 9.4% may be attributable to the transmission of IQ. The remaining 90.6% must be due to other types of factors. The off-diagonal elements explain how much of the familial comorbidity between two disorders is attributable to the familial transmission of IQ. For example, only 5.8% of the well-established familial comorbidity between alcohol abuse and antisocial personality is attributable to the familial transmission of intelligence. It is quite clear for antisocial behavior, alcohol, and drug abuse symptoms that the familial transmission of cognitive ability is only a very weak influence on the reason why these disorders run in families.

These results apply to a small, pilot sample, so substantive conclusions must be tempered accordingly. The methods, however, illustrate how genetic studies are moving away from establishing the *fact* of heritability and toward explaining the *how* of heritability. These same mathematical techniques of genetic epidemiology will eventually be used with molecular genetic data, where they will give much more powerful tests than those in current use. For example, simply substitute the genotype for, say, a 5HT receptor for IQ in Figure 23.1 and test the model. There are four advantages to this strategy: (a) it controls for population stratification; (b) it can truly estimate the extent to which the serotonin receptor (or any other genotypic marker) explains familial resemblance for antisocial behavior; (c) when used with multiple phenotypes, such as antisocial behavior, alcohol abuse, and substance abuse, the method also can address how much the serotonin receptor gene is associated with the comorbidity among the disorders; and (d) the model may be expanded to include simultaneous analysis of many genetic markers. Clearly, as more genes are

Figure 23.1 *Testing direction of causality with sibling data.*

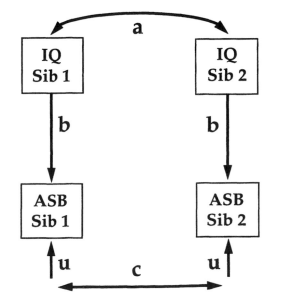

TABLE 23.3 Percentage of the Familial Transmission Variance and Covariance Among Drug Abuse, Alcohol Abuse, and Antisocial Personality Disorder Attributable to Vocabulary and Block Design IQ

	Drug Abuse	Alcohol Abuse	Antisocial Personality
Drug abuse	9.4	7.0	7.8
Alcohol abuse	7.0	2.2	5.8
Antisocial personality	7.8	5.8	6.7

added to the model and more phenotypes are studied, genetics well may provide a key role for understanding not only antisocial behavior but many of its correlates.

REFERENCES

Arora, R. C., & Meltzer, H. Y. (1989). 3H-imipramine binding in the frontal cortext of suicides. *Psychiatry Research, 30*(2), 125–135.

Asberg, M., Traskman, L., & Thoren, P. (1976). 5-HIAA in cerebral spinal fluid: A biochemical suicide predictor? *Archives of General Psychiatry, 33,* 1193–1997.

Asghari, V., Schoots, O., Van Kats, S., O'Hara, K., Jovanovic, V., Guan, H. C., Bunzow, J. R., Petronis, A., & Van Tol, H. H. M. (1994). Dopamine D4 receptor repeat: Analysis of different native and mutant forms of the human and rat genes. *Molecular Pharmacology, 46,* 364–373.

Baker, L. A. (1986). Estimating genetic correlations among discontinuous phenotypes: An analysis of criminal convictions and psychiatric hospital diagnoses in Danish adoptees. *Behavior Genetics* [Special issue: Multivariate behavioral genetics and development] *16,* 127–142.

Baker, L. A., Mack, W., Moffitt, T. E., & Mednick, S. (1989). Sex differences in property crime in a Danish adoption cohort. *Behavior Genetics, 19,* 355–370.

Bandura, A., & Walters, R. H. (1959). *Adolescent aggression.* New York: Ronald Press.

Benjamin, J., Li, L., Patterson, C., Greenberg, B. D., Murphy, D. L., & Hamer, D. H. (1996). Population and familial association between the D4 dopamine receptor gene and measures of Novelty Seeking. *Nature Genetics, 12,* 81–84.

Blumstein, A., Cohen, J., Roth, J. A., & Visher, C. A. (1986). *Criminal careers and "career criminals."* Washington, DC: National Academy Press.

Bohman, M. (1971). A comparative study of adopted children, foster children and children in their biological environment born after undesired pregnancies. *Acta Paediatrica Scandinavica, 60,* 5–38.

Bohman, M. (1978). Some genetic aspects of alcoholism and criminality: A population of adoptees. *Archives of General Psychiatry, 35,* 269–276.

Bohman, M. (1983). Alcoholism and crime: Studies of adoptees. *Substance and Alcohol Actions/Misuse, 4,* 137–147.

Bohman, M., Cloninger, C. R., Sigvardsson, S., & von Knorring, A.-L. (1982). Predisposition to petty criminality in Swedish adoptees: I. Genetic and environmental heterogeneity. *Archives of General Psychiatry, 39,* 1233–1241.

Bouchard, T. J., Jr., & McGue, M. (1981). Family studies of intelligence: A review. *Science, 212,* 1055–1059.

Brunner, H. G., Nelen, M., Breakfield, X. O., Ropers, H. H., & Van Oost, B. A. (1993). Abnormal behavior associated with a point mutation in the structural gene for monoamine oxidase A. *Science, 262,* 578–580.

Brunner, H. G., Nelen, M. R., van Zandvoort, P., Abeling, N. G. G. M., Van Gennip, A. H., Wolters, E. C., Kuiper, M. A., Ropers, H. H., & VanOost, B. A. (1993). X-linked borderline mental retardation with prominent behavioral disturbance: Phenotype, genetic localization, and evidence for disturbed monoamine metabolism. *American Journal of Human Genetics, 52,* 1032–1039.

Cadoret, R. J. (1978). Psychopathology in adopted-away offspring of biologic parents with antisocial behavior. *Archives of General Psychiatry, 35,* 176–184.

Cadoret, R. J., & Cain, C. A. (1980). Sex differences in predictors of antisocial behavior in adoptees. *Archives of General Psychiatry, 37,* 1171–1175.

Cadoret, R. J., Cain, C. A., & Crowe, R. R. (1983). Evidence for a gene-environment interaction in the development of adolescent antisocial behavior. *Behavior Genetics, 13,* 301–310.

Cadoret, R. J., Cunningham, L., Loftus, R., & Edwards, J. (1975). Studies of adoptees from psychiatrically disturbed biologic parents: II. Temperament, hyperactive, antisocial, and developmental variables. *Journal of Pediatrics, 87,* 301–306.

Cadoret, R. J., O'Gorman, T., Troughton, E., & Heywood, E. (1985). Alcoholism and antisocial personality: Interrelationships, genetic and environmental factors. *Archives of General Psychiatry, 42,* 161–167.

Cadoret, R. J., & Stewart, M. A. (1991). An adoption study of attention deficit/hyperactivity/aggression and their relationship to adult antisocial personality. *Comprehensive Psychiatry, 32*(1), 73–82.

Cadoret, R. J., Troughton, E., O'Gormon, T. W., & Heywood, E. (1986). An adoption study of genetic and environmental factors in drug abuse. *Archives of General Psychiatry, 43,* 1131–1136.

Cadoret, R. J., Yates, W. R., Troughton, E., Woodworth, G. (1995). Adoption study demonstrating two genetic pathways to drug abuse. *Archives of General Psychiatry, 52*(1), 42–52.

Carey, G. (1992). Twin imitation for antisocial behavior: Implications for genetic and family environment research. *Journal of Abnormal Psychology, 101,* 18–25.

Carey, G. (1993). Multivariate genetic relationships among drug abuse, alcohol abuse and antisocial personality. *Psychiatric Genetics, 3,* 141.

Carey, G. (1994a). The genetic association study in psychiatry: Analytical evaluation and a recommendation. *American Journal of Medical Genetics, 54,* 311–317.

Carey, G. (1994b). Genetics and violence. In A. J. Reiss, Jr. & J. A. Roth (Eds.), *Understanding and preventing violence. Vol. 2. Biobehavioral influences on violence* (pp. 21–58). Washington, DC: National Academy Press.

Carey, G. (1996). Family and genetic epidemiology of aggressive and antisocial behavior. In D. M. Stoff & R. D. Cairns (Eds.), *Aggression and violence: Genetic, neurobiological, and biosocial perspectives* (pp. 3–22). Hillsdale, NJ: Erlbaum.

Carey, G., & DiLalla, D. L. (1994). Personality and psychopathology: Genetic perspectives. *Journal of Abnormal Psychology, 103,* 32–43.

Carey, G., & Williamson, J. (1991). Linkage analysis of quantitative traits: Increased power by using selected samples. *American Journal of Human Genetics, 49*(4), 786–796.

Caspi, A., & Moffitt, T. E. (1995). The continuity of maladaptive behavior: From description to understanding in the study of antisocial behavior. In D. Chichetti & D. J. Cohen (Eds.), *Developmental psychopathology, Volume 2: Risk, disorder and adaption* (pp. 472–511). New York: Wiley.

Caspi, A., Moffitt, T. E., Silva, P. A., Stouthamer-Loeber, M., Krueger, R. F., & Schmutte, P. S. (1994). Are some people crime-prone? Replications of the personality-crime relationship across countries, genders, races, and methods. *Criminology, 32*, 163–195.

Catalano, M., Nobile, M., Novelli, E., Nothen, M. M., & Smeraldi, E. (1993). Distribution of a novel mutation in the first exon of the human D4 receptor gene in psychotic patients. *Biological Psychiatry, 34*, 459–464.

Christiansen, K. O. (1968). *Threshold of tolerance in various population groups illustrated by results from Danish criminological twin study.* London: J. & A. Churchill Ltd.

Christiansen, K. O. (1970). Crime in a Danish twin population. *Acta Geneticae Medicae Gemellologicae: Twin Research, 19*, 323–326.

Christiansen, K. O. (1974). *Seriousness of criminality and concordance among Danish twins.* London: Heinemann.

Christiansen, K. O. (1977). *A review of studies of criminality among twins.* New York: Gardner.

Cloninger, C. R., Christiansen, K. O., Reich, T., & Gottesman, I. I. (1978). Implications of sex differences in the prevalences of antisocial personality, alcoholism, and criminality for familial transmission. *Archives of General Psychiatry, 35*, 941–951.

Cloninger, C. R., & Gottesman, I. I. (1987). *Genetic and environmental factors in antisocial behavior disorders.* New York: Cambridge University Press.

Cloninger, C. R., Sigvardsson, S., Bohman, M., & von Knorring, A.-L. (1982). Predisposition to petty criminality in Swedish adoptees: II. Cross-fostering analysis of gene-environment interaction. *Archives of General Psychiatry, 39*, 1242–1247.

Coccaro, E. F., Siever, L. J., Klar, H. M., Maurer, G., Cooper, T. B., & Mohs, R. C. (1989). Serotonergic studies in patients with affective and personality disorders. Correlates with suicidal and impulsive aggressive behaviour. *Archives of General Psychiatry, 46*(7), 587–599.

Costa, P. T. J., & McCrae, R. R. (1985). *The NEO Personality Inventory manual.* Odessa, FL: Psychological Assessment Resources.

Crowe, R. R. (1972). The adopted offspring of women criminal offenders: A study of their arrest records. *Archives of General Psychiatry, 27*, 600–603.

Crowe, R. R. (1974). An adoption study of antisocial personality. *Archives of General Psychiatry, 31*, 785–791.

Crowe, R. R. (1993). Candidate genes in psychiatry: An epidemiological perspective. *American Journal of Medical Genetics, 48*, 74–77.

Dalgard, O. S., & Kringlen, E. (1976). A Norwegian twin study of criminality. *British Journal of Criminology, 16*, 213–232.

Duffy, D. L., & Martin, N. G. (1994). Inferring the direction of causation in cross-sectional twin data: Theoretical and empirical considerations. *Genetic Epidemiology, 11*(6), 483–502.

Eaves, L. J., Silberg, J. L., Hewitt, J. K., Rutter, M., Meyer, J. M., Neale, M. C., & Pickles, A. (1993). Analyzing twin resemblance in multi-symptom data: Genetic applications of a latent class model for symptoms of conduct disorder in juvenile boys. *Behavior Genetics, 23*, 5–19.

Ebstein, R. P., Novick, O., Umansky, R., Priel, B., Osher, Y., Blaine, D., Bennett, E. R., Nemanov, L., Katz, M., & Belmaker, R. H. (1996). Dopamine D4 receptor (D4DR) exon III polymorphism associated with the human personality trait of Novelty Seeking. *Nature Genetics, 12*, 78–80.

Eysenck, H. J. (1977). *Crime and personality* (rev. ed.). London: Routledge and Kegan Paul.

Falk, C. T., & Rubenstein, P. (1987). Haplotype relative risks: An easy reliable way to construct a control sample for risk calculations. *Annals of Human Genetics, 51*, 227–233.

Gabrielli, W. F., Jr., & Mednick, S. A. (1983). Genetic correlates of criminal behavior: Implications for research, attribution, and prevention. *American Behavioral Scientist, 27*, 59–74.

Gabrielli, W. F., Jr., & Mednick, S. A. (1984). Urban environment, genetics, and crime. *Criminology, 22*, 645–652.

Goddard, H. H. (1914). *Feeble-mindedness: Its causes and consequences.* New York: Macmillan.

Goldman, D. (1996). Interdisciplinary perceptions of genetics and behavior. *Politics and Life Sciences, 15*, 97–98.

Goldman, D., Brown, G. L., Albaugh, B., Robin, R., Goodson, S., Trunzo, M., Akhtar, L., Lucas-Derse, S., Long, J., Linnoila, M., & Dean, M. (1993). DRD2 dopamine receptor genotype, linkage disequilibrium and alcoholism in Americans and other populations. *Alcohol Clin Exp Res, 17*, 199–204.

Goldman, D., Lappalainen, J., & Ozaki. (1996). Direct analysis of candidate genes in impulsive behaviors. *CIBA Foundation Symposium 194. Genetics of Criminal and Antisocial Behavior.* Chichester: Wiley.

Goldsmith, H. H., & Gottesman, I. I. (Eds.). (in press). *Heritable variability and variable heritability in developmental psychopathology.* Oxford: Oxford University Press.

Goring, C. (1913). *The English convict: A statistical study.* London: Darling and Son.

Gottesman, I. I., Carey, G., & Hanson, D. H. (1983). *Pearls and perils in epigenetic psychopathology.* New York: Raven Press.

Gottesman, I. I., & Goldsmith, H. H. (1994). Developmental psychopathology of antisocial behavior: Inserting genes into its ontogenesis and epigenesis. In C. A. Nelson (Ed.), *Threats to optimal development: Integrating biological, psychological and social risk factors* (pp. 69–104). Hillsdale, NJ: Erlbaum.

Grove, W. M., Eckert, E. D., Heston, L. L., Bouchard, T. J., Jr., Segal, N., & Lykken, D. T. (1990). Heritability of substance abuse and antisocial behavior: A study of monozygotic twins raised apart. *Biological Psychiatry, 27*, 293–304.

Hauser, P., Zametkin, A. J., Martinez, P., Vitiello, B., Matochik, J. A., Mixson, A. J., & Weintraub, B. B. (1993). Attention deficit disorder in people with generalized resistance to thyroid hormone. *New England Journal of Medicine, 328*, 997–1001.

Heath, A. C., Kessler, R. C., Neale, M. C., Hewitt, J. K., Eaves, L. J., & Kendler, K. S. (1993). Testing hypotheses about direction of causation using cross-sectional family data. *Behavioral Genetics, 23*(1), 29–50.

Hutchings, B. (1972). *Environmental and genetic factors in psychopathology and criminality.* Unpublished master's dissertation, University of London.

Hutchings, B., & Mednick, S. A. (1971). *Criminality in adoptees and their adoptive and biological parents: A pilot study.* New York: Gardner.

Hutchings, B., & Mednick, S. A. (1975). *Registered criminality in the adoptive and biological parents of registered male criminal adoptees.* Baltimore: Johns Hopkins University Press.

Kidd, K. K. (1993). Associations of disease with genetic markers: Deja vu all over again. *American Journal of Medical Genetics, 48*, 71–73.

Lappalainen, J., Zhang, L., Dean, M., Oz, M., Ozaki, N., Yu, D.-H., Virkkunen, M., Weight, F., Linnoila, M., & Goldman, D. (1995). Identification, expression and pharmacology of a cys23-ser23 substitution in the human 5-HT2C receptor gene. *Genomics, 27*, 274–279.

Lewontin, R. C., Rose, S., & Kamin, L. J. (1984). *Not in our genes: Biology, ideology, and human nature.* New York: Pantheon Books.

Lichter, J. B., Barr, C. L., Kennedy, J. L., Van Tol, H. H. M., Kidd, K. K., & Livak, K. J. (1993). A hypervariable segment in the human D4 receptor (DRD4) gene. *Human Molecular Genetics, 2,* 767–773.

Linnoila, M., Virkunnen, M., & Scheinin, M. (1983). Low cerebrospinal fluid 5-hydroxyindole acetic acid concentration differentiates impulsive from non-impulsive violent behaviour. *Life Sciences, 33,* 2609–2614.

Loehlin, J. C., & Nichols, R. C. (1976). *Heredity, environment, and personality: A study of 850 sets of twins.* Austin: University of Texas Press.

Lykken, D. T. (1995). *The antisocial personalities.* Hillsdale, NJ: Erlbaum.

Lynam, D., Moffitt, T., & Stouthamer-Loeber, M. (1993). Explaining the relation between IQ and delinquency: Class, race, test motivation, school failure, or self-control? *Journal of Abnormal Psychology, 102*(2), 187–196.

Lyons, M. J. (1996). A twin study of self-reported criminal behavior. In C. Foundation (Ed.), *Genetics of criminal and antisocial behavior* (pp. 61–69). Chichester, UK: Wiley.

Lyons, M. J., Eaves, L., Tsuang, M. Y., Eisen, S. E., Goldberg, J., & True, W. T. (1993). Differential heritability of adult and juvenile antisocial traits. *Psychiatric Genetics, 3,* 117.

Lyons, M. J., True, W. R., Eisen, S. A., Goldberg, J., Meyer, J. M., Faraone, S. V., Eaves, L. J., & Tsuang, M. T. (1995). Differential heritability of adult and juvenile antisocial traits. *Archives of General Psychiatry, 52,* 906–915.

MacMillan, J., & Kofoed, L. (1984). Sociobiology and antisocial personality. *Journal of Nervous and Mental Disease, 172,* 701–706.

Mealey, L. (1995). The sociobiology of sociopathy: An integrated evolutionary model. *Behavioral and Brain Sciences, 18*(3), 401–477.

Mednick, S. A., Brennan, P., & Kandel, E. (1988). Predisposition to violence. *Aggressive Behavior* [Special issue: Current theoretical perspectives on aggressive and antisocial behavior] *14,* 25–33.

Mednick, S. A., & Finello, K. M. (1983). Biological factors and crime: Implications for forensic psychiatry. *International Journal of Law and Psychiatry, 6,* 1–15.

Mednick, S. A., Gabrielli, W. F., Jr., & Hutchings, B. (1983). *Genetic influences in criminal behavior: Evidence from an adoption cohort.* Boston: Kluwer-Nijhoff.

Mednick, S. A., Gabrielli, W. F., Jr., & Hutchings, B. (1984). Genetic influences in criminal convictions: Evidence from an adoption cohort. *Science, 224,* 891–894.

Mednick, S. A., Gabrielli, W. F., Jr., & Hutchings, B. (1987). *Genetic factors in the etiology of criminal behavior.* New York: Cambridge University Press.

Miczek, K. A., Haney, M., Tidey, J., Vivian, J., & Weerts, E. (1994). Neurochemistry and pharmacotherapeutic management of aggression and violence. In A. J. Reiss, K. A. Miczek, & J. A. Roth (Eds.), *Understanding and preventing violence:* Vol. 2: *Biobehavioral influences* (pp. 245–514). Washington, DC: National Academy Press.

Miles, D. R., & Carey, G. (1997). The genetic and environmental architecture of human aggression. *Journal of Personality and Social Psychology, 72,* 207–217.

Moffitt, T. E. (1987). Parental mental disorder and offspring criminal behavior: An adoption study. *Psychiatry, 50,* 346–360.

Moffitt, T. E. (1993). Adolescent-limited and life-course-persistent antisocial behavior: A developmental taxonomy. *Psychological Review, 100*(4), 674–701.

Moffitt, T. E., Gabrielli, W. F., Mednick, S. A., & Schulsinger, F. (1981). Socioeconomic status, IQ, and delinquency. *Journal of Abnormal Psychology, 90,* 152–156.

Moffitt, T. E., & Silva, P. A. (1988). IQ and delinquency: A direct test of the differential detection hypothesis. *Journal of Abnormal Psychology, 97*(3), 330–333.

Neale, M. C., Walters, E., Health, A. C., Kessler, R. C., Perusse, D., Eaves, L. J., & Kendler, K. S. (1994). Depression and parental bonding: Cause, consequence, or genetic covariance? *Genetic Epidemiology, 11*(6), 503–522.

Nielsen, D. A., Goldman, D., Virkkunen, M., Tokola, R., Rawlings, R., & Linnoila, M. (in press). Letter to the Editor, Serotonergic traits associate with a tryptophan hydroxylase polymorphism. *Archives of General Psychiatry.*

Nielsen, D. A., Goldman, D., Virkkunen, M., Tokola, R., Rawlings, R., Markku, & Linnoila, M. (1994). Suicidal behavior and 5-hydroxyindoleacetic acid concentration associated with tryptophan hydroxylase polymorphism. *Archives of General Psychiatry, 51,* 34–38.

Nothen, M. M., Cichon, S., Hemmer, Hebebrand, J., Remschmidt, H., Lehmkuhl, G., Poustka, F., Schmidt, M., Catalano, M., Fimmers, R., Korner, J., Rietschel, M., & Propping, P. (1994). Human dopamine D4 receptor gene: Frequent occurrence of a null allele and observation of homozygosity. *Human Molecular Genetics, 3,* 2207–2212.

Plomin, R., Owen, M. J., & McGuffin, P. (1994). The genetic basis of complex human behaviors. *Science, 264,* 1733–1739.

Pogue-Geile, M., Ferrell, R., Deka, R., Debeski, T., & Masnuck, S. (1996). *Novelty-seeking and polymorphisms in the D4 dopamine receptor gene: A twin and association study.* Paper presented at the annual meeting of the Society for Research in Psychopathology, Atlanta, GA.

Raine, A. (1993). *The psychopathology of crime: Criminal behavior as a clinical disorder.* New York: Academic Press.

Risch, N., & Zhang, H. (1995). Extreme discordant sib pairs for mapping quantitative trait loci in humans. *Science, 268,* 1584–1589.

Rowe, D. C. (1983). Biometrical genetic models of self-reported delinquent behavior: A twin study. *Behavior Genetics, 13,* 473–489.

Rowe, D. C. (1985). Sibling interaction and self-reported delinquent behavior: A study of 265 twin pairs. *Criminology, 23,* 223–240.

Rowe, D. C. (1986). Genetic and environmental components of antisocial behavior: A study of 265 twin pairs. *Criminology, 24,* 513–532.

Roy, A., & Linnoila, M. (1990). *Monoamines and suicidal behaviour.* New York: Brunner/Mazel.

Seeman, P., Ulpian, C., Chouinard, G., Van Tol, H. H. M., Dwosh, H., Liberman, J. A., Siminovitch, K., Liu, I. S. C., Waye, J., Voruganti, P., Hudson, C., Serjeant, G. R., Masibay, A. S., & Seeman, M. V. (1994). Dopamine D4 receptor variant, D4 glycine 194, in Africans but not in Caucasians: No association with schizophrenia. *American Journal of Medical Genetics, 54,* 384–390.

Sherry, S. T., Rogers, A. R., Harpending, H., Soodyall, H., Jenkins, T., & Stoneking, M. (1994). Mismatch distributions of mtDNA reveal recent human populations expansions. *Human Biology, 66,* 761–775.

Sigvardsson, S., Cloninger, C. R., Bohman, M., & von Knorring, A.-L. (1982). Predisposition to petty criminality in Swedish adoptees: III. Sex differences and validation of the male typology. *Archives of General Psychiatry, 39,* 1248–1253.

Simonsson, P., Traskman-Bendz, L., Alling, C., Oreland, L., Regnell, G., & Ohman, R. (1991). *European Neuropsychopharmacol, 1*(4), 503–510.

Stanley, M., Virggilio, J., & Gershon, S. (1982). Tritiated imipramine binding sites are decreased in the frontal cortex of suicides. *Science, 216,* 1337–1339.

Tellegen, A. (1985). *Structures of mood and personality and their relevance to assessing anxiety, with an emphasis on self-report.* Hillsdale, NJ: Erlbaum.

Tellegen, A., Lykken, D. T., Bouchard, T. J., Jr., Wilcox, K. J., Segal, N. L., & Rich, S. (1988). Personality similarity in twins reared apart and together. *Journal of Personality and Social Psychology, 54,* 1031–1039.

Tu, G.-C., & Israel, Y. (1995). Alcohol consumption by Orientals in North America is predicted largely by a single gene. *Behavior Genetics, 25,* 59–65.

Van Tol, H. H. M., Wu, C. M., Guan, H. C., Ohara, K., Bunzow, J. R., Civelli, O., Kennedy, J., Seeman, P., Niznik, H. B., & Jovanovic, V.

(1992). Multiple dopamine D4 receptor variants in the human population. *Nature, 358,* 149–152.

White, J. L., & Moffitt, T. E. (1989). A prospective replication of the protective effects of IQ in subjects at high risk for juvenile delinquency. *Journal of Consulting and Clinical Psychology, 57*(6), 719–724.

Wilson, J. Q., & Herrnstein, R. J. (1985). *Crime and human nature.* New York: Simon & Schuster.

Yoshida, A., Huang, I. Y., & Ikawa, M. (1984). Molecular abnormality of an inactive aldehyde dehydrogenase variant commonly found in Orientals. *Proceeding of the National Academy of Science U.S.A., 81,* 258–261.

CHAPTER 24

Ethological Models for Examining the Neurobiology of Aggressive and Affiliative Behaviors

CRAIG F. FERRIS and GEERT J. DE VRIES

Aggression is a normal part of mammalian behavior (Huntingford & Turner, 1987). There is an adaptive advantage to defending a territory, fighting for limited resources, competing for mates, and protecting young. This presumably was true in early human history. With the advent of civilization, we have other ways to acquire resources and settle disputes. In contemporary societies, only when the aggressive response is perceived as being out of context or excessive in its implementation does it take on the quality of violence. Despite great efforts to understand and develop intervention strategies to control violence, no simple solutions have been found because of the complex nature of the behavior. The etiology of violence involves multiple factors. Aggression by an individual is dependent on "hereditary and environmental factors determining his ontogenetic development ... and by the situational determinants to which the individual responds at the moment." (Lagerspetz, 1964, p. 12)

A violent act, like any other behavior, is envisioned to be organized and controlled by a neural network(s), that is, subsets of interconnected neurons conveying sensory and motor information to and from sites of integration (Delgado, 1980). Whereas the motor components or execution of a violent act has an "innate" quality (Johansson, 1981), the perception of a challenging or threatening stimulus that may precipitate the motor activity requires the synthesis of sensory information with past experience and present mood. Indeed, unprovoked, violent outbursts in some individuals may be a natural response to an imagined or perceived challenge or threat in their environment (Tardiff, 1992). If neural networks control behavior and behavior is modified by environmental conditions and learning, then neural networks must be plastic, subject to subtle neurochemical and neuroanatomical changes that can predispose an individual to violent behavior. Therefore, any attempt to develop psychosocial and psychopharmacological intervention strategies requires an understanding of how environmental and biological factors interact to predispose an organism to violent behavior.

Efforts to develop psychopharmacological intervention strategies for controlling violent behavior in psychiatric patients have been less than successful as most treatments are nonspecific and

arrest aggression by diminishing general activity (see Karper & Krystal, Chapter 41, this volume). For example, neuroleptics are routinely employed to control violent behavior (Soloff, 1987). By blocking a specific subtype of the dopamine receptor, neuroleptics can decrease aggression; however, the patient is quite often physically inactive and socially withdrawn. Consequently, psychiatric patients treated with neuroleptics are not always amenable to psychological and behavioral therapies. Can drugs be developed that block violent impulses but do not interfere with other behaviors? These hypothetical drugs, which have been called *serenics* (Olivier & Mos, 1990), should reduce or delay the rapid onset of anger, helping belligerent individuals to control their temper and allowing them to cope with problems in a less destructive, more socially acceptable way. Serenics should not impair initiative, interfere with normal social relations, or prevent people from adequately defending themselves from challenges or threats. Any development of serenics, however, requires a thorough understanding of the neuroanatomy and neurochemical control of aggression.

Pharmacology can be used to unravel the complex neurochemical control of aggression. For example, if animals treated with a drug that blocks the activity of a particular neurotransmitter show diminished fighting, then one might be inclined to suppose a role for that transmitter in the facilitation of aggression. In many early studies, however, drug treatments were not very specific and displayed mixed activities; consequently, the importance of any particular neurotransmitter system in the control of aggression was unclear. In recent years, this problem has been circumvented by the development of highly selective receptor agonists and antagonists. In addition, more scientists are defining the neurochemical control of aggression by administering drugs to specific sites of the brain that contain particular neural network(s) governing agonistic behavior.

Another area of research that has advanced the understanding of the neurochemical control of aggression is the use of ethologically valid animal models (Mos & Olivier, 1991). Some of the traditional animal models employed to study aggression were artificial, employing adverse stimuli to elicit responses that occurred out of context of normal aggressive behavior. For example, electrical shock or central nervous system injury to a rat maintained in isolation increases the likelihood that the animal will attack an inanimate object presented by the experimenter. In this instance, the resulting

This chapter was completed with the support of NIMH grant MH52280 to Craig F. Ferris and NSF IBN 9421658 to Geert J. De Vries.

behavior is fragmented and limited and occurs without the normal temporal and sequential pattern characteristic of agonistic responding in natural or seminatural conditions. Moreover, biting an inanimate object lacks the interactive quality that highlights agonistic encounters that normally occur between conspecifics (i.e., animals of the same species) as it relates to establishing dominance hierarchies, defining territorial limits, and protecting young. It is at best difficult, and may be impossible, to ascertain an understanding of the neurochemical regulation of aggression from pharmacological manipulations of artificial models.

More recent studies have focused on the neurobiological mechanisms that direct an animal to attack a conspecific during a social interaction. Because some of these mechanisms have been revealed, one now can examine how environmental and emotional insults alter these mechanisms to elicit an aggressive response that is out of context or excessive. Other studies have focused on the neurobiological mechanisms involved in affiliative behavior, that is, behavior associated with pair-bonding, cooperative familial interactions, and parental care. That approach also may be useful to understand the neurobiology of inappropriate aggressive behavior. A violent act may be due to alterations in those mechanisms that normally promote nurturing and protective behavior. Promoting prosocial behavior is one approach to interceding in the cycle of violence (see Hawkins, Arthur, & Olson, Chapter 34, this volume). In this chapter, we describe models of aggressive and affiliative behavior and the neurobiological mechanisms contributing to each. In addition, we discuss the environmental and endocrine factors that can affect neuronal plasticity and influence the different social behaviors.

DEFINING AGGRESSION

We define *aggression* as any behavior by which one animal attacks or bites another animal. Aggression is not to be confused with agonistic behavior, which comprises all the different response elements such as attack, retreat, submission, and flight that occur during conflict situations (Scott & Fredericson, 1951). Although *aggression* and *violence* may appear to be synonymous, *violence* connotes greater intensity and destruction. Violence is more commonly associated with descriptions of human behavior. In many cases, aggressive encounters between mammalian conspecifics in the wild are ritualized; who wins and loses is decided by posturing and threats (Eibl-Eibesfeldt, 1961). When overt aggression does occur, it usually is not life threatening. However, in some mammalian species, aggression can escalate to the level of serious injury and death, particularly during the mating season (Wilkinson & Shank, 1976).

CONTEXT-DEPENDENT AGGRESSION

In a seminal publication appearing in 1968, Moyer presented a comprehensive review of the different forms of aggression and their neural and endocrine regulation. This was one of the first attempts to synthesize the vast amount of data on aggression collected over the previous 3 decades. Moyer subdivided aggression according to the "stimulus situation" that elicited the behavior:

Predatory aggression, stimulated by the presence of a natural object of prey.

Intermale aggression, stimulated by the presence of a novel male conspecific in a neutral arena.

Fear-induced aggression, stimulated by threat and always preceded by escape attempts.

Irritable aggression, stimulated by presence of any attackable object. The tendency to display irritable aggression is enhanced by any stressor, such as isolation, electrical shock, food deprivation.

Territorial aggression, stimulated by the presence of an intruder in the home territory of a resident.

Maternal aggression, stimulated by a threatening stimulus in the proximity of the dam's young.

Instrumental aggression, stimulated by any of the situations already described but strengthened by learning.

Moyer's classification underscores the context-dependent nature of aggression and the diversity of stimulating situations.

A rat can be triggered to attack by many of these stimulus situations. Aggression can be evoked by pairing isolated males, *intermale aggression* (Davis, 1935; Seward, 1945); exposing grouped and paired males to unavoidable foot shock, *irritable-aggression* (O'Kelly & Steckle, 1939; Ulrich & Azrin, 1962); introducing an unfamiliar intruder into the home cage of a male resident, *territorial aggression* (Adams, 1976; Grant & Mackintosh, 1963); or killing a mouse, *predatory aggression* (Karli, 1956). However, the underlying neurobiological mechanisms for each type of aggression appear to be different. Tricyclics antidepressants that elevate catecholamines increase irritable aggression (Eichelman & Barchas, 1975) but inhibit predatory aggression (Katz, 1978). Lesions in the ventromedial hypothalamus enhance shock-induced and predatory aggression but have no effect on territorial aggression (Adams, 1971; Panksepp 1971a).

Equally diverse are the neurobiological mechanisms controlling aggression between species. For example, lesions in the midbrain central gray matter in the cat but not the rat blocks aggression triggered by hypothalamic stimulation (Mos, Kruk, Van der Poel, & Meelis, 1982). Septal lesions in the mouse (Slotnick & McMullen, 1972) and rat (Lau & Miczek, 1977) diminish attack behavior, but septal lesions in the hamster enhance aggression (Sodetz & Bunnell, 1970; Potegal, Blau, & Glusman, 1981). Injection of cholinergic agonists into the midbrain central gray matter in the cat elicits aggression, but similar treatments in the rat have no effect (Baxter, 1968; Carrive, Schmitt, & Karli, 1986). Although it is logical to assume different biological mechanisms may be responsible for each type of aggression within and between species, it is possible that the disparate results are due primarily to the artificial nature of many of the experimental conditions.

TOPOGRAPHY OF AGGRESSION

Given the diverse nature of the stimulus situations, the response patterns, and neural and endocrine controls, Moyer (1968, p. 65) surmised it was "fruitless to search for the physiological basis of aggression." Could aggressive behavior be conceptualized in a way that would allow neuroscientists to identify a common biological mechanism? A glimpse of the future was provided by Moyer when he suggested that a detailed ethological analyses of the response patterns or topography may be another way to differentiate and classify aggressive behavior.

Careful studies by Caroline Blanchard and Robert Blanchard (1977) revealed that domestic laboratory rats have attack and defensive behaviors similar to feral rats during comparable agonistic interactions. Introduction of an intruder into a colony of laboratory rats elicits specific attack behavior from the dominant male of the group. The α male begins the agonistic encounter by approaching and sniffing the intruder. This investigation leads to piloerection, an autonomic response by the α male that invariably leads to attack. The recipient of the attack, the intruder, seldom piloerects. The fight begins with a "lateral attack," a strategy by which the α male pushes its flanks toward the intruder followed by an "intention movement" of darting around the intruder to bite the back. The intruder tries to neutralize the attack by assuming an upright "boxing" stance while moving constantly to keep the attacker away from its back. The attacker may also assume an upright boxing stance in response to the intruder's behavior. The remainder of the attack strategy of the α male is determined by the defensive posture of the intruder. If the intruder assumes a supine (on-the-back) position, the α male launches attacks while standing on top of the intruder. Despite the vulnerability of the exposed ventral surface, the α male still directs the bites toward the back and shoulders of the stranger. If the intruder flees, the α male gives chase, attacking the exposed back and rump. Eventually the intruder freezes, lying on its back in a submissive posture or crouched low to the floor. Any movement by the intruder usually precipitates renewed attack by the α male. Wounds to the intruder are common in this setting; however, it is rare that the stranger bites the α male. Any bites by the intruder toward the α male occur on its face and are considered defensive and only in response to the biting of the α male. If the intruder remains in the cage of the colony for several days, it is likely to be killed.

The agonistic behavior between α males and intruders in colonies of wild rats (Barnett, 1958) is similar to that in the laboratory rat and dispels the notion that the latter is not qualified to participate in aggression studies because it has become "domesticated." The Blanchards not only established that the laboratory rodent is appropriate for the study of aggression but introduced a new classification for aggression (Blanchard & Blanchard, 1977). Attack behavior could be described as conspecific or *offensive attack, defensive attack,* or *predatory attack.* Each attack form had it own ethogram, that is, response pattern. For example, offensive attack was always preceded by piloerection and lateral attack. This response pattern is unique and dissimilar to defensive and predatory attack. When the different types of aggression outlined by Moyer are reevaluated for their response pattern, they fall into one of these three attack categories. It has been argued that predation should not be included as a form of aggression (O'Boyle, 1974), as the absence of affective behavior in a social context and the overlap with appetitive behavior makes it difficult to integrate the neurobiology of predation with that of other types of aggression. Therefore, agonis-

tic behavior is now classified as either offensive or defensive aggression (Adams, 1979; Albert & Walsh, 1984). *Offensive* aggression is characterized by the aggressor initiating an attack on an opponent; *defensive* aggression lacks the active approach. Classification based on response pattern is a conceptual lodestone, directing neuroscientists interested in studying the neurobiology of aggression away from the morass of context-dependent aggression.

The stimuli that elicit offensive and defense attack are different, as are the sequences of behaviors that accompany each agonistic response (Blanchard & Blanchard, 1977; Brain, 1981). Offensive and defensive aggression have been hypothesized to have their own neural networks, making it possible to design drugs to interact with critical synaptic connections that could inhibit one behavior while keeping the other intact (Olivier & Mos, 1990). Studies involving lesions in different brain areas suggest separate systems for offensive and defensive aggression (Adams, 1979; Albert & Walsh, 1984). Although much of the empirical data supporting the notion of unique offensive and defensive neural networks have been collected from animal models, human aggression has interesting and compelling similarities that suggest a similar neural organization (Blanchard, 1984).

GENES AND AGGRESSION

As noted at the beginning of the chapter, aggression is best viewed as the confluence of environmental and biological factors. Genes play a role in aggression because there is an inherited variation in aggressive behavior (see Carey & Goldman, Chapter 23, this volume). Mice routinely have been studied and characterized for strain differences in intraspecific aggression (Scott, 1942; Simon, 1979; Hahn & Haber, 1982). In 1959 at the University of Turku, Finland, Lagerspetz (1964) began the first efforts at selective breeding for aggressive behavior in mice and succeeded in establishing two lines of mice with high and low aggression referred to as Turku aggressive (TA) and Turku nonaggressive (TNA). Since then there have been several other successful attempts to breed for aggression in mice (Ebert & Hyde, 1976; Van Oortmerssen & Bakker, 1981). Cairns, MacCombie, and Hood (1983) designed an elegant study to examine the interaction between development, learning, and the heritability of aggression. Mice were bred selectively for high and low aggression. Genetic selection occurred within the first few generations and favored low aggression when tested at early maturity; that is, selection produced mice that were less likely than their ancestors to attack as young adults. However, the aggressive behavior between the two lines converged with age and experience. Experience had a strong influence, as a single test had a carryover effect on aggressive behavior examined months later. Thus, the confluence of experimental and developmental factors can mask the heritable effects of social behavior.

Characterization of strain differences and selective breeding offer an exciting approach to understanding the neurobiology of aggression. With a robust predictable behavior, it becomes easier to trace the biological differences between strains that may contribute to the behavioral differences. For example, the Turku mice of Lagerspetz differed in their urine odors. The urine odor from the Turku aggressive mice elicits attack from intermediately aggressive mice when placed on a castrated control, whereas the urine from the nonaggressive mice has no such effect (Sandnabba, 1986). In another example, Simon and coworkers identified three outbred strains of male mice coded CF-1, CD-1, and CFW that show different sensitivities to the aggression-promoting effects of gonadal steroids (Simon & Gandelman, 1978; Simon & Whalen, 1986; Simon & Masters, 1987). The CF-1 strain responds to estrogen and androgen treatment, the CFW strain to estrogen, and the CD-1 strain to androgen only. These model systems allow examination of sexual differentiation and steroid dependency of aggression. With respect to steroid influences on aggression, Van Oortmerssen, Dijk, and Schourman (1987) noted that adult mice bred for short attack latency had higher testosterone levels and testosterone sensitivity compared to controls.

Characterizing the neurobiological link between genes and aggression is not trivial. Can a single allele substitution at a given genetic locus influence aggressive responding? Analysis of a large kindred revealed that several human males affected by borderline mental retardation and impulsivity showed markedly disturbed monoamine metabolism due to the absence of monamine oxidase A (Brunner, Nelen, Breakefield, Ropers, & van Oost, 1993). Afflicted individuals show a tendency toward aggressive outbursts, associated with anger, fear, or frustration. Affected individuals show diminished levels of urinary monoamine metabolites, presumably reflecting altered central nervous system (CNS) metabolism of dopamine, norepinephrine, and serotonin. In another case, homozygous mutant mice lacking the gene encoding the 5-HT$_{1B}$ receptor were developed (Saudou et al., 1994). Male mutant mice showed enhanced aggression toward a wild-type intruder placed into their home cage. The latency to attack was shorter and the number of attacks greater than in control animals. Mice lacking the 5-HT$_{1B}$ receptor were more aggressive in the resident-intruder paradigm.

HYPOTHALAMIC AGGRESSION

Hess and Brugger (1943) reported that electrical stimulation in the hypothalamus could elicit agonistic response patterns in the freely moving cat. Electrical stimulation of the medial hypothalamus from the preoptic area to the ventrolateral nucleus causes piloerection, arching of the back, and hissing (Flynn, 1967; Fuchs, Edinger, & Siegal, 1985; Shaikh, Barret, & Siegel, 1987; Wasman & Flynn, 1962). This defensive behavior observed with hypothalamic stimulation is similar to the defensive behavior that occurs naturally when a cat is threatened. In addition, the defense reaction caused by electrical stimulation is stimulus bound, as the animal will direct its aggression toward specific objects in the environment. Electrical stimulation of the lateral hypothalamus elicits quiet biting attack characterized by a stalking movement and biting the back of the neck of a stimulus animal (A. Siegel & Pott, 1988; Wasman & Flynn, 1962). Unlike defensive aggression, this quiet biting attack or predatory aggression is not stimulus bound, as the animal will attack objects that do not normally elicit attack.

Consequently, a wealth of literature has been accumulated on the neuroanatomical and neurochemical control of defensive and predatory aggression in the cat associated with electrical stimula-

tion of the hypothalamus (for reviews, see Bandler, 1988; Glusman, 1985; A. Siegel, 1990). Studies on the electrical stimulation of the cat brain pioneered the neurobiology of aggression and continue to provide an ideal system for examining the neural networks controlling agonistic behavior (A. Siegel, 1990). This is not a practical model for studying the interactive effect of environment on brain plasticity and aggressive responding because of the size of the animal and the invasive nature of the experimental paradigm. Moreover, defensive aggression presumably is motivated by fear, whereas a quiet biting attack is judged to be predatory behavior and separate from aggression in a social context. Thus, neither of these forms of hypothalamic aggression fits the behavioral and contextual criteria defining offensive aggression.

Since the late 1960s, numerous investigators have reported attack behavior elicited by electrical stimulation of the hypothalamus of the rat (Albert, Nanji, Brayley, & Madryga, 1979; King & Hoebel, 1968; Koolhaas, 1978; Kruk, Van der Poel, & De Vos-Frerichs, 1979; Panksepp, 1971b; Panksepp & Trowill, 1969; Vergnes & Karli, 1970; Woodworth, 1971). Kruk and coworkers have thoroughly characterized the behavior, neuroanatomy, and neuropharmacology of hypothalamic aggression in the rat (Kruk, 1991). Electrical stimulation with movable electrodes has defined an "aggressive zone area," extending from the lateral ventromedial hypothalamus to the anterior hypothalamus (Kruk et al., 1983; Lammers, Kruk, Meelis, & Van der Poel, 1988). Initially it was thought that different areas controlled different types of aggression, but these results were dependent on the intensity of the electrical stimulation and not the placement of the electrode; that is, different intensities elicited different response patterns at the same site. Electrical stimulation of the aggressive zone area can elicit attack in both males and females and in different strains of rats (Kruk, Van der Lann, Van der Poel, Van Erp, & Meelis, 1990), whereas lesions placed within the aggressive zone area reduce aggression provoked by an intruder in a resident intruder paradigm (Adams, 1971; Olivier, 1977). This aggression zone area is not defined by any neuroanatomical boundaries. Hypothalamic aggression begins seconds after the onset of stimulation and ceases immediately after stimulation is halted. During stimulation there is little if any investigatory behavior. A stimulated animal may leap across the cage at a target directing bites to the head and neck. This "attack jump" is defensive and normally used by cornered rats. The aggression is stimulus bound, as objects that do not resemble provoking cues are not attacked. However, attacks are not constrained by the sex or social status of the target. For example, a subordinate animal will never attack the α male of a colony; yet, if driven by hypothalamic stimulation, it will readily attack and defeat the dominant conspecific (Koolhaas, 1978; Kruk et al., 1979).

The major advantage of hypothalamic aggression induced by electrical stimulation in the rat is its application to ethopharmacology. Olivier and Mos (1990) have systematically examined the pharmacological control of offensive aggression in different animal models, including hypothalamic aggression. However, one major drawback to using hypothalamic aggression as a model system is that the attack behavior does not conform to the normal ethogram of offensive aggression. For example, there is no lateral attack. Instead, they exhibit jump attack, which is not a common strategy employed by a males in a colony setting. In addition, many of the attacks occur to the head and face and not the back. Hence, electrical stimulation of the hypothalamus in the rat triggers attack releasing mechanisms, promoting the execution phase of fighting that may appear out of context.

ETHOLOGICAL MODELS OF OFFENSIVE AGGRESSION

Resident-Intruder Paradigm Using Small Rat Colonies

In the early 1970s Miczek (1974) employed the use of resident-intruder model to examine the effects of amphetamine on aggression in rats. This work was particularly significant because it employed a model that precluded the use of aversive stimuli. Rats were housed in small colonies of two males and two females. After the first litter had been raised and removed, an unfamiliar male rat was introduced into the home cage of the colony. The repeated presentation of the intruder would elicit an attack by one of the male residents. The offensive behavior by the resident male and the defensive behavior by the intruder fit the behavior observed in feral animals and the behavior described by the Blanchards. Miczek had established an ethologically valid model: He could routinely elicit offensive aggression characteristic of normal behavior that had been observed in wild rodents and in larger colony settings. In addition, it was possible to observe other nonagonistic social and solitary behaviors in this seminatural environment. With this model system, drugs could be applied to the resident male in the colony box or the intruder.

Miczek, Weerts, Tornatzky, Debold, and Vatne (1992) continued to expand on the resident-intruder model to include a complete quantitative ethological analysis of agonistic behavior. Not only could aggression be reported by the traditional measures of mean latency to attack, number of attacks, and the like, the individual could be examined for its own aggressive pattern, determining the probability of the sequences of specific acts and postures. For example, if a resident pursues an intruder, the probability is high that the resident will subsequently show a sideways threat. If a sideways threat is displayed, it is also highly probable that an attack bite will follow. With this type of ethological analysis, it was discovered that low doses of ethanol do not change the sequence of the elements of offensive aggression, but they increase the frequency and duration of an aggressive burst.

Resident-Intruder Paradigm Using Individually Housed Hamsters

The resident-intruder model has also been successfully employed to study offensive aggression in the golden hamster (*Mesocrecitus auratus*). The first detailed description of agonistic behavior between hamsters was provided by Grant and Mackintosh (1963) and later refined and extended by other investigators (Floody & Pfaff, 1977; Johnston, 1985; Lerwill & Makings, 1971). In the hamster resident-intruder paradigm, male hamsters are kept in separate cages because isolation enhances the aggression of a resident toward an intruder (Brain, 1972; Payne, 1973). This isolation is not unnatural as adult hamsters are not communal and maintain individ-

ual, solitary nest sites in the wild. They are maintained on a reverse light:dark cycle of 14:10 and filmed under dim red illumination because hamsters are nocturnal and their aggression is greatest during the dark phase of the circadian cycle (Landau, 1975; Lerwill & Making, 1971). In addition to isolation and circadian timing, numerous other factors can affect aggression. For example, housing and testing in smaller cages enhances aggression (Lawlor, 1963); older animals are more aggressive (Whitsett, 1975); smaller intruders are most likely to elicit attack as compared to larger animals (Payne & Swanson, 1972). The social histories of the intruders and residents are also important factors. For example, residents that are experienced fighters and intermittently used as breeders show short attack latencies (Ferris, unpublished observation).

Female hamsters are notoriously aggressive, particularly during lactation and in the presence of their pups (H. I. Siegel, Giordano, Mallafre, & Rosenblatt, 1983). Whereas male-male encounters do not normally result in physical injury, females will kill male and female intruders that enter their home cage during lactation. Potegal and coworkers (Potegal, 1992; Potegal & Popken, 1985; Potegal & ten Brink, 1984) have used this robust, reliable aggressive behavior of female hamsters to study attack readiness that occurs in animals during a short-term agonistic encounter. Potegal developed a model in which a female resident is first allowed a single attack on a conspecific intruder. This initial encounter decreases the latency and increases the probability of attack on a second intruder presented minutes later. The phenomenon was termed *attack priming*. Using this behavioral paradigm, Potegal, Huhman, Moore, Meyerhoff, and Skaredoff (1996) identified key populations of neurons in the amygdaloid complex that are selectively activated during attack priming and, therefore, appear to be part of the neural network controlling aggressive arousal. These neurons were identified by staining sections of the brain for fos protein, a marker of cellular activation.

NEUROCHEMICAL CONTROL OF OFFENSIVE AGGRESSION

Myriad reports implicate different neurotransmitters in the facilitation or inhibition of aggression (for reviews, see Eichelman, 1990; Mandel, 1980). However, as much of these data were obtained from studies on mouse-killing, shock-induced fighting in rodents and hypothalamic aggression in rats and cats, it is difficult to evaluate their relevance to offensive aggression as defined in a resident-intruder paradigm. With the use of ethologically valid models, it was discovered that many of the pharmacological agents used to affect aggressive responding are nonspecific and impair other behaviors. Dopamine receptor antagonists such as haloperidol aimed at the D_1 and D_2 receptor subtypes nonspecifically reduce aggressive behavior (Miczek et al., 1994). Low doses of benzodiazepine receptor agonists like diazepam enhance resident attack on an intruder, whereas higher doses reduce aggression, together with other behaviors (Miczek, 1974; Mos, Olivier, & Van der Poel, 1987).

Norepinephrine has been implicated in the facilitation of offensive aggression by a resident toward an intruder. Yoshimura, Kihara, and Ogawa (1987) reported that the centrally active β adrenergic receptor antagonist *l*-propranolol suppresses the offensive aggression of resident mice toward intruders in a dose-dependent manner. Indeed, numerous clinical reports have shown propranolol is effective in the treatment of aggression associated with damage to the central nervous system (Connor, 1993; Elliott, 1977; Yudofsky, Williams, & Gorman, 1987). However, propranolol's action on aggression may not be mediated by norepinephrine neurotransmission. Propranolol has an affinity for serotonin (5-HT) receptors, including the autoreceptor that regulates 5-HT release from presynaptic terminals (Middlemis 1984). Thus, propranolol may inhibit aggression by elevating synaptic 5-HT levels.

Serotonin and Offensive Aggression

A vast literature indicates an inverse relationship between 5-HT function in the CNS and aggressive behavior in many species, including humans (for reviews, see Brown & Linnoila, 1990; Eichelman, 1990; and Berman, Kavoussi, & Coccaro, Chapter 28, this volume). For example, male rats treated with selective neurotoxins that deplete brain 5-HT levels assume dominant positions in colonies of rats (Ellison, 1976). Resident rats with site-specific depletion of 5-HT in the lateral hypothalamus by microinjection of a neurotoxin that specifically causes lesions in 5-HT neurons show elevated offensive behavior toward intruders (Vergnes, Depaulis, Boehrer, & Kempf, 1988). Conversely, attacks, bites, and other agonistic behaviors that are part of the ethogram of offensive aggression can be reduced significantly with pharmacological manipulation that increases 5-HT levels or stimulates 5-HT$_1$ receptors. For example, resident hamsters show a significant increase in the latency to bite and a decrease in the number of bites toward an intruder when treated with fluoxetine, a serotonin-specific reuptake inhibitor (Ferris & Delville, 1994; Ferris, Melloni, Abbott, & Delville, 1995). As noted previously, offensive aggression is enhanced in homozygous mutant mice lacking the 5-HT$_{1B}$ receptor (Saudou et al., 1994). Eltropazine, a 5-HT $_{1a/1b}$ agonist (Sijbesma et al., 1990) produces a dose-dependent decrease in offensive aggression in a rat resident-intruder model (Olivier et al., 1987). Eltroprazine does not block defensive aggression, making it a potential candidate for development as a serenic (Olivier & Mos, 1990).

The relationship between low 5-HT function and high impulsivity was recently corroborated in a study of nonhuman primates examining species-typical agonistic behaviors in a natural setting (Mehlman et al., 1994). Twenty-six adolescent male rhesus macaques from Morgan Island, South Carolina, were captured, sampled for blood and cerebrospinal fluid (CSF), and fitted with radio transmitters to aid in tracking their whereabouts during behavioral observations. Animals were released back into a free-ranging population of 4,500 macaques and agonistic behavior was followed for 3 months. Risk taking was assessed by the distance animals leapt from tree branches. Approximately 8% of all leaping behavior was classified as "long leaping," from a human perspective, and deemed to be risky. An aggressive encounter was judged to be "intense" if it was punctuated by chase and physical assault. Approximately 10% of all agonistic encounters escalated into intense aggression. Adolescent monkeys with the highest aggression and greatest risk taking showed the lowest levels of 5-HIAA

concentrations in the CSF. The authors note that only the most severe forms of aggression and risk taking were correlated with low levels of 5-HT metabolite in CSF.

Vasopressin and Offensive Aggression

Studies on hamsters and rats indicate a role for arginine vasopressin (AVP) in the modulation of offensive aggression. In hamsters, an AVP receptor antagonist, microinjected into the anterior hypothalamus, causes a dose-dependent inhibition of offensive aggression of a resident male toward an intruder (Ferris & Potegal, 1988). Whereas treatment with AVP receptor antagonist increases bite latency and decreases the total number of bites toward the intruder, it acts like a serenic, because other social behaviors, general activity, and sexual behavior are unaffected. Conversely, microinjection of AVP into the anterior hypothalamus of resident hamsters significantly increases the number of biting attacks on intruders (Ferris et al., 1997). AVP receptor antagonists has also been tested in animals paired together in a neutral arena (Potegal & Ferris, 1990). Although this model is more complex than the resident-intruder paradigm and includes elements of both offensive and defensive aggression, the results are similar. AVP receptor antagonist injected into the anterior hypothalamus significantly depresses attacks and bites when either one or both members of the pair are treated with antagonist. The ability of AVP to modulate offensive aggression is not limited to the anterior hypothalamus. Microinjecting AVP into the ventrolateral hypothalamus (VLH) of the hamster facilitates offensive aggression (Delville, Mansour, & Ferris, 1996b; Ferris & Delville, 1994). Interestingly, in the golden hamster, AVP receptor binding within the VLH is androgen dependent (Delville et al., 1996a). This raises the possibility that the diminished offensive aggression noted in castrated hamsters (Ferris, Axelson, Martin, & Roberge, 1989; Payne & Swanson, 1972; Vandenbergh, 1971; Whitsett, 1975) is caused by a loss of AVP responsiveness in the VLH.

Unlike hamsters, rats show no steroid-sensitive binding sites for AVP. Infusion of AVP into the amygdala or lateral septum facilitates offensive aggression in castrated rats (Koolhaas, Moor, Heimstra, & Bohus, 1991; Koolhaas, Van den Brink, Roozendal, & Boorsma, 1990). The ability of AVP to affect offensive aggression at multiple sites in the CNS is evidence that this neurochemical system may play a broad physiological role in enhancing arousal during aggressive interactions.

It was discovered by chance that AVP injected into the anterior hypothalamus of the golden hamster triggers flank marking (Ferris, Albers, Wesolowski, Goldman, & Leeman, 1984), a stereotypic motor pattern used by hamsters to disseminate pheromones (Johnston, 1985). Flank marking cannot be elicited by the microinjection of other peptides, excitatory amino acids, pituitary hormones, or the classical neurotransmitters and is mediated through a V1$_a$ AVP receptor (Albers, Pollock, Simmons, & Ferris, 1986; Ferris, Singer, Meenan, & Albers, 1988). Microinjecting a V1$_a$-receptor antagonist into the anterior hypothalamus temporarily inhibits odor-induced flank marking triggered by the scents of other male hamsters (Ferris et al., 1988). Hence, flank marking, like offensive aggression, can be facilitated and inhibited by the administration of AVP agonists and antagonists, respectively.

Vasopressin-Serotonin Interactions

The search for mechanisms and anatomical substrates underlying interactions between functionally opposed neurotransmitter systems is an important aspect of the neurobiology of agonistic behavior. Ferris and coworkers have focused on the notion that AVP promotes aggression and dominant behavior by enhancing the activity of the neural network controlling agonistic behavior that is normally restrained by 5-HT (Ferris, 1992; Ferris & Delville, 1994; Ferris et al., 1997). This hypothesis is supported by four recent findings in the golden hamster: (a) The anterior hypothalamus has a high density of 5-HT_{1B} binding sites and receives a dense innervation of 5-HT fibers and terminals; (b) AVP neurons in the anterior hypothalamus appear to be preferentially innervated by 5-HT; (c) intraperitoneal injection of fluoxetine blocks offensive aggression facilitated by the microinjection of AVP in the anterior hypothalamus and VLH; and (d) intraperitoneal administration of fluoxetine causes a threefold increase in 5-HT levels coincident with a dramatic decrease in AVP levels in the anterior hypothalamus. These data suggest that 5-HT may act at pre- and postsynaptic sites to antagonize the actions of the AVP system. These preclinical studies examining the interaction between AVP and 5-HT are particularly exciting because a recent clinical study by Cocarro, Kavoussi, Berman, and Ferris (1997) indicates a similar reciprocal relationship in human studies. Personality disordered subjects with a history of fighting and assault show a negative correlation for prolactin release in response to a d-fenfluramine challenge, indication of a hyposensitive 5-HT system. Moreover, these same subjects show a positive correlation between CSF levels of AVP and aggression. Thus, in humans, a hyposensitive 5-HT system may result in enhanced CNS levels of AVP and the facilitation of aggressive behavior.

SOCIAL CONFLICT, OFFENSIVE AGGRESSION, AND NEURAL PLASTICITY

Dominant-Subordinate Relationships

By knowing much about the neuroanatomical and neurochemical control of offensive aggression in the golden hamster, it is feasible to study how environmental stress may affect brain plasticity to alter agonistic behavior. One environmental stressor that is particularly relevant to agonistic behavior is the social subjugation that accompanies the establishment and maintenance of dominant-subordinate relationships. Hamsters readily establish social status with a minimum of interactions (Lerwill & Makings, 1971). Ferris, Axelson, Shinto, and Albers (1987) examined the temporal and sequential pattern of agonistic and communicative behavior in pairs of male hamsters establishing social status. Hamsters were matched together in a neutral arena for 15 minutes each day for 5 consecutive days. The social status of each combatant appears to be determined by the level of overt aggression. Once the dominance relationship is determined, the level of overt aggression diminishes with each subsequent social encounter. Ultimately, animals show little if any overt aggression. However, with each encounter both the dominant and subordinate animals show enhanced flank marking behavior. Dominant and submissive animals do not flank mark equally. The dominant member of a pair will routinely flank mark three times more than its submissive partner. Flank marking is used to communicate social status and minimize the level of overt aggression, because removal of the flank glands is associated with constant fighting during each social encounter. Establishing and maintaining dominant-subordinate relationships in this experimental model is very simple, and the behavior highly predictable. The dominant-subordinate relationships are long lasting as animals show little if any aggression, high levels of flank marking, and no reversal in social status when introduced after a long period of isolation. More aggressive hamsters who flank mark more than other male conspecifics, more often are chosen as mates by receptive females as compared with subordinate partners (Huck, Lisk, & Gore, 1985). Thus, this model system can be used to examine neurobiological changes in dominant and subordinate animals and the endocrine factors that contribute to their change in behavior.

Adolescent Abuse

In humans, adolescence is defined as a period of pronounced physical, cognitive, and emotional growth. This period usually begins just before puberty and ends in early adulthood with sexual maturity, social awareness, and independence. The golden hamster has a developmental period analogous to adolescence. In the wild, hamsters wean around postnatal day 25 (p-25), leave the home nest, forage on their own, establish nest sites, and defend their territory. Hamsters can begin to establish dominance hierarchies as early as p-35 and have a minimal breeding age of 42 days. Androgen levels start to rise dramatically between p-28 and p-35.

Subjecting adolescent hamsters to daily threat and attack affects agonistic behavior in early adulthood (Ferris et al., 1995). Placing a smaller hamster into their home cage elicits more bites and a shorter latency to attack as compared to litter mates raised under control conditions. However, this enhanced aggression is context dependent because, when confronted by an intruder of equal size, they are much less aggressive than their control litter mates and are often very timid. This model system can be used to study the long-term behavioral and biological consequences of physical and emotional abuse in subadult animals.

Gonadal and Adrenal Steroids

A vast literature reports on steroid modulation of agonistic behavior (see Brain & Susman, Chapter 29, this volume). Testosterone implanted in the septum and medial preoptic area can enhance offensive aggression in castrated male mice (Owen, Peters, & Bronson, 1974) and rats (Albert, 1987). In hamsters, high levels of testosterone facilitate offensive aggression, whereas absence of testosterone diminishes initiated attacks and bites (Ferris et al., 1990; Payne & Swanson, 1972; Vandenbergh, 1971; Whitsett, 1975). As noted previously, one possible mechanism of action for testosterone in hamsters is the maintenance of AVP receptors in the VLH.

The role of glucocorticoids in offensive aggression is not as clear as that of testosterone. Depending on testing conditions and the duration of treatment used, glucocorticoids can produce opposite effects on agonistic behavior in rats, mice, and hamsters. Defeat in mice results in elevated corticosterone levels that appear to promote submissive behavior (Leshner, Korn, Mixon, Rosenthal, & Besser, 1980; Louch & Higginbotham, 1967). In the golden hamster, cortisol was shown to exert site-, context-, and dose-dependent effects on agonistic behavior (Hayden-Hixson & Ferris, 1991a, 1991b). In dominant hamsters, cortisol implanted in the anterior hypothalamus facilitates the display of submissive behavior in the presence of other dominant animals while promoting high levels of aggressive behavior in the presence of submissive animals. The mechanisms regulating these effects are unclear but could involve interaction with AVP or 5-HT. For instance, as glucocorticoids regulate AVP neurons (Swanson, 1991), they also facilitate the synthesis of 5-HT by enhancing brain levels of tryptophan hydroxylase, the rate-limiting enzyme in the formation of 5-HT (Azmitia & McEwen, 1974; Sze, Neckers, & Towle, 1976). In addition, there is evidence that glucocorticoids can act at nerve terminals to increase 5-HT synthesis by increasing tryptophan uptake (Necker & Sze, 1975). Furthermore, chronic stress activates glucocorticoid receptors in 5-HT neurons within the dorsal raphe nucleus (Kitayama et al., 1989).

Brain-Steroid Interactions

Neuronal plasticity is normally associated with early development or response to injury (reactive synaptogenesis); however, recent studies provide strong evidence for synaptic remodeling in the adult mammalian CNS, particularly in response to gonadal steroids (Frankfurt et al., 1990; Matsumoto, Micevych, & Arnold, 1988). Are there synaptic changes during the acquisition of submissive behavior following defeat?

Defeated mice display less offensive aggression and more submissive behavior (Frishknecht, Seigfried, & Waser, 1982; Williams & Lierle, 1988). Rats consistently defeated by more aggressive conspecifics show a behavioral inhibition characterized by less social initiative and offensive aggression as well as an increase in defensive behavior (Van de Poll, DeJonge, Van Oyen, & Van Pelt, 1982). Repeatedly defeated male hamsters respond in a submissive manner when confronted by a nonaggressive intruder (Potegal, Huhman, Moore, & Meyerhoff, 1993). Could social subjugation, that is, repeated defeat by more aggressive opponents, result in plastic changes in the AVP and 5-HT systems that could predispose subjugated animals to be less aggressive in subsequent social encounters? In support of this notion are reports that the development of submissive behavior is accompanied by an increase in the activity of the 5-HT system (Yodyingyuad, De la Riva, Abbott, Herbert, & Keverne, 1985). In addition, a decrease in AVP immunoreactivity has been observed within select populations of neurons in the anterior hypothalamus in continuously defeated, castrated hamsters (Ferris et al., 1989). This depletion of AVP immunoreactivity in subjugated animals is associated with a decrease in fighting and flank marking. However, changes in the AVP system were observed only in subjugated animals; no effect was recorded in dominant animals.

Hence, social conflict can have a significant effect on the neurotransmitters that affect aggressive responding. What possible mechanisms may contribute to this neural plasticity? In many species,

defeat and subjugation are associated with changes in plasma levels of gonadal and adrenal steroid hormones. In both combatants, aggressive encounters produce an elevation of glucocorticoid levels, possibly as a response to the stress caused by the confrontation (Schuurman, 1980). Following the encounter, glucocorticoids levels return to basal values. During subsequent aggressive encounters, higher levels of glucocorticoids are observed in the defeated, submissive animal, and these levels remain elevated for a longer period of time (Bronson & Eleftheriou, 1964; Eberhart, Keverne, & Meller, 1983; Ely & Henry, 1978; Huhman, Moore, Ferris, Mougey, & Meyerhoff, 1991; Louch & Higgenbotham, 1967; Raab et al., 1986). Furthermore, changes in testosterone levels coincide with the changes in glucocorticoids. Elevated levels of testosterone are observed in victorious animals and low levels in defeated males (Coe, Mendoza, & Levine, 1979; Eberhart, Keverne, & Meller, 1980; Rose et al., 1975; Sapolsky, 1985).

It should be noted, however, that animals maintained on constant or high levels of testosterone still can be defeated and display submissive behavior (Maruniak, Desjardins, & Bronson, 1977; Van de Poll, Smeets, Van Oyen, & Van der Swan, 1982). Conversely, castrated, testosterone-deficient animals still can fight and win (Maruniak et al., 1977; Whitsett, 1975). It may not be the presence or absence of testosterone alone that determines the level of offensive aggression but the ratio of glucocorticoids and androgens. Therefore, we propose that acute and prolonged changes in blood levels of both glucocorticoids and testosterone are responsible, in part, for AVP and 5-HT system changes that predispose defeated animals to behave in a submissive manner. Indeed, stabilizing adrenal and gonadal steroid levels has been reported to increase resistance to social subjugation in mice (Nock & Leshner, 1976).

ETHOLOGICAL MODELS OF AFFILIATIVE BEHAVIOR

Affiliative behavior offers an alternative way to study the neural mechanisms that regulate aggressive behavior. Animals that establish groups or join existing groups often display aggression toward animals that are not part of that group. The same is seen in monogamous animals, which after forming an often lifelong association with their mate, fiercely defend their territory from intruders (Kleiman, 1977). Therefore, understanding the mechanisms involved in forming social affiliations may help to understand how the brain controls aggression toward conspecifics.

Pair-bonding in rodents offers a particularly useful model to study affiliative behavior, including its aggressive component. Changes in affiliative behavior are closely correlated to changes in the reproductive status that follow pair-bonding; these changes easily can be timed. For example, male gerbils, California mice, and prairie voles stay with their mates throughout the gestation period and, following the birth of pups, engage in parental activities such as grooming, crouching over, and retrieving pups (Dewsbury, 1981; Elwood, 1977; Ergen, 1976; Getz & Hofmann, 1986; Gubernick & Albers, 1987). In gerbils and California mice, sexually naive males often attack or ignore pups; males are prepared for paternal behavior through mating and cohabitation with a pregnant female (Alberts & Gubernick, 1990; Elwood, 1977).

Sexually naive prairie vole males often show spontaneous parental responsiveness; mating, however, considerably increases it (Bamshad, Novak, & De Vries, 1994). Although no information is available on the possible neural mechanisms involved in affiliation of gerbils and California mice, comparative studies on voles suggest that central oxytocinergic and vasopressinergic systems may be involved. The great variability in patterns of social behavior among vole species enables one to compare these systems in closely related subspecies that show different patterns of social behavior. For example, prairie voles (*Microtus ochrogaster*) and pine voles (*Microtus pinetorum*) are monogamous. Fathers as well as mothers provide parental care. Montane voles (*Microtus montanus*) and meadow voles (*Microtus pennsylvanicus*) are promiscuous; only mothers provide parental care (McGuire & Novak, 1984; Oliveras & Novak, 1986). This difference appears to be reflected in the distribution of oxytocin and AVP receptors in the brain. For example, the monogamous prairie and pine voles have fewer AVP binding sites in the lateral septum than the promiscuous montane and meadow voles have (Insel & Shapiro, 1992; Insel, Wang, & Ferris, 1994).

Vasopressin and Paternal Behavior

The role of the central AVP in various affiliative behaviors may vary by sex. In comparing sexually naive male prairie and meadow voles with experienced voles 6 days after the birth of their first litter, we found the density of the AVP-immunoreactive innervation of the lateral septum and lateral habenular nucleus was lower in parental male prairie voles than in sexually naive males (Bamshad, Novak, & De Vries, 1993). A follow-up experiment showed that the density of the AVP-immunoreactive projections in prairie vole males decreased after mating, then increased gradually during the gestation period, only to decrease again after the birth of pups (Bamshad et al., 1994). The initial drop in AVP-immunoreactive fiber density in the lateral septum and lateral habenular nucleus after pairing may reflect an increase in AVP release, because it coincides with higher levels of AVP messenger RNA in the bed nucleus of the stria terminalis, the most probable source of septal and habenular AVP (Wang, Smith, Major, & De Vries, 1994). None of these changes were seen in meadow vole males or in the females of both species (Bamshad et al., 1993, 1994; Wang et al., 1994).

A number of pharmacological experiments suggest that the changes in AVP innervation may indeed be related to changes in social behaviors. For example, AVP may stimulate paternal behavior, because injections of AVP into the lateral septum of sexually naive male prairie voles stimulated grooming, crouching over, and contacting pups—the most prominent paternal activities displayed by parental prairie voles. In addition, injections of a $V1_a$ receptor antagonist blocked these behaviors (Wang et al., 1994) in an apparently site-specific manner. Injections of AVP into other areas or into the ventricles did not stimulate paternal behavior.

Vasopressin may also play a role in pair-bonding and the concomitant change in aggressive behavior directed toward unfamiliar conspecifics. Injections of a $V1_a$ receptor antagonist prior to mating blocked the mating-induced increase in male aggression and pair-bonding (Winslow, Hastings, Carter, Harbaugh, & Insel,

1993). Although this finding suggests that the antagonist blocked endogenous AVP, it does not identify the septum as the site where AVP is released. In rats, however, injections of the same $V1_a$ receptor antagonist have implicated the AVP innervation of the lateral septum and the amygdala in intermale aggression (Koolhaas et al., 1990, 1991).

Testosterone Effects on the Vasopressin System

The AVP innervation of these areas may mediate effects of testosterone on aggressive behavior. In rats, both the lateral septum and the amygdala receive their AVP innervation from the bed nucleus of the stria terminalis (De Vries & Buijs, 1983). The AVP production in this nucleus completely depends on the presence of gonadal steroids (De Vries, Buijs, Van Leeuwen, Caffi, & Swaab, 1985; Miller, Urban, & Dorsa, 1989). Because testosterone influences this system similarly in prairie voles and because testosterone levels increase after mating (Gaines et al., 1985; Wang et al., 1994), mating may influence aggressive behavior in part by the stimulating influence of testosterone on vasopressin neurotransmission.

Although gonadal hormone levels are also increased after mating in females (Carter et al., 1989), it is unclear whether these hormones influence female aggressive behavior. But, even if they do, the low levels of AVP peptide and *m*RNA in the bed nucleus of female compared to male prairie voles suggest that AVP does not play an important role in social behavior in female prairie voles (Bamshad et al., 1993, 1994; Wang et al., 1994). However, oxytocin rather than AVP appears to influence pair-bonding in female prairie voles (Williams, Insel, Harbaugh, & Carter, 1994; Winslow et al., 1993). Whether oxytocin influences mating-induced aggression is not known.

The species differences in affiliative behaviors may not result merely from differences in genetic endowment. The social conditions under which the animals are raised influence affiliative behavior displayed in adulthood. For example, male meadow voles cross-fostered by prairie vole parents tend to show more paternal behavior than their counterparts fostered by meadow vole parents (McGuire, 1988). Whether such early-rearing conditions also affect other hallmarks of monogamous behavior, such as the mating-induced aggressiveness to unfamiliar conspecifics, and whether such conditions influence central AVP and oxytocin pathways has to be determined. If they do, voles would offer an attractive model to study the effects of social conditions during development on aggressive behavior displayed in adulthood.

SUMMARY

The study of aggressive behavior has evolved from using models such as brain lesion and electric shock to ethological models such as the social behavior in voles. The early brain lesion and stimulation studies showed that distinct neural circuits control aggressive behavior. The artificial conditions under which these observations were conducted, however, made these studies less well suited to identify the factors that regulate the timing, organization, and intensity of aggressive behavior. The development of the ethological models has been much more productive in helping to identify the roles of endogenous factors such as genes, neurotransmitters, hormones, sex, and age and exogenous factors such as social status or the ingestion of toxicants such as ethanol. These models have provided the tools to develop drugs for intervention in humans with impulsive, violent behavior. Finally, the emergence of comparative studies on aggressive and affiliative behaviors will help to identify the social and environmental conditions in early development and adulthood that precipitate aggressive behavior. The comparative aspect of these studies is of most importance because only by studying different species are we able to understand the similarities and differences in control mechanisms and thereby estimate the boundaries in which aggressive behavior is regulated in humans. The combination of all these approaches facilitates and expands the development of interventions strategies.

REFERENCES

Adams, D. B. (1971). Defense and territorial behavior dissociated by hypothalamic lesions in the rat. *Nature, 232,* 573–574.

Adams, D. B. (1976). The relationship of scent-marking, olfactory investigation, and specific postures in the isolation-induced fighting of rats. *Behavior, 56,* 286–297.

Adams, D. B. (1979). Brain mechanisms for offense, defense and submission. *Behavioral Brain Sciences, 2,* 201–241.

Albers, H. E., Pollock J., Simmons, W. H., Ferris, C. F. (1986). A V1-like receptor mediates vasopressin induced flank marking behavior within the hamster hypothalamus. *Journal of Neuroscience, 6,* 2085–2089.

Albert, D. J. (1987). Intermale social aggression:reinstatement in castrated rats by implants of testosterone proprionate in the medial hypothalamus. *Physiology and Behavior, 39,* 555–560.

Albert, D. J., Nanji, N., Brayley, N., Madryga, F. J. (1979). Hyperreactivity as well as mouse killing is induced by electrical stimulation of the lateral hypothalamus in the rat. *Behavioral Neural Biology, 27,* 59–71.

Albert, D. J., & Walsh, M. L. (1984). Neural systems and the inhibitory modulation of agonistic behavior: a comparison of mammalian species. *Neuroscience and Behavioral Reviews, 8,* 5–24.

Alberts, J. R., & Gubernick, D. J. (1990). Functional organization of dyadic and triadic parent-offspring systems. In N. A. Krasnegor & R. S. Bridges (Eds.), *Mammalian parenting* (pp. 416–440). New York: Oxford University Press.

Azmitta, E. C., & McEwen, B. S. (1994). Adrenalcortical influence on rat brain tryptophan hydroxylase activity. *Brain Research, 78,* 291–302.

Bamshad, M., Novak, M. A., & De Vries, G. J. (1993). Sex and species differences in the vasopressin innervation of sexually naive and parental prairie voles, *Microtus ochrogaster,* and meadow voles, *Microtus pennsylvanicus. Journal of Neuroendocrinology, 5,* 247–255.

Bamshad, M., Novak, M. A., & De Vries, G. J. (1994). Cohabitation alters vasopressin innervation and paternal behavior in Prairie voles, *Microtus ochrogaster. Physiology and Behavior, 56,* 751–758.

Bandler, R. (1988). Brain mechanisms of aggression as revealed by electrical and chemical stimulation: Suggestion of a central role for the midbrain periaqueductal grey region. *Progress in Psychology and Physiological Psychology, 13,* 67–135.

Barnett, S. A. (1958). An analysis of social behavior in wild rats. *Proceedings of the Zoological Society, London, 130,* 107–152.

Baxter, B. L. (1968). Elicitation of emotional behavior by electrical or chemical stimulation applied at the same loci in cat mesencephalon. *Experimental Neurology, 21,* 1–10.

Blanchard, D. C. (1984). Applicability of animal models to human aggression. *Progress in Clinical and Biological Research, 169,* 49–74.

Blanchard, R. J., & Blanchard, D. C. (1977). Aggressive behaviour in the rat. *Physiology and Behavior 1,* 197–224.

Brain, P. F. (1972). Effects of isolation/grouping on endocrine function and fighting behavior in male and female golden hamsters (*Mesocricetus auratus Waterhouse*). *Behavioral Biology, 7,* 349–357.

Brain, P. F. (1981). Differentiating types of attack and defense in rodents. In P. F. Brain & D. Benton (Eds.), *Multidisciplinary approaches to aggression research* (pp. 53–77). New York: Elsevier.

Bronson, F. H., & Eleftheriou, B. F. (1964). Chronic physiological effects of fighting in mice. *General Comparative Endocrinology, 4,* 9–14.

Brown, G. L., & Linnoila, M. I. (1990). CSF serotonin metabolite (5-HIAA) studies in depression, impulsivity, and violence. *Journal of Clinical Psychiatry, 51* (4, suppl.), 31–41.

Brunner, H. G., Nelen, M., Breakefield, X. O., Ropers, H. H., & van Oost, B. A. (1993). Abnormal behavior associated with a point mutation in the structural gene for monoamine oxidase A. *Science, 262,* 578–580.

Cairns, R. B., MacCombie, D. J., & Hood, K. E., (1983). A developmental-genetic analysis of aggressive behavior in mice: I. Behavioral outcomes. *Journal of Comparative Psychology, 1,* 69–89.

Carrive, P., Schmitt, P., & Karli, P. (1986). Flight induced by microinjection of d-tubocurarine or a-bungarotoxin into medial hypothalamus or periaqueductal gray matter: Cholinergic or GABAergic mediation. *Behavioral Brain Research, 22,* 233–248.

Carter, C. S., Witt, D. M., Thompson, E. G., & Caristead, K. (1988). Effects of hormonal, sexual, and social history on mating and pair bonding in the prairie vole. *Physiology and Behavior, 44,* 691–697.

Coccaro, E. F., Kavoussi, R. J., Hauger, R. L., & Ferris, C. F. (1997). Cerebrospinal fluid vasopressin concentration correlates with indices of aggression and serotonin function in human subjects. (submitted for publication)

Coe, C. L., Mendoza, S. P., & Levine, S. (1979). Social status contrains the stress response in the squirrel monkey. *Physiology and Behavior, 23,* 633–638.

Connor, D. F. (1993). Beta blockers for aggression: A review of the pediatric experience. *Journal of Child and Adolescent Psychopharmacology, 3,* 99–114.

Davis, F. C. (1935). The measurement of aggressive behavior in laboratory rats. *Journal of Genetic Psychology, 4,* 213–217.

Delgado, J. M. R. (1980). Neuronal constellations in aggressive behavior. In I. Valzelli & I. Morgese (Eds.), *Aggression and violence: A psychobiological and clinical approach* (pp. 82–97). Milan, Italy: Edizione Saint Vincent.

Delville, Y., Mansour, K. M., & Ferris, C. F. (1996a). Testosterone facilitates aggression by modulating vasopressin receptors in the hypothalamus. *Physiology and Behavior, 60,* 25–29.

Delville, Y., Mansour, K. M., & Ferris, C. F. (1996b) Serotonin blocks vasopressin-facilitated offensive aggression: Interactions within the ventrolateral hypothalamus of golden hamsters. *Physiology and Behavior, 59,* 813–816.

De Vries, G. J., & Buijs, R. M. (1983). The origin of the vasopressinergic and oxytocinergic innervation of the rat brain with special reference to the lateral septum. *Brain Research, 273,* 307–317.

De Vries, G. J., Buijs, R. M., Van Leeuwen, F. W., Caffi, A. R., & Swaab, D. F. (1985). The vasopressinergic innervation of the brain in normal and castrated rats. *Journal of Comparative Neurology, 233,* 236–254.

Dewsbury, D. A. (1981). An exercise in the prediction of monogamy in the field from laboratory data on 42 muroid rodents. *The Biologist, 63,* 138–162.

Eberhart, J. A., Keverne, E. B., & Meller, R. E. (1980). Social influences on plasma testosterone levels in male talapoin monkeys. *Hormones and Behavior, 14*, 247–266.

Eberhart, J. A., Keverne, E. B., & Meller, R. E. (1983). Social influences on circulating levels of cortisol and prolactin in male talapoin monkeys. *Physiology and Behavior, 30*, 361–369.

Ebert, P. D., & Hyde, J. S. (1976). Selection for agonistic behavior in wild female *Mus musculus*. *Behavioral Genetics, 6*, 291–304.

Eibl-Eibesfeldt, I. (1961). The fighting behavior of animals. *Scientific American, 205*, 470–482.

Eichelman, B. S. (1990). Neurochemical and psychopharmacologic aspects of aggressive behavior. *Annual Review of Medicine, 41*, 147–158.

Eichelman, B. S., & Barchas, J. (1975). Facilitated shock-induced aggression following antidepressive medication in the rats. *Pharmacology, Biochemistry and Behavior, 3*, 601–604.

Elliott, F. A. (1977). Propranolol for the control of belligerent behavior following acute brain damage. *Annals of Neurology, 1*, 489–491.

Ellison, G. (1976). Monoamine neurotoxins: Selective and delayed effects on behavior in colonies of laboratory rats. *Brain Research, 103*, 81–92.

Elwood, R. W. (1977). Changes in the responses of male and female gerbils *(Meriones unguiculatus)* towards test pups during the pregnancy of the female. *Animal Behaviour, 25*, 46–51.

Ely, D. L., & Henry, J. P. (1978). Neuroendocrine response patterns in dominant and subordinate mice. *Hormones and Behavior, 10*, 156–169.

Ergen, G. (1976). Social and territorial behaviour in the Mongolian gerbil *(Meriones unguiculatus)* under seminatural conditions. *Biology and Behavior, 1*, 267–285.

Ferris, C. F. (1992). Role of vasopressin in aggressive and dominant/subordinate behaviors. In *Oxytocin and maternal, sexual, and social behaviors*. C. A. Pedersen, J. D. Caldwell, G. F. Jirikowski, & T. R. Insel (Eds.), *Annals of the New York Academy of Sciences, 652*, 212–226.

Ferris, C. F., Albers, H. E., Wesolowski, S. M., Goldman, B. D., & Leeman, S. E. (1984). Vasopressin injected into the hypothalamus triggers a stereotypic behavior in golden hamsters. *Science, 224*, 521–523.

Ferris, C. F., Axelson, J. F., Martin, A. M., & Roberge, L. R. (1989). Vasopressin immunoreactivity in the anterior hypothalamus is altered during the establishment of dominant/subordinate relationships between hamsters. *Neuroscience, 29*, 675–683.

Ferris, C. F., Axelson, J. F., Shinto, L., & Albers, H. E. (1987). Scent marking and the maintenance of dominant/subordiate status in male golden hamster. *Physiology and Behavior, 40*, 661–664.

Ferris, C. F., & Delville, Y. (1994). Vasopressin and serotonin interactions in the control of agonistic behavior. *Psychoneuroendocrinology, 19*, 593–601.

Ferris, C. F., Melloni, R. H., Jr., Abbott, M. A., & Delville, Y. (1995). *Behavioral and neurobiological consequences of adolescent abuse in golden hamsters*. San Diego: abstract 664.3, Society for Neuroscience.

Ferris, C. F., Melloni, R. H., Jr., Perry, K. W., Koppel, G., Fuller, R. W., & Delville, Y. (1997). Vasopressin/serotonin interaction in the anterior hypothalamus control aggressive behavior in golden hamsters. *Journal of Neuroscience*.

Ferris, C. F., & Potegal, M. (1988). Vasopressin receptor blockade in the anterior hypothalamus suppresses aggression in hamsters. *Physiology and Behavior, 44*, 235–239.

Ferris, C. F., Singer, E. A., Meenan, D. M., & Albers, H. E. (1988). Inhibition of vasopressin-stimulated flank marking behavior by V_1-receptor antagonists. *European Journal of Pharmacology, 154*, 153–159.

Floody, O. R., & Pfaff, D. W. (1977). Aggressive behavior in female hamsters. The hormonal basis for fluctuations in female aggressiveness correlated with estrous state. *Journal of Comparative and Physiological Psychology, 91*, 443–464.

Flynn, J. P. (1967). The neural basis of aggression in cats. In D. C. Glass (Ed.), *Neurophysiology and Emotion* (pp. 40–60). Rockefeller University Press and Russell Sage Foundation.

Frankfurt, M., Gould, E., Wooley, C. S., & McEwen, B. S. (1990). Gonadal steroids modify dendritic spine density in ventromedial hypothalamic neurons: A Golgi study in the adult rat. *Neuroendocrinology, 51*(5), 530–535.

Frishknecht, H. R., Seigfried, B., & Waser, P. G. (1982). Learning of submissive behavior in mice: A new model. *Behavioral Processes, 7*, 235–245.

Fuchs, S. A. G., Edinger, H. M., & Siegel, A. (1985). The organization of the hypothalamic pathways mediating affective defensive behavior in the cat. *Brain Research, 330*, 77–92.

Gaines, M. S., Fugate, C. L., Johnson, M. L., Johnson, D. C., Hisey, J. R., & Quadagno, D. M. (1985). Manipulation of aggressive behavior in male prairie voles *(Microtus ochrogaster)* implanted with testosterone in Silastic tubing. *Canadian Journal of Zoology, 63*, 2525–2528.

Getz, L. L., & Hofmann, J. E. (1986). Social organization in free-living prairie voles, *Microtus ochrogaster. Behavioral and Ecological Sociobiology, 18*, 275–282.

Glusman, M. (1985). Brain mechanisms and aggressive behavior in the cat. *International Journal of Neurology, 19*, 163–185.

Grant E. C., & Mackintosh, J. H. (1963). A comparison of the social postures of some common laboratory rodents. *Behavior, 21*, 246–259.

Gubernick, D. J., & Albers, J. R. (1987). The biparental care system of the California mouse, *Peromyscus californicus. Journal of Comparative Psychology, 101*, 169–177.

Hahn, M. E., & Haber, S. B. (1982). The inheritance of agonistic behavior in male mice: A diallel analysis. *Aggressive Behavior, 8*, 19–38.

Hayden-Hixson, D. M., & Ferris, C. F. (1991a). Steroid-specific regulation of agonistic responding in the anterior hypothalamus of male hamsters. *Physiology and Behavior, 50*, 793–799.

Hayden-Hixson, D. M., & Ferris, C. F. (1991b). Cortisol exerts site-, context-, and dose-specific effects on the agonistic behaviors of male golden hamsters. *Journal of Neuroendocrinology, 3*, 613–622.

Hess, W. R., & Brugger, M. (1943). Das susbkortikale Zentrum der affecktiven Abwehrreaktion. *Helvetica Physiologica Acta, 1*, 33–52.

Huck, U. W., Lisk, R. D., & Gore, A. C. (1985). Scent marking and mate choice in golden hamsters. *Physiology and Behavior, 35*, 389–393.

Huhman, K. L., Moore, T. O., Ferris, C. F., Mougey, E. H., & Meyerhoff, J. L. (1991). Acute and repeated exposure to social conflict in male golden hamsters: Increases in plasma POMC-peptides and cortisol and decreases in plasma testosterone. *Hormones and Behavior, 25*, 206–216.

Huntingford, F. A., & Turner, A. K. (1987). *Animal conflict*. New York: Chapman and Hall.

Insel, T. R., & Shapiro, L. E. (1992). Oxytocin receptor distribution reflects social organization in monogamous and polygamous voles. *Proceedings of the National Academy of Sciences USA, 89*, 5981–5985.

Insel, T. R., Wang, Z., & Ferris, C. F. (1994). Patterns of vasopressin receptor distribution associated with social organization in monogamous and non-monogamous microtine rodent. *Journal of Neuroscience, 14*, 5381–5392.

Johansson, G. G. (1981). Neural stimulation as a means of generating standardized threat under laboratory conditions. In P. F. Brain & D. Benton

(Eds.), *Multidisciplinary approaches to aggression research* (pp. 93–100). Amsterdam: Elsevier/North-Holland Biomedical Press.

Johnston, R. E. (1985). Communication. In H. I. Siegel (Ed.), *The hamster reproduction and behavior* (pp. 121–154). New York: Plenum.

Karli, P. (1956). The Norway rat's killing response to the white mouse. An experimental analysis. *Behaviour, 10,* 81–103.

Katz, R. J. (1978). Catecholamines in predatory behavior: A review and critique. *Aggressive Behavior, 4,* 153–172.

King, M. B., & Hoebel, B. G. (1968). Killing elicited by brain stimulation in rats. *Communications in Behavioral Biology, 2,* 173–177.

Kitayama, I., Cintra, A., Janson, A. M., Fuxe, K., Agnati, L. F., Eneroth, P., Aronsson, M., Harfstrand, A., Steinbush, H. W. M., Visser, T. J., Goldstein, M., Vale, W., & Gustafsson, J.-A. (1989). Chronic immobilization stress: Evidence for decreases of 5-hydroxy-tryptamine immunoreactivity and for increases of glucocorticoid receptor immunoreactivity in various brain regions of the male rat. *Journal of Neural Transmissions, 77,* 93–130.

Kleiman, D. (1977). Monogamy in mammals. *Quarterly Review of Biology 52,* 339–369.

Koolhaas, J. M. (1978). Hypothlamically induced intraspecific aggressive behavior in the rat. *Experimental Brain Research 32,* 365–375.

Koolhaas, J. M., Moor, E., Hiemstra, Y., & Bohus, B. (1991). The testosterone-dependent vasopressinergic neurons in the medial amygdala and lateral septum: Involvement in social behaviour of male rats. In S. Jard & R. Jamison (Eds.), *Vasopressin* (pp. 213–219). Paris-Londres: INSERM/John Libbey Eurotext Ltds.

Koolhaas, J. M., Van den Brink, T. H. C., Roozendal, B., & Boorsma, F. (1990). Medial amygdala and aggressive behavior: Interaction between testosterone and vasopressin. *Aggressive Behavior 16,* 223–229.

Kruk, M. R. (1991). Ethology and pharmacology of hypothalamic aggression in the rat. *Neuroscience and Biobehavioral Reviews, 15,* 527–538.

Kruk, M. R., Van der Lann, C. E., Van der Poel, A. M., Van Erp, A. M. M., & Meelis, W. (1990). Strain differences in attack patterns elicited by electrical stimulation in the hypothalamus of male CP-BWEzob and CPBWI rats. *Aggressive Behavior, 16,* 177–190.

Kruk, M. R., Van der Poel, A. M., & De Vos-Frerichs, T. P. (1979). The induction of aggressive behavior by electrical stimulation in the hypothalamus of male rats. *Behaviour, 70,* 292–322.

Kruk, M. R., Van der Poel, A. M., Meelis, W., Hermans, J., Mostert, P. G., Mos, J., & Lohman, A. H. M. (1983). Discriminate analysis of the localization of aggression-inducing electrode placements in the hypothalamus of male rats. *Brain Research, 260,* 61–97.

Lagerspetz, K. (1964). Studies on the aggressive behavior of mice. *Annales Academie Scientiarum Fennice,* (B) *131,* 1–131.

Lammers, J. H. C. M., Kruk, M. R., Meelis, W., & Van der Poel, A. M. (1988). Hypothalmaic substrates for brain stimulation-induced attack, teethchattering and social grooming in the rat. *Brain Research, 449,* 311–327.

Landau, I. T. (1975). Light-dark rhythms in aggressive behavior of the male golden hamster. *Physiology and Behavior, 14,* 767–774.

Lau, P., & Miczek, K. A., (1977). Differential effects of septal lesions on attack and defensive-submissive reactions during intraspecies aggression in rats. *Physiology and Behavior, 18,* 479–486.

Lawlor, M. (1963). Social dominance in the golden hamster. *Bulletin of the British Psychological Society, 16,* 1–14.

Lerwill, C. J., & Makings, P. (1971). The agonistic behavior of the golden hamster *Mesocricetus auratus (Waterhouse). Animal Behaviour, 19,* 714–721.

Leshner, A. I., Korn, S. J., Mixon, J. F., Rosenthal, C., & Besser, A. K. (1980). Effects of corticosterone on submissiveness in mice: Some temporal and theoretical considerations. *Physiology and Behavior, 24,* 283–288.

Louch, C. D., & Higginbotham, M. (1967). The relation between social rank and plasma corticosterone levels in mice. *General Comparative Endocrinology, 8,* 441–444.

Mandel, P. (1980). Neurochemistry of experimental aggression. In I. Valzelli & I. Morgese (Eds.), *Aggression and violence: A psychobiological and clinical approach* (pp. 61–71). Milan, Italy: Edizione Saint Vincent.

Maruniak, J. A., Desjardins, C., & Bronson, F. H. (1977). Dominant-subordinate relationships in castrated male mice bearing testosterone implants. *American Journal of Physiology, 2(6),* E495–E499.

Matsumoto, A., Micevych, P. E., & Arnold, A. P. (1988). Androgen regulates synaptic input to motoneurons of the adult rat spinal cord. *Journal of Neuroscience, 8,* 4168–4176.

McGuire, B. (1988). Effects of cross-fostering on parental behavior of meadow voles *(Microtus pennsylvanicus). Journal of Mammalogy, 69,* 332–341.

McGuire, B., & Novak, M. (1984). A comparison of maternal behavior in the meadow vole *(Microtus pennslyvanicus),* prairie vole *(M. ochrogaster)* and pine vole *(M. pinetorum). Animal Behaviour, 32,* 1132–1141.

Mehlman, P. T., Higley, J. D., Faucher, I., Lilly, A. A., Taub, D. M., Vickers, J., Suomi, S. J., & Linnoila, M. (1994). Low CSF 5-HIAA concentration and severe aggression and impaired impulse control in nonhuman primates. *American Journal of Psychiatry, 151,* 1485–1491.

Miczek, K. A. (1974). Intraspecies aggression in rats: Effects of d-amphetamine and chlordiazepoxide, *Psychopharmacologia, 39,* 275–301.

Miczek, K. A., Weerts, E., Haney, M., & Tidey, J. (1994). Neurobiological mechanisms controlling aggression: Preclinical developments for pharmacotherapeutic interventions. *Neuroscience and Biobehavioral Reviews, 18,* 97–110.

Miczek, K. A., Weerts, E. M., Tornatzky, W., Debold, J. F., & Vatne, T. M. (1992). Alcohol and "bursts" of aggressive behavior: Ethological analysis of individual differences in rats. *Psychopharmacology, 107,* 551–563.

Middlemis, Ð. N. (1984). Stereoselective blockade at [3H]5-HT binding sites and at the 5-HT autoreceptor by propranolol. *European Journal of Pharmacology, 101,* 289–293.

Miller, M. A., Urban, J. A., & Dorsa, D. M. (1989). Steroid dependency of vasopressin neurons in the bed nucleus of the stria terminalis by in situ hybridization. *Endocrinology, 125,* 2335–2340.

Mos, J., Kruk, M. R., Van der Poel, A. M., & Meelis, W. (1982). Aggressive behaviour induced by electrical stimulation in the midbrain central gray of male rats. *Aggressive Behavior, 8,* 261–284.

Mos, J., Olivier, B., & Van der Poel, A. M. (1987). Modulatory actions of benzodiazepines receptor ligands on agonistic behaviour. *Physiology and Behavior, 41,* 265–278.

Mos, J., & Olivier, B. (1991). Concepts in animal models for pathological aggressive behaviour in humans. In B. Olivier, J. Mos, & J. L. Slangen (Eds.), *Animal models in psychopharmacology, advances in pharmacological sciences* (pp. 297–316). Birkhauser Verlag.

Moyer, K. E. (1968). Kinds of aggression and their physiological basis. *Communications in Behavioral Biology, 2,* 65–87.

Neckers, L., & Sze, P. Y. (1975). Regulation of 5-Hydroxytryptamine metabolism in mouse brain by adrenal glucocorticoids. *Brain Research, 93,* 123–132.

Nock, B. L., & Leshner, A. I. (1976). Hormonal mediation of the effects of defeat on agonistic responding in mice. *Physiology and Behavior, 17,* 111–119.

O'Boyle, M. (1974). Rats and mice together: The predatory nature of the rat's mouse-killing response. *Psychological Bulletin, 891,* 261–269.

O'Kelly, L. I., & Steckle, L. C. (1939). A note on long enduring emotional responses in the rat. *Journal of Psychology, 8,* 125–131.

Oliveras, D., & Novak, M. (1986). A comparison of paternal behaviour in the meadow vole, *Microtus pennsylvanicus,* the pine vole, *M. pinetorum,* and the prairie vole, *M. ochrogaster. Animal Behaviour, 34,* 519–526.

Olivier, B. (1977). The ventromedial hypothalamus and aggressive behavior in rats. *Aggressive Behavior, 3,* 47–56.

Olivier, B., & Mos, J. (1990). Serenics, serotonin and aggression. [Review] *Progress in Clinical and Biological Research, 361,* 203–230.

Olivier, B., Mos, J., van der Heyden, J., Schipper, J., Berkelmans, B., Tulp, M. T. M., & Bevan, P. (1987). Serotonergic modulation of agonistic behavior. In B. Olivier, J. Mos, & P. F. Brain (Eds.), *Ethopharmacology of agonistic behavior in animals and humans* (pp. 162–186). Dordrectht, The Netherlands: Martinus Nijhoff.

Owen, K., Peters, P. J., & Bronson, F. H. (1974). Effects of intracranial implants of testosterone proprionate on intermale aggression in the castrated male mouse. *Hormones and Behavior, 5,* 83–92.

Panksepp, J. (1971a). Effects of hypothalmaic lesions on mouse-killing and shock-induced fighting in rats. *Physiology and Behavior, 6,* 311–316.

Panksepp, J. (1971b). Aggression elicited by electrical stimulation of the hypothalamus in albino rats. *Physiology and Behavior, 6,* 321–329.

Panksepp, J., & Trowill, J. (1969). Electrically induced affective attack from the hypothalamus of the albino rat. *Psychonomic Science, 16,* 118–119.

Payne, A. P. (1973). A comparison of the aggressive behavior of isolated intact and castrated male golden hamsters towards intruders introduced into the home cage. *Physiology and Behavior, 10,* 629–631.

Payne, A. P., & Swanson, H. H. (1970). Agonistic behavior between pairs of hamsters of the same and opposite sex in a neutral observation area. *Behavior, 36,* 259–269.

Payne, A. P., & Swanson, H. H. (1972). The effect of sex hormones on the agonistic behavior of the male golden hamster *(Mesocricetus auratus Waterhouse). Physiology and Behavior, 8,* 687–691.

Potegal, M. (1992). Aggression and aggressiveness in female golden hamsters. In K. Bjorkqvist & P. Niemela (Eds.), *Of mice and women: Aspects of female aggression* (pp. 329–350). San Diego: Academic Press.

Potegal, M., Blau, A., & Glusman, M. (1981). Effects of anteroventral septal lesions on intraspecific aggression in male hamsters. *Physiology and Behavior, 26,* 407–412.

Potegal, M., & Ferris, C. F. (1990). Intraspecific aggression in male hamsters is inhibited by intrahypothalamic VP-receptor antagonist. *Aggressive Behavior, 15,* 311–320.

Potegal, M., Ferris, C. F., Hebert, M., Meyerhoff, J., & Skaredoff, L. (1996). Attack priming in female Syrian golden hamsters is associated with a c-fos coupled process within the corticomedial amygdala. *Journal of Neuroscience, 75,* 869–880.

Potegal, M., Huhman, K., Moore, T., & Meyerhoff, J. (1993). Conditioned defeat in the syrian golden hamster *(Mesocricetus auratus). Behavioral and Neural Biology, 60,* 93–102.

Potegal, M., & Popken, J. (1985). The time course of attack priming effects in female golden hamsters. *Behavioral Processes, 11,* 199–208.

Potegal, M., & ten Brink, L. (1984). Behavior of attack-primed and attack-satiated female golden hamster *(Mesocricetus auratus). Journal of Comparative Psychology, 98,* 66–75.

Raab, A., Dantzer, R., Michaud, B., Mormede, P., Taghzouti, K, Simon, H., & Le Moal, M. (1986). Behavioral, physiological and immunological consequences of social status and aggression in chronically coexisting resident-intruder dyads of male rats. *Physiology and Behavior, 36,* 223–228.

Reis, D. J. (1974). Central neurotransmitters in aggression. *Research Publications of the Association for Research in Nervous and Mental Disease, 52,* 119–148.

Rose, R., Bernstein, I., & Gordon, T. (1975). Consequences of social conflict on plasma testosterone levels in Rhesus monkeys. *Psychosomatic Medicine, 37,* 50–61.

Sandnabba, N. K. (1986). Differences between two strains of mice, selectively bred for high and low aggressiveness, in the capacity of male odors to affect aggressive behavior. *Aggressive Behavior, 12,* 103–110.

Sapolsky, R. M. (1985). Stress-induced suppression of testicular function in the wild baboon: Role of glucocorticoids. *Endocrinology, 116,* 2273–2278.

Saudou, F., Amara, D. J., Dierich, A., LeMeur, M., Ramboz, S., Segu, A., Buhot, M.-C., & Hen, R. (1994). Enhanced aggressive behavior in mice lacking 5-HT$_{1B}$ receptor. *Science, 265,* 1875–1878.

Schuurman, T. (1980). Hormonal correlates of agonistic behavior in adult male rats. *Progress in Brain Research, 53,* 415–420.

Scott, J. P. (1942). Genetic differences in the social behavior of inbred strains of mice. *Journal of Heredity, 33,* 11–15.

Scott, J. P., & Fredericson, E. (1951). The causes of fighting in mice and rats. *Physiological Zoology, 24,* 273–309.

Seward, J. P. (1945). Aggressive behavior in the rat: I. General characteristics, age and sex differences. *Journal of Comparative Psychology, 38,* 175–196.

Shaikh, M. B., Barret, J., & Siegel, A. (1987). The pathways mediating affective defense and quiet biting attack from the midbrain central gray. *Brain Research, 437,* 9–25.

Siegel, A. (1990). Neural substrates of aggression and rage in the cat. *Progress in Psychobiological and Physiological Psychology, 14,* 135–233.

Siegel, A., & Pott, C. B. (1988). Neural substrate of aggression and flight in the cat. *Progress in Neurobiology, 31,* 261–283.

Siegel, H. I., Giordano, A. L., Mallafre, C. M., & Rosenblatt, J. S. (1983). Maternal aggression in hamsters: Effects of stage of lactation, presence of pups, and repeated testing. *Hormones and Behavior, 17,* 86–93.

Sijbesma, H., Schipper, J., & De Kloet, E. R. (1990). The anti-aggressive drug eltoprazine preferentially binds to 5-HT$_{1A}$ and 5-HT$_{1B}$ receptor subtypes in rat brain: sensitivity to guanine nucleotides. *European Journal of Pharmacology, 187,* 209–223.

Simon, N. G. (1979). The genetics of inter-male aggressive behavior in mice: Recent research and alternative strategies. *Neuroscience and Biobehavioral Reviews, 3,* 97–106.

Simon, N. G., & Gandleman, R. (1978). Aggression-promoting and aggression-eliciting properties of estrogen in male mice. *Physiology and Behavior, 21,* 161–164.

Simon, N. G., & Masters, D. (1987). Activation of male-typical aggression by testosterone but not its metabolites in C57BL/6J female mice. *Physiology and Behavior, 41,* 405–407.

Simon, N. G., & Whalen, R. E. (1986). Hormonal regulation of aggression: Evidence for a relationship among genotype, receptor binding, and behavioral sensitivity to androgen and estrogen. *Aggressive Behavior, 12,* 255–266.

Slotnick, B. M., & McMullen, M. F. (1972). Intraspecific fighting in albino mice with septal forebrain lesions. *Physiology and Behavior, 8,* 333–337.

Sodetz, F. J., & Bunnell, B. N. (1970). Septal ablation and the social behavior of the golden hamster. *Physiology and Behavior, 5,* 79–88.

Soloff, P. H. (1987). Emergency management of the violent patient. In R. E. Hales & A. J. Frances (Eds.), *American Psychiatric Association annual review* (Vol. 6, pp. 510–536). Washington, DC: American Psychiatric Press.

Swanson, L. W. (1991). Biochemical switching in hypothalamic circuits mediating responses to stress. *Progress in Brain Research, 87,* 181–200.

Sze, P. Y., Neckers, L., & Towle, A. C. (1976). Glucocorticoids as a regulatory factor for brain tryptophan hydroxylase. *Journal of Neurochemistry, 26,* 169–173.

Tardiff, K. (1992). The current state of psychiatry in the treatment of violent patients. *Archives of General Psychiatry, 49,* 493–499.

Ulrich, R. E., & Azrin, N. H. (1962). Reflexive fighting in response to aversive stimulation. *Journal of Experimental and Analytical Behavior, 5,* 511–520.

Vandenbergh, J. G. (1971). The effects of gonadal hormones on the aggressive behaviour of adult golden hamsters *(Mesocricetus auratus). Animal Behaviour, 19,* 589–594.

Van de Poll, N. E., DeJonge, F., Van Oyen, H. G., & Van Pelt, J. (1982). Aggressive behaviour in rats: Effects of winning or losing on subsequent aggressive interactions. *Behavioural Processes, 7,* 143–155.

Van de Poll, N. E., Smeets, J., Van Oyen, H. G., & Van der Swan, S. M. (1982). Behavioral consequences of agonistic experience in rats: Sex differences and the effects of testosterone. *Journal of Comparative and Physiological Psychology, 96,* 893–903.

Van Oortmerssen, G. A., & Bakker, T. C. M. (1981). Artificial selection for short and long attack latencies in wild *Mus musculus domesticus. Behavioral Genetics, 11,* 115–126.

Van Oortmerssen, G. A., Dijk, D. J., & Schourman, T. (1987). Studies in wild house mice. II. Testosterone and aggression. *Hormones and Behavior, 21,* 139–152.

Vergnes, M., Depaulis, A., Boehrer, A., & Kempf, E. (1988). Selective increase of offensive behavior in the rat following intrahypothalamic 5,7–DHT-induced serotonin depletion. *Behavioral Brain Research, 29,* 85–91.

Vergnes, M., Karli, P. (1970). Declenchement d'un comportement d'agression par stimulation electrique de l'hypothalmaus median chez le rat. *Physiology and Behavior, 4,* 1427–1430.

Wang, Z. X., Smith W., Major D. E., & De Vries G. J. (1994). Sex and species differences in the effects of cohabitation on vasopressin messenger RNA expression in the bed nucleus of the stria terminalis in prairie voles *(Microtus ochrogaster)* and meadow voles *(Microtus pennsylvanicus). Brain Research, 650,* 212–218.

Wasman, M., & Flynn, J. P. (1962). Direct attack elicited from the hypothalamus. *Archives of Neurology, 6,* 220–227.

Whitsett, J. M. (1975). The development of aggressive and marking behavior in intact and castrated male hamsters. *Hormones and Behavior, 6,* 47–57.

Wilkinson, P. F., & Shank, C. C. (1976). Rutting fight mortality among musk oxen on the Banks Island, Northwest Territories, Canada. *Animal Behaviour, 24,* 756–758.

Williams, J. R., Insel, T. R., Harbaugh, C. R., & Carter, C. S. (1994). Oxytocin administered centrally facilitates formation of a partner preference in female prairie voles *(Microtus ochrogaster). Journal of Neuroendocrinology, 6,* 247–250.

Williams, J. R., & Lierle, D. M. (1988). Effects of repeated defeat by a dominant conspecific on subsequent pain sensitivity, open-field activity, and escape learning. *Animal Learning and Behavior, 16,* 477–485.

Winslow, J. T., Hastings, N., Carter, C. S., Harbaugh, C. R., & Insel, T. R. (1993). A role for central vasopressin in pair bonding in monogamous prairie voles. *Nature, 365,* 545–548.

Woodworth, C. H. (1971). Attack elicited in rats by electrical stimulation of the lateral hypothamus. *Physiology and Behavior, 6,* 345–353.

Yodyingyuad, U., De la Riva, C., Abbott, D. H., Herbert, J., & Keverne, E. B. (1985). Relationship between dominance hierarchy, cerebrospinal fluid levels of amine transmitter metabolites (5-hydroxyindole acetic acid and homovanillic acid) and plasma cortisol in monkeys. *Neuroscience, 16,* 851–858.

Yoshimura, H., Kihara, Y., & Ogawa, N. (1987). Psychotropic effects of adrenergic β-blockers on agonistic behavior between resident and intruder mice. *Psychopharmacology, 91,* 445–450.

Yudofsky, S., Williams, D., & Gorman, J. (1981). Propranolol in the treatment of rage and violent behavior in patients with chronic brain syndromes. *American Journal of Psychiatry, 138,* 218–220.

CHAPTER 25

Medical Histories of Antisocial Individuals

PATRICIA A. BRENNAN and SARNOFF A. MEDNICK

The application of the medical model to antisocial and criminal behavior is a controversial issue. Most individuals would reject the notion that the majority of criminals commit antisocial acts because they suffer from a physical or biological illness. This is because the assumptions of free will and criminal responsibility are deeply ingrained in our society. Criminals are seen as having freely chosen their way of life and as fully deserving of retribution. Exceptions to the rule of criminal responsibility are made only in extreme cases of biological or mental disability. Most criminals are assumed to be relatively free of physical or biological deficits, and most physical health factors are assumed to play an insignificant role in criminal outcome. There is, however, a growing area of research suggesting that myriad physical health conditions may be causally related to antisocial behavior through the mediating factor of central nervous system dysfunction. These medical or physical health factors vary in their level of severity—from relatively minor nutritional imbalances to more serious perinatal complications and head injuries. Several other chapters in Part III of this handbook address the relationship between central nervous system processes and antisocial behavior (e.g., Henry & Moffitt, Chapter 26; Raine, Chapter 27, both this volume). In this chapter we review the research examining the relationship between physical health factors and antisocial behavior, and we discuss the implications of this research for theory and public policy.

DEVELOPMENTAL RISK AND ANTISOCIAL OUTCOME

Current theories on the role of medical factors and crime are much more complex than the historical proposition of Lombroso (1911) that a criminal was the simple product of a set genetic profile. Current theorists suggest that persistent antisocial behavior occurs as a result of an intricate interaction of medical and social factors over the course of development (Buikhuisen, 1988; Moffitt, 1993). Moffitt's (1993) life-course persistent offender theory, described

in detail elsewhere in this volume (see Henry & Moffitt, Chapter 26, this volume), exemplifies this approach. According to Moffitt, life-course persistent antisocial outcomes result from a transactional, developmental process that limits prosocial alternatives and "ensnares" individuals into criminal careers. She theorizes that congenital factors—heredity and perinatal complications—produce neuropsychological deficits in the infant's nervous system. These neuropsychological deficits manifest themselves as temperament difficulties, cognitive deficits, and motor delays in the child. Children with these biological deficits often find themselves in deficient social environments that might actually cause perinatal complications, poor nutrition, or early child abuse. The result is biological deficits in the child. Children who are unfortunate enough to have both biological and social deficits are theorized to be at the highest risk for persistent antisocial behavior.

Moffitt's developmental biosocial theory suggests that medical factors occurring early in the life span will have the greatest effect on serious antisocial outcome. In the broader context of developmental risk research, studies have been focused on biological risks occurring within three early childhood developmental periods: the prenatal (conception to seventh month of pregnancy), the perinatal (seventh month of pregnancy to 28 days after birth), and the postnatal (age 1 month and after). Prenatal risks include genetic and teratogenic factors that influence the fetus. Perinatal risks include delivery complications, prematurity, and low birth weight. Postnatal medical risks include infections, accidents, head injuries, toxicity, and nutritional deficiencies.

The term *developmental risk* applies to biological conditions that increase the risk for cognitive, behavioral, emotional, and physical problems (Kopp & Krakow, 1983). Research on the outcome of children at developmental risk has had a relatively short history. Prior to the major advances in medical care in the last century, most children suffering from developmental risk factors died in infancy or very early childhood. However, advances in medical care, improvements in social conditions, and an increased focus on pediatrics resulted in a significantly lower mortality rate for children who had suffered early developmental insults. By the 1950s, these children were the focus of widespread concern. Public health physicians began to suggest that prevention programs focus on children along the entire "continuum of reproduc-

This research was supported by National Institute of Mental Health Research Scientist Award MH00619 to Sarnoff A. Mednick.

tive casualty," which ranged from cerebral palsy and epilepsy to learning disabilities and behavior disturbances (Pasamanick & Knobloch, 1960, p. 304).

Prenatal and perinatal insults were hypothesized to lead to this continuum of disorders through the mediating factor of brain damage. This hypothesis formed the basis of several major longitudinal perinatal projects throughout the world, including the Collaborative Perinatal Project of the National Institute of Neurological Diseases and Blindness (Broman, Nichols, & Kennedy, 1975), the Kauai Island studies (Werner, Bierman, & French, 1971), and Drillien's preterm development studies (Drillien, 1964). These large-scale studies yielded three major findings. First, researchers discovered that developmental risks had additive negative effects on child outcome. Those children with the highest numbers of perinatal insults were found to evidence the most deviant outcomes. Second, most infants who suffered from perinatal complications developed into normally functioning children. Most deficits in functioning noted early in development were no longer apparent when the children reached school age. Third, those children who did evidence long-term negative outcomes following perinatal complications more often than not came from socially disadvantaged backgrounds. In other words, the environment of the child had a significant effect on the child's outcome and could either overcome or heighten the ill effects of early physical or biological insults.

The finding that the environment played such a significant role in the outcome of children at developmental risk was of major importance. It led researchers to point out that alongside the continuum of reproductive casualty there exists an equally important "continuum of caretaking casualty" (Sameroff & Chandler, 1975). It was recognized that a child's outcome also could be affected by postnatal insults. These postnatal insults include factors such as head injuries, poor nutrition, physical abuse, and exposure to toxins. These insults have environmental causes but may also have biological effects. Again, it is hypothesized that these postnatal developmental risk factors may affect antisocial outcome through the mediating role of central nervous system deficits.

GAPS BETWEEN THEORY AND EMPIRICAL RESEARCH

Theoretical conceptualizations of developmental risk and antisocial outcome are more complex than empirical studies that exist to date (Cicchetti & Richters, 1993). First, whereas empirical research is largely outcome oriented, developmental theory is process oriented. For example, developmental theorists focus on the process of how a mother's reaction to perinatal complications, when combined with other stresses, might lead to overindulgence of the child and a lack of discipline, which in turn might cause the child to adopt coercive behavior strategies in coping with his or her environment. Developmental theorists also suggest that it is paramount to consider the developmental capacities and demands that exist at each stage of life, and how a particular factor can have a greater or lesser effect depending on the child's stage of development. For example, nutritional deficiencies or lead toxicity may be more harmful to behavior development if they occur during a developmental stage in which rapid cognitive growth occurs. Empirical

research has not examined differential risks of postnatal factors occurring at different stages of development. Another important theoretical concept that has not yet been the focus of empirical research on antisocial outcomes is *organizational development* (Waters & Sroufe, 1983). Organizational development refers to the effect of adaptation at a preceding stage of development in leading to adaptation at a current stage of development. A child who evidences poor behavioral adaptation during one developmental stage will have more difficulty in adapting at later developmental stages, or a continuity may be noted between adaptation strategies at different levels of development. This concept may help to explain the relationship between earlier behavioral disorders such as temper tantrums and later behavioral disorders such as delinquency.

The two developmental risk concepts that are the most important to consider in an examination of the medical histories of antisocial individuals are the concepts of *transactional influence* (Sameroff & Chandler, 1975) and *protective factors* (Rutter, 1990). Biological and social factors are considered to have transactional influences on one another throughout development. In other words, the biological functioning of the child responds to the environment, and in turn the environment responds to the behavior that is generated by the biological functioning of the child. Environment and biological factors continually influence and change one another in the ongoing process of development. Although current empirical research on medical factors and antisocial outcome does not directly address transactional influences, some researchers in the field are beginning to examine basic interactions between biological and social variables in predicting antisocial outcome. This is the first step in understanding the transactional processes that underlie the development of antisocial behavior. Examinations of biosocial interactions also have suggested the important role of vulnerability and protective factors in the long-term outcomes of developmental risk. It is important to consider the mechanisms that protect those children who although at-risk develop into normal adolescents and adults. Empirical research on medical factors and antisocial outcome is just beginning to explore this important conceptual issue.

EMPIRICAL FINDINGS: REVIEW AND METHODOLOGICAL CRITIQUE

Recent advances in the focus of empirical research include the increasing attention to potential biosocial interactions, the recognition that biological risk may be related to certain types of antisocial behavior and not others, and the examination of how medical risk factors may affect the functioning of the central nervous system, which in turn may increase the propensity for antisocial behavior. A review of the research on prenatal, perinatal, and postnatal medical factors and antisocial outcome reflects these empirical advances and suggests the challenges that remain for future research.

Prenatal Factors and Antisocial Outcome

Prenatal biological risk factors include those that occur before birth through the seventh month of gestation (Kopp & Krakow, 1983). Genetic risk is included in this developmental time period;

we refer readers to Carey and Goldman (Chapter 23, this volume) for a review of genetic factors and antisocial behavior. We focus on other developmental risk factors that impinge on the fetus during pregnancy. These risk factors include illnesses of the mother during pregnancy (e.g., hypertension), eclampsia, and bleeding during pregnancy. For the purposes of this review, prematurity is included in the category of perinatal factors.

Few researchers have examined pregnancy complications apart from other perinatal complications as a factor in the development of antisocial behavior. Those studies that have made a distinction between prenatal and perinatal factors in predicting behavioral outcome have typically focused on childhood behavioral disorders in general rather than on delinquency or antisocial behavior in particular (e.g., McNeil, Wiegerink, & Dozier, 1970; Stott, 1972). These studies have yielded mixed results. For example, Pasamanick and his colleagues examined 1,151 children referred to Baltimore clinics with behavioral disturbances (Pasamanick, Rogers, & Lilienfeld, 1956). These children were compared with 902 controls matched by gender, race, age, and socioeconomic status. The behavior disordered children were found to have significantly higher rates of pregnancy complications (40%) than the controls (32%). It was noted that "mechanical" difficulties of delivery, in contrast, did not show an association with behavior disorders. Stott (1972) also found a relationship between prenatal stresses (maternal ill health) and behavior disorders characterized by impulsivity. He noted that delivery complications (including prematurity) were not significantly related to these behavioral disturbances. In contrast, McNeil and colleagues (1970) noted that perinatal and postnatal risk factors were more strongly related to behavioral disturbances than were prenatal factors such as maternal anemia or pre-eclampsia.

One reason for the mixed findings in studies of prenatal risk factors may be the heterogeneity of behavioral disorders in childhood. Clinic-referred samples will differ in the types of behavior problems included, and prenatal factors may be related to only certain types of behavioral disorders. Evidence for such a differential relationship is noted in a study linking prenatal alcohol exposure to behavioral outcome in childhood (Brown et al., 1991). This study examined the behavioral functioning of 68 five-year-old children with varying levels of prenatal exposure to alcohol. Externalizing behaviors, such as aggressiveness and overactivity, were found to be related to prenatal alcohol exposure. In contrast, internalizing behaviors such as anxiety and depression were not related to this prenatal risk factor. The results of this study suggest that in prenatal risk research, children with different behavioral disorders should be studied as distinct groups. The combination of different types of behavior disordered children into one outcome group may lead to confounded results. It is also important to note that the types of behavior disorders that have been found to be related to prenatal risk factors are impulsivity and aggression—the types of behavior disorders that are consistent with antisocial outcome in adulthood.

Only one study to date has made a direct comparison of the utility of prenatal risk factors versus perinatal risk factors in the prediction of adult antisocial outcome (Kandel & Mednick, 1991). This study examined 216 subjects drawn from a Danish perinatal birth cohort. Prenatal and perinatal complications were recorded during pregnancy and at the time of delivery by fully trained obstetricians. Weighted pregnancy and delivery scales were used to divide the subjects into high and low complication groups. The national police register was searched when the subjects were 20 to 22 years of age. The results of this study revealed that prenatal complications were not significantly related to antisocial outcome. Delivery (or perinatal) complications, in contrast, were found to be related to violent offending (80% of the violent offenders had high levels of delivery complications compared to 47% of the controls). One possible explanation for these results is the argument that delivery complications relate to antisocial outcome because they are more likely than prenatal complications to cause central nervous system dysfunction. However, this interpretation is contradicted by research linking prenatal complications to neurological deficits (e.g., Chen & Hsu, 1994; Lou et al., 1994).

Another possible explanation for Kandel and Mednick's failure to find a relationship between prenatal complications and antisocial outcome is methodological. Compared to the direct observational measures of delivery complications, measures of prenatal complications are subjective and often retrospective. Therefore, prenatal complication measures may not be reliable or valid. One prenatal complication measure, however, can be reliably and objectively measured. This is a count of small aberrations in external physical characteristics known as minor physical anomalies (MPAs). As an example of how such MPAs occur, consider the fetal development of the ears. In fetal life, the ears begin low on the neck of the fetus and slowly drift upward into their proper position. If a noxious event or substance impinges itself on the fetus, the development may be slowed or stopped and the ears' drift upward may end prematurely, resulting in low-seated ears—an observable MPA. The same agents that cause the formation of externally visible MPAs may also alter critical central nervous system development. The presence of many MPAs suggests repeated interference with neurological development.

Minor physical anomalies have been found to be related to aggression, attentional problems, and hyperactive behavior in children (Firestone & Peters, 1983; Fogel, Mednick, & Michelsen, 1985; LaVeck, Hammond, & LaVeck, 1980; Paulhus & Martin, 1986; Waldrop, Bell, McLaughlin, & Halverson, 1978). Researchers in the field of hyperactivity have hypothesized that prenatal insults influence the formation of MPAs and central nervous system abnormalities that produce a predisposition for impulsive behavior (Quinn & Rapoport, 1974). This same impulsiveness may increase the risk for antisocial outcome in adolescence or adulthood.

Preliminary evidence exists for a relationship between MPAs and violent offending. A longitudinal study of 129 males (Kandel, Brennan, Mednick, & Michelsen, 1989) examined the relationship between MPAs measured at age 12 and criminal arrests through the age of 21. Although this study found no relationship between MPAs and property offending, MPAs were found to be significantly related to violent criminal arrest. The relationship was especially strong in the case of recidivistic violent offending. Although this study is impaired by several limitations including a nonrepresentative sample and a small number of violent offenders, it does tentatively support the hypothesis that prenatal risk factors are related to criminal outcome.

Perinatal Factors and Antisocial Outcome

In 1861, W. J. Little observed that "the act of birth does occasionally imprint upon the nervous and muscular systems of the nascent infantile organism very serious and peculiar evils" (p. 294). It was not until 1934, however, that Rosanoff and his coworkers suggested that some types of adult behavioral deviance might be a consequence of perinatal events. Several researchers have since found increased rates of perinatal problems in the histories of acting out, aggressive, and criminal individuals. Mungas (1983) noted a relationship between perinatal factors and violence in a sample of neuropsychiatric patients. Litt (1971) studied perinatal disturbances in a birth cohort of 1,944 individuals in Denmark born between January 1, 1936, and September 30, 1938. He discovered that perinatal trauma predicted impulsive criminal offenses in adulthood.

Not all researchers have noted a significant relationship between perinatal factors and antisocial outcome. In a study of psychopathology in adolescence, perinatal factors were not found to be related to conduct disorder or oppositional defiant disorder (Cohen, Velez, Brook, & Smith, 1989). In a more recent retrospective study, perinatal and medical histories were found to be similar for arrested delinquent offenders and controls (Kendall, Andre, Pease, & Boulton, 1992). In the context of a prospective study of 5,966 males in Finland, low birth weight and premature delivery were studied as risk factors for adult crime (Rantakallio, Koiranen, & Moettoenen, 1992). Neither of these perinatal complications significantly predicted to criminal outcome.

Mixed results in this area of research may be explained by a closer examination of the types of antisocial outcomes that were assessed. The relationship between perinatal factors and antisocial behavior may be particular to violent offending or persistent offending, rather than property offending or delinquency. As noted earlier, Kandel and Mednick (1991) compared the differential effects of delivery complications on violent and property offending in young adulthood. They found that violent offenders, especially recidivistic violent offenders, had experienced significantly more delivery complications than controls or property offenders. Many studies that have failed to show a relationship between perinatal problems and antisocial outcome did not examine offenders according to specific types of crimes committed (e.g., Kendall et al., 1992; Szatmari, Reitsma, & Offord, 1986).

A series of studies by Lewis and her colleagues further supports the hypothesis that perinatal factors may be related to more serious types of antisocial outcomes. In 1977, Lewis and Shanok examined the perinatal histories of 109 delinquents and 109 matched controls. They reported no differences between delinquents' and nondelinquents' perinatal histories. Later they compared 84 nonincarcerated delinquents with 84 incarcerated delinquents and discovered a positive relationship between more serious offending and perinatal difficulties (Lewis, Shanok, & Balla, 1979). In this study of incarcerated males, they also found that *violent* criminals were particularly likely to have a history of perinatal problems. In a separate examination of 21 homicidally aggressive males and 34 controls, Lewis, Shanok, Grant, and Rituo (1983) noted that one of the factors that distinguished the homicidally aggressive males from the controls was a history of

perinatal complications. The finding that higher levels of perinatal risk are related to serious delinquency has also been replicated in females (Shanok & Lewis, 1981; Werner & Smith, 1992).

The social environment may also play an important role in determining the effects of perinatal complications on criminal outcome. In a prospective longitudinal study in Kauai, Werner (1987) found that the effects of perinatal stress on delinquent outcome were strongest for children exposed to a disruptive family environment. A disruptive family environment was defined by Werner as separation from the mother, marital discord, absence of the father, illegitimacy of the child, or parental mental health problems. Most of the research linking prematurity and low birth weight to behavioral deviance has also been biosocial in nature. Escalona (1982) aptly described children with both perinatal and social risk factors in their background as "babies at double-hazard." Drillien (1964) was the first to note a biosocial interaction between prematurity and familial stress in predicting to adverse behavior in school. This finding has been replicated in a number of studies of low birth weight and small-for-gestation babies (e.g., McGauhey, Starfield, Alexander, & Ensminger, 1991; Neligan, Kolvin, Scott, & Garside, 1976; Ross, Lipper, & Auld, 1990). The "double-hazard" of perinatal risk and social disadvantages increases the risk for deviant behavioral outcome.

Most examinations of biosocial interaction have not explored specific types of social risks in interaction with perinatal factors in predicting deviant outcomes. Most biosocial studies have used either a composite scale of social risk or the general social factor of socioeconomic status. Such studies do not inform us about the processes underlying the biosocial interaction. One exception to this rule is Raine, Brennan, and Mednick (1994), who found that delivery complications, when combined with maternal rejection of the child, predisposed to adult violent crime. This study was carried out in the context of a birth cohort of 4,269 males born between September 1959 and December 1961 at Rigshospitalet in Copenhagen, Denmark. Delivery complications, such as forceps extraction, breech delivery, umbilical cord prolapse, and pre-eclampsia, were recorded at birth by a Danish obstetrician. Delivery complications were interpreted as a reflection of perinatal neurological damage. Maternal rejection was operationalized as unwanted pregnancy, attempt to abort the fetus, and public institutional care of the infant. (It is important to note that the two risk factors of maternal rejection and delivery complications were not correlated in this sample.) Criminal status was assessed at age 18 through a check of the Danish official police register. An individual was considered to be a violent offender if he or she had been arrested for one or more violent crimes. In this study, a significant and specific interaction was noted between maternal rejection and delivery complications in predicting *violent* crime. The combination of both maternal rejection and delivery complications was found to lead to an exponential increase in violence. In addition, whereas maternal rejection interacted with delivery complications to produce violence, the social class measure did not. The results of this study suggest that maternal rejection may be a particularly hazardous component in a child's social environment. This finding is consistent with other research that has linked disruption in the mother-infant bonding process to psychopathic criminal behavior (Rutter, 1982) and suggests an underlying process of antisocial development.

Overall, the results of the Raine et al. (1994) study are consistent with Moffitt's (1993) biosocial theory. As Moffitt theorized, perinatal complications can lead to neurological deficits that cause school failure, occupational failure, and an adult criminal lifestyle. The effects of the neurological deficits might be exacerbated by a negative early psychosocial environment. On the other hand, a consistent and nurturing psychosocial environment could inhibit aggressive and antisocial behavior.

The Raine et al. study overcomes many of the weaknesses of other research examining the relationship between perinatal factors and antisocial or deviant outcomes. Previous studies examining the effect of perinatal factors on crime often have been restricted by retrospective measures (e.g., Lewis & Shanok, 1977), the use of maternal interviews (e.g., Cohen et al., 1989), small sample sizes or missing data (e.g., Szatmari et al., 1986), failure to differentiate types of antisocial behavior (e.g., Kendall et al., 1992), and a lack of attention to social or demographic factors that might interact to predict antisocial outcome.

One other major weakness of perinatal research is the incomplete understanding of the mechanism by which perinatal factors increase the risk for antisocial outcome. As stated previously, it is assumed that perinatal factors influence antisocial behavior through the mediating factor of neurological or central nervous system dysfunction. It is important to note that this assumption is never directly tested in the studies linking perinatal factors and antisocial outcome. There is, however, some evidence to support this assumption in the more general field of perinatal risk research. In their review of low birth weight studies, McCormick and Marie (1985) note that low birth weight infants are three times as likely as controls to evidence adverse neurological sequelae. Similarly, Fitzhardinge and Steven (1972) noted very high rates of minimal brain dysfunction and electroencephalogram abnormalities in infants who were small-for-gestation. A longitudinal study by Hertzig (1982) revealed that neurological dysfunction is apparent through middle childhood for those children who evidenced perinatal complications. This research provides support for the theory that perinatal factors influence antisocial outcome through the mediating factor of central nervous system dysfunction. However, research is needed that will test this proposition more directly.

Postnatal Risk Factors and Antisocial Outcome

Research on postnatal health factors and antisocial outcome also assumes a mediational role of central nervous system dysfunction. Head injuries, mineral toxicity, and dietary factors are the postnatal health factors that have been examined most frequently in relation to antisocial behavior. Although results from these areas of research have been provocative, methodological concerns must be taken into account when considering their potential utility for public policy.

Head Injury and Antisocial Outcome

Aggression is one of the most common behavioral sequelae to follow traumatic brain injuries (Miller, 1994). The most common aggressive syndromes observed after brain injury are episodic dyscontrol and frontal lobe disinhibition. Episodic dyscontrol syndrome is a pattern of violent outbursts that occur without apparent provocation from the environment. Elliott (1982) describes the clinical features of episodic dyscontrol as explosive rage, irrational thinking, and extreme physical aggression. These attacks of rage appear to be elicited or activated by abnormal electrophysiological activity in the brain. Frontal lobe disinhibition, in contrast, reflects a failure of a part of the brain to inhibit rage and aggression. Miller (1994) points out that the most typical head injuries include damage to the frontal lobes, which are responsible for the executive functions of planning and the inhibition of impulsive behavior. Therefore, damage to the frontal lobes will often result in increased impulsive behavior and concomitant aggression in the face of external provocation.

Given the nature of the clinically described syndromes following traumatic brain injury, it is hypothesized that postnatal head injury is related to antisocial outcomes, especially physical aggression and violence. There is some evidence for this hypothesis in research on marital aggression and head injury. In a sample of 31 men referred to therapy as wife batterers, 61% were found to have a history of serious head injury (Rosenbaum & Hoge, 1989). The authors of this study compare that rate with a general population rate of 6%. In a second study of head injury and marital aggression, 52% of wife batterers were found to have a history of head injury compared to 22% of controls (Rosenbaum, 1991). In a third study on marital aggression, 33 head-injured men were found to be more likely than controls to be irritable and argumentative and to lose their temper. In this study, no significant differences were noted in physical aggression toward partners; however, a very low base rate was reported for this behavior (three head-injured males compared with zero controls).

Several samples of especially violent individuals have been found to have high numbers of postnatal head injuries in their medical history. For example, in a sample of 62 habitually violent male prisoners, 61% self-reported a history of head injury (Bach-y-rita & Veno, 1974). In a sample of 14 juvenile males on death row, 57% were found to have serious head injuries (Lewis, Pincus et al., 1988). In a second death row study, 100% of a sample of 15 adult inmates were noted to have a history of head injuries (Lewis, Pincus, Feldman, Jackson, & Bard, 1986). Self-reports of these head injuries were confirmed by evidence from scars, cranium indentation, neurological deficits, CAT scans, and medical documentation. The results of these studies support the hypothesized relationship between developmental risk of head injury and antisocial outcome, particularly violent behavior.

Postnatal head injury, however, does *not* seem to be significantly related to *nonviolent* antisocial behavior. In a large cohort study of 1,647 delinquent offenders, no differences were found between delinquents and controls in history of admissions or outpatient contacts for head injuries (Kendall et al., 1992). These authors note that the results of the study may have been different if they were able to examine subtypes of offenders based on types of crimes committed. In another large cohort study of 5,966 males in Finland, delinquents were found to have more skull fractures and concussions in their medical history than were nondelinquents (Rantakallio et al., 1992). However, when the delinquents were divided into violent and nonviolent subgroups, an increased rate of postnatal head injury was found only for the violent delinquents in the sample. In another large sample of 1,055 subjects, medium security prisoners were not found to have higher rates of self-reported head injuries than controls (Templer et al., 1992). These authors did not report the types of offenses that the prisoners had committed; however, the level of medium security suggests that a substantial proportion may not have been violent offenders. Finally, in a direct comparison of violent and nonviolent criminals, Lewis and her colleagues noted that murderers and violent criminals had higher rates of head injuries than did nonviolent criminal controls (Lewis, Lovely, et al., 1988).

Research evidence suggests that a relationship exists between antisocial behavior, especially violent antisocial behavior, and a postnatal history of head trauma. There are methodological problems with the studies that have been reviewed, however, and there is minimal evidence to date for a causal relationship between head injury and antisocial outcome. Methodological problems include the failure to use control groups (e.g., Bach-y-rita & Veno, 1974), failure to match controls on demographic variables (e.g., Lewis, Lovely et al., 1988), reliance on self-report for medical histories (e.g., Rosenbaum & Hoge, 1989), and use of interviewers who were not blind to violence status (e.g., Lewis, Pincus et al., 1988). Furthermore, the retrospective nature of these studies makes causal inference difficult. Even in cases in which a significant relationship is noted between head injury and antisocial behavior, it cannot be determined from a retrospective study which factor caused the other. It seems plausible, for example, that violent or antisocial individuals may be at an increased risk for head injury because of their lifestyle. In the only prospective study to examine criminal activity before and after head trauma (Kreutzer, Wehman, Harris, Burns, & Young, 1991), the rates of criminal activity before the injury were found to be higher than those following the injury. Unfortunately, no conclusions can be drawn from this study because it did not have a control group and did not control for differential periods of risk.

Raine (1993) makes several cogent arguments in support of the causal pathway *from* head injury *to* antisocial behavior. He points out that (a) the peak risk period for head injury is younger than that for violent behavior and (b) the majority of head injuries are caused by factors other than interpersonal violence, such as falls or accidents. Although these arguments do support the hypothesis that head injury predisposes to violence, prospective research is needed to test this causal pathway more directly. Prospective, longitudinal studies are also needed to assess the role of factors such as perinatal trauma, alcohol abuse, or child abuse, which might predispose children to both head injuries and antisocial outcome (Kraus, Rock, & Hemyari, 1990; Kreutzer, Doberty, Harris, & Zasler, 1990). Until these and other confounding factors are controlled, the nature of the relationship between head injury and antisocial behavior remains incomplete.

Mineral Toxicity and Antisocial Outcome

Another potential postnatal risk factor for antisocial outcome is mineral toxicity. Toxic levels of lead and other minerals have been found to be related to brain lesions and neurological dysfunction (Chandra & Srivastava, 1970; Needleman et al., 1979), which may, in turn, increase the risk for antisocial outcome. Although lead is the mineral that historically has been studied in relation to behavioral outcome, recent research suggests that cadmium and manganese levels may also be related to antisocial and criminal behavior (Gottschalk, Rebello, Buchsbaum, Tucker, & Hodges, 1991; Marlowe et al., 1985; Pihl & Ervin, 1990).

Low-level lead toxicity has been found to be related to lowered IQ scores, poor school achievement, and increased risk for attention deficit disorder (Needleman, 1990). In a sample of 166 children living near leadworks in London, IQ was found to be negatively correlated with blood lead levels even when socioeconomic status was controlled (Yule, Lansdown, Millar, & Urbanowicz, 1981). In another comparison of 58 children with high dentine lead levels and 100 children with low dentine lead levels (Needleman et al., 1979), children with higher levels of lead evidenced lower IQ scores and higher levels of teacher-rated behavioral disturbances, including hyperactivity (aggressive behavior was not rated by the teachers). A prospective study of the effects of lead exposure also found a relationship between lead and self-reported delinquency in a sample of 132 adolescents (Needleman, Schell, Bellinger, Leviton, & Allred, 1990). In another study of 80 elementary school children, high levels of lead were found to interact with high levels of cadmium in predicting acting-out behavior (Marlowe et al., 1985). This lead-cadmium correlation with behavioral disturbance was noted after controlling for parents' age at birth, history of immunizations, hospital admissions since birth, separation from parents, and socioeconomic status. Several of the studies noting ill effects of lead exposure found that negative outcomes were apparent even for children whose lead levels fell within acceptable government standards of exposure (e.g., Marlowe et al., 1985).

A recently published study by Needleman and his colleagues (Needleman, Riess, Tobin, Biesecker, & Greenhouse, 1996) provides further evidence for the relationship between lead levels and delinquency. This study examined the teacher-, parent-, and child-reported behavior problems of 301 males at ages 7 and 11. In this sample, bone lead levels were found to be related to aggressive and delinquent behavior at age 11. This relationship remained significant when maternal intelligence, socioeconomic status, quality of child rearing, and rates of aggression at age 7 were entered as covariates in the analysis.

These studies of mineral toxicity were focused on samples of children and adolescents. Very few studies to date have examined the postnatal risk factor of mineral toxicity in relation to adult antisocial behavior. One case study of an adult male arrested for burglary revealed very high levels of lead in his system and a reduction in behavior problems following treatment for lead poisoning (Schauss, 1981). Another study of 30 incarcerated violent offenders and 19 incarcerated nonviolent controls found that violent behavior was correlated with higher levels of cadmium and lead (Pihl & Ervin, 1990). The study of hair trace elements has found mineral manganese to be related to antisocial outcome in adults (Gottschalk et al., 1991). Incarcerated male offenders and violent offenders had higher levels of manganese when compared to controls. In contrast to the previously noted studies, criminal groups in Gottschalk's study were not found to have higher levels of lead or cadmium than controls.

The results of studies of adult antisocial behavior and mineral toxicity are not consistent. In addition, they are limited by methodological flaws including single case study designs

(Schauss, 1981) or cross-sectional designs (Gottschalk et al., 1991), failure to include a normal control group (Pihl & Ervin, 1990), exclusive use of hair analysis measures (which may be inaccurate because of metals and minerals left behind by hair care products; Gottschalk et al., 1991; Pihl & Ervin, 1990), and lack of attention to other related nutritional imbalances. The lack of attention to other nutritional factors is problematic because evidence exists linking several dietary factors and antisocial outcome.

Dietary Factors and Antisocial Outcome

An excellent review of the relationship between nutrition and violence has been provided by Kanarek (1994). Our review focuses on antisocial behavior in general. The connection between dietary factors and antisocial behavior was first popularized by reports linking high sugar intake with hyperactive, irritable, and aggressive behavior (Dufty, 1975). The application of dietary interventions with antisocial populations soon followed these initial reports. One of the first dietary intervention studies reported that vitamin-supplemented diets improved personality functioning in adult jail inmates (D'Asaro, Groesbeck, & Nigro, 1975). However, the results of this study may be biased due to a dropout rate of 57% of the subjects. A dietary intervention study carried out with drug-dependent criminal offenders in Florida revealed that reduced carbohydrate intake led to decreased maladaptive behavior in a subset of offenders defined as hypoglycemic.

Schoenthaler and his colleagues have carried out a series of dietary intervention studies that have shown impressive results in institutionalized populations of offenders (Schoenthaler, 1991). In one such study (Schoenthaler, 1982), 24 juvenile males who received a reduced sugar diet were compared to 34 males institutionalized before the dietary change. The males who received the modified diet demonstrated less rule violations than the controls. A follow-up demonstrated that the initial results were not due to confounds such as race, age, gender, and type of offender (Schoenthaler, 1983a). In a separate intervention study using a quasi-experimental design, the aggressive and violent behaviors of 276 institutionalized juveniles decreased substantially following the introduction of a nutritionally superior diet (Schoenthaler & Doraz, 1983). Another dietary intervention study also revealed a 25% within-individual reduction in rule violations following the implementation of a low sugar diet (Schoenthaler, 1983b). Dietary changes consisting of the replacement of sucrose and food additives with complex carbohydrates were next implemented and examined at nine separate juvenile institutions throughout the United States. As reported by Schoenthaler (1983c), a reduction of behavior problems was noted in all nine of the institutions in which these dietary changes were implemented.

Although Schoenthaler's dietary intervention studies have highly consistent results, they can be criticized on methodological grounds (see Fishbein & Pease, 1994; Gray, 1986). Although the researchers stated that the procedures were double blind, the change in diet was substantial enough to be noticed by the offenders. There was also a failure to control for other institutional changes that occurred concomitantly with the new diet. These institutional changes included the implementation of counseling groups (Schoenthaler, 1982) and the admittance of females into the facility (Schoenthaler, 1983a), both of which may have acted

to reduce overall levels of institutional aggression. Results of within-individual comparisons may also be confounded by the tendency for individual behavior to improve over the course of institutionalization (Schoenthaler, 1983b). Schoenthaler's studies also can be criticized for statistical flaws and nonsophisticated approaches to design, but perhaps the greatest weakness is one that Schoenthaler himself points out (Schoenthaler, 1991), the lack of a well-developed theory that would explain why changes in diet would lead to decreased aggressive behavior. An examination of specific dietary factors and their relationship to brain functioning suggests that the mediating factor may be neurological dysfunction. Studies linking dietary factors to cognitive functioning provide some support for this contention (Schoenthaler et al., 1991). Another physiological process by which dietary factors may influence antisocial outcomes is through the mediating factor of hormones. Low blood glucose levels result in release of hormones such as adrenalin that are associated with increased irritability and agitation (Knopf, Cresto, Dujovne, Ramos, & deMajo, 1977) and therefore increase risk for antisocial behavior. Still another process by which diet may influence aggressive and antisocial behavior is through hypoglycemia and associated alcohol abuse.

Hypoglycemia, or chronic low blood sugar, is a diet-induced condition. If the brain is deprived of adequate levels of glucose, irritability and aggression may result (Marks, 1981). Blood glucose levels have been found to be related to hostility in normal unselected populations (Benton, Kumari, & Brain, 1982). In addition, a series of studies by Virkkunen have noted that violent offenders display reactive hypoglycemia in glucose tolerance tests (e.g., Virkkunen, 1983a, 1986a, 1986b). Virkkunen points out that abnormal glucose-insulin findings for violent offenders are consistent with the finding of low serum cholesterol levels in this same population. In a meta-analysis of six studies examining the effects of therapy to lower cholesterol, a relationship was noted between cholesterol-lowering therapies (drug and dietary) and increased rates of violent and suicidal behavior in males (Muldoon, Manuck, & Matthews, 1990). Low serum cholesterol levels have also been directly observed in homicidal offenders (Virkkunen, 1983b) and in individuals with the diagnoses of conduct disorder (Virkkunen & Penttinen, 1984) and antisocial personality disorder (Virkkunen, 1979). Alcohol abuse may be a mediating factor in this process. A bi-directional relationship has been observed between hypoglycemia and excessive alcohol use (Sereny, Endrenyi, & Devenyi, 1975; Williams, 1981), and alcohol abuse has a noticeable direct effect on violent and antisocial outcomes (Bushman & Cooper, 1990).

We have suggested several processes that may underlie the relationship between postnatal dietary risk factors and antisocial behavior. Future research examining these processes will help to refine and expand this model and to suggest appropriate intervention strategies related to diet and antisocial behavior.

THEORETICAL AND POLICY IMPLICATIONS

This review of developmental medical risk factors and antisocial outcome suggests several implications for theory and public policy. First, the research results are consistent with Moffitt's theory of life-course persistent offending (1993). Developmental medical risk factors seem to be particularly related to violent or persistent offending. In addition, those studies that have examined these medical risk factors in the context of different levels of social risk have provided support for biosocial interactions predicting antisocial outcomes. Moffitt theorizes that central nervous system dysfunction plays a mediating role between developmental risk factors and antisocial outcome. Research that directly tests this hypothesis is still needed; there is, however, no evidence to date that contradicts this mediational hypothesis.

An overall model of the relationship between medical risk factors and antisocial outcome is presented in Figure 25.1. This model suggests the following developmental process leading to antisocial outcome. Prenatal, perinatal, and postnatal factors cause neurological deficits in the child, and concomitant neglect and abuse compound the damage. During childhood these neurological deficits evidence themselves as lack of impulsivity control and cognitive deficits. Cognitive deficits lead to eventual school failure. Continued impulsive behavior combined with a lack of consistent external controls in the family or school result in eventual antisocial outcome.

The model presented in Figure 25.1 suggests a developmental perspective and a biosocial interaction in the prediction of antisocial outcome. What this model fails to represent is the transactional nature of this process as it occurs in development. For example, bi-directional relationships exist between many of the factors in the model. Just as neurological deficits may result in less consistent external behavioral controls, a lack of consistent external behavioral controls may lead to further neurological deficits (through further accidents or injury). This model also reflects a gap in our understanding of what types of factors might protect those individuals at medical risk for antisocial outcome. Increased knowledge about such protective factors would help provide the basis for interventions with children at high medical risk for criminal and aggressive behavior.

Given our current understanding of the relationship between medical risk factors and antisocial outcome, what are the implications for public policy? The biosocial interactions described earlier in this chapter suggest that biology is not "destiny" and that intervention and prevention strategies may reduce the outcome of criminal behavior in children who are at high levels of medical risk. To exemplify this point, consider the finding that perinatal factors may interact with unstable family environments in predicting antisocial outcome. A prevention strategy suggested by this finding would be the strengthening of the social environment for those children who may be biologically vulnerable. Children who have suffered from perinatal complications could be targeted for parent training interventions or school enrichment programs that would help to ameliorate the effects of their biological deficits.

The direct relationship between medical risk factors and antisocial outcome also suggests potential public health prevention strategies. These strategies might include the provision of intensive prenatal health care to mothers as well as education concerning the effects of alcohol and drug use during pregnancy. Parent training focused on nonphysical modes of discipline also may help reduce the prevalence of head injuries in children, and parent education focused on nutrition may help reduce cases of medical toxicity or hypoglycemia. These prevention strategies may result in a reduction of the notably high levels of antisocial behavior in U.S. society. Considering the substantial negative impact of violent behavior on our society, these prevention strategies have a relatively low cost and a potential for substantial benefit.

SUMMARY

This chapter has provided a review of the literature on potentially relevant causal factors in the medical histories of antisocial individuals. According to our review, prenatal, perinatal, and postnatal physical health factors may be particularly related to violent, early onset, or persistent antisocial behavior. In addition, the social context was found to play an important role in the outcomes of children who suffered these physical health risks. The "dual-hazard" of biological and social risks was found to result in an increased rate of antisocial behavior, and a healthy social environment was found to protect individuals at physical or medical risk for antisocial outcome. Future research is necessary to better elucidate the biological, social, and biosocial processes by which medical histories influence antisocial outcome.

REFERENCES

Bach-y-rita, G., & Veno, A. (1974). Habitual violence: A profile of 62 men. *American Journal of Psychiatry, 131,* 1015–1017.

Benton, D., Kumari, N., & Brain, P. F. (1982). Mild hypoglycemia and questionnaire measures of aggression. *Biological Psychology, 14,* 129–135.

Broman, S. H., Nichols, P. L., & Kennedy, W. A. (1975). *Preschool IQ: Prenatal and early developmental correlates.* Hillsdale, NJ: Erlbaum.

Brown, R., Coles, C. D., Smith, I. E., Platzman, K. A., Silverstein, J., Erickson, S., & Falek, A. (1991). Effects of prenatal alcohol exposure at school age: II. Attention and behavior. *Neurotoxicology and Teratology, 13,* 369–376.

Buikhuisen, W. (1988). Chronic juvenile delinquency: A theory. In W. Buikhuisen & S. A. Mednick (Eds.), *Explaining criminal behavior* (pp. 27–50). Leiden, The Netherlands: E. J. Brill.

Bushman, B. J., & Cooper H. M. (1990). Effects of alcohol on human aggression: An integrative research review. *Psychological Bulletin, 107,* 341–354.

Figure 25.1 *Medical risk factors and antisocial outcome from a developmental, biosocial perspective.*

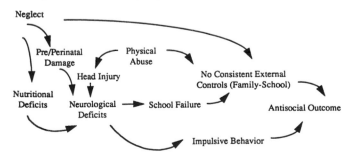

Chandra, S. V., & Srivastava, S. P. (1970). Experimental production of early brain lesions in rats by parenteral administration of manganese chloride. *Acta Pharmacologica Toxicology, 28,* 177–183.

Chen, Y. J., & Hsu, C. C. (1994). Effects of prenatal exposure to PCBS on the neurological function of children. *Developmental Medicine and Child Neurology, 36,* 312–320.

Cicchetti, D., & Richters, J. E. (1993). Developmental considerations in the investigation of conduct disorder. *Development and Psychopathology, 5,* 331–344.

Cohen, P., Velez, C., Brook, J., & Smith, J. (1989). Mechanisms of the relation between perinatal problems, early childhood illness and psychopathology in late childhood and adolescence. *Child Development, 60,* 701–709.

D'Asaro, B., Groesbeck, C., & Nigro, C. (1975). Diet vitamin program for jail inmates. *Orthomolecular Psychiatry, 4,* 212–222.

Drillien, C. M. (1964). *The growth and development of the prematurely born infant.* Edinburgh: Livingstone.

Dufty, W. (1975). *Sugar blues.* New York: Warner.

Elliott, F. A. (1982). Neurological findings in adult minimal brain dysfunction and the dyscontrol syndrome. *Journal of Nervous and Mental Disease, 170,* 680–687.

Escalona, S. K. (1982). Babies at double hazard: Early development of infants at biologic and social risk. *Pediatrics, 70,* 670–676.

Firestone, P., & Peters, S. (1983). Minor physical anomalies and behavior in children: A review. *Journal of Autism and Developmental Disorders, 13,* 411–425.

Fishbein, D. H., & Pease, S. E. (1994). Diet, nutrition and aggression. *Journal of Offender Rehabilitation, 21,* 117–144.

Fitzhardinge, P. M., & Steven, E. M. (1972). The small for date infant: II. Neurological and intellectual sequelae. *Pediatrics, 50,* 50–57.

Fogel, C. A., Mednick, S. A., & Michelsen, N. (1985). Hyperactive behavior and minor physical anomalies. *Acta Psychiatrica Scandinavica, 75,* 551–556.

Gottschalk, L. A., Rebello, T., Buchsbaum, M. S., Tucker, H. G., & Hodges, E. L. (1991). Abnormalities in hair trace elements as indicators of aberrant behavior. *Comprehensive Psychiatry, 32,* 229–237.

Gray, G. E. (1986). Diet, crime and delinquency: A critique. *Nutritional Reviews, 44,* 89–94.

Hertzig, M. E. (1982). Neurological "soft signs" in low birth weight children. *Annual Progress in Child Psychiatry and Child Development,* pp. 509–524.

Kanarek, R. B. (1994). Nutrition and violent behavior. In A. J. Reiss, K. A. Miczek, & J. A. Roth (Eds.), *Understanding and preventing violence: Volume 2. Biobehavioral influences* (pp. 515–539). Washington, DC: National Academy Press.

Kandel, E., Brennan, P. A., Mednick, S. A., & Michelsen, N. M. (1989). Minor physical anomalies and recidivistic adult violent offending. *Acta Psychiatrica Scandinavica, 79,* 103–107.

Kandel, E., & Mednick, S. A. (1991). Perinatal complications predict violent offending. *Criminology, 29,* 519–529.

Kendall, K., Andre, G., Pease, K., & Boulton, A. (1992). Health histories of juvenile offenders and a matched control group in Saskatchewan, Canada. *Criminal Behaviour and Mental Health, 2,* 269–286.

Knopf, C. J., Cresto, J. C., Dujovne, J. L., Ramos, O., & deMajo, S. F. (1977). Oral glucose tolerance test in 100 normal children. *Acta Diabetologica Latina, 14,* 95–99.

Kopp, C. B., & Krakow, J. B. (1983). The developmentalist and the study of biological risk: A view of the past with an eye toward the future. *Child Development, 54,* 1086–1108.

Kraus, J. F., Rock, A., & Hemyari, P. (1990). Brain injuries among infants, children, adolescents and young adults. *American Journal of Diseases of Children, 144,* 684–691.

Kreutzer, J. S., Doherty, K. R., Harris, J. A., & Zasler, N. D. (1990). Alcohol use among persons with traumatic brain injury. *Journal of Head Trauma Rehabilitation, 5,* 9–20.

Kreutzer, J. S., Wehman, P. H., Harris, J. A., Burns, C. T., & Young, H. F. (1991). Substance abuse and crime patterns among persons with traumatic brain injury referred for supported employment. *Brain Injury, 5,* 177–187.

LaVeck, B., Hammond, M. A., & LaVeck, G. D. (1980). Minor congenital anomalies and behavior in different home environments. *Journal of Pediatrics, 96,* 940–943.

Lewis, D. O., Lovely, R., Yeager, C., Ferguson, G., Friedman, M., Sloane, G., Friedman, H., & Pincus, J. H. (1988). Intrinsic and environmental characteristics of juvenile murderers. *Journal of the American Academy of Child and Adolescent Psychiatry, 27,* 582–587.

Lewis, D. O., Pincus, J. H., Bard, B., Richardson, E., Prichep, L. S., Feldman, M., & Yeager, M. A. (1988). Neuropsychiatric, psychoeducational and family characteristics of 14 juveniles condemned to death in the United States. *American Journal of Psychiatry, 145,* 584–589.

Lewis, D. O., Pincus, J. H., Feldman, M., Jackson, L., & Bard, B. (1986). Psychiatric, neurological and psychoeducational characteristics of 15 death row inmates in the United States. *American Journal of Psychiatry, 143,* 838–845.

Lewis, D. O., & Shanok, S. S. (1977). Medical histories of delinquent and nondelinquent children: An epidemiological study. *American Journal of Psychiatry, 134,* 1020–1025.

Lewis, D. O., Shanok, S. S., & Balla, D. A. (1979). Perinatal difficulties, head and face trauma, and child abuse in the medical histories of seriously delinquent children. *American Journal of Psychiatry, 136,* 419–423.

Lewis, D. O., Shanok, S. S., Grant, M., & Rituo, E. (1983). Homicidally aggressive young children: Neuropsychiatric and experimental correlates. *American Journal of Psychiatry, 140,* 148–153.

Litt, S. M. (1971). *Perinatal complications and criminality.* Unpublished doctoral dissertation, University of Michigan.

Little, W. J. (1861). On the influence of abnormal parturition, difficult labours, premature birth and asphyxia neonatorum on the mental and physical condition of the child, especially in relation to deformities. *Transactions of the Obstetrical Society of London, 3,* 293–344.

Lombroso, C. (1911). *Crime, its causes and remedies.* Boston: Little Brown.

Lou, H. C., Hansen, D., Nordentoft, M., Pryds, O., Jensen, F., Nim, J., & Hemingsen, R. (1994). Prenatal stressors of human life affect fetal brain development. *Developmental Medicine and Child Neurology, 36,* 826–832.

Marks, V. (1981). The regulation of blood glucose. In V. Marks & F. C. Rose (Eds.), *Hypoglycemia* (pp. 64–83). Oxford: Blackwell.

Marlowe, M., Cossairt, A., Moon, C., Errera, J., MacNeel, A., Peak, R., Ray, J., & Schroeder, C. (1985). Main and interaction effects of metallic toxins in classroom behavior. *Journal of Abnormal Child Psychology, 13,* 185–198.

McCormick, M. (1985). The contribution of low birth weight to infant mortality and childhood morbidity. *New England Journal of Medicine, 312,* 82–90.

McGauhey, P. J., Starfield, B., Alexander, C., & Ensminger, M. E. (1991). Social environment and vulnerability of low birth weight children: A social–epidemiological perspective. *Pediatrics, 88,* 943–953.

McNeil, T. F., Wiegerink, R., & Dozier, J. E. (1970). Pregnancy and birth complications in the births of seriously, moderately, and mildly behaviorally disturbed children. *Journal of Nervous and Mental Disease, 151*, 24–34.

Miller, L. (1994). Traumatic brain injury and aggression. *Journal of Offender Rehabilitation, 21*, 91–103.

Moffitt, T. E. (1993). Adolescence-limited and life-course-persistent antisocial behavior: A developmental taxonomy. *Psychological Review, 100*, 674–701.

Muldoon, M., Manuck, S., & Matthews, K. (1990). Lowering cholesterol concentrations and mortality: A review of primary prevention trials. *British Medical Journal, 301*, 309–314.

Mungas, D. (1983). An empirical analysis of specific syndromes of violent behavior. *Journal of Nervous and Mental Disease, 171*, 354–361.

Needleman, H. L. (1990). The future challenge of lead toxicity. *Environmental Health Perspectives, 89*, 85–89.

Needleman, H. L., Gunnoe, C., Leviton, A., Reed, R., Peresie, H., Maher, C., & Barrett, P. (1979). Deficits in psychologic and classroom performance of children with elevated dentine lead levels. *New England Journal of Medicine, 300*, 689–695.

Needleman, H. L., Riess, J. A., Tobin, M. J., Biesecker, G. E., & Greenhouse, J. B. (1996). Bone lead levels and delinquent behavior. *Journal of the American Medical Association, 275*, 363–369.

Needleman, H. L., Schell, A., Bellinger, D., Leviton, A., & Allred, E. M. (1990). The long-term effects of exposure to low doses of lead in childhood: An eleven year follow-up report. *The New England Journal of Medicine, 322*, 83–88.

Neligan, G. A., Kolvin, I., Scott, D. M., & Garside, R. F. (1976). *Born too soon or born too small*. Philadelphia: J. B. Lippincott.

Pasamanick, B., & Knobloch, H. (1960). Brain and behavior: Session I. Symposium 1959. 2. Brain damage and reproductive casualty. *American Journal of Orthopsychiatry, 30*, 298–305.

Pasamanick, B., Rogers, M. E., & Lilienfeld, A. M. (1956). Pregnancy experience and the development of behavior disorders in children. *American Journal of Psychiatry, 112*, 613–618.

Paulhus, D. L., & Martin, C. L. (1986). Predicting adult temperament from minor physical anomalies. *Journal of Personality and Social Psychology, 50*, 1235–1239.

Pihl, R. O., & Ervin, F. (1990). Lead and cadmium levels in violent criminals. *Psychological Reports, 66*, 839–844.

Quinn, P. O., & Rapoport, J. L. (1974). Minor physical anomalies and neurological status in hyperactive boys. *Pediatrics, 53*, 742–747.

Raine, A. (1993). *The psychopathology of crime*. San Diego: Academic Press.

Raine, A., Brennan, P. A., & Mednick, S. A. (1994). Birth complications combined with early maternal rejection at age 1 year predispose to violent crime at age 18 years. *Archives of General Psychiatry, 51*, 984–988.

Rantakallio, P., Koiranen, M., & Moettoenen, J. (1992). Association of perinatal events, epilepsy, and central nervous system trauma with juvenile delinquency. *Archives of Disease in Childhood, 67*, 1459–1461.

Rosanoff, A. J., Handy, L. M., & Plessett, I. R. (1934). The etiology of manic-depressive syndrome with special reference to their occurrence in twins. *American Journal of Psychiatry, 91*, 247–286.

Rosenbaum, A. (1991). The neuropsychology of marital aggression. In J. S. Milner (Ed.), *Neuropsychology of aggression* (pp. 167–180). Boston: Kluwer.

Rosenbaum, A., & Hoge, S. K. (1989). Head injury and marital aggression. *American Journal of Psychiatry, 146*, 1048–1051.

Ross, G., Lipper, E. G., & Auld, P. A. (1990). Social competence and behavior problems in premature children at school age. *Pediatrics, 86*, 391–397.

Rutter, M. (1982). *Maternal deprivation reassessed*. Harmondsworth, England: Penguin.

Rutter, M. (1990). Psychosocial resilience and protective mechanisms. In J. Rolf, A. S. Masten, D. Cicchetti, K. H. Nuechterlein, & S. Weintraub (Eds.), *Risk and protective factors in the development of psychopathology* (pp. 181–214). New York: Cambridge University Press.

Sameroff, A. J., & Chandler, M. J. (1975). Reproductive risk and the continuum of caretaker casualty. In F. D. Horowitz, E. M. Hetherington, S. Scarr-Salapatek, & G. Siegel (Eds.), *Review of child development research* (pp. 187–244). Chicago: University of Chicago Press.

Schauss, A. G. (1981). Utilizing hair trace element analysis in the treatment of violent juvenile and adult offenders. *International Journal of Biosocial Research, 2*, 42–49.

Schoenthaler, S. J. (1982). The effects of sugar in the treatment and control of antisocial behavior on an incarcerated juvenile population. *International Journal of Biosocial Research, 3*, 1–9.

Schoenthaler, S. J. (1983a). Diet and crime: An empirical examination of the value of nutrition in the control and treatment of incarcerated juvenile offenders. *International Journal of Biosocial Research, 4*, 25–39.

Schoenthaler, S. J. (1983b). The northern California diet behavior program: An empirical evaluation of 3000 incarcerated juveniles in Stanislaus County Juvenile Hall. *International Journal of Biosocial Research, 5*, 99–106.

Schoenthaler, S. J. (1983c). Diet and delinquency: A multi-state replication. *International Journal of Biosocial Research, 5*, 70–78.

Schoenthaler, S. J. (1991). Abstracts of early papers on the effects of vitamin and mineral supplementation on IQ and behavior. *Personality and Individual Differences, 12*, 335–341.

Schoenthaler, S. J., Amos, S. P., Doraz, W. E., Kelly, M. A., & Wakefield, J. (1991). Controlled trial of vitamin-mineral supplementation on intelligence and brain function. *Personality and Individual Differences, 12*, 343–350.

Schoenthaler, S. J., & Doraz, W. E. (1983). Types of offenses which can be reduced in an institutional setting using nutritional intervention: A preliminary empirical evaluation. *International Journal of Biosocial Research, 4*, 74–84.

Sereny, G., Endrenyi, L., & Devenyi, P. (1975). Glucose intolerance in alcoholism. *Journal of Studies on Alcohol, 36*, 359–364.

Shanok, S. S., & Lewis, D. O. (1981). Medical histories of female delinquents. *Archives of General Psychiatry, 38*, 211–213.

Stott, D. H. (1972). The congenital background to behavioral disturbance. In M. Roff, L. Robins, & M. Pollack (Eds.), *Life history research in psychopathology* (186–198). Minneapolis: University of Minnesota Press.

Szatmari, P., Reitsma, S. M., & Offord, D. R. (1986). Pregnancy and birth complications in antisocial adolescents and their siblings. *Canadian Journal of Psychiatry, 31*, 513–516.

Templer, D. I., Kasiraj, J., Trent, N. H., Trent, A., Hughey, B., Keller, W. J., Orling, R. A., & Thomas-Dobson, S. (1992). Exploration of head injury without medical attention. *Perceptual and Motor Skills, 75*, 195–202.

Virkkunen, M. (1979). Serum cholesterol in antisocial personality. *Neuropsychobiology, 5*, 27–30.

Virkkunen, M. (1983a). Insulin secretion during the glucose tolerance test in antisocial personality. *British Journal of Psychiatry, 142*, 598–604.

Virkkunen, M. (1983b). Serum cholesterol levels in homicidal offenders. *Neuropsychobiology, 10,* 65–69.

Virkkunen, M. (1986a). Insulin secretion during the glucose tolerance test among habitually violent and impulsive offenders. *Aggressive Behavior, 12,* 303–310.

Virkkunen, M. (1986b). Reactive hypoglycemic tendency among habitually violent offenders. *Nutrition Reviews, 44,* 94–103.

Virkkunen, M., & Penttinen, H. (1984). Serum cholesterol in aggressive conduct disorder: A preliminary study. *Biological Psychiatry, 19,* 435–439.

Waldrop, M. F., Bell, R. Q., McLaughlin, B., & Halverson, C. F. (1978). Newborn minor physical anomalies predict short attention span, peer aggression and impulsivity at age 3. *Science, 199,* 563–565.

Waters, E., & Sroufe, L. A. (1983). Competence as a developmental construct. *Developmental Review, 3,* 79–97.

Werner, E. E. (1987). Vulnerability and resiliency in children at risk for delinquency: A longitudinal study from birth to adulthood. In J. D. Burchard & S. N. Burchard (Eds.), *Primary prevention of psychopathology* (pp. 16–43). Newbury Park, CA: Sage Publications.

Werner, E. E., Bierman, J. M., & French, F. E. (1971). *The children of Kauai: A longitudinal study from the prenatal period to age ten.* Honolulu: University of Hawaii Press.

Werner, E. E., & Smith, R. S. (1992). *Overcoming the odds: High risk children from birth to adulthood.* London: Cornell University Press.

Williams, R. J. (1981). *The prevention of alcoholism through nutrition.* New York: Bantam Books.

Yule, W., Lansdown, R., Millar, I. B., & Urbanowicz, M. (1981). The relationship between blood lead concentrations, intelligence and attainment in a school population: A pilot study. *Developmental Medicine and Child Neurology, 23,* 567–576.

CHAPTER 26

Neuropsychological and Neuroimaging Studies of Juvenile Delinquency and Adult Criminal Behavior

BILL HENRY and TERRIE E. MOFFITT

The belief that brain deficits are among the causes of antisocial behavior is a very old one. Benjamin Rush (1812) referred to the "total perversion of the moral faculties" in people who displayed "innate preternatural moral depravity." Rush proposed that "there is probably an original defective organization in those parts of the body which are occupied by the moral faculties of the mind" (p. 360). Since Rush's day, quite a bit of research has been done to put his "hypothesis" to the scientific test. Contemporary research methods have improved our ability to understand the role of neuropsychological factors in the antisocial behavior problems of children and adults. Neuropsychological researchers have labored to understand whether people with antisocial behavior problems do differ in "faculties of the mind." Some progress has been made and that work is described in this chapter.

This chapter covers several topics. First, theory and data relating to the relation between neuropsychological deficit and the development of antisocial behavior among juveniles is reviewed. The broad topic of neuropsychological deficit is broken into the two specific deficits that have received the most empirical support to date: language deficits and executive deficits. Second, the extension of neuropsychological research to adult criminal behavior, including the psychopathic personality, is examined. Data from a promising new branch of research, neuroimaging studies, is also reviewed. The final section is a discussion of methodological issues and possible directions for future research. Our purpose here is to identify for the reader the broad trends and major issues within the field and to provide a starting point for the interested reader who wishes to pursue a particular issue further. Additional reviews of this field are provided by Moffitt and Henry (1991), Moffitt and Lynam (1994), and Raine (1993).

This work was supported by a grant from the Violence and Traumatic Stress Branch of the National Institute of Mental Health (MH-45070) to Terrie E. Moffitt.

NEUROPSYCHOLOGICAL STUDIES OF JUVENILE DELINQUENCY

Verbal Deficits and Risk for Delinquency

Theoretical Perspectives

Several theoretical issues arise when examining the relation between verbal deficit and antisocial behavior. First, by what means are these deficits related to antisocial behavior? Direct effects models emphasize the role of verbally based inhibitory mechanisms in interrupting and preventing antisocial behavior. These models posit a very direct and immediate relation between individuals' inability to control behavior and their involvement in antisocial behavior—in other words, poor verbal skills would be seen as a proximal contributor to antisocial behavior. For example, Wilson and Herrnstein (1985) suggest that low verbal intelligence contributes to a present-oriented cognitive style that, in turn, fosters irresponsible and exploitative behavior. Normal language development is viewed as an essential ingredient in prosocial processes such as delaying gratification, anticipating consequences, and linking belated punishments with earlier transgressions.

In contrast, Tarter and his colleagues (Tarter, Hegedus, Winsten, & Alterman, 1984, 1985) offer an indirect effects model in which language deficits set in motion some other mechanism that is the more proximal contributor to antisocial behavior. They hypothesize that children with poor communication skills may elicit less positive interaction and more physical punishment from their parents, especially if the family is distressed. It follows from Tarter's speculation that poor verbal abilities may act indirectly by hindering the development of healthy parent-child relationships that might forestall conduct problems.

A second theoretical issue involves whether it is the deficits in verbal skills per se that contribute to antisocial behavior. Because language functions are subserved by the left cerebral hemisphere in almost all individuals (see Benson & Zaidel, 1985), the relationship between antisocial behavior and verbal deficit also has been interpreted as evidence for dysfunction of the left cerebral hemisphere. For example, Nachshon (1988) argued that a generalized left-hemisphere dysfunction contributes to the hemisphere's normal control over impulsive behavior.

Finally, the issue arises as to whether verbal deficits might apply particularly to a subgroup of antisocial individuals. Moffitt (1993a) has proposed a model in which neuropsychological deficits (in both language and executive functions) contribute both directly and indirectly to antisocial behavior, but only for those subgroups of offenders who exhibit a life-course persistent pattern of antisocial behavior. This theory highlights the importance of examining potential sources of heterogeneity among offenders when attempting to link antisocial behavior to specific patterns of neuropsychological deficit.

Empirical Evidence for a Verbal Deficit

Relations between verbal deficits and antisocial behavior have been found using traditional intelligence tests as well as specialized neuropsychological measures. These results hold whether the antisocial subjects being examined are incarcerated, clinic-referred, or nonincarcerated community samples. The results also hold after appropriate controls are applied for variables such as socioeconomic status, race, academic achievement, detection by police, and motivation to take verbal tests (Lynam, Moffitt, & Stouthamer-Loeber, 1993). Verbal deficits have been shown to precede the onset of delinquent behavior and are strongest for the subgroup of delinquents who have a past history of attention deficit/hyperactivity disorder (ADHD).

Ever since Wechsler (1944) remarked on the diagnostic utility of a Performance IQ score to identify delinquents, a plethora of studies has been published on the "PIQ > VIQ" sign in delinquency (Haynes & Bensch, 1981; Lynam et al., 1993; Prentice & Kelly, 1963; Walsh, Petee, & Beyer, 1987; West & Farrington, 1973). This impressively replicable finding has been taken as strongly supporting a specific deficit in language manipulation for delinquents.

Almost all of the neuropsychological studies reviewed for this chapter provided some evidence of deficit on language-based tests for delinquents. The majority of the studies conducted in this area have compared incarcerated teens with nondelinquent controls (Berman & Siegal, 1976; Karniski, Levine, Clarke, Palfrey, & Meltzer, 1982; Sobotowicz, Evans, & Laughlin, 1987; Wolff, Waber, Bauermeister, Cohen, & Ferber, 1982). However, Lahey et al. (1995) examined the persistence of conduct disorder (CD) symptoms in a group of 171 clinic-referred boys and found that the combination of verbal intelligence scores below 100 and a biological parent who met criteria for antisocial personality disorder predicted an increase in the number CD symptoms across a 4-year span.

Language-based measures were found to be more strongly associated with self-reported delinquency than were nonlanguage measures in our own longitudinal project in New Zealand. The neuropsychological findings from this prospective longitudinal study have been reported in several papers to date (Frost, Moffitt, & McGee, 1989; Henry, Moffitt, & Silva, 1992; Moffitt, 1990a, 1990b, 1993b; Moffitt & Henry, 1989; Moffitt & Silva, 1988a, 1988b, 1988c; White, Moffitt, Earls, Robins, & Silva, 1990; White, Moffitt, & Silva, 1989, 1992).

In the New Zealand project, delinquent versus nondelinquent group differences were substantially greater for the verbal and auditory-verbal memory tests than for tests representing visual-motor integration and visual-spatial and mental flexibility functions. Specific language-based measures on which delinquents scored poorly relative to the sample norm were the Rey Auditory Verbal Learning Test (memorization of a word list), Verbal Fluency (rapid generation of a class of words), and the WISC-R VIQ subtests of Information, Similarities, Arithmetic, and Vocabulary.

A subgroup of delinquents with past histories of ADHD showed especially poor performance on the verbal and verbal memory factors, scoring a full standard deviation below nondelinquents. Apparently, these deficits emerged very early; at ages 3 and 5 these boys had scored more than a standard deviation below the age norm for boys on the Bayley and McCarthy tests of motor coordination and on the Stanford Binet test of cognitive performance. In addition, the comorbid cases had histories of extreme antisocial behavior with physical aggression that remained stable from age 3 to age 15 (Moffitt, 1990a). As adolescents, their law-breaking acts were more aggressive than the acts of other delinquents who did not have a history of neuropsychological deficits and school failure. Later follow-up of the sample (Moffitt, Lynam, & Silva, 1994) revealed that low neuropsychological test scores at age 13 predicted which boys would escalate into recidivistic criminal conviction by age 18. Boys with preadolescent problem behavior and neuropsychological deficits constituted 12% of the sample but accounted for 59% of the sample's 255 convictions.

Executive Dysfunctions and Risk for Delinquency

Theoretical Perspectives

Verbal deficits are not the only neuropsychological correlates of antisocial behavior. Antisocial behavior may also be associated with deficiencies in the brain's self-control functions. These mental functions are commonly referred to by neuropsychologists as "executive" functions, and they include sustaining attention and concentration; abstract reasoning and concept formation; formulating goals; anticipating and planning; programming and initiating purposive sequences of behavior; self-monitoring and self-awareness; inhibiting unsuccessful, inappropriate, or impulsive behaviors; and interrupting ongoing behavior patterns in order to shift to a more adaptive alternative behavior.

One historical rationale for neuropsychological research with delinquents was the apparent resemblance between criminal behavior and the disinhibited antisocial symptoms of patients with injury to the frontal lobes of the brain (Elliott, 1992). Pontius (1972), Gorenstein (1982), and Yeudall (1980) have developed theories based on the observed similarity between the behavior of delinquents and "pseudopsychopathic" patients with frontal lobe brain injuries. Gorenstein and Newman (1980) described *functional* similarities between disinhibited antisocial human behavior and experimental animal models of damage to the structures of the frontal lobes and limbic system of the brain. More recently, Newman and colleagues (e.g., Newman & Wallace, 1993; Patterson & Newman, 1993) have extended this model, further clarifying the nature of "disinhibitory psychopathology" (see also Quay, 1993).

Raine and Venables (1992) highlighted the need for careful consideration of the nature of frontal deficits that may be linked to antisocial behavior. Rather than referring to a general frontal dysfunction, these authors argued that the location of the frontal deficit determined the nature of the psychopathology exhibited. Psychopathic behavior was hypothesized to be associated with deficits in the orbitofrontal region; deficits in the dorsolateral region, on the other hand, were hypothesized to be associated with schizotypal behavior. Individuals unfortunate enough to have deficits in both areas were expected to exhibit both types of psychopathology and would thus appear as schizotypal psychopaths.

Empirical Evidence for an Executive Deficit

Evidence of the relation between executive deficits and aggression has been found among incarcerated subjects, among normal subjects in laboratory situations, and among nonselected populations. This relationship holds when controlling for intelligence and appears to be especially strong for a subgroup of offenders characterized by both antisocial behavior and ADHD.

Several studies that have applied batteries of formal tests of executive functions to delinquent subjects have shown that the test scores can discriminate between antisocial and nonantisocial adolescents (see Moffitt, 1990b; Moffitt & Henry, 1991, for reviews). In addition, there is some evidence that the persistent and impulsive behaviors characteristic of conduct-disordered children and adults with antisocial personality disorder may be associated with executive deficits, particularly in attention modulation (Newman, 1987; Newman & Howland, 1989; Newman & Kosson, 1986; Raine, 1988; Shapiro, Quay, Hogan, & Schwartz, 1988).

Skoff and Libon (1987) reported that one third of their incarcerated subjects scored in the impaired range on a battery composed of the Wisconsin Card Sort Test, Porteus Mazes, Trails B, Verbal Fluency, and four additional executive tasks. Other studies, although not focusing specifically on executive functions, have reported data from individual measures typically included in frontal lobe batteries (Berman & Siegal, 1976; Krynicki, 1978; Wolff et al., 1982). Five studies showed that delinquents score poorly on various tests requiring sequencing of motor behavior (Brickman, McManus, Grapentine, & Alessi, 1984; Hurwitz, Bibace, Wolff, & Rowbotham, 1972; Karniski et al., 1982; Lueger & Gill, 1990; Miller, Burdg, & Carpenter, 1980).

Two recent studies have examined the relationship between executive neuropsychological function and aggression among a nondelinquent population in a laboratory setting. Giancola and Zeichner (1994) reported that performance on the Conditional Association Task (hypothesized to assess functioning of the posterior dorsolateral area of the frontal cortex) was associated with intensity of shocks administered to a fictitious opponent under conditions of provocation. This result was replicated by Lau, Pihl, and Peterson (1995).

In our New Zealand study, adolescent boys who exhibited symptoms of both conduct disorder and ADHD scored more poorly on neuropsychological tests of executive functions than their peers who had either CD or ADHD (Moffitt & Henry, 1989; Moffitt & Silva, 1988c). In our companion study of executive functions and conduct problems in the Pittsburgh Youth Study, a longitudinal study of delinquency in Black and White inner-city boys (White et al., 1994), data were gathered on self-control and impulsivity using multiple tests and measures for 430 12-year-old boys. The impulsivity measures were strongly related to the 3-year longevity of antisocial behavior, even after controlling for intelligence and social class. Taken together, the New Zealand and Pittsburgh longitudinal studies suggest that neuropsychological dysfunctions that manifest themselves as poor scores on tests of self-control (and as the inattentive and impulsive symptoms of ADHD) are linked with the early onset of conduct disorder and with its subsequent persistence.

NEUROPSYCHOLOGICAL AND NEUROIMAGING STUDIES OF ADULT CRIMINAL BEHAVIOR

Persistent Adult Criminality

Neuropsychological Studies

Given that the evidence reviewed here linking juvenile antisocial behavior with individual differences in neuropsychological functioning and the fact that adult antisocial behavior is strongly predicted by juvenile antisocial behavior (see Lahey & Loeber, Chapter 5, this volume), one might expect to find similar neuropsychological impairments in adult offenders. Unfortunately, the state of the literature on neuropsychology and adult antisocial behavior makes evaluation of this hypothesis difficult. The literature is sparse and inconsistent, not yet pointing toward any consensus.

The most certain conclusion that might be drawn from the adult literature is that *persistent adult criminals* show the same general impairments on intelligence tests and neuropsychological test batteries as do juvenile delinquents. Adult criminals have been reported to manifest lower IQ scores, generally, and possibly a greater VIQ < PIQ split, specifically, on standard intelligence tests than do controls (Valliant, Asu, Cooper, & Mammola, 1984; Yeudall & Wardell, 1978; Yeudall, Fedora, Fedora, & Wardell, 1981). Additionally, this relation may be stronger in violent than in nonviolent offenders (DeWoffe & Ryan, 1984; Heilbrun, 1982; Heilbrun & Heilbrun, 1985; Holland & Holt, 1975; Holland, Beckett, & Levi, 1981). Results from studies using standard neuropsychological tests were much the same; persistent serious offenders showed the greatest deficits (Bryant, Scott, Golden, & Tori, 1984; Fedora & Fedora, 1983; Malloy, Noel, Longabaugh, & Beattie, 1990; Spellacy, 1978; Yeudall, 1977; Yeudall et al., 1981). Foster, Hillbrand, and Silverstein (1993) reported that a battery of neuropsychological measures, which included the Wisconsin Card Sorting Test, was related to aggression among a group of 23 violent forensic patients. This literature is not without disconfirming instances; for example, Hare, Frazelle, Bus, and Jutai (1980) failed to find neuropsychological deficits in a sample of male prison inmates on the Comprehensive Ability Battery (for other failures, cf. Sutker, Moan, & Allain, 1974; Virkkunen & Luukkonen, 1977).

Summarizing across studies on juvenile and adult criminal behavior, this research has pointed to two neuropsychological functions (verbal and executive) in which deficits are found. The effect sizes across studies with significant findings range from small to moderate (Cohen, 1992), but they appear to be robust. Verbal deficits have been empirically and theoretically linked to malfunction in the left hemisphere of the brain, and executive deficits have been similarly linked to the brain's frontal cortex (Kolb & Whishaw, 1985). In view of these anatomical links, technologies capable of generating images of the brain should reveal abnormalities in the left hemisphere and frontal cortex. We now turn to a brief review of studies of this kind.

Neuroimaging Studies

An emerging area of research involves the use of neuroimaging techniques to examine patterns of brain functioning associated with antisocial behavior. Broadly, neuroimaging techniques can be divided into those assessing structural characteristics of the brain (e.g., computerized tomography, magnetic resonance imaging) and those assessing functional characteristics of the brain (e.g., positron emission tomography). Both approaches have been used in assessing the brain function of antisocial individuals. Interested readers are referred to Raine (1993) for a more detailed discussion of the technical aspects of these assessment techniques.

All of the studies reviewed here used adult populations; many were specifically focused on sexual offenders. Results vary across studies, but when significant findings do emerge, they generally involve dysfunction in the temporal and frontal regions among offenders, a pattern partially supportive of results found in studies using performance tests. However, variability in results, coupled with small sample sizes and reliance upon incarcerated samples, suggests that caution is needed when attempting to draw conclusions.

Seven studies using computerized tomography to assess brain structure were conducted by Langevin and colleagues (Hucker et al., 1988; Hucker et al., 1986; Langevin, Ben-Aron, Wortzman, Dickey, & Handy, 1987; Langevin, Wortzman, Dickey, Wright, & Handy, 1988; Langevin, Wortzman, Wright, & Handy, 1989; Langevin, Lang, Wortzman, Frenzel, & Wright, 1989; Wright, Nobrega, Langevin, & Wortzman, 1990). Six of these studies compared sexual offenders to a nonviolent, nonsexual offender control group; one compared violent offenders to a nonviolent control group.

Results across the seven studies are mixed. In three of the studies, no significant differences in brain structure were found between offender groups. When differences were found, they tended to be in the form of greater abnormalities in the temporal region for the sex offender groups, particularly for those sex offenders who were also violent. For example, Langevin et al. (1988) reported that 17% of incest offenders, compared to 13% of controls, exhibited temporal lobe abnormalities (this difference was not significant). However, dividing the incest offenders on the basis of a history of violence revealed that 35% of violent incest offenders, compared to 13% of nonviolent incest offenders, exhibited temporal lobe abnormalities.

It should be noted that the failure to find consistent significant differences between offender groups in these studies does not suggest that structural abnormalities are not related to antisocial behavior; failure to include a nonoffender control group in these studies prohibits such a conclusion. Further, the samples used in these studies were generally small, decreasing statistical power and increasing the likelihood of failing to identify genuine differences between groups.

Five of the studies described earlier used both neuropsychological and neuroimaging techniques (Hucker et al., 1986; Hucker et

al., 1988; Langevin et al., 1987; Langevin et al., 1988; Langevin, Wortzman et al., 1989). In only two of these studies (Hucker et al., 1986; Hucker et al., 1988) were significant differences between groups found on both the neuropsychological assessments and the computerized tomography scans. Even in these studies, very few subjects showed both structural and functional impairment; for example, Hucker et al. (1986) reported that only 8% of their subjects showed impairment on both computerized tomography scans and the Reitan neuropsychological battery.

Three other studies have examined the relation between brain structure and antisocial behavior. Herzberg and Fenwick (1988) used computerized tomography to compare the brain structure of aggressive versus nonaggressive temporal lobe epileptics; they reported no significant differences between groups. In contrast, Tonkonogy (1991) compared 14 violent psychiatric patients with nine nonviolent psychiatric patients and found a significantly greater prevalence of temporal lobe abnormalities among the violent patients. Blake, Pincus, and Buckner (1995) reported CT and MRI abnormalities in 9 of 19 murderers assessed. These researchers also reported neuropsychological abnormalities (primarily frontal deficits) in 8 of 17 murderers assessed.

Fewer neuroimaging studies have attempted to link measures of functional brain characteristics to antisocial behavior. Volkow and Tancredi (1987) used positron emission tomography scans to examine brain function among four hospitalized, violent males. All four cases exhibited decreased cerebral blood flow in the temporal region; two of the cases exhibited decreased cerebral blood flow in the frontal cortex. Hendricks et al. (1988) found reduced cerebral blood flow, particularly over anterior regions, among a group of 16 child molesters compared to noncriminal controls; however, they failed to identify any significant differences in brain structure between groups using computerized tomography. Goyer et al. (1994) reported a significant negative relationship between cerebral glucose metabolism in the frontal cortex and a history of aggression among a group of 17 personality disorder patients. Raine, Buchsbaum et al. (1994) compared cerebral glucose metabolism among 22 murderers and 22 noncriminal controls. These authors reported decreased glucose metabolism in the lateral and medial prefrontal cortex among murderers.

Integration of Neuropsychological and Neuroimaging Studies

In summary, studies using measures of brain structure and brain function have yielded a different pattern of results. Studies of brain structure tend to find a relationship between temporal lobe abnormalities and antisocial behavior (particularly sexual offending); studies of brain function tend to highlight the role of the frontal region. When used together, dissociation between measures of brain structure and function appears to be the general rule rather than the exception.

Neuropsychological tests and neural imaging technologies play complementary roles in the study of antisocial behavior. Neuropsychological tests are relatively imprecise as indexes of the location of dysfunction in the brain, but they are very sensitive measures of how efficiently a brain performs mental functions thought to control behavior, including antisocial behavior. Imaging technologies are sensitive measures of what part within an antisocial individual's brain is performing poorly or has some sort of structural abnormality. However, as demonstrated earlier, deficits in structure and function need not co-occur. Function can be retained even in the presence of structural abnormality, and function can be lost in a structure that appears normal, given the constraints of contemporary imaging technology.

One strategy for further clarifying and integrating results from studies using both neuroimaging and neuropsychological assessment techniques is to use the imaging techniques to assess functioning in particular brain regions while those regions are being "challenged" by neuropsychological tests. Although this strategy has not yet been extensively used in the study of antisocial individuals, it has proven useful in examining the neural underpinnings of other disorders such as schizophrenia (e.g., Berman, Illowsy, & Weinberger, 1988; Weinberger, Berman, & Zec, 1986). Raine, Buchsbaum et al. (1994) used the continuous performance task (CPT) as a frontal challenge task in their comparison of murderers and noncriminals. Specific hypotheses generated from the neuropsychological literature could be tested by using as challenge tasks those neuropsychological measures that have been found to differentiate between antisocial and nonantisocial individuals.

Although some trends have emerged from the study of structural and functional brain deficits among adult criminals, this literature is far from complete. Reliance on small sample sizes, failure to consistently use noncriminal control groups, and use of a wide variety of types of offenders preclude drawing any firm conclusions. A very tentative suggestion is that the results of neuroimaging studies are consistent with results from tests of neuropsychological function. However, the two literatures are not integrated, and much future research is needed to more fully explore these issues.

Psychopathy

Psychopathy represents a special case of adult antisocial behavior. Several authors have attempted to link psychopathy with neuropsychological functioning, specifically with left hemisphere or frontal lobe functioning. Quite simply, some have found psychopathy-related deficits whereas others have not. Despite early successes, Yeudall and his colleagues failed to demonstrate that left hemisphere dysfunction was specific to psychopaths (Yeudall, 1977; Yeudall et al., 1981). Early studies by Schalling and her colleagues that found psychopathy-related deficits using the Porteus Maze Test and the Necker Cube (Lidberg, Levander, Schalling, & Lidberg, 1978; Schalling & Rosen, 1968) have failed to replicate reliably; the same was true for Gorenstein's (1982) initial findings of frontal lobe dysfunction in psychopaths (for failures, cf. Hare, 1984; Hoffman, Hall, & Bartsch, 1987; Sutker & Allain, 1987; Sutker, Moan, & Swanson, 1972). More recently, Hart, Forth, and Hare (1990) failed to find significant differences between psychopathic and nonpsychopathic criminals on a large battery of neuropsychological tests. This result, however, is contradicted by the results of an even more recent study by Smith, Arnett, and Newman (1992), who found that low-anxious psychopaths scored more poorly than low-anxious nonpsychopaths on several tasks tapping frontal lobe function (Trail Making Test-B and Block Design).

Some of the inconsistency in findings across studies may be due to the varied, and sometimes unreliable, diagnostic procedures used to define psychopathy. Whereas some investigators have defined psychopathy in terms of persistent criminality, others have defined it using personality measures such as the MMPI or the Socialization Scale of the California Personality Inventory. Still others have used the Psychopathy Checklist, an operationalization of Cleckley's (1976) clinical description that takes into account both behavior and personality (Hare, 1985a; see Hart & Hare, Chapter 3, this volume). These varied methods do not produce identical subject groups (Hare, 1985b); therefore, in comparing studies, we may be comparing apples and oranges.

METHODOLOGICAL CONSIDERATIONS

Generally speaking, research from a variety of perspectives has yielded a coherent picture of the relationship between brain function and antisocial behavior. As was seen in the case of psychopathy, however, the field is not without its complexities. Many of these complexities are closely tied to methodological issues. Thus, we close by drawing attention to five ways in which methodological concerns have hampered our efforts to understand the relation between brain function and antisocial behavior.

First, a major difficulty in interpreting research on antisocial behavior lies in attaining homogeneous samples. Offenders, particularly adolescent offenders, represent a very heterogeneous group. Recent efforts to subtype offenders have focused on the distinction between chronic and nonchronic patterns (e.g., Moffitt, 1993a). As described earlier, reports from the New Zealand study indicate a different pattern of neuropsychological performance for delinquents who had exhibited a long-term pattern of antisocial behavior compared with those whose antisocial behavior emerged in adolescence (Moffitt et al., 1994). Failure to recognize this source of heterogeneity in a sample may result in inconsistent or contradictory findings. A sample composed primarily of adolescent-limited delinquents will yield one pattern of neuropsychological performance; the performance of a group composed primarily of life-course persistent offenders may be dramatically different.

A second difficulty in interpreting results of these studies is the substantial difference in how antisocial behavior is defined. Some studies define antisocial behavior in terms of official police or court records whereas others rely on self-reports. Some studies focus on aggression or violence whereas others define antisocial behavior in terms of both violent and property crime. Some studies focus on individuals who have committed sexual crimes whereas others use samples of offenders who have committed nonsexual crimes.

This limitation is particularly apparent in the neuroimaging studies reviewed earlier, which have relied primarily on incarcerated subjects. Research on the neuropsychological deficits associated with antisocial behavior has been aided by inclusion of subjects from the general population identified as antisocial on the basis of self-report measures. Similar progress may be made by including these individuals in neuroimaging studies.

Third, it should be noted that studies have not consistently matched the control and experimental groups on variables that are known to influence performance on neuropsychological tasks, that is, race, age, and previous substance use. On the other hand, some studies control for variables that may not be necessary. For example, some authors have included education in their lists of relevant control variables (Hare, 1984; Hart et al., 1990). Excluding subjects who failed to achieve a certain level of education can lead to two problems: First, such designs may exclude neuropsychologically impaired subjects, thus throwing the baby out with the bathwater. Second, such designs may create a select and unrepresentative sample of prisoners, thus compromising generalization. Requiring that subjects meet a minimum level of reading ability may have the same confounding effects as requiring a minimum level of education.

Fourth, many studies have failed to include informative control groups. Some studies compared offenders with nonoffenders whereas others compared one type of offender (e.g., sex offenders) with a different type of offender (e.g., property offenders). Although a case may be made for either of these control groups, depending on the hypotheses of the study, inclusion of both control groups will advance most quickly our knowledge of the relation between brain function and antisocial behavior.

Finally, although neuroimaging techniques represent an important advance in assessment technology, they are not without their limitations. Computerized tomography has the disadvantage of relatively poor resolution, particularly for small brain regions. In addition, subjects are exposed to potentially dangerous X rays. Although such problems are not present with magnetic resonance imaging and positron emission tomography, the primary disadvantage of these techniques is that they are extremely expensive and time and labor intensive. As a result, their use with large representative samples of the population seems unlikely. In addition, studies that have used these techniques often report results in the form of case studies, without reporting tests of statistical significance. Finally, the criteria used in some studies to identify brain abnormalities are often not clearly defined. Thus, whereas these techniques are important advances in the field, they are not panaceas, and results generated in these studies still need to be viewed with caution.

DIRECTIONS FOR FUTURE RESEARCH

This chapter has reviewed evidence from neuropsychological and neuroimaging studies that brain dysfunction is a correlate of antisocial behavior. Unfortunately, the elucidation of theory in this field has not kept up with the collection of empirical data. The traditional notion that brain dysfunction influences antisocial behavior in the moment preceding each individual act may not be a complete explanation. For example, although the relationship between verbal intelligence and delinquency is robust, it is also quite modest; overall, the correlation between VIQ and delinquency is about .22, and group differences are about .5 standard deviation. Given this modest relationship, it is probable that verbal deficits exert their influence in the context of interactions between person and environment over the course of development. We need theories that specify the links in developmental chains between early brain function and later antisocial syndromes. Such theories can be most helpful if they integrate variability in brain function with other known risk factors for conduct problems, such as family adversity, antisocial personality traits, school failure, and poverty.

The recent emergence of imaging technologies has provided the opportunity to synthesize findings from these studies with findings from studies using neuropsychological measures. Such efforts can contribute to the construct validation of these performance measures and assist in the localization of test scores to specific brain regions and systems. It is clear that speaking of antisocial behavior being related to frontal lobe deficits is at best a crude description. Using both performance measures and imaging techniques may assist in developing a much more precise, fine-grained understanding of this relationship.

As indicated earlier, all of the studies of antisocial individuals that have used neuroimaging techniques have used adult populations. Reliance solely on adult populations is problematic for several reasons. Examining structural or functional deficits in adult criminals prevents analysis of the relation between these deficits and the onset and trajectory of the criminal career. Prospective longitudinal studies beginning in late childhood or early adolescence would be helpful in further clarifying the role played by these deficits in the emergence of antisocial behavior.

Finally, the etiology of these brain deficits, and the relation between these deficits and other individual difference characteristics, needs to be examined. Previous research has indicated that disruption in the ontogenesis of the fetal brain can occur as the result of many factors, such as maternal drug abuse, poor prenatal nutrition, or prenatal or postnatal exposure to toxic agents (Needleman & Beringer, 1981; Rodning, Beckwith, & Howard, 1989; Stewart, 1983); child abuse or neglect (Lewis, Shanok, Pincus, & Glaser, 1979); or birth complications (Kandel & Mednick, 1991). In addition, recent research has highlighted the relation between antisocial outcomes and infant characteristics such as perinatal problems (Kandel & Mednick, 1991; Raine, Brennan, & Mednick, 1994) and difficult toddler temperament (Tremblay, Pihl, Vitaro, & Dobkin, 1994; Henry, Caspi, Moffitt, & Silva, 1996). Longitudinal research that examines the linkages between early childhood characteristics, brain function, and antisocial behavior is still needed.

REFERENCES

Benson, D. F., & Zaidel, E. (1985). *The dual brain.* New York: Guilford.

Berman, A., & Siegal, A. W. (1976). Adaptive and learning skills in juvenile delinquents: A neuropsychological analysis. *Journal of Learning Disabilities, 9,* 51–58.

Blake, P., Pincus, J., & Buckner, C. (1995). Neurologic abnormalities in murderers. *Neurology, 45,* 1641–1647.

Brickman, A. S., McManus, M. M., Grapentine, W. L., & Alessi, N. (1984). Neuropsychological assessment of seriously delinquent adolescents. *Journal of the American Academy of Child Psychiatry, 23,* 453–457.

Bryant, E. T., Scott, M. L., Golden, C. J., & Tori, C. D. (1984). Neuropsychological deficits, learning disability and violent behavior. *Journal of Consulting and Clinical Psychology, 52,* 323–324.

Cleckley, H. (1976). *The mask of sanity.* St. Louis: Mosby.

Cohen, J. (1992). A power primer. *Psychological Bulletin, 112,* 155–159.

DeWolfe, A. S., & Ryan, J. J. (1984). Wechsler Performance IQ Verbal IQ index in a forensic sample: A reconsideration. *Journal of Clinical Psychology, 40,* 291–294.

Elliott, F. A. (1992). Violence: The neurologic contribution. *Archives of Neurology, 49*, 595–603.

Fedora, O., & Fedora, S. (1983). Some neuropsychological and psychophysiological aspects of psychopathic and nonpsychopathic criminals. In P. Flor-Henry & J. Gruzelier (Eds.), *Laterality and psychopathology* (pp. 41–58). Amsterdam: Elsevier.

Foster, H., Hillbrand, M., & Silverstein, M. (1993). Neuropsychological deficit and aggressive behavior: A prospective study. *Progress in Neuropsychopharmacology and Biological Psychiatry, 17*, 939–946.

Frost, L. A., Moffitt, T. E., & McGee, R. (1989). Neuropsychological function and psychopathology in an unselected cohort of young adolescents. *Journal of Abnormal Psychology, 98*, 307–313.

Giancola, P., & Zeichner, A. (1994). Neuropsychological performance on tests of frontal-lobe functioning and aggressive behavior in men. *Journal of Abnormal Psychology, 103*, 832–836.

Gorenstein, E. E. (1982). Frontal lobe functions in psychopaths. *Journal of Abnormal Psychology, 91*, 368–379.

Gorenstein, E. E., & Newman, J. P. (1980). Disinhibitory psychopathology: A new perspective and a model for research. *Psychological Review, 87*, 301–315.

Goyer, P., Andreason, P., Semple, W., Clayton, A., King, A., Compton-Toth, B., Schulz, S. C., & Cohen, R. (1994). Positron-emission tomography and personality disorders. *Neuropsychopharmacology, 10*, 21–28.

Hare, R. D. (1984). Performance of psychopaths on cognitive tasks related to frontal lobe function. *Journal of Abnormal Psychology, 93*, 133–140.

Hare, R. D. (1985a). *The Psychopathy Checklist*. Unpublished manuscript.

Hare, R. D. (1985b). Comparison of procedures for the assessment of psychopathy. *Journal of Consulting and Clinical Psychology, 53*, 7–16.

Hare, R. D., Frazelle, J., Bus, J., & Jutai, J. W. (1980). Psychopathy and structure of primary mental abilities. *Journal of Behavioral Assessment, 2*, 77–88.

Hart, S. D, Forth, A. E., & Hare, R. D. (1990). Performance of criminal psychopaths on selected neuropsychological tests. *Journal of Abnormal Psychology, 99*, 374–379.

Haynes, J. P., & Bensch, M. (1981). The P V sign of the WISC-R and recidivism in delinquents. *Journal of Consulting and Clinical Psychology, 49*, 480–481.

Heilbrun, A. B. (1982). Cognitive models of criminal violence based upon intelligence and psychopathy levels. *Journal of Clinical and Consulting Psychology, 50*, 547–557.

Heilbrun, A. B., & Heilbrun, M. R. (1985). Psychopathy and dangerousness: Comparison, integration and extension of two psychopathic typologies. *British Journal of Clinical Psychology, 24*, 181–195.

Hendricks, S., Fitzpatrick, D., Hartmann, K., Quaife, M., Stratbucker, R., & Graber, B. (1988). Brain structure and function in sexual molesters of children and adolescents. *Journal of Clinical Psychiatry, 49*, 108–112.

Henry, B., Caspi, A., Moffitt, T. E., & Silva, P. A. (1996). Temperamental and familial predictors of violent and non-violent criminal convictions: From age 3 to age 18. *Developmental Psychology, 32*, 614–623.

Henry, B., Moffitt, T. E., & Silva, P. A. (1992). Disentangling delinquency and learning disability: Neuropsychological function and social support. *International Journal of Clinical Neuropsychology, 13*, 1–6.

Herzberg, J., & Fenwick, P. (1988). The aetiology of aggression in temporal-lobe epilepsy. *British Journal of Psychiatry, 153*, 50–55.

Hoffman, J. J., Hall, R. W., & Bartsch, T. W. (1987). On the relative importance of "Psychopathic" personality and alcoholism on neuropsychological measures of frontal lobe function. *Journal of Abnormal Psychology, 96*, 158–160.

Holland, T. R., Beckett, G. E., & Levi, M. (1981). Intelligence, personality, and criminal violence: A multivariate analysis. *Journal of Consulting and Clinical Psychology, 49*, 106–111.

Holland, T. R., & Holt, N. (1975). Prisoner intellectual and personality correlates of offense severity and recidivism probability. *Journal of Clinical Psychology, 31*, 667–672.

Hucker, S., Langevin, R., Dickey, R., Handy, L., Chambers, J., Wright, S., Bain, J., & Wortzman, G. (1988). Cerebral damage and dysfunction in sexually aggressive men. *Annals of Sex Research, 1*, 33–47.

Hucker, S., Langevin, R., Wortzman, G., Bain, J., Handy, L., Chambers, J., & Wright, S. (1986). Neuropsychological impairment in pedophiles. *Canadian Journal of Behavioral Science, 18*, 440–448.

Hurwitz, I., Bibace, R. M. A., Wolff, P. H., & Rowbotham, B. M. (1972). Neurological function of normal boys, delinquent boys, and boys with learning problems. *Perceptual and Motor Skills, 35*, 387–394.

Kandel, E., & Mednick, S.A. (1991). Perinatal complications predict violent offending. *Criminology, 29*, 519–529.

Karniski, W. M., Levine, M. D., Clarke, S., Palfrey, J. S., & Meltzer, L. J. (1982). A study of neurodevelopmental findings in early adolescent delinquents. *Journal of Adolescent Health Care, 3*, 151–159.

Kolb, B., & Whishaw, I. Q. (1985). *Fundamentals of human neuropsychology*. New York: Freeman.

Krynicki, V. E. (1978). Cerebral dysfunction in repetitively assaultive offenders. *Journal of Nervous and Mental Disease, 166*, 59–67.

Lahey, B., Loeber, R., Hart, E., Frick, P., Applegate, B., Zhang, Q., Green, S., & Russo, M. (1995). Four-year longitudinal study of conduct disorder in boys: Patterns and predictors of persistence. *Journal of Abnormal Psychology, 104*, 83–94.

Langevin, R., Ben-Aron, M., Wortzman, G., Dickey, R., & Handy, L. (1987). Brain damage, diagnosis, and substance abuse among violent offenders. *Behavioral Sciences and the Law, 5*, 77–94.

Langevin, R., Lang, R., Wortzman, G., Frenzel, R., & Wright, P. (1989). An examination of brain damage and dysfunction in genital exhibitionists. *Annals of Sex Research, 2*, 77–87.

Langevin, R., Wortzman, G., Dickey, R., Wright, P., & Handy, L. (1988). Neuropsychological impairment in incest offenders. *Annals of Sex Research, 1*, 401–415.

Langevin, R., Wortzman, G., Wright, P., & Handy, L. (1989). Studies of brain damage and dysfunction in sex offenders. *Annals of Sex Research, 2*, 163–179.

Lau, M., Pihl, R., & Peterson, J. (1995). Provocation, acute alcohol intoxication, cognitive performance, and aggression. *Journal of Abnormal Psychology, 104*, 150–156.

Lewis, D. O., Shanok, S., Pincus, J., & Glaser, G. (1979). Violent juvenile delinquents: Psychiatric, neurological, psychological and abuse factors. *Journal of the American Academy of Child Psychiatry, 2*, 307–319.

Lidberg, L., Levander, S. E., Schalling, D., & Lidberg, V. (1978). Necker Cube reversals, arousal, and psychopathy. *British Journal of Social and Clinical Psychology, 17*, 355–361.

Lueger, R. & Gill, K. (1990). Frontal-lobe cognitive dysfunction in conduct disorder adolescents. *Journal of Clinical Psychology, 46*, 696–706.

Lynam, D., Moffitt, T. E., & Stouthamer-Loeber, J. (1993). Explaining the relation between IQ and delinquency: Race, class, test motivation, school failure, or self-control. *Journal of Abnormal Psychology, 102*, 187–196.

Malloy, P., Noel, N., Longabaugh, R., & Beattie, M. (1990). Determinants of neuropsychological impairment in antisocial substance abusers. *Addictive Behaviors, 15*, 431–438.

Miller, L. J., Burdg, N. B., & Carpenter, D. (1980). Application of recategorized WISC-R scores of adjudicated adolescents. *Perceptual and Motor Skills, 51,* 187–191.

Moffitt, T. E. (1990a). Juvenile delinquency and attention-deficit disorder: Developmental trajectories from age 3 to 15. *Child Development, 61,* 893–910.

Moffitt, T. E. (1990b). The neuropsychology of delinquency: A critical review of theory and research. In N. Morris & M. Tonry (Eds.), *Crime and Justice* (Vol. 12, pp. 99–169). Chicago: University of Chicago Press.

Moffitt, T. E. (1993a). Adolescence-limited and life-course-persistent antisocial behavior: A developmental taxonomy. *Psychological Review, 100,* 674–701.

Moffitt, T. E. (1993b). The neuropsychology of conduct disorder. *Development and Psychopathology, 5,* 135–151.

Moffitt, T. E., & Henry, B. (1989). Neuropsychological assessment of executive functions in self-reported delinquents. *Development and Psychopathology, 1,* 105–118.

Moffitt, T. E., & Henry, B. (1991). Neuropsychological studies of juvenile delinquency and violence: A review. In J. Milner (Ed.), *The neuropsychology of aggression* (pp. 67–91). Norwell, MA: Kluwer.

Moffitt, T. E., & Lynam, D. (1994). The neuropsychology of conduct disorder and delinquency: Implications for understanding antisocial behavior. In D. Fowles, P. Sutker, & S. Goodman (Eds.), *Psychopathy and antisocial personality: A developmental perspective: Vol. 18. Progress in experimental personality and psychopathology research.* New York: Springer.

Moffitt, T. E., Lynam, D., & Silva, P. A. (1994). Neuropsychological tests predict persistent male delinquency. *Criminology, 32,* 101–124.

Moffitt, T. E., & Silva, P. A. (1988a). IQ and delinquency: A direct test of the differential detection hypothesis. *Journal of Abnormal Psychology, 97,* 330–333.

Moffitt, T. E., & Silva, P. A. (1988b). Neuropsychological deficit and self-reported delinquency in an unselected birth cohort. *Journal of the American Academy of Child and Adolescent Psychiatry, 27,* 233–240.

Moffitt, T. E., & Silva, P. A. (1988c). Self-reported delinquency, neuropsychological deficit, and history of attention deficit disorder. *Journal of Abnormal Child Psychology, 16,* 553–569.

Nachshon, I. (1988). Hemisphere function in violent offenders. In T. E. Moffitt & S. A. Mednick (Eds.), *Biological contributions to crime causation* (pp. 55–67). Dordrecht, Holland: Martinus Nijhoff.

Needleman, H., & Beringer, D. (1981). The epidemiology of low-level lead exposure in childhood. *Journal of Child Psychiatry, 20,* 496–512.

Newman, J. P. (1987). Reaction to punishment in extroverts and psychopaths: Implications for the impulsive behavior of disinhibited individuals. *Journal of Research in Personality, 21,* 464–480.

Newman, J. P., & Howland, E. (1989). The effect of incentives on Wisconsin Card Sorting Task performance in psychopaths. Unpublished manuscript.

Newman, J. P., & Kosson, D. S. (1986). Passive avoidance learning in psychopathic and nonpsychopathic offenders. *Journal of Abnormal Psychology, 95,* 257–263.

Newman, J., & Wallace, J.(1993). Diverse pathways to deficient self-regulation: Implications for disinhibitory psychopathology in children. *Clinical Psychology Review, 13,* 699–720.

Patterson, C. M., & Newman, J. (1993). Reflectivity and learning from aversive events: Toward a psychological mechanism for the syndromes of disinhibition. *Psychological Review, 100,* 716–736.

Pontius, A. A. (1972). Neurological aspects in some type of delinquency, especially among juveniles: Toward a neurological model of ethical action. *Adolescence, 7,* 289–308.

Prentice, N. M., & Kelly, F. J. (1963). Intelligence and delinquency: A reconsideration. *Journal of Social Psychology, 60,* 327–337.

Quay, H. (1993). The psychobiology of undersocialized aggressive conduct disorder: A theoretical perspective. *Development and Psychopathology, 5,* 165–180.

Raine, A. (1988). Evoked potentials and antisocial behavior. In T. Moffitt & S. Mednick (Eds.), *Biological contributions to crime causation* (pp. 14–39). Dordrecht: Martinus Nijhoff.

Raine, A. (1993). *The psychopathology of crime.* New York: Academic Press.

Raine, A., Brennan, P., & Mednick, S. A. (1994). Birth complications combined with early maternal rejection at age 1 year predispose to violent crime at age 18 years. *Archives of General Psychiatry, 51,* 984–987.

Raine, A., Buchsbaum, M., Stanley, J., Lottenberg, S., Abel, L., & Stoddard, J. (1994). Selective reductions in prefrontal glucose metabolism in murderers. *Biological Psychiatry, 36,* 365–373.

Raine, A., & Venables, P. (1992). Antisocial behavior: Evolution, genetics, neuropsychology, and psychophysiology. In A. Gale & M. Eysenck (Eds.), *Handbook of individual differences: Biological perspectives.* London: Wiley.

Rodning, C., Beckwith, L., & Howard, J. (1989). Characteristics of attachment organization and play organization in prenatally drug-exposed toddlers. *Development and Psychopathology, 1,* 277–289.

Rush, B. (1812). *Medical injuries and observations upon the diseases of the mind.* Philadelphia: Kimber & Richardson.

Schalling, D., & Rosen, A. (1968). Porteus Maze differences between psychopathic and non-psychopathic criminals. *British Journal of Social and Clinical Psychology, 7,* 224–228.

Shapiro, S. K., Quay, H. C., Hogan, A. E., & Schwartz, K. P. (1988). Response perseveration and delayed responding in undersocialized aggressive conduct. *Journal of Abnormal Psychology, 97,* 371–373.

Skoff, B. F., & Libon, J. (1987). Impaired executive functions in a sample of male juvenile delinquents. *Journal of Clinical and Experimental Neuropsychology, 9,* 60.

Smith, S. S., Arnett, P. A., & Newman, J. P. (1992). Neuropsychological differentiation of psychopathic and nonpsychopathic criminal offenders. *Personality and Individual Differences, 13,* 1233–1243.

Sobotowicz, W., Evans, J. R., & Laughlin, J. (1987). Neuropsychological function and social support in delinquency and learning disability. *International Journal of Clinical Neuropsychology, 9,* 178–186.

Spellacy, F. (1978). Neuropsychological differentiation between violent and nonviolent men. *Journal of Clinical Psychology, 34,* 49–52.

Stewart, A. (1983). Severe perinatal hazards. In M. Rutter (Ed.), *Developmental neuropsychiatry* (pp. 15–31). New York: Guilford.

Sutker, P. B., & Allain, A. N. (1987). Cognitive abstraction, shifting, and control: Clinical sample comparisons of psychopaths and nonpsychopaths. *Journal of Abnormal Psychology, 96,* 73–75.

Sutker, P. B., Moan, C. E., & Allain, A. N. (1974). WAIS performance in unincarcerated groups of MMPI-defined sociopaths and normal controls. *Journal of Consulting and Clinical Psychology, 28,* 307–308.

Sutker, P. B., Moan, C. E., & Swanson, W. C. (1972). Porteus Maze Test qualitative performance in pure sociopaths, prison normals and antisocial psychotics. *Journal of Clinical Psychology, 28,* 349–353.

Tarter, R. E., Hegedus, A. M., Winsten, N. E., & Alterman, A. I. (1984). Neuropsychological, personality, and familial characteristics of physically abused delinquents. *Journal of the American Academy of Child Psychiatry, 23,* 668–674.

Tarter, R. E., Hegedus, A. M., Winsten, N. E., & Alterman, A. I. (1985). Intellectual profiles and violent behavior in juvenile delinquents. *Journal of Psychology, 119,* 125–128.

Tonkonogy, J. (1991). Violence and temporal lobe lesion: Head CT and MRI data. *Journal of Neuropsychiatry and Clinical Neurosciences, 3,* 189–196.

Tremblay, R., Pihl, R., Vitaro, F., & Dobkin, P. (1994). Predicting early onset of male antisocial behavior from preschool behavior. *Archives of General Psychiatry, 51,* 732–739.

Valliant, P. M., Asu, M. E., Cooper, D., & Mammola, D. (1984). Profile of dangerous and nondangerous offenders referred for pre-trial psychiatric assessment. *Psychological Reports, 54,* 411–418.

Virkkunen, M., & Luukkonen, P. (1977). WAIS performance in antisocial personality. *Acta Psychiatrica Scandinavica, 55,* 220–224.

Volkow, N., & Tancredi, L. (1987). Neural substrates of violent behaviour. *British Journal of Psychiatry, 151,* 668–673.

Walsh, A., Petee, T. A., & Beyer, J. A. (1987). Intellectual imbalance and delinquency: Comparing high verbal and high performance IQ delinquents. *Criminal Justice and Behavior, 14*(3), 370–379.

Wechsler, D. (1944). *The measurement of adult intelligence* (3rd ed.). Baltimore: Williams & Wilkins.

Weinberger, D., Berman, K., & Zec, R. (1986). Physiologic dysfunction of dorsolateral prefrontal cortex in schizophrenia: Regional cerebral blood flow evidence. *Archives of General Psychiatry, 43,* 114–124.

West, D. J., & Farrington, D. P. (1973). *Who becomes delinquent?* London: Heinemann Educational Books.

White, J., Moffitt, T. E., Caspi, A., Jeglum, D., Needles, D., & Stouthamer-Loeber, M. (1994). Measuring impulsivity and examining its relation to delinquency. *Journal of Abnormal Psychology, 103,* 192–205.

White, J., Moffitt, T. E., Earls, F., Robins, L. N., & Silva, P. A. (1990). How early can we tell? Preschool predictors of boys' conduct disorder and delinquency. *Criminology, 28,* 507–533.

White, J., Moffitt, T. E., & Silva, P. A. (1989). A prospective replication of the protective effects of IQ in subjects at high risk for juvenile delinquency. *Journal of Clinical and Consulting Psychology, 57,* 719–724.

White, J., Moffitt, T. E., & Silva, P. A. (1992). Specific arithmetic disability: Neuropsychological and socio-emotional correlates. *Archives of Neuropsychology, 7,* 1–16.

Wilson, J. Q., & Herrnstein, R. J. (1985). *Crime and human nature.* New York: Simon & Schuster.

Wolff, P. H., Waber, D., Bauermeister, M., Cohen, C., & Ferber, R. (1982). The neuropsychological status of adolescent delinquent boys. *Journal of Child Psychology and Psychiatry, 23,* 267–279.

Wright, P., Nobrega, J., Langevin, R., & Wortzman, G. (1990). Brain density and symmetry in pedophilic and sexually aggressive offenders. *Annals of Sex Research, 3,* 319–328.

Yeudall, L. T. (1977). Neuropsychological assessment of forensic disorders. *Canadian Mental Health, 25,* 7–15.

Yeudall, L. T. (1980). A neuropsychological perspective of persistent juvenile delinquency and criminal behavior. *Annals of the New York Academy of Science, 347,* 349–355.

Yeudall, L. T., & Wardell, D. M. (1978). Neuropsychological correlates of criminal psychopathy: Part II. Discrimination and prediction of dangerous and recidivistic offenders. In L. Beliveau, C. Canepa, & D. Szabo (Eds.), *Human aggression and its dangerousness.* Montreal: Pinel Institute.

Yeudall, L. T., Fedora, O., Fedora, S., & Wardell, D. (1981). Neurosocial perspective on the assessment and etiology of persistent criminality. *Australian Journal of Forensic Science, 13,* 131–159, *14,* 20–44.

CHAPTER 27

Antisocial Behavior and Psychophysiology: A Biosocial Perspective and a Prefrontal Dysfunction Hypothesis

ADRIAN RAINE

Since the 1940s, interest in the psychophysiological correlates of antisocial behavior has increased; and as the computer revolution promises to make psychophysiological research increasingly easier, it is predicted that there will be a substantial increase in psychophysiological research on antisocial behavior. Psychophysiological research has enormous potential to illuminate the etiology of antisocial behavior because it lies at the interface between clinical science, cognitive science, and neuroscience (Dawson, 1990). Psychophysiology is more suited than almost any other area of research to help explore the interplay between social and psychological processes on the one hand, and biological processes on the other, in relation to antisocial behavior.

There have been numerous reviews of the psychophysiology of antisocial behavior in the past decades (e.g., Hare, 1978; Mednick, Pollock, Volavka, & Gabrielli, 1982; Siddle & Trasler, 1981; Raine, 1988) with the most recent ones being Raine (1993), Fowles (1993), and Raine (1996). Consequently, this chapter attempts to highlight some of the most important issues, theories, and questions surrounding past research and to give attention to newly emerging ideas that have received little or no previous discussion. Nevertheless, the interested reader is referred to the reviews just mentioned for a more in-depth analysis of specific issues in the psychophysiology of antisocial behavior, to Patrick (1994) for newly emerging research on the startle blink reflex, and to Mealey (1995) for the psychophysiology of antisocial behavior in the context of sociobiological theory.

Similarly, extensive introductions on psychophysiological methodology are not given here. The reader is referred to Raine (1993) for brief reviews of psychophysiological methodology in relation to antisocial behavior; more detailed introductions to psychophysiological instrumentation, recording techniques, and other methodological issues may be found in Cacioppo, Tassinary, and Fridlund (1991); Coles, Donchin, and Porges (1986); Dawson,

Schell, and Filion (1991); and Ray (1990). This chapter provides an update and extension of the previous review made of the psychophysiology of antisocial behavior (Raine, 1993). In particular, special attention is paid to the theoretical context of this work and controversial issues that need to be addressed in future research.

Two key overarching concepts are developed in this chapter. The first concerns the prefrontal dysfunction hypothesis that is used as a heuristic, overarching framework to help better understand and integrate the diverse arousal, orienting, and reduced stress reactivity findings in antisocials. The second conceptual approach concerns the critical importance of a biosocial perspective on antisocial behavior, which illustrates both how the environment influences psychophysiological functioning and also how social processes interact with psychophysiological processes in mediating antisocial behavior. Before these perspectives are discussed, the empirical data on the psychophysiology of antisocial behavior is described.

AROUSAL THEORY

One influential psychophysiological theory of antisocial behavior is that antisocial individuals are chronically underaroused. Traditional psychophysiological measures of arousal include heart rate (HR), skin conductance (SC) activity, and electroencephalogram (EEG) measured during a "resting" state. Low HR and SC activity, and a more excessive slow-wave EEG (delta, theta, and slow alpha) indicate generalized underarousal. Most studies tend to employ single measures of arousal, although studies that employ multiple measures of the same construct of arousal are in a stronger position to test an arousal theory of antisocial behavior.

Electroencephalograms

There have probably been hundreds of studies assessing EEGs in criminals, delinquents, psychopaths, and violent offenders. Reviews of these studies may be found in Ellingson (1954), Hare (1970), Syndulko (1978), Mednick et al. (1982), Blackburn (1983), Volavka (1987), Venables (1988), Venables and Raine (1987), Milstein (1988), and Raine (1993). Because extensive

This chapter was written while the author was supported by National Institute of Mental Health Grant No. RO1 MH46435-02 and an NIMH Research Scientist Development Award (1 KO2 MH01114-01).

reviews exist, this section briefly summarizes the main points and generates additional observations.

A large number of studies implicate EEG abnormalities in violent recidivistic offending. As examples, Bach-y-Rita, Lion, Climent, and Ervin (1971) and Hill and Pond (1952) examined large samples of violent offenders and observed EEG abnormalities in about 50% of the cases. These findings have been supported by studies of murderers and other violent offenders (e.g., Mark & Ervin, 1970; Williams, 1969). More recently, Fishbein, Herning, Pickworth, and Haertzen (1989) in a sample of 124 adult male drug abusers found that aggression was associated with increased theta and decreased alpha. Convit, Czobar, & Volavka (1991) observed the same pattern within a sample of psychiatric inpatients; the number of instances of violence on wards was related to increased levels of delta activity and lower levels of alpha. Drake, Hietter, and Pakalnis (1992) found that whereas none of 24 depressed patients and only 1 of 20 headache control patients had abnormal EEGs, 7 of 23 patients with either intermittent explosive disorder or episodic dyscontrol had diffuse or focal slowing in EEG. These latter two studies were able to rule out medication levels, drowsiness, and degree of institutionalization as potential contaminants.

Mednick et al. (1982) conclude their review with the statement that "A high prevalence of EEG abnormalities exists among persons convicted of violent crimes; this is especially true of recidivistic offenders" (p. 67) and argue that the bulk of this research implicated the anterior regions of the brain, areas that regulate executive functions such as planning and decision making. They also suggest that the prevalence of EEG abnormalities in violent individuals ranges from 25% to 50%, with the rate of abnormalities in normals estimated as ranging from 5% to 20%. Similar conclusions are drawn by Volavka (1987) and Milstein (1988) for crime in general and violent crime in particular. In contrast, it is important to note that psychopathic behavior per se does not seem to be clearly associated with excessive slow-wave EEG (Blackburn, 1975; Fishbein et al., 1989; Harpur, Williamson, Forth, & Hare, 1986; Syndulko, 1978).

Skin Conductance Levels

A review of arousal studies since 1978 has been conducted by Raine (1993) (see also Fowles, 1993). Since 1978, arousal has been assessed by measurement during an initial "rest" period of either skin conductance levels (SCLs) or nonspecific fluctuations (NSFs). Four of the ten studies found significant effects, with three of these four finding differences for NSFs. Only one of the four found effects for SCLs, although another of these studies found trends for lower SCLs (Raine, Venables, & Williams, 1990a). NSFs may produce stronger support for SC underarousal in antisocials relative to SCLs because the latter are more influenced by factors such as local peripheral conditions of the skin and the thickness and hydration of the stratum corneum (Venables & Christie, 1973), factors that are unrelated to autonomic arousal.

An interesting finding is that of Buikhuisen, Bontekoe, Plas-Korenhoff, and Host (1985), who found effects specific to type of crime; that is, underarousal characterizes crimes of evasion (e.g., customs offenses) but not other forms of crime. It could be that autonomic underarousal is particularly conducive to escaping detection for covert, evasive crime. Regarding psychopathy, all

three studies of this subgroup of criminals failed to find group differences (Raine, 1993).

An important prospective study not reviewed by Raine (1993) found lower SC arousal to be related to antisocial behavior. Kruesi, Hibbs, Zahn, and Keysor (1992) found low SCLs measured at age 11 years to be predictive of institutionalization 2 years later in 29 children with disruptive behavioral disorders. It should be noted, however, that low SCLs did not predict arrest, although as noted by the authors a more long-term follow-up period may yet yield significant effects for this variable.

In conclusion, therefore, not all studies find lower autonomic arousal in antisocials. In particular, psychopaths do not appear to be characterized by low SC arousal (Fowles, 1993). However, for antisocial behavior in general, there is a clear indication that antisocials are characterized by low SCLs and fewer nonspecific SC responses during rest.

Heart Rate Levels

Data on resting HR provide striking support for underarousal in antisocials. Indeed, the findings for heart rate levels (HRLs) on noninstitutionalized antisocials is probably the strongest and best replicated finding in the field of the psychophysiology of antisocial behavior. A detailed review of these studies and theoretical and methodological considerations are given in Raine (1993). Fourteen studies on noninstitutionalized conduct disordered, delinquent, and antisocial children and adolescents showed significant effects in the predicted direction of lower resting heart rates in antisocial children. Effect sizes were substantial and averaged 0.84. Findings could not easily be attributed to a number of possible artifacts (Raine, 1993).

In contrast to noninstitutionalized populations, research on institutionalized criminals and psychopaths has consistently failed to find significant group differences. As with the literature on EEGs and SC, therefore, lower HR is a common predisposition to antisocial behavior in general and not institutionalized psychopathic criminal behavior in particular.

Prospective Psychophysiological Research on Arousal and Antisocial Behavior

One of the major difficulties in trying to draw conclusions on the psychophysiological basis of criminal behavior is that most studies conducted to date have been nonprospective and have used institutionalized populations. In addition, most studies report results from only one of the three most commonly measured psychophysiological response systems (electrodermal, cardiovascular, cortical). Prospective longitudinal research allows for much more powerful statements to be made about predispositions for criminal behavior and to elucidate cause-effect relationships, but because prospective research is more difficult to execute, there are few such studies.

Regarding HRLs, Wadsworth (1976) found that lower resting heart rate in unselected 11-year-old schoolboys predicted delinquency measured from ages 8 to 21. The very lowest HRLs were found in those who committed nonsexual violent criminal offenses as adults. Similarly, Farrington (1987) found that resting HR measured at ages 18 to 19 years in noninstitutionalized males predicted violent criminal offending at age 25. With respect to EEGs, two separate studies have shown that slow alpha frequency predicts to adult thievery in a sample of 129 Danish 13-year-old boys (Mednick, Volavka, Gabrielli, & Itil, 1981) and 571 Swedish 1- to 15-year-old boys (Petersen, Matousek, Mednick, Volavka, & Polloch, 1982). Regarding SC activity, Loeb and Mednick (1977) found that six of seven criminals aged 20 to 29 years had lower resting SCLs than did their matched normal controls when tested several years earlier at age 16 to 20 years, but this trend did not quite reach statistical significance. Similarly, as noted earlier, Kruesi et al. (1992) found that reduced SCLs predicted severity of aggression and institutionalization in 6- to 17-year-old children with disruptive behavior disorder.

As with most other studies, evidence in these prospective studies for prediction to antisocial behavior is based on only one measure of arousal. A 9-year prospective study of crime by Raine et al. (1990a) has shown, however, that HRLs, NSFs, and excessive theta EEGs measured at age 15 years in normal unselected schoolboys predicted criminal behavior at age 24 years. These three measures correctly classified 74.7% of all subjects as criminal or noncriminal, a rate significantly greater than chance (50%). In the total population, the three arousal measures were statistically independent; the fact that they all independently predicted to criminal behavior indicates strong support for an arousal theory of criminal and antisocial behavior (although this finding also cautions against the use of a simplistic, unitary arousal concept in explaining crime). Group differences in social class, academic ability, and area of residence were not found to mediate the link between underarousal and antisocial behavior. This is the first study providing evidence for underarousal in an antisocial population in all three psychophysiological response systems.

Interpretations of Low Arousal: Fearlessness and Stimulation-Seeking Theories

There are two main theoretical interpretations of reduced arousal in antisocials. Fearlessness theory indicates that low levels of arousal are markers of low levels of fear (Raine, 1993, 1996). For example, particularly fearless individuals such as bomb disposal experts who have been decorated for their bravery have particularly low heart rate levels and reactivity (Cox, Hallam, O'Connor, Rachman, 1983; O'Connor, Hallam, & Rachman, 1985) as do the British paratroopers decorated in the Falklands war (McMillan & Rachman, 1987). A fearlessness interpretation of low arousal levels assumes that subjects are not actually at "rest," but that instead the rest period of psychophysiological testing represents a mildly stressful paradigm and that low arousal during this period indicates lack of anxiety and fear. Lack of fear would predispose to antisocial and violent behavior because such behavior (e.g., fights and assaults) requires a degree of fearlessness to execute, whereas lack of fear, especially in childhood, would help explain poor socialization because low fear of punishment would reduce the effectiveness of conditioning. Fearlessness theory receives support from the fact that autonomic underarousal also provides the underpinning for a fearless or uninhibited temperament (see later discussion).

A second theory explaining reduced arousal is stimulation-seeking theory (Eysenck, 1964; Quay, 1965; Raine, 1993, 1996). This theory argues that low arousal represents an aversive physiological state and that antisocials seek out stimulation to increase their arousal levels to an optimal or normal level. Antisocial behavior is viewed as a form of stimulation seeking in that committing a burglary, assault, or robbery could be stimulating for some individuals.

Future research in this area needs to test differential predictions between these two theories. For example, stimulation-seeking theory would predict that low arousal would characterize antisocials in a "truly" resting state (i.e., a non-anxiety-provoking, neutral condition) because it is presumed that antisocials have a trait of underarousal that is not state-dependent. On the other hand, fearlessness theory would predict that group differences are maximized in those conditions that are anxiety provoking to the individual. To date, these two theories have not been tested against each other. A second direction for future research is to assess why not all underaroused individuals become antisocial. For example, in the discriminant function analysis conducted by Raine et al. (1990a), 23% of those who were predicted to become criminal by virtue of having low arousal did not in fact have an official conviction for a criminal offense. Some of these false positives may be due to error in that these underaroused subjects were "successful offenders" who did indeed commit offenses but were not caught by the police. Alternatively, whether underaroused individuals turn to crime to obtain their "arousal jag" in life may be a function of their social milieu. For example, those brought up in delinquent neighborhoods and exposed to delinquent peers or who have antisocial parents as models may turn to crime to increase arousal levels, whereas those who have high IQ and are brought up in a noncriminogenic environment may obtain their stimulation from a career in politics or academic research. There have been no such tests of these diverging outcomes, but future biosocial research needs to tackle why not all underaroused individuals embark on a criminal career.

Before leaving arousal theory, the possibility has to be considered that fearlessness theory and stimulation-seeking theory may be complementary theories rather than competing ones. That is, low levels of arousal may predispose to crime because it produces some degree of fearlessness and also encourages antisocial stimulation seeking. The synergistic effect of these two influences may be more important in explaining antisocial behavior than the consideration of the single influence of only one of these causal processes.

Crider (1993) has suggested that reduced NSFs are related to an antagonistic personality type (impulsive, hostile, unsocialized, irresponsible), whereas high arousal relates to an agreeable personality. This analysis is consistent with lower arousal in more antisocial personalities. Crider further argued that schizoid personality (shy, withdrawn, emotionally detached) is related to low SC lability. It could be speculated, therefore, that reduced SC activity is particularly related to antisocials with a schizoid personality, and this notion will be returned to later.

Disinhibited Temperament and Psychophysiological Underarousal

The prospective research previously mentioned highlights the potential importance of underarousal as a psychophysiological predisposition for violence. Findings to be reviewed in this section in turn suggest that such underarousal may predispose to a disinhibited temperament that in itself may act as one early predispositional factor for criminal and violent behavior. Prospective, longitudinal studies are essential for the examination of this proposition. To date, such studies have been limited, focusing on relatively early years. Extension into adult years could establish whether a disinhibited temperament does predispose to violence. Existing studies are briefly reviewed, because there are interesting parallels between the psychophysiological correlates of crime and the psychophysiological correlates of a disinhibited temperament.

In most of the early work in this area (Kagan, 1989, Kagan, Resnick, & Snidman, 1988; Reznick et al., 1986) children classified as either inhibited or uninhibited at 21 months were also found to be inhibited or disinhibited at ages 4, 5.5, and 7.5 years. Consequently, early temperament (as measured by a tendency to withdraw or interact across a variety of experimental situations) appears to show some developmental stability.

Some support for the notion that temperament may show stability across time has been put forward by Scerbo, Raine, Venables, and Mednick (1995). The assumption that behavioral inhibition/disinhibition may be a stable temperament was tested using a cohort of 1,795 Mauritian children tested longitudinally at ages 3, 8, and 11 years. Subjects were rated on theoretically relevant behaviors of inhibition such as approach-avoidance, fearfulness, verbalizations, crying behavior, and sociability. An inhibition index was calculated and used to classify children as extremely inhibited, middle, or extremely uninhibited at each age. Results indicated that subjects classified as uninhibited at age 3 had higher disinhibition scores at age 8 years ($p < .01$). Subjects who were uninhibited at both ages 3 and 8 (stably uninhibited) were more likely to remain uninhibited at age 11 years ($p < .02$). These results were independent of sex and ethnicity, replicated from one sample to another, and provide cross-cultural generalizability for the findings of Kagan and colleagues (Kagin, Reznick, & Snidman, 1988).

There is growing evidence that inhibited and disinhibited children differ in terms of their physiological responsiveness to novel stimuli; in particular, uninhibited children have been found to have lower HRLs. Low HR and increased vagal tone measured at age 4 were correlated with disinhibited behavior at age 5.5 years, whereas those with relatively low fetal heart rates had lower levels of motoric activity and crying at age 4 months (Kagan, 1989; Snidman, Kagan, & McQuilkin, 1991). Similarly, Fox (1989) found that 5-month-old infants with high vagal tone (associated with increased heart rate variability and low HRLs and indicating increasing parasympathetic tuning of the ANS) were more sociable and exploratory at 14 months, whereas Stifter and Fox (1990) found that increased vagal tone at 5 months was associated with high activity levels and a lack of fear to a novel stimulus.

A confirmation and extension of the link between HR and disinhibition have been provided in the Mauritius longitudinal study (Scerbo, Raine, Venables, & Mednick, in press). Lower heart rate and skin conductance measured at age 3 were associated with disinhibition at age 3 ($p < .0001$), whereas those who remained stably disinhibited from ages 3 to 8 years were also found to have lower resting HRs ($p < .002$). Again, these results replicated from one sample to another. In addition, children who remained stably disinhibited from ages 3 to 8 years were twice as likely to have lower HR *and* lower SCLs measured at age 3 years. Again, these findings were found to replicate from one half of the sample to the other. It is important to note that group differences in HR could not be attributable to group differences in height, weight, or respiratory complaints.

A disinhibited temperament appears to be relatively consistent across time and determined in part by lower HR and possibly lower SC activity. The interesting possibility is that reduced autonomic arousal may in infancy predispose to exploratory behavior and fearlessness and in childhood to a disinhibited temperament. This temperament may later predispose a child to externalizing behavior problems such as socialized aggression and hyperactivity and in early adulthood to criminal and violent behavior. Studies conducted to date have only laid the basis for the hypothesis that a disinhibited temperament may predispose to adult violence and that both are underpinned by low autonomic arousal; confirmation and extension in other prospective studies are required. Nevertheless, these early findings linking underarousal to a disinhibited temperament are conceptually consistent with the body of research reviewed earlier linking autonomic underarousal (especially low HR) to the development of later criminal behavior.

ORIENTING DEFICITS IN ANTISOCIAL INDIVIDUALS

Main Findings

Key findings from nine studies that have assessed SC orienting to neutral stimuli in antisocial groups has been reviewed by Raine (1993); McBurnett and Lahey (1994) also have reviewed SC orienting, specifically in conduct disordered and delinquent children. Five out of nine studies find evidence for an orienting deficit as indicated by reduced frequency of SCRs to orienting stimuli. Frequency measures of SC orienting appear to produce stronger findings in these studies, perhaps because frequency measures tend to be more reliable than amplitude measures; this in turn may be because amplitude is more affected by non-autonomic nervous system factors such as the number and size of sweat glands (Venables & Christie, 1973).

Fowles (1993) in a review of SC and antisocial behavior commented on the attention deficit hypothesis proposed by Raine and Venables (1984). This hypothesis argued that antisocials were characterized by a fundamental deficit in the ability to allocate attentional resources to environmental events. In evaluating this hypothesis, Fowles (1993) suggested that there may be two attentional deficits, one deficit with respect to attending to neutral stimuli and one deficit with respect to the anticipation of aversive events. It is acknowledged that Fowles may be correct and that there may be multiple attentional deficits in antisocials that may or may not be related. For example, although antisocials have attentional deficits in paradigms in which they must passively attend or respond in anticipation of an aversive stimulus, the event-related potential literature indicates that they have *better* attention to events of interest (Raine, 1989). Research in this area needs to explore further the relationships between these types of deficits and to address the issue of heterogeneity in the behavior of antisocials, as described in the next section.

Passive Attention Deficit in Schizoid Antisocials

The most striking finding drawn from the review by Raine (1993) of orienting deficits in antisocials is that reduced SC orienting appears to be specific to psychopathic, criminal, and antisocial individuals with schizoid or schizotypal features. For example, Raine and Venables (1984) found SC nonresponding characterized antisocial adolescents who had schizoid tendencies (introversion, psychoticism, and anxiety), whereas Raine (1987) found that reduced SC orienting characterized criminals with high schizotypal personality scores. Similarly, Blackburn (1979) reported that reduced frequency and amplitude of the SC orienting response and faster SC habituation characterized secondary psychopaths with schizoid features (high MMPI schizophrenia scores, high anxiety, socially withdrawn). As noted earlier, Crider (1993) has also argued for a link between antisocial personality and schizotypal personality with respect to reduced frequency of nonspecific SC responses.

The notion that schizoid antisocials in particular are characterized by passive attentional deficits, as indicated by autonomic indexes of orienting, also receives some support from central nervous system (CNS) measures of information processing deficits and arousal. For example, Howard (1984) found that it was a schizoid subgroup of offenders (those who were more withdrawn and anxious) who had the most atypical EEGs. Blackburn (1979) found that secondary schizoid psychopaths had the excessive EEG theta activity, indicating CNS underarousal. Krakowski, Convit, Jaeger, and Lin (1989) found that violent schizophrenics had the highest degree of neurological and neuropsychological abnormalities.

In summary, there is growing evidence that a schizotypal subgroup of antisocials is particularly characterized by psychophysiological deficits. In addition, there is some evidence that schizotypal antisocials may represent that subgroup of antisocials who are particularly characterized by prefrontal dysfunction (see Raine, 1993, pp. 112–113 for a more detailed discussion). Although in the past a more extraverted, nonanxious, nonpsychosis-prone subgroup of offenders (i.e., "primary" psychopaths) has been the focus of psychophysiological research, the previous analysis suggests that a different personality profile (viz. schizotypal psychopaths) are particularly worthy of future study.

PSYCHOPHYSIOLOGICAL PROTECTIVE FACTORS AGAINST CRIME DEVELOPMENT

All psychophysiological research to date has attempted to ask the question, "What psychophysiological factors predispose to crime?," and consequently has focused exclusively on risk factors for crime development. A potentially more important question to be posed, however, is "What factors protect a child predisposed to crime from becoming criminal?" Understanding protective factors against crime development is of critical conceptual importance because it can more directly inform intervention and prevention of antisocial behavior. The first lines of early research in this area are outlined next.

Protective Factors in Adults

The principal finding to emerge from the first work in this area is that *higher* autonomic activity during adolescence may act as a protective factor against crime development. Raine, Venables, and Williams (1995, 1996) report on a 14-year prospective study in which autonomic and CNS measures of arousal, orienting, and classical conditioning were taken in 101 unselected 15-year-old

male schoolchildren. Of these, 17 adolescent antisocials who desisted from adult crime (Desistors) were matched on adolescent antisocial behavior and demographic variables with 17 adolescent antisocials who had became criminal by age 29 (Criminals), and 17 nonantisocial, noncriminals (Controls). Desistors had significantly higher heart rate levels, higher SC arousal (measured by nonspecific SC responses—see Figure 27.1), and higher SC orienting, better SC conditioning, and faster half-recovery time of the SC response relative to Criminals (see Figure 27.2). Findings suggest that individuals predisposed to adult crime by virtue of showing antisocial behavior in adolescence may be protected from crime by heightened levels of autonomic arousal and reactivity. Such protection was specific to autonomic arousal in that groups did not differ in terms of resting EEG.

Protective Factors in Adolescents

Findings from a second study on adults provides some support for this initial finding in adolescents. Brennan et al. (in press) report on a study of protective factors in 50 men predisposed to crime by virtue of having a seriously criminal father who had been imprisoned. Twenty-four of these men developed a criminal record and were imprisoned themselves, whereas the other group of 26 did not

Figure 27.1 *Adolescents who desist from adult crime (desistors) but who are just as antisocial at age 15 as those who become criminal at age 24 (criminals) are characterized by significantly higher resting heart rate and increased skin conductance arousal (frequency of nonspecific skin conductance responses) measured at age 15 years.*

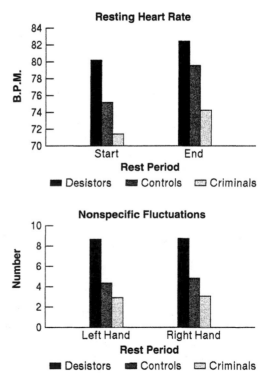

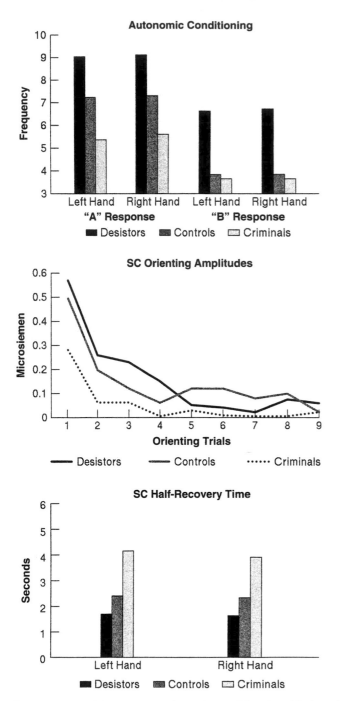

Figure 27.2 *Adolescents who desist from adult crime (desistors) but who are just as antisocial at age 15 as those who become criminal at age 24 (criminals) are characterized by significantly better classical conditioning, higher SC orienting, and faster SC half-recovery times measured at age 15 years.*

show any criminal offending. SC and HR measures of reactivity to 14 orienting tones were measured at age 35 years. The group who desisted from crime were found to have significantly higher levels of SC and HR orienting relative to those who exhibited criminal behavior and also relative to a noncriminal control group who had noncriminal fathers (see Figure 27.3).

Interpretation of Findings

An important question in these two studies concerns how enhanced autonomic activity in desistors against crime should be interpreted. Regarding increased orienting, it is possible that this indicant of enhanced information processing observed in desistors against crime is accounted for by higher intelligence (IQ), because high IQ has been found to protect against crime development (Kandel, Mednick, Kirkegaard-Sorenson, & Hutchings, 1988). This does not seem to be the case for two reasons. First, the desistors in the study of Raine et al. (1995) did not differ in terms of academic ability from those who broke down for crime. Second, Brennan et al. (in press) partialed out the effects of group differences in IQ and still found that desistors had significantly higher orienting. Better orienting in desistors may, therefore, reflect a

Figure 27.3 *Those at risk for crime by virtue of having a severely criminal father, but who themselves desist from crime (black bar), are characterized by significantly increased SC orienting and increased HR orienting relative to noncriminal sons with noncriminal fathers (neither criminal), criminal sons with noncriminal fathers (only son criminal), and criminal sons with criminal fathers (both criminal).*

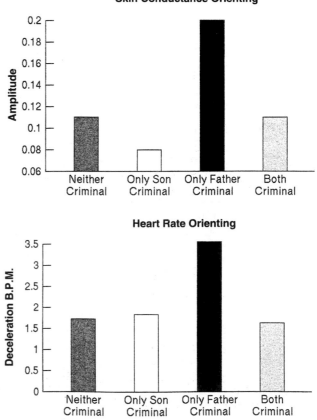

more fundamental, preattentive or automated information processing superiority in desistors as opposed to the more controlled attentional processing reflected in traditional IQ measures. The faster half-recovery times in desistors is also broadly consistent with this interpretation because fast recovery has been thought of as indicating an "open" attentional stance to the environment (Hare, 1978; Siddle & Trasler, 1981; Venables, 1974). The superior conditioning is viewed as facilitating desistence because better conditioning facilitates the development of a conscience, construed as consisting of a set of classically conditioned emotional responses (Eysenck, 1977; Raine & Venables, 1981). In other words, desistors seem to have a nervous system particularly sensitive to forming associations between signals of punishment (CS) and the punishment itself (UCS). In a similar fashion, higher resting HRs in desistors may be interpreted as indicating higher levels of fearfulness in these individuals.

Overall, the initial profile that is being built up on the psychophysiological characteristics of the desistor is one of heightened fundamental attentional abilities (better orienting), greater responsivity to environmental stimuli in general (fast recovery), greater sensitivity to cues predicting punishment in particular (better classical conditioning), and higher fearfulness (high HR levels). The importance of research on psychophysiological protective factors such as these is that they offer suggestions on possible intervention and prevention strategies for crime development.

EVENT-RELATED POTENTIALS

The review so far has focused on psychophysiological abnormalities in a diverse group of antisocials that are indicative of underarousal and a deficit in attention, whereas psychopathic criminals in particular are not characterized by deficits in arousal or responsivity to neutral orienting stimuli. In contrast, event-related potential (ERP) research has indicated, perhaps surprisingly, that antisocials are characterized by *enhanced* attentional processing to events of interest.

ERPs are recorded from electrodes placed at various locations on the scalp from where they record the electrical activity of the brain in response to discrete experimental stimuli, usually tones or light flashes. In general, larger ERP amplitudes reflect greater information processing to the stimulus in question. One of the most frequently cited ERPs is the P300, a positive-going wave that peaks approximately 300 to 350 ms. after stimulus onset and is thought to reflect a variety of complex cognitive processes ranging from selective attention to the resolution of uncertainty.

Tripartite Event-Related Potential Model of Antisocial Behavior

A detailed review of 21 ERP studies of antisocial groups is presented in Raine (1989, 1993). Only a brief summary of this review can be given here. ERP studies of antisocials can conceptually be broken down into early-, middle-, and late-latency ERP studies. A tripartite model was generated to account for these data and is shown in Figure 27.4.

EP COMPONENT	EMPIRICAL FINDING	PSYCHOLOGICAL PROCESS	BEHAVIOURAL CONSEQUENCE
EARLY	↑ BAER LAT	↓ AROUSAL/ ↑ FILTERING	STIMULUS DEPRIVATION ↓
MIDDLE	↑ VEP	VISUAL AUGMENTING	SENSATION SEEKING ↓
LATE	↑ P3	↑ ATTENTION	ATTENTION TO STIMULATING EVENTS ↓
			ANTISOCIALITY

Figure 27.4 *A tripartite ERP model of antisocial behavior based on findings from 21 ERP studies of antisocial populations broken down into early-, middle-, and late-latency ERPs. BAER = brainstem average evoked response; VEP = visual evoked potential.*

Early ERP studies observed long latency brain stem averaged evoked responses (BAERs), which psychologically can be interpreted as indicating reduced arousal and excessively high filtering of environmental stimuli. The behavioral consequence of such underarousal and filtering would be stimulus deprivation and chronically low levels of arousal (see first component of Figure 27.4). Findings for middle-latency ERPs were more equivocal, but it was speculated that antisocials appear to show increased ERP amplitudes to stimuli of increasing intensity (visual cortical augmenting), a phenomena that has been linked to sensation seeking (see second component of Figure 27.4). Results from late-latency ERPs were much more consistent and indicated, surprisingly, that psychopaths gave *enhanced* P300 amplitudes to stimuli that have to be selectively attended to (see third component of Figure 27.4); this was interpreted as indicating enhanced attention to stimuli of interest that require active attention (as opposed to the type of passive attention required in orienting paradigms involving neutral stimuli).

The behavioral consequences of findings from these three ERP levels (stimulus deprivation, sensation seeking, and attention to stimulating events) were argued to be causally linked (see right-hand column, Figure 27.4). That is, individuals with chronically low levels of arousal (possibly caused by excessive filtering of stimuli) seek out stimulating events to increase their levels of arousal to more optimal levels. This stimulation seeking may partly account for the enhanced attention shown to events of interest, as reflected in enhanced P300 ERPs to target stimuli in selective attention paradigms. Potentially dangerous and risky situations in which acts of violence and crime are facilitated may, therefore, represent situations to which such antisocial personalities become particularly attracted.

As with many biological theories of violence, this tripartite ERP model is only a partial explanation of violent behavior. Whether the proposed biological predisposition to violence manifests itself in antisocial personality, crime, and violence may be very dependent on the environmental circumstances in which an individual is placed. For example, given an appropriately high IQ, adequate parenting, and rearing in a family of high socioeconomic status, this risk-taking and stimulation-seeking bent may manifest itself in careers such as those involving risky business ventures, the armed forces, or automobile racing rather than crime and violence. An unusual feature of this model is the argument based on late ERP findings that antisocials are capable of *enhanced* attentional processing to task-relevant events. This enhancement contradicts established views of criminal behavior in the biological literature that almost universally emphasize *deficits* with respect to such populations.

New Research Findings

An important question concerns whether new studies not included in the review by Raine (1989) have supported or negated the three elements of the ERP model of antisocial and psychopathic behavior. Regarding BAERs, Fishbein et al. (1989), in a sample of 124 drug abusers, showed that those who were overtly aggressive had significant delays in the latency of the BAER. The fact that they also showed more EEG delta activity supports the interpretation by Raine (1989) that delayed latencies of BAERs reflect underarousal. Juvenile delinquents also show the BAER latency effect. Herning, Hickey, Pickworth, and Jaffe (1989) showed that 12 noninstitutionalized male delinquents had a delay in latency in wave V of the BAER relative to 13 age-matched nondelinquents. These two studies provide further support for the first stage of the ERP model indicating reduced arousal and increased filtering of stimuli as indicated by slower BAER latencies. However, such filtering deficits, although characterizing antisocial behavior in general, do not appear to characterize antisocial personality disorder or intermittent explosive disorder in particular (Fishbein et al., 1989; Drake, Hietter, & Pakalnis, 1992).

Regarding the second stage of the model dealing with ERP augmenting-reducing and antisocial behavior, Raine and Venables (1990) found no differences between psychopathic and nonpsychopathic criminals on ERP augmenting-reducing. On the other hand, new data presented here indicate that criminals as a group do differ from normal controls. The 32 male adult criminals tested in Raine and Venables (1990) were compared on visual ERP augmenting-reducing (recorded at Cz, a central site of the 10-20 system) to 27 noncriminal male controls assessed using the same experimental procedures as reported in Raine and Venables (1990). A significant group (criminal vs. noncriminal) x intensity (20, 80, 200, and 400 foot lamberts) x component (P1-N1 vs. N1-P2) interaction was observed for amplitudes, $F(3,171) = 4.8$, $p < .003$. A breakdown of this interaction is shown in Figure 27.5 and reveals that for N1-P2 amplitudes the noncriminal controls do not show increased amplitudes as stimulus intensity increases ($p > .80$), whereas criminals show a strong augmenting profile of increased amplitudes with increasing intensity ($F (3,93) = 7.0$, $p < .001$). For P1-N1 amplitudes, neither the controls nor criminals showed significant augmenting.

Although there appear to be no other studies of ERP augmenting-reducing in criminals, Dykman et al. (1992) have shown that hyperactive children are more likely to be classified as ERP augmenters relative to reading disabled controls. As such, these new findings, when taken together, provide some support for ERP aug-

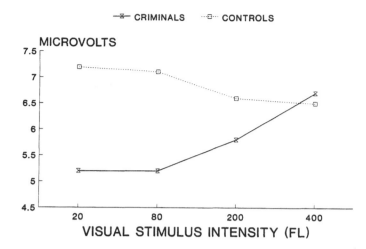

N1-P2 AMPLITUDE RECORDED AT Cz

Figure 27.5 *The group X component X intensity interaction (p < .003) indicated that for the N1-P2 component, amplitudes increased across stimulus intensities in the 32 Criminals but not in the 27 Controls, indicating greater ERP augmenting in criminals.*

menting for criminal behavior per se and for antisocial-related disorders, but not for psychopathy per se, a conclusion similar to that drawn for the review on arousal reported earlier.

Regarding later ERP components related to attentional processing, the five analyses that obtained evidence for enhanced P300 ERPs in the review by Raine (1989) are supported by results of six new studies on antisocial populations. Raine, Venables, and Williams (1990b) showed that 15-years-olds who had developed a criminal record by age 24 were characterized by faster P300 latency and a larger N100 amplitude to a warning stimulus predicting punishment relative to normals; these data are consistent with the notion of enhanced attention to events that demand attention in antisocials.

Regarding the other five studies, the review of late ERPs by Raine (1989) did not include data on the contingent negative variation (CNV), but it is of interest that larger CNVs have been reported in five studies of antisocial populations in forewarned reaction time tasks (Fenton, Fenwick, Ferguson, & Lam, 1978; Forth & Hare, 1989; Howard, Fenton, & Fenwick, 1984; Raine & Venables, 1987; Raine et al., 1990b). The CNV is a slow, negative-going potential that builds up during the interval between a warning stimulus and a second stimulus occurring a few seconds later that must be responded to in some way. As such, the CNV is thought to reflect attentional processes related to expectancy and motor preparation. Because larger CNVs indicate greater expectancy and attentional processing to the stimulus warning of an aversive event, these data are consistent with the notion that antisocials are capable of enhanced attentional processing to events of significance and interest. To be set against these five significant findings on CNV is a study by Drake et al. (1992) that found longer (not shorter) P300 latencies in habitually violent offenders.

McBurnett and Lahey (1994) reviewed data on delinquency and ERPs and noted that generally findings appear to fit the proposed ERP model. This model is also capable of helping to explain seemingly inconsistent findings. For example, Satterfield and Schell (1984) found that hyperactives who were also delinquent had more normal EEGs than hyperactives who were not delinquent. As pointed out by McBurnett and Lahey (1994), however, the EEG was recorded while children watched a cartoon show and the aggression and stimulation derived from cartoons may be thought to be of particular interest to antisocial children. As such, the more normal EEGs of delinquent hyperactives is consistent with the previously discussed model that shows information processing proficiencies in antisocials in conditions that demand active attention.

Conclusions on ERP Research

In conclusion, the studies in the past 5 years have generally supported the tripartite ERP model of antisocial behavior proposed by Raine (1989). As with the findings on underarousal, this model appears to be a somewhat better explanation of antisocial behavior per se rather than psychopathic behavior in particular. The advantage of the model is that it also can be used to incorporate the strong findings on both autonomic and cortical underarousal in antisocial populations reviewed earlier. Furthermore, it also explains the attentional deficits shown by antisocials in orienting paradigms because stimuli have no significance or interest and do not need to be attended to. At the same time, it can help explain the enhanced attention of antisocials during active attention paradigms. Because this tripartite model suggests that antisocials may under certain circumstances be capable of enhanced attentional abilities, it also opens up implications for intervention and treatment.

DEVELOPMENTAL PERSPECTIVES ON THE PSYCHOPHYSIOLOGY OF ANTISOCIAL BEHAVIOR

Many studies of antisocial behavior have been conducted on adults. An important question concerns the extent to which the same psychophysiological profile of adult antisocials can be found in childhood and adolescence. Most of the prospective longitudinal research on psychophysiology described earlier tested subjects during adolescence and this research generally supports the findings observed in adults.

With respect to conduct disorder and antisocial behavior in childhood, the most detailed review to date has been written by McBurnett and Lahey (1994). They conclude that whereas it is difficult to make definitive statements because of the sparsity of empirical studies, conduct disordered children who are aggressive and undersocialized are characterized by low arousal and reactivity. The strongest effects were obtained for reduced heart rate levels in conduct disordered children, confirming the findings for antisocial behavior throughout the life span.

One conceptual point made by McBurnett and Lahey (1994) is worth reiterating; that is, it is quite possible that subgroups of conduct disordered children can show quite different psychophysiological profiles. One recently published empirical study not reviewed by McBurnett and Lahey (1994) clearly illustrates and amplifies

this point. Zahn and Kruesi (1993) in a study of 11-year-old boys with disruptive behavior disorder found that boys who *lacked* a diagnosis of conduct disorder had *high* resting HR. Zahn and Kruesi (1993) speculate that the boys in their sample were referred by those parents who had difficulty managing their sons and that "this inclusion criterion could bias the sample toward having anxious, uptight, and/or easily stressed parents, which in turn might contribute to the relatively high HR" (p. 611). In contrast, other studies finding low resting HR have been conducted on unselected populations or those referred by school systems for treatment. On the other hand, findings on SC reactivity by Zahn and Kruesi (1993) were generally consistent with the literature on antisocial behavior; that is, boys with disruptive behavior disorder generally showed significantly reduced autonomic nervous system reactivity (particularly to signal tones in a reaction time task). The issue of heterogeneity with antisocial populations will be returned to later.

There is an important empirical gap in the literature with respect to the psychophysiological characteristics of children under the age of 10 years. The literature on temperament reviewed earlier does nevertheless extend the notion of underarousal and low reactivity to infants and young children with a disinhibited temperament, but more studies are needed on young children in which more direct measures of antisocial and aggressive behavior are taken. It must be borne in mind that major developmental changes that may mask or occlude the type of findings observed in adolescence and adulthood take place early in childhood. These issues are currently being explored by the author in the context of the Mauritius Child Health Project in which psychophysiological measures taken at age 3 in 1,795 3-year-old Mauritian children are being related to measures of crime and violence taken at age 25 years.

A PREFRONTAL DYSFUNCTION THEORY OF ANTISOCIAL BEHAVIOR

An important conceptual need in future psychophysiological research is to progress from interpretations of single psychophysiological measures and associated findings to more overarching models of antisocial behavior. A related issue concerns attempts to understand the wider significance of psychophysiological findings and to relate such findings to other fields of research.

The Theory

Prefrontal dysfunction theory represents one feasible theoretical account of antisocial behavior that can help account for some of the psychophysiological findings on antisocial behavior in addition to other findings. The basic idea underpinning this theory is that damage to the frontal lobe can predispose to antisocial and violent behavior. A modification to this theory proposed here is that (a) damage is localized within the frontal lobe to the prefrontal cortex and that (b) prefrontal dysfunction could explain the psychophysiological arousal and orienting deficits observed in antisocials. Evidence for these two propositions is based in part on brain imaging research, a methodology that may be viewed as psychophysiological in nature because it involves relating physiological functioning with psychological processes.

Supporting Evidence

With respect to localization of damage specifically to the prefrontal cortex, the primary evidence comes from a brain imaging study of murderers using positron emission tomography (PET). Raine et al. (1994) found reduced glucose metabolism in 22 murderers relative to 22 age- and sex-matched normal controls to be specific to prefrontal cortex; no glucose reductions were observed in more posterior frontal areas. Two other PET studies have found reduced frontal glucose metabolism to be related to aggressive and violent behavior (Goyer et al., 1994; Goyer & Semple, 1996; Volkow & Tancredi, 1987). This modification to frontal dysfunction theory is in keeping with the notion that it is the prefrontal region of the brain in particular that is centrally involved in the regulation of emotional, social, cognitive, and behavioral processes.

Regarding the notion that prefrontal dysfunction may help explain arousal and orienting deficits in antisocials, brain imaging studies have demonstrated that reduced SC orienting is related to damage or dysfunction to the prefrontal cortex (see Raine & Lencz, 1993, for a detailed review). Raine, Reynolds, and Sheard (1991) found that the number of SC orienting responses correlated between .44 and .60 with the area of prefrontal cortex as measured by magnetic resonance imaging (MRI) in a normal sample. The direction of the effects (reduced orienting associated with reduced medial and lateral prefrontal area) is consistent with the notion that prefrontal cortex plays an important role in mediating orienting. Similarly, Hazlett, Dawson, Buchsbaum, and Nuechterlein (1993) found significant associations between reduced glucose metabolism in frontal cortex (measured by PET) and SC orienting. Damasio, Tranel, and Damasio (1990) showed that sociopaths with bilateral lesions to the orbital frontal and lower medial prefrontal cortex showed reduced skin conductance response (SCR) amplitudes to the socially meaningful stimuli when compared to six control patients with nonfrontal lesions. New data from Damasio's laboratory confirm the notion that damage to the ventromedial region of the prefrontal cortex results in deficits in SC orienting (Tranel & Damasio, 1994). These brain imaging and neurological studies indicate that dysfunction to the prefrontal cortex may represent the source of the orienting deficits observed in antisocials.

Brain imaging, neurophysiological, and animal studies all suggest a link between arousal and the prefrontal area. With respect to structural brain imaging, Raine et al. (1991) found that SCLs correlated between .24 and .65 with the area of prefrontal cortex as measured by MRI in a normal sample. The direction of the effects (reduced arousal associated with reduced prefrontal area) is consistent with the notion that prefrontal dysfunction may contribute to reduced arousal. With respect to functional brain imaging, experimental studies have shown that experimental manipulations that increase arousal lead to an increase in regional cerebral blood flow in the frontal lobes, indicating that arousal and frontal functioning are related (Mathew, 1989). With respect to neurophysiological studies, Hellige (1993) reviews data that indicate that the right prefrontal cortex plays a role in mediating alertness. Phasic arousal as measured neurophysiologically in humans has been associated with right frontal activity (Asenbaum, Lang, Egkher, & Lindinger, 1992). Regarding animals, studies of dorsal frontal lesions in rats have indicated that the frontal cortex modulates

arousal by inhibiting the brain stem mechanisms that are responsible for reticular formation arousal (Kinghorn & Fleming, 1985; Kinghorn, Fleming, & Anderson, 1987). Evidence from three sources, therefore, supports the view that prefrontal dysfunction may, in part, underlie reduced physiological arousal, possibly via its reciprocal relationships with the reticular activating system.

Prefrontal dysfunction theory may also account for psychophysiological findings of lack of fear in antisocials and reduced reactivity to stressors (Fowles, 1993; Raine, 1993). Lesions of the ventral medial frontal cortex in rats result in reduced stress responses (Frysztak & Neafsey, 1991). Undergraduates with reduced frontal arousal (as indicated by excessive frontal EEG theta activity) have both reduced trait anxiety and reduced anxiety during an arithmetic stress task (Mizuki, Kajimura, & Kai, 1992). One- and 2-year-old infants who have higher right frontal activity (as indicated by EEG) are more likely to cry in response to the stress of maternal separation (Fox, Bell, & Jones, 1992), thus linking frontal activation with increased stress responsivity. In addition, neuropsychological case studies have frequently reported that patients with lesions to the prefrontal cortex are less reactive to stressors and have reduced anxiety levels (Beaumont, 1983; Stuss & Benson, 1986). Studies on rats indicate that even mildly stressful environmental events are associated with increased neurotransmitter activity in the medial frontal cortex (Cenci, Kalen, & Mandel, 1992). Taking these human and animal studies together, there is reason to believe that prefrontal dysfunction may underlie the reduced stress reactivity observed in antisocials.

Given the complexity of antisocial behavior, it is unlikely that any single theoretical perspective will fully account for antisocial behavior. Nevertheless, because a prefrontal dysfunction theory can also incorporate personality (e.g., high impulsivity), cognitive (e.g., response perseveration, loss of intellectual flexibility), and social (e.g., impaired social skills) characteristics of antisocials in addition to the previously mentioned psychophysiological characteristics, it represents a potentially important theoretical perspective on antisocial behavior that is worthy of further consideration.

BIOSOCIAL PSYCHOPHYSIOLOGICAL RESEARCH ON ANTISOCIAL BEHAVIOR

One of the major challenges for future psychophysiological research on antisocial behavior is to integrate psychophysiological mechanisms with social and psychological processes that are of importance to antisociality. Biological factors do not operate in a vacuum, and it is quite possible that the interplay between psychophysiological and social risk factors for antisocial behavior are more important than either factor in isolation. Despite this, there has been surprisingly little biosocial research on antisocial behavior, and in particular there has been little psychophysiological biosocial research. A review of research from a broad social psychophysiological perspective on antisocial behavior may be found in Raine (1988). Rather than repeat the issues in this review, this section instead focuses on three increasingly important and interrelated issues that have not received much attention and that impact the biosocial approach to crime: (a) psychophysiological characteristics of child abusers, (b) possible effects of child abuse on psychophysiological functioning, and (c) studies that show the moderating effect of the social environment on antisocial-psychophysiological relationships.

Psychophysiological Characteristics of Child Abusers

There is a growing literature on the psychophysiological characteristics of adults who abuse children or who are prone to child abuse. What is particularly dramatic about this literature is that child abusers show a very different psychophysiological profile to antisocial behavior in general, showing not reduced autonomic activity and arousal but *increased* reactivity and arousal. Wolfe, Fairbank, Kelly, and Bradlyn (1983) found that mothers who abused their children, relative to nonabusive mothers, showed increased SC response amplitudes to videotaped scenes of stressful behavior in children; respiratory data also showed them to be more aroused to scenes of both stressful and nonstressful child behavior. Pruitt and Erickson (1985) similarly showed that subjects with a greater potential for child abuse (measured by the Child Abuse Potential Checklist) were more aroused to videotaped presentations of infants smiling, crying, or in a quiescent state as indicated by SC. Crowe and Zeskind (1992) likewise showed greater HR and SC reactivity to high-pitched infant cries relative to controls.

These data show that child abusers have greater psychophysiological reactivity to stressful child stimuli, but an important question is whether child abusers are more responsive because they have been sensitized to child stimuli per se. That is, are such individuals generally hyperreactive to all forms of stimuli, or are they hyperreactive only to child stimuli? In this respect, Casanova, Domanic, McCanne, and Milner (1992) showed that mothers with a higher potential for child abuse showed greater and more prolonged sympathetic activation (measured by SC and HR) during a cold pressor stressor and a stressful film depicting industrial accidents than controls. These data indicate that child abusers are hyperresponsive to nonchild stressors also, which in turn suggests that such individuals possess a hyperresponsive autonomic system preceding child abuse, and that such hyperresponsivity predisposes some individuals to overreact in an abusive fashion to their children during times of stress. Nevertheless, prospective longitudinal research is needed to better tease out the temporal relationship between hyperresponsivity and child abuse to help resolve this complex causal issue.

There are two provocative issues posed by this small but growing literature on the psychophysiological characteristics of child abusers. First, it illustrates the great importance of the issue of heterogeneity in antisocial behavior (see McBurnett & Lahey, 1994). Most previous studies have assessed general antisocial behavior. Future studies must address the heterogeneity issue more directly; specifically, are orienting and arousal deficits most strongly found in antisocials who do not abuse children? Second, this initial literature on the psychophysiology of child abusers poses the question of why this group shows such a radically different psychophysiological profile than most of the antisocial population in general. One speculative answer is made in the next section, with reference to the effects of traumatic stress on psychophysiological functioning.

Effect of Traumatic Environmental Stressors on Psychophysiological Responsivity

Assuming that these findings on autonomic hyperreactivity in child abusers are replicable and genuine, why do such individuals show the *reverse* psychophysiological profile that has been identified in antisocials in general? One speculative answer is that such individuals may have been abused in turn as children, and that the effect of such abuse is to alter autonomic functioning in the direction of hypersensitivity to environmental stimuli.

With respect to the effects of child abuse on psychophysiological reactivity, Hill, Bleichfeld, Brunstetter, & Hebert (1989) have shown that 7- to 15-year-old hospitalized children who had been abused showed greater HR deceleratory responses to videotaped scenes of everyday events relative to nonhospitalized normal control children. They also had more negative feelings to these everyday scenes and reported more negative outcomes to them. Although findings in this field are to date sparse, the speculation being advanced is that the trauma of child abuse may lead to hyperresponsive autonomic functioning. To the extent that individuals who are abused as children are more likely to abuse children in adulthood, such a scenario could account for the hyperresponsivity reported above for child abusers.

It is certainly known that traumatic life experiences can result in (or at least are correlated with) increased autonomic responsivity to both neutral and stressful events. For example, adults with post-traumatic stress disorder (PTSD) have repeatedly been shown to have increased SC and HR responding to stimulation (Pitman & Orr, 1993; Shalev & Rogel, 1993) and consistently show higher autonomic arousal levels at rest (Blanchard, 1990; McFall, Murburg, Roszell, & Veith, 1989). What is less certain, however, is whether individuals who are genetically hyperresponsive are more likely to respond to stressful life events by developing PTSD or whether the traumatic event itself produces alterations in autonomic functioning. Less traumatic but nevertheless stressful experiences such as having both parents high on expressed emotionality have also been associated with increased resting arousal in 11- to 16-year-old children (Hibbs, Zahn, Hamburger, Kruesi, & Rapoport, 1992).

The stress literature has potentially important implications for psychophysiological research on antisocial behavior. As one example, in a pilot study Steiner (1994) found that juvenile delinquents who also had a diagnosis of PTSD had significantly higher resting HRs than delinquents without this diagnosis, implicating that although antisocials as a whole have lower arousal and responsivity than normals, there may exist a subgroup who have experienced a traumatic event, who have particularly high autonomic activity, and who generate significant heterogeneity with respect to psychophysiological profiles of antisocials. It is likely that antisocial populations contain a relatively high proportion of individuals who have experienced traumatic stress. If so, there is considerable scope for clarifying the psychophysiological basis of antisocial behavior by taking the potential effects of prior abuse and other trauma into account. Again, prospective longitudinal research is critical for helping to disentangle the question of whether trauma changes autonomic functioning or whether those with a certain nervous system are in some way more predisposed to experiencing trauma.

It is possible that experiencing environmental stress in early childhood (rather than later traumatic stress in adolescence or adulthood) results in *reduced* autonomic arousal. For example, coming from a broken home by age 4 years is associated with lower resting HR at age 11 years (Wadsworth, 1976). Experiencing stress such as maternal separation or physical abuse at a very early stage in life could conceivably inoculate the individual, making him or her more resistant to later life stress. At a prenatal level, it has been long known that stress during pregnancy in rodents results in offspring that are less emotionally reactive to stressful stimuli (e.g., Adler & Conklin, 1963; Keeley, 1962). Antisocials may have lower resting HRs and be less fearful in a rest period prior to experimental stimulation because, relative to the very harsh situations they have experienced throughout their lives, such an event is not particularly stressful. Conversely, highly socialized individuals who have generally been protected from life's stressors may be more reactive to a mild stressor.

It is also possible that the psychophysiological fearlessness observed in antisocials is in part a learned phenomenon. For example, Fenz and Epstein (1967) have argued that the low HRs observed in experienced parachute jumpers is a learned response, and there also have been reports that watching violent films results in lowering of HR by as much as 10 to 15 beats per minute (Carruthers & Taggart, 1973). Although the relatively high heritability of HRLs suggests that fearlessness in antisocials may be, in part, genetically mediated, we must not discount the possibility that stressful experiences, desensitization experiences, and learning experiences may also contribute in important ways to the development of this psychophysiological trait, and as such may be modifiable.

In summary, there is a major need for this gap in the literature to be filled in future research. In particular, the timing of the experience of stress and abuse may have crucial effects on latter psychophysiological reactivity. Proximal trauma may result in hyperresponsivity whereas having experienced distal trauma may result in hyporesponsivity and "inoculation" to stress.

Interactions Between Social and Psychophysiological Processes

If social factors do impact on the links between psychophysiology and antisocial behavior, what is the nature of such interactions? Few people have investigated this issue, but the evidence available to date suggests that stronger and more consistent psychophysiology–antisocial behavior relationships may be found in those individuals who come from benign home backgrounds (Raine, 1988; Raine & Mednick, 1989). Evidence for this view is derived from both studies of resting HR and studies of SC activity.

With respect to resting HR, although HRL is generally lower in antisocials, it is a particularly strong characteristic of antisocials from higher social classes and those from intact homes. For example, Raine and Venables (1984) found lower HRLs to be associated with antisocial behavior in adolescents from high social classes, but not in those from lower social classes. Similarly, Wadsworth (1976) found lower HRL at age 11 years predicted criminal behavior in adulthood in those from intact homes, but not in those from broken homes. Maliphant, Hume, & Furnham (1990) found partic-

ularly strong links between lower resting HRL and antisocial behavior in girls from privileged middle class backgrounds attending private schools in England (Maliphant et al., 1990).

Regarding skin conductance activity, a similar pattern of findings have emerged. Reduced SC conditioning characterizes antisocial adolescents from high but not low social classes (Raine & Venables, 1981). Similarly, schizoid criminals from intact home environments show reduced SC orienting, whereas schizoid criminals from broken homes do not (Raine, 1987). Similarly, criminals *without* a childhood history broken by parental absence and disharmony show poorer SC conditioning (Hemming, 1981), whereas privileged (high socioeconomic status) offenders who commit crimes of evasion show reduced SC arousal and reactivity (Buikhuisen, Bontekoe, Plas-Korenhoff, & Buuren, 1985). Again, reduced SC arousal and reactivity in these studies are found particularly in antisocials from benign home backgrounds.

One explanation for this pattern of results is that when the "social push" toward antisocial behavior is lower (high socioeconomic status, intact homes), psychophysiological determinants of antisocial behavior assume greater importance (Raine & Venables, 1981). Conversely social causes of criminal behavior may be more important explanations of antisociality in those exposed to adverse early home conditions. In support of this proposition, Satterfield (1987) found that in the higher social classes, biological high-risk subjects were up to 28 times more likely than biologically low-risk subjects to be criminal, whereas such rates were much lower in the lower social classes (sevenfold increase in crime in biologically at-risk subjects).

Although this biosocial perspective may be a plausible initial hypothesis, there are several other possible ways in which social and psychophysiological risk factors for antisocial behavior may interact. For example, it may be that antisocial behavior is greatest in those who have both psychophysiological *and* social risk factors. Future research in this area needs to explore this latter possibility, attempt to confirm or refute the stronger psychophysiology-antisocial links in those from benign home backgrounds, and map out precise biosocial interactions for violent crime in particular.

SUMMARY

This chapter reviewed the psychophysiological correlates of antisocial behavior and attempted to integrate these data using a theoretical approach based on prefrontal dysfunction theory and a conceptual approach based on a biosocial perspective. Findings of studies on resting EEGs, SC, and HR indicate that antisocials are characterized by underarousal; these findings suggest that antisocials are stimulation seekers who are relatively fearless. Underarousal also typifies infants and young children with a disinhibited temperament, which is thought to be a predisposition to juvenile delinquency. Deficits in the orienting response, a measure of attention allocation, also predispose to later antisocial and criminal behavior, particularly in a subgroup of schizoid antisocials who are anxious and withdrawn. Initial studies have shown that particularly high levels of orienting and arousal may protect against crime development in those predisposed to antisocial behavior. A tripartite event-related potential model of antisocial behavior suggests that (a) underarousal and excessive filtering of stimuli (indicated by increased brain stem ERP latencies) results in stimulus deprivation that leads to (b) stimulation seeking (indicated by ERP augmenting to increasing stimulus intensity) that in turn leads to (c) increased attention to stimulating events (reflected by larger P300 amplitudes to targets), and hence antisocial stimulation seeking. In developmental terms, these psychophysiological correlates of adult antisocial behavior are generally found in antisocial children, although heterogeneity and developmental change are viewed as having considerable influence on psychophysiological processes. A prefrontal dysfunction model of antisocial behavior is developed as one overarching heuristic framework within which to view the psychophysiology of antisocial behavior, in which it is argued that prefrontal dysfunction results in arousal, orienting, and anticipatory fear deficits (in addition to personality and cognitive deficits) that in turn predispose to antisocial behavior. Finally, the critical importance of adopting a biosocial perspective is emphasized. Specifically, an initial working hypothesis is developed that suggests that the paradoxically increased autonomic responsiveness of adult child abusers may be a function of such adults having suffered traumatic stress during childhood, resulting in alterations of autonomic nervous system functioning in the direction of hyperresponsivity. It is also hypothesized that the psychophysiological correlates of antisocial behavior may be greatest in those from more benign home backgrounds in which the psychosocial push toward crime is relatively weaker.

REFERENCES

Adler, R., & Conklin, P. M. (1963). Handling of pregnant rats: Effects on emotionality of their offspring. *Science, 142,* 411–412.

Asenbaum, S., Lang, W., Egkher, A., & Lindinger, G. (1992). Frontal DC potentials in auditory selective attention. *Electroencephalography and Clinical Neurophysiology, 82,* 469–476.

Bach-y-Rita, G., Lion, J. R., Climent, C. E., & Ervin, F. (1971). Episodic dyscontrol : A study of 139 violent patients. *American Journal of Psychiatry, 127,* 1473–1478.

Beaumont, J. G. (1983). *Introduction to neuropsychology.* Oxford: Blackwell.

Blackburn, R. (1975). Aggression and EEG: A quantitative analysis. *Journal of Abnormal Psychology, 84,* 358–365.

Blackburn, R. (1979). Cortical and autonomic responses arousal in primary and secondary psychopaths. *Psychophysiology, 16,* 143–150.

Blackburn, R. (1983). Psychopathy, delinquency and crime. In A. Gale & J. A. Edwards (Eds.), *Physiological correlates of human behavior* (Vol. 3, pp. 187–205). London: Academic Press.

Blanchard, E. B. (1990). Elevated basal level of cardiovascular responses in Vietnam veterans with PTSD: A health problem in the making? *Journal of Anxiety Disorders, 4,* 233–237.

Brennan, P., Raine, A., Schulsinger, F., Kierkegaard-Sorensen, L., Knop, J., Hutchins, B., Rosenberg, R., & Mednick, S. A. (in press). Psychophysiological protective factors for males at high risk for crime. *American Journal of Psychiatry.*

Buchsbaum, M. S., Nuechterlein, K. H., Haier, R. J., Wu, J., Sicotte, N., Hazlett, E., Asarnow, R., Potkin, S., & Guich, S. (1990). Glucose metabolic rate in normals and schizophrenics during the continuous performance test assessed by positron emission tomography. *British Journal of Psychiatry, 156,* 216–227.

Buikhuisen, W., Bontekoe, E. H. M., Plas-Korenhoff, C. D., & Buuren, S. (1985). Characteristics of criminals: The privileged offender. *International Journal of Law and Psychiatry, 7,* 301–313.

Buikhuisen, W., Eurelings-Bontekoe, E. H. M., & Host, K. B. (1989). Crime and recovery time: Mednick revisited. *International Journal of Law and Psychiatry, 12,* 29–40.

Cacioppo, J., Tassinary, L., & Fridlund, A (1991). *Principles of psychophysiology: Physical, social and inferential elements.* Cambridge: Cambridge University Press.

Carruthers, M., & Taggart, P. (1973). Vagotonicity of violence: Biochemical and cardiac response to violent films and television programmes. *British Medical Journal, 2,* 383–389.

Casanova, G. M., Domanic, J., McCanne, T. M., & Milner, J. S. (1992). Physiological responses to non-child-related stressors in mothers at risk for child abuse. *Child Abuse and Neglect, 16,* 31–44.

Cenci, M. A., Kalen, P., & Mandel, R. J. (1992). Regional differences in the regulation of dopamine and noradrenaline release in medial frontal cortex, nucleus accumbens and caudate-putamen: A microdialysis study in the rat. *Brain Research, 581,* 217–228.

Coles, M. P. G., Donchin, E., & Porges, S. W. (1986). *Psychophysiology: Systems, processes, and applications.* New York: Guilford.

Convit, A., Czobor, P., & Volavka, J. (1991). Lateralized abnormality in the EEG of persistently violent psychiatric inpatients. *Biological Psychiatry, 30,* 363–370.

Cox, D., Hallam, R., O'Connor, K., & Rachman, S. (1983). An experimental study of fearlessness and courage. *British Journal of Psychology, 74,* 107–117.

Crider, A. (1993). Electrodermal response lability—stability: Individual difference correlates. In J. C. Roy, W. Boucsein, D. C. Fowles, & J. Gruzelier (Eds.), *Electrodermal activity: From physiology to psychology* (pp. 173–186). New York: Plenum.

Crowe, H., & Zeskind, P. S. (1992). Psychophysiological and perceptual responses to infant cries varying in pitch: Comparison of adults with low and high scores on the Child Abuse Potential Inventory. *Child Abuse and Neglect, 16,* 19–29.

Damasio, A. R., Tranel, D., & Damasio, H. (1990). Individuals with sociopathic behavior caused by frontal damage fail to respond autonomically to social stimuli. *Behavioral Brain Research, 41,* 81–94.

Davies, J. G. V., & Maliphant, R. (1971). Autonomic responses of male adolescents exhibiting refractory behavior in school. *Journal of Child Psychology and Psychiatry, 12,* 115–127.

Dawson, M. E. (1990). Psychophysiology at the interface of clinical science, cognitive science, and neuroscience: Presidential address (1989). *Psychophysiology, 27,* 243–255.

Dawson, M. E., Schell, A. M., & Filion, D. (1991). The electrodermal system. In J. T. Cacioppo, L. G. Tassinary, & A. Fridlund (Eds.), *Principles of psychophysiology: Physical, social and inferential elements* (pp. 295–324). Cambridge: Cambridge University Press.

Drake, M. E., Hietter, S. A., & Pakalnis, A. (1992). EEG and evoked potentials in episodic-dyscontrol syndrome. *Neuropsychobiology, 26,* 125–128.

Dykman, R. A., Ackerman, P. T., & Oglesby, D. M. (1992). Heart rate reactivity in attention deficit disorder subgroups. *Integrative Physiological and Behavioral Science, 27,* 228–245.

Ellingson, R. J. (1954). The incidence of EEG abnormality among patients with mental disorders of apparently nonorganic origin: A critical review. *American Journal of Psychiatry, 111,* 262–275.

Eysenck, H. J. (1964). *Crime and personality.* London: Methuen.

Eysenck, H. J. (1977). *Crime and personality* (3rd ed.). St. Albans: Paladin.

Farrington, D. P. (1987). Implications of biological findings for criminological research. In S. A. Mednick, T. E. Moffitt, & S. A. Stack (Eds.), *The causes of crime: New biological approaches* (pp. 42–64). New York: Cambridge University Press.

Fenton, G. W., Fenwick, P. B. C., Ferguson, W., & Lam, C. T. (1978). The contingent negative variation in antisocial behavior: A pilot study of Broadmoor patients. *British Journal of Psychiatry, 132,* 368–377.

Fenz, W. D., & Epstein, S. (1967). Gradients of physiological arousal in parachutists as a function of an approaching jump. *Psychosomatic Medicine, 29,* 33–51.

Fishbein, D. H., Herning, R. I., Pickworth, W. B., & Haertzen, C. A. (1989). EEG and brainstem auditory evoked response potentials in adult male drug abusers with self-reported histories of aggressive behavior. *Biological Psychiatry, 26,* 595–611.

Forth, A., & Hare, R. D. (1989). The contingent negative variation in psychopaths. *Psychophysiology, 26,* 676–682.

Fowles, D. C. (1980). The three arousal model: Implications of Gray's two-factor learning theory for heart rate, electrodermal activity, and psychopathy. *Psychophysiology, 17,* 87–104.

Fowles, D. C. (1993). Electrodermal activity and antisocial behavior. In J. C. Roy, W. Boucsein, D. C. Fowles, & J. Gruzelier (Eds.), *Electrodermal activity: From physiology to psychology* (pp. 223–238). New York: Plenum.

Fox, N. A. (1989). Psychophysiological correlates of emotional reactivity during the first year of life. *Developmental Psychology, 25,* 364–372.

Fox, N. A., Bell, M. A., & Jones, N. A. (1992). Individual differences in response to stress and cerebral asymmetry. *Developmental Neuropsychology, 8,* 161–184.

Frysztak, R. J., & Neafsey, E. J. (1991). The effect of medial frontal cortex lesions on respiration, "freezing," and ultrasonic vocalizations during conditioned emotional responses in rats. *Cerebral Cortex, 1,* 418–425.

Goyer, P. F., Andreason, P. J., Semple, W. E., Clayton, A. H., King, A. C., Compton-Toth, B. A., Schulz, S. C., & Cohen, R. M. (1994). Positron-emission tomography and personality disorders. *Neuropsychopharmacology, 10,* 21–28.

Goyer, P. F., & Semple, W. E. (1996). PET studies of aggression in personality disorder and other nonpsychotic patients. In D. M. Stoff & R. F. Cairns (Eds.), *The neurobiology of clinical aggression* (pp. 219–236). Hillsdale, NJ: Erlbaum.

Hare, R. D. (1970). *Psychopathy: Theory and practice.* New York: Wiley & Sons.

Hare, R. D. (1978). Electrodermal and cardiovascular correlates of psychopathy. In R. D. Hare & D. Schalling (Eds.), *Psychopathic behavior: Approaches to research* (pp. 107–144). New York: Wiley.

Harpur, T. J., Williamson, S. E., Forth, A., & Hare, R. D. (1986). A quantitative assessment of resting EEG in psychopathic and non-psychopathic criminals. *Psychophysiology, 23,* 439.

Hazlett, E., Dawson, M., Buchsbaum, M. S., & Nuechterlein, K. (1993). Reduced regional brain glucose metabolism assessed by PET in electrodermal nonresponder schizophrenics: A pilot study. *Journal of Abnormal Psychology, 102,* 39–46.

Hellige, J. B. (1993). *Hemisphere asymmetry: What's right and what's left.* Cambridge, MA: Harvard University Press.

Hemming, J. H. (1981). Electrodermal indices in a selected prison sample and students. *Personality and Individual Differences, 2,* 37–46.

Herning, R. I., Hickey, J. E., Pickworth, W. B., & Jaffe, J. N. (1989). Auditory event-related potentials in adolescents at risk for drug abuse. *Biological Psychiatry, 25,* 598–609.

Hibbs, E. D., Zahn, T. P., Hamburger, S. D., Kruesi, M. P. J., & Rapoport, J. L. (1992). Parental expressed emotion and psychophysiological reactivity in disturbed and normal children. *British Journal of Psychiatry, 160,* 504–510.

Hill, D., & Pond, D. A. (1952). Reflections on 100 capital cases submitted for electroencephalography. *Journal of Mental Science, 98,* 23–43.

Hill, S. D., Bleichfeld, B., Brunstetter, R. D., & Hebert, J. E. (1989). Cognitive and physiological responsiveness of abused children. *Journal of the American Academy of Child and Adolescent Psychiatry, 28,* 219–224.

Howard, R. C. (1984). The clinical EEG and personality in mentally abnormal offenders. *Psychological Medicine, 14,* 569–580.

Howard, R. C., Fenton, G. W., & Fenwick, P. B. (1984). The contingent negative variation, personality and antisocial behaviour. *British Journal of Psychiatry, 144,* 463–474.

Kagan, J. (1989). Temperamental contributions to social behavior. *American Psychologist, 44,* 668–674.

Kagan, J., Reznick, J. S., & Snidman, N. (1988). Biological bases of childhood shyness. *Science, 240,* 167–171.

Kandel, E., Mednick, S. A., Kirkegaard-Sorensen, L., & Hutchings, B. (1988). IQ as a protective factor for subjects at high risk for antisocial behavior. *Journal of Consulting and Clinical Psychology, 56,* 224–226.

Keeley, K. (1962). Prenatal influences on behavior of offspring of crowded mice. *Science, 143,* 44–45.

Kinghorn, E. W., & Fleming, D. E. (1985). The effects of frontal lesions on brain hyper-synchronous bursting and behavioral activity. *Physiology and Behavior, 35,* 261–265.

Kinghorn, E. W., Fleming, D. E., & Anderson, R. H. (1987). The effects of bilateral and unilateral frontal lesions on visual cortical hyper-synchronous bursting and behavioral activity. *Physiology and Behavior, 39,* 297–301.

Krakowski, M. I., Convit, A., Jaeger, J., & Lin, S. (1989). Neurological impairment in violent schizophrenic inpatients. *American Journal of Psychiatry, 146,* 849–853.

Kruesi, M. J., Hibbs, E. D., Zahn, T. P., & Keysor, C. S. (1992). A 2-year prospective follow-up study of children and adolescents with disruptive behavior disorders: Prediction by cerebrospinal fluid 5-hydroxyindoleacetic acid, homovanillic acid, and autonomic measures? *Archives of General Psychiatry, 49,* 429–435.

Kruesi, M. J., Rapoport, J. L., Hamburger, S., & Hibbs, E. D. (1990). Cerebrospinal fluid monoamine metabolites, aggression, and impulsivity in disruptive behavior disorders of children and adolescents. *Archives of General Psychiatry, 47,* 419–426.

Larsen, P. B., Schneiderman, N., & Pasin, R. D. (1986). Physiological bases of cardiovascular psychophysiology. In M. G. H. Coles, E. Donchin, & S. W. Porges (Eds.), *Psychophysiology: Systems, processes, and application* (pp. 122–165). New York: Guilford.

Loeb, J., & Mednick, S. A. (1977). A prospective study of predictors of criminality: 3. Electrodermal response patterns. In S. A. Mednick & K. O. Christiansen (Eds.), *Biosocial bases to criminal behavior* (pp. 245–254). New York: Gardner.

McBurnett, K., & Lahey, B. B. (1994). Biological correlates of conduct disorder and antisocial behavior in children and adolescents. In D.C. Fowles (Ed.), *Progress in experimental personality and psychopathology research.* New York: Springer.

McFall, M. E., Murburg, M. M., Roszell, D. K., & Veith, R. C. (1989). Psychophysiologic and neuroendocrine findings in posttraumatic stress disorder: A review of theory and research. *Journal of Anxiety Disorders, 3,* 243–257.

McMillan, T. M., & Rachman, S.-J. (1987). Fearlessness and courage: A laboratory study of paratrooper veterans of the Falklands War. *British Journal of Psychology, 78,* 375–383.

Maliphant, R., Hume, F., & Furnham, A. (1990). Autonomic nervous system (ANS) activity, personality characteristics and disruptive behavior in girls. *Journal of Child Psychology and Psychiatry, 31,* 619–628.

Mark, V. H., & Ervin, F. R. (1970). *Violence and the brain.* New York: Harper & Row.

Mathew, R. J. (1989). Hyperfrontality of regional cerebral blood flow distribution in normals during resting wakefulness: Fact or fiction? *Biological Psychiatry, 26,* 717–724.

Mealey, L. (1995). The sociobiology of sociopathy: An integrated evolutionary model. *Behavioral and Brain Sciences, 18,* 523–599.

Mednick, S. A., Pollock, V., Volavka, J., & Gabrielli, W. F. (1982). Biology and violence. In M. Wolfgang & N. A. Weiner (Eds.), *Criminal violence* (pp. 21–80). Beverly Hills: Sage Publications.

Mednick, S. A., Volavka, J., Gabrielli, W. F., & Itil, T. (1981). EEG as a predictor of antisocial behavior. *Criminology, 19,* 219–231.

Milstein, V. (1988). EEG topography in patients with aggressive violent behavior. In T. E. Moffitt & S. A. Mednick (Eds.), *Biological contributions to crime causation* (pp. 40–54). Dordrecht, The Netherlands: Kluwer.

Mizuki, Y., Kajimura, N., & Kai, S (1992). Differential responses to mental stress in high and low anxious normal humans assessed by frontal midline theta activity. *International Journal of Psychophysiology, 12,* 169–178.

O'Connor, K., Hallam, R., & Rachman, S. (1985). Fearless and courage: A replication experiment. *British Journal of Psychology, 76,* 187–197.

Ohman, A. (1981). Electrodermal activity and vulnerability to schizophrenia: A review. *Biological Psychology, 12,* 87–145.

Patrick, C. J. (1994). Emotion and psychopathy: Startling new insights. *Psychophysiology, 31,* 319–330.

Petersen, I., Matousek, M., Mednick, S. A., Volavka, J., & Pollock, V. (1982). EEG antecedents of thievery. *Criminology, 19,* 219–229.

Pitman, R. K., & Orr, S. P. (1993). Psychophysiologic testing for post-traumatic stress disorder: Forensic psychiatric application. *Bulletin of the American Academy of Psychiatry and Law, 21,* 37–52.

Pruitt, D. L., & Erickson, M. T. (1985). The Child Abuse Potential Inventory: A study of concurrent validity. *Journal of Clinical Psychology, 41,* 104–111.

Quay, H. C. (1965). Psychopathic personality as pathological stimulation-seeking. *American Journal of Psychiatry, 122,* 180–183.

Raine, A. (1987). Effect of early environment on electrodermal and cognitive correlates of schizotypy and psychopathy in criminals. *International Journal of Psychophysiology, 4,* 277–287.

Raine, A. (1988). Antisocial behavior and social psychophysiology. In H. Wagner (Ed.), *Social psychophysiology and emotion: Theory and clinical application* (pp. 231–253). London: Wiley.

Raine, A. (1989). Evoked potentials and psychopathy. *International Journal of Psychophysiology, 8,* 1–16.

Raine, A. (1993). *The psychopathology of crime: Criminal behavior as a clinical disorder.* San Diego: Academic Press.

Raine, A. (1996). Autonomic nervous system activity and violence. In D. M. Stoff & R. F. Cairns (Eds.), *The neurobiology of clinical aggression* (pp. 145–168). Hillsdale, NJ: Erlbaum.

Raine, A., Buchsbaum, M. S., Stanley, J., Lottenberg, S., Abel, L., & Stoddard, J. (1994). Selective reductions in pre-frontal glucose metabolism in murderers. *Biological Psychiatry, 36,* 365–373.

Raine, A., & Lencz, T. (1993). The neuroanatomy of electrodermal activity. In J. C. Roy (Ed.), *Electrodermal activity: From physiology to psychology* (pp. 115–136). New York: Plenum.

Raine, A., & Mednick, S. A. (1989). Biosocial longitudinal research into antisocial behavior. *Review d'Epidemiologie et de Sante Publique, 37,* 515–524.

Raine, A., Reynolds, G. P., & Sheard, C. (1991). Neuroanatomical mediators of electrodermal activity in normal human subjects: A magnetic resonance imaging study. *Psychophysiology, 28,* 448–558.

Raine, A., & Venables, P. H. (1981). Classical conditioning and socialization—A biosocial interaction? *Personality and Individual Differences, 2,* 273–283.

Raine, A., & Venables, P. H. (1984). Electrodermal non-responding, schizoid tendencies, and antisocial behavior in adolescents. *Psychophysiology, 21,* 424–433.

Raine, A., & Venables, P. H. (1987). Contingent negative variation, P3 evoked potentials, and antisocial behavior. *Psychophysiology, 24,* 191–199.

Raine, A., & Venables, P. H. (1990). Evoked potential augmenting-reducing in psychopaths and criminals with poor smooth-pursuit eye movements. *Psychiatry Research, 31,* 85–98.

Raine, A., Venables, P. H., & Williams, M. (1990a). Relationships between CNS and ANS measures of arousal at age 15 and criminality at age 24. *Archives of General Psychiatry, 47,* 1003–1007.

Raine, A., Venables, P. H., & Williams, M. (1990b). Relationships between N1, P300 and CNV recorded at age 15 and criminal behavior at age 24. *Psychophysiology, 27,* 567–575.

Raine, A., Venables, P. H., & Williams, M. (1995). High autonomic arousal and electrodermal orienting at age 15 years as protective factors against criminal behavior at age 29 years. *American Journal of Psychiatry, 152,* 1595–1600.

Raine, A., Venables, P. H., & Williams, M. (1996). Better autonomic conditioning and faster electrodermal half-recovery time at age 15 years as protective factors against crime at age 29 years. *Developmental Psychology, 32,* 624–630.

Ray, W. J. (1990). The electrocortical system. In J. T. Cacioppo, L. G. Tassinary (Eds.), *Principles of psychophysiology* (pp. 385–412). Cambridge: Cambridge University Press.

Reznick, J. S., Kagan, J., Snidman, N., Gersten, M., Baak, K., & Rosenberg, A. (1986). Inhibited and uninhibited children: A follow-up study. *Child Development, 57,* 660–680.

Satterfield, J. H. (1987). Childhood diagnostic and neurophysiological predictors of teenage arrest rates: An eight-year prospective study. In S. A. Mednick, T. E. Moffitt, & S. Stack (Eds.), *The causes of crime: New biological approaches* (pp. 146–167). Cambridge: Cambridge University Press.

Satterfield, J. H., & Schell, A. M. (1984). Childhood brain function differences in delinquent and non-delinquent hyperactive boys. *Electroencephalography and Clinical Neurophysiology, 57,* 199–207.

Scerbo, A., Raine, A., Venables, P. H., & Mednick, S. A. (1995). Stability of temperament from ages 3 to 11 years in Mauritian children. *Journal of Abnormal Child Psychology, 23,* 607–618.

Scerbo, A. S., Raine, A., Venables, P. H., & Mednick, S. A. (in press). Heart rate and skin conductance in behaviorally inhibited Mauritian children. *Journal of Abnormal Psychology.*

Shalev, A. Y., & Rogel, F. Y. (1993). Psychophysiology of posttraumatic stress disorder: From sulphur fumes to behavioral genetics. *Psychosomatic Medicine, 55,* 413–423.

Siddle, D. A. T., & Trasler, G. (1981). The psychophysiology of psychopathic behavior. In M. J. Christie & P. G. Mellett (Eds.), *Foundations of psychosomatics* (pp. 283–303). Chichester, England: Wiley.

Snidman, N., Kagan, J., & McQuilkin, A. (1991). Fetal heart rate as a predictor of infant behavior. *Psychophysiology, 28*, 51.

Steiner, H. (1994). Heart rate in conduct disordered adolescents with and without PTSD. Manuscript submitted for publication.

Stern, R. M., Ray, W. J., & Davis, C. M. (1980). *Psychophysiological recording*. New York: Oxford University Press.

Stifter, C. A., & Fox, N. A. (1990). Infant reactivity: Physiological correlates of newborn and 5-month temperament. *Developmental Psychology, 26*, 582–588.

Stuss, D. T., & Benson, D. F. (1986). *The frontal lobes*. New York: Raven Press.

Syndulko, K. (1978). Electrocortical investigations of sociopathy. In R. D. Hare & D. Schalling (Eds.), *Psychopathic behavior: Approaches to research* (pp. 145–156). Chichester, England: Wiley.

Tranel, D., & Damasio, H. (1994). Neuroanatomical correlates of electrodermal skin conductance responses. *Psychophysiology, 31*, 427–438.

Venables, P. H. (1974). The recovery limb of the skin conductance response. In S. A. Mednick, F. Schulsinger, J. Higgins, & B. Bell (Eds.), *Genetics, environment and psychopathology* (pp. 117–133). Oxford: North-Holland.

Venables, P. H. (1987). Autonomic and central nervous system factors in criminal behavior. In S. A. Mednick, T. Moffitt, & S. Stack (Eds.), *The causes of crime: New biological approaches* (pp. 110–136). New York: Cambridge University Press.

Venables, P. H. (1988). Psychophysiology and crime: Theory and data. In T. E. Moffitt & S. A. Mednick (Eds.), *Biological contributions to crime causation* (pp. 3–13). Dordrecht, The Netherlands: Martinus Nijhoff.

Venables, P. H., & Christie, M. J. (1973). Mechanisms, instrumentation, recording techniques, and quantification of responses. In W. F. Prokasy & D. C. Raskin (Eds.), *Electrodermal activity in psychological research* (pp. 1–124). New York: Wiley.

Venables, P. H., & Raine, A. (1987). Biological theory. In B. McGurk, D. Thornton, & M. Williams (Eds.), *Applying psychology to imprisonment: Theory and practice* (pp. 3–28). London: HMSO.

Volavka, J. (1987). Electroencephalogram among criminals. In S. A. Mednick, T. E. Moffitt, & S. Stack (Eds.), *The causes of crime: New biological approaches* (pp. 137–145). Cambridge: Cambridge University Press.

Volkow, N. D., & Tancredi, L. (1987). Neural substrates of violent behavior: A preliminary study with positron emission tomography. *British Journal of Psychiatry, 151*, 668–673.

Wadsworth, M. E. J. (1976). Delinquency, pulse rate and early emotional deprivation. *British Journal of Criminology, 16*, 245–256.

Williams, D. (1969). Neural factors related to habitual aggression: Consideration of those differences between those habitually aggressive and others who have committed crimes of violence. *Brain, 92*, 503–520.

Wolfe, D. A., Fairbank, J. A., Kelly, J. A., & Bradlyn, A. S. (1983). Child abusive parents' physiological responses to stressful and non-stressful behavior in children. *Behavioral Assessment, 5*, 363–371.

Zahn, T. P. (1986). Psychophysiological approaches to psychopathology. In M. G. H. Coles, E. Donchin, & S. W. Porges (Eds.), *Psychophysiology: Systems, processes, and applications* (pp. 508–609). New York: Guilford.

Zahn, T. P., & Kruesi, M. J. (1993). Autonomic activity in boys with disruptive behavior disorders. *Psychophysiology, 30*, 605–614.

CHAPTER 28

Neurotransmitter Correlates of Human Aggression

MITCHELL E. BERMAN, RICHARD J. KAVOUSSI, and EMIL F. COCCARO

The human brain is an extraordinarily intricate organ system containing about 100 billion neuron cells, with each neuron forming up to 15,000 connections with other cells. Despite this complexity, substantial progress has been made in the past 20 years toward understanding how neurotransmitter functioning is related to human aggression. This chapter provides an overview of the strategies used to assess neurotransmitter activity, the evidence for a relation between neurotransmitter functioning and aggressive behavior in humans, and the limitations of existing studies. Theoretical mechanisms for how neurotransmitter functioning may affect aggressive behavior and the recent use of experimental methodologies in this research area are also discussed.

NEUROTRANSMITTER ACTION

Neurons convey information to other neurons by generating impulses known as action potentials down the neuronal cell body (the axon), which are then converted to chemical signals at the synapse, or contact point, between neurons. These chemical signals result from the release of neurotransmitter molecules from neuronal structures called terminal buttons. Released neurotransmitters diffuse across the synapse and bind to receptors on the membranes of adjacent neurons, generating action potentials in these postsynaptic neurons. Receptor stimulation stops when neurotransmitter molecules in the synapse are taken back up into the terminal buttons of the presynaptic neuron, a process known as re-uptake, or are metabolized and eliminated from the system. Receptor elements also exist on presynaptic neurons. Stimulation of presynaptic receptors can influence the synthesis of neurotransmitters by neurons, the firing rate of action potentials, or the release of neurotransmitters into the synapse.

Neurotransmitter activity is determined by several factors, including (a) the biologic availability of precursor substances necessary for the production of neurotransmitters in neuronal cells; (b) the activity of enzymes regulating the synthesis and metabolism of neurotransmitters; (c) pre- and postsynaptic receptor functioning; and (d) the storage, release, and re-uptake activity of neuronal cells. Indexes of these various factors provide different ways to view neurotransmitter activity.

Although between 50 and 100 molecules are known or suspected neurotransmitters, only the monoamines (i.e., serotonin [5-HT], norepinephrine [NE], and dopamine [DA]) have been systematically studied with respect to human aggression. Of the monoamines, the most extensive human literature exists for serotonin and aggression. The relation between aggressive behavior and other neurotransmitter systems (e.g., acetylcholine and gamma amino butyric acid [GABA]) has been examined in lower animal species but not in humans (see Miczek, Weerts, Haney, & Tidey, 1994, for a review). This chapter focuses on human aggression, which directs the discussion to the role of the monoamines.

MEASUREMENT OF NEUROTRANSMITTER ACTIVITY

Among the first considerations when studying neurotransmitter functioning and aggressive behavior in humans is selecting a strategy to measure neurotransmitter activity. Studies of neurotransmitters and human aggression have employed three general strategies for assessing neurotransmitter activity: (a) central neurochemical measures, (b) challenge of neuroregulatory systems with pharmacological agents, and (c) peripheral measures. Each strategy provides indexes of neurotransmitter activity that can be correlated with dimensional measures of aggression (e.g., self- or other-rating scales) or used to discriminate groups of individuals characterized by aggressive behavior (e.g., violent criminal offenders, children with conduct disorder, adults with antisocial personality disorder).

Neurochemical Measures

Central neurochemical measures provide an opportunity to study substances that come in direct contact with the central nervous system, including the brain, by examining metabolites of neurotransmitters in cerebrospinal fluid (CSF). The cost and invasiveness of removing CSF through a puncture in the lumbar sack is a disadvantage of this assessment strategy. Also, neurochemical measures provide no information about neuronal activity in specific regions of the brain. A final disadvantage of this strategy is that CSF metabolites are thought to reflect presynaptic activity, or the amount of neurotransmitter substances available for release into the synapse, and provide no information about the functioning of postsynaptic neurotransmitter receptors.

Pharmacochallenge Measures

In pharmacochallenge measurement techniques, a drug ("probe") that targets one or more neurotransmitter systems is administered, and hormonal (e.g., cortisol, prolactin) or behavioral (e.g., self-reported subjective mood states) responses to the drug are observed. Because hormonal output is controlled, in part, through neurotransmitter activity in the brain, elevated or lowered hormonal responses to a probe are thought to reflect abnormal neurotransmitter functioning. Hormonal responses to probes can reflect either postsynaptic or "net" (pre- and postsynaptic) functioning, depending on the probe used. A criticism of pharmacochallenge measures is that no probe specifically activates a single neurotransmitter or receptor subtype system. It is also difficult to determine if hormonal responses result from the stimulation of brain neurons (which would be an index of neurotransmitter functioning) or if the effects are produced by the direct activation of the glands that manufacture specific hormones (see Coccaro & Kavoussi, 1994, for a fuller discussion of these issues). Additionally, infusion of drug probes may produce uncomfortable side effects, such as nausea or dysphoria.

Peripheral Measures

Peripheral measurement strategies involve assaying blood or urine samples. Blood or urine may be examined for substances necessary for the production of neurotransmitters in the brain, metabolites produced by the breakdown of neurotransmitter material, or enzymes associated with neurotransmitter metabolism. The concentration of these substances in blood or urine putatively reflects presynaptic neurotransmitter activity.

Another peripheral strategy involves the study of neurotransmitter receptors occurring on blood platelet cells. These elements appear to be similar to those in the brain and have been used as indexes of either pre- or postsynaptic central neurotransmitter receptor functioning (e.g., Cook et al., 1994). Advantages of peripheral measures in general are that they are minimally invasive, costly, and time consuming (on the part of the subject). They are especially useful for subject populations in which use of more invasive procedures may be undesirable, such as children. Because differences between neurotransmitter activity in the periphery and central nervous systems exist, such approaches are considered the least informative source about central neurotransmitter functioning (Coccaro & Kavoussi, 1994).

SEROTONIN (5-HT) AND HUMAN AGGRESSION

Serotonin (5-HT) is perhaps the most widely distributed monoamine neurotransmitter system in the mammalian brain. Primarily an inhibitory neurotransmitter (i.e., inhibits the production of postsynaptic action potentials), 5-HT plays a role in the regulation of sexual behaviors, analgesia, appetite, sleep, and mood. Evidence also exists to support the idea that serotonergic functioning is associated with aggressive behaviors. Both presynaptic (e.g., CSF 5-HT metabolite) and postsynaptic (e.g., pharmacochallenge) indexes have been associated with aggression in humans, and most central neurochemical and challenge studies indicate that 5-HT activity is inversely correlated with the level of aggressive behavior exhibited. This relationship has been found in personality-disordered patients, "normal" research volunteers, and criminal offenders. However, the magnitude and direction of the relationship may be affected by such subject characteristics as developmental stage, presence of specific psychiatric disorders (e.g., substance abuse, anxiety disorders, specific personality disorder, or depression), the form of aggression (impulsive vs. premeditated), and the indexes of aggressive behavior and serotonergic functioning used. In contrast to pharmacochallenge and neurochemical studies, studies using peripheral measures have provided more conflicting results.

Neurochemical Measures

The majority of neurochemical studies report that aggressive behavior is inversely related to CSF 5-HIAA (5-hydroxyindoleacetic acid, a major metabolite of 5-HT) concentrations. Brown and colleagues, in their investigations of men with personality disorders, were among the earliest researchers to demonstrate this relationship (G. L. Brown et al., 1982; G. L. Brown, Goodwin, Ballenger, Goyer, & Major, 1979). These findings have been replicated in a number of criminal and clinical samples. Inverse relationships between CSF 5-HIAA and aggressive or violent behavior have been found in abstinent alcoholics (Limson et al., 1991), male and female research volunteers without psychopathology (Roy, Adinoff, & Linnoila, 1988), and men who murder their sexual partners (Lidberg, Tuck, Åsberg, Scalia-Tomba, & Bertilsson, 1985). Impulsive violent offenders (most diagnosed with either antisocial personality disorder or intermittent explosive disorder) have also been found to have lower CSF 5-HIAA concentrations than offenders who commit nonimpulsive, premeditated acts of violence (Linnoila et al., 1983), showing that 5-HT functioning may be principally associated with an impulsive or reactive subtype of aggressive behavior. Other studies, however, have failed to find that CSF 5-HIAA concentrations are inversely correlated with aggressive behavior in male (Coccaro, 1992) or female (Gardner, Lucas, & Cowdry, 1990) personality-disordered patients.

Examining central neurotransmitter indexes in children may provide important information about the biological development of aggressive behavior. Because of the invasive nature of the procedure, few CSF aggression studies of children have been conducted. Kruesi, Rapoport, Hamburger, Hibbs, and Potter (1990) reported that children with disruptive behavior disorders (i.e., attention deficit disorder, oppositional defiant disorder, and conduct disorder) had lower CSF 5-HIAA concentrations compared with adolescents with obsessive-compulsive defiant disorder. CSF 5-HIAA concentrations were also inversely correlated with ratings of aggressive behavior in this study. At 2-year follow-up, initial 5-HIAA levels were found to be a robust predictor of aggressive behavior (Kruesi et al., 1992). To date, however, no study has repeatedly assessed neurotransmitter activity, environmental influences, and aggressive behaviors across the life span. Such data would be required to provide conclusive support for the idea that childhood neurotransmitter organization influences future aggressive behavior.

The central neurochemical strategy has also been used to demonstrate that 5-HT activity in some aggressive individuals may be genetically determined (see Carey & Goldman, Chapter 23, this volume, for a review of the relation of genetics to antisocial behavior). Nielsen et al. (1994) examined the gene responsible for tryptophan hydroxylase production in a Finnish sample of violent criminals and arsonists. Tryptophan hydroxylase is a rate-limiting enzyme that controls 5-HT metabolism. Lower levels of CSF 5-HIAA were related to a specific tryptophan hydroxylase genotype, but only for a subgroup of impulsive offenders who committed unpremeditated and unprovoked crimes. Thus, for some impulsively aggressive individuals, reduced 5-HT functioning may be genetically determined.

Pharmacochallenge Studies

Most challenge studies also support the idea that central 5-HT functioning is inversely related to aggressive behavior. However, the direction or magnitude of the relation between challenge indexes of 5-HT and aggression may be affected by the presence of depression (Coccaro et al., 1989), substance abuse (Fishbein, Lozovsky, & Jaffe, 1989), or anxiety disorders (Wetzler, Kahn, Asnis, Korn, & van Praag, 1991). Coccaro and his colleagues examined aggressive behavior and 5-HT in males with either personality disorders or major depression using fenfluramine, a probe that stimulates postsynaptic receptors by both releasing 5-HT and blocking its re-uptake (Coccaro et al., 1989). Compared with normal controls, prolactin response to fenfluramine was lower ("blunted") in both depressed and personality-disordered subjects. However, ratings of aggressive behavior were inversely correlated with hormonal response to the probe only in the personality-disordered subjects. Thus, a relation between aggression and indexes of 5-HT functioning may not appear in all subject populations.

Blunted hormonal response to fenfluramine challenge also has been found in violent criminal offenders compared with healthy controls (O'Keane et al., 1992). An inverse relation between prolactin response to fenfluramine and aggressive behavior, however, has not been universally replicated. For example, a positive association between prolactin response to fenfluramine and self-reported aggressive and impulsive behaviors in substance abusers has been reported (Fishbein et al., 1989). No comparison groups were included in this last study, which limits the generalizability of the findings.

Prolactin response to fenfluramine challenge (both the d= and d,1 isomers of this probe) provides an index of net (pre- and postsynaptic) 5-HT functioning, rather than information about the functioning of specific postsynaptic receptors. Agonist probes that specifically stimulate postsynaptic receptors also have been used to examine aggressive behavior. For example, prolactin response to challenge with buspirone, an agonist that stimulates postsynaptic 5-HT$_{1a}$ receptors, has been inversely correlated with self-

reported aggressive tendencies (e.g., Coccaro, Gabriel, & Siever, 1990). Reduced prolactin response to m-CPP (meta-chlorophenylpiperazine), another postsynaptic probe, has been shown to discriminate antisocial personality–disordered males from controls (Moss, Yao, & Panzak, 1990). Wetzler et al. (1991), however, found no differences in prolactin response to m-CPP in aggressive patients with panic disorder or depression compared with nonaggressive patients. Besides differences in subject characteristics (antisocial personality disorder vs. anxious or depressed patients), the conflicting m-CPP findings may be due to the use of different dosages across studies (a lower dose was used in the nonsignificant Wetzler et al., 1991, study).

As with central neurochemical studies, few pharmacochallenge investigations of children have been conducted. In contrast to studies in adults, pharmacochallenge data do not support an inverse relation between 5-HT and aggressive behavior in children. Stoff et al. (1992), in a study of prepubertal and adolescent males with disruptive behavior disorders (i.e., conduct disorder, attention deficit/hyperactivity disorder [ADHD], oppositional defiant disorder), found no relation between hormonal response to fenfluramine challenge and aggressive behavior. Halperin et al. (1994), however, reported a positive relationship, with fenfluramine producing higher prolactin response in aggressive boys with ADHD compared with nonaggressive ADHD boys. Stoff et al. (1992) suggested that pharmacochallenge studies of aggression in children may produce results different from those in adults because of age-related differences in neuroregulation of hormonal systems.

Pharmacochallenge techniques also have been used to examine familial patterns of aggression, impulsivity, and alcoholism. Coccaro, Silverman, Klar, Horvath, and Siever (1994) reported that personality-disordered males with blunted prolactin response to fenfluramine challenge had a significantly greater proportion of first-degree relatives with impulsive personality traits. Reduced 5-HT functioning in probands also tended to be associated with alcoholism in family members. Surprisingly, questionnaire measures of aggression in probands (i.e., historical interviews, self-reports) were not associated with increased risk of problem behaviors in family members. The results of Coccaro et al. (1994) indicate that a biological marker (5-HT status) may be a better predictor of impulsive behavior problems in first-degree relatives than questionnaire measures of aggressive behavior.

Peripheral Measures

Monoamine oxidase (MAO) is an enzyme that is involved in the breakdown of neurotransmitter substances in the synaptic gap of central neurons and thus is related to the amount of neurotransmitter available for the stimulation of postsynaptic receptors. MAO activity assessed in platelets has been used as an index of central presynaptic serotonergic functioning in impulsive or aggressive individuals. The results of MAO studies in both children and adults are conflicting. In children, for example, MAO has been positively (Stoff et al., 1989), negatively (Bowden, Deutsch, & Swanson, 1987), and not at all (Pliszka, Rogeness, & Medrano, 1988) associated with aggressive or impulsive behaviors. Some studies of adults have reported an inverse relation between MAO indexes and aggressive behavior in men (Belfrage, Lidberg, &

Oreland, 1992) and women (Soloff, Cornelius, Foglia, George, & Perel, 1991), but these results have not been universally replicated (Castrogiovanni, Capone, Maremmani, & Marazziti, 1994; Hallman, Knorring, Edman, & Oreland, 1991).

Platelet [³H]imipramine binding site density has also been studied in regard to human aggressive and antisocial behavior, primarily in children. The imipramine binding site appears to be among several structures that play a role in the transport of serotonin from the exterior to the interior of the platelet cell, a process known as uptake. ADHD children with comorbid conduct disorder have been reported to have reduced imipramine binding site density compared with ADHD children without conduct symptoms (Stoff, Pollock, Vitiello, Behar, & Bridger, 1987). Imipramine binding parameters have also been shown to be inversely correlated with ratings of aggression, hostility, and externalizing behavior in children (Birmaher et al., 1990). In contrast to these findings are studies of adolescent boys (Stoff et al., 1991) and normal adults (Castrogiovanni et al., 1994) that have failed to demonstrate a relation between imipramine binding parameters and aggressive behavior. Imipramine binding parameters are not directly correlated with serotonin uptake (Wood, Suranyi-Cadotte, Nair, LaFaulle, & Schwartz, 1983) or CSF 5-HIAA concentrations (Stoff, Goldman, Bridger, Jain, & Pylypiw, 1990), limiting this measure's use as an index of central 5-HT functioning.

As with MAO and imipramine binding, the results of studies using other platelet uptake or receptor binding indexes are conflicting. An inverse relation between platelet uptake of 5-HT and aggressive behavior has been reported in both child (Modai et al., 1989) and adult psychiatric patients (C. S. Brown et al., 1989). Platelet 5-HT$_2$ receptor binding has also been shown to be lower in delinquent adolescents incarcerated for violent crimes compared with matched controls (Blumensohn et al., 1995). In contrast to these findings, other studies have reported either no relation or a positive relation between serotonin markers in blood and aggressive behavior (Halperin et al., 1994; Mann, McBride, Anderson, & Mieczkowski, 1992; Pliszka, Rogeness, Renner, Sherman, & Broussard, 1988). It is important to note that peripheral measures of 5-HT functioning may be minimally, or not at all, related to central 5-HT measures (e.g., Mann, McBride, Brown et al., 1992). For this reason, peripheral measures may provide limited information on central 5-HT activity.

Neurobiological studies of human aggression, in general, have suffered from the use of relatively small clinical or forensic samples with highly idiosyncratic characteristics, making both cross-study comparisons and generalization of findings difficult. Moffitt and her colleagues recently conducted a revealing epidemiological study that addresses these methodological limitations. These investigators examined whole blood serotonin and aggressive behavior in a birth cohort of 781 21-year-old male and female New Zealanders (Moffitt et al., in press). Whole blood serotonin was shown to be positively related to violence (but not general criminality) in males but not females. This relationship was found even when potential confounding variables were controlled, such as diet, use of psychiatric medications, body mass, number of suicide attempts, alcohol use, intelligence, and socioeconomic status. The unique combination of epidemiological and neurobiological methodologies used in this study provides support for the idea that whole blood 5-HT may be positively related to aggressive behavior in community samples. This study appears to contradict neurochemical and pharmacochallenge studies that generally show an inverse relation between 5-HT indexes and aggressive behavior. However, high whole blood serotonin concentration is thought to be associated with decreased central 5-HT functioning (Anderson, Freedman, & Cohen, 1987; Hanna, Yuwiler, & Cantwell, 1991).

Experimental Studies

Thus far, the studies discussed involve nonexperimental methodology ("correlational" designs) in which neurotransmitter functioning is not manipulated. Neurotransmitter indexes are passively observed, usually at one point in time, and are then correlated with dimensional measures of aggression or used to discriminate individuals with diagnoses associated with aggressive behavior (e.g., antisocial personality disorder). Such nonexperimental designs prohibit drawing causal inferences regarding neurotransmitter activity and aggressive behavior.

Neurotransmitter activity is not static and is influenced by a variety of environmental factors. Early social influences have been shown to produce enduring changes in neurotransmitter activity in both nonhuman primates (Higley, Suomi, & Linnoila, 1991; Kraemer, Ebert, Schmidt, & McKinney, 1989) and humans (Galvin et al., 1991; Gerra et al., 1993). Combined with the nonexperimental studies of neurotransmitter activity and aggression reviewed earlier, these data could be interpreted to mean that early social environment affects neurotransmitter organization, which in turn is causally related to a propensity to engage in antisocial acts. It could also be argued that unstable early social environments produce both behavioral (i.e., aggressive behavior) and biological (i.e., neurotransmitter functioning) changes that may be statistically associated but not causally related. To determine if neurotransmitter activity is causally related to aggressive behavior in humans requires the use of experimental methodology.

Investigators have begun to use experimental methodology (i.e., manipulation of neurotransmitter activity and random assignment to treatment conditions) to examine potential causal relations between neurotransmitter functioning and aggressive behavior. These studies have focused exclusively on the 5-HT system of normal research volunteers with no discernible psychiatric disorders. The earliest experimental study involved manipulation of central 5-HT by either increasing or decreasing the amount of tryptophan in participants' diets (Smith, Pihl, Young, & Ervin, 1986). Tryptophan is an amino acid necessary for the synthesis of central 5-HT. Tryptophan supplements have been shown to increase CSF 5-HIAA in humans (Young & Gauthier, 1981), and tryptophan-deficient diets reduce central CSF 5-HIAA concentrations in lower primates (Young, Ervin, Pihl, & Finn, 1989). Smith et al. (1986) found that manipulating dietary tryptophan did not affect aggressive behavior, with aggression defined as the intensity and duration of shock delivered to a fictitious subject in another room. Smith et al. (1986) suggested that their nonsignificant results may have been due to the failure of a provocation manipulation to elicit retaliatory aggressive behavior in subjects. In a follow-up study, this group used a laboratory task that incorporated high levels of provocation by a fictitious adversary (Pihl et al., 1995). In this second study, subjects in a tryptophan-depleted group tended to set higher shocks for a moderately provocative adversary than subjects who received a tryptophan-augmented diet. In another recent study, Cleare and Bond (1995) found that tryptophan-elicited aggressive behavior was dependent on individual differences in aggressive disposition. Specifically, high-trait aggressive individuals tended to behave more aggressively after a tryptophan-depletion procedure compared with high-trait aggressives receiving a tryptophan-augmented diet. Low-trait aggressives showed the opposite effect, with a tryptophan-augmented diet increasing aggression compared with a tryptophan-depleted diet. Although suggestive, the results of these dietary tryptophan studies were found in posthoc examinations of nonsignificant trends. Moreover, tryptophan-manipulation studies of aggression have not included pharmacologically inactive placebo control conditions, limiting the conclusions that can be drawn from these findings.

Other recent experimental studies have used agonist probes to manipulate central 5-HT. Bond, Feizollah, and Lader (1995) reported that fenfluramine produced modest self-reported antiaggressive effects in males and females. Cherek, Spiga, and Creson (1995) found that eltoprazine, a putative $5-HT_{1A}$ and $5-HT_{1B}$ agonist, reduced aggressive responding during a laboratory task in five male participants. However, the drug also reduced responding on a topographically similar nonaggressive response option, raising the question of whether the drug has specific antiaggressive effects or merely suppresses ongoing behavior.

In general, experimental studies have provided qualified evidence that manipulating central 5-HT alters aggressive behavior in humans, with changes in 5-HT functioning being inversely related to aggressive behavior. The effects found in experimental studies are modest, which may be due to the use of individuals without documented personality pathology or a significant history of aggressive behavior. However, some support for a causal role for serotonin functioning in the aggressive behavior of psychiatric patients is provided by controlled pharmacotherapy treatment studies (see Karper & Krystal, Chapter 41, this volume).

Potential Mechanisms for 5-HT and Aggression

Although a full consensus has not yet been reached, neurochemical, pharmacochallenge, and experimental studies provide evidence for an inverse relation between 5-HT activity and aggressive behavior in humans. How 5-HT activity influences aggressive behavior in humans, however, is not yet known. It has been proposed that decreases in serotonergic activity predispose an organism to engage in behaviors that are normally suppressed (e.g., Depue & Spoont, 1986). That is, serotonin appears to play a role in behavioral inhibition. This model has been expanded to include impulsive or reactive aggressive behavior, whereby reduced central 5-HT may predispose an organism to engage in aggressive responses that would otherwise be constrained (Coccaro, 1989).

Although reduced 5-HT activity may predispose an organism to aggress, the actual expression of aggressive behavior may depend on threat or provocation. Marks, O'Brien, and Paxinos (1977) observed that chemical lesioning of 5-HT neurons increased mouse-killing behavior in rats, an effect that was reduced when the rats were exposed to mice prior to the destruc-

tion of 5-HT neurons. Rats likely habituated to the presence of mice during the pre-exposure procedure, decreasing the provocative characteristics of this stimulus. Further support for the role of provocation in 5-HT associated aggression comes from a study of vervet monkeys placed on a tryptophan-depletion diet (Chamberlain, Ervin, Pihl, & Young, 1987). Male primates with central 5-HT reduced in this manner behaved aggressively primarily under provocative conditions (competition for food). In humans, 5-HT activity has been correlated primarily with impulsive violent behavior, presumably elicited by provocative contextual cues in the immediate social environment (Linnoila et al., 1983; Virkkunen et al., 1994). Additionally, attack or provocation appears to be necessary for eliciting aggressive behavior when 5-HT activity is experimentally decreased in humans (Cleare & Bond, 1995; Pihl et al., 1995). The results of these animal and human studies indicate that the effect of 5-HT on aggressive behavior may be moderated by provocation. That is, decreased 5-HT activity may heighten perception of, or responsivity to, provocation or attack. In the absence of provocative stimuli, decreased 5-HT functioning may have little effect on the level of aggressive behavior exhibited by humans (Smith et al., 1986). However, a complete understanding of how environmental events, cognitive processes, and neurotransmitter functioning interact in the expression of aggression awaits further study.

OTHER MONOAMINE NEUROTRANSMITTERS AND HUMAN AGGRESSION

Compared to serotonin, the relation between both dopamine and norepinephrine and human aggression is less clear. Some evidence for an inverse relation between dopamine and aggression in humans has been reported. Given that indexes of dopamine and 5-HT functioning are often positively correlated, it is not yet known whether dopamine activity affects aggression separately from 5-HT in humans. Studies of norepinephrine activity and human aggression have produced conflicting results. In adults, central and pharmacochallenge studies tend to support a positive relation between norepinephrine and aggressive behavior. In children, peripheral measures support an inverse relationship between norepinephrine and conduct problems.

Norepinephrine (NE)

The norepinephrine (NE) system has been hypothesized to affect both arousal and degree of sensitivity an organism displays toward the environment, which may prepare an organism to respond aggressively to novel or threatening environmental stimuli (Siever et al., 1991). Evidence for a preparatory role for NE in human aggression comes from positive correlations between NE indexes and questionnaire measures of sensation-seeking, extraversion, and risk-taking behaviors in humans (Buchsbaum, Muscettola, & Goodwin, 1981; Kuperman, Kramer, & Loney, 1988; Roy, DeJong, & Linnoila, 1989) and from animal data that show a positive correlation between NE activity and aggressive behavior (e.g., Higley et al., 1992). In humans, CSF MHPG (3-methoxy-4-hydroxyphenylglycol), a central NE metabolite, has been positively associated with a history of aggression in males (G. L. Brown et al., 1979). However, a relation between MHPG and aggression in humans has not always been found (G. L. Brown et al., 1982; Kruesi et al., 1992; Lidberg et al., 1985; Roy et al., 1988; Virkkunen, Nuutila, Goodwin, & Linnoila, 1987).

Few pharmacochallenge investigations of NE functioning and aggression have been conducted. Coccaro et al. (1991) found a positive correlation between growth hormone response to challenge with clonidine (an alpha-2 NE agonist) and irritability in personality-disordered patients and normal controls. Growth hormone response was not correlated with prolactin response to fenfluramine challenge in these subjects, indicating that the effects of NE on irritability may be independent of those exerted by serotonin on aggressive behavior.

In contrast to the perspective that NE activity should facilitate aggressive behavior due to its sensitizing effects, it has also been proposed that the anxiogenic effects associated with elevated NE should act as an inhibitor of aggressive behavior (Rogeness, Javors, Maas, & Macedo, 1989; Rogeness, Javors, & Pliszka, 1992). Evidence for this position comes primarily from studies of children using peripheral measures of NE functioning. Indexes of NE activity have been positively associated with behavioral inhibition in children (Kagan, Reznick, & Snidman, 1987), and other studies have demonstrated that children classified as high in conduct symptoms and low in anxiety symptoms tend to have lower peripheral MHPG (Pliszka, Rogeness, & Medrano, 1988), and lower dopamine-β-hydroxylase (DβH), an enzyme involved in the production of NE and a putative index of NE activity (Rogeness et al., 1989). Similar results have been reported in a study of ADHD boys, in which a subgroup with conduct disorder (CD) behavior problems was found to have lower DβH compared with boys diagnosed as ADHD without CD and matched controls (Bowden et al., 1987). Other studies, however, have failed to find a relation between conduct disorder and peripheral measures of NE functioning in children (Halperin et al., 1994; Pliszka, Rogeness, & Medrano, 1988; Pliszka, Rogeness, Renner et al., 1988).

Dopamine (DA)

Dopamine (DA) is considered to play a role in behavioral activation, reward mechanisms, and goal-directed behavior. Results from animal studies indicate that increased DA functioning is usually associated with increases in shock-induced or defensive aggression (see Netter & Rammsayer, 1991; Spoont, 1992, for reviews). It also has been suggested that DA activity may be positively associated with aggressive or impulsive behavior in humans (e.g., Rogeness et al., 1992). Results of central neurochemical studies of humans, however, generally parallel those of serotonin, indicating that DA activity is inversely correlated with aggressive behavior. For example, CSF homovanillac acid (HVA), a dopamine metabolite, has been found to be negatively correlated with a life history of aggression (Limson et al., 1991). In addition, low levels of CSF HVA appear to discriminate recidivist violent criminal offenders from nonrecidivists (Virkkunen, DeJong, Bartko, Goodwin, & Linnoila, 1989) and incarcerated offenders with antisocial personality disorder from those with paranoid or passive-aggressive personality disorders (Linnoila et al., 1983). No adequate theoretical frame-

work exists to explain the disparate findings from the human and animal literature. However, serotonin functioning may control dopamine turnover in humans (Ågren, Mefford, Rudorfer, Linnoila, & Potter, 1986), which may account for the similar findings for serotonin and dopamine neurochemical studies.

LIMITATIONS AND FUTURE DIRECTIONS

The molecular mechanisms by which neurotransmitter systems influence the expression of human aggression are not yet known. The observation that a particular index of neurotransmitter activity is blunted or elevated in aggressive individuals provides little information in this regard. Using 5-HT as an example, the observation that CSF 5-HIAA is reduced in impulsively aggressive individuals could have several meanings at the molecular level. It could indicate a decrease in the rate of synthesis or release of 5-HT into the synapse. Alternatively, it could indicate a reduction in 5-HT neurons. 5-HT activity is also inextricably linked with the functioning of other neurotransmitter systems (e.g., GABA, DA). Given these complexities, a full understanding of the role of neurotransmitter functioning in human aggressive behavior at the molecular level will depend on future investigations.

The focus of human studies of aggression has been on the monoamine neurotransmitters, despite promising preclinical data that implicate other neurotransmitter systems (e.g., acetylcholine, GABA). This does not mean that other systems play a trivial role in the expression of human aggression. Research efforts are frequently guided by existing findings, personal experience and expediency, and the preferences of funding agencies. Studies of GABA and aggression, which have been fruitful in lower animal species, may prove as valuable in humans.

At the micro level, work remains to elucidate the roles of specific pre- and postsynaptic receptors, as well as the combined effects of different neurotransmitter systems, on human aggression. At the macro level, the potential moderating effects of contextual variables, such as provocation, have not been systematically studied. For this reason, it is not yet known how environmental events and changes in neurotransmitter functioning interact to influence aggressive behavior in humans. Laboratory methodologies have been used to examine the combined role of situational variables and other biological variables (e.g., testosterone, ethanol) on human aggressive behavior (Berman, Gladue, & Taylor, 1993; Taylor & Leonard, 1983). If adopted for use in future studies, such laboratory approaches may help clarify the role of neurotransmitter activity in human aggression. Finally, no longitudinal study of neurotransmitter functioning and aggressive behavior from childhood to adulthood has been conducted. Although costly, such studies would provide information about how the organization and activation of neurotransmitter functioning changes across the life span, the role of early childhood environment in these changes, and how these factors affect the development and maintenance of aggressive behaviors.

The results of the investigations discussed in this chapter should not be interpreted to mean that neurotransmitter abnormalities are responsible for all forms of human aggression, or that aggressive behavior should be universally treated with agents that alter neurotransmitter activity. No biologic factor has yet been shown to be either a necessary or a sufficient cause of aggressive behavior. Indeed, many forms of violent behavior, such as premeditated violence, seem to be unrelated to abnormalities in neurotransmitter functioning (e.g., Linnoila et al., 1983). Although studies of neurotransmitter functioning provide one avenue to understanding human aggression, economic, political, and cultural factors are clearly important in the development and expression of violent behavior, perhaps more so than individual differences in biology.

REFERENCES

Ågren, H., Mefford, I. N., Rudorfer, M. V., Linnoila, M., & Potter, W. Z. (1986). Interacting neurotransmitter systems. A nonexperimental approach to the 5HIAA-HVA correlation in human CSF. *Journal of Psychiatry Research, 20,* 175–193.

Anderson, G. M., Freedman, D. X., & Cohen, D. J. (1987). Whole blood serotonin in autistic and normal subjects. *Journal of Child Psychology and Psychiatry, 28,* 885–900.

Belfrage, H., Lidberg, L., & Oreland, L. (1992). Platelet monoamine oxidase activity in mentally disordered violent offenders. *Acta Psychiatrica Scandinavica, 85,* 218–221.

Berman, M., Gladue, B., & Taylor, S. (1993). The effects of hormones, Type A behavior pattern, and provocation on aggression in men. *Motivation and Emotion, 17,* 125–138.

Birmaher, B., Stanley, M., Greenhill, L., Twomey, J., Gavrilescu, A., & Rabinovich, H. (1990). Platelet imipramine binding in children and adolescents with impulsive behavior. *Journal of the American Academy of Child and Adolescent Psychiatry, 29,* 914–918.

Blumensohn, R., Ratzoni, G., Weizman, A., Israeli, M., Greuner, N., Apter, A., Tyano, S., & Biegon, A. (1995). Reduction in serotonin 5HT$_2$ receptor binding on platelets of delinquent adolescents. *Psychopharmacology, 118,* 354–356.

Bond, A. J., Feizollah, S., & Lader, M. H. (1995). The effects of d–Fenfluramine on mood and performance, and on neuroendocrine indicators of 5-HT function. *Journal of Psychopharmacology, 9,* 1–8.

Bowden, C. L., Deutsch, C. K., & Swanson, J. M. (1987). Plasma dopamine-β-hydroxylase and platelet monoamine oxidase in attention deficit disorder and conduct disorder. *Journal of the American Academy of Child and Adolescent Psychiatry, 27,* 171–174.

Brown, C. S., Kent, T. A., Bryant, S. G., Gavedon, R. M., Campbell, J. L., Felthous, A. R., Barratt, E. S., & Rose, R. M. (1989). Blood platelet uptake of serotonin in episodic aggression. *Psychiatry Research, 27,* 5–12.

Brown, G. L., Ebert, M. H., Goyer, P. F., Jimerson, D. C., Klein, W. J., Bunney, W. E., & Goodwin, F. K. (1982). Aggression, suicide, and serotonin: Relationships to CSF amine metabolites. *American Journal of Psychiatry, 139,* 741–746.

Brown, G. L., Goodwin, F. K., Ballenger, J. C., Goyer, P. F., & Major, L. F. (1979). Aggression in humans correlates with cerebrospinal fluid amine metabolites. *Psychiatry Research, 1,* 131–139.

Buchsbaum, M. S., Muscettola, G., & Goodwin, F. K. (1981). Urinary MHPG, stress response, personality factors, and somatosensory evoked potentials in normal subjects and patients with major affective disorders. *Neuropsychobiology, 7,* 212–224.

Castrogiovanni, P., Capone, M. R., Maremmani, I., & Marazziti, D. (1994). Platelet serotonergic markers and aggressive behaviour in healthy subjects. *Biological Psychiatry, 29,* 105–107.

Chamberlain, B., Ervin, F. R., Pihl, R. O., & Young, S. N. (1987). The effect of raising or lowering tryptophan levels on aggression in vervet monkeys. *Pharmacology, Biochemistry, & Behavior, 28,* 503–510.

Cherek, D. R., Spiga, R., & Creson, D. L. (1995). Acute effects of eltoprazine on aggressive and point-maintained responding of normal male participants: Phase I study. *Experimental and Clinical Psychopharmacology, 3,* 287–293.

Cleare, A. J., & Bond, A. J. (1995). The effect of tryptophan depletion and enhancement on subjective and behavioural aggression in normal male subjects. *Psychopharmacology, 118,* 72–81.

Coccaro, E. F. (1989). Central serotonin and impulsive aggression. *British Journal of Psychiatry, 155* (Suppl. 8), 52–62.

Coccaro, E. F. (1992). Impulsive aggression and central serotonergic system function in humans: An example of a dimensional brain-behavior relationship. *International Clinical Psychopharmacology, 7,* 3–12.

Coccaro, E. F., Gabriel, S., & Siever, L. J. (1990). Buspirone challenge: Preliminary evidence for a role for central 5-HT$_{1a}$ receptor function in impulsive aggressive behavior in humans. *Psychopharmacology Bulletin, 26,* 393–405.

Coccaro, E. F., & Kavoussi, R. J. (1994). Neuropsychopharmacologic challenge in biological psychiatry. *Clinical Chemistry, 40,* 319–327.

Coccaro, E. F., Lawrence, T., Trestman, R., Gabriel, S., Klar, H. M., & Siever, L. J. (1991). Growth hormone responses to intravenous clonidine challenge correlate with behavioral irritability in psychiatric patients and healthy volunteers. *Psychiatry Research, 39,* 129–139.

Coccaro, E. F., Siever, L. J., Klar, H. M., Maurer, G., Cochrane, K., Cooper, T. B., Mohs, R. C., & Davis, K. L. (1989). Serotonergic studies in patients with affective and personality disorders: Correlates with suicidal and impulsive aggressive behavior. *Archives of General Psychiatry, 46,* 587–599.

Coccaro, E. F., Silverman, J. M., Klar, H. K., Horvath, T. B., & Siever, L. J. (1994). Familial correlates of reduced central serotonergic system function in patients with personality disorders. *Archives of General Psychiatry, 51,* 318–324.

Cook, E. H., Fletcher, K. E., Wainwright, M., Marks, N., Yan, S., & Leventhal, B. L. (1994). Primary structure of human platelet serotonin 5-HT$_{2A}$ receptor: Identity with frontal cortex serotonin 5-HT$_{2A}$ receptor. *Journal of Neurochemistry, 63,* 465–469.

Depue, R. A., & Spoont, M. R. (1986). Conceptualizing a serotonin trait: A behavioral dimension of constraint. *Annals of the New York Academy of Sciences, 487,* 47–62.

Fishbein, D. H., Lozovsky, D., & Jaffe, J. H. (1989). Impulsivity, aggression, and neuroendocrine responses to serotonergic stimulation in substance abusers. *Biological Psychiatry, 25,* 1049–1066.

Galvin, M., Shekhar, A., Simon, J., Stilwell, B., Ten Eyck, R., Laite, G., Karwisch, G., & Blix, S. (1991). Low dopamine-beta-hydroxylase: A biological sequela of abuse and neglect? *Psychiatry Research, 39,* 1–11.

Gardner, D. L., Lucas, P. B., & Cowdry, R. W. (1990). CSF metabolites in borderline personality disorder compared with normal controls. *Biological Psychiatry, 28,* 247–254.

Gerra, G., Caccavari, R., Delsignore, R., Passeri, M., Fertonani Affini, G., Maestri, D., Monica, C., & Brambilla, F. (1993). Parental divorce and neuroendocrine changes in adolescents. *Acta Psychiatrica Scandinavica, 87,* 350–354.

Hallman, J., Knorring, L. V., Edman, G., & Oreland, L. (1991). Personality traits and platelet monoamine oxidase activity in alcoholic women. *Addictive Behaviors, 16,* 533–541.

Halperin, J. M., Sharma, V., Siever, L. J., Schwartz, S. T., Matier, K., Wornell, G., & Newcorn, J. H. (1994). Serotonergic function in aggressive and nonaggressive boys with attention deficit hyperactivity disorder. *American Journal of Psychiatry, 151,* 243–248.

Hanna, G., Yuwiler, A., & Cantwell, D. P. (1991). Whole blood serotonin in juvenile obsessive-compulsive disorder. *Biological Psychiatry, 29,* 738–744.

Higley, J. D., Mehlman, P. T., Taub, D. M., Higley, S. B., Suomi, S. J., Linnoila, M., & Vickers, J. H. (1992). Cerebrospinal fluid monoamine and adrenal correlates of aggression in free-ranging rhesus monkeys. *Archives of General Psychiatry, 49,* 436–441.

Higley, J. D., Suomi, S. J., & Linnoila, M. (1991). CSF monoamine metabolite concentrations vary according to age, rearing, and sex, and are influenced by the stressor of social separation in rhesus monkeys. *Psychopharmacology, 103,* 551–556.

Kagan, J., Reznick, J. S., & Snidman, N. (1987). The physiology and psychology of behavioral inhibition in children. *Child Development, 58,* 1459–1473.

Kraemer, G. W., Ebert, M. H., Schmidt, D. E., & McKinney, W. T. (1989). A longitudinal study of the effect of different social rearing conditions on cerebrospinal fluid norepinephrine and biogenic amine metabolites in rhesus monkeys. *Neuropsychopharmacology, 2,* 175–189.

Kruesi, M. J. P., Hibbs, E. D., Zahn, T. P., Keysor, C. S., Hamburger, S. D., Bartko, J. J., & Rapoport, J. L. (1992). A 2-year prospective follow-up study of children and adolescents with disruptive behavior disorders. *Archives of General Psychiatry, 49,* 429–435.

Kruesi, M. J., Rapoport, J. L., Hamburger, S., Hibbs, E., & Potter, W. Z. (1990). Cerebrospinal fluid monoamine metabolites, aggression, and impulsivity in disruptive behavior disorders of children and adolescents. *Archives of General Psychiatry, 47,* 419–426.

Kuperman, S., Kramer, J., & Loney, J. (1988). Enzyme activity and behavior in hyperactive children grown up. *Biological Psychiatry, 24,* 375–383.

Lidberg, L., Tuck, J. R., Åsberg, M., Scalia-Tomba, G. P., & Bertilsson, L. (1985). Homicide, suicide, and CSF 5-HIAA. *Acta Psychiatrica Scandinavica, 71,* 230–236.

Limson, R., Goldman, D., Roy, A., Lamparski, D., Ravitz, B., Adinoff, B., Linnoila, M. (1991). Personality and cerebrospinal fluid monoamine metabolites in alcoholics and controls. *Archives of General Psychiatry, 48,* 437–441.

Linnoila, M., Virkkunen, M., Scheinin, M., Nuutila, A., Rimon, R., & Goodwin, F. K. (1983). Low cerebrospinal fluid 5-hydroxyindoleacetic acid concentration differentiates impulsive from nonimpulsive violent behavior. *Life Sciences, 33,* 2609–2614.

Mann, J. J., McBride, P. A., Anderson, G. M., & Mieczkowski, T. A. (1992). Platelet and whole blood serotonin content in depressed inpatients: Correlations with acute and lifetime psychopathology. *Biological Psychiatry, 32,* 243–257.

Mann, J. J., McBride, P. A., Brown, R. P., Linnoila, M., Leon, A. C., DeMeo, M., Mieczkowski, T., Myers, J. E., & Stanley, M. (1992). Relationship between central and peripheral serotonin indexes in depressed and suicidal psychiatric inpatients. *Archives of General Psychiatry, 49,* 442–446.

Marks, P. C., O'Brien, M., & Paxinos, G. (1977). 5,7-DHT-induced muricide: Inhibition as a result of exposure of rats to mice. *Brain Research, 135,* 383–388.

Miczek, K. A., Weerts, E., Haney, M., & Tidey, J. (1994). Neurobiological mechanisms controlling aggression: Preclinical developments for pharmacotherapeutic interventions. *Neuroscience and Biobehavioral Reviews, 18,* 97–110.

Modai, I., Apter, A., Meltzer, M., Tyano, S., Walevski, A., & Jerushalmy, Z. (1989). Serotonin uptake by platelets of suicidal and aggressive adolescent psychiatric inpatients. *Neuropsychobiology, 21,* 9–13.

Moffitt, T. E., Brammer, G. L., Caspi, A., Fawcett, J. P., Raleigh, M., Yuwiler, A., & Silva, P. (in press). Whole blood serotonin relates to violence in an epidemiological study. *Biological Psychiatry.*

Moss, H. B., Yao, J. K., & Panzak, G. L. (1990). Serotonergic responsivity and behavioral dimensions in antisocial personality disorder with substance abuse. *Biological Psychiatry, 28,* 325–338.

Netter, P., & Rammsayer, T. (1991). Reactivity to dopaminergic drugs and aggression related personality traits. *Personality and Individual Differences, 12,* 1009–1017.

Nielsen, D. A., Goldman, D., Virkkunen, M., Tokola, R., Rawlings, R., & Linnoila, M. (1994). Suicidality and 5-hydroxyindoleacetic acid concentration associated with tryptophan hydroxylase polymorphism. *Archives of General Psychiatry, 51,* 34–35.

O'Keane, V., Moloney, E., O'Neill, H., O'Connor, A., Smith, C., & Dinan, T. G. (1992). Blunted prolactin responses to *d*-Fenfluramine in sociopathy: Evidence for subsensitivity of central serotonergic function. *British Journal of Psychiatry, 160,* 643–646.

Pihl, R. O., Young, S., Harden, P., Plotnick, S., Chamberlain, B., & Ervin, F. R. (1995). Acute effect of altered tryptophan levels and alcohol on aggression in normal human males. *Psychopharmacology, 119,* 353–360.

Pliszka, S. R., Rogeness, G. A., & Medrano, M. A. (1988). DBH, MHPG, and MAO in children with depressive, anxiety, and conduct disorders: Relationship to diagnosis and symptom ratings. *Psychiatry Research, 24,* 35–44.

Pliszka, S. R., Rogeness, G. A., Renner, P., Sherman, J., & Broussard, T. (1988). Plasma neurochemistry in juvenile offenders. *Journal of the American Academy of Child and Adolescent Psychiatry, 27,* 588–594.

Rogeness, G. A., Javors, M. A., Maas, J. W., & Macedo, C. A. (1989). Catecholamines and diagnoses in children. *Journal of the American Academy of Child and Adolescent Psychiatry, 29,* 234–241.

Rogeness, G. A., Javors, M. A., & Pliszka, S. R. (1992). Neurochemistry and child and adolescent psychiatry. *Journal of the American Academy of Child and Adolescent Psychiatry, 31,* 765–781.

Roy, A., Adinoff, B., & Linnoila, M. (1988). Acting out hostility in normal volunteers: Negative correlation with levels of 5HIAA in cerebrospinal fluid. *Psychiatry Research, 24,* 187–194.

Roy, A., DeJong, J., & Linnoila, M. (1989). Extraversion in pathological gamblers: Correlates with indexes of noradrenergic function. *Archives of General Psychiatry, 46,* 679–861.

Siever, L. J., Kahn, R. S., Lawlor, B. A., Trestman, R. L., Lawrence, T. L., & Coccaro, E. F. (1991). II. Critical issues in defining the role of serotonin in psychiatric disorders. *Pharmacological Reviews, 43,* 509–525.

Smith, S. E., Pihl, R. O., Young, S. N., & Ervin, F. R. (1986). Elevation and reduction of plasma tryptophan and their effects on aggression and perceptual sensitivity in normal males. *Aggressive Behavior, 12,* 393–407.

Soloff, P. H., Cornelius, J., Foglia, J., George, A., & Perel, J. M. (1991). Platelet MAO in borderline personality disorder. *Biological Psychiatry, 29,* 499–502.

Spoont, M. R. (1992). Modulatory role of serotonin in neural information processing: Implications for human psychopathology. *Psychological Bulletin, 112,* 330–350.

Stoff, D. M., Friedman, E., Pollock, L., Vitiello, B., Kendall, P. C., & Bridger, W. H. (1989). Elevated platelet MAO is related to impulsivity in disruptive behavior disorders. *Journal of the American Academy of Child and Adolescent Psychiatry, 28,* 754–760.

Stoff, D. M., Goldman, W., Bridger, W. H., Jain, A. K., & Pylypiw, A. (1990). No correlation between platelet imipramine binding and CSF 5-HIAA in neurosurgical patients. *Psychiatry Research, 33*, 323–326.

Stoff, D. M., Ieni, J., Friedman, E., Bidger, W. H., Pollock, L., & Vitiello, B. (1991). Platelet ^{3}H-imipramine binding, serotonin uptake, and plasma ∞_1 acid glycoprotein in disruptive behavior disorders. *Biological Psychiatry, 29*, 494–498.

Stoff, D. M., Pasatiempo, A. P., Yeung, J., Cooper, T. B., Bridger, W. H., & Rabinovich, H. (1992). Neuroendocrine responses to challenge with *dl*-fenfluramine and aggression in disruptive behavior disorders of children and adolescents. *Psychiatry Research, 43*, 263–276.

Stoff, D. M., Pollock, L., Vitiello, B., Behar, D., & Bridger (1987). Reduction of (^{3}H)-imipramine binding sites on platelets of conduct-disordered children. *Neuropsychopharmacology, 1*, 55–62.

Taylor, S., & Leonard, K. (1983). Alcohol and human physical aggression. In R. Geen & E. Donnerstein (Eds.), *Aggression: Theoretical and empirical reviews: Vol. 2. Issues in research* (pp. 77–101). New York: Academic Press.

Virkkunen, M., DeJong, J., Bartko, J., Goodwin, F. K., & Linnoila, M. (1989). Relationship of psychological variables to recidivism in violent offenders and impulsive fire setters. *Archives of General Psychiatry, 46*, 600–603.

Virkkunen, M., Nuutila, A., Goodwin, F. K., & Linnoila, M. (1987). Cerebrospinal fluid monoamine metabolite levels in male arsonists. *Archives of General Psychiatry, 44*, 241–247.

Virkkunen, M., Rawlings, R., Tokola, R., Poland, R. E., Guidotti, A., Nemeroff, C., Bissette, G., Kalogeras, K., Karonen, S., & Linnoila, M. (1994). CSF biochemistries, glucose metabolism, and diurnal activity rhythms in alcoholic, violent offenders, fire setters, and healthy volunteers. *Archives of General Psychiatry, 51*, 20–27.

Wetzler, S., Kahn, R. S., Asnis, G. M., Korn, M., & van Praag, H. M. (1991). Serotonin receptor sensitivity and aggression. *Psychiatry Research, 37*, 271–279.

Wood, P. L., Suranyi-Cadotte, B. E., Nair, N. P. V., LaFaulle, F., & Schwartz, G. (1983). Lack of association between ^{3}H-imipramine binding sites and uptake of serotonin in control, depressed, and schizophrenic patients. *Neuropsychopharmacology, 22*, 1211–1214.

Young, S. N., Ervin, F. R., Pihl, R. O., & Finn, P. (1989). Biochemical aspects of tryptophan depletion in primates. *Psychopharmacology, 98*, 508–511.

Young, S. N., & Gauthier, S. (1981). Effect of tryptophan administration on tryptophan, 5-hydroxyindoleacetic acid, and indoleacetic acid in human lumbar and cisternal cerebrospinal fluid. *Journal of Neurology, Neurosurgery and Psychiatry, 44*, 323–327.

CHAPTER 29

Hormonal Aspects of Aggression and Violence

PAUL F. BRAIN and ELIZABETH J. SUSMAN

The links between endocrine secretions (hormones) and human violence are much more subtle and complex than had been thought. A formerly widely held view was that many forms of human hostility were consequences of "raging hormones" and could be treated by manipulations that included castration or therapy with antiandrogens (compounds that block "male" sex hormones), estrogens ("female" sex hormones), or progesterone derivatives. Clinically, excessive hostility was linked, in certain cases, to perinatal exposure to sex steroids or to the adult development of an endocrine disorder. It should be self-evident that there are considerable dangers in seeking to equate *all* examples of human aggression to medical disorders. If disordered hormones have roles, they are likely to be of relevance to only *some* forms of interpersonal behavior, not group activities such as riots and wars, which clearly have a sociocultural basis.

There are, however, dangers in assuming that hormonal factors have negligible roles in all human behavior. The fact that one cannot establish that hormones *cause* human aggression does not suggest that one should seek complete explanations of violence in other biological systems (genes or the brain), in early social experiences, or in cultural values. A case-by-case approach is needed to explain the complex interactions between the genetic and physiological characteristics of the individual and the environmental factors influencing individual development. Although hormones as causal influences predominate in the existing literature on antisocial and violent behavior, the effects of behavior and affective experiences on hormone concentrations are now also considered (Booth, Shelley, Mazur, Tharp, & Kittok, 1989; Brooks-Gunn, Graber, & Paikoff, 1994; Mazur, Booth, & Dabbs, 1992; Susman, Worrall, Murowchick, Frobose, & Schwab, 1996).

Reciprocal influences of hormones and behavior are considered but not generally examined in current research. A viewing of hormones as *consequences* as well as *causes* of behavior merits attention in studies of hormone-behavior interactions across the life span. This integration is needed as organizational influences during prenatal development and activational influences throughout development are purely biological components of antisocial and violent behavior. Clearly, such complex behaviors are also influenced by other factors.

DEFINING THE VARIABLES AND THE NATURE OF THE RELATIONSHIP

Recent literature reviews reveal a more complex but more useful explanation of antisocial and violent behavior. Human aggression is a much more difficult and nebulous concept (theoretical construct) than was formerly believed. Further, hormones clearly can no longer be regarded as chemicals that simply switch behavior on or off. In specific cases, they change the probability that certain verbal and physical responses that can be labeled "aggression" will be generated in particular situations by individuals with specific accumulated experiences. When they have a role, hormones are more like the risk factors involved in, for example, coronary heart disease than the causes of specific diseases. There are obvious parallels with the attempts to relate human aggression to factors such as alcohol ingestion (Brain, 1986). Having said this, there is good evidence that a range of hormones act on human behavioral potential prenatally (the so-called organizing actions), at puberty (a developmental stage characterized by profound endocrine and behavioral changes), and in adulthood (the so-called activational effects) to alter levels of human aggressive behavior. Our review focuses on the roles of hormones on aggression in these three periods of human life. It outlines the essentials of the modern syntheses of the hormone-human aggression data (e.g., Brain, 1994a, 1994b) but updates the account with recently published material.

A major point that should be reiterated is that aggression and violence are concepts and not actual entities, and this makes definitions elusive. Behaviors falling under these headings generally will have the potential for harm or damage to their target, be intentional (rather than accidental) acts, often involve arousal, and be clearly aversive to the victim or recipient of the act. It is further acknowledged that aggression may serve a variety of different functions in infrahuman animals. Brain and Haug (1992) examined attempts to link hormones to aggression in rats and mice (the majority of studies) and concluded that the situations used to assess aggression actually tap a diverse range of motivations including offense, defense, and predation. Different tests showed varying responses to common manipulations of sex and adrenal steroids, confirming that these paradigms do not measure the same thing. This means that there will *not* be a distinct endocrinology of all forms of aggression. These animal models do elucidate the ways in which particular hormonal factors may be involved in mechanisms (direct and indirect) modulating the probability of eliciting (in response to particular stimuli) classes of behavior in specific environments. Many rodent models of aggression are, however, based on clearly adaptive behaviors, concerned with competition for mates, territory, food, or social status, whereas many examples of human aggression result from the breakdown of social conventions (indeed, some involve hyper-defensiveness). Indeed, predatory responses in animals may have some affinities with human psychopathic behavior as both are characterized by low levels of emotional arousal. In addition, defensive behaviors have resonance to some activities evident in disturbed individuals in clinical settings.

The situations linking hormones to aggression in humans are at least as confused as in infrahuman animals. Dent (1983) pointed out some of the difficulties of relating aggressive behavior in our own species to endocrine functioning. He also maintained that there was often an inadequate defining of aggression, an overreliance on the Buss-Durkee Hostility Inventory, and a failure to appreciate the complex secretory patterns of hormones. Assays based on a single blood sample are of very limited utility. These conclusions have been amplified by Brain (1994b) and others (Chaiken, Chaiken, & Rhodes, 1994) who emphasized the heterogeneous nature of human aggression and violence, such that the same crime (e.g., assault and battery, homicide, or verbal aggression) may have several etiologies.

Perhaps the most useful definition of violent human behavior is that offered by the Panel on the Understanding and Control of Violent Behavior (Reiss & Roth, 1993), namely, "behaviors by individuals that intentionally threaten, attempt or inflict physical harm on others" (p. 2). This definition concentrates more on physical acts than on verbal threats or responses and is still open to the charge that the same event can be (and often is) viewed differently by the various participants and external observers of actions. Behavior is a result of complex interactions between biological factors (including hormones), situational determinants (the context), and accumulated experiences (learning). These factors are difficult to disentangle, especially in the case of antisocial and violent behavior. The major components of the endocrine system that are generally linked to human aggression are the hormones associated with the gonads and the adrenal cortex, although other endocrine factors (notably the thyroid and the adrenal medulla) have been correlated with some direct and indirect hostile actions.

Taking up Dent's (1983) criticisms of the literature, it is important to know

1. whether a hormone titer is increasing or decreasing and whether it is elevated or depressed with relation to a baseline,

2. the distribution of the hormone in the different body compartments,

3. the population sizes of hormone receptors and their degree of occupation by bound hormone,

4. interactions with other hormones, and

5. whether the particular endocrine factor shows rhythms of change related to season, time of day, or menstrual cycle.

Brain (1989) has presented a model of the relationship between hormones and behavior, emphasizing the following:

1. Endocrine glands "crosstalk" or interact with each other.

2. Hormones may be metabolically changed to other chemicals in a variety of locations, providing a number of discrete messages.

3. Hormones can target the CNS, sensory systems, social cue producers (e.g., the body surface or odor-producing glands), or other endocrine glands to produce their effects.

4. These varied targets will change a number of behavioral elements that interact in a complex way.

5. The experiences derived from the behavioral output provide feedback to influence the endocrine target's metabolic conversion processes and its consequent activities.

The Brain (1994b) review separately provides data on nonprimates, infrahuman primates, and humans, but this present account is largely limited to humans.

PRENATAL ORGANIZATIONAL INFLUENCES

Good evidence from studies on rats, mice, and primates indicates that the presence of sex steroids in prenatal life subtly modifies the brain circuitry from the basic female to that of the male condition. As a result of exposure to sex steroids, actual neural architecture appears to be changed, as well as populations of hormonal binding sites and the brain's subsequent responsiveness to hormones of the hypothalamic-pituitary-gonadal system. The classic experiment on the effects of hormones on behavior consisted of administering gonadal steroids (estrogens, progesterone, or testosterone) to pregnant mothers and then observing the sexual behavior of male and female guinea pigs after the attainment of adulthood (Phoenix, Goy, Gerall, & Young, 1959). The hypothesis was that gonadal hormones, androgens or estrogens, reaching animals during prenatal life, have an *organizing action* that would be reflected in the character of adult sexual behavior. Organizational influences refer to major structural changes that occur during pre- and perinatal development. In the postnatal period, gonadal hormones are responsible for bringing to expression the patterns of behavior previously organized by genes.

In humans, the hormone effects theory states that the presence of gonadal steroids during prenatal life causes structural and organizational changes that masculinize and defeminize the brain, a process referred to as *androgenization* (Meyer-Bahlberg et al., 1995) that results in sexual dimorphisms in behavior (where the male and the female show distinct behavioral patterns). A wide repertoire of reproductive and nonreproductive behaviors is presumed to be influenced by gonadal steroid–induced sexual dimorphisms. Nonreproductive behaviors considered to be affected by prenatal organizational influences include spatial cognition, sex-typed behavior (e.g., activity level), and sexual orientation. The research approach adopted for detecting organizational influences on behavior consists of showing the degree of masculine or feminine responses on cognitive or behavioral measures. The samples generally consist of individuals exposed to atypical concentrations of endogenous (e.g., changed by an endocrine disorder) or exogenously administered hormones (injected or implanted) during prenatal development (Hines & Shipley, 1984; Reinisch, Ziemba-Davis, & Sanders, 1991). Sexual dimorphisms in spatial cognition have been a popular focus in studies of early influences of androgenization. Greater androgenization in brain development may explain the generally reported advantage of males in spatial abilities in both atypical populations and individuals undergoing normative development.

Prenatal hormone influences on sex-typed behavior and sexual orientation were first examined by Money and Ehrhardt (1972), who reported more tomboy behavior in girls exposed to excessive androgens prenatally than in nonexposed counterparts. Well-designed studies have looked at the effects of prenatal exposure to high concentrations of androgens via the mother's congenital adrenal hyperplasia (a condition in which the mother's adrenal gland is hyperactive) on childhood sex-typed activity and playmate preferences (Berenbaum & Hines, 1992; Berenbaum & Snyder, 1995). These childhood behaviors may predict later gender orientation. Girls exposed to excessive androgens would be expected to display more masculine sex-typed behavior and to prefer male playmates. The hypothesis was supported in preschool children for sex-typed behavior but not for playmate preference. Early androgen exposure appears to have a major effect on childhood boy-typical activity preference (Berenbaum & Snyder, 1995). Girls from mothers with congenital adrenal hyperplasia preferred to play with boys' toys, but early androgen exposure did not influence playmate preference. Girls did not prefer to play with boys. The authors conclude that hormone influences on sexual orientation are complex and in need of further study.

In studies attempting to link prenatal hormones' effects and behavior, it must be recognized that there are multiple sociocultural influences on behavior in addition to those attributable to hormones. For instance, the validity of prenatal influences on sexual dimorphic spatial cognition is questionable because gender differences exist even before puberty when differences should be most pronounced because of the activational influence of gonadal steroids at this time (Linn & Petersen, 1985). Socialization processes can contribute to or override the influence of hormones on behavior at multiple points in development. For each succeeding year of life, socialization influences may have more pronounced effects on cognition and behavior than during early development.

PUBERTAL INFLUENCES

In terms of their effects around puberty, there have been numerous claims relating gonadal hormones to "rebellious attitude." It should be noted that Hays (1981) concludes the following:

1. Mood changes produced by hormones (including factors unrelated to the gonadal system) may be consequences of the instigation of drives with no socially acceptable outlets in young people.

2. Development may involve changes in behavioral sensitivities to hormones as well as changes in hormones per se.

3. Circadian rhythms are important considerations in relating hormones and behavior at puberty as hormonal concentrations may covary with moods and behaviors.

4. Interactions between hormones may prove more important than titers of single hormones.

Gonadal steroids in postpubertal male and female mammals bring to expression the patterns of behavior previously organized or determined by genetic and experiential factors. In addition to the direct effects, gonadal hormones also may influence behavior indirectly by affecting somatic development primarily via the development of secondary sexual characteristics at puberty (Meyer-Bahlburg et al., 1995; Petersen & Taylor, 1980). The existing literature tends to focus on activational (as opposed to organizational) influences of hormones on healthy child and adolescent behavior.

Previous reviews of hormones and violence have not considered the notion that antisocial behavior, emotions, and cognition are linked. These three behavioral components, as well as hormone concentrations, change rapidly during puberty. The activational influence of hormones at puberty is a basis for the storm and stress theory of adolescence (Hall, 1904). Although the hypothesis that pubertal hormones affect antisocial behavior has been around for decades, actual concentrations of hormones in adolescents and problem behaviors have only recently been examined concurrently. In the last 2 decades, circulating concentrations of hormones have begun to be examined in studies of activational influences of these factors in healthy adolescent samples (see Buchanan, Eccles, & Becker, 1992; Susman & Petersen, 1992, for reviews). Adults were generally the focus in previous studies, and behaviors examined tended to be aggressive or antisocial in nature (Archer, 1991). The addition of studies of adolescents is important for theoretical reasons. Adolescence is the developmental period when hormones may be expected to be related to behavior because of the activational influences of rising hormones around puberty. Adolescence is also the time when antisocial behavior and delinquency increases. Thus, androgens have been considered an etiological factor in this rise of antisocial behavior in young adolescents. The behaviors included in studies of the impact of hormones on antisocial behavior and aggression have been increased in breadth as it is evident that emotions and antisocial behavior may be developmental precursors to antisocial and violent behavior. The extended range of behaviors includes problem behaviors and conduct disorders (Constantino et al., 1993; Scerbo & Kolko, 1994), emotions (Brooks-Gunn & Warren, 1989; Susman, Dorn, & Chrousos, 1991; Susman et al., 1985), and health behaviors (smoking; Bauman, Foshee, Koch, Haley, & Downton, 1989). The age-diverse samples and the range of behaviors in existing studies increase the difficulty of making generalizations about hormone-behavior interactions across studies and developmental periods. Nonetheless, a strength of the last decade of hormone-behavior research with adolescents is that the hormonal profile and behavior are assessed simultaneously, facilitating more definitive conclusions regarding the reciprocal influences of hormone-behavior interactions.

AGGRESSIVE AND ANTISOCIAL BEHAVIOR

The theoretical basis for considering gonadal steroids (specifically androgens) and aggressive/antisocial behavior is based on the following rationale: Males have both higher concentrations of androgens and higher levels of aggressive behavior than females. Therefore, androgens are suggested to be involved in the etiology of aggressive behavior.

The association between circulating testosterone (T) and aggressive behavior in adolescents was first examined in 15- to 17-year-old Swedish males (Olweus, Mattsson, Schalling, & Low, 1980). Testosterone was related to self reports of physical and verbal aggression resulting from provocation. In another report from the same study, the causal role of T in provoked and unprovoked aggression was examined (Olweus, Mattsson, Schalling, & Low, 1988). Path analysis findings from Grade 6 to Grade 9 indicated a direct causal effect of T on provoked aggressive behavior. The findings were somewhat different for unprovoked aggressive behavior for which an indirect effect of T was mediated by low frustration tolerance at Grade 9. The overall findings indicate that androgens have both direct and indirect effects on antisocial behavior.

Androgens as causes or consequences of behavior do not operate in isolation from other hormone actions. Stress hormones secreted in response to exposure to stressful circumstances influence the secretion of gonadal hormones in both animals and humans. Higher levels of cortisol (the major adrenocortical stress steroid) in subhuman primates are related to lower concentrations of T (Sapolsky, 1991). In human adolescents, antisocial behavior is associated with a profile of lower gonadal steroid and higher adrenal androgen concentrations (Nottelmann et al., 1987; Susman et al., 1987). The connection between stress, cortisol, and T has led to the hypothesis that cortisol mediates the T-aggression link. In disruptive behavior-disordered children, this was not the case (Scerbo & Kolko, 1994). Testosterone and rated aggression were related positively; there was also a negative relationship between cortisol and rated inattention/overactivity; but there was *no* relation between T and cortisol. The failure to find interactions between T and cortisol could be attributed to the psychiatric disorders of children enrolled in the study. Cortisol is positively related to internalizing behavior, a finding consistent with that for adults with depression (Gold, Goodwin, & Chrousos, 1988a, 1988b). The normative interaction between the adrenocortical and gonadal axes may be overridden by the endocrine components of a psychiatric disorder such as conduct disorder. The association between T and aggressive behavior problems in disruptive children was not found in 4- to 10-year-old children with diagnoses of conduct problems (Constantino et al., 1993) or healthy pubertal age adolescents (Susman et al., 1987). Failures to find consistency in T-aggressive relations across adult and adolescent studies reflect the diversity of methodologies and age groups. It is noteworthy that the associations between antisocial behavior and T are not apparent in studies that include children and younger adolescents (Brooks-Gunn & Warren, 1989; Constantino et al., 1993; Nottelmann et al., 1987; Susman et al., 1987). Conversely, the association does exist in older adolescents (Olweus et al., 1980, 1988) and adults (see review by Archer, 1991). The developmental

differences in these sets of findings indicate that elevated T and antisocial behavior may be a consequence (as opposed to a cause) of aggressive behavior during adulthood (Constantino et al., 1993; Susman, Dorn, Inoff-Germain, Nottelman, & Chrousos, in press).

Although testosterone has been the hormone most generally associated with aggressive behavior, low cortisol levels are associated with aggressive behavior in children and adults in a number of studies. In general, low cortisol is associated with greater antisocial behavior. In an early study, Virkkunen (1985) showed that habitually violent offenders had low levels of cortisol. In a later study, Virkkunen et al. (1994) showed that cerebrospinal fluid adrenocorticotropin hormone was low in a similar population of substance abusers and offenders. In males with a violent history of abusing others, cortisol levels were lower than levels in comparison males (Bergman & Brismar, 1994). The findings of hyporesponsivity of cortisol and antisocial behavior are reported in children as well as in adults. In preadolescent boys, saliva cortisol was associated with greater conduct disorder symptoms counts (Vanyukov et al., 1993). In the Vanyukov et al., (1993) study, cortisol levels were lower in sons whose fathers had conduct disorder as children and who subsequently developed antisocial personality compared to cortisol levels in sons whose fathers did not have an Axis I psychiatric disorder or who did not develop antisocial behavior. Lower levels of cortisol also were reported in prepubertal children of parents with a psychoactive substance use disorder (PSUD; Moss, Vanyukov, & Martin, 1995). Boys at high risk for PSUD secreted less salivary cortisol than controls in anticipation of a stressful task. Prepubertal and pubertal boys and girls with lower levels of plasma cortisol at the beginning of a stressful situation (a phlebotomy procedure) that increased across the time of the procedure (40 min) had significantly more symptoms of conduct disorder (Susman et al., in press) than other groups of adolescents. The other groups of adolescents either did not change in cortisol levels or decreased in levels across the time of the procedure. Hypothalamic-pituitary-adrenal (HPA) axis hyporesponsivity and aggressive behavior correspond to the cardiovascular system underarousal and aggressive behavior observed in adolescents and adults (Raine, 1996). The collective findings indicate that hyporesponsivity of the HPA axis is a significant risk factor for antisocial and aggressive behavior in children, adolescents, and adults.

Emotions

The reciprocal interactions among emotions, antisocial behavior, and hormones remain an almost uncharted territory, although since the mid-1980s, these processes have begun to receive attention (see Brooks-Gunn et al., 1994; Brooks-Gunn & Warren, 1989; Susman et al., 1991; Susman et al., 1987). Self-reports of emotions and aggressive affect or self-reported aggressive behaviors tend to be the preferred methodology for examining emotions and antisocial or aggressive tendencies. Obtaining valid behavioral observations of emotions in aggressive encounters presents formidable logistic, economic, and conceptual problems. Nonetheless, relations between emotions, aggressive affect and attributes, and hormones have been established. Brooks-Gunn and Warren (1989) reported that self-reports of aggressive affect were negatively related to the adrenal androgen dehydroepiandrosterone sulphate (DHEAS) but not to T in 10- to 14-year-old girls. The interaction between negative life events and DHEAS and aggressive affect also was significant. Girls with lower concentrations of DHEAS and who experienced negative life events had more aggressive affect than girls with fewer negative life events. The relationship did not occur at the higher levels of DHEAS. The importance of considering the impact of the social context on hormone-aggressive processes is supported by these findings.

Hypotheses regarding relations between hormones, emotions, and aggressive behavior also were tested in boys and girls in a study of biosocial development during puberty (Nottelmann et al., 1987; Susman et al., 1987). One hypothesis was that higher concentrations of gonadal androgens (T) and adrenal androgens (dehydroepiandrosterone [DHEA] and DHEAS) would be related to aggressive attributes. A second hypothesis was that negative emotions would mediate the pathway between hormone levels and aggressive behavior. For boys, higher levels of emotional tone (sad and anxious affect) were related to lower T-to-estradiol (E_2) ratio, T-E_2-binding globulin (a protein that removes sex steroids from the circulation), and higher levels of androstenedione (an androgen from the adrenal cortex). Delinquent behavior problems were related to lower levels of E_2 and higher levels of androstenedione. Emotions did not mediate the path between hormones and aggressive attributes, although anxious affect and delinquent behavior problems were positively related. These existing studies suggest that there are complex links among emotions, aggressive behavior, and hormones; but a cohesive theoretical perspective on these connections remains elusive.

Models for examining interactions between, and mediators of, hormones and antisocial behavior are needed to address conceptual issues regarding the little understood interactive biosocial processes. Emotions are likely to vary with hormone changes; aggressive/antisocial behaviors are likely to change with hormone changes; and emotions are likely to change prior to or following an antisocial act. Because emotions may be affected by both hormones and antisocial behavior, the role of hormones should be pursued as contributors to antisocial behavior.

Smoking

Smoking has been viewed as being highly correlated with both antisocial behavior and negative health consequences in current Western societies. The onset of smoking in early adolescence is coincident with the increase in T and various forms of rebellious and antisocial behavior. In a study of 12 to 14-year-olds, salivary T was positively associated with cigarette smoking (Bauman et al., 1989). Indeed, smoking may now be part of the general construct of social deviance in some societies. Interactions between smoking, T, and peer smoking also have been reported. In males, relations between friend smoking and adolescent smoking were stronger at the higher levels than at the lower levels of T. Stronger relationships existed between T and adolescent smoking for males whose friends smoke than for males whose friends do not smoke (Bauman, Foshee, & Haley, 1992). For girls, the significant interactions were between adolescent smoking and adolescent T, and there were stronger relationships between mother and adolescent smoking for the highest T

levels. The interactions between T and peer and family relations, in conjunction with gender differences, attest to the importance of constructing models that include socialization as well as endocrine influences on even minor antisocial behavior.

There appears to be an inverse relationship between epinephrine excretion by 13-year-olds and their delinquency at ages 18 to 26 (Magnusson, 1987), a relationship accounted for by motor restlessness. Longitudinal developmental studies involving multiple measures of hormones and varied ratings of aggression are currently yielding fruitful data.

The developmental data are complicated by the observation by Bjorkqvist, Osterman, and Lagerspetz (1994) that, although it is generally assumed that boys frequently use physical aggression whereas girls use verbal responses, Finnish boys and girls show few differences up to 8 years of age. After this time, boys were more prone to use direct aggression (both physical and verbal), whereas girls were more likely to use indirect aggression (such as backbiting, gossiping, and subtle manipulations).

Truscott (1992) has provided evidence supporting the view that violence is transmitted intergenerationally from parents to their adolescent offspring and that psychological mechanisms (perhaps including hormones) play a role in this phenomenon. Hammock and Richardson (1992) found that early established aggressive tendencies were predictive factors in adult unprovoked and provoked aggression in a laboratory test.

Buchanan et al. (1992) reviewed the data implicating the activational effects of hormones on moods and behavior in adolescents in Western cultures. Their conclusion is that a range of neural and peripheral changes (e.g., T-binding globulin, melatonin, and adrenocortical hormones) may influence mood and behavior in such individuals.

HORMONES AND ADULT VIOLENCE

Hormones potentially play a role in several areas of violence in adult humans. These are looked at under a number of traditional headings.

Sexual Dimorphism and Aggression

Sexual dimorphisms in adult human aggression often are claimed to be related to physiological processes and learning experience in development. Evidence summarized by Maccoby and Jacklin (1974, 1980) influentially suggests that males are biologically predisposed toward aggressive behavior. Kruttschnitt (1994) reviewed the evidence that sex differences in human aggression are real, concluding, however, that "the most challenging issues appear in the area of understanding how social, situational or cultural factors ameliorate or aggravate aggressive or violent behavior patterns in males and females" (p. 325).

Campbell, Muncer, and Coyle (1992) and Campbell, Muncer, and Gorman (1993) suggest that physical aggression is viewed rather differently by males and females. They suggest that females generally view aggression as resulting from a failure at self-control, whereas males often regard it as instrumental (i.e., an exercise of control over others). Bjorkqvist, Lagerspetz, and Kaukiainen (1992) demonstrated in a Finnish study that, in adulthood, both males and females develop skills in subtly different covert (indirect) aggression by which they attempt to disguise aggressive interactions. They provide confirmation that physical aggression is actually a relatively rare form of adult, interpersonal social interaction and that some workers are inclusive in the activities they will list under the heading of aggression.

Hammock and Richardson (1992) found in a laboratory study involving delivery of electric shocks to 200 subjects that unprovoked aggression was best predicted by a model including sex of the target (males delivered and received stronger shocks than females), masculinity, and aggressive tendencies. Provoked aggression (by angering the subject) was best predicted by a model including provocation, masculinity, and aggressive tendencies.

Harris (1992) suggests that attempts to analyze sex differences in human aggression have been confounded in many studies by studying subjects who are married or dating. In a study of 416 U.S. undergraduate students, it was found that males were generally likely to have received and exhibited more forms of aggressive behavior than females.

Van Goozen, Frijda, and van de Poll (1994) suggest that "anger proneness" is a better focus than aggression for looking at male versus female differences in behavior. They point to evidence that factors that affect anger disposition and anger arousal differ in men and women (Eagly & Steffen, 1986). Subsequently, Van Goozen et al., (1994) compared women who took part in aggressive sports (e.g., kick boxing, wrestling, and rugby) with recreational swimmers. All subjects had normal menstrual cycles and reportedly did not take performance-enhancing drugs. There was no evidence that these groups differed in their anger proneness. Clearly, the simple view that males and females show obvious differences in their adult aggression has come under attack from several directions.

Castration and Human Aggression

Castration (as carried out in venerable and not especially well-controlled studies in ancient Egyptian, Scandinavian, and American populations) has been associated with impressively low levels of recidivism in the case of sexually aggressive rapists, but the impacts of aging, concomitant counseling, and bodily self-image have not been fully evaluated. Certainly, humans are less immediately behaviorally changed by this surgery in adulthood than are laboratory rodents.

Estrogen Therapies

Brain (1994b) has reviewed the therapies involving natural and synthetic estrogens and aggressive behavior. These compounds are associated with many difficult side effects (e.g., gynecomastia [development of breasts] and phlebothrombosis [blood clots]), but they do appear to reduce aggressive and sexual drive in males with excessive libido (defined on the basis of being involved in sex crimes). The precise way in which these compounds act is, however, very confusing. Possible mechanisms involve blocking the production of endogenous androgens or occupying the binding sites.

Treatment With Antihormones

Antiandrogens have debatable effects on human aggression, but there has been more success with the long-acting progesterone derivatives (A-norprogesterone and medroxy-progesterone acetate). It is still unclear *which* forms of aggressive behavior are modified by these compounds. Antiandrogens also influence the neural androgen receptors and may additionally change the enzyme activities and steroid transformations that occur in the brain. Leventhal and Brodie (1981) concluded that antiandrogenic agents may be effective in treating human hostility because of their anesthetic actions.

Currently, there is an apparent reduction in the enthusiasm for "treating" human violence by castration or administration of antiandrogens, estrogens, or progesterone derivatives.

Testosterone and Human Aggression

There were many early attempts to correlate levels of T with human aggression in populations of prisoners and others with a known history of antisocial behavior. These were often confounded by the unreliability of the behavioral measures. Offenses based on the sentence of the courts were generally divorced in time from the endocrine measures. Often a single plasma determination for T was obtained, and other important factors, such as homosexual activity and alcohol consumption, were not considered. In spite of this, Miczek, Mirsky, Carey, DeBold, and Raine (1994) concluded that "steroid and peptide hormones as well as peptides and biogenic amines are critically important in the neural and physiologic mechanisms initiating, executing and coping with violent behavior" (p. 1). They caution, however, that there is "no simple relationship between steroids and aggression, much less violence" (p. 8) and confirm that androgens both influence and are influenced by aggressive behavior.

Archer's (1991) meta-analysis provides a reasonable starting point for studies that have attempted to associate measures of aggressive behavior obtained on the Buss-Durkee Hostility Inventory to plasma T titers. The social environment is more closely associated with T levels than scores on the Buss-Durkee. External (rather than self) assessments of the subject's behavior were more useful, and it was noted that the Buss-Durkee scale measures aggressive feelings rather than aggressive actions. In spite of this, there was a low but positive relationship between T levels and the overall inventory score for 230 males tested over five studies.

The self-perceptions of aggressive offenders rarely accord well with other people's views of their behavior. Canadian data (e.g., Bain, Langevin, Dickey, Hucker, & Wright, 1988; Langevin et al., 1985) suggest that sexually aggressive men have lower baseline levels of DHEAS and luteinizing hormone than controls. It appears that focusing on a particular subcategory of aggressive behavior is important. In a variety of tests (e.g., athletic, examination, and laboratory tasks), "winners" have been shown to have higher overall T levels than losers (Booth et al., 1989; Mazur et al., 1992). The hormonal change appears to be a consequence of altered mood and apparent status. Brain (1994b) concluded that "it seems unlikely that androgens have a simple causal effect on human aggression and violence but the patterns of sex steroids do appear to alter several factors (e.g., 'aggressive feelings,' self image and social signaling) that predispose individuals towards carrying out actions that can receive this label" (p. 221). Reiss and Roth (1993) reported that the Panel on the Understanding and Control of Violent Behavior strongly advocated saliva measures of gonadal and adrenal hormones in such studies but also suggested that measures in the brain were likely to be more useful than peripheral measures in providing biological markers of violent behavior.

What are the current views? A pessimistic evaluation is provided by Benton (1992). Testosterone has, he concludes at best, a limited role in the expression of human, male aggression. He points out (not unreasonably) that repeated studies on highly aggressive individuals (e.g., young, unintelligent individuals lacking social skills) could account for the apparent link. Benton (1992) argues that such findings do not indicate that T plays a role in aggression in the majority of the population. In spite of this, Christiansen and Knussman (1987) showed that serum concentrations of T and dihydrotestosterone (DHT, an androgen that mainly exerts effects on the body) as well as saliva T determined in 117 healthy, young (20- to 30-year-old) German men were both positively correlated with self-ratings of spontaneous aggression. Dominance was positively related only to the serum hormone measures, and the DHT to T ratio was negatively correlated with sexual aggression.

Gladue (1991) studied groups of U.S. male and female homosexuals and heterosexuals who completed a self-report Aggression Inventory after giving blood samples to assay resting levels of T and E_2. Groups were matched (cf. earlier studies) in terms of age, education, vocational interests, and stage of the menstrual cycle where appropriate. Sexual orientation appeared to have little effect on aggression, but males showed positive correlations between total (but not unbound to plasma globulins) T and physical, verbal, and impulsive aggression and between E_2 and physical, verbal, and impatient aggression. Conversely, females showed negative correlations between total T and physical, verbal, and impatient aggression and between E_2 and physical and impulsive aggression and avoidance behavior.

Christiansen and Winkler (1992) attempted to correlate physical aggression (based on previous injuries) to hormonal changes in 114 male Namibian bushmen. They found no differences between an arbitrary violent and a nonviolent group but significant positive correlations between frequency of violent behavior and serum DHT level, saliva T level, and the saliva to serum ratio of T. The serum T, E_2, and serum DHT to T ratios were only weakly positively correlated with the frequency of violent behavior. More violent men had higher mean values on measures of physical robustness, which suggests an indirect effect of androgens on human aggression.

Lindman, von der Pahlen, Ost, and Eriksson (1992) looked at the serum T, cortisol, glucose, and ethanol values in Finnish males arrested for spouse abuse. At the time of arrest, values of T tended to be reduced and cortisol elevated compared with the same individuals when sober, but there was little evidence that levels were different from those for nonviolent drinkers. Cortisol may have been elevated somewhat by the "stress" of being arrested. Neither T nor ethanol intoxication was the sole cause of aggression, but the authors speculated that higher T played a role in the development of aggressive coping mechanisms before alcohol abuse.

Dabbs, Frady, Carr, and Besch (1987) obtained single saliva samples from 18- to 23-year-old male U.S. prisoners that were analyzed for free T and related this measure to the violence involved in the crimes for which they were convicted. There appeared to be a relationship between T and the severity of the violence, especially at the extreme values. Inmates rated by their peers as "tougher" had higher T values, but inmates convicted of nonviolent crimes with high T levels had longer times to serve before parole and more punishments for discipline problems. All these individuals lived in a difficult environment where violence was the norm. The Dabbs et al. (1987) study demonstrates the efficacy of using saliva to determine hormone concentrations.

Bjorkqvist, Nygren, Bjorklund, and Bjorkqvist (1994) looked at the claim that taking anabolic steroids could be linked to some impressive examples of human violence (including homicide). In a double-blind study, male Finns were given T (40 mg/day), a placebo, or no treatment over a week. Subjective and observer-assessed mood estimations were conducted before and after treatment. The placebo group scored higher than both the T and the no-treatment groups on self-estimated anger, irritation, impulsivity, and frustration. The observer-assessment results were similar. The lower response in the T group might be due to suppression of the body's own hormone secretion. Androgen usage causes changed expectations rather than an increase in actual aggressiveness. The results agree with two other double blind studies involving anabolic androgens and mood change but differ from a third study in which the hormones increased hostility as well as resentment and aggression. Ehlers, Rickler, and Hovey (1980) suggested that women who displayed more aggressive behavior had significantly higher T levels than women lower in aggressiveness, but the groups on which this analysis was based were very different in terms of their neurological diagnoses. Van Goozen et al. (1994) studied 22 young female-to-male transsexuals who all were in good health and with initially normal menstrual cycles and a normal range of hormonal variables. These individuals were tested just before and 3 months after T (250 mg of Testoviron depot, usually intramuscular every 2 months). Anger proneness (but not overt aggression) was increased by T treatment.

Other Hormones and Hostility

It is worth reminding ourselves that other hormonal systems (e.g., the adrenomedullary axis) have been related in complex ways to human aggression (Brain, 1994b). Branscombe and Wann (1992) used responses to the film *Rocky IV* to show that sports competitions can elevate physiological arousal (possibly involving medullary adrenal release) in female U.S. undergraduates, which could potentially facilitate the conversion of hostile inclinations into aggressive behavior. Elevations in blood pressure were much more obvious in individuals who frequently reported pride in their U.S. identity than in individuals with a lower identification.

CONCLUDING REMARKS

It is certainly true the hormones may exert effects on some forms of human aggression by acting during prenatal life, at puberty, or in adulthood. However, the actions produced are considerably more subtle (and limited) than was assumed by pioneers in this area. Having said this, increased sophistication in the rating of violence and the sensitivity and accuracy of endocrine measures used are providing valuable insights to the nature of the linkages. A case-by-case approach is clearly needed for determining the relevance of particular hormones in particular individuals exhibiting specific behaviors.

Theoretical and Methodological Considerations

The perspective that hormones act as exclusive causes of antisocial behavior seems excessively limited. Antisocial behavior is multicausal, involving a complex of cognitive, emotional, social, and contextual factors. Models for research on hormones and behavior now tend to consider hormones as causes, consequences, or mediators of transactions between individuals and their environment (Brooks-Gunn et al., 1994; Susman et al., 1996). The belief that hormones are major causal influences on behavior grew out of animal models and the emphasis on organizational influences of hormones during fetal life. Activational influences were thought to involve only subtle modifications in synaptic neurochemistry that did not involve changes in neuronal morphology (Arnold & Gorski, 1984). New evidence suggests that adult neural regions can respond to hormonal manipulations with dramatic structural changes (Gould, Woolley, & McEwen, 1991). Research on hormone-structural changes has focused primarily on the hippocampal formation, specifically the sexually dimorphic circuitry of the avian song system (DeVoogd, 1991), the mammalian spinal cord (e.g., DeVoogd, Nixdorf, & Nottebohm, 1985), and the hypothalamus (Bloch & Gorski, 1988). A finding with potentially important implications for understanding human behavior is that hormone-induced changes in reproductive behavior correlate with hormone-induced morphologic changes, both developmentally and in adulthood (Gould et al., 1991). It is likely then that hormone-induced structural changes are at least partially responsible for functional changes and, in turn, behavioral changes in postfetal life. Structural changes in brain development in humans may lie at the core of changes in cognition, affective expression, and aggressive behavior during the menstrual cycle, at puberty, and at the menopause. Hormone-induced structural brain changes in childhood and adulthood and the effects of these changes on behavior are largely unexplored. These changes may be a product of both endogenous cyclical hormone change and exogenous environmental processes.

Environmental Circumstances and Their Effects on Endocrine Processes

The interaction of individuals and their development are only beginning to be examined. Environments characterized by poverty, crime, pollution, and neurotoxins (e.g., lead) may contribute to hormone-induced functional brain changes. Research that integrates hormones and behavioral measures is seldom based on highly developed theories and models. Integrations tend to be at an empirical level with findings from one level (biological) related to findings from another level of analysis (behavioral) using correlational statistical procedures. Theories are urgently needed to guide and integrate future studies on hormones and antisocial/violent behavior. Well-expressed theories on how environmental processes affect neuroendocrine processes are especially needed, in as much as it is now known that the contexts of human development affect the expression of genes and related neuroendocrine processes. Contextual processes that are known to affect neuroendocrine development in subhuman species may provide fodder for developing hypotheses to be tested in humans. The effects of the environment and experience, winning and losing (Booth et al. 1989; Mazur et al., 1992), on hormone concentrations attest to the power of environmental manipulations. If the environment can be shown to affect hormone-behavior processes and antisocial behavior, then science has provided the possibility of designing environmental interventions to promote development in pathways less conducive to antisocial behavior.

REFERENCES

Archer, J. (1991). The influence of testosterone on human aggression. *British Journal of Psychology, 82,* 1–28.

Arnold, A., & Gorski, R. (1984). Gonadal steroid induction of structural sex differences in the central nervous system. *Annual Review of Neuroscience, 7,* 413–442.

Bain, J., Langevin, R., Dickey, R., Hucker, S., & Wright, P. (1988). Hormones in sexually aggressive men: I. Baseline values for eight hormones. II. The ACTH test. *Annals of Sex Research, 1,* 63–78.

Bauman, K. E., Foshee, V. A., & Haley, N. J. (1992). The interaction of sociological and biological factors in adolescent cigarette smoking. *Addictive Behavior, 17,* 459–467.

Bauman, K. E., Foshee, V. A., Koch, G. G., Haley, N. J., & Downton, M. I. (1989). Testosterone and cigarette smoking in early adolescence. *Journal of Behavioral Medicine, 12,* 425–433.

Benton, D. (1992). Hormones and human aggression. In K. Bjorkqvist & P. Niemela (Eds.), *Of mice and women* (pp. 37–48). San Diego: Academic Press.

Berenbaum, S. A., & Hines, M. (1992). Early androgens are related to childhood sex-typed toy preferences. *Psychological Science, 3,* 203–206.

Berenbaum, S. A., & Snyder, E. (1995). Early hormonal influences on childhood sex-typed activity and playmate preferences: Implications for the development of sexual orientation. *Developmental Psychology, 31,* 31–42.

Bergman, B., & Brismar, B. (1994). Hormone levels and personality traits in abusive and suicidal male alcoholics. *Alcoholism, Clinical and Experimental Research, 18,* 311–316.

Bjorkqvist, K., Lagerspetz, K. M. J., & Kaukiainen, A. (1992). Do girls manipulate and boys fight? Developmental trends in regards to direct and indirect aggression. *Aggressive Behavior, 18,* 117–127.

Bjorkqvist, K., Nygren, T., Bjorklund, A.-C., & Bjorkqvist S.-E. (1994). Testosterone intake and aggressiveness: Real effect or anticipation? *Aggressive Behavior, 20,* 17–26.

Bjorkqvist, K., Osterman, K., & Lagerspetz, K. M. J. (1994). Sex differences in covert aggression among adults. *Aggressive Behavior, 2,* 27–33.

Bloch, G., & Gorski, R. (1988). Estrogen/progesterone treatment in adulthood affects the size of several components of the medial preoptic area in the male rat. *Journal of Comparative Neurology, 190,* 613–622.

Booth, A., Shelley, G., Mazur, A., Tharp, G., & Kittok, R. (1989). Testosterone and winning and losing in human competition. *Hormones and Behavior, 23,* 556–571.

Brain, P. F. (Ed.). (1986). *Alcohol and aggression.* London: Croom-Helm.

Brain, P. F. (1989). An ethoexperimental approach to behavioral endocrinology. In R. J. Blanchard, P. F. Brain, D. C. Blanchard, & S. Parmigiani (Eds.), *Ethoexperimental approaches to the study of behavior* (pp. 539–557). Dordrecht, The Netherlands: Kluwer.

Brain, P. F. (1994a). Biological-psychological. In M. Hersen, R. T. Ammerman, & L. A. Sisson (Eds.), *Handbook of aggressive and destructive behavior in psychiatric patients* (pp. 3–16). New York: Plenum.

Brain, P. F. (1994b). Hormonal aspects of aggression and violence. In A. J. Reiss Jr., K. A. Miczek, & J. I. Roth (Eds.), *Understanding and preventing violence: Vol. 2. Biobehavioral influences* (pp. 173–244). Washington, DC: National Academy Press.

Brain, P. F., & Haug, M. (1992). Hormonal and neurochemical correlates of various forms of animal aggression. *Psychoneuroendocrinology, 17,* 537–551.

Branscombe, N. R., & Wann, D. L. (1992). Physiologic arousal and reactions to out group members during competitions that implicate an important social identity. *Aggressive Behavior, 18,* 85–93.

Brooks-Gunn, J., Graber, J., & Paikoff, R. (1994). Studying links between hormones and negative affect: Models and measures. *Journal of Research on Adolescence, 4,* 469–486.

Brooks-Gunn, J., & Warren, M. (1989). Biological and social contributions to negative affect in young adolescent girls. *Child Development, 60,* 40–55.

Buchanan, C. M., Eccles, J. S., & Becker, J. B. (1992). Are adolescents the victims of raging hormones: Evidence for activational effects of hormones on moods and behavior at adolescence. *Psychological Bulletin, 111,* 62–107.

Campbell, A., Muncer, S., & Coyle, F. (1992). Social representation of aggression as an explanation of gender differences: A preliminary study. *Aggressive Behavior, 18,* 95–108.

Campbell, A., Muncer, S., & Gorman, B. (1993). Sex and social representations of aggression: A communal-agenetic analysis. *Aggressive Behavior, 19,* 125–135.

Chaiken, J., Chaiken, M., & Rhodes, W. (1994). Predicting violent behavior and classifying violent offenders. In A. J. Reiss Jr. & J. A. Roth (Eds.), *Understanding and preventing violence: Vol. 4. Consequences and control* (pp. 217–295). Washington, DC: National Academy Press.

Christiansen, K., & Knussman, R. (1987). Androgen levels and components of aggressive behavior in men. *Hormones and Behavior, 21,* 170–180.

Christiansen, K., & Winkler, E.-M. (1992). Hormonal, anthropometrical, and behavioral correlates of physical aggression in !Kung San Men of Namibiaq. *Aggressive Behavior, 18,* 271–289.

Constantino, J. N., Grosz, S., Saenger, P., Chandler, D. W., Nandi, R., & Earls, F. J. (1993). Testosterone and aggression in children. *Journal of the American Academy of Child and Adolescent Psychiatry, 32,* 1217–1222.

Dabbs, J. M., Frady, R. L., Carr, T. S., & Besch, N. F. (1987). Saliva, testosterone, and criminal violence in young adult male prisoners. *Psychosomatic Medicine, 49,* 174–182.

Dent, R. R. M. (1983). Endocrine correlates of aggression. *Progress in Neuro-Psychopharmacology and Biological Psychiatry, 7,* 525–528.

DeVoogd, T. J. (1991). Endocrine modulation of the development and adult function of the avian song system. *Psychoneuroendocrinology, 16,* 41–66.

DeVoogd, T. J., Nixdorf, B., & Nottebohm, F. (1985). Synaptogenesis and changes in synaptic morphology related to acquisition of a new behavior. *Brain Research, 329,* 304–338.

Eagly, A. H., & Steffen, V. J. (1986). Gender and aggressive behavior. A meta-analytic review of the social psychological literature. *Psychological Bulletin, 100,* 309–330.

Ehlers, C. L., Rickler, K. C., & Hovey, J. E. (1980). A possible relationship between plasma, testosterone, and aggressive behavior in a female outpatient population. In M. Girgis & L. G. Kiloh (Eds.), *Limbic epilepsy and the dyscontrol syndrome* (pp. 183–194). New York: Elsevier/North-Holland Biomedical Press.

Gladue, B. A. (1991). Aggressive behavioral characteristics, hormones, and sexual orientation in men and women. *Aggressive Behavior, 17,* 313–326.

Gold, P. W., Goodwin, F. K., & Chrousos, G. P. (1988a). Clinical and biochemical manifestations of depression: Relation to the neurobiology of stress (first of two parts). *New England Journal of Medicine, 319,* 349–353.

Gold, P. W., Goodwin, F. K., & Chrousos, G. P. (1988b). Clinical and biochemical manifestations of depression: Relation to the neurobiology of stress (second of two parts). *New England Journal of Medicine, 319,* 413–420.

Gould, E., Woolley, C. S., & McEwen, B. S. (1991). The hippocampal formation: Morphological changes induced by thyroid, gonadal, and adrenal hormones. *Psychoneuroendocrinology, 16,* 67–84.

Hall, G. S. (1904). *Adolescence.* New York: Appleton.

Hammock, G. S., & Richardson, D. R. (1992). Predictors of aggressive behavior. *Aggressive Behavior, 18,* 219–229.

Harris, M. B. (1992). Sex, race, and experiences of aggression. *Aggressive Behavior, 18,* 201–217.

Hays, S. E. (1981). The psychoendocrinology of puberty and adolescent aggression. In D. A. Hamburg & M. B. Trudeau (Eds.), *Biobehavioral aspects of aggression* (pp. 107–119). New York: Alan R. Liss.

Hines, M., & Shipley, C. (1984). Prenatal exposure to diethylstilbestrol (DES) and the development of sexually dimorphic cognitive abilities and cerebral lateralization. *Developmental Psychology, 20,* 56–80.

Kruttschnitt, C. (1994). Gender and interpersonal violence. In A. J. Reiss Jr. & J. A. Roth (Eds.), *Understanding and preventing violence: Vol. 3. Social influences* (pp. 293–376). Washington, DC: National Academy Press.

Langevin, R., Bain, J., Ben-Aron, M., Coulhard, R., Day, D., Handy, L., Heasman, G., Hucker, S., Purins, J., Roger, V., Russan, A., Webster, C., & Wortzman, G. (1985). Sexual aggression: Constructing a predictive equation. In R. Langevin (Ed.), *Erotic preference, gender identity, and aggression in men* (pp. 50–93). Hillsdale, NJ: Erlbaum.

Leventhal, B. L., & Brodie, H. K. H. (1981). The pharmacology of violence. In D. A. Hamburg & M. B. Trudeau (Eds.), *Biobehavioral aspects of aggression* (pp. 85–106). New York: Alan R. Liss.

Lindman, R., von der Pahlen, B., Ost, B., & Eriksson, C. J. P. (1992). Serum testosterone, cortisol, glucose, and ethanol in males arrested for spouse abuse. *Aggressive Behavior, 18,* 393–400.

Linn, M. C., & Petersen, A. C. (1985). Emergence and characterization of sex differences in spatial ability: A meta analysis. *Child Development, 56,* 1479–1498.

Maccoby, E. E., & Jacklin, C. N. (1974). *The psychology of sex differences.* Stanford: Stanford University Press.

Maccoby, E. E., & Jacklin, C. N. (1980). Sex differences in aggression: A rejoinder and reprise. *Child Development, 51,* 964–980.

Magnusson, D. (1987). Adult delinquency in the light of conduct and physiology at an early age: A longitudinal study. In D. Magnusson & A. Ohman (Eds.), *Psychopathology: An international perspective* (pp. 221–234). Orlando, FL: Academic Press.

Mazur, A., Booth, A., & Dabbs, J. (1992). Testosterone and chess competition. *Social Psychology Quarterly, 55*, 70–77.

Meyer-Bahlberg, H. F. L., Ehrhardt, A. A., Rosen, L. R., Gruen, R. S., Veridiano, N. P., Vann, F. H., & Neuwalder, H. F. (1995). Prenatal estrogens and the development of homosexual orientation. *Developmental Psychology, 31*, 12–21.

Miczek, K. A., Mirsky, A. F., Carey, G., DeBold, J., & Raine, A. (1994). An overview of biological influences on violent behavior. In A. J. Reiss Jr., K. A. Miczek, & J. A. Roth (Eds.), *Understanding and preventing violence: Vol. 2. Biobehavioral influences* (pp. 1–20). Washington, DC: National Academy Press.

Money, J., & Ehrhardt, A. A. (1972). *Man and woman. Boy and girl.* Baltimore: Johns Hopkins University Press.

Moss, H. B., Vanyukov, M. M., & Martin, C. S. (1995). Salivary cortisol responses and the risk for substance abuse in prepubertal boys. *Biological Psychiatry, 38*, 547–555.

Nottelmann, E. D., Susman, E. J., Dorn, L. D., Inoff-Germain, G. E., Cutler, G. B., Jr., Loriaux, D. L., & Chrousos, G. P. (1987). Developmental processes in American early adolescents: Relationships between adolescent adjustment problems and chronological pubertal stage and puberty-related serum hormone levels. *Journal of Pediatrics, 110*, 473–480.

Olweus, D., Mattsson, A., Schalling, D., & Low, H. (1980). Testosterone, aggression, physical, and personality dimensions in normal adolescent males. *Psychosomatic Medicine, 42*, 253–269.

Olweus, D., Mattsson, A., Schalling, D., & Low, H. (1988). Circulating testosterone levels and aggression in adolescent males: A causal analysis. *Psychosomatic Medicine, 50*, 261–272.

Petersen, A. C., & Taylor, B. (1980). The biological approach to adolescence: Biological change and psychosocial adaptation. In J. Adelson (Ed.), *Handbook of the psychology of adolescence* (pp. 115–155). New York: Wiley.

Phoenix, C. H., Goy, R. W., Gerall, A. A., & Young, W. C. (1959). Organizing action of prenatally administered testosterone propionate on the tissues mediating mating behavior in the female guinea pig. *Endocrinology, 65*, 369–382.

Raine, A. (1996, May). *The interaction of social and psychophysiological factors.* Paper presented at the NATO Advanced Study Institute, Biosocial bases of violence: Theory and research, Rhodes, Greece.

Reinisch, J. M., Ziemba-Davis, M., & Sanders, S. A. (1991). Hormonal contributions to sexually dimorphic behavioral development in humans. *Psychoneuroendocrinology, 16*, 213–278.

Reiss, A. J., & Roth, J. A. (1993). *Understanding and preventing violence.* Washington, DC: National Academy Press.

Rodrigues-Sierra, J. F. (1986). Extended organizational effects of estrogen at puberty. *Annals of the New York Academy of Sciences, 474*, 293–307.

Sapolsky, R. M. (1991). Testicular function, social rank, and personality among wild baboons. *Psychoneuroendocrinology, 16*, 281–293.

Scerbo, A. S., & Kolko, D. J. (1994). Salivary testosterone and cortisol in disruptive children: Relationship to aggressive, hyperactive, and internalizing behaviors. *Journal of the American Academy of Child Psychiatry, 33*, 1174–1184.

Susman, E. J., Dorn, L. D., & Chrousos, G. P. (1991). Negative affect and hormone levels in young adolescents: Concurrent and longitudinal perspectives. *Journal of Youth and Adolescence, 20*, 167–190.

Susman, E. J., Dorn, L. D., Inoff-Germain, G., Nottelmann, E. D., & Chrousos, G. P. (in press). Cortisol reactivity, distress behavior, behavior problems, and emotionality in young adolescents: A longitudinal perspective. *Journal of Research on Adolescence.*

Susman, E. J., Nottelmann, E. D., Inoff-Germain, G. E., Dorn, L. D., Cutler, G. B., Loriaux, D. L., & Chrousos, G. P. (1985). Hormones, emotional dispositions, and aggressive attributes in young adolescents. *Child Development, 58*, 1114–1134.

Susman, E. J., & Petersen, A. C. (1992). Hormones and behavior in adolescence. In E. R. McAnarney, R. E. Kreipe, D. P. Orr, & G. D. Comerci (Eds.), *Textbook of adolescent medicine* (pp. 125–130). New York: Saunders.

Susman, E. J., Worrall, B. K., Murowchick, E., Frobose, C., & Schwab, J. (1996). Experience and neuroendocrine parameters of development: Aggressive behavior and competencies. In D. Stoff & R. Cairns (Eds.), *Neurobiological approaches to clinical aggression research* (pp. 267–289). Hillsdale, NJ: Erlbaum.

Truscott, D. (1992). Intergenerational transmission of violent behavior in adolescent males. *Aggressive Behavior, 18*, 327–335.

Van Goozen, S., Frijda, N., & van de Poll, N. (1994). Anger and aggression in women: Influence of sports choice and testosterone administration. *Aggressive Behavior, 20*, 213–222.

Vanyukov, M. M., Moss, H. B., Plail, J. A., Blackson, T., Mezzick, A. C., & Tarter, R. E. (1993). Antisocial symptoms in preadolescent boys and in their parents: Associations with cortisol. *Psychiatric Research, 46*, 9–17.

Virkkunen, M. (1985). Urinary free cortisol secretion in habitually violent offenders. *Acta Psychiatria Scandinevica, 72*, 40–44.

Virkkunen, M., Rawlings, R., Tokola, R., Poland, R. E., Guidotti, A., Nemeroff, C., Bissette, G., Kalogeras, K., Karonen, S. L., & Linnoila, M. (1994). CSF biochemistries, glucose metabolism, and diurnal activity rhythms in alcoholic, violent offenders, impulsive fire setters, and healthy volunteers. *Archives of General Psychiatry, 51*, 20–27.

Williams, C. L. (1986). A reevaluation of the concept of separable periods of organizational and activational actions of estrogens in development of brain and behavior. *Annals of the New York Academy of Sciences, 474*, 282–292.

CHAPTER 30

Conceptual Models of the Nervous System: Implications for Antisocial Behavior

JOSEPH P. NEWMAN

An organism responds in a particular way to a particular situation because of the state in which it currently finds itself. That state can only be contained as a physical specification of the cells which constitute the organism, above all, as a specification of the neuro-endocrine system. Thus, both genetic and environmental factors and interactions between them must act by altering the *physiological* basis of behaviour. (Gray, 1972, pp. 372–373, emphasis in original)

To the extent that this statement is correct, knowledge about the entire array of factors governing antisocial behavior is likely to be advanced by a good working model of the neuroendocrine system. Moreover, by relating the diverse influences of genetic, developmental, and situational variables to a unitary context (i.e., the neuroendocrine system), a working model of this type encourages investigators to conceptualize these variables in a more integrated fashion. Such working models have been referred to by Gray (1972) and others (e.g., Hebb, 1955) as *conceptual nervous system* (cNS) models.

In essence, the cNS is a theory about the real nervous system (CNS). The significance of the cNS derives from our incomplete understanding of the real nervous system. Without such understanding, we can only speculate about how its functions are achieved and how it influences behavior. Thus, cNS models are hypothetical constructs that may be found useful or wanting and will probably require revision as knowledge about the real nervous system continues to evolve. In light of this uncertainty, it is essential to recognize that a cNS model may limit as well as facilitate research by determining which psychological processes and dimensions of behavior are examined and how.

Recognizing the shortcomings of an earlier cNS model, Hebb (1955) noted that the cNS "of 1930 was evidently like the gin that was being drunk about the same time; it was homemade and none too good." Continuing in the same vein, he proposed, "If we *must* drink we can now get better liquor; likewise, the conceptual nervous system of 1930 is out of date and—if we must neurologize— let us use the best brand of neurology we can find" (p. 243). The new brand of neurology espoused by Hebb related to then recent advances relating the brain stem structures to learning and motivation via the concept of *arousal.* Based on more recent discoveries

relating the septo-hippocampal system (SHS) to learning and motivation via a more elaborate understanding of the brain's arousal systems, Gray (1972, 1987) appears to have uncorked a vintage cNS model (see also, Fowles, 1980).

Although cNS models are based on and constrained by knowledge of the actual nervous system, the cNS models employed by psychologists are heavily influenced by behavioral data. Indeed, Gray (1987) proposed that "the structure of the neuro-endocrine system *inferred* by the psychologist from purely behavioural data may be at certain points in advance of physiological knowledge" (p. 241, emphasis in original). The cNS, then, is a hypothetical construct informed by physiology on the one hand and elaborated by psychology on the other. Its purpose is to guide theorizing about causal influences on behavior and to enhance understanding of both psychological and physiological processes by integrating the two.

Owing to the complexity of CNS functioning, cNS modeling may be attempted at various levels. At the physiological level, cNS models might involve any of a wide variety of cortical, subcortical, or neurotransmitter systems. At the psychological level, cNS models might target learning, emotion, attention, or a range of other factors that influence behavior regulation, propensity to antisocial behavior, or both. Whereas one cNS model may focus on the implications of the ascending reticular activating system (ARAS) for arousal regulation (Eysenck, 1967), another may be concerned with the implications of the septo-hippocampal system (SHS) for behavioral inhibition (Gray, 1987), and a third model may highlight the implications of serotonergic pathways for impulsive aggression (see Berman, Kavoussi, & Coccaro, Chapter 28, this volume). Thus, the number of potential cNS models may be quite large.

The hypothetical nature of cNS models implies that no one cNS model can lay claim to being correct. How, then, should we select or evaluate alternative cNS models? cNS models are essentially heuristic devices; therefore, the metric for evaluating them rests, to a large extent, on their utility. The utility of a cNS model, in turn, is likely to depend on a number of factors, including, but not limited to, (a) the accuracy and clarity with which the cNS model reflects the physiological system modeled; (b) the applicability of its biopsychological constructs to behavioral syndromes of interest (e.g., antisocial behavior); (c) the ease with which the model's biopsychological constructs connect with other relevant constructs so that it is useful for organizing related theory and evidence; and (d) the extent to which the model generates novel and valid predictions that promote hypothesis testing and advance understanding.

Although these criteria are reasonable and suggest a standard for evaluating cNS models, it would be premature to compare alternative cNS models of antisocial behavior at this time. With the notable exception of Eysenck's (1967) model, the use of cNS models to elucidate antisocial behavior is relatively new, and there is a dearth of evidence by which to judge alternative models. Complicating matters further, cNS models often focus on different biopsychological systems and aspects of antisocial behavior (e.g., aggression, sensation seeking, and lack of responsiveness to social sanctions).

Rather than comparing and contrasting diverse cNS models, this discussion employs a more limited and fundamental strategy. Specifically, this chapter focuses on the application of one well-developed cNS model to a single, especially significant form of antisocial behavior—psychopathy. By this means, I hope to clarify the nature of cNS models, convey their potential utility, and highlight a number of important issues that arise in their application. In adopting this strategy, I neglect other cNS models of antisocial behavior (e.g., Gorenstein, 1991) as well as other manifestations of antisocial behavior (e.g., Coccaro & Kavoussi, 1995), including emerging cNS models of childhood and adolescent conduct disorder (e.g., Quay, 1993). On the other hand, this "case study" approach permits a more detailed analysis of the issues that arise in applying cNS models to antisocial behavior, which, in turn, may advance application of cNS models more generally.

THEORETICAL CONTEXT AND CONTROVERSIAL ISSUES

To illustrate the use of cNS models to elucidate antisocial behavior, I focus on the application of Gray's cNS model to psychopathy. Gray (e.g., 1972) is an articulate proponent of the cNS approach, and his model provides a particularly useful context for theorizing about psychopathy (e.g., Fowles, 1980; Fowles & Missel, 1994; Lykken, 1995; Newman & Wallace, 1993a, 1993b; Patterson & Newman, 1993).

Eysenck's Model

Before describing the specifics of Gray's cNS model, I briefly discuss Eysenck's (1967, 1981) theoretical framework because it provides an important context for Gray's model and the cNS modeling of antisocial behavior more generally. Eysenck's cNS model provides an excellent example of this approach to antisocial behavior (Eysenck, 1981; Eysenck & Eysenck, 1978; Eysenck & Gudjonsson, 1989). According to the model, genetic factors contribute to individual differences in physiological processes (e.g., ascending reticular activating system [ARAS]) that, in turn, drive fundamental psychological processes (e.g., motivation, learning) that give rise to stable differences in personality (e.g., introversion-extraversion [I-E]) and, ultimately, influence a person's social behavior and risk for psychopathology (e.g., antisocial personality disorder).

A common confusion that arises when considering biological influences on social behavior relates to whether particular behaviors, such as driving under the influence of alcohol or committing an armed robbery, can be rooted in our biology. Are there really genetic or physiological processes responsible for such specific behaviors? In most cases, scientists investigating the biological basis of antisocial behavior are searching for characteristics that predispose a person to such behavior rather than direct causal relationships.

This predisposing role of physiological factors is intrinsic to Eysenck's (1981) model. Specifically, personality is employed as an intervening variable. Rather than relating individual differences in physiological functioning to antisocial behavior directly, Eysenck links them to general personality styles, which, in turn, make antisocial behavior more or less likely. In contrast to the diversity that characterizes antisocial behavior, personality dimensions are relatively homogeneous. Thus, linking personality to specific biopsychological processes seems more plausible. In addition, situating personality constructs between a physiological predisposition and antisocial behavior clarifies why particular predispositions do not always become manifested as antisocial behavior. Lykken (1982), for example, has proposed that a biologically based trait of fearlessness may predispose a person to heroic or antisocial deeds, depending on their socialization.

Within Eysenck's (1981) model, the relation between personality and antisocial behavior is mediated by psychological processes such as perception, motivation, emotion, and cognition, which, in turn, influence learning, development, and social adjustment. To the extent that personality does, in fact, influence a person's risk for antisocial behavior by systematically influencing that person's reaction to environmental events, the contribution of personality to antisocial behavior must be understood in light of myriad person by situation interactions that shape an individual's response to the environment. Accordingly, the significance of personality-based explanations of antisocial behavior depends on the extent to which the personality constructs invoked implicate specific psychological processes. Eysenck's use of the ARAS to achieve this specificity provides a classic example of a cNS model.

Though recognizing the crucial role of experience in shaping behavior, Eysenck's (1981) model focuses on the role of biopsychological processes in mediating one's transactions with the environment. His general framework provides a model for other investigators interested in the development and application of cNS models. Recognizing its virtues, Gray (1981) has adopted Eysenck's theoretical framework to develop his own cNS model. Whereas Eysenck's cNS model is predicated on the ARAS, Gray's (1987) model is based primarily on the septo-hippocampal system.

Gray's Model

As shown in Figure 30.1, Gray's model has three interacting systems: the behavioral activation system (BAS), the behavioral inhibition system (BIS), and the nonspecific arousal system (NAS). Each system plays a crucial role in the regulation of behavior. The BAS is sensitive to cues for reward and active avoidance and functions to (a) increase NAS activity, (b) inhibit activity in the BIS, and (c) initiate motor behavior in the service of approach or active avoidance. The BIS is sensitive to cues for punishment and nonreward and serves to (a) increase NAS activity, (b) interrupt ongoing or anticipated motor behavior, and (c) direct attention to significant stimuli. The NAS receives inputs from both the BAS and the BIS and acts to increase the intensity (i.e., speed and force) of behavior. As indicated by the two switches in the decision mechanism that "turn on" approach behavior or the stop/inspect response, the BAS and BIS compete to influence the focus of behavior. If BAS activation is stronger, people will maintain their focus and initiate goal-directed behavior, whereas they will pause and redirect attention to environmental cues (i.e., initiate passive avoidance) if BIS activity predominates. NAS activity, on the other hand, influences qualitative rather than directional aspects of behavior. In addition to increasing the speed and force of whatever behavior eventually occurs, as proposed by Gray, increases in NAS activity will tend to increase the focus of attention and speed with which behavior is initiated, thus limiting the amount of time and concomitant processing accorded to the simultaneous evaluation of BAS and BIS inputs (see Wallace, Bachorowski, & Newman, 1991; Wallace & Newman, in press).

Although schematic representations of Gray's model are often limited to the three systems described earlier (e.g., Fowles, 1980; Newman & Wallace, 1993), an additional system—the fight/flight system (FFS)—has been receiving increased attention (Gray, 1987), especially with regard to reactive aggression (e.g., Gray, 1991; Quay, 1993) and panic disorder (Fowles, 1993a). In contrast to the BAS and BIS, which respond to conditioned stimuli, the FFS is activated by unconditioned aversive stimuli such as pain and the termination or omission of reward. Once activated, the

FFS is associated with extreme autonomic nervous system activity and intense motor activity of the type associated with frantic struggle, fleeing an aggressor, or lashing out in counterattack.

Evaluation of the Eysenck/Gray Model

With regard to the first criterion for evaluating CNS models, the accuracy and clarity with which the cNS model reflects the physiological system modeled, Gray's model is based primarily on the implications of the septo-hippocampal system (SHS), although it is also informed by the effects of antianxiety drugs and, to a lesser extent, other CNS pathways (see Gray, 1994). The psychological counterpart of the SHS is the BIS. Gray has been developing the implications of SHS functioning for behavioral inhibition and anxiety for more than 25 years (see Gray, 1970). A detailed critique of his proposals regarding the physiology of anxiety and behavioral inhibition is beyond the scope of this chapter. Although there is no consensus regarding the exact functions of the SHS or the physiological substrate of anxiety, Gray's proposals are consistent with a great deal of experimental evidence concerning the consequences of lesioning the SHS as well as with the evidence concerning the effects of antianxiety drugs (see Gray, 1982, 1987). Although Gray acknowledges that his formulations will require additional modification, his characterization of SHS functioning is plausible, comprehensive, and up-to-date (see also, Gray, 1991, 1994).

With regard to (b), the applicability of the model to relevant behavioral syndromes, Fowles (1988, 1993b) has provided numerous examples of the applicability of Gray's model to psychopathological syndromes, including psychopathy. Supporting the applicability of the model to antisocial behavior, numerous investigators have used Gray's model as a framework for describing their perspective on antisocial behavior (Fowles, 1980; Kilzieh & Cloninger, 1993; Lykken, 1995; McBurnett, 1991; Milich, Hartung, Martin, & Haigler, 1994; Newman & Wallace, 1993a, 1993b; Quay, 1993; Walker et al., 1991).

The third criterion for cNS models noted earlier relates to (c), the ease with which the model's biopsychological constructs connect with other relevant constructs so that it is useful for organizing related theory and evidence. Investigators of antisocial behavior have offered a variety of proposals concerning the behavioral, personality, psychophysiological, and biochemical correlates of antisocial behavior. For example, numerous investigators have identified deficient passive avoidance learning as a key correlate of psychopathy as well as criminality and weak socialization more generally (Lykken, 1957; Patterson & Newman, 1993; Trasler, 1978). Passive avoidance involves the inhibition of specific behaviors that have been associated with punishment. Passive avoidance is integral to Gray's model and has been used by Gray to label the output of the BIS (e.g., 1987). Because any of the factors characterized in Gray's model could influence the output of the BIS, the model provides a rich source of hypotheses concerning passive avoidance deficits (see Newman & Wallace, 1993a).

With regard to personality, antisocial behavior has been linked to a wide variety of personality traits and other traitlike individual difference variables, including, but not limited to, aggressiveness, impulsivity, sensation seeking, thought disorder, low anxiety/harm avoidance, low arousal, low intelligence, lack of empathy, poor

Figure 30.1 *An adaptation of Gray and Smith's model for conflict and discrimination learning.*

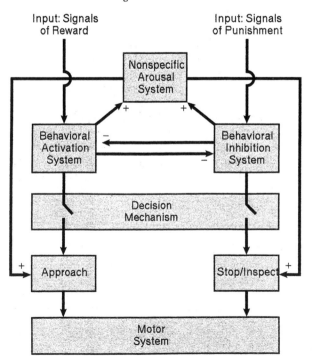

conditionability, and impaired executive functioning. Though these characteristics are quite diverse, it is possible to conceptualize them as (a) driving motor activity (e.g., aggressiveness, impulsivity, sensation seeking), (b) weakening inhibition (e.g., poor fear conditioning, lack of empathy, low anxiety/harm avoidance), or (c) interfering with judgment/information processing (e.g., intelligence, thought disorder, impaired executive functioning). Moreover, these traitlike correlates of antisocial behavior have been linked to the three major factors that emerge consistently in factor analytic studies of personality. These factors are typically labeled extraversion, neuroticism, and psychoticism (e.g., Eysenck & Eysenck, 1978); impulsivity, anxiety, and socialization (Barratt & Patton, 1983); novelty seeking, harm avoidance, and reward dependence (Cloninger, 1987); or positive emotionality, negative emotionality, and constraint (Tellegen, 1985).

As was the case with passive avoidance, Gray's model has been linked to the major dimensions of personality and, thus, may be suitable for conceptualizing the biopsychological correlates of antisocial behavior at this level as well. The association between Gray's BAS (i.e., behavioral approach) and impulsivity is quite straightforward as is the relation of Gray's BIS (i.e., behavioral inhibition) to anxiety/negative emotionality (see Gray, 1991; Larsen & Ketelaar, 1989).

The significance of Gray's model for the third dimension of personality, sometimes described as psychoticism, psychopathy, socialization, constraint, conformity, and reward dependence, is less clear. Both Gray (1991) and Fowles (1993a) associate psychopathy with a weak BIS, thus positing that anxiety and psychopathy anchor opposite ends of the same continuum (see Gray, 1991). In identifying psychopathy with low anxiety and a weak BIS, however, this strategy does little to distinguish the third dimension of personality. Toward this end, Gray (1991) relates psychoticism to the FFS and, though acknowledging potential problems, he also associates Tellegen's (1982) constraint factor with the FFS. Fowles and Missel (1994), however, propose a different strategy for distinguishing the anxiety and constraint factors. They relate the constraint factor, which includes a fear/harm avoidance component, to the BIS, and they map the more reactive aspects of anxiety onto the FFS. Concerning this proposal, it is worth noting that Fowles and Missel relate psychopathy to low constraint (i.e., a weak BIS) rather than low anxiety (see also, Lykken, 1995).

The uncertain applicability of Gray's model to the socialization/constraint dimension is ironic given the model's immediate bearing on passive avoidance learning—a process regarded as fundamental to the socialization process. Within Gray's model, the most obvious explanation for poor passive avoidance learning involves the direct effects of the BIS because passive avoidance is the behavioral output of this system. Though psychopathy is associated with poor passive avoidance, it remains to be established whether passive avoidance learning is more closely linked with the anxiety/negative emotionality (e.g., Gray, 1991) or socialization/constraint dimensions (e.g., Fowles & Missel, 1994). Alternatively, as discussed in the section on current findings, individuals with low levels of anxiety and constraint may display weak passive avoidance for different reasons—a possibility with important implications for the relation of Gray's model to socialization/constraint.

Gray's biopsychological constructs also have been associated with numerous psychophysiological and biochemical correlates of antisocial behavior. A relatively large number of investigators have reported that psychopaths display less electrodermal activity in anticipation of aversive events, whereas their heart rate (HR) is equal to or greater than that of nonpsychopathic controls (Hare, 1978). In a thoughtful and thorough analysis of the relation of Gray's model to psychophysiological indexes of arousal, Fowles (1980) proposed that electrodermal activity may be associated with Gray's BIS, whereas HR is often associated with BAS activity.

Concerning the biochemical evidence on antisocial individuals, the relation between Gray's cNS model and antisocial behavior has been the subject of several reviews (e.g., Lewis, 1991; McBurnett, 1991; Quay, 1993; Rogeness, Javors, & Pliszka, 1992). Although recognizing the inherent complexity of neurotransmitter systems and the pitfalls involved in mapping neurochemistry to neuroanatomy and behavior, the authors have offered tentative proposals concerning the relation of dopamine (DA), norepinephrine (NE), and serotonin (5-HT) to processes specified by Gray's model. In brief, there appears to be good agreement that DA is involved in BAS functioning because of its association with the localization of rewarding and punishment stimuli and mobilization of active behavior to approach or avoid them (Cloninger, 1987; Depue, Luciana, Arbisi, Collins, & Leon, 1994). According to Rogeness et al. (1992, p. 771), "Regulation of the septohippocampal system [i.e., BIS] appears to be noradrenergic with additional regulation from serotonergic projections from the median raphe." More specifically, NE appears to be instrumental in regulating DA-dependent behaviors (i.e., BAS activity), whereas "serotonergic mechanisms appear stronger in inhibiting irritable, aggressive behavior" associated with the fight/flight system (FFS; Rogeness et al., 1992, p. 772; cf. Spoont, 1992).

The last criterion enumerated earlier concerns the extent to which a cNS model generates novel and valid predictions, thus promoting hypothesis testing and enhanced understanding. At a general level, Gray's model appears to accommodate many of the major factors that have guided research on the psychobiological underpinnings of antisocial behavior. Indeed, numerous chapters and journal articles have been written on the good "fit" or applicability of Gray's model to a wide variety of personality types and psychopathological conditions (e.g., Fowles, 1988, 1993b). Though such presentations promote the *potential* utility of Gray's model, they do not necessarily document its ability to advance the field.

In order to realize the contribution of Gray's cNS model for antisocial behavior, it is important for investigators to be clearer about the interrelated but distinct issues of *applicability,* involving the breadth and coverage of the model, and *utility,* stemming from the model's ability to generate specific, testable, and novel hypotheses. Although the applicability of a cNS model contributes to its potential utility, investigators must go beyond post hoc mapping of personality and psychopathological constructs onto Gray's model to realize this potential. Breadth and flexibility are important, but if the model is so broad and flexible that it can explain just about any finding after the fact, then the validity of the "explanations" must be suspect.

Consider the predisposition to impulsive behavior. By one account, impulsivity may reflect a strong BAS, conferring enhanced sensitivity to reward cues and a bias toward behavioral approach as opposed to avoidance (Gray, 1981; Gray, Owen, Davis, & Tsaltas, 1983). Alternatively, a weak BIS may diminish inhibitory control over response inclinations from the BAS, resulting in a tendency to act quickly without adequate regard for negative consequences (Fowles, 1980). A third explanation highlights the role of NAS activity in promoting the rapid initiation and intense maintenance of goal-directed behavior (Wallace et al., 1991). Finally, a fourth explanation focuses on the reciprocal inhibition of the BAS and BIS (Newman & Wallace, 1993a). Given the range of potential "explanations," Gray's model can account for impulsive behavior in diverse ways, but the etiology of specific instance of the behavior remains obscured.

This example raises an important issue concerning the distinction between applicability and utility. Though the broad applicability and provision of multiple pathways to dysregulation are strengths of Gray's model, investigators must be careful not to accept ostensibly compelling explanations without critically evaluating alternative ones. Relatedly, they must resist attributing phenotypically similar behaviors (e.g., impulsive behavior) to identical mechanisms without explicit examination of the potential pathways. It is possible to generate and test specific explanations for particular behaviors using Gray's model, but this generally requires the manipulation or measurement of multiple components of the model (see the next section on methodological issues). Overall, Gray's model appears to be broad enough to accommodate a wide range of behaviors, elaborate enough to suggest multiple explanations, and detailed enough to allow specific hypothesis testing.

Paralleling this discussion of impulsivity, a fundamental controversy emerging from the literature on cNS models of antisocial behavior concerns the extent to which psychopathy and other antisocial syndromes may be conceptualized as exaggerated approach behavior (e.g., strong BAS), low anxiety (e.g., weak BIS), or some other biopsychological process (e.g., low constraint, poor response modulation).

METHODOLOGICAL ISSUES

Sample Characteristics

To the extent that investigators hypothesize specific biopsychological predispositions to antisocial behavior, obtaining meaningful results depends on the homogeneity of the sample identified. In light of the heterogeneity that characterizes antisocial individuals, it is crucial to define subject groups carefully. Many investigators (e.g., Blackburn, 1983; Raine & Venables, 1981; Trasler, 1978) regard antisocial behavior as a failure of socialization influenced by a combination of biological and environmental factors. However, some cases of antisocial behavior appear to reflect environmental factors primarily, whereas biological factors seem to be paramount in others. If one's goal is to identify a biological predisposition, it is important to study subjects whose antisocial behavior is likely to have important biological determinants.

Though strategies for achieving homogeneous groups have not, as yet, been well elaborated, they may involve (a) eliminating subjects with strong environmental inducements to antisocial behavior, (b) focusing on subjects with especially chronic or extreme forms of antisocial behavior, (c) focusing on subtypes with a demonstrated family history, or (d) identifying and using biological/cognitive markers or personality traits to identify more homogeneous groups.

Laboratory Measures

As noted earlier, investigators have related the components of Gray's model to various biochemical, psychophysiological, behavioral, and self-report measures. Examination of this work suggests that each of these measures contributes a relatively unique and complementary perspective on Gray's cNS model, although the relation of these measures to specific components of Gray's model is inferential. Thus, investigators must exercise caution in using any one of these measures to draw conclusions about which aspect of Gray's model has been assessed.

For example, Fowles (1980) offers a compelling argument concerning the association of Gray's BIS with EDA, but the link between BIS functioning and EDA is, itself, only a hypothesis. In outlining his proposal, Fowles (1980) stated, "It is not necessarily being argued that EDA responds only to stimuli which activate the BIS. . . . EDA is seen in response to a wide range of stimuli" (p. 93). Thus, there is reason to be cautious in attributing group differences in EDA to BIS functioning in particular. Even when subjects' reactions to aversive events are assessed under well-controlled laboratory conditions, individual differences in EDA may relate to a variety of factors, including some that are independent of BIS functioning (e.g., active avoidance; Miller, 1979; Spziler & Epstein, 1976). Thus, low EDA per se is not sufficient to identify psychopathy with a weak BIS.

Interpreting the biochemical evidence on antisocial individuals using Gray's model has been the subject of several reviews (e.g., Gray, 1991; Lewis, 1991; McBurnett, 1991; Quay, 1993; Rogeness et al., 1992). Although there appears to be some consensus regarding the relation of Gray's subsystems to the major neurotransmitter systems, the proposals are quite tentative and exceedingly complex. Although recent efforts to bridge the biochemical and behavioral domain using Gray's model as a framework represent an exciting development, the use of biochemical manipulations or measures to draw conclusions about group differences in BAS or BIS functioning is also premature.

A third means of assessing the components of Gray's model involves behavioral performance under well-controlled laboratory conditions. For example, evaluating the probability and intensity of responding for reward provides a reasonable index of BAS activity; the probability and amount of response suppression in response to punishment cues affords a measure of BIS activity; and a bias toward approach or avoidance under mixed-incentive conditions provides information about the balance between the systems (see Arnett, Smith, & Newman, in press; Newman & Wallace, 1993a; Quay, 1993). Moreover, there is some evidence that response speed and, to a smaller degree, attentional focus are informative with regard to NAS activity (Wallace et al., 1991; Wallace & Newman, in press).

Here too, it would be hazardous to draw conclusions without assessing other elements of the model. As already noted, the components of Gray's model are interactive and, thus, yield multiple pathways to a given outcome. Impulsive behavior may reflect intense BAS activation, high NAS reactivity, or a weak BIS. Although laboratory research on passive avoidance learning in psychopaths is often attributed to individual differences in the strength of the BIS, it too may reflect multiple mechanisms. The behavioral outputs of Gray's model (i.e., approach, passive avoidance) reflect the resolution of a go/no-go conflict with multiple factors influencing the outcome (Newman & Wallace, 1993a). Multiple pathways notwithstanding, an advantage of behavioral measures concerns their face validity owing to Gray's behavioral description of each system's function.

Investigators have also proposed using self-report measures of personality and affect to characterize the psychological processes contributing to antisocial behavior using Gray's model. Based on Tellegen's mapping of positive emotionality to the BAS and negative emotionality to the BIS, for instance, it may be informative to assess positive and negative affect in antisocial offenders to draw inferences about BAS- and BIS-related processes, respectively (see Fowles, 1987). More recently, Fowles and Missel (1994) proposed that measures such as Schalling's (1978) psychic anxiety and somatic anxiety scales may be useful for assessing BIS and FFS activity, respectively. Here too, however, investigators must be cautious because trait differences may reflect diverse psychological processes, including the cumulative effects of diverse experiences that are influenced by personality-related response inclinations (see Fowles, 1987; Frick, in press).

Overall, it appears that biochemical, psychophysiological, behavioral, and self-report measures may be used as rough estimates of BAS and BIS functioning suitable for characterizing antisocial individuals as BAS or BIS dominant. Despite the global nature of this distinction, it represents an important step in recognizing the diverse processes contributing to antisocial behavior and provides a context for integrating the correlates of antisocial behavior across multiple measurement domains.

On the other hand, a major thesis of this chapter is that cNS models offer the opportunity for greater precision in specifying the psychological processes underlying antisocial behavior; and, in this regard, the distinction between BAS and BIS dominant styles seems short of the mark. Indeed, the position advocated in this chapter is that realizing the unique potential of Gray's model involves moving beyond the classification of antisocial syndromes according to the major components of his model. In my opinion, the unique contribution of cNS models relates to their ability to generate testable hypotheses with a degree of novelty and specificity that would not be possible without the detailed perspective that they provide (see Gorenstein & Newman, 1980).

CURRENT FINDINGS

This section reviews a select literature on the psychopath as a means of exploring the application of Gray's model to antisocial behavior. In particular, I attempt to evaluate alternative mechanisms for psychopathic behavior derived from Gray's model. This strategy is intended to highlight methodological issues pertaining to diverse interpretations, particularly the importance of using experimental manipulations and multiple measures. Among other reasons, psychopathy was selected because it is generally regarded as the prototypical antisocial syndrome (Gorenstein & Newman, 1980), it appears to have important psychobiological underpinnings (Hare, 1991; Hart & Hare, Chapter 3, this volume), and there is considerable evidence that it may be assessed reliably and validly using Hare's Psychopathy Checklist (PCL; Hare, 1991). Moreover, evidence suggests that the PCL identifies a relatively homogeneous and extremely antisocial group with regard to number and range of crimes, frequency of violent and sex crimes, degree of substance abuse, and risk for recidivism (see Hare, 1991, for a review). Given the reliability of the PCL, its ability to identify a relatively homogeneous group of subjects, and the prolific antisocial behavior of the subjects identified, PCL-defined psychopaths represent a good sample for evaluating the application of Gray's model to antisocial behavior.

The Weak BIS Hypothesis

In a particularly influential review of the implications of Gray's model for psychopathy, Fowles (1980) proposed that many symptoms of psychopathy are "interpretable as a direct manifestation of a weak or deficient BIS" (p. 96). According to Fowles (1980), a weak BIS could explain psychopaths' absence of anxiety and difficulty inhibiting behavior in the presence of punishment cues, problems learning from past punishments (passive avoidance) and nonreward (extinction), strong reward-seeking behavior, tendency toward unsocialized active-avoidance (which, like reward, is mediated by the BAS), and their low tolerance for alcohol.

With regard to experimental evidence, Fowles (1980, 1993a) relies on pre-existing psychophysiological, behavioral, and personality data to link psychopathy and the BIS. Numerous studies document psychopaths' weaker electrodermal (EDA) in response to stimuli that have been paired with aversive events and in anticipation of aversive events (Hare, 1978). If Fowles's assumption linking EDA and BIS activity is correct, then such evidence is consistent with a weak BIS. With regard to behavioral evidence, Fowles (1988) cites laboratory studies demonstrating deficient passive avoidance learning (e.g., Lykken, 1957; Newman & Kosson, 1986; Newman, Widom, & Nathan, 1985) and extinction (Newman, Patterson, & Kosson, 1987; Siegel, 1978) as evidence of deficient BIS functioning in psychopaths. The weak BIS hypothesis is also consistent with clinical characterizations of psychopaths emphasizing "absence of nervousness or psychoneurotic manifestations" (Cleckley, 1976, p. 224).

Fowles's (1980) paper has been important for demonstrating the applicability of Gray's model to psychopathy and antisocial behavior more generally (see also Fowles, 1988). To advance understanding, however, investigators must use the weak BIS hypothesis as a springboard to generate and test more specific alternative hypotheses rather than evaluating the global hypothesis.

The BIS carries out numerous functions related to checking stimuli, interrupting behavior, shifting the focus of attention, and initiating passive avoidance, all of which are subserved by different physiological systems (Gray, 1987, 1991). If the multicomponent nature of the BIS is granted, then it is important for proponents of the weak BIS hypothesis to be clear about which aspect of BIS functioning is presumed dysfunctional in psychopaths or, alternatively, whether psychopaths are deficient in all aspects of BIS functioning. In the latter case, it would be useful to specify whether (a) some integrative dysfunction is presumed to render all of the separate processes comprising the BIS ineffective, (b) a problem at the input stage (e.g., insensitivity to punishment cues) precludes enactment of other BIS functions (i.e., the interruption of approach and redirection of attention), or (c) some other process (e.g., exaggerated approach) is presumed responsible for psychopaths' failures to stop, reflect, and initiate passive avoidance.

Such elaboration might also clarify the extent to which the weak BIS hypothesis represents an advance over the low-fear theory. In discussing what he calls the Fowles-Gray-Lykken theory, Lykken (1995) stated that it "assimilates the Lykken low-fear theory, now the 'weak-BIS' theory" (p. 163). Using Gray's model to recast long-standing theory and research involving psychopaths' insensitivity to fear stimuli exercises the broad applicability of the model but may do little to advance the field. The utility of Gray's model involves its ability to generate alternative hypotheses about the psychological processes contributing to inhibitory deficits—processes that may then be tested and further elaborated to increase understanding.

An example of the need for greater specificity concerns the common assumption that psychopaths' poor passive avoidance learning supports a weak BIS interpretation. Psychopaths do not display a global deficit in passive avoidance learning (Newman & Kosson, 1986; Schmauk, 1970). Available evidence suggests that psychopaths fail to master passive avoidance contingencies when they are latent (Lykken, 1957) or otherwise require subjects to suspend goal-directed behavior to process secondary contingencies (Newman & Wallace, 1993b). When passive avoidance contingencies are salient from the outset of a task, so that subjects do not need to alter the focus of their goal-directed behavior to process them, then psychopaths perform as well as controls (Newman & Wallace, 1993b). Relatedly, psychopaths perform passive avoidance tasks as well as controls when trials are well spaced, allowing ample time to suspend goal-directed behavior and process punishment feedback (Arnett, Howland, Smith, & Newman, 1993; Newman et al., 1987).

Similar evidence exists regarding the situation specificity of psychopaths' EDA (Arnett et al., in press). Low-anxious psychopaths displayed significantly less EDA than low-anxious nonpsychopaths in response to punishment cues while they were responding for rewards even though their EDA to the same cues was nonsignificantly *greater* than that of controls in the absence of reward cues.

The situation-specific nature of psychopaths' deficient passive avoidance and EDA indicates that they are not globally insensitive to punishment cues. Deficient passive avoidance is seen most clearly on tasks in which subjects must alter a pre-established or otherwise dominant response set to process punishment feedback. Such evidence is not consistent with a global, weak BIS hypothesis or with proposals targeting the BIS input (i.e., sensitivity to punishment cues). More specifically, the data suggest a problem with the BIS interrupt function or some other process responsible for updating a person's response strategy (see Damasio, 1994; Newman et al., in press; Patterson & Newman, 1993).

The BAS Dominance Hypothesis

The same year that Fowles (1980) related Gray's SHS model (i.e., the BIS) to psychopathy, Gorenstein and Newman (1980) proposed a "septal lesion" model for psychopathy and other syndromes of disinhibition. Although this model has been misrepresented as positing a "brain defect" (Lykken, 1995, p. 180), Gorenstein and Newman (1980) stated unambiguously that "in suggesting such an analogy, we do *not* imply that human disinhibition can be traced to septal dysfunction. Rather, we suggest that behavioral analysis of the septal syndrome can elucidate basic psychological components of human disinhibition" (p. 302). On this basis, Gorenstein and Newman (1980) proposed that "one may hypothesize that hypersensitivity to rewards . . . characterizes human disinhibition and in turn plays a significant role in sustaining the known avoidance deficits" (p. 312). A more elaborate version of the reward dominance hypothesis has been set out by Quay (1988, 1993) with regard to the behavior problems of children with conduct and attention deficit disorder.

To explore this hypothesis, Newman and Kosson (1986) examined passive avoidance learning under conditions involving monetary punishments only or a combination of reward and punishment incentives. Although the tasks used in the two conditions were identical, psychopaths' deficient passive avoidance was specific to the condition requiring them to inhibit reward seeking to avoid punishment (see also, Moses, Ratliff, & Ratliff, 1979; Newman et al., 1985; Scerbo et al., 1990; Thornquist & Zuckerman, 1995). Replicating and extending earlier work by Siegel (1978), Newman et al. (1987) found that psychopaths also perseverated responding for reward in a card-playing task despite the fact that their excessive reward seeking resulted in their earning significantly less money than controls (see also, S. K. Shapiro, Quay, Hogan, & Schwartz, 1988).

Arnett et al. (in press), employed a combination of behavioral and psychophysiological measures to evaluate BAS-related activity in psychopaths and nonpsychopathic offenders during a serial-reaction-time task. Subjects earned 5 cents each time that their response rate for five consecutive responses exceeded a criterion. As predicted by the strong BAS hypothesis, low-anxious psychopaths responded significantly faster than controls, but this effect was qualified by a higher order interaction indicating that support was due primarily to response rate during later trials. Because the reward-only trials were interspersed with reward-punishment trials, response speed during the later reward-only trials may have been influenced by factors other than reward.

Whereas the findings for passive avoidance and response perseveration are consistent with proposals that reward seeking has overshadowed avoidance, they provide little or no evidence that hypersensitivity to reward per se is responsible for this response style. Because weak inhibition may reflect multiple pathways in Gray's model, establishing such influences requires more focused experimental manipulations. To examine sensitivity to reward cues more directly, Newman, Patterson, Howland, and Nichols (1990) employed a pattern-matching task involving reward-only and punishment-only incentives. Unlike impulsive college students, low-anxious psychopaths did not appear to be differentially activated by reward cues. Newman, Kosson, and Patterson (1992) examined delay of gratification under reward-only and reward-punishment conditions. Here too, low-anxious psychopaths appeared no more impulsive than controls in the reward-only condition. Similarly, low-anxious psychopathic delinquents performed as well as controls on a reward-only version of the passive avoidance task described earlier (e.g., Newman et al., 1985).

Gray (1987; see also, Lykken, 1995) has proposed that the disinhibited behavior of primary or low-anxious psychopaths may reflect a weak BIS, whereas the behavior problems of high-anxious or neurotic psychopaths reflect exaggerated approach (i.e., a strong BAS). This review has focused on the evidence for hypersensitivity to reward cues in primary (low-anxious) psychopaths and, therefore, does not contradict proposals relating this mechanism to other disinhibited groups (see also, Newman & Wallace, 1993a).

The Response Modulation Hypothesis

Whereas the previous hypotheses focus on whole systems (e.g., the BIS) or their relative dominance, Gray's model also provides a useful framework for investigating a variety of specific processes that may hamper self-regulation (see Newman & Wallace, 1993a, 1993b; Nichols & Newman, 1986). The response modulation hypothesis provides a good example. The term *response modulation* was used by McCleary (1966) to describe the tendency of animals with septal and hippocampal lesions to persist in "dominant" responses despite punishment, extinction, or contingency reversal (i.e., response perseveration). Thus, response perseveration was viewed as a failure to revise response strategies based on new or unexpected information rather than an imbalance between reward and punishment motivation. Similarly, the response modulation hypothesis attributes the self-regulatory problems of psychopaths to a reduced capacity to shift attention from the effortful organization and implementation of goal-directed behavior to its evaluation/modification (Newman et al., 1987, 1990; Patterson & Newman, 1993; see also, Damasio, 1994). Patterson and Newman (1993) proposed a four-stage model to elucidate response modulation and distinguish it from the insensitivity to punishment emphasis entailed by the weak BIS hypothesis (see also, Newman, 1987). At Stage 1 of the model, a person allocates attentional and motor resources to achieving a particular goal. If the goal-directed behavior is successful, then the sequence ends. However, if the person perceives proprioceptive or environmental feedback indicating that the goal-directed behavior is unsuitable, then such information produces an increase in nonspecific arousal and a "call for processing" in Stage 2. Stage 3 involves the person's reaction to the call for processing. In one scenario, the person suspends goal-directed behavior and reorients attention (i.e., displays reflectivity) in which case the increase in arousal subserves cognitive processing of the unexpected/revised circumstances. In another, the person fails to alter his or her ongoing (dominant) response set with the result that the arousal fuels active responding (i.e., disinhibition) related to the original goal-directed behavior. Stage 4 involves the consequences of the response style displayed at Stage 3. Whereas pausing to reflect on the arousal-eliciting event enables a person to adjust his or her

response strategy and learn from experience, the disinhibited reaction facilitates active coping but reduces encoding of the stimulus conditions and behavior that gave rise to the problem. Although it is difficult to rule out problems associated with Stages 1 and 2, Patterson and Newman (1993) have proposed that the poor passive avoidance learning and other poorly regulated behavior of psychopaths relate to processes connected with Stage 3 of the model, which, in turn, interferes with consolidation of information at Stage 4 (see also, Newman & Wallace, 1993b).

Most, if not all, of the behavioral data cited in support of the weak BIS and BAS dominance hypotheses are also consistent with the poor response modulation hypothesis (i.e., psychopaths fail to suppress approach behavior despite punishment). Distinguishing among the alternative explanations requires careful analysis of the *situations* in which psychopaths display inhibitory failures as well as detailed assessment of the model's multiple components.

Although such studies are scarce, Newman and Wallace (1993b) suggest that available evidence is most consistent with the response modulation hypothesis. First, there is little evidence that psychopaths display regulatory deficits in reward- or punishment-only situations (Newman et al., 1990). Even though the EDA of psychopaths is distinctive in punishment-only situations, their disinhibited behavior is relatively specific to situations requiring subjects to suspend approach behavior in reaction to cues for punishment (Newman & Wallace, 1993b). Second, even in situations involving approach-avoidance conflict, psychopaths tend to perform as well as controls when the demands for response modulation are minimized by making the avoidance contingency salient from the outset (Newman et al., 1990; Newman, Wallace, Schmitt, & Arnett, in press) or providing subjects with ample time to process negative feedback (Arnett, Howland, Smith, & Newman, 1993). Third, psychopaths often display a paradoxical increase in response speed in reaction to punishment cues, suggesting that they are normally responsive to the arousing, though not the inhibiting, properties of such cues (Arnett et al., in press). Finally, psychopaths seem to be less influenced by contextual cues even when they are unrelated to punishment (Newman, in press; Newman et al., in press).

In addition, the response modulation hypothesis suggests an explanation for poor socialization and lack of constraint that is largely independent of reward and punishment sensitivity and, thus, the impulsivity and anxiety/negative emotionality dimensions (see also, Depue & Spoont, 1986; Lynam, 1996). In its general form, the response modulation hypothesis holds that once engaged in effortful goal-directed behavior, psychopaths are relatively unaffected by contextual cues that automatically prime associations and enhance perspective in controls. Such perspective taking may be essential for good judgment, affective depth, impulse control, interpersonal commitment, and self-regulation more generally (Newman, in press; Newman & Wallace, 1993b; D. Shapiro, 1965).

Although the response modulation hypothesis was not derived from Gray's model, the framework helped form specific a priori hypotheses about the nature of the problem and its consequences for self-regulation (Patterson & Newman, 1993). According to Gray (1987), the SHS is instrumental in comparing stimulus inputs from the environment with predictions based on knowledge of (a) past environmental regularities (acquired via Pavlovian conditioning), (b) the next intended behavior, and (c) the anticipated consequences of such behavior on the environment (inferred from instrumental conditioning). For the most part, this complex integrative process occurs in a relatively automatic fashion. However, "if there is discordance between actual and expected stimuli or if the predicted stimulus is aversive—conditions that are jointly termed 'mismatch'—the septo-hippocampal system takes direct control over behaviour and now functions in 'control mode'" (Gray, 1987, p. 294). One interpretation of psychopaths' laboratory performance is that the (automatic) shift to control mode occurs less readily.

With regard to the neurochemistry underlying these processes, Gray (1987) proposes the following:

> Under appropriate conditions, the ascending noradrenergic input to the SHS prompts this into applying its computational powers to the analysis of anxiogenic stimuli; while the serotonergic input prompts it to inhibit motor behaviour. At the same time, the locus coeruleus system increases the activity of a number of other regions widely distributed in the brain (so exercising its general arousal function). (p. 313)

Finally, Gray (1987) notes that ascending serotonergic projections are especially important in mediating behavioral inhibition in response to "high-intensity anxiety" (p. 313; i.e., cues for punishment) as opposed to stimuli for nonreward (see also, Spoont, 1992).

Given this formulation, one may speculate that the laboratory performance of low-anxious psychopaths is related to the ascending serotonergic projections. Accordingly, cues for punishment would tend to elicit active as opposed to passive solutions without necessarily altering the arousal component of their response to punishment cues. Such individuals would also be more likely to emit dominant responses without sufficient processing of the relatively automatic associations primed by "mismatches." Moreover, laboratory evidence of disinhibited responding in psychopaths has been found principally in reaction to punishment cues rather than cues for nonreward[1] and while subjects are engaged in task relevant approach behavior (e.g., Newman et al., 1985, 1990, 1992). Although space limitations preclude elaboration, this brief consideration of the implications of Gray's model for psychopathy suggests a number of interesting questions and hypotheses relating to response modulation, serotonergic projections, and personality (e.g., constraint) with general implications for antisocial behavior (see also, Lynam, 1996).

---

[1]The reward-only control conditions employed in our research entail "frustrative nonreward" when subjects respond to the no-go cues. That is, the expected reward is omitted. The reward-only conditions are identical to the reward-punishment conditions with the exception that responses to no-go cues are followed by punishment in the latter case. Notably, this one difference is sufficient to determine whether we obtain group differences in passive avoidance learning and other measures of response inhibition.

SUMMARY, CONCLUSIONS, AND FUTURE DIRECTIONS

It has been proposed that cNS models are valuable for organizing and integrating findings from diverse literatures in relation to specific processes of relevance to antisocial behavior. This chapter focuses on Gray's model, which has been used increasingly for this purpose. The model provides a broad framework and encompasses a variety of physiological, motivational, learning, and cognitive factors of relevance to antisocial behavior. However, the literatures subsumed by these factors are themselves extensive and complex. It stands to reason, therefore, that a schematic version of Gray's model such as the one commonly applied in personality and psychopathology research (e.g., Figure 30.1) is necessarily superficial. Proper use of the model would seem to require investigators to become conversant with the research literatures being represented by the model (e.g., see Gray, 1987) in order to provide a meaningful analysis of the processes being modeled. Gray's model is especially valuable for clarifying the psychological implications of these literatures and highlighting potential interactions among the implied processes, but it cannot, without terrific loss of meaningful detail, substitute for the content of these literatures. To the extent that investigators reify the hypothetical constructs in Gray's model using broad notions such as approach-avoidance or reward sensitivity–punishment sensitivity, we lose the opportunity to advance our understanding of these complex, multidimensional processes.

These comments notwithstanding, there is evidence that Gray's model has proven useful at the level of schematic-based formulations. Such formulations are useful for demonstrating the applicability of Gray's model (e.g., a dysfunctional BIS could explain many symptoms of psychopathy); for conceptualizing competing hypotheses (e.g., the disinhibited behavior of particular antisocial syndromes may involve exaggerated BAS processes, weak BIS processes, or some combination of the two); for suggesting interactions that may moderate disinhibited behavior (e.g., high anxiety and, presumably, a strong BIS may moderate the expression of conduct disorder in children; Frick, in press; Walker et al., 1991); as well as for identifying psychological processes in need of more detailed analysis (e.g., Does the disinhibited behavior of psychopaths reflect BIS-mediated increases in NAS arousal?). The point emphasized throughout this chapter is that such formulations are valuable to the extent that they clarify the processes contributing to antisocial behavior. Given a literature linking electrodermal hyporeactivity to psychopathy, it is pointless to propose that EDA indexes the BIS and then use this evidence to conclude that a relationship between psychopathy and BIS functioning has been demonstrated. The significance of linking EDA to BIS functioning is that EDA may then be used to test more specific hypotheses. For example, to what extent is the evidence for weak BIS functioning (EDA) affected by BAS activation?

In conclusion, a thorough understanding of the predisposition to antisocial behavior appears to require integrating findings from the physiological, neuroendocrine, psychophysiological, behavioral, cognitive, emotional, and personality domains. As knowledge increases in each of these domains, so will the need for heuristic devices to conceptualize these diverse influences and their interactions. cNS models can serve this important function. Gray's model was used as an example to illustrate this function. The model demonstrates terrific potential for relating diverse influences on antisocial behavior as well as for identifying relatively unique processes contributing to the development of such behavior problems. However, to realize the potential of Gray's and other cNS models, it is essential that we do not reify hypothetical constructs nor lose sight of the complex physiological processes underlying them. The purpose of a cNS model is to increase the depth and specificity of our formulations. Used properly, they should stimulate specific hypotheses about the biopsychological processes underlying antisocial behavior, clarify the distinct biopsychological processes contributing to the antisocial behavior of diverse subgroups, and provide a means of conceptualizing the role of environmental factors in moderating antisocial response inclinations.

REFERENCES

Arnett, P. A., Howland, E. W., Smith, S. S., & Newman, J. P. (1993). Autonomic responsivity during passive avoidance in incarcerated psychopaths. *Personality and Individual Differences, 14,* 173–185.

Arnett, P. A., Smith, S. S., & Newman, J. P. (in press). Approach and avoidance motivation in incarcerated psychopaths during passive avoidance. *Journal of Personality and Social Psychology.*

Barratt, E. S., & Patton, J. H. (1983). Impulsivity: Cognitive, behavioral, and psychophysiological correlates. In M. Zuckerman (Ed.), *Biological bases of sensation seeking, impulsivity, and anxiety* (pp. 77–116). Hillsdale, NJ: Erlbaum.

Blackburn, R. (1983). Psychopathy, delinquency, and crime. In A. Gale & J. A. Edwards (Eds.), *Physiological correlates of human behavior* (pp. 187–203). New York: Academic Press.

Cleckley, H. (1976). *The mask of sanity* (5th ed.). St. Louis: Mosby.

Cloninger, C. R. (1987). Neurogenetic adaptive mechanisms in alcoholism. *Science, 23,* 410–415.

Coccaro, E. F., & Kavoussi, R. J. (1995). Neurotransmitter correlates of impulsive aggression. In D. M. Stoff & R. B. Cairns (Eds.), *The neurobiology of clinical aggression.* Hillsdale, NJ: Erlbaum.

Damasio, A. R. (1994). *Descartes' error: Emotion, reason, and the human brain.* New York: Putnam (Grosset Books).

Depue, R. A., Luciana, M., Arbisi, P., Collins, P., & Leon, A. (1994). Dopamine and the structure of personality: Relation of agonist-induced dopamine activity to positive emotionality. *Journal of Personality and Social Psychology, 67,* 485–495.

Depue, R. A., & Spoont, M. R. (1986). Conceptualizing a serotonin trait: A behavioral dimension of constraint. *Annals of the New York Academy of Sciences, 487,* 47–62.

Eysenck, H. J. (1967). *The biological basis of personality.* Springfield, IL: Charles C Thomas.

Eysenck, H. J. (1981). General features of the model. In H. J. Eysenck (Ed.), *A model for personality* (pp. 1–37). New York: Springer-Verlag.

Eysenck, H. J., & Eysenck, S. B. G. (1978). Psychopathy, personality, and genetics. In R. D. Hare & D. Schalling (Eds.), *Psychopathic behavior: Approaches to research* (pp. 197–223). New York: Wiley.

Eysenck, H. J., & Gudjonsson, G. H. (1989). *The causes and cures of criminality.* New York: Plenum.

Fowles, D. C. (1980). The three arousal model: Implications of Gray's two-factor learning theory for heart rate, electrodermal activity, and psychopathy. *Psychophysiology, 17,* 87–104.

Fowles, D. C. (1987). Application of a behavioral theory of motivation to the concepts of anxiety and impulsivity. *Journal of Research in Personality, 21,* 417–435.

Fowles, D. C. (1988). Psychophysiology and psychopathology: A motivational approach. *Psychophysiology, 25,* 373–391.

Fowles, D. C. (1993a). Electrodermal activity and antisocial behavior: Empirical findings and theoretical issues. In J. C. Roy, W. Boucsein, D. Fowles, & J. Gruzelier (Eds.), *Progress in electrodermal research* (pp. 223–237). London: Plenum.

Fowles, D. C. (1993b). A motivational theory of psychopathology. In W. Spaulding (Ed.), *Nebraska symposium on motivation: Integrated views of motivation, cognition, and emotion* (Vol. 41). Lincoln: University of Nebraska Press.

Fowles, D. C., & Missel, K. (1994). Electrodermal hyporeactivity, motivation, and psychopathy: Theoretical issues. In D. Fowles, P. Sutker, & S. Goodman (Eds.), *Psychopathy and antisocial personality: A developmental perspective: Vol. 17. Progress in experimental personality and psychopathology research* (pp. 263–284). New York: Springer, 1994.

Frick, P. J. (in press). Callous-unemotional traits and conduct problems: Applying the two-factor model of psychopathy to children. In R. D. Hare, D. Cooke, & A. Forth (Eds.), *Psychopathy theory: research and implications for society.*

Gorenstein, E. E. (1991). A cognitive perspective on antisocial personality. In P. A. Magaro (Ed.), *Annual review of psychopathology: Cognitive bases of mental disorders* (Vol. 1; pp. 100–133). Newbury Park, CA: Sage Publications.

Gorenstein, E. E., & Newman, J. P. (1980). Disinhibitory psychopathology: A new perspective and a model for research. *Psychological Review, 87,* 301–315.

Gray, J. A. (1970). The psychophysiological basis of introversion-extraversion. *Behavior Research & Therapy, 8,* 249–266.

Gray, J. A. (1972). Learning theory, the conceptual nervous system, and personality. In V. D. Nebylitsyn & J. A. Gray (Eds.), *Biological bases of individual behavior* (pp. 182–205). New York: Academic Press.

Gray, J. A. (1981). A critique of Eysenck's theory of personality. In H. J. Eysenck (Ed.), *A model for personality* (pp. 246–276). New York: Springer-Verlag.

Gray, J. A. (1982). *The neuropsychology of anxiety.* New York: Oxford University Press.

Gray, J. A. (1987). *The psychology of fear and stress.* New York: Cambridge University Press.

Gray, J. A. (1991). Neural systems, emotion, and personality. In J. Madden IV (Ed.), *Neurobiology of learning, emotion, and affect* (pp. 273–396). New York: Raven Press.

Gray, J. A. (1994). Framework for a taxonomy of psychiatric disorder. In S. H. M. van Goozen, N. E. Van de Poll, & J. A. Sergeant (Eds.), *Emotions: Essays on emotion theory* (pp. 29–60). Hillsdale, NJ: Erlbaum.

Gray, J. A., Owen, S., Davis, N., & Tsaltas, E. (1983). Psychological and physiological relations between anxiety and impulsivity. In M. Zuckerman (Ed.), *Biological bases of sensation seeking, impulsivity, and anxiety* (pp. 189–217). Hillsdale, NJ: Erlbaum.

Hare, R. D. (1978). Electrodermal and cardiovascular correlates of psychopathy. In R. D. Hare & D. Schalling (Eds.), *Psychopathic behavior: Approaches to research* (pp. 107–143). New York: Wiley.

Hare, R. D. (1991). *The Hare Psychopathy Checklist–Revised.* Toronto: Multi-Health Systems.

Hebb, D. O. (1955). Drives and the C.N.S. (conceptual nervous system). *Psychological Review, 62,* 243–254.

Kilzieh, N., & Cloninger, C. R. (1993, Spring). Psychophysiological antecedents of personality. *Journal of Personality Disorders, Supplement,* 100–117.

Larsen, R. J., & Ketelaar, T. (1989). Extraversion, neuroticism, and susceptibility to positive and negative mood induction procedures. *Personality and Individual Differences, 10,* 1221–1228.

Lewis, C. E. (1991). Neurochemical mechanisms of chronic antisocial behavior (psychopathy): A literature review. *Journal of Nervous and Mental Disease, 179,* 720–727.

Lykken, D. T. (1957). A study of anxiety in the sociopathic personality. *Journal of Abnormal and Social Psychology, 55,* 6–10.

Lykken, D. T. (1982, September). Fearlessness: Its carefree charm and deadly risks. *Psychology Today,* pp. 20–28.

Lykken, D. T. (1995). *The antisocial personalities.* Hillsdale, NJ: Erlbaum.

Lynam, D. R. (1996). Early identification of chronic offenders: Who is the fledgling psychopath? *Psychological Bulletin, 120,* 209–234.

McBurnett, K. (1991). Psychobiological approaches to personality and their applications to child psychopathology. In A. Kazdin & B. Lahey (Eds.), *Advances in clinical child psychology* (Vol. 14). New York: Plenum.

McCleary, R. A. (1966). Response-modulating function of the limbic system: Initiation and suppression. In E. Stellar & J. M. Sprague (Eds.), *Progress in physiological psychology* (Vol. 1, pp. 209–271). New York: Plenum.

Milich, R., Hartung, C. M., Martin, C. A., & Haigler, E. D. (1994). Behavioral disinhibition and underlying processes in adolescents with disruptive behavior disorders. In D. K. Routh (Ed.), *Disruptive behavior disorders in childhood* (pp. 109–138). New York: Plenum.

Miller, S. M. (1979). Controllability and human stress: Method, evidence, and theory. *Behavior Research and Therapy, 17,* 287–304.

Moses, J. A., Ratliff, R. G., & Ratliff, A. R. (1979). Discrimination learning of delinquent boys as a function of reinforcement contingency and delinquent subtype. *Journal of Abnormal Child Psychology, 7,* 443–453.

Newman, J. P. (1987). Reaction to punishment in extraverts and psychopaths: Implications for the impulsive behavior of disinhibited individuals. *Journal of Research in Personality, 21,* 464–485.

Newman, J. P. (in press). Psychopathic behavior: An information processing perspective. In R. D. Hare, D. Cooke, & A. Forth (Eds.), *Psychopathy theory: research and implications for society.*

Newman, J. P., & Kosson, D. S. (1986). Passive avoidance learning in psychopathic and nonpsychopathic offenders. *Journal of Abnormal Psychology, 95,* 257–263.

Newman, J. P., Kosson, D. S., & Patterson, C. M. (1992). Delay of gratification in psychopathic and nonpsychopathic offenders. *Journal of Abnormal Psychology, 101,* 630–636.

Newman, J. P., Patterson, C. M., Howland, E. W., & Nichols, S. L. (1990). Passive avoidance in psychopaths: The effects of reward. *Personality and Individual Differences, 11,* 1101–1114.

Newman, J. P., Patterson, C. M., & Kosson, D. S. (1987). Response perseveration in psychopaths. *Journal of Abnormal Psychology, 96,* 145–148.

Newman, J. P., Schmitt, W. A., & Voss, W. (in press). The impact of motivationally neutral cues on psychopaths: Assessing the generality of the response modulation hypothesis. *Journal of Abnormal Psychology.*

Newman, J. P., & Wallace, J. F. (1993a). Diverse pathways to deficient self-regulation: Implications for disinhibitory psychopathology in children. *Clinical Psychology Review, 13,* 690–720.

Newman, J. P., & Wallace, J. F. (1993b). Psychopathy and cognition. In P. C. Kendall & K. S. Dobson (Eds.), *Psychopathology and Cognition* (pp. 293–349). New York: Academic Press.

Newman, J. P., Wallace, J. F., Schmitt, W. A., & Arnett, P. A. (in press). Behavioral inhibition system functioning in anxious, impulsive, and psychopathic individuals. *Personality and Individual Differences.*

Newman, J. P., Widom, C. S., & Nathan, S. (1985). Passive-avoidance in syndromes of disinhibition: Psychopathy and extraversion. *Journal of Personality and Social Psychology, 48,* 1316–1327.

Nichols, S. L., & Newman, J. P. (1986). Effects of punishment on response latency in extraverts. *Journal of Personality and Social Psychology, 50,* 624–630.

Patterson, C. M., & Newman, J. P. (1993). Reflectivity and learning from aversive events: Toward a psychological mechanism for the syndromes of disinhibition. *Psychological Review, 100,* 716–736.

Quay, H. C. (1988). The behavioral reward and inhibition system in childhood behavior disorder. In L. M. Bloomingdale (Ed.), *Attention deficit disorder* (Vol. 3; pp. 176–186). New York: Spectrum.

Quay, H. C. (1993). The psychobiology of undersocialized aggressive conduct disorder: A theoretical perspective. *Development and Psychopathology, 5,* 165–180.

Raine, A., & Venables, P. (1981). Classical conditioning and socialisation—A biosocial interaction. *Personality and Individual Differences, 2,* 273–283.

Rogeness, G. A., Javors, M. A., & Pliszka, S. R. (1992). Neurochemistry and child and adolescent psychiatry. *American Academy of Child and Adolescent Psychiatry, 31,* 765–781.

Scerbo, A., Raine, A., O'Brien, M., Chan, C., Rhee, C., & Smiley, N. (1990). Reward dominance and passive avoidance learning in adolescent psychopaths. *Journal of Abnormal Child Psychology, 18,* 451–463.

Schalling, D. (1978). Psychopathy-related personality variables: The psychophysiology of socialization. In R. D. Hare & D. Schalling (Eds.), *Psychopathic behavior: Approaches to research* (pp. 85–106). New York: Wiley.

Schmauk, F. J. (1970). Punishment, arousal, and avoidance learning in sociopaths. *Journal of Abnormal Psychology, 76,* 325–335.

Shapiro, D. (1965). *Neurotic styles.* New York: Basic Books.

Shapiro, S. K., Quay, H. C., Hogan, A. E., & Schwartz, K. P. (1988). Response perseveration and delayed responding in undersocialized aggressive conduct disorder. *Journal of Abnormal Psychology, 97,* 371–373.

Siegel, R. A. (1978). Probability of punishment and suppression of behavior in psychopathic and nonpsychopathic offenders. *Journal of Abnormal Psychology, 87,* 514–522.

Spoont, M. R. (1992). Modulatory role of serotonin in neural information processing: Implications for human psychopathology. *Psychological Bulletin, 112,* 330–350.

Spziler, J. A., & Epstein, S. (1976). Availability of an avoidance response as related to autonomic arousal. *Journal of Abnormal Psychology, 85,* 73–82.

Tellegen, A. (1985). Structures of mood and personality and their relevance to assessing anxiety, with an emphasis on self-report. In A. H. Tuma & J. D. Maser (Eds.), *Anxiety and anxiety disorders* (pp. 681–706). Hillsdale, NJ: Erlbaum.

Thornquist, M. H., & M. Zuckerman, M. (1995). Psychopathy, passive-avoidance learning and basic dimensions of personality. *Personality and Individual Differences, 19,* 525–534.

Trasler, G. (1978). Relations between psychopathy and persistent criminality—Methodological and theoretical issues. In R. D. Hare & D. Schalling (Eds.), *Psychopathic behavior: Approaches to research* (pp. 273–298). New York: Wiley.

Walker, J. L., Lahey, B. B., Russo, M. F., Frick, P. J., Christ, A. G., McBurnett, K., Loeber, R., Stouthamer-Loeber, M., & Green, S. M. (1991). Anxiety, inhibition, and conduct disorder in children: I. Relations to social impairment. *Journal of the American Academy of Child and Adolescent Psychiatry, 30,* 187–191.

Wallace, J. F., Bachorowski, J., & Newman, J. P. (1991). Failures of response modulation: Impulsive behavior in anxious and impulsive individuals. *Journal of Research in Personality, 25,* 23–44.

Wallace, J. F., & Newman, J. P. (in press). Attentional processes mediating the breakdown of self regulation: Effects of neuroticism and stimulus significance. *Personality and Individual Differences.*

Wallace, J. F., & Newman, J. P. (in press). Neuroticism and the attentional mediation of dysregulatory psychopathology. *Cognitive Therapy and Research.*

CHAPTER 31

On the Psychobiology of Antisocial Behavior

MARKKU LINNOILA

BIOLOGICAL PSYCHIATRY AS A FRAMEWORK TO INVESTIGATE ANTISOCIAL PERSONALITY DISORDER

Using biological methods to study the brain and behavior has been hampered by the relative crudity of the available tools. The situation is changing at a breathtaking pace, however, because of advances in structural and functional imaging techniques, molecular biology, and molecular genetics. Two interesting consequences of the refinement of the biological methods are that the artificial division of psychiatry into biological and psychosocial components is disappearing, and understanding the role of genes is rapidly becoming necessary to delineate the specific role of environment in the development of psychiatric disorders. For the first time, there is evidence that a powerful pharmacological treatment and psychotherapy, when successful, can lead to similar changes in the activity of central nervous system circuits (Baxter et al., 1992).

All too often, the importance of the results of sophisticated biological studies has been diminished by a lack of sophistication in the clinical characterization of the study populations. This is unfortunate because the psychiatric knowledge base together with a high level of clinical skills in the area of diagnosis can be combined with the new techniques to ensure a more comprehensive and precise understanding of clinical conditions such as antisocial personality disorder.

DIAGNOSIS AND COURSE OF ANTISOCIAL PERSONALITY DISORDER

Antisocial personality disorder (ASPD), as defined in *DSM-IV,* has an early onset. The diagnostic criteria require that patients fulfill at least some of the criteria for conduct disorder prior to age 15 (American Psychiatric Association, 1994). Antisocial personality disorder is diagnosed much more often in men than in women, and it is particularly prevalent among alcohol and other substance abusing populations (American Psychiatric Association, 1994). ASPD, however, may not be life long. Many patients have been reported to remit if they survive until their 40s (Robins, 1966).

Antecedents of Antisocial Personality Disorder

Tarter, McBride, Buonpane, and Schneider (1977) were among the first to point out that men with early onset alcoholism and antisocial behavioral traits often had a history of attention deficit disorder. Later, Mannuzza, Klein, Bessler, Malloy, and La Padula (1993), in a longitudinal follow-up study, demonstrated that boys with attention deficit disorder, even without prominent features of conduct disorder, developed antisocial personality disorder much more often than boys without attention deficit disorder.

More recently, a Finnish follow-up study on a cohort of elementary school students in a small city found that early aggressiveness among boys preceded the development of conduct disorder, which, in turn, preceded early onset alcohol abuse with antisocial traits (Pulkkinen & Pitkanen, 1994). The role of early aggressiveness and a family history positive for paternal aggressiveness in the development of antisocial personality traits have also been emphasized by Moss, Vanyukov, and Martin (1995).

Common Comorbidities of Antisocial Personality Disorder

Alcohol dependence is a disorder that is very often comorbid with ASPD. Cloninger, Bohman, and Sigvardsson (1981) in their adoption study in Sweden defined two types of alcoholism. Type II had an early onset, the vulnerability was transmitted from fathers to sons, and the disorder was associated with antisocial personality traits. Cloninger et al.'s study was based on a general population sample. In a clinical sample, Irwin, Schuckit, and Smith (1990) examined Cloninger et al.'s criteria for subgrouping of alcoholics and found that the age at onset explained most of the variance in the course and symptomatology of alcoholism. Other criteria used by Cloninger et al. (1981) to define Type II alcoholism turned out to be superfluous. Furthermore, Anthenelli, Smith, Irwin, and Schuckit (1994), again in a clinical sample, found that 73% of patients with Cloninger et al.'s Type II alcoholism had primary antisocial personality disorder.

Schuckit, Pitts, Reich, King, and Winokur (1969) for a long time have applied a primary-secondary classification to alcoholism research. This classification depends on the relative times of onset of alcohol dependence and other mental disorders. It has proven to be very successful in clinical research. However, it may be problematic for genetic studies. The age-dependent expression of a genetic vulnerability to a type of alcoholism often associated with antisocial personality traits during childhood and early adolescence may be attention deficit or conduct disorder. This set of circumstances may complicate attempts to define homogeneous groups of patients for molecular genetic studies. This is because according to the primary-secondary classification an individual with a history of conduct disorder or attention deficit disorder, who later develops alcoholism with antisocial personality traits, is given the diagnosis of secondary alcoholism.

Polysubstance abuse is common among patients with ASPD and those with early-onset alcoholism (Schmitz et al., 1993). Clearly, molecular genetic studies are needed to decipher whether common genetic vulnerabilities predispose an individual to attention deficit, conduct, and antisocial personality disorders and to early-onset alcoholism and polysubstance abuse with and without antisocial personality disorder. The question is whether these conditions represent a spectrum of disorders based on the same genetic vulnerability variables or discrete disorders within the spectrum with discrete genetic vulnerability variables.

PSYCHIATRIC GENETICS OF ANTISOCIAL PERSONALITY DISORDER

Recent studies of twins (Lyons et al., 1995) and adoptees (Cadoret, Yates, Troughton, Woodworth, & Stewart, 1995) on antisocial personality disorder yielded interesting results. The main finding of Lyons et al. was that adult antisocial behavior has a significantly stronger genetic contribution than adolescent antisocial behavior. Cadoret et al. convincingly demonstrated an additive interaction between a genetic vulnerability and adverse adoptive home environment for the development of aggressivity and conduct disorder but not antisocial personality disorder. Yet, strong genetic and lesser environmental contributions were found to the vulnerability to develop ASPD. The Cadoret et al. (1995) results are difficult to reconcile with the findings of Pulkkinen and Pitkanen (1994) and Lyons et al. (1995). However, no obvious methodological deficiencies in the study explain the apparent discrepancies (Kendler, 1995). Furthermore, the results of Cadoret et al. (1995) also seemingly contradict postulates concerning transient adolescent limited antisociality as contrasted to life-course-persistent antisocial behavior described by Moffitt (1993). Again, molecular genetics may hold the key for understanding the more specific gene-environment interactions involved in the development of antisocial personality disorder and its predecessors, as pointed out by Carey and Goldman (Chapter 23, this volume).

Ethological Models of Aggressive and Affiliative Behaviors

Ethological models of behavior have contributed extensively to our understanding of the functioning of various neuronal circuits and neurotransmitters in controlling aggressive and affiliative behaviors (Ferris & De Vries, Chapter 24, this volume). Despite the elegance of many of the described studies in rodents, they have been relatively uninformative concerning antisocial behavior per se in humans.

This circumstance may be related to the lengthy developmental period that is important in humans but whose duration is compacted and whose content reduced in complexity among rodents. To simulate assortative mating among humans, nonhuman primates can be bred for certain heritable biochemical outcomes, such as low cerebrospinal fluid 5-hydroxyindoleacetic acid (5-HIAA) concentration. The selective breeding can be combined with parental neglect during critical developmental periods. These manipulations produce an animal model with face validity for antisocial personality traits. Nonhuman primates that have undergone these manipulations have a propensity to abuse alcohol when provided access to a palatable alcohol solution (Higley, Suomi, & Linnoila, 1996). Additional studies using operant techniques are needed to investigate the validity of this nonhuman primate model for alcoholism, substance abuse, and antisocial behavioral traits. Molecular genetic studies will elucidate vulnerability genes conducive to reduced central serotonin turnover rate in the animals.

MEDICAL HISTORIES OF ANTISOCIAL INDIVIDUALS

In the United States, individuals with antisocial personality disorder often are characterized by less than optimal pre- and perinatal care (Brennan & Mednick, Chapter 25, this volume). Undoubtedly, this set of circumstances contributes to lifelong adverse consequences and improving pre- and perinatal care in the United States should reduce the number of adults with antisocial personality disorder. It has to be noted, however, that Scandinavian countries, which have outstanding, mandatory pre- and perinatal care and very extensive social services, continue to have their fair share of adults with ASPD.

The role of head trauma in the development of antisocial personality disorder must not be overlooked. We recently have completed a study of young adults who, after a primarily frontal brain injury, developed the "pseudosociopathic syndrome" (P. Andreason et al., unpublished observations). These previously normal individuals, after recovering from the trauma, clinically resembled patients with ASPD. Similar to violent impulsive alcoholics who abuse their spouses, they had orbital, frontal, thalamic, and head of the candate nucleus deficits in neuronal activity revealed by deoxyglucose positron emission tomography (PET) scans (W. A. Williams et al., unpublished observations). More subtle brain injuries sustained early during development could be conducive to deviant development, for example, by impairing impulse control beginning in early childhood. This possibility is compatible with hypotheses put forward by Brennan and Mednick (Chapter 25, this volume).

Neuroimaging Studies

As reviewed by Henry and Moffitt (Chapter 26, this volume) and Raine (Chapter 27, this volume), the results of neuroimaging clearly point to frontotemporal neuronal activity deficits among patients with antisocial personality disorder. Consistent with these findings in imaging studies, neuropsychological studies have found indications of subtle frontal lobe function deficits among patients with ASPD (H. Weingartner et al., unpublished observations). Our finding of low 3-methoxy-4-hyphoxyphenyl glycol (MHPG) concentrations in the cerebrospinal fluid (CSF) of violent, alcoholic patients with antisocial personality disorder (Virkkunen, Eggert, Rawlins, & Linnoila, 1996) is compatible with Raine's reports (reviewed in Raine, Chapter 27, this volume) of reduced sympathetic arousal among recidivist criminals. We (D. T. George et al., unpublished observations) have completed a psychobiological study on spouse and child abusers, many of whom had alcohol dependence and antisocial personality traits. According to Raine's hypothesis, they showed abnormal cardiovascular reactivity to an intravenous lactate infusion as compared to healthy volunteers. Perhaps surprisingly and apparently different from Raine's postulate, the largest difference between the offenders and comparison subjects was in the vagal rather than the sympathetic regulation of the heart.

Neurotransmitter Correlates

The neurotransmitter correlates of antisocial personality disorder are complex. Reduced frontal serotonin turnover rate, as indexed by low CSF 5-HIAA concentration (Stanley, Traskman-Benz, & Dorovine-Zis, 1985) is common among impulsive, violent patients with antisocial personality disorder (Berman, Kavoussi, & Coccaro, Chapter 28, this volume). The clinical characteristics most commonly associated with the low CSF 5-HIAA concentrations are impaired impulse control (Linnoila et al., 1983), irritability (Virkkunen, Kallio et al., 1994; Berman et al., Chapter 28, this volume) hyperactivity, and abnormal day-night activity rhythms (Virkkunen, Rawlings et al., 1994).

Among rhesus monkey infants CSF 5-HIAA is highly heritable (Higley et al., 1993). Parental neglect during early development exacerbates the reduction in CSF 5-HIAA concentrations, which precedes and coincides with puberty (Higley, Suomi, & Linnoila, 1996). Adolescent male rhesus monkeys with low CSF 5-HIAA concentrations have impaired impulse control as indicated by long leaps at great heights in response to an interesting target, and they persevere in an intense activity once engaged. In the context of aggressive encounters, the perserverence often leads to "escalated aggression," which is conducive to physical injury and even death (Higley, Mehlman, Taub et al., 1996; Mehlman et al., 1995).

As reviewed earlier, antisocial, alcoholic, violent offenders also have low central and peripheral noradrenergic activity as indicated by low CSF MHPG concentrations (Virkkunen, Rawlings et al., 1994). Their main CSF dopamine metabolite, homovanillic acid (HVA), concentrations, however, have not been different from healthy volunteers in most of our studies.

Hormonal Correlates of Aggressive Behavior

Alcoholic, violent offenders diagnosed with antisocial personality disorder have been found to have high CSF free-testosterone and low CSF corticotropin concentrations (Virkkunen, Rawlings et al.,

1994). Early on, Virkkunen (1985) had discovered low urinary free-cortisol output among antisocial, alcoholic violent offenders. Similar to these findings, Moss, Vanyukov, and Martin (1995) reported low salivary free-cortisol concentrations among delinquent boys with conduct disorder (Brain & Susman, Chapter 29, this volume).

Contrary to Coccaro et al.'s unpublished results reviewed in Berman et al. (Chapter 28, this volume), we have not found low CSF argininevasopressin concentrations among alcoholic violent offenders as compared to controls (Virkkunen, Rawlings et al., 1994).

Among rhesus macaques, high CSF free-testosterone concentrations generally are associated with competitive aggressiveness and assertiveness necessary to maintain dominance. However, when a high CSF free-testosterone concentration is combined with a low CSF 5-HIAA concentration, the result is increased physical aggressiveness (Higley, Mehlman, Poland et al., 1996).

Pharmacotherapies of Violent Behavior

The common denominator of pharmacotherapies for violent behavior is a functional agonistic effect on the serotonin system. This is true for serotonin receptor agonists such as eltoprazine and serotonin uptake inhibitors. Beta-blockers are efficacious in aggression reduction in much higher doses and after longer periods of time than needed for beta receptor blockade. Their mechanism for reducing aggression most likely is inhibition of presynaptic serotonin autoreceptors. Lithium and carbamazepine, which in controlled studies also have reduced the incidence of aggressive behavior, are functional serotonin agonists in humans. (For a review, see Linnoila & Virkkunen, 1991; Karper & Krystal, Chapter 41, this volume).

PSYCHOSOCIAL TREATMENTS FOR ANTISOCIAL BEHAVIORAL TRAITS

Teaching coping skills has turned out to be an efficacious psychotherapeutic modality to treat early-onset alcoholics with antisocial traits (Litt, Babor, Del Boca, Kadden, & Cooney, 1992). Perhaps the therapeutic modality could be modified to serve patients with ASPD and be combined with serotonergic pharmacotherapies for maximal efficacy.

CONCLUSION

Antisocial personality disorder has an inherited vulnerability component that can be compounded by adverse developmental environment. The patients are characterized by a subtle frontal lobe functional deficit conducive to impaired impulse control and perseveration. Biochemically, impulsive, alcoholic, violent patients with ASPD are characterized by high CSF free-testosterone and low 5-HIAA and corticotropin concentrations. They often are physically hyperactive or have desynchronized day-night activity rhythms. Irritability and monotony avoidance are personality characteristics typical of alcoholic violent patients with antisocial personality disorder. If impulsive, alcoholic patients with ASPD survive until their 40s, many stop their alcohol abuse and, in this context, seem to reduce or stop their antisocial behaviors (Robins, 1966; Virkkunen & Linnoila, unpublished observations).

FUTURE DIRECTIONS

Well-designed molecular genetic studies are necessary to define the gene-environment interactions conducive to the development of ASPD. Understanding at the fundamental level is required to institute specific and, ideally, effective prevention strategies. Pathophysiological studies await the development of new ligands for brain imaging that will visualize transmitter turnover rates, receptor densities and affinities, and aspects of intracellular signal transduction mechanisms. Treatment studies based on manual-driven psychosocial interventions in combination with placebo controlled pharmacotherapeutic trials are needed to provide a rational means to reduce morbidity and mortality among patients with antisocial personality disorder.

Ironically, for the future studies to yield meaningful data, despite their technical sophistication, an exquisitely careful clinical description of patient populations remains one of the most critical variables.

REFERENCES

American Psychiatric Association. Committee on Nomenclature and Statistics. (1994). *Diagnostic and statistical manual of mental disorders* (4th ed.). Washington, DC: Author.

Anthenelli, R. M., Smith, T. L., Irwin, M. R., & Schuckit, M. A. (1994). A comparative study of criteria for subgrouping alcoholics: The primary/secondary diagnostic scheme versus variations of the Type 1/Type 2 criteria. *American Journal of Psychiatry, 151,* 1468–1474.

Baxter, L. R., Schwartz, J. M., Bergman, K. S., Szuba, M. P., Guze, B. H., Mazziotta, J. C., Alazraki, A., Selin, C. E., Ferng, H. K., Munford, B., & Phelphs, M. E. (1992). Caudate glucose metabolic rate changes with both drug and behavior theraphy for obsessive-compulsive disorder. *Archives of General Psychiatry, 49,* 681–689.

Cadoret, R. J., Yates, W. R., Troughton, E., Woodworth, G., & Stewart, M. A. (1995). Genetic environmental interaction in the genesis of aggressivity and conduct disorders. *Archives of General Psychiatry, 52,* 916–924.

Cloninger, C. R., Bohman, M., & Sigvardsson, S. (1981). Inheritance of alcohol abuse: Cross-fostering analysis of adopted men. *Archives of General Psychiatry, 38,* 861–867.

Higley, J. D., Mehlman, P., Poland, R., Taub, D., Vickers, D., Suomi, S. J., Linnoila, M. (1996). CSF 5-HIAA and CSF free testosterone correlate with different types of aggressive behaviors in a nonhuman primate model of violent behavior. *Biological Psychiatry, 40,* 1067–1082.

Higley, J. D., Mehlman, P., Taub, D., Higley, S., Vickers, D., Lindell, S., Suomi, S., & Linnoila, M. (1996). Excessive mortality in young free-ranging male non-human primates with low CSF 5HIAA concentrations. *Archives of General Psychiatry, 53,* 537–543.

Higley, J. D., Suomi, S. J., & Linnoila, M. (1996). A nonhuman primate model of Type II excessive alcohol consumption? (Part 1): Low CSF-5HIAA concentrations and diminished social competence correlate with excessive alcohol consumption. *Alcoholism Clinical and Experimental Research, 20,* 629–642.

Higley, J. D., Thompson, W. T., Champoux, M., Goldman, D., Hasert, M. F., Kraemer, G. W., Scalan, J. M., Suomi, S. J., & Linnoila, M. (1993). Paternal and maternal genetic and environmental genetic and environmental contributions to CSF monoamine metabolite concentrations in rhesus monkeys (macaca mulata). *Archives of General Psychiatry, 80,* 615–623.

Irwin, M., Schuckit, M. A., & Smith, T. L. (1990). Clinical importance of age at onset in Type 1 and 2 primary alcoholics. *Archives of General Psychiatry, 47,* 320–324.

Kendler, K. S. (1995). Genetic epidemiology in psychiatry. *Archives of General Psychiatry, 52,* 895–899.

Linnoila, M., & Virkkunen, M. (1991). Monoamines, glucose metabolism and impulse control. In M. Sandler, A. Coppen, & S. Harnett (Eds.), *5-hydroxytryptamine in psychiatry* (pp. 258–278). New York: Oxford University Press.

Linnoila, M., Virkkunen, M., Scheinin, M., Nuutila, D., Rimon, R., & Goodwin F. K. (1983). Low cerebrospinal fluid 5-hydroxy-indoleacetic acid concentration differentiates impulsive from nonimpulsive violent behavior. *Life Science, 33,* 2609–2614.

Litt, M. D., Babor, T. F., Del Boca, F. K., Kadden, R. M., & Cooney, N. L. (1992). Types of alcoholics II. Application of an empirically derived typology to treatment matching. *Archives of General Psychiatry, 49,* 609–614.

Lyons, M. J., True, W. R., Eisen S. A., Goldberg, J., Meyer, J. M., Faraone, S. V., Eaves, L. J., & Tsuang, M. J. (1995). Differential heritability of adult and juvenile traits. *Archives of General Psychiatry, 52,* 906–915.

Mannuzza, S., Klein, R. G., Bessler, A., Malloy, P., & La Padula, M. (1993). Adult outcome of hyperactive boys. *Archives of General Psychiatry, 50,* 565–576.

Mehlman, P., Higley, J. D., Fancher, B., Lilly, A., Taub, D., Vickers, D., Suomi, S., & Linnoila, M. (1995). Correlation of CSF 5-HIAA concentrations with sociality and the timing of emigration in free-ranging primates. *American Journal of Psychiatry, 152,* 907–913.

Mofitt, T. E. (1993). Adolescence-limited and life-course persistent antisocial behavior: A developmental taxonomy. *Psychological Review, 100,* 67–701.

Moss, H. B., Mezzich, A., Yao, J. K., Gavaler, J., & Martin, C. S. (1995). Aggressivity among sons of substance-abusing fathers: Association with psychiatric disorder in the father and son, paternal personality, pubertal development and socioeconomic status. *American Journal of Drug and Alcohol Abuse, 21,* 195–208.

Moss, H. B., Vanyukov, M. M., & Martin, C. S. (1995). Salivary cortisol responses and the risk for substance abuse in prepubertal boys. *Biological Psychiatry, 38,* 547–555.

Pulkkinen, L., & Pitkanen, T. (1994). A prospective study of the precursors to problem drinking in young adulthood. *Journal of Studies on Alcohol, 55,* 578–587.

Robins, L. N. (1966). *Deviant children grow up: A sociological and psychiatric study of sociopathic personality.* Baltimore: Williams & Wilkins.

Schmitz, J., DeJong, J., Roy, A., Garnett, D., Moore, V., Lamparski, D., Waxman, R., & Linnoila, M. (1993). Substance abuse among subjects screened out from an alcoholism research program. *American Journal of Drug and Alcohol Abuse, 19,* 359–368.

Schuckit, M. A., Pitts, F. N., Reich, J., King, L. J., & Winokur, G. (1969). Alcoholism I: Two types of alcoholism in women. *Archives of General Psychiatry, 20,* 301–306.

Stanley, M., Traskman-Benz, L., & Dorovini-Zis, K. (1985). Correlations between aminergic metabolites simultaneously obtained from human CSF and brain. *Life Science, 37,* 2609–2614.

Tarter, R. E., McBride, H., Buonpane, N., & Schneider, D. V. (1997). Differentiation of alcoholics. *Archives of General Psychiatry, 34,* 761–768.

Virkkunen, M. (1985). Urinary free cortisol secretion in habitually violent offenders. *Acta Psychiatry Scandinavica, 72,* 40–44.

Virkkunen, M., Eggert, M., Rawlings, R., & Linnoila, M. (1996). A prospective follow-up study of alcoholic violent offenders and fire setters. *Archives of General Psychiatry, 53,* 523–529.

Virkkunen, M., Kallio, E., Rawlings, R., Tokola, R., Poland, R., Guidotti, A., Nemeroff, C., Bissette, G., Kalogeras K., Karonen, S., & Linnoila, M. (1994). Personality profiles and state aggressiveness in Finnish alcoholics, violent offenders. *Archives of General Psychiatry, 51,* 28–33.

Virkkunen, M., Rawlings, R., Tokola, R., Poland, R., Guidotti, A., Nemeroff, C., Bissette, G., Kalogeras, K., Karonen, S. L., & Linnoila, M. (1994). CSF biochemistries, glucose metabolism, and diurnal activity rhythms in alcoholic violent offenders, fire setters and healthy volunteers. *Archives of General Psychiatry, 51,* 20–28.

PART FOUR

Prevention, Treatment, and Management

CHAPTER 32

The Prevention of Antisocial Behavior: Some Considerations in the Search for Effective Interventions

JOHN B. REID and J. MARK EDDY

THE SOCIAL CONTEXT IN WHICH THE DEVELOPMENT OF VIABLE PREVENTION PROGRAMS MUST BE DEVELOPED AND EVALUATED

In considerations of antisocial behavior within the United States, violence and the fear of violence have become highly charged flash points for political debate, scientific inquiry, dramatic changes in budget priorities at federal and local levels, and vigorous demonstrations of public dissatisfaction with the government. This level of concern seems justified. Compared with other industrialized and well-educated countries, the U.S. homicide rate is about twice that of the nearest competitor (see Potter & Mercy, Chapter 1, this volume). The homicide rate for males 15 to 24 years of age is over four times that of the runner up, with about half of those arrests involving persons age 21 years and younger (Cairns & Cairns, 1994; Fingerhut & Kleinman, 1990; World Health Organization, 1992). Since 1987, the rate of homicides by young adolescents has shown a disturbing and well-publicized increase (Greenwood, Model, Rydell, & Chiesa, 1996). Although, certainly, the current public and political outcries for decisive actions against criminals have been fueled by increasing fear and anger over seemingly random and violent street crimes, surprisingly (or perhaps not so surprisingly), the vast majority of violent acts in the United States are perpetrated by family members and friends (Zimring & Hawkins, 1995). Thus, in many ways, the nature of the problem is not quite what the debate would make it seem.

As is quite common in families, the response of the public and policy makers to the problem of antisocial behavior has been to "crack down" with strict sanctions. Since 1967, the public has been getting increasingly more punitive in its attitude about crime and punishment, with clear majorities across ethnic and economic groups now favoring the death penalty, mandatory sentencing for serious juvenile as well as adult offenders, and stiff sentences for recidivists (DiIulio, 1995; Mayer, 1992; U.S. Bureau of Justice Statistics, 1993). During the 1980s, such intensification in public

attitude, coupled with a marked increase in the "get tough" rhetoric of politicians, occasioned a massive increase in adult prison populations across the country. Even though national crime rates did not increase significantly during this period, in most states, incarceration rates increased over 300% (Greenwood et al., 1994). Although getting tough may provide private citizens with some sense of fairness and justice and politicians with enough votes to get reelected, it is quite an expensive proposition.

The prime example of legislation that has led to increases in incarceration is California's Three Strikes law. Enacted in 1994, Three Strikes is one of the most severe "get tough" laws in the United States, mandating that persons found guilty of a third felony be imprisoned for 25 years to life following convictions for two previous and serious felonies. The third felony need not be serious or violent for imposition of the mandated sentence. Brief consideration of some preliminary findings on the costs and benefits of the Three Strikes law provides a useful perspective for discussion of some of the major challenges that must be met if we are to develop strategies for the prevention of antisocial behavior that are scientifically, politically, *and* economically viable.

When Three Strikes went into effect in 1994, the Department of Corrections (DOC) budget in California was $2.6 billion, or 7% of total state spending. If the new law is fully enforced, by the year 2000 the corrections budget will swell to about $5.5 billion, or 20% of the projected state budget (Greenwood et al., 1994; Petersilia, 1995). According to Petersilia (1995), unless state or federal taxes are increased markedly, the money to cover this mandated program must come from other state programs. Because funding for primary and secondary education is guaranteed by the state constitution and spending for health and welfare currently also is mandated, the money needed for Three Strikes will likely come from and exhaust funds currently allocated for nonmandated programs, such as higher education and early child and family intervention and assistance programs. In other words, if current funding trends continue, there will likely be a scarcity of funds for any *additional* programs aimed to *prevent* the development of violent and antisocial behavior in the first place.

As the California experience demonstrates, given no increases in resources, additional money spent on prison services will diminish the funds available for prevention programs, even if such programs

Support for work on this chapter was provided by grants nos. P50 MH 46690 and R01-54248 from the Prevention Research Branch, NIMH, US. Public Health Service.

are demonstrated to be effective. The problem is further compounded by the simultaneous increase in incarceration as the solution of choice for youth violence. In Oregon, for example, voters recently passed a law to mandate incarceration for youngsters age 15 years and older who are convicted of a variety of felonies. This law quickly led to allocation of scarce juvenile corrections funds for the construction of four new secure facilities for youngsters.

Despite the enthusiasm over incarceration, little evidence indicates that the increased use of incarceration over the last decade has had any effect on the rate of violent crime (Greenwood et al., 1994; Reis & Roth, 1993). Recent studies modeling the costs and benefits of the Three Strikes program (Greenwood et al., 1996; Petersilia, 1995) indicate that the California adult prison population (currently more than 130,000) and the annual DOC budget (currently more than $2.5 billion) will double over the next 5 years. According to a recent projection, each crime prevented by the Three Strikes program will cost about $16,000, with a maximum reduction of 25% in the U.S. crime rate if the program were fully implemented nationally (Greenwood et al., 1996). As indicated previously, such a reduction, if achieved, would not change our international rank as number one in the rate of violent crime. Unless more economical and more effective alternative interventions can be developed, it will take more money than is available to reduce the U.S. homicide rate to the point that it does not far exceed that of other industrialized countries.

LIFE-COURSE DEVELOPMENT AND PREVENTION

A tremendous amount of basic research activity over the last two decades has studied the antecedents, development, maintenance, and the epidemiology of antisocial behavior. We now know that the serious, chronic, and violent antisocial behavior patterns discussed in the previous section are predictable mileposts along developmental pathways that can be traced back to early childhood or before. Once begun, it appears that developmental trajectories toward more serious antisocial behavior tend to be quite stable (Olweus, 1979); and the earlier these trajectories start, the greater is the risk for the most serious outcomes (Moffitt, 1993; Patterson, DeBaryshe, & Ramsey, 1989). The more generalized or diversified the antisocial behaviors demonstrated by children along these paths, the greater is the risk for a lifetime antisocial career (Loeber et al., 1993). Most important, we know that antisocial behaviors are not inert, but rather their coercive nature nearly guarantees that they will be perpetuated and intensified through the responses they generate in others (Dodge, 1983; Patterson, Reid, & Dishion, 1992; Reid, 1993).

We also know a great deal about the contextual factors and proximal antecedents along these paths that mediate the relationships between early and later child antisocial behaviors. Although significant contextual antecedents of antisocial behavior can be traced back even to previous generations (Caspi & Elder, 1988), a variety of preventable or malleable environmental risk factors that exist in the prenatal environment and onward have been identified. These environmental, or *contextual,* risk factors are many, and like individual behavioral risk factors, they are laid out along developmental paths, with exposure to a risk factor at one point in devel-

opment usually increasing the risk of being exposed to or affected by other risk factors at later points in development.

It is important to note that the developmental outcomes that follow from contextual and behavioral antecedents often are neither linear nor simply additive but dynamic, conditional, and interactive. Caspi, Elder, and Bem (1987) provide an excellent example of this sort of developmental complexity in their studies of the relationships of childhood ill-temperedness and occupational status in adulthood. They found no direct effect from early ill-temper to later occupational status, but they found a strong relationship between ill-temper and subsequent low educational attainment and between educational attainment and occupational status. Thus, in this instance, it is not just that the early conduct problems simply mature into problems in getting and holding good jobs, but rather that the early antecedent puts the child at risk for a second, more proximal, antecedent and so on, with the occurrence of each antecedent increasing the risk of poor adjustment during adulthood. Such sequences of contextual and behavioral risk factors, like mine fields, can be entered through any number of risk exposures. Conceptualizations such as cumulative disadvantage (Sampson & Laub, 1993) and interactional and cumulative continuities (Caspi & Moffit, 1995) have been articulated to describe the linkage of successive antecedents and the accumulation of risk over the life course.

Numerous examples of such interactional continuities have been documented in the developmental literature on antisocial behavior. Economic disadvantage, for example, is a powerful contextual antecedent of antisocial developmental trajectories, but its relationship to later delinquency is mediated by the extent to which it disrupts consistent and constructive parenting (Larzelere & Patterson, 1990). Coercive interaction between parent and child, characterized by ineffective and abusive discipline by the parent and noncompliance and aggressiveness by the child, is one of the earliest and strongest antecedents of antisocial behavior (Loeber & Dishion, 1983). But such difficulties in early parent-child interaction significantly increase the risk of conflict with both classmates and teachers in elementary school (Reid, 1993). In turn, each of these problems is a powerful antecedent of adolescent antisocial behavior in its own right (Patterson et al., 1992).

The rapidly expanding knowledge base about the development of antisocial behavior has major implications for how we conceptualize strategies for its prevention. Recently, two experienced groups of scientists, policy makers, and advocates conducted audits of the field of prevention and issued consensus reports on the current status and future directions of prevention science in mental health. Both the Institute of Medicine Report (IOM; Mrazek & Haggerty, 1994) and the National Institute of Mental Health Prevention Research Steering Committee Report (NIMH, 1993) underlined the necessity that the next generation of preventive interventions be carefully informed by data-driven life-course models, that the relationships of developmental antecedents to maladaptive outcomes be carefully articulated and specifically targeted for intervention, and that the key antecedent and mediating variables be measured.

A powerful prevention model should lay out the major antecedents of a target outcome and their dynamic relationships to one another across the life course. As used here, a preventive strategy is one that targets one or more of the significant antecedents, and its effectiveness needs to be assessed at two levels. The first level of effects are the immediate or *proximal* impacts of the prevention program on the antecedent(s) targeted. For example, to what extent did the specific parenting variables targeted in a preventive intervention improve as a function of the parent training? The second level of effects are the more *distal* impacts of the prevention program on either nontargeted, concurrent antecedents or subsequent antecedents that are specified by the developmental-epidemiological model, and their impacts on targeted symptoms or on the actual disorder. For example, did the child's improved identification of feelings lead to less rejection by classmates later in the year? Did improved parenting in the first grade lead to less truancy and greater academic success in middle school? Did observed changes in both the immediate and distal antecedents have any impact on subsequent juvenile arrest rates? The earlier in the life course the preventive intervention is implemented, the more important it is to specify and measure immediate impacts on targeted antecedents and subsequent hypothesized mediating variables as well as long-term outcomes. Such a focus ensures that each study of the efficacy of a prevention program serves not only as an experimental test of the program itself but also of the underlying theoretical model.

As indicated by a careful reading of other chapters in this volume and the brief examples described earlier, we are now in the position to develop life-course models of antisocial behavior that are of the type recommended by the IOM and the NIMH advisory committees. The basic elements of one plausible developmental model are presented here as a device to illustrate how the designs of some of the most promising recent preventive intervention and assessment strategies relate to recent developmental and methodological studies.

A DEVELOPMENTAL MODEL OF ANTISOCIAL BEHAVIOR

The illustrative model in Figure 32.1 is not an attempt to present a comprehensive model of the development of antisocial behavior. In accord with the discussion to this point, the model depicts a life-course trajectory toward antisocial behavior and serious delinquency that can begin to gain momentum even before birth and that increases in velocity and intensity through successive antecedents during childhood and adolescence. Four other important considerations are highlighted by the model. First, some of the antecedents are active only for a short time (e.g., maternal smoking and drug use during pregnancy) whereas others are active for years (e.g., parental discipline or monitoring, poor school performance, and association with delinquent peers). Such information is critical in deciding on the duration of preventive interventions. If an intervention is terminated before the targeted antecedent has diminished in importance (e.g., parental supervision through middle and high school), then a developmental model would not predict a long-term preventive impact unless there was reason to believe that the intervention had long-term persistence effects on the antecedent (e.g., parents independently continue to apply sufficient monitoring skills once taught) or follow-up booster intervention procedures were in place to ensure persistence.

Second, the settings in which the *proximal* antecedents exert their influence vary across development. Before birth, for example, most proximal antecedents reside in the fetus or within the mother, with the more distal contextual antecedents affecting the fetus to the extent that the mother's health, diet, substance use, and stress level are affected. During this period, comprehensive interventions could be designed that focus only on the pregnant mother. During early childhood, interactions between the child and key socialization agents such as parents, day care workers, and siblings serve as the most powerful antecedents to later behavior problems (see Shaw & Winslow, Chapter 15, this volume). Thus, interventions that focus on improving and supporting the prosocial "family management" skills (i.e., tracking, discipline, positive reinforcement, problem solving) of parents and day care workers most actively address the proximal antecedents. By the time the child has made the transition to elementary school, powerful antecedents can be found in at least three settings (i.e., home, classroom, and peer groups). Unless there are clear reasons for predicting why an intervention conducted in one setting will affect antecedents in the others, a multisetting intervention is likely required.

Third, the developmental model in Figure 32.1 provides a road map for measurement. As argued previously, each intervention trial should be not only an outcome study but also be an experimental test of the underlying theoretical model. This is the case particularly for early preventive interventions for antisocial behavior in which the distal outcome of *ultimate* interest (e.g., serious crimes against persons) may not be observable for 1 or 2 decades after the intervention. By carefully measuring the fidelity and dosage of implementation, the immediate impact of intervention on the targeted and nontargeted concurrent antecedents, and the more distal impacts on subsequent antecedents, mediators, and outcomes, we can determine (a) the degree and specificity to which the intervention was implemented, (b) the extent to which antecedents were immediately changed, and (c) the extent to which the immediate impacts were related to beneficial long-term changes. Collected on a regular basis across the field, such data would certainly help us to more efficiently improve both our theory and our implementation strategies.

Fourth, the model clearly highlights that many of the antecedents to serious antisocial behavior along the life course in themselves are significant public health problems that are costly in terms of both human suffering and public money. In the first year of life, premature and low-birth-weight deliveries as well as subsequent physical abuse are not just antecedents of later conduct problems but may lead to a variety of infant and child physical and mental health problems and further can be extremely expensive due to intensive medical care and social service needs. During the school years, educational problems, special educational services, and school dropout all have both personal and economic costs, as do such antecedents as early cigarette use and drug use and early sexual activity and parenting. To the extent that the immediate antecedents targeted by preventive interventions also are significant problems and preventable in their own right, such effects warrant measurement in terms of both individual outcomes and societal costs and benefits. Given that preventive interventions for antisocial behavior sometimes are pitted against incarceration and human services for limited funds, it will be critical to measure the benefits of the interventions as comprehensively as possible.

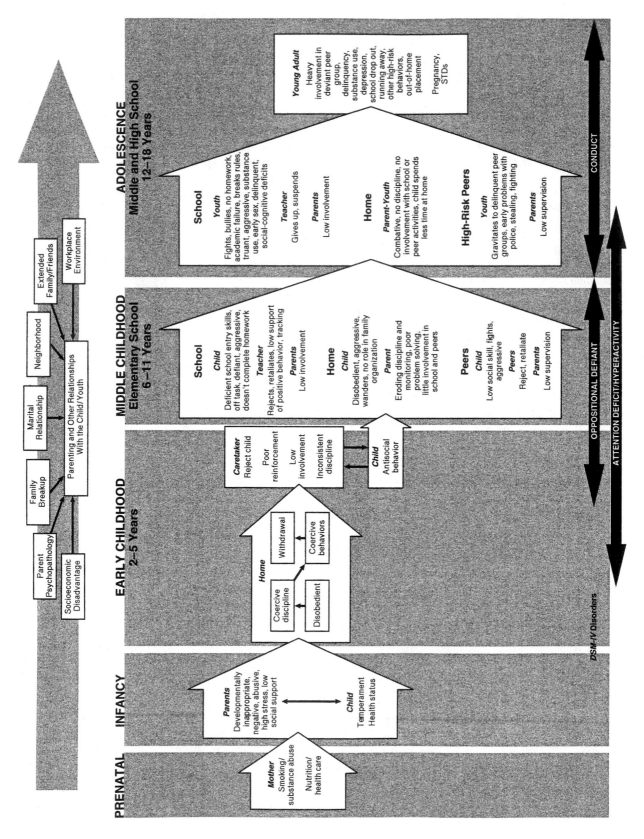

Figure 32.1 *Illustrative developmental model of child antisocial behavior.*

PREVENTIVE INTERVENTIONS ACROSS THE LIFE COURSE

Given a life-course developmental model of the same general sort as presented in this chapter, the idea of the *prevention of antisocial behavior* needs to be clarified. It would be difficult to use Figure 32.1 to chose one or even several points at which the child first develops a serious antisocial problem. The developmental process is not only highly stable (Olweus, 1979); it seems nearly seamless across the young life course. As illustrated in Figure 32.1, the sequential diagnostic classifications that mirror the developmental process reveal a process of more and more serious *disorders.* Although the point of onset is thus arbitrary, what is not arbitrary is the continued progress of the developmental trajectory once begun.

For the purposes of this chapter, *preventive interventions* refer to attempts to effect positive changes in the trajectories of youngsters at any point in the developmental process, as evidenced by at least one of the following: (a) a reduction of antecedents targeted during the intervention, (b) a reduction in the probability that subsequent antecedent risk factors will be demonstrated, or (c) a reduction in the risk of long-term, socially significant outcomes (e.g., delinquency, incarceration, violence). From consideration of these three criteria, two further definitional elements follow. First, preventive interventions can be mounted at any point along the life course. Second, as articulated by Kellam and Rebok (1992), the baseline for evaluating the effectiveness of preventive interventions is not a preintervention measure, as in some clinical and drug trials. Rather, the baseline is the *developmental trajectory* for youngsters of comparable risk status who are not exposed to the intervention.

In the next sections, examples of interventions at various points along the life course are discussed in terms of the extent to which the interventions target key active antecedents of antisocial behavior, their immediate impacts on targeted and subsequent antecedents, their impacts on long-term outcomes if available, their costs and benefits (if such information is available), and their implications for the next generation of preventive interventions.

INTERVENTIONS THAT TARGET THE PRENATAL AND EARLY CHILDHOOD ENVIRONMENT

Ziegler, Taussig, and Black (1992) wrote an excellent review article on the value of early interventions for the prevention of antisocial behavior and delinquency. Several long-term follow-up studies of early childhood prevention programs designed to promote overall child development, health, and competence showed remarkable power in reducing subsequent levels of antisocial and delinquent behavior. The reviewers considered the findings surprising but attributed the promising effects in reducing delinquency to the various programs embracing an "ecological view of child development by treating children through their broad environment rather than through isolated intervention" (p. 997). They argued that the interventions shared the focus of strengthening the families of the children and improving the interactions of families with the larger social systems in which they were embedded, thereby helping the child to learn effective coping skills in a vari-

ety of social contexts. By improving the social competence of the children, the authors argued that the children were less likely to engage in any number of socially incompetent activities, including juvenile delinquency.

These early interventions targeted many of the specific antecedents of antisocial behavior illustrated in Figure 32.1. If, in fact, risk is cumulative and early exposure to risk factors increases the probability of being exposed to more risk factors later, then the earlier the intervention, the more effective it should be in changing long-term developmental trajectories. Many of the interventions reviewed were initiated during pregnancy and targeted such factors as maternal nutrition (Lally, Mangione, & Honig, 1988), maternal health and smoking reduction (Olds, 1988), and family problem-solving skills (Provence & Naylor, 1983). As indicated in Figure 32.1, these are central antecedents for temperamental and cognitive difficulties at birth, which in turn are antecedent to poor patterns of parent-child positive interaction, which are antecedent to tantrums, aggression, and noncompliance by the child and coercive abusive and rejecting parenting during the toddler years, and so on.

Illustrative Early Interventions

A closer look at one of the most rigorous of the early intervention prevention studies cited previously is enlightening. In a randomized set of trials beginning in the 1970s, David Olds and his colleagues (Olds, Henderson, Chamberlin, & Tatelbaum, 1986; Olds, Henderson, Tatelbaum, & Chamberlin, 1986) tested the effects of early intervention and assistance for a sample of 400 poor, first-time mothers enrolled before the 30th week of pregnancy. In the most intense condition, the mothers were visited biweekly during pregnancy by a public health nurse, weekly for 6 weeks after birth, and on a progressively leaner schedule through age 24 months. The interventions stressed improving maternal health and cessation of drugs, particularly cigarettes. The child's health was an additional focus after birth, as well as the mother's care of the infant; her utilization of services; development of support systems; and family, educational, and occupational planning. The intervention was practical in nature, focusing on direct day-by-day care of the baby and better relationships with and utilization of opportunities in the larger community. Over the first 4 years of life, the babies born to control group mothers were exposed to many of the early proximal parenting and contextual antecedent risk factors of antisocial developmental trajectories, including high rates of referrals for physical abuse and neglect, high rates of health encounters for injuries and ingestions, low levels of maternal warmth and contingent punishment, and more emotional and health problems in general for the mothers. The infants themselves demonstrated early behavioral indications of trajectories toward antisocial behavior, including higher incidence of premature births and low birth weights, parent-rated fussiness at birth, and cognitive delays.

Olds and coworkers carefully measured the experimental groups on all these proximal risk factors repeatedly over the course of the studies. Large and significant intervention effects were observed on all these (and many other) early and proximal antecedents for antisocial behavior. For example, relative to comparison groups, the smoking mothers in the intervention groups significantly reduced their smoking during pregnancy; the incidence of child abuse and neglect during the first 2 years was 4% compared to 19% for the comparison group; and the mothers provided significantly more stimulating environments for their children. Further, the children were significantly less likely to require emergency room care, and their mental quotients significantly and steadily improved through age 3 to 4 years. Not only were there significant effects on most of the very early antecedents in Figure 32.1, but in many cases, the antecedents were neutralized over the entire developmental span during which our model indicates that they actually increase the risk of antisocial development.

As argued earlier, we think such developmental-span targeting is a *critical* ingredient to effective prevention trials. Smoking during pregnancy, which is clearly linked to postnatal temperament and cognitive problems, is an antecedent that becomes nearly inconsequential after birth. Although desirable, it is not essential to stop the mother from smoking forever, just for a few months to lower the risk of insults to the child's central nervous system. The vast majority of serious injuries and death from physical abuse occur before age 2 (American Humane Society, 1981), probably because babies are so fragile during this phase of development and because they can neither run away from parents nor complain to neighbors. If serious abuse can be effectively prevented during that period, as was demonstrated by Olds and his group, then one should expect major dividends in changing the developmental trajectories of very young children at risk for antisocial behavior. As will be described later, as the children reach preschool age, effective and well-evaluated interventions are available for remediating or preventing coercive, abusive, and incompetent parental discipline, which constitute a major set of antecedents at that period of development.

In addition to these proximal antecedents, the intervention had significant effects on a number of contextual antecedents as well. First, the mothers in the intensive intervention group showed a reduction in subsequent pregnancies of more than 40% compared to the control group and an increase in paid employment of more than 80% (Olds, Henderson, & Kitzman, 1994). The concomitant reductions in dependence on AFDC represent real cash savings to mandated entitlement programs. In fact, Olds et al. estimated the costs of the program to be just over $3,000 (in 1980 U.S. dollars) and calculated that those costs were recovered (by a calculation of reduced government expenditures relative to families in the control group) within 4 years (Olds, Henderson, Phelps, Kitzman, & Hanks, 1993). In addition, it will be possible to document the savings due to reduced reliance on welfare, fewer subsequent births, and increased payment of income taxes, as the follow-up study unfolds. Finally, it is probable that this study eventually will demonstrate significant cost effectiveness in terms of reduced crime and incarceration. In the current climate of tight money for preventive services, it is of critical importance to collect and report such data.

Because of its rigorous design and the measurement of both proximal and distal outcomes, Olds et al.'s work gives theoretical meaning to the findings of scores of other less rigorous early prevention studies that showed "surprisingly" effective results on subsequent delinquency. The next generation of early prevention trials must intensify efforts to unpack the specific active ingredients of the intervention strategies. Olds reported a number of analyses to indicate that nicotine reduction during pregnancy

reduced early childhood cognitive deficits (Olds, Henderson, & Tatelbaum, 1994). This is probably true; however, it would be useful to rule out alternative explanations. For example, perhaps, mothers who smoked socialized with other adults who smoked and who used other drugs. A significant number may have changed their socializing patterns to facilitate smoking reduction, such as by avoiding contact with other smokers. Just the social precautions taken to quit smoking might affect the level of peer antisocial influences to which the mother is exposed.

For the next generation of rigorous long-term studies, it will be useful to have broader input into the initial design of the research strategies. The studies conducted by Olds and his group, for example, originally were formulated and designed by experts in pediatric public health. As the cohort continues to develop, the range of developmental, theoretical, and measurement issues becomes increasingly complex. To get the maximum benefits from such expensive studies, it seems essential to utilize long-term consultation from multidisciplinary advisory boards.

INTERVENTIONS THAT TARGET THE FAMILY ENVIRONMENT

In the developmental model presented in Figure 32.1, it is argued that after school entry, the development of antisocial behavior is affected increasingly by behavioral, social, and contextual variables in multiple settings outside the home. However, a substantial body of longitudinal studies documents the contention that parents can serve critical protective functions across the social domains of risk active during the school years (i.e., the family, school, and peer group). In a program of studies by Patterson and his colleagues, effective parental discipline and supervision have been shown to significantly moderate the relationship of social and economic disadvantage to later delinquency (Larzelere & Patterson, 1990), to be predictive of better academic achievement and lower association with delinquent peers (Patterson et al., 1992), and to reduce the risk of subsequent drug use (Chilcoate, Dishion, & Anthony, 1995).

As the child gets older and spends more time outside the home, however, the preventive role of the parents becomes more distal or indirect. With the approach of adolescence, the most proximal antecedents of serious antisocial behavior are to be found outside the home, in association with delinquent peers, school failure and dropout, and drug use (Dishion, Capaldi, Spracklen, & Li, 1995; Elliot, Huizinga, & Ageton, 1985; Patterson et al., 1992). During this developmental period, the key parental variables have to do with monitoring and influencing the youngsters' exposure to risk in these domains. As the complexity of the socialization tasks increases, the goals of parent interventions change and become more difficult. In addition, the importance of antecedent variables such as parental supervision interact with the level or number of risk factors to which the youngster is exposed outside the home.

Such relationships are well illustrated by an analysis by Stoolmiller and Eddy (1994). Using repeated measures for 206 at-risk boys, taken when they were 10, 12, 14, and 16 years of age, they examined the predictive relationships among exposure to delinquent peers, unsupervised wandering, and detainment (i.e., the equivalent of an adult arrest) by police. Figure 32.2 displays the trivariate relationship between unsupervised wandering, delinquent peers, and the average number of detainments (i.e., arrests) by police per 2 years. As can be seen in Figure 32.2, there is a huge interaction between the number of delinquent peers and the amount of unsupervised wandering in the prediction of arrests by the police. The importance and the challenge of supervising young adolescents is critical in contexts or neighborhoods in which the risk of delinquent peer association is high; it may be trivial in other neighborhoods (see Thornberry & Krohn, Chapter 21, this volume). Unfortunately, the risk factors typically are correlated, and the parents under most stress often live in neighborhoods with a high prevalence of delinquency.

The proximal antecedents that need to be specifically targeted in interventions with parents before or during the transition to school are shown in Figure 32.1. These include development of noncoercive discipline, positive strategies for teaching and encouraging social and educational development, strategies for increasing and improving parental involvement in school and peer activities, and problem-solving strategies. A substantial literature now exists to document the feasibility of aiming a variety of interventions at this set of parental antecedents, depending on the developmental level of the child, the seriousness of the conduct problems, and the presence or absence of a variety of protective and risk factors.

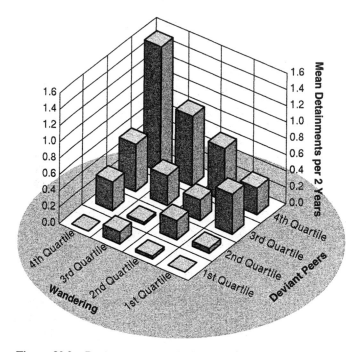

Figure 32.2 *Deviant peer association, wandering, and detainment of at-risk boys (from age 10 to 16 years).*

Illustrative Interventions on Early Parent and Child Antecedents

In randomized studies using flexible parent training protocols and materials, Webster-Stratton (e.g., Webster-Stratton, 1989) demonstrated immediate and consistent effectiveness with young children showing early signs of conduct problems. Using carefully crafted parent training programs, her interventions were precisely aimed at play skills, increasing positive parent-child interactions and parental praise, and teaching nonpunitive and effective discipline strategies. The effects persisted over a 3-year follow-up period (e.g., Webster-Stratton, 1989). Although the effects were marked and long lasting, the effects were most stable for children whose families were not exposed to multiple domains of risk.

In another randomized study of parent training with oppositional preschoolers, McNeil, Eyberg, Eisenstadt, Newcomb, and Funderbunk (1991) found not only strong effects on coercive behavior in the home setting but strong generalization to preschool settings. Taken together, these studies indicate that it is quite possible to change key and proximal antecedents during the transition to school that actually change the developmental trajectory of antisocial behavior across both time and settings. The follow-up by Webster-Stratton indicates that in situations in which multiple risk factors in the environment are continuously undermining the parents' ability to raise and socialize the child successfully, the singular focus on parenting antecedents at one early and critical point in time may not be sufficient to achieve persistent preventive impacts. Indeed, as the antecedents, moderators, and mediators of risk rapidly increase in number and complexity over childhood and adolescence, it becomes less and less likely that any one intervention in any one setting will effectively change the developmental course of antisocial behavior.

Parent training programs conducted during early childhood have the potential to be extremely cost-effective in reducing future serious crime (Webster-Stratton, 1989). Unfortunately, very little data are available on the cost effectiveness, particularly if considered broadly. There are reasons to believe that in addition to directly reducing antisocial behavior, such interventions may have an impact on a number of subsequent antecedents of future antisocial behavior, many of which are significant public health or social problems in their own right (e.g., physical abuse or problems in school). In the next generation of studies, it will be of critical importance to more thoroughly document these proximal gains through systematic studies of costs and benefits. However, evidence at this time shows parent training is a cost-effective deterrent to serious crime. In their analyses of several early intervention strategies, Greenwood et al. (1996) found such parent training strategies to compare very favorably to the Three Strikes program in preventing serious crime. Based on reasonable estimates of program implementation costs and outcome, Greenwood and colleagues estimated that for each $1 million spent, Three Strikes could prevent about 60 crimes, compared to over 150 crimes prevented by parent training.

Illustrative Parenting Interventions on Later Parent and Child Antecedents

In light of the lessening of direct parental influence and the increase of proximal risk factors in extra-home settings over the elementary, middle, and high school years, it is remarkable that even with older children and adolescents, family or parent training interventions often are quite powerful in reducing and preventing the development of antisocial behavior. Patterson, Dishion, and Chamberlain (1993) reviewed a large number of intervention studies to demonstrate reasonably consistent and positive effects of family interventions of various types with antisocial children and adolescents. In their review, however, they demonstrated that interventions with families of pre-elementary-school-aged children were more effective and less labor intensive than interventions with families of older youngsters.

Even with serious juvenile offenders, intensive and multifaceted parent training can be cost effective in interrupting the development of chronic criminal lifestyles. For example, Bank, Marlowe, Reid, Patterson, and Weinrott (1991) carried out a randomized study with chronic juvenile offenders that compared parent training to intensive family and adolescent services delivered by the juvenile court. The parent training was focused on a range of middle childhood and early adolescent antecedents shown in Figure 32.1. It was not time limited and concentrated on training and encouraging parents to better supervise their youngsters, to monitor their peer relationships, to negotiate behavioral contracts, and to encourage their school participation and homework completion. Compared to the group treated by the juvenile court, the parent training group showed marked reductions in court reported offenses over a 3-year follow-up period. Although most of the difference in offending rates was due to a sharp interruption in arrests for youths of the parent training group during the year following referral, the program had a cumulative effect on incarceration rates. Over the 3-year follow-up period, the youths exposed to parent training spent a third fewer days in out-of-home placements. As can be seen in Figure 32.3, the cumulative difference in costs was not trivial.

The interventions delivered in both conditions in this study averaged approximately 50 hours per family, including frequent "boosters" after initial termination. Bank and colleagues concluded that the level of effort needed to achieve these effects might be an obstacle to the wide implementation of the program. As argued up to this point, it is clear from the relevant developmental and intervention studies that parents have a critical role to play in the prevention of antisocial child and adolescent behavior, but their power to directly influence this developmental process is progressively limited as the youngster spends more and more time in high-risk and out-of-home settings. Although effective interventions are available to amplify the influence of parental influence over the developmental process, comprehensive prevention of antisocial behavior after the child's entry to school probably will require coordinated interventions in multiple risk settings.

INTERVENTIONS THAT TARGET THE SCHOOL ENVIRONMENT OR SIMULTANEOUSLY TARGET MULTIPLE ENVIRONMENTS

In terms of the developmental model presented earlier in this chapter (i.e., Figure 32.1), the parents, or for that matter any adult who is serving as a socialization agent, retain a central role in the prevention of antisocial behavior through adolescence. Before birth, the mother's emotional and physical health, abstinence from tobacco and drugs, and utilization of prenatal care are critical in

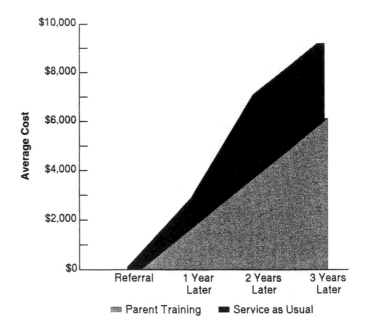

Figure 32.3 *Comparison of average cost of incarceration between the parent training and service-as-usual groups.*

preventing the earliest antecedents of conduct problems. During infancy, the parent's development of a nurturing, stimulating, positive, and contingent relationship with the child sets the groundwork for avoiding the beginnings of the coercive processes that start with early behavior problems and ineffective discipline. During the preschool years, the family teaches the emotional regulation, impulse control, and social and attentional skills that are critical as the child moves into the school and peer settings. From that point onward, the family provides a secure and consistent base, a laboratory for the development of more complex social, academic, and problem-solving skills and the opportunity for mentoring as the child confronts risks and challenges outside the home. However, the parents' ability to directly alter the child's transactions with risky situations and agents outside the home diminishes rapidly over the school years. In disorganized families living in impoverished, transient neighborhoods, this ability may decrease even before the elementary school years. However, even with a diminished opportunity for direct influence, the interventions described to this point indicate that parents, if they choose to accept and are able to complete the assignment, remain powerful agents in the prevention of antisocial behavior. Unfortunately, the more risk factors there are in out-of-home settings, the less the parents will be able to develop a protective cocoon that will adequately protect the developing child from risk.

In many respects, the proximal risk factors within school and peer settings are quite similar to those within the family. Antisocial children are perceived as negative and coercive by both teachers and peers. On the playground and in the classroom, their rates of disruptive and noncompliant and aggressive behaviors are elevated (Walker, Steiber, Ramsey, & O'Neill, 1990), and there is evidence that teachers and nonantisocial peers retaliate coercively (Trachenberg & Viken, 1994; Walker & Buckley, 1973). Therefore, it is clear that an important set of antecedents to be targeted in peer and classroom interventions has to do with training adults in effective management skills for the immediate social setting, such as clarity and appropriateness of rules, clear and fair and immediate consequences, the general organization of activities, and the amount of adult supervision and follow through. Training for peers similarly would target the development of problem-solving skills, including how to effectively monitor and appropriately react to child antisocial behavior in the pertinent settings.

Although this sounds rather straightforward and not that different than the previously discussed family interventions, the structural aspects of intervening in the classroom and peer settings make such attempts much more complicated than those that intervene in the home. When interventions are focused in the family setting, a relatively small number of adults need to learn new ways of dealing with the child. In terms of sibling conflict, a relatively small and fixed number of children can be targeted. Once the basic issues of structuring and monitoring activities, setting rules and consequences, following through with clear expectations, and developing ways of troubleshooting problems as they come up are all dealt with, it is necessary only to track and fine tune the preventive solutions for months and in some cases for years. One can think in terms of "the intervention" and perhaps of "booster shots."

In contrast, such simplicity does not exist in school and peer settings. For example, how many teachers does the child have contact with each day? If, in fact, the very proximal reactions of others to child antisocial behavior have powerful effects on their maintenance, then do we have to coordinate the activities of all teachers around issues of antisocial behavior? How about the school bus driver, the playground monitor, or the cafeteria supervisor? Given such issues, the simple logistics of carrying out behavioral programs in school or peer settings appears daunting. The complexity increases when one considers that inconsistent teacher reactions to aggression will be just as serious in the third grade as in the first. How do we develop a strategy to deal with such proximal antecedents year after year? Yet another complication to this already overwhelming set of issues is the mobility of families with young children. If a prevention program is located in one school in a district but not in others and high-risk families move frequently between schools, the program simply will not be delivered in full to most high-risk families. Unfortunately, this is a particular problem with low-income families. For example, in an elementary school located in one of the most impoverished areas in our town, it is not uncommon for there to be more than a 150% attrition rate during the first grade year.

Given such issues, whereas prevention strategies for families can be designed at the individual child level (because in most cases the family and the child form one or at least a small set of units), when designing stand-alone school-level preventive interventions, one should probably think in terms of school districts or even entire communities (Biglan, 1993) as the unit of universal interventions. And, if one thinks of such large and complex organizations as units, then the idea of having all administrators, teachers, counselors, and school boards agree on specific behavioral strategies seems somewhat problematic in the real world. Because of such problems, large-scale prevention programs need to target very general antecedents that are appropriate across all, or at least most,

of the schools in a definable geographic area of migration (i.e., the region within which most at-risk families who move locally are moving). For example, yearly classes that teach basic skills such as discipline, monitoring, and problem solving to parents and problem-solving skills to children and districtwide programs for administrators that work toward common policies and practices around school organization, rules, and data collection, storage, and sharing are all appropriate candidates for such general programs. On the other hand, school-based interventions aimed at specific proximal antecedents of antisocial behavior probably are best conceptualized and utilized as interventions *tailored* to specific problems encountered and acknowledged in individual schools or even classrooms within schools. Whether a general or more specific approach is taken, if such interventions are conducted in the context of other programs, they should be carefully integrated with those programs (e.g., parent-focused interventions).

Fortunately, a host of powerful interventions can be used to modify school environments to reduce aggressive behavior and bullying; to increase academic organization; to support academic success; and to teach positive peer relations, social skills, and social cognitive competencies (see Walker, Colvin, & Ramsey, 1995, for a comprehensive review). More specifically, in the context of the developmental model of antisocial behavior presented in this chapter, three sorts of school-based interventions seem most useful, albeit to varying degrees, for creating preventive effects: first, stand-alone programs that target specific antecedents in the school setting such as peer relations, social and educational skills, and day-to-day classroom discipline strategies; second, collaborative programs that join parents and teachers in reducing risks and neutralizing interpersonal antecedents of antisocial behavior; and third, restructuring programs that change the ecology of schools to reduce the number of systemic antecedents of antisocial behavior present in the environment.

Illustrative Stand-Alone Interventions

In a series of large-scale epidemiologically based randomized controlled trials, Kellam and colleagues tested the efficacy of two low-cost interventions, the Good Behavior Game (GBG; Barrish, Saunders, & Wolfe, 1969) and Mastery Learning (ML; Block & Burns, 1976; Dolan, 1986; Guskey, 1985). Briefly, the GBG is a classroom team-based behavior management program that attempts to promote prosocial child behavior by rewarding groups of children who keep their negative behaviors to a minimum. In contrast, ML is a group-paced math and reading skills educational program that requires the majority of children to demonstrate mastery of a specified set of skills prior to the class moving on to the next set of skills. Each of these prevention program components has demonstrated some positive long-term effects (Dolan et al., 1993; Kellam, Rebok, Ialongo, & Mayer, 1994). For example, aggressive first-grade boys who were randomly assigned to a 2-year GBG-only condition tended to reduce their aggressive behaviors across elementary and early middle school. First graders assigned to a 2-year ML-only condition demonstrated significant short-term improvement in standardized reading achievement (Dolan et al., 1993), and some beneficial effects were apparent through at least the end of the fifth grade year (Crijnen, Feehan, &

Kellam, 1996). Thus, both the GBG and ML managed to have a successful impact on key antecedents (i.e., aggressive behavior in early elementary school and low academic achievement) of later, more serious conduct problems. Unfortunately, cost-benefit information is not yet available on these programs.

Illustrative Collaborative Interventions

In contrast to stand-alone interventions, collaborative interventions simultaneously target antecedents in multiple settings (e.g., Hawkins et al., 1992; Tremblay, Kurtz, Masse, Vitaro, & Pihl, in press). Although often interventions focused in one social domain have some implications for, if not actual procedures to influence, other social domains of risk (e.g., Blechman, 1985; Patterson, Reid, Jones, & Conger, 1975), collaborative interventions involve a great deal more in the way of theory-driven integrated interventions. For example, the Linking Interests of Families and Teachers (LIFT) program (Reid, 1996) was designed to address key antecedents present during the elementary school years (see Figure 32.1). Child behaviors were targeted via interventions within three settings: home (i.e., a 6-session group parent training), classroom (i.e., a 20-session social and problem-solving skills training), and the peer group (i.e., the GBG discussed previously). The three interventions were integrated via common curricula, homework exercises that spanned settings, and a communication systems set up within and across each setting (e.g., classroom telephone line, newsletters). Delivered together, the interventions were designed to simultaneously provide support for the child's prosocial behavior and to take away support for the child's antisocial behavior within each setting.

In a randomized trial of the LIFT program, the entire first or fifth grade classes in elementary schools located in at-risk urban and suburban neighborhoods were randomly assigned to either a control or intervention condition. Neighborhood risk status was determined by high levels of juvenile crime in the school catchment area relative to levels in the community at large. At the completion of the 1-year program, intervention as compared to control children exhibited significant decreases in aggressive and other antisocial behaviors as reported by their teachers, their parents, their peers, and trained observers who coded peer interactions on the playground during recess (Reid, Eddy, Bank, & Fetrow, 1994). Many of the significant differences actually indicated fall to spring increases in problem behaviors for the control as compared to the intervention children; such differences may truly reflect *preventive* intervention.

In contrast to a relatively "low-dose" (i.e., short-term, low-intensity) intervention such as LIFT, a "high-dose" intervention currently in progress is the Fast Track prevention program (Bierman et al., 1993). Kindergarten students attending at-risk schools who demonstrated high levels of disruptive behavior and poor peer relations based on *both* parent and teacher reports were recruited for FAST Track. The FAST Track intervention also involved home, classroom, and peer components but at a much more intensive level than the LIFT program. Parent training began in the first year with a 22-session group experience that was supplemented by home visits and phone contacts and continued with contacts across the summer and group meetings and contacts across the following year. In the classroom, a multiyear teacher-delivered classroom

program (Kusche & Greenberg, 1990) targeted the development of self-control skills, emotional awareness abilities, and interpersonal problem-solving skills of children. As part of the program, teachers also were taught skills for the effective management of disruptive behavior in the classroom, and parents were given updates on the information their children were being presented at school. The final two components of FAST Track pulled the child out of the regular classroom for enrichment activities. The first, a phonics-oriented reading skills tutoring program, occurred three times per week, and an effort was made to have at least one parent attend one session per week. The second, a peer-pairing program, was held once a week for 30 minutes. During this period, children participated in a guided-play session with a classroom peer who was not currently exhibiting disruptive behaviors.

In a randomized controlled trial of the FAST Track program that is currently in progress, the impact of the first year of the intervention program on hypothesized antecedents of later conduct problems appears promising. For example, in contrast to the control group, by the end of the school year, children in the intervention group received fewer peer nominations for aggressiveness and more were reported by peers to be well liked (Coie, 1996). Further, children in the intervention group are demonstrating improved reading skills (e.g., better word attack skills) and their parents are exhibiting greater levels of involvement in the child's schoolwork. Because collaborative programs such as LIFT and FAST Track are still in the implementation or early follow-up phases, cost-benefit information is not yet available.

Illustrative Restructuring Interventions

Stand-alone and collaborative programs tend to focus on changing antecedents in key "micro" environments (i.e., the behavioral contingencies in effect between the child and other children and adults in the home or school) within which a child learns. In contrast, restructuring programs take a "macro" approach by making changes in the general school environment hypothesized to decrease the number of antecedents present. For example, in the School Transitional Environment Project (STEP; Felner et al., 1993), children are kept together in teams throughout most of the day, and each team has classes only within a particular part of the school building. Homeroom teachers take on the additional role of guidance counselor, including acting as an active liaison between the school and parent. Thus, STEP targets several of the antecedents listed in Figure 32.1, including teacher behavior (e.g., monitoring, involvement) and parent involvement in school, which in turn are hypothesized to affect child antisocial behaviors.

The outcome of STEP has been evaluated in several randomized trials. In the first, the adjustment of students entering an urban high school setting with or without STEP were compared across a 5-year period. In the short run, STEP students exhibited better academic and social adjustment (Felner, Ginter, & Primavera, 1982). By the end of the first year, control students showed marked decreases in grades and attendance relative to STEP students. In the long run, the most striking finding was that students in the control group had significantly higher dropout rates than students in the STEP: From the second year forward, the dropout rates of the control group were twice that of the STEP group (43%

vs. 24%). Several replications of this initial effort have demonstrated similar results (Felner et al., 1993).

A newer restructuring program that appears to have some promise, the Quantum Opportunity Program (Hahn, Leavitt, & Aaron, 1994; Taggart, 1995), provides learning, development, and service opportunities to at-risk youths during high school. An important component of the program is using cash and scholarship incentives to reward achievement and graduation. Such opportunities and incentives had a significant impact on antisocial behavior: Arrest rates for students who received the program were 30% of those who did not receive the program. If such decreases can be replicated in other studies, Greenwood et al. (1996) estimate that relative to a variety of currently available options, including early intervention programs (i.e., home visits and day care) and parent training, cash incentives may be one of the most cost effective ways to reduce juvenile crime, with 258 serious crimes prevented for every $1 million spent.

Illustrative Preventive Interventions That Do Not Appear to Work

Each of the aforementioned school-based prevention programs has demonstrated promise, however preliminary, in terms of producing some preventive effects. In contrast to these programs, several programs might reasonably be conducted within the context of a school that have demonstrated *iatrogenic* effects. Unfortunately, the most noteworthy of such programs utilized ideas that at present tend to be quite popular in society at large, such as pairing an at-risk child with a prosocial nonfamily member adult (i.e., so-called mentoring) or congregating at-risk children into groups for treatment.

In the Cambridge-Somerville prevention program (McCord, 1992), preadolescent boys living in impoverished, high-crime neighborhoods were targeted for intervention. The premise of the intervention was that the trajectory of at-risk boys could be diverted away from delinquency and toward prosocial participation in society if "a devoted individual outside [their] own family [gave] consistent emotional support, friendship, and timely guidance" (Allport, 1951, p. vi). In a longitudinal outcome study of the program, each member of a demographically matched pair of 12-year-old boys was randomly assigned to either receive guidance and assistance from a social worker or to a no-attention control group. On average, treated boys were visited by social workers two times per month for 5½ years. The boys also received a variety of other as-needed services, such as academic tutoring.

In initial follow-ups, it appeared that the program had no effect, but in the most recent follow-up, when the men were now approaching the age of 50 years, the program appears to have had an adverse effect, with those treated exhibiting a variety of more problematic outcomes than those who were untreated. Further, and even more troubling, adverse effects were most apparent in men whose families were viewed as cooperating with the program. McCord (1992) concluded that the negative effects of the program might be due to a "critical error" in the original conceptualization of the program: "A child rejected by parents may not be best served by someone else who tries to take the role of parent" (p. 203). This statement should be qualified by the extent to which such a role is taken, how the role is played, and what happens with the child's parents in the meantime. For example, joint foster care and family therapy programs seem to hold promise for changing the trajectory of some children displaying high levels of antisocial behavior (e.g., Chamberlain, 1994).

Studies have also found negative effects when children with problem behaviors were grouped together for treatment. For example, in a recent study that contrasted the effectiveness of a group parent training intervention, a peer-group intervention, and a parent training and peer-group combined intervention for families with adolescents identified as at-risk for substance use and other problem behaviors, those who received the peer-group intervention used more tobacco and were rated by teachers as having more behavior problems than children who received no intervention (Dishion & Andrews, 1995). Such escalation of problems follows from the model in Figure 32.1: Deviant peer group association during adolescence is associated with increased displays of antisocial behavior. Even though the deviant peers were spending time during the treatment program in groups with responsible adults, the program could not supervise them outside the group, and if lack of supervision and association with deviant peers were problems prior to the program, the program may have simply provided at-risk children a venue for increasing their networks of association with other at-risk children. These two studies highlight the importance of randomized clinical trials paired with long-term follow-up periods in furthering our knowledge of prevention. In both cases, it seemed quite reasonable at the time of conception that the conducted interventions would be beneficial to the participants involved, yet such was not the case. Unfortunately, this likely would not have been as clear without the benefit of a control group and long-term follow up data.

SOME FINAL COMMENTS

An attempt has been made in this chapter to provide an overview of the rapidly growing knowledge base about the specific developmental paths leading to serious antisocial behavior and our increasing ability to profitably use that base to develop powerful prevention efforts at just about any point along the young life course. An attempt also has been made to describe the increasing tension between these advances in prevention science, on the one hand, and growing impatience by the public for quick and decisive action, increasing demands for documentation of the concrete benefits of preventive interventions, and decreasing available resources, on the other hand. Numerous examples have been given to demonstrate that carefully crafted interventions can be effective not only in terms of long-term antisocial outcomes but also can be shown profitable in terms of short-term effects on serious antecedent milestones.

The theory-driven interventions described here demonstrate the synergism possible as basic scientists and methodologists add their expertise to the search for new prevention strategies. Not only do such collaborations result in more powerful interventions, the intervention studies result in experimental tests of basic developmental models. We hope that the next generation of preventive trials will reap the benefits of even greater collaboration. As preventionists rely ever more heavily on the basic sciences, it becomes absolutely clear that every chapter in this volume represents a critical piece of the puzzle to be solved in our search for effective preventive strategies for antisocial behavior. It also is clear that clinical and prevention researchers no longer can ignore the economics of the problems at hand. Our society is currently waging a battle that pits ever-increasing rates of pathology against exponentially increasing costs to society, and scientists need to join the battle anew with a complete, multidisciplinary arsenal.

Despite the successes theoretically based prevention programs have had, the enormity of the problems posed by the antecedents of antisocial behavior must not be underemphasized. As the ambient level of youth violence increases across the country, as our school environments continue to deteriorate in both the academic and behavioral domains, and as gangs increase in their ability to proactively socialize youngsters into patterns of antisocial behavior, the power of parents and other adults to successfully monitor and mentor their children's social development both during and after school is seriously jeopardized. And, as usual, the families whose internal functioning is under the most social, economic, and environmental stress tend to live in neighborhoods that present children with a high density of risk factors, both inside and outside school. Without also focusing our scientific and preventive energies on developing strategies that modify these broader social domains, even the best conceived family- or school-based interventions are unlikely to succeed.

REFERENCES

Allport, G. (1951). Foreword. In E. Powers & H. Witmer (Eds.), *An experiment in the prevention of delinquency: The Cambridge-Somerville Youth Study* (pp. vii–xiv). New York: Columbia University Press.

American Humane Society. (1981). *Child protective division, annual report, 1980: National analysis of official child neglect and abuse reporting.* Denver: Author.

Bank, L., Marlowe, J. H., Reid, J. B., Patterson, G. R., & Weinrott, M. R. (1991). A comparative evaluation of parent-training interventions for families of chronic delinquents. *Journal of Abnormal Child Psychology, 19,* 15–33.

Barrish, H. H., Saunders, M., & Wolfe, M. D. (1969). Good behavior game. Effects of individual contingencies for group consequences and disruptive behavior in a classroom. *Journal of Applied Behavior Analysis, 2,* 119–124.

Bierman, K. L., Coie, J. D., Dodge, K. A., Greenberg, M. T., Lochman, J. E., & McMahon, R. J. (1992). A developmental and clinical model for the prevention of conduct disorder: The Fast Track program. *Development and Psychopathology, 4,* 509–527.

Biglan, A. (1993). A functional contextualist framework for community interventions. In S. C. Hayes, L. J. Hayes, H. W. Reese, & T. R. Sarbin (Eds.), *Varieties of scientific contextualism* (pp. 251–276). Reno, NV: Context Press.

Blechman, E. A. (1985). *Solving child behavior problems at home and school.* Champaign, IL: Research Press.

Block, J., & Burns, R. (1976). Mastery learning. In L. Shulman (Ed.), *Review of research in education* (Vol. 4, pp. 3–49). Itasca, IL: F. E. Peacock.

Cairns, R. B., & Cairns, B. D. (1994). *Lifelines and risks: Pathways of youth in our times.* Cambridge: Cambridge University Press.

Caspi, A., & Elder, G. H. (1988). Childhood precursors of the life course: Early personality and life disorganization. In E. M. Hetherington, R. M. Lerner, & M. Perimutter (Eds.), *Child development in life-span perspective* (pp. 115–142). Hillsdale, NJ: Erlbaum.

Caspi, A., Elder, G. H., & Bem, D. J. (1987). Moving against the world: Lifecourse patterns of explosive children. *Developmental Psychology, 23,* 308–313.

Caspi, A., & Moffitt, T. E. (1995). The continuity of maladaptive behavior: From description to understanding in the study of antisocial behavior. In D. Chicchetti & D. Cohen (Eds.), *Developmental psychopathology: Vol. 2. Risk, disorder and adaptation* (pp. 472–511). New York: Wiley.

Chamberlain, P. (1994). *Family connections: A treatment foster care model for adolescents with delinquency.* Eugene, OR: Castalia.

Chilcoate, H., Dishion, T. J., & Anthony, J. C. (1995). Parent monitoring and the incidence of drug sampling in urban elementary school children. *American Journal of Epidemiology, 141*(1), 25–31.

Coie, J. D. (1996, May). *Effectiveness trials: An initial evaluation of the FAST Track program.* Paper presented at the Fifth National Institute of Mental Health National Conference on Prevention Research, Washington, DC.

Crijnen, A. A. M., Feehan, M., & Kellam, S. G. (1996). *The course and malleability of reading achievement in elementary school.* Paper submitted for publication.

DiIulio, J. J. (1995, May). *Net repairing: Rethinking incarceration and intermediate sanctions. A comment on Professor Joan R. Petersilia, "Diverting nonviolent prisoners to intermediate sanctions."* Paper presented at the Conference on the Future of Criminal Justice Policy in California, Berkeley, CA.

Dishion, T. J., & Andrews, D. W. (1995). Prevention escalation in problem behaviors with high-risk young adolescents: Immediate and 1-year outcome. *Journal of Consulting and Clinical Psychology, 63,* 538–548.

Dishion, T. J., Capaldi, D., Spracklen, K. M., & Li, F. (1995). Peer ecology of male adolescent drug use. *Development and Psychopathology, 7,* 803–824.

Dodge, K. A. (1983). Behavioral antecedents of peer social status. *Child Development, 54,* 1386–1399.

Dolan, L. J. (1986). Mastery learning as a preventive strategy. *Outcomes, 5,* 20–27.

Dolan, L. J., Kellam, S. G., Brown, C. H., Werthamer-Larsson, L., Rebok, G. W., Mayer, L. S., Laudoff, J., Turkkan, J., Ford, C., & Wheeler, L. (1993). The short-term impact of two classroom-based preventive interventions on aggressive and shy behaviors and poor achievement. *Journal of Applied Developmental Psychology, 14,* 317–345.

Elliot, D. S., Huizinga, D., & Ageton, S. S. (1985). *Explaining delinquency and drug use.* Beverly Hills, CA: Sage Publications.

Felner, R. D., Brand, S., Adan, A. M., Mulhall, P. F., Flowers, N., Sartain, B., & DuBois, D. L. (1993). Restructuring the ecology of the school as an approach to prevention during school transitions: Longitudinal follow-ups and extensions of the school transitional environment project (STEP). L. A. Jason, K. E. Danner, & K. S. Kurasaki (Eds.), *Prevention and school transitions* (pp. 103–136). Binghamton, NY: Haworth.

Felner, R. D., Ginter, M., & Primavera, J. (1982). Primary prevention during school transitions: Social support and environmental structure. *American Journal of Community Psychology, 10,* 277–290.

Fingerhut, L. A., & Kleinman, J. C. (1990). International and interstate comparisons of homicides among young males. *Journal of the American Medical Association, 263,* 3292–3295.

Greenwood, P. W., Model, K. E., Rydell, C. P., & Chiesa, J. (1996). *Diverting children from a life of crime: Measuring costs and benefits*. Santa Monica, CA: RAND, MR699.0-UCB/RC/IF.

Greenwood, P. W., Rydell, C. P., Abrahamse, A. F., Caulkins, J. P., Chiesa, J., Model, K. E., & Klein, S. P. (1994). *Three strikes and you're out: Estimated benefits and costs of California's new mandatory sentencing law*. Santa Monica, CA: RAND, MR-509-RC.

Guskey, T. (1985). *Implementing mastery learning*. Belmont, CA: Wadsworth.

Hahn, A., Leavitt, T., & Aaron, P. (1994). *Evaluation of the Quantum Opportunities Program (QOP): Did the program work? A report on the postsecondary outcomes and cost-effectiveness of the QOP program (1989–1993)*. Waltham, MA: Brandeis University Press.

Hawkins, J. D., Catalano, R. F., Morrison, D. M., O'Donnell, J., Abbot, R. D., & Day, L. E. (1992). Seattle Social Development Project: Effects of the first four years on protective factors and problem behaviors. In J. McCord & R. E. Tremblay (Eds.), *Preventing antisocial behavior: Interventions from birth through adolescence* (pp. 139–161). New York: Guilford.

Kellam, S. G., & Rebok, G. W. (1992). Building developmental and etiological theory through epidemiologically based preventive intervention trials. In J. McCord & R. E. Tremblay (Eds.), *Preventing antisocial behavior: Interventions from birth through adolescence* (pp. 162–195). New York: Guilford.

Kellam, S. G., Rebok, G. W., Ialongo, N., & Mayer, L. S. (1994). The course and malleability of aggressive behavior from early first grade into middle school: Results of a developmental epidemiologically-based preventive trial. *Journal of Child Psychology and Psychiatry, 35*, 259–281.

Kusche, C. A., & Greenberg, M. T. (1990). *The PATHS curriculum*. Seattle: EXCEL.

Lally, R. J., Mangione, P. L., & Honig, A. S. (1988). The Syracuse University Family Development Research Program: Long range impact of an early intervention program with low-income children and their families. In D. Powell (Ed.), *Parent education as early childhood intervention: Emerging directions in theory, research and practice* (pp. 79–104). Norwood, NJ: Ablex.

Larzelere, R. E., & Patterson, G. R. (1990). Parental management: Mediators of the effect of socioeconomic status on early delinquency. *Criminology, 28*, 301–323.

Loeber, R., & Dishion, T. (1983). Early predictors of male delinquency: A review. *Psychological Bulletin, 94*, 68–99.

Loeber, R., Wung, P., Keenan, K, Giroux, B., Stouthamer-Loeber, M., Van Kammen, W. B., & Maughan, B. (1993). Developmental pathways in disruptive child behavior. *Development and Psychopathology, 5*, 103–133.

Mayer, W. G. (1992). *The changing American mind*. Ann Arbor: University of Michigan Press.

McCord, J. (1992). The Cambridge-Somerville study: A pioneering longitudinal experimental study of delinquency prevention. In J. McCord & R. E. Tremblay (Eds.), *Preventing antisocial behavior: Interventions from birth through adolescence* (pp. 196–206). New York: Guilford.

McNeil, C. B., Eyberg, S., Eisenstadt, T. H., Newcomb, K., & Funderburk, B. (1991). Parent-child interaction therapy with behavior problem children: Generalization of treatment effects to the school setting. *Journal of Clinical Child Psychology, 20*, 140–151.

Moffitt, T. E. (1993) Adolescence-limited and life-course-persistent antisocial behavior: A developmental taxonomy. *Psychological Review, 100*, 674–701.

Mrazek, P. G., & Haggerty, R. J. (Eds.). (1994). *Reducing risks for mental disorders: Frontiers for preventive intervention research*. Washington, DC: National Academy Press.

National Institute of Mental Health (NIMH), Prevention Research Steering Committee (1993). *The prevention of mental disorders: A national research agenda*. Bethesda, MD: Author.

Olds, D. L. (1988). The prenatal/early infancy project. In E. L. Cowan, R. P. Lorion, & J. Ramos-McKay (Eds.), *Fourteen ounces of prevention: A handbook for practitioners* (pp. 9–22). Washington, DC: American Psychological Association.

Olds, D. L., Henderson, C., Chamberlin, R., & Tatelbaum, R. (1986). Preventing child abuse and neglect: A randomized trial of nurse home visitation. *Pediatrics, 78*, 65–78.

Olds, D. L., Henderson, C. R., & Kitzman, H. (1994). Does prenatal and infancy nurse home visitation have enduring effects on qualities of parental caregiving and child health and 25 to 50 months of life? *Pediatrics, 93*, 89–98.

Olds, D. L., Henderson, C. R., Phelps, C., Kitzman, H., & Hanks, C. (1993). Effects of prenatal and infancy nurse home visitation on government spending. *Medical Care, 3*, 1–20.

Olds, D. L., Henderson, C., & Tatelbaum, R. (1994). Prevention of intellectual impairment in children of women who smoke cigarettes during pregnancy. *Pediatrics, 93*, 228–233.

Olds, D. L., Henderson, C. R., Tatelbaum, R., & Chamberlin, R. (1986). Improving the delivery of prenatal care and outcomes of pregnancy: A randomized trial of nurse home visitation. *Pediatrics, 77*, 16–28.

Olweus, D. (1979). Stability of aggressive reaction patterns in males: A review. *Psychological Bulletin, 86*(4), 852–875.

Patterson, G. R., Chamberlain, P., & Reid, J. B. (1984). A comparative evaluation of a parent training program. *Behavior Therapy, 13*, 638–650.

Patterson, G. R., DeBaryshe, B. D., & Ramsey, E. (1989). A developmental perspective on antisocial behavior. *American Psychologist, 44*, 329–335.

Patterson, G. R., Dishion, T. J., & Chamberlain, P. (1993). Outcomes and methodological issues relating to treatment of antisocial children. In T. R. Giles (Ed.), *Handbook of effective psychotherapy* (pp. 43–88). New York: Plenum.

Patterson, G. R., Reid, J. B., & Dishion, T. J. (1992). *A social learning approach: 4. Antisocial boys*. Eugene, OR: Castalia.

Patterson, G. R., Reid, J. B., Jones, R. R., & Conger, R. E. (1975). *Families with aggressive children*. Eugene, OR: Castalia Publishing.

Petersilia, J. R. (1995, May). *Diverting nonviolent prisoners to intermediate sanctions*. Paper presented at the Conference on the Future of Criminal Justice Policy in California, Berkeley, CA.

Provence, S., & Naylor, A. (1983). *Working with disadvantaged parents and children: Scientific issues and practice*. New Haven, CT: Yale University Press.

Reid, J. B. (1993). Prevention of conduct disorder before and after school entry: Relating interventions to development findings. *Journal of Development and Psychopathology, 5*, 243–262.

Reid, J. B. (1996, May). *Efficacy trials in the prevention of conduct disorder*. Paper presented at the Fifth National Institute of Mental Health National Conference on Prevention Research, Washington, DC.

Reid, J. B., Eddy, J. M., Bank, L., & Fetrow, R. A. (1994, November). *Preliminary findings from a universal prevention program for conduct disorder*. Paper presented at the Fourth National Institute of Mental Health National Conference on Prevention Research, Washington, DC.

Reis, A. J., & Roth, J. A. (Eds.). (1993). *Understanding and preventing violence*. Washington, DC: National Academy Press.

Sampson, R. J., & Laub, J. H. (1993). *Crime in the making: Pathways and turning points through life.* Cambridge, MA: Harvard University Press.

Stoolmiller, M., & Eddy, J. M. (1994, November). *The role of unsupervised wandering and delinquent peers in male adolescent delinquent behavior.* Paper presented at the Fourth National Institute of Mental Health National Conference on Prevention Research, Washington, DC.

Taggart, R. (1995). Quantum Opportunity Program. Philadelphia: Opportunities Industrialization Centers of America.

Trachenberg, S., & Viken, R. J. (1994). Aggressive boys in the classroom: Biased attributions or shared perceptions? *Child Development, 65,* 829–835.

Tremblay, R. E., Kurtz, L., Masse, L. C., Vitaro, R., & Pihl, R. O. (in press). A bimodal preventive intervention for disruptive kindergarten boys: Its impact through mid-adolescence. *Journal of Consulting and Clinical Psychology.*

U.S. Bureau of Justice Statistics. (1993). *Sourcebook of criminal justice statistics.* Washington, DC: Author.

Walker, H. M., & Buckley, N. K. (1973). Teacher attention to appropriate and inappropriate classroom behavior: An individual case study. *Focus on Exceptional Children, 5,* 5–11.

Walker, H. M., Colvin, G., & Ramsey, E. (1995). *Antisocial behavior in school: Strategies and best practices.* Pacific Grove, CA: Brooks/Cole.

Walker, H. M., Steiber, S., Ramsey, E., & O'Neill, R. E. (1990). School behavioral profiles of arrested versus nonarrested adolescents. *Exceptionality, 1,* 249–265.

Webster-Stratton, C. (1989). Systematic comparison of consumer satisfaction of three cost-effective parent training programs for conduct problem children. *Behavior Therapy, 20*(1), 103–116.

Webster-Stratton, C., Kolpacoff, M., & Hollingsworth, T. (1988). Self-administered videotape therapy for families with conduct-problem children: Comparison with two cost-effective treatments and a control group. *Journal of Consulting and Clinical Psychology, 56*(4), 558–566.

World Health Organization. (1992). *Annual report on homicide.* Geneva, Switzerland: Author.

Ziegler, E., Taussig, C., & Black, K. (1992). Early childhood intervention: A promising preventative for juvenile delinquency. *American Psychologist, 47*(8), 997–1006.

Zimring, F., & Hawkins, G. (1995). *Incapacitation: Penal confinement and the restraint of crime.* New York: Oxford University Press.

CHAPTER 33

Bridging Development, Prevention, and Policy

DAVID R. OFFORD

The aim of this chapter is to indicate what implications can be drawn from current knowledge of antisocial behavior to influence policy aimed at reducing antisocial behavior. The chapter begins by reviewing selected epidemiological findings and their relevance to intervention strategies. It then outlines policy-relevant issues germane to interventions and contrasts three different intervention strategies. The chapter ends by suggesting needed policy initiatives in the field.

MAJOR EPIDEMIOLOGICAL FINDINGS

Epidemiological studies are of two types, descriptive and experimental (Robins, 1978). In the former, the investigator observes only and collects data; in the latter, the researcher initiates interventions and attempts to evaluate their effects. Relevant findings from each type of study are covered in turn.

Descriptive Studies

Descriptive studies have made three major contributions pertinent to the intervention initiative in antisocial behavior. First, they have described the burden of suffering that indicates the importance of the condition as a focus for intervention efforts. Second, they have provided data that have allowed the identification of subgroups of antisocial children whose behaviors probably have different etiologies, natural histories, and responses to interventions. Third, they have presented findings that have pointed to certain variables as being potential risk factors and data suggesting different pathways for the development of antisocial behavior.

The term *burden of suffering* has three dimensions relevant to describing the importance of a condition or disorder: frequency, morbidity, and cost. On all three dimensions, antisocial behavior ranks extremely high. For example, in the Ontario Child Health Study, a large community survey of children 4 to 16 years of age, the 6-month prevalence of conduct disorder was 5.5% (Offord et al., 1987). The prevalence of one or more disorders was 18.1%. Therefore, conduct disorder was present in more than 30% of children classified as having at least one disorder. Further, the rate of severe antisocial behavior including violent acts is greater among youths than in any other age group (Osgood, O'Malley, Bachman, & Johnston, 1989; Silverman et al., 1988). Adolescence also is the age group at greatest risk for victimization (Centers for Disease Control, 1992a). For example, in a 1992 study, 50% of the boys and 25% of the girls reported being physically attacked by someone at school (Centers for Disease Control, 1992b). In terms of morbidity, the life quality of children with antisocial behavior is lowered not only because of their symptoms and behaviors but also because of associated impairments; for example, in social relationships with their peers, parents, and teachers and in satisfactory achievement in school (Offord et al., 1989; Sanford, Offord, Boyle, Peace, & Racine, 1992). Further, the onset of antisocial behavior in childhood often is followed by a lifetime of serious psychosocial problems. For example, almost half of all clinically identified antisocial youngsters becomes antisocial adults (Robins, 1966, 1970). Last, the costs of antisocial behavior in children and adolescents are immense. They include not just health-related costs but, for example, direct costs in the educational, child welfare, and juvenile justice systems and indirect costs, primarily those related to lost lifetime earnings due to associated disabilities (Institute of Medicine, 1989). Even if one limits the consideration of costs to those of maintaining juvenile correctional facilities, the costs are enormous with more than $1 billion spent in 1985 (U.S. Department of Justice, 1986).

The data on burden of suffering of antisocial behavior from descriptive epidemiologic studies have two major implications for intervention initiatives. First, the prevalence of antisocial behavior is so high that it is most unlikely that the clinical enterprise alone, dealing with identified cases, can ever make a major dent in reducing the burden of suffering from this condition. Historically, clinical services have not been a major factor in improving the health status of populations (McKeown, 1976, 1988). What are needed are programs for *groups* of children and adolescents that are effective in preventing the onset of antisocial behavior or curtailing its severity and duration. Second, the immense burden of suffering from antisocial behavior dictates that large resources, both human and fiscal, be brought to bear to discover ways of lessening this burden of suffering.

357

Subgroups

Many different attempts have been made to describe either categories of antisocial behavior or subgroups of antisocial children. An example of the former is the description of four patterns of adolescent violence (Elliott, Huizinga, & Morse, 1986; Tolan & Guerra, 1994). The first pattern is related to specific situations. These situational influences may heighten an individual's predisposition toward violence or increase the seriousness of the violent acts that occur. Among the many examples of such influences are the availability of handguns, alcohol and drug use, extreme heat, poverty, social discrimination, and oppression. The second pattern of adolescent violence, relationship violence, occurs between persons with ongoing relationships, such as family members and friends. The third pattern is termed predatory violence. The violent acts are situational and carried out as part of a chronic pattern of criminal or antisocial behavior. Robberies, muggings, and gang assaults are common examples. The fourth and last pattern of violence, psychopathological violence, although rare, usually is severe and appears to be the result of a combination of neurological dysfunction and severe psychological trauma. These types of violence appear to differ in prevalence, course, etiology, and very likely in effective interventions.

A current example of subgrouping antisocial children and adolescents centers on age of onset. Early-onset antisocial behavior is characterized by male preponderance, physical violence, comorbid hyperactivity, and the presence of learning problems and family pathology (Moffitt, 1993). Late- or adolescent-onset antisocial behavior is characterized primarily by association with deviant peers. There is evidence that the antisocial behavior of the early-onset group is distinguished by greater severity and persistence than the later-onset group (Farrington, Loeber, & Van Kammen, 1990; Tolan & Thomas, 1995). This finding has led to Moffitt's naming of the two types as *life-course persistent* and *adolescence limited.*

Subgrouping has two main implications for policy. First, it emphasizes the heterogeneous nature of antisocial behavior and the children and adolescents who carry it out. When, for example, the data are firm that there are subgroups of antisocial children with different associated features and natural histories, it is probable that their antisocial behaviors have different etiologies and may require different interventions. The second implication is that knowledge of the magnitude and seriousness of different subgroups should influence the relative emphasis given to intervention initiatives aimed at reducing antisocial behavior. For example, the emphasis given to prevention efforts with the early-onset subgroup could be justified because of the seriousness and relatively poor long-term prognosis of this subgroup. However, the late-onset subgroup is much more common (Farrington, 1983; Moffitt, 1993; Offord et al., 1992), and the data are incomplete on its seriousness and long-term prognosis (Coie, 1996). If the two groups do not differ on these latter two characteristics, then, based on prevalence data alone, the late-onset group would deserve much increased emphasis as a focus for intervention initiatives.

Risk Factors and Developmental Pathways

Descriptive longitudinal studies can provide data on risk factors and developmental pathways for antisocial behavior. They are well suited to identify risk factors for antisocial behavior from among those variables that are correlates of the condition. A risk factor is one special type of correlate that requires documentation of precedence (Kraemer et al., 1997; Mrazek & Haggerty, 1994). Thus, a risk factor for antisocial behavior must precede the onset of the behavior. It is important to distinguish among different types of risk factors (Kraemer et al., 1997). A risk factor that can change or be changed in a child is termed a *variable risk factor.* A risk factor that cannot be demonstrated to change can be called a *fixed marker* (e.g., gender, age). Fixed markers for antisocial behavior are important in that they can identify children at high risk for the condition. For effective intervention efforts, it is a necessity to identify those risk factors that are causal and show that they can be manipulated, and when manipulated, it can be demonstrated that the risk for antisocial behavior is reduced. Descriptive longitudinal studies can identify risk factors, but they are not a strong design to identify *causal* risk factors (Department of Clinical Epidemiology and Biostatistics, McMaster University Health Sciences Centre, 1981). Experimental studies are better suited for this purpose.

One other aspect of causal risk factors deserves mention, that is, their relative strength or importance. The critical concept here is attributable risk (Lipman, Offord, & Boyle, 1996; Streiner, Norman, & Munroe Blum, 1989). It indicates the maximum reduction in the incidence of a condition or disorder that could be expected if the effects of a causal risk factor could be eliminated. Again, experimental studies provide the strongest design to determine the attributable risk of a causal risk factor. However, descriptive studies can give helpful estimates of the magnitude of this parameter for hypothesized causal risk factors. Risk factor research has important implications for efforts to reduce the incidence of antisocial behavior. For example, focusing efforts on changing noncausal risk factors for antisocial behavior cannot result in a reduction of the incidence of the condition. Similarly, centering intervention initiatives on causal risk factors with a low attributable risk, even if successful, will not produce a meaningful diminution in the incidence of antisocial behavior. The magnitude of attributable risk is dependent on two factors: the strength of the relationship between the risk variable and the outcome, and the frequency of the risk variable in the population. So, for example, whereas low birth weight may have a strong independent causal relationship with antisocial behavior, its frequency in most populations is low. Therefore, even though reducing the incidence of low birth weight is a worthwhile endeavor, it cannot be expected to result in an important reduction in antisocial behavior.

Studies in descriptive epidemiology also can identify developmental pathways through which groups of children proceed on their way to serious antisocial behavior. An example of this endeavor is the work of Loeber and colleagues (1993). They have described three pathways to antisocial behavior, which they have termed *overt, covert,* and *authority conflict.* Such work can influence prevention efforts by identifying different groups of children on the basis of the onset and course of the antecedent behaviors to serious antisocial behavior. For each identified developmental pathway, it will be necessary to determine the proportion of antisocial children who take this pathway and discover at what point it is most efficient to intervene on known causal risk factors. Ideally, intervention efforts should center on interrupting developmental pathways that account for a significant proportion of antisocial children and those with known causal risk factors with high attributable risks, when there is evidence that these can be modified. As mentioned previously, descriptive studies can contribute suggestive data only on these latter issues.

Summary

Descriptive epidemiological studies can contribute important information to aid and direct intervention efforts. They can provide data on the burden of suffering, which can be helpful to policy makers and others in justifying the scope of the intervention and evaluation enterprise required to advance our knowledge about how to prevent antisocial behavior. Information on subgroups, risk factors, and developmental pathways can help target prevention programs both in terms of who receives them and what should be the elements of such programs. However, descriptive epidemiology has marked limits in informing prevention initiatives. It can identify promising leads and rule out others. Only by actually attempting to intervene can one come up against important issues, for example, in compliance and delivery, that never could have been identified by descriptive studies. Therefore, an issue that deserves attention is the relative proportion of limited research funds that should be devoted to descriptive studies compared with intervention projects. At the very least, one can argue that justification for funding descriptive studies should be based, in part, on the specific contributions they can make to prevention efforts.

Experimental Studies

The results of intervention studies aimed at preventing antisocial behavior and criminality recently have been reviewed (Tremblay & Craig, 1995) as has the literature on reducing adolescent violence (Tolan & Guerra, 1994). The findings in the former indicate that early childhood interventions can have a positive effect on the three most important risk factors for juvenile delinquency: disruptive behavior, deficits in cognitive skills, and poor or inadequate parenting. Studies of the prevention of disruptive behavior have focused on preschool and elementary school-aged children, whereas those aimed at preventing cognitive deficits have used samples of infants and toddlers. Projects in which parenting was the major outcome of interest generally focused on mothers of high-risk children during the perinatal period. In terms of the prevention of adolescent violence, most approaches have not been well evaluated. Basic knowledge is lacking about what is effective, with what population, and for what type of violence. However, for each level of intervention—namely, individual, proximal interpersonal systems (family, peers), proximal social settings (school, neighborhood or community, residential institutions), and societal macrosystem—there are examples of effective programs, although the vast majority of evaluated programs target individual-level influences (Tolan & Guerra, 1994).

SELECTED POLICY-RELEVANT ISSUES

A number of issues in prevention research have direct relevance to policy. They are organized under the subheadings of design, intervention, evaluation, and dissemination and maintenance in other settings.

Design

Strength

The Canadian Task Force on the Periodic Health Examination (1979) has developed a classification of study designs to rank the strength of scientific evidence supporting the effectiveness of interventions. From strongest to weakest, it includes well-designed randomized controlled trials, well-designed controlled trials without randomization, well-designed cohort or case-control analytic studies, comparisons between times and places with or without intervention, and opinions of respected authorities. The stronger the design, the more credence one can give to the findings and their policy implications.

Effectiveness versus Efficacy

Effectiveness centers on whether or not an intervention does more good than harm to those to whom it is offered (Sackett, 1980; Tugwell, Bennett, Haynes, & Sackett, 1985). Efficacy, on the other hand, is concerned with whether or not an intervention does more good than harm under ideal circumstances. Components of these ideal circumstances can include choosing subjects with the greatest potential to respond to the intervention, using as deliverers of the intervention personnel who have had extensive periods of training, and paying no attention to costs. Small efficacy studies are helpful as prerequisites to launching effectiveness trials. However, policy recommendations to prevent antisocial behavior will have to be based on the results of effectiveness studies, not efficacy ones.

Intervention

Multiple Elements Included and Described

Some programs to prevent antisocial behavior rely on a single intervention element (e.g., Cunningham, 1996; Lochman & Wells, 1996). However, most preventive interventions now include multiple elements (Tremblay & Craig, 1995). For example, FAST Track, a large-scale multisite prevention demonstration project aimed at preventing antisocial behavior in young children, has seven integrated components in its intervention: parent training, home visits, enhancement of the parent-child relationship, academic tutoring, a universal prevention curriculum used by teachers, a social-skill training group program for targeted high-risk children, and a peer-pairing program (Bierman, Greenberg, & CPPRG, 1996). Because the occurrence of antisocial behavior is dependent on the presence of multiple causal risk factors, prevention programs with more than one intervention element will almost certainly have the greatest chance of success (Tremblay & Craig, 1995). Further, it is essential that the individual elements of an intervention be described in detail. Such a description not only allows monitoring program integrity but also provides a necessary prerequisite for the intervention to be widely disseminated.

Implementation

Preventive interventions no matter how specifically described cannot be highly effective without carefully developed delivering systems. The delivery systems must do two things: identify the targets for the intervention and provide the intervention to the entire population of interest. If the delivery system results in only a small proportion of the targeted population receiving the intervention, this will curtail its effectiveness for the population as a whole. Compliance from both the deliverers of the program and the members of the population of interest is required. Last, as noted in the section on effectiveness versus efficacy, a prevention program that has been shown to do more good than harm only under special conditions that never could be widely present has a limited value in reducing the burden of suffering from antisocial behavior.

Evaluation

Independent Outcomes

Outcome data collected from informants that are not blind to the intervention status of the groups at issue are highly suspect. Outcome information independent of these informants, for example, ratings from independent observers, is needed if policy makers are to have confidence in the validity of the results.

Impact

Several elements of impact are important from a policy perspective. First, although process or proximal variables tied tightly to an element of an intervention are necessary to determine whether or not that element has had an immediate effect, more convincing outcome variables in relation to the prevention of antisocial behavior are those that operationalize the behavior itself. For example, although it could be important to know whether or not parent management training improved parents' interactions with their children, the real test of the intervention from a policy perspective is the extent to which it results in reducing antisocial behavior or preventing its onset. Therefore, in measuring impact, changes in outcome variables are preferable to changes in process variables. Second, the social importance of outcomes is of concern. For example, the demonstration of reduction in antisocial behavior as measured on checklist data is not nearly as convincing as showing that an intervention results in reductions in antisocial behavior as measured by vandalism rates, police calls, and false-alarm fire calls. These are real-life outcomes that, of course, have direct cost implications. Third, other important aspects of impact include the magnitude of the changes resulting from an intervention and their timing and sustainability. Timing is the interval between the start of the intervention and the appearance of the beneficial outcomes; sustainability addresses the issue of the duration of the beneficial effects of an intervention.

Cost

Any serious effort to prevent antisocial behavior in *groups* of children and youth must be reasonably priced, and the costs of the intervention must be known. In a recent edited book on preventing childhood disorders, substance abuse, and delinquency (Peters & McMahon, 1996), costs were mentioned in only one chapter (Peters & Russell, 1996). Thus, it was impossible to know what the approximate costs would be to apply a specific prevention program to large groups of children.

Dissemination and Maintenance

A prevention program that is to play an important role in reducing the burden of suffering from antisocial behavior must not only be shown to be effective in one setting but also will have to be widely disseminated and maintained in other settings. This aim will have to succeed against the background that most successful interventions in the child mental health field are never disseminated successfully to other settings and, indeed, are usually not maintained in their original setting (Jones, in press). There are a number of reasons for this, and four will be mentioned.

Cost

A policy maker interested in widely disseminating an effective program will want to know what the costs will be. Such data are a necessary prerequisite before any serious thoughts of dissemination can be entertained.

Feasibility

To be successfully spread, a prevention program must be acceptable to both the deliverers and the target population. If its effectiveness has been demonstrated under conditions of highly complex administrative arrangements and intense demands on the deliverers of the intervention, it is unlikely that it will be taken up in other settings.

Program Originates Outside the Setting

When a prevention program has been launched in a particular setting by persons who are not members of that setting, the chances of its being maintained there are slight. It is one thing for academics to evaluate existing programs in the community and quite another for them not only to evaluate a program but also launch and carry out the intervention. For example, Kolvin et al.'s (1981) demonstration project in the Newcastle schools was a product of a university setting and carried out by university personnel. As one might suspect, once the funding ran out and the study was finished, the school system showed no interest in continuing the program even though elements of it had been shown to be effective.

Reliance on Exceptional People

Prevention programs, especially those that have been shown to be effective often are the work of one or a small group of exceptional and perhaps charismatic people. It is difficult or impossible to duplicate them. The more the effectiveness of a prevention program for antisocial behavior is dependent on exceptional people, the less likely it will ever be successful in preventing antisocial behavior in children other than those in the original sample.

Summary

Policy initiatives in the prevention of antisocial behavior need the results of studies in which the findings are based on a strong design, the intervention was directed at effectiveness not efficacy, the intervention consisted of multiple elements all of which were clearly described, the delivery system was feasible and the intervention reached the entire target population, the evaluation included independent socially important outcomes, and data were available on the timing, sustainability, and cost of the intervention. Further, it can be argued that the prevention field in the antisocial domain needs not just more effective programs but ones that, if effective, could be widely disseminated and maintained in other settings. Issues of cost, feasibility, the extent to which the program belongs to the population of interest or has originated from outside, and its dependence on exceptional people are all critical issues within this last concern.

THREE DIFFERENT INTERVENTIONS

When considering the policy options for reducing antisocial behavior, it becomes clear that only three strategies or types of programs can be employed: clinical, targeted, and universal. Each approach has advantages and disadvantages; these trade-offs have been discussed in detail elsewhere (Offord et al., submitted) and are summarized here.

Clinical Programs

The major characteristic of clinical programs is that the family perceives the child as having a problem and seeks help. Even a cursory consideration of the magnitude of the problem of antisocial behavior in children and youths leaves one with the inescapable conclusion that the clinical enterprise can never play a major role in reducing the burden of suffering from antisocial behavior. It is much too expensive, there are difficulties with obtaining adequate coverage of a population and compliance, and the results are discouraging (Kazdin, 1993; Tolan & Guerra, 1994). Most of the funds for controlling and curtailing antisocial behavior are given to the clinical enterprise, and most of the evaluations also are directed at clinical programs (Tolan & Guerra, 1994).

Targeted Programs

In a targeted program, individual families and their children do not seek help. They are identified as needing help because it is determined that they are at increased risk for future problems. The target population is established by two strategies: identifying groups of children based on characteristics outside the child (e.g., family is on social assistance) or identifying members of the high-risk sample because they have distinguishing characteristics (e.g., mild antisocial behavior).

A major advantage of a targeted program is that it is potentially efficient if the target population can be shown to be at much increased risk for antisocial behavior. There are several disadvantages to this approach, however. The first one concerns the screening itself. The costs associated with screening may be high. Further, it can be expected that the refusal rate for participation in the screening procedure will be highest among those at greatest risk for antisocial behavior (Rose, 1985; Rutter, Tizard, & Whitmore, 1970). Second, it is difficult to screen accurately for future disorder (see Figure 33.1). There are always trade-offs between the positive predictive value of a screen and its sensitivity. The former is concerned with the proportion of children identified by the screen who actually will end up with antisocial behavior at a later date. When the positive predictive value is low, far more children will be identified as being at-risk than end up with the outcome of interest. When attempts are made to increase the positive predictive value, the sensitivity falls. That is, the proportion of children with the outcome who are identified by the screen will be reduced. When the positive predictive value is low, any intervention offered to the screen-positive children must be inexpensive and nonstigmatizing, because the majority of children receiving the intervention are not at-risk for the outcome. On the other hand, if the positive predictive value is high and the sensitivity low, even if the preventive intervention is effective with the screen-positive children, it will not result in a sizable reduction of the outcome because most children with the outcome will not be identified by the screen. A recent publication on the performance of the screen in the FAST Track project illustrates the limits of the accuracy of a screening procedure. The screening procedure used a combination of teacher and parent data in kindergarten and the prediction was of problem outcomes in the fall and spring of grade 1. The positive predictive value of the screen was 70.4%, but the sensitivity was only 50.9% (Lochmann & CPPRG, 1995).

A second disadvantage of the targeted approach is that a large number of children at small risk will give rise to more cases of the disorder of interest than the small number of children who are at high risk (Rose, 1985). The implication is that any particular targeted program, even if successful, will not result in a sizable reduction in the burden of suffering for a condition such as antisocial behavior. A series of targeted programs would be needed to fulfill this aim. A third disadvantage of the targeted approach is that it does not consider as candidates for intervention causal risk factors that put entire populations at risk. Rather, the targeted approach focuses its efforts on reducing the effects of causal risk factors that distinguish the high-risk group from the rest of the population. However, the important causal risk factors (those with the highest attributable risks) may be ones that apply to the population as a whole. These could include widespread marital discord or academic underachievement. A final disadvantage of the targeted approach is the possibility of labeling or stigmatizing the high-risk population. Labeling becomes particularly unfortunate if the screening procedure results in identifying large numbers of false positive children.

Universal Programs

In these initiatives, all children (and their families) in a geographic area or a setting (e.g., a school) receive the intervention. Individual families do not seek help and no one is singled out for the intervention. An obvious advantage to this approach is that there is no labeling or stigmatization of any members of a population.

The universal approach has several disadvantages, however, and two will be mentioned. First, it may be unnecessarily expensive because most of the children receiving the intervention will not be at-risk for the outcome. Second, universal programs may have their greatest effect on children who are at lowest risk for the outcome of interest (Jones, in press). Programs such as free public libraries and state-subsidized higher education are universal, yet those who take advantage of them are primarily middle class.

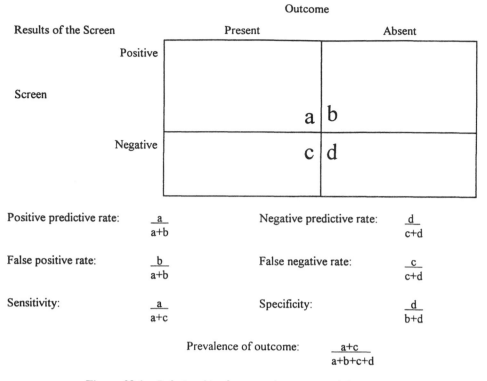

Figure 33.1 *Relationships between the screen and the outcome.*

Summary

Clearly, there are trade-offs among clinical, targeted, and universal programs. All three are needed to reduce antisocial behavior. The optimal mix of these three approaches will change as knowledge accumulates about effectiveness and costs of various interventions. Combinations of all three will be needed. Universal programs cannot be expected to prevent all children from developing antisocial personality disorder, but they may prevent some children from developing it. Targeted programs could be expected to further reduce antisocial behavior in those children who did not respond to the universal programs. Given these two types of programs in place, the clinical enterprise would be much more manageable. In the absence of effective universal and targeted programs, clinical programs will continue to be overwhelmed and not accurately directed at children most in need of them.

FUTURE POLICY INITIATIVES

Two policy issues confronting the research enterprise concerned with reducing and preventing antisocial behavior center on descriptive versus experimental epidemiology and efficacy versus effectiveness. With limited research funds, decisions will have to be made about the payoff of supporting expensive descriptive studies rather than devoting these funds to promising intervention efforts. A further set of discussions is needed about supporting expensive efficacy studies that, even if successful, could not be implemented widely, compared with supporting intervention efforts that, from the beginning, if they are successful, could be disseminated and maintained in a variety of settings. Last, it will be necessary to fund intervention studies in the antisocial domain in a balanced fashion so that progress can be made in discovering the effectiveness of interventions of all three types of programs: clinical, targeted, and universal. A major initiative could be to evaluate combinations of these three types of programs in different community settings.

It should be noted that a major challenge in formulating a policy for reducing antisocial behavior is that it occurs in a variety of settings, most of which do not see antisocial behavior as their primary concern. For the serious forms of antisocial behavior, the justice system has the primary responsibility. Otherwise, the responsibility is widely dispersed among, for example, public health, welfare, education, social services, and mental health systems. Prevention programs, to have widespread beneficial effects, will have to be shown to be acceptable and effective in the multiple systems that are relevant to them.

REFERENCES

Bierman, K. L., Greenberg, M. T., & The Conduct Problems Prevention Research Group (CPPRG). (1996). Social skill training in the FAST Track program. In R. D. Peters & R. J. McMahon (Eds.), *Preventing childhood disorders, substance abuse, and delinquency* (pp. 65–89). Thousand Oaks, CA: Sage Publications.

Canadian Task Force on the Periodic Health Examination. (1979). The periodic health examination. *Canadian Medical Association Journal, 121,* 3–45.

Centers for Disease Control. (1992a). Physical fighting among high school students—United States, 1990. *Morbidity and Mortality Weekly Report, 41,* 91.

Centers for Disease Control. (1992b). *Proceedings of the third national injury control conference.* Atlanta: Author.

Coie, J. D. (1996). The prevalence of violence and antisocial behavior. In R. D. Peters & R. J. McMahon (Eds.), *Preventing childhood disorders, substance abuse, and delinquency* (pp. 1–18). Thousand Oaks, CA: Sage Publications.

Cunningham, C. C. (1996). Promising directions in the design of parent training programs for children with disruptive behavior disorders: Improving availability, utilization and cost-efficacy. In R. D. Peters & R. J. McMahon (Eds.), *Preventing childhood disorders, substance abuse, and delinquency* (pp. 144–160). Thousand Oaks, CA: Sage Publications.

Department of Clinical Epidemiology and Biostatistics, McMaster University Health Sciences Centre. (1981). How to read clinical journals: IV. To determine etiology and causation. *Journal of Canadian Medical Association, 124,* 985–990.

Elliott, D. S., Huizinga, D., & Morse, B. (1986). Self-reported violent offending: A descriptive analysis of juvenile violent offenders and their offending careers. *Journal of Interpersonal Violence, 4,* 472–514.

Farrington, D. P. (1983). Offending from 10 to 25 years of age. In K. Van Dusen & S. A. Mednicks (Eds.), *Prospective studies of crime and delinquency* (pp. 17–38). Boston: Kluwer-Nijhoff.

Farrington, D., Loeber, R., & Van Kammen, W.B. (1990). Long-term criminal outcomes of hyperactivity-impulsivity-attention deficit and conduct problems in childhood. In L. Robins & M. Rutter (Eds.), *Straight and devious pathways from childhood to adulthood* (pp. 62–81). Cambridge, England: Cambridge University Press.

Institute of Medicine. (1989). *Research on children and adolescents with mental, behavioral and developmental disorders: Mobilizing a national initiative.* Washington, DC: National Academy Press.

Jones, M. B. (in press). Undoing the effects of poverty on children: Non-economic initiatives. In *Proceedings of the inaugural symposium of the Centre for Studies of Children at Risk: Improving the life quality of children; options and evidence.* Hamilton, Ontario: Centre for Studies of Children at Risk.

Kazdin, A. E. (1993). Treatment of conduct disorder: Progress and directions in psychotherapy research. *Development and Psychopathology, 5,* 277–310.

Kolvin, T., Garside, R. F., Nicol, A. R., MacMillan, A., Wolstenhome, I., & Leitch, I. M. (1981). *Help starts here: The maladjusted child in the ordinary school.* New York: Tavistock.

Kraemer, H. C., Kazdin, A. E., Offord, D. R., Kessler, R. C., Jensen, P. S., & Kupfer, D. J. (1997). Coming to terms with the terms of risk. *Archives of General Psychiatry, 54,* 337–343.

Lipman, E. L., Offord, D. R., & Boyle, M. H. (1996). What if we could eliminate child poverty. The theoretical effect on child psychosocial morbidity. *Social Psychiatry and Psychiatric Epidemiology, 31,* 303–307.

Lochman, J. E., & The Conduct Problems Prevention Research Group (CPPRG). (1995). Screening of child behavior problems for prevention programs at school entry. *Journal of Consulting and Clinical Psychology, 63,* 549–559.

Lochman, J. E., & Wells, K. C. (1996). A social-cognitive intervention with aggressive children: Prevention effects and contextual implemen-

tation issues. In R. D. Peters & R. J. McMahon (Eds.), *Preventing childhood disorders, substance abuse and delinquency* (pp. 111–143). Thousand Oaks, CA: Sage Publications.

Loeber, R., Wung, P., Keenan, K., Giroux, B., Stouthamer-Loeber, M., Van Kammen, W. B., & Maughan, B. (1993). Developmental pathways in disruptive child behavior. *Developmental and Psychopathology, 5,* 101–131.

McKeown, T. (1976). *The modern rise of population.* New York: Academic Press.

McKeown, T. (1988). *The origins of human disease.* New York: Basil Blackwell.

Moffitt, T. E. (1993). Adolescent-limited and life-course-persistent antisocial behavior: A developmental taxonomy. *Psychological Review, 100,* 674–701.

Mrazek, P. J., & Haggerty, R. J. (Eds.). (1994). *Reducing risks for mental disorders: Frontiers for preventive intervention research.* Washington, DC: National Academy Press.

Offord, D. R., Boyle, M. H., Fleming, J. E., Munroe Blum, H., & Rae-Grant, N. I. (1989). Ontario Child Health Study: Summary of selected results. *Canadian Journal of Psychiatry, 34,* 483–491.

Offord, D. R., Boyle, M. H., Racine, Y. A., Fleming, J. E., Cadman, D. T., Munroe Blum, H., Byrne, C., Links, P., Lipman, E. L., MacMillan, H. L., Rae-Grant, N. I., Sanford, M. N., Szatmari, P., Thomas, H., & Woodward, C. A. (1992). Outcome, prognosis and risk in a longitudinal follow-up study. *Journal of the American Academy of Child and Adolescent Psychiatry, 31,* 60–67.

Offord, D. R., Boyle, M. H., Szatmari, P., Rae-Grant, N. I., Links, P. S., Cadman, D. T., Byles, J. A., Crawford, J. W., Munroe Blum, H., Byrne, C., & Woodward, C. A. (1987). Ontario Child Health Study: Six-month prevalence of disorder and rates of service utilization. *Archives of General Psychiatry, 44,* 832–836.

Offord, D. R., Kraemer, H. C., Kazdin, A. E., Jensen, P. S., Kessler, R. C., & Kupfer, D. J. (submitted). Reducing the burden of suffering from child mental disorders: Trade-offs among clinical, targeted and universal programs.

Osgood, D. W., O'Malley, P. M., Bachman, J. G., & Johnston, L. D. (1989). Time trends and age trends in arrests and self-reported illegal behavior. *Criminology, 27,* 389–417.

Peters, R. D., & McMahon, R. J. (Eds.). (1996). *Preventing childhood disorders, substance abuse and delinquency.* Thousand Oaks, CA: Sage Publications.

Peters, R. D., & Russell, C. C. (1996). Promoting development and preventing disorder. The Better Beginnings, Better Futures Project. In R. D. Peters & R. J. McMahon (Eds.), *Preventing childhood disorders, substance abuse and delinquency* (pp. 19–47). Thousand Oaks, CA: Sage Publications.

Robins, L. N. (1966). *Deviant children grown up.* Baltimore: Williams & Wilkins.

Robins, L. N. (1970). The adult development of the antisocial child. *Seminars in Psychiatry, 6,* 420–434.

Robins, L. N. (1978). Psychiatric epidemiology. *Archives of General Psychiatry, 35,* 697–702.

Rose, G. (1985). Sick individuals and sick populations. *International Journal of Epidemiology, 14,* 32–38.

Rutter, M., Tizard, J., & Whitmore, K. (1970). *Education, health and behavior.* London: Longman.

Sackett, D. S. (1980). Evaluation of health services. In J. Last (Ed.), *Preventive medicine and public health* (pp. 1800–1823). New York: Appleton Century Crofts.

Sanford, M. N., Offord, D. R., Boyle, M. H., Peace, A., & Racine, Y. A. (1992). Ontario Child Health Study: Social and school impairments in children aged 6 to 16 years. *Journal of the American Academy of Child and Adolescent Psychiatry, 31,* 60–67.

Silverman, M. M., Lalley, T. L., Rosenberg, M. L., Smith, J. C., Parron, D., & Jacobs, J. (1988). Control of stress and violent behavior: Mid-course review of the 1990 health objectives. *Public Health Reports, 103,* 38–49.

Steiner, D. L., Norman, G. R., & Munroe Blum, H. (1989). *Epidemiology.* Toronto: B. C. Decker.

Tolan, P., & Guerra, N. (1994). *What works in reducing adolescent violence: An empirical review of the field.* Boulder: Center for the Study and Prevention of Violence, Institute for Behavioral Sciences, University of Colorado.

Tolan, P. H., & Thomas, P. (1995). The implications of age of onset for delinquency risk: II. Longitudinal data. *Journal of Abnormal Child Psychology, 23,* 157–181.

Tremblay, R. E., & Craig, W. M. (1995). Developmental crime prevention. In M. Tonry & D. P. Farrington (Eds.), *Building a safer society: Strategic approaches to crime prevention* (Vol. 19, pp. 151–236). Chicago: University of Chicago Press.

Tugwell, P. T., Bennett, K. J., Haynes, R. B., & Sackett, D. L. (1985). The measurement iterative loop: A framework for the critical appraisal of need, benefits and costs of health interventions. *Journal of Chronic Diseases, 38,* 339–351.

U.S. Department of Justice. (1986). *Source book of criminal justice statistics—1985 (NCS-100899).* Washington, DC: Government Printing Office.

CHAPTER 34

Community Interventions to Reduce Risks and Enhance Protection Against Antisocial Behavior

J. DAVID HAWKINS, MICHAEL W. ARTHUR, and JEFFREY J. OLSON

Crime and substance abuse are serious, costly social problems that touch every community in this country. Fortunately, the knowledge base for developing effective interventions to prevent antisocial behavior among children and adolescents has expanded dramatically in recent years (Howell, Krisberg, Hawkins, & Wilson, 1995; Institute of Medicine [IOM], 1994). Longitudinal research has revealed a consistent set of predictors of the development of antisocial behavior (Hawkins, Arthur, & Catalano, 1995). Interventions targeting these predictors have been successful at reducing the prevalence of antisocial behavior in the populations so targeted (Howell et al., 1995; IOM, 1994). Using this knowledge to assist communities in reducing the prevalence of antisocial behavior is a pressing social policy objective (Biglan, 1995).

Risk factors that predict increased likelihood of antisocial behavior have been identified at the individual, family, school, peer group, and community levels (Brewer, Hawkins, Catalano, & Neckerman, 1995; Farrington, 1996; Loeber, 1990). Individual risk factors include low birth weight, prenatal drug exposure, perinatal complications, brain damage, hyperactivity and lack of impulse control, sensation seeking, rebelliousness, early initiation of antisocial behavior, and favorable attitudes toward delinquency and drug use (Brennan & Mednick, Chapter 25, this volume; Dishion & Patterson, Chapter 20, this volume). Family risk factors include poor family management practices such as a lack of supervision and excessively harsh or inconsistent discipline (including child abuse or neglect), high levels of family conflict, a family history of antisocial behavior, and favorable parental attitudes toward and involvement in crime, violence, and drug use (Shaw & Winslow, Chapter 15, this volume; Widom, Chapter 16, this volume). School risk factors include early and persistent antisocial behavior during the early elementary grades, academic failure beginning in the late elementary grades, and low commitment to school (Farrington, 1996; Maguin & Loeber, 1995). Association with peers who engage in drug use, delinquency, and violence is a strong and con-

sistent predictor of antisocial behavior (Cairns, Cadwallader, Estell, & Neckerman, Chapter 19, this volume) and of progressing to more serious and chronic levels (Thornberry & Krohn, Chapter 21, this volume). Community-level risk factors include neighborhood social disorganization, high rates of mobility, severe economic deprivation, availability of drugs or firearms, permissive laws, lax enforcement of laws, norms favorable to antisocial behavior, and frequent media portrayals of violence (Brewer et al., 1995; Hawkins, Arthur, & Catalano, 1995; Huesmann, Moise, & Podolski, Chapter 18, this volume; Sampson, 1994).

Different risk factors appear to be particularly salient at different developmental stages (Bell, 1986). Family and individual factors are the earliest consistent predictors of adolescent problem behaviors (Baumrind, 1985; Loeber & Stouthamer-Loeber, 1987), whereas school factors become significant predictors during the middle- to late elementary school years (Gottfredson, 1988). Early exposure to multiple risk factors predicts early involvement in serious delinquency and drug use (Huizinga, Loeber, & Thornberry, in press; Newcomb, Maddahian, & Bentler, 1986). In turn, an early initiation to these behaviors predicts greater likelihood of frequent and persistent involvement in serious problem behavior (Elliott, 1994; IOM, 1994). This evidence suggests that delaying the onset of delinquency, violence, and drug use should be a primary preventive goal.

The research also indicates that the likelihood of serious antisocial behavior is greatest among those exposed to multiple risk factors (IOM, 1994; Newcomb et al., 1986; Howell, 1995). These reviews and others (e.g., Coie et al., 1993; Dryfoos, 1990; Hawkins, 1995) reveal that many of the same risk factors predict adolescent delinquency, violence, and substance abuse and also predict dropping out of school, early sexual involvement, and teen pregnancy. Moreover, the research indicates that a small proportion of youth account for roughly two thirds to three quarters of the violent crimes committed by their age cohort (Elliott, 1994; Huizinga et al., in press) and that these youth typically have multiple risk factors and few protective factors, display consistently higher rates of a variety of antisocial behaviors than their peers at each age, and initiate criminal activity at a young age (Howell, 1995). Preventive actions that address predictors in multiple domains and are sustained through childhood may be required to prevent serious antisocial behavior among those at greatest risk

---

The authors gratefully acknowledge support from the Center for Substance Abuse Prevention, Substance Abuse and Mental Health Services Administration, and the National Institute on Drug Abuse in the preparation of this chapter.

due to exposure to multiple risk factors (Hawkins, Arthur, & Catalano, 1995; Wilson & Howell, 1993).

Studies have revealed, however, that many children avoid serious involvement in antisocial behavior despite exposure to multiple risk factors (e.g., Rutter, 1979; Werner & Smith, 1992). These studies have explored protective factors that appear to buffer against or mitigate the negative effects of risk exposure. Protective factors have been identified within individuals and within the social environment. Individual protective factors against antisocial behavior include female gender, high IQ, a resilient temperament, and a positive social orientation (Garmezy, 1985). Social protective factors include warm, supportive relationships and social bonding to adults (Rutter, 1979; Werner & Smith, 1992), recognition for involvement in positive extracurricular activities (Rae, Grant, Thomas, Offord, & Boyle, 1989), and social institutions such as peer groups, schools, and communities that emphasize positive social norms, prosocial behavior, and educational success (Brewer et al., 1995; Rutter, Maughan, Mortimore, Ouston, & Smith, 1979). Preventive interventions should focus on enhancing protective factors while reducing risk factors.

The research suggests that interventions that reduce multiple risk factors while enhancing protective factors in the family, school, peer and community environments over the course of infant, childhood, and adolescent development hold promise for preventing multiple adolescent health and behavior problems. A current challenge is to apply this knowledge to reducing the prevalence of adolescent antisocial behavior in communities throughout this country (Biglan, 1995; Hawkins, Catalano, & Associates, 1992; Howell, 1995). Multifaceted interventions that support enduring community-level change to reduce risk and develop protective factors to mitigate the influences of risk exposure may be required to achieve sustained reductions in the prevalence of antisocial behavior (Brewer et al., 1995; IOM, 1994). A comprehensive community approach to prevention would include intensive and sustained indicated prevention services for the small proportion of youths who initiate serious antisocial behavior at an early age embedded within selective interventions for high-risk populations and universal interventions aimed at the entire community (IOM, 1994). Such multilayered prevention strategies could have synergistic effects by reducing risk and enhancing protective processes across multiple domains.

The community's responsibility for preventing juvenile delinquency and drug abuse has become firmly entrenched in current policies and practice (Howell, 1995). For instance, Title V of the Juvenile Justice and Delinquency Prevention Amendments of 1992, the Center for Substance Abuse Prevention's Community Partnership Demonstration Program, and the Robert Wood Johnson Foundation's Fighting Back and Healthy Nations initiatives all emphasize community involvement in planning comprehensive strategies to prevent antisocial behavior; these represent a significant investment in community prevention efforts. A survey of community drug prevention activities in the United States identified more than 1,250 coalitions representing communities in every state (Join Together, 1992). Since the late 1980s, the increase in community prevention programs has created a demand for information about effective intervention models and strategies.

This chapter reviews knowledge about the effectiveness of community interventions to reduce risks and enhance protection against adolescent antisocial behavior and identifies promising leads for research and intervention. Of specific interest here are community mobilization, media, and policy interventions that seek to reduce risk factors and enhance protective factors in order to reduce the prevalence of adolescent antisocial behavior. For the purposes of this chapter, antisocial behavior includes conduct problems, violence, delinquency, and substance abuse in recognition of the interrelationships among these problems and the risk and protective factors that predict them. First, current issues in community-level prevention are discussed; next, community interventions that have shown promising results in studies employing experimental or quasi-experimental designs are reviewed. These are followed by a summary of methodological issues in studying and evaluating community interventions. Finally, conclusions about the state of the field and directions for further research and intervention are discussed.

ISSUES IN COMMUNITY PREVENTIVE INTERVENTIONS

Focus on the Individual Versus the Environment

The first challenge a community faces in trying to prevent antisocial behavior is arriving at a shared understanding of the sources or causes of the problem in the community. Problem definition shapes the types of responses considered. For example, if antisocial behavior is thought to be caused by individual characteristics such as impulsiveness and lack of self-control, then interventions that target individuals and teach impulse control are logical options. If, on the other hand, antisocial behavior is viewed as a response to social conditions such as poverty, social disorganization, and racism, then strategies that focus on empowering disenfranchised groups and community organizing are more likely to be pursued. Without a clear and shared understanding of the sources of the problem, it is difficult for communities to develop a coordinated array of prevention services that are likely to reduce risk and enhance protection at multiple levels and thus reduce the prevalence of antisocial behavior.

This issue is apparent in both current theories of antisocial behavior and attempts to prevent antisocial behavior. Several theorists have proposed that antisocial behavior is primarily the result of individual differences in the ability to regulate behavior and delay gratification (e.g., Gottfredson & Hirschi, 1990; Rowe, 1996; Wilson & Herrnstein, 1985), whereas others have emphasized social disorganization (e.g., Bursik & Grasmick, 1996; Sampson, 1994) or situational aspects of the environment (Clarke, 1995) as important causal factors. Paralleling these diverging theoretical models, community approaches to preventing antisocial behavior also have tended to follow diverging tracks. Many prevention programs focus on individuals, teaching self-regulation and social problem-solving skills (e.g., Kellam & Rebok, 1992). In contrast, others focus on community mobilization (e.g., Fawcett, Paine, Francisco, & Vliet, 1993; Hawkins et al., 1992), and still others apply "target hardening" approaches that change community environments to reduce situational opportunities and inducements to engage in antisocial activity (e.g., Clarke, 1995).

In fact, longitudinal research indicates that individual, social, and environmental factors all influence antisocial behavior. It is likely that antisocial behavior results from transactions between individuals with different propensities toward antisocial behavior and their physical and social environments, which also differ in their motivating versus inhibiting properties (Catalano & Hawkins, 1996; Farrington, 1996; Thornberry & Krohn, Chapter 21, this volume). For example, Moffitt (1990) reported that youths diagnosed with attention deficit disorder who had little family adversity (including low parental IQ, education, income and occupational status; teen mother; single parent; large family size; and poor family relations) had little risk for delinquency, although similar youths who experienced high levels of family adversity were at high risk for developing chronic antisocial and violent behavior. To achieve sustained reductions in the prevalence of antisocial behavior, theoretical models are needed that can integrate the individual, social, environmental, and situational factors involved at multiple levels to organize and guide the design of multilevel interventions (Catalano & Hawkins, 1996; Petraitis, Flay, & Miller, 1995; Thornberry, 1987). Likewise, intervention models are needed that address the organizational and implementation issues in developing a coordinated array of community responses that address risk and protective factors at multiple levels, particularly for those exposed to multiple risks and few protective factors, while balancing the community's multiple objectives (Howell, 1995; IOM, 1994).

Community Mobilization and Intervention Implementation

Reduction of risk in multiple social domains requires that interventions be implemented widely with sufficient fidelity and intensity to change community norms, conditions, and behaviors. To enhance their impact, community intervention strategies frequently involve mobilizing community members to participate actively in planning and implementing prevention activities (e.g., Fawcett et al., 1993; Hawkins et al., 1992). Community mobilization is believed to increase the impact of the interventions by reducing social disorganization, promoting strong community norms against antisocial behavior, and creating community ownership and investment in prevention activities. Therefore, community members need the tools to select promising intervention strategies and implement them effectively and to monitor the impact of their efforts.

However, there are gaps in knowledge regarding community mobilization approaches to prevention. For example, little is known about the factors that influence communities to select effective prevention strategies or to implement selected strategies with enough fidelity, intensity, and duration to achieve the desired risk reduction. Little research has been conducted to examine the factors that influence a community's readiness to implement comprehensive community prevention initiatives effectively (Arthur, Brewer, Graham, Shavel, Tremper, & Hawkins, 1996; Oetting et al., 1995). Further study of factors related to citizen participation in community prevention initiatives, community selection of prevention strategies, and community readiness to implement comprehensive prevention strategies effectively is needed to expand the knowledge base for community prevention initiatives (Biglan, 1995).

Despite these gaps in knowledge about processes related to community prevention implementation, progress has been made recently in designing successful community prevention initiatives. Efforts to prevent antisocial behavior through comprehensive community interventions, through mass media interventions, and through policy changes have shown positive results in a growing number of studies. These studies are reviewed briefly in the next section. Interventions were included in this review if they explicitly addressed empirically established predictors of antisocial behavior, were implemented at a community level to change the normative context for development within the community, and had shown evidence of effectiveness at reducing targeted risk factors and enhancing targeted protective factors using a quasi-experimental or experimental research design. Though limited by the methodological challenges confronting the evaluation of community interventions (Connell, Kubisch, Schorr, & Weiss, 1995), these studies indicate that community interventions have the potential to reduce the prevalence of antisocial behavior.

COMMUNITY INTERVENTIONS TO REDUCE RISKS AND ENHANCE PROTECTION AGAINST ANTISOCIAL BEHAVIOR

The most promising current community prevention models have been adapted from the field of public health (Hawkins, Arthur, & Catalano, 1995; IOM, 1994). Comprehensive communitywide programs focused on reducing risk factors for heart and lung disease have demonstrated positive effects on health behaviors and significant reductions in risk factor levels within the targeted populations (Farquhar, Fortmann, & Flora, 1990; Perry, Kelder, Murray, & Klepp, 1992). Given the success of these community interventions at reducing risk factors for heart disease, community interventions designed to reduce risk factors for violence, delinquency, and drug abuse currently are being implemented (Hawkins et al., 1992; Howell, 1995).

Comprehensive Community Interventions

The Midwestern Prevention Project (Pentz et al., 1989) was a multilevel community intervention to prevent substance abuse. The project was initiated in 1984 in 42 public middle and junior high schools in 15 school districts in the Kansas City area. Using a quasi-experimental design, 8 schools were randomized to experimental or control conditions, 20 schools were able to reschedule existing programming to participate and were assigned to the intervention condition, and 14 schools were unable to reschedule their programming and so were assigned to the control condition. Project components included (a) mass media programming, (b) school based drug resistance skills curricula, (c) parent education and organization, (d) community organization, and (e) health policy. These components were introduced sequentially over 4 years, starting with the mass media, school curricula, and parent interventions during the middle or junior high school years (Pentz et al., 1989).

After the first year of mass media and school-based intervention, prevalence rates for monthly and weekly use of cigarettes, alcohol, and marijuana were significantly lower for the intervention schools than for schools in the control condition that received the media intervention only. The net increase in drug use prevalence among intervention schools was half that of delayed intervention (control) schools (Pentz et al., 1989). In analyses examining only the eight schools randomly assigned to the study condition 3 years following initiation of the interventions, significant differences between conditions were found for cigarette and marijuana use but not alcohol use. The Midwestern Prevention Project was effective at preventing the onset of substance use among both high-risk and general population students (Johnson et al., 1990).

Another series of studies of comprehensive community interventions to prevent adolescent smoking and alcohol use has been conducted by Perry and her colleagues (Perry et al., 1992; Perry et al., 1993). The Class of 1989 study was part of the Minnesota Heart Health Program (MHHP), a research and demonstration project to reduce cardiovascular disease in three communities from 1980 to 1993 (Perry et al., 1992). The Class of 1989 study was designed to evaluate the combined impact of a classroom-based social influences smoking prevention curriculum delivered to the Class of 1989 during their sixth, seventh, and eighth grades and the communitywide cardiovascular health promotion activities of the MHHP. Communitywide activities included seven strategies: (a) cardiovascular risk factor screening for adults, (b) grocery and restaurant point-of-purchase food labeling for health education, (c) community mobilization for annual risk factor education campaigns, (d) continuing education of health professionals to promote community awareness of cardiovascular disease risk factors and prevention, (e) mass media education campaigns, (f) adult education, and (g) youth education. Using a quasi-experimental design, a single-intervention community was matched with a reference community. The intervention community received both the communitywide intervention to improve diet, exercise, and smoking patterns among the entire population and the school-based social influences curriculum; the reference community received neither.

The interventions were evaluated using annual surveys of the cohort of students who were in sixth grade in 1983. Identifying information was collected at each survey administration, allowing the data to be analyzed as a longitudinal cohort design for students present at multiple years or as repeated cross-sectional designs including all students present at each time point. Analyses of both the cohort and cross-sectional data revealed significant differences in smoking prevalence between the intervention and comparison communities. When the students were seniors in high school, 14.6% of the cohort in the intervention community smoked compared to 24.1% of the cohort in the reference community (Perry et al., 1992). The findings suggest that the combined school and community interventions produced a significant reduction in smoking prevalence among middle and high school youths. However, the findings are limited by the study design, which used a single pair of communities and relied on data analysis at the individual rather than community level.

A second project, Project Northland, is using a similar combination of community-based and classroom interventions, along with a parent intervention component, to prevent alcohol use among adolescents in several small communities in northeastern Minnesota. This section of the state was targeted because of the high prevalence of alcohol-related problems in the region (Perry et al., 1993). The project recruited 24 school districts and their surrounding communities to participate. Four small, adjacent districts were combined, and the resulting 20 districts were blocked by size and randomized to treatment and delayed-treatment control conditions (Perry et al., 1993; Perry et al., 1996). The project is being evaluated using surveys of all students in the sixth-grade cohort conducted in the fall of 1991 (baseline), and in the spring of 1992, 1993, and 1994.

After 3 years of intervention, students in the intervention school districts reported significantly lower scores on a Tendency to Use Alcohol scale and significantly lower prevalence of monthly and weekly alcohol use (Perry et al., 1996). Significant differences in the hypothesized direction were also observed for survey scales measuring peer influences to use alcohol, perceived norms regarding teen alcohol use, parents communicating sanctions for their child's alcohol use, and reasons for teens not to use alcohol (Perry et al., 1996). These effects on alcohol-related attitudes and behaviors are noteworthy, given the wide prevalence of alcohol use among adolescents and the strong research design of the study. Differences between the intervention and comparison groups in cigarette use, smokeless tobacco use, marijuana use, perceived self-efficacy, and perceived access to alcohol were not significant.

Policy Change Interventions

A second communitywide prevention strategy that has shown some evidence of effectiveness at preventing antisocial behavior is to change policies and laws governing the availability, sale, and use of alcohol, cigarettes, and firearms. Changes in state policies regarding liquor taxes (Levy & Sheflin, 1985), liquor sales outlets (Wagenaar & Holder, 1991), and the legal drinking age (Saffer & Grossman, 1987) have been shown to influence rates of alcohol consumption and alcohol-related traffic accidents (O'Malley & Wagenaar, 1991). Given the correlational nature of many of these studies it is impossible to infer causality, yet the consistency of the observed relationships suggests that policy interventions to reduce availability and communicate norms against teen alcohol use can be an effective prevention strategy.

Some studies of the impact of firearm regulations have revealed positive results (Brewer et al., 1995). Loftin, McDowell, Wiersema, and Cottey (1991) evaluated a 1977 Washington, DC, ordinance that prohibited the purchase, sale, transfer, and possession of handguns by civilians unless they already owned a handgun. A multiple time-series design was used to examine monthly frequencies of firearm homicides in Washington, DC, and in adjacent metropolitan areas in Virginia and Maryland from 1968 to 1987. The analysis revealed that homicides in Washington, DC, decreased by 25% after institution of the law, and the reduction was maintained through 1987. It should be noted, however, that the homicide rate in Washington, DC, more than doubled between 1987 and 1993 (Dobrin, Wiersema, Loftin, & McDowell, 1996), suggesting that the presence of other factors, such as gun violence associated with the spread of crack cocaine dealing, overwhelmed the positive impact of the handgun ordinance. Jung and Jason (1988) also used a time-series design to examine a similar change in the law in Evanston, Illinois, compared to Rock Island, Illinois, a city that did not change its laws. Firearm assaults in Evanston decreased significantly during the preintervention period, attributed to intensive media coverage of the new law, but showed no change in the postintervention period, whereas firearm assaults did not change significantly in Rock Island.

In contrast, however, McDowall, Lizotte, and Wiersema (1991) found no impact on rates of assault following passage of a 1981 Morton Grove, Illinois, law that banned the sale of handguns as well as their possession by private citizens. A time-series analysis was conducted on arrest data beginning 5 years before and ending 5 years after passage of the law, which showed no change in assault rates. The authors cited minimal enforcement of the law in interpreting the lack of impact on assaults. The conflicting findings suggest that laws and policies influence behavior by communicating the community's norms. Thus, these strategies are less effective when they are not enforced or when they are not supported by community members. For example, efforts to reduce the availability of firearms, cigarettes, and alcohol through regulations and tax increases have been opposed in many communities by the merchants that sell these products and the community members who purchase them. Community mobilization can help to generate the visible support needed to make policy changes work.

For example, Rogers, Feighery, Tencati, Butler, and Weiner (1995) used a quasi-experimental design to assess a project developed to address the problem of point-of-purchase tobacco advertising. An existing sign control ordinance that set limits on store window coverage and sidewalk signs was used by residents in a community mobilization and media campaign to reduce the level of tobacco advertising in the community (Rogers et al., 1995). Community organizers used presentations and media advocacy efforts to inform residents about the ordinance and violations involving tobacco advertising. Residents were mobilized to file complaints with the city's code enforcement office when neighborhood stores were not in compliance with the ordinance. Compared to the baseline, significant reductions in campaign-related tobacco advertising were observed in the targeted stores after the campaign, whereas no changes were observed over the same period in four reference communities.

Media Interventions

A third community-level prevention strategy that has shown positive effects is use of the media to change public attitudes, educate community residents, and support other community interventions. For example, the Partnership for a Drug Free America has used advertising to encourage negative attitudes toward the use of illegal drugs (e.g., "This is your brain on drugs"). Mall intercept surveys indicated significant changes in norms and attitudes toward marijuana and cocaine in markets receiving saturation advertising compared to other markets (Black, 1989). In general, media campaigns have shown limited effectiveness as isolated strategies (Schilling & McAlister, 1990) but have been found to enhance the effects of related school- and community-based prevention programs (Flynn et al., 1992; Perry et al., 1992) and to increase participation and exposure to parent training programs (Hawkins, Catalano, & Kent, 1991).

Bauman, LaPrelle, Brown, Koch, and Padgett (1991) evaluated the effects of three different mass media smoking cessation programs. One program used 30-second radio messages that focused on seven expected consequences of smoking. The second program was similar but also included a 60-second radio message that invited persons 12 to 15 years old to enter an "I Won't Smoke Sweepstakes." The third program was similar to the second but included television broadcast of the sweepstakes offer. Results indicated that participants in the radio intervention condition reported significantly more negative expected consequences of smoking and lower perceived friend's approval of smoking. Findings also suggested that the programs involving television were no more effective than those with radio alone and that a peer-involvement component was not effective at changing attitudes. None of the interventions had a significant effect on smoking behavior (Bauman et al., 1991).

Flynn et al. (1992; Flynn, Worden, Secker-Walker, Badger, & Geller, 1995), evaluated the effectiveness of a combined school and mass media intervention to prevent cigarette smoking in four widely separated communities. Over the course of 4 years, students in two communities received both interventions while students in two other matched communities received only the school intervention. The school intervention consisted of grade-specific curricula delivered in grades 5 through 10. The media program consisted of radio and television messages addressing the same objectives as the classroom curricula and designed to appeal to six target age and gender groups. The results indicated that significantly fewer students in the combined media and school intervention condition than in the school intervention only condition initiated smoking by the end of the intervention (Flynn et al., 1992) and by the 2-year follow-up (Flynn et al., 1995). Moreover, students in the combined intervention condition reported less favorable norms and attitudes toward smoking than students in the school intervention only condition.

Thus, studies of community interventions to reduce risk and enhance protection against antisocial behavior have demonstrated positive effects of community mobilization, policy change, and media interventions. Generally, these interventions have targeted risk factors including availability of firearms and drugs, community disorganization, and favorable attitudes toward antisocial behavior and protective factors of social bonding and clear norms against antisocial behavior. However, the promising findings of these interventions are constrained by a number of methodological concerns. These issues and emerging methods for addressing them are discussed in the following section.

METHODOLOGICAL ISSUES IN THE STUDY OF COMMUNITY INTERVENTIONS TO PREVENT ANTISOCIAL BEHAVIOR

A number of issues that pertain to community prevention research should be considered when weighing the evidence, individually and cumulatively, from the studies available. Community intervention research involves study designs that must address threats posed by measurement constraints, mixed units of analysis, and implementation integrity as well as the interpretive challenge presented by heterogeneous effects across populations and along the developmental life course. Careful theoretical specification, multiple measurement sources, and multiple and varied statistical analysis techniques can be employed to meet these challenges.

Measurement Issues

Much of the research on antisocial behavior has focused on the individual as the unit of measurement. This is appropriate for intervention and research designs that focus on creating and documenting changes in individuals or their perception of their environment. However, for interventions and research that emphasize changes in social environments and community systems, community-level measures are needed to assess such changes adequately. Moreover, it is important that the same core measures are measured consistently across all intervention and control communities (Peterson, Hawkins, & Catalano, 1992). Recently, work has been done to develop and validate community-level indicators of important risk and protective factors and behavioral outcomes (e.g., Coulton, 1995). Since 1993, the authors have been collaborating with a consortium of six states to identify, collect, and validate standardized survey and archival indicators of risk and protective factors for drug abuse and other antisocial behavior, with funding from the Center for Substance Abuse Prevention. This effort reflects a triangulation approach to the measurement of risk and protective factors at the community, peer group, school, family, and individual levels. Triangulation, using multiple different measures of the same set of constructs, is used to reduce the bias inherent in any single measurement strategy.

Mixed Units of Analysis

Studies of comprehensive community initiatives often include interventions that operate simultaneously at multiple ecological levels, such as the community (e.g., mobilization, media, and policy change strategies), school or classroom (e.g., strategies changing school management structures or classroom teaching practices), family (e.g., parent training strategies), and individual (e.g., social competence promotion strategies). Many published studies of prevention programs violate a basic premise of experimental design—that the unit randomized to experimental condition is the unit of analysis. Communities, schools, or classrooms often are the unit of random assignment to experimental or control condition, but analyses of the impact of the intervention often use the individual student as the unit of analysis. Community, school, or classroom differences are, thus, confounded with program effects on individuals (Biglan & Ary, 1985).

Some studies have addressed this problem by assigning multiple communities, schools, or classrooms to each condition, then analyzing at the same level at which randomization occurs (Biglan et al., 1987; Perry et al., 1993). Even so, analysis using small numbers of randomized communities limits the study's power to detect significant effects because statistics are less stable with small numbers of analysis units (Koepsell et al., 1991; Murray & Hannan, 1990). However, mixed model analyses of variance (Koepsell et al., 1991), hierarchical linear modeling (Bryk & Raudenbush, 1992), and generalized estimating equations (Liang & Zeger, 1986) can be used to estimate both the individual- and group-level components of variation and therefore increase statistical power. Alternatively, multiple investigators conducting similar studies with different populations in comparable or contrasting communities could build a collective case for the effectiveness of a given approach. Clear specification of the relevant features of the settings and careful attention to implementation integrity are critical elements of this approach.

Heterogeneity of Effect Across Different Populations

Existing prevention studies have shown differential effectiveness with different demographic groups. Such differences can mask the effects of community-level interventions delivered to diverse populations. When sample sizes are sufficiently large, researchers can investigate directly the differential effects of preventive interventions on different groups. When subgroups are not large enough for such analysis, Dwyer et al. (1989) have proposed statistical methods using combined logistic and multiple regression models to estimate interaction effects between intervention condition and baseline risk levels. Although this solution is proposed for assessing differential effects across baseline levels of the outcome measures, it may be applicable to other quantifiable risk factors as well. Oversampling of smaller demographic groups also can be used to generate large enough samples to investigate differential program impact. Ultimately, replication studies are needed to confirm the utility of specific prevention strategies with different populations.

Intervention Implementation Integrity and Intensity

Prevention studies also should investigate the effects of differential intervention implementation integrity and intensity (IOM, 1994; Peterson et al., 1992). Given the multiple factors likely to influence community prevention program implementation, this issue is particularly important for community prevention studies. By randomly and independently selecting samples of residents in intervention communities at each measurement point, factors hypothesized to influence the impact of the intervention may be examined (e.g., length of exposure, level of teacher training, variety of media employed). In our own prevention studies, we have proposed and used three steps in examining implementation: (a) collecting data to assess the degree of implementation, (b) reporting data on implementation for each dimension of the intervention, and (c) including implementation data in the tests of efficacy (Hawkins, Abbott, Catalano, & Gillmore, 1991).

A major challenge for community prevention research at this time is to overcome theoretical and methodological weaknesses. Evaluations of comprehensive community-based strategies to reduce risk and enhance protection employing evaluation designs that are multiyear and quasi-experimental or experimental are rare. The primary reason for this is that community-based outcome research is expensive (Mittelmark, Hunt, Heath, & Schmid, 1993). However, despite this obstacle, much work to improve methods for evaluating community interventions is proceeding along the lines just described (e.g., Connell et al., 1995).

CURRENT DIRECTIONS AND IMPLICATIONS FOR FUTURE WORK

Despite the challenges inherent in evaluating communitywide preventive interventions, the research suggests that community mobilization, policy change, and media interventions can reduce risk factors, enhance protective factors, and prevent adolescent antisocial behavior. These interventions appear to have the greatest impact when multiple strategies are employed simultaneously in a coordinated fashion. The current challenge for community prevention is to expand the knowledge base needed to guide communities in the design, implementation, and evaluation of comprehensive, coordinated, multicomponent prevention strategies.

The community's role and responsibility for prevention efforts highlights the importance of attending to diversity in communities, so that all groups participate in preventive activities. The preventive interventions included in risk reduction and protective factor enhancement strategies require the involvement of individuals, parents, neighborhood members, educators, community health and social service providers, law enforcement personnel, business and media representatives, and others. Cultural perspectives of different groups, classes, ethnicities, and races affect their views on parenting, teaching, and antisocial behavior as well as the prevalence of antisocial behavior among their members (Catalano et al., 1993). To be adopted and used by a community, the preventive strategy must be acceptable to community members. This is best accomplished when community leaders and opinion shapers have the opportunity to take ownership of the strategy and make it their own, and when diverse community members are involved in tailoring the intervention to the community (Marin, 1993).

Based on the community intervention findings and prevention principles described in this chapter, we have developed a model called Communities That Care (CTC) for comprehensive community intervention to reduce risks and enhance protection (Developmental Research and Programs, 1994; Hawkins, Catalano, & Associates, 1992). The CTC strategy consists of three phases. In the first phase, key community leaders are provided a half-day orientation to the project. If they commit to implementing it, they decide as a group to become the oversight body for the project and to appoint a prevention board of diverse members of their community. During the second phase, the community prevention board is constituted and trained to conduct a community risk and resource assessment. Over a 6-month period the board gathers archival and survey data on indicators of the risk and protective factors for adolescent health and behavior problems in the community. Based on these results, the board ranks risk factors for preventive action. The board then designs its prevention strategy to address targeted risk factors and enhance protective factors, selecting preventive interventions from a menu of programs and strategies that have shown positive effects in quasi-experimental and controlled studies. (For reviews of these programs and their results, see Hawkins, Arthur, & Catalano, 1995; Hawkins, Catalano, & Associates, 1992; Hawkins, Catalano, & Miller, 1992; Brewer et al., 1995; Developmental Research and Programs, 1996). In the third phase, the board implements and evaluates the preventive strategy, using task forces composed of community members with a stake in the outcome, to ensure implementation of each component. Baseline risk assessment data serve as the benchmark against which to judge community progress in risk reduction in subsequent years.

The Communities That Care process activates both the community leadership and grassroots community sectors to take ownership of the prevention planning strategy. The strategy involves assessing risk and protective factors in the community to identify risk factors that are elevated or trending in an undesirable direction over time, protective resources already in place in the community, and gaps in resources needed to reduce risks and build protection against them. Communities select and implement specific preventive interventions shown to be efficacious at addressing their high-priority risk and protective factors. Communities monitor the results of the preventive interventions they have implemented by periodically reassessing the levels and trends in the targeted risk and protective factors and adjust the interventions as needed to achieve greater effects.

Pilot studies of the CTC strategy have indicated that communities can be mobilized to adopt the model, conduct risk and resource assessments using epidemiological data, rank risk and protective factors to address, and select and implement promising prevention strategies (Arthur, Ayers, Graham, & Hawkins, 1996; Harachi, Ayers, Hawkins, Catalano, & Cushing, 1995). Our experience in working with communities has revealed the importance of ongoing training and proactive technical assistance during the first years of the community mobilization process to ensure the institutionalization of risk- and protection-focused prevention. It also has indicated the importance of developing epidemiological methods for assessing risk and protective factors in the community to guide the ranking of targets for preventive intervention. We currently are collaborating with six states in the development of standardized archival indicators and student and household survey measures of risk and protective factors and antisocial behavior outcomes that can be used to compare risk and protective factors across diverse communities. We also have encountered strong demand from communities for information about efficacious prevention strategies to address their high-priority risk and protective factors. Our team's reviews of risk reduction interventions have led to the identification of a set of effective interventions for risk reduction that simultaneously enhance protective factors (see Brewer et al., 1995; Developmental Research and Programs, 1996; Hawkins, Catalano, & Associates, 1992; Hawkins, Catalano & Brewer, 1995). These approaches have been included in CTC to enable communities to select efficacious preventive interventions for inclusion in their comprehensive risk reduction and protective factor enhancement strategies.

Our experience suggests the utility of this approach, which combines community mobilization and epidemiologically based social planning approaches, for empowering communities to develop theory-based, empirically grounded prevention systems that coordinate multiple prevention strategies at multiple levels and that address the specific epidemiological risk and protective factor profiles of each community. An experimental evaluation of the effects of this approach on communities' levels of risk and protective factors and prevalence of antisocial behavior remains to be conducted (Peterson et al., 1992).

If communities are to become protective environments for healthy development, community members ultimately will have to take responsibility for identifying, ranking, and addressing risks in the community as well as for implementing strategies to reduce salient risks and enhance the development of social integration and bonding to the community and its standards. Preventive interventions seeking to reduce the prevalence of antisocial behavior among those at greatest risk must include a focus on the successful development of cognitive and social skills and social bonding from an early age, as well as on the promotion of strong normative standards in opposition to antisocial behavior across the community. Recent advances in prevention science and health epidemiology are providing tools communities can use to plan and implement strategic, outcome-focused plans for reducing the prevalence of antisocial behavior among adolescents and young adults.

REFERENCES

Arthur, M. W., Ayers, C. D., Graham, K. A., & Hawkins, J. D. (1996). *Mobilizing communities to reduce risks for substance abuse: A comparison of two strategies.* Unpublished manuscript.

Arthur, M. W., Brewer, D. D., Graham, K. G., Shavel, D. A., Tremper, M., & Hawkins, J. D. (1996). *Assessing state and community readiness for prevention.* Unpublished manuscript.

Bauman, K. E., LaPrelle, J., Brown, J. D., Koch, G. G., & Padgett, C. A. (1991). The influence of three mass media campaigns on variables related to adolescent cigarette smoking: Results of a field experiment. *American Journal of Public Health, 81,* 597–604.

Baumrind, D. (1985). Familial antecedents of adolescents drug use: A developmental perspective. In C. L. Jones & R. J. Battjes (Eds.), *Etiology of drug abuse: Implications for prevention* (NIDA Research Monograph 56, pp. 13–14). Washington, DC: U.S. Government Printing Office.

Bell, R. Q. (1986). Age-specific manifestations in changing psychosocial risk. In D. C. Farran & J. D. McKinney (Eds.), *The concept of risk in intellectual and psychosocial development.* New York: Academic Press.

Biglan, A. (1995). Translating what we know about the context of antisocial behavior into a lower prevalence of such behavior. *Journal of Applied Behavior Analysis, 28,* 479–492.

Biglan, A., & Ary, D. V. (1985). Current methodological issues in research on smoking prevention. In C. Bell & R. J. Battjes (Eds.), *Prevention research: Deterring drug abuse among children and adolescents* (NIDA Research Monograph no. 63, pp. 170–195). Washington, DC: U.S. Government Printing Office.

Biglan, A., Severson, H., Ary, D., Faller, C., Gallison, C., Thompson, R., Glasgow, R., & Lichtenstein, E. (1987). Do smoking prevention programs really work? Attrition and the internal and external validity of an evaluation of a refusal skills training program. *Journal of Behavioral Medicine, 10,* 159–171.

Black, G. S. (1989). *Changing attitudes toward drug use.* Rochester, NY: Gordon S. Black Corp.

Brewer, D. D., Hawkins, J. D., Catalano, R., & Neckerman, H. (1995). Preventing serious, violent, and chronic juvenile offending: A review of evaluations of selected strategies in childhood, adolescence, and the community. In J. C. Howell, B. Krisberg, J. D. Hawkins, & J. H. Wilson (Eds.), *Sourcebook on serious, violent, and chronic juvenile offenders* (pp. 61–141). Thousand Oaks, CA: Sage Publications.

Bryk, A. S., & Raudenbush, S. W. (1992). *Hierarchical linear models: Applications and data analysis methods.* Newbury Park, CA: Sage Publications.

Bursik, R. J., Jr., & Grasmick, H. G. (1996). The use of contextual analysis in models of criminal behavior. In J. D. Hawkins (Ed.), *Delinquency and crime: Current theories* (pp. 236–267). New York: Cambridge University Press.

Catalano, R. F., & Hawkins, J. D. (1996). The social development model: A theory of antisocial behavior. In J. D. Hawkins (Ed.), *Delinquency and crime: Current theories* (pp. 149–197). New York: Cambridge University Press.

Catalano, R. F., Hawkins, J. D., Krenz, C., Gillmore, M., Morrison, D., Wells, E., & Abbott, R. (1993). Using research to guide culturally appropriate drug abuse prevention. *Journal of Consulting and Clinical Psychology 61,* 804–811.

Clarke, R. V. (1995). Situational crime prevention. In M. Tonry & D. P. Farrington (Eds.), *Building a safer society: Strategic approaches to crime prevention: Vol. 19. Crime and justice: A review of research* (pp. 91–150). Chicago: University of Chicago Press.

Coie, J. D., Watt, N. F., West, S. G., Hawkins, J. D., Asarnow, J. R., Markman, H. J., Ramey, S. L., Shure, M. B., & Long, B. (1993). The science of prevention: A conceptual framework and some directions for a national research program. *American Psychologist, 48,* 1013–1022.

Connell, J. P., Kubisch, A. C., Schorr, L. B., & Weiss, C. H. (Eds.). (1995). *New approaches to evaluating community initiatives: Concepts, methods, and contexts.* Washington, DC: The Aspen Institute.

Coulton, C. J. (1995). Using community-level indicators of children's well-being in comprehensive community initiatives. In J. P. Connell, A. C. Kubisch, L. B. Schorr, & C. H. Weiss (Eds.), *New approaches to evaluating community initiatives: Concepts, methods, and contexts.* Washington, DC: The Aspen Institute.

Developmental Research and Programs. (1994). *Communities That Care planning kit.* Seattle: Author.

Developmental Research and Programs. (1996). *Communities That Care prevention strategies: A research guide to what works.* Seattle: Author.

Dobrin, A., Wiersema, B., Loftin, C., & McDowall, D. (Eds.). (1996). *Statistical handbook on violence in America.* Phoenix: Oryx Press.

Dorfman, L., & Wallack, L. (1993). Advertising health: The case for counter-ads. *Public Health Reports, 108*(6), 716–726.

Dryfoos, J. G. (1990). *Adolescents at risk: Prevalence and prevention.* New York: Oxford University Press.

Dwyer, J. H., MacKinnon, D. V., Pentz, M. A., Flay, B. R., Hansen, W. B., Wang, E. Y. I., & Johnson, C. A. (1989). Estimating intervention effects in longitudinal studies. *American Journal of Epidemiology, 130,* 781–795.

Elliott, D. S. (1994). Serious violent offenders: Onset, developmental course, and termination: The American Society of Criminology 1993 Presidential Address. *Criminology, 32,* 1–21.

Farquhar, J. W., Fortmann, S. P., & Flora, J. A. (1990). Effects of community-wide education on cardiovascular disease risk factors: The Stanford Five-City Project. *Journal of the American Medical Association, 264,* 359–365.

Farrington, D. P. (1996). The explanation and prevention of youthful offending. In J. D. Hawkins (Ed.), *Delinquency and crime: Current theories* (pp. 68–148). New York: Cambridge University Press.

Fawcett, S. B., Paine, A. L., Francisco, V. T., & Vliet, M. (1993). *Promoting health through community development.* Binghamton, NY: Haworth.

Flynn, B. S., Worden, J. K., Secker-Walker, R. H., Badger, G. J., & Geller, B. M., (1995). Cigarette smoking prevention effects of mass media and school interventions targeted to gender and age groups. *Journal of Health Education, 26*(2), S-45–S-51.

Flynn, B. S., Worden, J. K., Secker-Walker, R. H., Badger, G. J., Geller, B. M., & Costanza, M. C. (1992). Prevention of cigarette smoking through mass media intervention and school programs. *American Journal of Public Health, 82*(6), 827–834.

Garmezy, N. (1985). Stress-resistant children: The search for protective factors. In J. E. Stevenson (Ed.), *Recent research in developmental psychopathology* (pp. 213–233). Elmsford, NY: Pergamon.

Gottfredson, D. C. (1988). *Issues in adolescent drug use.* Unpublished final report to the U.S. Department of Justice. Baltimore, MD: Johns Hopkins University, Center for Research on Elementary and Middle Schools.

Gottfredson, M. R., & Hirschi, T. (1990). *A general theory of crime.* Stanford, CA: Stanford University Press.

Harachi, T. W., Ayers, C. D., Hawkins, J. D., Catalano, R. F., & Cushing, J. (1995). Empowering communities to prevent adolescent substance abuse: Results from a risk- and protection-focused community mobilization effort. *Journal of Primary Prevention, 16,* 233–254.

Hawkins, J. D. (1995, August). Controlling crime before it happens: Risk-focused prevention. *National Institute of Justice Journal,* pp. 10–18.

Hawkins, J. D., Abbott, R., Catalano, R. F., & Gillmore, M. R. (1991). Assessing effectiveness of drug abuse prevention: Long-term effects and replication. In C. Leukfeld & W. Bukoski (Eds.), *Drug abuse prevention research: Methodological issues* (NIDA Research Monograph 107, DHHS publication no. ADM 91-1761, pp. 195–212). Washington, DC: U.S. Government Printing Office.

Hawkins, J. D., Arthur, M. W., & Catalano, R. F. (1995). Preventing substance abuse. In M. Tonry & D. P. Farrington (Eds.), *Building a safer society: Strategic approaches to crime prevention* (pp. 343–427). Chicago: University of Chicago Press.

Hawkins, J. D., Catalano, R. F., & Associates. (1992). *Communities That Care: Action for drug abuse prevention.* San Francisco: Jossey-Bass.

Hawkins, J. D., Catalano, R. F., & Brewer, D. D. (1995). Preventing serious, violent, and chronic juvenile offending: Effective strategies from conception to age 6. In J. C. Howell, B. Krisberg, & J. D. Hawkins (Eds.), *A sourcebook: Serious, violent, and chronic juvenile offenders.* (pp. 47–60). Thousand Oaks, CA: Sage Publications.

Hawkins, J. D., Catalano, R. F., & Kent, L. A. (1991). Combining broadcast media and parent education to prevent teenage drug abuse. In L. Donohew, H. E. Sypher, & W. J. Bukoski (Eds.), *Persuasive communication and drug abuse prevention* (pp. 283–342). Hillsdale, NJ: Erlbaum.

Hawkins, J. D., Catalano, R. F., & Miller, J. Y. (1992). Risk and protective factors for alcohol and other drug problems in adolescence and early adulthood: Implications for substance abuse prevention. *Psychological Bulletin, 112,* 64–105.

Howell, J. C. (Ed.). (1995). *Guide for implementing the comprehensive strategy for serious, violent, and chronic juvenile offenders.* Washington, DC: U.S. Department of Justice, Office of Juvenile Justice and Delinquency Prevention.

Howell, J. C., Krisberg, B., Hawkins, J. D., & Wilson, J. J. (Eds.). (1995). *A sourcebook: Serious, violent, and chronic juvenile offenders.* Thousand Oaks, CA: Sage Publications.

Huizinga, D., Loeber, R., & Thornberry, T. P. (in press). *The prevention of serious delinquency and violence: Implications from the program of research on the causes and correlates of delinquency.* Washington, DC: U.S. Department of Justice, Office of Juvenile Justice and Delinquency Prevention.

Institute of Medicine (IOM), Committee on Prevention of Mental Disorders. (1994). P. J. Mrazek & R. J. Haggerty (Eds.), *Reducing risks for mental disorders: Frontiers for preventive intervention research.* Washington, DC: National Academy Press.

Johnson, C. A., Pentz, M. A., Weber, M. D., Dwyer, J. H., Baer, N. A., MacKinnon, D. P., Hansen, W. B., & Flay, B. R. (1990). Relative effectiveness of comprehensive community programming for drug abuse prevention with high-risk and low-risk adolescents. *Journal of Consulting and Clinical Psychology, 58,* 447–456.

Join Together. (1992). *Who is really fighting the war on drugs?* Boston: Trustees of Boston University.

Jung, R. S., & Jason, L. A. (1988). Firearm violence and the effects of gun control legislation. *American Journal of Community Psychology, 16,* 515–524.

Kellam, S. G., & Rebok, G. W. (1992). Building developmental and etiological theory through epidemiologically based preventive intervention trials. In J. McCord & R. E. Tremblay (Eds.), *Preventing antisocial behavior: Interventions from birth through adolescence* (pp. 162–195). New York: Guilford.

Koepsell, T. D., Martin, D. C., Diehr, P. H., Psaty, B. M., Wagner, E. H., Perrin, E. B., & Cheadle, A. (1991). Data analysis and sample size issues in evaluations of community-based health promotion and disease prevention programs: A mixed model analysis of variance approach. *Journal of Clinical Epidemiology, 44,* 701–713.

Levy, D., & Sheflin, N. (1985). The demand for alcoholic beverages: An aggregate time-series analysis. *Journal of Public Policy and Marketing, 4,* 47–54.

Liang, K. Y., & Zeger, S. L. (1986). Longitudinal data analysis using generalized linear models. *Biometrika, 73,* 13–22.

Loeber, R. (1990). Development and risk factors of juvenile antisocial behavior and delinquency. *Clinical Psychology Review, 10,* 1–41.

Loeber, R., & Stouthamer-Loeber, M. (1987). Prediction. In H. C. Quay (Ed.), *Handbook of juvenile delinquency* (pp. 325–382). New York: Wiley.

Loftin, C., McDowell, D., Wiersema, B., & Cottey, T. I. (1991). Effects of restrictive licensing of handguns on homicide and suicide in the District of Columbia. *New England Journal of Medicine, 325,* 1615–1620.

Maguin, E., & Loeber, R. (1995). Academic performance and delinquency. *Crime and Justice: A Review of Research, 20,* 145–264.

Marin, G. (1993). Defining culturally appropriate community interventions: Hispanics as a case study. *Journal of Community Psychology, 21,* 149–161.

McDowell, D., Lizotte, A. J., & Wiersema, B. (1991). General deterrence through civilian gun ownership: An evaluation of the quasi-experimental evidence. *Criminology, 29,* 541–559.

Mittelmark, M. B., Hunt, M. K., Heath, G. W., & Schmid, T. L. (1993). Realistic outcomes: Lessons from community-based research and demonstration programs for the prevention of cardiovascular diseases. *Journal of Public Health Policy, 14*(4), 437–462.

Moffitt, T. E. (1990). Juvenile delinquency and attention deficit disorder: Boys' developmental trajectories from age 3 to age 15. *Child Development, 61*(3), 893–910.

Murray, D. M., & Hannan, P. J. (1990). Planning for the appropriate analysis in school-based drug-use prevention studies. *Journal of Consulting and Clinical Psychology, 58,* 458–468.

Newcomb, M. D., Maddahian, E., & Bentler, P. M. (1986). Risk factors for drug use among adolescents: Concurrent and longitudinal analyses. *American Journal of Public Health, 76,* 525–530.

Oetting, E. R., Donnermeyer, J. F., Plested, B. A., Edwards, R. W., Kelly, K., & Beauvais, F. (1995). Assessing community readiness for prevention. *International Journal of the Addictions, 30,* 659–683.

O'Malley, P. M., & Wagenaar, A. C. (1991). Effects of minimum drinking age laws on alcohol use, related behaviors and traffic crash involvement among American youth: 1976–1987. *Journal of Studies on Alcohol, 52,* 478–491.

Pentz, M. A., Dwyer, J. H., MacKinnon, D. P., Flay, B. R., Hansen, W. B., Wang, E. Y. I., & Johnson, C. A. (1989). A multi-community trial for primary prevention of adolescent drug abuse: Effects on drug use prevalence. *Journal of the American Medical Association, 261,* 3259–3266.

Perry, C. L., Kelder, S. H., Murray, D. M., & Klepp, K.-I. (1992). Communitywide smoking prevention: Long-term outcomes of the Minnesota Heart Health Program and Class of 1989 study. *American Journal of Public Health, 82,* 1210–1216.

Perry, C. L., Williams, C. L., Forster, J. L., Wolfson, M., Wagenaar, A. C., Finnegan, J. R., McGovern, P. G., Veblen-Mortenson, S., Komro, K. A., & Anstine, P. S. (1993). Background, conceptualization and design of a community-wide research program on adolescent alcohol use: Project Northland. *Health Education Research, 8,* 125–136.

Perry, C. L., Williams, C. L., Veblen-Mortenson, S., Toomey, T. L., Komro, K. A., Anstine, P. S., McGovern, P. G., Finnegan, J. R., Forster, J. L., Wagenaar, A. C., & Wolfson, M. (1996). Project Northland: Outcomes of a community-wide alcohol use prevention program during early adolescence. *American Journal of Public Health, 86*(7), 956–965.

Peterson, P. L., Hawkins, J. D., & Catalano, R. F. (1992). Evaluating comprehensive community drug risk reduction interventions: Design challenges and recommendations. *Evaluation Review, 16,* 579–602.

Petraitis, J., Flay, B. R., & Miller, T. Q. (1995). Reviewing theories of adolescent substance use: Organizing pieces of the puzzle. *Psychological Bulletin, 117*(1), 67–86.

Rae-Grant, N., Thomas, B. H., Offord, D. R., & Boyle, M. H. (1989). Risk, protective factors, and the prevalence of behavioral and emotional disorders in children and adolescents. *Journal of the American Academy of Child and Adolescent Psychiatry, 28,* 262–268.

Rogers, T., Feighery, E. C., Tencati, E. M., Butler, J. L., & Weiner, L. (1995). Community mobilization to reduce point-of-purchase advertising of tobacco products. *Health Education Quarterly, 22*(4), 427–442.

Rowe, D. C. (1996). An adaptive strategy theory of crime and delinquency. In J. D. Hawkins (Ed.), *Delinquency and crime: Current theories* (pp. 268–314). New York: Cambridge University Press.

Rutter, M. (1979). Protective factors in children's responses to stress and disadvantage. In M. W. Kent & J. E. Rolf (Eds.), *Primary prevention of psychopathology: Vol. 3. Social competence in children* (pp. 49–74). Hanover, NH: University Press of New England.

Rutter, M., Maughan, B., Mortimore, P., Ouston, J., & Smith, A. (1979). *Fifteen thousand hours: Secondary schools and their effects on children.* Cambridge, MA: Harvard University Press.

Saffer, H., & Grossman, M. (1987). Beer taxes, the legal drinking age, and youth motor vehicle fatalities. *Journal of Legal Studies, 16,* 351–374.

Sampson, R. J. (1994, February). *Community-level factors in the development of violent behavior: Implications for social policy.* Paper presented at the Aspen Institute Conference on Children and Violence, Boca Raton, FL.

Schilling, R., & McAlister, A. (1990). Preventing drug use in adolescents through media interventions. *Journal of Consulting and Clinical Psychology, 58,* 416–424.

Thornberry, T. P. (1987). Toward an interactional theory of delinquency. *Criminology 25,* 863–891.

Wagenaar, A. C., & Holder, H. D. (1991). A change from public to private sale of wine: Results from natural experiments in Iowa and West Virginia. *Journal of Studies on Alcohol, 52,* 162–173.

Werner, E. E., & Smith, R. S. (1992). *Overcoming the odds: High risk children from birth to adulthood.* Ithaca, NY: Cornell University Press.

Wilson, J. J., & Howell, J. C. (1993). *A comprehensive strategy for serious, violent, and chronic juvenile offenders: Program summary.* Washington, DC: U. S. Department of Justice, Office of Juvenile Justice and Delinquency Prevention.

Wilson, J. Q., & Herrnstein, R. J. (1985). *Crime and human nature.* New York: Simon & Schuster.

CHAPTER 35

Prevention of Aggression and Violence Among Inner-City Youths

NANCY G. GUERRA, BETH ATTAR, and ROGER P. WEISSBERG

In this chapter we characterize and critique the current status of violence prevention efforts in inner-city communities. A central issue is how conditions in the inner city increase risk and limit intervention effectiveness and which programs hold the most promise under these conditions. First, we describe the challenges facing preventive interventions in the inner city. We then consider risk and protective factors that provide a commonly used framework for programming. Following this, we review selected preventive interventions, noting key principles of the most effective programs. Finally, we suggest directions for future research and practice and discuss how to link basic and applied research to inform practice in these communities.

THE INNER CITY AS A CONTEXT
FOR PREVENTIVE INTERVENTIONS

There is a general consensus that inner cities in the United States are characterized by chronic poverty, social problems, and high concentrations of ethnic minorities. The social milieu has been portrayed as one in which disorganization, dislocation, and isolation prevail. As Wilson (1987, p. 58) notes:

> The communities of the underclass are plagued by massive joblessness, flagrant and open lawlessness, and low-achieving schools, and therefore tend to be avoided by others. Consequently, the residents of these areas, whether women and children of welfare families or aggressive street criminals, have become increasingly socially isolated from mainstream patterns of behavior.

Within inner cities, community institutions are often in a state of chaos due to budgetary constraints and staff turnover. Organizations that normally promote prosocial behavior, such as youth clubs, community centers, and after-school programs, are often inadequate or nonexistent. Schools are plagued by lack of funding, teacher strikes, high absenteeism, conflicts between administration and teachers, and the feelings of alienation that are held by many parents toward schools (Comer, 1988). One striking example of

disorganization in the public school system in the inner cities is the instability of teaching staff. In the Chicago Public Schools, approximately 5,700 children arrive at school each day to find that they have no teacher (Kozol, 1991).

This systemwide disorganization is frequently paralleled by high levels of family instability. Often, the very composition of the family is in a state of constant flux—members may enter and leave the home, mothers' boyfriends may join households and sometimes take a paternal role in the absence of fathers, and teenage births swell the ranks of family membership, particularly for minority youths. The instability of families is associated with poverty, as median family incomes among unmarried mothers is almost half that of divorced mothers and five times less than that of two-parent families.

In addition to scarce economic resources, systemwide disorganization, and family instability, violence has become a fact of life in many inner-city communities. The ready availability of guns means that violence can and does have deadly consequences. Firearms are being used increasingly in violent crimes, as gunshots account for approximately 70% of homicides nationwide (Uniform Crime Reports, 1992), and death by gunshot is the leading cause of death among African American male adolescents (Centers for Disease Control, 1991). Furthermore, the acceleration in the distribution of crack cocaine since the mid-1980s and the widespread use of guns among drug dealers has increased the embeddedness of violence in these communities.

Violent environments can impact children's aggression and violence in multiple ways. To begin with, serious violence becomes more normative as children regularly observe violent acts. In a study of eighth-grade inner-city children, Shakoor and Chalmers (1991) found that 55% of boys and 45% of girls reported having seen someone *shot* in the preceding year. Because of the prevalence of violence in the inner cities, daily activities are often organized around avoiding violence. Children learn to take cover from stray gunfire in apartment hallways and under furniture and must cope with a constant fear of violence. As one survey of inner-city youth found, 42% of males reported that their lives had been threatened (Gladstein, Slater-Rusonis, & Heald, 1992). In another study, 60% of inner-city elementary school children reported having to stay inside due to fear of violence, and 40% reported having to hide because of neighborhood shootings in the past year (Attar, Guerra, & Tolan, 1994). Although some children may respond to this increasing danger by staying out of harm's way, for other children, guns become the preferred method of self-protection.

Children also must cope with the psychological consequences of violence exposure as they see their neighbors, friends, and relatives fall victim to both intentional and random acts of violence. Today's inner cities have been compared to war zones (Garbarino, Kostelny, & Dubrow, 1991). In the words of an eighth-grade boy describing life in an inner-city housing project (*Chicago Tribune,* September 5, 1993):

> People get shot over silly things
> In my book it's called killing town
> People get killed for just walking around
> It's like a massacre that will not stop
> Black on Black killing all around the clock.

As the level of violence increases, this behavior is often woven into the fabric of social interaction. For example, Anderson (in press) describes a "code of violence" whereby violence becomes both a necessary and desirable behavior.

Violence is also closely connected to the proliferation of gangs in inner cities. Whereas 25 years ago, gangs were formed to protect neighborhoods and were governed by particular codes of conduct (Papajohn, 1994), today's street gangs are deeply involved in the drug trade and are increasingly well armed and violent. In some cities, it is estimated that approximately 50% of all homicides are gang related, and the increase in urban violence during the 1990s has been linked to the upsurge in gang involvement in the crack cocaine market and to the resulting gun culture (Jencks, 1992). Gangs often extend their snares to recruit children, who serve as drug runners, lookouts, and commit murder in the place of older gang members.

Developing and conducting preventive interventions in the most disadvantaged urban settings pose challenges not encountered in more privileged environments. First, environmental factors such as chronic stress and exposure to violence increase the general level of risk for aggression across the population. Second, the conditions that exist in the inner-city compound individual risk, and children growing up in this environment experience a type of double jeopardy. Third, such environmental conditions may reduce receptivity to intervention efforts. Some individuals may simply be unable to benefit from psychological or educational programs until their basic problems are resolved. Fourth, although some programs may be potent enough at a given point in time to produce enduring effects, the conditions in the inner city make it less likely that intervention effects will be sustained. Fifth, the inner-city setting often makes program implementation more difficult. For example, neighborhood violence significantly affects both the willingness of agencies to provide services in a community and the residents' ability to participate in such programs. In addition, programs developed for White, middle-class youth must be adapted to reflect the norms, values, and practices of children

and families from diverse ethnic background (see Yung & Hammond, Chapter 45, this volume).

RISK AND PROTECTIVE FACTORS IN THE DEVELOPMENT OF AGGRESSION

The approach most frequently used in developing preventive interventions relies on specification of individual and contextual factors shown to put certain children at-risk for future violence and those factors that protect against such risk. Interventions strive to reduce risk, to thwart the potential negative effects of individual risk factors, or to promote protective factors that reduce the likely impact of risk. A complete review of the literature on risk factors and protective factors is beyond the scope of the present chapter, but they will be discussed in the context of specific intervention approaches.

Specifically, *risk factors* refer to aspects of the individual or environment that make it more likely that a person will engage in aggression or violence. A large body of research has illuminated specific characteristics of individual children, families, peer groups, schools, and communities that are associated with the development and maintenance of aggression and are often targeted by preventive interventions. As the previous discussion of the inner-city environment illustrates, because of a number of factors including stress and exposure to violence, inner-city communities can be characterized as "risky environments," wherein children's healthy emotional, behavioral, and intellectual development may be compromised and aggression and violence are more likely. Recent risk factor studies have also looked specifically at the interaction of individual risk and environmental risk in disadvantaged urban populations. For example, Attar et al. (1994) found that stressful life events (e.g., divorce, illness) predicted children's aggression only in the most disadvantaged environments characterized by chronic environmental stress (e.g., poverty, unemployment).

In addition to intervening with risk factors in order to inhibit or prevent the development of aggression, interventions may also focus on enhancing aspects of the individual and environment that promote prosocial behavior and mental health. This approach forms the cornerstone of broad-based youth development or healthy human development programs. In some cases, interventions attempt to single out those *protective factors* that specifically buffer the effects of risk, although the precise link to a particular risk factor or set of risk factors is infrequently delineated. In fact, few studies have examined protective factors or their buffering effects in the context of specific risk. In particular, the protective factors necessary to buffer the effects of the socioeconomic and environmental context of the inner city generally have not been compared with those that benefit children in other settings.

EFFECTIVENESS OF CURRENT PREVENTION PROGRAMS

In this chapter, we discuss preventive intervention studies that target risk factors related to violence, include relevant behavioral outcome measures, focus on economically disadvantaged children and youth, and are conducted in urban settings.[1] Because onset of serious violent behavior does not usually occur until adolescence, we include programs for children targeting behavioral variables that predict later violence (e.g., early aggression), although in most cases long-term effects on violent behavior were not measured. This review is not exhaustive but rather is intended to provide examples of different programs in order to highlight key principles and activities that provide a framework for violence prevention in the inner city. Although many programs target multiple contexts, they are grouped according to their primary focus: the individual child or the child's family, peers, and school.

Child-Centered Interventions

Child-centered interventions cluster around four areas of risk: early physical development and health, cognitive functioning and academic performance, social-behavioral skills; and social-cognitive processes. Some programs provide services directly to children through trained professionals, whereas others train specific caregivers (e.g., teachers) to stimulate children's development. Programs generally fall into one of four categories related to developmental timing: prenatal/postnatal services to families, preschool enrichment programs, interventions during the elementary years, and programs for adolescents.

Prenatal/Postnatal Services to Families

To prevent child problems associated with poor maternal health (e.g., low birth weight, birth trauma) and inadequate postnatal care, prenatal/postnatal programs provide broad-based educational and support services to mothers with known risk factors such as poverty, single-parent status, and young age. These problems have flourished in disadvantaged areas, although most research studies have been conducted in poor rural and semirural areas.

A program for mothers raising young children in high-risk environments, the Yale Child Welfare Research Program, was carried out by Provence and Naylor (1983). This program relied on home visits by a social worker during the prenatal and early infancy period to help mothers with medical, financial, and support services. The goal was to reduce the negative impact of the multiple stressors experienced by disadvantaged mothers on children's well-being. In a follow-up study (Seitz, Rosenbaum, & Apfel, 1985), both mothers and children in the intervention program fared better on several variables when compared to a matched nonintervention control group. Specifically, the intervention mothers were more likely to report a positive emotional atmosphere in the family and were more involved in their children's education. Looking at children's subsequent behavior, the intervention children were rated by teachers as less aggressive than the control children.

Although this study is significant in demonstrating an impact on aggressive behavior and is frequently cited as an example of the effectiveness of early intervention programs, the findings must be interpreted cautiously. Intervention subjects volunteered to participate in the program, and they were compared with a matched nonintervention control group. Because not all subjects had volunteered and assignment to treatment and control groups was not random, it is quite likely that subjects in the intervention condition were more motivated to provide a supportive environment for their children than subjects in the matched nonintervention groups. These initial differences, rather than intervention effects, could be responsible for differing outcomes. Nevertheless, given the sharp increase in births to teenage and unwed mothers in urban settings who are often ill-prepared for the demands of caring for their infants, this program provides the best data available on the potential power of early intervention.

Preschool Enrichment Programs

The best-known preventive intervention for poor urban children is the Head Start program. Although not restricted to inner cities, it is one of the few programs that has taken hold in urban areas throughout the United States. Begun during the War on Poverty as a brief summer preschool experience for economically disadvantaged children, Head Start is now more comprehensive in service, begins earlier, and lasts longer. It has also spawned a number of experimental evaluation studies to determine its impact on intellectual and social outcomes. These studies (e.g., Lee, Brooks-Gunn, Schnur, & Liaw, 1990) generally have reported positive short-term intellectual and social gains, with most effects disappearing by elementary school, although more global outcome measures (e.g., high school graduation) generally have favored Head Start children. One explanation for the washout of many early gains was that brief inoculation could not prevent future deprivation and disadvantage, suggesting that such programs should be continued over the course of children's development, particularly in the most disadvantaged communities (Zigler, 1987).

Two landmark preschool enrichment studies, the Perry Preschool Project and the Houston Parent-Child Development Center, have reported an encouraging long-term impact on aggression and delinquency among disadvantaged minority youth using an intensive, well-articulated preschool program. Both projects randomly assigned subjects to intervention or control conditions and collected extensive data on participants.

The Perry Preschool Project targeted low-income African American children in a mid-size midwestern city. Preschoolers determined to be at high risk for school failure were randomly assigned to treatment or control groups. Treatment children received 1 to 2 years of academically oriented preschool education between ages 3 and 5, accompanied by frequent parent meetings and home visits. Positive academic gains were found following the intervention, although this boost was lost after a few years. However, long-term benefits were still apparent, as intervention children fared better than control children on a number of outcome measures in early adulthood. They received better grades, scored better on standardized achievement tests, had better high school graduation rates (67% vs. 49%) higher employment, fewer acts of misconduct, and a lower arrest rate (Berreuta-Clement, Schweinhart, Barnett, Epstein, & Weikart, 1984).

---

[1]We did not include programs that targeted one or several risk factors for aggression but did not measure outcomes in terms of impact on aggression or violence. Also, although we included only studies that specifically focused on disadvantaged urban youth, we realize that there is some variation across studies and cohorts in terms of actual levels of community disadvantage and the extent to which the sample was drawn from the most distressed inner-city settings.

The Houston Parent-Child Development Center provided both preschool enrichment and postnatal family services to low-income Mexican American children from disadvantaged urban areas. The goals of the program were to foster academic development and prevent behavioral problems. At age 1, children were randomly assigned to the intervention or control group. The 2-year intervention (when children were between 1 and 3 years of age) included home visits and a 1-year preschool program. Follow-up studies conducted when the children were in elementary school revealed that intervention children were less aggressive and more prosocial than control children (Johnson, 1988).

Even the promising results of these projects, however, are clouded by small sample size, high attrition rates, and actual impact on violent behavior. It is also unclear whether the positive results of programs such as the Perry Preschool Project, conducted more than 2 decades ago, would extend to children living in most inner cities today. These data do support the claim that short-term academic gains are possible in even the most disadvantaged settings. What is less clear is whether short-term academic gains also translate into long-term reductions in aggressive and violent behavior and whether precise timing and specific program content are important factors. Although poor academic performance is one risk factor for aggressive behavior, there are many other processes involved in the development of aggression. It may be that preschool enrichment programs also need to target directly the social-cognitive and behavioral correlates of aggression (Zigler & Trickett, 1978).

Programs that emphasize social and behavioral competencies assume that skills learned will generalize across situations and over time. Therefore, not only should such skills be maintained, they should provide children with a template for mastering stressful and problematic encounters in the future. A number of preschool social enrichment programs have been developed. Some programs have reported modest gains, although the findings have not been unequivocal.

For example, the pioneering work of Spivack and Shure (Shure & Spivack, 1979; Spivack & Shure, 1974) used a competence-building intervention. The main thrust was to promote the development of social problem-solving skills in inner-city preschool children, using Interpersonal Cognitive Problem-Solving Skills training (ICPS). In a series of studies, they found improvements in problem-solving skills *and* classroom behavioral adjustment (including reductions in aggression) for intervention children that were also evident at follow-up. These findings seemed to indicate that early social problem-solving training was an effective strategy for preventing antisocial behavior among inner-city children.

Given this initial success, a number of replication studies were conducted. The intervention techniques used were similar or even identical to the Spivack and Shure program, and several improvements in experimental methodology were often made, including random assignment of children to treatment and control groups, the use of unbiased raters of children's adjustment, and continued follow-up assessments. Unfortunately, the results of these subsequent studies were less encouraging. In general, although many researchers were able to demonstrate significant improvements in children's social problem-solving skills, these gains did not translate to behavioral improvements. For example, Rickel and Burgio (1982) attempted to replicate the ICPS training program with iden-tified high-risk African American inner-city preschool children. Using the exact training program, initial differences on social problem-solving skills indicated improvements for intervention versus control subjects. However, these improvements were not maintained at 2-year follow-up, and no behavioral improvements were noted either immediately following or 2 years after the intervention.

Interventions During the Elementary Years

A diverse portfolio of prevention programs exists for elementary school-age children, many evolving from the ICPS model. Although some programs have demonstrated modest gains in social problem solving and related improvements in adjustment, others have been less successful; and results have been discouraging for inner-city children. For example, in a classroom-based prevention study comparing the effects of social problem-solving training for middle-class suburban and inner-city third-grade children, Weissberg et al. (1981) provided both groups of children with a 52-session social problem-solving training program. The classroom curriculum was comprised of five major units: identifying feelings, identifying problems, generating solutions, considering consequences, and practicing behavioral strategies. In addition, six parent training sessions were offered to help parents reinforce children's problem-solving skills. Results for the suburban middle-class children showed that children from intervention classrooms outperformed children from control classrooms on a number of key social-cognitive skills and on seven of nine teacher-rated behavioral adjustment variables, including aggressive and antisocial behavior. In contrast, the adjustment of inner-city intervention children significantly declined on five of nine teacher-rated behavioral indexes and their aggressive behavior actually increased.

In another study with elementary school children, Hawkins and his colleagues (Hawkins, Von Cleve, & Catalano, 1991) used the ICPS classroom curriculum with first- and second-grade elementary school children from low-income urban schools. They also expanded the intervention program beyond problem-solving training to include teacher training in classroom management and interactive teaching as well as parent training in family management. Overall, children in the intervention classrooms were rated by teachers as less aggressive than children in the control classrooms at posttest. However, an examination of differences for African American and White children separately revealed that the intervention was only effective for White children.

Considering these mixed results, it is difficult to draw conclusions about the effectiveness of child-centered preventive interventions during the elementary school years in inner-city settings. However, one point is worth mentioning. In several replication studies conducted with low-income minority children, interventions did appear to be more effective for subsequent cohorts of children (Weissberg, Caplan, & Harwood, 1991). It may be that preventive interventions are simply more difficult to adapt and implement in settings characterized by high levels of economic and social stress and that repeated implementations are necessary before an effective matching of program and target children can be achieved. It may also be that in such settings, early inoculation cannot sustain changes; intervention beginning at the elementary school level is not sufficiently early to address risk; and programs must be extended into adolescence.

Programs for Adolescents

Most interventions for adolescents have been carried out as treatment programs involving adjudicated or incarcerated youths (for a review, see Goldstein, 1986; Guerra, Tolan, & Hammond, 1994). When prevention programs are offered, they typically are conducted in schools as part of a health education or social development curriculum. For example, Caplan et al. (1992) provided a 20-session curriculum, the Positive Youth Development Program, to sixth- and seventh-grade children from inner-city and suburban schools. The program focused on improving children's competencies in six areas: stress management, self-esteem, problem solving, substances and health information, assertiveness, and social networks. Intervention children were rated by their teachers as less impulsive and more adept at constructive conflict resolution than children in attention control classrooms. Self-report ratings showed gains in problem-solving skills and reductions in alcohol use. In general, the program was found to be beneficial for both inner-city and suburban students, although the long-term effects are still undetermined and effects on violence were not established.

Although this study was conducted with inner-city minority youths, it was not specifically tailored to a particular ethnic or cultural group. In contrast, Hammond (1991) developed a 20-session training program for African American adolescents. The program provides specific training in social skills, conflict resolution skills, and anger management. In a recent evaluation study (Hammond & Yung, 1993), 160 African American middle school youth (ages 13 to 15) were randomly assigned to treatment or control groups. The training was provided over the course of one school semester. Three-year follow-up data indicated that 17.6% of participating youth had subsequent juvenile court involvement, compared with 48.7% of control youth. Furthermore, control youth were significantly more likely than intervention youth to have been charged with a violent offense.

Family Interventions

Family interventions have as their main goal the modification of parent-child interactions. The most common type of program is parent training. Using a range of intervention modalities, these programs assume that children's behavior develops within the family context and that the focus of intervention should be at the level of the parent-child interaction rather than at the level of the individual child alone. Parent training is usually conducted with parents alone, who then use newly acquired parenting skills in the home.

In general, there is evidence to show that parent training is effective in the prevention and treatment of children's antisocial behavior (e.g., Dumas, 1989; Miller & Prinz, 1990). However, low-income families living under conditions of chronic and persistent stress appear to be least likely to benefit from these programs. For example, Dumas and Wahler (1983) conducted two studies using a standardized parent training program for families who differed both in socioeconomic status and in degree of social isolation. At follow-up assessment 1 year after the intervention, results indicated an increase in the probability of treatment failure for families that experienced economic disadvantage, social isolation, or both. Looking at these studies in the context of the parent

training literature, it seems that most of the successful parent training programs have been conducted with nonminority families who were not living under conditions of extreme stress.

Why have parent training programs been less effective for inner-city minority children and their families? One possible explanation is that models developed on nonminority middle-class families are simply not relevant for all families in all settings. In some cultures, respect for authority is paramount and children are not permitted, let alone encouraged, to discuss or participate in rule setting. Interventions promoting firm, clear, and understanding parenting might be readily dismissed by parents who do not subscribe to such normative beliefs about effective child-rearing practices. In addition to cultural differences, parents experiencing multiple stressors may simply be overwhelmed by day-to-day pressures. Even if interventions are able to bring about short-term changes in parenting practices, the behavior of children and their parents may ultimately respond to myriad powerful contextual factors that parent training cannot undo.

One intervention attempted to address many of these issues in a program for parents of first- and second-grade African American children living in South Central Los Angeles (Myers et al., 1992). The Effective Black Parenting Program (EBPP), a 15-session cognitive-behavioral parenting skills-building intervention, integrated both historical and contemporary sociocultural issues relevant to African American families. The program, led by African American professionals, included teaching skills such as using praise, time-out, incentives for good behavior, and the ignoring of bad behavior. At the same time, the role of traditional disciplinary practices (e.g., physical punishment and obedience) was discussed and contrasted with a more modern approach to discipline emphasizing helping children to internalize nonaggressive standards of behavior.

A postintervention assessment indicated that compared with controls, treatment parents showed reductions in rejection, felt more positive about relationships with their children, used less spanking, and reported reductions in children's disruptive behavior. At 1-year follow-up, some behavioral gains were maintained, specifically reductions in boys' withdrawn and hyperactive behaviors. These positive results were tempered, however, by findings that treatment parents were likely to regress to the use of coercive parenting and that girls evidenced increased disruptive behavior.

Peer-Focused Interventions

Child-centered interventions are often conducted in classrooms or small groups and hence involve children's peers in the intervention process. However, child-centered interventions primarily focus on improving children's social skills rather than on changing the nature of the peer group interaction. By contrast, peer-focused interventions directly target peer influences and peer processes as a means of modifying children's behavior. Because the influence of peers increases with age, these programs are usually designed for adolescents. Two primary models of peer-focused interventions have been evaluated: (a) peer leadership groups that bring together leaders from a variety of student groups to encourage conventional activities; and (b) programs that seek to prevent youths from affiliating with antisocial peer groups, particularly organized street gangs.

Peer Leadership Groups

A number of peer leadership groups have been derived from the Guided-Group Interaction (GGI) approach. Basically, GGI promotes conformity to conventional social rules through a series of free discussions in structured peer groups (Bixby & McCorkle, 1951). Several derivatives of GGI emerged, particularly in the 1970s and 1980s, including Positive Peer Culture, Peer Group Counseling, and Peer Culture Development. In general, these approaches all attempt to enhance the leadership skills and positive involvement of selected peers. In turn, it is expected that these leaders will influence their own peer groups to behave in a more conventional and positive manner.

As with most programs of this type, there have been very few controlled studies. One exception was a multiple-cohort evaluation of a Peer Culture Development (PCD) program, the School Action Effectiveness Study reported in Gottfredson (1987). The program was implemented in several elementary and high schools in low-income urban neighborhoods. The most comprehensive and scientifically rigorous evaluation was conducted with the third cohort of participants, after many initial programmatic difficulties had been worked out.

The overall goals of this particular PCD program were to alter peer interaction patterns to reduce negative peer influence, increase students' sense of responsibility for their actions, increase their belief in conventional social rules, promote attachment to school, increase their self-esteem, and reduce their alienation from conventional society. All eligible students were randomly assigned to either an intervention or control condition. Students in the intervention condition attended daily group meetings for a period of at least one semester. The groups included both troubled students (labeled "criterion" students) and students expected to be positive role models (labeled "noncriterion" students).

Intervention-control comparisons for elementary school students failed to show significant intervention effects on any of the multiple indicators of antisocial behavior that were assessed. Specifically, the intervention had no short-term effects on self-reports or teacher reports of problem behavior, and no effect on school referrals for disruptive behavior, tardiness, or absences. In a more disturbing finding, the high-school intervention had an *adverse* effect on participants. Compared to control children, the intervention youths showed significantly more tardiness, less attachment to parents, more "waywardness," and more self-reported delinquent behavior. In most cases these differences were due to the poorer performance of criterion children, but in some instances (e.g., school tardiness), it appears that the noncriterion children were most adversely affected by the intervention.

Interventions Directed at Juvenile Gangs

Since the emergence and identification of juvenile gang activity as a key urban social problem in the early part of this century, interventions targeting juvenile gangs have proliferated. Initially, these programs emphasized prevention, including efforts to redirect gang members toward more prosocial community activities and to reduce recruitment of new members. The available literature does not show much impact from preventive interventions alone. For example, Klein (1971) provided athletic and social events and academic tutoring to 800 members of four gangs. However, following intervention, increases in criminal behavior of participants were noted. Apparently, the activities increased the time gang members spent together, thereby increasing their criminal behavior. A subsequent program was somewhat more successful when time spent together was controlled. Overall results from this type of program were not encouraging, however. Efforts that have focused on preventing recruitment and initiation into gang activities have not demonstrated statistically significant results (e.g., Thompson & Jason, 1988).

In trying to enhance the effectiveness of antigang programs, an emphasis on increased surveillance and suppression of youth gangs emerged. Currently, the most promising strategies combine prevention, social intervention, treatment, suppression, and community mobilization in a communitywide effort (for a review, see Klein, 1995). For example, a gang reduction program in an economically disadvantaged Latino neighborhood of a large midwestern city that emphasizes targeted control of violent youth gang offenders and provision of a range of social services and opportunities for youths has demonstrated promising preliminary results. Compared to the preprogram period, participants report more than a 50% reduction in the number of serious crimes committed (Spergel & Grossman, 1994).

Interventions Focused on Classroom and School Environment

Classroom-based interventions attempt to change children's academic achievement and social behavior through modifying the classroom environment. Such interventions commonly target two areas of teacher skills: teacher practices and classroom management. By contrast, schoolwide interventions focus on characteristics of the school organization, including size, student groupings, parental involvement, management and governance, and school climate.

Teacher Practices and Classroom Management

Specific teacher practices can enhance children's classroom achievement. These include monitoring the entire class continuously, conducting multiple activities without breaking the flow of classroom events, moving activities at a good pace, and providing work at an appropriate level of difficulty. In addition, students who find academic tasks more difficult also appear to benefit from a slower pace combined with sufficient practice time as well as from considerable encouragement and praise from the teacher (Brophy, 1979). Unfortunately, teachers of low-income minority children tend to minimize interaction (Raudenbush, 1983) and provide less contingent praise (Fleischner & Van Acker, 1990).

One example of a method that concentrates on academic instruction and skills training is the Direct Instruction Model. This approach incorporates training in basic skills, systematic reinforcement for correct responses, and effective use of teaching time. Teachers who use this program follow a carefully sequenced curriculum, with specific methods for monitoring student progress. In a nationwide evaluation comparing this model with 12 other teaching strategies used with economically disadvantaged kindergarten through third-grade children, the Direct Instruct Model produced the greatest gains in academic (particularly language and math) and social (particularly self-esteem) skills (Becker & Carnine, 1980).

Cross-age tutoring also holds promise for improving student achievement. Most tutoring programs target students who experience academic and social difficulties, although some programs have involved entire classrooms (e.g., Jason, Frasure, & Ferone, 1981). In general, such programs result in improved academic performance on the part of both the children tutored and their tutors, although their impact on children's social skills and behaviors has yet to be demonstrated (see Cohen, Kulik, & Kulik, 1982, for a meta-analysis of tutoring studies).

In terms of classroom organization, cooperative learning groups promote higher student motivation, more successful mastery of tasks, and greater cultural understanding than individualistic classroom activities (Slavin, 1982). In cooperative learning groups, students of differing abilities work together as teams on selected activities so that the success of an individual student depends on the success of the other students in his or her group. Cooperative learning groups can also be effective in facilitating classroom management. Other classroom management strategies that have been shown to relate to reductions in student misbehavior include establishing clear rules for behavior, giving clear directions and maintaining consistent expectations, praising students for on-task behavior and good performance, and handling student misconduct in the least disruptive manner possible (Brophy, 1979; Hawkins & Weis, 1985).

Schoolwide Interventions

The organization of a school has a significant impact on student learning and behavior. Several interventions have been developed to impact organizational characteristics. However, few programs have systematically evaluated the effectiveness of school restructuring in urban and inner-city schools. Even when evaluations have been conducted, the focus has been on achievement gains, and measures of aggressive behavior are rarely included. Because achievement deficits constitute a risk factor for aggression, some of the more comprehensive programs are reviewed.

Felner and Adan (1988) report on the evaluation of a program designed to facilitate student transition into high school. The program was directed at low-income ninth-grade minority students entering a large urban high school. In essence, the program involved only a minimal reorganization focused on keeping students together in common groups and in close proximity and expanding the role of the homeroom teacher to include a variety of counseling and administrative functions. Even with these minor changes, when compared to matched control students, intervention students showed fewer decreases in academic performance and fewer absences. However, these differences did appear to diminish over time, and few differences were evident 2 to 3 years following the intervention, which is not surprising given the modest nature of the intervention.

In a more ambitious effort specifically tailored to predominantly African American inner-city elementary schools, the School Development Program (Comer, 1980, 1988) represents a comprehensive effort to change the organization and management of inner-city schools to make them more child oriented and more effective. Although the details of the Comer model are somewhat vague and unspecified, its major thrust involves the creation of three "teams." The school planning and management team is the governance and management body of the school. The second team, the mental health team, is charged with preventing behavior problems in the school, primarily by ensuring that policies and practices promote nurturing interpersonal relationships characterized by mutual respect. The third team, the parent program, uses existing parent organizations to increase parent participation in a range of school activities.

The program has other complexities, described in more detail elsewhere (e.g., Anson et al., 1991). A notable feature of the program in relation to inner-city schools is a prominent focus on the specific experiences of disadvantaged minority children. Significant efforts are made to organize classroom and school activities to promote both self-affirmation and validation of children's ethnic and cultural identities. Achievements of minority group members are emphasized and "mainstream" success is promoted. Although many evaluations of the program are still ongoing, initial data suggest gains in student achievement when school reorganization is consistent with the model (Comer, 1988).

SUMMARY AND CONCLUSIONS

We have reviewed a number of programs designed to reduce one or more risk factors for aggression and violence during different developmental periods and to promote healthy youth development. Some of these programs have yielded promising results, some have failed to produce change, and some have even been harmful. In most all cases, the impact on extreme and severe violent behavior has not been measured. Although some programs are broader in scope, few programs, to date, have provided multicomponent, multicontext services that impact the child, the family, the peer group, and the school simultaneously and address more systematically the effects of environmental stressors such as unemployment, unequal resource allocation, social policies, and the prevalence of violence. At present conclusions must be drawn from those circumscribed programs for which data are available.

What types of programs are recommended, in what socialization context, and at what points in time? To begin with, it is important to acknowledge that preventive interventions must do more than simply teach people how to cope with the difficult conditions that plague today's inner cities. Not only do such conditions increase population risk for aggression, compound individual risk, reduce receptivity to intervention, and interfere with long-term maintenance of related gains, they impede the healthy physical, intellectual, and social development of children growing up under such circumstances.

Although a number of intervention studies have been reviewed in this chapter, even the best research is compromised by concerns over nonrandom assignment to conditions, small sample size, rater bias, single outcome measures, and high attrition rates during follow-up. Any conclusions drawn from this literature are tentative and in need of further replication. In general, this literature suggests that prevention programs should focus on enhancing the physical, cognitive, social, and emotional development of children by providing broad-based services over the course of development. The most effective programs focus on increasing an individual's ability to meet the needs of a particular developmental stage that can, in turn, lay the groundwork for successful passage into subsequent developmental stages. Thus, early academic development provides an important building block for continued adaptation through childhood and adolescence. Similarly, to ease the transition into positive adult roles, programs for adolescents must provide skills such as job training and opportunities for employment.

Continued research is needed to examine risk and protective factors involved in the etiology of violence in the inner city, particularly those factors that are likely to inform "real-world" services. To ascertain the necessary and sufficient components of effective interventions, large-scale prevention research projects must be conducted, a number of which are currently underway (e.g., Conduct Problems Research Group, 1992; Guerra, 1994). In many cases, programs may need first to develop participant readiness to receive services—for instance, a drug-addicted mother will not benefit from parent training until she is drug free. Also, the interactions between participants and particular aspects of programs must be considered to create a "match" so that youths see the programs as personal resources (McLaughlin, Irby, & Langman, 1994). Although these programs are the most costly, it is likely that the most effective interventions will address multiple causal factors, be carried out in multiple contexts, and be extended over the course of development. Families, peers, schools, and communities must work in concert to provide opportunities for children to learn and practice prosocial behavior and to create environments in which prosocial behavior is both modeled and reinforced.

REFERENCES

Anderson, E. (in press). Violence and the inner-city poor. In J. McCord (Ed.), *Growing up violent*. Cambridge, England: Cambridge University Press.

Anson, A. R., Cook, T. D., Habib, F., Grady, M. K., Haynes, N., & Comer, J. P. (1991). The Comer school development program: A theoretical analysis. *Urban Education, 26*, 56–82.

Attar, B., Guerra, N. G., & Tolan, P. H. (1994). Neighborhood disadvantage, stressful life events, and adjustment in elementary school children. *Journal of Clinical Child Psychology, 23*, 394–400.

Becker, W. C., & Carnine, D. W. (1980). Direct instruction: An effective approach to educational intervention with the disadvantaged and low performers. In B. B. Lahey & A. E. Kazdin (Eds.), *Advances in clinical child psychology* (Vol. 3). New York: Plenum.

Berreuta-Clement, J. R., Schweinhart, L. J., Barnett, W. S., Epstein, A. S., & Weikart, D. P. (1984). *Changed lives: The effects of the Perry Preschool Program on youths through age 19* [Monographs of the High/Scope Educational Research Foundation, No. 8]. Ypsilanti, MI: High/Scope Press.

Bixby, F. L., & McCorkle, L. W. (1951). Guided group interaction and correctional work. *American Sociological Review, 16*, 455–459.

Brophy, J. E. (1979). Teacher behavior and its effects. *Journal of Educational Psychology, 71*, 733–750.

Caplan, M., Weissberg, R. P., Grober, J. S., Sivo, P. J., Grady, K., & Jacoby, C. (1992). Social competence promotion with inner-city and suburban young adolescents: Effects on social adjustment and alcohol use. *Journal of Consulting and Clinical Psychology, 60*, 56–63.

Centers for Disease Control. (1991). Forum on youth violence in minority communities: Setting the agenda for prevention. *Public Health Reports, 106*, 225–253.

Chicago Tribune, September 5, 1993.

Cohen, P. A., Kulik, J. A., & Kulik, C. C. (1982). Educational outcomes of tutoring: A meta-analysis of findings. *American Educational Research Journal, 19*, 237–248.

Comer, J. P. (1980). *School power: Implications of an intervention project*. New York: Free Press.

Comer, J. P. (1988). Educating poor minority children. *Scientific American, 256*, 42–48.

Conduct Problems Research Group. (1992). A developmental and clinical model for the prevention of conduct disorder: The FAST Track Program. *Development and Psychopathology, 4*, 509–527.

Dumas, J. E. (1989). Treating antisocial behavior in children: Child and family approaches. *Clinical Psychology Review, 9*, 197–222.

Dumas, J. E., & Wahler, R. G. (1983). Predictors of treatment outcome in parent training: Mother insularity and socioeconomic disadvantage. *Behavioral Assessment, 5*, 301–313.

Elliot, D. E. (1994, October). *Youth violence*. Presidential address at the annual meeting of the American Society of Criminology, Miami, FL.

Felner, R. D., & Adan, A. M. (1988). The school transitional environment project: An ecological intervention and evaluation. In R. H. Price, E. L. Cowen, R. P. Lorion, & J. Ramos-McKay (Eds.), *14 ounces of prevention: A casebook for practitioners* (pp. 111–122). Washington, DC: American Psychological Association.

Fleischner, J. E., & Van Acker, R. (1990). *Monograph on critical issues in special education: Implications for personnel preparation*. Denton: University of North Texas.

Garbarino, J., Kostelny, K., & Dubrow, N. (1991). What children can tell us about living in danger. *American Psychologist, 46*, 376–382.

Gladstein, J., Slater-Rusonis, E. J., & Heald, F. P. (1992). A comparison of inner-city and upper-middle class youths' exposure to violence. *Journal of Adolescent Health, 13*, 275–280.

Goldstein, A. P. (1986). Psychological skill training and the aggressive adolescent. In S. P. Apter & A. P. Goldstein (Eds.), *Youth violence* (pp. 89–119). Elmsford, NY: Pergamon.

Gottfredson, G. D. (1987). Peer group interventions to reduce the risk of delinquent behavior: A selective review and a new evaluation. *Criminology, 25*, 671–714.

Guerra, N. G. (1994). Violence prevention. *Preventive Medicine, 23*, 661–664.

Guerra, N. G., Tolan, P. T., & Hammond, R. (1994). Prevention of adolescent violence. In L. D. Eron, J. Gentry, & P. Schlegel (Eds.), *Reason to hope: A psychological perspective on violence and youth*. Washington, DC: American Psychological Association.

Hammond, R. (1991). *Dealing with anger: Givin' it, takin' it, workin' it out*. Champaign, IL: Research Press.

Hammond, R., & Yung, B. R. (1991). Preventing violence in at-risk African-American youth. *Journal of Health Care for the Poor and Underserved, 2*, 359–373.

Hammond, R., & Yung, B. (1993). *Evaluation and activity report: Positive adolescents choices training grant*. Unpublished grant report, U.S. Maternal and Child Health Bureau.

Hawkins, J. D., Von Cleve, E., & Catalano, R. F. (1991). Reducing early childhood aggression: Results of a primary prevention program. *Journal of the American Academy of Child and Adolescent Psychiatry, 30*, 208–217.

Hawkins, D., & Weis, J. G. (1985). The social development model: An integrated approach to delinquency prevention. *Journal of Primary Prevention, 6,* 73–97.

Jason, L. A., Frasure, S., & Ferone, L. (1981). Establishing supervising behaviors in eighth graders and peer-tutoring behaviors in first graders. *Child Study Journal, 11,* 201–219.

Jencks, C. (1992). *Rethinking social policy.* Cambridge: Harvard University Press.

Johnson, D. L. (1988). Primary prevention of behavior problems in young children: The Houston Parent-Child Development Center. In R. H. Price, E. L. Cowen, R. P. Lorion, & J. Ramos-McKay (Eds.), *14 ounces of prevention: A casebook for practitioners* (pp. 44–52). Washington, DC: American Psychological Association.

Kellam, S. (1992, September). *Evaluation of a school-based prevention program.* Paper presented at the workshop on Prevention of Conduct Disorders, National Institute of Mental Health, Washington, DC.

Klein, M. W. (1971). *Street gangs and street workers.* Englewood Cliffs, NJ: Prentice Hall.

Klein, M. W. (1995). *The American street gang.* New York: Oxford University Press.

Kozol, J. (1991). *Savage inequalities.* New York: Harper Perennial.

Lee, V. E., Brooks-Gunn, J., Schnur, E., & Liaw, F. (1990). Are Head Start effects sustained? A longitudinal follow-up comparison of disadvantaged children attending Head Start, no preschool, and other preschool programs. *Child Development, 61,* 495–507.

McLaughlin, M. W., Irby, M. A., & Langman, J. (1994). *Urban sanctuaries.* San Francisco: Jossey-Bass.

Miller, G. E., & Prinz, R. J. (1990). Enhancement of social learning family interventions for child conduct disorder. *Psychological Bulletin, 108,* 291–307.

Myers, H. F., Alvy, K. T., Arrington, A., Richardson, M. A., Marigna, M., Huff, R., Main, M., & Newcomb, M. D. (1992). The impact of a parent training program on inner-city African-American families. *Journal of Community Psychology, 20,* 132–147.

Papajohn, G. (1994, August 19). 'King' Wheat's killing mirrors change in gangs. *Chicago Tribune,* pp. 1, 14.

Provence, S., & Naylor, A. (1983). *Working with disadvantaged parents and children: Scientific issues and practice.* New Haven: Yale University Press.

Raudenbush, S. W. (1983). Utilizing controversy as a source of hypotheses for meta-analysis: The case of teacher expectancy's effect on pupil IQ. *Urban Education, 28,* 114–131.

Rickel, A. U., & Burgio, J. C. (1982). Assessing social competencies in lower income preschool children. *American Journal of Community Psychology, 10,* 635–645.

Seitz, V., Rosenbaum, L. K., & Apfel, N. H. (1985). Effects of family support intervention: A ten-year follow up. *Child Development, 56,* 376–391.

Shakoor, B. H., & Chalmers, D. (1991). Co-victimization of African-American children who witness violence: Effects on cognitive, emotional, and behavioral development. *Journal of the National Medical Association, 83,* 233–238.

Shure, M. B., & Spivack, G. (1979). Interpersonal cognitive problem-solving and primary prevention: Programming for preschool and kindergarten children. *Journal of Clinical Child Psychology, 8,* 89–94.

Slavin, R. E. (1982). *Cooperative learning groups: What the research says to the teacher.* Washington, DC: National Education Association.

Spergel, I. A., & Grossman, S. F. (1994, October). *Gang violence and crime theory: Gang violence reduction project.* Paper presented at the annual meeting of the American Society of Criminology, Miami, FL.

Spivack, G., & Shure, M. B. (1974). *Social adjustment of young children: A cognitive approach to solving real-life problems.* San Francisco: Jossey-Bass.

Thompson, D. W., & Jason, L. E. (1988). Street gangs and preventive interventions. *Criminal Justice and Behavior, 15,* 323–333.

Uniform Crime Reports. (1992). Washington, DC: Federal Bureau of Investigation.

Weissberg, R. P., Gesten, E. L., Rapkin, B. D., Cowen, E. L., Davidson, E., de Apodaca, R. F., & McKim, B. J. (1981). The evaluation of a social problem-solving training program for suburban and inner-city third grade children. *Journal of Consulting and Clinical Psychology, 49,* 251–261.

Weissberg, R. P., Caplan, M., & Harwood, R. L. (1991). Promoting competent young people in competence-enhancing environments: A systems-based perspective on primary prevention. *Journal of Consulting and Clinical Psychology, 59,* 830–841.

Wilson, W. J. (1987). *The truly disadvantaged: The inner city, the underclass and public policy.* Chicago: University of Chicago Press.

Zigler, E. F. (1987). Formal school for four-year-olds? *American Psychologist, 42,* 254–260.

Zigler, E. F., & Trickett, P. K. (1978). IQ, social competence, and evaluation of early childhood intervention programs. *American Psychologist, 33,* 789–798.

CHAPTER 36

Parent-Focused and Cognitive-Behavioral Treatments of Antisocial Youth

MICHAEL A. SOUTHAM-GEROW and PHILIP C. KENDALL

The importance of an examination of psychosocial interventions for antisocial behavior is manifold. Aggressive and antisocial behavior in children and adolescents represents a serious and perplexing problem to society. Although relatively few in number, those children who behave antisocially persist in their problem behaviors, often into adulthood, and often engage in criminal activity (Farrington, Loeber, & Van Kammen, 1990; Loeber, 1982; Olweus, 1979; Robins, 1966). Independent of the adult outcome, the children and adolescents who behave antisocially are often destructive and harmful in their youth and represent a significant proportion of the clinically referred population (Curry, Pelissier, Woodford, & Lochman, 1988; Horne & Sayger, 1990; Kazdin, 1987a; Patterson, 1982; Stewart, 1985). In addition, empirical examinations of interventions provide evidence for conceptual models, leading to a greater understanding of the processes involved in the development of antisocial and violent behavior. Although research has demonstrated some positive treatment effects, the intractability of the problem as well as the costs incurred (e.g., social, financial, human) indicate that work must continue (Lipsey, 1992). This chapter examines parent-focused and cognitive-behavioral treatments of antisocial and aggressive behavior in children and adolescents. First, we consider the conceptual bases for psychosocial treatment of antisocial youths. Second, we appraise the current state of the field by critiquing the prominent treatment modalities: cognitive-behavioral and parent training. Third, we examine important diagnostic and methodological issues pertinent to the study and evaluation of treatments for these youth. Finally, we consider future goals for research in the area.

CONCEPTUAL ISSUES

Treatment requires a strong conceptual basis. Efforts to explain the roots of antisocial behavior have generally fallen into three categories: *biological* approaches; *social and cognitive* approaches; and *family- and parent-based* approaches.

Biological Factors

Several other chapters in this volume review the research on biological factors of antisocial behavior; thus, we discuss only illus-

trative evidence suggesting a child-based biological component to the development of aggression (see Brennan & Mednick, Chapter 25, this volume; Carey & Goldman, Chapter 23, this volume; Berman, Kavoussi, & Coccaro, Chapter 28, this volume; Henry & Moffitt, Chapter 26, this volume; Raine, Chapter 27, this volume). In general, most work suggests a transactional model of the development of antisocial behavior (e.g., Lytton, 1990). Specifically, the data best support the notion of the importance of the development of the organism-environment interactional relationship. Genetic factors and early life events (e.g., perinatal trauma, obstetrical complications) have been linked to antisocial behavior (e.g., Brennan, Mednick, & Kandel, 1991). Raine, Brennan, and Mednick (1994) found that birth complications and early maternal rejection interacted to predispose 1-year-olds to violent crime at age 18 years. In a finding supporting a link between temperamental style and later antisocial behavior, Wootton, Frick, Shelton, and Silverthorn (1997) found that callous-unemotional child traits were related to child conduct problems independent of parenting practices. Research from developmental, neurophysiological, and clinical realms buttresses transactional notions (e.g., autonomic reactivity, MAO platelet level, genetic factors, temperament; see Bates, Bayles, Bennett, Ridge, & Brown, 1991; Pincus, 1987; Raine, Venables, & Williams, 1990; Stoff et al., 1989; Tremblay, Pihl, Vitaro, & Dobkin, 1994).

Cognitive and Social Factors

Several investigators have explored the ramifications of the antisocial child's understanding of the social milieu. For instance, Dodge described reactive children (i.e., aggressive in reaction to stimuli), distinguished by their overattention to hostile stimuli and their intention-cue detection error (i.e., perceiving hostile intention in others when cues are relatively ambiguous), and proactive children (i.e., aggressive without any apparent physical or social cue), whose approach is biased by their expectation of positive results from aversive/aggressive behavior and their inadequate or limited problem-solving skills (Coie, Dodge, & Coppotelli, 1982; Dodge, 1980, 1991). Other social processing problems emerge in aggressive children (e.g., Dodge & Newman, 1981; Guerra & Slaby, 1990). Aggressive boys value social goals of dominance and revenge more and social affiliation less than nonaggressive boys, and aggressive youths believe that aggressive acts will enhance their self-esteem and help them to avoid a negative image (Lochman, White, & Wayland, 1991; Slaby & Guerra, 1988). Aggressive children also do not appear to understand emotion in ways that nonaggressive children do, anticipating fewer feelings of sadness or fear when faced with difficult situations and yet coping poorly when they do experience emotional states (Garrison & Stolberg, 1983).

Cognitive-behavioral formulations have also been forwarded to explain aggressive behavior in children. Empirical evidence has indicated that both cognitive distortion (i.e., children process information in a distorted fashion, e.g., misinterpretation of the intentionality of others) and cognitive deficiencies (i.e., cognitive-processing ability is somehow deficient, leading to action that does not benefit from forethought) are present in the thinking of aggressive and antisocial children (see Kendall & MacDonald, 1993; Kendall, Ronan, & Epps, 1991). Along similar lines, Huesmann (1988) has described a script theory of aggressive behavior, suggesting that children, through enactive and observational learning, develop limited, aggressive scripts that they apply across situations. The work of social information processing and cognitive-behavioral theorists led to the several cognitive-behavioral interventions for aggressive children discussed in this chapter—treatments focusing on the antisocial youths' deficient problem-solving skills and biases toward agonistic solutions.

Parent and Family Characteristics

Considerable empirical work has supported the importance of family environment in the development of antisocial behavior (Eron, Huesmann, & Zelli, 1991; Frick, 1994; Gardner, 1992; Patterson, 1982). Patterson and his colleagues have outlined the coercive relationship between caregiver and child involving reciprocal reinforcement of gradually increasing coercive behaviors—a training leading to the child's rejection by peers, school failure, and deviant peer group membership (Patterson, 1982; Patterson, DeBaryshe, & Ramsey, 1989; Patterson, Reid, & Dishion, 1992). Additional research has indicated that other family factors are operative in the development of antisocial behaviors: poor parenting practices and negative parental discipline practices;[1] family transitions (e.g., divorce, remarriage); parental alcohol use; indiscriminate parenting practices (e.g., inconsistent limit setting); parental psychopathology (e.g., antisocial behavior); and familial adversity (Capaldi & Patterson, 1991; Frick et al., 1992; Haapasalo & Tremblay, 1994; McCord, 1993; Pelham & Lang, 1993; Vuchinich, Bank, & Patterson, 1992; Wahler & Dumas, 1989). Overall, the research suggests a complex, interactive relationship between parental and child behavior.

Patterson, Capaldi, and Bank (1991) described differential family environment, course, and prognosis for early starters versus late starters (cf. childhood-onset/adolescence-onset model; Hin-

shaw, Lahey, & Hart, 1993; aggressive-versatile/nonaggressive-antisocial; Loeber, 1988; life-course-persistent/adolescence-limited model; Moffitt, 1993). Early starters are children who receive early coercive training, evidence an earlier onset of coercive behaviors, and show more negative outcomes compared to late starters. Late starters—whose aversive behaviors began in middle adolescence and were learned in deviant peer groups—typically came from homes experiencing severe trauma (e.g., death or divorce, unemployment) during the child's middle adolescence, before which the home had been relatively stable.

Empirical findings support family- or parent-based approaches and have yielded several prominent treatment alternatives addressing the familial forces contributing to antisocial and aggressive behavior in children (e.g., Patterson, 1982). However, an accurate understanding of aggression in childhood and adolescence cannot be obtained by examining only parental and family factors. Biological, social-cognitive, and familial-parental factors all require consideration in the study and treatment of antisocial behavior in youths.

TREATMENT INTERVENTIONS

With varying degrees of adherence to methodologically preferred features of research, many paradigms have been used in the treatment of youth with antisocial behavior. Although gains from the treatments are often modest and the extended course of the disorder for a significant number of children is not interrupted, some effective treatments have been identified. Kazdin (1993) has described some criteria for determining the promise of a treatment, including that (a) the treatment is based on a theoretical conceptualization of the disorder, (b) the conceptualization has received support from research, (c) outcome evidence has supported the treatment's effectiveness, and (d) outcome is related to the processes identified in the conceptualization of the disorder. Although no treatments have adequately met all of these criteria, we concur with others that the social learning family interventions and the child-focused cognitive-behavioral/problem-solving skills training models represent the more promising interventions for the antisocial child (Kazdin, 1987b; Miller & Prinz, 1990). Several excellent reviews of the antisocial behavior treatment literature are available (Dumas, 1989; Kazdin, 1987b; 1993; Miller, 1994). Our review is illustrative rather than exhaustive and strives to identify research that serves as exemplars of the particular modality. Although many forms of treatment have been used with antisocial children,[2] our examination considers only cognitive-behavioral and parent training approaches.

---

[1]In addition, Vuchinich, Bank, and Patterson's (1992) study indicates that a child's antisocial behavior is related negatively with positive parental discipline practices, suggesting the child-effect discussed by Lytton (1990) and others.

[2]Such a limitation precludes discussion of other tested modalities. For example, the Teaching-Family model has received research attention and support (e.g., Bedlington, Braukmann, Ramp, & Wolf, 1988; Phillips, Phillips, Wolf, & Faxsen, 1973; Wolf, Braukmann, & Ramp, 1987). We refer interested readers to these papers as exemplars of the work done using this intervention. Additionally, psychopharmacological approaches have been used with antisocial children, often in an adjunctive role (see Hinshaw, 1992). Because another chapter in this volume addresses this form of treatment, it will not be described here (see Karper & Krystal, Chapter 41, this volume).

Cognitive-Behavioral Approach

A cognitive-behavioral (CB) approach to antisocial behavior in childhood addresses those cognitive deficiencies and distortions that prohibit the child from developing flexible problem-solving skills and that lead to limited social skills. CB therapy typically consists of multiple components: (a) social and problem-solving skills education, (b) a coping model, (c) role-playing, (d) in vivo experiences, (e) affective education, (f) homework assignments, and (g) response-cost contingencies (Kendall & Braswell, 1993; Kendall & Siqueland, 1989).

Evidence supporting CB interventions has been amassing, with results generally indicating at least modest gains. For example, Kolko, Loar, and Sturnick (1990) examined a group treatment with a sample of conduct-disordered children in an inpatient ward of a hospital. The treatment group evidenced pronounced improvements in areas of social competence as judged by the child and a clinical observer, with gains maintained at 1-year follow-up. In another study, Kendall, Reber, McLeer, Epps, and Ronan (1990) reported that teacher and child ratings of subjects' prosocial, self-control, and social competence all indicated significant beneficial effects from the CB therapy. Despite their strengths, both of these studies have weaknesses that require redressing. For example, an inpatient population may not represent the typical antisocial child, and longer follow-up assessments are needed.[3] In addition, measurement of home behavior and home environment were lacking in the studies despite their demonstrated relevance in antisocial behavior.

Kazdin and his colleagues (e.g., Kazdin, Bass, Siegel, & Thomas, 1989; Kazdin, Esveldt-Dawson, French, & Unis, 1987b) reported several excellent examinations of the effects of a CB treatment (problem-solving skills training [PSST]; a combination of the Kendall & Braswell, 1993, and Spivack & Shure, 1974, programs). Kazdin et al. (1987b) reported that the PSST elicited significant change compared with the other two conditions (relationship therapy and treatment-contact control), both at posttreatment and at 1-year follow-up. The improvement was marked on both measures of home (e.g., Child Behavior Checklist [CBCL]; Achenbach, 1991a) and school behavior (e.g., Child Behavior Checklist–Teacher's Report Form [TRF]; Achenbach, 1991b). In a subsequent study, Kazdin et al. (1989) attempted to differentiate the treatment effects among two forms of PSST and relationship therapy. One treatment consisted of PSST as described earlier (see Kazdin et al., 1987b). The second (PSST-P) included the same protocol plus in vivo homework assignments called "supersolvers," with which skills learned in a session

were practiced in a real setting outside of therapy time. Improvements were found across settings (home and school) and at both posttreatment and 1-year follow-up, though differences between the PSST and PSST-P conditions were, in general, nonsignificant.

CB interventions for antisocial youths represent a promising approach by effectively addressing youths' cognitive and social problems. The CB approach is based on research indicating social-cognitive and problem-solving deficits among antisocial youths. However, most treatments investigated do not measure these constructs, opting to examine the treatment's effectiveness at the impact level (see Kendall & Morris, 1991). Moreover, CB treatments, by focusing on the child, lack sufficient attention to the familial variables that have been implicated in the development and maintenance of antisocial behavior in children (e.g., Patterson, 1982). These home-based problems, unaddressed, may impede or disrupt the progress of a child or adolescent whose social and problem-solving skills have been enhanced.

Parent Training Approach

Parent training has been one of the most prevalent and tested approaches for the treatment of aggression in children and adolescents. Patterson and colleagues have tested and refined both their theoretical model (coercive family process) and their treatment approach. A parent training treatment protocol typically entails the systematic training to the parent(s) of the "target" child to perform four central tasks: (a) outline house rules, (b) enforce contingency consequences, (c) monitor and supervise the child when he or she is not in the home, and (d) use problem-solving strategies with the child (Patterson, 1982). Many variations of the parent training model have been implemented and evaluated.

Dumas's (1989) review of the parent training literature revealed several studies supporting the effectiveness of Patterson et al.'s program—with clinically significant gains posttreatment and at 1-year follow-up (e.g., Forgatch, 1991; Patterson, Chamberlain, & Reid, 1982). Forehand (see Forehand & Long, 1991) and his colleagues have used a behavioral approach to train parents to (a) attend to the target child, (b) praise appropriate behavior, (c) ignore minor inappropriate behavior, and (d) issue clear directions followed by praise for compliance or consequence for noncompliance. In one long-term follow-up study, Baum and Forehand (1981) reported that the treatment paradigm sustained gains on both parent-report measures and observational measures from 1 to $4\frac{1}{2}$ years after treatment completion. Although the study did not assess clinical significance of the changes (nor were diagnoses examined), the long-term gains suggest the efficacy of the treatment.

Webster-Stratton and her colleagues introduced a low-cost alteration of the parent training model by using videotaped modeling of various parent training strategies. Webster-Stratton, Kolpacoff, and Hollinsworth (1988) reported a randomized clinical trial of four treatment groups: a waiting-list control, a group discussion, a group discussion videotape modeling treatment (GDVM), and an individually administered videotape modeling treatment (IVM). In the two videotape modeling treatments, the majority of the parent training occurred through the viewing of a videotape containing explanation of an intended target skill and multiple examples of situations in which to employ the skill. All three treatment groups

---

[3]Lochman (1992) reported long-lasting effects (3-year follow-up) of an anger-coping prevention program for undiagnosed aggressive children. Although treated children's substance use was within normal ranges, and their self-esteem and social problem-solving skills were enhanced by the intervention, their general behavioral deviance (e.g., classroom disruption, delinquency rates) was only modestly impacted. However, participants who received booster sessions had better outcomes in terms of school behavior, suggesting the utility of longer-term treatment. The study lacks generalizability to the other studies reviewed here because of its reliance on a nonclinical sample; it is included in the review to highlight the importance of booster sessions.

exhibited significant effects compared to the waiting-list control group with few significant differences among the three treatments. The IVM treatment was found to be at least as potent as the group discussion format, indicating that IVM, though not as viable as other treatments, provides a low-cost, effective alternative to more intensive, more expensive, therapist-driven interventions. Webster-Stratton has reported subsequent success with the videotape modeling parent training approach (e.g., Webster-Stratton, 1994).

Because of its prominence in the field, the shortcomings of the parent training approach have been outlined. One criticism is that the approach relies on parents to implement the necessary intervention (Webster-Stratton, 1985). Often the parents are unable or unwilling to use the skills provided by treatment because of their own pathology (e.g., depression, antisocial patterns). Wahler and Dumas (1989; Wahler, 1980) have described the "insular mother" who possesses minimal social support because of her hostile/aversive interactions with the community and family members. Additionally, research has indicated that antisocial children's parents are often unreliable or resistant to treatment, which weakens the intervention's effectiveness (e.g., Patterson & Chamberlain, 1994). Stoolmiller, Duncan, Bank, and Patterson (1993) reported empirical evidence suggesting that families with "accelerating and chronically high levels of resistance . . . [and] families that show low levels of resistance from baseline to termination" (Stoolmiller et al., 1993, p. 927) are least likely to benefit from intervention. Families who are engaged in work with the therapist, who evidence increasing resistance, but are able to resolve their opposition have the best prognosis. Webster-Stratton (1985) found that although none of the potentially undermining variables could be considered a reliable predictor immediately posttreatment, two predictors of negative treatment outcome emerged at 1-year follow-up: the single parent family and general life stressors.

A related shortcoming of parent training is the prevalence of attrition among the families treated. Attrition rates are presumably high from these treatments because of the factors discussed earlier: The families involved are exposed to multiple stressors and parents often have their own psychological problems (e.g., substance use, depression, antisocial behavior). In addition, some work has revealed other predictors of attrition: age of child (with older children's families more likely to drop out of treatment) and child comorbid diagnosis of substance use (Dishion & Patterson, 1992; Kaminer, Tarter, Bukstein, & Kabene, 1992). In a study examining the effectiveness of a parent training program, Kazdin (1990) reported that those families classified as premature terminators were marked from the treatment completers by the (a) severity of the dysfunction of their child, (b) sources of maternal stress, and (c) severity of their socioeconomic disadvantage. Early identification of families at-risk becomes an important goal, with the consideration of additional treatment components a likely pathway for improvement on the difficult road for these high-risk families and their children.

Toward an Integrated Treatment Approach

In light of these findings, Miller and Prinz (1990) described possible avenues for improvement of the parent training paradigm: expansion of parent training and broadening of the treatment focus by adding treatment components to parent training. Expansion of parent training might include strengthening parenting skills already taught with additional sessions (i.e., lengthening treatment) or teaching additional skills for dealing with the child (e.g., conflict resolution skills, self-control skills). The second avenue offered by Miller and Prinz lay in a broader-based treatment model, advocating the addition of components to the current parent training paradigm to address parental concerns outside of the child's behavior (e.g., marital discord, maternal depression, substance abuse) as well as working on an individual basis with the child (e.g., social-skills training, anger management training).

Research has addressed the weaknesses of parent training largely via the second avenue (i.e., broadening traditional parent training). Dadds, Schwartz, and Sanders, (1987) found markedly better improvements, using both statistical tests and normative comparisons (see Kendall & Grove, 1988), for families who received parent training along with an adjunctive treatment that expanded the parents' problem-solving skills and encouraged the parents to support each other. Pfiffner, Jouriles, Brown, Etscheidt, and Kelly (1990) enhanced parent training for single-parent families by adding a problem-solving skills training component addressing topics other than child management. Pfiffner et al. (1990) reported success for both parent training alone and enhanced parent training, with the enhanced condition evidencing better overall results. Webster-Stratton (1994) added several parent-focused components to her videotape parent training paradigm. The additional components included personal self-control, communication skills, problem-solving skills between adults, teaching problem-solving skills to children, and strengthening social support and self-care. Results supported the effectiveness of the intervention, though long-term effects have yet to be reported. These studies—aimed to ameliorate problems ostensibly unrelated to the child—represent a positive and important step for the future.

Other work broadening the parent training paradigm has combined parent training and child-focused cognitive-behavioral treatment. Horne and Sayger (1990) described a treatment program for children with conduct disorder and oppositional defiant disorder that included (a) a comprehensive assessment of all problem areas for the target child and the family, (b) multisystemic involvement (parent, siblings, teacher, etc.), (c) an attempt to impact the environment and establish positive expectation for change, (d) parent training skills, (e) problem-solving skills training for the child, and (f) maintenance of skills through detailed follow-up procedures. Extensive in scope, the treatment has reported success in case study form only; a more rigorous study is needed to evaluate further the effectiveness of the treatment. Kazdin and colleagues have combined a parent training program with their cognitive-behavioral treatment PSST for the target child (Kazdin et al., 1987a; Kazdin, Siegel, & Bass, 1992). In the first of these studies, Kazdin et al. (1987a) found that the treatment group evidenced improved prosocial behavior and decreased externalizing behaviors (measured by the CBCL, parent and teacher report) compared to the control group at both posttreatment and 1-year follow-up. In a subsequent study, Kazdin et al. (1992) reported that the combined approach evidenced both clinical and statistical significance. Additionally, Webster-Stratton and Hammond (1997) found that a combined parent-training, child-training intervention evidenced the best outcomes at 1-year follow-up compared to either of the two treatments alone. These studies, whose goal lies in influencing both the parent's caretaking and the child's behavior, integrates findings from social-cognitive and family research. Finally, Henggeler's even broader multisystemic treatment, involving a "present-focused and action-oriented . . . [approach that] directly addresses intrapersonal (e.g., cognitive) and systemic (i.e., family, peer, school) factors that are known to be associated with adolescent antisocial behavior" (Borduin et al., 1995, p. 571) has shown some promising effects with juvenile delinquent populations (e.g., Henggeler, Melton, & Smith, 1992; Henggeler et al., 1986).

ISSUES IN THE TREATMENT OF ANTISOCIAL YOUTH

Overall, treatment of antisocial youth has occupied considerable research resources. Although some gains have been made, the stability of aggressive behavior and the continued failure of the extant treatments to retard or halt the course of some youths leaves substantial work for the future. To aid subsequent research, we now examine diagnostic and methodological topics relevant to the improvement of the treatment of antisocial children.

Diagnostic Issues

One major concern involves the changing set of diagnostic criteria used in treatment outcome studies. The *Diagnostic and Statistical Manual for Mental Disorders* (*DSM-IV;* American Psychiatric Association, 1994) provides explicit and arguably reliable criteria for establishing a diagnosis of conduct disorder (CD) in children. However, these clusters of symptoms change from revision to revision and not all research clinics follow the *DSM*'s diagnostic criteria nor its nosology. As a result, identified children are labeled antisocial, or aggressive, or conduct-disordered, or oppositional-defiant disordered, or delinquent with the consequence being uncertainty that any one researcher's sample is similar to another's. Although we do not advocate mandatory adoption of the *DSM* and its criteria for all treatment outcome researchers, we do believe that specification of diagnostic or inclusion criteria and careful descriptions of subject characteristics are needed in published outcome reports.

Comorbidity of child diagnoses has been a hotbed of research in recent years (Caron & Rutter, 1991; Kendall & Clarkin, 1992; Nottelmann & Jensen, 1995), with researchers in childhood psychopathology examining the co-occurrence of multiple disorders (e.g., Abikoff & Klein, 1992; Brady & Kendall, 1992). CD has figured prominently in the recent empirical work in relation to comorbidity, and current conclusions suggest that CD often co-occurs along with depression, substance abuse, or attention-deficit hyperactivity disorder.

Depression

Early work referred to the depression found concomitant with CD as "masked depression" due to the symptomatic dominance of CD (Carlson & Cantwell, 1980). Cole and Carpentieri (1990) found that a significant overlap between CD and depression existed, with

these comorbid children tending to be more socially rejected or controversial[4] compared to children with either of the disorders alone. Other investigations have supported this finding, indicating that aggressive children exhibit equivalent levels of internalized distress compared to matched nonaggressive clinical cases (Curry et al., 1988). Research has found that the family environments of CD and depressed youths are more aversive than the homes of youth with depression only (Dadds, Sanders, Morrison, & Rebgetz, 1992; Sanders, Dadds, Johnston, & Cash, 1992).

Substance Abuse

DeMilio (1989) and Milin, Halikas, Meller, and Morse (1991) both found relatively high rates of comorbidity between these two problem areas, with rates as high as 91% of a substance abuse group being also diagnosed with CD. Bukstein, Brent, and Kaminer (1989) concluded that CD and substance abuse frequently co-occur, citing studies indicating three possible paths that the association takes: (a) substance abuse preceding CD, (b) CD preceding substance abuse, or (c) the two disorders as independent developments (see White, Chapter 47, this volume).

Attention Deficit/Hyperactivity Disorder

Literature reviews have revealed that attention deficit/hyperactivity disorder (ADHD) and CD frequently occurred in tandem (e.g., between 30% to 50% of children and adolescents presenting with comorbid disorders), though each disorder was found to be present independently of the other in many cases and differentiating behavioral characteristics were discernible for the two disorders (Biederman, Newcorn, & Sprich, 1991; Hinshaw, 1987, 1992). For the child with ADHD alone, cognitive and achievement deficits are most notable, whereas for the child with CD alone, the differentiating characteristics seem to be antisocial parents, poor parental supervision, maternal rejection, parental substance abuse, family hostility, and low socioeconomic status. The child with CD often has better social skills and displays more on-task behavior than the child with ADHD, but he or she has worse behavioral and social outcomes. The combined disorder is marked by the amalgamation of the worst of both worlds: academic problems, more severe symptoms, greater levels of parental psychopathology, higher rates of peer rejection, and more familial disadvantages. In fact, Lynam (1996) identified hyperactivity-impulsivity-inattention and conduct problems as the constellation of symptoms most predictive of chronic criminal behavior and psychopathy. A good deal of empirical work has attempted to further define the differences between the two disorders, in terms of familial setting; later outcome; and social, emotional, and cognitive functioning (e.g., Abikoff & Klein, 1992; Frick, Kamphaus et al., 1991; Frick, Lahey, Christ, Loeber, & Green, 1991; Reeves, Werry, Elkind, & Zametkin, 1987; Szatmari, Boyle, & Offord, 1989; Walker, Lahey, Hynd, & Frame, 1987; Werry, Reeves, & Elkind, 1987; West & Prinz, 1987).

Comorbidity of childhood disorders represents a critical area for future work. The implications of the existence of a large per-

---

[4]Controversial children are characterized by their peers nominating them as both popular and disliked, suggesting a "controversy" about the child in question (Coie, Dodge, & Coppotelli, 1982).

centage of youths with multiple disorders among the general population are far-reaching. For example, a detailed analysis of the many subpopulations of CD youths (e.g., with ADHD or substance dependence) could lead to the adaptation of different treatment paradigms (e.g., medication, substance dependence treatment, social skills training).

Methodological Issues

Although there are discussions of preferred methods in treatment outcome research (e.g., Kazdin, 1992; Kendall & Norton-Ford, 1982), methodological rigor is not always followed. We will enumerate some of the important limitations and advances in clinical research methodology.

Long-Term Follow-Up

A foremost limitation is that child treatment outcome research has generally failed to assess long-term effectiveness. Although researchers have begun to report treatment maintenance at 1-year posttreatment (e.g., Kazdin, Siegel, & Bass, 1992), rigorous longer-term follow-up is almost nonexistent. Because the long-term prognosis for antisocial children is generally poor, long-term follow-ups represent a critical index of a treatment's impact. Many researchers have called for a "chronic disorder" conceptualization for CD and antisocial behavior in children, likening it to a problem requiring long-term care (e.g., Kazdin, 1987a; Miller, London, & Prinz, 1991; Wolf, Braukmann, & Ramp, 1987). In this light, it may be more productive to expect incremental improvements in a variety of domains (e.g., stealing, fighting, arrests, fires started, parent-child conflict, child distress) over longer periods of time rather than to anticipate a "cure," with absence of symptomatic behavior at one or two posttreatment assessment points.

Treatment Manuals

The use of flexibly applied manualized treatments has been an important tool in disseminating treatments that have documented effectiveness in research clinics, bridging the gap between science and practice (see Dobson & Shaw, 1988). Clinical researchers working with antisocial children have manualized their treatments (e.g., Phillips, Phillips, Fixsen, & Wolf, 1974), not only facilitating the transportability of treatment protocols, but also allowing for replication of clinical trials at different sites (Kendall & Southam-Gerow, 1995). We encourage the development and use of manuals in child-clinical outcome research with antisocial children.

Randomized Clinical Trials

Kendall and Morris (1991) noted that whereas "analog studies have a place within the scientific study of child treatments," (p. 779) randomized clinical trials must be used as the final test of a treatment's effectiveness. Unfortunately, rigorous randomized clinical trials are not always used in child clinical research. Such trials require carefully diagnosed subjects who are randomly assigned to either a treatment condition or a nontreatment (or a comparative treatment) condition. For the children in the treatment group, assignment to a therapist must also be done in a random fashion. In some instances, other considerations (e.g., severity of problem, expertise of a therapist) might be used to determine the assignment of a child to a condition and though these considerations may seem helpful, they undermine the science of the trial. The paucity of randomized clinical trials with antisocial youths requires remedy.

Control and Comparison Groups

The issue of control groups in clinical research has been controversial. Especially in the case of severely disordered children, is it unethical to deny treatment for any period of time? Many research clinics use a waiting-list control group, randomly placing children in an 8- to 12-week waiting period, at the end of which time treatment is provided. Although this arrangement successfully provides a test of treatment versus no-treatment hypotheses, it requires a child (and his or her family) in need of services to wait for several weeks. However, the short duration of waiting lists precludes any long-term statements about the course of an untreated disorder and also fails to rule out all threats to internal validity (e.g., maturation, simultaneous occurrence of important events). It may be more desirable to use comparison groups instead of control groups, especially given the preponderance of data suggesting the dire long-term course of antisocial youths who go untreated. In using more than one "active" treatment during the course of one study, additional youths may be helped while the effects of two (or more) treatments are evaluated.

Selection of Assessment Instruments

The assessment battery for antisocial children typically includes measures of aggressive and antisocial behavior as well as depressive and anxious symptomatology and other problem areas (e.g., substance abuse, attention deficit/hyperactivity problems) to achieve a full diagnostic picture. Kendall and Morris (1991) distinguish between the *specifying level* and the *impact level* in regard to dependent measures in child therapy research. An instrument strong at the specifying level assesses the exact skill(s) that are expected to be affected by treatment (e.g., number of aggressive acts). On the other hand, an instrument strong at the impact level measures the extent to which the treated individual's life is changed by the intervention, generally through examining the impact the individual has on people in her or his natural environment (e.g., peers, parents, teachers). A battery must aim at both of these levels to fully assess the effectiveness of a treatment. Many of the studies reviewed assessed both levels, generally emphasizing one over the other: Kazdin's work emphasizes the impact level; Patterson's work emphasizes the specifying level.

In addition, the selection of dependent measures is influenced by the theoretical orientation of the investigator(s). Family interventions will assess family variables (e.g., coercive process), whereas child-focused interventions will assess individual variables (e.g., cognitive self-talk). Comparative studies will need to include assessments of both sets of variables to best determine a treatment's relative effectiveness. Finally, developmental issues should be considered when dependent measures are selected. A meaningful measure of antisocial behavior for children at the age of 9 may not accurately assess the same target behavior for a child of 12. Issues of sensitivity (i.e., an instrument's ability to detect a problem when it is present) and specificity (i.e., an instrument's ability to discriminate between general difficulties and the particular difficulties—for example, family conflict—that the instrument purports to measure) are critical. Such considerations may require the formulation of new measures or the adaptation of current ones. In the end, compiling a thorough assessment battery is one of the more important tasks facing the researcher of treatment of antisocial behavior in children.

Clinical and Statistical Significance

Finally, the reporting of a treatment's effectiveness should be done in terms of both statistical and clinical significance. Statistical tests are necessary, as they provide evidence of a treatment gain that is beyond chance alone. However, such gains may not necessarily impact the life of each child. Kendall and Grove (1988) outlined the use of normative data to determine the clinical significance of a treatment gain. By assessing how many of the children fall within normative (nonclinical) levels on a particular measure (e.g., Child Behavior Checklist [CBCL]; Achenbach, 1991a), a researcher can report the posttreatment functioning of subjects relative to normative populations. Furthermore, by assessing the degree to which once-identified disordered children are now in the normal range according to measures of functioning provides an important gauge of a treatment's effectiveness.

With antisocial children, measures such as the CBCL may not assess the breadth of the child's difficulties. For example, examining recidivism rates (in cases in which the child has been engaged in illegal activity) becomes an important consideration with CD youths. In fact, given the perseverance of antisocial behavior, some have argued from the "chronic disorder" model that if the gravity of the crimes decreases, the treatment has been somewhat successful. Although the ultimate goals of treatments should continue to be the optimal adjustment for antisocial children, these smaller victories represent important steps on the journey.

Although several advances in methodology have been introduced into treatment outcome research in recent years, a good deal of work remains. Strong research can—and must—be conducted while remaining sensitive to clinical concerns.

CONCLUSIONS AND FUTURE DIRECTIONS

The field has made considerable progress toward the formulation of adequate treatments for antisocial behavior in youths; nevertheless the road remains an arduous one. Many critical arenas of knowledge are poorly understood. In this section, we offer comments and suggestions for future work.

Weisz, Weiss, and Donenberg (1992) identified that although work at research clinics has provided support for the efficacy of therapy with youths, similar research at general service clinics (GSC) has yielded more disappointing results. The transportability to these treatments shown to be effective at research clinics to GSCs stands as one of the largest challenges facing the field (see Kendall & Southam-Gerow, 1995). Kirigin, Braukmann, Atwater, and Wolf (1982) reviewed research on the Teaching-Family program, noting that the group home treatment has been transported to the community frequently (see also Chamberlain & Friman, Chapter 39, this volume). Fleischman and Szykula (1981) reported

an effective transport of Patterson's (1982) parent training program for antisocial children to a GSC; however, the study lacked a control group and did not consider attrition rates in analyzing its results. Future work must endeavor to buttress the bridge between research and practice.

Antisocial children are a heterogeneous group. A more detailed understanding of the extent and nature of the comorbidity of other disorders with aggressive and antisocial behavior will help formulate more sensitive treatment approaches. Careful assessment of the child's family and the child will provide the therapist with the necessary information to select appropriate components for a comprehensive treatment plan. Furthermore, the heterogeneity of family structures and the multicultural nature of our society necessitates the consideration of racial, ethnic, and cultural factors in the formulation of treatment approaches (e.g., Prinz & Miller, 1991; Szapocznik, Kurtines, Santisteban, & Rio, 1990). Additionally, the described prevalence of CD among boys when compared to girls (4 to 1) has been challenged by Zoccolillo and Rogers (1991) and others (see also Calhoun, Jurgens, & Chen, 1993; Giordano & Cernkovich, Chapter 46, this volume). If different symptom clusters (e.g., sexual promiscuity, alcohol abuse) predict CD-like outcomes in girls, are some girls being misdiagnosed?

Some researchers have advocated a chronic disease model for the antisocial aggressive child or adolescent to encourage longer-term care for these youths, noting the stability of aggression across the life span (Kazdin, 1987a; Miller, London, & Prinz, 1991; Wolf, Braukmann, & Ramp, 1987). We agree that such a model will increase treatment and prevention efforts (see Reid & Eddy, Chapter 32, this volume). By clarifying the disastrous course possible for antisocial children along with the difficulties inherent in treating them, preventive and treatment interventions may provide the most cost-effective way for society to deal with the chronic nature of antisocial behavior.

Parent training alone, or cognitive-behavioral approaches alone, will rarely suffice to treat all of the problems of antisocial youths. The integration of family and child-focused approaches (see Fauber & Kendall, 1992) along with one or more of the following will generally be indicated: academic remediation, support and psychotherapy for the parent(s), substance abuse treatment, psychopharmacologic treatment, and treatment for depression for the child, the parent(s) or both. Considering the chronic disorder model, longer-term treatment and scheduled "booster sessions," although now rarely investigated, represent additional avenues of treatment (e.g., Lochman, 1992). Although the costs of these approaches may seem prohibitive, we contend that the costs of failing to do so will be higher. Finally, broader models of antisocial behavior in youth—including biological, familial, social-cognitive, ecological, and developmental factors—need to be developed and evaluated (e.g., Tolan, Guerra, & Kendall, 1995).

Armed with the best possible treatment approaches, we may not solve all the problems suffered and posed by antisocial behavior in children. Aggression and antisocial behavior in children reflect, in part, the violence in society as a whole. Thus, in addition to addressing the antisocial children, we advocate examination of means to reduce aggression in society. This may result in preventive parent training and social-skills training interventions for at-risk youths. Webster-Stratton's (1994) videotape modeling provides one possible method of addressing this task. Finally, the identification and redressing of social factors leading to aggression and antisocial behavior (e.g., economic inequity, neighborhood violence) may provide a most attractive route to significant reduction of antisocial behavior in children. Current thought sometimes considers society's problems to be beyond remedy, but in pursuing the path toward their solution, we may yet discover the best treatment for antisocial behavior.

REFERENCES

Abikoff, H., & Klein, R. G. (1992). Attention-deficit hyperactivity and conduct disorder: Comorbidity and implications for treatment. *Journal of Consulting and Clinical Psychology, 60,* 881–892.

Achenbach, T. M. (1991a). *Manual for the Child Behavior Checklists/4-18 and 1991 profile.* Burlington: University of Vermont.

Achenbach, T. M. (1991b). *Manual for the Teacher's Report Form and 1991 profile.* Burlington: University of Vermont.

American Psychiatric Association. (1994). *Diagnostic and statistical manual of mental disorders* (4th ed.). Washington, DC: Author.

Bates, J. E., Bayles, K., Bennett, D. S., Ridge, B., & Brown, M. M. (1991). Origins of externalizing behavior problems at eight years of age. In D. J. Pepler & K. H. Rubin (Eds.), *The development and treatment of childhood aggression* (pp. 93–120). Hillsdale, NJ: Erlbaum.

Baum, C. G., & Forehand, R. (1981). Long term follow-up assessment of parent training by use of multiple outcome measures. *Behavior Therapy, 12,* 643–652.

Bedlington, M. M., Braukmann, C. J., Ramp, K. A., & Wolf, M. M. (1988). A comparison of treatment environments in community-based group homes for adolescent offenders. *Criminal Justice and Behavior, 15,* 349–363.

Biederman, J., Newcorn, J., & Sprich, S. (1991). Comorbidity of attention deficit hyperactivity disorder with conduct, depressive, anxiety, and other disorders. *American Journal of Psychiatry, 148,* 564–577.

Borduin, C. M., Mann, B. J., Cone, L. T., Henggeler, S. W., Fucci, B. R., Blaske, D. M., & Williams, R. A. (1995). Multisystemic treatment of serious juvenile offenders: Long-term prevention of criminality and violence. *Journal of Consulting and Clinical Psychology, 63,* 569–578.

Brady, E. U., & Kendall, P. C. (1992). Comorbidity of anxiety and depression in children and adolescents. *Psychological Bulletin, 111,* 244–255.

Brennan, P., Mednick, S., & Kandel, E. (1991). Congenital determinants of violent and property offending. In D. J. Pepler & K. H. Rubin (Eds.), *The development and treatment of childhood aggression* (pp. 81–92). Hillsdale, NJ: Erlbaum.

Bukstein, O. G., Brent, D. A., & Kaminer, Y. (1989). Comorbidity of substance abuse and other psychiatric disorders in adolescence. *American Journal of Psychiatry, 146,* 1131–1141.

Calhoun, G., Jurgens, J., & Chen, F. (1993). The neophyte female delinquent: A review of the literature. *Adolescence, 28,* 461–471.

Capaldi, D. M., & Patterson, G. R. (1991). Relation of parental transitions to boys' adjustment problems: I. A linear hypothesis. II. Mothers at risk for transitions and unskilled parenting. *Developmental Psychology, 27,* 489–504.

Carlson, G. A., & Cantwell, D. P. (1980). Unmasking masked depression in children and adolescents. *American Journal of Psychiatry, 137,* 445–449.

Caron, C., & Rutter, M. (1991). Comorbidity in child psychopathology: Concepts, issues and research strategies. *Journal of Child Psychology and Psychiatry, 32,* 1063–1080.

Coie, J. D., Dodge, K. A., & Coppotelli, H. (1982). Dimensions and types of social status: A cross-age perspective. *Developmental Psychology, 18,* 557–570.

Cole, D. A., & Carpentieri, S. (1990). Social status and the comorbidity of child depression and conduct disorder. *Journal of Consulting and Clinical Psychology, 58,* 748–757.

Curry, J. F., Pelissier, B., Woodford, D. J., & Lochman, J. E. (1988). Violent or assaultive youth: Dimensional and categorical comparisons with mental health samples. *Journal of the American Academy of Child and Adolescent Psychiatry, 27,* 226–232.

Dadds, M. R., Sanders, M. R., Morrison, M., & Rebgetz, M. (1992). Childhood depression and conduct disorder: II. An analysis of family interaction patterns in the home. *Journal of Abnormal Psychology, 101,* 505–513.

Dadds, M. R., Schwartz, S., & Sanders, M. R. (1987). Marital discord and treatment outcome in behavioral treatment of child conduct disorders. *Journal of Consulting and Clinical Psychology, 55,* 396–403.

DeMilio, L. (1989). Psychiatric syndromes in adolescent substance abusers. *American Journal of Psychiatry, 146,* 1212–1214.

Dishion, T. J., & Patterson, G. R. (1992). Age effects in parent training outcome. *Behavior Therapy, 23,* 719–729.

Dobson, K. S., & Shaw, B. F. (1988). The use of treatment manuals in cognitive therapy: Experience and issues. *Journal of Consulting and Clinical Psychology, 56,* 673–680.

Dodge, K. A. (1980). Social cognition and children's aggressive behavior. *Child Development, 51,* 162–170.

Dodge, K. A. (1991). The structure and function of reactive and proactive aggression. In D. J. Pepler & K. H. Rubin (Eds.), *The development and treatment of childhood aggression* (pp. 201–218). Hillsdale, NJ: Erlbaum.

Dodge, K. A., & Newman, J. P. (1981). Biased decision making processes in aggressive boys. *Journal of Abnormal Psychology, 90,* 375–379.

Dumas, J. E. (1989). Treating antisocial behavior in children: Child and family approaches. *Clinical Psychology Review, 9,* 197–222.

Eron, L. D., Huesmann, L. R., & Zelli, A. (1991). The role of parental variables in the learning of aggression. In D. J. Pepler & K. H. Rubin (Eds.), *The development and treatment of childhood aggression* (pp. 169–188). Hillsdale, NJ: Erlbaum.

Farrington, D. P., Loeber, R., & Van Kammen, W. B. (1990). Long-term criminal outcomes of hyperactivity-impulsivity-attention deficit and conduct problems in childhood. In L. N. Robins & M. Rutter (Eds.), *Straight and devious pathways from childhood to adulthood* (pp. 62–81). Cambridge: Cambridge University Press.

Fauber, R. L., & Kendall, P. C. (1992). Children and families: Integrating the focus of interventions. *Journal of Psychotherapy Integration, 2,* 107–123.

Fleischman, M. J., & Szykula, S. A. (1981). A community setting replication of a social learning treatment for aggressive children. *Behavior Therapy, 12,* 115–122.

Forehand, R., & Long, N. (1991). Prevention of aggression and other behavior problems in the early adolescent years. In D. J. Pepler & K. H. Rubin (Eds.), *The development and treatment of childhood aggression* (pp. 317–330). Hillsdale, NJ: Erlbaum.

Forgatch, M. S. (1991). The clinical science vortex: A developing theory of antisocial behavior. In D. J. Pepler & K. H. Rubin (Eds.), *The development and treatment of childhood aggression* (pp. 291–315). Hillsdale, NJ: Erlbaum.

Frick, P. J. (1994). Family dysfunction and the disruptive behavior disorders: A review of recent empirical findings. In T. H. Ollendick & R. J. Prinz (Eds.), *Advances in clinical child psychology* (Vol. 16, pp. 203–226). New York: Plenum.

Frick, P. J., Kamphaus, R. W., Lahey, B. J., Loeber, R., Christ, M. A. G., Hart, E. L., & Tannenbaum, L. E. (1991). Academic underachievement and the disruptive behavior disorders. *Journal of Consulting and Clinical Psychology, 59*, 289–294.

Frick, P. J., Lahey, B. B., Christ, M. A. G., Loeber, R., & Green, S. (1991). History of childhood behavior problems in biological relatives of boys with attention deficit hyperactivity disorder and conduct disorder. *Journal of Clinical Child Psychology, 20*, 445–451.

Frick, P. J., Lahey, B. B., Loeber, R., Stouthamer-Loeber, M., Christ, M. A. G., & Hanson, K. (1992). Familial risk factors to oppositional defiant disorder and conduct disorder: Parental psychopathology and maternal parenting. *Journal of Consulting and Clinical Psychology, 60*, 49–55.

Gardner, F. E. M. (1992). Parent-child interaction and conduct disorder. *Educational Psychology Review, 4*, 135–163.

Garrison, S. R., & Stolberg, A. L. (1983). Modification of anger in children by affective imagery training. *Journal of Abnormal Child Psychology, 11*, 115–130.

Guerra, N. G., & Slaby, R. G. (1990). Cognitive mediators of aggression in adolescent offenders: 2. Intervention. *Developmental Psychology, 26*, 269–277.

Haapasalo, J., & Tremblay, R. E. (1994). Physically aggressive boys from ages 6 to 12: Family background, parenting behavior, and prediction of delinquency. *Journal of Consulting and Clinical Psychology, 62*, 1044–1052.

Henggeler, S. W., Melton, G. B., & Smith, L. A. (1992). Family preservation using multisystemic therapy: An effective alternative to incarceration. *Journal of Consulting and Clinical Psychology, 60*, 953–961.

Henggeler, S. W., Rodick, J. D., Borduin, C. M., Hanson, C. L., Watson, S. M., & Urey, J. R. (1986). Multisystemic treatment of juvenile offenders: Effects on adolescent behavior and family interaction. *Developmental Psychology, 22*, 132–141.

Hinshaw, S. P. (1987). On the distinction between attentional deficits/hyperactivity and conduct problems/aggression in child psychopathology. *Psychological Bulletin, 101*, 443–463.

Hinshaw, S. P. (1992). Academic underachievement, attention deficits, and aggression: Comorbidity and implications for intervention. *Journal of Consulting and Clinical Psychology, 60*, 893–903.

Hinshaw, S. P., Lahey, B. B., & Hart, E. L. (1993). Issues of taxonomy and comorbidity in the development of conduct disorder. *Development and Psychopathology, 5*, 31–49.

Horne, A. M., & Sayger, T. V. (1990). *Treating conduct and oppositional defiant disorders in children.* Elmsford, NY: Pergamon.

Huesmann, L. R. (1988). An information processing model for the development of aggression. *Aggressive Behavior, 14*, 13–24.

Kaminer, Y., Tarter, R. E., Bukstein, O. G., & Kabene, M. (1992). Comparison between treatment completers and noncompleters among dually diagnosed substance-abusing adolescents. *Journal of the American Academy of Child and Adolescent Psychiatry, 31*, 1046–1049.

Kazdin, A. E. (1987a). *Conduct disorders in childhood and adolescence.* Newbury Park, CA: Sage Publications.

Kazdin, A. E. (1987b). Treatment of antisocial behavior in children: Current status and future directions. *Psychological Bulletin, 102*, 187–203.

Kazdin, A. E. (1990). Premature termination from treatment among children referred for antisocial behavior. *Journal of Child Psychology, Psychiatry, and Allied Disciplines, 31*, 415–425.

Kazdin, A. E. (1992). *Research designs in clinical psychology* (2nd ed.). Boston: Allyn & Bacon.

Kazdin, A. E. (1993). Treatment of conduct disorder: Progress and directions for psychotherapy research. *Development and Psychopathology, 5*, 277–310.

Kazdin, A. E., Bass, D., Siegel, T., & Thomas, C. (1989). Cognitive-behavioral therapy and relationship therapy in the treatment of children referred for antisocial behavior. *Journal of Consulting and Clinical Psychology, 57*, 522–535.

Kazdin, A. E., Esveldt-Dawson, K., French, N. H., & Unis, A. S. (1987a). Effects of parent management training and problem-solving skills training combined in the treatment of antisocial child behavior. *Journal of the American Academy of Child and Adolescent Psychiatry, 26*, 416–424.

Kazdin, A. E., Esveldt-Dawson, K., French, N. H., & Unis, A. S. (1987b). Problem-solving skills training and relationship therapy in the treatment of antisocial child behavior. *Journal of Consulting and Clinical Psychology, 55*, 76–85.

Kazdin, A. E., Siegel, T. C., & Bass, D. (1992). Cognitive problem-solving skills training and parent management training in the treatment of antisocial behavior in children. *Journal of Consulting and Clinical Psychology, 60*, 733–740.

Kendall, P. C., & Braswell, L. (1993). *Cognitive-behavioral therapy for impulsive children* (2nd ed.). New York: Guilford.

Kendall, P. C., & Clarkin, J. F. (1992). Introduction to Special Section: Comorbidity and treatment implications. *Journal of Consulting and Clinical Psychology, 60*, 833–835.

Kendall, P. C., & Grove, W. (1988). Normative comparisons in therapy outcome. *Behavioral Assessment, 10*, 147–158.

Kendall, P. C., & MacDonald, J. P. (1993). Cognition in the psychopathology of youth and implications for treatment. In K. S. Dobson & P. C. Kendall (Eds.), *Psychopathology and cognition* (pp. 387–432). San Diego: Academic Press.

Kendall, P. C., & Morris, R. (1991). Child therapy: Issues and recommendations. *Journal of Consulting and Clinical Psychology, 60*, 869–880.

Kendall, P. C., & Norton-Ford, J. D. (1982). Therapy outcome research methods. In P. C. Kendall & J. N. Butcher (Eds.), *Handbook of research methods in clinical psychology* (pp. 429–460). New York: Wiley.

Kendall, P. C., Reber, M., McLeer, S., Epps, J., & Ronan, K. R. (1990). Cognitive-behavioral treatment of conduct-disordered children. *Cognitive Therapy and Research, 14*, 279–297.

Kendall, P. C., Ronan, K. R., & Epps, J. (1991). Aggression in children/adolescents: Cognitive-behavioral treatment perspectives. In D. J. Pepler & K. H. Rubin (Eds.), *Development and treatment of childhood aggression* (pp. 341–360). Hillsdale, NJ: Erlbaum.

Kendall, P. C., & Siqueland, L. (1989). Child and adolescent therapy. In A. M. Nezu & C. M. Nezu (Eds.), *Clinical decision making in behavior therapy: A problem-solving perspective* (pp. 321–336). Champaign, IL: Research Press.

Kendall, P. C., & Southam-Gerow, M. A. (1995). Issues in the transportability of treatment: The case of anxiety disorders in youth. *Journal of Consulting and Clinical Psychology, 63*, 702–708.

Kirigin, K. A., Braukmann, C. J., Atwater, J. D., & Wolf, M. M. (1982). An evaluation of Teaching-Family (Achievement Place) group homes for juvenile offenders. *Journal of Applied Behavior Analysis, 15*, 1–16.

Kolko, D. J., Loar, L. L., & Sturnick, D. (1990). Inpatient social-cognitive skills training groups with conduct disordered and attention deficit disordered children. *Journal of Child Psychology, Psychiatry, and Allied Disciplines, 31*, 737–748.

Lipsey, M. W. (1992, October–November). *The effects of treatment on juvenile delinquents: Results from meta-analysis.* From NIMH Meeting for Potential Applicants for Research to Prevent Youth Violence, Bethesda, MD.

Lochman, J. E. (1992). Cognitive-behavioral intervention with aggressive boys: Three-year follow-up and preventive effects. *Journal of Consulting and Clinical Psychology, 60,* 426–432.

Lochman, J. E., White, J. E., & Wayland, K. K. (1991). Cognitive-behavioral assessment and treatment with aggressive children. In P. C. Kendall (Ed.), *Child and adolescent therapy: Cognitive-behavioral procedures* (pp. 25–65). New York: Guilford.

Loeber, R. (1982). The stability of antisocial and delinquent child behavior: A review. *Child Development, 53,* 1431–1446.

Loeber, R. (1988). Natural histories of conduct problems, delinquency, and associated substance use: Evidence for developmental progressions. In B. B. Lahey & A. E. Kazdin (Eds.), *Advances in clinical child psychology* (Vol. 11, pp. 73–124). New York: Plenum.

Lynam, D. R. (1996). Early identification of chronic offenders: Who is the fledgling psychopath? *Psychological Bulletin, 120,* 209–234.

Lytton, H. (1990). Child and parent effects in boys' conduct disorder: A reinterpretation. *Developmental Psychology, 26,* 683–697.

McCord, J. (1993). Conduct disorder and antisocial behavior: Some thoughts about processes. *Development and Psychopathology, 5,* 321–329.

Milin, R., Halikas, J. A., Meller, J. E., & Morse, C. (1991). Psychopathology among substance abusing juvenile offenders. *Journal of the American Academy of Child and Adolescent Psychiatry, 30,* 569–574.

Miller, G. E., London, L. H., & Prinz, R. J. (1991). Understanding and treating serious childhood behavior disorders. *Family and Community Health, 14,* 33–41.

Miller, G. E., & Prinz, R. J. (1990). Enhancement of social learning family interventions for childhood conduct disorder. *Psychological Bulletin, 108,* 291–307.

Miller, L. S. (1994). Preventive interventions for conduct disorders: A review. *Child and Adolescent Psychiatric Clinics of North America, 3,* 405–420.

Moffitt, T. E. (1993). Adolescence-limited and life-course-persistent antisocial behavior: A developmental taxonomy. *Psychological Review, 100,* 674–701.

Nottelmann, E. D., & Jensen, P. S. (1995). Comorbidity of disorders in children and adolescents: Developmental perspectives. In T. H. Ollendick & R. J. Prinz (Eds.), *Advances in clinical child psychology* (Vol. 17, pp. 109–155). New York: Plenum.

Olweus, D. (1979). Stability of aggressive reactive patterns in males: A review. *Psychological Bulletin, 86,* 852–875.

Patterson, G. R. (1982). *Coercive family process.* Eugene, OR: Castalia.

Patterson, G. R., Capaldi, D., & Bank, L. (1991). An early starter model for predicting delinquency. In D. J. Pepler & K. H. Rubin (Eds.), *The development and treatment of childhood aggression* (pp. 131–168). Hillsdale, NJ: Erlbaum.

Patterson, G. R., & Chamberlain, P. (1994). A functional analysis of resistance during parent training therapy. *Clinical Psychology: Science and Practice, 1,* 53–70.

Patterson, G. R., Chamberlain, P., & Reid, J. B. (1982). A comparative evaluation of a parent-training program. *Behavior Therapy, 13,* 638–650.

Patterson, G. R., DeBaryshe, B. D., & Ramsey, E. (1989). A developmental perspective on antisocial behavior. *American Psychologist, 44,* 329–335.

Patterson, G. R., Reid, J. B., & Dishion, T. J. (1992). *Antisocial boys.* Eugene, OR: Castalia.

Pelham, W. E., & Lang, A. R. (1993). Parental alcohol consumption and deviant child behavior: Laboratory studies of reciprocal effects. *Clinical Psychology Review, 13,* 763–784.

Pfiffner, L. J., Jouriles, E. N., Brown, M. M., Etscheidt, M. A., & Kelly, J. A. (1990). Effects of problem-solving therapy on outcomes of parent training for single-parent families. *Child and Family Behavior Therapy, 12,* 1–11.

Phillips, E. L., Phillips, E. A., Fixsen, D. L., & Wolf, M. M. (1974). *The teaching-family handbook.* Lawrence: University of Kansas Printing Service.

Phillips, E. L., Phillips, E. A., Wolf, M. M., & Fixsen, D. L. (1973). Achievement Place: Development of the elected manager system. *Journal of Applied Behavior Analysis, 6,* 541–561.

Pincus, J. H. (1987). A neurological view of violence. In D. H. Crowell, I. M. Evans, & C. R. O'Donnell (Eds.), *Childhood aggression and violence: Sources of influence, prevention, and control* (pp. 53–73). New York: Plenum.

Prinz, R. J., & Miller, G. E. (1991). Issues in understanding and treating childhood conduct problems in disadvantaged populations. *Journal of Clinical Child Psychology, 20,* 379–385.

Raine, A., Brennan, P., & Mednick, S. A. (1994). Birth complications combined with early maternal rejection at age 1 year predispose to violent crime at age 18 years. *Archives of General Psychiatry, 51,* 984–988.

Raine, A., Venables, P. H., & Williams, M. (1990). Relationships between CNS and ANS measures of arousal at age 15 and criminality at age 24. *Archives of General Psychiatry, 47,* 1003–1007.

Reeves, J. C., Werry, J. S., Elkind, G. S., & Zametkin, A. (1987). Attention deficit, conduct, oppositional, and anxiety disorders in children: II. Clinical characteristics. *Journal of the American Academy of Child and Adolescent Psychiatry, 26,* 144–155.

Robins, L. N. (1966). *Deviant children grown up: A sociological and psychiatric study of sociopathic personality.* Baltimore: Williams & Williams.

Sanders, M. R., Dadds, M. R., Johnston, B. M., & Cash, R. (1992). Childhood depression and conduct disorder: I. Behavioral, affective, and cognitive aspects of family problem-solving interactions. *Journal of Abnormal Psychology, 101,* 495–504.

Slaby, R. G., & Guerra, N. G. (1988). Cognitive mediators of aggression in adolescent offenders. 1. Assessment. *Developmental Psychology, 24,* 580–588.

Spivack, G., & Shure, M. B. (1974). *Social adjustment of young children.* San Francisco: Jossey-Bass.

Stewart, M. A. (1985). Aggressive conduct disorder: A brief review. *Aggressive Behavior, 11,* 323–331.

Stoff, D. M., Friedman, E., Pollock, L., Vitiello, B., Kendall, P. C., & Bridger, W. H. (1989). Elevated platelet MAO is related to impulsivity in disruptive behavior disorders. *Journal of the American Academy of Child and Adolescent Psychiatry, 28,* 754–760.

Stoolmiller, M., Duncan, T., Bank, L., & Patterson, G. R. (1993). Some problems and solutions in the study of change: Significant patterns in client resistance. *Journal of Consulting and Clinical Psychology, 61,* 920–928.

Szapocznik, J., Kurtines, W., Santisteban, D. A., & Rio, A. T. (1990). Interplay of advances between theory, research, and application in treatment interventions aimed at behavior problem children and adolescents. *Journal of Consulting and Clinical Psychology, 58,* 696–703.

Szatmari, P., Boyle, M., & Offord, D. R. (1989). ADDH and conduct disorder: Degree of diagnostic overlap and differences among correlates. *Journal of the American Academy of Child and Adolescent Psychiatry, 28,* 865–872.

Tolan, P. H., Guerra, N. G., & Kendall, P. C. (1995). A developmental-ecological perspective on antisocial behavior in children and adolescents: Toward a unified risk and intervention framework. *Journal of Consulting and Clinical Psychology, 63,* 579–584.

Tremblay, R. E., Pihl, R. O., Vitaro, F., & Dobkin, P. L. (1994). Predicting early onset of male antisocial behavior from preschool behavior. *Archives of General Psychiatry, 51,* 732–739.

Vuchinich, S., Bank, L., & Patterson, G. R. (1992). Parenting, peers, and the stability of antisocial behavior in preadolescent boys. *Developmental Psychology, 28,* 510–521.

Wahler, R. G. (1980). The insular mother: Her problems in parent-child treatment. *Journal of Applied Behavior Analysis, 13,* 207–219.

Wahler, R. G., & Dumas, J. E. (1989). Attentional problems in dysfunctional mother-child interactions: An interbehavioral model. *Psychological Bulletin, 105,* 116–130.

Walker, J. L., Lahey, B. J., Hynd, G. W., & Frame, C. L. (1987). Comparisons of specific patterns of antisocial behavior in children with conduct disorder with or without coexisting hyperactivity. *Journal of Consulting and Clinical Psychology, 55,* 910–913.

Webster-Stratton, C. (1985). Predictors of treatment outcome in parent training for conduct disordered children. *Behavior Therapy, 16,* 223–243.

Webster-Stratton, C. (1994). Advancing videotape parent training: A comparison study. *Journal of Consulting and Clinical Psychology, 62,* 583–593.

Webster-Stratton, C., Kolpacoff, M., & Hollinsworth, T. (1988). Self-administered videotape therapy for families with conduct-problem children: Comparison with two cost-effective treatments and a control group. *Journal of Consulting and Clinical Psychology, 56,* 558–566.

Webster-Stratton, C., & Hammond, M. (1997). Treating children with early-onset conduct problems: A comparison of child and parent training interventions. *Journal of Consulting and Clinical Psychology, 65,* 93–109.

Weisz, J. R., Weiss, B., & Donenberg, G. R. (1992). The lab versus the clinic: Effects of child and adolescent psychotherapy. *American Psychologist, 47,* 1578–1585.

Werry, J. S., Reeves, J. C., & Elkind, G. S. (1987). Attention deficit, conduct, oppositional, and anxiety disorders in children: I. A review of research on differentiating characteristics. *Journal of the American Academy of Child and Adolescent Psychiatry, 26,* 133–143.

West, M. O., & Prinz, R. J. (1987). Parent alcoholism and childhood psychopathology. *Psychological Bulletin, 102,* 204–218.

Wolf, M. M., Braukmann, C. J., & Ramp, K. A. (1987). Serious delinquent behavior as part of a significantly handicapping condition: Cures and supportive environments. *Journal of Applied Behavior Analysis, 20,* 347–359.

Wootton, J. M., Frick, P. J., Shelton, K. K., & Silverthorn, P. (1997). Ineffective parenting and childhood conduct problems: The moderating role of callous unemotional traits. *Journal of Consulting and Clinical Psychology, 65,* 301–308.

Zoccolillo, M., & Rogers, K. (1991). Characteristics and outcome of hospitalized adolescent girls with conduct disorder. *Journal of the American Academy of Child and Adolescent Psychiatry, 30,* 973–981.

CHAPTER 37

Culturally Competent Psychosocial Interventions With Antisocial Problem Behavior in Hispanic Youths

J. DOUGLAS COATSWORTH, JOSÉ SZAPOCZNIK, WILLIAM KURTINES, and DANIEL A. SANTISTEBAN

A major concern in the literature on antisocial problem behaviors has been the development and evaluation of interventions to prevent or reduce the occurrence of these problem behaviors in children and adolescents (Kazdin, 1987; Tolan, Guerra, & Kendall, 1995; see also Guerra, Attar, & Weissberg, Chapter 35, this volume). An important corollary of this concern is the increased need to identify or develop culturally competent interventions to serve ethnic minority populations (Kazdin, 1993; Sue, Zane, & Young, 1994; Tolan et al., 1995). The success of interventions with antisocial problem behavior youths may depend greatly on the social and physical context in which interventions are delivered (e.g., Bourdin et al., 1995). Ensuring that the context of the intervention and the method of service delivery are compatible with the expectations of the participants/clients increases the probability of a successful intervention. There is also recognition of how the major contexts for intervention—the family, school, or community—are each embedded within the context of culture (Szapocznik & Kurtines, 1993). Clearly, recognizing the influence of culture and considering its potential influence at all levels of an intervention, from theoretical background, to intervention design, to staffing and implementation, to evaluation, are critical to the overall success of the intervention.

Although progress has been made in studying the mental health needs of culturally diverse groups, research on the development and evaluation of culturally competent psychosocial interventions with culturally diverse populations is sparse (Sue et al., 1994). The construction of culturally competent interventions involves more than sensitivity to issues of culture. It reflects the

acquisition and mastery of knowledge and skills required to fully integrate a cultural perspective into an intervention in such a way that participants will accept it, the probability of success will increase, and the ensuing gains will be valued by the participants (Institute of Medicine, 1994; Orlandi, 1992). Culturally competent interventions are the result of the cumulative progress of knowledge in which advances in the theoretical domain contribute to innovative research, which in turn informs theory and guides the development of culturally competent interventions. Systematic programs of research create a unique context for the evolution of culturally competent interventions. The systematic nature of these research programs is such that advances are not always ground breaking, and lessons are frequently hard-won, but the cumulative knowledge gained and the diversity of the lessons create the setting from which culturally competent interventions emerge.

This chapter has two primary aims. The first is to provide the results of a review of the empirical literature on interventions with antisocial problem behavior Hispanic youths. The second, more general aim, is to discuss the process of developing and evaluating culturally competent interventions and several basic issues that must be addressed along the way.

A REVIEW OF THE LITERATURE ON CULTURALLY COMPETENT INTERVENTIONS WITH HISPANICS

A systematic search of the literature from 1974 to 1995 using the computerized PsychLit database was conducted to identify programs of intervention research with Hispanic antisocial and behavior problem youths that have yielded empirically tested, culturally competent interventions. The results of the search identified only two systematic programs of intervention research: one at the Hispanic Research Center at Fordham University (Rogler, Malgady, & Rodriguez, 1989; Malgady & Rodriguez, 1994), and the other, our own at the University of Miami's Spanish Family Guidance Center and the Center for Family Studies (Szapocznik et al., 1996). No randomized studies of intervention research with Hispanic antisocial youths were found outside of these programs. However, the literature search did identify a broad spectrum of work including an array of clinical reports, often presenting

This work was funded by Grant Number 3481 from the National Institute of Mental Health, Grant Number DA5334 from the National Institute on Drug Abuse, Grant Number 1H86 SPO2350 from the Center for Substance Abuse Prevention, Grant Number 1 HD7 TI00417 from the Center for Substance Abuse Treatment, Grant Number 90CL1111 from the Administration for Children, Youth and Families and Grant Number 90PD0211 from the Administration for Children and Families, Department of Health and Human Services to José Szapocznik, Center for Family Studies/Spanish Family Guidance Center, University of Miami; by Grant Number 1 P50 DA07697 to Howard Liddle, Ed.D.

descriptive observations of values, beliefs, and customs associated with Hispanic culture, small cross-cultural research studies comparing two or more ethnic/cultural groups, and clinicians' descriptions of Hispanic values and reflections on the implications for treatment. Despite this large literature, most of these observations have not been tested with controlled observations.

Empirical Studies of Interventions With Hispanic Youths

The Hispanic Research Center at Fordham University

Lloyd Rogler and his colleagues at the Hispanic Research Center have produced a systematic program of research investigating the nature and relationship between cultural factors and mental health in Hispanics (see Rogler et al., 1989; Malgady & Rodriguez, 1994). Although not specific to children and adolescents manifesting antisocial behavior problems, this program demonstrates the development and evaluation of culturally competent interventions and has implications for prevention and treatment of antisocial problem behaviors. The program of research has followed a conceptual framework that organized their work into five phases of research progressing from (a) the identification of factors associated with mental health problems in Hispanics to (b) help seeking efforts, to (c) evaluation and diagnosis of client disorders and problems, to (d) implementing therapeutic interventions, to (e) the client's resumption of postintervention social roles (Rogler et al., 1989). Building on prior phases, this research program has yielded several empirical studies investigating the efficacy of culturally competent treatment modalities for Puerto Rican children, adolescents, and adults (cf. Costantino, Malgady, & Rogler, 1986; Malgady, Rogler, & Costantino, 1990a, 1990b).

In their initial intervention study, Costantino, Malgady, and Rogler (1986) integrated Puerto Rican *cuentos* (folktales) to convey a cultural theme or moral within a framework of modeling therapy. One intervention used the *cuentos* in their natural form; a second adapted these *cuentos* to bridge Puerto Rican and American cultures. The design also included an art/play therapy condition and a no-intervention control. A total of 210 Puerto Rican children (grades kindergarten through 3; mean age = 7.45 years) were stratified by sex and grade and randomly assigned to one of the four intervention conditions.

Analyses revealed immediate treatment effects on anxiety symptoms, but only for first graders. First graders who participated in the adapted *cuento* modality demonstrated significantly lower levels of anxiety symptoms when compared with both control conditions. Children in the original *cuento* therapy showed lower anxiety compared to the no-treatment control group but were not significantly different from the art/play control group. However, 1-year follow-up treatment effects were evident for all grades, with both the original and adapted *cuento* groups showing reduced anxiety in comparison to the two control groups. Treatment effects for social judgment for both experimental treatments were evident only immediately following treatment and not at follow-up. In comparison to the art/play control group, both *cuento* interventions demonstrated reductions in conduct problems (aggression, disruptiveness, and inability to delay gratification). However, neither experimental intervention showed effects when compared to the no-treatment control group.

In their second intervention, modifications were made to develop a *cuento* therapy for high-risk Puerto Rican adolescents. Biographical stories of prominent Puerto Ricans were used to expose the youths to role models of achievement in an effort to promote ethnic pride, ethnic identity, and adaptive behaviors for coping with the stresses of poverty, discrimination, and urban life (Malgady et al., 1990b). By integrating themes of cultural conflict within the stories, Malgady and colleagues were able to highlight the real-life struggles of these adolescents attempting to bridge two cultures. Forty male and 50 female Puerto Rican adolescents in grades 8 and 9, identified to be at elevated risk by teacher ratings of behavior problems, were randomly assigned to either the experimental intervention or an attention control. Results indicated that the experimental intervention was more effective than the attention control in reducing anxiety symptoms and in increasing self-concept and ethnic identity. These results were moderated by sex and the father's presence in the family structure. In households in which the father was absent, treatment enhanced self-concept and ethnic identity. However, in households in which the father was present, treatment did not affect males' self-concept and ethnic identity but had a negative effect on adolescent girls' self-image.

This unexpected negative finding highlights the need for understanding the complex interactions between important aspects of the adolescents' social contexts, such as family composition or intrafamilial relationships, gender, and the broader context of culture. Even sophisticated culturally sensitive intervention models may have unintended effects. Given the complexity of the relations and processes interventions try to modify, it should not be surprising that they are not universally effective. Thus the ensuing research task becomes using these results to inform theory and future research endeavors that will yield improved interventions targeting newly recognized relations.

A third study from the same team investigated the storytelling modality based on pictorial stimuli rather than on verbal or written stimuli (Costantino & Rivera, 1994). Eight pictures from the Tell-Me-A-Story (TEMAS) thematic apperception test (Costantino, 1987), depicting a variety of multiracial Hispanic characters in culturally appropriate family school and urban settings, were used as the cultural content of the intervention. The treatment, conducted in a group format, involved three phases—producing a composite story about the picture, sharing personal experiences and feelings, and finally, role-playing and reinforcement of imitative behaviors. High-risk Hispanic children in grades 4 through 6 were recruited to participate and were screened using a diagnostic interview. Students were selected for the study if they were among the 30 most symptomatic in the diagnostic categories of conduct, anxiety, and phobic disorders. Students were stratified by grade and sex and randomized to experimental or attention control conditions. Results indicated that the experimental intervention produced immediate postintervention effects on anxiety and phobic symptoms and on behavioral conduct in school as rated by their teachers.

The theoretical notion underlying all three of these interventions is that cultural conflict is at the root of symptomatic behavior among Hispanic (Puerto Rican) children and adolescents (Malgady et al., 1990a; Malgady & Rodriguez, 1994). Given this idea as the primary theoretical structure, the research group has focused on developing culturally competent interventions with the resolution of cultural conflict as their primary goal. In designing culturally competent interventions, Rogler and his colleagues have used the client's cultural values as a "vehicle" for the therapeutic intervention (Costantino & Rivera, 1994). Results of these three outcome studies yielded findings suggesting that these intervention modalities were efficacious in reducing psychological symptoms or increasing self-image in Hispanic youths.

The Spanish Family Guidance Center/Center for Family Studies

The second major program of research culminating in the empirical evaluation of culturally competent interventions has been conducted by our own team of researchers from the Spanish Family Guidance Center/Center for Family Studies at the University of Miami. In describing our work, we illustrate the evolution of a systematic program of research for developing and evaluating prevention and treatment interventions with antisocial problem behavior Hispanic youths. To advance the investigation and the prevention and treatment of Hispanic adolescent antisocial problem behavior, we reframed the challenges inherent to culturally competent intervention research into research questions, the answers to which could be pursued within the framework of a rigorous program of systematic research. In translating these challenges into research questions, methodological issues had to be resolved, resulting in some of our most important breakthroughs in theoretical understanding. Likewise, advances in our theoretical understanding have resulted in progress in overcoming obstacles to resolving clinical problems as well as in some of our most important methodological advances (Szapocznik & Kurtines, 1989, 1993; Szapocznik, Kurtines, Perez-Vidal, Hervis, & Foote, 1990; Szapocznik, Perez-Vidal, Hervis, Brickman, & Kurtines, 1990). Thus, the evolution of our approach has been guided by the view that research must be both a final step in the completion of each stage of knowledge development and a solid foundation from which to pursue new theoretical and applied breakthroughs.

With respect to theory, our approach draws on both the structural (Minuchin, 1974; Minuchin & Fishman, 1981; Minuchin, Rosman, & Baker, 1978) and strategic (Haley, 1976; Madanes, 1981) traditions in family systems theory. With respect to application, our work has focused on developing prevention and treatment interventions for antisocial problem behavior and drug abuse among Hispanic children and adolescents. This research has involved the investigation of the cultural characteristics of our Hispanic population (primarily Cuban American in the 1970s and 1980s, but increasingly Nicaraguan, Columbian, Puerto Rican, Peruvian, and Salvadoran in the 1990s), the role that cultural factors may play in the process of prevention and treatment, and the role cultural factors may play in determining differential outcomes. Our efforts to develop and investigate novel, theoretically based, and culturally appropriate interventions that can be used in the prevention and treatment of behavior problems and drug abuse among Hispanic youths has led directly to a structural and family-based approach to working with Hispanic families (Szapocznik, Kurtines, & Santisteban, 1994; Szapocznik et al., 1996).

In 1972 the Spanish Family Guidance Center was established in Miami, Florida, in response to an alarming increase in the number of Hispanic adolescents with antisocial problem behaviors. One of the first challenges we encountered was to identify and develop a culturally appropriate and acceptable treatment intervention for antisocial problem behavior Cuban youths. Our starting point was to develop a better understanding of how the transplanted Cuban culture resembled, and differed from, the mainstream culture of the Miami area. To accomplish this, a comprehensive empirical study on value orientations was designed based on the pioneer work on worldviews by Kluckhohn and Strodtbeck (1961). The major study on value orientation (Szapocznik, Scopetta, Aranalde, & Kurtines, 1978) that ensued determined that a family-oriented approach in which therapists take an active, directive, present-oriented leadership role matched the expectations of our population. This was the first indicator that a structural and systemic approach to family therapy was particularly well suited for this population (Szapocznik, Scopetta, & King, 1978). The finding permitted us to articulate a culturally compatible theory of change that incorporated an understanding of both the transcultural therapeutic change processes and the culture-specific content required to intervene with this population.

A second area of inquiry that directed us in refining our theory of change and defining our intervention modality was our work investigating the strains of acculturation. These studies showed that different rates of acculturation among family members cause disruptions within the family that require direct intervention (Szapocznik & Kurtines, 1979; Szapocznik, Kurtines, & Fernandez, 1980; Szapocznik, Scopetta, Kurtines, & Aranalde, 1978). More specifically, we demonstrated that normal transcultural family processes may combine with acculturation processes to exaggerate intergenerational differences and exacerbate intrafamilial conflicts (Szapocznik, Santisteban, Kurtines, Perez-Vidal, & Hervis, 1984). A prototypical example can be found in the case of Hispanic immigrants who find themselves in a bicultural context. In this case, the adolescent's normal striving for independence combines with the adolescent's powerful acculturation to the American cultural value of individualism. The parent's normal tendency to preserve family integrity, on the other hand, combines with a tenacious adherence to the Hispanic cultural value on strong family cohesion and parental control. The combination of the intergenerational and cultural differences exacerbates intrafamilial conflict in which parents and adolescents feel alienated from each other. Results of these studies also suggested that structural family therapy was well suited for the treatment of these intergenerational/acculturational problems (Szapocznik, Scopetta, & King, 1978).

Structural family therapy is particularly well suited to address the kinds of problems observed in our population because it is possible to separate content from process. At the content level, the cultural and intergenerational conflicts can be the focus of attention and make the therapy particularly attuned to the Hispanic family. At the process level, structural family therapy seeks to modify the breakdown in communication resulting from these intensified cultural and intergenerational conflicts. More specifically, in treating Hispanic families, the *content* of therapy may be issues of cultural differences, differences in rates of acculturation, and parental adjustments to changes in their adolescent. Work at the *process* level promotes more adaptive communication between family members, thus dissolving barriers to discussion of topics such as those mentioned earlier. In this way, therapy can be tailored to the specific and unique cultural and intergenerational conflicts.

These theoretical advancements led directly to our initial efforts to investigate the therapeutic efficacy of a family-oriented intervention with Hispanic families. A series of pilot research studies (Scopetta et al., 1977) compared individual, conjoint family, and family ecological interventions. These pilot studies provided evidence that structural family therapy was compatible with the issues and problems of our Hispanic population. However, they also suggested the need to modify certain intervention components, such as making the modality strategic and time-limited. To distinguish the particular structural family therapy approach that emerged from this phase of our work, we termed it Brief Strategic Family Therapy (BSFT). Since 1975 we have conducted a large number of funded studies on BSFT and on its specialized applications (see Szapocznik, Kurtines, Santisteban, & Rio, 1990).

Bicultural Effectiveness Training and Family Effectiveness Training

Our first efforts at developing specialized applications of BSFT sought to address the impact that immigration and acculturation had on our families. Some families required an intervention designed specifically for this constellation of problems. As a result, we developed Bicultural Effectiveness Training (BET; Szapocznik et al., 1984), an intervention to enhance bicultural skills in two-generation Hispanic immigrant families that addresses family conflicts that arose from differential intergenerational acculturation rates and the consequent adolescent disruptive/conduct problems. BET, a 12-session psychoeducational intervention, is based on a strategy that provides families and family members with skills for effectively coping with manifestly conflicting cultural values and behavioral expectations. BET teaches families to feel enriched rather than stressed by the unique opportunities provided them in their daily transcultural existence.

A clinical trial was conducted to investigate the relative efficacy of BET in comparison to structural family therapy (Szapocznik, Santisteban, Rio, Perez-Vidal, Kurtines, & Hervis, 1986). Forty-one Cuban American families with a behavior problem adolescent were randomly assigned to either BET or a structural family therapy condition. The results of this study indicated that BET was as effective as structural family therapy in bringing about improvement in adolescent and family functioning. These findings suggested that BET could accomplish the goals of family therapy while focusing on the cultural content that made therapy attractive to Hispanic families.

Subsequently, we combined BSFT and BET into a prevention/intervention modality that we called Family Effectiveness Training (FET; Szapocznik, Santisteban, Rio, Perez-Vidal, & Kurtines, 1986). The efficacy of FET was evaluated in a study with 79 Hispanic families with children ages 6 to 11 presenting with emotional and behavioral problems (Szapocznik, Santisteban, Rio, Perez-Vidal, Santisteban, & Kurtines, 1989). Families were randomly assigned to FET or a Minimum Contact Control condition. The results indicated that families in the FET condition showed significantly greater improvement than did control families on dependent measures of structural family functioning, adolescent problem behaviors as reported by parents, and child self-

concept. Thus, the intervention was able to successfully improve functioning of both the child and the family. Furthermore, follow-up assessments indicated that the impact of the FET intervention was maintained.

Measurement Issues

Our efforts to evaluate culturally competent interventions forced us to make advancements in the area of culturally appropriate measures and methods. Our main research challenge was to develop a measure for Hispanic families that was appropriate for our structural theory, clinically relevant, and psychometrically sound.

To launch this work, we borrowed from the work of Minuchin and his colleagues with the Wiltwick Family Tasks (Minuchin et al., 1978), a structured procedure in which families are instructed to plan a menu, discuss their likes and dislikes about other family members, and discuss the last family argument. The tasks were useful as standard stimuli, but the scoring of these tasks presented problems of standardization and reliability. For this reason, we reorganized the scoring procedure into broad, theoretically and clinically important dimensions of structural family functioning; standardized the administration procedure (Hervis, Szapocznik, Mitrani, Rio, & Kurtines, 1991); developed a detailed manual with anchors and examples to enhance reliability and replicability of the scoring procedure; and obtained validational evidence for the usefulness and nonobtrusiveness of the procedure in family therapy outcome studies (Szapocznik, Rio, Hervis, Mitrani, Kurtines, & Faraci, 1991).

The Structural Family Systems Ratings (SFSR) developed in response to this research need defines family structure as the family's repetitive patterns of interactions along five interrelated dimensions. *Structure* is the basic and most important dimension and is a measure of leadership, subsystem organization, and communication flow. *Resonance* is a measure of the sensitivity of family members toward one another. It focuses on boundaries and emotional distance between family members. *Developmental stage* assesses the extent to which each family member's roles and tasks correspond with the developmental stage within the family. *Identified patienthood* assesses the extent to which the family operates as if the primary family problem is the fault of one member who exhibits the symptom. Last, *conflict resolution* is a measure of the family's style in managing disagreements and conflicts.

The psychometric properties of the SFSR were investigated using data from more than 500 Hispanic families participating in treatment. Both content and construct validity were explored (Szapocznik et al., 1991). Content validity was built into the SFSR by developing the scales to tap structural concepts. Construct validity was extensively examined revealing that the SFSR measures improvements resulting from structural family therapy and that it discriminates between interventions that are and are not expected to bring about structural family change. Data addressing the factor structure of the scales and interrater reliabilities were also obtained.

The SFSR represents one of the most important measurement advances of our program of research. The SFSR is a theoretically meaningful measure of structural family functioning that has become an essential tool for answering some of the critical questions posed by subsequent steps in our keep research. We have continued to refine the SFSR, extending its use to nonresearch clinical settings (cf. Szapocznik & Kurtines, 1989) and adapting it to the range of family constellations that occur in our minority communities of the 1990s, including single parent and extended kinships.

Engaging Families Into Treatment

Results from our intervention studies suggested an additional clinical/application challenge confronted us: engaging families into the intervention. In response, we developed a culturally competent intervention based on our structural and systems perspectives. The approach, Strategic Structural Systems Engagement (SSSE; Szapocznik, Perez-Vidal et al., 1990; Szapocznik & Kurtines, 1989), is based on the premise that whatever the initial presenting symptom may be, the initial obstacle to change is "resistance" to coming into treatment. When resistance is defined as the symptom to be targeted by the intervention, the structural systems model also defines it as a manifestation or symptom of the family's current pattern of interaction. Therefore, we have argued (Szapocznik, Perez-Vidal et al., 1990) that the same systemic and structural principles that apply to the understanding of family functioning and treatment also apply to the understanding and treatment of the family's resistance to engagement.

It follows from the strategic structural model that the solution to overcoming the undesirable "symptom" of resistance is to restructure the family's patterns of interaction that permit the symptom to exist. Once the first phase of the therapeutic process in which resistance is overcome and the family agrees to participate has been accomplished, it becomes possible to shift the focus of the intervention toward removing the presenting symptoms of problem behavior and drug abuse. A more recent reconceptualization of this work (Santisteban & Szapocznik, 1994) has refocused the locus of resistance to the therapist because it became clearer that when therapists changed their behavior (by using SSSE techniques) the family's resistance was overcome.

In a process similar to how theoretical advances in our structural family therapy intervention theory demanded progress in our measurement strategy, theoretical advances in understanding the nature of resistance to entering treatment and the concomitant advances in developing strategies for overcoming this type of resistance required a reconceptualization of our approach to treatment outcome measures. Because the problem to be addressed was that of getting the family into therapy, we had to move beyond the analysis of pre- to postoutcome measures to rates of engagement and maintenance through treatment completion as indexes of intervention efficacy.

In most treatment outcome studies, outcome is assessed for those subjects who complete the intervention or control conditions. Because so many studies suggest that there are no differential treatment effects among completers, differential retention/attrition rates may be a critically important measure that distinguishes between different types of interventions (Kazdin, 1986). Acknowledging that treatment outcome assesses efficacy on only a highly selected sample (treatment completers) highlights the enormous importance that attrition and retention have as complementary measures of efficacy. It follows that interventions should be assessed first in terms of their ability to engage and retain subjects/clients and, second, using the more conventional measures of outcome efficacy applied to treatment survivors.

The efficacy of SSSE in engaging and bringing to therapy completion Hispanic families with drug-abusing youths was tested in a major clinical trial (Szapocznik et al., 1988) in which 108 Hispanic families with behavior problem adolescents (who were also suspected of, or were observed, using drugs) were randomly assigned to one of two conditions: SSSE or an Engagement as Usual control condition. In this control condition, the clients were approached in a way that resembled as closely as possible the kind of engagement that usually takes place in outpatient centers. In the experimental condition, client-families were engaged using techniques developed specifically for use with families that resist therapy. Considerable work was done in developing a manual for the experimental condition (Szapocznik & Kurtines, 1989; Szapocznik, Kurtines, Santisteban et al., 1990) and in describing modality guidelines for both conditions to ensure standardization and replicability of the study.

There were two basic findings: First, SSSE demonstrated substantial efficacy in engaging and maintaining families in treatment. Whereas 57% of the families in the Engagement as Usual condition failed to engage into treatment, the rate was only 7% in the SSSE condition. Of those who engaged into treatment, 41% in the Engagement as Usual condition dropped out compared to 17% in the SSSE condition. Thus, of all of the cases that were initially assigned, 77% in the Structural Systems Engagement condition were successfully terminated compared to only 25% in the Engagement as Usual condition. Second, adolescents in both conditions showed significant decreases in problem behavior, and these changes were not significantly different across conditions. Therefore, the efficacy of the SSSE intervention was in extending the benefits of therapy to many more families by increasing the rate of engagement and retention in treatment.

A second study designed to replicate and extend these engagement findings was recently completed (Santisteban et al., 1996). This study was designed to provide for a more rigorously controlled experimental test of the engagement interventions by using a larger and more multicultural sample, a more stringent criterion for successful engagement, and two control conditions instead of one.

Large, statistically significant differences were found between the experimental engagement condition and the two control conditions for rates of engagement. In the experimental condition, 81% of the families were successfully engaged, compared with 60% of the control families. Although the overall rates of the second engagement study appear lower than those of the first study, this is due to the more stringent criteria for engagement used in the second study. When the rates of engagement in the second study were compared with those of the original study using the original criteria, the results indicated that there were no significant differences between the two experimental engagement conditions: 93% in the first study and 88% in the second.

We also studied whether culture/ethnicity might influence intervention efficacy within our multicultural Hispanic sample. The data indicated dramatically different rates of engagement across Hispanic groups. Among the non-Cuban Hispanics (composed primarily of Nicaraguan families but including also Colombian, Puerto Rican, Peruvian, and Mexican families) assigned to the experimental condition, the rate of engagement intervention failure was extremely low, 3%. In contrast, among the Cuban Hispanic sample assigned to the experimental condition, the rate of intervention failure was relatively high, 36%. A more fine-grained case-by-case analysis of these findings suggested that the very different histories and trajectories of these Hispanic subgroups within the same Dade County community may have resulted in different patterns of resistance to engaging into therapy. These findings allowed us to articulate in an exploratory way the mechanism by which culture/ethnicity and other subtle contextual factors may influence clinical processes (Santisteban et al., 1996, Szapocznik & Kurtines, 1993) related to engagement.

Comparison of Structural Family Therapy With Other Modalities

Our research up to this point had concentrated on the development, refinement, and testing of structural family theory and strategies for Hispanic families with antisocial problem behavior youth. However, the question of the relative efficacy of a structural family systems approach, when compared to other widely used clinical interventions, became our next challenge. This research question was addressed primarily in two outcome research studies.

The first outcome study compared BSFT and individual psychodynamic child therapy, with a recreational activity group as a control. An experimental design was achieved by randomly assigning sixty-nine 6- to 9-year-old Hispanic boys to the three intervention conditions (Szapocznik, Rio et al., 1989). With respect to treatment efficacy, the control condition was significantly less effective in retaining cases than the two treatment conditions, with more than two thirds of the dropouts occurring in the control condition. These attrition results support our earlier recognition that dropout rates are important outcome measures that may distinguish the efficacy of different intervention/control conditions. A second finding was that the two treatment conditions, structural family therapy and psychodynamic child therapy, were equivalent in reducing behavior and emotional problems based on parent- and self-reports. A third finding involves the greater efficacy of family therapy over child therapy in protecting family integrity in the long term. In this study, psychodynamic therapy was found to be efficacious in bringing about symptom reduction and improved child psychodynamic functioning; but it was also found to result in undesirable deterioration of family functioning. The findings provided support for the structural family therapy assumption that treating the whole family is important, because it improves the symptoms and protests the family, whereas treating only the child may result in deteriorated family functioning. A fourth important finding revealed that there is a complex relationship between specific mechanisms (family interaction vs. child psychodynamic functioning) and related outcome variables. Examination of the relationship between the putative etiological factors postulated by the two theoretical/clinical approaches, on the one hand, support some of the underlying assumptions of psychodynamic theory. On the other, it does not support some of the underlying assumptions

of family therapy, that is, that changes in family functioning are necessary for symptom reduction. Hence, there was considerable value to extending the investigation beyond a simple horse race to a study of postulated underlying mechanisms.

Our second major outcome study further extended our work by testing the efficacy of structural family therapy in reducing behavior problems and investigating whether changes in family functioning mediated reductions in antisocial problem behavior. In this study, 79 Hispanic families with an adolescent referred for conduct problems were randomly assigned to one of two treatment conditions—BSFT or a group therapy control condition.

Outcome data were analyzed using two complementary approaches. The first was by Repeated Measures Multivariate Analysis of Variance (MANOVA) and the second by analysis of reliable/clinically significant change as recommended by Jacobson and Traux (1991). The latter method complements the more commonly used analyses of group means by providing a case-by-case index of change. The MANOVA and follow-up univariate analyses revealed that our experimental group changed significantly and our control group did not on our two dependent variable indicators of antisocial problem behavior: parent report of Conduct Disorder and Socialized Aggression from the Revised Behavior Problem Checklist (Quay & Petersen, 1987). The results of the analyses of reliable/clinically significant change corroborated the multivariate approach, indicating that a substantially larger proportion of family therapy cases showed clinically significant improvement on the same outcome dimensions of Conduct Disorder and Socialized Aggression.

BASIC ISSUES IN THE EVOLUTION OF A CULTURALLY COMPETENT INTERVENTION

At the foundation of a maturing program of research is an understanding of the issues in conducting culturally competent work and a theoretical framework that helps guide the research efforts. It has been our experience that in the evolution of a culturally competent program of intervention research with Hispanics, several basic research issues that pertain to the clinical development of culturally competent interventions and to the evaluation of the interventions have to be addressed. With respect to developing interventions, primary issues entail articulating a theoretical model of both the transcultural processes and culture-specific content to be included in the intervention and formulating a framework for implementing the intervention in a culturally compatible manner (i.e., incorporating the relevant transcultural processes and culture-specific content). Primary issues for evaluating interventions include identifying, adapting, or developing culturally appropriate measures and methods for evaluating the interventions and actually conducting outcome studies that evaluate the efficacy of the intervention.

Basic to all culturally competent interventions is a theoretical model articulating the factors and processes that contribute to the development or maintenance of the problem behavior. This model is not necessarily culturally specific, but it attends to the general psychosocial mechanism and processes that are theoretically or empirically linked to the pattern of behavior targeted for change. In the case of our theoretical framework, which focuses on repetitive patterns of interactions, these processes are transcultural, with similar processes likely to be operating across ethnic/cultural groups. However, researchers must also be aware of how culture-specific processes may shape the developmental course of the problem behavior.

In our own work, and in that of Rogler and colleagues, the process of acculturation and its accompanying stress and conflict reflect a specific social/clinical process, experienced by the population we were working with, that also had to be integrated into the theoretical foundations of the intervention. For us, the process of differential acculturation was critical and evident in the strained and altered patterns of interaction in our clinical families.

Another excellent example of establishing a theoretical foundation for building a systematic program of culturally competent research with Hispanic antisocial and behavior problem youth is the theoretical model and research plan for preventing substance use in Hispanic adolescent outlined by Schinke and colleagues at Columbia University School of Social Work (Schinke, Moncher, Palleja, Zayas, & Schilling, 1988; Schinke, Schilling, Palleja, & Zayas, 1987). Using basic theories of stress, coping, and social support, the group frames a basic theoretical model linking substance use in adolescence to purportedly causal antecedent conditions. The model and research plan also suggest how Hispanic values, customs, and traditions could be integrated into the model to help guide culturally competent interventions. Simultaneously, it acknowledges the difficulties in transferring technologies across ethnic groups.

Once a general model of theoretical mechanisms is articulated, it must then be translated into a clinical intervention. At this stage the challenge is to formulate a framework for integrating the relevant transcultural *therapeutic* processes and the culture-specific content. In our work, we adopted the modality of structural family therapy, which contained core concepts, methods, and procedures compatible with our population's cultural views. This intervention also effectively targeted the mechanisms of family dysfunction that were articulated in our general theory of problem behavior development. Rogler and colleagues have argued for a slightly different approach, one that uses the client's cultural values as a beginning of the design of the intervention and then as a "vehicle" for therapeutic change (Costantino & Rivera, 1994; Rogler, Malgady, Costantino, & Blumenthal, 1987). However, many of the therapeutic techniques in their interventions—modeling; sharing personal experiences and feelings; role-playing and reinforcement of imitative behaviors; and the probable mechanisms of change, cognitive restructuring, and shaping behavior through modeling—are not intervention techniques or change mechanisms specific to Puerto Rican youths. Rather, they are transcultural processes that have been rendered more accessible to change through use of culturally compatible content.

Developing measures that are, as Kazdin (1986) recommended, theoretically appropriate, clinically relevant, and with psychometric properties adequate for use in research settings, is a critical step. This process involves ensuring that the measures and methods are psychometrically as well as linguistically comparable, that is, the extent to which the psychological and sociocultural concepts and constructs are comparable across populations.

Our efforts to investigate the effects of acculturation on the Cuban immigrant population of Miami required a great deal of

work designing and creating an adequate measure of acculturation that would reflect our view of biculturalism and be sensitive to the changes we expected in our interventions. From this need emerged the Behavioral Acculturation Scale (Szapocznik, Scopetta, Kurtines et al., 1978) and the Bicultural Involvement Questionnaire (Szapocznik et al., 1980). The use of both of these instruments in our clinical outcome studies helped to shed light on some of the complex processes by which culture affects individuals and families.

Our work with adapting the Revised Behavior Problem Checklist (Quay & Petersen, 1987) for use with Hispanic populations was slightly more complex. The first step in adapting this measure was to translate it into Spanish using the techniques of translation and back translation (Kurtines & Szapocznik, 1995). The second step involved collecting data using the Spanish language version and evaluating the cross-cultural consistency of the RBPC's factor structure with our population (Rio, Quay, Santisteban, & Szapocznik, 1989). The results of our factor analysis yielded a six-factor structure that was highly comparable with the original version. This work comprised an important step in our program of research, providing a cross-culturally validated measure for assessing antisocial problem behavior in Hispanic youths.

The final step in the evolution of a culturally competent intervention is conducting outcome studies that evaluate the efficacy of the intervention and interpretation. Evaluation of the program is also conducted in a culturally sensitive manner but is dictated just as much by basic research design and statistical analysis techniques. Ideally, this step of evaluation can highlight both the efficacy of the transcultural therapeutic change processes and the efficacy of any culture-specific processes or content. Results of this phase of the evolution of culturally competent interventions must yield information that can feed back to theory and clinical development. If the results suggest an ineffective program, researchers must be willing to consider possibilities of implementation failure or theory failure (Weiss, 1972). Implementation failure might occur for many reasons, including lack of intensity or fidelity/integrity to the intervention or lack of cultural compatibility with the views of the population. Theory failure might result from a misspecified theoretical model of transcultural or culture-specific developmental mechanisms.

Within a program of culturally competent research, each phase of the research endeavor must be couched within a basic understanding of cultural issues. Description of those issues can be found in the extensive literature, based mostly on observations that identify cultural characteristics of Hispanics, that is recommended for careful consideration.

Bernal, Bonilla, and Bellido (1995) capture some of the most important recommendations in their articulation of a framework for research that can be used as a guide for developing culturally sensitive interventions or adapting existing psychosocial treatments for Hispanic clients. Their framework consists of eight partially overlapping dimensions to which researchers developing a culturally competent intervention should attend. The first, and perhaps most basic is the dimension of *language*. Because language is the "carrier of the culture," culturally syntonic language is critical to ensuring that clients are receiving the intervention the therapist intends. The second dimension, *persons*, refers to the client-therapist match. Research has indicated that ethnic and racial similarities between therapist and client can improve therapeutic outcome (see Sue et al., 1994). The dimension of *metaphors* refers to the culturally consonant use of symbols and concepts in the intervention. The authors define the fourth dimension, *content*, as one of cultural knowledge. This dimension reflects the appreciation of cultural information about values, customs, and traditions. In developing a culturally competent intervention for Hispanics, researchers might start by familiarizing themselves with basic Hispanic values and consider also the uniqueness of the particular ethnic group participating in their intervention. The degree to which treatment concepts are consonant with the cultural context defines the fifth dimension—*concepts*. The manner in which problems are conceptualized and the treatment model is communicated must be consistent with the belief system of the clients. The *goals* of treatment represent the sixth dimension in their framework. Again, the goals of treatment must be presented in a manner consonant with the cultural values held by the client population. Establishing treatment goals or communicating goals in a manner that is discrepant with those held by the client reduces the likelihood of an effective outcome.

The methods by which the intervention is delivered is a critical issue for consideration. Although many different intervention modalities exist as options for developing an intervention for antisocial behavior problem youths, cultural knowledge may dictate the selection of one over all others. One example is the general recommendation for family therapy as the treatment modality of choice for Hispanic clients because this intervention modality is congruent with the dominant Hispanic worldview of "familism" (Sabogal et al., 1987). The eighth and final dimension to their framework is *context*. Context refers to the changing social, political, economic processes that create unique situations in each intervention.

This framework proposed by Bernal et al. (1995) represents a compilation of the issues that underlie culturally sensitive programs. But, as noted earlier, cultural competence encompasses more than cultural sensitivity. It also includes the mastery of knowledge and skills that comes most efficiently from progressive experience conducting a program of study that integrates theory, research, and application. Issues discussed in the framework must be applied to each of the basic research issues if a culturally competent intervention is to evolve.

FUTURE DIRECTIONS

The need to develop psychosocial interventions that can be used in contexts of cultural diversity takes on a larger significance in view of the broader social, political, and historical trends that are taking place. This is especially the case as we, in the United States, become an increasingly culturally diverse society. Projections indicate a dramatic shift in racial and ethnic composition of the U.S. population over the next few decades, with Hispanics surpassing African Americans as the largest "minority" (Yung & Hammond, Chapter 45, this volume). It is important that basic research on culture and the development of culturally competent interventions continue to evolve, and researchers must be cognizant of the dynamic nature of culture.

In addition to attending to the dynamic nature of culture, it is important that culturally competent interventions address the multitude of changing historical and social conditions and the multiple systems that have an impact on the target populations. Hence, in its latest evolution, our work has become more multisystemic as well as structural. This structural multisystemic family-focused approach based on Structural Ecosystems Theory (Szapocznik et al., 1996) now pervades our efforts to develop and evaluate culturally competent interventions at many levels, ranging from clinical interventions to neighborhood-based and school-based interventions.

REFERENCES

Bernal, G., Bonilla, J., & Bellido, C. (1995). Ecological validity and cultural sensitivity for outcome research: Issues for the cultural adaptation and development of psychosocial treatments with Hispanics. *Journal of Abnormal Child Psychology, 23*(1), 67–82.

Bourdin, C. M., Mann, B. J., Cone, L. T., Henggeler, S. W., Fucci, B. R., Blaske, D. M., & Williams, R. A. (1995). Multisystemic treatment of serious juvenile offenders: Long term prevention of criminality and violence. *Journal of Consulting and Clinical Psychology, 63,* 569–578.

Costantino, G. (1987). *TEMAS (Tell-Me-A-Story) Thematic Apperception Test.* Los Angeles: Western Psychological Services.

Costantino, G., & Rivera, C. (1994). Culturally sensitive treatment modalities for Puerto Rican children, adolescents, and adults. In R. G. Malgady & O. Rodriguez (Eds.), *Theoretical and conceptual issues in Hispanic mental health* (pp. 181–226). Malabar, FL: Krieger.

Costantino, G., Malgady, R. G., & Rogler, L. H. (1986). Cuento therapy: A culturally sensitive modality for Puerto Rican children. *Journal of Consulting and Clinical Psychology, 54,* 739–746.

Haley, J. (1976). *Problem-solving therapy.* San Francisco: Jossey-Bass.

Hervis, O. E., Szapocznik, J., Mitrani, V., Rio, A. T., & Kurtines, W. M. (1991). *Structural Family Systems Ratings: A revised manual.* Unpublished manuscript.

Institute of Medicine. (1994). *Reducing risk for mental disorders: Frontiers for preventive intervention research.* Washington, DC: National Academy Press.

Jacobson, N. S., & Traux, T. (1991). Clinical significance: A statistical approach to defining meaningful change in psychotherapy research. *Journal of Consulting and Clinical Psychology, 59*(1), 12–19.

Kazdin, A. E. (1986). Comparative outcome studies of psychotherapy: Methodological issues and strategies. *Journal of Consulting and Clinical Psychology, 54,* 95–105.

Kazdin, A. E. (1987). Treatment of antisocial behavior in children: Current status and future directions. *Psychological Bulletin, 102,* 187–203.

Kazdin, A. E. (1993). Adolescent mental health: Prevention and treatment programs. *American Psychologist, 48*(2), 127–141.

Kluckhohn, F. R., & Strodtbeck, F. L. (1961). *Variations in value orientations.* Evanston, IL: Row, Peterson.

Kurtines, W. M., & Szapocznik, J. (1995). Cultural competence in assessing Hispanic youths and families: Challenges in the assessment of treatment needs and treatment evaluation for Hispanic drug abusing adolescents. In E. Rahdert & D. Czechowicz (Eds.), *Adolescent drug abuse: Clinical assessment and therapeutic interventions.* (NIDA Research Monograph No. 156, NIH Publication No. 95-3908). Bethesda, MD: NIDA.

Madanes, C. (1981). *Strategic family therapy.* San Francisco: Jossey-Bass.

Malgady, R. G., & Rodriguez, O. (1994). *Theoretical and conceptual issues in Hispanic mental health.* Malabar, FL: Krieger.

Malgady, R. G., Rogler, L. H., & Costantino, G. (1990a). Culturally sensitive psychotherapy for Puerto Rican children and adolescents: A program of treatment outcome research. *Journal of Consulting and Clinical Psychology, 58*(6), 704–712.

Malgady, R. G., Rogler, L. H., & Costantino, G. (1990b). Hero/heroine modeling for Puerto Rican adolescents: A preventive mental health intervention. *Journal of Consulting and Clinical Psychology, 58*(4), 469–474.

Minuchin, S. (1974). *Families and family therapy.* Cambridge: Harvard University Press.

Minuchin, S., & Fishman, H. C. (1981). *Family therapy techniques.* Cambridge: Harvard University Press.

Minuchin, S., Rosman, B. L., & Baker, L. (1978). *Psychosomatic families: Anorexia nervosa in context.* Cambridge: Harvard University Press.

Orlandi, M. A. (1992). Defining cultural competence: An organizing framework. In M. A. Orlandi (Ed.), *Cultural competence for evaluators* (pp. 293–299). Washington, DC: Office of Substance Abuse Prevention: DHHS Pub. No. (ADM) 92-1884.

Quay, H. C., & Peterson, D. R. (1987). *Manual for the Revised Behavior Problem Checklist.* (Available from H. C. Quay, Department of Psychology, P. O. Box 248185, Coral Gables, Florida 33124.)

Rio, A. T., Quay, H. C., Santisteban, D. A., & Szapocznik, J. (1989). A factor analytical study of a Spanish translation of the Revised Behavior Problem Checklist. *Journal of Clinical Child Psychology, 18*(4), 343–350.

Rogler, L. H., Malgady, R. G., Costantino, G., & Blumenthal, R. (1987). What do culturally sensitive mental health services mean? The case of Hispanics. *American Psychologist, 42,* 565–570.

Rogler, L. H., Malgady, R. G., & Rodriguez, O. (1989). *Hispanics and mental health: A framework for research.* Malabar, FL: Krieger.

Sabogal, F., Marin, G., Otero-Sabogal, R., Marin, B., & Perez-Stable, E. (1987). Changes in Hispanic familism with acculturation (Technical report # 17). San Francisco: University of California.

Santisteban, D. A., & Szapocznik, J. (1994). Bridging theory, research and practice to more successfully engage substance abusing youth and their families into therapy. *Journal of Child and Adolescent Substance Abuse, 3*(2), 9–24.

Santisteban, D. A., Szapocznik, J., Perez-Vidal, A., Kurtines, W. M., Murray, E. J., & LaPerriere, A. (1996). Engaging behavior problem drug abusing youth and their families into treatment: An investigation of the efficacy of specialized engagement interventions and factors that contribute to differential effectiveness. *Journal of Family Psychology, 10,* 35–44.

Schinke, S. P., Schilling, R. F., Palleja, J., & Zayas, L. H. (1987). Prevention research among ethnic-racial minority group adolescents. *The Behavior Therapist, 10*(7), 151–155.

Schinke, S. P., Moncher, M. S., Palleja, J., Zayas, L. H., & Schilling, R. (1988). Hispanic youth, substance abuse, and stress: Implications for prevention research. *International Journal of the Addictions, 23*(8), 809–826.

Scopetta, M. A., Szapocznik, J., King, O. E., Ladner, R., Alegre, C., & Tillman, M. S. (1977). *Final Report: The Spanish drug rehabilitation research project* (NIDA Grant # HB1 DA01696). Miami: University of Miami, Spanish Family Guidance Center.

Sue, S., Zane, N., & Young, K. (1994). Research on psychotherapy with culturally diverse populations. In A. E. Bergin & S. L. Garfield (Eds.), *Handbook of psychotherapy and behavioral change* (pp. 783–817). New York: Wiley.

Szapocznik, J., & Kurtines, W. M. (1979). Acculturation, biculturalism and adjustment among Cuban Americans. In A. Padilla (Ed.), *Psychological dimensions on the acculturation process: Theory, models and some new findings.* Boulder, CO: Westview press. (Sponsored by the American Association for the Advancement of Science.)

Szapocznik, J., & Kurtines, W. M. (1989). *Breakthroughs in family treatment.* New York: Springer.

Szapocznik, J., & Kurtines, W. M. (1993). Family psychology and cultural diversity: Opportunities for theory, research and application. *American Psychologist, 48*(4), 400–407.

Szapocznik, J., Kurtines, W., & Fernandez, T. (1980). Biculturalism and adjustment among Hispanic youths. *International Journal of Intercultural Relations, 4,* 353–375.

Szapocznik, J., Kurtines, W., Perez-Vidal, A., Hervis, O., & Foote, F. (1990). One person family therapy. In R. A. Wells & V. A. Gianetti (Eds.), *Handbook of brief psychotherapies* (pp. 493–510). New York: Plenum.

Szapocznik, J., Kurtines, W. M., & Santisteban, D. A. (1994). The interplay of advances among theory, research and application in family interventions for Hispanic behavior problem youth. In R. G. Malgady & O. Rodriguez (Eds.), *Theoretical and conceptual issues in Hispanic mental health* (pp. 155–179). Malabar, FL: Krieger.

Szapocznik, J., Kurtines, W., Santisteban, D. A., Pantin, H., Scopetta, M., Mancilla, Y., Aisenberg, S., McIntosh, S., Perez-Vidal, A., & Coatsworth, J. D. (1996). The evolution of a multisystemic structural approach for working with Hispanic families in culturally pluralistic contexts. In J. Garcia & M. C. Zea (Eds.), *Psychological interventions and research with Latino populations* (pp. 166–190). Boston: Allyn & Bacon.

Szapocznik, J., Kurtines, W., Santisteban, D., & Rio, A. T. (1990). The interplay of advances among theory, research and application in treatment interventions aimed at behavior problem children and adolescents. *Journal of Consulting and Clinical Psychology, 58*(6), 696–703.

Szapocznik, J., Perez-Vidal, A., Brickman, A., Foote, F. H., Santisteban, D., Hervis, O., & Kurtines, W. H. (1988). Engaging adolescent drug abusers and their families into treatment: A Strategic Structural Systems approach. *Journal of Consulting and Clinical Psychology, 56,* 552–557.

Szapocznik, J., Perez-Vidal, A., Hervis, O., Brickman, A. L., & Kurtines, W. M. (1990). Innovations in family therapy: Overcoming resistance to treatment. In R. A. Wells & V. A. Gianetti (Eds.), *Handbook of brief psychotherapy* (pp. 93–114). New York: Plenum.

Szapocznik, J., Rio, A. T., Hervis, O. E., Mitrani, V. B., Kurtines, W. M., & Faraci, A. M. (1991). Assessing change in family functioning as a result of treatment: The structural family system ratings scale (SFSR). *Journal of Marital and Family Therapy, 17*(3), 295–310.

Szapocznik, J., Rio, A., Murray, E., Cohen, R., Scopetta, M., Rivas-Vasquez, A., Hervis, O., Posada, V., & Kurtines, W. (1989). Structural family versus psychodynamic child therapy for problematic Hispanic boys. *Journal of Consulting and Clinical Psychology, 57*(5), 571–578.

Szapocznik, J., Santisteban, D., Kurtines, W. M., Perez-Vidal, A., & Hervis, O. (1984). Bicultural Effectiveness Training (BET): A treatment intervention for enhancing intercultural adjustment. *Hispanic Journal of Behavioral Sciences, 6*(4), 317–344.

Szapocznik, J., Santisteban, D., Rio, A., Perez-Vidal, A., & Kurtines, W. M. (1986). Family effectiveness training for Hispanic families: Strategic structural systems intervention for the prevention of drug abuse. In H. P. Lefley & P. B. Pedersen (Eds.), *Cross cultural training for mental health professionals* (pp. 245–260). Springfield, IL: Charles C Thomas.

Szapocznik, J., Santisteban, D., Rio, A., Perez-Vidal, A., Kurtines, W., & Hervis, O. (1986). Bicultural Effectiveness Training (BET): An intervention modality for families experiencing intergenerational/intercultural conflict. *Hispanic Journal of Behavioral Sciences, 8*(4), 303–330.

Szapocznik, J., Santisteban, D., Rio, A., Perez-Vidal, A., Santisteban, D. A., & Kurtines, W. (1989). Family effectiveness training: An intervention to prevent problem behaviors in Hispanic adolescents. *Hispanic Journal of Behavioral Sciences, 11*, 4–27.

Szapocznik, J., Scopetta, M. A., Aranalde, M. A., & Kurtines, W. (1978). Cuban value structure: Clinical implications. *Journal of Consulting and Clinical Psychology, 46*(5), 961–970.

Szapocznik, J., Scopetta, M. A., & King, O. (1978). Theory and practice in matching treatment to the special characteristics and problems of Cuban immigrants. *Journal of Community Psychology, 6,* 112–122.

Szapocznik, J., Scopetta, M. A., Kurtines, W., & Aranalde, M. A. (1978). Theory and measurement of acculturation. *Interamerican Journal of Psychology, 12,* 113–130.

Tolan, P. H., Guerra, N. G., & Kendall, P. C. (1995). Introduction to special section: Prediction and prevention of antisocial behavior in children and adolescents. *Journal of Consulting and Clinical Psychology, 63,* 515–517.

Weiss, C. H. (1972). *Evaluation research.* Englewood Cliffs, NJ: Prentice Hall.

CHAPTER 38

Treatment of Juvenile Delinquency: Between Punishment and Therapy

PATRICK H. TOLAN and DEBORAH GORMAN-SMITH

The purpose of this chapter is to provide an understanding of current knowledge and practice in regard to the treatment of juvenile delinquency and the application of that knowledge in policies and programs. To do so is a formidable task because ascertaining which approaches are efficacious can be difficult, and determining how efficacious components are translated into effective service delivery is even more difficult (Tolan, 1996; Weisz, Donenberg, Han, & Kauneckis, 1995). This task is a more complicated judgment because juvenile delinquency treatment usually occurs because of involvement with the juvenile court and its ensuing legal complications. Complex and not necessarily obvious influences on service delivery and mediators of posttreatment outcome must be considered (Bortner, 1986; Fagan, Hartstone, Rudman, & Hansen, 1984). The nature of these complicating influences can be traced to several inherent paradoxes in the intended purpose of the juvenile court and the role of treatment within that system (Feld, 1992). Indeed, there has been considerable debate about whether treatment should be a central concern of the court. The inclusion of treatment as part of the role of the court has been criticized as potentially harmful to children (Rubin, 1985), antithetical to the constitutional protections provided in criminal procedures (Feld, 1992), a deceptive and coercive inculcation of mainstream values, and a confusion of immoral willful behavior with symptoms of psychopathology (Orlando & Crippen, 1992). Further, early reviews that suggested treatment was ineffective have fueled tension between the juvenile justice system as treatment provider and as legal processing system (Martinson, 1974).

Because juvenile delinquency is a legally defined status rather than a psychiatric disorder or specific behavioral problem, the treatment of juvenile delinquency is inherently embedded in ongoing organizational tensions within the juvenile justice system (Feld, 1992). It has never been clear whether the juvenile justice system is primarily intended to prosecute and punish children and adolescents committing crimes or to provide care, support, and treatment (Fagan, 1990). For example, do assaultive adolescents need treatment to overcome or manage their aggressive, impulsive behavior, or do they need due legal process leading to freedom restrictions as just deserts for failing in their social responsibility not to break laws? The juvenile court's history and, therefore, nature of juvenile delinquency programs can be characterized as an unhappy marriage between legal procedures designed to establish guilt and exact punishment and psychotherapeutic interventions designed to rehabilitate or to prevent progression to more serious and chronic offending.

These complexities, conflicts, and contradictions comprise a treatment service delivery structure that must be considered in the development of services as well as in the evaluation of the impact of services. This structure may influence treatment effects substantially and may even overshadow the pertinence of conclusions from controlled field trials and research-based demonstration projects (Tolan, 1996). However, the treatment delivery issues and their impact from the organizational tensions inherent in the juvenile justice system are rarely considered or evaluated. Too often the efficacy of model interventions is directly applied as a policy recommendation. This chapter discusses the nature and impact of organizational tensions that often constrain treatment of juvenile delinquency.

Several recent comprehensive reviews quite adequately summarize the evaluations of interventions and provide direction for the future (Guerra, Tolan, & Hammond, 1995; Hawkins, Catalano, & Brewer, 1995; Kazdin, 1993; Lipsey, 1992; Mulvey, Arthur, & Reppucci, 1993; Tolan & Guerra, 1994a, 1994b). Although there is some variance in the focus of these recent reviews, the general findings and conclusions are remarkably similar. Rather than repeating the contributions of these reviews, we limit our presentation to summarizing their major findings and conclusions. We then focus on the policy constraints, ambiguities, and contradictions involved in delivering juvenile delinquency treatment that compromise the utility and sufficiency of these findings.

Support for this work was provided by NIMH grants (R01 MH48248 and R18 MH48034) and the University of Illinois Great Cities Institute Faculty Scholars Program.

MAJOR FINDINGS AND RECOMMENDATIONS OF EFFICACY[1] REVIEWS

Early reviews of delinquency interventions commonly concluded that "nothing works" (e.g., Martinson, 1974). However, these reviews were often limited to the judgment of the reviewer, and many of the studies to that date had serious methodological flaws. In contrast, current reviews have a larger and sounder set of studies to rely on, as well as meta-analytic techniques to make statistical summaries across studies. These methods provide more reliable estimates of effects as well as greater power to detect effects (see Lipsey & Wilson, 1993). The reviews suggest juvenile delinquency rates can be affected through a variety of interventions. The most substantial evidence is for interventions that (a) improve behavior management at school (Bry, 1982; Gottfredson, 1987); (b) provide opportunities for "meaningful" roles (Jones & Offord, 1989; Schinke, Orlandi, & Cole, 1992; Shorts, 1986); (c) train social problem solving, particularly by including behavioral practice as well as skills education (Guerra & Slaby, 1990); and (d) improve parent management and family relationships (Henggeler, Melton, & Smith, 1992; Patterson, Reid, & Dishion, 1992; Webster-Stratton, Hollingsworth, & Kolpacoff, 1989).

In addition to these components, reviews also shed light on the effects of diverting delinquents from the legal procedures and official sanctions of the juvenile courts. The evidence for the effectiveness of diversion is mixed. Diversion programs had a modest positive effect for younger youths (ages 11 to 14), for those youths with more contact hours with the program, when family involvement was a component, and when the diversion activities were more structured (Gensheimer, Mayer, Gottschalk, & Davidson, 1986). However, no overall substantial positive effect was found.

Beyond these summary conclusions, more specific direction can be culled from Lipsey's (1992) meta-analysis of almost 500 evaluations of interventions for juvenile delinquents. This analysis is particularly comprehensive as it included unpublished as well as published studies. Sixty-four percent of the studies show positive treatment impact (some benefit for treatment compared with no-treatment groups), with a mean effect size difference from control groups of .10 standard deviation.[2] This is equivalent to an average 10% reduction in delinquency. This means that if the base rate of

recidivism or later delinquency is 50% on average, interventions reduce that rate to 45%. It should also be noted, however, that contrary to the view that interventions can only help, 30% of studies showed better outcome for control groups.

Large variability existed around this small average effect. Different approaches and different methods of service delivery related to the size of the effect observed. Also, using regression analyses, Lipsey showed that half of the explained variance in effect size was attributable to research methods such as how variables were measured, sources used, and analytic methods applied. Treatment design features were also influential. Summarizing across service delivery characteristics, Lipsey concluded that more structured treatments such as those using behavioral techniques and teaching skills show the largest delinquency reductions. This is consistent with meta-analyses of treatment reports for child psychopathology, which find the most effective treatments are highly structured (Weisz et al., 1995).

Among the types of treatments reviewed by Lipsey (1992) that are offered as part of the juvenile justice system, the specific category of employment training and opportunities produced the largest average impact on decreasing delinquency [effect size (ES) = .37 SD units]. Social-skills–oriented programs also showed a comparatively larger average effect size (ES = .32). Counseling programs overall were not effective (ES = .04, if within the juvenile justice system; ES = .07, if community based), and school tutoring had no effect on delinquency rate.

When only community-based programs were compared, the largest effect was for group counseling (ES = .18) and casework. This finding may seem surprising, given the negative effects reported by some for group interventions (Gottfredson, 1987) and the importance of peer relations as a harmful influence on delinquency (see Thornberry & Krohn, Chapter 21, this volume). However, there is a distinction in effects of groups depending on the mix of group participants and the structure of the group interaction (Tolan & Guerra, 1994b). Thus, although positive peer culture can have a negative effect (Feldman, 1992), structured peer counseling that leads to influence and association with prosocial peers and has strong structure and supervision by adults can be helpful (Tolan & Guerra, 1994a, 1994b).

When the location of the program was considered, the largest effect among programs occurred with community residential placement (ES = .16). Innovative programming in probation and restitution each had an average effect of .10 SD units. Insubstantial effects were found for community-based individual programs and employment counseling.

Negative effects (higher than base-rate recidivism) were found for vocational counseling (ES = −.18) and deterrence (ES = −.24). Given that deterrence (e.g., exposing delinquents to fear-inducing conditions of prisons or punishing delinquents) is at the heart of the punishment approach, its substantial negative effect is notable. If the base rate of recidivism was 50%, this effect size suggests deterrence would *increase* that rate to 62%.

Effect sizes were related to greater involvement of the experimenter in assuring treatment integrity, as well as amount of treatment (greater dose, duration, or intensity). Among reports reviewed, the median duration was 26 weeks and 100 contact hours. When covariation with other functional outcomes was con-

---

[1]*Efficacy* refers to demonstrated statistically significant effects of a treatment in a controlled field trial. *Effectiveness* refers to such differences in actual practice.

[2]There is much discussion about the meaning of small to moderate effect sizes for clinical significance (e.g., moving deviant persons to nondeviance). In this application, the key concern is preventing involvement (reducing prevalence), preventing rearrest (reducing subsequent incidence among high-risk groups), and reducing seriousness and chronicity of those already involved (decreasing length of criminal career or seriousness of crime). Because most studies rely on comparison of average differences between treatments and controls, few results can be readily judged for clinical significance. For public health problems, a 10% to 20% reduction suggests a powerful intervention. For clinical treatment trials, this may be insubstantial (see Kendall & Grove, 1988). The judgment rendered depends on the interest of the person making the judgment.

sidered, Lipsey (1992) found that delinquency improvement was most closely associated with school participation (represented by attendance and involvement in school activities). Delinquency improvement did not relate to academic performance improvement or psychological and interpersonal variables. Increase in school participation, however, was associated with improvements in psychological and interpersonal adjustment, suggesting some indirect link to improvement in delinquent behavior.

These results suggest a clear refutation of the conclusion that nothing works. This meta-analysis, however, in congruence with other recent reviews, suggests that the effects are modest to small for most interventions and that the methodology of the studies has as much influence on the results as the intervention approach. Also, many of these studies relied on pre- and postcomparisons, so the effects are of "during intervention" change. It is unclear how well these are maintained over time. Some substantial lasting effects have been demonstrated (Borduin et al., 1995), but such follow-up is still rare. Given the prevailing theories that a small portion of youths are life-course antisocial (see Moffitt, 1993) and in need of long-term management, the extent to which these effects last is a critical concern. These necessary qualifications of conclusions limit the authority of these findings for dictating policy. However, they do suggest preferred directions for designing future programs.

With these qualifications, the findings suggest the availability of efficacious treatments for delinquency. The categories of types of efficacious treatments are broad groupings, and the effect sizes vary substantially within categories; therefore, their application to specific programs may vary (Lipsey, 1992). For large-scale programs targeting at-risk youths, the strongest evidence is for programs that combine behavior management with social cognitive skills. This includes programs that improve parenting skills and management of the at-risk youths in school. Such programs may work through improving school involvement. Programs that combine skill-development with parent management and school-parent relationship building seem to have advantages over single-component programs.

For programs for those already identified and being treated within the juvenile justice system, the weight of the evidence favors community residential treatment and employment skills training over incarceration and psychological counseling. Multimodal programs seem most valuable. Deterrence programs (e.g., "Scared Straight," "Three-Strikes") seem to be ill advised despite their political appeal.

THREE EXAMPLES OF PROMISING INTERVENTIONS

Three examples of relatively new but empirically supported programs for juvenile delinquency illustrate the range of approaches that can meet the heterogeneous treatment needs among delinquent populations. Each focuses on a major risk factor, is theoretically driven, and utilizes multiple components.

Multisystemic Treatment (MST) was developed by Henggeler and colleagues (Henggeler & Borduin, 1990; Henggeler et al., 1992) and is based on family systems theory of behavior and behavior change. MST approaches delinquency from Bronfen-

brenner's theory of social ecology, which considers the individual as part of a number of interconnected systems (family, peer, school, neighborhood). In addition to problem-focused interventions within the family, MST helps the family manage each of these systems. Thus, a key distinction of MST is to see the family as the primary mediator of adolescent risk. The goal is to affect risk influences such as antisocial peers and poor school participation through improving family functioning.

An example of MST's demonstrated effectiveness is the 1992 study by Henggeler et al. Eighty-four serious juvenile offenders and their families were randomly assigned to MST or service-as-usual conditions. Each offender had at least one felony arrest and averaged 9.5 weeks of prior placement in correctional facilities. Following treatment, the youths receiving MST had fewer arrests and self-reported offenses and spent an average of 10 fewer weeks incarcerated than those receiving services as usual (Henggeler et al., 1992). Follow-up of these same subjects 2.4 years postreferral showed that youths receiving MST were less likely to be rearrested (39% of the MST group had not been rearrested compared with 20% of the group receiving usual services). The mean time to rearrest for youths receiving MST was 56.2 weeks, whereas the mean time for youths receiving usual services was 31.7 weeks (Henggeler, Melton, Smith, Schoenwald, & Hanley, 1993).

One limitation of multisystemic family treatment can be that youths must have families willing to participate. This is often not possible with delinquents. Chamberlain and colleagues report on the effectiveness of an alternative model to traditional residential or foster care treatment, called *Specialized Foster Care* (SFC; Chamberlain, 1990; Chamberlain & Friman, Chapter 39, this volume; Chamberlain & Reid, 1991). In the SFC approach, the foster parent plays a central role in the treatment and rehabilitation of the youths as part of a multicomponent model that includes (a) recruitment and screening of foster parents, (b) preservice training, (c) daily management of the youth in the home and community, (d) ongoing supervision and support for foster parents, (e) individual treatment for the youth, (f) family treatment, and (g) case management and community liaison services. The study's subjects had an average of 11.4 arrests prior to the program (Chamberlain & Friman, Chapter 39, this volume). Random assignment comparison to traditional residential facilities showed that youths participating in SFC had significantly lower reincarceration rates (38%) compared with those placed in residential facilities (88%) 1 year after completing treatment (see Chamberlain & Friman, Chapter 39, this volume, for more details about this intervention).

For youths unable to be released to specialized foster care or to be treated in community-based intervention, programs are needed to aid the transition out of institutions. The *Violent Juvenile Offender Program* (Fagan, 1990) was designed to aid in the reintegration of serious offenders into the community. This program provides intensive supervision and control of offenders in the community as well as services to teach youths strategies necessary for independent living in the community (not returning home or relying on dependable parental supervision). Like multisystemic treatment, the conceptual frame for the program is grounded in a theoretical model of the development of serious antisocial behavior (Elliott, Ageton, & Cantor, 1979). Three-year programs were tested in four states. Although some differences in results existed across sites, those sites with stronger implementation of the program demonstrated lower recidivism rates for participants than for control subjects. In the two states with strong adherence to the program, there were fewer rearrests and longer time to first arrest (Fagan, 1990).

Thus, these examples, the overall meta-analysis, and several other reviews suggest that there are efficacious interventions that have substantial but moderate effects on recidivism and self-reported delinquency, with greater impact realized when programs are well organized and structured and have multiple components (Tolan & Guerra, 1994b). However, these efficacy reports have limited meaning if not linked to an understanding of conflicts in purpose within the juvenile justice system that frame the realities of service delivery and public policy (Jacob, 1983). The remainder of this chapter focuses on how these important forces at least moderate, and may mediate, the efficacy of interventions and discusses key issues that need to be considered in evaluating the effectiveness of delinquency treatment, development and delivery of such interventions, and formulation of policy responses.

A BASIC INHERENT CONFLICT BETWEEN TREATMENT AND PUNISHMENT

The inherent conflicts that are part of any attempt to treat juvenile delinquency are generated from a basic contradiction between the two primary social functions assigned to the court: rehabilitation and punishment (Feld, 1992; Macallair, 1993). This philosophical conflict permeates service delivery and affects all aspects of intervention with juvenile delinquents from identification to sentencing. The differences begin with the assumptions about child and adolescent behavior and the psychology of each approach. A punishment model presumes that individuals make a conscious choice to act criminally, are responsible for that behavior, and should be held accountable regardless of age or cognitive development. The primary interest of intervention, based on this perspective, is establishing legal responsibility (guilt). The major procedural concerns are fairness and equity in application, and these are accomplished according to case precedents and principles based in constitutional, criminal procedural, and common law (Feld, 1992). Punishment is to be applied in accordance with the seriousness of the crime with limited consideration of extenuating circumstances, such as the age or level of understanding held by the defendant. Inherent in this model is the belief that punishment will serve as a deterrent for self and others in committing further criminal acts.

In contrast, a treatment approach assumes that juveniles are not committing crimes due to conscious choice but due to poor care, inept skills, limited opportunities, or poor judgment (Fagan, 1990; Feld, 1992). This approach assumes that society has a basic responsibility to provide adequate care to all children. Any criminal behavior by young children represents a failure of society to adequately function in its role as *parens patriae* (ultimate parent; Weischeit & Alexander, 1988). From this view, child and adolescent criminal behavior is due to limited judgment and carries limited or no responsibility for the act (Orlando & Crippen, 1992). This reasoning led to the separation of juvenile court from general criminal court and the use of civil rather than criminal procedures (see *In re Gault*, 1967, for a review of the juvenile court's development and purpose and McCarthy & Carr, 1980). Thus, the court is a benevolent overseer for those in its charge. There is no need to ensure proper criminal procedures and protection of constitutional rights. From this developmental view, the procedural concern is to ensure adequate attention and care. The goal is to prevent further development toward adult criminality and to provide needed aid to correct the mistakes of youth. Interceding in a child's life is justified by the court's benevolent interest in and responsibility for the well-being of the young of our society.

The *parens patriae* philosophy remains a substantial influence on juvenile justice despite several Supreme Court (e.g., *In re Gault*, 1967) and lower court rulings (*In re Seven Minors*, 1983; *In re D. F. B.*, 1988) that the nature of juvenile court proceedings is criminal prosecution. Increasingly, there are also legislative modifications of the procedures and dominion of the court, usually reflecting a move away from benevolent interaction toward increasing prosecution and imposing punishment. Despite these recent changes, juvenile justice systems continue to address issues of abuse and neglect (child well-being) as well as criminal proceedings of those under majority age. Court actions, particularly treatment program and staff decisions, continue to be influenced by the social and psychological history of the youths charged as well as criminal laws.

THE IMPACT OF CONTINUOUS REFORM

In addition to this basic conflict, policy regarding how the system should operate is often formulated or modified in response to concerns of the public or because of the emergence of some political concern. As a result, public policy and funding decisions regarding the processing and treatment of juvenile offenders are often made without due consideration of relevant scientific and historical information or consideration of the lasting implications of policy. For example, the current emphasis on having violent juvenile offenders tried in adult criminal court is not based on a careful discussion of the policy implications, empirical evidence of the likely impact on crime, or potential conflicts with other laws and procedures. In fact, based on empirical evidence of prevalence and incidence of delinquent behavior among adolescents, it is likely that the policy change will affect only a few defendants and will have no substantial impact on crime (Orlando & Crippen, 1992). This change in policy is symbolic and meant to communicate intolerance of youth crime and is presented as a solution to the burgeoning population of serious delinquents. It reassures the public that something is being done. Thus, many of the policy decisions guiding the court are not based on a legal or welfare basis but are responses to the immediate concerns.

Because of the political basis of reforms, potentially effective treatments (e.g., multisystemic family intervention) may not even be considered as a treatment option, whereas interventions that clearly do not work yet meet the criterion of pleasing the public (e.g., boot camps) become the treatment of choice. Rather than clarifying direction for the court, the reforms often constrain the quality, dependability, and rationality of how service delivery is determined. Because such reforms are often not sustained, they rarely affect most day-to-day operations. Like other social institutions such as schools, the juvenile justice system functions in a social ecology of constant reform but with no substantial or sustained direction (see Sarason, 1971, for a powerful, precise analysis of how system reforms can be compromised repeatedly).

QUESTIONS ARISING FROM THE INFLUENCE OF INHERENT CONFLICTS AND CONTINUOUS REFORM ON DELINQUENCY TREATMENT

Whether the intended approach of an intervention actually is implemented or sustained and its effect level can depend heavily on adequate consideration of these inherent conflicts between punishment and treatment and recognition of the difference between policy and procedures (Fagan, 1995). These considerations lead to five questions/dilemmas that need empirical direction. We discuss the nature of each question and note the empirical support for reasoned responses.

Does the Research Support a Treatment or a Justice Model?

During the 1970s, following several Supreme Court decisions extending criminal procedural guarantees and safeguards to juvenile proceedings as well as conclusions from reviews of treatment programs that nothing works, there was a decided increase in attempts to formalize court proceedings and to emphasize justice administration rather than treatment considerations (Fagan, 1990, 1995). Since that time, a number of states have adopted the justice model. As empirical evidence about the effects of the two approaches is accumulating, the findings generally support treatment over the justice approach (Fagan, 1990, 1995; Lipsey, 1992).

Two natural experiments that illustrate the relative value of each approach can be seen in the reforms of Washington and Massachusetts. In 1977, the state of Washington passed legislation implementing a justice model requiring all adjudicated offenders to serve specified time periods in correctional facilities for specific offenses. These changes were based on reports that juveniles committing more serious crimes such as armed robbery and murder were often staying in institutions for shorter periods of time than were juveniles committing minor or status offenses. The intent was not to increase the severity of punishment for offenders but rather to have a more uniform and equitable system with punishment graded according to the seriousness of the act rather than the circumstances or needs of the charged youths (Macallair, 1993; Schneider & Schram, 1983). Although there was an immediate overall reduction in the severity of sanctions imposed within the state, this reduction was short lived (Schneider & Schram, 1983). The change in policy resulted in more juveniles per capita being sent to institutions, although the average length of stay decreased from 388 days to 265 days. Since its institution in 1984, the average length of stay has increased every year, and state facilities are operating at more than 100% of capacity (Macallair, 1993). Thus, the approach has engendered problems that accompany overcrowding such as poorer population management and the inability

to provide needed services. Analyses evaluating decisions regarding punishment found that legal variables such as severity of offense and prior record did not predict disposition decisions prior to the policy change. After the policy change, these legal concerns were predictive of decisions, but at a moderate level ($R^2 = .15$). Contrary to the model, nonlegal factors such as age, race, and gender still significantly influenced decisions (Castellano, 1986). The most telling results, however, concerned the primary purpose of the change in policy: reducing recidivism and deterring new offenders. Schneider (1984) reported that recidivism did not change overall after the policy changes; and in some urban areas, the rates increased postpolicy. After reviewing the Washington system and the available evidence, Castellano (1986) concluded that "there is no evidence to suggest that the adoption of a 'just deserts' approach to juvenile offending has reduced juvenile delinquency" (p. 502).

One of the more powerful examples favoring treatment is from the other natural experiment resulting from a change in state policies. Massachusetts closed its five juvenile correctional training schools and replaced them with a network of small, community-based programs operating in neighborhoods throughout the state. The rationale was that the institutions were actually harmful to the children placed in them and that they failed to provide the care and treatment that was needed to reduce the likelihood of recidivism. Money was reallocated to be used by private agencies to provide comprehensive and individualized treatment. For youths who did not require secure custody, intensive outreach and tracking were provided in their own homes and neighborhoods (Krisberg, Austin, Joe, & Steele, 1987; Macallair, 1993). Notably, these changes were not accompanied by an increase in crime (Austin, Elms, Krisberg, & Steele, 1991). Austin et al. (1991) noted that "Massachusetts continues to have one of the lowest rates of juvenile crime in the nation" (p. 24).

Utah followed the same approach of closing its training schools and opening community-based programs. Evaluation of the effect of this policy indicated a 66% decline in the frequency of subsequent arrests during a 12-month follow-up (Krisberg et al., 1987). Other studies have found that youths treated in community-based programs had lower rates of recidivism than youths placed in training schools. In a comprehensive review of these programs, Fagan (1990) concludes that the weight of the evidence is that community-based programs do not increase risk to public safety, do result in similar or lower recidivism rates, and can do so at a much lower cost than training schools or incarceration. Thus, contrary to popular belief and current policy trends, the weight of the evidence does not favor a simple justice administration model.

How Should Service Eligibility and Provision Be Determined? Who Should Be Treated and When and on What Basis?

The evidence shows that treatment can be effective; therefore, one can assume that efforts should be made to identify and provide services. The issue that arises next is determining who should be treated and when. Should this decision be based on scientific prediction and early preventive intervention or require meeting legal criteria of proven guilt before imposing intervention?

Early Identification

Although there are many studies on identification as well as important scientific advances, the prediction of who will become delinquent and what involvement means for seriousness and chronicity of criminal behavior is still uncertain (Tolan & Loeber, 1993). The most robust findings are that there is a group of individuals who tend to show early aggression, are likely to have less able parents (poor monitoring, inconsistent discipline), and are likely to show poor impulse control early in life (Moffitt, 1993). As these individuals enter elementary school, they are likely to be rejected by peers, show poor interpersonal skills, lag academically, and gravitate toward delinquent peers (Patterson et al., 1992). This group is most at-risk to be involved early in criminal behavior, to develop serious criminal behavior during adolescence, and to continue such behavior beyond adolescence (Elliott, 1994). In most studies, this profile fits about 5% or 6% of the male population. Typically, they are responsible for about 50% of all crimes (Farrington, Ohlin, & Wilson, 1986). It should be noted that these findings have been replicated in many samples. However, the finding that a small proportion of youths are responsible for much of the delinquency does not mean that early, accurate identification of the small portion of adolescents is plausible or even the most desirable goal. First, the accuracy of identification is limited (see Stouthamer-Loeber & Loeber, 1988; Tolan, 1988). Second, criminal behavior is not limited to this early-onset, serious-offending group. Most adolescents report some delinquent behavior with about 25% reporting some serious crime (Elliott, 1994). These adolescents as a group are responsible for almost as much crime as the very active 5% to 8% (Tolan & Loeber, 1993). Overall, their crimes do tend to be less serious (Tracy, Wolfgang, & Figlio, 1990). However, comparisons of chronic offenders (those arrested at least five times) with others showed the nonchronics were responsible for 27.1% of index (serious) crimes. For example, 22.7% of aggravated assaults were committed by members not in this chronic group (Tracy et al., 1990). How these nonchronic but serious-offending youths differ in risk characteristics from those fitting the chronic pattern is still unclear, and how their intervention needs differ is virtually unexamined (Tolan & Thomas, 1990).

The recent formulations about the difference in prognosis for early- and late-initiating offenders may be a useful guide for legal system involvement (Moffitt, 1993; Tolan, 1988). A basic distinction between the two groups is that early starters have a greater tendency to be involved in serious criminal behavior chronically and to have life-course persistent criminal behavior (Moffitt, 1993; Tolan & Thomas, 1995). For example, in a national sample, Tolan and Thomas (1995) found those adolescents starting before age 12 were six to eight times more likely to commit serious felonies over 2 or more years than those starting later. However, the prognosis is such behavior will discontinue after adolescence even among the early starting and seriously involved. Thus, it is impractical, at present, to base imposed treatment on this distinction. The current scientific knowledge base about risk is too limited in power and accuracy to justify legally based action or to specify which intervention programs should be provided to which youths. This should improve as more refined developmental models are proposed and empirically validated (Loeber et al., 1993). Finally, analytic methods that permit consideration of multiple patterns and multiple dimensions of categorizing patterns of involvement are being applied.

The primary tension here is between the legal concern and the preventive interest. The legal concern is not to impose treatment or attach the social stigma of labeling someone as criminal-prone prior to such behavior, due process, and determination of guilt. The preventive interest is to identify those at-risk early and to provide intervention. The legal concern is with minimizing false positives (including those not truly at-risk) whereas the preventive concern is with false negatives (missing those at-risk). Our current knowledge base is too biased toward false positives to satisfy civil liberty and criminal process concerns. However, a useful alternative may be to use this distinction and related risk factors to alert parents, schools, and social service agencies of the likely value of voluntary referral. At present, inclusion decisions may be better based in risk/benefit analyses.

Risks/Benefits of Inclusion

There are risks and benefits of focusing efforts on either the early-onset, seriously, and chronically involved group or the group that starts later and is often less seriously and chronically involved. If one focuses on the more seriously and more persistently involved subject, then there is reason to believe more intensive and costly services will be needed and that a smaller proportion will respond (Gordon, 1983). However, the ultimate impact on crime from stopping or preventing development of chronic criminal behavior of each member of this group is greater. As a result, one can find compelling arguments for focusing the scarce resources of the juvenile court on early identification and treatment of the most serious, violent delinquents (Coates, 1984; Fagan & Hartstone, 1986). Because identification may only be accurate enough once repeated appearances before the court occur, the likelihood of full response at this late stage is limited. Expensive long-term management may be the realistic need (Mulvey et al., 1993).

Others suggest the limited efficacy of interventions with the chronic group shows that focusing resources on them would be dissipating the potential impact that could occur if the larger but less intensively involved portion of delinquents were treated (Lorion, Tolan, & Wahler, 1987). Less serious and chronic delinquents are more likely to respond and need less extensive and costly interventions, but this segment also has a high rate of "natural recovery." Thus, intervention benefits over nonintervention may be temporary or modest.

Present knowledge suggests that there is a practical trade-off of likely responsiveness to treatment with predictability of risk and seriousness of offending. The present scientific knowledge can guide but not fully direct. This judgment remains political. The need, however, is to better blend and balance the legal and scientific criteria.

Legal Versus Scientific Criterion for Inclusion

As already alluded to, an important consideration in deciding whom to target and include is the tension between preventive identification and legal due process. It has been argued that because all delinquency treatment occurs as part of a legal system and usually as a disposition of a criminal justice procedure, that participation is inherently coercive and, therefore, must be applied to only those shown to be criminally culpable (guilty). This argument imposes a different set of criteria and standards for inclusion decisions than occurs when empirical risk models are used. Accuracy is still of interest. Unlike most preventive approaches, however, legal principles weigh false positives as much more troublesome than false negatives. Two legal principles are influential: (a) Legal justification exists for infringement on freedom through intervention, and (b) indication exists that the treatment imposed will be beneficial (Saul & Davidson, 1983; Scull, 1984). Thus, any delinquency prevention or treatment program may need to consider these additional inclusion criteria to balance legal and scientific concerns.

As noted elsewhere, the legal criteria, although more justifiable in regard to criminal procedures, do not have empirical support for accuracy at identifying criminals or predicting future offending. Also, it is a false distinction to assume no intervention is needed simply because guilt has not been proven (Binder & Geis, 1984). Thus, program developers cannot confidentially rely on legal or scientific direction at this point. A careful balance of empirical, ethical, and political considerations is needed for judging the effectiveness of interventions.

What Are Reasonable Standards for Judging an Intervention Effective or Useful?

Potential Harm of Identification

From a policy perspective, we must consider that any identification as a delinquent or predelinquent carries stigma and a possible decrease in individual liberty (Ezell, 1992). Harm may result by simply identifying an individual as being at-risk or including that person in a group receiving treatment (McCord, 1978). Also, identification does not ensure one will receive beneficial treatment. Related to this are the implications from a finding that offering programs can lead to shifts in the identification procedures. Policies to limit the reach of the court may be undermined because under stricter inclusion criteria, children who might otherwise not be arrested are charged with more serious crimes because it is believed they may benefit from a diversion or prevention program (Saul & Davidson, 1983).

One common characteristic of all participates in delinquency treatment programs as a result of their involvement with the court is that their participation has been coerced to some extent. For some, participation may prevent further legal sanctions. For others, participation may be a requirement for fulfilling a sentence. For still others, it may be an unnegotiable part of an incarceration. This coercive base to all delinquency treatment may limit the ability to generalize efficacy judgments from volunteer-based demonstration projects (Scull, 1984). Some contend that because treatment is imposed as a legal sanction, this coercion increases the likelihood of further legal problems. For example, if a family is required to participate in family therapy but the father refuses to do so, the target child can face harsher sanctions, the parents may be cited with contempt, or the other children may be removed from the home (Blomberg, 1977).

The Unproven Value of Intervention Timing

It is generally believed that early identification and involvement in preventive treatment efforts will diminish risk for participation in antisocial and delinquent behavior. In fact, no test of the effects of timing of intervention on delinquency has been done. The closest test of such a principle was a parent-training program conducted by Patterson et al. (1992) for parents of children with conduct problems. These investigators found that program effects only occurred for the younger cohort. This does not imply that earlier intervention is better or that long-term impact will be greater. Another possibility is that rather than timing effects, programs are effective because they are intensive, organized, and comprehensive (see Borduin et al., 1995; Chamberlain & Friman, Chapter 39; Rice & Harris, Chapter 40, both this volume). This alternative explanation merits careful consideration because scientific evidence that early intervention is necessary for substantial impact is critical to its legal justification. If the problem is, instead, to bring adequate economic and personnel resources to high-risk youth, then timing may be less important.

Although there has not been any sufficient test of the value of early identification versus adequate intervention at the time of delinquency, early intervention may be compelling for other reasons. If (a) it is more difficult to treat the more seriously involved, (b) the level of seriousness seems to progress over time, and (c) the more seriously involved tend to start earlier than other children, then it follows that efforts should be made to identify at-risk individuals and involve them in programs as early as possible. Early involvement usually is less costly, and responsiveness usually is greater (Miller, 1994). As adolescent delinquents become more involved in serious delinquency and more embroiled in the juvenile justice system, their ability to respond to and sustain intervention benefits lessens (Ezell, 1992; Gensheimer et al., 1986). Thus, early intervention may block the iatrogenic effects of greater involvement in the legal system (Austin, Krisberg, & Joe, 1987).

Differential Impact of Interventions

Evidence is emerging that most programs do not have the same effect on all delinquents. Programs that work for one group of delinquents may not work for another. For example, intensive psychotherapy, although effective for violent adolescents in residential treatment (Hartstone & Cocozza, 1983), has demonstrated negative effects for other delinquent populations (Tolan & Guerra, 1994a, 1994b). Youths coming before the court are heterogeneous as to extent of problems, criminal involvement and persistence, and need for intervention. Thus, application of programs cannot be simply a matter of demonstrating some effect or meeting some legal criteria for inclusion. If identification and treatment are to be meaningful, they must aid in targeting subgroups that will benefit from particular interventions. Such identification requires greater sophistication than currently exists. In particular, there is a need for studies that can test for whom and under what circumstances delinquency treatment programs are substantially effective (Tolan, Kendall, & Beidel, 1996).

Each of the considerations can and should influence judgments about what is effective and the utility of programs, as well as the measured impact one finds. Program development and program operations need to include these factors. If not, evaluation of impact may be inaccurate or of little use.

How Should the Legal Principles of Equity and Uniformity of Justice Administration Be Balanced Against Maintaining Prescriptive Responses Sensitive to Each Situation?

Conflicts between the treatment and justice models are illustrated by legal interest in having all those committing a given crime receive the same punishment versus the rehabilitative interest in prescriptive responding based on the circumstances and background of the delinquent (Feld, 1983). The obvious conflict of these general principles can be complicated further by variations in procedures among juvenile courts (Fagan et al., 1984). Rates of referral and the characteristics influencing processing (e.g., type of crime, age, criminal history, ethnicity) vary substantially from court to court. Plea bargaining can shift the charges brought to trial. Equity becomes difficult to determine when some delinquents have plea bargained to less serious charges, whereas others have not been able to do so (Fagan et al., 1984). Further, the public now demands the management of delinquents to reduce the likelihood of a "dangerous" person being released. However, the ability to predict dangerousness remains quite low for scientific as well as clinical reasons (Mulvey et al., 1993). Thus, equity and dangerousness remain poorly articulated like other disposition-influencing concepts, and there is little understanding about the relative influence they should have on juvenile justice decisions. These terms and the principles and goals of juvenile justice they represent need more careful and explicit consideration in treatment programming. There is a need to recognize that tension will remain between uniformity and the specific needs of each case.

How Should Public Opinion Be Incorporated Into Policy Decisions? Should Court Procedures, Dispositions, and Intervention Methods and Provisions Be Reactive to Public Opinion?

A basic principle of our legal system is that court procedures and actions should not merely reflect majority rule. Courts should not be swayed by public opinion in the formation of policy but rather they should be guided by statutes, case precedents, and jurisprudence (McCarthy & Carr, 1980). As with any public institution, however, the juvenile court serves the public and, to some extent, reflects the democratic will. This constitutional role imposes constraints on juvenile delinquency treatment programs because they must be imposed in a manner consistent with the law but also with cognizance of the political ramifications of treatment decisions. Also, historical shifts occur in the demands made on the court related to beliefs about treatment, what type of crime is more serious, and how much judicial latitude is acceptable. Thus, program decisions may be related to many influences other than jurisprudence or scientific progress. For example, with the declared "war on drugs" during the late 1980s, there was an influx of drug cases (36% increase) into the court and minimal sentencing requirements were imposed (Krisberg, 1992). The mandate placed on the court was to get tough with drug dealers and users, although the accumulating evidence was that legal prosecution would have little effect on the market or on the users (Krisberg, 1992). The impact of these policy changes on administration of treatment programs and their effects

was probably great but not considered. Thus, even though a policy may not make empirical sense, its political importance is a major influence on court operations and treatment administration.

An important consideration in understanding juvenile delinquency treatment is how these shifts in policy tend to occur. For example, the current movement toward harsher penalties, retribution as a motive for sentencing, and the disbelief about rehabilitative efforts by the juvenile justice system has been attributed to the public's demand for these changes. This demand is based on the stated perception that youth crime is increasing in rate and seriousness (Krisberg, 1992). However, the perception about youth crime varies substantially from the best estimates of actual patterns of crime. For example, adults believed youth crime was increasing during the late 1970s when it was actually decreasing, and a similar discrepancy was evident in the mid-1980s (Krisberg, 1992). Public perception of youth crime is not always accurate.

In addition, politicians and the media do not always represent the prevailing beliefs of the public accurately, and this can mislead policy. Evidence exist that public sentiment does not fit a simplistic solution of getting tougher and transferring juveniles to adult court. A 1991 comprehensive public opinion survey of attitudes toward juvenile crime confirmed that a majority of respondents were very concerned about juvenile crime (Schwartz, 1992). Eighty-two percent of respondents believed that the amount of serious juvenile crime had increased in their state, and 78% indicated concern about becoming the victim of serious violent crime. However, 88% of the respondents believed that the primary purpose of the juvenile court should be to treat and rehabilitate offenders. Only 12% of those surveyed stated that the primary purpose of the court should be to punish offenders.

When the same respondents were asked how the court should treat juveniles who commit specific types of serious crimes, the responses showed variation by crime type. Ninety-nine percent believed that juveniles who commit serious violent crimes should be punished, and 68% stated that juveniles who commit violent crimes should be tried in adult courts. Although the public wants offenders to be punished for crimes committed, depending on the type of crime, between 88% and 95% of those surveyed supported rehabilitation if at all possible. Seventy-one percent indicated that they favored a system that relied on community-based services rather than a training school approach (Schwartz, 1992).

As noted by Schwartz (1992), these results suggest the public may not be as demanding of harsh punishment to the exclusion of rehabilitation as public officials have implied. Respondents wanted investment in programs in which offenders receive job training, have access to community-based educational opportunities, and receive counseling and intensive community-based supervision. The direction that would be taken from public opinion is more enlightened, compassionate, and probably more cost effective than many of the policies being offered as "public sentiment" and currently guiding the court (Schwartz, 1992).

CONCLUSIONS AND RECOMMENDATIONS

These many competing forces within the juvenile justice system influence the type of programs that can be developed, how they can operate, and what impact they ultimately have. Their importance and the ensuing organizational tensions may make it seem impossible to develop and deliver prototypic treatments that are effective. Rather than concluding that the system is too complex or too haphazard to permit viable planning, we believe it is important to recognize and incorporate these ongoing tensions in program planning, to expect them to be the context for how planned programs will actually function. Further, there is some empirical evidence that can immediately guide intervention and policy decisions.

What Works

The weight of the evidence is that punishment approaches and exclusive focus on legal procedures will not substantially affect delinquency. There is evidence for efficacy of several treatment approaches to delinquency (Lipsey, 1992; Mulvey et al., 1993; Tolan & Guerra, 1994a). In particular, programs that are structured and focus on behavioral change are most effective. Treatment programs that teach practical employment skills have relatively good effects. Programs that include parent training or family organization and those that focus on modifying beliefs and attitudes about aggression and violence seem most promising for preventing or curtailing involvement in delinquent behavior. In general, multicomponent programs are advised. Community and school-based programs also have been identified as effective (Tolan & Guerra, 1994b).

The weight of the evidence shows that community-based interventions are at least as effective as residential treatment or incarceration-based interventions. In fact, they may be more effective. However, community-based programs carry a potential of increasing negative public perceptions, particularly as any crime committed by those in community programs may be ascribed to the fact that they were not incarcerated. Similarly, the evidence supports more intensive programming that provides skills, support, and follow-up. However, such programs are labeled as coddling criminals or wasting tax money. The full cost/benefit ratios determined and the empirical evidence supporting these approaches need to be disseminated.

Three Areas in Need of Further Research and Policy Review

Although efficacious approaches and impressive demonstration programs can be found, the primary weakness is the generalizability of such findings to heterogeneous systems dealing with a wide variety of needs. To advance beyond this status, research and policy attention to three areas are required. First, the practical utility of the existing knowledge base for identification is too limited to guide action. Neither a legal criteria nor a statistical prediction approach can powerfully or accurately differentiate who is at-risk, who among those starting delinquency is likely to show serious or chronic criminality, or who is likely to respond to different types of programs. These questions need direct testing. Also, existing scientific evidence should not be ignored but should be incorporated judiciously as preferred approaches.

Second, many of the programs developed make little distinction of impact beyond reporting some overall statistical differences between two groups. As a result, the actual potential benefit is hard to discern. There is a need to provide results in terms that make the practical implications more obvious. Also, there is a need to disaggregate these findings to explain whom the program helps, hinders, and does not affect. In addition, there is a need to determine moderation of program impact due to behavioral characteristics (e.g., level of delinquency), circumstantial characteristics (e.g., family background, educational level), and operational integrity. Similarly, evaluations are needed that help determine what circumstances mediate program delivery and impact.

Finally, and perhaps most important, there is a need to link program impact to the organizational tensions outlined in this chapter. What are the juvenile justice system characteristics that promote successful program development and sustain programs? What are examples of a successful balance of the pressures of these various tensions? What are viable strategies for addressing public sentiment but maintaining an empirical and jurisprudent focus? How do we better blend legal and treatment goals and principles?

All of these questions need to be considered in future program development, intervention trials, and evaluation research. Otherwise, we are unlikely to make real progress in treating juvenile delinquency. We will be limited to producing experimental demonstrations that are not adopted in practice and to having programs that do not operate as they are planned; and we will periodically provide summary reviews that repeatedly suggest some approaches are efficacious, but we will know too little to conclude how to use this information.

REFERENCES

Austin, J., Elms, W., Krisberg, B., & Steele, P. A. (1991). *Unlocking juvenile corrections: Evaluating the Massachusetts Department of Youth Services.* San Francisco: National Council on Crime and Delinquency.

Austin, J., Krisberg, B., & Joe, K. (1987). *The impact of juvenile court intervention* [Monograph]. San Francisco: National Council on Crime and Delinquency.

Binder, A., & Geis, G. (1984). *Ad populum* argumentation in criminology: Juvenile diversion as rhetoric. *Crime and Delinquency, 30,* 624–647.

Blomberg, T. G. (1977). Diversion and accelerated social control. *Journal of Criminal Law and Criminology, 68,* 274–282.

Borduin, C. M., Mann, B. J., Cone, L. T., Henggeler, S. W., Fucci, B. R., Blaske, D. M., & Williams, R. A. (1995). Multisystemic treatment of serious juvenile offenders: Long-term prevention of criminality and violence. *Journal of Consulting and Clinical Psychology, 63,* 509–518.

Bortner, M. A. (1986). Traditional rhetoric, organizational realities: Remand of juveniles to adult court. *Crime and Delinquency, 32,* 53–73.

Bry, B. H. (1982). Reducing the incidence of adolescent problems through preventive intervention: One- and five-year follow-up. *American Journal of Community Psychology, 10,* 265–276.

Castellano, T. C. (1986). The justice model in the juvenile justice system: Washington State's experience. *Law and Policy, 8,* 479–506.

Chamberlain, P. (1990). Comparative evaluation of Specialized Foster Care for seriously delinquent youths: A first step. *Community Alternatives: International Journal of Family Care, 13,* 21–36.

Chamberlain, P., & Reid, J. B. (1991). Using a specialized foster care community treatment model for children and adolescents leaving the state mental hospital. *Journal of Community Psychology, 19,* 266–276.

Coates, R. B. (1984). Appropriate alternatives for the violent juvenile offender. In R. A. Mathias, P. DeMuro, & R. S. Allison (Eds.), *Violent juvenile offenders: An anthology*. San Francisco: National Council on Crime and Delinquency.

Elliott, D. S. (1994). Serious violent offenders: Onset, developmental course, and termination. The American Society of Criminology 1993 presidential address. *Criminology, 32*, 1–21.

Elliott, D. S., Ageton, S. S., & Cantor, R. J. (1979). An integrated theoretical perspective on delinquent behavior. *Journal of Research in Crime and Delinquency, 16*, 3–27.

Ezell, M. (1992). Juvenile arbitration: Net-widening and other unintended consequences. *Journal of Research in Crime and Delinquency, 26*, 358–377.

Fagan, J. A. (1990). Treatment and reintegration of violent juvenile offenders: Experimental results. *Justice Quarterly, 7*, 233–263.

Fagan, J. A. (1995). Separating the men from the boys: The comparative advantage of juvenile versus criminal court sanctions on recidivism among adolescent felony offenders. In J. C. Howell, B. Krisberg, J. D. Hawkins, & J. J. Wilson (Eds.), *A sourcebook: Serious, violent, & chronic juvenile offenders* (Chap. 8, pp. 238–260). Thousand Oaks, CA: Sage Publications.

Fagan, J. A., & Hartstone, E. (1986). *Innovation and experimentation in juvenile corrections: Implementing a community reintegration model for violent juvenile offenders*. Washington, DC: Office of Juvenile Justice and Delinquency Prevention.

Fagan, J. A., Hartstone, E., Rudman, C. J., & Hansen, K. V. (1984). System processing of violent juvenile offenders: An empirical assessment. In R. A. Mathias, P. DeMuro, & R. S. Allison (Eds.), *Violent juvenile offenders: An anthology*. San Francisco: National Council on Crime and Delinquency.

Farrington, D. P., Ohlin, L. E., & Wilson, J. Q. (1986). *Understanding and controlling crime: Toward a new research strategy*. New York: Springer-Verlag.

Feld, B. C. (1983). Delinquent careers and criminal policy: Just deserts and the waiver decision. *Criminology, 21*, 195.

Feld, B. C. (1992). Criminalizing the juvenile court: A research agenda for the 1990s. In I. M. Schwartz (Ed.), *Juvenile justice and public policy: Toward a national agenda*. New York: Lexington Books.

Feldman, R. A. (1992). The St. Louis experiment: Effective treatment of antisocial youths in prosocial peer groups. In J. McCord & R. Tremblay (Eds.), *Preventing antisocial behavior: Interventions from birth through adolescence* (pp. 233–252). New York: Guilford.

Gensheimer, L. K., Mayer, J. P., Gottschalk, R., & Davidson, W. S. (1986). Diverting youth from the juvenile justice system: A meta-analysis of intervention efficacy. In S. J. Apter & A. P. Goldstein (Eds.), *Youth violence: Programs and prospects* (pp. 39–57). Elmsford, NY: Pergamon.

Gordon, R. (1983). An operational definition of prevention. *Public Health Reports, 98*, 107–109.

Gottfredson, D. (1987). Peer group interventions to reduce the risk of delinquent behavior: A selective review and a new evaluation. *Criminology, 25*, 671–714.

Guerra, N. G., & Slaby, R. G. (1990). Cognitive mediators of aggression in adolescent offenders: II. Intervention. *Developmental Psychology, 26*, 269–277.

Guerra, N. G., Tolan, P. H., & Hammond, R. (1995). Interventions for adolescent violence. In L. G. Gentry, J. P. Schlagel, & L. Eron (Eds.), *Reason to hope: A psychosocial perspective on violence and youth* (pp. 383–404). Washington, DC: American Psychological Association.

Hartstone, E., & Cocozza, J. (1983). Violent youth: The impact of mental health treatment. *International Journal of Law and Psychiatry, 6*, 207–224.

Hawkins, J. D., Catalano, R. F., & Brewer, D. D. (1995). Preventing serious, violent, and chronic juvenile offending: Effective strategies from conception to age six. In J. C. Howell, B. Krisberg, & J. D. Hawkins (Eds.), *A Sourcebook: Serious, violent, and chronic juvenile offenders* (Chap. 3, pp. 47–60). Thousand Oaks, CA: Sage Publications.

Henggeler, S. W., & Borduin, C. M. (1990). *Family therapy and beyond: A multisystemic approach to treating the behavior problems of children and adolescents*. Pacific Grove, CA: Brooks/Cole.

Henggeler, S. W., Melton, G. B., & Smith, L. A. (1992). Family preservation using multisystemic therapy: An effective alternative to incarcerating serious juvenile offenders. *Journal of Consulting and Clinical Psychology, 60*, 953–961.

Henggeler, S. W., Melton, G. B., Smith, L. A., Schoenwald, M. A., & Hanley, J. H. (1993). Family preservation using multisystemic treatment: Long-term follow-up to a clinical trial with serious juvenile offenders. *Journal of Child and Family Studies, 2*, 283–293.

Jacob, H. (1983). Courts as organizations. In L. Mather & K. Boyum (Eds.), *Empirical theories about the courts* (pp. 191–215). White Plains, NY: Longman.

Jones, M. B., & Offord, D. R. (1989). Reduction of antisocial behavior in poor children by nonschool skill-development. *Journal of Child Psychology and Psychiatry, 30*(5), 737–750.

Kazdin, A. E. (1993). Treatment of conduct disorder: Progress and directions in psychotherapy research. *Development and Psychopathology, 5*, 277–310.

Kendall, P. C., & Grove, W. (1988). Normative comparisons in therapy outcome. *Behavioral Assessment, 10*, 147–158.

Krisberg, B. (1992). Youth crime and its prevention: A research agenda. In I. M. Schwartz (Ed.), *Juvenile justice and public policy: Toward a national agenda*. New York: Lexington Books.

Krisberg, B., Austin, J., Joe, K., & Steele, P. (1987). *The impact of juvenile court sanctions*. San Francisco: National Council on Crime and Delinquency.

Lipsey, M. W. (1992). Juvenile delinquency treatment: A meta-analytic inquiry into the variability of effects. In T. D. Cook, H. Cooper, D. S. Cordray, H. Harmann, L. D. Hedges, R. J. Light, T. A. Lewis, & F. Mosteller (Eds.), *Meta-analysis for explanation: A casebook*. New York: Russell Sage.

Lipsey, M. W., & Wilson, D. B. (1993). The efficacy of psychological, educational, and behavioral treatment: Confirmation from meta-analysis. *American Psychologist, 48*, 1181–1209.

Loeber, R., Wung, P., Keenan, K., Giroux, B., Stouthamer-Loeber, M., Van Kammen, W. B., & Maugham, B. (1993). Developmental pathways in disruptive child behavior. *Development and Psychopathology, 15*, 101–133.

Lorion, R. P., Tolan, P. H., & Wahler, R. G. (1987). Prevention. In H. C. Quay (Ed.), *Handbook of juvenile delinquency*. New York: Wiley.

Macallair, D. (1993). Reaffirming rehabilitation in juvenile justice. *Youth and Society, 25*, 104–125.

Martinson, R. (1974). What works? Questions and answers about prison reform. *Public Interest, 35*, 22–54.

McCarthy, F. B., & Carr, J. G. (1980). *Juvenile law and its processes*. New York: Bobbs-Merrill.

McCord, J. (1978). A thirty-year follow-up of treatment effects. *American Psychologist, 33*, 284–289.

Miller, L. (1994). Preventive interventions for conduct disorder. *Child and Adolescent Psychiatric Clinics, 3*(2) 405–420.

Moffitt, T. E. (1993). Adolescent-limited and life-course persistent antisocial behavior: A developmental taxonomy. *Psychological Review, 100*, 674–701.

Mulvey, E. P., Arthur, M. W., & Reppucci, N. D. (1993). The prevention and treatment of juvenile delinquency: A review of the research. *Clinical Psychology Review, 13*, 133–157.

Orlando, F. A., & Crippen, G. L. (1992). The rights of children and the juvenile court. In I. M. Schwartz (Ed.), *Juvenile justice and public policy: Toward a national agenda.* New York: Lexington Books.

Patterson, G. R., Reid, J. B., & Dishion, T. J. (1992). *Antisocial boys.* Eugene, OR: Castalia.

Rubin, H. T. (1985). *Juvenile justice: Policy, practice, and law* (2nd ed.). New York: Random House.

Sarason, S. B. (1971). *The culture of the school and the problem of change.* Boston: Allyn & Bacon.

Saul, J. A., & Davidson, W. S. (1983). Implementation of juvenile diversion programs: Cast your net on the other side of the boat. In J. R. Kluegel (Ed.), *Evaluating juvenile justice* (pp. 31–45). Beverly Hills, CA: Sage Publications.

Schinke, S. P., Orlandi, M. A., & Cole, K. C. (1992). Boys and girls clubs in public housing developments: Prevention services for youths at risk. *Journal of Community Psychology, 20*, 118–128.

Schneider, A. L. (1984). Sentencing guidelines and recidivism rates of juvenile offenders. *Justice Quarterly, 1*, 107–124.

Schneider, A. L., & Schram, D. (1983). *A comparison of intake and sentencing decision making under rehabilitation and justice models of the juvenile system: Vol. 5. An assessment of juvenile justice system reform in Washington State.* Institute of Policy Analysis.

Schwartz, I. M. (1992). Juvenile crime-fighting policies: What the public really wants. In I. M. Schwartz (Ed.), *Juvenile justice and public policy: Toward a national agenda.* New York: Lexington Books.

Scull, A. T. (1984). *Decarceration: Community treatment and the deviant— A radical view* (2nd ed.). New Brunswick, NJ: Rutgers University Press.

Shorts, I. D. (1986). Delinquency by association? Outcome of joint participation by at-risk and convicted youths in a community-based programme. *British Journal of Criminology, 26*(2), 156–163.

Stouthamer-Loeber, M., & Loeber, R. (1988). The use of prediction data in understanding delinquency. *Behavioral Sciences and the Law, 6*, 333–354.

Tolan, P. H. (1988). Socioeconomic, family, and social stress correlates of adolescents' antisocial and delinquent behavior. *Journal of Abnormal Child Psychology, 16*, 317–332.

Tolan, P. H. (1996). Characteristics shared by exemplary child clinical interventions for indicated populations. In M. C. Roberts (Ed.), *Model programs in service delivery in child and family mental health.* Hillsdale, NJ: Erlbaum.

Tolan, P. H., & Guerra, N. G. (1994a). Prevention of delinquency: Current status and issues. *Journal of Applied and Preventive Psychology, 3*, 251–273.

Tolan, P. H., & Guerra, N. G. (1994b). *What works in reducing adolescent violence: An empirical review of the field* [Monograph prepared for the Center for the Study and Prevention of Youth Violence]. Boulder: University of Colorado Press.

Tolan, P. H., Kendall, P. C., & Beidel, D. C. (1996). *A call for treatment comparison studies of child and adolescent interventions.* Manuscript submitted for publication.

Tolan, P. H., & Loeber, R. (1993). Antisocial behavior. In P. H. Tolan & B. J. Cohler (Eds.), *Handbook of clinical research and practice with adolescents* (pp. 207–331). New York: Wiley.

Tolan, P. H., & Thomas, P. (1988). Correlates of delinquency participation and persistence. *Criminal Justice and Human Behavior, 15*, 306–327.

Tolan, P. H., & Thomas, P. (1995). The implications of age of onset for delinquency risk: II. Longitudinal data. *Journal of Abnormal Child Psychology, 23*, 157–181.

Tracy, P. E., Wolfgang, M. E., & Figlio, R. M. (1990). *Delinquency careers in two birth cohorts.* New York: Plenum.

Webster-Stratton, C., Hollingsworth, T., & Kolpacoff, M. (1989). The long-term effectiveness and clinical significance of three cost-effective training programs for families with conduct-problem children. *Journal of Consulting and Clinical Psychology, 57*, 550–553.

Weischeit, R., & Alexander, D. (1988). Juvenile justice philosophy and the demise of parens patriae. *Federal Probation, 41*, 56–63.

Weisz, J. R., Donenberg, G. R., Han, S. S., & Kauneckis, D. (1995). Child and adolescent psychotherapy outcomes in experiments versus clinics: Why the disparity. *Journal of Abnormal Child Psychology, 23*, 83–106.

CASES CITED

In re D. F. B., 430 N.W. 2d. 476 (1988)

In re Gault, 387 v.s. 1 (1967)

In re Seven Minors, 99 Nev. 427, 664 P 2d 947 (1983).

CHAPTER 39

Residential Programs for Antisocial Children and Adolescents

PATRICIA CHAMBERLAIN and PATRICK C. FRIMAN

BACKGROUND

Placement in residential programs is a widely used, rapidly growing method of treating children and adolescents with severe conduct problems and antisocial behavior. In 1983 more than 19,000 children were in residential care. By 1986 that number had increased by 32% to more than 25,000 (Select Committee on Children, Youth, and Families, 1990). These data do not include for-profit residential treatment centers, so they underestimate the total number of youths in residential care. The American Public Welfare Association estimated that in 1990 there were 65,000 children and adolescents in residential care and the associated costs, when combined with costs for institutionalized care, comprised approximately 70% of the funding for children's mental health services (U.S. Department of Health and Human Services, 1995).

The proportion of these youths who have serious conduct problems and antisocial behavior is unknown, but it is likely that rates at least parallel the proportion of such cases referred to mental health clinics (i.e., two thirds of all referrals). A study comparing behavior problems in samples of youths from residential care and inpatient psychiatric care found no difference in levels of externalizing problems (Friman, Evans, Larzelere, Williams, & Daly, 1993).

Theoretical Underpinnings

Pioneers of theoretically based residential care treatments, such as Redl and Wineman (1952), described these settings as laboratories with the potential for gaining total therapeutic control over youth life. The goal of residential treatment was to create a therapeutic milieu in which everyday events were turned into corrective experiences and "healing through living" (Wells, 1991) could occur.

Support for this project was provided by Grant No. R01 MH47458 from the Center for Studies of Violent Behavior and Traumatic Stress, NIMH, U.S. PHS, and Grant No. P50 MH46690 from the Prevention Research Branch, NIMH, U.S. PHS.

Judy Boler prepared and edited the manuscript. Keith Flicker and Malcolm Tabor from the State of Oregon Office for Services to Children and Families were instrumental in permitting the conduct of the NIMH study.

Early accounts of "therapeutic milieus" for severely antisocial youngsters are informative in terms of the clinical issues addressed and staff effort and commitment required for success. Bettelheim (1982), in his address commemorating the 75th anniversary of the Hawthorne Cedar Knolls School, noted that as much could be learned from failures in residential care as from successes. He described early attempts to apply psychoanalytic practice directly to the institutional care of children. He suggested that "gangsters" of all ages learn better from lessons taught through daily experiences than from uncovering the unconscious like "nice neurotics, hysterics, and compulsive characters for whom psychoanalysis can be of value" (p. 57). This assumption has since been empirically supported in studies on the treatment of children and adolescents with conduct disorders (Kazdin, 1985; G. E. Miller & Prinz, 1990).

Influence of Public Policy on Residential Care

In the United States, the goal of the 1980 Adoption Assistance and Child Welfare Act was to keep children and their families together. The law allows for but discourages out-of-home placement in residential care or institutions and calls for returning children to family settings, biological or otherwise. Avoiding residential placement has also been advocated by various professional and advocacy groups that complain about its costs relative to its benefits and tout home-based and community corrections alternatives (e.g., Wolins, 1974). Whittaker (1990), in a summary of concerns about residential placement, wrote that it was intrusive, overused, potentially abusive and neglectful, highly variable in effectiveness, and costly. A prevalent related notion is that residential centers are highly resistant to change, regardless of input from community and professional sources. For these (and other) reasons, residential care can perpetuate the cycle of increasingly restrictive placements for troubled youths (Rothman, 1980).

Nonetheless, since the 1974 Juvenile Justice and Delinquency Prevention Act, there has been a large increase in community-based residential programs for adolescents. Although placement in residential care is seen as the last resort (prior to incarceration) for treatment of youths with severe antisocial behavior, such programs exist in every state. Furthermore, empirical studies, although directly relevant for managing antisocial behavior and conduct disorders, often have limited influence on treatments used in these programs.

Contemporary approaches to residential care are characterized by a broad range of placement settings, including institutional settings that use shift workers, family-style group homes in community settings, psychiatric hospitalization, wilderness programs, boot camps, training schools, and, more recently, treatment or therapeutic foster care. The theoretical foundations for these programs vary widely, ranging from those with virtually no underlying theory to guide program development to those known as much for their theory as for their accomplishments. Although the range of out-of-home placements used for antisocial children is broad, in this chapter we confine our review to findings from family-style residential care models.

In Table 39.1 we briefly review four representative program models. These are the Teaching Family Model (TFM), Project Re-ED, Positive Peer Culture (PPC), and Treatment Foster Care (TFC). The table summarizes each model's basic theoretical tenets, living setting characteristics, staffing patterns, and key treatment features. Even though these models are the most widely used and influential in the residential care field, systematic studies using well-controlled designs have been few and far between, especially for PPC and Project Re-ED. For example, the representative study on PPC was conducted in an Omaha education setting rather than in a residential setting (Siegel & Senna, 1988; Vorrath & Brendtro, 1985). Although evaluations of PPC have been conducted with youths in residential placement, the Omaha-based study is better known and more rigorously designed and used more concrete outcome variables than those conducted in residential settings. The only major evaluation on Project Re-ED has been criticized for being incomplete (Weinstein, 1974) and for using weak measures (Mordock, 1993). Evaluations of the TFM have been more frequent, comprehensive, and rigorous in terms of measures used and designs (Friman, Almquist, Soper, & Lucas, 1995). Studies on the efficacy of TFC have shown some promising results (Bryant & Snodgrass, 1992; Hawkins, Almeida, & Samet, 1990) but, with a few exceptions, have not included comparison or control groups (Chamberlain & Reid, 1991; Clark et al., 1994).

The empirical gap in research on residential placement is real and hard to explain, especially in light of the abundant research on interventions for childhood conduct problems, antisocial behavior, and aggression. This literature is probably more highly developed than for any other childhood disorder, with the possible exception of attention deficit disorder. Since the early 1960s, several controlled clinical trials have been conducted testing the efficacy of treatments and, more recently, of preventive interventions that target these problems.

Several studies have shown that environmentally mediated treatments based on a set of well-prescribed learning principles

TABLE 39.1 Characteristics of Four Residential Care Models

Program	Theory	Living Setting	Staffing Pattern	Treatment Features
Teaching Family Model	Operant Learning Theory	Family-style group home with 4 to 8 youths	Teaching parents	a. Token economy motivational system b. Self-government with youths having input into rules and structure c. Focus on teaching social skills d. Continuous evaluation of youth progress and TFM parents' performance e. Limited use of mental health services, emphasis on normalization
Project Re-ED	Ecological Transactional Learning Theory	Residential schools	Two teacher counselors for each group of 8 children	a. Targets treatment with youths and community b. Aims to improve fit between children and others in their social system c. Aims to improve support and instruction youngsters need for further development
Positive Peer Culture	Positive Peer Culture (peer group has the most influence over youths)	Varies widely from in-school programs to PPC for incarcerated youths	Groups are run by peers and supervised by adults	a. Guided group interaction b. Establishment of a coercive group process that aims to foster a subculture of caring, responsibility, and prosocial interactions c. Youth behavior evaluated against standard of whether it helps more than it hurts others
Treatment Foster Care	Social Learning Theory	One or 2 youths placed in each family	TFC parents are trained and supervised as members of a treatment team that includes a case manager and other treatment agents (family therapist, parole/probation)	a. TFC parents as primary change agents b. Structured treatment plan with clearly specified targets and daily expectations c. Mental health services added as necessary d. Close monitoring of youth adjustment in school e. Association with peers with similar problems minimized f. Family (biological/adoptive) treatment usually included

are effective in producing lasting, positive changes in child antisocial behavior (e.g., Kazdin, 1985; Reid & Patterson, 1976; Webster-Stratton & Hammond, 1990). These findings and others, obtained from studies in education and sociology, reflect the developmental course and treatment of childhood conduct problems and could increase the effectiveness of residential programming. But, with a few notable exceptions (e.g., the Teaching Family Model), the residential care field has failed to recognize or capitalize on this research.

Controversial Issues

Probably the most controversial issue in residential care is its limited demonstrated capacity to reduce postplacement problems (Friman et al., 1996; Jones, Weinrott, & Howard, 1981). Yet the most highly touted alternatives to residential placement (e.g., family preservation services) have not been shown to be superior in this regard. Controlled studies comparing residential placements to alternatives have yet to be conducted and could be difficult to design and ethically questionable. For example, should a youth who has a reasonable chance of living at home be subjected by random assignment to residential care? Controlled research could compare alternative models of care for youths placed out of their homes. Studies could also test the importance of targeting aftercare settings (e.g., family treatment), readily address important questions relating to outcomes, and identify key or salient features of treatments.

Yet how far treatment should extend or whether regular family contact and family treatment should be a part of residential treatment programs is a controversial issue within the residential care community. Logistical barriers can make family treatment for youths in care difficult to achieve, but it is also not reasonable to expect that in-placement behavior changes in youths with severe conduct problems will maintain in the postplacement environment without adult support. Ideally, parents or other aftercare persons would be trained to provide daily structure for youths, similar to that in residential care. This training would include comparable levels of supervision, discipline, and expectations for academic achievement and work skills. Failure to include parents in youth programs may be the single largest barrier to generalization of positive treatment effects postplacement. For example, highly antisocial youths in residential care are unlikely to naturally connect with or gravitate toward prosocial peers when they return home. Thus, relationships with adults and activities organized and supervised by adults become critical stabilizing components in the postplacement social world.

Garrett (1985) conducted a meta-analysis on types of treatments and their outcomes in residential care and found that individual and group therapies had no impact on recidivism, whereas family therapy appeared to be more effective. Borduin et al. (1995) also found that recidivism for institutionalized delinquents 15 months after release was significantly less for those who received family therapy (60%) than for those in the control group (93%).

Other prevalent controversies in the residential care field involve negative perceptions about the quality of youth life during placement (Clemmer, 1940; Pecora, Whittaker, Maluccio, Barth, & Plotnick, 1992). Whether these perceptions are valid is unknown because there has been little controlled research on these topics. However, they are important because American sentiment toward residential placement is increasingly suspicious, pessimistic, and hostile (Wells, 1991; Wolins, 1974).

Whereas there is extensive scientific evidence showing that youths' lives before placement are filled with failure and conduct problems (Small, Kennedy, & Bender, 1991), unlike the research on other special populations (e.g., geriatric—Williams, 1991; developmentally disabled—Schalock & Begab, 1990; mentally ill—Oliver & Mohamad, 1992), there is virtually no current research on quality of life for conduct problem youngsters in residential placement. This knowledge void has been filled by negative beliefs based on older, mostly descriptive literature (e.g., D'Amato, 1969; McEwen, 1978; Schur, 1973) and by precedent-setting court cases (e.g., *Donaldson v. O'Connor,* 1974; *Morales v. Turman,* 1973) and media influences.

Four prominent issues have characterized the quality of life controversy: (a) the lack of relevant treatment; (b) the potential for abuse or neglect from supervising adults; (c) the sense of isolation from family, friends, and community; and (d) contagion of problems from other youngsters in care (Oliver & Mohamad, 1992; Schalock & Begab, 1990; Williams, 1991).

Providing Appropriate Treatment

As indicated earlier, investigators from diverse fields have developed effective approaches for youth conduct problems. These approaches train parents, teachers, and other socializing adults to use behavior management strategies to reduce aggressive and hostile child behavior patterns. Strategies typically involve use of contingency-based management with high levels of reinforcement for appropriate child behavior, especially nonaggressive, noncoercive problem solving in difficult or challenging situations.

The concept of engineering a social environment to resocialize youths was promoted in the early 1960s by behavioral researchers (Patterson, Cobb, & Ray, 1973). The subsequent studies showed that, compared to traditional, individually focused psychotherapy, environmentally mediated treatments were more effective in changing aggressive behavior patterns. These early studies were extended and replicated by several investigators (G. E. Miller & Prinz, 1990).

Recent approaches to the prevention and treatment of conduct disorders prescribe ecologically based interventions in all of the child's key social settings (e.g., home, school, peer group; Reid, 1993). Prescriptions are based on the recognition that interventions in one setting alone are rarely sufficiently powerful to produce lasting, clinically significant change for these youths.

The best-known large-scale program using social learning principles is the Teaching Family Model (TFM). In the TFM, improvements in youth behavior are sought by programming positive parent and peer interactions and effective school performance within a family-style environment (Braukmann & Wolf, 1987). Numerous studies have demonstrated a variety of robust, positive in-program behavior changes. These include improvements in specific skill areas such as following instructions, homework completion, conversation skills, classroom behavior, and school grades (Phillips, 1968). But in-program successes of the TFM have not been matched by postplacement effects, a fact that underscores the need for intervention in multiple settings for conduct-disordered youths.

A recent study on youths at Boys Town, the largest program currently using the TFM, showed significant increases in a number of psychological variables (e.g., sense of control, relationships with adults, sense of isolation) and school performance measures (e.g., grade point average, years of school completed, graduation) for up to an 8-year period compared to youths in other residential programs (Friman et al., 1996). But previous studies of the TFM in other locations (e.g., Achievement Place) that focused on postprogram arrest rates did not find significant differences between youths in the TFM and youths in other programs (Kirigin, Braukmann, Atwater, & Wolf, 1982). Combining knowledge gained from these results and from their other extensive studies of serious delinquency, Wolf, Braukmann, and Ramp (1987) made a compelling case for categorizing chronic juvenile offending as part of a significant handicapping condition. Their aim was to provide a conceptual base for an argument similar to the one we are making here. Specifically, programs that do not target multiple settings (e.g., residential, foster, and in-home care) in multiple time frames (e.g., during and after placement) risk the loss of treatment gains following youth departure.

Relationship With Supervising Adults

It is commonly believed that the relationship between youths in placement and their supervising staff is adversarial, servile, or collusive. This is rooted in the notion of an inmate counterculture, which was vividly portrayed in Goffman's (1961) classic work *Asylums* and dates back at least to the work of Clemmer (1940). Some articles have concluded that most children entering a residential program already have negative perceptions of authority and that deprivation of their liberty can instigate resistance rather than cooperation (Empey & Stafford, 1991). These perspectives emphasize how enforcement of rules can damage the relationship between children and their care providers (Lundman, 1984).

Yet the relationship between youths and the adults with whom they live has been clearly identified in several studies as being a pivotal factor for successful child adjustment. For example, two mechanisms through which supportive adults exert their influence appear to be teaching new skills and providing supervision. Several longitudinal studies have reported that low parental supervision is a contributing variable in the development of delinquency (e.g., Farrington, 1978; Laub & Sampson, 1988). Additionally, low supervision has been associated with poor school achievement, negative peer relationships (Dishion, 1990), physical fighting (Loeber & Dishion, 1984), drug use (Baumrind, 1991), and antisocial behavior (Kazdin, 1985).

A related issue pertains to control strategies (i.e., discipline) used in residential care and who decides when controls are necessary. Social learning programs typically advocate setting clear limits and enforcing infractions with consistent mild discipline such as point/privilege loss (Coughlin & Shanahan, 1991). In these programs, limits are set and enforced by supervising adults. In peer-mediated approaches, the adolescents themselves have a much larger role in determining the need for and type of discipline (Vorrath & Brendtro, 1985). Studies on residential treatments for youngsters with serious conduct problems should examine the efficacy of discipline or control methods from the perspectives of both the caregiver and child/adolescent.

Isolation/Contagion

The common belief that residential placement produces an inexorable sense of isolation from family (Empey & Stafford, 1991;

Kiesler, 1982) has at least two sources. One is the logical conclusion that the all-encompassing nature of residential life and the presence of institutional barriers to outside contact can cause a sense of isolation. Another is based on case descriptions and first-hand accounts of life in residential settings that emphasize isolation and disconnection from family (D'Amato, 1969; Trieschman & Whittaker, 1972).

The literature suggests that the sense of isolation from family that youths experience is often matched by a sense of isolation from friends. Yet most youths referred to placement for severe conduct problems and delinquency were members of deviant peer groups prior to their placement, and isolating them from those peers may be part of successful program planning (Chamberlain, 1994). There is a growing body of evidence demonstrating the powerful role negative peer associations play in the development and maintenance of delinquent and other forms of antisocial behavior (e.g., substance abuse).

For example, the National Youth Survey (Elliott, Huizinga, & Ageton, 1985) showed the strength of the relationship between affiliation with a deviant peer group and escalation of delinquency. To the extent that youths associated with deviant peers, they had greater increases in delinquency over time than would have been predicted from their prior rates of offending. The risk for reoffending was nonsignificant for youths who had no association with delinquent peers, even if they had poor family relationships. These authors commented that it was ironic that most approaches for treatment of serious delinquents relied on group work that "may actually be contributing to the maintenance and enhancement of delinquent friendships and cliques" (p. 149). Data from street-worker programs have also suggested that the more intensive the intervention with groups, the greater the increase in delinquency (Klein, 1969, 1971; W. B. Miller, 1962).

More recently, Dishion and Andrews (1995) found iatrogenic effects of group work in their study aimed at prevention of conduct problems and substance use for at-risk teenagers. They compared effectiveness of interventions in five conditions (parent groups, adolescent groups, parent and adolescent groups combined, and two control groups). The parent group condition was superior to all of the others in producing reduced family conflict at termination and in teacher reports of reduced externalizing problems at 1-year follow-up. Conversely, teachers reported significantly higher externalizing scores for youths in the adolescent group condition at follow-up than for youths in any other condition. The question of whether negative peer influences on the behavior of antisocial youths placed together can be mitigated by the level and type of adult supervision or discipline they receive should be empirically tested. Thornberry and Krohn (Chapter 21, this volume) provide a clear and systematic consideration of relevant data on the role of peer influences on delinquency and drug use.

METHODOLOGY

In this section, some of the shortcomings of research on residential care are reviewed and recommendations are made for the design of future research.

The primary goal of residential programs is the provision of care for youths, and for most programs, outcome evaluation has been an afterthought. Three recommendations are made so that program development and evaluation can be more conjugal than orthogonal activities: (a) obtain accurate characterizations of the youths served; (b) establish explicit outcome goals; and (c) establish program planning, evaluation, standards, and practice simultaneously.

Characterizing Youths Served

Defining the population to be served in residential programs is a task that has been all but unattended, even by programs known for their high evaluation standards. For example, in the TFM, youths are typically described rather globally; they are delinquent, predelinquent, or juvenile offenders (Braukmann & Wolf, 1987). In Project Re-ED, youths are typically described as troubled or troubling (Mordock, 1993). In PPC, descriptions of youths range from truant to delinquent (Gold & Osgood, 1992). Program descriptions rarely include data on individual and family risk factors or on psychological variables that could enhance the more global characterizations given of the youths served. Such data would not only allow for comparability among programs but could also enhance the development of appropriate treatments and program evaluations (Gold & Osgood, 1992).

The usefulness of psychological variables was demonstrated by Gold and Osgood (1992), who analyzed outcomes for 300 youths in four facilities using PPC and showed that the interplay between personality and treatment variables significantly influenced outcomes. Youths with high levels of anxiety and depression did not benefit from treatment unless it was mediated by a nurturing adult in the program. The success of these youths outside of the program was also contingent upon the availability of such adults. Yet PPC emphasizes peer-mediated treatment; in fact, the program is based on that principle. Knowledge about the limits imposed on success from purely peer-mediated treatment for youths who are highly anxious or depressed underscores the benefit of expanded knowledge about the types of youths who are placed. Youths in placement have diverse mental health needs, no one treatment can fit all youths, and psychological and behavioral assessment should be an integral part of the treatment planning process.

Selecting Explicit Outcomes

Relevant outcomes should be linked to in-program treatment targets for youths and their families. To the extent that programs treat homogeneous populations (e.g., conduct-disordered youths), common outcome variables can be assessed for all participants. The presence of comorbid psychiatric conditions should also be considered in outcome evaluations. Four basic adjustment or outcome domains seem relevant to evaluating the effectiveness of residential placement for youths referred for severe antisocial and conduct problems: (a) restrictiveness of living; (b) level of educational/academic functioning; (c) level of antisocial, criminal, and drug-related behavior; and (d) presence/absence of psychiatric symptoms. Assessments in each domain at preplacement and discharge and in follow-up would allow for preliminary examination of the benefits of treatment. The following measures are suggested to assess these domains.

Restrictiveness of Living

The Restrictiveness of Living Environments Scale (ROLES) was developed by Hawkins, Almedia, Fabry, and Reitz (1992) through literature reviews and surveys of professionals familiar with placement options for children and adolescents. Restrictiveness of residential settings is measured on a scale ranging from least restrictive (independent living) to most restrictive (adult correctional facility). The ROLES has been shown to have good psychometric properties and is currently being used in federal evaluations of 11 Comprehensive Mental Health Services demonstration/research projects.

Academic Engagement/Functioning

At a minimum, school grades, attendance, and standardized test scores should be obtained. Increasingly, research is showing that conduct-disordered youths have significant reading difficulties that may exacerbate their problems (Cornwall & Bawden, 1992; Hinshaw, 1992). Thus, reading assessment at program admission could be an important programming aid. For example, all youths entering Boys Town are tested at admission with the Diagnostic Assessment of Reading (DAR) test (Roswell & Chall, 1992). The DAR is criterion referenced and is used to assess word recognition, oral reading of connected text, word meanings, silent reading comprehension, and spelling. Early results from Boys Town show that more than 25% of youths placed are at least two grade levels behind on all skills assessed with the DAR. Preliminary findings from interventions based on these assessments show that with just 36 weeks of placement-based reading instruction, most youths can make up their 2-year delay (Curtis, 1995).

Antisocial Behavior

For youths older than 12 years, official arrest data with details of each offense sorted according to the FBI Uniform Crime Reports (1980) can be obtained. The Elliott Behavior Checklist (EBC; Elliott, Ageton, Huizinga, Knowles, & Canter, 1983) is a confidential self-report of criminal activities that details the types of criminal activities the youth has engaged in and the setting and frequency of each type. The EBC has demonstrated good content and construct validity in a number of studies (e.g., Capaldi & Patterson, 1989).

Psychiatric Symptoms

One useful, efficient instrument for screening youths in placement is the Brief Symptoms Inventory (BSI; Derogatis & Spencer, 1982). The BSI is a 53-item standardized questionnaire that assesses several dimensions of mental health, including somatization, obsessive compulsive, interpersonal sensitivity, depression, anxiety, hostility, phobic anxiety, paranoid ideation, and psychoticism. The BSI has high convergent validity with the MMPI, good internal consistency, and test-retest stability.

Another useful instrument is the Diagnostic Interview Schedule for Children (DISC-R), which now is available in a user-friendly computerized version (C-DISC) that simplifies use and lessens the training required (Shaffer et al., 1993). The C-DISC provides a comprehensive symptomatic and diagnostic report of psychiatric problems. The C-DISC can also detect comorbidities, the ignorance of which can thwart effective treatment planning (Friman & Lucas, 1996). A voice version of the C-DISC

(V-DISC), now being evaluated at Boys Town, does not require the presence of an examiner, an innovation that increases the efficiency of the DISC even further. Also being evaluated at Boys Town is a shortened version of the DISC that can be used for screening (S-DISC) over the telephone.

Planning Program Evaluation in Concert With Service Development

Future studies on residential care should incorporate greater scientific rigor, including the use of fully randomized designs. Burns (1994) made a series of recommendations for conducting child mental health services research that applies to research on residential care. These were that the eligible population be well specified with clear inclusion/exclusion criteria, control and experimental interventions be clearly specified, both control and experimental conditions be acceptable to consumers and clinicians, and the measures used be understandable and clinically relevant. Other important considerations should include assessments of effects at follow-up, systematic documentation of whether the planned intervention actually occurred, data on attrition and dropouts, use of multiple indicators of outcomes, and use of measures that are sensitive to change and that include multiple perspectives of child adjustment in relevant domains.

Because of the widespread and growing use of residential care, the need for scientific testing of various models of care is critical. In the next section, we describe one such effort that used a randomized trial to compare processes and outcomes in two types of residential care for adolescents with severe conduct problems and delinquency.

A RANDOMIZED STUDY COMPARING EFFICACY OF TREATMENT FOSTER CARE TO GROUP CARE FOR BOYS WITH CHRONIC DELINQUENCY

In 1990, the Violence and Traumatic Stress Branch of the National Institute of Mental Health funded a study that compared two models of care for males being diverted from training school placement by the courts: Treatment Foster Care (TFC) and Group Care (GC). Boys designated by the court for out-of-home care were randomly assigned to placement and treatment in TFC or GC programs.

Subjects were assessed at baseline, 3 months after they had been placed in care, then at 6- (termination), 12-, 18-, and 24-month follow-ups. Outcomes assessed included antisocial behavior and delinquency, mental health and academic adjustment, and peer relations. The 3-month assessment targeted "mediators" or treatment practices hypothesized to predict outcomes, regardless of the placement condition (i.e., supervision, discipline, and association with/influence of delinquent peers).

Preliminary Results

At this time, 49 (of 80) participants have completed at least the 12-month assessment, and the findings are reported. Participating boys were chronic offenders with an average of more than 13 arrests and 4 felonies prior to referral. The average rate of self-reported criminal acts during the previous 6 months was just over 15. There were no differences between groups at baseline on rates or seriousness of criminal activity. There were also no differences on ethnic makeup, which was 85% European American, 3.5% African American, 8% Hispanic, and 1.6% other.

The Relationship of During-Treatment Practices and Outcomes

After 3 months of placement, the following variables were measured: (a) the amount and quality of supervision, (b) the discipline given and received, and (c) the patterns of association and degree of influence with delinquent peers. Multiple assessments (e.g., interviews, repeated telephone assessments, diaries) were obtained from multiple agents (i.e., the boy, his primary caretaker, his interviewer). Composite scores were computed for each variable. Table 39.2 shows the correlations of these mediators (for both groups combined) with official arrest data at 1-year follow-up when most boys had been out of treatment for 6 months.

Regardless of treatment condition, discipline and association with delinquent peers predicted total arrests at 1-year follow-up as well as the average seriousness of those arrests. During-program contact with delinquent peers also predicted an increase in the seriousness of offenses committed at follow-up. These findings clearly show that to the degree the boy associated with and was influenced by antisocial peers during his tenure in residential care, he was more likely to commit more and more serious crimes during follow-up. This result is in line with findings from studies reviewed earlier (Dishion & Andrews, 1995; Elliott et al., 1985).

A multivariate analysis of variance (MANOVA) was conducted to determine if there were differences in the two treatment groups on scores for the mediating variables. A significant difference was found ($p = .0001$) with TFC boys receiving higher scores on appropriate discipline and lower scores on association with deviant peers than boys in GC.

Results for self-reported criminal activity mirror the official arrest data; association with delinquent peers significantly predicted total criminal activity at 1-year follow-up, and discipline and association with delinquent peers predicted self-reports of serious violent offenses at 1 year.

Criminal Behavior

As shown in Figure 39.1, by 2-year follow-up, boys in the TFC condition had an average of two arrests whereas those in GC had

TABLE 39.2   Correlations of Mediators With Official Arrests

	Total Arrests	Seriousness of Arrests	Change in Seriousness Baseline–1 yr
Supervision	.15	.008	-.080
Discipline	-.330*	-.270*	-.160
Association with delinquent peers	.430**	.370***	.380**

$* = p < .06$; $** = p < .03$; $*** = p < .005$

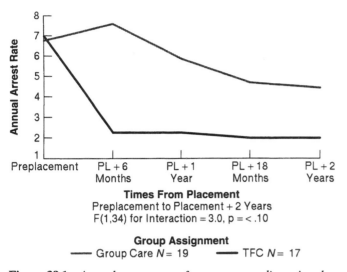

Figure 39.1   *Annual arrest rates of two groups mediators' study.*

an average of 4.5. If this trend continues, we expect to have clinically and statistically significant differences between the two groups once data from the entire sample have been obtained.

Incarceration and Runaway Rates

Incarceration rates and days spent as runaways were examined for the 12-month period following baseline. Table 39.3 presents the mean number of days in detention, training schools, and "on the run" for the two groups. There were significant differences between TFC and GC on days in detention ($p < .01$) and days "on the run" ($p < .01$).

CONCLUSIONS

During the past 30 years, positive changes have occurred in residential care. Many programs have made changes in their methods and goals with an eye toward improving quality of life. Many residential programs have moved away from the traditional training school/institutional format staffed by custodial shift workers to smaller group home formats with family-style, teacher-oriented, or peer-mediated structures. The fundamental goal of these programs has been to correct past problems by establishing humane, caring, habilitative environments for youths in trouble.

The effectiveness of these efforts, however, is limited and underresearched, especially given the widespread and increasing use of resi-

dential care as a treatment for children and adolescents with severe conduct problems. Our review leads us to make five recommendations:

1. More systematic research on residential care should be funded so that policy decisions at the federal and state levels may be better informed.

2. In-treatment as well as discharge and follow-up assessments are needed.

3. Evaluations should be tailored to measure those things the program targets for change; then these in-program targets should be related to long-term outcomes.

4. Better descriptions of program participants and components should be provided.

5. Researchers should provide technical assistance to community-based service programs so that studies are relevant and sensitive to the theory of treatment used in the program.

The lack of systematic study of the efficacy of group care coupled with the widespread use of this approach is an excellent example of the rift between clinical practice and research. If the substantial investments made in research are to realize positive effects, bridging this gap between research and practice should be a priority.

REFERENCES

Baumrind, D. (1991). Effective parenting during the early adolescent transition. In P. A. Cowan & E. M. Hetherington (Eds.), *Family transitions* (pp. 111–163). Hillsdale, NJ: Erlbaum.

Bettelheim, B. (1982). The necessity and value of residential treatment for severely disturbed children. *Family and Mental Health Journal, 8*(1 & 2), 55–61.

Borduin, C. M., Mann, B. J., Cone, L. T., Henggeler, S. W., Fucci, B. R., Blaske, D. M., & Williams, R. A. (1995). Multisystemic treatment of serious juvenile offenders: Long-term prevention of criminality and violence. *Journal of Consulting and Clinical Psychology, 63,* 569–578.

Braukmann, C. J., & Wolf, M. M. (1987). Behaviorally based group homes for juvenile offenders. In E. K. Morris & C. J. Braukmann (Eds.), *Behavioral approaches to crime and delinquency* (pp. 135–155). New York: Plenum.

Bryant, B., & Snodgrass, R. D. (1992). Foster family care applications with special populations: People Places, Inc. *Community Alternatives, 4,* 1–25.

Burns, B. J. (1994). The challenge of child mental health services research. *Journal of Emotional and Behavioral Disorders, 2*(4), 254–259.

Capaldi, D., & Patterson, G. R. (1989). *Psychometric properties of fourteen latent constructs from the Oregon Youth Study.* New York: Springer-Verlag.

Chamberlain, P. (1994). *Family connections.* Eugene, OR: Castalia.

Chamberlain, P., & Reid, J. B. (1991). Using a specialized foster care community treatment model for children and adolescents leaving the state mental hospital. *Journal of Community Psychology, 19,* 266–276.

Clark, H. B., Pange, M. E., Lee, B., Boyd, L. A., McDonald, B. A., & Stewart, E. S. (1994). Improving adjustment outcomes for foster children with emotional and behavioral disorders: Early findings from a controlled study on individualized services. *Journal of Emotional and Behavioral Disorders, 2,* 207–218.

TABLE 39.3   Means for Days in Detention, Training Schools, and On the Run

	TFC	GC
Days in detention	20.4 (26.6)	76.2 (50.1)
Days in training schools	34.4 (70.9)	23.1 (55.9)
Days on the run	10.1 (23.1)	32.5 (38.6)

Clemmer, D. (1940). *The prison community.* New York: Holt, Rinehart and Winston.

Cornwall, A., & Bawden, H. N. (1992). Reading disabilities and aggression: A critical review. *Journal of Learning Disabilities, 25,* 281–288.

Coughlin, D., & Shanahan, D. (1991). *Boys Town Family Home Program: Training manual* (3rd ed.). Boys Town, NE: Boys Town Press.

Curtis, M. E. (1995). Interventions for adolescents "at risk." In L. R. Putnam (Ed.), *How to be a better reading teacher* (pp. 231–239). Columbus, OH: Macmillan.

D'Amato, G. (1969). *Residential treatment for child mental health.* Springfield, IL: Charles C Thomas.

Derogatis, L. R., & Spencer, P. M. (1982). *The brief symptom inventory (BSI) administration, scoring, & procedures manual—I.* Baltimore: Clinical Psychometric Research.

Dishion, T. J. (1990). The peer context of troublesome child and adolescent behavior. In I. Leone (Ed.), *Understanding the troubled and troublesome child* (pp. 128–153). Beverly Hills, CA: Sage Publications.

Dishion, T. J., & Andrews, D. W. (1995). Preventing escalation in problem behaviors with high risk young adolescents: Immediate and 1-year outcomes. *Journal of Consulting and Clinical Psychology, 63,* 538–548.

Donaldson v. O'Connor, 493 F.2d 507 (5th Cir. 1974).

Elliott, D. S., Ageton, S. S., Huizinga, D., Knowles, B. A., & Canter, R. J. (1983). *The prevalence and incidence of delinquent behavior: 1975–1980.* Boulder, CO: Behavioral Research Institute.

Elliott, D. S., Huizinga, D., & Ageton, S. S. (1985). *Explaining delinquency and drug use.* Beverly Hills, CA: Sage Publications.

Empey, L. T., & Stafford, M. C. (1991). *American delinquency: Its meaning and construction* (3rd ed.). Belmont, CA: Wadsworth.

Farrington, D. P. (1978). The family backgrounds of aggressive youths. In L. A. Hersov, M. Berger, & D. Shaffer (Eds.), *Aggression and antisocial behavior in childhood and adolescence* (pp. 73–93). Elmsford, NY: Pergamon.

Friman, P. C., Almquist, J., Soper, S., & Lucas, C. (1995, November). *Using the C-DISC to assess adolescents entering residential care.* Proceedings of the 28th Annual Convention of the Association for the Advancement of Behavior Therapy.

Friman, P. C., Evans, J., Larzelere, R., Williams, G., & Daly, D. L. (1993). Correspondence between child dysfunction and program intensiveness: Evidence of a continuum of care across five child mental health programs. *The Journal of Community Psychology, 21,* 227–233.

Friman, P. C., Osgood, D. W., Shanahan, D., Thompson, R. W., Larzelere, R., & Daly, D. L. (1996). A longitudinal evaluation of prevalent negative beliefs about residential placement for troubled adolescents. *Journal of Abnormal Child Psychology, 24,* 299–324.

Garrett, C. J. (1985). Effects of residential treatment on adjudicated delinquents: A meta-analysis. *Journal of Research in Crime and Delinquency, 22,* 287–308.

Goffman, E. (1961). *Asylums.* Garden City, NY: Anchor.

Gold, M., & Osgood, D. (1992). *Personality and peer influence in juvenile corrections.* Westport, CT: Greenwood Press.

Hawkins, R. P., Almeida, M. C., Fabry, B., & Reitz, A. L. (1992). A scale to measure restrictiveness of living environments for troubled children and youths. *Hospital and Community Psychiatry, 43,* 54–58.

Hawkins, R. P., Almeida, M. C., & Samet, M. (1990). Comparative evaluation of foster family-based treatment and five other choices: A preliminary report. In A. Algarin, R. M. Friedman, A. J. Duchnowksi, K. Kutash, S. Silver, & M. K. Johnson (Eds.), *Second annual conference proceedings on children's mental health services and policy: Building a research base* (pp. 91–111). Tampa: University of South Florida, Florida Mental Health Institute, Research and Training Center for Children's Mental Health.

Hinshaw, S. P. (1992). Externalizing behavior problems and academic underachievement in childhood and adolescence: Causal relationships and underlying mechanisms. *Psychological Bulletin, 111,* 127–155.

Jones, R. R., Weinrott, M. R., & Howard, J. R. (1981). *The national evaluation of the teaching family model.* (Final Rep., Grants MH25631 & MH31018). Eugene, OR: Evaluation Research Group.

Kazdin, A. E. (1985). *Treatment of antisocial behavior in children and adolescents.* Homewood, IL: Dorsey Press.

Keisler, C. A. (1982). Noninstitutionalization as potential public policy for mental patients. *American Psychologist, 37,* 349–360.

Kirigin, K. A., Braukmann, C. J., Atwater, J., & Wolf, M. M. (1982). An evaluation of Achievement Place (Teaching-Family) group homes for juvenile offenders. *Journal of Applied Behavior Analysis, 15,* 1–16.

Klein, M. W. (1969). Gang cohesiveness, delinquency, and a street work program. *Journal of Research in Crime and Delinquency, 6,* 135–166.

Klein, M. W. (1971). *Street gangs and street workers.* Englewood Cliffs, NJ: Prentice Hall.

Laub, J. H., & Sampson, R. J. (1988). Unraveling families and delinquency: A reanalysis of the Gluecks' data. *Criminology, 26,* 355–379.

Loeber, R., & Dishion, T. J. (1984). Boys who fight at home and in school: Family conditions influencing cross-setting consistency. *Journal of Consulting and Clinical Psychology, 52,* 759–768.

Lundman, R. J. (1984). *Prevention and control of juvenile delinquency.* New York: Oxford University Press.

McEwen, C. A. (1978). *Designing correctional environments for youths: Dilemmas of subculture development.* Cambridge, MA: Ballinger.

Miller, G. E., & Prinz, R. J. (1990). Enhancement of social learning family interventions for childhood conduct disorder. *Psychological Bulletin, 108,* 291–307.

Miller, W. B. (1962). The impact of a "total community" delinquency control project. *Social Problems, 10,* 168–191.

Morales v. Turman, 364 F. Supp. 166 (E.D. Tex. 1973), rev'd on other grounds, 562 F.2d 993 (5th Cir. 1977) (St. Stat. 4.25, 4.34, 10.20).

Mordock, J. B. (1993). Evaluating treatment effectiveness. In C. E. Schaefer & A. J. Swanson (Eds.), *Children in residential care* (pp. 149–179). Northvale, NJ: Jason Aronson.

Oliver, J. P., & Mohamad, H. (1992). The quality of life of the chronically mentally ill: A comparison of public, private, and voluntary residential provisions. *British Journal of Social Work, 22,* 391–404.

Patterson, G. R., Cobb, J. A., & Ray, R. S. (1973). A social engineering technology for retraining the families of aggressive boys. In H. E. Adams & I. P. Unikel (Eds.), *Issues and trends in behavior therapy* (pp. 139–224). Springfield, IL: Charles C Thomas. (Also: In S. Steinmetz & M. Straus [Eds.], *Violence in the family* [pp. 309–314]. New York: Dodd, Mead & Co.)

Pecora, P. J., Whittaker, J. K., Maluccio, A. N., Barth, R. P., & Plotnick, R. D. (1992). *The child welfare challenge.* New York: Aldine.

Phillips, E. L. (1968). Achievement place: Token reinforcement procedures in a home-style rehabilitation for pre-delinquent boys. *Journal of Applied Behavior Analysis, 1,* 213–223.

Redl, F., & Wineman, D. (1952). *Controls from within: Techniques for the treatment of the aggressive child.* Glencoe, IL: The Free Press.

Reid, J. B. (1993). Prevention of conduct disorders before and after school entry: Relating intervention to developmental findings. *Journal of Development and Psychopathology, 5,* 243–262.

Reid, J. B., & Patterson, G. R. (1976). The modification of aggression and stealing behavior of boys in the home setting. In A. Bandura & E. Ribes (Eds.), *Behavior modification: Experimental analyses of aggression and delinquency* (pp. 123–145). Hillsdale, NJ: Erlbaum.

Roswell, F. G., & Chall, J. S. (1992). *Diagnostic assessments of reading.* Chicago: Riverside.

Rothman, D. J. (1980). *Conscience and convenience: The asylum and its alternatives in progressive America.* Boston: Little, Brown.

Schalock, R. L., & Begab, M. J. (1990). *Quality of life: Perspectives and issues.* Albany, NY: American Association on Mental Retardation.

Schur, E. M. (1973). *Radical nonintervention.* Englewood Cliffs, NJ: Prentice Hall.

Select Committee on Children, Youth, and Families, U.S. House of Representatives. (1990). *No place to call home: Discarded children in America.* Washington, DC: Government Printing Office.

Shaffer, D., Schwab-Stone, M., Fisher, P., Cohen, P., Piacentini, J., Davies, M., Conners, K., & Regier, D. (1993). The Diagnostic Interview Schedule for Children–Revised Version (DISC-R): I. Preparation, field testing, interrater reliability, and acceptability. *Journal of the American Academy of Child and Adolescent Psychiatry, 32,* 643–650.

Siegel, L. J., & Senna, J. J. (1988). *Juvenile delinquency* (3rd ed.). St. Paul: West Publishing.

Small, R., Kennedy, K., & Bender, B. (1991). Critical issues for practice in residential treatment: The view from within. *American Journal of Orthopsychiatry, 61,* 327–338.

Trieschman, A. E., & Whittaker, J. K. (Eds.). (1972). *Children away from home: A source book of residential treatment.* Chicago: Aldine.

U.S. Department of Health and Human Services. (1995). *Evaluating children's mental health systems* (Guidance for Applicants No. SM 95-02). Rockville, MD: Author.

Vorrath, H., & Brendtro, L. K. (1985). *Positive peer culture.* Chicago: Aldine.

Webster-Stratton, C., & Hammond, M. (1990). Predictors of treatment outcome in parent training for families with conduct problem children. *Behavior Therapy, 21,* 319–337.

Weinstein, L. (1974, December). *Evaluation of a program for re-educating disturbed children: A follow up comparison with untreated children.* Washington, DC: HEW, Bureau for the Education of the Handicapped.

Wells, K. W. (1991). Long-term residential treatment for children: Introduction. *American Journal of Orthopsychiatry, 61,* 324–327.

Whittaker, J. (1990). *Challenges for residential treatment.* Unpublished manuscript.

Williams, D. (1991). Developing environmental interventions to enhance quality of life for elders and their providers in adult residential care: An overview. *Adult Residential Care Journal, 5,* 185–198.

Wolf, M. M., Braukmann, C. J., & Ramp, K. A. (1987). Serious delinquent behavior as part of a significantly handicapping condition: Cures and supportive environments. *Journal of Applied Behavior Analysis, 20,* 347–359.

Wolins, M. (1974). *Group care: Explorations in the powerful environment.* New York: Aldine.

CHAPTER 40

The Treatment of Adult Offenders

MARNIE E. RICE and GRANT T. HARRIS

The idea that systematic intervention could induce criminals to stop antisocial conduct is a modern one. Rehabilitation and treatment were fundamental to the evolution of prisons, which began as a test of American theories about crime causation. Changed ideas about the causes of crime led to changes in how prisons operated. Throughout history, many theories about the causes of (and effective remedies for) crime have been abandoned without reasonable test. This chapter traces the history of attempts to treat adult offenders, examines the empirical evidence, and suggests directions for future research.

THE HISTORY OF REHABILITATION FOR ADULT OFFENDERS

Before the 18th century, dungeons and jails were primarily used to hold persons awaiting trial or punishment; the modern concept of prison as a consequence, in itself, for crime did not exist (Morris, 1974). Until the American Revolution, communities dealt with wrongdoers as sinners. Fines, shaming, flogging, banishment,[1] and hanging were used to deal with criminals (the primary means still in much of the world). Though most of these now seem brutal, until 1770, North American communities had no other ways to combat crime.

Out of revolutionary fervor and a desire to be rid of all things British, Americans concluded that the cause of crime was the punishment prescribed by law. Harsh punishment hardened offenders to commit the very offenses punishment was supposed to prevent. Harsh penalties made judges and juries flinch from imposing them, permitting offenders to go unpunished and thus encouraging misdeeds. The old array of penalties was too cruel and too inconsistent to deter crime. Prisons began as a theory-based interven-

tion: Statutes that offered certain, graded, and humane penalties would deter offenders and (nearly) eliminate crime. A crucial piece of this system was the prison, but little thought was given to how life inside should be organized. The fact of prison, not its internal routine, was to accomplish correction (Rothman, 1971).

These ideas were soon, albeit temporarily, abandoned. Examination of the lives and circumstances of criminals seemed to show that the failure of the family to provide guidance and discipline was the basis of crime. The remedy was straightforward: Rather than reforming the statutes, the criminals must be reformed by removing them from corrupt influences and placing them in a model society in which discipline and constructive activities were paramount. The first attempt to implement such ideas occurred at New York's Auburn Prison in 1823, and Pennsylvania's Walnut Street Prison quickly followed in 1826. A penitentiary founded on the same principles opened in Upper Canada at Kingston in 1835 (Curtis, Graham, Kelly, & Patterson, 1985). By the 1830s, dignitaries and ordinary tourists from all over the world regularly visited North American penitentiaries, and they frequently served as models for other prisons. In the Auburn (or congregate) system, prisoners slept alone in their cells but labored and ate together; they were forbidden, however, to exchange words or even glances. The rival Pennsylvania system completely isolated prisoners at all times. It is important to realize that, for all their apparent harshness, these new prison routines were driven by a spirit of reform, experimentation, and philanthropy, with the expectation that society as a whole would be improved (Rothman, 1971).

Soon, however, things began to break down. Harsh punishments were needed to prevent prisoners from communicating and to make them work hard. Wardens had to rely on money generated by convict labor. Overcrowding ended the use of individual cells. There was an unanticipated preponderance of "hardened" violent criminals unamenable to reform. Corruption permitted prisoners financial and personal exchange with the outside. Sentences were fixed and could not be extended even for those who had not (yet) reformed. Protracted incarceration in silence began to seem cruel. It was also clear, even in the absence of formal evaluation, that prison did not eliminate crime. By the 1860s, what began as an experiment in treatment ended in resignation to mere custody. The

---

[1]For over a century, Britain used transportation to Botany Bay (Australia) as a primary means to combat crime. Eighteenth-century Britons might also have employed graded sanctions in prison to deter crime (plus execution, of course) had they not had the unique option of banishment to a place so distant that return was impossible (Hughes, 1988).

ideal of reformation and rehabilitation was abandoned in favor of the idea that the unpleasantness of prison would deter criminals (Rothman, 1971).

In the 1870s, however, new reformers called for educational programs and an end to cruel and arbitrary punishment. Reforms also included modernization of cells and, especially, a system of earned remission of sentence (Curtis et al., 1985; Ekstedt & Griffiths, 1990). In the 1870s and 1880s, a new North American view of crime placed the cause of deviance in broad social factors. Slums, poverty, and degradation were the substrate, and careful analysis revealed the path of each offender's fall into criminality. This new progressive movement called for probation, parole, and indeterminate sentencing to meet and remedy each offender's crime-producing circumstances. By this system, probation would simultaneously monitor and control the offender's activities and provide firm, friendly counsel. Indeterminate confinement would permit officials to gauge that moment when each prisoner was ready for release and ensure that each engaged in wholehearted self-correction. Reformers wanted prisons to be more like hospitals in which psychiatrists would diagnose and remedy the defects of each prisoner (cf. Fink, Derby, & Martin, 1969). Prisons were to be humanized with recreation, education, and vocational programs. Finally, parole boards and parole officers would fulfill a role similar to probation in guiding, befriending, and advising the reforming offender (Rothman, 1980).

By 1910, probation, indeterminate sentencing, and parole were widespread across the continent. These methods were adopted partly because they allowed punishments to vary and greatly enhanced the discretionary power of judges, prison administrators, parole officials, and the police. They also quickly came under attack when parolees and probationers committed new crimes and because it seemed that criminals were escaping punishment. As in the previous century, the reforms were never fully implemented. Chronic underfunding meant huge caseloads and perfunctory, superficial, and arbitrary service. Plea bargaining and blatant discrimination undermined the possibility that probation and parole could actually reform offenders. Psychiatrists spent all of their time diagnosing and classifying and never developed treatments. Educational programs were underfunded, and vocational training was again subverted into the use of convict labor to provide money to run the institutions. Correctional staff were poorly trained and, most important, continued to rely on physical punishment to maintain order and make prisoners work. That is, in contrast to the ideals, probation, prison, and parole exercised only the most rudimentary community supervision or merely held offenders in custody (Rothman, 1980).

Again, despite the high hopes and reforming zeal at the turn of the century, by the 1930s and 1940s few believed in probation, prison, and parole, in themselves, as the means to rehabilitate offenders. By World War II, correctional services were again viewed as punitive custody whose mere existence would deter crime. Of course, probation, prison (with some recreational, vocational, and educational programs), and parole persist. In themselves, they are rarely perceived to have rehabilitative effects. There is evidence, however, from outside North America that consistent punishment in the form of criminal sanctions can reduce criminal behavior as is predicted by learning theory (Brennan & Mednick, 1994). In North America (and particularly the United States), however, criminal justice sanctions, perhaps because of their severity, have never been consistently applied. Meta-analyses based primarily on North American studies show that variations in criminal sanctions have no effect on subsequent criminal conduct (Andrews et al., 1990). Furthermore, compared to community sanctions, prisons may even increase the likelihood of recidivism (Andrews et al., 1990; Petersilia, Turner, & Peterson, 1986).

The 1960s and 1970s saw yet another resurgence in prison reform and in the idea that treatment could change the defective personal qualities that led to crime. Based on Jones's (1953) ideas, therapeutic communities were common. Although there were important differences among programs, there were also common clinical factors. Peer support was emphasized, often by employing program graduates as lead therapists. Treatment was insight oriented and emotionally evocative, featuring psychodynamic counseling, group encounter sessions, and defense-disrupting therapy. Finally, therapeutic communities were radical reforms. They sought to fundamentally alter the custodial and punitive institutional environment and thereby make changes in offenders' character and behavior—changes that would lead to improved psychological well-being and reductions in crime (Barker, 1980; Gunn & Robertson, 1982; Harris, Rice, & Cormier, 1994; Ogloff, Wong, & Greenwood, 1990; Weisman, 1995). Therapeutic communities for adult offenders were established in the United States (e.g., Bale et al., 1980; Wexler, Falkin, & Lipton, 1990), Canada (e.g., Ogloff et al., 1990; Rice, Harris, & Cormier, 1992), Britain (Cooke, 1989; Copas & Whiteley, 1976; Gunn & Robertson, 1982), and Western Europe (van der Hoeven Clinic in the Netherlands and other programs in West German prisons; Dolan & Coid, 1993).

Beginning even more recently, social learning approaches to treating adult offenders have been implemented. Token economies (e.g., Milan, 1987; Milan & McKee, 1976), cognitive-behavioral training in anger management (e.g., Stermac, 1986), social problem solving (e.g., Ross & Fabiano, 1985), and attempts to change procriminal attitudes through differential association (e.g., Andrews, Keissling, Robinson, & Mickus, 1986) have been reported.

In addition to the modest resurgence in offender treatment beginning in the 1960s and 1970s, there has been a claim that "nothing works." Martinson (1974) asserted that "the rehabilitative efforts that have been reported so far have had no appreciable effect on recidivism" (p. 25). The adoption of this position by some policy makers (also motivated by the desire to reduce costs) has led to the development of new forms of deterrence-oriented punishments. Shock incarceration ("Scared Straight" programs), boot camps, fixed determinate sentences, the abolition of parole, intensive supervision programs, and a resurgence of capital punishment in the United States all reflect a return to deterrence as the means to control crime. At the present time, on the grounds that prisoners cannot victimize the general public, there are increasing calls to use prison as incapacitation, incarcerating as many criminals as possible for as long as possible. Compared with a century ago, however, we now have many more tools to evaluate the efficiency of incapacitation in preventing crime (for a good example, see Greenwood, 1994).

THEORETICAL CONTEXT AND CONTROVERSIAL ISSUES

We note a fundamental metatheoretical controversy about crime. Some commentators (usually sociologists) regard crime as the manifestation of such societal phenomena as social injustice and unequal distribution of wealth. By such views, studies of the characteristics of criminals and, especially, treatment for offenders are misguided and even perpetuate social injustice (e.g., Kamin, 1993). The contrasting view asserts that, compared to sociocultural variables, personal characteristics account for much more variability in criminal behavior, and, therefore, the appropriate unit of scientific analysis is the individual (Andrews & Bonta, 1994). This chapter's topic presupposes a focus on the individual, but we note that individual differences in criminal conduct could reflect large-scale social forces. Individual propensities toward crime, regardless of their ultimate cause, *might* be most effectively treated not by intervening on an individual basis, but by such large-scale policies as social assistance for poor families or specialized education programs in high-risk neighborhoods (cf. Zigler & Muenchow, 1992).

Other chapters of this volume demonstrate that there is, as yet, nothing approaching an agreed-upon theory of crime. Crime is variously attributed to social factors, subcultural phenomena, physiological defects, personality differences, conditioning history, and faulty beliefs and attitudes. It has even been argued that crime is a disorder itself (cf. Raine, 1993). Unlike many areas of medicine, for example, where the pathogens are determined, there is no clear cause of the problem (yet) and, therefore, no obvious treatment.

Also, crime or criminal behavior is not a well-defined psychological construct. Such constructs as intelligence, extraversion, and even schizophrenia are comparatively well understood by the operations that measure them and relate them to similar but different constructs. There is cross-cultural variation about which acts are crimes; consumption of alcohol, narcotic use, bigamy, prostitution, gambling, and producing pornography are all crimes in some jurisdictions and not in others. Indeed, if America were to abandon the "war on drugs" and address substance abuse as a mental health problem, hundreds of thousands of prisoners would immediately change status from criminals to patients. As Andrews and Bonta (1994) put it, "How can we have a science of activities whose quality appears so dependent upon the evaluation of an audience?" (p. 25). Fortunately, as Andrews and Bonta point out, much of the "cultural relativism" in defining criminality disappears as one focuses on more serious crimes such as assault, robbery, and murder.

The clearest theme of our historical review is the swing between two ideologies: The first is that prison or the threat of punishment will reduce crime; the second is that crime is due to factors (e.g., injustices in society, failures in family life, faulty early experiences, or physical development) that produce remediable defects in offenders. The first ideology led to the establishment of prisons as we now know them. The second has led repeatedly to the notion that prisoners can be reformed. Perhaps driven by cycles of liberal and conservative thinking, Western society has repeatedly abandoned one idea in favor of the other.

The second theme is the theoretical and practical weakness of these social experiments. Exactly how the stark isolation of early 19th-century prisons was supposed to change a wrongdoer's character was never specified; and exactly how living in a slum caused people to become criminals was not clear. Reform ideologies gave wardens no clues about how to keep order within prisons while prisoners underwent rehabilitation. Even if it is completely correct, no theory about crime can eliminate it. The reformers failed to put their ideas into effective practice. Administrative expediency, chronic overcrowding and underfunding, and lack of training repeatedly meant that reforms were quickly subverted. More to the point, useful data on the effects of reform (or, indeed, the effects of punishment) were never collected. The absence of facts permitted change to be driven by ideology and opinion.

Programs and evaluations based on poorly articulated theories (or no theory) are unlikely to make contributions (G. D. Gottfredson, 1984). In addition to holding theories that were too simplistic, the efforts of successive generations of progressive reformers foundered because they lacked both effective treatments and tools to evaluate them. As this volume attests, modern theories of antisocial behavior are more sophisticated (and certainly more numerous). As never before, psychologists and social scientists have available a wider range of both treatment and evaluation technologies. Consequently, we now turn to the current evidence on the efficacy of treatments for adult offenders. Sadly, it is still true that almost all offender programs lack a theoretical rationale. Programs seem to be employed because they are familiar, are the accepted thing to do, are easily implemented, and require little or no staff training (Elliott, 1980).

METHODOLOGICAL ISSUES

Theoretical Rationale for Treatment Programs

Elliott (1980) outlines a multistep program development evaluation (PDE) approach for delinquency intervention. The first step is the articulation of a theory that specifies how a set of variables is logically related to criminal behavior. Because the literature on risk factors suggests that offending is best explained by multiple factors, rehabilitation efforts that focus on more than a single cause are indicated (e.g., Borduin et al., 1995). The second step is the design of program components to produce measurable changes in the causal variables. Next, there must be process evaluation to determine that program activities actually occur and that program objectives are met. Then, if positive change in process measures is demonstrated, outcome information must be obtained to determine whether achieving the program objectives affects offending as expected by the theory. Finally, the process and outcome evaluations should be used to modify the program to increase positive outcome. A good example of the use of the PDE approach in the juvenile delinquency area is provided in D. C. Gottfredson and Gottfredson (1992).

Program Integrity

An essential component of PDE and of any treatment evaluation is ensuring that treatment is delivered as planned. One way to increase program integrity is to use program manuals with step-by-step instructions (e.g., Liberman, Kopelowicz, & Young, 1994; see also, Hinshaw & Zupan, Chapter 4, this volume). The strongest method of assessing program integrity is time sampling of staff behaviors (e.g., Menditto et al., 1996; Paul & Lentz, 1977). Other methods include program supervisors or evaluators observing therapy sessions (or recordings of sessions) to ensure that therapists follow prescribed procedures (e.g., Andrews, 1980). The critical importance of supervision was exemplified by Bassett and Blanchard (1977), who showed that lack of supervision rapidly turned a well-designed prison token economy into a program that may have done more harm than good. The importance of program integrity is also well illustrated in a study by Fagan (1990). Positive treatment effects were found for juvenile offenders assigned to a well-implemented behavioral program. At one of four sites, however, the behavioral program was so poorly implemented for the "treatment group" that more therapeutic elements were in effect for the control group, which exhibited lower recidivism.

Measuring Outcome

The primary goal of treatment for offenders is a reduction in the rate and severity of reoffending, but it is not simple to operationally define this goal. First, what is a reoffense? Are we interested only in officially reported recidivism, or should we include criminal behavior for which the offender was never apprehended? Although most would agree that both are important, there is no completely satisfactory way to gather these data. Elliott and colleagues (Elliott, 1994; Elliott, Huizinga, & Ageton, 1985) established the validity of self-report measures in a national probability sample of youths. Respondents were guaranteed confidentiality via a certificate of confidentiality from the U.S. Department of Health, Education and Welfare. However, the validity of self-report measures among adult offender populations (especially in the absence of a certificate of confidentiality) is yet to be established. Moreover, locating subjects to obtain self-reports of recidivism can be extremely difficult, and dropout rates are likely to be high (Fagan, 1990). Official report measures (arrests or, to an even greater extent, convictions) are known to underestimate both the rate and the severity of reoffending. However, because higher effect sizes have been obtained using official versus self-reported delinquency (Farrington, 1985), and because they can be relatively easily obtained, official data may be more valid for evaluating treatment when the comparison of recidivism rates between treated and untreated offenders is more important than determining absolute levels of reoffending.

Several additional measures of outcome have been used, including admissions (or readmissions) to psychiatric hospitals or secure psychiatric settings for offenses that could have resulted in criminal charges (e.g., Rice et al., 1992) and police reports about offenses believed to have happened (Marshall & Barbaree, 1988). Because no one measure is completely satisfactory, it is safest to gather multiple outcomes. However, official recidivism should always be reported separately.

A related issue pertains to what reoffenses should be counted. Some treatments may target general reductions in crime; others may target specific offenses (sex offenses or violent offenses). For specific offenses, sexual or violent reoffenses are often reduced by plea bargaining to nonsexual, nonviolent convictions. In such cases, police reports (including victim and witness statements) are required. Of course, such data are much harder to gather. Also, the more restricted the range of offenses counted as recidivism, the lower is the base rate of reoffending, and the more difficult it is to obtain differences between treated and untreated groups.

Also important is the time course of reoffending and the length of follow-up. The longer the follow-up, the greater is the recidivism rate (e.g., Rice & Harris, 1995b). Follow-ups must be long enough to permit detection of differences between treated and untreated groups. Event history analyses permit investigators to examine the time course of recidivism and allow for differential opportunity to reoffend (Singer & Willett, 1991).

Recidivism is not the only important outcome. Institutional, community, psychological, vocational, and academic adjustment has also been used, generally with somewhat higher success rates (Lipsey, 1992). In an era of public sector financial constraints, cost effectiveness must also be considered in any outcome evaluation. Without denying the importance of these other outcomes, our focus here is primarily on recidivism.

Control Groups

Without a credible control group, inferences about treatment are impossible, as many variables besides a treatment program can affect outcome. For example, crime rates are known to decline with age during adulthood (though less so with increasing age; see Farrington, 1986; Hoffman & Beck, 1984). The strongest designs are those with random assignment to treatment or nontreatment (or alternative treatment) conditions. Randomized designs can frequently be justified on grounds that limited resources preclude offering an unproven treatment to all and the fairest way to determine who gets treatment is randomly (cf. Elliott, 1980). Ideally, at least one alternate treatment would be included to evaluate placebo effects and to evaluate the contribution of specific components. In the absence of a randomized design, a quasi-experimental design with comparison and treatment groups matched on major risk factors is essential. Treatment dropouts must be included in at least some analyses. Otherwise, the comparability of the two groups is compromised, and lower recidivism for treatment completers than for untreated subjects indicates little about the effectiveness of treatment. Assigning treatment dropouts or refusers to a comparison group (e.g., DeLeon, 1984; Dutton, 1986; Marshall & Barbaree, 1988) is especially problematic.

In a study of sex offender treatment, the outcome of treatment completers and treatment dropouts was compared to a randomly selected untreated control group (all of whom volunteered for treatment) as well as to a group of nonvolunteers matched on some risk variables (Marques, Day, Nelson, & West, 1993). When treatment dropouts were included in the treatment group, recidivism rates of all three groups were equivalent. Very high recidivism rates were obtained for the dropouts. The finding that the highest risk offenders are most likely to drop out of treatment has been noted by others (e.g., Abel, Mittelman, Becker, Rathner, &

Rouleau, 1988; Ogloff et al., 1990). Dropout rates are also very high in programs for drug-abusing offenders (Anglin & Hser, 1990) and in pharmacological treatments for sex offenders (Langevin et al., 1979). Analyses of those who stayed in treatment may be most useful in establishing the importance of the various process measures in predicting outcome, as well as determining the characteristics of participants most likely to accept treatment.

Although between-subjects controlled designs are the most practical, the rates of offending for some offenders (e.g., opiate abusers) are so high that within-subjects repeated measures designs may be feasible. For example, methadone maintenance programs for narcotic-addicted offenders have been evaluated by examining property crimes committed on and off the program (Hser, Anglin, & Chou, 1988). The design must include enough timepoints (on and off the program) to permit strong conclusions. Furthermore, if, during the reversal phase, the offending rate returns to near pretreatment levels, many theories would consider that as evidence of program failure.

Sample Selection

Treatments are most likely to be effective (as well as most cost effective) when they target relatively high-risk offenders (Andrews & Bonta, 1994). Intensive treatment for low-risk offenders may increase recidivism (Andrews et al., 1986). An objective measure of risk should be reported (see Bonta, 1996), and the risk levels of the treatment and comparison samples should be reported. Psychopaths may constitute an extremely high-risk group, and even very intensive treatment may not be effective for this group. Thus, it may be advisable to report subjects' scores on a measure of psychopathy (e.g., the Psychopathy Checklist–Revised; Hare, 1991; Hart & Hare, Chapter 3, this volume).

Another important consideration pertains to the sample size required to demonstrate a treatment effect. Given that the mean effect sizes obtained in the offender treatment area are low, power analyses (Cohen, 1969) should be conducted to ensure that the design includes enough participants to detect at least a small to moderate effect.

Meta-Analysis

The most controversial issue regarding offender treatment has been (and, in nonscientific circles, still is) whether any treatment reduces criminal recidivism. Despite positive reviews of the literature (e.g., Basta & Davidson, 1988; Cullen & Gendreau, 1989; Gendreau & Ross, 1979), critics can cite numerous negative findings, identify methodological flaws in studies reporting positive findings, and conclude that there is no convincing evidence of effective treatment (e.g., Martinson, 1974; Sechrest, White, & Brown, 1979). Fortunately, meta-analysis addresses many problems with narrative reviews by combining data from many studies, permitting the examination of effect sizes as well as determining which variables influence them. To index effect size, we refer here to Cohen's d, the difference (in SDs) between the means of the treatment and control groups. According to accepted standards (cf. Cohen, 1969), ds of .20 are small, .50 moderate, and .80 large.

CURRENT FINDINGS

The most comprehensive meta-analysis examined 443 studies of offenders aged 12 to 21 (Lipsey, 1992; see Tolan & Gorman-Smith, Chapter 38, this volume, for more detail). At the top of this range, the offenders would be adults in most jurisdictions; offenders over 21 were included in some of the studies, as long as the majority were younger. Lipsey included only studies for which there was at least one quantitative measure of delinquency outcome and a comparison group described in sufficient detail to ascertain its pretreatment similarity to the treated group. Lipsey included studies from several previous meta-analyses (see Lipsey & Wilson, 1993, for a comprehensive list); thus, his meta-analysis rendered earlier ones largely obsolete. The number of studies allowed Lipsey to examine several moderator variables.

Lipsey's meta-analysis, as well as all of the earlier meta-analyses, found a positive overall effect size. However, many earlier meta-analyses included too few studies to enable rejection of the null hypothesis of no overall effect of treatment on recidivism. Even though effect sizes were substantial (ranging from ds of .13 to .52), several early meta-analysts concluded that there was little evidence that correctional treatment altered recidivism. Lipsey found $d = .17$, somewhat lower than most other meta-analyses but was able to strongly reject the null hypothesis that nothing works. The most influential moderator variables indicated that more specific and structured treatments (e.g., behavioral and skills training) and multimodal treatments were more effective than less structured, less specific treatments (e.g., counseling). Treatment effectiveness was positively related to risk, community (vs. institutional) setting, and higher levels of involvement by researchers. More intensive community treatment (longer duration, more frequent treatment contacts) was associated with larger effects. Negative effect sizes were obtained for the treatment intervention in about one third of the studies, confirming that some treatments can do harm and emphasizing the need for evaluation.

Although Lipsey found no differential effect sizes attributable to age, almost all subjects were juveniles, as were the subjects in all earlier meta-analyses, except that by Andrews et al. (1990), which included both adults and juveniles. Of the 154 comparisons between treated and comparison subjects in that meta-analysis, 23 or 15% (from 13 separate studies) were from programs run in the adult versus juvenile justice system. Andrews et al. also found no differences for programs run for adults compared to juveniles. Before analysis, Andrews et al. categorized studies as to how well they followed three principles of effective correctional service: risk, need, and responsivity. First, they argued intensive service should be reserved for high-risk cases and minimal service for low-risk cases. Second, treatment to reduce recidivism must target dynamic risk factors or criminogenic needs—treatment must address changeable factors empirically related to criminal conduct. The most promising targets are antisocial attitudes and peer associations, chemical dependencies, identification with antisocial models, social skills and self-control, and self-management. Third, generally offenders are most responsive to behavioral, social learning programs delivered by therapists using "firm but fair" approaches while modeling and rewarding anticriminal thoughts, feelings, and actions. A few highly verbal, self-reflective offenders might benefit from nonbehavioral, evocative, less structured programs. Andrews et al. further categorized studies according to whether they used (a) criminal sanctions without treatment; (b) inappropriate correctional service (e.g., service to low-risk offenders; nondirective, relationship-dependent, psychodynamic therapy; milieu therapy and group approaches emphasizing communication); (c) appropriate service (e.g., service to higher risk cases; all behavioral programs unless to low-risk cases; and structured nonbehavioral treatments targeting criminogenic needs); or (d) unspecified service. Andrews et al. found a small overall effect ($d = .20$), but appropriate service yielded larger effects than all others, cutting recidivism by more than 50%. Similarly, Lipsey (1992) concluded that the best treatment produced decreases of 20% to 40%, and the best treatments were, by and large, the same as those classed by Andrews et al. as appropriate.

The only meta-analysis of treatment for adult offenders (Lösel & Koferl, 1989) included only nine studies (by four investigators) that measured recidivism. All programs were described as "social therapy," located in the Federal Republic of Germany, and published, if at all, in German. For recidivism, d was approximately .21, very close to the overall means obtained by Lipsey (1992) and Andrews et al. (1990). Unfortunately, too few details were given to classify programs by Andrews et al.'s principles of effective correctional service.

Lipsey and Wilson (1993) reviewed 290 meta-analytic studies on the efficacy of psychological, educational, and behavioral treatments for all populations and all types of outcomes. They found, overall, a moderate positive effect size of .50, an effect substantially higher than effects on mortality obtained for such common medical treatments as chemotherapy for breast cancer and aortocoronary bypass surgery. They found that one group, pre-post treatment designs, overestimated treatment effects and that among studies that included both a placebo-treatment control group and a no-treatment control group, the effect size was an average of approximately .20 higher for the comparison of the treatment of interest and the no-treatment control than for the treatment of interest and the placebo treatment. Thus, they concluded that an effect size in the order of .20 could represent a "placebo" effect rather than a true treatment effect.

Is it just a coincidence, then, that the overall effect size in the offender treatment area is .20, exactly the amount that Lipsey and Wilson conclude could be a placebo effect? Of course, many would argue that content-nonspecific or "placebo" effects should be considered legitimate parts of psychological treatment (e.g., Wilkins, 1986). In any event, the much larger effect sizes obtained in the meta-analyses for "appropriate correctional service" cannot be dismissed as placebo.

THERAPEUTIC COMMUNITIES

Unfortunately, very few studies of therapeutic communities (TCs) were included in these meta-analyses, perhaps because TCs have been more popular for adults than for juveniles; few evaluations included a comparison group; and many of the subjects were addicts or psychiatric patients for whom criminal histories or out-

comes were not reported. Craft, Stephenson, and Granger (1964) studied the recidivism of young probationers admitted randomly to either a TC or a more authoritarian program with individual therapy. In a 3-year follow-up, the TC was associated with slightly (but not significantly) more reoffenses and significantly more serious offenses than the comparison therapy. Gunn and Robertson (1982) compared the 2-year postdischarge recidivism rates of men in a TC with those of matched untreated prisoners. Slight nonsignificant differences favored the untreated men.

We reported on the 10-year recidivism rates of violent offenders treated in a maximum security psychiatric hospital TC compared to matched incarcerated subjects (Rice et al., 1992). There was no overall difference in recidivism between the groups. However, for psychopaths, those who participated in the TC were more likely to reoffend than those from prison; whereas for nonpsychopaths, the opposite result was obtained.

Some reports of TCs for substance-abusing offenders have been critically reviewed elsewhere (Smart, 1976). Bale et al. (1980) found that when treatment dropouts were included, treatment had no effect on recidivism. Those who completed treatment, however, were less likely than untreated subjects to be convicted as of the 1-year follow-up. Treatment may be effective for persons who receive sufficient amounts; or remaining in treatment may serve as a "filter," detecting persons of low pretreatment risk. Very large dropout rates characterize more recent studies of TCs for substance-abusing offenders (see Anglin & Hser, 1990). Wexler et al. (1990) report positive results from a prison TC for substance-abusing offenders when all subjects who terminated treatment were included in the treatment group. Control subjects had either volunteered for treatment but could not be accommodated or participated in other programs. TC subjects had significantly fewer arrests than subjects in the other two groups but also had significantly less time at risk.

Careful examination of the outcome data for therapeutic communities for adult offenders yields scant evidence of effectiveness, especially for the groups for which they are frequently recommended—psychopaths and substance-abusing offenders. TCs are primarily insight oriented, with high levels of intensive group psychotherapy, and are usually not skills based or behavioral. In addition, lack of programmatic structure and reliance on clinical intuition is likely to impair effectiveness (Wilson, 1997). Few, if any, would meet the Andrews et al. (1990) criteria for appropriate correctional service.

EXAMPLES OF POSITIVE OUTCOME STUDIES
FOR ADULT OFFENDERS

Andrews et al. (1990) listed eight studies of adult offenders with positive results. We now describe those published studies with stronger designs to give the reader a flavor for the best evidence for the effectiveness of treatment for adult offenders.

Probationers (Andrews, 1980) were randomly assigned to probation officers who had been administered measures of empathy and socialization, both hypothetically relevant to outcome. Program managers, officers, clients, and researchers were "blind" to scores on these measures. Treatment was one-to-one counseling explicitly focused on modeling problem-solving and anticriminal attitudes. Program integrity was checked using probationers' and program managers' ratings of the probation officers. Program managers gave more positive evaluations to officers high in empathy, and probationers rated officers high in empathy as more open and warm than low-empathy officers. During recorded sessions, researchers counted anticriminal statements by the officers and the number of times officers rewarded anticriminal statements and disapproved of procriminal statements. Officers high in socialization emitted more of these desirable behaviors. Probationers assigned to officers high in both empathy and socialization had lower recidivism—defined as events that occurred during the program rather than afterward. Of course, officers who were more socialized and empathic might have been less likely to report probationers' offenses. Also, recidivism rates were "adjusted" for probationer age and sex and professional status of the officer. Unadjusted results yielded the same pattern, but significance was not reported.

In a U.S. Navy correctional institution (Grant & Grant, 1959), recruits court-martialed for offenses ranging from unauthorized absence to murder were assigned to treatment groups according to interpersonal maturity. Some groups consisted of men high in interpersonal maturity, some had only men low in maturity, and some included both. Each group also had one of three sets of three supervising officers. The three supervisory teams were ranked on their predicted effectiveness in reducing criminal attitudes. Treatment was group therapy to increase social maturity by forcing offenders to "work through" anxiety caused by the close relationships in closed groups. Treatment also included work, educational, and recreational experiences. Recidivism was indicated by success on restoration to duty. There was an interaction between offenders' maturity and the quality of supervision such that mature offenders did better than immature offenders only when they had been assigned to consistent, high-quality supervision. By contrast, low-maturity subjects had worse outcomes when they had been assigned to high-quality, consistent supervision. Andrews et al. (1990) categorized the immature subjects assigned to high-quality, consistent supervisors as inappropriate service; mature subjects assigned to the same supervisors were classed as appropriate.

Ross, Fabiano, and Ewles (1988; see also, Ross & Fabiano, 1985) specially trained probation officers to provide social skills training, problem solving, values education, assertion training, negotiation skills training, and social perspective taking. The 80-hour program was taught to groups of four to six probationers randomly assigned to probation plus the cognitive program, attention-placebo control group, or probation alone. Probationers were all assessed as high risk. Those assigned to the cognitive training program had lower rates of program-concurrent recidivism.

These studies represent some of the strongest evidence that treatment for adult offenders can be effective. Outcome measures in all were weak: None included postprogram criminal offending. Although all were listed as embodying the principles of appropriate correctional service, it is not immediately apparent how. Thus, for example, the Grant and Grant (1959) study meets those criteria only after the invocation of a specific responsivity principle: For high-functioning offenders, nonstructured, insight-oriented therapies are most effective. It could be argued that in some studies "treatment" was simply skillful and intensive application of sanctions.

Three reasonably well-controlled studies reporting lower recidivism for treated adult offenders were not included in the Andrews et al. (1990) meta-analysis. Bloom and Singer (1979) found positive, significant, but very small (especially considering the cost) effects from an intensive, long-lasting, eclectic, milieu therapy program that included counseling, individual and group psychotherapy, pharmacological treatments, academic and vocational education, work assignments, and recreation. The program also included a graded system of privilege levels.

Pearson (1988) evaluated intensive supervision for nonviolent offenders. The program required employment, provided frequent community contacts between officers and offenders, and included random drug tests. Most offenders received specialized counseling, and offenders were matched to community sponsors and others who provided help, guidance, and anticriminal modeling. Compared to matched offenders who did not participate, the intensively supervised offenders had less recidivism, and the program cost substantially less than the usual program.

Palmer, Brown, and Barrera (1992) evaluated treatment for men convicted of abusing their female partners. The program consisted of 10 weekly sessions described as relatively unstructured but involved modeling of anticriminal values, skills teaching, and other components that Andrews et al. (1990) would classify as appropriate service. Compared with randomly assigned control subjects, treated men (including dropouts) had lower rates of recidivism in a 1- to 2-year follow-up.

As a final caution on meta-analyses, we note Hall's (1995) meta-analysis of 12 sex offender treatment evaluations. There was a small but statistically significant overall effect of treatment (Cohen's $d = .24$), and Hall observed no significant variability in effect size that could be attributed to the studies' methodological quality. This conclusion was, however, related to the mischaracterization of some studies. For example, the control subjects in a study of castration were said to be men "not granted castration by a committee of two physicians and a lawyer" (Hall, 1995, Table 1, p. 805). In fact, the original report said something quite different:

> Fifty-three applications for castration were submitted, of which only 17 cases were not granted by the authoritative commission. The larger number was cancelled by the applicants themselves before the decision of the commission was made and, in 6 cases, after the commission had given permission. (Wille & Beier, 1989, pp. 111–112)

At least 68% of the control subjects were "treatment" refusers. We, therefore, reexamined the 12 original reports. In seven studies, all or most of the control group were men who refused or dropped out of treatment. Of the other five studies, three employed random assignment, one a matching design, and, in one, the control group included men from an earlier cohort or some who did not participate for administrative reasons. Mean effect sizes (Cohen's d) for the two sets of studies were .49, $p < .05$, and -.01, ns, respectively. Hall's (1995) result, therefore, provides an estimate of the nonspecific effect of volunteering for and persisting with treatment upon sexual recidivism.

Based on the size of this methodological artifact, the appropriate inferential test for studies employing treatment refusers as the control group might be to reject the null hypothesis that the confidence interval for d includes .50 (instead of the usual criterion of zero). We note finally that Hall (1995) compared three classes of treatment—behavioral, cognitive behavioral, and hormonal (including castration)—and reported superiority for the latter two over the first. Because it seemed to contradict more comprehensive meta-analyses of treatment (Lipsey, 1992; Lipsey & Wilson, 1993), this conclusion warranted further examination. The accurate classification of control groups yielded a more plausible explanation: *None* of the evaluations of behavioral treatment but *all* of the evaluations of hormonal interventions used the treatment-refusers-as-control design. Hall's (1995) conclusions are thus compromised by the confounding of study quality and treatment type.

CONCLUSIONS

Reviewing the research leaves one in a dilemma. History shows that attempts to reform prisons and justice systems to rehabilitate or treat criminals have been repeatedly abandoned when effective methods to bring about change were found lacking. There is little doubt that harsher penalties, executions, and deterrence will fail as effective social policies.

On the other hand, the available evidence, when closely examined, does not yet permit a firm conclusion that we have developed effective treatments for adult offenders. Meta-analyses based on juvenile offenders provide strong evidence of positive treatment effects. Treatments with the most promise are skills based and behavioral provided to higher risk offenders in the community. Age has not been related to treatment efficacy, although it has not been subjected to a strong test. The literature on effective treatments for adult offenders is exceedingly sparse, and almost all existing studies reporting positive results for adult offenders have significant problems. Somewhat surprisingly, Lipsey (1992) and Lipsey and Wilson (1993) found that few methodological details affected effect size, but these findings cannot be taken as license to ignore research design. Meta-analyses must include some methodologically strong studies to be useful. Clearly, practical considerations and the huge problems involved in changing institutional and bureaucratic routines make implementing programs with high integrity extremely difficult. To say that no treatment for adult offenders has been shown to be effective is not to say that treatments have been shown to be ineffective. Unfortunately, policy makers and the public are prone to confuse these two different conclusions—one arguably correct and the other certainly false. For the moment, we must conclude that effective treatment for adult offenders is, at best, in its infancy.

FUTURE RESEARCH

Because so few high-quality studies have been conducted with adult offenders, it is premature to limit our evaluative efforts exclusively to treatments found most promising for juveniles. Some treatments with positive results for adult offenders do not seem particularly structured, behavioral, or skills based. Future

treatment efforts should include some that do not necessarily follow from the juvenile literature. Pharmacological treatments, for example, have very rarely been tested. It is extremely important that there be a careful evaluation of treatment effectiveness so that a future meta-analysis can examine the effects of different forms of treatment.

Finally, we believe that considerable research effort should be spent on treatment for psychopaths (Hart & Hare, Chapter 3, this volume). Treatment for adult offenders might be generally less effective than treatment for juveniles because the proportion of psychopaths among adult offenders is higher than among juvenile offenders, and that proportion may increase as the severity and frequency of crime increases. We have provided evidence that adult offender populations are composed of two distinct subgroups: psychopaths and nonpsychopaths, rather than a continuum on which psychopaths represent one extreme. That is, psychopathy reflects a taxon: a fundamental dysjunction in nature between psychopaths and nonpsychopaths (Harris, Rice, & Quinsey, 1994). Furthermore, we suggest that the psychopathy taxon is genetically based and is not a disorder but is, in the evolutionary sense, an adaptation (Harris et al., 1994; Mealey, 1995; Quinsey & Lalumière, 1995). By this view, psychopathic mental and behavioral characteristics conferred a reproductive advantage in ancestral environments characterized by social instability and scarcity of resources, especially when the proportion of psychopaths in the population was fairly low.

According to these speculations, interventions that alter the antisocial behavior of psychopaths bear no necessary similarity to those that are effective for other offenders. Thus, treatment might be more successful among youthful offenders because it induces the relatively large proportion of nonpsychopaths to desist criminal behavior earlier (Quinsey, Harris, & Rice, in press). To the extent that offender populations include psychopaths, treatment effects will be difficult to obtain. Because psychopaths are not disordered, there is nothing for therapy to fix. Interventions aimed at remediation of skill deficits, raising low self-esteem, reducing substance abuse, strengthening the superego, and improving intimacy might all, to varying degrees, reduce the recidivism of nonpsychopaths. They will not, according to our speculations, however, affect the antisocial conduct of psychopaths (even if they can be shown to change proximal measures of those constructs), because they are irrelevant to the root causes of antisocial conduct among psychopaths. As an example, in follow-up studies of released offenders, alcohol abuse history (though worse among psychopaths) was related to recidivism only among nonpsychopaths; among psychopaths, alcohol abuse and recidivism were unrelated (Rice & Harris, 1995).

By this view, treatments that affect rates of criminal recidivism among psychopaths will be those that increase the detection of and reduce the payoff for deception, exploitation, and antisocial conduct. By the same token, treatments targeting psychopathic characteristics empirically related to recidivism (e.g., irresponsibility, impulsivity; Harris et al., 1994) might also be effective. Based on these speculations, we recommend that future research include measures of psychopathy. Interesting and potentially fruitful questions include: What predicts criminal and violent recidivism among psychopaths? To what extent does the proportion of psychopaths in a population of offenders attenuate treatment effects? To what extent is psychopathy a predictor of treatment response? What experimental conditions increase the probability of cooperative behavior by psychopaths? Do very high doses of "appropriate correctional service" affect the recidivism of psychopaths? It is our view that attention to these issues has the potential to lead to new and effective interventions to reduce the recidivism of a group of particularly dangerous individuals.

REFERENCES

Abel, G. G., Mittelman, M., Becker, J. V., Rathner, J., & Rouleau, J. L. (1988). Predicting child molesters' response to treatment. In R. A. Prentky & V. L. Quinsey (Eds.), *Human sexual aggression: Current perspectives* (pp. 223–234). New York: New York Academy of Sciences.

Andrews, D. A. (1980). Some experimental investigations of the principles of differential association through deliberate manipulations of the structure of service systems. *American Sociological Review, 45,* 448–462.

Andrews, D. A., & Bonta, J. (1994). *The psychology of criminal conduct.* Cincinnati: Anderson.

Andrews, D. A., Kiessling, J. J., Robinson, D., & Mickus, S. (1986). The risk principle of case classification: An outcome evaluation with young adult probationers. *Canadian Journal of Criminology, 28,* 377–384.

Andrews, D. A., Zinger, I., Hoge, R. D., Bonta, J., Gendreau, P., & Cullen, F. T. (1990). Does correctional treatment work? A clinically relevant and psychologically informed meta-analysis. *Criminology, 28,* 369–404.

Anglin, M. D., & Hser, Y. I. (1990). Treatment of drug abuse. In M. Tonry & J.O. Wilson (Eds.), *Crime and justice: An annual review of research: Vol. 13. Drugs and Crime* (pp. 393–460). Chicago: University of Chicago Press.

Bale, R. N., Van Stone, W. W., Kuldau, J. M., Engelsing, T. M., Elashoff, R. M., & Zarcone, V. P. (1980). Therapeutic communities vs. methadone maintenance. *Archives of General Psychiatry, 37,* 179–193.

Barker, E. T. (1980). The Penetanguishene program: A personal review. In H. Toch (Ed.), *Therapeutic communities in corrections* (pp. 73–81). New York: Praeger.

Bassett, J. E., & Blanchard, E. B. (1977). The effect of the absence of close supervision on the use of response cost in a prison token economy. *Journal of Applied Behavior Analysis, 10,* 375–379.

Basta, J. M., & Davidson, W. S. (1988). Treatment of juvenile offenders: Study outcomes since 1980. *Behavioral Sciences & the Law, 6,* 355–384.

Bloom, H. S., & Singer, N. M. (1979). Determining the cost-effectiveness of correctional programs. In L. Sechrest, S. G. West, M. A. Phillips, R. Redner, & W. Yeaton (Eds.), *Evaluation studies: Review Annual* (pp. 552–568). Beverly Hills, CA: Sage Publications.

Bonta, J. (1996). Risk-needs assessment and treatment. In A. Harland (Ed.), *Choosing correctional options that work* (pp. 18–32). Thousand Oaks, CA: Sage Publications.

Borduin, C. M., Mann, B. J., Cone, L. T., Henggeler, S. W., Fucci, B. R., Blaske, D. M., & Williams, R. A. (1995). Multisystemic treatment of serious juvenile offenders: Long-term prevention of criminality and violence. *Journal of Consulting and Clinical Psychology, 63,* 569–578.

Brennan, P. A., & Mednick, S. A. (1994). Learning theory approach to the deterrence of criminal recidivism. *Journal of Abnormal Psychology, 103,* 430–440.

Cohen, J. (1969). *Statistical power analysis for the behavioral sciences.* New York: Academic Press.

Cooke, D. J. (1989). Containing violent prisoners: An analysis of the Barlinnie Special Unit. *British Journal of Criminology, 29,* 129–144.

Copas, J. B., & Whiteley, J. S. (1976). Predicting success in the treatment of psychopaths. *British Journal of Psychiatry, 129,* 388–392.

Craft, M., Stephenson, G., & Granger, C. (1964). A controlled trial of authoritarian and self-governing regimes with adolescent psychopaths. *American Journal of Orthopsychiatry, 64,* 543–554.

Cullen, F. T., & Gendreau, P. (1989). The effectiveness of correctional rehabilitation. In L. Goodstein & D. MacKenzie (Eds.), *The American prison: Issues in research and policy* (pp. 23–44). New York: Plenum.

Curtis, D., Graham, A., Kelly, L., & Patterson, A. (1985). *Kingston Penitentiary: The first hundred and fifty years: 1835–1985.* Ottawa: Ministry of Supply and Services.

DeLeon, G. (1984). *The therapeutic community: Study of effectiveness.* Washington, DC: Government Printing Office.

Dolan, B., & Coid, J. (1993). *Psychopathic and antisocial personality disorders: Treatment and research issues.* London: Gaskell.

Dutton, D. G. (1986). The outcome of court-mandated treatment for wife assault: A quasi-experimental evaluation. *Violence and Victims, 1,* 163–175.

Ekstedt, J. W., & Griffiths, C. T. (1990). Correctional treatment programs. In N. Z. Hilton, M. A. Jackson, & C. D. Webster (Eds.), *Clinical criminology: Theory, research, and practice* (pp. 607–624). Toronto: Canadian Scholars' Press, Inc.

Elliott, D. S. (1980). Recurring issues in the evaluation of delinquency prevention and treatment programs. In D. Shichor & D. H. Kelly (Eds.), *Critical issues in juvenile delinquency* (pp. 237–262). Lexington: D.C. Heath and Company.

Elliott, D. S. (1994). Serious violent offenders: Onset, developmental course, and termination—The American society of criminology 1993 presidential address. *Criminology, 32,* 1–21.

Elliott, D. S., Huizinga, D., & Ageton, S. S. (1985). *Explaining delinquency and drug use.* Beverly Hills, CA: Sage Publications.

Fagan, J. A. (1990). Treatment and reintegration of violent delinquents: Experimental results. *Justice Quarterly, 7,* 233–263.

Farrington, D. P. (1985). Predicting self-reported and official delinquency. In D. P. Farrington & R. Tarling (Eds.), *Prediction in criminology* (pp. 150–173). Albany: State University of New York Press.

Farrington, D. P. (1986). Age and crime. In M. Tonry & N. Morris (Eds.), *Crime and justice: An annual review of research* (pp. 189–250). Chicago: University of Chicago Press.

Fink, L., Derby, W. N., & Martin, J. P. (1969). Psychiatry's new role in corrections. *American Journal of Psychiatry, 126,* 124–128.

Gendreau, P., & Ross, R. R. (1979). Effective correctional treatment: Bibliotherapy for cynics. *Crime & Delinquency, 25,* 463–489.

Gottfredson, D. C., & Gottfredson, G. D. (1992). Theory-guided investigation: Three field experiments. In J. McCord & R. E. Tremblay (Eds.), *Preventing antisocial behavior: Interventions from birth through adolescence* (pp. 311–329). New York: Guilford.

Gottfredson, G. D. (1984). A theory-ridden approach to program evaluation. *American Psychologist, 39,* 1101–1112.

Grant, J. D., & Grant, M. Q. (1959). A group dynamics approach to the treatment of nonconformists in the Navy. In T. Sellin (Ed.), *Prevention of juvenile delinquency* (pp. 126–135). Philadelphia: The American Academy of Political and Social Science.

Greenwood, P. W. (1994). *Three strikes and you're out: Estimated costs and benefits of California's new mandatory-sentencing law.* RAND Corporation (MR-509-RC). Santa Monica, CA: RAND.

Gunn, J., & Robertson, G.R. (1982). An evaluation of Grendon Prison. In J. Gunn & D. P. Farrington (Eds.), *Abnormal offenders, delinquency, and the criminal justice system* (pp. 285–305). New York: Wiley.

Hall, G. C. N. (1995). Sex offender recidivism revisited: A meta-analysis of recent treatment studies. *Journal of Consulting and Clinical Psychology, 63,* 802–809.

Hare, R. D. (1991). *The Revised Psychopathy Checklist.* Toronto: Multihealth Systems.

Harris, G. T., Rice, M. E., & Cormier, C. A. (1994). Psychopaths: Is a therapeutic community therapeutic? *Therapeutic Communities, 15,* 283–300.

Harris, G. T., Rice, M. E., & Quinsey, V. L. (1994). Psychopathy as a taxon: Evidence that psychopaths are a discrete class. *Journal of Consulting and Clinical Psychology, 62,* 387–397.

Hoffman, P. B., & Beck, J. L. (1984). Burnout—Age at release from prison and recidivism. *Journal of Criminal Justice, 12,* 617–623.

Hser, Y. I., Anglin, M. D., & Chou, C. P. (1988). Evaluation of drug abuse treatment: A repeated measures design assessing methadone maintenance. *Evaluation Review, 12,* 547–570.

Hughes, R. (1988). *Fatal shore: The epic of Australia's founding.* New York: Random.

Jones, M. (1953). *The therapeutic community.* New York: Basic Books.

Kamin, L. (1993). The temper of the times. [Review of the book *Understanding and preventing violence.*] *Readings: A Journal of Reviews and Commentary in Mental Health, 8,* 4–7.

Langevin, R., Paitich, D., Hucker, S., Newman, S., Ramsay, G., Pope, S., Geller, G., & Anderson, C. (1979). The effect of assertiveness training, provera, and sex of therapist in the treatment of genital exhibitionism. *Journal of Behavior Therapy and Experimental Psychiatry, 10,* 275–282.

Liberman, R. P., Kopelowicz, A., & Young, A. S. (1994). Biobehavioral treatment and rehabilitation of schizophrenia. *Behavior Therapy, 25,* 89–107.

Lipsey, M. W. (1992). Juvenile delinquency treatment: A meta-analytic inquiry into the variability of effects. In R. S. Cook, H. Cooper, D. S. Cordray, H. Hartmann, L. V. Hedges, R. J. Light, T. A. Louis, & F. Mosteller (Eds.), *Meta-analysis for explanation* (pp. 83–125). New York: Russell Sage.

Lipsey, M. W., & Wilson, D. B. (1993). The efficacy of psychological, educational, and behavioral treatment. *American Psychologist, 48,* 1181–1209.

Lösel, F., & Koferl, P. (1989). Evaluation research on correctional treatment in West Germany: A meta-analysis. In H. Wegener, F. Lösel, & J. Haisch (Eds.), *Criminal behavior and the justice system: Psychological perspectives* (pp. 334–355). New York: Springer-Verlag.

Marques, J. K., Day, D. M., Nelson, C., & West, M. A. (1993). Findings and recommendations from California's experimental treatment program. In G. C. N. Hall, R. Hirschman, R. Graham, & M. S. Zaragoza (Eds.), *Sexual aggression: Issues in etiology and assessment and treatment* (pp. 197–214). Washington, DC: Taylor & Francis.

Marshall, W. L., & Barbaree, H. E. (1988). The long-term evaluation of a behavioral treatment program for child molesters. *Behavior Research and Therapy, 26,* 499–511.

Martinson, R. (1974). What works? Questions and answers about prison reform. *Public Interest, 35,* 22–84.

Mealey, L. (1995). The sociobiology of sociopathy: An integrated evolutionary model. *Behavioral and Brain Sciences, 18,* 523–541.

Menditto, A. A., Beck, N. C., Stuve, P., Fisher, J. A., Stacy, M., Longue, M. B., & Baldwin, L. J. (1996). Effectiveness of clozapine and a social learning program for severely disabled psychiatric inpatients. *Psychiatric Services, 47,* 46–51.

Milan, M. A. (1987). Token economy programs in closed institutions. In E. K. Morris & C. J. Braukmann (Eds.), *Behavioral approaches to crime and delinquency: A handbook of application, research, and concepts* (pp. 195–222). New York: Plenum.

Milan, M. A., & McKee, J. M. (1976). The cellblock token economy: Token reinforcement procedures in a maximum security correctional institution for adult male felons. *Journal of Applied Behavior Analysis, 9,* 253–275.

Morris, N. (1974). *The future of imprisonment.* Chicago: University of Chicago Press.

Ogloff, J. R. P., Wong, S., & Greenwood, A. (1990). Treating criminal psychopaths in a therapeutic community program. *Behavioral Sciences and the Law, 8,* 181–190.

Palmer, S. E., Brown, R. A., & Barrera, M. E. (1992). Group treatment program for abusive husbands: Long-term evaluation. *American Journal of Orthopsychiatry, 62,* 276–283.

Paul, G. L., & Lentz, R. J. (1977). *Psychosocial treatment of chronic mental patients.* Cambridge: Harvard University Press.

Pearson, F. S. (1988). Evaluation of New Jersey's intensive supervision program. *Crime and Delinquency, 34,* 437–448.

Petersilia, J., Turner, S., & Peterson, J. (1986). *Prison versus probation in California.* Santa Monica, CA: RAND.

Quinsey, V. L., Harris, G. T., & Rice, M. E. (in press). *Violent offenders: Appraising and managing risk.* Washington, DC: American Psychological Association Press.

Quinsey, V. L., & Lalumière, M. (1995). Psychopathy is a nonarbitrary class. *Behavioral and Brain Sciences, 18,* 570.

Raine, A. (1993). *The psychopathology of crime.* New York: Academic Press.

Rice, M. E., & Harris, G. T. (1995a). Psychopathy, schizophrenia, alcohol abuse, and violent recidivism. *International Journal of Law and Psychiatry, 18,* 333–342.

Rice, M. E., & Harris, G. T. (1995b). Violent recidivism: Assessing predictive validity. *Journal of Consulting and Clinical Psychology, 63,* 737–748.

Rice, M. E., Harris, G. T., & Cormier, C. (1992). Evaluation of a maximum security therapeutic community for psychopaths and other mentally disordered offenders. *Law and Human Behavior, 16,* 399–412.

Ross, R. R., & Fabiano, E. A. (1985). *Time to think: A cognitive model of delinquency prevention and offender rehabilitation.* Johnson City, TN: Institute of Social Science and Arts.

Ross, R. R., Fabiano, E. A., & Ewles, C. D. (1988). Reasoning and rehabilitation. *International Journal of Offender Therapy and Comparative Criminology, 32,* 29–35.

Rothman, D. J. (1971). *The discovery of the asylum: Social order and disorder in the new republic.* Boston: Little, Brown.

Rothman, D. J. (1980). *Conscience and convenience: The asylum and its alternatives in progressive America.* Boston: Little, Brown.

Sechrest, L., White, S. O., & Brown, E. D. (1979). *The rehabilitation of criminal offenders: Problems and prospects.* Washington, DC: National Academy Press.

Singer, J. D., & Willett, J. B. (1991). Modeling the days of our lives: Using survival analysis when designing and analyzing longitudinal studies of duration and the time of events. *Psychological Bulletin, 110,* 268–290.

Smart, R. G. (1976). Outcome studies of therapeutic community and halfway house treatment for addicts. *International Journal of Addictions, 11,* 143–159.

Stermac, L. E. (1986). Anger control treatment for forensic patients. *Journal of Interpersonal Violence, 1,* 446–457.

Weisman, R. (1995). Reflections on the Oak Ridge experiment with psychiatric offenders, 1965–1968. *International Journal of Law and Psychiatry, 18,* 265–290.

Wexler, H. K., Falkin, G. P., & Lipton, D. S. (1990). Outcome evaluation of a prison therapeutic community for substance abuse treatment. *Criminal Justice and Behavior, 17,* 71–92.

Wilkins, W. (1986). Rhetoric and irrelevant criteria that disguise behavior therapy efficacy: Historical and contemporary notes. *Journal of Behavior Therapy and Experimental Psychiatry, 17,* 83–89.

Wille, R., & Beier, K. M. (1989). Castration in Germany. *Annals of Sex Research, 2,* 103–133.

Wilson, G. T. (1997). Treatment manuals in clinical practice. *Behavior Research and Therapy, 35,* 205–210.

Zigler, E., & Muenchow, S. (1992). *Head Start: The inside story of America's most successful educational experiment.* New York: Basic Books.

CHAPTER 41

Pharmacotherapy of Violent Behavior

LAURENCE P. KARPER and JOHN H. KRYSTAL

The pharmacologic treatment of violent behavior is a significant part of the practice of clinical psychiatry and an active area of current research. This chapter presents an overview of the treatment of violent behavior, a review of the methodology of treatment studies, a summary of the current state of the art of pharmacotherapy, and directions for future research. In this review, the focus is on the pharmacologic treatment of individuals whose violent behavior is directed at other persons or property.

Many psychiatric diagnoses may be associated with violent behavior including personality disorders, attention deficit/hyperactivity disorder, conduct disorder, personality change due to a medical condition, and impulse-control disorders (American Psychiatric Association, 1994). In addition, violent behavior is a frequent concomitant of schizophrenia, bipolar disorder, dementia, delirium, and substance abuse (Tardiff, 1992). Recent work (see Monahan, 1992; Monahan, Chapter 9, this volume) suggests that psychotic symptoms rather than specific psychiatric diagnoses may be a better predictor of the occurrence of violent behavior. Approximately 10% of psychiatric patients who are admitted for treatment have a recent history of aggressive behavior (Tardiff, 1992), and approximately 50% of incarcerated individuals can be diagnosed with a psychiatric condition (most commonly, personality disorders and substance abuse; Dietz, 1992).

THEORETICAL CONTEXT: PRINCIPLES AND CAVEATS

The treatment of individuals with violent behavior is complex and the prognosis often is considered poor, with the passage of time being the best treatment (Widiger, Corbitt, & Millon, 1992). The treatment of chronically antisocial individuals requires a multidisciplinary and multidimensional approach (Reid & Burke, 1989). Integration of pharmacologic and psychosocial interventions may succeed by treating both maladaptive temperament and character (Cloninger, Svrakic, & Przybeck, 1993). Subtyping violent behavior on the basis of "predatory" versus "affective" may provide valuable neurobiological clues to plan treatment (Kruesi et al., 1994; Vitiello, Behar, Hunt, Stoff, & Ricciuti, 1990). "Affective"

or impulsive violence may be more amenable to pharmacologic interventions, whereas "predatory" or planned violence may be better treated by psychosocial and behavioral means. Research on the neurobiological classification of violent behavior could lead to improved treatment strategies. Other subtyping approaches include instrumental versus hostile aggression (Atkins & Stoff, 1993) and over- versus undercontrolled hostility (Hershorn & Rosenbaum, 1991). Pharmacologic treatment in the absence of a consistent psychosocial intervention, particularly in children (Stewart, Myers, Burket, & Lyles, 1990), rarely is satisfactory. Current practice is to use both pharmacologic and psychosocial interventions in a comprehensive treatment program.

The first step in developing a pharmacologic treatment plan for an individual with violent behavior is to perform a diagnostic evaluation, including a detailed review of any problematic behavior and symptoms. If the evaluation occurs during a violent episode in an emergency room, a complete medical and psychiatric history should be obtained as soon as possible. Obtaining a complete evaluation may be difficult in an emergency room setting because of the urgent and disruptive nature of violent episodes. However, elicitation of information regarding allergies, previous medications, and history of any neuropsychiatric or medical illness should be attempted from the patient or a significant other. Physical evidence of drug abuse, anticholinergic toxicity, neurologic signs, or disorientation are indications of reversible causes of aggressive behavior. The most common contributing factor to violence is drug-induced intoxication (Reid, 1988). Alcohol, opiates, PCP, cocaine, and amphetamines can precipitate violence in a vulnerable individual or can cause delirium during intoxication or withdrawal. Neuropsychological testing and neurological examination, as well as an assessment for abuse, are particularly important in the evaluation of children with aggressive or criminal behavior (Mandoki, Sumner, & Matthews-Ferrari, 1992).

No medication has been approved by the Food and Drug Administration specifically for the treatment of violent behavior. Psychotropic medication cannot eliminate important environmental influences of behavior, such as parental psychopathology or disruptive living situations. The treatment of violence begins with an evaluation for and then treatment of any psychiatric or medical disorders, if present. A pharmacotherapeutic trial always should be coupled with objective ratings of behavior and target symptoms. One of the most commonly used rating scales for the measurement of violent behavior in pharmacologic studies is the Overt Aggression Scale (Yudofsky, Silver, Jackson, Endicott, & Williams, 1986). Other scales, such as the Brief Psychiatric Rating Scale (Overall & Gorham, 1962) for the assessment of psychosis, also can be used to measure symptoms and to document efficacy. The lack of discrimination between sedation, amelioration of psychiatric symptomatology, and the specific reduction of violence is a limitation of the available research literature. More needs to be known about the neurobiology of violent behavior to develop more efficacious treatments with fewer side effects.

METHODOLOGY

Research on the pharmacologic treatment of violent behavior has employed animal models of aggression, pharmacologic challenge studies, and clinical treatment studies. Experiments utilizing animal models have delineated the neurochemical basis of the modulation of aggression and irritability and provided hypotheses that can be tested in pharmacologic treatment trials. Some of the first animal studies to evaluate aggressive behavior occurred between 1930 and 1938 (Valzelli, 1967). Subsequent work using animal paradigms to induce aggressiveness found that several classes of psychotropic agents reduced the aggressive behavior (Valzelli, Giacalone, & Garattini, 1967). An important methodological question concerns whether the doses used in the animal models impair motor responses or cause analgesia (Valzelli, 1967). If that is the case, it is not the specific antiaggressive properties of the drugs but the analgesic or sedative properties that reduce aggressiveness. These concerns also are useful in evaluating the efficacy of pharmacologic agents in clinical studies in humans.

Several critical methodological issues must be considered when evaluating clinical trials of antiaggressive medications. These include accurate diagnosis, patient selection, and the confounding influence of time and multiple medications (De Koning & Mak, 1991). The specificity of the diagnostic assessment is central to the applicability of the results of the study. Experimental control for placebo effects and random allocation of patients to experimental and standard therapies help to reduce bias and distinguish medication response from the effects of time, hospitalization, or chance. Studies utilizing the crossover design have the advantage of testing two or more therapies on the same patient. Crossover experiments can provide tests of treatment matching hypotheses. One limitation of this method is that the effectiveness of a drug may continue after it is withdrawn. Studies of antiaggressive agents often are uncontrolled open-label trials, because of the difficulty of conducting experimental trials with violent patients. In spite of the methodological limitations of many of the studies reviewed here, they do provide useful information on clinical treatment and can provide preliminary data for later controlled trials.

CURRENT FINDINGS

Antidepressants

Antidepressants can be useful in depressed and irritable aggressive adults (Fava et al., 1993). Research also has indicated a role for antidepressants in the treatment of depression with agitation and attention deficit/hyperactivity disorder in children and adolescents (Ambrosini, Bianchi, Rabinovich, & Elia, 1993a, 1993b; Stewart et al., 1990). Antidepressant efficacy may be related to the enhancement of serotonin neurotransmission or down-regulation of noradrenergic receptors (Nelson, 1991). The antiaggressive effects of antidepressants may be related to their effects on these neurotransmitter systems. Studies of human cerebrospinal fluid metabolites (Insel, Zohar, Benkelfat, & Murphy, 1990) as well as platelet monoamine oxidase activity (Stoff et al., 1989) have suggested that serotonergic function is reduced in subjects with impulsive aggressive and self-injurious behavior.

Trazodone and fluoxetine, antidepressants with selective serotonergic activity, have been reported to be helpful in open trials in diagnostic groups with aggression problems, including children with disruptive behavior (Zubieta & Alessi, 1992), patients with a personality disorder (Coccaro, Astill, Herbert, & Schut, 1990), and brain-injured patients (Pinner & Rich, 1988). Given the success of serotonergic antidepressants such as clomipramine, fluoxetine, and fluvoxamine in obsessive-compulsive disorder, these agents have been utilized in compulsive behaviors associated with sexual obsessions (Stein et al., 1992) and paraphilic coercive disorder (Kafka, 1991). Placebo-controlled, double-blind studies differentiating the effects of these agents on the symptoms of depression or obsessive-compulsive disorder and violent behavior will be necessary to delineate whether these agents are specifically reducing violent behavior or improving the underlying psychiatric symptomatology.

Cases have been reported of suicidality and violence emerging after treatment has begun with fluoxetine and other antidepressants (e.g., Teicher, Glod, & Cole, 1990), and they have received much media attention. Large-scale studies, however, do not support the notion that the selective serotonin re-uptake inhibitors are more likely than other antidepressants to cause suicidal ideation (Molcho & Stanley, 1992). In a meta-analysis involving 3,992 patients, Heiligenstein, Beasley, and Potvin (1993) found no increase in aggression in patients treated with fluoxetine as compared to a placebo. Fluoxetine is less lethal in overdose than other antidepressants, and this is particularly important in the treatment of impulsive or aggressive patients.

Lithium

Lithium is used in the treatment of bipolar disorder, schizophrenia, and schizoaffective disorder (Cohen & Lipinski, 1986; Schou, 1989; Stewart et al., 1990). Although the mechanism of action of lithium is not known, its efficacy in reducing violence may be because it increases brain serotonin function (Linnoila, Virkkunen, Roy, & Potter, 1990). The initial studies documenting the antiaggressive efficacy of lithium were conducted in the 1970s by Sheard (Sheard, 1975; Sheard, Marini, Bridges, & Wagner, 1976) and Tupin et al. (1973). These investigators studied the effects of lithium in groups of aggressive prisoners. Sheard evaluated the efficacy of high- and low-dose lithium on aggressive incidents in male prisoners 16 to 24 years old. This study demonstrated that lithium reduced episodes of violent behavior. Long-term treatment with lithium reduced aggression in a diagnostically diverse group of patients, a subset of which had a history of abnormal EEGs and brain injury (Tupin et al., 1973). Females with "emotionally unstable character disorder" had reductions in impulsivity, combativeness, and hostility during lithium treatment (Rifkin, Quitkin, Carrillo, Blumberg, & Klein, 1972). Lithium was effective for the control of aggression and mood lability in a double-blind trial in the mentally handicapped (Craft et al., 1987). Lithium also has been shown to reduce aggression in children and adolescents with conduct disorder, bipolar disorder, episodic dyscontrol, and mental retardation (Campbell, Gonzalez, & Silva, 1992; Mandoki et al., 1992; Stewart et al., 1990). A recent double-blind, placebo-controlled trial of lithium in aggressive children with conduct disorder supports its use in this patient group (Campbell et al., 1995).

A combination of lithium, antipsychotic drugs, and anticonvulsants is used to control violence and labile mood in schizophrenia, schizoaffective disorder, bipolar disorder, and organic mood disorders. This combination can reduce the dosage levels of antipsychotic medications needed. Lithium should be used with caution in individuals with epilepsy or organic mental disorders, because it can lower the seizure threshold. Lithium may cause a toxic neurological reaction at therapeutic doses and therefore must be titrated carefully. Contraindications to the use of lithium are renal, thyroid, and cardiovascular disease. Laboratory evaluation of renal and thyroid function as well as lithium levels must be routinely performed by the prescribing physician.

Antihypertensive Agents

Beta-blockers (β-adrenergic receptor antagonists) and clonidine, an α_2-adrenergic receptor partial agonist decrease noradrenergic functioning, which may result in decreased aggression (Eichelman, 1987). The β-adrenergic receptor antagonists (such as propranolol, nadolol, pindolol, and metoprolol) are used to treat hypertension, angina, and cardiac arrhythmias. Propranolol reduced aggressive behavior in adults with both acute and chronic neurological impairments (Silver, Hales, & Yudofsky, 1990) as well as in children and adolescents (Mandoki et al., 1992). Double-blind, placebo-controlled studies have found propranolol (Greendyke, Kanter, Schuster, Verstreate, & Wootton, 1986) and pindolol (Greendyke & Kanter, 1986) helpful in reducing violent behavior in patients with chronic organic brain syndromes. Propranolol also has been used to treat aggression associated with mental retardation (Luchins & Dojka, 1989; Stewart et al., 1990). Beta-blockers have fewer neurological side effects than neuroleptics and so therefore may be better tolerated in patients with organic mental disorders.

Impulsive symptoms in intermittent explosive disorder, conduct disorder, and attention deficit disorder may improve with beta-blockers (Campbell et al., 1992; Mattes, 1990; Stewart et al., 1990). Double-blind, placebo-controlled studies have demonstrated that beta-blockers can reduce both psychotic symptoms

and aggression (e.g., Ratey et al., 1992). The antipsychotic efficacy may be related to an increase in antipsychotic blood levels or the treatment of side effects such as akathisia (Lipinski, Keck, & McElroy, 1988). Beta-blockers are contraindicated in patients with a history of cardiovascular or peripheral vascular disease, asthma or chronic lung disease, or diabetes and may worsen or cause depression (Silver et al., 1990).

Clonidine may have modest efficacy in reducing impulsivity and aggression in children (Kemph, DeVane, Levin, Jarecke, & Miller, 1993). Controlled trials in well-defined population groups are needed to assess adequately the clinical efficacy of clonidine.

Stimulants

Attention deficit/hyperactivity disorder is often associated with aggressive or antisocial behavior that may respond to pharmacologic treatment (Shaffer, 1994). Stimulant medications (such as amphetamine, pemoline, and methylphenidate) may be helpful in treating the impulsivity and aggressiveness associated with conduct disorder and attention deficit/hyperactivity disorder in children and adolescents (Campbell et al., 1992; Kaplan, Busner, Kupietz, Wassermann, & Segal, 1990; Stewart et al., 1990). The stimulants may be abused and can lead to paranoia and aggressive or violent behavior.

Dopamine Receptor Antagonists

Neuroleptics block dopamine receptors in the brain and have been used in the acute management of aggressive and violent behavior for more than 4 decades. The rationale for the efficacy of these agents in reducing violence is that elevations in brain dopamine by drugs such as L-dopa and apomorphine can cause aggression in animals (Eichelman, 1987). The primary indication for neuroleptic drugs is the treatment of psychotic symptoms in schizophrenia, psychotic depression, acute mania, delusional disorder, schizophreniform disorder, and schizoaffective disorder (Kane, 1989). Neuroleptic drugs are especially useful in the acute treatment of patients with agitated or aggressive behavior in the context of an acute psychotic decompensation. Violent behavior in psychotic patients may be related to paranoid delusions, excitement, command auditory hallucinations, or thought disorder. Treatment of the psychosis reduces the agitation and violent behavior associated with it.

The management of chronic violent behavior with neuroleptic drugs rarely should be instituted in nonpsychotic patients. Patients with borderline personality disorder may benefit from long-term treatment with antipsychotics (Cowdry & Gardner, 1988). Other medications should be tried first and proven ineffective prior to chronic treatment with neuroleptic drugs, because of the aversive and potentially irreversible side effect of tardive dyskinesia. This disfiguring disorder occurs in approximately 15% to 20% of patients treated with neuroleptic drugs (American Psychiatric Association Task Force on Tardive Dyskinesia, 1992).

Neuroleptic drugs can be given to rapidly reduce violent behavior in the emergency room setting. High-potency neuroleptic drugs such as haloperidol are used frequently because of a favorable cardiovascular side effect profile (Donlon, Hopkin, Schaffer, & Amsterdam, 1979). The availability of intramuscular and oral elixir forms provide for convenient and rapid absorption. Low-potency drugs such as chlorpromazine can cause a sterile abscess when given via the intramuscular route and can result in hypotension and anticholinergic toxicity (Tardiff, 1989). Because neuroleptic drugs lower the threshold for having a seizure, they should not be used in the acute treatment of drug intoxication and withdrawal or in cases of known or suspected neurological illness (such as epilepsy). Medically compromised and elderly patients also are at risk for increased side effects such as anticholinergic toxicity.

The initial dosing studies of intramuscular neuroleptic drugs utilized a technique known as *rapid neuroleptization*. This strategy employed multiple repeated injections of neuroleptic drugs resulting in very high daily doses (haloperidol dosages up to 100 mg/24 hours; Donlon, Hopkin, & Tupin, 1979). Subsequent studies demonstrated that more modest doses (haloperidol doses of 10 to 30 mg/24 hours) were as effective with fewer side effects (Tardiff, 1989). It should be noted that some patients may require higher doses because of poor absorption or severity of illness. Yesavage (1982) found that haloperidol levels were inversely correlated with violence, supporting the use of blood-level measurement in refractory patients.

Noncompliance is a critical issue in the pharmacologic treatment of aggression in schizophrenia (Young, Zonana, & Shepler, 1986). Neuroleptic drug side effects (particularly akathisia, a subjective sense of anxiety that may be mistaken for increasing agitation due to psychosis, and dysphoria) are a major factor in noncompliance (Young et al., 1986). Depot neuroleptic drugs, an injectable long-acting form of the medication, can improve compliance (Kane, 1985). Compliance can be monitored by measuring blood levels of the neuroleptic drug or prolactin, a hormone that is elevated in people who are taking neuroleptic drugs, except for clozapine (Young et al., 1986). For patients with persistent noncompliance, certain jurisdictions allow outpatient commitment (Miller, 1991). Outpatient commitment is a court-ordered civil commitment that mandates a patient to comply with an outpatient treatment plan. Outpatient commitment can be used to ensure compliance with injectable medications. Thirty-five states and the District of Columbia allow outpatient commitment at this time (Torrey & Kaplan, 1995). Research is needed to assess the effectiveness of outpatient commitment to enhance compliance and reduce violent behavior.

The neurological side effects of neuroleptics limit their usefulness. The optimal control of these side effects is necessary to effectively use these agents. Dystonias and Parkinsonism (tremors, stiffness, shuffling gait) occur frequently with high-potency antipsychotics. The treatment of these side effects include anticholinergic agents such as benztropine. Akathisia can cause violent (Crowner et al., 1990) or suicidal behavior (Drake & Erhrlich, 1985). Benzodiazepines or beta-blockers are the most effective treatments for akathisia (Fleischhacker, Roth, & Kane, 1990).

Clozapine is an atypical antipsychotic that is more effective in refractory patients than conventional neuroleptic drugs (Kane, Honigfeld, Singer, & Meltzer, 1988), and it has fewer Parkinsonian side effects. However, fatal agranulocytosis and seizures are two of its adverse reactions. Clozapine is reserved for patients who are refractory to conventional treatment because of its side effect pro-

file and cost. It is more than ten times as expensive as typical neuroleptic drugs, but the use of clozapine can result in dramatic cost savings because its increased efficacy leads to decreases in hospitalization rates (Meltzer, 1996). Clozapine cannot be used for rapid control of aggression because it can cause severe hypotension. When clozapine is part of a treatment program including weekly hematological monitoring (for agranulocytosis), there have been documented reductions in the need for restraints and violent behavior in state hospital patients (Wilson, 1992) and in severely ill forensic patients (Maier, 1992). Clozapine may reduce aggression even in patients who continue to have significant psychotic symptoms (Ratey, Leveroni, Kilmer, Gutheil, & Swartz, 1993).

The Benzodiazepines

Benzodiazepines can be used to produce sedation rapidly after violent behavior occurs. The use of benzodiazepines to reduce agitation can lessen the likelihood of behavioral escalation (Tardiff, 1989). Benzodiazepines enhance the functioning of the γ-aminobutyric acid neurotransmitter system, which results in sedation; it also may be why they are useful in reducing aggression (Eichelman, 1988). Benzodiazepines have a wide therapeutic index and are well tolerated; they are used extensively in the treatment of panic disorder and generalized anxiety disorder (Shader & Greenblatt, 1993).

Benzodiazepines increase seizure threshold and have few neurological or medical side effects and, therefore, are the preferred treatment for the emergency management of agitation or violent behavior. They are the medications of first choice in alcohol withdrawal and other causes of agitation that may predispose patients to seizures. In difficult or unclear diagnostic situations, benzodiazepines are used until a definitive evaluation can be completed.

Clinical research has demonstrated the efficacy of benzodiazepines in the treatment of acute psychosis (Cohen & Lipinski, 1986), manic agitation (Lenox, Newhouse, Creelman, & Whitaker, 1992), and episodic temper outbursts (Griffith, 1985).

In patients with extreme psychotic agitation, neuroleptic drugs can be administered along with benzodiazepines. This combination is well tolerated and quite effective, and it appears to manage agitation better than either agent alone (Garza-Trevino, Hollister, Overall, & Alexander, 1989). Treatment regimens including both of these drugs result in decreased doses of neuroleptic drugs and fewer side effects.

The side effects of benzodiazepines include sedation, ataxia, memory disturbances, confusion, hypotension, and respiratory depression. Long-acting benzodiazepines, such as diazepam, chlordiazepoxide, and flurazepam, may be especially likely to cause confusion or prolonged sedation and therefore should be avoided in the elderly or those suffering from liver dysfunction. Disinhibition with benzodiazepines is an uncommon but serious adverse reaction in approximately 1% of patients treated with benzodiazepines (Dietch & Jennings, 1988). Patients with borderline personality disorder may be at a higher risk for this reaction (Gardner & Cowdry, 1985). Chronic treatment with benzodiazepines carries the risk of tolerance and abuse, especially in patients with substance abuse histories (American Psychiatric Association Task Force on Benzodiazepine Dependency, 1990).

Anticonvulsants

The primary use of the anticonvulsants carbamazepine and valproic acid in psychiatry is in the treatment of bipolar disorder (Pope, McElroy, Keck, & Hudson, 1991). The mechanism of action of these agents is not yet clear; however, several neurotransmitter systems as well as their anticonvulsive properties have been suggested (Post, 1987).

The first studies to document the efficacy of carbamazepine in the reduction of aggression were in patients with abnormal EEGs or neuropsychological impairments (e.g., Foster, Hillbrand, & Chi, 1989; Neppe, 1983). An open label study (Mattes, 1990) suggested that carbamazepine was effective in reducing rage outbursts in patients with intermittent explosive disorder. Cowdry and Gardner (1988), in a controlled study, found that carbamazepine reduced impulsive aggression in the treatment of borderline personality disorder.

There is a paucity of double-blind studies with anticonvulsants in children. An open pilot study (Kafantaris et al., 1992) suggested that treatment with carbamazepine reduces violent behavior in conduct disorder. Some children may symptomatically worsen during a carbamazepine trial (Campbell et al., 1992), perhaps because of reductions in neuroleptic blood levels (Jann et al., 1985). The main side effects of carbamazepine are agranulocytosis, hyponatremia, and liver function abnormalities.

There have been no double-blind, placebo-controlled studies with valproic acid in the treatment of violent behavior. Open studies have been tried with some success in reducing agitation and aggressiveness in patients with dementia (Mellow, Solano-Lopez, & Davis, 1993), mental retardation (Mattes, 1992), organic mental disorders (Mazure, Druss, & Cellar, 1992), and borderline personality disorder (Stein, Simeon, Frenkel, Islam, & Hollander, 1995). Double-blind, placebo-controlled trials in defined patient groups are necessary to guide treatment with this drug.

Medroxyprogesterone Acetate

Medroxyprogesterone acetate is a testosterone-depleting hormone that has been used in the treatment of male sex offenders (Levine, 1989). In a double-blind, placebo-controlled study, medroxyprogesterone acetate has had some efficacy in inhibiting sexual desire and reducing recidivism in pedophiles and sex offenders (Cooper, Sandhu, Losztyn, & Cernovsky, 1992), but numerous side effects resulted in patient noncompliance.

VIOLENCE AND THE SEROTONERGIC SYSTEM: A POSSIBLE OVERARCHING THEORY

Even though no definitive treatment is available for violent behavior, a common neurobiological pathway for its expression may exist. Disturbances in the serotonin neurotransmitter system have been associated with violent behavior. This relationship has been investigated by evaluating the levels of 5-hydroxyindoleacetic acid, a serotonin metabolite, in the cerebrospinal fluid as a measure of the synthesis or turnover of serotonin in the brain. This

line of research has led to the finding that low concentrations of cerebrospinal fluid 5-hydroxyindoleacetic acid are associated with impulsivity and violence (Roy, Virkkunen, & Linnoila, 1991; see also Berman, Kavoussi, & Coccaro, Chapter 27, this volume). In particular, the lack of impulse control may be strongly linked to low cerebrospinal fluid concentrations of 5-hydroxyindoleacetic acid (Virkkunen et al., 1994). In a study of violent offenders and fire setters, reduced central serotonin turnover rate was related to recidivist impulsive behavior (Virkkunen, Eggert, Rawlins, & Linnoila, 1996). Studies also have found the association of low central serotonin function and impulsivity in nonhuman primates with similar results (Mehlman et al., 1994). Low central nervous system serotonin activity, through its influence on the suprachiasmatic nucleus, may lead to disturbances in impulse control and therefore may predispose individuals to violence (Roy et al., 1991; Virkkunen et al., 1994).

In light of the evidence for the dysregulation of the serotonergic neurotransmitter system in individuals with histories of impulsivity and violence, the mechanism of action of pharmacologic agents that reduce violence may be related to their effects on the serotonin system. Each of the pharmacologic agents reviewed here affects the function of several different neurotransmitter systems. Many have significant effects on the serotonin system. Antidepressants, especially the selective serotonin re-uptake inhibitors, affect primarily the serotonin system. These agents increase central nervous system serotonin activity. Lithium and carbamazepine, although affecting several neurotransmitter systems, may share a common propensity to increase central nervous system serotonin activity (Post, Weiss, & Chuang, 1992). Less clear is the effect on the central nervous system of antihypertensive agents such as propranolol that bind to several serotonin receptor subtypes. There is no doubt that the serotonergic neurotransmitter system plays a critical role in modulating impulsivity. It seems clear, however, that other neurotransmitter systems as well as genetic and environmental factors are involved in the etiopathogenesis and treatment of the complex behaviors that lead to violence.

CONCLUSIONS

The pharmacologic agents used in the treatment of violence act on the serotonergic, noradrenergic, γ-aminobutyric acid, and dopamine neurotransmitter systems. Evidence suggests that pharmacologic effects on the serotonin system may be a common mechanism of action for drugs that reduce impulsivity and therefore the propensity for violence. Antidepressants, stimulants, neuroleptics, benzodiazepines, beta-blockers, anticonvulsants, and lithium are the most frequently used pharmacologic agents for the treatment of violent behavior. The decisive factors in choosing a particular psychopharmacologic agent are the diagnosis of the patient, ease of use, and the ability of the patient to tolerate side effects. The best place to begin is to use a medication appropriate for treating any underlying psychiatric or medical illness (Eichelman, 1988).

Benzodiazepines are useful for short-term or emergency treatment because they are well tolerated and generally safe, with few side effects. Their use is limited by patient tolerance and the potential for abuse. Antidepressant drugs should be used in the context of depression or attention deficit/hyperactivity disorder. Tricyclic antidepressants are considerably more lethal than the selective serotonin re-uptake inhibitors in an overdose. Anticonvulsants and beta-blockers are the first choice in the chronic treatment of aggression and impulsivity in individuals with organic mental disorders, especially in those with an underlying seizure disorder. Lithium has been the most studied antiaggressive agent and is particularly effective in individuals with mood lability, excitement, and impulsivity. Neuroleptics are effective in individuals with psychotic symptoms. Stimulants have a limited role in the treatment of aggression. Because of their high potential for abuse as well as their propensity to cause violence in vulnerable individuals, stimulants are used in patients with clearly defined psychiatric syndromes (attention deficit/hyperactivity disorder) who have a documented response after a therapeutic trial.

The psychopharmacologic agents reviewed here, when used appropriately, can reduce the incidence of violent behavior. However, there are no a priori pharmacologic solutions for the problem of violence. The treatment plan must take into account the complex details that initiate and maintain violent behavior. Pharmacologic treatment is most likely to be efficacious when used in conjunction with appropriate psychosocial and behavioral interventions (see Chamberlain & Friman, Chapter 28; Guerra, Attar, & Weissberg, Chapter 35; Hawkins, Arthur, & Olson, Chapter 34; Rice & Harris, Chapter 40; Tardiff, Chapter 42; Southam-Gerow & Kendall, Chapter 36, all in this volume).

FUTURE WORK

Even though some medications can reduce violent behavior, much work needs to be done in this critical field. Research into the neurobiological and psychosocial subtypes of violent behavior would provide more meaningful subsets of patients for treatment studies. This would enable clinicians to provide more rational and less trial-and-error pharmacotherapy. Expanding the focus of treatment studies to types of violence rather than psychiatric diagnoses would improve the relevance of pharmacology to the social dimensions of violence. In terms of new pharmacological approaches, the development and testing of new nonsedating antiaggressive agents, such as the serenics (Olivier, Mos, & Rasmussen, 1990), should be a high priority, because sedation and other side effects of currently available medications limit compliance and the rehabilitation potential of patients. Given the biological evidence for the relationship between decreased central nervous system serotonin activity and impulsivity, future work on the function of this neurotransmitter system and the many serotonin receptor subtypes may lead to improved pharmacologic treatments. A serious lacuna in the research literature is the paucity of studies on clearly defined populations employing a standardized combination of medication and psychosocial treatment. These studies are complex to analyze and more difficult to complete than a single-medication trial; however, they are necessary to improve the success of combination treatments. Multisite studies also would be helpful in improving the applicability of the results of studies to general treatment settings.

REFERENCES

Ambrosini, P. J., Bianchi, M. D., Rabinovich, H., & Elia, J. (1993a). Antidepressant treatments in children and adolescents: I. Affective disorders. *Journal of the American Academy of Child and Adolescent Psychiatry, 32,* 1–6.

Ambrosini, P. J., Bianchi, M. D., Rabinovich, H., & Elia, J. (1993b). Antidepressant treatments in children and adolescents: II. Anxiety, physical, and behavioral disorders. *Journal of the American Academy of Child and Adolescent Psychiatry, 32,* 483–493.

American Psychiatric Association. (1994). *Diagnostic and statistical manual of mental disorders* (4th ed.). Washington, DC: Author.

American Psychiatric Association Task Force on Benzodiazepine Dependency. (1990). *Benzodiazepine dependence, toxicity, and abuse.* Washington, DC: American Psychiatric Association.

American Psychiatric Association Task Force on Tardive Dyskinesia. (1992). *Tardive dyskinesia: A task force report of the American Psychiatric Association.* Washington, DC: American Psychiatric Association.

Atkins, M. S., & Stoff, D. M. (1993). Instrumental and hostile aggression in childhood disruptive behavior disorders. *Journal of Abnormal Child Psychology, 21,* 165–178.

Campbell, M., Adams, P. B., Small, A. M., Kafantaris, V., Silva, R. R., Shell, J., Perry, R., & Overall, J. E. (1995). Lithium in hospitalized aggressive children with conduct disorder: A double-blind and placebo-controlled study. *Journal of the American Academy of Child and Adolescent Psychiatry, 34,* 445–453.

Campbell, M., Gonzalez, N. M., & Silva, R. R. (1992). The pharmacologic treatment of conduct disorders and rage outbursts. *Psychiatric Clinics of North America, 15,* 69–85.

Cloninger, C. R., Svrakic, D. M., & Przybeck, T. R. (1993). A psychobiological model of temperament and character. *Archives of General Psychiatry, 50,* 975–990.

Coccaro, E. F., Astill, J. L., Herbert, J. L., & Schut, A. G. (1990). Fluoxetine treatment of impulsive aggression in *DSM-III-R* personality disorder patients. *Journal of Clinical Psychopharmacology, 10,* 373–375.

Cohen, B. M., & Lipinski, J. F. (1986). Treatment of acute psychosis with non-neuroleptic agents. *Psychosomatics, 27* (suppl.), 7–16.

Cooper, A. J., Sandhu, S., Losztyn, S., & Cernovsky, Z. (1992). A double-blind placebo controlled trial of medroxyprogesterone acetate and cyproterone acetate with seven pedophiles. *Canadian Journal of Psychiatry—Revue Canadienne de Psychiatrie, 37,* 687–693.

Cowdry, R. W., & Gardner, D. L. (1988). Pharmacotherapy of borderline personality disorder: Alprazolam, carbamazepine, trifluoperazine and tranylcypromine. *Archives of General Psychiatry, 45,* 111–119.

Craft, M., Ismail, I. A., Krishnamurti, D., Mathews, J., Regan, A., North, P. M., & Seth, R. V. (1987). Lithium in the treatment of aggression in mentally handicapped patients: A double-blind trial. *British Journal of Psychiatry, 150,* 685–689.

Crowner, M. L., Douyon, R., Convit, A., Gaztanaga, P., Volavka, J., & Bakall, R. (1990). Akathisia and violence. *Psychopharmacology Bulletin, 26,* 115–117.

De Koning, P., & Mak, M. (1991). Problems in human aggression research. *Journal of Neuropsychiatry and the Clinical Neurosciences, 3,* S61–S65.

Dietch, J. T., & Jennings, R. K. (1988). Aggressive dyscontrol in patients treated with benzodiazepines. *Journal of Clinical Psychiatry, 49,* 184–189.

Dietz, P. E. (1992). Mentally disordered offenders: Patterns in the relationship between mental disorder and crime. *Psychiatric Clinics of North America, 15,* 539–551.

Donlon, P. T., Hopkin, J., Schaffer, C. B., & Amsterdam, E. (1979). Cardiovascular safety of rapid treatment with intramuscular haloperidol. *American Journal of Psychiatry, 136,* 233–234.

Donlon, P. T., Hopkin, J., & Tupin, J. P. (1979). Overview: Efficacy and safety of the rapid neuroleptization method with injectable haloperidol. *American Journal of Psychiatry, 136,* 273–278.

Drake, R. E., & Erhrlich, J. (1985). Suicide attempts associated with akathisia. *American Journal of Psychiatry, 142,* 499–501.

Eichelman, B. (1987). Neurochemical and psychopharmacologic aspects of aggressive behavior. In H. Y. Meltzer (Ed.), *Psychopharmacology: The third generation of progress* (pp. 697–704). New York: Raven Press.

Eichelman, B. (1988). Toward a rational pharmacotherapy for aggression. *Hospital and Community Psychiatry, 39,* 21–39.

Fava, M., Rosenbaum, J. F., Pava, J. A., McCarthy, M. K., Steingard, R. J., & Bouffides, E. (1993). Anger attacks in unipolar depression: Part I. Clinical correlates and response to fluoxetine treatment. *American Journal of Psychiatry, 150,* 1158–1163.

Fleischhacker, W. W., Roth, S. D., & Kane, J. M. (1990). The pharmacologic treatment of neuroleptic-induced akathisia. *Journal of Clinical Psychopharmacology, 10,* 12–21.

Foster, H. D., Hillbrand, M., & Chi, C. C. (1989). Efficacy of carbamazepine in assaultive patients with frontal lobe dysfunction. *Progress in Neuro-Psychopharmacology and Biological Psychiatry, 13,* 865–874.

Gardner, D. L., & Cowdry, R. W. (1985). Alprazolam-induced dyscontrol in borderline personality disorder. *American Journal of Psychiatry, 142,* 98–100.

Garza-Trevino, E. S., Hollister, L. E., Overall, J. E., & Alexander, W. F. (1989). Efficacy of combinations of intramuscular antipsychotics and sedative-hypnotics for control of psychotic agitation. *American Journal of Psychiatry, 146,* 1598–1601.

Greendyke, R. M., & Kanter, D. R. (1986). Therapeutic effects of pindolol on behavioral disturbances associated with organic brain disease: A double-blind study. *Journal of Clinical Psychiatry, 47,* 423–426.

Greendyke, R. M., Kanter, D. R., Schuster, D. B., Verstreate, S., & Wootton, J. (1986). Propranolol treatment of assaultive patients with organic brain disease. A double-blind crossover, placebo-controlled study. *Journal of Nervous and Mental Disease, 174,* 290–294.

Griffith, J. L. (1985). Treatment of episodic behavioral disorders with rapidly absorbed benzodiazepines. *Journal of Nervous and Mental Disease, 173,* 312–315.

Heiligenstein, J. H., Beasley, C. M., Jr., & Potvin, J. H. (1993). Fluoxetine not associated with increased aggression in controlled clinical trials. *International Clinical Psychopharmacology, 8,* 277–280.

Hershorn, M., & Rosenbaum, A. (1991). Over- vs. undercontrolled hostility: Application of the construct to the classification of maritally violent men. *Violence and Victims, 6,* 151–158.

Insel, T. R., Zohar, J., Benkelfat, C., & Murphy, D. L. (1990). Serotonin in obsessions, compulsions, and the control of aggressive impulses. *Annals of the New York Academy of Sciences, 600,* 574–585.

Jann, M. W., Ereshefsky, L., Saklad, S. R., Seidel, D. R., Davis, C. M., Burch, N. R., & Bowden, C. L. (1985). Effects of carbamazepine on plasma haloperidol levels. *Journal of Clinical Psychopharmacology, 5,* 106–109.

Kafantaris, V., Campbell, M., Padron-Gayol, M. V., Small, A. M., Locascio, J. J., & Rosenberg, C. R. (1992). Carbamazepine in hospitalized aggressive conduct disorder children: An open pilot study. *Psychopharmacology Bulletin, 28,* 193–199.

Kafka, M. P. (1991). Successful treatment of paraphilic coercive disorder (a rapist) with fluoxetine hydrochloride. *British Journal of Psychiatry, 158,* 844–847.

Kane, J. M. (1985). Compliance issues in outpatient treatment. *Journal of Clinical Psychopharmacology, 5*(suppl.) 22S–27S.

Kane, J. M. (1989). The current status of neuroleptic therapy. *Journal of Clinical Psychiatry, 50,* 322–328.

Kane, J., Honigfeld, G., Singer, J., & Meltzer, H. (1988). Clozapine for the treatment resistant schizophrenic: A double-blind comparison with chlorpromazine. *Archives of General Psychiatry, 45,* 789–796.

Kaplan, S. L., Busner, J., Kupietz, S., Wassermann, E., & Segal, B. (1990). Effects of methylphenidate on adolescents with aggressive conduct disorder and ADDH: A preliminary report. *Journal of the American Academy of Child and Adolescent Psychiatry, 29,* 719–723.

Kemph, J. P., DeVane, C. L., Levin, G. M., Jarecke, R., & Miller, R. L. (1993). Treatment of aggressive children with clonidine: Results of an open pilot study. *Journal of the American Academy of Child and Adolescent Psychiatry, 32,* 577–581.

Kruesi, M. J. P., Hibbs, E. D., Hamburger, S. D., Rapoport, J. L., Keysor, C. S., & Elia, J. (1994). Measurement of aggression in children with disruptive behavior disorders. *Journal of Offender Rehabilitation, 21,* 159–172.

Lenox, R. H., Newhouse, P. A., Creelman, W. L., & Whitaker, T. M. (1992). Adjunctive treatment of manic agitation with lorazepam versus haloperidol: A double-blind study. *Journal of Clinical Psychiatry, 53,* 47–52.

Levine, S. B. (1989). Hypoactive sexual desire and other problems of sexual desire. In American Psychiatric Association, *Treatments of psychiatric disorders: A task force report of the American Psychiatric Association* (pp. 2264–2279). Washington, DC: American Psychiatric Association.

Linnoila, M., Virkkunen, M., Roy, A., & Potter, W. Z. (1990). Monoamines, glucose metabolism and impulse control. In H. M. Van Praag, R. Plutchik, & A. Apter (Eds.), *Violence and suicidality: Perspectives in clinical and psychobiological research* (pp. 218–241). New York: Brunner/Mazel.

Lipinski, J. F., Jr., Keck, P. E., Jr., & McElroy, S. L. (1988). Beta-adrenergic antagonists in psychosis: Is improvement due to treatment of neuroleptic-induced akathisia? *Journal of Clinical Psychopharmacology, 8,* 409–416.

Luchins, D. J., & Dojka, D. (1989). Lithium and propranolol in aggression and self-injurious behavior in the mentally retarded. *Psychopharmacology Bulletin, 25,* 372–375.

Maier, G. J. (1992). The impact of clozapine on 25 forensic patients. *Bulletin of the American Academy of Psychiatry and the Law, 20,* 297–307.

Mandoki, M. W., Sumner, G. S., & Matthews-Ferrari, K. (1992). Evaluation and treatment of rage in children and adolescents. *Child Psychiatry and Human Development, 22,* 227–235.

Mattes, J. A. (1990). Comparative effectiveness of carbamazepine and propranolol for rage outbursts. *Journal of Neuropsychiatry and Clinical Neurosciences, 2,* 159–164.

Mattes, J. A. (1992). Valproic acid for nonaffective aggression in the mentally retarded. *Journal of Nervous & Mental Disease, 180,* 601–602.

Mazure, C. M., Druss, B. G., & Cellar, J. S. (1992). Valproate treatment of older psychotic patients with organic mental syndromes and behavioral dyscontrol. *Journal of the American Geriatrics Society, 40,* 914–916.

Mehlman, P. T., Higley, J. D., Faucher, I., Lilly, A. A., Taub, D. M., Vickers, J., Suomi, S. J., & Linnoila, M. (1994). Low CSF 5-HIAA concentrations and severe aggression and impaired impulse control in nonhuman primates. *American Journal of Psychiatry, 151,* 1485–1491.

Mellow, A. M., Solano-Lopez, C., & Davis, S. (1993). Sodium valproate in the treatment of behavioral disturbance in dementia. *Journal of Geriatric Psychiatry & Neurology, 6,* 205–209.

Meltzer, H. Y. (1996). Cost-effectiveness of clozapine treatment. *Journal of Clinical Psychiatry Monograph, 14*(no. 2), 16–17.

Meltzer, H. Y., & Cola, P. A. (1994). The pharmacoeconomics of clozapine: A review. *Journal of Clinical Psychiatry, 55*(suppl. B), 161–164.

Miller, R. D. (1991). Involuntary civil commitment. In R. I. Simon (Ed.), *Review of clinical psychiatry and the law* (Vol. 2, pp. 95–172). Washington DC: American Psychiatric Press.

Molcho, A., & Stanley, M. (1992). Antidepressants and suicide risk: Issues of chemical and behavioral toxicity. *Journal of Clinical Psychopharmacology, 12,* 13S–18S.

Monahan, J. (1992). Mental disorder and violent behavior: perceptions and evidence. *American Psychologist, 4,* 511–521.

Nelson, J. C. (1991). Current status of tricyclic antidepressants in psychiatry, their pharmacology and clinical applications. *Journal of Clinical Psychiatry, 52,* 193–200.

Neppe, V. M. (1983). Carbamazepine as adjunctive treatment in nonepileptic chronic inpatients with EEG temporal lobe abnormalities. *Journal of Clinical Psychiatry, 44,* 326–331.

Olivier, B., Mos, J., & Rasmussen, D. (1990). Behavioural pharmacology of the serenic, eltoprazine. *Drug Metabolism and Drug Interactions, 8,* 31–83.

Overall, J. E., & Gorham, D. R. (1962). The brief psychiatric rating scale (B.P.R.S.). *Psychological Reports, 10,* 799–812.

Pinner, E., & Rich, C. L. (1988). Effects of trazodone on aggressive behavior in seven patients with organic mental disorders. *American Journal of Psychiatry, 145,* 1295–1296.

Pope, H. G., Jr., McElroy, S. L., Keck, P. E., Jr., & Hudson, J. I. (1991). Valproate in the treatment of acute mania: A placebo-controlled study. *Archives of General Psychiatry, 48,* 62–68.

Post, R. M. (1987). Mechanism of action of carbamazepine and related anticonvulsants in affective illness. In H. Y. Meltzer (Ed.), *Psychopharmacology: The third generation of progress* (pp. 567–576). New York: Raven Press.

Post, R. M., Weiss, S. R. B., & Chuang, D. M. (1992). Mechanisms of action of anticonvulsants in affective disorders: Comparisons with lithium. *Journal of Clinical Psychopharmacology, 12,* 23S–35S.

Ratey, J. J., Leveroni, C., Kilmer, D., Gutheil, C., & Swartz, B. (1993). The effects of clozapine on severely aggressive psychiatric inpatients in a state hospital. *Journal of Clinical Psychiatry, 54,* 219–223.

Ratey, J. J., Sorgi, P., O'Driscoll, G. A., Sands, S., Daehler, M. L., Fletcher, J. R., Kadish, W., Spruiell, G., Polakoff, S., Lindem, K. J., Bemporad, J. R., Richardson, L., & Rosenfeld, R. (1992). Nadolol to treat aggression and psychiatric symptomatology in chronic psychiatric inpatients: A double-blind, placebo-controlled study. *Journal of Clinical Psychiatry, 53,* 41–46.

Reid, W. H. (1988). Clinical evaluation of the violent patient. *Psychiatric Clinics of North America, 4,* 527–537.

Reid, W. H., & Burke, W. J. (1989). Antisocial personality disorder. In American Psychiatric Association, *Treatments of psychiatric disorders: A task force report of the American Psychiatric Association* (pp. 2742–2749). Washington, DC: American Psychiatric Association.

Rifkin, A., Quitkin, F., Carrillo, C., Blumberg, A. G., & Klein, D. F. (1972). Lithium carbonate in emotionally unstable character disorder. *Archives of General Psychiatry, 27,* 519–523.

Roy, A., Virkkunen, M., & Linnoila, M. (1991). Serotonin in suicide, violence, and alcoholism. In E. Coccaro & D. Murphy (Eds.), *Serotonin in major psychiatric disorders* (pp. 187–208). Washington, DC: American Psychiatric Association.

Schou, M. (1989). Lithium prophylaxis: Myths and realities. *American Journal of Psychiatry, 146,* 573–576.

Shader, R. I., & Greenblatt, D. J. (1993). Drug therapy: Use of benzodiazepines in anxiety disorders. *New England Journal of Medicine, 328,* 1398–1405.

Shaffer, D. (1994). Attention deficit hyperactivity disorder in adults. *American Journal of Psychiatry, 151,* 633–638.

Sheard, M. H. (1975). Lithium in the treatment of aggression. *Journal of Nervous and Mental Disease, 160,* 108–118.

Sheard, M. H., Marini, J. L., Bridges, C. I., & Wagner, E. (1976). The effect of lithium in impulsive aggressive behavior in man. *American Journal of Psychiatry, 133,* 1409–1413.

Silver, J. M., Hales, R. E., & Yudofsky, S. C. (1990). Psychiatric consultation to neurology. In A. Tasman, S. M. Goldfinger, & C. A. Kaufmann (Eds.), *American Psychiatric Press review of psychiatry* (Vol. 9, pp. 433–465). Washington, DC: American Psychiatric Press.

Stein, D. J., Hollander, E., Anthony, D. T., Schneier, F. R., Fallon, B. A., Liebowitz, M. R., & Klein, D. F. (1992). Serotonergic medications for sexual obsessions, sexual addictions, and paraphilias. *Journal of Clinical Psychiatry, 53,* 267–271.

Stein, D. J., Simeon, D., Frenkel, M., Islam, M. N., & Hollander, E. (1995). An open trial of valproate in borderline personality disorder. *Journal of Clinical Psychiatry, 56,* 506–510.

Stewart, J. T., Myers, W. C., Burket, R. C., & Lyles W. B. (1990). A review of the pharmacotherapy of aggression in children and adolescents. *Journal of the American Academy of Child and Adolescent Psychiatry, 29,* 269–277.

Stoff, D. M., Friedman, E., Pollock, L., Vitiello, B., Kendall, P. C., & Bridger, W. H. (1989). Elevated platelet MAO is related to impulsivity in disruptive behavior disorders. *Journal of the American Academy of Child and Adolescent Psychiatry, 28,* 754–760.

Tardiff, K. (1989). *Assessment and management of violent patients.* Washington, DC: American Psychiatric Press.

Tardiff, K. (1992). The current state of psychiatry in the treatment of violent patients. *Archives of General Psychiatry, 49,* 493–499.

Teicher, M. H., Glod, C., & Cole, J. O. (1990). Emergence of suicidal preoccupation during fluoxetine treatment. *American Journal of Psychiatry, 147,* 207–210.

Torrey, E. F., & Kaplan, R. J. (1995). A national survey of the use of outpatient commitment. *Psychiatric Services, 46,* 778–784.

Tupin, J. P., Smith, D. B., Clanon, T. L., Kim, L. I., Nugent, A., & Groupe, A. (1973). The long-term use of lithium in aggressive prisoners. *Comprehensive Psychiatry, 14,* 311–317.

Valzelli, L. (1967). Drugs and aggressiveness. *Advances in Pharmacology, 5,* 79–108.

Valzelli, L., Giacolone, E., & Garattini, S. (1967). Pharmacological control of aggressive behavior in mice. *European Journal of Pharmacology, 2,* 144–146.

Virkkunen, M., Eggert, M., Rawlings, R., & Linnoila, M. (1996). A prospective follow-up study of alcoholic violent offenders and fire setters. *Archives of General Psychiatry, 53,* 523–529.

Virkkunen, M., Rawlings, R., Tokola, R., Poland, R., Guidotti, A., Nemeroff, C., Bissette, G., Kalogeras, K., Karonen, S. L., & Linnoila, M. (1994). CSF biochemistries, glucose metabolism, and diurnal activity rhythms in alcoholic, violent offenders, fire setters, and healthy volunteers. *Archives of General Psychiatry, 51,* 20–27.

Vitiello, B., Behar, D., Hunt, J., Stoff, D., & Ricciuti, A. (1990). Subtyping aggression in children and adolescents. *Journal of Neuropsychiatry and Clinical Neurosciences, 2,* 189–192.

Widiger, T. A., Corbitt, E. M., & Millon, T. (1992). Antisocial personality disorder. In A. Tasman & M. B. Riba (Eds.), *American Psychiatric Press review of psychiatry* (Vol. 11, pp. 63–79). Washington, DC: American Psychiatric Press.

Wilson, W. H. (1992). Clinical review of clozapine treatment in a state hospital. *Hospital and Community Psychiatry, 43,* 700–703.

Yesavage, J. A. (1982). Inpatient violence and the schizophrenic patient: An inverse correlation between danger-related events and neuroleptic blood levels. *Biological Psychiatry, 17,* 1331–1337.

Young, J. L., Zonana, H. V., & Shepler, L. (1986). Medication noncompliance in schizophrenia: Codification and update. *Bulletin of the American Academy of Psychiatry and the Law, 14,* 105–122.

Yudofsky, S. C., Silver, J. M., Jackson, W., Endicott, J., & Williams, D. (1986). The overt aggression scale: An operationalized rating scale for verbal and physical aggression. *American Journal of Psychiatry, 143*(1, suppl.), 35–39.

Zubieta, J. K., & Alessi, N. E. (1992). Acute and chronic administration of trazodone in the treatment of disruptive behavior disorders in children. *Journal of Clinical Psychopharmacology, 12,* 346–351.

CHAPTER 42

Evaluation and Treatment of Violent Patients

KENNETH TARDIFF

The study of violence among psychiatric patients has grown enormously over the past 20 years, as has the concern about violence in our society. Prior to that time period, the involvement of psychiatrists and other mental health professionals in the problem of violence was at the level of philosophy regarding causes of aggression. Since then, large systematic studies of patients have assessed the risk of violence in psychiatric hospitals, violence just before hospitalization, and violence in the community (Craig, 1982; Krakowski, Volavka, & Brizer, 1986; Rossi et al., 1985; Tardiff, 1984a; Tardiff & Koenigsberg, 1985; Tardiff & Sweillam, 1980, 1982). Case reports have been published on the effectiveness of medications for mentally disordered violent psychiatric patients (Campbell et al., 1984; Luchins, 1984; Yudofsky, Williams, & Gorman, 1981). Some of these studies of medications were controlled (Craft et al., 1987; Mattes, Rosenberg, & Mays, 1984; Okuma et al., 1989). Additional work in the 1980s involved building a consensus on the use of other means to control violence among psychiatric patients, namely, seclusion, restraint, and behavioral treatment (Tardiff, 1984b). Treatment of violent patients has moved into the community with the development of models of monitoring persons found not guilty by reason of insanity and models of involuntary outpatient treatment for civil patients who were formerly violent (Bloom, Williams, & Bigelow, 1991; Geller, 1990; Wiederanders & Choate, 1994).

CONTROVERSIAL ISSUES

A number of controversial issues are involved in the management of violent patients. The first is the proper role or scope of involvement for mental health professionals. Psychiatrists and other mental health professionals have expertise in the management of violence for a group of persons designated as patients but not for violence at large in society (Tardiff, 1992). Violence in society is related to factors such as economics, culture, criminal behavior, drug dealing, mass media, and the availability of weapons. These factors are not within the usual realm of psychiatric expertise, although such factors must be considered in the treatment of an individual patient and are public health concerns. Psychiatric and medical techniques of assessment, diagnosis, and treatment of patients with violent behavior parallel the techniques used for other clinical problems of patients.

There is disagreement as to whether mental health professionals can predict violence among psychiatric patients. Earlier writings were not supportive; however, now there is more confidence in our ability to predict violence (Klassen & O'Connor, 1989; Lidz, Mulvey, & Gardner, 1993; Monahan & Steadman, 1994a; Tardiff, 1989a). Yet, much of the research supporting the prediction of violence is fragmented and not comprehensive. Accuracy in predicting violence may not be as important as attempting to predict violence to protect potential victims (Beck, 1988).

We have developed guidelines for the safe use of physical controls such as restraint and seclusion, yet there remains concern about the impact of the techniques on patients (Soliday, 1985). The effectiveness of seclusion, restraint, and medications has not been studied in controlled protocols for obvious reasons, namely, the danger involved in not using these methods with violent patients.

Despite the controversies that remain and the work that lies ahead, the management of violent patients has progressed over the past two decades.

EVALUATION OF THE VIOLENT PATIENT

When faced with a patient who speaks of violence or has been violent, clinicians may become anxious or experience other emotions that cause them to veer from the assessment routine followed for other psychiatric problems (Lion & Pasternak, 1973). More recent writings on the evaluation of violent patients should remind clinicians of standard clinical practice. These principles are summarized in this chapter (Reid & Balis, 1987; Tardiff, 1992, 1996).

The evaluation of the patient who presents problems of violence should include an assessment of the chief complaint, history of the present illness, family history, personal and developmental history, medical history, mental status, physical examination, laboratory tests, and imaging. In gathering information about the patient, the clinician should use as many sources of information as possible.

This includes information from the patient, the police, relatives, the patient's therapist, and the primary care physician as well as previous medical and criminal records. The history of the present illness, that is, the history of the patient's violence, should be assessed in great detail, and the areas to be covered are discussed later in this chapter under the short-term prediction of violence.

The patient's medical history should be reviewed extensively, because medical disorders can manifest themselves with violence. These disorders also are mentioned later in the section on the short-term prediction of violence. The physical examination may reveal signs of underlying medical disorders that have been associated with violence. Signs of alcohol or drug intoxication may be present, such as slurred speech, lack of coordination, unsteady gait, nystagmus, dilated or constricted pupils, and elevated blood pressure and heart rate. Withdrawal from alcohol and some drugs may produce tremors, increased autonomic activity, and even seizures.

In addition to the usual laboratory testing and procedures, an electroencephalogram (EEG) should be part of the routine evaluation of the violent patient. The routine EEG should be augmented with nasopharyngeal leads as well as a sleep EEG. Blood and urine for alcohol and drug assays should be monitored. One should use imaging for violent patients, with a preference for magnetic resonance imaging because of its superiority over computed tomography in detecting temporal lobe pathology. If a specific medical disorder is suspected, other laboratory tests are indicated, such as determination of arterial blood gas levels, testing for human immunodeficiency virus antibodies, glucose tolerance tests, determination of ceruloplasmin and copper levels in urine and serum, determination of urine porphobilinogen levels, heavy metal screening, determination of antinuclear antibodies, and lumbar puncture, if intracranial pressure is not elevated.

SHORT-TERM PREDICTION OF VIOLENCE

An evaluation of a patient's potential for violence is done in the emergency room or the outpatient office when a decision must be made about admitting a patient to a hospital or when the clinician has the duty to protect potential victims of that patient. This evaluation also is made when considering giving a patient a pass or discharging a patient from the hospital.

A psychiatrist or other mental health professional should attempt to assess a patient's short-term violence potential using techniques analogous to the short-term predictors of suicide potential. *Short-term* is defined as a period of a few days or a week at most, until the patient is seen for the next therapy session or aftercare or follow-up appointment. Beyond that time, many factors could intervene, such as a stabilized schizophrenic patient stopping antipsychotic medication or new stressors in the patient's life.

Along the same lines as the evaluation of suicide potential, evaluation of the potential for violence includes how well-planned the threat is. Vague threats of killing someone are not as serious, all things being equal. As with suicide, the availability of a means of inflicting injury is important. For example, if the patient has recently purchased or owns a gun, obviously the threat should be taken more seriously. If a weapon can be confiscated, this reduces the potential for homicide.

A past history of violence or other impulsive behavior is often predictive of future violence. One should ask about injuries to other persons, destruction of property, suicide attempts, reckless driving, reckless spending, criminal offenses, sexual acting out, and other impulsive behaviors. Studies of violent patients admitted to hospitals have found that they were more likely than nonviolent patients to have a history of prior violence (Craig, 1982; Tardiff, 1984a; Tardiff & Sweillam, 1980; Yesavage, 1983a). Furthermore, a history of prior suicide attempts was found in a greater proportion of violent patients than nonviolent patients.

One should assess the degree of past injuries (e.g., broken bones and lacerations), as well as toward whom violence has been directed and under what circumstances. Often a pattern emerges of past violent behavior in specific circumstances (e.g., escalation of a dispute between a husband and wife about issues of money, esteem, or sexuality). Unlike suicide, the presence of others at home may not tip the balance toward safety but rather increase the propensity toward violence unless the dynamics of past violent episodes are explored and prevented.

A past history of being abused as a child or being in a family in which physical abuse occurred should be considered important. Being abused as a child is related to becoming a physically abusive adult. There is evidence that not only is being abused as a child related to adult violence but so is witnessing intrafamily violence (e.g., spouse abuse).

A number of studies have found that schizophrenic patients are overly represented in groups of patients who are violent toward other people just before or during psychiatric hospitalization. Studies link violence to paranoid delusional thinking and hallucinations in schizophrenia (Craig, 1982; Lindquist & Allebeck, 1990; Planansky & Johnson, 1977; Tardiff, 1984a; Tardiff & Sweillam, 1980; Taylor & Gunn, 1984). These patients believe that people are threatening, persecuting, or in some other way trying to harm them. Violence is a reaction to these perceived threats. Often the theme of the delusion is consistent over time. However, when one looks at groups of patients in less acute settings or when patients stay for long periods of time in a hospital, the nonparanoid schizophrenic is even more likely than the paranoid schizophrenic to be violent. In these cases, rather than from paranoid delusional thinking, violence comes from psychotic disorganization or general excitability. Some patients may have difficulty delaying gratification and a low tolerance for frustration, with violent consequences.

Sometimes, violence is due to factors other than the schizophrenic process per se. For example, violence can be an indirect complication of antipsychotic medication when patients with akathisia restlessly move around on the inpatient unit and bump into other patients. It is important to keep in mind that schizophrenic patients may have another disorder primarily responsible for violence, such as neurological impairment or mental retardation (Krakowski et al., 1989). Finally, violence by schizophrenic patients may be due to personality disorders, alcohol or drug abuse, or reasons not related to psychiatric impairment, for example, retaliation or self-defense.

Manic patients have been found to have sudden severe violent episodes (Binder & McNiel, 1990; Tardiff, 1984a; Tardiff & Sweillam, 1980; Yesavage, 1983a). Often violence erupts in the early phase of treatment of the acute manic state. Such a patient may respond violently to any form of containment or limit setting, be it physical or otherwise, for example, when a nurse insists that the patient should take medication.

Personality disorders have been found to be associated with increased risk of violence, particularly by antisocial and borderline patients (Bland & Orn, 1986; Hare & McPherson, 1984; Tardiff, 1984a; Tardiff & Koenigsberg, 1985). Violence manifested by persons with antisocial personality disorder is just one of many antisocial behaviors. These patients repeatedly get into physical fights and manifest a number of other antisocial behaviors, such as stealing, lying, and reckless driving. The patient shows no guilt or remorse for violence and other antisocial behavior. In the case of the borderline personality disorder, the violence often is related to perceived rejection and impulsivity. In addition to frequent displays of anger and recurrent physical violence toward others, the borderline personality patient manifests a number of other behavioral and severe psychological problems.

These disorders should be differentiated from another nonpsychotic episodic violence disorder that has a better prognosis in regard to treatment. Intermittent explosive disorder is manifested by recurrent outbursts of violence that are grossly out of proportion to any precipitating psychosocial stressor. Following a violent episode there often is remorse. In the intervening period between these violent episodes, there is little evidence of other behavioral problems.

Episodic nonpsychotic violence usually involves family members, usually a man battering a woman and less often a parent abusing a child. The pattern of violence repeats itself in a predictable way. For example, spouse battering characteristically involves a man who has low self-esteem and financial, sexual, or other conflicts that are expressed physically rather than verbally. The woman victim feels helpless, guilty, ashamed, and afraid to take action to stop the violence. Arguments escalate in a repetitive fashion, often fueled by alcohol, and culminate in physical violence toward the woman.

Substance abuse is associated with violence. Alcoholism as a primary disorder or in conjunction with other psychiatric disorders can result in violence (Bland & Orn, 1986; Kay, Wolkenfeld, & Murrill, 1988; Taylor & Gunn, 1984). This often is the result of disinhibition, particularly in the early phase of intoxication, as well as emotional lability and impaired judgment. A number of other substances also have been associated with violence (Lowenstein et al., 1987; Swanson, Holzer, Ganju, & Jono, 1990). Stimulants, particularly cocaine, can be dangerous. The early phase of cocaine intoxication is manifested by euphoria, which quickly can turn to irritability, agitation, suspicion, and violence, especially with crack or intravenous cocaine. With continued use of cocaine in a binge as well as chronic amphetamine use, suspicion may turn to paranoid delusional thinking and violence. Heavy cocaine use has caused maniclike delirium with severe violence. The craving for cocaine also may result in violence, as the addict desperately seeks more cocaine or the money to purchase it. Hallucinogens, particularly phencyclidine, which is a dissociative anesthetic, are known to cause violence, suicide, and bizarre behavior (Budd & Lindstrom, 1982). Hallucinogens can produce impaired judgment and cause perceptual changes and delusional thinking.

Studies have demonstrated that organic brain disease can result in violence (Kay et al., 1988; Tardiff, 1984a; Tardiff & Sweillam, 1980). Violence in temporal lobe epilepsy is not frequent, but when it occurs, it may occur during the ictal period and, if so, often is purposeless (Weiger & Bear, 1988). Head trauma and other neurological and medical disorders can have an impact on the brain and produce violent behavior (Reid & Balis, 1987). Infections of the brain, including viral encephalitis, AIDS, tuberculosis and fungal meningitis, syphilis, and herpes simplex can be associated with violent behavior. Other diseases of the brain associated with violence include normal pressure hydrocephalus, cerebrovascular diseases, tumors, Huntington's chorea, multiple sclerosis, Pick's disease, multi-infarct dementia, Alzheimer's disease, Parkinson's disease, and Wilson's disease as well as postanoxic or posthypoglycemic states with brain damage. Organic impairment of the brain may produce violence through general dyscontrol or through psychosis, as in the case of senile dementia, with which paranoid delusions or misidentifications can occur (Deutsch et al., 1991; Petrie, Lawson, & Hollander, 1982). These elderly patients can be quite dangerous, especially when armed with weapons to resist what they perceive as forces that will hurt them or deprive them of property or other possessions.

A wide range of medical illnesses have been found to be associated with violent behavior (Lidz et al., 1993; Reid & Balis, 1987), many of which are treatable and reversible. These disorders include hypoxia; electrolyte imbalances; hepatic disease; renal disease; vitamin deficiencies (such as B-12, folate, or thiamine); systemic infections; hypoglycemia; Cushing's disease; hyperthyroidism; hypothyroidism; systemic lupus erythematosus; poisoning by heavy metals, insecticides, and other substances; and porphyria.

Last, the potential for violence should consider the patient's compliance or noncompliance with treatment. Whether a patient keeps clinic appointments, returns after hospital passes, and takes medication regularly goes into the formula on the risk of violence in the future. On this point, for schizophrenic patients or other psychotic patients with a history of violence, acceptance of depot antipsychotic medication is very reassuring for the staff.

In summary, the assessment of violence potential for the short term (i.e., in days or a week) is analogous to the assessment for suicide potential. The clinician must consider the following: subtle questioning of the patient if violence is not mentioned; appearance of the patient; how well planned is the threat of violence; available means of inflicting injury; past history of violence and impulsive behavior with attention to frequency, degree of past injuries to others and self, toward whom, and under what circumstances; alcohol and drug use; the presence of other organic mental disorders; the presence of schizophrenia, mania, or other psychosis; the presence of certain personality and impulse control disorders; and noncompliance with treatment in the past.

All of these factors are weighed in the final assessment of whether the patient poses a significant risk to others so that some action is necessary by the evaluator. Such action may include changing the treatment plan, hospitalizing the patient, keeping the patient in the hospital, or warning the intended victim or the police. All of the data on which the decision that the patient is or is not a risk for violence must be documented in writing; the thinking process through which the decision was made should be evident in the written documentation. Reassessment of the potential for violence should be made at short intervals (e.g., from visit to visit or every few days) if the patient is to continue to be treated outside the hospital or other institution. Reassessment should be done before passes or discharge from the hospital. Clinicians have not been faulted for inaccurate prediction but for failure to collect the data necessary for the prediction of violence and to use the data logically to make a prediction (Beck, 1988).

ATTACKS ON CLINICIANS

The prediction of a risk for violence is important to prevent injuries to persons in proximity to potentially violent patients, including staff members. A number of studies have surveyed clinicians as to whether they have been attacked by patients and, if so, what were the circumstances of these attacks. Roughly 40% of psychiatrists have been attacked by patients some time in their careers (Hatti, Dubin, & Weiss, 1982; Madden, Lion, & Penna, 1976; Tardiff & Maurice, 1977; Whitman, Armao, & Dent, 1976). Studies of psychiatric residents show that from 28% to 48% of residents report attacks while in residency (Chaimowitz & Moscovitch, 1991; Fink, Shoyer, & Dubin, 1991; Grey, 1989). Surveys of nurses show they are more likely than psychiatrists to be attacked, often on multiple occasions, by psychiatric patients (Carmel & Hunter, 1989; Lanza & Kayne, 1991). Social workers and psychologists are less likely than psychiatrists to be attacked by patients (Bernstein, 1981). A task force of the American Psychiatric Association has reviewed the literature, interviewed clinicians who have been attacked, and formulated guidelines for safety (American Psychiatric Association, 1992).

EMERGENCY MANAGEMENT OF VIOLENCE

In managing violence by patients, one must consider the balance between medication, seclusion, and restraint. An ineffective type or dose of medication increases the risk of violence or the use of other physical means of control such as seclusion and restraint. Patients should not be in prolonged seclusion or restraints because of inadequate medication. On the other hand, patients should not be overmedicated to keep them out of seclusion or restraints. Instead, the treatment plan must be reviewed with consideration to changing the medication or adding other treatment, such a behavioral therapy.

Seclusion and Restraint

From 1981 to 1985, a task force of the American Psychiatric Association studied the literature on the psychiatric uses of seclusion and restraint, surveyed states by mail regarding guidelines, and developed minimal standards for the use of seclusion and restraint. An expanded text describes the use of seclusion and restraint to manage violent patients and these guidelines are summarized later in this chapter (American Psychiatric Association, 1995; Tardiff, 1984b). Although the APA task force did address the use of seclu-

sion and restraint for children, a more recent mail survey of states found that seclusion and restraint guidelines for children generally conform to those of adults (Fassler & Cotton, 1992).

Seclusion and restraint are procedures to prevent harm to the patient or other persons when other controls are not effective or appropriate or to prevent serious disruption of the treatment program or significant damage to the physical environment. In addition, seclusion may be used to decrease the stimulation a patient receives, possibly at the patient's request.

The decision on whether to use seclusion, restraint, medication, or any combination of these controls is made on the basis of the clinical needs of the individual case. For example, if the etiology of the violent behavior is unknown, restraint may be indicated so as to maintain the patient drug free for evaluation. In addition, a violent patient may be preferentially managed in seclusion and restraint because of medical illness or drug allergies that would preclude the use of certain medications to control violent behavior.

Another issue for seclusion and restraint is whether these controls should be used only once a patient is actually in the process of manifesting dangerous behavior, as opposed to whether the staff may use these procedures in anticipation of imminent dangerous behavior by the patient. Once they are familiar with a particular patient, staff members may rely on past patterns of verbal or nonverbal phenomena that have occurred before violent episodes. The use of previous patterns of behavior to justify preventive seclusion or restraint must be documented clearly. The same parameters for physician orders and staff monitoring apply when imminent violence is the indication for seclusion or restraint. The regulations of each institution and state may not allow seclusion or restraint to be used in this manner.

There are contraindications to the use of seclusion and restraint. They should never be used for punishment when no danger exists to the patient or others. Seclusion or restraint may be contraindicated because the patient's medical condition may require monitoring and close physical proximity of staff members. Restraint may be useful in delirium and dementia, where reduced sensory input from seclusion may lead to worsening of the clinical state.

Release from seclusion or restraint occurs when the patient's behavior is under control and no longer poses a danger to self or others. Ability to control one's behavior and cooperate is evaluated throughout the seclusion or restraint episode. For example, during each visit, the patient's ability to respond to a verbal request should be judged. Release from seclusion is a gradual process. The first step may be opening the seclusion room door for brief periods of time, followed by complete opening of the seclusion room door, and the patient spending time alone in his or her room, until the patient can be released to the general ward environment. Any evidence of loss of control or lack of cooperation should result in movement back to more restrictive steps in the procedure. The restrained patient may be transferred to seclusion when there appears to be adequate self-control and stabilization. The same process of gradual release from seclusion is used at the appropriate time. Following the episode of seclusion or restraint, the patient should be allowed to voice his or her feelings about the episode and should be questioned as to what led up to the behavior requiring seclusion or restraint, as well as what could have been done to prevent it.

A possible alternative to seclusion or restraint to prevent violence is continuous one-to-one observation of the patient by a staff member. This procedure rarely has been studied. The best study took place in Canada, where 102 inpatients who received continuous observation were compared to 102 control inpatients (Shugar & Rehaluk, 1990). Continuous observation was most effective when it was used for less than 72 hours for the management of violence and suicidal behavior.

Use of Emergency Medication

Emergency medication is useful for psychotic, violent patients; it often is used in conjunction with seclusion or restraint. Emergency medication may be indicated for nonpsychotic, violent patients when verbal intervention may not be appropriate or effective. It may be used instead of seclusion or restraint. On the other hand, it may be used with seclusion or restraint during severe agitation or violence to minimize the detrimental effects violence may have on patients even though they are secluded or restrained.

Antipsychotic medication should be used primarily for the management of violent patients who manifest psychotic symptomatology. Occasionally it may be indicated for patients who are not psychotic but are violent, as in the case of patients with dementia or other organic brain dysfunction, for whom anxiolytic agents or sedatives may exacerbate the clinical picture (Coccaro et al., 1990). In the emergency situation, antipsychotic medication often is given intramuscularly depending on the circumstances, for example, if the psychotic patient is completely out of control.

Although this author favors the use of high-potency antipsychotic drugs with or without concurrent lorazepam, the choice of strategy also should take into consideration the patient's history and physical status. One should attempt to review the patient's previous responses to medication as well as the presence of medical illnesses that may predispose to or be exacerbated by extrapyramidal side effects or orthostatic hypotension. If extrapyramidal side effects are less acceptable, low-potency antipsychotics should be used. If orthostatic hypotension and related side effects are less acceptable, then high-potency antipsychotics are indicated. The physician, of course, should be free to change strategy as the patient's medical condition is monitored.

The benzodiazepines can be used very effectively in emergency situations if violence is occurring or is imminent. Benzodiazepines may be used with the antipsychotic medications for schizophrenics, manics, and patients in other psychotic states (Garza-Trevino, Hollister, Overall, & Alexander, 1989; Salzman et al., 1991). They may be used alone for the management of nonpsychotic patients. For patients who appear to have some degree of control, they may be offered as oral medication. However, in most emergency situations, benzodiazepines are used intramuscularly.

Lorazepam is the benzodiazepine of choice for use in emergencies because it is reliably and rapidly absorbed from injection sites, unlike diazepam or chlordiazepoxide. Lorazepam also is useful because it produces sedation for a longer period of time than diazepam, and it remains in circulation rather than being absorbed into tissues. On the other hand, the half-life of lorazepam is 12 hours, much shorter than diazepam, so that accu-

mulation is not as problematic as it is with diazepam. Lorazepam, given by intramuscular injection, rapidly begins to enter the circulation system and produces sedation within an hour. The oral administration of lorazepam produces more gradual effects, with sedation occurring usually more than 1 hour and less than 4 hours after administration.

LONG-TERM MEDICATION

A large literature is available on psychopharmacology and the management of violent patients. This chapter will not cover the topic extensively because it is covered in Karper and Krystal (Chapter 41, this volume). The antipsychotics diminish violence due to delusions, hallucinations, and other psychotic symptomatology. The long-acting injected depot forms of haloperidol and fluphenazine are very helpful in assuring compliance because they have to be administered only every several weeks. Two studies suggest that clozapine can diminish violence by schizophrenic patients beyond its effects on psychosis per se (Ratey, Leveroni, Kilmer, Guthiel, & Swartz, 1993; Volavka, Zito, & Vitrai, 1993). Clozapine and the other new antipsychotics may have specific effects on hostility, agitation, and physical violence.

The anticonvulsants have been studied for the long-term management of violence based on the belief that some episodic violence is caused by neurophysiologic dysfunction (Monroe, 1970). The most frequently studied anticonvulsant for the management of violence is carbamazepine. There are few controlled studies but numerous case reports, particularly for carbamazepine (Foster, Hillbrand, & Chi, 1989; Luchins, 1984; Patterson, 1987; Young & Hillbrand, 1994). Many of these studies involve violent schizophrenics, without seizure disorders, who were on concurrent antipsychotic medication. In fact, one of the only controlled studies involved concurrent antipsychotic medication (Okuma et al., 1989).

Propranolol is the most frequently studied beta-blocker for the management of violence. Only one study has been controlled (Greendyke et al., 1986). Clinical studies of small numbers of patients have found that propranolol does decrease violence in a variety of mental and neurological disorders, including head trauma (Yudofsky et al., 1981), dementia (Yudofsky, Silver, & Hales, 1990), Huntington's disease (Stewart, Mounts, & Clark, 1987), and autism (Ratey et al., 1987). Propranolol has been used effectively for the control of violence in schizophrenia along with antipsychotics (Sorgi, Ratey, & Polakoff, 1986; Whitman, Maier, & Eichelman, 1987). Another beta-blocker, nadolol, was found effective in decreasing violence in schizophrenia in a double-blind, controlled study (Ratey et al., 1992). Pindolol was studied in a double-blind, placebo study and was found effective in decreasing aggression in demented patients (Greendyke & Kanter, 1986).

Lithium has been found to be beneficial in diminishing violence in a number of mental disorders when there is no evidence of mania. A double-blind, controlled study found it effective with mentally retarded adults (Craft et al., 1987). Other studies have found that lithium diminished aggression among children with conduct disorder (Campbell et al., 1984; Siassi, 1982). A double-blind, controlled study showed that lithium decreased violence in prisoners without major mental disorders except for personality disorders (Sheard et al., 1976).

LONG-TERM PSYCHODYNAMIC PSYCHOTHERAPY

Psychotherapy has received little attention in terms of empirical research, although it does have a place in the treatment of selected patients. Most of the literature formulates principles of therapy with violent patients with particular attention to transference and countertransference issues (Lion & Pasternak, 1973; Tardiff, 1996).

Long-term psychotherapy can be useful for violent patients who are not psychotic and have primarily personality disorders or intermittent explosive disorders. In spousal abuse, couples sessions may be indicated only if the spouse's safety can be ensured. The first goal of therapy is to evaluate whether the patient really is motivated. The patient must identify patterns of escalation in violence and learn to disengage at an early phase. Often an early phase of a violent episode involves a physical feeling as anger builds, for example, flushing of the face. The patient should be taught to recognize early warning signs and disengage before physical violence occurs. The therapist should monitor transference and be prepared to deal with negative thoughts or threats by the patients. Countertransference must be monitored, because violence can evoke inappropriate feelings and reactions to patients. Psychotherapy should provide insight as to why the patient must use violence as a means of expression. Often these patients have difficulty verbally expressing their feelings and conflicts. Themes common in the treatment of violent patients often involve low self-esteem.

BEHAVIORAL TREATMENT

Behavioral therapy is an effective but complex and rigorous approach to the management of violent behavior in severely impaired institutional populations. This approach may be used for severely impaired patients (e.g., chronic schizophrenics, mentally retarded patients) in conjunction with other treatment approaches. The basic principles outlined in this chapter have been drawn from the work of Liberman and Wong (Liberman & Wong, 1984; Wong, Woolsey, Innocent, & Liberman, 1988). The basic goal of the behavioral treatment program is to convert an unstructured hospital setting, which may promote violent behavior among patients, into a structured setting that will provide stimuli aimed at decreasing violent behavior and increasing prosocial behavior.

A trained experienced behavioral analyst should be responsible for planning a behavioral treatment program on an inpatient unit. Behavioral treatment programs should be reviewed periodically by persons other than the ward personnel to ensure their quality and ethical standards. In addition, the patient should be involved as much as possible in the formulation of the plan. Informed written consent should be obtained if the patient is competent to do so. The goals and process of the treatment program should be discussed with the patient, and an assessment should be made of the patient's desires in terms of privileges and rewards that may be used to motivate positive behavior.

The behavioral program should include specification of the target behaviors that will be addressed. Behavioral responses or techniques involve positive ways of influencing a patient's behavior. For violent patients, often reinforcement for nonviolent behavior must be given in the early phase of treatment at the end of very short intervals (e.g., every few seconds or every few minutes). As the program continues and the patient becomes more cooperative, reinforcement can be spaced out over longer periods of time, eventually resulting in a token economy program.

In conjunction with these positive reinforcement approaches, the patient, once under control, may be taught social skills as alternatives to aggressive and destructive behavior. Clearly disturbed patients may become violent because they are unable to use social skills (e.g., persuasion and negotiation). Social skills training can teach alternatives to violent behavior, including appropriate affect, facial expressiveness, proper posture, direct eye contact, appropriate expression of frustration, and requests for the listener to change his or her behavior.

In contrast to the types of programs discussed so far, some programs use negative stimuli or withholding or withdrawing positive stimuli to decrease violent and other undesirable behaviors. This involves the patient losing privileges or being fined in terms of tokens. Other programs remove the patient from the environment or treatment program for varying periods of time. Moving to more restrictive procedures is considered seclusionary time-out or time-out from reinforcement. This involves placing the patient in a special area with no reinforcements following violent or other inappropriate behavior and may actually involve a seclusion room. Unlike seclusion used for the emergency situations described earlier, seclusionary time-out is administered immediately following the display of a specific target behavior, whether it is of immediate danger to others or not. Another more restrictive procedure is contingent restraint, which involves immobilizing some part of a patient's body by some device (e.g., soft ties, restraint chair, cuffs, posey jacket) following the occurrence of a specific violent act. Unlike the use of seclusion and restraints in an emergency situation, their use in behavior programs is brief, lasting as little as 5 minutes and rarely longer than 1 hour.

COMMUNITY TREATMENT AND MONITORING

Release of mentally abnormal offenders, whether they were found not guilty by reason of insanity (NGRI) or merely treated as civil patients in hospitals, is an important area of study. In Oregon, California, and a number of other states, programs that monitor NGRI released patients have been effective in protecting the public while decreasing the cost of hospitalization and ensuring the liberty of properly treated patients (Bloom et al., 1991; Wiederanders & Choate, 1994). For example, in Oregon, the Psychiatric Security Review Board functions independently of the court system. Once a patient is assigned to its jurisdiction, the board assumes the sole authority to determine placement in the community or a hospital, based on what is best for the patient, while protecting society from the danger of violence by the patient.

As with NGRI released patients, formerly violent civil patients have been managed in programs of involuntary community treatment provided proper patient selection and rigorous monitoring exist (Geller, 1990; Slobogin, 1994). Research shows that monitoring formerly violent patients in the community is not enough. There must be intensive case management with strong links to agencies providing mental health services and social services and proper attention to families and social networks of the formerly violent patient (Estroff, Zimmer, Lachicotte, & Benoit, 1994; Monahan & Steadman, 1994b).

CONCLUSIONS

Violence by persons with mental disorders is more frequent than among persons with no mental disorders. The disorders with higher risk of violence include schizophrenia, mania, substance abuse, other organic disorders and some personality disorders, particularly the antisocial and borderline types.

The evaluation of the violent person must be comprehensive in that it must assess psychopathology as well as medical abnormalities. It must use laboratory and other diagnostic procedures as indicated. The psychopathological and physiological processes leading to violence must be seen in relation to the environment as one assesses the causes of violence and plans treatment.

There is growing confidence that experienced, trained clinicians can predict the potential for violence in the short term. This is important not only to satisfy their legal obligations but for the safety of others in society as well. Attacks by patients on staff members have received more and more attention. Guidelines for the prevention and management of such violence have begun to be formulated.

Acute management of violence by psychiatric patients has become more effective and safer because of guidelines developed on the psychiatric use of seclusion and restraint and by the availability of rapidly acting, safe, injectable drugs such as lorzepam. The long-term management of violence by refractory schizophrenic patients has improved with the use of clozapine and other new antipsychotics. Older antipsychotics, such as haloperidol and fluphenazine, particularly in injected long-acting depot form, still remain the first line of treatment. Medications developed for use in disorders not related to violence per se, for example, anticonvulsants, lithium, and beta-blockers, have been studied in the long-term management of violence, predominantly by means of noncontrolled case studies.

Behavioral therapy has been developed for the management of violence in institutions in which medication is not effective or indicated. Psychotherapy, on the other hand, can be used widely in outpatient settings for a group of patients with no psychosis or other incapacitating psychopathology. The treatment of mentally abnormal offenders in the community has used monitored conditioned release programs, involuntary outpatient treatment programs, and intensive case management programs.

FUTURE WORK

More attention must be given to the safety of staff members in health care settings. The needs of staff members for security vary according to the setting, from the emergency room, psychiatric inpatient unit, general hospital, or outpatient office. Security issues should be part of the accreditation process for health care institutions and for training programs such as residencies and other professional education programs.

Research on prediction of violence must be comprehensive but practical. The clinician must think in terms of the number and types of variables that form the basis of a clinical decision as to whether a patient poses a risk of violence and, if so, what intervention is indicated. Studies should be prospective in nature and clearly define independent and dependent variables. Prediction must be targeted to the short term, that is, days or a week at most, because that time period is most crucial in clinical situations such as the time between visits or in a decision to hospitalize or discharge from a hospital.

Studies of new and existing medications for the treatment of violent patients should follow standard protocols, including placebo controls. Rating instruments should establish a baseline of violence in a quantitative manner. Other factors related to violence, for example, staff members in hospitals or the behavior of others around the violent patient, must be taken into consideration in medication studies.

Use of seclusion and restraint in institutions must be monitored to avoid the inappropriate or prolonged use of these techniques beyond the time they are needed. This should be a regular part of quality assurance protocols for all types of institutions from public to private and from psychiatric to general medical institutions.

Future research on the etiology of violence will involve the use of neuroimaging that assesses the function of the brain as well as anatomic structures and new techniques not conceived at this time. Studies of the classification and phenomenology of violence must parallel our use of more sophisticated technology in the study of violence. We must develop structured, quantitative, and clinically relevant measures of violence.

Ideally, funding for research on violence and its victims will increase as our concern about violence continues to do so.

REFERENCES

American Psychiatric Association. (1985). *Seclusion and restraint: The psychiatric uses. Task force report no. 22.* Washington, DC: Author.

American Psychiatric Association. (1992). *Clinician safety: Task force report no. 33.* Washington, DC: Author.

Asnis, G. M., Kaplan, M. L., van Praag, H. M., & Sanderson, W. C. (1994). Homicidal behaviors among psychiatric outpatients. *Hospital and Community Psychiatry, 45,* 127–132.

Beck, J. C. (1988). The therapist's legal duty when the patient may be violent. *Psychiatric Clinic of North America, 11,* 665–679.

Bernstein, H. A. (1981). Survey of threats and assaults directed toward psychotherapists. *American Journal of Psychotherapy, 35,* 542–549.

Binder, R. L., & McNiel, D. E. (1990). The relationship of gender to violent behavior in acutely disturbed psychiatric patients. *Journal of Clinical Psychiatry, 51,* 110–114.

Bland, R., & Orn, H. (1986). Family violence and psychiatry. *Canadian Journal of Psychiatry, 31,* 129–137.

Bloom, J. D., Williams, M. H., & Bigelow, D. A. (1991). Monitoring conditional release of persons found not guilty by reason of insanity. *American Journal of Psychiatry, 148,* 444–448.

Budd, R. D., & Lindstrom, D. M. (1982). Characteristics of victims of PCP-related deaths in Los Angeles County. *Journal of Toxicology and Clinical Toxicology, 19,* 997–1004.

Campbell, M., Small, A. M., Green, W. H., Jennings, S. J., Perry, R., Bennett, W. G., & Anderson, L. (1984). Behavioral efficacy of haloperidol and lithium carbonate. A comparison in hospitalized aggressive children with conduct disorder. *Archives of General Psychiatry, 41,* 650–656.

Carmel, H., & Hunter, M. (1989). Staff injuries from inpatient violence. *Hospital and Community Psychiatry, 40,* 41–46.

Chaimowitz, G. A., & Mocovitch, A. (1991). Patient assaults against psychiatric residents: The Canadian experience. *Canadian Journal of Psychiatry, 36,* 107–111.

Coccaro, E. F., Kramer, E., Zemishlany, Z., Thorne, A., Rice, C. M., Giordani, B., Duvvi, K., Patel, B. M., Torres, J., Nora, R., Neufeld, R., Mohs, R. C., & Davis, K. L. (1990). Pharmacologic treatment of noncognitive behavioral disturbances in elderly demented patients. *American Journal of Psychiatry, 147,* 1640–1645.

Craft, M., Ismail, I. A., Krishnamurti, D., Mathews, J., Regan, A., Seth, R. V., & North, P. M. (1987). Lithium in the treatment of aggression in mentally handicapped patients. A double-blind trial. *British Journal of Psychiatry, 150,* 685–689.

Craig, T. J. (1982). An epidemiologic study of problems associated with violence among psychiatric patients. *American Journal of Psychiatry, 139,* 1262–1266.

Deutsch, L. H., Bylsma, F. W., Rovner, B. W., et al. (1991). Psychosis and physical aggression in probable Alzheimer's disease. *American Journal of Psychiatry, 148,* 1159–1163.

Dubin, W. R. (1989). The role of fantasies, countertransference, and psychological defenses in patient violence. *Hospital and Community Psychiatry, 40,* 1280–1283.

Dvoskin, J. A., & Steadman, H. J. (1994). Using intensive case management to reduce violence by mentally ill persons in the community. *Hospital and Community Psychiatry, 45,* 679–684.

Estroff, S. E., Zimmer, C., Lachicotte, W. S., & Benoit, J. (1994). The influence of social networks and social support on violence by persons with serious mental illness. *Hospital and Community Psychiatry, 45,* 669–678.

Fassler, D., & Cotton, N. (1992). A national survey on the use of seclusion in the psychiatric treatment of children. *Hospital and Community Psychiatry, 43,* 370–374.

Fink, D. L., Shoyer, B., & Dubin, W. R. (1991). A study of assaults against psychiatric residents. *Academic Psychiatry, 15,* 94–99.

Foster, H. G., Hollbrand, M., & Chi, C. C. (1989). Efficacy of carbamazepine in assaultive patients with frontal lobe dysfunction. Progress neuropsychopharmacology. *Biological Psychiatry, 13,* 865–874.

Garza-Trevino, E. S., Hollister, L. E., Overall, J. E., & Alexander, W. F. (1989). Efficacy of combinations of intramuscular antipsychotics and sedative-hypnotics for control of psychotic agitation. *American Journal of Psychiatry, 146,* 1598–1601.

Geller, J. L. (1990). Clinical guidelines for the use of involuntary outpatient treatment. *Hospital and Community Psychiatry, 41,* 749–755.

Greendyke, R. M., & Kanter, D. R. (1986). Therapeutic effects of pindolol on behavioral disturbances associated with organic brain disease: A double-blind study. *Journal of Clinical Psychiatry, 47,* 423–426.

Greendyke, R. M., Kanter, D. R., Schuster, D. B., Verstreate, S., & Wootton, J. (1986). Propranolol treatment of assaultive patients with organic brain disease. *Journal of Nervous and Mental Disorder, 174,* 290–294.

Grey, G. E. (1989). Assaults by patients against residents at a public psychiatric hospital. *Academic Psychiatry, 13,* 81–86.

Hare, R., & McPherson, L. (1984). Violent and aggressive behavior by criminal psychopaths. *International Journal of Law Psychiatry, 7,* 35–50.

Hatti, S., Dubin, W. R., & Weiss, K. J. (1982). A study of the circumstances surrounding patient assaults on psychiatrists. *Hospital and Community Psychiatry, 33,* 660–661.

Karson, C., & Bigelow, L. B. (1987). Violent behavior in schizophrenic inpatients. *Journal of Nervous and Mental Disorders, 175,* 161–164.

Kay, S. R., Wolkenfeld, F., & Murrill, L. M. (1988). Profiles of aggression among psychiatric patients. *Journal of Nervous and Mental Disorders, 176,* 547–557.

Klassen, D., & O'Connor, W. (1989). Assessing the risk of violence in released mental patients. *Psychological Assessment, 1,* 75–81.

Krakowski, M., Convit, A., Jaeger, J., & Volavka, J. (1989). Neurological impairment in schizophrenic patients. *American Journal of Psychiatry, 146,* 849–853.

Krakowski, M., Volavka, J., & Brizer, D. (1986). Psychopathology and violence: A review of literature. *Comprehensive Psychiatry, 27,* 131–148.

Lanza, M. L., & Kayne, H. (1991). Staff and environment characteristics related to patient assault. *Issues in Mental Health Nursing, 12,* 253–266.

Liberman, R. P., & Wong, S. E. (1984). Behavioral analysis and therapy procedures related to seclusion and restraint. In K. Tardiff (Ed.), *The psychiatric uses of seclusion and restraint.* Washington, DC: American Psychiatric Press.

Lidz, C. W., Mulvey, E. P., & Gardner, W. (1993). The accuracy of predictions of violence to others. *Journal of the American Medical Association, 269,* 1007–1011.

Lindquist, P., & Allebeck, P. (1990). Schizophrenia and crime: A longitudinal follow-up of 644 schizophrenics in Stockholm. *British Journal of Psychiatry, 157,* 345–350.

Lion, J. R., & Pasternak, S. A. (1973). Countertransference reactions to violent patients. *American Journal of Psychiatry, 130,* 207–210.

Lion, J. R., Tardiff, K. (1987). The long-term treatment of the violent patient. In R. E. Hales & A. J. Frances (Eds.), *The American Psychiatric Association annual review* (Vol. 6, pp. 537–548). Washington, DC: American Psychiatric Press.

Lowenstein, D. H., Massa, S. M., Rowbotham, M. C., Collins, S. D., McKinney, H. E., & Simon, R. P. (1987). Acute neurologic and psychiatric complications associated with cocaine abuse. *American Journal of Medicine, 83,* 841–846.

Luchins, D. I. (1984). Carbamazepine in psychiatric syndromes: Clinical and neuropharmacological properties. *Psychopharmacology Bulletin, 20,* 569–571.

Madden, D. J., Lion, J. R., & Penna, M. W. (1976). Assaults on psychiatrists by patients. *American Journal of Psychiatry, 133,* 422–425.

Mattes, J. A., Rosenberg, J., & Mays, D. (1984). Carbamazepine versus propranolol in patients with uncontrolled rage outbursts: A random assignment study. *Psychopharmacology Bulletin, 20,* 98–100.

Monaham, J., & Steadman, H. (1994a). Toward a rejuvenation of risk assessment research. In J. Monahan & H. Steadman (Ed.), *Violence and mental disorder: Developments in risk assessment.* Chicago: University of Chicago Press.

Monahan, J., & Steadman, H. (1994b). *Violence and mental disorders: Developments in risk assessment.* Chicago: University of Chicago Press.

Monroe, R. R. (1970). *Episodic behavioral disorders.* Cambridge, MA: Harvard University Press.

Okuma, T., Yamashita, I., Takahashi, R., Iloh, H., Otsuki, S., Watanbe, S., Sarai, K., Hazama, H., & Inanaga, K. (1989). A double-blind study of the adjunctive carbamazepine versus placebo on excited states of schizophrenia and schizoaffective disorders. *Acta Psychiatrica Scandinavica, 80,* 250–259.

Patterson, J. F. (1987). Carbamazepine for assaultive patients with organic brain disease: An open pilot study. *Psychosomatics, 28,* 579–581.

Petrie, W. M., Lawson, E. C., & Hollender, M. H. (1982). Violence in geriatric patients. *Journal of the American Medical Association, 248,* 443–444.

Planansky, K., & Johnston, R. (1977). Homicidal aggression in schizophrenic men. *Acta Psychiatrica Scandinavica, 55,* 65–73.

Ratey, J. J., Leveroni, C., Kilmer, D., Gutheil, C., & Swartz, B. (1993). The effects of clozapine on severely aggressive psychiatric inpatients in a state hospital. *Journal of Clinical Psychiatry, 54,* 219–223.

Ratey, J. J., Mikkelsen, E., Sorgi, P., Zuckerman, H. S., Polakoff, S., Bemporad, J., Beck, P., & Kadish, W. (1987). Autism: The treatment of aggressive behaviors. *Journal of Clinical Psychopharmacology, 7,* 35–41.

Ratey, J. J., Sorgi, P., O'Driscoll, G. A., Sands, S., Doehler, M. L., Fletcher, J. R., Kadish, W., Sprurell, G., Polakoff, S., & Lindem, K. J. (1992). Nadolol to treatment aggression and psychiatric symptomatology in chronic psychiatric inpatients: A double-blind, placebo-controlled study. *Journal of Clinical Psychiatry, 53,* 41–46.

Reid, W. H., & Balis, E. U. (1987). Evaluation of the violent patient. In R. E. Hales & A. J. Frances (Eds.), *American Psychiatric Association annual review* (Vol. 6, pp. 491–509). Washington, DC: American Psychiatric Press.

Rossi, A. M., Jacobs, M., Monteleone, M., Olsen, R., Surber, R. W., Winkler, E. L., & Wommack, A. (1985). Violent or fear-inducing behavior associated with hospital admission. *Hospital and Community Psychiatry, 36,* 643–647.

Salzman, C., Solomon, D., Miyawaki, E., Glassman, R., Rood, L., Flowers, E., & Thayer, S. (1991). Parenteral lorazepam versus parenteral haloperidol for the control of psychotic disruptive behavior. *Journal of Clinical Psychiatry, 52,* 177–180.

Sheard, M. H., Marini, J. L., Bridges, C. I., & Wagner, E. (1976). The effects of lithium on impulsive aggressive behavior in man. *American Journal of Psychiatry, 133,* 1409–1413.

Shugar, G., & Rehaluk, R. (1990). Continuous observation for psychiatric inpatients: A critical evaluation. *Comprehensive Psychiatry, 30,* 48–55.

Siassi, I. (1982). Lithium treatment of impulsive behavior in children. *Journal of Clinical Psychiatry, 43,* 482–484.

Slobogin, C. (1994). Involuntary community treatment of people who are violent and mentally ill: A legal analysis. *Hospital and Community Psychiatry, 45,* 685–689.

Soliday, S. M. (1985). A comparison of patient and staff attitudes toward seclusion. *Journal of Nervous and Mental Disorders, 173,* 282–291.

Sorgi, P. J., Ratey, J. J., & Polakoff, S. (1986). Beta-adrenergic blockers for the control of aggressive behaviors in patients with chronic schizophrenia. *American Journal of Psychiatry, 143,* 775–776.

Stewart, J. T., Mounts, M. L., & Clark, R. L., Jr. (1987). Aggressive behavior in Huntington's disease: Treatment with propranolol. *Journal of Clinical Psychiatry, 48,* 106–108.

Swanson, J. W., Holzer, C. E., Ganju, V. K., & Jono, R. T. (1990). Violence and psychiatric disorder in the community: Evidence from the Epidemiologic Catchment Area survey. *Hospital and Community Psychiatry, 41,* 761–770.

Tardiff, K. (1984a). Characteristics of assaultive patients in private hospitals. *American Journal of Psychiatry, 141,* 1232–1235.

Tardiff, K. (Ed.). (1984b). *The psychiatric uses of seclusion and restraint.* Washington, DC: American Psychiatric Press.

Tardiff, K. (1989a). A model for the short-term prediction of violence potential. In D. A. Brizer & M. Crowner (Eds.), *Current approaches to the prediction of violence.* Washington, DC: American Psychiatric Press.

Tardiff, K. (1996). *Assessment and management of violent patients* (2nd ed.). Washington, DC: American Psychiatric Press.

Tardiff, K. (1992). The current state of psychiatry in the treatment of violent patients. *Archives General Psychiatry, 49,* 493–499.

Tardiff, K., & Koenigsberg, H. W. (1985). Assaultive behavior among psychiatric outpatients. *American Journal of Psychiatry, 142,* 960–963.

Tardiff, K., & Maurice, W. L. (1977). The care of violent patients by psychiatrists: A tale of two cities. *Canadian Psychiatric Association Journal, 22,* 83–86.

Tardiff, K., & Sweillam, A. (1980). Assault, suicide and mental illness. *Archives of General Psychiatry, 37,* 164–169.

Tardiff, K., & Sweillam, A. (1982). Assaultive behavior among chronic inpatients. *American Journal of Psychiatry, 139,* 312–315.

Taylor, P. J., & Gunn, J. (1984). Violence and psychosis. *British Medical Journal, 288,* 1945–1949.

Volavka, J., Zito, J. M., & Vitrai, J. (1993). Clozapine effects on hostility and aggression in schizophrenia. *Journal of Clinical Psychopharmacology, 13,* 287–289.

Weiger, B., & Bear, D. (1988). An approach to the neurology of aggression. *Journal of Psychiatric Research, 22,* 85–98.

Whitman, J. R., Maier, G. J., & Eichelman, B. (1987). Beta-adrenergic blockers for aggressive behavior in schizophrenia [letter]. *American Journal Psychiatry, 144,* 538–539.

Whitman, R. M., Armao, B. B., & Dent, O. B. (1976). Assault on the therapist. *American Journal of Psychiatry, 133,* 426–431.

Wiederanders, M. R., & Choate, P. A. (1994). Beyond recidivism: Measuring community adjustments of conditionally released insanity acquittees. *Psychological Assessment, 1,* 61–66.

Wong, S. E., Woolsey, J. E., Innocent, A. J., & Liberman, R. P. (1988). Behavioral treatment of violent patients. In K. Tardiff (Ed.), *The violent patient* (Vol. 1). Philadelphia: W. B. Saunders.

Yesavage, J. A. (1983a). Bipolar illness: Correlates of dangerous inpatient behavior. *British Journal of Psychiatry, 143,* 554–557.

Yesavage, J. A. (1983b). Inpatient violence and the schizophrenic patient. *Acta Psychiatrica Scandinavica, 67,* 353–357.

Young, J. L., & Hillbrand, M. (1994). Carbamazepine lowers aggression: A review. *Bulletin of the American Academy of Psychiatry and the Law, 22,* 53–62.

Yudofsky, S. C., Silver, J. M., & Hales, R. E. (1990). Pharmacologic management of aggression in the elderly. *Journal of Clinical Psychiatry, 51*(10, suppl.), 22–28.

Yudofsky, S. C. Williams, D., & Gorman, J. (1981). Propranolol in the treatment of rage and violent behavior in patients with chronic brain syndrome. *American Journal of Psychiatry, 138,* 218–220.

CHAPTER 43

Themes for Consideration in Future Research on Prevention and Intervention With Antisocial Behaviors

EDWARD P. MULVEY and JENNIFER L. WOOLARD

The chapters in this section have provided a rich overview of what is known and what needs to be known about prevention and intervention with antisocial behaviors. The authors provided a wealth of information about approaches that have proven successful and the lessons that have been learned in efforts to find these approaches. This chapter highlights some consistent themes that appear across the chapters and raises some questions that might be considered in future research in this area.

It is worth noting first that preventing or treating antisocial behaviors is often frustrating for even the most knowledgeable professionals. It is often hard to know exactly which particular approach is supported by sound research. As has been pointed out repeatedly in this part these behaviors (a) are caused and maintained by numerous, interacting factors; (b) are socially, culturally, and developmentally bound; and (c) are rarely, if ever, adequately explained by a single theoretical orientation. These realities make the accumulation and application of empirical information about effective interventions in this area a daunting task.

This is not to say that we know nothing. Particular things can be said with some certainty about the developmental patterns of antisocial behavior (e.g., age of onset is an important consideration in identifying children at high risk for later antisocial behavior; Blumstein, Farrington, & Moitra, 1985; Farrington et al., 1990), and there are several specific intervention strategies with accumulated records of some success (e.g., social cognitive approaches paired with family intervention; Kazdin, 1993; Southam-Gerow & Kendall, Chapter 36, this volume). There are numerous "known" facts in this area; often, it just takes considerable work to find them.

This is partially the result of the segregation of findings into pools of information about different aspects of particular antisocial behaviors. Whole literatures exist on the development of delinquency careers, the consistency of conduct disorder symptoms, and the effects of neighborhood environment on crime and drug use. Researchers working in one subarea recognize the relevance of the other existing lines of investigation but are rarely able to conduct studies that reflect the breadth of issues related to the development and patterns of antisocial behaviors (see Farrington, Chapter 22, this volume). This leaves individuals doing intervention studies in this area and policy makers in a difficult situation. They have bits and pieces of information to guide their efforts, but there is also an overwhelming sense of the complexity of the phenomenon being addressed.

In response, individuals mounting interventions usually take one of two approaches. They may try to be truly comprehensive, providing a broad set of services to effect change in both the individual and his or her surroundings. If this approach is taken, one must confront the difficulties of demonstrating consistency and replicability as well as face the possibility of explaining complicated, differential outcomes. Alternatively, they may narrowly specify the individuals enrolled in the program or the behaviors targeted for change, choosing only to address a particular setting or set of behaviors. Taking this second approach requires a demonstration that behaviors or settings with strong effects on an individual's developmental trajectory have been targeted for change and that a focused intervention of the sort tested will have broad applicability outside of its controlled demonstration. Neither approach is wholly satisfactory, and the tension between ambitious, "shotgun" efforts and myopic, controlled studies is a consistent undercurrent to intervention research in the area.

This disparate nature of the literature on prevention and intervention about antisocial behaviors also muddies public debate. Programmers and policy experts often pick and choose among disjointed findings until they find some that match their broad purposes. Prevention strategies aimed at preserving families or training parents, for example, justify their approach at least partially on information about the importance of family environments as buffers against the development of antisocial behavior and of the harm to children from placement out of the home. Similarly, both sides of the debate on the reasonableness of retributive approaches in juvenile justice often use simplistic generalizations about the predictability of offending careers and the effectiveness of intervening with seriously antisocial adolescents (Tate, Reppucci, & Mulvey, 1995).

This chapter highlights three basic issues that researchers and programmers in this field must consider if we are to provide a more cohesive picture in our next generation of studies on antisocial behavior. These issues emerge repeatedly in the chapters here but have often been blurred or sidestepped. Debating them and considering them in our formulation of new research agendas are necessary steps toward a more integrated view of how to think about and address antisocial behaviors.

WHAT DO WE MEAN BY RISK FACTORS?

As emphasized by Offord (Chapter 33, this volume), little effort is usually paid to pursuing the distinction between *fixed risk markers* and *variable risk factors* (Compas, Hinden, & Gerhardt, 1995; Kraemer et al., in press). Risk markers are those correlates of an antisocial behavior that precede the occurrence of the behavior of interest but cannot be changed (e.g., gender). Risk factors not only precede and correlate with the behavior of interest, but they also have been shown to have a causal relationship to the behavior (i.e., their removal or reduction will reduce the likelihood or intensity of the antisocial behavior). The causal relationship is best shown through an experimental manipulation, rather than longitudinal research, because the latter is best suited for description rather than demonstration of causal pathways. Risk markers are useful because they inform methods for identifying individuals appropriate for special programming before the maladaptive behavior is exhibited. Risk factors are important because they indicate where programming resources should be concentrated to be most effective. Systematic research on risk factors can also provide valuable information about how much relative impact can be expected from focusing on the reduction of particular risk factors (Offord, Chapter 33, this volume).

Unfortunately, longitudinal research can easily be interpreted as finding strong risk factors when it really may have found useful risk markers. Association with delinquent peers provides an example. Although association with delinquent peers has been shown to be related to continued delinquency in mid-adolescence (e.g., Farrington, 1995; Jessor, Van Den Bos, Vanderryn, Costa, & Turbin, 1995), the evidence that removing an adolescent from delinquent peers is an effective method for altering individual propensities for continued offending is less clear (see Chamberlain & Friman, Chapter 39, this volume). Nevertheless, many programmers and policy makers have interpreted the strong association between delinquent peers and continued offending as evidence for the necessity to do group level interventions with delinquents, despite demonstrations of negative effects from such approaches (Klein, 1983). It would seem incumbent upon researchers to both generate the research results needed to make the distinction between risk markers and causal risk factors found in longitudinal research and to make this subtle distinction understandable to program planners and policy makers.

In refining the presentation of what longitudinal research does and does not show, it would also be useful to examine the effects of sampling on the power of risk factors. Longitudinal research is often viewed as a method of taking different moving pictures of basically the same phenomenon, that is, the developmental patterns of antisocial lifestyles, with the expectation that results should be generally the same across the different samples. To continue the movie analogy, the movie actors change, but the script should stay the same. In reality, however, the particular troupe of actors making the movie has much more impact on the way the script unfolds than we commonly assume. Sampling differences might make one factor appear very powerfully associated with antisocial behavior in one study and only marginally related in another. Reviewing contradictory research on age of onset and delinquency risk, Tolan and Thomas (1995) reveal sampling differences across studies on key dimensions that have implications for the generalizability of onset age as a risk factor, including the marker of onset (e.g., conviction vs. other reports), the type of characteristics assessed (e.g., stable individual and family characteristics vs. dynamic situational characteristics) and the nature of the samples (e.g., high-risk males vs. other groups). Accounting for the sampling differences across studies is rarely done systematically, however, and the observed differences are instead interpreted usually as evidence that a particular factor must not be a robust, stable predictor of future antisocial behavior.

This consideration is particularly important as research moves toward examination of neighborhood and community effects, because sampling restrictively in these types of studies can have an impact on the conclusions. A neighborhood level variable (e.g., level of social disorganization) may exert a strong influence on the prevalence of antisocial behavior in a community, with some neighborhoods high on that measure having markedly higher prevalence rates. Yet in studies in which subjects are drawn overwhelmingly from neighborhoods uniformly either low or high on this variable, its influence will appear relatively weak (Rose, 1985).

The scope of the sampling done for developmental cohort studies thus greatly affects how strongly the relationship between neighborhood factors and individual outcomes will emerge. As more and more targeted sampling strategies are used to respond to policy concerns (e.g., adolescents from low-income, urban neighborhoods), the broad impact of neighborhood variables should diminish. Such sampling strategies introduce unintentional yet systematic sample selection bias at the context level. Although it is possible to model these contextual selection effects (Berk, 1983; Winship & Mare, 1992), statistically compensating for them may not be adequate, given the real-world implications of such research. Interindividual differences can be expected to emerge as more powerful, explanatory variables, and the leap to policy arguments about the potential utility of individual-level approaches for intervention can be made all too easily.

Guerra, Attar, and Weissberg's (Chapter 35, this volume) discussion of intervention in inner-city environments illustrates this point. The contextual influences of an urban environment are powerful factors, but the contribution of "urbanness" to variance in outcomes will be diminished if all youths in a particular study come from an urban context. Interventions based on these results may then focus on individual strategies for coping rather than on changing aspects of the context. Obviously, comparisons of the relative influence of individual and neighborhood effects can only be done very carefully, accounting for the different sampling strategies used in the studies examined.

Taking community-level sample selection effects seriously means that researchers must also then take on the challenge of identifying theoretically and empirically critical factors at the levels of neighborhood and community. To meet this challenge, general demographic characterizations must give way to more complex characterizations at the community level. Research on problem behaviors, including antisocial behavior, is beginning to examine the role and process by which community factors affect negative (or healthy) outcomes in adolescents as well as the impact of such factors on intervention techniques (Blyth & Leffert, 1995; Brooks-Gunn, Duncan, Klebanov, & Sealand, 1993; Coulton, Korbin, Su, & Chow, 1995; Hawkins, Arthur, & Olson, Chapter 34, this volume; Kupersmidt, Griesler, DeRosier, Patterson, & Davis, 1995). For example, patterns of community structure based on indicators of social organization have been related systematically to the prevalence of behavioral outcomes such as child maltreatment, violent crime, and juvenile delinquency (Coulton et al., 1995).

These larger effects must not only be identified but also should be considered sources of variance; we must move beyond a tendency to "control" for these factors in the statistical sense. Transactional and interactionist perspectives on development have begun to emphasize the links between the individual and larger ecosystems, raising interesting theoretical questions and difficult methodological issues such as measuring multifactorial outcomes and directionality effects (Caprara & Rutter, 1995). Recent advances in statistical modeling have resulted in techniques that allow macro-level variables such as neighborhood or community characteristics to have an impact on individual-level variables as well as interaction terms (e.g., DiPrete & Forristal, 1994; Hox & Kreft, 1994). Continued use of these techniques will eventually have implications for study design methods, such as the number of individuals and contexts to sample to ensure adequate statistical power (Martin, Diehr, Perrin, & Koepsell, 1993; West, Aiken, & Todd, 1993).

Using recent statistical advances to pursue research on contextual effects would seem to be more useful than clarifying the relative power of one risk marker over another. There is some evidence that cumulative risk (the total number of risk factors that a child has, regardless of their type) may be a powerful predictor of later difficulties (Jessor et al., 1995; Rutter, 1979). In addition, there is a sound argument that risk status produces a cascading effect over time; the presence of a large number of risk markers at one developmental period greatly increases the chances of the next developmental risk marker being present through indirect cumulative chain effects (Caprara & Rutter, 1995). Given this, one can question the utility of further refining information about the interrelationship and relative power of risk markers. A consideration of overall cumulative risk might do a perfectly acceptable job of identifying vulnerable populations of children for policy and programmatic purposes.

Knowing which of these risk markers are actually risk factors, however, would be very valuable and could have far-reaching effects for the design of interventions. As Reid and Eddy (Chapter 32, this volume) point out, the ideal target for intervention is a risk factor at one developmental period that has the most direct causal relationship to a risk factor at the next developmental period. If these chains of risk factors can be isolated, then targeted interventions at each developmental period could be expected to have long-lasting effects. In addition, emerging research on the role of protective factors in the etiology and developmental course of antisocial behavior could assist in the development of a two-pronged strategy aimed at reducing risk factors while enhancing protective factors. Although less developed than work on risk factors, recent findings on protective factors suggest that protective factors may have a stronger association with changes in problem behaviors than existing risk factors (Jessor et al., 1995). As Rutter (1990) emphasized, the concepts of risk and protection are not fixed attributes with global characteristics. Rather, attention should focus on the mechanisms by which risk and protection factors operate; it is changes in the mechanisms that ultimately may alter the developmental trajectories of various problem behaviors. Until we make clear distinctions about what we mean by risk markers and factors and produce research that allows us to tell the difference, however, we will never be able to tap the full potential of longitudinal approaches for targeting and framing intervention.

WHEN SHOULD WE BE SEARCHING FOR A TECHNOLOGY FOR INTERVENTION?

There is an implicit quest for technology behind much of the applied research on antisocial behaviors. It is hoped that systematic intervention approaches can be fashioned through a clear statement of program mission and operations and that this strategy can then be transferred to other locales for successful implementation. In much the same way that we have come to rely on scientific advances to provide devices such as microwaves that can be plugged into any kitchen, we strive toward social scientific advances to produce a method for addressing antisocial behaviors that can be applied in almost all clinics, schools, or neighborhoods. We are, in essence, searching for a systematic approach for intervention that is robust to different service provider and community realities.

This assumption is rarely examined for its reasonableness before mounting and testing an intervention, even though the history of interventions with antisocial behavior is littered with demonstration programs that never survived the difficult process of replication (e.g., Rappaport, Seidman, & Davidson, 1979). It is generally assumed that the lack of subsequent, positive results arises because the original, successful program was not done "correctly" on "properly identified" clients; if it had been, there would have been positive effects. Unfortunately, in most of these situations, it is not determined whether the theoretical formulation of the problem was incorrect, the integrity of the replication effort was lacking, or some set of client characteristics in the new setting reduced the likelihood for success. In short, there is surprisingly little work done on institutionalizing programs in ways that ensure high fidelity of the intervention (see, however, the Teaching Family and Therapeutic Foster Care Models reviewed by Chamberlain & Friman, Chapter 39, this volume, for notable exceptions). Instead, we strive to develop "better, faster, stronger" versions of the same interventions to overcome the lack of replication.

It may be, however, that some programs will never be transportable to another setting precisely because contextual factors greatly affect their success. We may never see these instances, though, as long as we assume that context is a nonissue, something to be overcome rather than incorporated into the science itself. As Rice and Harris (Chapter 40, this volume) note, one of the most influential factors predicting successful interventions in juvenile justice is whether the intervention was applied "appropriately" (cf. Andrews et al., 1990). Yet we rarely document or examine the local historical, daily operational, or community contextual factors that support the initiation and maintenance of successful programs, even though these factors may be highly influential in the success of an intervention approach (Felner, Phillips, DuBois, & Lease, 1991; Munoz, Snowden, Kelly, & Associates, 1979; Sarason, 1978; Trickett, 1991).

Aside from the influence of context, whether an approach may be ready for transport to another setting may also depend on the form of antisocial behavior addressed or the type of intervention. Certain types of behavior (e.g., aggressive acts) at delimited developmental periods (e.g., latency age) in targeted samples (e.g., clinically referred children) may be uniform or intraindividually determined enough to be addressed consistently by particular approaches (e.g., social cognitive training supported by either a family or classroom environment; see Southam-Gerow & Kendall, Chapter 36, this volume). Similarly, certain approaches, such as the pharmacological interventions outlined by Karper and Krystal (Chapter 41, this volume), may be sufficiently resistant to environmental influences to make their systematic exploration as a transferable technology reasonable.

However, other forms of behavior (e.g., school violence) at other developmental periods (e.g., mid-adolescence) in more broadly defined samples (e.g., students in high-risk neighborhoods) may be so contextually based that the development of uniformly applicable interventions may be unlikely. The factors supporting the continued problem might not be amenable to an approach that is translatable across settings or samples. The contextual nature of these problems may instead necessitate intervention at the setting level. In these situations, the process and strategy of intervention may be the key to transportability, rather than the content of the intervention (see Hawkins, Arthur, & Olson, Chapter 34, this volume). Ultimately, a balance between program fidelity and implementation adaptability must be developed (Institute of Medicine, 1994), but we rarely invest much in striking this balance.

Our implicit search for an intervention technology to serve all different problem situations can have two effects. First, it often spawns frustration among applied researchers with the complexities of community influences. Some of this frustration seems evident in the chapters by Tolan and Gorman-Smith (Chapter 38) and Guerra, Attar, and Weissberg (Chapter 35) in this volume. As pointed out by these investigators, the effects of juvenile justice decision making or community mores can often overshadow whatever program effects might be produced or measured (for a historical view of these changing social forces, see Rice & Harris, Chapter 40, this volume). Even interventions that are targeted at changing institutional and contextual influences for program participants often result in minor or no changes within the existing system.

Second, our implicit acceptance of the search for a technology can often bias our measurement of program effects toward an undue concern with the content, rather than the process, of service delivery. Because we are often looking for an intervention that can be transported to another site, we often focus on the easily documented mechanics of the intervention rather than the "gestalt" of the intervention. How many group sessions make up the interven-

tion package or whether the protocol for case management followed a particular format for brokering services may be considered very important things to measure; ethnographic information about how the program developed or how it was viewed by consumers may be considered "fluff."

This bias toward measurement of program mechanics, however, may prove shortsighted. Programs often fail or take hold because of factors related to the community's readiness, receptivity, or acceptance, and development of these aspects of an intervention may be as critical as a concern with the mechanics of program delivery. Such work, however, requires a commitment to active engagement and to collaboration with key members of the community (Guba & Lincoln, 1989; Walsh, 1987), and researchers are often less prone to take on this long view of the process of intervention.

Certainly documentation of program integrity is important if we are to accumulate comparable information about successful program approaches. At this point, however, we do not know enough about the influence of program context on implementation (Tolan & Gorman-Smith, Chapter 38, this volume), and there is little emphasis among researchers on evaluating interventions across communities that differ on key characteristics hypothesized to affect implementation (Hawkins et al., Chapter 34, this volume). The point stressed here is simply that the measurement of program implementation could often go beyond the most easily measurable aspects of program delivery to include dimensions of programming that are rarely addressed (e.g., see Felner et al., 1991; Kelly, 1986; Munoz et al., 1979; Trickett, 1991). Whether a program fosters a learning environment among staff, what its values are about sticking with a client through life changes, or how political pressures of a community are handled by program administrators may all be very relevant considerations for understanding how to replicate a successful program. Yet aspects of program functioning like these are rarely examined, largely because we have thought of program implementation as something that must be achievable in spite of, rather than in conjunction with, larger situational influences.

WHAT ARE THE APPROPRIATE SUBGROUPS?

As pointed out repeatedly in this section, an adequate system for classifying subgroups of individuals who engage in antisocial behavior is critical to the development of successful interventions. It is unrealistic to expect that the same general prevention and intervention approaches will have a significant impact across the spectrum of individuals who engage in antisocial behaviors. Future advancements in theoretical and practical knowledge depend on our ability to disaggregate groups of antisocial individuals into homogeneous subgroups with either common etiologies or reactions to intervention.

Classification of antisocial individuals is a complicated undertaking, however, mainly because of the myriad interrelationships of different behaviors and the changes in patterns of behavior over time. Many individuals who display a particular form of antisocial behavior (e.g., aggression) often display other forms of antisocial behavior (e.g., drug use), but the presence of one is never a guarantee that the other behavior is also there. Also, individuals who display a particular antisocial behavior at one time in their development may or may not later display that behavior. They may, however, display another form of antisocial, or at-risk, behavior. There may be an underlying risk status responsible for different developmental manifestations, but the exact link between the earlier behavior and the later one may not be evident (Bell, 1986).

There are three basic approaches to the classification of antisocial individuals into subgroups. First, there are taxonomic systems based on observable behavior. Using this approach, individuals can be put into categories depending on the types of behaviors they have engaged in, with the idea that particular constellations of involvement indicate an underlying severity. Often times the history of prior treatments is also considered in an attempt to account for a dimension of amenability to certain interventions.

Systems relying on patterns of antisocial behavior and prior treatment are used primarily by service providers or courts to provide guidance for decision making about specific intervention alternatives (usually institutional placement; see Wiebush, Baird, Krisberg, & Onek, 1995). These approaches provide a way to systematize community or service provider values about the allocation of resources or the application of retribution, with the assumption that individuals having higher risk of reoffending should be given more intensive supervision or intervention. Approaches based on a single type of behavior have historically been inadequate methods for establishing these sorts of taxonomies. Burglars, for instance, might not be clearly much different from armed robbers, or children with school problems might not be that distinct from those with peer relationship issues. More multidimensional approaches are now pursued, often considering the breadth of adjustment difficulties as well as the intensity and severity of antisocial behaviors in different settings (Coie & Dodge, in press).

Second, there are clinical, diagnostic systems. In these approaches, individuals can be classified into groups based on the presence or absence of a particular pattern of behaviors or symptoms, not all of which are antisocial behaviors per se. Children meeting the criteria for conduct disorder or attention deficit disorder or adults having certain personality disorders or exhibiting psychopathy might be examined for their differential responses to particular intervention approaches (e.g., Rice & Harris, Chapter 40, this volume). The logic behind this approach is that the individuals falling into these different categories share some underlying, dispositional characteristics that should make their responses to interventions relatively uniform. By finding reliable methods for determining when someone fits these categories and determining which interventions show an effect with these individuals, adequate knowledge toward differential diagnosis and treatment can be accumulated and applied. Unfortunately, not all researchers use the same criteria, whether examining antisocial behavior in adolescents (e.g., Chamberlain & Friman, Chapter 39, this volume; Southam-Gerow & Kendall, Chapter 36, this volume) or adults (e.g., Karper & Krystal, Chapter 41, this volume; Tardiff, Chapter 42, this volume).

Third, there are classification strategies based on developmental pathways. These approaches are most useful for identifying children and adolescents who might respond differentially to intervention, based on the likely outcomes at their next stage in their movement toward an adult antisocial career. Perhaps the distinctions receiving the most attention currently are between early and late starters (Nagin & Farrington, 1992; Tolan & Thomas, 1995) and adolescent limited versus high-level and low-level chronics (Nagin, Farrington, & Moffitt, 1995). Considerable statistical work still needs to be done before different trajectories of the development of antisocial behavior can be clearly identified (Blumstein et al., 1985; Elliott, 1994; Moffitt, 1993).

Although these three approaches are widely used, it is rare for researchers making these distinctions to be clear about why they have chosen a particular strategy for determining subgroups of interest. Instead, investigators often simply divide their samples according to the distinctions that make the most sense to their disciplinary audience. Diagnostic groups are often examined separately, for example, without clear theoretical justification on why these groups should be expected to respond differently to the treatment offered. Overall developmental trajectories are often examined with little concern for the possible influences of case characteristics on these patterns of offending. General categories of more or less serious delinquents are examined without consideration for where they are in their "careers" of antisocial behavior. Although it is broadly acknowledged that analysis of subgroups is essential to knowing how to prevent or intervene with antisocial individuals, there is little integration of the different approaches to this task.

Future studies could be more useful if the purposes of subgroup analyses were considered in the original sampling and instrument development stages of research design. Studies looking at intervention effects with early starters having particular clinical characteristics such as attention deficit disorder, for example, could greatly increase our understanding of both etiology and effectiveness. Similarly, studies on adolescent samples of high policy interest (e.g., serious offenders transferred to adult court) could be more useful if they systematically varied their sampling according to age. To be truly useful, future studies will have to move beyond the simple recognition that subgroup analyses can be informative. They will have to move toward integrating these different methods for creating subgroups so that a fuller picture of specific effects can emerge.

CONCLUSION

Much valuable information is presented in the chapters in this part, and the authors provide an overview of prevention and intervention with antisocial behavior that cannot be found elsewhere. Nonetheless, this area of investigation remains rather disjointed. Bodies of highly developed research exist literally side-by-side in the literature, with limited integration of the insights of one area into the practice of the other.

This chapter has highlighted three issues that seem to pervade these sometimes disparate reviews and called for explicit consideration of these issues in future research. Specifically, we are hoping that future researchers expend effort on clarifying what is meant by risk factors, assessing when it is appropriate to search for technology, and deciding what are appropriate subgroups.

Increased clarity on these issues would promote more focused research in several of the areas reviewed as well as a more coherent, next generation of research findings. The development of more effective prevention and intervention strategies would benefit from such an effort.

Finally, it is worth noting that a call for such an integration of approaches is within the spirit of Saleem Shah, to whom this collection is dedicated. Anyone familiar with Saleem personally or with his writings realizes that what he brought to the research endeavor was a continuing call to look beyond one's own disciplinary and practice boundaries. He brought people together and challenged ideas in light of what other researchers' work had shown. His was a call to learn from what others had done and to keep an eye on the potential utility of whatever one might do. We would do well to heed his advice in fashioning our next generation of research on antisocial behavior.

REFERENCES

Andrews, D., Zinger, I., Hoge, R., Bonta, J., Gendreau, P., & Cullen, F. (1990). Does correctional treatment work? A clinically relevant and psychologically informed meta-analysis. *Criminology, 28,* 369–404.

Bell, R. Q. (1986). Age-specific manifestations in changing psychosocial risk. In D. C. Farran & J. D. McKinney (Eds.), *The concept of risk in intellectual and psychosocial development* (pp. 124–138). New York: Academic Press.

Berk, R. (1983). An introduction to sample selection bias in sociological data. *American Sociological Review, 48,* 386–398.

Blumstein, A., Farrington, D. P., & Moitra, S. (1985). Delinquency careers: Innocents, desisters, and persisters. In M. Tonry & N. Morris (Eds.), *Crime and Justice* (Vol. 6, pp. 187–222). Chicago: University of Chicago Press.

Blyth, D. A., & Leffert, N. (1995). Communities as contexts for adolescent development: An empirical analysis. *Journal of Adolescent Research, 10,* 64–87.

Brooks-Gunn, J., Duncan, G. J., Klebanov, P. K., & Sealand, N. (1993). Do neighborhoods influence child and adolescent development? *American Journal of Sociology, 99,* 383–395.

Caprara, G. V., & Rutter, M. (1995). Individual development and social change: Time trends and their causes. In M. Rutter & D. J. Smith (Eds.), *Psychosocial disorders in young people* (pp. 35–66). New York: Wiley.

Coie, J., & Dodge, K. (in press). Aggression and antisocial behavior. In W. Damon (Ed.), *Handbook of child psychology: Vol. 3. Social, emotional, and personality development* (5th ed.). New York: Wiley.

Compas, B. E., Hinden, B. R., & Gerhardt, C. A. (1995). Adolescent development. Pathways and processes of risk and resilience. *Annual Review of Psychology, 46,* 265–293.

Coulton, C. J., Korbin, J. E., Su, M., & Chow, J. (1995). Community level factors and child maltreatment rates. *Child Development, 66,* 1262–1276.

DiPrete, T. A., & Forristal, J. D. (1994). Multilevel models: Methods and substance. *Annual Review of Sociology, 20,* 331–357.

Elliott, D. S. (1994). Serious violent offenders: Onset, developmental course, and termination—The American Society of Criminology 1993 presidential address. *Criminology, 32,* 1–21.

Farrington, D. P. (1995). The challenge of teenage antisocial behavior. In M. Rutter (Ed.), *Psychosocial disturbances in young people* (pp. 83–130). Cambridge: Cambridge University Press.

Farrington, D. P., Loeber, R., Elliott, D. S., Hawkins, J. D., Kandel, D. B., Klein, M. W., McCord, J., Rowe, D. C., & Tremblay, R. E. (1990). Advancing knowledge about the onset of delinquency and crime. In B. B. Lahey & A. E. Kazdin (Eds.), *Clinical child psychology* (Vol. 13, pp. 283–342). New York: Plenum.

Felner, R. D., Phillips, R. S. C., DuBois, D., & Lease, A. M. (1991). Ecological interventions and the process of change for prevention: Wedding theory and research to implementation in real world settings. *American Journal of Community Psychology, 19,* 379–387.

Guba, E. G., & Lincoln, Y. S. (1989). *Fourth generation evaluation.* Newbury Park, CA: Sage Publications.

Hox, J. J., & Kreft, I. G. (1994). Multilevel analysis methods. *Sociological Methods and Research, 22,* 283–299.

Jessor, R., Van Den Bos, J., Vanderryn, J., Costa, F. M., & Turbin, M. S. (1995). Protective factors in adolescent problem behavior: Moderator effects and developmental change. *Developmental Psychology, 31,* 923–933.

Kazdin, A. E. (1993). Treatment of conduct disorder: Progress and directions in psychotherapy research. *Development and Psychopathology, 5,* 277–310.

Kelly, J. G. (1986). Content and process: An ecological view of the interdependence of practice and research. *American Journal of Community Psychology, 14,* 581–589.

Klein, M. W. (1983). Where juvenile justice meets social service. Social intervention with troubled youth. In E. Seidman (Ed.), *Handbook of social intervention* (pp. 362–384). Beverly Hills, CA: Sage Publications.

Kraemer, H., Kazdin, A., Offord, D., Kessler, R., & Kupfer, D. (in press). Coming to terms with the terms of risk. *Archives of General Psychiatry.*

Kupersmidt, J. B., Griesler, P. C., DeRosier, M. E., Patterson, C. J., & Davis, P. W. (1995). Childhood aggression and peer relations in the context of family and neighborhood factors. *Child Development, 66,* 360–375.

Martin, D. C., Diehr, P., Perrin, E. B., & Koepsell, T. D. (1993). The effect of matching on the power of randomized community intervention studies. *Statistics in Medicine, 12,* 329–338.

Moffitt, T. E. (1990). The neuropsychology of delinquency: A critical review of theory and research. In N. Morris & M. Tonry (Eds.), *Crime and justice* (Vol. 12, pp. 99–169). Chicago: University of Chicago Press.

Moffitt, T. E. (1993). Adolescence-limited and life-course-persistent antisocial behavior: A developmental taxonomy. *Psychological Review, 100,* 674–701.

Munoz, R. F., Snowden, L. R., Kelly, J. G., & Associates (Eds.). (1979). *Social and psychological research in community settings.* San Francisco: Jossey-Bass.

Nagin, D., & Farrington, D. P. (1992). The onset and persistence of offending. *Criminology, 30,* 501–523.

Nagin, D., Farrington, D., & Moffitt, T. (1995). Life course trajectories of different types of offenders. *Criminology, 33,* 111–139.

Rappaport, J., Seidman, E., & Davidson, W. S. (1979). Demonstration research and manifest versus true adoption: The natural history of a research project to divert adolescents from the legal system. In R. F. Munoz, L. R. Snowden, J. G. Kelly, & Associates (Eds.), *Social and psychological research in community settings* (pp. 101–144). San Francisco: Jossey-Bass.

Rose, G. (1985). Sick individuals and sick populations. *International Journal of Epidemiology, 14,* 32–38.

Rutter, M. (1979). Protective factors in children's response to stress and disadvantage. In W. M. Ken & J. E. Rolf (Eds.), *Primary prevention of psychopathology* (Vol. 3, pp. 49–74). Hanover, NH: University Press of New England.

Rutter, M. (1990). Psychosocial resilience and protective mechanisms. In J. E. Rolf, A. S. Masten, D. Cicchetti, K. H. Nuechterlein, & S. Weintraub (Eds.), *Risk and protective factors in the development of psychopathology* (pp. 181–214). New York: Cambridge University Press.

Sarason, S. B. (1978). The nature of problem solving in social action. *American Psychologist, 33,* 370–380.

Tate, D., Reppucci, N. D., Mulvey, E. P. (1995). Violent juvenile delinquents: Treatment effectiveness and implications for future action. *American Psychologist, 50,* 777–782.

Tolan, P. H., & Thomas, P. (1995). The implications of age of onset for delinquency risk: II. Longitudinal data. *Journal of Abnormal Child Psychology, 23,* 157–181.

Trickett, E. J. (1991). Paradigms and the research report: Making what actually happens a heuristic for theory. *American Journal of Community Psychology, 19,* 365–370.

Walsh, R. (1987). The evolution of the research relationship in community psychology. *American Journal of Community Psychology, 15,* 773–788.

West, S. G., Aiken, L. S., & Todd, M. (1993). Probing the effects of individual components in multiple component prevention programs. *American Journal of Community Psychology, 21,* 571–606.

Wiebush, R. G., Baird, C., Krisberg, B., & Onek, D. (1995). Risk assessment and classification for serious, violent, and chronic juvenile offenders. In J. C. Howell, B. Krisberg, J. D. Hawkins, & J. J. Wilson (Eds.), *A sourcebook on serious, violent, and chronic juvenile offenders* (pp. 171–212). Thousand Oaks, CA: Sage Publications.

Winship, C., & Mare, R. D. (1992). Models for sample selection bias. *Annual Review of Sociology, 18,* 327–350.

PART FIVE

Special Issues and Special Populations

CHAPTER 44

Cross-Cultural Perspectives on Antisocial Behavior

NORMAN G. DINGES, MERA M. ATLIS, and GINA M. VINCENT

This chapter develops a framework for a cross-cultural understanding of antisocial behavior. We approach this topic by focusing primarily on the history and current applications of the concept of antisocial personality disorder and secondarily by reviewing the related research on precursor behaviors such as delinquency. This strategy is necessitated by a notable gap in the cross-cultural literature on conduct disorder, as indicated by recent reviews (Blue & Griffith, 1995). We consider the history of the antisocial personality concept with reference to cultural and ethnic issues, examine the theoretical context and controversial issues involved in its definition and clinical application, and review and critique the empirical research.

Despite caution on the contextual issues associated with cultural and ethnic issues in cross-cultural settings (Hinton & Kleinman, 1993), there has been surprisingly little attention given their use in the diagnosis of antisocial personality. Perhaps this reflects the limited attention to cultural and ethnic factors that has characterized the general approach to psychiatric nosology and the Axis II personality disorders in particular. Or this neglect may reflect the trend over the last few decades to discover the biological etiology of mental disorders while continuing to use descriptive symptom criteria to increase the reliability of psychiatric diagnoses. It is surprising, nonetheless, that diagnoses that, at least on the surface, appear so clearly fraught with socially evaluative symptom criteria (e.g., lack of remorse, deceitfulness) should not have been at the forefront of the cross-cultural debate about the uses of psychiatric diagnoses. By contrast, the diagnoses of schizophrenia and depression, both of which are hypothesized to be more biologically based in their etiology, have received far more cross-cultural attention (Berry, Poortinga, Segall, & Dassen, 1992; Maser & Dinges, 1993).

THE HISTORY OF ANTISOCIAL PERSONALITY DISORDER

The precursor of the modern concept of the antisocial personality disorder (ASPD) dates from the late 1700s, when Pinel (1801/1977) observed a group of white "madmen" suffering from what he called *manie sans delire* ("insanity without delirium").

The concept of *manie sans delire* has evolved through a series of clinical descriptors and diagnostic criteria to become what we now classify as antisocial personality disorder on Axis II of the *Diagnostic and Statistical Manual of Mental Disorders* (*DSM-IV*; American Psychiatric Association, 1994). Although the criteria for this diagnosis have continually evolved, the reference samples on which they were established typically have been comprised primarily of the populations of white males of Western descent on whom until quite recently the overall modern psychiatric nomenclature has been based (Hinton & Kleinman, 1993). Questions about the cross-cultural validity of the diagnosis of ASPD have suffered a fate similar to other psychiatric diagnoses insofar as the core behavioral characteristics and the distinguishing symptom criteria have been assumed to be universally applicable.

As a means of providing some historical background by which to assess the cross-cultural validity of antisocial personality disorder, we placed the symptom criteria from the most widely accepted diagnostic frameworks and instruments into three content-based categories of intrapersonal characteristics (traits), interpersonal behaviors, and criminal behaviors (Cleckley, 1955; American Psychiatric Association, 1952, 1968, 1980, 1987, 1994); *International Classification of Diseases and Related Health Problems* (*ICD-10*; World Health Organization, 1990); Hare Psychopathy Checklist–Revised (PCL-R; Hare, 1991). *Criminal behaviors* refer to observable conflicts with legal norms, such as aggression that leads to physical fights or assault, failure to honor financial obligations, juvenile delinquency, and failure to conform to social norms. *Interpersonal characteristics* refer to behaviors exhibited within the individual's social environment that brings him or her into conflict with others. The interpersonal category includes social interactions such as unreliability, dishonesty, callousness, and an inability to maintain consistent work behavior or intimate relationships or to function as a parent. *Intrapersonal characteristics* involve inferred, nonobservable, processes that have traditionally been seen as internal, such as a lack of judgment, impulsivity, an inability to feel remorse or guilt, an inability to learn from punishment, and rationalizing or blaming others for one's behavior. In terms of cross-cultural validity, it might be argued that symptoms of criminal and interpersonal behaviors are less discriminative because of their varying definitions in different cultural settings. By contrast, intrapersonal characteristics, such as the thought processes and motivations underlying antisocial behaviors, might be amenable to greater cross-cultural consensus and presumptive universality.

As Figure 44.1 indicates, Cleckley (1955) first enumerated the diagnostic criteria for the disorder he originally termed *sociopathy,* and later, *psychopathy.* Based on observations of white, middle-class, male patients in a mental hospital setting, Cleckley's criteria focused largely on the intrapersonal symptomology of these men, with no mention of their criminal behavior patterns. Derived from largely the same clinical population, the *DSM-I* diagnosis for sociopathic personality disturbance: antisocial reaction (American Psychiatric Association, 1952), and the *DSM-II* diagnosis of antisocial personality disorder (American Psychiatric Association, 1968) retained much of Cleckley's original diagnostic concept and symptom content, with the exception of the introduction of a few criminal behaviors. However, as the *DSM-II* cautioned, "A mere history of repeated criminal or social offenses is not sufficient to justify this diagnosis" (American Psychiatric Association, 1968, as cited in Hare, 1991).

The diagnosis of ASPD was transformed with the publication of the *DSM-III* (American Psychiatric Association, 1980) and *DSM-III-R* (American Psychiatric Association, 1987). Formerly defined by symptoms that were primarily considered psychological in nature, the diagnosis now was based almost entirely on criminal acts and inappropriate interpersonal behaviors. Moreover, it also became necessary for an individual to have shown evidence of a conduct disorder, based almost entirely on participation in criminal

acts such as truancy, theft, and vandalism before age 15 in order to receive the antisocial personality disorder diagnosis as an adult. As critically reviewed by Widiger and Corbitt (1995), this form of the ASPD definition has engendered a number of criticisms, not the least of which is an overemphasis on overt criminal acts and related behaviors and a general neglect of personality traits.

The contemporary context uses three classification approaches to diagnosing antisocial personality disorder, the *DSM-IV* (American Psychiatric Association, 1994), *ICD-10,* (World Health Organization, 1990), and the PCL-R (Hare, 1991). Each has been shaped to some degree by explicit or implicit considerations of cross-cultural applicability. Although cross-cultural validity was a priority in the construction of the *ICD-10* as an international system of diagnosis, the symptom criteria were still defined largely by Western ideals of conduct. However, the *ICD-10* conceptualization of *dyssocial personality disorder* emphasizes intrapersonal and interpersonal symptoms rather than criminal acts and thus indicates a shift toward a "personality-based" definition of ASPD. Similarly, out of disappointment in the shift toward criminal behavior criteria in the *DSM-III,* Hare (1990) developed the PCL and later, the PCL-R (Hart, Hare, & Harpur, 1992). Hare attributes much of the clinical basis for the PCL-R to Cleckley's concept of the *psychopath.* Consequently, the majority of items in the PCL-R load on two factors: Factor 1 is characterized by interpersonal and affective characteristics, and Factor 2 is described by characteristics reflecting an impulsive, antisocial, and unstable lifestyle. Although the PCL-R retained some criminal behaviors among its diagnostic criteria, the

Figure 44.1 *Historical changes in antisocial personality disorder symptom criteria classified as intrapersonal, interpersonal, or criminal.*

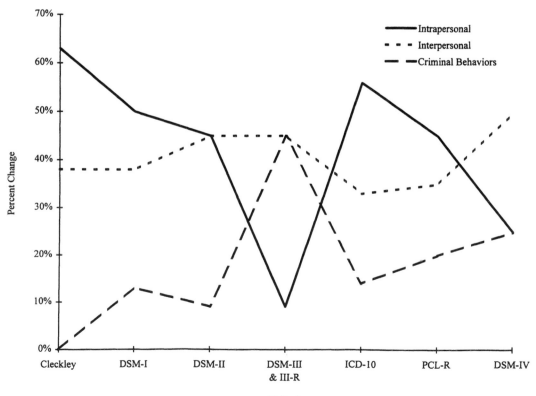

interpersonal and intrapersonal symptomologies must be present to elicit the antisocial personality diagnosis.

Perhaps reflective of implicit cross-cultural validity concerns, the *DSM-IV* also appears to have returned, at least partially, to more traditional concepts of antisocial personality disorder. Most notably, the *DSM-IV* was the first edition to formally indicate that the diagnosis of ASPD may be applied inappropriately to individuals from settings in which "seemingly antisocial behavior" could be the result of a protective survival strategy. The *DSM-IV* compensates for this problem by asking clinicians "to consider the social and economic context in which the behaviors occur" (American Psychiatric Association, 1994, p. 647) before applying the diagnosis.

Although the *DSM-IV* is a step toward a more cross-culturally valid system of diagnosis for ASPD, it continues to contain a large component of criminal behaviors as the dominant diagnostic criteria. One reason for this transition from the criteria in the *DSM-I* and *DSM-II* to the modern criteria of the *DSM-III* and *DSM-IV* has been the need to shift to more objective signs and symptoms. According to Robins (1995), the *DSM-I* was constructed "mainly to give hospitals a common coding system" (p. 135). With the advent of the *DSM-III* and particularly the *DSM-IV*, it was also necessary to have a reliable instrument that met the needs of insurance companies and researchers. In the interest of reliability, intrapersonal criteria were sacrificed for observable behaviors. However, this change may mask potentially more cross-culturally discriminative symptom criteria from the intrapersonal and interpersonal domains. Assuming that the diagnosis of antisocial personality disorder awaits future empirical demonstration of its cross-cultural validity, the content of the *ICD-10* and PCL-R criteria provides more balanced symptom domains and is potentially more sensitive to cross-cultural variations in what may indeed turn out to be a universally recognized mental disorder.

THEORETICAL CONTEXT AND CONTROVERSIAL ISSUES

Since the mid-1970s, there has been a period of dynamic growth in the refined conceptualization and instrumentation with which to examine the role of culture in causing and shaping the course of psychopathology (Alarcon, 1995). During the same period, the standard psychiatric nomenclature has shown a dramatic increase in both the number of diagnostic entities defined for classification and the emergence of the multiaxial system that characterizes *DSM-IV* and its precursors *DSM-III* and *DSM-III-R*. Unfortunately, these two rapidly developing areas have proceeded along parallel pathways with limited cross-fertilization, as exemplified by the relatively minor attention given to potential cross-cultural misuses of psychiatric classification when applied to members of ethnic minorities or non-Western societies (Hinton & Kleinman, 1993).

The limited interaction of these parallel areas of development ended with the formation of the National Institute of Mental Health (NIMH) Working Group on Culture and *DSM-IV*. This group was formed later than other *DSM-IV* working groups. Consequently, its contribution occurred relatively late in the process of creating the *DSM-IV*. Although the extensive recommendations of the group on the role of culture in diagnosis and classification

were dramatically downsized in relation to other components of the *DSM-IV*, there have been several noteworthy additions. Among the additions to the *DSM-IV* manual are the following: (a) introductory material on culture, (b) sections on culture for each diagnostic category, (c) an appendix describing the process of creating a cultural case formulation, (d) a glossary of "culture-bound" syndromes, and (e) a forthcoming sourcebook on culture and diagnosis. Of particular note was the omission of the recommended illustrative cross-ethnic and cross-cultural cases for each section of the *DSM-IV Casebook*. Despite rather pointed criticisms of the limited attention given to cultural issues in the *DSM-IV* (Alarcon, 1995), the stage appears to have been set for more attention to cultural content in future revisions.

A cross-cultural perspective on antisocial personality disorder is nested within the ongoing debate on the sociocultural influences on the etiology, symptoms, and course of mental disorders in general, and the rapidly developing area of cross-cultural and international psychopathology classification in particular (Hinton & Kleinman, 1993). Although space limitations do not permit a full review of these developments, it is important to recognize several recurrent and often controversial themes that have characterized this debate.

1. One major theme has focused on the distinction between the *universal* (found in all cultures) and the *particular* (found in only some cultures) nature of various mental disorders. There appears to be empirical support for the universal nature of some mental disorders, such as schizophrenia and depression, albeit with considerable controversy about their phenomenology as well as their core and peripheral symptoms (Manson, 1995). Considerable controversy surrounds other disorders. For example, Paris (1991) asserts the universality of antisocial personality disorder, whereas others have called its universality into question or pointed to its limited clinical utility due to grossly overdiagnosing specific populations such as inner-city Black males (Mezzich et al., 1992).

2. A corollary issue (assuming universal occurrence) is whether ASPD would maintain an *invariant factor structure* insofar as the symptom criteria were similarly grouped and weighted in other cultures or ethnic groups. As our description of the historical shifts in symptom criteria indicates, and as our later review of research findings shows, precious little evidence exists to support an assertion of cross-cultural or cross-ethnic invariant factor structure for ASPD.

3. Another key theme has been the *implicit monocultural evaluative framework* that guides the construction and classification of the *DSM*. Nuckolls (1992) and Agich (1994) provide an extensive philosophical critique of the social and evaluative underpinnings of the personality disorders in general and antisocial personality disorder in particular. Agich (1994) contends that irrespective of their defining criteria, judgments of antisocial personality should not be treated as context-independent (and by extension value-neutral) prototype judgments. In terms of the historical debate on the personal pathology versus social deviance nature of ASPD, Agich (1994) is squarely in the social deviance camp by asserting the dependence of diagnostic judgments on an evaluative framework of behavioral appropriateness that cannot be justified without due regard for the specific circumstances and the context of the behaviors.

4. Yet another theme regards the definition of the self on a continuum emphasizing a more *egocentric orientation* (attending to self and maintaining independence from others) or *sociocentric orientation* (attending to others, fitting in, harmonious interdependence; Schweder & Bourne, 1984). Definitions of the self along this continuum have obvious implications for the behavioral thresholds and intrapersonal symptom criteria that could be used in assessing antisocial behavior. Fuller consideration of this issue also concerns definitions of the individual locus (psychopathology) as opposed to social group locus (social pathology) of antisocial behavior explanations. This issue has been discussed more fully in the cross-cultural examination of other mental disorders (Lutz, 1985) and should be examined at greater length with respect to the diagnosis of antisocial personality disorder.

5. As anticipated by (4), perhaps the most important theme has been the contention that antisocial personality does not define a *concept of personality* at all, but rather a *concept of social deviance.* Thus it fails to account for contextual information needed to make normative judgments of its acceptability or rejection by culturally different communities (Agich, 1994). For example, personality disorders are typically defined by the pervasiveness of the behaviors that characterize a particular diagnostic subtype and are considered highly resistant to change. This view fails to account for community dysfunctions that may promote and reward criminal and other antisocial behaviors. It also fails to account for the acculturative pressures on recent immigrant and refugee groups in which their enclave of socialization temporarily (or perhaps permanently) sanctions criminal and antisocial behaviors as a necessary antecedent to attaining economic stability in the host culture. Such phenomena are especially likely to be seen in refugee groups containing significant numbers of former members of the military or criminal class from the culture of origin.

In addition to these concerns, Hinton and Kleinman (1993), Kleinman and Fabrega (1992), and Alarcon (1995) argue for the very problematic nature of ASPD on cross-cultural clinical utility grounds. In this light, it is somewhat surprising that the most recent review of other controversial aspects of antisocial personality disorder did not specifically consider any of the cross-cultural issues discussed earlier (Widiger & Corbitt, 1995).

CROSS-CULTURAL METHODOLOGICAL ISSUES

We turn now to a review of the empirical studies of antisocial behavior, beginning first with a brief summary of some methodological problems that have characterized cross-cultural psychopathology research. These same problems are present throughout consideration of the cross-cultural applicability of the antisocial personality disorder construct.

In a frequently cited paper, Good and Good (1986) described several cross-cultural methodological concerns that required attention when using definitions of psychopathology and standardized diagnostic measures with populations other than the predominantly White, middle-class, North American populations for whom they were originally designed. The cautionary note of these methodological problems is equally applicable for informed understanding of putatively antisocial behaviors in cross-cultural settings.

The problem of *normative uncertainty* addresses interpretation of the type, level, and duration of symptoms that require assump-

tions about definitions of the normal and abnormal from culture to culture. Figure 44.1 depicts the shifting nature of the intrapersonal, interpersonal, and criminal behaviors that have been used to define antisocial personality disorder according to different classification systems used in North America. Despite the shifting nature of the symptomatology, a high degree of confidence in the diagnostic criteria led to ASPD being the only personality disorder included in the Epidemiological Catchment Area (ECA) studies. But there was little prior evidence that the threshold and core symptoms were similarly defined and equally weighted for severity across the different ethnic minorities included in the ECA sample. In contrast to the discussion of the many issues of symptom array and clinical judgment complexity that went into the final criteria for *DSM-IV* antisocial personality disorder, questions on the cross-cultural validity of the diagnosis went unaddressed (Widiger & Corbitt, 1995).

The process used to obtain agreement about the final diagnostic criteria for antisocial personality disorder in different versions of the *DSM* appears to reflect the problem of *centricultural bias.* As the research findings that follow indicate, it may be possible to qualify individuals from different cultures for a diagnosis of antisocial personality disorder using *DSM-III* and *DSM-III-R* criteria. However, because the diagnostic criteria were developed and validated without concern for cross-cultural applications, a number of other symptoms of equal or greater importance may have been omitted in determining what constitutes antisocial behavior from an indigenous culture's perspective. Some of the criminal behaviors included in the diagnostic criteria may have received little, if any, weight from other cultural perspectives that view such acts as part of social protest or profit-oriented behaviors in an environment of limited social recognition or economic opportunity. Indeed, many of the current diagnostic criteria assume an economic opportunity structure that supports individual and family social stability as a normative expectancy for ethnic minority communities. This expectancy is obviously at odds with the reality of recent immigrant and refugee populations as well as more established ethnic groups. Centricultural bias also may have precluded the identification of symptoms and behaviors that would be readily identified by ethnic community members as more valid indicators of pathological antisocial behavior. Consequently, although there may be universal recognition of the "antisocial personality" construct, distinctly different sets of behaviors may comprise its definition for different ethnic populations.

There is empirical support for the problem of *indeterminacy of meaning,* as indicated by the relatively modest levels of interrater reliability for some of the more trait-based antisocial personality symptom criteria, such as "lacks empathy," that were part of the development of *DSM-IV* (Widiger & Corbitt, 1995). As studies of other diagnostic entities have indicated, symptom criteria often lack semantic equivalence (as well as functional and metric equivalence) when applied cross culturally (Manson, 1995). This is particularly problematic when internal emotional states such as guilt, shame, and sinfulness are being represented (Manson, Shore, & Bloom, 1985). For example, an item such as "lack of remorse" might be particularly problematic when applied in shame cultures (e.g., many sociocentric Asian cultures) as opposed to more egocentric-oriented Western cultures based on Judeo-Christian concepts of individual "sin." Similarly, "deceitfulness" may have a culturally different meaning in decidedly unequal social power exchanges or in situations of potential embarrassment, and "irresponsibility" may be problematic when viewed in the context of frequent job changes or absenteeism resulting from culturally prescribed role obligations to one's family. Consequently, reluctance to admit to profoundly embarrassing or extremely shameful behaviors might be construed as dissembling or evasive and thus deceitful. Similarly, frequent work absences because of prepotent culturally prescribed attendance at extended grief ceremonies or the need to provide transportation for members of a large extended family may convey the strong impression of a person who has little concern for job responsibilities.

Finally, the problem of *category validity* refers to applying a category created for one culture to others for which it may not be applicable. Although the universality of the ASPD category has been posited, there are no formal investigations to directly test this assumption. Diagnosis of antisocial personality disorder among Black or Hispanic groups using current *DSM-IV* symptom criteria may be due more to the methods used than to the cross-cultural validity of the antisocial personality category. The authors of this chapter accept that something like antisocial personality disorder probably occurs in most, if not all, American ethnic minorities, but not that it is adequately or even necessarily defined by the *DSM-IV* criteria. An approach that first determined the semantic equivalence across cultures of *DSM-IV* criteria and then combined these criteria with indigenous criteria for antisocial behavior, including associated motivational and emotional characteristics, would undoubtedly provide a more complete, valid, and clinically useful cross-cultural category of ASPD.

CURRENT FINDINGS

The following is a brief review of current research related to ethnic group differences in antisocial behavior and includes: (a) epidemiological studies that used large, representative samples to examine ethnic differences in antisocial personality disorder; (b) studies that used convenience samples from institutionalized populations for similar comparisons; and (c) select cross-cultural and cross-ethnic studies of delinquent behavior that are included because they lend perspective to cultural and ethnic influences on antisocial behavior (see Cloninger, Bayon, & Przybeck, Chapter 2, this volume; Widiger & Corbitt, Chapter 7, this volume).

Epidemiological Studies

Several epidemiological studies reported prevalence rates for antisocial personality disorder and delinquency among different ethnic groups (see Table 44.1). Four of these used portions of the ECA sample of 19,182 individuals from five different sites around the United States (i.e., St. Louis, Baltimore, New Haven, Los Angeles, and Durham), including individuals residing in institutions such as prisons and psychiatric hospitals. Based on *DSM-III* symptom criteria obtained through the NIMH Diagnostic Interview Schedule (Robins & Regier, 1991), these studies found no significant differences in the prevalence rates of ASPD across White, Black, and Hispanic groups within the United States (Burnam et al., 1987; Robins et al., 1984; Robins, Tipp, & Przybeck, 1991). A similar lack of difference in ethnic group prevalence rates was also found

in the National Comorbidity Survey (Kessler et al., 1994). By contrast, the National Vietnam Veterans Readjustment Study (NVVRS), which matched war theater veterans and civilian counterparts for ethnicity and sex, found that lifetime prevalence rates for ASPD were significantly higher overall for Vietnam veterans compared to civilians, and 6 months prevalence rates were significantly higher among Blacks versus White/Other and Black versus Hispanic veterans (Kulka et al., 1990).

In addition, the National Longitudinal Survey of Youth (NLSY) found that White females reported higher levels of delinquency than Black females (Windle, 1990). Conversely, significantly more Black males have committed a serious violent offense by age 17 than White males, and nearly twice as many Black males continued their violent offenses into their 20s. Interestingly, there were no racial differences in the likelihood of having a violent career for males between the ages of 18 and 20 who were employed or living with a partner (Elliot, 1994).

Of particular interest are differences in the content of the antisocial personality diagnosis and its common external correlates across ethnic groups within the United States. Robins et al. (1991), for example, found content differences when trying to explain why minority groups were overrepresented in arrested and incarcerated populations yet did not have significantly higher diagnosis rates for ASPD (see Yung & Hammond, Chapter 45, this volume). Two reasons were offered to account for this discrepancy. First, in the nondiagnosed portion of the sample, Blacks were more likely than Whites to have used weapons in their criminal offenses. It is possible that there is a greater acceptance of weapon use in the Black community, increasing their risk for imprisonment regardless of their rate of antisocial personality disorder. Second, it was suggested that arrested Blacks tended to be more normal than Whites with the same arrest history. Other differences were found in the childhood behavior problems that are typically viewed as precursor symptoms predictive of adult antisocial personality disorder. For example, Black adolescent males who were suspended or expelled from school were significantly less likely to receive a diagnosis of adult ASPD than were White male or Black female adolescents exhibiting the same behavior patterns (Robins et al. 1991).

Interesting ethnic group differences in the correlates of antisocial personality disorder have also been noted for substance abuse, intelligence, and intimate relationship problems. Consistent with the differential diagnosis problem associated with the high comorbidity between ASPD and psychoactive substance abuse (Widiger & Corbitt, 1995), Windle (1990) found non-Black adolescents were more likely than Black adolescents to have substance abuse problems. Moreover, the relationship between ASPD and lower intelligence was found to be much stronger for Whites than for Blacks or Hispanics, and multiple divorces and separations were more strongly related to ASPD for Whites and Hispanics than Blacks (Windle, 1990).

Studies of Institutionalized Populations

A few studies investigated adult ethnic differences in antisocial personality disorder within institutionalized populations such as prison inmates and forensic psychiatric hospital patients. Teplin (1994), for example, found that in jail detainees, White men had a

TABLE 44.1   Epidemiological Studies Citing Prevalence Rates for Antisocial Personality Disorder

Authors	Method	Findings
Epidemiological Catchment Area (ECA) studies		

Robins et al. (1984)	*ECA Sample: N* = 9,543 adults
	New Haven—5,060, 10% Black, 90% non-Black
	Baltimore—3,560, 34% Black, 66% non-Black
	St. Louis—3,200, 19% Black, 81% non-Black
	Instruments: Diagnostic Interview Schedule
	    (DIS; *DSM-III*)
		Differences between Blacks and Whites were modest and not consistent across sites. The lifetime prevalence rates of ASPD were
		    New Haven: Black (1.7%), non-Black (2.1%)
		    Baltimore: Black (2.3%), non-Black (2.7%)
		    St. Louis: Black (3.9%), non-Black (3.1%)

Burnam et al. (1987)	*ECA Sample: N* = 3,125 adults Los Angeles—42% White, 40% Mexican American	Sex and ethnicity were not significant predictors of antisocial personality disorder. The prevalence of ASPD was slightly higher in Mexican Americans (1.2%) than in Whites (0.4%) and was their fifth most common disorder.
Compton et al. (1991)	*Sample: N* = 18,320 adults 60% Taiwanese (metropolitan, small towns, and rural) 40% American (community residence ECA samples)	The lifetime prevalence rate of ASPD was significantly lower for Taiwanese (0.10%–0.22%) than Americans (1.49%–5.66%).
Robins et al. (1991)	*ECA Sample: N* = 19,182 adults Durham: 4,101; 63% White, 36% Black, 0.5% Hispanic Los Angeles: 3,261; 51% White, 5% Black, 45% Hispanic St. Louis, New Haven, and Baltimore (see Robins et al., 1984)	Rates of ASPD were not significantly different between ethnic groups. As compared to Whites: Black arrestees and weapon users less often met criteria for ASPD; Black weapon users were less likely to have had childhood behavior problems; most childhood behaviors were less predictive of ASPD; multiple divorces and separations were associated less with ASPD.
The National Vietnam Veterans Readjustment Study (NVVRS)		

Kulka et al. (1990)	*Sample: N* = 2,980 veterans
	18% Hispanic, 18% Black, and 34% Other men,
	    30% females
	Instruments: DIS
		Six months prevalence rates for ASPD were significantly higher among Blacks vs. Whites/Other and Blacks vs. Hispanics. Lifetime prevalence rates for ASPD are higher in veterans than in civilians and ECA sample.
		    Black men: Theater veterans (13%), civilian counterparts (8.5%)
		    Hispanic men: Theater veterans (9.2%), civilian counterparts (0.8%)
		    White/Other men: Theater veterans (9.1%), civilian counterparts (3.7%)

National Longitudinal Survey of Youth (NLSY)		
Windle (1990)	*Sample: N* = 2,411 youths 52% male, 48% female 57% White, 25% Black, 18% Hispanic *Instruments:* 20 antisocial behavior Likert-scale items	Men commit delinquent acts more frequently than women, with the exception of running away. White females reported higher levels of delinquency than Black females. Non-Black status was predictive of late-adolescent substance use and dependency symptoms.
National Youth Survey (NYS)		
Elliot (1994)	*Sample: N* = 1,725 youths *Instruments:* Self-report measure of serious violent offense	Thirty-six percent of Black and 25% of White males have committed a serious violent offense by age 17. The onset of a serious violent career is one year younger for Blacks. Nearly twice as many Blacks as Whites continue their violent offenses into their 20s, but differences disappear between 18 and 20 for those living with a partner or having employment.
National Comorbidity Survey (NCS)		
Kessler et al. (1994)	*Sample: N* = 8,098 adults 75.3% White, 11.5% Black, 9.7% Hispanic, 3.5% Other *Instruments:* Composite International Diagnostic Interview	Prevalence rates of ASPD were not significantly different between ethnic groups. Blacks had lower prevalence of all disorders than Whites.

significantly higher prevalence rate of the ASPD diagnosis than either Blacks or Hispanics. This conflicts with findings from the ECA sample that indicated no difference in prevalence rates across ethnic groups in community settings.

The 10 normative samples used in the development of the PCL came from incarcerated White males (Hare, 1991), with the exception of two samples of Blacks and one sample of Canadian Indians. According to Hare (1991), the reliability of PCL and PCL-R total scores do not differ between the racial groups studied thus far, differences in mean scores appear to be small in practical terms, and the external correlates of the PCL and PCL-R total scores are similar for racial groups. However, Kosson, Smith, and Newman (1990) found that although the PCL was reliable with Blacks, there were differences in the distribution of PCL scores and the factor structure between Whites and Blacks. In addition, Black inmates received significantly higher psychopathy ratings overall and were charged with significantly more violent crimes (mainly because of a higher proportion of robberies). Interestingly, in Black inmates, impulsivity, one of the main external correlates of psychopathy, was not significantly related to the existence of psychopathy.

Cross-Cultural Studies of Delinquency and Acculturative Influences

Although they do not focus specifically on diagnostic issues, selected studies of delinquency and acculturative influences are summarized here. Such studies may be heuristic for future investigations of antisocial behavior in which better understanding of contextual factors can be achieved when examining the more limited set of symptom criteria used in diagnosing ASPD. They may also be useful insofar as antisocial personality disorder requires a diagnosis of conduct disorder, and delinquent behaviors are often part of that diagnosis. Studies that have focused more specifically on acculturative influences may also enhance our understanding of culturally mediated antisocial behaviors.

The findings from a number of studies of adolescents in juvenile detention centers suggest that Whites display more antisocial behaviors. Specifically, White delinquents reported significantly higher rates of illicit drug use (Dembo, La Voie, Schmeidler, & Washborn, 1987), psychological dysfunction, and troubled family backgrounds (Dembo, Williams, & Schmeidler, 1994) than their Black counterparts. White adjudicated minors also demonstrated more generalized delinquency patterns than Hispanic Americans (Lyon, Henggeler, & Hall, 1992). Other studies of cross-cultural differences in delinquency found that racial mistrust toward Whites was predictive of delinquent behaviors and a disposition to deviance in Black adolescent boys (Taylor, Biafora, & Warheit, 1994). As measured by self-report questions reflecting a disposition to engage in various deviant behaviors, African American and Haitian Black adolescent boys reported a greater willingness than White boys to violate the law; yet, no significant differences were found within groups of African American, Haitian, and Caribbean Island Black boys in their disposition to deviance (Taylor et al., 1994).

Other studies have found no ethnic differences in delinquency or predisposition to deviance when other factors are taken into account. For example, two studies controlling for the type of neighborhood residence demonstrated that ethnic differences were only apparent when one's neighborhood (i.e., underclass) was not accounted for (Maguin, Loeber, & LeMahieu, 1993; Peeples & Loeber, 1994). Those residing in an underclass environment were more likely to participate in delinquent behavior, regardless of race. In a study of potential cross-cultural significance, the social ecology of delinquency was examined by looking at the effects of parental authoritativeness. This was done by categorizing adolescents according to ethnicity, socioeconomic status, and two-parent versus single-parent households, thus creating what were referred to as "ecological niches" (Steinberg, Mounts, Lamborn, & Dornbusch, 1991). The results indicated that whether one's parents were authoritative or not transcended differences in ethnicity. Specifically, those with authoritative parents were significantly less likely to participate in delinquent behavior, an effect that was strongest in Whites and Asians. Finally, using regression analyses, Fridrich and Flannery (1995) found that the relationship between parental monitoring and delinquency was mediated by susceptibility to antisocial peer pressure for both White and Mexican American early adolescents, regardless of ethnicity or level of acculturation.

Acculturative influences also appear to play a key role with respect to antisocial behaviors (see Yung & Hammond, Chapter 45, this volume). Some studies have demonstrated that the more integrated adolescents are with their traditional culture, or the less acculturated they are in general, the less likely they are to participate in delinquent behaviors. This finding was demonstrated in Mexican American adolescents (Buriel, Calzada, & Vasquez, 1982; Jessor, Graves, Hanson, & Jessor, 1968; Vigil, 1979) and with Moroccan, Turkish, and Surinamese adolescent boys in the Netherlands (Junger & Polder, 1992). Among Puerto Rican adolescent boys, acculturation was positively associated with participation in interpersonal violence and theft (Sommers, Fagan, & Baskin, 1993), and acculturated Hispanic adolescents were more susceptible than unacculturated Hispanic adolescents to antisocial peer pressure (Wall, Power, & Arbona, 1993).

These results suggest that rates of deviant behavior in Hispanic culture are higher among the less acculturated than among the more acculturated groups. This difference is attributed to the stress experienced when the former group is exposed to conflicting values of the new culture without the knowledge and resources needed to obtain the goals valued in the new culture (Vega, Hough, & Miranda, 1985). Others have argued that the strong family orientation characteristic of Hispanic culture results in less antisocial behavior among the unacculturated (Buriel et al., 1982).

CRITIQUE

Study Design

Cross-sectional designs have characterized the studies reviewed here, even though it might have been possible to conduct a longitudinal examination of antisocial behaviors (e.g., Windle, 1990). This is a particularly problematic design issue because ASPD is the only personality disorder that requires a specific childhood diagnosis of conduct disorder as a criteria for the adult diagnostic framework. From a cross-cultural perspective, it would be interesting to know, for example, the relative percentages of different ethnic populations that progress from conduct disorder to adult antisocial personality disorder. The large epidemiological studies are certainly adequate for size and inclusion of prison populations, as well as oversampling of ethnic populations to increase statistical power. However, ethnicity was typically treated as a static variable defined by self-identification as an ethnic group member, and acculturative differences within ethnic groups were only minimally addressed. Comparisons were made on the nominal status of Black, White, or Hispanic group membership without concern for the wide variation within groups, or comparisons were made on a post hoc basis using institutionalized populations of different ethnic groups.

In light of the considerable heterogeneity within ethnic populations, it is surprising that few studies appear to have given much thought to acculturative differences involving different generations, waves of immigration, or the historical aspects of majority/minority social relations within study communities. From the standpoint of construct validity, it might be particularly informative to examine antisocial personality disorder among different ethnic populations with reference to their socializing enclaves and the behavioral incentives to which they are exposed. Examination is also indicated of the social ecology in which ethnic minorities attempt to establish socially rewarded identities, occupy valued roles, and achieve status within their respective communities. This approach would permit more careful examination, from an ethnic community perspective, of the criminal behavior components of antisocial personality disorder. It would also encourage study designs that might more adequately address etiological issues by which links between community, personality, and pathological behaviors could be examined. For example, rather than simply using race as a nominal variable, Steinberg et al. (1991) categorized subjects by ecological niches. Using the concept of the ecological niche, each subject was consequently defined by ethnicity, socioeconomic status (working class vs. middle class based on the parents' education level), and family structure (two-parent biologically intact vs. nonintact with one parent or a stepfamily).

Sampling Issues

With the exception of the epidemiological surveys summarized in Table 44.1, most studies of antisocial behavior in community populations have used convenience samples lacking control for proportional representation of ethnic minority populations. Moreover, those few studies that purposely oversampled Blacks, Hispanics, or economically disadvantaged groups did not make within-group sampling distinctions within the nominal ethnic groupings (e.g., Caribbean Blacks vs. Urban American Blacks). School populations of unknown representativeness commonly have been used, typically studying males, but not females, and having limited ethnic group variation in the total sample. The lack of inclusion of school dropouts for comparative study with school populations apparently has not been considered a serious sampling problem, even though important differences in the type, frequency, and severity of antisocial behaviors between these two groups are likely.

Institutionalized or incarcerated male populations have received considerable focus for specific study of antisocial personality dis-

order. For example, Hare (1991) describes 10 normative samples used in developing and standardizing the PCL and PCL-R. Two of these samples were Black and one was composed of Canadian Indians (Wong, 1986, cited in Hare, 1991). Both Black and Canadian Indian ethnicity were studied without distinction for subgroup differences, such as the reservation-based or urban residence of the Canadian Indian group. Asian and Pacific Islanders and American Indian populations have not been studied to date, but this deficiency may be remedied in forthcoming research that is replicating the National Vietnam Veterans Readjustment Study with these populations (S. M. Manson, personal communication, February 1996). It is also notable that little attention has been given to sampling behavior settings as well as individuals, and that there has been a pronounced trend to "study down" by using incarcerated populations rather than obtaining samples from among community dwelling, affluent groups such as lawyers or stockbrokers.

Measurement and Instrumentation

The polythetic nature of the symptom criteria for antisocial personality disorder nested within the categorical measurement structure of *DSM-IV* has not been examined thoroughly enough to determine symptom clusters that might more reliably discriminate different ethnic populations. This approach has probably blurred ethnic distinctions by focusing on the criminal behaviors that were characteristic of those versions of the *DSM* symptom criteria used to make diagnoses in the ECA and the National Comorbidity studies. Perhaps because it is considered a diagnosis for which the defining criteria are well agreed upon, antisocial personality disorder seems not to have received as much attention as other *DSM* diagnoses with respect to ethnic variations in symptomatology. As our examination of the fluctuating composition of the symptom criteria (depicted in Figure 44.1) indicates, this seems to be a disorder of considerable complexity that deserves more refined measurement. For example, dimensional measures that could be administered more easily and cost effectively in organizational settings such as schools might be used for early detection of nascent antisocial behaviors of considerable social consequence for different communities.

One of the major problems with instruments for examining antisocial behavior in general and antisocial personality in particular is the lack of consistency and commonly agreed criteria. With few exceptions, however, instrument content typically has not been factor-analytically derived and issues of cross-cultural equivalence (semantic, functional, and metric) have not been formally considered. Although Hare (1991) reports similar reliability and relatively small mean differences for the normative samples included in the development of the PCL and PCL-R, the ethnic samples to date are limited to incarcerated Blacks and Canadian Indians. Hare cautions that current data do not permit determination of whether the factor structure is the same for other groups as it is for Whites.

Interpretation of Findings

The data from epidemiological studies indicate that antisocial personality disorder has roughly the same prevalence rate across ethnic groups. However, these rates are based on *DSM* criteria that were heavily weighted for criminal behaviors and deemphasized assessment of personality traits that some have claimed are very difficult for clinicians to make (Hare, 1991). It is possible that the selection of symptom criteria to achieve higher interrater reliability has resulted in decreasing cross-cultural validity. The increasing homogenization of symptoms and a case definition heavily loaded on criminal behavior may effectively reduce cross-cultural research to a comparison of symptom frequencies. If the personality traits that are part of the more traditional conceptualization of antisocial personality were included in the diagnostic criteria, reliability might decline, but a more cross-culturally valid diagnosis of greater clinical utility also might result. In addition, this approach might achieve a better balance between the descriptive and evaluative aspects of the diagnosis (Agich, 1994).

By contrast with community samples, the ethnic group differences among incarcerated populations indicated that Whites have higher rates of antisocial personality than other ethnic groups. Whites also appeared to engage in more delinquent behaviors in the communities represented in the studies reviewed. This difference may be due as much to the criteria used in determining incarceration of different ethnic groups as it is to ethnic differences in antisocial personality diagnosis. Controlling for type and severity of criminal behaviors would help to clarify the difference in rates of ASPD. It is quite possible that incarcerated Whites are characterized by greater personality disturbances and more severe crimes, whereas other ethnic group members are incarcerated for lesser offenses with less accompanying personality pathology.

Examination of contextual factors has contributed significantly to the cross-cultural understanding of antisocial behaviors. For example, ethnic differences in antisocial personality or the lack thereof have been illuminated by an analysis of the demographic factors and associated variables that provide a more complete picture of the social patterns involved (Robins et al., 1991). Greater attention to acculturative influences and variations in the ecological niches that promote or constrain antisocial behaviors have also added to cross-cultural understanding.

SUMMARY AND FUTURE RESEARCH AGENDA

An incomplete picture of antisocial behavior still remains with respect to cross-culturally appropriate definitions, thresholds of tolerance, normative standards, and attributed personality pathology. Compared to other diagnostic entities that have been addressed by cross-cultural psychopathology research, in general the Axis II disorders have been conspicuously neglected. Although antisocial personality disorder has been a frequently cited example of a cross-culturally problematic personality disorder, it is nonetheless one of the few to receive empirical research attention with respect to ethnic minorities. It is also perhaps one of the better personality disorders to use as a research prototype for the challenging future that lies ahead for cross-cultural psychopathology research.

Conceptual and theoretical issues abound with respect to cross-cultural views of antisocial behavior and the universality of ASPD. A thorough reexamination of the way in which ASPD is defined and interpreted from different cross-cultural perspectives would be instructive for both theoretical and empirical purposes. A related

concern is the locus of antisocial behaviors and their putative pathological form that exists in antisocial personality disorder. Thus, reexamination of conceptual and theoretical issues seems indicated because the current *DSM-IV* definition of mental disorder excludes deviant behavior or conflicts between the individual and society unless they are symptoms of dysfunction *within* the person.

Increased application of the Cultural Formulation Outline that has been incorporated into the appendices of *DSM-IV* could prove useful in dealing with a number of the conceptual issues noted earlier. Combined with the standard multiaxial diagnostic formulation, the more idiographic content of the cultural formulation addresses a number of important cultural factors in completing a comprehensive diagnosis. Mezzich (1995) has suggested that a second generation of contextualized epidemiological methods might be derived from systematic use of the cultural formulation approach.

More fundamental descriptive research is clearly needed on the cross-cultural variations in antisocial behaviors that are perceived as exceeding the boundaries of normality from different cultural perspectives and levels of acculturation. Ethnomethodological approaches that identify problem behaviors from the perspective of ethnic communities are recommended for identifying the environmental forces and factors that may invalidate or sharpen diagnostic accuracy. In addition, this type of research will contribute to a cross-culturally meaningful diagnostic category for clinical purposes.

Expanding the categorical diagnosis of antisocial personality disorder to incorporate more dimensional measures based on a larger pool of cross-culturally representative personality traits would significantly advance our understanding of antisocial behavior and its empirically determined pathological forms. A factor-analytically derived dimensional approach to measurement that systematically examined the factor structure of antisocial personality disorder across a number of ethnic minority populations would be a major advance in resolving issues of normative uncertainty. It would also be particularly appropriate for the cross-cultural content validity of the symptoms and the cross-cultural construct validity of ASPD.

A related problem concerns the overlap of ASPD symptoms with those of other personality disorders, as well as its diagnostic comorbidity with Axis I disorders. Although personality disorders are based on pervasive personality traits, fundamental research on the cross-cultural variations in the presence, strength, and dispersion of personality traits is inadequate to inform the larger question of their pathological manifestations. Adequate research on the structural invariance of personality traits lacks cross-cultural representativeness, so there may be significant limitations on how rapidly such research could be accomplished. As for issues of comorbidity with Axis I disorders, clinical experience suggests that the typically high correlation between psychoactive substance abuse and antisocial personality disorder may vary from culture to culture and needs to be empirically verified.

As indicated in the critique section of this chapter, research on the developmental course and natural history of antisocial personality disorder for different ethnic minorities could prove useful with respect to possible differences in the associated etiological factors. Of particular concern is the increasingly earlier age of psychoactive substance abuse and the related delinquent behaviors that may be the result of differential early exposure, and consequently greater risk, for ethnic minorities such as American Indians and Alaska Natives. Cross-cultural replication of longitudinal studies of adolescents employing various predictive models would provide a welcome contribution to the current dearth of research on the cultural or ethnic variables related to the developmental precursors of antisocial behavior and its adult pathological forms (e.g., Dishion & Patterson, 1993; Elliot, 1994).

REFERENCES

Agich, G. J. (1994). Evaluative judgment and personality disorder. In J. Z. Sadler, O. P. Wiggins, & M. A. Schwartz (Eds.), *Philosophical perspectives on psychiatric diagnostic classification* (pp. 233–245). Baltimore: Johns Hopkins University Press.

Alarcon, R. D. (1995). Culture and psychiatric diagnosis: Impact on *DSM-IV* and *ICD-10*. *The Psychiatric Clinics of North America: Cultural Psychiatry, 18*(3), 449–467.

American Psychiatric Association. (1952). *Diagnostic and statistical manual of mental disorders*. Washington, DC: Author.

American Psychiatric Association. (1968). *Diagnostic and statistical manual of mental disorders* (2nd ed.). Washington, DC: Author.

American Psychiatric Association. (1980). *Diagnostic and statistical manual of mental disorders* (3rd ed.). Washington, DC: Author.

American Psychiatric Association. (1987). *Diagnostic and statistical manual of mental disorders* (3rd ed., rev.). Washington, DC: Author.

American Psychiatric Association. (1994). *Diagnostic and statistical manual of mental disorders* (4th ed.). Washington, DC: Author.

Berry, J. W., Poortinga, Y. H., Segall, M. H., & Dansen, P. R. (1992). *Cross-cultural psychology: Research and applications*. Cambridge: Cambridge University Press.

Blue, H. C., & Griffith, E. H. (1995). Sociocultural and therapeutic perspectives on violence. *The Psychiatric Clinics of North America: Cultural Psychiatry, 18*(3), 571–587.

Buriel, R., Calzada, S., & Vasquez, R. (1982). The relationship of traditional Mexican American culture to adjustment and delinquency among three generations of Mexican American male adolescents. *Hispanic Journal of Behavioral Sciences, 4*(1), 41–55.

Burnam, M. A., Hough, R. L., Escobar, J. I., Karno, M., Timbers, D. M., Telles, C. A., & Locke, B. Z. (1987). Six-month prevalence of specific psychiatric disorders among Mexican Americans and non-Hispanic Whites in Los Angeles. *Archives of General Psychiatry, 44*, 687–694.

Cleckley, H. (1955). *The mask of sanity*. Saint Louis: Mosby.

Compton, W. M., Helzer, J. E., Hai-Gwo, H., Eng-Kung, Y., McEvoy, L., Tipp, J. E., & Spitznagel, E. L. (1991). New methods in cross-cultural psychiatry: Psychiatric illness in Taiwan and the United States. *American Journal of Psychiatry, 148*, 1667–1704.

Dembo, R., La Voie, L., Schmeidler, J., & Washborn, M. (1987). The nature and correlates of psychological/emotional functioning among a sample of detained youths. *Clinical Justice and Behavior, 14*(3), 311–334.

Dembo, R., Williams, L., & Schmeidler, J. (1994). Psychosocial, alcohol/other drug use, and delinquency differences between urban Black and White male high risk youth. *International Journal of the Addictions, 29*(4), 461–483.

Dishion, T. J., & Patterson, G. R. (1993). Antisocial behavior: Using a multiple gating strategy. In M. I. Singer, L. T. Singer, & T. M. Anglin (Eds.), *Handbook for screening adolescents at psychosocial risk* (pp. 375–399). New York: Lexington Books/Macmillan.

Elliot, D. S. (1994). Serious violent offenders: Onset, developmental course, and termination—the American Society of Criminology 1993 presidential address. *Criminology, 32*, 1–21.

Fridrich, A. H., & Flannery, D. J. (1995). The effects of ethnicity and acculturation on early adolescent delinquency. *Journal of Child and Family Studies, 4*(1), 69–87.

Good, B. J., & Good, M. J. B. (1986). The cultural context of diagnosis and therapy: A view from medical anthropology. In M. R. Miranda & H. H. L. Kitano (Eds.), *Mental health research and practice in minority communities: Development of culturally sensitive programs* (pp. 1–27, DHHS Publication No. ADM 86-1466). Washington, DC: Government Printing Office.

Hare, R. D. (1990). *The Hare Psychopathy Checklist (PCL)*. New York: Multi-Health Systems.

Hare, R. D. (1991). *The Hare Psychopathy Checklist–Revised (PCL-R)*. New York: Multi-Health Systems.

Hart, S. D., Hare, R. D., & Harpur, T. J. (1992). The Psychopathy Checklist–Revised (PCL-R): An overview for researchers and clinicians. In J. C. Rosen & P. McReynolds (Eds.), *Advances in psychological assessment* (Vol. 8, pp. 103–130). New York: Plenum.

Hinton, L., & Kleinman, A. (1993). Cultural issues and international psychiatric diagnosis. In J. A. Costa e Silva & C. C. Nadelson (Eds.), *International review of psychiatry* (Vol. 1, pp. 111–129). Washington, DC: American Psychiatric Press.

Jessor, R., Graves, T. D., Hanson, R. C., & Jessor, S. (1968). *Society, personality, and deviant behavior: A study of a tri-ethnic community*. New York: Holt, Reinhart and Winston.

Junger, M., & Polder, W. (1992). Some explanations of crime among four ethnic groups in the Netherlands. *Journal of Quantitative Criminology, 8*(1), 51–77.

Kessler, R. C., McGonagle, K. A., Zhao, S., Nelson, C. B., Hughes, M., Eshleman, S., Wittchen, H., & Kendler, K. S. (1994). Lifetime and 12-month prevalence of *DSM-III-R* psychiatric disorders in the United States: Results from the National Comorbidity Survey. *Archives of General Psychiatry, 51*, 8–19.

Kleinman, A., & Fabrega, H. (1992, April). Introduction to manual. In J. E. Mezzich, A. Kleinman, H. Fabrega, B. Good, G. Johnson-Powell, K. Lin, S. M. Manson, & D. Parron, *Cultural proposals for* DSM-IV: Submitted to the *DSM-IV* Task Force by the Steering Committee, NIMH-Sponsored Group on Culture and Diagnosis.

Kosson, D., Smith, S. S., & Newman, J. P. (1990). Evaluating the construct validity of psychopathy in Black and White male inmates: Three preliminary studies. *Journal of Abnormal Psychology, 99*(3), 250–259.

Kulka, R. A., Schlenger, W. E., Fairbank, J. A., Hough, R. L., Jordan, B. K., Marmar, C. R., & Weiss, D. S. (1990). *The National Vietnam Veterans Readjustment Study: Tables of findings and technical appendices*. New York: Brunner/Mazel.

Lutz, K. (1985). Depression and translation of emotional worlds. In A. Kleiman & B. Good (Eds.), *Culture and depression: Studies in the anthropology and cross-cultural psychiatry of affect and disorder* (pp. 63–100). Berkeley: University of California Press.

Lyon, J., Henggeler, S., & Hall, J. A. (1992). The family relations, peer relations, and criminal activities of Caucasian and Hispanic-American gang members. *Journal of Abnormal Child Psychology, 20*(5), 439–449.

Maguin, E. M., Loeber, R., & LeMahieu, P. G. (1993). Does the relationship between poor reading and delinquency hold for males of different ages and ethnic groups? *Journal of Emotional and Behavioral Disorders, 1*(2), 88–100.

Manson, S. M. (1995). Culture and major depression: Current challenges in the diagnosis of mood disorders. *Psychiatric Clinics of North America: Cultural Psychiatry, 18*(3), 487–503.

Manson, S. M., Shore, J. H., & Bloom, J. D. (1985). The depressive experience in American Indian communities: A challenge for psychiatric theory and diagnosis. In A. Kleinman & B. Good (Eds.), *Culture and depression: Studies in the anthropology and cross-cultural psychiatry of affect and disorder* (pp. 331–368). Berkeley: University of California Press.

Maser, J. D., & Dinges, N. G. (1993). Comorbidity: Meaning and uses in cross-cultural clinical research. *Culture Medicine and Psychiatry, 16*(4), 409–425.

Mezzich, J. E. (1995). Cultural formulation and comprehensive diagnosis: Clinical and research perspectives. *Psychiatric Clinics of North America: Cultural Psychiatry, 18*(3), 649–658.

Mezzich, J. E., Kelinman, A., Fabrega, H., Good, B., Johnson-Powell, G., Lin, K., Manson, S. M., & Parron, D. (1992, April). *Cultural proposals for* DSM-IV. Submitted to the *DSM-IV* Task Force by the Steering Committee, NIMH-Sponsored Group on Culture and Diagnosis.

Nuckolls, C. W. (1992). Toward a cultural history of the personality disorders. *Social Science and Medicine, 35*(1), 37–47.

Paris, J. (1991). Personality disorders, parasuicide, and culture. *Transcultural Psychiatric Research Review, 28*, 25–39.

Peeples, F., & Loeber, R. (1994). Do individual factors and neighborhood context explain ethnic differences in juvenile delinquency? *Journal of Quantitative Criminology, 10*(2), 141–154.

Pinel, P. (1977). A treatise on insanity. In D. N. Robinson (Ed.), *Significant contributions to the history of psychology, 1750–1920.* Washington, DC: University Publications of America. (Original work published 1801)

Robins, L. N. (1995). Commentary on antisocial personality disorders. In W. J. Livesley (Ed.), *The* DSM-IV *personality disorders.* New York: Guilford.

Robins, L. N., Helzer, J. E., Weissman, M. M., Orvaschel, H., Gruenberg, E., Burke, J. D., & Regier, D. A. (1984). Lifetime prevalence of specific psychiatric disorders in three cities. *Archives of General Psychiatry, 41*, 949–958.

Robins, L. N., & Regier, D. A. (Eds.). (1991). *Psychiatric disorders in America: The Epidemiological Catchment Area study.* New York: Free Press.

Robins, L. N., Tipp, J., & Przybeck, T. (1991). Antisocial personality. In L. N. Robins & D. A. Regier (Eds.), *Psychiatric disorders in America: The Epidemiological Catchment Area study* (pp. 258–291). New York: Free Press.

Schweder, R. A., & Bourne, E. G. (1984). Does the concept of the person vary cross-culturally? In A. J. Marsell & G. M. White (Eds.), *Cultural conceptions of mental health and therapy* (pp. 97–140). Boston: Reidel Publishing.

Sommers, I., Fagan, J., & Baskin, D. (1993). Sociocultural influences on the explanation of delinquency for Puerto Rican youths. *Hispanic Journal of Behavioral Sciences, 15*(1), 36–62.

Steinberg, L., Mounts, N. S., Lamborn, S. D., & Dornbusch, S. M. (1991). Authoritative parenting and adolescent adjustment across varied ecological niches. *Journal of Research on Adolescence, 1*(1), 19–36.

Taylor, D. L., Biafora, F. A., & Warheit, G. J. (1994). Racial mistrust and disposition to deviance among African American, Haitian, and other Caribbean island adolescent boys. *Law and Human Behavior, 18*(3), 291–303.

Teplin, L. (1994). Psychiatric and substance abuse disorders among male urban jail detainees. *American Journal of Public Health, 84*(2), 290–293.

Vega, W., Hough, R., & Miranda, M. (1985). Modeling cross-cultural research in Hispanic mental health. In W. Vega & M. Miranda (Eds.), *Stress and Hispanic mental health: Relating research to service delivery* (pp. 1–29, DHHS Publication No. ADM 85-1410). Washington, DC: Government Printing Office.

Vigil, D. (1979). Adaptation strategies and cultural life styles of Mexican American adolescents. *Hispanic Journal of Behavioral Sciences, 1*(4), 375–392.

Wall, J. A., Power, T. G., & Arbona, C. (1993). Susceptibility to antisocial peer pressure and its relation to acculturation in Mexican-American adolescents. *Journal of Adolescent Research, 8*(4), 403–418.

Widiger, T. A., & Corbit, E. M. (1995). Antisocial personality disorder. In W. J. Livesley (Ed.), *The* DSM-IV *personality disorders* (pp. 103–126). New York: Guilford.

Windle, M. (1990). A longitudinal study of antisocial behaviors in early adolescence as predictors of late adolescent substance use: Gender and ethnic group differences. *Journal of Abnormal Psychology, 99*(1), 86–91.

World Health Organization. (1990). *International classification of diseases and related health problems* (10th ed.). Geneva: Author.

CHAPTER 45

Antisocial Behavior in Minority Groups: Epidemiological and Cultural Perspectives

BETTY R. YUNG and W. RODNEY HAMMOND

In 20th-century American society, young men of ethnic minority cultures historically have been overrepresented as the perpetrators and victims of violent crime, as gang members, as substance abusers, and as sellers of illicit drugs. They also have been the group most frequently arrested for robberies, burglaries, and motor vehicle thefts. Recent decreases in the overall levels of property, drug-related, and violent crimes in our country have not held true for male African American and Hispanic adolescents and young adults. In fact, in most categories of antisocial and delinquent behavior, their participation rates are escalating at near-epidemic proportions (Council on Crime in America, 1996; Jones & Krisberg, 1994). We have much less complete information on antisocial behavior among Native American and Asian American youth. However, self-report survey data suggest that particular subgroups of male and female Native American high school students have higher rates of alcohol use, shoplifting, vandalism, and assaultive behavior than their Caucasian or African American peers (Gruber, Anderson, & DiClemente, 1994; Gruber, DiClemente, & Anderson, 1994; Newcomb, Fahy, & Skager, 1990). Similarly, certain Asian American adolescent subgroups, particularly recent refugees and young men of lower socioeconomic status, appear to have elevated risk for substance abuse, gang membership, theft, and violence (Chesney-Lind et al., 1992; Huff, 1993; Monti, 1993; Rockhill et al., 1993; White, Homma-True, Golden, Gramp, & Lee, 1995).

Nor are young ethnic minority women immune to this pattern. Although aggressive and other antisocial behavior continues to be concentrated within male groups, there is a growing involvement of these female adolescents in acts of violence and in the formation of their own gangs (Chen & True, 1994; DuRant, Pendergrast, & Cadenhead, 1994; Goldstein & Soriano, 1994; Monti, 1993).

Despite a burgeoning literature that has examined the strong correlation between ethnicity and certain types of antisocial behavior, at present we lack adequate etiological explanations for this disproportionality. The relationship between ethnic minority status and the interwoven social, economic, cultural, institutional, and interpersonal influences that either encourage or suppress antisocial behavior is poorly understood. In fact, all too often there has been a failure to distinguish appropriately between ethnicity and adverse social and economic factors such as poverty, unemployment, and neighborhood disorganization that are overprevalent in ethnic minority communities and that are independently associated with violence, substance abuse, and other health and behavior problems (Hill, Soriano, Chen, & LaFromboise, 1994). Unfortunately, this has sometimes resulted in the perception that the predisposing risk factors for antisocial behavior are embedded within the cultural characteristics of the ethnic minority group rather than in associated environmental conditions, individual traits, or family influences.

In the past the lack of differentiation between race and ethnicity and socioeconomic status made it easier to advance pejorative theories of ethnic minority antisocial behavior and criminality, including views of biological or genetic inferiority or deviant cultural values shared across entire ethnic/cultural groups (see discussions in Flowers, 1988; Hawkins, 1990; Stark, 1993). Now largely discounted, for many years such assumptions influenced much of the research on racial/ethnic behavioral differences (National Center for Health Statistics [NCHS], 1991; Nickens, 1991). It was a step forward when the role of economic deprivation and the accompanying stressors experienced by many ethnic minority families began to be recognized as major contributors to the perpetration of violence, the use and sale of drugs, and the commission of property crimes (Attar, Guerra, & Tolan, 1994; DuRant, Pendergrast, & Cadenhead, 1994; Reynolds, Weissberg, & Kaprow, 1992). However, many studies still consider ethnicity "as a proxy variable . . . that takes the place of the more complex set of life circumstances that are associated with race" (Fairchild, Yee, Wyatt, & Weizmann, 1995, p. 46). The confounding of variables makes it difficult to disentangle the independent effects of ethnicity, poverty status, and other socioeconomic conditions on antisocial behavior (Hill et al., 1994; NCHS, 1991). In addition, there is a relative scarcity of research examining the resiliency factors influencing the proportionally larger numbers of ethnic minority adolescents (including poor youngsters living in disadvantaged high crime neighborhoods) who are not violent, delinquent, or drug abusing.

Contemporary research is slowly making progress toward a better understanding of the epidemiology of antisocial behavior among ethnic minority adolescents, continuing research needs, related risk factors, and, to a lesser degree, protective factors mitigating against indulgence in such behavior. This chapter explores the prevalence of antisocial behavior among African American, Hispanic American, Native American, and Asian American youths, focusing primarily on aggressive and violent behavior, substance abuse, membership in gangs, and general involvement in delinquency. It includes discussion of related risk and resiliency factors for each group and each problem behavior. Violence victimization is addressed only as a contributory factor for antisocial behavior, and discussion of suicide, sexual violence, and violence related to major mental illness is excluded. Wherever possible, gender differences and interethnic comparisons are highlighted, and throughout the narrative, attention is called to gaps in our current knowledge. The reader is cautioned that some topics are covered more fully than others. This is primarily related to the amount of available research on the ethnic group or the particular problem behavior as manifested by that group. In addition, because of space limitations, this review is intended to be representative rather than exhaustive. The reader interested in a more anthropological, cross-cultural approach is referred to Dinges, Atlis, and Vincent (Chapter 44, this volume).

The chapter begins with a description of the present demographic profile and projected trends in the ethnic composition of the U.S. population and then proceeds to a discussion of the challenges related to collecting and analyzing information on antisocial behaviors among ethnic minority youths. These sections are followed by a description of each ethnic group, highlighting what is reported about the prevalence of particular conduct problems, the factors contributing to their onset and trajectory, and the special issues related to acquiring additional knowledge about such problems and planning culturally relevant and effective interventions to address them. The chapter's conclusions stress the need for improved research as a foundation for culturally informed prevention and intervention program design.

DEMOGRAPHIC TRENDS

As we approach the 21st century, the racial and ethnic composition of the U.S. population is shifting in proportion, and the projections for the coming decades entail still more dramatic changes. Figure 45.1 illustrates the 1990 census profile and the anticipated changes in population composition in the year 2050.

It should be noted that the 1990 figures for the non-White population in the United States are reflective of better classification systems for race and ethnicity. For example, in 1990 only 69% of U.S. children were classified as White, non-Hispanic, down from 86% so classified in 1950. However, the apparent increase in the non-White proportion of the population is partially attributable to the creation of the Hispanic and Asian/Pacific Islander ethnic identifiers because previously many individuals in these groups were counted as White (Lewit & Baker, 1994).

Changes in data collection and reporting methods do not fully account for the changing American demographics. Immigration patterns and higher birth rates among some ethnic minority groups are important contributors to changes in the relative representation

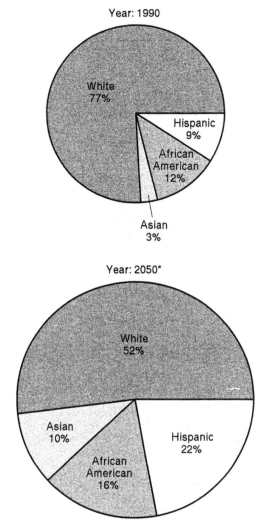

*Projected. Native Americans represented 1% of the total U.S. population. Although expected to double in number by 2050, their population share will remain at about 1%.

Figure 45.1 *Racial and ethnic composition of U.S. population.*
Source: McKenny & Bennett (1994). Issues regarding data on race and ethnicity, the Census Bureau experience. *Public Health Reports,* 109, 16–25.

of non-White and White people in the country's population (Lewit & Baker, 1994; McKenney & Bennett, 1994).

Growth rates are particularly high for Asian/Pacific Islanders, largely due to increased immigration of Southeast Asians fueled by political turmoil in their countries and by changes in the U.S. immigration law and policy that began in the mid-1960s. Between 1980 and 1990, the size of this population doubled, with increases of more than 125% for Asian Indians, Koreans, and Vietnamese. The Asian/Pacific Islander population is expected to expand from its present level of 7 million to 40 million in 2050. The Hispanic origin population is also increasing rapidly, with more than half of the growth rate coming from continued immigration from Mexico and other Latin American countries. The number of U.S. Hispanics grew at a rate of 53% during the 1980s and is expected to exceed 80 million by the mid-21st century. Native Americans are also experiencing substantial growth but at a slower rate than Hispanics or Asian/Pacific Islanders. Between 1980 and 1990, the size of the Native American population grew 38% to nearly 2 million and is projected to double by 2050. The African American population, presently the largest ethnic minority group, is growing at a still slower pace (up 13% between the 1980 and 1990 censuses). Growth of this population comes primarily from natural increase (i.e., birth rate) with smaller contributions from immigration. Expected to increase to 62 million by the year 2050, the African American population will be substantially below Hispanic numbers at mid-century (Lewit & Baker, 1994; McKenney & Bennett, 1994).

The effects of these demographic shifts will be profound. In the coming century, the historical "majority" group of White persons of European origin will barely exceed half of the American population (see Figure 45.1). This increasing heterogeneity presents us with a variety of challenges.

We must find ways to ensure the full and equitable participation of all children and adolescents in the "good life" promised in American society. This must involve not only enhancing the status and acceptance of ethnic diversity within the larger culture but improving the often dismal environmental conditions in which many African American, Hispanic, Native American, and Asian American youngsters live. Removal of the barriers of discrimination and lack of access to educational opportunities and economic resources ultimately will help us to substantially reduce the exposure to risks that contribute to antisocial behavior among ethnic minority youths. As a first step in this process, we must confront the critical research issues that limit our present understanding of the problem and our ability to conceptualize culturally appropriate interventions.

PROBLEMS AND LIMITATIONS OF CURRENT RESEARCH

Our knowledge of the extent of the antisocial behavior of ethnic minority youths and the associated constellations of related risks is hampered by the same constraints that limit our complete understanding of the prevalence and etiology of this behavior among all American youths. At the national level there is no completely reliable source of data on substance abuse, delinquent activity, gang membership, and violence (except for homicide victimization). National data sources such the Youth Risk Behavior Survey, the National Youth Survey, the National Youth Gang Survey, and the NIDA Monitoring the Future Survey provide valuable estimates and insights. However, as self-report instruments they are subject to the limitations of all such tools, that is, potential underreporting or overreporting of behaviors resulting from memory failure, deception, miscoding, differing definitions of problem behavior, missing data, and reluctance to self-identify as

a person who engages in antisocial activity (Barham, 1992; Flowers, 1988; Menard, 1992). Official records such as juvenile offender statistics from the Office of Juvenile Justice and Delinquency Prevention do not obtain data on antisocial behavior that has not come to the attention of the criminal justice system, thus excluding a vast number of unreported episodes of violent and other antisocial acts (Elliott, Huizinga, & Morse, 1986; National Committee for Injury Prevention and Control [NCIPC], 1989). Prevalence estimates based on the National Youth Survey, a prospective longitudinal study using a self-reported measure of violent offending, have been substantially higher than arrest data indicate (Elliott et al., 1986).

Accurate data on the number, composition, and activities of youth gangs are particularly difficult to obtain because there is no national reporting system. In addition, because there is no agreed-upon definition for gangs, local law enforcement officials—the major source of information about gang prevalence in most American cities—use their own criteria and may easily exaggerate or underestimate the problem in their localities (Goldstein & Glick, 1994).

Problems in the collection of prevalence information are exacerbated in the case of ethnic minority youths. There are additional issues related to access, ethnic/racial classification methods, sampling, instrumentation, and data analysis that make it considerably more difficult to gather data and develop the knowledge base needed for understanding the behavior of different ethnic minority youth groups (Hughes, Seidman, & Williams, 1993; Vega, 1992). Hughes et al. (1993) call attention to the diverse "points at which culture intersects major phases of the research enterprise—problem formulation, population definition, concept and measurement development, research design, methodology, and data analysis—and influences and constrains what researchers deem worthy of investigation and how they interpret what they observe" (p. 687).

Issues of specific concern include the following:

1. *General lack of data on ethnic minority health and behavior problems.* National surveys often gather data on ethnicity but exclude less numerous ethnic groups from data analysis because their numbers in a given sample may be too few for statistically valid analysis (NCHS, 1991). In the alternative, these diverse groups may be lumped together in a metacategory of "Other" that, although it does permit qualitative data analysis, compromises our ability to discriminate ethnic differences among the aggregated groups (Vega, 1992; Yu & Liu, 1992). Oversampling (i.e., modification of a random probability sample to include greater numbers of the target group than would have been selected based on their representation within the total survey universe) has been recommended as a technique to study the characteristics of these "rare" groups in greater detail (Sugarman, Brenneman, LaRoque, Warren, & Goldberg, 1994).

2. *Lack of data on ethnic subgroups.* There is tremendous intra-ethnic diversity among African American, Hispanic, Native American, and Asian American/Pacific Islander populations in terms of language, customs, values, worldview, levels of acculturation, socioeconomic status, geographic concentration patterns, and length of residence in the United States (see sections on each group to follow). However, it is still quite rare to find studies that report data by ethnic subgroupings, making it difficult to evaluate

risk factors and behavior patterns that may vary widely from group to group (NCHS, 1991). For example, Uehara, Takeuchi, and Smukler (1994) found that combining diverse Asian American subpopulations into a single ethnic category concealed significant within-group differences in mental health functioning status.

3. *Problems of classification.* Comparing data from different sources can be problematic because of varying methods of identifying and classifying ethnicity. These methods include self-identification, observation by a researcher or service provider, identification by next of kin, or judgment based on surname. Research examining the consequences of diverse classification schemes for establishing ethnicity has found that there is significant disparity when the same population is categorized using different methods of identification (Sugarman, Soderberg, Gordon, & Rivara, 1993; Yu & Liu, 1992; Zimmerman et al., 1994). In addition, this issue is complicated by the increasing numbers of individuals who have mixed ethnic ancestry and whose self-identification decisions and feelings of ethnic affiliation may be based on very personal factors (McKenney & Bennett, 1994; NCHS, 1991).

4. *Problems of access.* Unique geographic dispersement patterns among the diverse ethnic minority groups may create sampling technique problems (McGraw, McKinlay, Crawford, Costa, & Cohen, 1992). National survey sampling methods often target "known" ethnic communities and census tracts. However, this may have unintended consequences, including capturing only a particular ethnic subgroup rather than a broader population of individuals from different countries of origin and life circumstances (Flack et al., 1995). In addition, this method fails to include the responses of ethnic minority individuals living in communities with a low representation of their particular group (NCHS, 1991).

Access, however, is a much broader concern than simply locating individuals to be surveyed. There are particular needs for improving data collection for hard-to-reach ethnic minority groups such as urban Native Americans, undocumented immigrants and refugees, migrant workers, and homeless individuals (NCHS, 1991). In addition, much research on adolescents is carried out in school settings, automatically excluding absent, dropout, and runaway youths, a population in which ethnic minority adolescents are overrepresented (Yung & Hammond, 1997). In nonschool settings, even if the researcher is able to locate out-of-school youths, it may be difficult to convince them to participate in research, particularly if they are engaging in high-risk behavior such as prostitution or drug trafficking (Chavez, Edwards, & Oetting, 1989). Rates of refusal to participate in survey research are higher for ethnic minority boys and young men who may be concerned that responses about their health practices or antisocial behavior will be disclosed to "authorities" (McGraw et al., 1992). Chavez et al. (1989) found that refusal rates decreased when interviewers stopped asking their young dropout subjects for social security numbers. Other special efforts to ensure confidentiality and to establish rapport may be helpful in overcoming this prudent reluctance. In addition, it may be necessary to modify methods of approaching and engaging Native American and Asian American individuals and communities in research enterprises. Hostility or refusals may result if cultural customs are not respected, including gaining entry into the community by approaching its formal and informal leaders and accepting ritual drinks or gifts (Darou, Hum, & Kurtness, 1993; Pernice, 1994).

5. *Lack of study of key risk variables.* Although recent research has made advances in distinguishing between socioeconomic variables and ethnicity in behavioral research on adolescents, there is considerable room for improvement. An issue of continuing concern is the development of adequate indicators of socioeconomic status for ethnic minority populations. Economic factors such as income and educational level or occupation of parents and in school-based research eligibility for free or reduced lunch are often used to establish poverty or disadvantaged status of adolescents. However, there are noneconomic aspects of social deprivation unique to ethnic minorities that are rarely incorporated into current measurement concepts. For example, racially based residential segregation places many ethnic minority youths in communities with poorer schools, higher crime rates, scarcer job opportunities, lower levels of police protection, and fewer resources to prevent crime. Yet the impact of this form of isolation and marginalization on problems such as homicide has been given limited attention in the research literature (Peterson & Krivo, 1993). Although the sociocultural context of the lives of ethnic minority youths is an acknowledged source of influence on violent and other aberrant behaviors, present methods of conceptualizing and measuring the related variables are oversimplified and inconsistent across studies (American Psychological Association [APA], 1994; Fairchild et al., 1995). Another area needing additional research attention is the potential effects of acculturation levels, family/adolescent cultural conflicts, and length of residence in the United States on deviant and delinquent behavior (Brindis, Wolfe, McCarter, Ball, & Starbuck-Morales, 1995; Oetting & Beauvais, 1991; Vega, Gil, Warheit, Zimmerman, & Apospori, 1993). At present few studies have examined these issues.

6. *Instrumentation.* One of the most frequently used methods for collecting information on antisocial behavior is the self-report survey. With ethnic minority children and adolescents, the use of such instruments may be problematic because of literacy levels, linguistic issues, concerns about confidentiality, and differential response patterns to common formats for survey questions. For youngsters who speak English as a second language, there may be a need for translation of the instrument—a process fraught with difficulties including uncertainty about the transferability of constructs across different languages (Pernice, 1994; Vega, 1992). If translators are used for face-to-face interviews, there are additional complications related to willingness to disclose personal behaviors and habits to someone who may be a member of the adolescent's own community (Pernice, 1994). In addition, there may be ethnic differences in responses to survey questions and self-rating scales. Studies suggest that Hispanics are more likely than Caucasian respondents to give socially desirable responses on Likert scales. Asian Americans, particularly those from refugee and recent immigrant populations who may be unacquainted with survey methods, are also more prone to give answers reflecting politeness and a desire to please the interviewer (Pernice, 1994). In contrast, African Americans are more likely than Caucausian subjects to use the extreme response categories on Likert scale instruments (Hughes et al., 1993; McGraw et al., 1992).

7. *Data analysis and interpretation of results.* Whether the research results being examined are from self-report surveys, observations and ratings of behavior by others, or review of archival records, interpretation of what the data means must take into account the cultural and environmental contexts in which the behavior of interest occurs. Hughes et al. (1993) note that ratings of parenting practices related to permitting adolescent autonomy need to consider the amount of environmental danger faced by the youth. In high crime neighborhoods, it may be competent, positive, and appropriate parenting to restrict adolescent freedom for independent activity outside the home at levels of severity that might, in other circumstances, be considered overly protective or rigid. Similarly, Prinz and Miller (1991) assert:

> A pattern of child behavior that is labeled as "aggressive" may in some contexts be interpreted as normative and adaptive. Children who live in an impoverished neighborhood replete with high crime and frequent challenges develop survival skills to manage their environment. Verbal and physical aggression can be necessary to survival and coping . . . Rather than viewing aggression as maladaptive, an alternative conceptualization is that some aggressive behaviors play an important part in maintaining a peer group that is a major source of social support, learning, and perhaps economic opportunity. (p. 380)

The authors do caution that care must be taken not to confuse these more minor forms of verbal aggression and fighting with serious delinquent acts of stealing, aggravated assault, or vandalism. Studies that match diverse groups living in similar situations would enable separation of ethnic effects and environmental influences.

The need for attention to culturally attuned interpretation of research results extends to the analysis of archival information from national data sets. Juvenile justice records indicate that ethnic minority youths, particularly African American and Hispanic male adolescents, are consistently overrepresented in correctional facilities. Although a simplistic explanation for this disparity is that ethnic minority youths have arrest rates that are higher than their Caucasian peers, additional research yields evidence of discriminatory treatment based on ethnicity. African American and Hispanic youths are more likely to be detained in secure pretrial confinement (and for longer periods of time) than Caucasian youths arrested for similar offenses, even controlling for factors such as gender, family circumstances, and prior offense records. They also typically receive harsher dispositions, including commitment to state institutions, than Caucasian youths with similar profiles who have been charged with the same types of crime (Jones & Krisberg, 1994). Much self-report data on substance use and violent behavior contradict the prevalence rates suggested by arrest and incarceration records (Huizinga & Elliott, 1985; Stark, 1993; see also sections on Hispanic and African American youth to follow). However, in many studies interpretation of crime trends tends to focus exclusively on these official records sources and does not consider confounding circumstances.

Because of these limitations, the descriptions of antisocial behavior in populations of Hispanic, Asian American, Native American, and African American adolescents that follow should be interpreted with caution and should be considered only as a very early foundation for the knowledge base needed.

ANTISOCIAL BEHAVIOR PATTERNS IN EACH ETHNIC MINORITY GROUP

HISPANICS

Profile of the Population

Although U.S. Hispanics share a common language, they represent a heterogeneous population in terms of countries of origin, English proficiency, acculturation, cultural norms, and racial background (Rosado & Elias, 1993; Soriano, 1994). The largest subgroups of Hispanics are Mexican Americans, Puerto Ricans, Cubans, and other individuals from many different Central and South American countries, accounting for 63%, 11%, 5%, and 22%, respectively, of the total U.S. Hispanic population (Rosado & Elias, 1993; Soriano, 1994). The greatest concentrations of these groups are in California, Texas, New York, and Florida with a smaller but still sizable presence in New Jersey, New Mexico, Arizona, and Colorado (Rosado & Elias, 1993).

Socioeconomic profiles vary somewhat by ethnic subgroup but reflect by many indicators a disadvantaged status. Poverty levels are high for Hispanic families. Puerto Rican and Mexican American families are on the average about three times more likely to fall below federal poverty guidelines than White non-Hispanic families. Hispanic high school completion rates of 50.9% compare unfavorably to those of African Americans (64.6%) and White non-Hispanics (78.4%) (Flack et al., 1995). Within the Hispanic population, a subgroup with particularly poor living conditions is the migrant and seasonal farm worker whose average annual income is about $5,500 and whose family frequently resides in substandard housing and has poor access to support resources (Martin, Gordon, & Kuperschmidt, 1995).

Delinquency

According to the National Council on Crime and Delinquency, in 1991, the overall rate of incarceration for Hispanic adolescents was 60% greater than that of Caucasian youths although less than half that of African American youths (Jones & Krisberg, 1994). A similar pattern was shown in a study of juvenile first time offenders in the San Francisco Bay area. The number of African American delinquent offenders was more than double that of Hispanic youth, although the percentage increase of juvenile court contacts between 1988 and 1992 was greater for Hispanic youth (66%) than for African Americans (27%; White et al., 1995). Earlier FBI reports indicated that between 1985 and 1989, Hispanic adolescents accounted for a disproportionate share of arrests for murder, rape, robbery, and aggravated assault (cited in Ewing, 1990).

Delinquency is generally higher among dropout youth, and Hispanic youth, particularly those with limited English proficiency, are at higher than average risk for school dropout (Chavez et al., 1989; Chavez, Oetting, & Swaim, 1994). In a study that examined the delinquent behavior of dropout youth, Mexican American dropouts were found to have lower rates of minor delinquent activity (shoplifting, threatening with a weapon, and driving under the influence) but higher rates of serious deviant behavior including violent assaults with weapons, auto theft, burglary, and purchase of stolen goods than their Caucasian dropout counterparts (Chavez et al., 1994).

Gang Involvement

By a national survey on gang membership, Hispanic adolescents have been estimated to represent the second largest population of U.S. gang members (Spergel, 1989, cited in Soriano, 1994). However, in certain cities, they constitute the largest proportion. In Los Angeles, Hispanics account for 58% of the street gang population (Hutson, Anglin, & Pratt, 1994) and in Chicago, there are an estimated 50 Hispanic gangs, the largest number in the city (Ribisl & Davidson, 1993).

There is considerable variation in the degree and seriousness of antisocial and violent behavior carried out as part of the gang activity of Hispanic youths (Moore, 1987; Vigil, 1987). Hispanic gangs in Los Angeles are frequently involved in drive-by shootings that result in death or serious injury (Hutson et al., 1994). Violent assault and threats of physical attack by Hispanic gangs in Chicago's public schools have been widespread and have been identified by students who are not in gangs as a major reason for their dropping out of school (Hutchison & Kyle, 1993). On the other hand, investigation of Chicano gangs in smaller cities including Phoenix and Milwaukee found that Hispanic gang members in these locations had no greater likelihood than other youths with similar profiles to fight or to commit assaults (Moore, 1987).

Ethnic differences in the patterns of gang activities have been identified. Hispanic groups are believed to be more prone to engage in violence related to protection of territory or "turf" whereas other ethnic minority gangs may be more involved in robbery, vandalism, or drug trafficking (Ribisl & Davidson, 1993). Vigil (1987) described a Chicano gang norm which encourages its members to think and act like " 'vatos locos' [crazy dudes], moving in and out of . . . wild adventures, showing fearlessness, toughness, daring, and especially unpredictable forms of destructive behavior" (p. 237).

Substance Abuse

Recent survey data have found with much consistency that rates of use and abuse of alcohol and other drugs are generally lower among Hispanic adolescents in comparison to Caucasian youths (Boles, Casas, Furlong, Gonzalez, & Morrison, 1994; Brindis et al., 1995; Catalano et al., 1993; Newcomb et al., 1990; Oetting & Beauvais, 1991; Rodriguez & Recio, 1992; U.S. Department of Health and Human Services [USDHHS], 1995; Vanderschmidt, Lang, Knight-Williams, & Vanderschmidt, 1993). An exception is found in the report of Kann and colleagues (1995) on the results of the 1993 Youth Risk Behavior Survey. In this study both male and female Hispanic high school students were significantly more likely to report lifetime marijuana, cocaine, and crack use. In addition, Hispanic males also admitted to episodic heavy drinking more frequently than did Caucasian or African American male adolescents. Gender and ethnic subgroup differences in drinking and drug use patterns were evident in these studies as well. Hispanic youths who were recent immigrants demonstrated lower rates of alcohol and marijuana use than those of native-born Hispanic adolescents (Brindis et al., 1995; White et al., 1995). Oetting and Beauvais (1991) came to a similar conclusion, noting that youths who self-identified as Spanish American (whose families had been in the United States for a longer period of time) had significantly higher rates across all categories of substance use than more recently arrived Mexican American adolescents.

In all the studies reported here, Hispanic male adolescent rates of alcohol and drug use were found to be higher than rates for Hispanic females. One study indicated that the lowest levels of substance use and the highest levels of total abstinence among all gender and ethnic groups were reported by Mexican American female adolescents (Boles et al., 1994). Another investigation found that Hispanic female rates for alcohol and other drug use were lower than those of Caucasian males and non-Hispanic White females but were higher than those of African American female adolescents (USDHHS, 1995). By most accounts, the extent of substance use for young Hispanic women was low, and this held true even among the school dropout population (Chavez et al., 1994).

These findings appear to be inconsistent with other research that suggests high prevalence rates of substance abuse among older Hispanic adolescents and young adults (Oetting & Beauvais, 1991). However, it is notable that with the exception of the USDHHS study (1995) and the work of Chavez and colleagues (1989, 1994), the studies cited in this section are based on in-school surveys that, by virtue of the high dropout, school absence, and incarceration rates of Hispanic youths, probably underrepresent the population most at-risk for this problem. Because out-of-school youth are much more likely to engage in drug use and other antisocial behavior (Chavez et al., 1994; Watts & Wright, 1990), their exclusion likely means that the actual extent of substance abuse by Hispanic youth is underestimated in these studies.

Violence

Research on the perpetration of violence by Hispanic adolescents is much less prolific than studies on this problem in the African American youth population. In general, there is a lack of detailed information on overall prevalence and extent of violence committed by this group. In addition, there are very few studies that have included intra- and interethnic comparison data. Most available research suggests that Hispanic adolescents are responsible for a greater amount of violent behavior than Caucasian adolescents but less than their African American peers. During the 1980s, Hispanic youth accounted for almost 25% of the total juvenile arrests for murder at a time when their representation in the U.S. population was about 8% (Ewing, 1990). This rate, however, was lower than that of African American adolescents who made up roughly half of those arrested for homicide.

Data on the commission of nonfatal violence by Hispanic youths shows a similar trend. The Youth Risk Behavior Survey (YRBS) system developed by the Centers for Disease Control provides data on self-reported fighting behavior and carrying of weapons (as well as information on other health behavior concerns including substance abuse). The YRBS, now conducted biennially, includes national, state, territorial, and local school-based surveys of high school students (Kann et al., 1995). Various YRBS reports indicate that Hispanic male adolescents have higher rates of fighting than Caucasian youths. They also estimate that rates of these behaviors for young Hispanic women have been lower than for all males but higher than for female Caucasian adolescents (Kann et al., 1995; Rodriguez & Brindis, 1995; USDHHS, 1995). Reported rates of Hispanic youths carrying a weapon have varied, ranging from 17.2% (USDHHS, 1995) to 41.1% (Rodriguez & Brindis, 1995). Comparisons with non–African American minority groups were not available in these surveys nor were they reported for African Americans in all categories of violent behavior indicators; where reported, two showed somewhat lower rates for Hispanic youth (Kann et al., 1995; USDHHS, 1995), although an earlier YRBS report found that Hispanic male adolescents carried weapons more frequently than African American male teens (Centers for Disease Control [CDC], 1991).

For out-of-school youths, there is still less information on violent behavior patterns. The USDHHS (1995) study included Hispanic dropout youths in its survey population but did not report on response differences for in-school versus dropout youths. Chavez et al. (1994) found a high incidence of violence perpetration by the young Mexican American dropouts in their study population. They reported that almost 1 in 5 Mexican American dropout youths had cut someone with a knife. They also determined that the incidence of violence perpetration for Mexican American dropouts was somewhat higher than that of Caucasian dropouts and significantly higher than a comparison group of Mexican American and Caucasian youths who were still in school.

Risk and Resiliency Factors

The behaviors related to substance abuse, violence, gang membership, and delinquency are so frequently interconnected that engaging in any one of them has to be considered a risk factor for becoming involved in any or all of the others. In addition, other sources of risk have been identified in the research on the antisocial behavior patterns of Hispanic adolescents. Some of the identified factors appear to be common across all youth groups. For example, Soriano, Soriano, and Jimenez (1994) listed the following as potential contributors to gang involvement: high levels of family stress, conflict, and domestic violence; alcohol and drug abuse; low self-esteem; poor communication skills; poor parental disciplinary practices and lack of involvement with the child's school; and low expectations of parent and teacher. Sheline, Skipper, and Broadhead (1994) also highlighted the adverse effects of harsh disciplinary methods and infrequent parental expression of affection on aggression in Hispanic elementary school boys. The work of Chavez and colleagues (1989, 1994) called attention to the positive influence of staying in school as a protective factor against violent and delinquent behavior. These risk and resiliency factors are somewhat "generic" in that they would have applicability as positive or negative influences for adolescents of any ethnicity. We can easily identify other contributors in the same category (e.g., poverty, unemployment, interpersonal skill deficits, association with deviant peers). Rather than covering the more universal risk factors in depth, this section focuses primarily on the behavioral influences more unique to Hispanic children and adolescents.

Cultural factors such as ethnic affiliation, ethnic identity, and acculturation levels may be significant contributors to the Hispanic youths' behavioral choices. Length of stay in the United States has been associated with levels of alcohol and drug use; that is, native-born Hispanic youths are more prone to substance use and abuse than newcomer immigrant youths (Brindis et al., 1995; White et al., 1995). Of course, length of residence may not accurately reflect one's level of acculturation. However, at minimum, a longer period of residence clearly presents the ethnic minority adolescent with greater opportunities to observe the mainstream culture's norms and behaviors. In some communities these norms include not only acceptance of substance use but peer pressure actively encouraging this behavior. Because Hispanic youth with longer exposure to these expectations and practices appear to move closer to Anglo substance use patterns, it is possible that a Hispanic youth's fuller assimilation into the majority culture, perhaps accompanied by a loss of identification with his or her own ethnic culture, may constitute a risk factor for use and abuse of alcohol and other drugs. There is modest empirical support for this proposition. Oetting and Beauvais (1991) found that higher levels of identification with Hispanic culture had a positive effect on substance use and that identification with Anglo culture had the opposite outcome.

For Hispanic adolescents, the straddling of two cultures presents additional risks. Studies by Szapocznik, Kurtines, Santiesteban, and Rio (1990) suggested that bicultural conflicts between Cuban children and their parents, based on differing levels of acculturation, led these children to be more easily influenced by substance-abusing, antisocial peers. The Puerto Rican Youth Survey of male adolescents in New York City (Pabon, Rodriguez, & Gurin, 1992) examined more closely the connection between delinquent behaviors and associations with deviant peers. This study found positive correlations between these variables but only in relation to time spent with delinquent peers in the evenings. The authors also found that delinquent peer group relationships were characterized by emotional estrangement such as feelings of loneliness. They proposed a possible explanation from earlier research (Edelman, 1984, cited in Pabon, Rodriguez, & Gurin, 1992) that suggested that bonding of delinquent Hispanic youths emerged more from a desire for protection against neighborhood violence than from a search for emotional attachment.

Certain family factors are key influences on whether a youth will follow a conventional or delinquent path, and they appear to be an especially critical influence on the behavior of Hispanic youths (Murata, 1990; Rodriguez & Recio, 1992; Smith & Krohn, 1995; Soriano et al., 1994; Vega, Gil et al., 1993). Risk for joining a gang is increased for Hispanic males when there are intergenerational role models in the family and bicultural family conflicts (Soriano et al., 1994). Male Puerto Rican adolescents were more likely than others in a national sample to engage in hard drug use when there was a lesser degree of parental involvement in school (Rodriguez & Recio, 1992). Smith and Krohn (1995) found that strong family solidarity, cohesion, and attachment were greater influences promoting nondelinquent behavior for Hispanic male adolescents than for African American and Caucasian male youths. However, for Hispanic youths, direct parental control and discipline exerted a lesser influence.

Although family variables represent critically important risk or protective factors, they are not exclusive determinants of the Hispanic youths' behavioral pathway. Association with acting-out peers, prior drug use, and tolerance for deviance have also been found to be strongly related to hard drug use (Rodriguez & Recio, 1992). Vega, Gil et al. (1993) found acculturation variables to be of similar importance in the behavioral choices of Cuban American adolescents. Their study concluded that an absence of family protective variables (family pride, respect, cohesion, parental support, and disposition to deviance) created risk for the Cuban American adolescent but that, once created, acculturation strain variables (birthplace, language conflict, acculturation conflict, and perception of discrimination) had a stronger role in actually producing the negative behavior.

Many Hispanic children and adolescents lack access to school and community resources that might prevent the onset and maintenance of antisocial behavior. Boles and her colleagues (1994) reported that Mexican American and Mexican youths (the latter term refers to youngsters born in Mexico but now living in the United States) had participated less frequently in substance abuse prevention programs than their fellow Caucasian high school students. The experiences of other Hispanic subgroups are similar. Children of migrant and seasonal farm workers, a predominantly Hispanic population, demonstrate high levels of emotional and behavioral problems. However, they seldom receive preventive psychological treatment because of logistical, attitudinal, or structural barriers such as parents' transportation difficulties, fear or dislike of health professionals, or language incompatibilities (Martin et al., 1995). Comparable barriers to preventive services also affect many urban Hispanic youths, including those living in distressed neighborhoods where there is chronic exposure to community violence, a major risk factor for future violence perpetration and other antisocial behaviors (Attar, Guerra, & Tolan, 1994). The reader is referred to Coatsworth, Szapocznik, Kurtines, and Santisteban (Chapter 37, this volume) for a review of culturally competent psychosocial interventions with Hispanic youths.

Although good school adjustment clearly functions as a protective factor against antisocial behavior for Hispanic and all other youths, there are unusual risks that threaten the ability of Hispanic immigrant and other young people with limited English language skills to make educational progress. It is especially difficult for Hispanic newcomer children to do well and remain in school. They report feelings of marginalization, fears of deportation, shock at the behavior of U.S. students (e.g., drugs and weapons in schools, racial hate violence, lack of respect for teachers), and verbal and physical victimization. Their educational advancement is often hampered by the lack of culturally competent teachers, textbooks that are not written from a multicultural perspective, and difficulties in placing them at the appropriate grade level. In addition, if not proficient in English, they may receive insufficient English language instruction to allow them to participate meaningfully in regular academic courses (White et al., 1995).

ASIAN AMERICANS

Profile of the Population

Asian Americans are an extremely heterogeneous group with wide diversity in their languages, national and racial origins, religious beliefs, lifestyles, cultural traditions, and health behaviors (Chen & True, 1994). Asian Americans in the United States represent 28 different ethnic groups including, in order of population size, Chinese, Filipino, Japanese, Asian Indian, and Koreans. The highest concentrations of Asian Americans reside in California, Hawaii,

New York, Texas, and Illinois. The Asian American population includes Pacific Islanders, an ethnically diverse group comprised of Native Hawaiians, Samoans, Guanamanians, Tongans, and Fijians (Chen & True, 1994; Flack et al., 1995). Some of the continental U.S. Asian American population includes people of Chinese, Japanese, and Filipino descent who have been in the country for more than a century. However, more recently arrived Southeast Asian immigrants and refugees now make up a sizable portion of the Asian American population (Chen & True, 1994; Lee, 1988).

There is wide variation in the demographic profiles of Asian Americans. Although generally perceived to be more affluent and better educated than other ethnic minority groups, these characteristics typically apply to those who have lived in the country longer or those who were wealthy at the time of entry. Later-arriving refugees and immigrants are generally of lower socioeconomic status. Muecke (1983) noted that the waves of Southeast Asian refugees arriving in the early to mid-1970s were generally well-educated and familiar with Western culture. However, most of the refugee and immigrants entering the country in the 1980s and 1990s have had little or no formal education; have lived in rural and remote locations; have experienced extended periods of malnutrition, stress, and transitional living arrangements prior to their U.S. arrival; and have fled under dire circumstances rather than making a studied personal choice to immigrate. Thus, although overall rates for income level and educational attainment are generally higher for Asian Americans than for non-Hispanic White families, there are ethnic subgroups (in particular, the newcomer Southeast Asians) that have high poverty and school dropout rates. In some locations dropout rates for Laotian and Filipino students are around 50%. There are also significant numbers of Asian Americans and Pacific Islanders living in poverty; their overall below-poverty rates of 14% are about twice that of non-Hispanic Whites (Chen & True, 1994).

Delinquency

There is virtually no data available on general levels of delinquent behavior among Asian American youth. In official statistics and self-report surveys, Asian American children and adolescents are most frequently aggregated into the "Other" category, which makes it impossible to distinguish their unique behavior patterns (NCHS, 1991). From the scarce available data, it appears that their rates of delinquency are lower than for other ethnic minority groups (Chen & True, 1994). However, antisocial conduct problems and juvenile court involvement are exhibited by certain ethnic subgroups of Asian American youths. Williams (1989) has noted behavior problems, including lying, cheating, stealing, and prostitution among some Southeast Asian refugee adolescents, especially unaccompanied minors and Amerasian youths (generally those born to Asian mothers and American soldiers). A San Francisco study found that although overall rates of delinquent offending were lower for Asian American youths than for Hispanic, African American, and Caucasian adolescents, their arrests began to increase in 1988, so that by 1992, the numbers of Asian Americans involved in the juvenile justice system had come close to that of Hispanic youths, the second highest offender group (White et al., 1995).

Data on delinquent behavior among the ethnically diverse adolescents in Hawaii are available through statewide studies conducted by the Center for Youth Research at the University of Hawaii (Chesney-Lind et al., 1992; Rockhill et al., 1993). Trends described in these studies did not indicate a pattern of overall increase in delinquency during the 1980s. Arrests for serious violent crime such as homicide, rape, and robbery declined. However, cases of aggravated assault nearly quadrupled and status offenses such as running away from home increased by 179%. Similar to national patterns, the majority of juvenile crime among Pacific Islander youth was committed by male adolescents (Chesney-Lind et al., 1992). Self-report surveys of antisocial behavior using questions extrapolated from the National Youth Survey suggested that there was variation in delinquent activity by island of residence and by neighborhood. Youths from Neighbor Islands and Maui reported more antisocial behavior than did adolescent residents of Oahu, including shoplifting, creating graffiti, drug dealing, gang fighting, drug use, weapons carrying, and vandalism in spite of the fact that demographic profiles were similar. Other data collected from local schools and service agencies on Oahu found higher rates of antisocial activity among the portion of the Hawaiian youth population living in poor communities (Rockhill et al., 1993).

Gangs

Asian American gangs constitute a small proportion of the total gang population in the United States. Their numbers have been estimated at 2,000 members (Huff, 1993). It is likely that this is an undercount. In San Francisco alone, 14 Filipino and 10 multiethnic (Southeast Asian and Chinese) gangs have been identified by law enforcement sources (White et al., 1995). Asian American gangs are reported to be involved in very serious crime including heroin and other drug trafficking, victimization of local businesses, and robbery. Concerns have been raised that their numbers are growing, with particular increases among Southeast Asian youth (Conly, Kelly, Mahanna, & Warner, 1993; Huff, 1993). Gang growth in Hawaii has been evident in recent years. In 1988 the Honolulu Police Department identified 22 gangs with a membership of about 450. By 1991, the official count had grown to 45 gangs with an estimated 1,020 members, primarily Filipino, 47.4%; Samoan, 18%; or Native Hawaiian, 14.4% (Chesney-Lind et al., 1992). Self-reports of gang contact by Hawaiian youth indicated that a high proportion of these adolescents have regular association with gang members, with 51% reporting having friends who are gang members, 27% having family members in gangs, and 12% of the reporting youth themselves belonging to gangs (Rockhill et al., 1993).

Intraethnic differences are notable among Asian American gangs. Chinese gangs have been reported to be more involved with organized crime and to include more adults in their membership (Chen & True, 1994; Conly et al., 1993; Huff, 1993). Vietnamese gangs attract less educated and urbanized youth whose activities include criminally motivated robberies and assaults in their own communities; certain Vietnamese cultural norms (e.g., distrust of banks and tendency to keep valuables at home) make neighborhood residents vulnerable to muggings and assaults by these

young gang members (Huff, 1993). Hawaiian youth gang members report high levels of alcohol and drug use, and 67% report routinely carrying a concealed weapon. Female adolescent Hawaiian gang members report less delinquent activity than their fellow male gang members but a significantly greater incidence of drug use, weapons carrying, and vandalism than their female peers who are not in gangs (Rockhill et al., 1993).

Substance Abuse

There is little research that reports on Asian American adolescent patterns of substance abuse. As in other health and behavior areas, on national surveys Asian American youths are generally excluded from analysis because of small numbers or the data are impossible to analyze because of aggregation practices (Oetting & Beauvais, 1991). The scarce existing data suggest that alcohol and other drug use rates are lower than those of Caucasian youths or children and adolescents of other ethnicities (Oetting & Beauvais, 1991; White et al., 1995). A low alcohol usage pattern is also reflected among Asian American adults who are underrepresented in admissions to alcohol treatment programs (USDHHS, 1990). The study of newcomer youths in the San Francisco area also found that Chinese American adolescents had lower rates of lifetime cocaine and other illegal drug use but called attention to the fact that drinking rates of Chinese American youths who had been in the United States for a longer period of residence were higher than those of newcomer Chinese American high school students (White et al., 1995). An earlier study of more than 1,900 Asian/Pacific Islander students by the U.S. Department of Education reported relatively high incidence of occasional alcohol use by Asian American adolescents at rates of 43.7% for males and 34.2% for females (cited in Chen & True, 1994). Although these rates are still substantially lower than ones generally reported for Caucasian or other ethnic minority youths (compare, for example, Kann et al., 1995), these studies suggest that alcohol use among Asian American and Pacific Islander adolescents may not be an inconsequential problem.

Violence

Similar to other behavior risk categories, there is little information on Asian American youths as perpetrators of violence. Homicide perpetration rates appear to be the lowest for all Asian Americans than for all other groups. In 1988, Asian American youths accounted for only 1.3% of the total homicides in the United States. It is of some concern, however, that this proportion represented a substantial increase from their 1984 rate of 0.4% (Ewing, 1990). In a school-based survey in San Francisco that measured self-reported carrying of weapons and fighting, Chinese American youths reported lower rates of such behaviors than did all other respondents (cited in White et al., 1995). On the other hand, within the general population of Asian American youths, gang members are a subgroup more prone to committing acts of violence. The Hawaii self-report survey documented high levels of weapons carrying, gang fighting, and other assaultive behavior by both male and female gang members (Rockhill et al., 1993). However, arrest records for Hawaiian gang members suggested more involvement in property crimes than in murders or assault (Chesney-Lind et al., 1992).

Risk and Resiliency Factors

Like all youths, Asian American adolescents are at higher risk for antisocial behavior if they live in inner city neighborhoods where they are routinely exposed to street violence, the drug trade, gang activity, and robbery (Chesney-Lind et al., 1992). There are other risk and protective factors that are culturally specific to adolescents of this ethnicity. For example, one explanation for their apparently low participation in substance use may be the influence of parental abstinence as it appears that there is also little alcohol and drug use among adult Asian Americans (USDHHS, 1990). In addition, a survey population of Asian American youths reported holding cognitive beliefs about substance use that would support avoidance of this behavior. Specifically, they endorsed the views that marijuana is harmful and that use of drugs might lead to addiction more frequently than did Hispanic or African American youths or adolescents of other ethnic groups. They also indicated that they were less inclined to use drugs because of fear of punishment and because they believed that using drugs would make them feel disappointed in themselves (Newcomb et al., 1990). It would be worthwhile to investigate how these beliefs originated.

Traditional Asian American values of harmony, pacifism, and impulse control may also serve as a protective mechanism for youths, buffering them against the conditions that encourage violent and aggressive behavior. In addition, the traditional Asian family roles requiring strict obedience to parental authority may also inhibit these types of behavior (Hill et al., 1994).

On the other hand, when cultures clash, the resulting conflicts can be a source of vulnerability for Asian American youths. Lee (1988) has described the multidimensional sources of acculturative stress experienced by Southeast Asian refugee adolescents when they come into contact with American culture. She identified five separate cultures (Southeast Asian, American, refugee, American adolescent, and Asian refugee adolescent) into which these youngsters must try to integrate successfully. The engendered stress is believed to be related to the high incidence of behavioral and emotional problems among many Southeast Asian refugee youths.

For refugee and immigrant youths, the quality of their postmigration experiences will help to determine their adjustment to American life and their progress on a number of dimensions, including school performance and the development of friendships, both of which can serve as protective forces against taking behavioral risk (Lee, 1988). A study of Vietnamese adolescents in Connecticut found that youngsters who did not establish friendships with American peers were at greater risk for emotional and behavioral problems than their peers who formed this bond (cited in Lee, 1988). Unfortunately, many newcomer children report that their initial experiences are quite negative and that they find American culture unwelcoming, particularly in the school environment (White et al., 1995). Asian American adolescents in Minneapolis surveyed as part of the Minnesota Adolescent Health Survey indicated the highest levels of concern of any ethnic group about "being treated unfairly because of my race" (Rode & Bellfield, 1992).

The assimilation process for Asian American adolescents is also a frequent source of intergenerational conflict between these youngsters and their parents (Huang, 1994; Lee, 1988). If Asian American adolescents adopt the mainstream American adolescent values of greater independence and autonomy and less restrained emotional expression, conflict with parents can result (Yau & Smetana, 1993). Bicultural family stress has been identified as a risk contributor for gang membership (Chen & True, 1994; Huang, 1994; Soriano et al., 1994). Huang (1994) cites research indicating that many Chinese adolescents in serious conflict with their families over such issues have coped with a loss of family support by joining gangs.

There appear to be few prevention programs that specifically target the Asian American adolescent population. In a recent review of community-based health promotion programs for ethnic minority adolescents, only one of the 19 programs identified was serving a predominantly Asian American youth population (Yung & Hammond, 1997). Such programs could serve as a protective influence against an environment of risk, and their development has been particularly recommended for the Southeast Asian refugee population (Williams & Berry, 1991).

NATIVE AMERICANS

Profile of the Population

The Native American population is composed of many tribes and subpopulations of diverse cultural orientations and characterized by different lifestyles, language families, states of acculturation, and residency (e.g., reservations, rural communities, or cities). Native Americans have been described as the "smallest and perhaps most diverse of all American minority groups" (Nickens, 1991, p. 29). In the United States, there are at least 124 major federally recognized tribes and bands with larger but undetermined numbers of subgroupings (estimated at around 500) such as pueblo units or villages, each with distinct traditions and customs (Johnson et al., 1995).

Among identified Native Americans, the largest concentrations are found within the Western and Pacific regions of the lower 48 states of the continental United States, with approximately 47% residing in four states: California, Oklahoma, Arizona, and New Mexico (Ho, 1992). In Alaska the indigenous people include Eskimos, Aleuts, and the Athabascans of the eastern sector of the state; these groups comprise about 16% of the state's population (Ho, 1992; Trimble, 1990). An increasing trend toward moves from reservations to urban locations has been notable since 1970, with only about an estimated one fourth of the Native American population currently living on 278 federal and state reservations (Ho, 1992). This dispersement throughout the general U.S. population isolates Native Americans from their indigenous political and cultural institutions and traditions and also removes them further geographically from federal service programs designed to meet their health and other resource needs (Johnson et al., 1995).

By many indicators, the Native American population does not enjoy a status of parity and well-being in American society. Native

Americans are two to three times more likely to live at poverty level than non-Native American groups (Johnson et al., 1995). School dropout rates for Native American youths have been estimated to be as high as 50% (Shafer, 1995).

Delinquency

Native American youth delinquency has received relatively little attention in research literature. A majority of the research has been directed to the study of substance abuse and suicide, which represent the problems of greatest concern among Native American youths. McShane (1988) listed eight studies conducted primarily during the 1970s that examined delinquent behavior such as petty theft and misdemeanors in relation to family disorganization, drug use, and forced attendance at boarding school. The Office of Technology Assessment (OTA, 1990) cited research that suggested that when alcohol-related offenses were factored out, Native American youth delinquency rates were comparable to those of other adolescent groups.

The best recent source of information on Native American delinquency comes from the self-reports of the Minnesota Adolescent Health Survey given to approximately 14,000 Native American youths across the country (Blum, Harmon, Harris, Bergeisen, & Resnick, 1992; Blum, Harmon, Harris, Resnick et al., 1992). In addition to the valuable information it provides on Native American gangs, substance use, and violence (see subsections to follow), the survey also captured information on other delinquent behavior. Nearly 20% of the survey respondents said they had stolen money from their parents in the last year. About 23% of the male students and about 14% of the females admitted to damaging or vandalizing property. About 1 in 5 males and 16% of female respondents said they had shoplifted within the past year. Female rates of running away from home at 10% were slightly higher than male rates of 8% (Blum, Harmon, Harris, Resnick et al., 1992). For these particular behaviors, there was no information on comparative rates for Caucasian or other ethnic minority youths, although such comparisons were described for other dimensions of antisocial behavior such as substance abuse.

Gangs

Information on Native American gangs is also available through the Minnesota Adolescent Health Survey. Among both males and females, about 15% of the respondents identified themselves as belonging to gangs. Survey results also showed that Native American youths who were gang members were more likely to report being involved in multiple episodes of violent behavior, with 18% claiming they had hit or beaten someone up three or more times during the past year and a similar percentage indicating they had been in three or more group fights in this same time frame. In addition, gang members were more likely than nongang members to be routine users of alcohol and other drugs (Blum, Harmon, Harris, Resnick et al., 1992).

Substance Abuse

Substance abuse among Native American youths has been a longstanding concern. Reviews have generally demonstrated over many years that Native American adolescents and adults have high rates of alcohol and other drug use, typically at levels far exceeding those of Caucasians and all other ethnic groups (Moncher, Holden, & Trimble, 1990; Rodriguez & Recio, 1992). However, two recent studies reported opposite findings. Sellers, Winfree, and Griffiths (1993) did not find differences in alcohol consumption patterns among older male Native American and non-Native American youths. They did find that all youths in their sample had high consumption rates and that Native American youths were significantly more likely to have permissive attitudes toward marijuana use. The Minnesota study found that in comparison with a rural Caucasian sample, Native American survey respondents reported lower rates of routine alcohol use. However, they also discovered that the rates of heavy drinking for Native American 12th graders and the rates of use of all other drugs for all Native American subjects were significantly higher than for the comparison group (Blum, Harmon, Harris, Resnick et al., 1992). Empirical studies on Native American child and adolescent substance use also have consistently shown that use of tobacco, alcohol, and other drugs is initiated at earlier ages among Native American children and adolescents than among any other group (Blum, Harmon, Harris, Resnick et al., 1992; Moncher et al., 1990; Segal, 1994).

Violence

There is little research that has focused specifically on the problem of Native American youth violence perpetration or victimization (Hampton & Yung, 1995; Yung & Hammond, 1995b). Rates of homicide perpetration by Native Americans of all ages appear to be the lowest for all ethnic minority groups, standing at 0.7% in 1990 (National Research Council, 1993), although an earlier study found that youth-committed homicides were lower for Native Americans than for Hispanics and African Americans but higher than for Asian American youths (Ewing, 1990). In addition, Native American youths are overrepresented in arrests for aggravated nonfatal and other assaults (National Research Council, 1993). Data from the Minnesota study support the view that there are substantial problems with fighting and bullying in this population. The study reported that nearly 40% of Native American adolescents had hit or beat someone up during the past year, with the highest rates among male middle school students. An average of 25% of these youths said they had been in a group fight at least once in the past year. Overall group fighting was more prevalent among males than females.

Risk and Resiliency Factors

Similar to patterns for other ethnic minority groups, it appears to be the accumulation of risk factors that predisposes some Native American adolescents toward antisocial behavior. Moncher et al. (1990) empirically tested the proposition that Native American children exposed to a greater number of risk factors would have the highest incidence of substance use, and their findings supported this hypothesis. Among the fourth and fifth grade children in their sample, those with 10 or more of 16 identified risk factors (including various measures of school adjustment, school absenteeism, and parental and peer smoking) were currently using beer or wine (at a 90% rate) or marijuana (at an 80% rate). Native American children and adolescents who live on reservations face other community-level risks created by the conditions associated with poverty and lack of economic and recreational opportunities (Johnson et al., 1995).

Native American cultural values should function as a powerful protective force and mitigator of risk for a variety of problem behaviors. Of particular importance is the tradition of Native American dependence "on relational networks that support and nurture bonds of mutual assistance and affection and emphasize the importance of personal respect" (Hill et al., 1994, p. 83). Such support systems can serve to alleviate stress, work through difficult problems, provide material assistance, and contribute to feelings of self-esteem and security, all of which might help adolescents refrain from self-destructive behavior and function better in a sometimes hostile environment. However, under present conditions of geographic dispersement, social isolation, and distancing from indigenous traditions, this source of support is often lacking (Johnson et al., 1995). Urban Native American adolescents living in Minnesota reported lower feelings of family, school, and community connectedness and a lesser belief that school personnel or church leaders cared about their welfare than their Caucasian or other ethnic minority peers. Nearly 20% of the boys and 7% of the girls said that they would not seek help from anyone if they were feeling depressed or angry or were experiencing relationship problems (Rode & Bellfield, 1992).

The issue of cultural identification is particularly complex for Native American youths. Oetting and Beauvais (1991) cite research that suggests that greater identification with Native American culture works as a risk rather than a protective factor. In fact, they found that Native American youths with the highest levels of identification with their own culture also had the highest levels of substance abuse. LaFromboise, Coleman, and Gerton (1993) have advanced the viewpoint, supported by empirical research, that Native American adolescents who have a bicultural orientation may have better general levels of psychological functioning and enhanced protection from behavioral risks. The development of such bicultural competence as a positive force against involvement in antisocial behavior bears further investigation as to specific effects on substance abuse, violence perpetration, gang membership, and delinquency (Hill et al., 1994; LaFromboise et al., 1993).

The development of prosocial skills has been established as an important mediator for all children and youths against various types of problem behavior, including violence, substance abuse, and gang membership. Because of high rates of adult substance abuse in Native American families, some Native American children may have less exposure to the modeling of abstinence and the development of related prosocial skills and attitudes. Mail (1995) reported on her observations of a class of Native American second graders who were pretending to be drunk. Their play included a make-believe drive in a truck weaving about because of the intoxication of the "driver." The children's teacher indicated that many of the parents of these children were problem drinkers and remarked on the fact that the children did not mimic the negative aspects of drinking, only amusement at a loss of physical and mental control. It may be especially important to expose young Native American youths to positive social learning influences that present models for skills of refusal, resistance to peer pressure, problem solving, and negotiation, which might help them to attain and maintain safe and drug-free behavior.

Positive bonding to school is a well-recognized protective factor that can help to shape feelings of self-worth and competence as well as improve future prospects for employment and a comfortable material life. Unfortunately, many Native American youths have negative attitudes toward school, which is reflected in poor attendance and academic performance. Nearly one third of the Native American junior high school students surveyed as part of the Minnesota Adolescent Health Survey reported that they disliked school; those who reported these feelings had lower grades and higher incidence of truancy, and their rates were higher than their Caucasian and other peers. At senior high level, however, a lower percentage of Native American students reported dislike of school. For this group, grades were higher, attendance was better, and more concern about academic progress was expressed. A possible explanation for the difference between junior and senior level students is that the more dissatisfied and poorer performing students may drop out before reaching high school. Combined with other data confirming high dropout rates among Native American youths, these findings underscore the importance of designing early preventive interventions that will reduce alienation from school, improve academic performance, and lower the probability of noncompletion. In addition, it also points to the need for secondary prevention services to improve the potential for retaining at-risk students still in school as well as to develop educational and vocational programming for those who have already dropped out.

AFRICAN AMERICANS

Profile of the Population

Presently African Americans represent the largest ethnic minority group in the United States. In America most persons of this ethnicity share the common heritage of their ancestors having entered the nation as slaves brought in from different African countries. Because of their identifiable physical characteristics of darker skin and their shared legacy of experiences in American society, African Americans are often considered to be a relatively homogeneous group. However, there is considerable within-group diversity on many dimensions, including country of ancestral origin and present life circumstances on a broad range of social, economic, educational, geographic residence, and lifestyle variables. The U.S. African American population also includes immigrants from Africa and the Caribbean (Hammond & Yung, 1994).

There continue to be disparities in the overall status of African Americans in the United States with regard to income, employment, level of educational attainment, health, and other indicators of general welfare. In the 1990 census, the average rate of poverty for African Americans was 32.7% compared with 11.3% for White non-Hispanic individuals. For children the poverty rate was 46% (Flack et al., 1995). Substantial numbers of the African American population live in poor inner-city communities that are characterized by environmental risks such as neighborhood crime, overcrowding, substandard housing, overt drug trafficking, poor schools, and other adverse conditions frequently associated with lower socioeconomic status (Johnson et al., 1995).

African American adolescents, particularly males, have high rates of school dropout and are less likely to find employment after school whether they complete school or drop out (National Center for Education Statistics, 1995). The leading causes of morbidity and early mortality among African Americans include preventable conditions that are often responsible for the untimely deaths of African American children and adolescents, including infant mortality, AIDS, substance abuse, unintentional injury, and violence (Hammond & Yung, 1993; Johnson et al., 1995; Yee et al., 1995).

Attention has been particularly focused on the plight of African American boys and young men who lead all other groups in rates of homicide victimization, perpetration, arrests, convictions, incarceration, and gang involvement as well as being disproportionately represented in alternative schools and special education classes and among school dropouts and the unemployed (Eisenman, 1995; Prothrow-Stith, 1991). The spotlight on endangered African American males has sometimes obscured the similar risk profile of their female counterparts who place second in risk for premature deaths by homicide as well as their vulnerability for other health and behavior problems (Hammond & Yung, 1993; Prothrow-Stith, 1991). National Youth Survey data suggest a 3 to 1 (African American to Caucausian) ratio for young women who are serious violent offenders—an ethnic difference larger than that for males whose Black-to-White differential is 3 to 2 (Elliott, 1994a, 1994b).

Delinquency

Across all age, gender, and ethnic groups, African Americans are overrepresented in virtually all categories of arrests in great disproportion to their representation within the total population (Blumstein, 1995; Council on Crime in America, 1996; Jones & Krisberg, 1994; National Research Council, 1993; U.S. Department of Justice [USDOJ], 1991).

Within the youth population, African American adolescents are five times more likely than Caucasian youths to be arrested for violent crime, including murder, rape, robbery, and assault, and their rates of detention and incarceration are more than three times greater (Office of Juvenile Justice and Delinquency Prevention [OJJDDP], 1993; Jones & Krisberg, 1994). They are also more likely to receive harsher sentences (Jones & Krisberg, 1994). In recent years arrest trends for offenses related to heroin and crack cocaine use and sale have been particularly alarming. During the 1980s Caucasian youth arrests for this type of crimes increased 250%. For African American youths the rate of increase was 2000% (OJJDDP, 1993). Murder arrest rates have shown similar patterns (see section on violence to follow).

Aggravating factors that contribute to the higher delinquency rates of African American youths have been identified. Among these is differential attention by the law enforcement systems to African Americans, particularly with regard to drug activity (Blumstein, 1995; Jones & Krisberg, 1994). Blumstein (1995) also commented on the fact that within the African American community, drug sellers tend more often to operate in the street so that they are more vulnerable to apprehension and arrest. In contrast, Caucasian dealers carry out their trade in less visible locations. Blumstein and others also have implicated the diminishing job opportunities in inner cities as a factor in the greater involvement of African American youths in drug trafficking (Blumstein, 1995; National Research Council, 1993; Weisz, Martin, Walter, & Fernandez, 1991).

Similar explanations, also rooted in economic conditions, have been advanced to account for the higher rates of African American arrests for property crimes. African American male adolescents and adults are more likely than Caucasians to be arrested for robbery. However, Caucasian males are somewhat more likely to be arrested for committing burglaries or other types of theft (USDOJ, 1991). Studies suggest that the commission of property crimes is closely correlated to unemployment and school dropout at a risk level more pronounced than for non-Caucasians (Weisz et al., 1991). Because African American and other economically disadvantaged ethnic minority youths have poorer prospects for completion of education and for employment, they are more likely to turn to illegal means to get their material needs met (Elliott et al., 1986; Weisz et al., 1991).

Gangs

Earlier estimates from the 1980s calculated that there were more than 1,400 gangs in the United States with a membership exceeding 120,000 and that 55% of all gang members were African American (Soriano, 1993). This is undoubtedly a drastic underestimate of current gang membership. In Los Angeles alone, law enforcement officials now claim that there are more than 100,000 Crips and Bloods in the greater metropolitan area, with a continual creation of new loosely affiliated subgangs (Huff, 1993). In addition, whereas in the past the gang problem was concentrated within the largest U.S. cities (primarily New York, Los Angeles, and Chicago), in recent years gang presence has become visible in medium and even smaller size cities throughout the country (Huff, 1993; Monti, 1993). Again it is important to keep in mind that definitions of gangs (and thus gang count) vary widely according to local standards. In some localities, organized crime groups in the drug-trafficking business (which may include youths as part of their distribution network) are also counted as gangs (Huff, 1993).

In spite of these identification issues, it appears that by any accounting system, gang membership has increased and gang activity now includes more drug involvement and more violence using lethal weapons (Goldstein & Soriano, 1994; Huff, 1993; Monti, 1993). Mobility of gang members has been implicated in the establishment of the newer gangs as has the cultural influence of gangster models spread through media influences including television, film, and rap music (Huff, 1993). Economic adversity has also played a strong role. Moore (1993) has described the formation and development of new African American gangs in Milwaukee in the 1980s. Their creation coincided with the disappearance of factory jobs, the loss of other employment opportunities, and a substantial increase in dependence on public welfare. The new African American gangs in this city modeled themselves after established gangs in terms of colors and symbols, but in their early stages, they did not engage in whole-group delinquent or violent acts although members were usually involved as individuals in thefts, acts of vandalism, or other antisocial behaviors. As these gangs evolved, they became more territorial and began to move into the business of drug trafficking.

Gangs routinely engage in a variety of antisocial and delinquent behavior that may include drug use and sale, "missions" of drive-by shootings in rival gang neighborhoods, theft, vandalism, and assault (Goldstein & Soriano, 1994; Huff, 1993). Much of the violence in which the gang is involved occurs over protection of turf, including territory for drug sales and provocations. Goldstein and Soriano (1994) list some of the provocation triggers to include: "bad looks, rumors, territorial boundary disputes, disputes over girls, out-of-neighborhood parties, drinking or using illegal drugs, and ethnic tensions" (p. 321). Cummings (1993) also describes youth group-initiated "wilding sprees" (i.e., extremely violent acts with no apparent provocation). Several of the more notorious incidents such as the 1989 attack and rape of a jogger in Central Park have involved African American youths. Such high-profile acts have been widely covered in the news media and have created public panic and outrage. However, it is unclear how frequently wilding violence occurs, whether it is perpetrated more frequently by one ethnic minority group than by others, and if those who participate in it are actually part of an established gang.

Although most gangs are composed primarily of ethnic minority members, the exact role of ethnicity in enticing young people to join and to stay in gangs is not well understood. It appears that gangs of different ethnicities engage in different activity patterns. For example, Asian American gangs are more likely to be involved in property crimes whereas African American gangs more commonly traffic in drugs (Ribisl & Davidson, 1993). The acquisition of resources, unavailable through legal means, has been hypothesized to be a major contributor to gang involvement, along with a general adolescent need for peer solidarity, excitement, and enhancement of self-image (Goldstein & Soriano, 1994). However, many of these same influences also extend to low-income Caucasian youths who have a much lesser propensity than ethnic minority adolescents to establish or belong to gangs. For African American and other ethnic minority youths, it appears that there are additional contributors related to urban underclass status such as neighborhood disorganization, the need for self-protection, intergenerational role models, and the opportunity to wield power (Cummings & Monti, 1993; Goldstein & Soriano, 1994).

Substance Abuse

Many studies have found lower rates of alcohol and other drug use among African American children and adolescents who are in school in comparison to Caucasian classmates. In addition, where data are available, African American youth substance use rates have been lower than for those of their Native American and Hispanic peers (Catalano et al., 1993; Gruber et al., 1994; Kann et al., 1995; Oetting & Beauvais, 1991; Rode & Bellfield, 1992; USDHHS, 1995; Valois, McKeown, Garrison, & Vincent, 1995). These studies included surveys conducted in urban, rural, and suburban locations. Catalano et al. (1993) also cite research that establishes that with the exception of Native American youths, early initiation of substance use is more prevalent among Cau-

casian children and adolescents than among African American and other ethnic minority youngsters.

These data are not consistent with the higher prevalence rates of alcohol and other substance abuse (particularly crack cocaine) among older African American adolescents and young adults, as suggested by arrest and drug treatment rates. This may be partially accounted for by differential attention by the law enforcement and justice systems to ethnic minority youths (Jones & Krisberg, 1994). In addition, the cited surveys were school-based and thus excluded the higher risk populations of dropout, truant, runaway, homeless, and incarcerated African American youths (Oetting & Beauvais, 1991). Incarcerated African American youths, in particular, have been found to have rates of substance abuse far exceeding those of in-school African American and other youths although these findings are not universal. One study determined that the rates of drug abuse among African American youths in detention were lower than Caucasian male detainees with similar offense profiles (Dembo, Williams, & Schmeidler, 1994). In addition, studies that have compared the adult alcohol use patterns of African Americans to those of Caucasians have found comparable or lower rates for both African American men and women (Myers, Kagawa-Singer, Kumanyika, Lex, & Markides, 1994).

Violence

Although adult homicide arrest rates have been going down since 1980, juvenile homicides have been on the rise. Growth has been particularly evident for young ethnic minority men. Between 1985 and 1992, homicide arrests for non-Caucasian males increased by 123% in comparison to a 50% increase for young Caucasian men (Blumstein, 1995; Council on Crime in America, 1996). For African American male adolescents ages 14 to 17, the rate of increase was 300% (Council on Crime in America, 1996). The profile of homicide offenders in 1992 reflects this disproportion. Of the some 25,000 murderers arrested during this year, 90% were male, 50% were between the ages of 15 and 24, and 55% were African American (USDOJ, 1994).

African Americans were also overrepresented in the 1992 victim population, as they have been for at least the last three decades. African American males had the highest homicide victimization rate at 72 per 100,000, followed by African American females (14 per 100,000), Caucasian males (9 per 100,000), and Caucasian females (4 per 100,000). It is important to highlight that in addition to being the subgroup most likely to commit murders, young African American men 15 to 24 were also the most likely to be killed by violent means, with their homicide rates standing at 159 per 100,000 in 1992 and showing almost continual year-to-year increases (USDOJ, 1994).

Varying ethnic and gender patterns are reflected in studies of nonlethal violence among youths. Typically these studies track self-reported incidence of physical fighting and carrying of weapons; some also include fighting-related injuries, use of weapons, and other law-violating behavior as well. The National Youth Survey (NYS) on a national probability sample of adolescents found significant racial/ethnic differences in the prevalence of African American and Caucasian serious violent offending, with African Americans generally having higher rates. However, this research also indicated that differences were relatively modest during the adolescent years and decreased when controls for socioeconomic status were considered (Elliott, 1994a).

The Youth Risk Behavior Survey (YRBS) provides another source of information on these behaviors as reported by youths who are in school. Several of the YRBS studies have found that African American male adolescents exceed their male and female peers in carrying of guns on and off school property, at rates ranging from 12.6% to 20.9% (Kann et al., 1995; USDHHS, 1995; Valois et al., 1995). All three of these studies found slightly higher rates of fighting among African American male adolescents than among Caucasian boys. Two of them found more pronounced differences among young women; African American female adolescent fighting rates, although lower than those of any male groups, were nearly 1.5 times greater than those of their Caucasian female classmates (Kann et al., 1995; Valois et al., 1995). These findings are similar to NYS data that also found more significant differences in violent offending among African American and Caucausian female perpetrators than among their male peers (Elliott, 1994a).

However, this pattern of higher rates of weapons carrying and fighting for African American youths was not consistent across all studies. An early Youth Risk Behavior Survey study found the highest rates of weapons carrying among Hispanic males although African American male rates of such behavior were considerably above the Caucasian males in the sample (CDC, 1991). Two other school-based studies collapsed violence variables into a single category of violence risk-taking behavior and included interethnic comparisons. One found slightly higher rates of violence perpetration among Caucasian middle school youths than among African American youths, with Hispanic adolescents having the lowest rates (Vanderschmidt et al., 1993). The other found that self-reported violent behaviors occurred more frequently among Native American male youths, followed by African American males, Caucasian males, Native American females, African American females, and Caucasian females (Gruber et al., 1994).

With the exception of the USDHHS research, these studies focused on a within-school population. The USDHHS study that included a sample of 22% out-of-school youths did not, however, report on differential response patterns by school status. In addition, these studies, for the most part, reported on national or statewide samples. Although their samples included urban, disadvantaged ethnic minority students, they did not distinguish the effects of socioeconomic status on the demonstration of violent behaviors. Other studies have focused primarily or exclusively on African American children and adolescents living in low-income inner-city neighborhoods. Typically, they have found higher rates of weapons carrying and fighting among these high-risk youths than in the general adolescent population (DuRant et al., 1994; Kulig, Valentine, & Steriti, 1994; Sheley, McGee, & Wright, 1992; Webster, Gainer, & Champion, 1993). Two of these studies reported that approximately 40% of their inner-city respondents routinely carried guns (DuRant et al., 1994; Webster et al., 1993); this is nearly twice as high as the highest rate reported in the national samples. Within this research, studies that examined socioeconomic factors as a contributing variable found that other risk factors appeared to have a stronger correlation (DuRant et al., 1994; Sheley et al., 1992), although other studies have pointed to

conditions associated with socioeconomic status as strong correlates of aggressive and delinquent behavior (e.g., Attar et al., 1994; Smith & Krohn, 1995).

Related Risk and Resiliency Factors

Because African American youths have long been recognized to be disproportionately involved in antisocial behavior, there is substantially more literature on the risk factors for this population. Recent increased awareness of the prevalence of violence perpetration and victimization among African American adolescents has generated an especially prolific body of research on this health behavior problem. This subsection provides only a compressed review of the many available studies on risk and resiliency factors related to violence and other antisocial behaviors among African American youths.

In examining this research, the first conclusion we reach is that deviant behaviors co-occur for African American adolescents (as indeed for all adolescents), making it difficult to tease out which behaviors or tendencies are antecedent to the others. Gang membership co-varies with risk for committing assaultive violence, including homicide (Busch, Zagar, Hughes, Arbit, & Bussell, 1990). Arrests for drug crimes are associated with a higher incidence of carrying weapons, particularly guns (Black & Ricardo, 1994; Busch et al., 1990; Sheley, 1994; Vanderschmidt et al., 1993; Webster et al., 1993). Associations with deviant peers are positively correlated with substance use (Catalano et al., 1993), and poor school adjustment is predicted by early manifestations of childhood aggression (Coie, Lochman, Terry, & Hyman, 1992). However, it is often a chicken-and-egg dilemma to determine the directional influence or order of occurrence of these behaviors. Is the aggressively inclined adolescent more likely to join a gang because of the potential opportunities to act out hostilities, or is it instead that gang activities are inherently violent and that all gang members, whether or not they were initially predisposed toward aggression, are naturally drawn into aggressive acts because they are a primary focus of the gang? Some research has concluded that involvement with delinquent peers is most likely an antecedent to the onset of delinquent behavior and represents the most common path to chronic, serious offending (Elliott, 1994b; see also discussion in Thornberry & Krohn, Chapter 21, this volume).

It appears that some adolescents display a broad array of antisocial behaviors and that many of these behaviors are mutually influential and reinforcing (Guerra, Tolan, & Hammond, 1994). Integrated conceptual models that combine social learning, social control, and economic deprivation/strain theories are useful in examining the general pathways to antisocial behavior. However, these models have rarely been applied to ethnic minority youths, and it is critically important to consider unique ethnic and sociocultural influences affecting these youngsters (Rodriguez & Recio, 1992). For African American youths, influences that tend to support or mitigate against antisocial behavior fall into the broad categories of environmental/structural factors, family variables, and individual cognitive beliefs and attitudes.

It is also important to stress here the cumulative effects of multiple risk factors. In examining youth vulnerability for substance use, Catalano et al. (1993) found few ethnic differences in the significance of any one risk factor in predicting early substance use initiation but concluded that African American children had a greater overall level of exposure to risk factors than did the Caucasian children in their sample. Similarly, Vega, Zimmerman, Warheit, Apospori, and Gil (1993) found that in comparison to White non-Hispanic, Cuban American, and other Hispanic youths, African American children were less likely to have no risk factors. In addition, they had the highest mean number of risk factors of all groups surveyed. However, the subsample of African American children with the highest total risk scores reported lesser illicit drug use than other groups in the sample, leading the research team to conclude that there was a greater subcultural resiliency among certain high-risk African American youngsters. Although the Vega study did not investigate the source of this resiliency, the Catalano study found that African American children in their sample were more likely to report proactive family management strategies by their parents that appeared to buffer against early substance use initiation, including gateway drugs such as tobacco and alcohol.

Environmental risks and structural barriers to educational and job opportunities appear to be particularly strong contributors to antisocial behavior among African American children and adolescents. Various investigators have noted that the higher prevalence rates of African American youth violence and property crime perpetration may have less to do with racial/ethnic effects than with academic failure, school dropout, and the resulting socioeconomic disadvantage (Black & Ricardo, 1994; Dembo et al., 1994; Weisz et al., 1991). However, low income in itself cannot fully account for a propensity toward antisocial behavior because the majority of African Americans and other individuals living in poverty do not engage in such behaviors (Hammond & Yung, 1993). Instead, most research highlights the conditions frequently associated with poverty such as limited resources, high crime rates, family stress, and adverse future prospects as significant contributors (Attar et al., 1994; Reynolds et al., 1992; Smith & Krohn, 1995). Attar et al. (1994) empirically tested the effects of neighborhood disadvantage and community-level stress on aggressive behavior in young African American and Hispanic children residing in inner cities. They determined that these urban ethnic minority children were exposed to multiple stressful life events, that the highest levels of neighborhood disadvantage increased chronic stress levels, and that such stressors were significantly related to aggressive behavior by these youngsters.

In combination with other risk variables related to the individual and the family, conditions of economic and social disadvantage may tend to point a young person toward an antisocial path (Kagan, 1991). Once they have moved in that direction, interactions with other factors such as differential arrest rates, scarcity of job opportunities, and social factors such as the involvement of friends or family members in crime and perceived peer support for drug use, drug trafficking, or other antisocial behaviors make it more difficult for African American youth to break the bonds of this lifestyle (Carmichael, 1990; Dembo et al., 1994; Elliott, 1994a; Rodriguez & Recio, 1992; Weisz et al., 1991).

One of the most negative influences in disadvantaged African American neighborhoods is acute and prolonged exposure of children and adolescents to community violence. In addition to its adverse psychological effects, violence exposure and victimization have been significantly correlated with behavioral consequences such as frequent fighting, weapon carrying, missing school because of fear of attack, and performing poorly in school (Attar et al., 1994; DuRant et al., 1994; Jenkins & Bell, 1994; Kann et al., 1995; Martin, Sadowski, Cotton, & McCarraher, 1996; Shapiro, Dorman, Welker, Burkey, & Clough, 1992; Sheley et al., 1992). Most studies cite higher levels of violence exposure and victimization for African American youths than for other children and adolescents (see reviews in Hammond & Yung, 1994, and Hampton & Yung, 1995). Fear or threats of future victimization are an especially important influence in the decision to carry a gun. More frequently than other youths, African American adolescents cite motives of self-protection as a primary reason for arming themselves (Martin et al., 1996; Shapiro et al., 1992; Webster et al., 1993). However, these youths' own explanations for why they carry guns may not be a completely accurate picture. Weapons carriers are also more likely than nonarmed youths to be involved in assaultive and other delinquent behaviors, to have been arrested for drug-related charges, and to be failing in school (Black & Ricardo, 1994; Sheley et al., 1992; Webster et al., 1993).

Chronic exposure to violence and early tendencies to act aggressively or engage in other deviances may also support the development of dysfunctional cognitive beliefs and ways of processing social information that can cyclically breed more violence or other antisocial behaviors (Coie, Dodge, Terry, & Wright, 1991; Dembo et al., 1994; Webster et al., 1993). Coie and his colleagues (1991) found that among aggressive 7- and 9-year-old African American boys, there was a tendency to assume hostile intent of their peers, even when an event was neutral rather than provocative. Dodge, Price, Bachorowski, and Newman (1990) discovered similar biases in a population of severely aggressive incarcerated African American adolescents. This may be an adaptive process developed by these children and adolescents to help them cope in a world that is dangerous (Prinz & Miller, 1991). Whatever the source, hostile attribution bias helps to create an environment in which African American youths who are disposed to this belief may fight over the most trivial of incidents. Unfortunately, in today's world, these fights may involve deadly weapons (Hammond & Yung, 1994; Prothrow-Stith, 1991; Yung & Hammond, 1995b; see also Fagan & Wilkinson, Chapter 50, this volume).

Dembo et al. (1994) offer additional insight into belief systems that contribute to the perpetuation of violent and other antisocial behavior. They conducted an empirical investigation testing a sociocultural conceptual framework that considers delinquent behavior among urban ethnic minority adolescents as peer-oriented and subculturally embedded. In examining differences among Caucasian and African American youths detained for property offenses, they found that Caucasian youths had higher degrees of emotional/psychological dysfunction and more troubled family backgrounds. In contrast, African American detainees indicated a higher level of involvement with friends who were delinquent. They also identified more strongly with the "criminal class" and held views of illegal activities as acceptable and even socially valued. Similar findings were reported by Carmichael (1990). In his study of African American delinquents in custody, juvenile respondents ranked drug dealers, assailants, and murderers as types of criminals they respected highly, frequently citing the need to earn a living; to avenge a wrong; or to protect self, family, or drug sale territory as justification for their respect for these "professions." Again it is apparent that environmental influences help to shape attitudes and values that in turn may promote future destructive behavior. For a more complete discussion of cross-cultural differences in diagnoses of antisocial personality disorder, see Dinges et al. (Chapter 44, this volume).

Several family variables stand out as important potential sources of support for, or protection from, negative behaviors among African American children and adolescents. Stronger parental control, including establishing clear rules, expecting and requiring obedience, and monitoring of activities is positively associated with freedom from antisocial behavior (Catalano et al., 1993; Smith & Krohn, 1995). Positive family/child attachment and communication have also been found to discourage African American youngsters from drug use, aggressive behavior, and delinquent activity (Black & Ricardo, 1994; Catalano et al., 1993; Smith & Krohn, 1995). Involvement of African American parents in their children's schooling has been identified as a key factor related to better attendance and less frequent in-school problem behavior (Reynolds et al., 1992). On the negative side, high levels of family conflict, including witnessing of domestic violence between other family members and physical violence between parent and child, have been associated with aggressive behavior and carrying guns among African American adolescents living in public housing projects (DuRant et al., 1994). Poor parental role modeling, particularly abusing drugs and participating in criminal violence, has been significantly related to the perpetration of homicide and other assaults and to chemical dependency for exposed youngsters (Black & Ricardo, 1994; Busch, Zagar, Hughes, Arbit, & Bussell, 1990).

Despite the comparative wealth of literature on antisocial behavior among African American youths, there are many areas of potential influence that have had only limited exploration, making it difficult to determine their generalizability. For example, although Afrocentric values and beliefs have been widely proposed as a conceptual foundation for prevention and intervention programs directed to a variety of health and behavior problems, there has been limited empirical research validating this approach (Belgrave et al., 1994). Further study of this concept may be a productive research direction because this study found that an Afrocentric value system contributed a small but significant positive influence on African American children's attitudes toward drug use. Church attendance and religious behavior have also been suggested as protective agents for African American children and youths. However, DuRant et al. (1994) found no association between these factors and violence perpetration by African American youths. In a similar vein, Jenkins and Bell (1994) found that church attendance did not mitigate distress symptoms in African American girls or behavior problems in African American boys who were witnesses to violence. In general, for African American as for other ethnic minority youths, a stronger focus has been placed on identifying risk rather than protective factors, leaving us with a significant knowledge gap in our understanding of resiliency.

CONCLUSIONS

The limitations of current research on antisocial behavior among Asian American, Hispanic, Native American, and African American youths were apparent throughout this review. Every general and ethnic-specific research issue mentioned in the introductory section of this chapter surfaced as a concern and an impediment to accurate knowledge of prevalence and etiology of delinquency, violence, substance abuse, and gang participation among these ethnic minority children and adolescents. The lack of comprehensive, standardized national databases on antisocial behavior causes reliance on local and regional studies that neither provide a reliable estimate of the extent of these problems nor reflect the behavior patterns of most youth. National surveys are not likely to do so either because they do not usually describe differences in responses to variables such as metropolitan versus rural residence—factors that may contribute greatly to environmental risk. For example, the national Youth Risk Behavior Survey of general samples of American adolescents invariably reported lesser average incidence of youth weapon carrying than the extent reported in surveys of ethnic minority youths living in poor inner-city neighborhoods.

Most data on antisocial behavior among ethnic minority adolescent populations come from self-report, arrest or treatment sources or law enforcement official reports or estimates. Each data source has built-in limitations and the sources often do not agree with one other. In the Hawaii studies, for example, there was a wide variation in the estimated ethnic subgroup composition of gangs, the extent of gang membership, and the nature of antisocial behavior in which gangs participated when police records and youth self-reports were compared (Chesney-Lind et al., 1992; Rockhill et al., 1993). There was also a disparity between the self-reported prevalence of substance abuse for African American and Hispanic youths and their drug-related arrests. This may be due to underreporting by surveyed youths, failure to capture the responses of the highest risk subgroups, or a greater propensity for law enforcement to focus on this problem in low-income ethnic minority communities.

There was a general lack of information on problem behavior among Asian American youths, and when they were compared to other ethnic minorities, there was rarely any distinction made between the extremely diverse ethnic subgroups, potentially masking significant behavioral differences in the higher risk populations such as Southeast Asian youngsters of low socioeconomic status. Even the Hawaii studies (Chesney-Lind et al., 1992; Rockhill et al., 1993) provided little data on ethnic differences in antisocial behavior although they focused on a population that was quite heterogeneous. There was a similar lack of information on subpopulation differences among Native American youths (e.g., by tribal affiliation or by urban/rural or reservation/nonreservation residence). Although there were several studies that provided data on Mexican American, Puerto Rican, and Cuban American adolescents, there were few that covered all subgroups of Hispanic youths and most were dealing only with single behavior issues such as substance abuse. It was thus difficult to make intraethnic comparisons across multiple behavioral dimensions. For African American youths, there was little attention to heterogeneity in the population. There were also few studies that compared the behaviors of African American city dwellers with those of African

American youths living in rural locations, suburbs, or small cities. Nor were there studies that focused on newer immigrant youths from Africa or the Caribbean.

Many studies we reviewed did not describe how ethnic/racial classifications were determined. This is an important issue because variations in a range of 12% to 68% have been found when the same population is classified by different methods (Sugarman et al., 1993; Zimmerman et al., 1994). Many adolescent surveys such as the Youth Risk Behavior Survey use self-identification as the basis for determining ethnicity. However, the Census Bureau receives a substantial number of inquiries during its data collection periods from adults who are unsure how to respond to this question (McKenney & Bennett, 1994). If this is a difficult issue for adults, it is surely much harder for children and adolescents, especially if they have mixed ancestry.

Access to certain ethnic minority populations and subpopulations was clearly a problem in many of these studies. The relative lack of data on Asian American, Native American, and Hispanic youths may be reflective of their patterns of geographic concentration or dispersement, which creates sampling technique problems. In the case of Asian American youths, the lack of research may also result from investigator perception of lower risk for this population (Chen & True, 1994). Also notably absent from most studies was the population of out-of-school youths who were not incarcerated. An exception was the work of Chavez and his colleagues on Mexican American dropouts (Chavez et al., 1989; Chavez et al., 1994). Their work clearly demonstrates that this is an extremely high-risk population that needs greater attention from both the research and interventionist communities.

Instrumentation and selection of variables to be examined were problematic in some studies as well. Adolescent health surveys that included data on carrying weapons typically made no distinction between carrying them to use for self-defense or violent purposes and legitimate reasons such as hunting or target practice (DuRant, Getts, Cadenhead, & Woods, 1995). Additionally, many studies examined only ethnicity and not socioeconomic status or neighborhood distress as variables. In contrast, the study by Attar et al. (1994) stood out as an excellent example of a well-conceived effort to avoid confounding ethnicity with certain environmental conditions. There is a need for greater attention to the operational parameters of socioeconomic status variables and to the creation of new measures of disadvantagement, perhaps including school quality, segregation patterns, access to prevention resources, police/resident relationships, and other community characteristics (APA, 1994; Fairchild et al., 1995; Peterson & Krivo, 1993). Because of its rich detail of contextual conditions that may influence antisocial behavior among ethnic minority youths, ethnographic research such as that of Anderson (1994) may be a particularly valuable resource to help in generating new hypotheses. Using the methods of urban anthropology, Anderson studied street norms of African American youths living in dangerous environments, furthering our understanding of the informal rules governing the use of violence, concepts of masculinity, unique sources of disputes and conflicts among young women, self-identity development, and the parental role in the behavioral regulation of violence. Additional studies of violence or other antisocial behaviors among different ethnic minority groups would contribute research questions for empirical testing that are particularly salient because of their generation from real-world contexts.

We found that many of the risks faced by ethnic minority adolescents are common across all youth cultures, for example, poor academic performance, school dropout, ineffective parental disciplinary and family management practices, low parental involvement in the child's education, neighborhood crime, environmental risk, bonding with deviant peers, and individual cognitive beliefs and processes. However, some risks were clearly ethnic specific. For recently arrived immigrant youths, the stresses of assimilation and bicultural adjustment often create a vulnerability for both emotional and behavioral problems. Even among ethnic minority youths whose families have resided in the United States long-term, issues of integration into mainstream culture continue to be a difficult and hazardous proposition for many.

Although not included as a research construct in the studies described in this chapter, racism was a common underlying element contributing to risk for the participation of ethnic minority youths in a variety of antisocial behaviors. In the study of San Francisco newcomer youths (White et al., 1995), negative stereotyping, verbal and physical abuse by schoolmates, perception of danger at school/fear of hate crime, and unequal resources created tremendous school adjustment problems for young refugees and immigrants. Structural barriers to mobility, combined with institutional discrimination by the law enforcement and juvenile justice systems, help to create and maintain an underclass status, particularly for African American and Hispanic youths (Blumstein, 1995; Elliott et al., 1986; Hill et al., 1994; Jones & Krisberg, 1994). Outgroup status and perceptions of a lack of power may be especially significant motivators for the banding together of ethnic minority gangs (Cummings & Monti, 1993; Goldstein & Soriano, 1994).

Pick any subtopic that we have discussed in this chapter and you will find a need for further research. It was particularly disappointing that the research on risk factor identification was so much better developed than that on protective factors although the studies of the impact of ethnic-specific family variables on delinquency (Smith & Krohn, 1995) and on substance use (Vega, Gil et al., 1993) presented sophisticated prototypes that should be replicated. The majority of ethnic minority youths are not members of gangs, do not abuse alcohol or other drugs, do not commit acts of violence, and do not indulge in other problem behaviors. This includes many disadvantaged youngsters who are subject to comparable individual, family, or community-based risks that have influenced antisocial behavior in their similarly exposed peers. Before we can mount appropriate and effective prevention and intervention programs, we must not only understand the factors that moderate risks but also the dynamic interactions between risk and resiliency factors. Lacking this knowledge, we are in danger of wasting resources on programs that may fail to produce positive results or, still worse, contribute to adverse outcomes.

REFERENCES

American Psychological Association. (1994). *Violence and youth: Psychology's response. Volume I: Summary report of the American Psychological Association Commission on Violence and Youth.* Washington, DC: Author.

Attar, B., Guerra, N., & Tolan, P. (1994). Neighborhood disadvantage, stressful life events, and adjustment in urban elementary-school children. *Journal of Clinical Child Psychology, 23,* 391–400.

Barham, J. (1992, July). *Has violent crime really increased? A comparison of violence rates reported by the two U.S. Department of Justice Data Sets.* Presentation to the American Psychological Association Commission on Youth and Violence, Washington, DC.

Belgrave, F., Cherry, V., Cummingham, D., Walwyn, S., Letlaka-Rennert, K., & Phillips, F. (1994). The influence of Africentric values, self-esteem, and black identity on drug attitudes among African American fifth graders: A preliminary study. *Journal of Black Psychology, 20,* 143–156.

Black, M., & Ricardo, I. (1994). Drug use, drug trafficking, and weapon carrying among low-income African-American, early adolescent boys. *Pediatrics, 93,* 1065–1072.

Blum, R., Harmon, B., Harris, L., Bergeisen, L., & Resnick, M. (1992). American Indian–Alaska Native youth health. *JAMA, 267,* 1637–1644.

Blum, R., Harmon, B., Harris, L., Resnick, M., Stutelberg, K., & Robles, A. (1992). *The state of Native American youth health.* Minneapolis: University of Minnesota, Division of General Pediatrics and Adolescent Health.

Blumstein, A. (1995). Violence by young people: Why the deadly nexus? *National Institute of Justice Journal, 229,* 2–9.

Boles, S., Casas, M., Furlong, M., Gonzalez, G., & Morrison, G. (1994). Alcohol and other drug use patterns among Mexican-American, Mexican, and Caucasian adolescents: New directions for assessment and research. *Journal of Clinical Child Psychology, 23,* 39–46.

Brindis, C., Wolfe, M., McCarter, V., Ball, S., & Starbuck-Morales, S. (1995). The associations between immigrant status and risk-behavior patterns in Latino adolescents. *Journal of Adolescent Health, 17,* 99–105.

Busch, K., Zagar, R., Hughes, J., Arbit, J., & Bussell, R. (1990). Adolescents who kill. *Journal of Clinical Psychology, 46,* 472–485.

Carmichael, B. (1990). An exploratory study of values and attitudes of black delinquents in custody. *Journal of Crime and Justice, 13,* 66–85.

Catalano, R., Hawkins, D., Krenz, C., Gillmore, M., Morrison, D., Wells, E., & Abbott, R. (1993). Using research to guide culturally appropriate drug abuse prevention. *Journal of Consulting and Clinical Psychology, 61,* 804–811.

Centers for Disease Control. (1991). Weapon-carrying among high school students. *Journal of the American Medical Association, 266,* 2342.

Chavez, E., Edwards, R., & Oetting, E. (1989). Mexican American and white American school dropouts' drug use, health status, and involvement in violence. *Public Health Reports, 104,* 594–604.

Chavez, E., Oetting, E., & Swaim, R. (1994). Dropout and delinquency: Mexican-American and Caucasian non-Hispanic youth. *Journal of Clinical Child Psychology, 23,* 47–55.

Chen, A., & True, R. (1994). Experience of violence: Asian Americans. In L. Eron, J. Gentry, & P. Schlegel (Eds.), *Reason to hope: A psychosocial perspective on violence and youth* (pp. 133–144). Washington, DC: American Psychological Association.

Chesney-Lind, M., Marker, N., Rodriguez Stern, I., Yap, A., Song, V., Reyes, H., Reyes, Y., Stern, J., & Taira, J. (1992). *Gangs and delinquency in Hawaii.* Honolulu: University of Hawaii, Center for Youth Research.

Coie, J., Dodge, K., Terry, R., & Wright, V. (1991). The role of aggression in peer relations: An analysis of aggression episodes in boys' play groups. *Child Development, 62,* 812–826.

Coie, J., Lochman, J., Terry, R., & Hyman, C. (1992). Predicting early adolescent disorder from childhood aggression and peer rejection. *Journal of Consulting and Clinical Psychology, 60,* 783–792.

Conly, C., Kelly, P., Mahanna, P., & Warner, L. (1993). *Street gangs: Current knowledge and strategies.* Washington, DC: U.S. Department of Justice.

Council on Crime in America. (1996). *The state of violent crime in America.* Washington, DC: New Citizenship Project.

Cummings, S. (1993). The anatomy of a wilding gang. In S. Cummings & D. Monti (Eds.), *Gangs: The origins and impact of contemporary youth gangs in the United States* (pp. 49–73). Albany: State University of New York Press.

Cummings, S., & Monti, D. (1993). Public policy and gangs: Social science and the urban underclass. In S. Cummings & D. Monti (Eds.), *Gangs: The origins and impact of contemporary youth gangs in the United States* (pp. 305–320). Albany: State University of New York Press.

Darou, W., Hum, A., & Kurtness, J. (1993). An investigation of the impact of psychosocial research on a native population. *Professional Psychology: Research and Practice, 24,* 325–329.

Dembo, R., Williams, L., & Schmeidler, J. (1994). Psychosocial, alcohol/other drug use, and delinquency differences between urban black and white male high risk youth. *The International Journal of the Addictions, 29,* 461–483.

Dodge, K., Price, J., Bachorowski, J., & Newman, J. (1990). Hostile attributional biases in severely aggressive adolescents. *Journal of Abnormal Psychology, 99,* 385–392.

DuRant, R., Pendergrast, R., & Cadenhead, C. (1994). Exposure to violence and victimization and fighting behavior by urban Black adolescents. *Journal of Adolescent Health, 15,* 311–318.

Eisenman, R. (1995). Why psychologists should study race. *American Psychologist, 50,* 42–43.

Elliott, D. (1994a). Serious violent offenders: Onset, developmental course, and termination—The American Society of Criminology 1993 Presidential Address. *Criminology, 32,* 1–21.

Elliott, D. (1994b). Longitudinal research in criminology: Promise and practice. In E. Weitekamp & H. Kerner (Eds.), *Cross-national longitudinal research on human development and criminal behavior* (pp. 189–201). Netherlands: Kluwer.

Elliott, D., Huizinga, D., & Morse, B. (1986). Self-reported violent offending: A descriptive analysis of juvenile violent offenders and their offending careers. *Journal of Interpersonal Violence, 1,* 472–514.

Ewing, P. (1990). *When children kill children: Dynamics of juvenile homicide.* Lexington, MA: Lexington Books.

Fairchild, H., Yee, A., Wyatt, G., & Weizmann, F. (1995). Readdressing psychology's problems with race. *American Psychologist, 50,* 46–47.

Flack, J., Amaro, H., Jenkinds, W., Kunitz, S., Levy, J., Mixon, M., & Yu, E. (1995). Panel I: Epidemiology of minority health. *Health Psychology, 14,* 592–600.

Flowers, R. (1988). *Minorities and criminality.* Westport, CT: Greenwood Press.

Goldstein, A., & Glick, B. (1994). *The prosocial gang: Implementing aggression replacement training.* Thousand Oaks, CA: Sage Publications.

Goldstein, A., & Soriano, F. (1994). Juvenile gangs. In L. Eron, J. Gentry, & P. Schlegel (Eds.), *Reason to hope: A psychosocial perspective on violence and youth* (pp. 315–331). Washington, DC: American Psychological Association.

Gruber, E., Anderson, M., & DiClemente, R. (1994). Alcohol-specific problem behavior among Native American, Black and White adolescents in a midwestern state. *Journal of Adolescent Health, 15,* 59. Abstract of a presentation at the annual meeting of the Society for Adolescent Medicine, March 16–20, 1994.

Gruber, E., DiClemente, R., & Anderson, M. (1994). Differences in risk-taking behavior among Native American, Black and White adolescents in a midwestern state. *Journal of Adolescent Health, 15,* 59. Abstract of a presentation at the annual meeting of the Society for Adolescent Medicine, March 16–20, 1994.

Guerra, N., Tolan, P., & Hammond, R. (1994). Prevention and treatment of adolescent violence. In L. Eron, J. Gentry, & P. Schlegel (Eds.), *Reason to hope: A psychosocial perspective on violence and youth* (pp. 383–403). Washington, DC: American Psychological Association.

Hammond, R., & Yung, B. (1993). Psychology's role in the public health response to assaultive violence among young African-American men. *American Psychologist, 48,* 142–154.

Hammond, R., & Yung, B. (1994). Experience of violence: African-Americans. In L. Eron, J. Gentry, & P. Schlegel (Eds.), *Reason to hope: A psychosocial perspective on violence and youth* (pp. 105–118). Washington, DC: American Psychological Association.

Hampton, R. L., & Yung, B. (1995). Violence in communities of color: Where we were, where we are, where we need to be. In T. Gullotta, R. Hampton, & P. Jenkins (Eds.), *When anger governs: Preventing violence in America* (pp. 53–86). Newbury Park, CA: Sage Publications.

Hawkins, D. F. (1990). Explaining the Black homicide rate. *Journal of Interpersonal Violence, 5,* 151–163.

Hill, H., Soriano, F., Chen, A., & LaFromboise, T. (1994). Sociocultural factors in the etiology and prevention of violence among ethnic minority youth. In L. Eron, J. Gentry, & P. Schlegel (Eds.), *Reason to hope: A psychosocial perspective on violence and youth* (pp. 59–97). Washington, DC: American Psychological Association.

Ho, M. (1992). *Minority children and adolescents in therapy.* Newberry Park, CA: Sage Publications.

Huang, L. (1994). An integrative approach to clinical assessment and intervention with Asian-American adolescents. *Journal of Clinical Child Psychology, 23,* 21–31.

Huff, R. (1993). Gangs in the United States. In A. Goldstein & R. Huff, *The gang intervention handbook* (pp. 3–20). Champaign, IL: Research Press.

Hughes, D., Seidman, E., & Williams, N. (1993). Cultural phenomena and the research enterprise: Toward a culturally anchored methodology. *American Journal of Community Psychology, 21,* 687–703.

Huizinga, D., & Elliott, D. (1985). *Juvenile offenders' prevalence, offender incidence and arrest rates by race.* Boulder, CO: Institute of Behavioral Science.

Hutchison, R., & Kyle, C. (1993). Hispanic street gangs in Chicago's Public Schools. In S. Cummings & D. Monti (Eds.), *Gangs: The origins and impact of contemporary youth gangs in the United States* (pp. 113–136). Albany: State University of New York Press.

Hutson, R., Anglin, D., & Pratt, M. (1994). Adolescents and children injured or killed in drive-by shootings in Los Angeles. *New England Journal of Medicine, 330,* 324–327.

Jenkins, E., & Bell, C. (1994). Violence among inner city high school students and post-traumatic stress disorder. In S. Friedman (Ed.), *Anxiety disorders in African Americans* (pp. 76–88). New York: Springer.

Johnson, K., Anderson, N., Bastida, E., Kramer, J., Williams, D., & Wong, M. (1995). Panel II: Macrosocial and environmental influences on minority health. *Health Psychology, 14,* 601–612.

Jones, M., & Krisberg, B. (1994). *Images and reality: Juvenile crime, youth violence and public policy.* San Francisco: National Council on Crime and Delinquency.

Kagan, J. (1991). Etiologies of adolescents at risk. *Journal of Adolescent Health, 12,* 591–596.

Kann, L., Warren, C., Harris, W., Collins, J., Douglas, K., Collins, M., Williams, B., Ross, J., & Kolbe, L. (1995). Youth Risk Behavior Surveillance—United States, 1993. *Journal of School Health, 65,* 163–170.

Kulig, J., Valentine, J., & Steriti, L. (1994). A correlational analysis of weapon-carrying among urban high school students: Findings from a cross-sectional survey. *Journal of Adolescent Health, 15,* 61. Abstract of a presentation at the annual meeting of the Society for Adolescent Medicine, March 16–20, 1994.

LaFromboise, T., Coleman, H., & Gerton, J. (1993). Psychological impact of biculturalism: Evidence and theory. *Psychological Bulletin, 114,* 395–412.

Lee, E. (1988). Cultural factors in working with Southeast Asian refugee adolescents. *Journal of Adolescence, 11,* 167–179.

Lewit, E., & Baker, L. (1994). Race and ethnicity—Changes for children. *Critical Health Issues for Children and Youth, 4,* 134–144.

Mail, P. (1995). Early modeling of drinking behavior by Native American elementary school playing drunk. *International Journal of the Addictions, 30,* 1187–1197.

Martin, S., Gordon, T., & Kuperschmidt, J. (1995). Survey of exposure to violence among the children of migrant and seasonal farm workers. *Public Health Reports, 110,* 268–276.

Martin, S., Sadowski, L., Cotten, N., & McCarraher, D. (1996). Response of African-American adolescents in North Carolina to gun carrying by school mates. *Journal of School Health, 66,* 23–26.

McGraw, S., McKinlay, J., Crawford, S., Costa, L., & Cohen, L. (1992). Health survey methods with minority populations: Some lessons from recent experiences. In D. Becker, D. Hill, J. Jackson, D. Levine, F. Stillman, & S. Weiss (Eds.), *Health behavior research in minority populations: Access, design, and implementation* (pp. 149–167). NIH Publication No. 92-2965. Washington, DC: U.S. Department of Health and Human Services.

McKenney, N., & Bennett, C. (1994). Issues regarding data on race and ethnicity: The Census Bureau experience. *Public Health Reports, 109,* 16–25.

McShane, D. (1988). An analysis of mental health research with American Indian youth. *Journal of Adolescence, 11,* 87–116.

Menard, S. (1992). Residual gains, reliability, and the UCR-NCS relationship: A comment on Blumstein, Cohen, and Rosenfeld. *Criminology, 30,* 105–113.

Moncher, M., Holden, G., & Trimble, J. (1990). Substance abuse among Native-American youth. *Journal of Consulting and Clinical Psychology, 58,* 408–415.

Monti, D. (1993). Origins and problems of gang research in the United States. In S. Cummings & D. Monti (Eds.), *Gangs: The origins and impact of contemporary youth gangs in the United States* (pp. 3–25). Albany: State University of New York Press.

Moore, J. (1987). Variations in violence among Hispanic gangs. In J. Kraus, S. Sorenson, & P. Juarez (Eds.), *Research conference on violence and homicide in Hispanic communities* (pp. 215–230). Los Angeles: UCLA Publication Services.

Moore, J. (1993). Gangs, drugs, and violence. In S. Cummings & D. Monti (Eds.), *Gangs: The origins and impact of contemporary youth gangs in the United States* (pp. 27–46). Albany: State University of New York Press.

Muecke, M. (1983). Caring for Southeast Asian refugee patients in the USA. *American Journal of Public Health, 73,* 431–438.

Murata, J. (1990). Father's family violence and son's delinquency: Conflict tactics, bonding, and serious juvenile crime in the Mexican-American family. *Western Journal of Nursing Research, 12,* 61–71.

Myers, H., Kagawa-Singer, M., Kumanyika, S., Lex, B., & Markides, K. (1994). Panel III: Behavioral risk factors related to chronic diseases in ethnic minorities. *Health Psychology, 14,* 613–621.

National Center for Education Statistics. (1995). *The pocket condition of education 1995.* NCES 95-817. Washington, DC: U.S. Department of Education.

National Center for Health Statistics (1991). *Setting a research agenda: Challenges for the Minority Health Statistics Grant Program.* Washington, DC: U.S. Department of Health and Human Services.

National Committee for Injury Prevention and Control. (1989). *Injury prevention: Meeting the challenge.* New York: Oxford University Press.

National Research Council. (1993). A. Reiss & J. Roth (Eds.), *Understanding and preventing violence.* Washington, DC: National Academy Press.

Newcomb, M., Fahy, B., & Skager, R. (1990). Reasons to avoid drug use among teenagers: Associations with actual drug use and implications for prevention among different demographic groups. *Journal of Alcohol and Drug Education, 36,* 53–81.

Nickens, H. (1991). The health status of minority populations in the United States. *Western Journal of Medicine, 155,* 27–32.

Oetting, E., & Beauvais, F. (1991). Orthogonal cultural identification theory: The cultural identification of minority adolescents. *International Journal of the Addictions, 25,* 655–685.

Office of Juvenile Justice and Delinquency Prevention. (1993). *Juveniles and violence: Juvenile offending and victimization.* Fact Sheet #3, July 1993. Washington, DC: U.S. Department of Justice.

Office of Technology Assessment. (1990). *Indian adolescent mental health.* OTA-H-446. Washington, DC: Government Printing Office.

Pabon, E., Rodriguez, O., & Gurin, G. (1992). Clarifying peer relations and delinquency. *Youth and Society, 24,* 149–165.

Pernice, R. (1994). Methodological issues in research with refugees and immigrants. *Professional Psychology: Research and Practice, 25,* 207–213.

Peterson, R., & Krivo, L. (1993). Racial segregation and black urban homicide. *Social Forces, 71,* 1001–1026.

Prinz, R., & Miller, G. (1991). Issues in understanding and treating childhood conduct problems in disadvantaged populations. *Journal of Clinical Child Psychology, 20,* 379–385.

Prothrow-Stith, D. (1991). *Deadly consequences: How violence is destroying our teenage population and a plan to begin solving the problem.* New York: HarperCollins.

Reynolds, A., Weissberg, R., & Kaprow, W. (1992). Prediction of early social and academic adjustment of children from the inner city. *American Journal of Community Psychology, 20,* 599–624.

Ribisl, K., & Davidson, W. (1993). Community change interventions. In A. Goldstein & R. Huff (Eds.), *The gang intervention handbook* (pp. 333–355). Champaign, IL: Research Press.

Rockhill, A., Chesney-Lind, M., Allen, J., Batalon, N., Garvin, E., Joe, K., & Spina, M. (1993). *Surveying Hawaii's youth: Neighborhoods, delinquency and gangs.* Honolulu: University of Hawaii, Center for Youth Research.

Rode, P., & Bellfield, K. (1992). *The next generation: The health and well being of young people of color in the Twin Cities. A report based on the Minnesota Adolescent Health Survey.* Minneapolis, MN: Urban Coalition of Minneapolis.

Rodriguez, M., & Brindis, C. (1995). Violence and Latino youth: Prevention and methodological issues. *Public Health Reports, 110,* 260–267.

Rodriguez, O., & Recio, J. (1992). The applicability of the integrated social control model to Puerto Rican drug use. *Journal of Crime and Justice, 15,* 1–23.

Rosado, J., & Elias, M. (1993). Ecological and psychocultural mediators in the delivery of services for urban, culturally diverse Hispanic clients. *Professional Psychology: Research and Practice, 24,* 450–459.

Segal, B. (1994). Urban-rural comparisons of drug-taking behavior among Alaskan youth. *International Journal of the Addictions, 29,* 1029–1044.

Sellers, C., Winfree, T., & Griffiths, C. (1993). Legal attitudes, permissive norm qualities, and substance use: A comparison of American Indian and non-Indian youth. *The Journal of Drug Issues, 23,* 493–513.

Shafer, M. (1995). Transition and Native American youth: A follow-up study of school leavers on the Fort Apache Indian Reservation. *Journal of Rehabilitation, 61,* 60–65.

Shapiro, J., Dorman, R., Welker, C., Burkey, W., & Clough, J. (1992). *Youth attitudes toward guns and violence: Relations with sex, age, ethnic group, and exposure.* Cleveland, OH: The Guidance Centers.

Sheley, J. (1994). Drug activity and firearms possession and use by juveniles. *The Journal of Drug Issues, 24,* 363–382.

Sheley, J., McGee, Z., & Wright, J. (1992). Gun-related violence in and around inner-city schools. *American Journal of Diseases of Childhood, 146,* 677–682.

Sheline, J., Skipper, B., & Broadhead, E. (1994). Risk factors for violent behavior in elementary school boys: Have you hugged your child today? *American Journal of Public Health, 84,* 661–663.

Smith, C., & Krohn, M. (1995). Delinquency and family life among male adolescents: The role of ethnicity. *Journal of Youth and Adolescence, 24,* 69–93.

Soriano, F. (1993). Cultural sensitivity and gang intervention. In A. Goldstein & R. Huff, *The gang intervention handbook* (pp. 441–461). Champaign, IL: Research Press.

Soriano, F. (1994). Experience of violence: U.S. Latinos. In L. Eron, J. Gentry, & P. Schlegel (Eds.), *Reason to hope: A psychosocial perspective on violence and youth* (pp. 119–132). Washington, DC: American Psychological Association.

Soriano, M., Soriano, F., & Jimenez, E. (1994). School violence among culturally diverse populations: Sociocultural and institutional considerations. *School Psychology Review, 23,* 215–235.

Stark, E. (1993). The myth of black violence. *Social Work, 38,* 485–490.

Sugarman, J., Brenneman, G., LaRoque, W., Warren, C., & Goldberg, H. (1994). The urban American Indian oversample in the 1988 National Maternal and Infant Health Survey. *Public Health Reports, 109,* 243–250.

Sugarman, J., Soderberg, R., Gordon, J., & Rivara, F. (1993). Racial misclassification of American Indians: Its effect on injury rates in Oregon, 1989 through 1990. *American Journal of Public Health, 83,* 681–684.

Szapocznik, J., Kurtines, W., Santisteban, D., & Rio, A. (1990). Interplay of advances between theory, research, and application in treatment interventions aimed at behavior problem children and adolescents. *Journal of Consulting and Clinical Psychology, 58,* 696–703.

Trimble, J. (1990). Application of psychological knowledge for American Indians and Alaska Natives. *Journal of Training and Practice in Professional Psychology, 4,* 45–63.

Uehara, E., Takeuchi, D., & Smukler, M. (1994). Effects of combining disparate groups in the analysis of ethnic differences: Variations among Asian American mental health service consumers in level of community functioning. *American Journal of Community Psychology, 22,* 83–99.

U.S. Department of Health and Human Services. (1990). *Alcohol and health*. Seventh Special Report to the U.S. Congress. Washington, DC: Author.

U.S. Department of Health and Human Services. (1995). *Vital and health statistics. Health-risk behaviors among our nation's youth, 1992.* Series 10. Data from the National Health Interview Survey, No. 192. DHHS Publication No. (PHS) 95–1520.

U.S. Department of Justice. (1991). *Tracking offenders, 1988.* Washington, DC: Bureau of Justice Statistics.

U.S. Department of Justice. (1994). *Violent crime.* NCJ-147486. Washington, DC: Bureau of Justice Statistics.

Valois, R., McKeown, R., Garrison, C., & Vincent, M. (1995). Correlates of aggressive and violent behaviors among public high school students. *Journal of Adolescent Health, 16,* 26–34.

Vanderschmidt, H., Lang, J., Knight-Williams, V., & Vanderschmidt, F. (1993). Risks among inner-city young teens: The prevalence of sexual activity, violence, drugs, and smoking. *Journal of Adolescent Health, 14,* 282–288.

Vega, W. (1992). Theoretical and pragmatic implications of cultural diversity for community research. *Journal of Community Psychology, 20,* 375–391.

Vega, W., Gil, A., Warheit, G., Zimmerman, R., & Apospori, E. (1993). Acculturation and delinquent behavior among Cuban American adolescents: Toward an empirical model. *American Journal of Community Psychology, 21,* 113–125.

Vega, W., Zimmerman, R., Warheit, G., Apospori, E., & Gil, A. (1993). Risk factors for early adolescent drug use in four ethnic and racial groups. *American Journal of Public Health, 83,* 185–189.

Vigil, J. (1987). Street socialization, locura behavior, and violence among Chicano gang members. In J. Kraus, S. Sorenson, & P. Juarez (Eds.), *Research conference on violence and homicide in Hispanic communities* (pp. 231–242). Los Angeles: UCLA Publication Services.

Watts, D., & Wright, L. (1990). The relationship of alcohol, tobacco, marijuana, and other illegal drug use to delinquency among Mexican-American, Black, and White adolescent males. *Adolescence, 25,* 171–181.

Webster, D., Gainer, P., & Champion, H. (1993). Weapon carrying among inner-city junior high school students: Defensive behavior vs. aggressive delinquency. *American Journal of Public Health, 83,* 1604–1608.

Weisz, J., Martin, S., Walter, B., & Fernandez, G. (1991). Differential prediction of young adult arrests for property and personal crimes: Findings of a cohort follow-up study of violent boys from North Carolina's Willie M Program. *Journal of Child Psychology and Psychiatry, 32,* 783–792.

White, J., Homma-True, R., Golden, B., Gramp, H., & Lee, R. (1995). *Newcomer children in San Francisco: Their health and well-being.* A report by the Child Health Initiative for Immigrant/Refugee Newcomers Project. San Francisco: San Francisco Department of Public Health.

Williams, C. (1989). Prevention programs for refugees: An interface for mental health and public health. *Journal of Primary Prevention, 10,* 167–186.

Williams, C., & Berry, J. (1991). Primary prevention of acculturative stress among refugees: Application of psychological theory and practice. *American Psychologist, 46,* 632–641.

Yau, J., & Smetana, J. (1993). Chinese-American adolescents' reasoning about cultural conflicts. *Journal of Adolescent Research, 8,* 419–438.

Yee, B., Castro, F., Hammond, R., John, R., Wyatt, G., & Yung, B. (1995). Panel IV: Risk-taking and abusive behaviors among ethnic minorities. *Health Psychology, 14,* 622–631.

Yu, E., & Liu, W. (1992). U.S. national health data on Asian Americans and Pacific Islanders: A research agenda for the 1990's. *American Journal of Public Health, 82,* 1645–1662.

Yung, B., & Hammond, R. (1995a). Experience of violence: Native Americans. In L. Eron, J. Gentry, & P. Schlegel (Eds.), *Reason to hope: A psychosocial perspective on violence and youth* (pp. 133–144). Washington, DC: American Psychological Association.

Yung, B., & Hammond, R. (1995b). *PACT. Positive Adolescent Choices Training: A model for violence prevention groups with African-American youth. Program guide.* Champaign, IL: Research Press.

Yung, B., & Hammond, R. (1997). Community-based interventions. In D. Wilson, J. Rodrigue, & W. Taylor (Eds.), *Health promotion for minority adolescents* (pp. 269–297). Washington, DC: American Psychological Association.

Zimmerman, R., Vega, W., Gil, A., Warheit, G., Apospori, E., & Biafora, F. (1994). Who is Hispanic? Definitions and their consequences. *American Journal of Public Health, 84,* 1985–1987.

CHAPTER 46

Gender and Antisocial Behavior

PEGGY C. GIORDANO and STEPHEN A. CERNKOVICH

Males tend to engage in more antisocial behavior than their female counterparts. This gender difference holds up fairly consistently across historical periods, geographic regions, age categories, and socioeconomic strata (see, e.g., Cernkovich & Giordano, 1979a; McCord, 1993; Robins, Tipp, & Przybeck, 1991; Steffensmeier & Streifel, 1993). Male predominance in antisocial behavior has long justified a heavier research emphasis on male offenders. Research on females was for many years either nonexistent or hampered by serious conceptual, sampling, and measurement problems, but since the 1970s there has been a marked increase in research on both adolescent and adult women. This chapter considers theory and research that has focused on (a) why most females do not evidence antisocial behavior patterns, but especially on (b) why some do. After a brief historical overview, we concentrate on the period since the 1970s, when the pace of research on these questions began to accelerate.

Early Conceptions of the Female Criminal

Early explanations for both discrepancies in rates of antisocial behavior by gender and for females' involvement emphasized constitutional factors. Cesare Lombroso, the Italian physician, and other early writers stressed how the basic physiological and psychological makeup of women largely precluded participation in criminal and aggressive behaviors. Females' infrequent forays into antisocial territory were seen as anomalies or perversions in a more general picture of passivity and interest in domestic concerns (see Chesney-Lind & Shelden, 1992; Klein, 1973; Leonard, 1982, for excellent reviews of the work of early theorists such as Lombroso [Lombroso & Ferrero, 1916; Pollack, 1950; Thomas, 1928]). Although most of this work is now considered outmoded, stereotypic, and even sexist, some of these early themes reappear in more recent theory and research. Two of these are particularly persistent:

1. Antisocial behavior is more consistent with the active, dominant, and acquisitive role repertoire of men (Berger, 1989; Schur, 1984; Widom, 1984). Consequently, it has been suggested that the crimes of females are more aberrant or serious when they do occur. Lombroso, in support of this view, quotes an Italian proverb: "Rarely is a woman wicked, but when she is she surpasses the man" (Lombroso & Ferrero, 1916, p. 147). That female antisocial behavior is statistically more rare in itself suggests the possibility of a greater level of disturbance on the part of female offenders in comparison to male criminals (Robins, 1986).

Although theories of male deviance shifted over time away from an exclusive focus on individual or deficit explanations, increasingly incorporating social and structural factors into explanatory models, the assumption of psychological disturbance or personal problems has held a strong foothold in the female crime literature (see the review by Widom, 1984). Until the 1970s, even when social variables such as family or peers were examined, the interpretation was generally consistent with a deficit perspective. For example, Barker and Adams (1962) proposed that many females' delinquent acts were psychological reaction formations to absent or inadequate fathers, and Reige (1972) emphasized the loneliness and low self-concept of many delinquent girls.

2. A different and somewhat contradictory portrait emphasizes that even when females engage in delinquency or criminal activity, their involvement is of a less serious nature than that of males. Generally consistent with a different-styles-of-pathology argument (men externalize, women internalize; see, e.g., Horwitz & White, 1987; Ostrov, Offer, & Howard, 1989), females are seen as criminal lightweights who confine themselves to a narrow band of status offenses or petty larcenies, especially shoplifting. An important subtext of this position underscores the sexual nature of much of women's offending. This connection was made by early writers such as Thomas (1928), but this emphasis on girls' and women's sexuality has continued to the present. As Herksovitz boldly put it, "the predominant expression of delinquency among females in our society is promiscuous sexual behavior" (cited in Bartollas, 1993, p. 237).

Even when females commit more "masculine" kinds of crimes, their level of involvement is assumed to be minor, and their motivations are believed to be different. Describing what he termed the occasional female criminal, Lombroso asserted, "These are not like men. They do not commit crimes out of evil passions, but to please their lovers. They steal or compromise themselves for men's sakes, without having sometimes any direct interest in the act" (Lombroso & Ferrero, 1916, p. 196). This idea is still found in modern reviews. For example, Steffensmeier and Allan (1995) reiterate the widely held belief that "most women in prison would not be there if they had not gotten romantically involved" (p. 88).

The "New" Female Offender

These themes and contradictions coexisted in the relatively small body of research on female crime that had accumulated by the early 1970s. It is conventional to associate an increased interest in females' antisocial behavior at this time with apparent *changes* in females' levels of involvement. For example, Berger (1989) noted the emergence of the belief that "female crime and delinquency had been rising and that a new type of female offender had emerged who was more violent and aggressive than her predecessors" (p. 376). Although there were indeed a flurry of articles and books concerned with change issues (Ageton, 1983; Simon, 1975; Steffensmeier, 1978, 1980; Steffensmeier & Steffensmeier, 1980), it is likely that more research attention would have been directed to an understanding of females' behavior even without this impetus. The disparity in knowledge concerning males and females was quite glaring, and there was increased recognition of the need for research to counter the "gender gap" in relation to many kinds of health-related outcomes, including antisocial behavior. The National Institute of Mental Health funded at least three projects on female delinquency and crime prior to the publication of Adler's 1975 book, *Sisters in Crime*—a work that is generally considered to have turned the spotlight on the "new" female criminal. Regardless of the origins of this increased attention, there is little question that the period of the 1970s to the present has seen an exponential increase in research and theorizing on the relationship between gender and antisocial behavior.

The Application of Male-Based Theories to Female Crime

The belief in an increase in females' criminal involvement did more than foster a number of articles tracing trends (although it did this as well). Another effect was to open ways of thinking about women's criminality: If rates had changed significantly over time, how could individualistic "personal problems" or even psychological disturbance theories explain this? At this point, a number of studies began to examine the relevance of variables derived from classic sociological theories to an understanding of female criminality. These are often referred to as "male" theories because they had been developed with a focus on males and had been tested with exclusively male samples. There were two ways in which concepts from these theories were incorporated into the study of female crime. First, it became increasingly unacceptable to exclude females from large-scale research efforts. Thus, even if gender was not a major focus, it became customary to design projects that included female as well as male subjects. For example, the National Youth Survey (a prospective interview-based longitudinal study of deviant behavior from adolescence into early adulthood) was designed this way at the outset. The substantive aspects of these studies included attention to such factors as family and school attachment, peer influence, and economic strain, not just loneliness or low self-esteem.

Although these studies have been criticized as a mere "add women and stir" approach (Chesney-Lind, 1989), they represented a significant advance over the male-only sampling strategies that had been standard procedure for decades.

A second group of researchers began to conduct studies in which female delinquency was a central focus (Campbell, 1981, 1984; Cernkovich & Giordano, 1979a, 1979b; Giordano, 1978; Giordano & Cernkovich, 1979; Norland, Wessel, & Shover, 1981). These studies also examined social and structural influences, but here gender was more than a demographic control or dummy variable. In this research, conceptualization and measurement reflected a focus on females. Peer influences were studied, but it was recognized that the dynamics/mechanisms might be somewhat distinct for females. For example, although same-gender networks figure centrally in the delinquent involvement of boys, females were found most likely to commit acts of law violation when in mixed-gender groups (Giordano & Cernkovich, 1979).

The idea of investigating common themes as well as the potential for variations by gender was also found in the work of psychologists whose research focused on basic developmental processes. Cairns, Cairns, Neckerman, Ferguson, and Gariépy (1989) studied network influences on aggression but often focused descriptive and theoretical attention on how gender influenced processes as well as outcomes. For example, some female networks were characterized by hostile and aggressive actions, but the behavioral manifestations tended to be more indirect, involving ostracism, rumors, and the like, as well as directly aggressive behaviors (see also, Hood, 1994).

Feminist Perspectives

Investigators also have increasingly explored the potential of feminist concepts and theories to inform gender-crime issues (see especially Carlen, 1985; Chesney-Lind, 1989; Messerschmidt, 1986; Simpson, 1989; Smart, 1976). Feminist perspectives have highlighted some of the limitations of the "male-derived" approaches. Early papers critiqued the ways in which the classic delinquency theorists summarily dismissed consideration of females (Klein, 1973; Leonard, 1982; Smart, 1976). Later analyses took issue with the basic content and logic of these theories and generally concluded that they may be limited in their ability to adequately explain either women's conformity or their acts of rebellion (Daly & Chesney-Lind, 1988). Consequently, new paradigms are required, ones that break in fundamental ways from the male-oriented theories.

Another important contribution of feminist scholarship has been increased attention to the role of agents of social control, including parents who construct and enact definitions of what is incorrigible or out-of-control behavior, and of police and other justice personnel whose decision-making strategies are fundamentally connected to the image the general public has of female crime. For example, the belief that much of the delinquency of females has a sexual character can be traced to the behaviors, fears, and emphases of these formal and informal control agents (Chesney-Lind, 1989; Schlossman & Cairns, 1991; Schlossman & Wallach, 1978).

Feminist research also can be seen as increasingly forging links between women's experiences of victimization and their patterns of offending. The role of early physical and sexual abuse has been highlighted, as has the necessity of placing many female acts of aggression within the larger context of male patterns of violence and control (see especially Chesney-Lind & Shelden, 1992; Daly & Chesney-Lind, 1988; Messerschmidt, 1987; Shelden, 1981).

Finally, feminist critiques have emphasized the need to open up the field to a variety of different methodologies, including qualitative ones. In the process of delving "more deeply into the social worlds of girls and women" (Daly & Chesney-Lind, 1988, p. 519), a more comprehensive and fully contextualized account of female crime will result (Carlen, 1985).

THEORETICAL ISSUES/CONTROVERSIES

As the previous review indicates, some contradictory conceptions of the female offender emerged in the early research, and these sometimes inconsistent themes continue in more modern literature. Although a variety of issues have not been fully resolved, we highlight four continuing areas of controversy.

Do Females Commit Similar or Different Kinds of Crimes Than Males?

That females commit *fewer* acts of antisocial behavior is not in question, but beyond this, consensus declines. Whether female *patterns* of offending are distinct from those of males is not simply or merely a "descriptive" issue because these varied portraits relate directly to the kinds of theoretical models that are then advanced to explain them. This issue is also connected to sampling and measurement strategies, as will be reviewed in the following section.

The notion that females commit fundamentally different types of crimes—especially that they are disproportionately involved in status offenses (behaviors, such as truancy, that are illegal only for juveniles)—derives principally from studies relying on official statistics. Especially prior to legislative changes relating to the deinstitutionalization of status offenders, the trends were clear: Females were much more likely than males to be arrested for status offenses. Males were also arrested for these offenses but contributed disproportionately to the total arrests for both serious and less serious personal and property crimes. Sexual activity figured prominently in females' involvement with the justice system, either directly or under the guise of such categories as incorrigibility and running away.

This situation appears to be changing. For example, Schwartz, Steketee, and Schneider (1990), analyzing incarceration of males and females in public training schools and detention centers, trace a dramatic decline between 1971 and 1986 in the "number and percentage of youths confined for status offenses in public juvenile training schools with a particularly dramatic decline for females" (1990, p. 506). Using a different methodological strategy, Schlossman and Cairns (1991) reach a similar conclusion: Females in the Carolina Longitudinal Survey were rarely found to have been arrested for status offenses across many years of follow-up. Nevertheless, some scholars conclude that this is still a common route into the system for many young women (Chesney-Lind & Shelden, 1992). Rhodes and Fischer (1993), for example,

examined the patterns of referral to a diversion (i.e., nonjudicial) program in California and echoed the traditional theme. Females were likely to be referred to the program because of status offenses and personal problems, males for violations of the law.

The advent of self-report delinquency scales made it possible to examine the nature and extent of gender differences in antisocial behavior without the confounding influences of processing biases, legal and social changes, and other inconsistencies. Although self-reports have their own biases and limitations, studies using these instruments present a different picture of offending patterns. Investigators have generally concluded that males and females commit similar offenses—females simply commit them on a less frequent basis. When the range of behaviors comprising delinquency scales is considered, the rank order of offenses is remarkably similar for males and females. Most males do not engage in serious acts of antisocial behavior, and these are also the least frequent behaviors among females. High-frequency offense categories across gender include such status offenses as drinking and disobeying parents (Figueira-McDonough, Barton, & Sarri, 1981; see also, Cernkovich & Giordano, 1979a), as well as minor property offenses. The findings that have emerged using the self-report methodology do not offer strong support for the distinct patterns hypothesis.

Are Theories Used to Explain Male Antisocial Behavior Relevant to an Understanding of Female Crime and Delinquency?

The so-called generalizability issue (Are the causes of female and male involvement in antisocial behavior similar or distinct?) is also an area of continuing controversy. Although the very early view of female offenders as "seriously disturbed" or wicked has largely been rejected, a recurring theme is that females need a greater or even different sort of "push" than males in order to engage in antisocial behaviors. Distinctively female push variables include the notion of a liberated or nontraditional set of gender role attitudes or of excessive masculinity. A number of researchers have investigated whether these attitudes or personality attributes are associated with females' involvement and, in general, have not found much support for a masculinization or liberation effect (see Berger, 1989; Giordano & Cernkovich, 1979; Norland, Wessel, & Shover, 1981; Widom, 1984; but see Heimer, 1991). Feminist theorists, although also skeptical of the idea of a direct link between liberated attitudes and women's experiences of crime, nevertheless call for a move away from traditional male-based theories (Daly & Chesney-Lind, 1988). This is, in effect, a call for a bifurcation of theory. As yet, however, new feminist theories of crime have not been fully developed or tested. As a result, the bulk of the recent empirical work in this area can be considered, conceptually and in terms of measurement, derivative from aspects of the "classic" (male) theories of crime and delinquency. Specific findings from this body of research are reviewed in the current findings section of this chapter.

Is Female Crime Increasing?

The idea that there have been dramatic increases in female crime has not received widespread support. Nevertheless, there have been many attempts to determine whether apparent shifts in official statistics represent real trends, changes in official processing, or some combination of the two. Unfortunately, self-report methods were not widely used until the 1960s, and the development of self-report instruments that included attention to serious offenses is an even more recent phenomenon. Most analyses of long-term changes have used official sources of data. Some researchers have identified what they argue are significant increases in female involvement (Austin, 1993), but others question the methodologies involved. Steffensmeier, for example, argues that increases are slight, primarily resulting from shifts in property offense involvement, especially shoplifting (Steffensmeier, 1978; Steffensmeier & Streifel, 1992, 1993). One problem in attempting to capture the nature and significance of trends is the issue of what constitutes an appropriate measure of change. Steffensmeier (1978) contends that the proper unit of analysis should be the percentage of female involvement relative to the total volume of crime (i.e., the gender ratio). Although this is an important consideration, our own view is that this definition imposes a limited perspective on what comprises a significant change. For example, even if females' level of involvement increased exponentially, the conclusion would necessarily be that not much of interest had occurred if males' criminality evidenced a similar increase. It is important to understand more about how women's present behavior compares to that in earlier eras, as well as the somewhat different concern of convergence of male-female rates.

Further complicating matters, Feeley and Little (1991) recently analyzed a much older data set, which encompassed the years 1675 to 1880. In their study of London court registries, these researchers documented that there was actually a significant amount of female crime during those years, followed by an eventual *decline* over the period examined. They linked this decrease to the capitalist mode of production, which had the effect of marginalizing females' roles in the household and the economy (i.e., making it difficult for women to find employment). These kinds of analyses that cover a broad time frame are an important adjunct to more typical trend studies because they may provide insight into potential shifts in gendered behavior patterns that may be gradual and incremental rather than sudden or dramatic.

Is the Long-Term Prognosis More Favorable for Female Than for Male Offenders?

Given the inconsistent portraits in the existing literature, it is possible to construct a plausible rationale for each of three competing hypotheses relating to the long-term prospects of female in contrast to male offenders.

1. Female offenders will tend to evidence more favorable outcomes over the long term than will their male counterparts. Even if females do evidence significant early antisocial tendencies, the weight of "nurturant role obligations" (Robbins, 1989, p. 119) and stronger pressures in the direction of conformity confronting all women (Scarr-Salapatek & Salapatek, 1973; Schur, 1984) lead us to predict that females will mature out of such behaviors earlier and at a higher rate than males.

2. Female offenders will evidence more problematic outcomes, including continued involvement in antisocial behavior,

greater psychological distress, and more difficulty adapting to such prosocial adult roles as that of parent or spouse (see Lewis et al., 1991; Zoccolillo & Rogers, 1991). For example, Tremblay (1991, p. 76) believes that a primary rationale for studying conduct-disordered girls is that they would tend to "quickly become mothers who start a new generation of highly disruptive conduct-disordered boys." Robins (1986) found that in following up a sample of girls originally diagnosed for conduct disorder in childhood/adolescence, a high percentage continued to evidence a wide range of problems as they matured. The overall low base rate of involvement for females could suggest a greater level of "seriousness" when it does occur. This notion of seriousness could encompass several related areas: (a) The behavior itself may be more firmly entrenched/chronic (a là Lombroso's "wickedness" proverb); (b) it may be symptomatic of an enduring psychological trait or constellation/syndrome of psychological disorders (Crites, 1976; Ross & Fabiano, 1986; Widom, 1984) and problem life events; and (c) the greater social stigma attached to female in contrast to male involvement in antisocial behavior may be more limiting to females' life chances and opportunities for a return to conventional roles, quite apart from a particular level of pathology.

3. Few gender differences will be found in long-term prognosis, the processes linked to desistance and the likelihood of desistance. Researchers who emphasize the generalizability of explanatory models across gender offer support for this hypothesis, whereas those who call for distinct theoretical models might predict a difference in the nature of long-term outcomes.

METHODOLOGY

At least part of the reason for continued inconsistencies in the existing literature is that the research base in this area is still less than ideal. In this section, we review certain aspects of sampling and methodology that are limiting to the knowledge base about the causes, course, and consequences of antisocial behavior among adolescent and adult women.

No Data, Small Ns, or No Comparison Group

Several investigators have produced monographs focusing on the female offender; however, many of these are essentially reviews of the literature, with little or no original data being presented (Heidensohn, 1985; Leonard, 1982; Ross & Fabiano, 1986; Schur, 1984; Smart, 1976; Weisheit & Mahan, 1988). Several important qualitative studies—for example, Campbell's (1981, 1984) observational analyses of female gang members in New York and Miller's (1986) study of female prostitutes in Milwaukee—have been extremely useful sources for theory building, but it is difficult to generalize from these studies because of their reliance on small samples and because they lack a male comparison group. Carlen's (1985) work also develops a number of interesting hypotheses relating to gender, but it is difficult to draw definitive conclusions based on her analysis of the lives of four criminal women in England. We cannot be certain whether the patterns she emphasized would be characteristic of a larger, more heterogeneous sample.

Limitations of Official Data Sources

A popular source of crime data includes such official statistics as the Uniform Crime Reports, an annual compilation of police statistics gathered and published by the Federal Bureau of Investigation. Although studies based on official crime statistics (e.g., Adler, 1975; Simon, 1975; Steffensmeier, 1978, 1980, 1993; Steffensmeier & Steffensmeier, 1980; Steffensmeier & Streifel, 1992; Widom, 1988) have been useful, particularly in sorting out trends/shifts in patterns of involvement, such data also have serious shortcomings. The biases and limitations of official crime statistics are well known, especially the tendency of these data to reflect such confounding influences as gender, race, and class bias more than the actual amount and distribution of antisocial behavior. These biases become especially problematic as we try to understand more about the extent and nature of female crime and delinquency. There is a sizable research literature on differential justice system processing by gender that shows that females are treated more harshly than males for some offenses but less harshly for others (see, e.g., Boritch, 1992; Chesney-Lind, 1989; Crew, 1991; Erez, 1992). Although there is continuing debate regarding whether the justice system over- or underpunishes females, it seems certain that official crime statistics fail to accurately represent the full range of female offending. Research based on official data has made important contributions, but these data must be supplemented with unofficial data sources if we wish to examine the full range of female antisocial behavior and to answer more specific questions about this behavior.

Lack of Longitudinal Designs

Prospective longitudinal designs have become an increasingly popular alternative to officially derived sources of data. Unfortunately, many of the most important contributions to our knowledge focus exclusively on follow-ups of young boys; even those studies that include females have focused most analyses on males (Loeber, Stouthamer-Loeber, Van Kammen, & Farrington, 1991; McCord, 1983; Patterson, 1982; Sampson & Laub, 1990; Wolfgang, Thornberry, & Figlio, 1987). It may be that insights from these studies of male delinquents will generalize to the experiences of female offenders, but this has not been shown conclusively. For example, longitudinal research demonstrates that most individuals who have engaged in antisocial behavior during adolescence desist on reaching adulthood (Blumstein & Cohen, 1987; Gottfredson & Hirschi, 1990; Hirschi & Gottfredson, 1983). At the same time, a small number continue offending at a relatively high rate (Farrington, Ohlin, & Wilson, 1986; Shannon, 1988) and contribute disproportionately to the total volume of antisocial and violent behavior. Sampson and Laub (1990), in a long-term follow-up of delinquent males using data previously collected by Glueck and Glueck (1950), found that strong bonds of marital attachment in adulthood and job stability were linked to desistance. However, it is not known whether these factors would be equally salient for understanding the process of maturing in a sample of highly delinquent young women. We simply do not know whether females with an early and significant history of involvement in antisocial behavior continue to evidence this pattern or begin to assume more socially

productive roles as they mature. We do not know whether patterns of female persistence/desistance follow the same trajectory as that of males. It is critical to determine whether the specific factors found to be important in the male-based desistance literature are also important to an understanding of the criminal career histories of female offenders.

The few available longitudinal studies are limited in other ways. Warren and Rosenbaum (1986), for example, followed the criminal careers of 159 females incarcerated as adolescents in order to determine whether they continued to experience problems as adults. This study is important in documenting that a high percentage were found to have an adult criminal record. However, analysis is restricted to data derived from institutional records at both Time 1 and follow-up. This restriction limits the potential utility of such a sample, particularly in trying to understand more about patterns of variation in persistent criminality. From the available records, the investigators concluded that virtually all the females had problem families. Thus, variations in family functioning/quality (which likely would have emerged had the researchers been able to interview the subjects) could not be examined for their effects on long-term outcomes (Rosenbaum, 1989). In addition, the analysis was limited to the presence or absence of a criminal arrest as an adult; neither degree of criminality nor other behavioral outcomes were examined.

Robins's (1966, 1986) research also included follow-ups with females and males seen at a psychiatric clinic for antisocial behavior in childhood or adolescence. Although data at Time 1 consist of only official records, Time 2 data include follow-up interviews as well as records analyses. This study is generally consistent with Warren and Rosenbaum's (1986) conclusions in that there is continuity to the antisocial behavior problems of the females in the study, although it also indicates the importance of including attention to outcomes other than crime/antisocial behavior. While Robins's research illustrates the utility of combining official and unofficial data sources, more recent longitudinal analyses are essential, especially given the changes since the 1970s in the factors that bring females to the attention of public agencies. For example, Robins notes how many of the females in her sample were referred because of "sex offenses." Although this undoubtedly still occurs, such referrals are increasingly less likely in more recent decades (Schlossman & Cairns, 1991).

Problems "Capturing" the Serious Female Offender

Although neighborhood and school-based surveys have become increasingly popular alternatives to official data, such surveys have their limitations as well. Although there are several recent well-designed longitudinal studies with adequate representation of female respondents, these unselected cohort designs (Stattin, Magnusson, & Reichel, 1989; White, Moffitt, Earls, Robins, & Silva, 1990) and national probability samples (Elliott, Huizinga, & Menard, 1989; Osgood, Johnston, O'Mally, & Bachman, 1988) do not include sufficiently large numbers of seriously delinquent girls to allow meaningful analysis. For example, Stattin, Magnusson, and Reichel (1989) followed up 1,393 pupils in Sweden and found that only 15 females had official crime records as juveniles. Similarly, only 15 of the 484 females in our neighborhood youth survey (Cernkovich, Giordano, & Pugh, 1985) had ever been picked up by the police, and only 3 had been picked up more than once. Wolfgang, Thornberry, and Figlio (1987) reported that 1.9% of the females in their large cohort study had committed a violent offense resulting in injury to a victim. Only 2 females from the National Youth Survey qualified as serious violent offenders—defined as those youths who exhibited a high offending rate for more than 1 year (Huizinga, Morse, & Elliott, 1992). Cairns and colleagues (Cairns, Cairns, Neckerman, Ferguson, & Garièpy, 1989; Schlossman & Cairns, 1991) found that only 6% of their female sample had at least one serious arrest charge by age 18.

Perhaps the most important lesson to be learned from such data is that gender socialization is, in general, very powerful—the average female is just not very delinquent/criminal. Although this generalization does make it difficult to study criminal careers that have never really "taken off" to begin with, there is no question that a subset of adolescent and adult women does engage in antisocial and aggressive behavior that is sufficiently chronic or serious to warrant official intervention. A recent Bureau of Justice Statistics report indicates that during the period of 1980 to 1989, "the number of women in prison has grown at a faster rate than that of men. In a year-to-year comparison, the percentage of women is now the highest it has ever been, beginning with the first annual collection of prison statistics in 1926" (Greenfeld & Minor-Harper, 1991, p. 1). Between 1986 and 1991, the number of women incarcerated in state prisons increased 75%, compared to 53% for males. The 1980 to 1989 rate of arrest for "selected serious crimes" (i.e., murder, nonnegligent manslaughter, robbery, aggravated assault, rape, and burglary) as a percentage of all arrests increased more rapidly for women than for men. The total number of females arrested between 1986 and 1991 increased 24%, compared to only 13% for males (Greenfeld & Minor-Harper, 1991; Snell, 1994; also see Culliver, 1993).

There is no question that serious female offenders exist, yet their low base rates and relatively small absolute number make it unlikely that they will be captured using traditional survey sampling procedures. This has important theoretical implications because the causal processes and desistance patterns associated with routine crime and delinquency and those evidenced by serious offenders may be quite similar, or they may be very different (see Dishion & Patterson, Chapter 20, this volume). To the extent that general samples have omitted or underrepresented chronic offenders, this important question has gone untested empirically. The data in Table 46.1, comparing the offending levels of an institutional and a neighborhood sample of youths (Cernkovich, Giordano, & Pugh, 1985), illustrate this problem in reference to several selected offenses.

The first four columns of the table compare all neighborhood and all institutional girls in the sample. In all cases, institutional girls are considerably more delinquent than their neighborhood counterparts. This is true for both serious and relatively minor offenses. For example, whereas only 4% of neighborhood girls report any involvement in grand theft, 64% of institutional girls report involvement. The differences in mean rates (based on frequency codes ranging from never = 0 to 2 to 3 times a week or more = 130) are from 3 to 51 times greater for the institutional as compared to the neighborhood respondents. For example, institutional females report an average of 24 grand theft incidents compared to 0.57 for neighborhood youths.

The last four columns of the table represent only those youths whose offending levels qualify them as chronic offenders (5 or more self-reported major offenses during the 12-month reference period). Chronic offenders comprise only 10% of the neighborhood sample but 65% of the institutional sample. The various comparisons indicate that institutional chronic offenders are significantly more delinquent than their neighborhood counterparts. For example, 31% of neighborhood chronic offenders report involvement in grand theft, but 80% of institutional offenders admit involvement. Similarly, comparison of incidence rates shows that institutional chronic offenders report rates that are from 1.25 to 8 times greater than those reported by neighborhood chronic offenders. Additional analysis (not shown) reveals that the differences are quite large for total self-reported delinquency (mean levels of involvement of 1,178 vs. 450 for institutional and neighborhood chronic offenders, respectively) as well as for the specific subscales (e.g., property offenses: 194 vs. 49; violent

TABLE 46.1 Prevalence (%) and Incidence (Mean) of Female Involvement in Selected Offenses

Offense	All Neighborhood		All Institutional		Neighborhood Chronic		Institutional Chronic	
	%	Mean	%	Mean	%	Mean	%	Mean
Grand Theft	4	0.57	64	24.22	31	5.44	80	36.33
Run Away	10	1.41	70	28.55	25	9.96	67	28.38
Concealed Weapon	10	5.30	52	41.96	31	20.08	62	50.22
Petty Theft	17	1.93	52	20.30	35	8.52	60	26.77
Gang Fights	16	1.91	45	22.95	48	11.79	53	30.32
Sold Marijuana	7	2.96	60	53.05	25	14.88	74	73.98
Simple Assault	62	19.81	93	58.02	96	53.02	98	66.07
Sold Hard Drugs	1	0.63	38	32.10	15	6.38	56	49.43
Unarmed Robbery	4	1.22	28	14.63	25	12.12	39	22.56
Theft $5–$50	8	1.18	68	21.40	31	7.81	83	31.05
Breaking & Entering	1	0.29	42	14.09	8	2.83	57	21.18
Drug Use	20	6.97	80	79.03	38	24.21	89	99.45

offenses: 160 vs. 117; status offenses: 407 vs. 159; drug-related offenses: 374 vs. 100).

Such data make it clear that institutionalized youths are not only more delinquent than the "average kid" in the general youth population but also considerably more delinquent than the *most delinquent* youths identified in the typical self-report survey. Although studies of the general youth population are useful, it also is important to locate the chronic delinquent offender, to compare the behavior of this youth with that of others along the behavioral continuum, and to identify those factors and processes associated with this extreme level of delinquency involvement.

Limitations of "Male-Based" Measures

In our view, it is not necessary or even desirable to develop entirely "new" concepts, scales, and other measures in an attempt to better understand female criminality. We disagree with the view that the classic (male-based) theories are irrelevant to understanding female antisocial behavior. Instead, these offer a logical conceptual and measurement starting point. Classic theorists have written volumes and have studied thousands of offenders. In the process, they have identified life domains and influences that have been rather consistently associated with the onset and continuation of antisocial patterns of behavior. It is unlikely that one would identify a sphere of life (e.g., family, school, economic) that had not been considered by the classic theorists. The use of common measurement space (addressing similar questions to males as well as females) also helps in the task of specifying areas of convergence or divergence in the causal processes of interest. It is very difficult to determine whether women face unique concerns/issues without the presence of comparable male data.

This does not mean that the classic male-based theories/concepts must necessarily be transplanted wholesale. Theories of female crime may combine variables in a different way or suggest a different balance or emphasis. For example, Hagan's power-control theory relies on variables examined in previous research on delinquency (supervision, taste for risk, maternal employment) but combines them in a unique way in order to explain convergence/divergence in female and male deviance (Hagan, Gillis, & Simpson, 1985; Hagan, Simpson, & Gillis, 1987).

CURRENT FINDINGS

In this section, we review recent research on a variety of causal mechanisms as they have been linked to disparities in male-female rates and to variations in females' involvement in antisocial behavior.

Biological and Psychological Factors

Although we concentrate on some of the advances and limitations in our knowledge about social factors, the period from the 1970s to the present also produced a literature exploring biological and psychological influences on female antisocial behavior. In a review, Fishbein (1992) highlighted the role of psychobiological processes, as these are thought to influence not only males' generally higher levels of aggression but also the smaller subset of women who engage in these kinds of behaviors. Fishbein (1992) contends that "the incidence of psychopathology ... is high among female offenders" (p. 103; see also, Lewis et al., 1991) but also points to the potential importance of other biochemical processes. Her review suggests links between female aggression and mesomorphic body type, premenstrual difficulties, and hypothalmic function.

Another set of studies emphasizes the role of early maturation. Stattin and Magnusson (1990) found that early maturing girls in a large Swedish cohort tended to engage in more norm violations and precocious sexual activity than did later maturing girls. In an analysis of data from the Dunedin, New Zealand, longitudinal study, Caspi, Lynam, Moffitt, and Silva (1993) also found an effect of early maturation. These studies represent something of a departure from earlier treatments of biology or sexuality, however, because the researchers have an interest in the social consequences of some of these physical changes. For example, Caspi et al. (1993) point out that in mixed-sex school settings, the early maturing girl faces particular pressure to behave in more mature ways. Stattin and Magnusson (1990) also point out the behavioral consequences of dating and associating with older males.

Some longitudinal projects stress the continuity of aggression and other antisocial behavior over time, a perspective that has biological and individual differences implications. Moffitt (1992), for example, identified a life-course persistent delinquent type, characterized by an early and continuing history of behavior problems, and found this type among both males and females. In a longitudinal study of children referred to a child guidance clinic because of antisocial behavior, Robins (1966) also found that females were likely to develop antisocial personality disorders or other psychiatric problems in their adult years. More recently, using data from the Epidemiological Catchment Area study, Robins (1986) examined the nature and extent of reported childhood symptoms as these related to externalizing and other disorders in adulthood. Females who reported an early history of behaviors associated with conduct disorder were also more likely to develop externalizing as well as internalizing disorders. Robins concluded that at least part of the reason that some studies have shown a more favorable long-term prognosis for females (e.g., Kellam, Simon, & Ensminger, 1983; Lefkowitz, Eron, Waldron, & Huesmann, 1977) may be that these studies examined only continuities in aggression, rather than assessing a broader range of outcomes.

Widom (1984) has pointed out some of the problems involved in attempting to establish linkages between gender, psychopathology, and crime. From an early age individuals receive strong messages regarding what will be considered gender-appropriate conduct; therefore, it is likely that these scripts will also figure into patterns of deviance. In addition, those who react to various kinds of behavioral output are also influenced by gender stereotypes and assumptions. This will tend to confound attempts to sort out what may be "real" gender differences and what may be socially constructed or amplified. For example, Ventura (1991) analyzed police decision making concerning the appropriate disposition of violent misdemeanors. Police were given discretion to take the individual to a local mental health facility or to the city jail. Being female was significantly associated with the decision to refer to the mental health rather than the criminal justice system.

Family Factors

To the extent that females are more strongly bonded to the family than males, it often is argued that familial influences are more salient in the genesis of female as compared to male antisocial behavior (see, e.g., Baskin & Sommers, 1993; Cernkovich & Giordano, 1987; Morash & Chesney-Lind, 1991; Rosenbaum, 1987; Smith & Paternoster, 1987). Of all the family factors thought to contribute to crime and delinquency, none has received more attention than the broken home. Broken homes are thought to have their effect on delinquency primarily through reduced supervision and control and the resultant increased association with peers (Austin, 1992; Hirschi, 1969; Matsueda & Heimer, 1987). Datesman and Scarpitti (1975) found that female offenders are somewhat more likely than males to come from broken homes. Rosenbaum's (1989) follow-up study of institutionalized juvenile females into adulthood found that only 7% came from intact families. Canter (1982), however, found that broken homes had at least as great an effect on boys as on girls, and our own research (Cernkovich & Giordano, 1987) found no broken home effect for either males or females. We agree with Canter that such results are not so surprising when one considers that much of the evidence showing that family factors have a greater effect on females than on males derives from studies of official delinquency. It may be that youths from broken homes are not necessarily more delinquent than those from intact homes but that the former (especially girls) are more likely to be arrested, processed through the court system, and incarcerated (see Johnson, 1986).

A more consistent body of research findings relates to the nature and quality of family relationships (Cernkovich & Giordano, 1987; Gove & Crutchfield, 1982; Hirschi, 1969; Kruttschnitt & Krmpotich, 1990; Lauritsen, 1993). Persistent, long-term family disruptions and negative relationships are especially likely to produce chronic delinquency (Loeber, 1982). Parental rejection of children and children's rejection of parents have been shown to be associated with delinquency and aggression in most studies (Loeber & Stouthamer-Loeber, 1986, pp. 54–55). Conflict, hostility, minimal parental involvement with children, lack of warmth and affection, and lack of attachment and supervision are all strong correlates of delinquency and other behavior problems (Cernkovich & Giordano, 1987; Laub & Sampson, 1988; Loeber & Stouthamer-Loeber, 1986; Rosenbaum, 1989). Norland, Shover, Thornton, and James (1979) found that family conflict had a greater effect on female than male involvement in status, property, and aggressive offenses; and Rosenbaum's (1989) study of institutionalized delinquent girls found that most came from environments in which family conflict was the norm. Henggeler, Edwards, and Borduin (1987) found that families of female delinquents were more dysfunctional than those of male delinquents, supporting the supposition that because societal sanctions against female misbehavior are so strong, severe familial problems must exist in order to generate delinquent conduct among girls.

Research on levels of supervision and control has shown that delinquency is most likely in families that impose few rules and do not effectively discipline or supervise their children. The evidence is overwhelming that inconsistent, punishment-oriented, and extreme forms of discipline (lax or harsh) are associated with antisocial behavior. Because girls historically have been the objects of greater levels of parental supervision, control, and discipline than have boys, this is thought by many to be responsible for their comparatively low rates of antisocial behavior. For example, Baskin and Sommers (1993) and Rosenbaum (1989) found poor familial supervision to be characteristic of the serious female offenders they studied.

Abuse and neglect of children have both been shown to lead to a variety of maladies: delinquency and adult criminality, emotional problems, developmental difficulties, problems in establishing and maintaining intimate relationships, running away from home, difficulties at school, drug and alcohol abuse, and violence within and outside of the family (Chesney-Lind & Rodriguez, 1983; Gelles & Cornell, 1985; Widom, 1988, 1989a, 1989b; J. Q. Wilson & Herrnstein, 1985, pp. 256–263). Even when such variables as gender and race are controlled, the odds of having a criminal record are almost two times higher for abused/neglected subjects when compared to nonabused subjects (Widom, 1989b). Because girls are more likely than boys to be abuse victims, such experiences are thought to be more salient for females and often are viewed as primary causes of much antisocial behavior (Chesney-Lind & Shelden, 1992; also see Browne & Finkelhor, 1986; Chesney-Lind & Rodriguez, 1983; Widom, 1988, Chapter 16, this volume). Because so much abuse remains hidden, however, it is difficult to draw firm conclusions regarding its effect. In addition, although being abused appears to increase the odds of subsequent antisocial behavior, the majority of abuse victims (70%) do not go on to have adult criminal records (Widom, 1989b; also see Zingraff, Leiter, Myers, & Johnsen, 1993).

Peer Influences

The literature on peer influences on female behavior is much less well developed than the body of research relating to family factors. This likely stems from the long-held belief that, compared with males, females remain more closely tied to family and domestic concerns. Although this is accurate, there is also a rather sizable literature that finds that females forge stronger and more intimate bonds with friends than males do during virtually every phase in the life cycle. Adolescent friendships, in particular, have been shown to be particularly intimate and all encompassing (Berndt, 1982; Rawlins, 1992; see also, Thornberry & Krohn, Chapter 21, this volume). In an early study of the peer associations of delinquent girls, we interviewed institutionalized as well as high school youth and found that delinquent girls were strongly embedded in friendship networks that encouraged their delinquent behavior. Results suggested that the perception of approval for law violations from other females was especially important, although the mixed-sex clique was the most common context in which delinquency actually occurred (Giordano, 1978; Giordano & Cernkovich, 1979).

A second study (Giordano, Cernkovich, & Pugh, 1986) examined the peer context of female (and male) delinquency in much greater detail. This research provided a stronger test of what has been called the "social disability" hypothesis—the notion that female as well as male delinquents are likely to experience deficits in peer relations. The issue of the level of attachment within delinquent peer groups is pivotal in theory development: To the degree that delinquents' relationships are found not to be in any real sense primary, cohesive, or solidary, the significance of group processes in the etiology of delinquent behavior is believed to be minimized. This has been a major contention of control theory, whose proponents have argued that because delinquents are less strongly attached to conventional adults than are nondelinquents, they are less likely to be attached to each other: "The idea that delinquents have comparatively warm, intimate social relations with each other (or with anyone) is a romantic myth" (Hirschi, 1969, p. 159). This kind of argument is especially evident in the early work on female crime, in which female delinquents were often described as "lone wolves" (Wattenberg, 1956) and as incapable of having friendships with contemporaries (Konopka, 1966). There is also a well-developed research tradition that has emphasized the role of early peer rejection in the development of oppositional-defiant disorders (Kupersmidt & Coie, 1990; Parker & Asher, 1987). Our research presented a contrast to this view, documenting that female adolescents (and their male counterparts) with different levels of involvement in delinquency appeared to be quite *similar* in the ways in which they experienced their friendship relations. Levels of perceived caring, self-disclosure, frequency of interaction and identity support were not significantly associated with the nature or extent of involvement in delinquency (see also, Campbell, 1990; Matsueda, 1992; Morash, 1986).

The Carolina Longitudinal Study (a prospective longitudinal study of social development following two cohorts over a 14-year period) also has shown that aggressive youths—both male and female—tend to be solid members of peer clusters. Cairns, Cairns, Neckerman, Gest, and Garièpy (1988) collected data from peers and teachers and found that although aggressive individuals were frequently disliked or considered less popular by the broader peer group, they were about as likely as less delinquent youths to have reciprocated friendships. These investigators also documented high levels of similarity in the aggressive tendencies of individuals within particular social networks, which offers additional support for a social influence/social learning framework.

School Factors

School and school-related variables assume prominent roles in most major theories of delinquency, but there is some debate as to whether school problems are a cause or an effect of involvement in delinquent behavior (see, e.g., Hirschi, 1969; Kelly, 1974; Liska & Reed, 1985; Phillips & Kelly, 1979; Polk & Schafer, 1972). Although there is a large body of basic research on school variables, there has been little attempt to examine gender variation in the impact of school factors on antisocial behavior. Rather, most criminologists study only boys or assume that boys and girls are similarly affected by school-related factors (Rosenbaum & Lasley, 1990). There is some evidence suggesting that the relationship between school factors and delinquency may be gender specific under certain conditions, but the overall literature is both equivocal and contradictory (Cairns, Cairns, & Neckerman, 1989; Rosenbaum, 1987; Rosenbaum & Lasley, 1990; also see, e.g., Elliott & Voss, 1974; Hindelang, 1973; Johnson, 1979; Krohn & Massey, 1980; Smith & Paternoster, 1987).

The assumptions of social control theory are most compatible with a hypothesis of little or no gender variation in the influence of school factors (see, e.g., Elliott & Voss, 1974; Hindelang, 1973; Hirschi, 1969; Smith & Paternoster, 1987). Rosenbaum and Lasley (1990) believe, however, that power-control theory—which predicts gender variability in the influence of school factors—is a viable theoretical alternative. Their research supports the power-control model in showing that male delinquency tends to be associated with academic variables (such as grades and achievement attitudes), whereas female delinquency is more likely to be related to nonacademic factors (such as involvement in extracurricular activities and attitudes toward teachers). They conclude that this is consistent with the notion that girls and boys have different orientations toward school: Girls approach it from an affective and boys from an achievement perspective (Rosenbaum & Lasley, 1990). Consequently, they believe gender-specific explanations may be necessary to account for the relationship between school and delinquency.

Economic and Community-Level Factors

There is quite a disparity in our knowledge about the impact of economic and other opportunity variables on female as contrasted with male crime and antisocial behavior. The rationale for the neglect of such variables is similar to that discussed with regard to school factors—"status striving" is considered the province of males, whereas females are seen as motivated primarily by relationship issues and concerns. However, our research suggests that this kind of bifurcation of theoretical directions is misleading. For example, we found that females who perceived blocked educational and occupational opportunities were significantly more delinquent than those who did not (Cernkovich & Giordano, 1979b). We also examined the perception of gender-based blocked opportunity (the belief that certain legitimate avenues of success are closed or restricted on the basis of gender), which can be considered a variation on the liberation-causes-delinquency theme that gained prominence in the 1970s. It is interesting that only the traditional blocked opportunity scale (derived from male-oriented literature) was significantly correlated with self-reported delinquency.

In an observational study of "hustling" in Milwaukee, Miller (1986) found that prostitution was but one of a number of legitimate, quasi-legitimate, and illegitimate strategies for survival employed by economically marginal young women. She also found an effect for family relationships but conceptualized family influence differently than is typically the case. Instead of emphasizing a lack of attachment, Miller suggested that many of the young women in her sample were strongly embedded in domestic kin networks and were actually introduced to these kinds of activities by network members. Family members such as cousins and young aunts were an important source of social learning about techniques, motivations, and details of involvement in some of these illegal behaviors. Other recent qualitative research also has emphasized the linkages between adolescent/young adults' increasingly tenuous connections to the labor force and their movement into criminal and sometimes aggressive activities. Unfortunately there is almost no mention of females in these works (see, e.g., Gaines, 1991; Jankowski, 1991; Sullivan, 1989). Figueira-McDonough (1992) notes a similar problem with community-level factors: Most theories and studies do not include attention to gender issues. Although her own analysis does not include empirical data, Figueira-McDonough does show how certain community characteristics, especially poverty and high rates of instability, may affect the gender ratio (the relative participation of females in criminal activities), through variation in gender ideologies and other informal social control processes.

Contextual Factors

It is important to understand more about the context in which females participate in illegal activities. Traditional theories are tied to certain images of female offending—that is, the idea of the female as a "helpless and pitiful victim," as a passive accomplice to male offenders, or as a mere ornamental appendage (see, e.g., Steffensmeier & Allan's, 1995, discussion of these images). Motivational states are also assumed, many times in the absence of empirical evidence, for example, the notion that females, in comparison to males, are rather uninterested in financial gain or do not become involved in violent activities because of pecuniary motivations. In order to explore the validity of these kinds of images, Pettiway (1987) examined how various domestic living arrangements were linked to specific crime patterns. He found considerable heterogeneity in women's involvement with crime partners. Although some females committed crimes with a boyfriend, those who committed them alone, with other females, or in the context of a mixed-sex group accounted for about 75% of the sample. His analysis documented that the various crime partnerships were directly related to variations in women's domestic living arrangements.

Other researchers have focused on the specific characteristics of property as well as violent offenses committed by women. Sommers and Baskin (1993), in a study of robbery and aggravated assault, found that utilitarian or monetary interests were common among property offenders, supporting the view that female motivations are not necessarily distinct from those of their male counterparts. In contrast, in a study of female embezzlers, Zietz (1981) found that women's rationalizations for their fraudulent activities were different from those of males. Whereas previous studies have shown "borrowing" to be a dominant justification among male embezzlers, Zietz found that this was only one of many among females: Equally important were rationalizations based on their role responsibilities as wives, mothers, and daughters. Jurik and Gregware (1992) recently documented that gender had a significant impact on the processes that built up to an eventual homicide. Dominant theories of homicide (largely developed through research on male offenders) place emphasis on interactional/situational "triggers," but analysis of the content of presentence reports suggests that many females had a long history of abuse, or at least a long sequence of previous negative interactions with the victim, that typically preceded the homicide incident. These kinds of contextual data are extremely valuable as we attempt to build theory and develop intervention strategies that take gender into account.

Issues of Ethnicity

Although our discussion has emphasized areas of similarity and contrast between male and female offenders, there also has been increased attention to the role played by ethnicity in structuring causal mechanisms, as well as the distribution of outcomes. Hill and Crawford (1990), relying on data from the 1979 to 1980 youth cohort surveys of the National Longitudinal Surveys, concluded that social psychological factors were somewhat more important in explaining the behavior of white females, whereas structural/deprivation variables (e.g., proximity to the central city, discrepancies between educational aspirations and achievements, and a lack of educational achievement) explained more of the variance among black females.

Although our previous research was designed with a primary emphasis on gender, our sampling plan also overrepresented African American youths, ensuring race-sex subgroups approximately equal in size, distributed across a variety of socioeconomic categories, enabling us to examine the effects of race and race-by-sex interactions. This research revealed areas of similarity as well as some differences by respondent ethnicity. For example, an analysis of school factors (Cernkovich & Giordano, 1992) suggested that such variables as attachment and commitment to school operated in a similar fashion for both Black and White females. However, in other analyses (Cernkovich & Giordano, 1987; Giordano, Cernkovich, & Pugh, 1986), Black youths had somewhat less intense or intimate relationships with friends, while scoring significantly higher on family intimacy across the adolescent period (see also, Giordano, Cernkovich, & DeMaris, 1993). A greater tolerance for heterogeneity also characterized the Black youths in our sample (see also, Tolson & Urberg, 1993). This led us to theorize that although peer influences are likely important to all youths, Black adolescents may be less susceptible to direct peer pressures. We also found that family variables explained a somewhat greater amount of the variance in delinquency among the White females in the sample when compared to their African American counterparts.

Other researchers have focused on how ethnicity affects rates of involvement. Black females have been found to have higher rates of involvement in violent crimes, but few ethnic differences are found for property, sex-related, and drug or drinking offenses (Steffensmeier & Allan, 1988). Our own research has shown that Black females report more violent offenses than do Whites but that White females report greater involvement in minor status, minor property, and drug-related offenses (Cernkovich & Giordano, 1979a; see also, Ageton, 1983; Laub & McDermott, 1985). Although the idea that there is a "subculture of violence" has been rejected by many criminologists, there is increased attention to some of the cultural as well as structural underpinnings of these behavior patterns. High levels of disadvantage, cultural isolation, and everyday situational contingencies may contribute to the production of behaviors that are not in themselves seen as valued or desirable (Simpson, 1991; Sullivan, 1989; W. J. Wilson, 1987).

CONCLUSIONS

This review does not present an entirely consistent portrait of either the factors implicated in females' lower rates of antisocial behavior or those connected to such behaviors when they do occur. Some of the apparent inconsistencies in the literature stem from the sampling and methodological problems outlined in the methodology section. For example, scholars who have emphasized the important role of sexual abuse have tended to rely on samples of street youths or prostitutes, for whom the connection might be hypothesized to be especially prevalent (see Chesney-Lind, 1989). On the other hand, neighborhood youth surveys also offer a limited perspective because they necessarily focus on a more restricted range of antisocial outcomes. But although samples, measurement strategies, and the existing research base are not entirely comprehensive, the following kind of conclusion seems somewhat premature:

> Theoretical criminology is unable to explain adequately the phenomenon of women and crime. Theories that are frequently hailed as explanations of human behavior are, in fact, discussions of male behavior and male criminality. In addition, . . . this oversight regarding women is not easily remedied. We cannot simply apply these theories to women, nor can we modify them with a brief addition or subtraction here and there. They are biased to the core, riddled with assumptions that relate to a male—not a female—reality. (Leonard, 1982, p. 181)

Although theory and research in this area may need more than a brief addition here or a subtraction there, the findings discussed in this chapter generally support the idea that family, peer, school, and economic variables are appropriate foci for additional research.

FUTURE RESEARCH

More female-based research is needed on all the theoretical domains traditionally examined for their relevance to male antisocial behavior. We know very little about how living in marginal or economically disadvantaged circumstances affects female involvement in antisocial behavior, although there is a wealth of information on how structural constraints affect male misbehavior. Females may have been sheltered historically, but these circumstances may now be more personally devastating to females who are maturing in large urban centers that offer few economic opportunities; such women may be feeling the brunt of economic deprivation more directly now than in the past. Similarly, the idea that school failure is not an important correlate of female misbehavior presupposes that achievement and success in this area are not important to young women as they attempt to make their way in the world. It is an oversimplification to assume, as has been the case traditionally, that women's identities and concerns revolve entirely around family and relationship issues.

At the same time, numerous studies have shown that females have been socialized to be more sensitive to others and to place a higher value on interpersonal intimacy. It is, therefore, important to explore further the impact of significant others—including family, peers, and male partners—as we attempt to understand how young women become involved in antisocial behavior. The need for a more complete understanding of the role of romantic and other male-female relationships is especially great. Currently, the inferences in the literature regarding this domain are based largely on stereotypes and conventional wisdom.

Research designs developed to address some of these gaps in the literature should include serious female offenders as well as those young women likely to be captured via traditional sampling strategies. Our own longitudinal study involves a follow-up of a sample of neighborhood respondents as well as a sample of females who were incarcerated in a state facility. This should enable some basic comparisons regarding causal processes and long-term outcomes and should increase our understanding about how particular types of sampling strategies affect our knowledge about gender differences. Qualitative studies, on their own and in combination with quantitative approaches, also will be an important part of research that seeks to place female crime within a broader frame of reference. More general research focused on gender also is quite relevant and can be an important source for theory building and the development of appropriate measurement instruments. Although future research can benefit from a primary focus on females, in our view male comparison samples and some areas of common measurement are essential if we are to make informed statements about what is unique to or shared by each gender. This would also provide a more secure base from which to design gender-sensitive prevention and treatment strategies.

Existing research also points up the need to assess a variety of behavioral and mental health outcomes in addition to antisocial tendencies. This strategy of including multiple outcomes in study designs is useful in relation to male behavior but may be critical when it comes to understanding patterns of variation in problem outcomes within a sample of females.

Given that most of the studies reviewed in this chapter are cross-sectional, there is a special need to determine how females with early antisocial tendencies fare in the long run. There is suggestive evidence that females with an early history of antisocial tendencies continue to evidence problems throughout the life course, but these studies are far from definitive and are much more limited in number and scope when compared to the body of research into male careers or trajectories.

REFERENCES

Adler, F. (1975). *Sisters in crime.* New York: McGraw-Hill.

Ageton, S. S. (1983). The dynamics of female delinquency, 1976–1980. *Criminology, 21,* 555–584.

Austin, R. (1992). Race, female headship, and delinquency: A longitudinal analysis. *Justice Quarterly, 9,* 585–607.

Austin, R. L. (1993). Recent trends in official male and female crime rates: The convergence controversy. *Journal of Criminal Justice, 21,* 447–466.

Barker, G. H., & Adams, W. T. (1962). Comparison of the delinquencies of boys and girls. *Journal of Criminal Law, Criminology, and Police Science, 53,* 470–475.

Bartollas, C. (1993). *Juvenile delinquency* (3rd ed.). New York: Macmillan.

Baskin, D., & Sommers, I. (1993). Females' initiation into violent street crime. *Justice Quarterly, 10,* 559–583.

Berger, Ronald J. (1989). Female delinquency in the emancipation era: A review of the literature. *Sex Roles, 21,* 375–399.

Berndt, T. J. (1982). The features and effects of friendship in early adolescence. *Child Development, 53,* 1447–1460.

Blumstein, A., & Cohen, J. (1987). Characterizing criminal careers. *Science, 237,* 985–991.

Boritch, H. (1992). Gender and criminal court outcomes: An historical analysis. *Criminology, 30,* 293–325.

Browne, A., & Finkelhor, D. (1986). Impact of child sexual abuse: A review of research. *Psychological Bulletin, 99,* 66–77.

Cairns, R. B., Cairns, B. D., & Neckerman, H. J. (1989). Early school dropout: Configurations and determinants. *Child Development, 60,* 1437–1452.

Cairns, R. B., Cairns, B. D., Neckerman, H. J., Ferguson, L. L., & Garièpy, J.-L. (1989). Growth and aggression: I. Childhood to early adolescence. *Child Development, 25,* 320–330.

Cairns, R. B., Cairns, B. D., Neckerman, H. J., Gest, S. D., & Garièpy, J.-L. (1988). Social networks and aggressive behavior: Peer support or peer rejection? *Developmental Psychology, 24,* 815–823.

Campbell, A. (1981). *Girl delinquents.* New York: St. Martin's Press.

Campbell, A. (1984). *The girls in the gang.* Oxford: Basil Blackwell.

Campbell, A. (1990). On the invisibility of the female delinquent peer group. *Women and Criminal Justice, 2,* 41–62.

Canter, R. J. (1982). Family correlates of male and female delinquency. *Criminology, 20,* 149–167.

Carlen, P. (Ed.). (1985). *Criminal women.* Cambridge, England: Polity Press.

Caspi, A., Lynam, D., Moffitt, T. E., & Silva, P. A. (1993). Unraveling girls' delinquency: Biological, dispositional, and contextual contributions to adolescent misbehavior. *Developmental Psychology, 29,* 19–30.

Cernkovich, S. A., & Giordano, P. C. (1979a). A comparative analysis of male and female delinquency. *Sociological Quarterly, 20,* 131–145.

Cernkovich, S. A., & Giordano, P. C. (1979b). Delinquency, opportunity, and gender. *Journal of Criminal Law and Criminology, 70,* 145–151.

Cernkovich, S. A., & Giordano, P. C. (1987). Family relationships and delinquency. *Criminology, 25,* 295–321.

Cernkovich, S. A., & Giordano, P. C. (1992). School bonding, race, and delinquency. *Criminology, 30,* 261–291.

Cernkovich, S. A., Giordano, P. C., & Pugh, M. D. (1985). Chronic offenders: The missing cases in self-report delinquency research. *Journal of Criminal Law and Criminology, 76,* 705–732.

Chesney-Lind, M. (1989). Girl's crime and woman's place: Toward a feminist mode of female delinquency. *Crime and Delinquency, 35,* 5–29.

Chesney-Lind, M., & Rodriguez, N. (1983). Women under lock and key. *Prison Journal, 63,* 47–65.

Chesney-Lind, M., & Shelden, R. G. (1992). *Girls, delinquency, and juvenile justice.* Pacific Grove, CA: Brooks/Cole.

Crew, B. K. (1991). Sex differences in criminal sentencing: Chivalry or patriarchy. *Justice Quarterly, 8,* 59–83.

Crites, L. (Ed.). (1976). *The female offender.* Lexington, MA: Heath.

Culliver, C. (1993). *Female criminality: The state of the art.* New York: Garland.

Daly, K., & Chesney-Lind, M. (1988). Feminism and criminology. *Justice Quarterly, 5,* 497–538.

Datesman, S. K., & Scarpitti, F. R. (1975). Female delinquency and broken homes: A re-assessment. *Criminology, 13,* 33–55.

Elliott, D. S., Huizinga, D., & Menard, S. (1989). *Multiple problem youth: Delinquency, substance use, and mental health problems.* New York: Springer-Verlag.

Elliott, D., & Voss, H. (1974). *Delinquency and dropout.* Lexington, MA: Heath.

Erez, D. (1992). Dangerous men, evil women: Gender and parole decision-making. *Justice Quarterly, 9,* 105–126.

Farrington, D. P., Ohlin, L., & Wilson, J. Q. (1986). *Understanding and controlling crime.* New York: Springer-Verlag.

Feeley, M., & Little, D. L. (1991). The vanishing female: The decline of women in the criminal process, 1687–1912. *Law and Society Review, 25,* 719–757.

Figueira-McDonough, J. (1992). Community structure and female delinquency rates: A heuristic discussion. *Youth and Society, 24,* 3–30.

Figueira-McDonough, J., Barton, W. H., & Sarri, R. (1981). Normal deviance: Gender similarities in adolescent subcultures. In M. Q. Warren (Ed.), *Comparing female and male offenders* (pp. 17–45). Beverly Hills, CA: Sage Publications.

Fishbein, D. (1992). The psychobiology of female aggression. *Criminal Justice and Behavior, 19,* 99–126.

Gaines, D. (1991). *Teenage wasteland: Suburbia's dead end kids.* New York: Harper.

Gelles, R., & Cornell, C. P. (1985). *Intimate violence in families.* Beverly Hills, CA: Sage Publications.

Giordano, P. C. (1978). Guys, girls, and gangs: The changing social context of female delinquency. *Journal of Criminal Law and Criminology, 69,* 126–132.

Giordano, P. C., & Cernkovich, S. A. (1979). On complicating the relationship between liberation and delinquency. *Social Problems, 26,* 467–481.

Giordano, P. C., Cernkovich, S. A., & DeMaris, A. (1993). The family and peer relations of black adolescents. *Journal of Marriage and the Family, 55,* 277–287.

Giordano, P. C., Cernkovich, S. A., & Pugh, M. D. (1986). Friendships and delinquency. *American Journal of Sociology, 91,* 1170–1202.

Glueck, S., & Glueck, E. (1950). *Unraveling juvenile delinquency.* New York: The Commonwealth Fund.

Gottfredson, M., & Hirschi, T. (1990). *A general theory of crime.* Stanford, CA: Stanford University Press.

Gove, W., & Crutchfield, R. (1982). The family and juvenile delinquency. *The Sociological Quarterly, 23,* 301–319.

Greenfeld, L. A., & Minor-Harper, S. (1991). *Women in prison* (Special Report). Washington, DC: Bureau of Justice Statistics, U.S. Department of Justice.

Hagan, J., Gillis, A. R., & Simpson, J. (1985). The class structure of gender and delinquency: Toward a power control theory of common delinquent behavior. *American Journal of Sociology, 90,* 1151–1178.

Hagan, J., Simpson, J., & Gillis, A. R. (1987). Class in the household: A power-control theory of gender and delinquency. *American Journal of Sociology, 92,* 788–816.

Heidensohn, F. (1985). *Women and crime.* New York: New York University Press.

Heimer, K. (1991, November). *Gender, conflict, and delinquency: A process of intimate oppression.* Paper presented at the annual meeting of the American Society of Criminology, San Francisco, CA.

Henggeler, S., Edwards, J., & Borduin, C. (1987). The family relations of female juvenile delinquents. *Journal of Abnormal Child Psychology, 15,* 199–209.

Hill, G. D., & Crawford, E. M. (1990). Women, race, and crime. *Criminology, 28,* 601–626.

Hindelang, M. (1973). Causes of delinquency: A partial explication and extension. *Social Problems, 20,* 471–487.

Hirschi, T. (1969). *Causes of delinquency.* Berkeley: University of California Press.

Hirschi, T., & Gottfredson, M. (1983). Age and the explanation of crime. *American Journal of Sociology, 89,* 552–584.

Hood, K. E. (1994). Intractable tangles of sex and gender in developing women's aggressive behavior: An optimistic view. In D. M. Stoff & R. B. Cairns (Eds.), *Aggression and violence: Neurobiological, biosocial, and genetic perspectives.* Hillsdale, NJ: Erlbaum.

Horwitz, A. V., & White, H. R. (1987). Gender role orientations and styles of pathology among adolescents. *Journal of Health and Social Behavior, 28,* 158–170.

Huizinga, D., Morse, B. J., & Elliott, D. S. (1992). *The National Youth Survey: An overview and description of recent findings* (National Youth Survey Project Report No. 55). Boulder, CO: Institute of Behavioral Science, University of Colorado.

Jankowski, M. S. (1991). *Islands in the street: Gangs and American urban society.* Berkeley: University of California Press.

Johnson, R. E. (1979). *Juvenile delinquency and its origins.* Cambridge, England: Cambridge University Press.

Johnson, R. E. (1986). Family structure and delinquency: General patterns and gender differences. *Criminology, 24,* 65–80.

Jurik, N. C., & Gregware, P. (1992). A method for murder: The study of homicides by women. In G. Miller & J. Holstein (Eds.), *Perspectives on social problems* (Vol. 4). Greenwich, CT: JAI Press.

Kellam, S., Simon, M., & Ensminger, M. (1983). Antecedents in first grade of teenage substance use and psychological well being. In D. Ricks & B. Dohrenwend (Eds.), *Origins of psychopathology* (pp. 17–42). New York: Cambridge University Press.

Kelly, D. (1974). Track position and delinquent involvement: A preliminary analysis. *Sociology and Social Research, 58,* 380–386.

Klein, D. (1973). The etiology of female crime: A review of the literature. *Issues in Criminology, 8,* 3–30.

Konopka, G. (1966). *The adolescent girl in conflict.* Englewood Cliffs, NJ: Prentice Hall.

Krohn, M., & Massey, J. (1980). Social control and delinquent behavior: An examination of the elements of the social bond. *Sociological Quarterly, 21,* 529–543.

Kruttschnitt, C., & Krmpotich, S. (1990). Aggressive behavior among female inmates: An exploratory study. *Justice Quarterly, 7,* 371–389.

Kupersmidt, J. B., & Coie, J. D. (1990). Preadolescent peer status, aggression, and school adjustment as predictors of externalizing problems in adolescence. *Child Development, 61,* 1350–1362.

Laub, J., & McDermott, M. (1985). An analysis of serious crime by young black women. *Criminology, 23,* 81–97.

Laub, J., & Sampson, R. (1988). Unraveling families and delinquency: A reanalysis of the Gluecks' data. *Criminology, 26,* 355–379.

Lauritsen, J. (1993). Sibling resemblance in juvenile delinquency: Findings from the National Youth Survey. *Criminology, 31,* 387–409.

Lefkowitz, M., Eron, L., Waldron, L., & Huesmann, L. (1977). *Growing up to be violent.* Elmsford, NY: Pergamon.

Leonard, E. (1982). *Women, crime, and society: A critique of theoretical criminology.* New York: Longman.

Lewis, D., Yeager, C., Cobham-Portorreal, C., Klein, N., Showalter, C., & Anthony, A. (1991). A follow-up of female delinquents: Maternal contributions to the perpetuation of deviance. *Journal of the American Academy of Child and Adolescent Psychiatry, 30,* 197–201.

Liska, A., & Reed, M. (1985). Ties to conventional institutions and delinquency: Estimating reciprocal effects. *American Sociological Review, 50,* 547–560.

Loeber, R. (1982). The stability of antisocial and delinquent child behavior: A review. *Child Development, 53,* 1431–1446.

Loeber, R., & Stouthamer-Loeber, M. (1986). Family factors as correlates and predictors of juvenile conduct problems. In M. Tonry & N. Morris (Eds.), *Crime and justice: An annual review of research* (Vol. 7). Chicago: University of Chicago Press.

Loeber, R., Stouthamer-Loeber, M., Van Kammen, W., & Farrington, D. P. (1991). Initiation, escalation, and desistance in juvenile offending and their correlates. *The Journal of Criminal Law and Criminology, 82,* 36–82.

Lombroso, C., & Ferrero, W. (1916). *The female offender.* New York: Philosophical Society.

McCord, J. (1983). A longitudinal study of aggression and antisocial behavior. In K. T. VanDusen & S. A. Mednick (Eds.), *Prospective studies of crime and delinquency* (pp. 269–276). Boston: Kluwer-Nijhoff.

McCord, J. (1993). Gender issues. In C. Culliver (Ed.), *Female criminality: The state of the art* (pp. 105–118). New York: Garland.

Matsueda, R. L. (1992). Reflected appraisals, parental labeling, and delinquency: Specifying a symbolic interactionist theory. *American Journal of Sociology, 97,* 1577–1611.

Matsueda, R. L., & Heimer, K. (1987). Race, family structure, and delinquency: A test of differential association and social control theories. *American Sociological Review, 52,* 826–840.

Messerschmidt, J. (1986). *Capitalism, patriarchy, and crime.* Totowa, NJ: Rowman and Littlefield.

Messerschmidt, J. (1987). Feminism, criminology, and the rise of the female sex delinquent, 1880–1930. *Contemporary Crises, 11,* 243–263.

Miller, E. (1986). *Street women.* Philadelphia: Temple University Press.

Moffitt, T. E. (1992). *Adolescence-limited and life-course persistent antisocial behavior: A developmental taxonomy.* Unpublished manuscript.

Morash, M. (1986). Gender, peer group experiences, and seriousness of delinquency. *Journal of Research in Crime and Delinquency, 23,* 43–67.

Morash, M., & Chesney-Lind, M. (1991). A reformulation and partial test of power control theory of delinquency. *Justice Quarterly, 8,* 347–377.

Norland, S., Shover, N., Thornton, W. E., & James, J. (1979). Intrafamily conflict and delinquency. *Pacific Sociological Review, 22,* 223–240.

Norland, S., Wessel, R. C., & Shover, N. (1981). Masculinity and delinquency. *Criminology, 19,* 421–433.

Osgood, D., Johnston, L., O'Mally, P., & Bachman, J. (1988). The generality of deviance in late adolescence and early adulthood. *American Sociological Review, 53,* 81–93.

Ostrov, E., Offer, D., & Howard, K. (1989). Gender differences in adolescent symptomatology: A normative study. *Journal of American Academy Child Adolescent Psychiatry, 28,* 394–398.

Parker, J. G., & Asher, S. R. (1987). Peer relations and later personal adjustment: Are low-accepted children at risk? *Psychological Bulletin, 102,* 357–389.

Patterson, G. R. (1982). *Coercive family process.* Eugene, OR: Castalia.

Pettiway, L. E. (1987). Participation in crime partnerships by female drug users: The effects of domestic arrangements, drug use, and criminal involvement. *Criminology, 25,* 741–766.

Phillips, J., & Kelly, D. (1979). School failure and delinquency: What causes which? *Criminology, 17,* 194–207.

Polk, K., & Schafer, W. (1972). *Schools and delinquency.* Englewood Cliffs, NJ: Prentice Hall.

Pollack, O. (1950). *The criminality of women.* New York: Barnes.

Rawlins, W. (1992). *Friendship matters: Communication, dialectics, and the life course.* New York: Aldine de Gruyter.

Reige, M. G. (1972). Parental affection and juvenile delinquency in girls. *British Journal of Criminology, 12,* 55–73.

Rhodes, J. E., & Fischer, K. (1993). Spanning the gender gap: Gender differences in delinquency among inner-city adolescents. *Adolescence, 28,* 879–889.

Robbins, C. (1989). Sex differences in psychosocial consequences of alcohol and drug abuse. *Journal of Health and Social Behavior, 30,* 117–130.

Robins, L. N. (1966). *Deviant children grown up.* Baltimore: Williams & Wilkins.

Robins, L. N. (1986). The consequences of conduct disorder in girls. In D. Olweus, J. Block, & M. Radkey-Yarrow (Eds.), *Development of antisocial and prosocial behavior* (pp. 385–414). Orlando: Academic Press.

Robins, L. N., Tipp, J., & Przybeck, T. (1991). Antisocial personality. In L. N. Robins & D. A. Regier (Eds.), *Psychiatric disorders in America* (pp. 258–290). New York: The Free Press.

Rosenbaum, J. L. (1987). Social control, gender, and delinquency: An analysis of drug, property, and violent offenders. *Justice Quarterly, 4,* 117–132.

Rosenbaum, J. L. (1989). Family dysfunction and female delinquency. *Crime and Delinquency, 35,* 31–44.

Rosenbaum, J. L., & Lasley, J. R. (1990). School, community context, and delinquency: Rethinking the gender gap. *Justice Quarterly, 7,* 493–514.

Ross, R. R., & Fabiano, E. A. (1986). *Female offenders: Correctional afterthoughts.* Jefferson, NC: McFarland and Company.

Sampson, R., & Laub, J. H. (1990). Crime and deviance over the life course: The salience of adult social bonds. *American Sociological Review, 55,* 609–627.

Scarr-Salapatek, S., & Salapatek, P. (Eds.). (1973). *Socialization.* Columbus, OH: Merrill.

Schlossman, S., & Cairns, R. B. (1991). Problem girls: Observations on past and present. In G. H. Elder Jr., R. D. Park, & J. Modell (Eds.), *Children in time and place: Relations between history and developmental psychology* (pp. 110–130). New York: Cambridge University Press.

Schlossman, S., & Wallach, S. (1978). The crime of precocious sexuality: Female juvenile delinquency in the progressive era. *Harvard Educational Review, 48,* 65–94.

Schur, E. (1984). *Labeling women deviant.* New York: Random House.

Schwartz, I., Steketee, M., & Schneider, V. (1990). Federal juvenile justice policy and the incarceration of girls. *Crime and Delinquency, 36,* 503–520.

Shannon, L. (1988). *Criminal career continuity: Its social context.* New York: Human Sciences Press.

Shelden, R. (1981). Sex discrimination in the juvenile justice system: Memphis, Tennessee, 1900–1917. In M. Q. Warren (Ed.), *Comparing female and male offenders* (pp. 55–72). Beverly Hills, CA: Sage Publications.

Simon, R. (1975). *Women and crime.* Lexington, MA: Lexington Books.

Simpson, S. (1989). Feminist theory, crime, and justice. *Criminology, 27,* 607–631.

Simpson, S. (1991). Caste, class, and violent crime: Explaining differences in female offending. *Criminology, 29,* 115–135.

Smart, C. (1976). *Women, crime, and criminology: A feminist critique.* London: Routledge and Kegan Paul.

Smith, D., & Paternoster, R. (1987). The gender gap in theories of deviance: Issues and evidence. *Journal of Research in Crime and Delinquency, 24,* 140–172.

Snell, T. (1994). *Bureau of Justice statistics special report: Women in prison.* Washington, DC: U.S. Department of Justice, Office of Justice Programs, Bureau of Justice Statistics.

Sommers, I., & Baskin, D. R. (1993). The situational context of violent female offending. *Journal of Research in Crime and Delinquency, 30,* 136–162.

Stattin, H., & Magnusson, D. (1990). *Pubertal maturation in female development.* Hillsdale, NJ: Erlbaum.

Stattin, H., Magnusson, D., & Reichel, H. (1989). Criminal activity at different ages. *British Journal of Criminology, 29,* 368–385.

Steffensmeier, D. (1978). Crime and the contemporary woman: An analysis of changing levels of female property crime, 1960–1975. *Social Forces, 57,* 566–584.

Steffensmeier, D. (1980). Sex differences in patterns of adult crime, 1965–1977: A review and assessment. *Social Forces, 58,* 1080–1109.

Steffensmeier, D. (1993). National trends in female arrests, 1960–1990: Assessment and recommendations for research. *Journal of Quantitative Criminology, 9,* 411–441.

Steffensmeier, D., & Allan, E. (1988). Sex disparities in arrests by residence, race, and age: An assessment of the gender convergence/crime hypothesis. *Justice Quarterly, 5,* 53–80.

Steffensmeier, D., & Allan, E. (1995). Criminal behavior: Gender and age. In J. F. Sheley (Ed.), *Criminology: A contemporary handbook* (pp. 83–113). Belmont, CA: Wadsworth.

Steffensmeier, D. J., & Steffensmeier, R. H. (1980). Trends in female delinquency: An examination of arrest, juvenile court, self-report, and field data. *Criminology, 18,* 62–85.

Steffensmeier, D., & Streifel, C. (1992). Time-series analysis of the female percentage of arrests for property crimes, 1960–1985: A test of alternative explanations. *Justice Quarterly, 9,* 77–103.

Steffensmeier, D., & Streifel, C. (1993). Trends in female crime, 1960–1990. In C. Culliver (Ed.), *Female criminality: The state of the art* (pp. 63–101). New York: Garland.

Sullivan, M. (1989). *Getting paid: Youth crime and work in the inner city.* Ithaca, NY: Cornell University Press.

Thomas, W. I. (1928). *The unadjusted girl.* Boston: Little, Brown.

Tolson, J., & Urberg, K. (1993). Similarity between adolescent best friends. *Journal of Adolescent Research, 8,* 274–288.

Tremblay, R. E. (1991). Aggression, prosocial behavior, and gender: Three magic words but no magic wand. In D. J. Pepler & K. H. Rubin (Eds.), *The development and treatment of childhood aggression* (pp. 71–78). Hillsdale, NJ: Erlbaum.

Ventura, L. (1991). *Patient or prisoner? Police disposition of the violent mentally ill.* Doctoral dissertation, Bowling Green State University, Bowling Green, OH.

Warren, M. Q., & Rosenbaum, J. L. (1986). Criminal careers of female offenders. *Criminal Justice and Behavior, 13,* 393–418.

Wattenberg, W. (1956). Differences between girl and boy repeaters. *Journal of Educational Psychology, 47,* 137–146.

Weisheit, R., & Mahan, S. (1988). *Women, crime, and criminal justice.* Cincinnati, OH: Anderson.

White, J. L., Moffitt, T. E., Earls, F., Robins, L. N., & Silva, P. A. (1990). How early can we tell?: Predictors of childhood conduct disorder and adolescent delinquency. *Criminology, 28,* 507–533.

Widom, C. S. (1984). Sex roles, criminality, and psychopathology. In C. Spatz Widom (Ed.), *Sex roles and psychopathology* (pp. 183–217). New York: Plenum.

Widom, C. S. (1988). Sampling bias and implications for child abuse research. *American Journal of Orthopsychiatry, 58,* 260–270.

Widom, C. S. (1989a). Child abuse, neglect, and adult behavior: Research design and findings on criminality, violence, and child abuse. *American Journal of Orthopsychiatry, 59,* 355–367.

Widom, C. S. (1989b). Child abuse, neglect, and violent criminal behavior. *Criminology, 27,* 251–271.

Wilson, J. Q., & Herrnstein, R. (1985). *Crime and human nature.* New York: Simon & Schuster.

Wilson, W. J. (1987). *The truly disadvantaged.* Chicago: University of Chicago Press.

Wolfgang, M. E., Thornberry, T. P., & Figlio, R. M. (1987). *From boy to man: From delinquency to crime.* Chicago: University of Chicago Press.

Zietz, D. (1981). *Women who embezzle or defraud: A study of convicted felons.* New York: Praeger.

Zingraff, M., Leiter, J., Myers, K., & Johnsen, M. (1993). Child maltreatment and youthful problem behavior. *Criminology, 31,* 173–202.

Zoccolillo, M., & Rogers, K. (1991). Characteristics and outcomes of hospitalized adolescent girls with conduct disorder. *Journal of American Academy of Child Adolescent Psychiatry, 30,* 973–981.

CHAPTER 47

Alcohol, Illicit Drugs, and Violence

HELENE RASKIN WHITE

The relationship between alcohol use and violence is well documented. Similarly, it is well accepted that illicit drug use is connected to violence. However, whether alcohol or other psychoactive drugs have a direct causal effect on violence has been debated. This chapter reviews the literature that addresses this question.

Although alcohol and many drugs share similar statistical relationships with violence, the mechanisms and processes that account for their associations may be different. That is, alcohol use is presumed to contribute to violence because of the psychopharmacological properties of the drug, as well as the expectancies and societal norms surrounding these properties. On the other hand, illicit drug use is assumed to contribute to violence primarily because of the conditions of the illegal drug market. Thus, the alcohol and illicit drug models differ in their causal propositions and in their implications for social policy. This chapter explores differences, as well as similarities, in the various models of substance use and violence. First, the historical context of research on alcohol/drugs and violence is discussed. Then the theoretical models that have been proffered to explain these relationships are presented, followed by a discussion of selected methodological issues in this field of research. Finally, the chapter concludes with a summary of the existing data and recommendations for future research. In the space limitations of this chapter, all the relevant literature cannot be covered; the reader is referred to several excellent reviews for greater detail (e.g., Chaiken & Chaiken, 1990; Fagan, 1990; Miczek et al., 1994; Osgood, 1994).

HISTORICAL CONTEXT AND CONTROVERSIAL ISSUES

Until recently, it had been proffered that alcohol use is associated with violent crime, whereas other drug use is associated with a high proportion of property crime. Proponents of the alcohol-violence model emphasized the psychopharmacological effects of alcohol intoxication as the cause for violent behavior (Fagan, 1990). The drug–property crime model was based principally on the notion that heroin (and other drug) addicts commit crimes in order to secure money for drugs (Ball, Rosen, Flueck, & Nurco, 1981). It is interesting that proponents of the alcohol-violence model did not give weight to the fact that a substantial proportion of inmates convicted of property crimes were under the influence of alcohol at the time of the offense (Bureau of Justice Statistics, 1994a). Similarly, only since the mid-1980s have drug–property crime model proponents given weight to the fact that heroin- and cocaine-addicted individuals are often involved in violent crimes, typically committed over drug possession and sale (see Goldstein, 1985).

Much of the attention on reduction of alcohol-related violence focuses on limiting availability of alcohol through strategies such as increasing taxes, raising the drinking age, and limiting hours of sale. However, extreme limits on legal access might create an illicit market for alcohol, which, as was seen during Prohibition, could increase violence (Woodiwiss, 1988) or could expose drinkers to deviant subcultures in which violence is reinforced. The reduction of drug-related violence focuses on a legal model, sometimes referred to as the "War on Drugs." Proponents of this approach favor increased punishment for drug users and dealers and interdiction of the flow of drugs to the United States. In both of these models, the focus is on substances and not on the individual. That is, these models do not address other sources of violence within individual offenders and within society, such as an aggressive temperament or economic hardship. An alternative strategy, harm reduction, has also received a lot of attention. Proponents of the harm reduction model believe that attention should be focused on treatment for those with alcohol and drug problems and on prevention of alcohol and drug use among youths. The harm reduction model also focuses primarily on reducing alcohol and drug use rather than on addressing other causes of violence within individuals. This chapter explores the direct and spurious relationships between substance use and violence and examines individual differences in these relationships. (For details on the history of the drug-violence relationship, see Goldstein, 1989; Lindesmith, 1940; McBride, 1981; for details on violence during Prohibition, see Woodiwiss, 1988.)

The author would like to express appreciation to Drs. Marsha Bates, Dennis Gorman, and Allan Horwitz for their comments and suggestions on earlier drafts. Preparation of this chapter was supported, in part, by grants from the National Institute on Drug Abuse (#DA/AA-03395) and the Alcoholic Beverage Medical Research Foundation.

THEORETICAL ISSUES

There are four basic explanatory models for the relationship between alcohol/drug use and violence: (a) Substance use causes violence; (b) violence leads to substance use; (c) the relationship is reciprocal; and (d) the relationship is spurious; that is, it is coincidental or explained by a set of common causes (see White, 1990). Each model may be applicable to different subgroups of the population or to different incidents of alcohol- and drug-related violence. The following sections describe the models, and later sections present the empirical data that both support and refute them.

Substance Use Causes Violent Behavior

One causal model posits that alcohol and drug use lead to violence because of either the psychopharmacological properties of the drugs, the economic motivation to get drugs, or the systemic violence associated with the illegal drug market (Goldstein, 1985). The *psychopharmacological model* proposes that the effects of intoxication (including disinhibition, cognitive-perceptual distortions, attention deficits, bad judgment, and neurochemical changes) cause aggressive behavior (Collins, 1981; Fagan, 1990). In addition, chronic intoxication may also contribute to subsequent aggression as a result of factors such as withdrawal, sleep deprivation, nutritional deficits, impairment of neuropsychological functioning, or enhancement of psychopathologic personality disorders (Virkkunen & Linnoila, 1993).

The *economic motivation model* assumes that drug users need to generate illicit income to support their drug habit. Thus, they engage in crimes to get drugs or the money to buy drugs. Some of these crimes can involve violence, for example, armed robbery or the unexpected presence of a homeowner during a burglary. This model is applicable to illicit drugs but not to alcohol.

More recently, attention has focused on the *systemic model* (Goldstein, 1985). This model suggests that the system of drug distribution and use is inherently connected with violent crime. The systemic types of crimes surrounding drug distribution include fights over organizational and territorial issues; enforcement of rules; punishments of and efforts to protect buyers and sellers; transaction-related crimes, such as robberies of drugs and money from dealers or buyers; assaults to collect debts; and resolution of disputes over quality or amount (Miczek et al., 1994). Given that there is no legal mechanism to resolve these disputes, violence or the threat of violence is used to enforce rules in the illicit market. In addition, there is often third party violence, such as bystander shootings or assaults on prostitutes who sell drugs (Miczek et al., 1994). Further, the drug market can create community disorganization, which, in turn, affects the norms and behaviors of individuals who live in the community. This community disorganization may be associated with increases in violence that are not directly related to drug selling (see Blumstein, 1995). Greater detail on these three models is presented in the current findings section.

Violence Leads to Alcohol and Drug Use

This model is based on the assumption that aggressive individuals are more likely than nonaggressive individuals to select (or be pushed into) social situations and subcultures in which heavy drinking and drug use are condoned or encouraged. According to this explanation, involvement in a violent subculture provides the context, the reference group, and the definitions of the situation that are conducive for subsequent involvement with drugs (White, 1990). For example, rather than a need for a drug compelling an individual to commit a robbery, the income generated from a robbery might provide the individual with extra money to secure drugs and place the individual in an environment that is supportive of drug use (Collins, Hubbard, & Rachal, 1985).

It also has been suggested that several aspects of the professional crime lifestyle are conducive to heavy drinking and drug use, such as working periodically, partying between jobs, being unmarried, and being geographically mobile (Collins & Messerschmidt, 1993). In addition to subcultural and lifestyle explanations, it has been proposed that aggressive individuals may use drugs in order to self-medicate (Khantzian, 1985) or to give themselves an excuse to act aggressively (Collins, 1993).

The Relationship Is Reciprocal

It is also possible that both of the previous models are correct and that the relationship between substance use and violence is reciprocal. That is, substance use and violence may be causally linked and mutually reinforcing; thus, drinking and drug use may lead to more violence, and violent behavior may lead to more drinking and drug use (Collins, 1986; Fagan & Chin, 1990). For example, when an addict has an easy opportunity to commit robbery, he or she will commit it and then buy drugs with the money gained, not out of a compulsion but rather as a consumer expenditure. Conversely, when the need for drugs is great, users will commit crimes, including violent crimes, to get money to buy drugs (Goldstein, 1981; see also, Chaiken & Chaiken, 1990). Although reciprocity is not a well-developed area, it may hold promise in clarifying causal relationships.

The Relationship Is Spurious

The spurious model postulates that substance use and violence do not have a direct causal link. Rather, they are related either coincidentally or because they share common causes, such as genetic or temperamental traits, antisocial personality disorder, parental modeling of heavy drinking and violence, and poor relations with parents (White, 1990; White, Brick, & Hansell, 1993). (Greater detail is presented in the current findings section.) For example, young males account for a disproportional share of violent incidents and are also the heaviest drinkers and drug users. In addition, subcultural norms may reinforce both violence and substance use. That is, heavy drinkers and illicit drug users are considered deviant and may be forced into subcultures in which violence is condoned, or certain subcultures may promote both violence and heavy drinking as proof of masculinity, which would spuriously inflate the relationship (Fagan, 1990; see Gorman & White, 1995, and Thornberry & Krohn, Chapter 21, this volume, for a discussion of peer influences on drug use and delinquency).

From a routine activities perspective, violence occurs most often when and where people are drinking, such as at bars and sports stadiums, at night, and on weekends (see Fagan, 1993b). Proponents of this perspective argue that bars are "ideal" places for violent crime because customers carry cash and are often too intoxicated to defend themselves, there are weakened social controls, and the bar atmosphere intensifies competition. Thus, situational factors contribute to a spurious relationship between alcohol use and violence (for greater detail, see Fagan, 1993b; Roncek & Maier, 1991). (For a review of the social and physical characteristics of bars that increase the likelihood of violence, see Graham, Schmidt, & Gillis, 1995.)

Obviously, no one model can account for all individuals or all types of violence. Further, several factors may be operating simultaneously to connect substance use and violence. The causal and spurious models described here are relatively simplistic; more complicated interactive models also have been postulated (see Collins, 1981). Clearly, when one takes into account the intrapersonal, interpersonal, and environmental influences on the substance use–violence relationship, more complex mediation and moderation models need to be considered, and they are discussed in the current findings section (for greater detail on these models, see Collins, 1981; Fagan, 1990; White, 1990). Some of the methodological issues in examining the relationship between substance use and violence follow.

METHODOLOGICAL ISSUES

There are numerous methodological issues involved in studying the alcohol/drug use–violence nexus. They involve definitions, measures, subjects, experimental designs, and analyses. Several of the more important issues are highlighted (see also, Fagan, 1993a).

Definitions

One problem has to do with the lack of uniformity in definitions. The distinctions between violent and property crime are often arbitrary. Burglary is considered a property crime and robbery a violent crime. Yet both are acquisition crimes and are more relevant to an economic motivation theory than to a psychopharmacological theory. In addition, property crimes may escalate into violent crimes because of unforeseen circumstances (e.g., a homeowner returns unexpectedly during a burglary).

Drug-related crime means different things in different studies. For example, drug-related homicide can include murders related to drug distribution, murders committed while using drugs, murders committed in the act of a crime to get money for drugs, and accidental murders in a high drug use neighborhood. Which of the categories is included in rates of drug-related homicide varies from one municipality to another, so data from different studies are often incompatible. Also, some statistics include alcohol in drug-related crimes, and others do not. It appears that the rate of drug-related homicides doubles when alcohol is included (Brownstein & Goldstein, 1990). In addition, a robbery to get money for groceries because the grocery money was spent on drugs is often overlooked as a drug-related crime. Similarly, when a man beats his wife for taking his drugs, it may or may not count as a drug-related crime (Miczek et al., 1994).

Measures

Most of the survey research on the alcohol/drug–violence connection has relied on self-report data. Self-reports are generally accepted as reliable and valid indicators of criminal behavior and alcohol and drug use. In addition, self-reports provide a more direct, sensitive, and complete measure of various forms of deviant behavior than do measures based on official law enforcement and institutional records and avoid the problem of false negatives (i.e., "hidden" cases; for greater detail and supporting studies, see Elliott, Huizinga, & Menard, 1989). Of course, there are many caveats for using self-report data, such as respondents' inability to remember past events, misunderstanding the questions, and efforts to conceal or exaggerate (Chaiken & Chaiken, 1990). For example, offenders may exaggerate the role of alcohol and drugs prior to an offense in order to justify their behavior.

In addition, there often are problems with the operationalization and measurement of alcohol and drug use. Few studies collect blood, breath, saliva, or urine samples to determine alcohol and drug levels. Those that do collect information on drug use only at the time of arrest and not at the time of the offense, which could be days earlier. Homicide studies using autopsy results collect data only from the victim. If the victim did not die immediately, then drugs such as alcohol could be metabolized out of the system prior to the autopsy (for greater details, see Roizen, 1993).

Measurement of alcohol and drug use varies greatly across studies. Some studies measure acute use, and others measure chronic use. Also, researchers often measure frequency but not quantity of use; however, quantity (especially binge drinking) may be more important for violence (Collins, 1993). There also are issues of measurement in terms of using simple dichotomies or trichotomies, arbitrary terms such as *often* or *occasionally,* and aggregate drug use scales (for greater detail, see White, 1990). Studies that rely on police or victim indications of alcohol or drug involvement often underestimate such involvement because of either inability to identify signs of intoxication or, in the case of police, failure to write it on the arrest report (Roizen, 1993). (For a discussion of additional measurement errors inherent in official records, see Fagan, 1993a.) Operationalization of the violence measures is also problematic. Findings differ depending on whether one measures threat of force or use of force, injury or no injury, and use or no use of a weapon. Therefore, more complete data on intensity of violence, duration in time, rate of episodes, and physical consequences are needed (Roizen, 1993).

Studies of substance use and violence often examine the comorbidity of various psychiatric diagnoses including alcohol dependence, drug dependence, and antisocial personality disorder. Yet caution must be used when examining data on the degree of overlap of diagnoses (Bukstein, Brent, & Kaminer, 1989; Smith & Newman, 1990). Often, diagnostic criteria overlap from one disorder to another inflating rates of comorbidity. Further, rates of overlap differ dramatically if one uses self-report instruments as compared to intensive interviews and clinician ratings (Bukstein et al., 1989). Sample selection also can seriously affect rates of comorbidity. The fact that people in drug treatment are often mandated by the court might inflate the overlap with antisocial personality disorders (Yates, Fulton, Gabel, & Brass, 1989). Also, the high rates of comorbidity between two disorders in hospital or clinic samples may occur because patients with comorbid conditions are more likely to seek treatment than those with only one disorder (Bukstein et al., 1989). (For greater detail on the methodological issues related to studying comorbidity, see Bukstein et al., 1989.)

Samples

Some researchers have relied on captive samples in prisons or in treatment programs to study the alcohol/drug–violence relationship. Such samples have the advantage of providing a pool of subjects who exhibit high frequencies of the behaviors of interest, but the relationships observed may not be generalizable to the general population and may overestimate the degree of co-occurrence. For example, research indicates that heavy drug users and problem drinkers are more likely to be arrested and that high-rate offenders who do not get caught are usually not frequent drug users (Chaiken & Chaiken, 1990; Collins, 1986). Similarly, poor battered women may go to shelters where they are enlisted as research subjects in studies of domestic violence, whereas wealthier women have the resources to remain undetected (Roizen, 1993). Without proper controls and knowledge of base rates of the behaviors of interest, it is difficult to accurately describe relationships.

On the other hand, samples drawn from general populations have limited numbers of individuals engaging in drug use or violence. Many general surveys of youths are administered in schools and omit dropouts who are known to have higher rates of drug use. Further, delinquents are harder to contact than nondelinquents and when contacted are less likely to participate in research (see White, 1990).

Experimental Designs

Laboratory research on aggression and drug use has its own set of methodological problems. Most of this research with human subjects has been on alcohol use; however, in many cases, the criticisms are applicable to other drugs as well. It is questionable whether the results from laboratory experiments are generalizable to the "real world." First, these studies have relied principally on samples of college students. Second, laboratory subjects usually achieve much lower blood alcohol levels than the levels reached by violent assailants in the community. Further, subjects are usually tested within 1 hour of drinking rather than after several hours (or days) of drinking, which is more typical of alcohol-related violent incidents. There also is a question of how well one can fool subjects in the placebo and antiplacebo conditions. Further, there often are no alternatives to an aggressive response in laboratory studies, whereas in real life one can walk away (Bushman & Cooper, 1990; Cohen, Lipsey, Wilson, & Derzon, 1994). On the other hand, it should be noted that the validity (with respect to measuring aggression) and reliability (test-retest) of these studies have been well established (Gustafson, 1993).

Analyses

One problem with laboratory research has been the tendency to analyze group statistics. Given the large degree of individual vari-

ation in the reaction to alcohol and other drugs, researchers need to analyze individuals separately (Miczek, Weerts, & DeBold, 1993). Another problem in estimating the extent of overlap between drug use and violence results from differences in classification schema and analytic strategies. Researchers often fail to control for age in their analyses. Given that drug use and violence are age dependent, failure to take account of this phenomenon can lead to spurious findings. In addition, cross-sectional or retrospective studies do not allow for the prospective analysis of the temporal sequencing of drug use and violence.

The issues raised here provide a sample of the many conceptual and methodological ambiguities that characterize the alcohol/drug–violence literature; the following review of the literature should be interpreted within these limitations.

CURRENT FINDINGS

This section discusses some of the important research findings as they relate to the theoretical models discussed earlier. First, the studies that support an association between alcohol/drug use and violence are described, and then data that address causal and spurious relationships are presented.

Degree of Association

Alcohol and Drug Use at the Time of the Offense

Statistics on rates of alcohol use by offenders at the time of an offense provide strong support for the alcohol-violence relationship. The rates vary greatly across studies. In general, however, studies indicate that more than half of all homicides and assaults are committed when the offender, victim, or both have been drinking (see Collins & Messerschmidt, 1993; Roizen, 1993). However, in one study, although more than 50% of the assaultive offenders reported drinking at the time of their offense, 59% of those drinking did not think the drinking was relevant to the offense (Collins & Messerschmidt, 1993). Approximately one third to three fourths of all sexual assaults involve alcohol use by either the offender, the victim, or both (Collins & Messerschmidt, 1993). Rates of alcohol use in sexual assaults depend on offense characteristics, such as location, relationship of victim to offender, amount of force, and degree of spontaneity (see also, Roizen, 1993).

Although alcohol is present in about one fourth to one half of all incidents of domestic violence, empirical studies suggest that the relationship of alcohol use to domestic violence episodes depends on individual characteristics, such as social class, hostility level, and approval of violence (Kaufman Kantor & Straus, 1987; Leonard, 1993). In a large national probability study, most incidents of spousal abuse (76%) did not involve alcohol, and most occasions of alcohol use did not result in domestic violence (Kaufman Kantor & Straus, 1987). On the other hand, studies have consistently demonstrated that excessive drinking patterns (of husbands and, in some studies, of wives) are related to rates of wife abuse, after controls for other confounding variables (Leonard, 1993). In contrast to domestic violence, Collins and Schlenger (1988) found that it was acute episodes rather than chronic patterns of alcohol use that better predicted other types of violent offending. Note, however, that studies indicate that offenders drink no differently on the day they commit a crime than they do on any other day (Roizen, 1993). (For greater detail, see Leonard, 1993, and Widom, 1993, respectively, on the link of alcohol use to spousal and child abuse; and Collins & Messerschmidt, 1993, and Roizen, 1993, on alcohol-violence statistics.)

Rates of alcohol use at the time of a property offense also are high. Approximately one third of all property offenses are committed by individuals under the influence of alcohol. In fact, more burglaries and car thefts than robberies are committed under the influence of alcohol (Roizen, 1993). Alcohol involvement is less likely when the crime is planned rather than spontaneous and when it is committed alone rather than in a group (Wright, 1993). Alcohol consumption also increases the risks of being a victim of a robbery (Collins & Messerschmidt, 1993).

Rates of alcohol-related violent offenses appear higher for males than for females and are highest in the 20- to 30-year-old age group as compared with younger or older samples (Collins & Messerschmidt, 1993). Gender-by-age interactions are also noteworthy (e.g., rates of alcohol-related homicides increase for females but decrease for males from age 20 to 50; Streifel, 1993). The data on ethnic differences in alcohol-related violence are inconsistent (Collins & Messerschmidt, 1993) and also indicate complex gender-by-ethnicity interactions (Streifel, 1993).

Self-report studies in the community (e.g., victimization studies) also provide empirical support for the alcohol-violence relationship, although the rates vary considerably and are somewhat lower than offender self-reports. Pernanen's (1991) study of the town of Thunder Bay in Canada indicates that 54% of all incidents of violence (which also included nonserious types of violence such as pushing and shoving) were alcohol related (51% assailant, 30% victim). Conversely, data from the U.S. National Crime Victimization Survey indicate that only 28% of all violent crimes were alcohol related (Gramckow, Stinson, Williams, Bertolucci, & Martin, 1995). Cohen et al. (1994) conducted a meta-analysis of cross-sectional studies examining the alcohol-violence relationship. They found significant, although very modest, effect sizes. They also found that the associations between alcohol and violent crime were weaker than those between alcohol and nonviolent crime. The relationships were stronger in criminal and psychiatric samples than in general population samples.

Research on adolescent offenders indicates very low rates of alcohol use at the time of violent offenses (Collins, 1993; for a review, see Cohen et al., 1994). Only 8% of all youths in custody in state institutions reported that they were under the influence of only alcohol when they committed a violent offense (Bureau of Justice Statistics, 1994a). In addition, self-report studies of adolescent alcohol use and violence find very low (although significant) correlations (coefficients below .2), indicating that most of the variance between the two behaviors is not shared (Osgood, 1994; White, 1990). Among adolescents, the correlations with violence are the same for other drugs as for alcohol, and the correlations with alcohol are higher for property crime than for violence (Osgood, 1994).

In three national studies, approximately one half of juvenile and adult inmates reported that they committed a property or violent crime while under the influence of alcohol, drugs, or both (Bureau of Justice Statistics, 1994a). Rates of alcohol/drug-related crime were higher for property than violent crime for youths and prison inmates and higher for violent crime among jail inmates. Overall, the data demonstrate that alcohol and drug use were equally involved in both property and violent crimes. In terms of specific drugs, adult inmates most often cited crack or cocaine, followed by marijuana and then heroin/opiates (Bureau of Justice Statistics, 1993).

In city studies, about one fourth to one half of all homicides are drug related (Bureau of Justice Statistics, 1992). However, one national study estimated that only 10% of the homicides and assaults are the result of drug use (Goldstein, 1989). Some of the difference may reflect definitional issues discussed earlier, as well as whether alcohol is or is not included as a drug in these studies. Drug-related homicides appear to involve young (late teens through 20s) men, especially African Americans and Hispanics (Blumstein, 1995; Bureau of Justice Statistics, 1992). Other studies suggest that about half of all victims of homicide have drugs (usually cocaine or a cocaine metabolite) in their body (Bureau of Justice Statistics, 1992). In a state prison survey, 30% of the inmates reported that their victims in violent offenses were under the influence of alcohol or drugs (Bureau of Justice Statistics, 1993).

Some research indicates that drug-related violence is increasing for women. There is debate, however, whether women's violent crime rates are increasing or whether official labeling of females is increasing (Goldstein, 1989). In general, data from community samples of adolescents do not provide strong support for a direct association between alcohol/drug use and violence (Carpenter, Glassner, Johnson, & Loughlin 1988; White, 1997). After a review of the literature on alcohol, drugs, and violence among youths, Osgood (1994, p. 33) concludes that there is little evidence that substance use makes "an independent contribution to adolescent violence."

Alcohol and Drug Use by Violent Offenders

Criminal justice statistics indicate that violent offenders are heavier drinkers than the rest of the population. The Epidemiologic Catchment Area (ECA) study found that 19% to 29% of those living in the community were diagnosed with alcohol abuse or dependence at some time in their lives as compared with more than 56% of prisoners (Collins, 1993). In a study of state correctional facilities, 40% of the property offenders and 35% of the violent offenders were classified as "very heavy drinkers" as compared to national household estimates of 11% (Wright, 1993). Further, 40% of the offenders drank daily as compared with 6% in national household surveys.

In a Drug Use Forecasting (DUF) program study of male and female arrestees across 24 cities, 38% to 85% tested positive for any drug (Bureau of Justice Statistics, 1994b). More than 60% of males and females arrested for robbery tested positive for illicit drugs. Similar percentages were found for burglary, larceny-theft, and motor vehicle theft. Almost half the males and 65% of the females arrested for homicide tested positive for drugs (Bureau of Justice Statistics, 1994b). These rates reflect drug use at the time of the arrest, not necessarily the offense, and are indicative of a heavy drug-using population. Similarly, self-report data from incarcerated juvenile and adult offenders indicate much higher levels of prior drug involvement than reported in household surveys (Bureau of Justice Statistics, 1993).

Although research on adolescents does not provide strong support for a direct relationship between alcohol/drug use and violence, the data suggest that drug users as opposed to nonusers are more likely to be delinquent and more likely to be involved in violence (Osgood, 1994). Yet violence is concentrated among only a few youths (Carpenter et al., 1988; Johnson, Wish, Schmeidler, & Huizinga, 1986). Carpenter and colleagues (1988) found that those youths involved in violence were also more involved in delinquency and drug use than their peers. Not only were those heavily involved individuals more often perpetrators, but also they were more often victims of violence. The spurious model probably accounts for the association of drug use with violence among youths and is discussed in greater detail later (see also, White, 1997).

In sum, the statistics, especially on adults, indicate that there is a much higher-than-chance association between alcohol/drug use and the commission of violent offenses and also that there are higher rates of alcoholism and heavy drinking and drug use among violent offenders compared with the general population. One problem with these statistics is that we do not have data on regular patterns of drinking and drug use among violent offenders. That is, we do not know what percentage of the time these same individuals are intoxicated when they are not acting aggressively (Pernanen, 1991). Thus, violent behavior may not be seriously influenced by drinking or drug use at the time of the event, but rather violent offenders may simply be heavy drinkers and drug users (Roizen, 1993).

Cross-Cultural Comparisons

Although the association between alcohol use and violent crime has been identified in many Western cultures, anthropological studies indicate that there are cultural differences in the nature of the relationship and, therefore, that the relationship depends on individual and environmental factors rather than solely on the pharmacological properties of alcohol (MacAndrew & Edgerton, 1969). Wet cultures (cultures in which alcohol use is well integrated into society, such as France and Italy) have much lower rates of alcohol-related violence than dry cultures (such as Finland) and mixed cultures (such as the United States; Parker, 1993). This difference could be due to variability in drinking patterns. That is, binge drinking is more common in dry cultures, whereas high frequency–low quantity drinking is more common in wet cultures. Violence appears to be related to high-quantity consumption (Collins, 1993).

Studies of Alcohol Availability and Violence

Rates of homicide and other forms of violence are related to alcohol availability and per capita consumption in international, as well as in U.S. state, comparisons, although the strength of the relationship is reduced when other variables, such as poverty, are controlled (Parker, 1993). Further, efforts to reduce drinking have been shown to decrease violent crime. For example, during a strike of the Norwegian alcohol monopoly, a consumption decrease of 20% to 30% was accompanied by a 22% reduction in domestic disturbances and a 15% reduction in acts of violence

against persons (see Cook & Moore, 1993). In a comparison of states in the United States, an increase in the beer tax was associated with a significant decrease in robberies and rapes but not in homicides (Cook & Moore, 1993). A recent study in Los Angeles County also found a geographical association between assaultive violence and density of on-sale and off-sale alcohol outlets after controlling for confounding variables, such as socioeconomic status, race/ethnicity, unemployment, and city size (Scribner, MacKinnon, & Dwyer, 1995). Overall, this area of research suggests that moderate restrictions on availability may reduce violence (Cook & Moore, 1993).

Although the research presented here indicates that a high rate of violence is committed by individuals while they are under the influence of alcohol or by those who are heavy drug and alcohol users, and that violent crime is related to alcohol availability in certain localities, substance use does not necessarily cause violence. As Fagan (1993a) states, to assign a causal role to alcohol or drugs requires proof that the behavior would not have occurred had the individual been sober. The next section discusses some of the empirical support for both causal and spurious models.

Causal Models

Several longitudinal studies have attempted to establish a causal order between drug use and violence. Researchers have applied developmental models similar to Kandel's Stage or Gateway model of drug use (Kandel, Yamaguchi, & Chen, 1992), which demonstrate that alcohol and cigarette use precedes the use of marijuana, which, in turn, is followed by other illicit drug use. Among those who engage in both delinquency and drug use, delinquent behavior (including aggressive delinquency) developmentally precedes the use of drugs (Elliott et al., 1989; see also, White, 1990, for a review). Studies also have demonstrated that childhood antisocial behavior (usually defined as delinquent or aggressive behavior) is consistently related to the later development of alcohol problems in adolescence (for a review, see Zucker, 1991) and adulthood (for a review, see Zucker & Gomberg, 1986). Thus, from a temporal-ordering perspective, substance use does not lead to the initiation of crime or violence.

In a longitudinal analysis, White, Brick, and Hansell (1993) examined the relationships between alcohol use and aggressive behavior among males from early adolescence into late adolescence. The findings indicated that early aggressive behavior as compared to alcohol use was a better predictor of later alcohol-related aggression. These results suggest that males who engage in alcohol-related aggression are aggressive from early adolescence and behave aggressively whether or not they use alcohol. Further, the data indicated that early aggression led to increases in alcohol use, but alcohol use did not lead to increases in aggressive behaviors. In a later paper, White and Hansell (1996) found that gender moderated the alcohol-aggression relationship and that aggression was a better predictor of alcohol-related aggression for males but that alcohol use was a better predictor for females.

Loeber's (1988) review of the literature indicates that nonaggressive as compared to aggressive antisocial behaviors in childhood better predict later substance use (see also, White, 1992), but aggressive behavior predicts more serious forms of multiple drug use. However, Loeber notes that a large proportion of adult addicts and heavy drug users were not aggressive as children or adolescents, whereas most violent offenders were highly aggressive as youngsters. Although research indicates that conduct disorders and delinquency precede the initiation into drug use, studies also show that increases in property crime and acquisitive violence occur subsequent to regular use of hard drugs among adolescents (Loeber, 1988). In addition, heavy drug use appears to predict maintenance of delinquent behavior in late adolescence (Elliott et al., 1989). In sum, the longitudinal research indicates that initiation into violence precedes drug use; however, changes in drug use affect changes in violence (see also, Chaiken & Chaiken, 1990). Although the data indicate that, for most people, aggressive behavior precedes initiation into drug use, it does not mean that acute or chronic use of drugs does not lead to subsequent violent behavior. The data supporting a causal relationship are reviewed separately for the psychopharmacological, economic motivation, and systemic models.

The Psychopharmacological Model

The psychopharmacological model has gained greater support in the alcohol literature than it has for other drugs. Support for this model comes from laboratory studies of animals and humans. Although studies of animals demonstrate that low to moderate doses of alcohol increase aggressive responding, there are many problems in generalizing from animal aggression to human violence (Ferris & DeVries, Chapter 24, this volume; Miczek et al., 1994). This section discusses only studies of humans.

Bushman and Cooper (1990) conducted a meta-analysis of the best-controlled laboratory studies and concluded that it is the interaction of both alcohol and expectancies that leads to aggressive behavior in laboratory situations, rather than either variable alone. Controlled studies have consistently found that acute intoxication (below sedating levels) is related to aggression when the subject is provoked (Bushman & Cooper, 1990). However, it also has been demonstrated that the relationship between alcohol use and aggression is moderated by subject characteristics (e.g., gender, aggressive tendencies, cognitive abilities), experimental design conditions (e.g., provocation, nonaggressive response alternative, peer pressure, normative standards), and beverage characteristics (e.g., dose, type; Gustafson, 1993; Ito, Miller, & Pollack, 1996; Pihl, Peterson, & Lau, 1993; Taylor & Chermack, 1993).

The psychopharmacological explanation for the drug-violence association has largely been refuted in the literature with regard to heroin and marijuana but has received strong support for barbiturates and tranquilizers and occasionally for other drugs such as amphetamines, PCP (phencyclidine), and LSD (lysergic acid diethylamide). (For an extensive review of specific drug effects on aggression in animals and humans, see Miczek et al., 1994.) Laboratory studies indicate that marijuana and opiates have the opposite effect of alcohol in that moderate doses temporarily inhibit aggression and violence, although withdrawal from opiates increases aggression. There is some research to indicate that chronic use of marijuana, opiates, and amphetamines does increase the risk of violent behavior (Miczek et al., 1994). Accord-

ing to a large review of existing research, there is no proof that violence is related to acute or chronic cocaine powder use (Miczek et al., 1994). Researchers are currently questioning whether there may be a unique pharmacological effect of crack resulting from its route of administration (i.e., smoking), yet no conclusive evidence in humans or animals has been reported (Miczek et al., 1994). There has been no evidence (except anecdotal and small samples) in humans that acute use of PCP or LSD is associated with violent behavior, except when use enhances already existing psychopathology (Miczek et al., 1994; see also, Fagan, 1990; McBride, 1981). Similarly, cocaine and amphetamine use can increase paranoia, which might result in violence. However, the intoxicating effects of all of these drugs account for very little of drug-related violent crime. In a study in New York City of all the drug-related homicides, only 14% were classified as psychopharmacological (Goldstein, Brownstein, Ryan, & Bellucci, 1989). Whereas all of the homicides committed while the offender was using alcohol but no other drug were classified as psychopharmacological, very few cases involving the use of another drug without alcohol were so classified (Goldstein, Brownstein, Ryan, & Bellucci, 1989).

Numerous biological and neurological mechanisms have been proffered to explain how alcohol use causes violence. For example, heavy drinking is known to cause hypoglycemia, sleep disturbances, and withdrawal symptoms, all of which are related to aggression. In addition, the effects of alcohol on aggressive behavior may be mediated by a number of neurotransmitter systems, such as gamma-aminobutyric acid (GABA) or serotonin (5-HT). However, much of the research on alcohol and neurotransmitters has been inconsistent and suggests that individual differences in levels of aggression may moderate these relationships (for details, see Miczek et al., 1993; Pihl & Peterson, 1993b). It also has been demonstrated that neurological disturbances, such as frontal lobe disorder, which are sometimes attributable to heavy drinking and drug use, are related to violent tendencies (Fagan, 1990; Pihl & Peterson, 1993a).

There has not been strong support for a global alcohol disinhibition theory, although specific disinhibition may have explanatory promise. That is, alcohol may inhibit cues that normally control one's behavior (Pihl & Peterson, 1993a). It may be that alcohol use reduces one's fear of retaliation and breaking rules and, thus, disinhibits one's willingness to act aggressively. In addition, in low doses alcohol arouses behavior and thus may potentiate aggressive behavior. Further, alcohol influences the ability to judge the degree of threat in a social situation (for greater detail, see Pihl et al., 1993). Alcohol intoxication may also reduce attentional capacity so that the individual can direct attention only on the most salient external cues. Thus, if provocative cues are salient, an individual will behave aggressively (Gustafson, 1993). In fact, laboratory research has shown that aggressive behavior can be averted by providing cues that facilitate self-reflection about actions, such as the subject hearing the opponent say, "I will not set high shocks" (Taylor, 1993; see also Ito et al., 1996).

The cognitive effects of intoxication on interpersonal interactions may also account for alcohol's effect on violence. That is, alcohol causes cognitive impairment in information processing and communication and interferes with the ability of individuals to interact with each other. Alcohol affects speech, eye movement, facial expressions, and motor coordination (Pernanen, 1993). Those who interact with a drinker may interpret the drinker as signaling disrespect and rudeness, which increases the risk of conflict and aggression. In addition, the intoxicated individual may misperceive the cues from other individuals as either hostile or threatening and thus respond aggressively. This cognitive impairment effect may explain the high rates of alcohol use among victims (who often initiate the violent incident). These cognitive-interactional explanations could also be applicable to certain illicit drugs that may interfere with interpersonal communication. In addition, alcohol and drug use put an individual at risk for victimization because intoxicated individuals may place themselves in situations and contexts in which the risk of violence is high and yet may be unable to appropriately assess risks that might be apparent to a sober person (Collins & Messerschmidt, 1993). Further, the effects of alcohol and drugs on emotions could affect aggressive responding. Substance use may intensify emotions such as hate and rage, which are associated with aggression, or use may suppress guilt or shame, which typically inhibit aggression (Reiss & Roth, 1993).

Although the laboratory research on alcohol expectancy effects is equivocal (Gustafson, 1993), it is hypothesized that social and cultural definitions of drinking affect people's behavior. Many Americans believe that alcohol produces or facilitates aggressive responding (Lang, 1993). Similarly, some people think that being drunk reduces one's accountability for violent acts. Thus, it is possible that individuals act aggressively when they are intoxicated because of these expectancies or because they expect to be judged or punished less harshly (for greater detail, see Lang, 1993). Fagan (1990) refers to this as the "learned disinhibition model." He suggests that subjects who consume alcohol simply behave consistently with their expectancy that alcohol use will cause aggression. Thus, in certain cultures, the belief that one is intoxicated is itself a cue to act aggressively.

Research that has examined the role of alcohol and other drugs in violent crime indicates that the psychopharmacological model predominates for females and the predominant drug is alcohol. Alcohol is also the predominant drug in the psychopharmacological model for males; however, the systemic model predominates for males (Spunt, Goldstein, Bellucci, & Miller, 1990). In addition, the psychopharmacological model has received little support in the adolescent literature (Carpenter et al., 1988; White, 1990). In sum, the psychopharmacological model appears relevant for explaining a potential causal relationship between alcohol and violence among adults but little of the relationship between drugs and violence.

Economic Motivation Model

Evidence for the economic motivation model comes from literature on heroin addicts that indicates that raising or lowering the frequency of substance use among addicts raises or lowers their frequency of crime, including violent crime (e.g., Ball et al., 1981; Chaiken & Chaiken, 1990). Although heroin use may not initiate crime, addiction is often a key point in the acceleration of an existing criminal career (Chaiken & Chaiken, 1990). Heavily involved daily drug users account for a disproportionate share of criminal acts, and the containment of drug use through treatment and close supervision leads to dramatic reductions in both drug use and crime, including violent crime (Clayton & Tuchfeld, 1982). But research suggests that this reduction occurs only for individuals with previously low levels of criminal activity (Nurco, Hanlon, Kinlock, & Duszynski, 1988).

In a study of state correctional facilities, only 12% of the jail and prison inmates reported that they committed a violent crime (predominantly robbery) to get money to pay for drugs (Bureau of Justice Statistics, 1993). Also, in a study of homicides in New York City, only 4% of all drug-related homicides were classified as economically motivated (Goldstein et al., 1989). There is less economically motivated crime related to crack than there had been to heroin in the 1970s and 1980s. In fact, in Washington, DC, there was a decline in property crime with the crack epidemic. Because there is more money in crack distribution than in previous illegal drug markets, drug dealing may obviate the need to commit property crimes and income-generating violent crimes (Miczek et al., 1994). Yet some of the robberies that have been categorized as systemic violence probably involve an economic motivation. Therefore, the economic motivation model most likely accounts for a share of drug-related violent crimes, especially acquisition crimes.

Studies of female addicts suggest that they tend to commit primarily nonviolent income-generating crimes, especially prostitution, drug selling, and shoplifting (Chaiken & Chaiken, 1990). But interviews with women who do commit violent street crime indicate that most commit robbery in order to get money, especially for drugs (Sommers & Baskin, 1993). The economic motivation explanation has not been supported among adolescents. Intensive drug users and highly delinquent youths do not report committing crimes to raise money for drugs (Johnson et al., 1986). Adolescents in the community report committing crimes for fun, to obtain valued goods, or to get money. They claim to be able to obtain drugs within their usual budgets and that other commodities are more important to purchase from the profits of crime (Carpenter et al., 1988). The current involvement of many youths in the crack market may provide enough income to reduce their need for economically motivated crime (see the next section).

The Systemic Model

The systemic model explains drug-related violence as resulting from negative interactions in the illegal drug market. This model probably accounts for most of the violence related to illicit drug use, especially drug-related homicides, which have increased since the appearance of crack in 1985 (Blumstein, 1995; Fagan & Chin, 1990; Goldstein et al., 1989). In a study in New York City, the majority of drug- (including alcohol) related homicides were systemic (74%), and the major drug of involvement was crack followed by cocaine (Goldstein et al., 1989). Only 3 out of 218 homicides involved heroin. Although most research reports that only a small proportion of females are perpetrators of systemic violence, studies suggest that women's roles in the illicit drug market are increasing, and, hence, we will see higher rates of drug-related systemic violence among them (see Fagan, 1994; Goldstein, 1989). Drug sellers are often victims of assaults, robberies, and homicides. In addition, police, potential witnesses, and informants are often victims of violence (Bureau of Justice Statistics, 1992). (For a list of all the types of violence related to drug distribution, see Bureau of Justice Statistics, 1992; for greater detail on violence in the illegal drug market, see Fagan & Chin, 1990.)

Studies conducted in the 1980s suggested that the systemic model was not applicable to the majority of youthful drug users because few were involved in distribution at a high enough level (see White, 1990). More recent studies suggest that the systemic model can probably account for a significant amount of drug-related violence among youths in inner cities (Fagan & Chin, 1990; Inciardi & Pottieger, 1991). The crack market has attracted a younger group of sellers than previous drug markets, possibly because the demand for crack makes dealing easy and profitable, the business provides the opportunity for advancement and feelings of achievement, and dealing creates a challenge for youths (Inciardi & Pottieger, 1991). Research on drug dealing within youth gangs also provides partial support for the systemic model (see Fagan, 1989).

Van Kammen and Loeber (1994) demonstrated that previous involvement in violent crime increased the risk of drug dealing for male adolescents, as did previous involvement in property crime. Thus, individuals who are drawn to dealing are already violent and delinquent individuals. Once individuals got involved in drug use or dealing, their level of violent crime increased as did their possession of weapons. These data on adolescents support the spurious model and suggest that violent individuals are attracted to drug selling rather than drug selling initially causing individuals to become violent. This model is now discussed in greater detail.

The Spurious Model

Evidence supporting the spurious model comes from adolescent samples in which relatively nonserious forms of substance use appeared to occur simultaneously with relatively minor and infrequent forms of delinquent behavior. This type of association led Jessor and Jessor (1977) to identify a problem behavior syndrome in which cigarette use, precocious sexual behavior, problem drinking, use of marijuana and other drugs, stealing, and aggression clustered together. This cluster of behaviors was explained by the same set of environmental and personality variables and was negatively related to conventional behavior. Other researchers, however, argue that problem behaviors constitute several distinct factors rather than a single construct (for a review, see White & Labouvie, 1994). Overall, the literature suggests that substance use and violence share several common causes or predictors, although there are also specific factors (e.g., coping styles) that determine which adolescents will specialize in each behavior. Given that problem behaviors share several common causes, the same individuals would be expected to engage in both substance use and violent crime. For example, many of the childhood risk factors for violence identified in the National Research Council report on violence (Reiss & Roth, 1993) have also been identified as risk factors for teenage drug use and for adult alcoholism (see Hawkins, Cata-

lano, & Miller, 1992). Some of the common risk factors are hyperactivity, impulsivity, attention deficit disorder, risk taking, inability to delay gratification, abuse or rejection in family, lack of parental nurturance, early school failure, and peer rejection.

Clinical and community data clearly support a comorbidity between alcohol/drug abuse and antisocial personality disorder (ASPD). For example, data from the ECA study indicate that 84% of respondents identified with ASPD also had some form of substance abuse and those with ASPD had more severe types of substance abuse (Regier et al., 1990). In addition, individuals diagnosed with alcohol and other drug disorders reported symptoms of ASPD at a substantially higher rate than those without disorders. These individuals also had high rates of anxiety and affective disorders. Rates of comorbidity are especially high among prison populations (Collins, Schlenger, & Jordan, 1988) and alcoholism treatment populations (Hesselbrock, Hesselbrock, & Stabenau, 1985). Further, studies indicate that the risks of violent behavior are especially elevated among individuals diagnosed with ASPD who also abuse alcohol and other illicit drugs (Miczek et al., 1994).

These data on comorbidity suggest that individuals with ASPD are likely to be heavily involved with alcohol and drugs and those with drug and alcohol disorders are often diagnosed with ASPD. Yet they do not suggest that one disorder causes the other. Rather, a set of predisposing personality or temperament factors (e.g., impulsivity) or family background factors (e.g., parental alcoholism) may contribute to both. Certain of these factors may even have a genetic basis, although more research is needed to provide conclusive evidence. For example, Type II alcoholism has been demonstrated to have a high heredity liability, and the majority of alcoholics diagnosed with ASPD are classified as Type II (Virkkunen & Linnoila, 1993). Type II alcoholics have onset before age 25 and are characterized as impulsive, high-sensation seekers with a history of aggression and violence. In addition, ASPD has been shown to have a genetic component (Miczek et al., 1994).

A spurious model can also explain some of the systemic violence in the illicit drug trade. Drug users are often violence-prone individuals, and drug markets attract high-risk seekers who carry guns (Miczek et al., 1994). Fagan and Chin (1990) found that crack sellers were violent more often than other drug sellers but that their violence was not confined to the drug-selling context. Rather, crack sellers were involved in a host of illegal activities. The researchers argue that it would be unwise to conclude that the drug business makes people violent; instead, drug selling provides a context that facilitates violence. They suggest that the participation of violent individuals in the crack trade and the decreased controls and increased opportunities in these areas may account for the increased violence in the crack market. In sum, the spurious model probably accounts for a large proportion of alcohol/drug-related violence, especially among youths.

CONCLUSIONS AND FUTURE RESEARCH

The data presented in this chapter indicate that substance use and violence are related both causally and spuriously. From a causal perspective, the illicit drug market increases violence because of the inability to settle disputes legally as well as other aspects of its illegal nature. However, it has also been demonstrated that violent individuals are attracted to the illegal drug market. In addition, acute incidents of alcohol intoxication probably cause some amount of violence due to effects on neurotransmitter and cognitive functioning, although the research demonstrates that the effects of alcohol on aggression are more prominent among those who already have an elevated inclination to be aggressive (for a review, see Lang, 1993). Thus, even these possible causal relationships may be moderated by the spurious association between substance use and violence. There are individuals who are inherently aggressive, and these individuals engage in violent behavior with and without the use of alcohol or drugs. Many are also alcohol and drug abusers. This overlap results primarily because many of the same individual, family, and situational variables increase the risk of both substance abuse and violence. Hence, it is just as important for future research to examine the processes that account for how aggressiveness promotes heavy alcohol and drug use as for how alcohol and drug use intensify aggressive responding.

One promising area for research is to identify the situational factors that enhance the potential for violence. The more we understand about the processes and mechanisms that account for the relationship between substance use and violence, the better able we will be to design sound intervention strategies. For example, changing the environment in bars (e.g., lighting, guardianship, glassware) may be an effective strategy to reduce alcohol-related injury (Fagan, 1993b; Shepherd, 1994). We need more in-depth studies that focus on violent incidents (e.g., observations in bars or intensive interviews with violent offenders and victims) to describe the escalation of violence in various situations and the role of alcohol and other drugs in that process. In addition, we should investigate comparable incidents that do not result in violence to ascertain the factors that account for its absence.

There appear to be at least two types of individuals who are involved in alcohol-related violence: (a) those who are aggressive whether or not they drink and who drink heavily most of the time (e.g., repetitive violent offenders and those diagnosed with antisocial personality disorder); and (b) those for whom the state of intoxication, the setting, and the provocation interact on a specific occasion to cause an isolated incident of aggressive behavior. Obviously, prevention and intervention policies would differ depending on which type of violent actor we are trying to reach. Targeted interventions to reduce aggressive tendencies would be most promising for the former group. Responsible drinking campaigns aimed at reducing high-quantity consumption would be most appropriate for the latter group.

On the other hand, reduction of violence related to illicit drug use would have to focus on the illegal drug market. Legalization of drugs is one recommended strategy (although quite controversial in the United States) because it would take away the profit in drug dealing (Trebach, 1993). Without profits, dealers would leave the business and no longer "push" drugs on young people. Further, disputes related to illegal distribution would be eliminated. Tighter control of drug importation and distribution is an alternative strategy, although it does not seem to be currently working to curtail violence, and such efforts would need dramatic changes to be effective (Nadelmann, 1989). Demand reduction through preven-

tion of and treatment for drug abuse might also be effective in reducing systemic violence (see McBride & Swartz, 1990).

Given that homicides among young inner-city African American males account for most of the recently observed increases in violent crime, Blumstein (1995) claims that reductions in the illegal market would lead to less gun possession and, thus, reduce homicide rates among this population. However, Osgood (1994) argues that even if we were to eliminate the drug economy, we would not necessarily reduce most of the violence because a large part of the drug-related violence results from the recruitment of violent individuals and occurs in violent communities. It is also possible that if the drug market were reduced or eliminated, some criminals who financially profit from the drug trade would revert to alternative crimes to get money, including violent crimes such as robbery (Bureau of Justice Statistics, 1992).

Efforts may be better spent concentrating on violent individuals and the sources of their violence. As already stated, intoxication facilitates aggression in those individuals already inclined to aggression, and many of the individuals involved in systemic drug-related violence are individuals who are also violent outside of the drug market. Further, most violent offenders were aggressive as children. Therefore, we need to develop interventions to reduce aggressiveness and violence in individuals (see Part IV of this volume). These interventions should be based on research findings and should be properly evaluated. In addition to individual-level approaches, changes in the inner cities also are needed. These changes entail providing youths with nonviolent routes to social status, including better paying jobs, better schools, and more opportunities, as well as remedying community disorganization and economic hardships.

According to the National Institute on Justice, most crimes result from a variety of factors. Even when drugs are a cause, they are likely to be only one among many causes (Bureau of Justice Statistics, 1994b). We need, therefore, to focus our efforts on the multiple sources of violence and recognize that alcohol and drugs are only a part of the problem.

REFERENCES

Ball, J. C., Rosen, L., Flueck, J. A., & Nurco, D. N. (1981). The criminality of heroin addicts: When addicted and when off opiates. In J. A. Inciardi (Ed.), *The drugs-crime connection* (pp. 39–65). Beverly Hills, CA: Sage Publications.

Blumstein, A. (1995). Youth violence, guns, and the illicit-drug industry. In C. Block & R. Block (Eds.), *Trends, risks, and interventions in lethal violence* (pp. 3–15). Washington, DC: National Institute of Justice.

Brownstein, H. H., & Goldstein, P. J. (1990). A typology of drug-related homicides. In R. Weisheit (Ed.), *Drugs, crime, and the criminal justice system* (pp. 171–192). Cincinnati, OH: ACJS/Anderson.

Bukstein, O. G., Brent, D. A., & Kaminer, Y. (1989). Comorbidity of substance abuse and other psychiatric disorders in adolescents. *American Journal of Psychiatry, 146*, 1131–1141.

Bureau of Justice Statistics. (1992). *Drugs, crime, and the justice system.* Washington, DC: U.S. Department of Justice.

Bureau of Justice Statistics. (1993). *Drugs and crime facts, 1993.* Washington, DC: U.S. Department of Justice.

Bureau of Justice Statistics. (1994a). *Fact sheet: Drug data summary.* Washington, DC: U.S. Department of Justice.

Bureau of Justice Statistics. (1994b). *Fact sheet: Drug-related crime.* Washington, DC: U.S. Department of Justice.

Bushman, B. J., & Cooper, H. M. (1990). Effects of alcohol on human aggression: An integrative research review. *Psychological Bulletin, 107,* 341–354.

Carpenter, C., Glassner, B., Johnson, B. D., & Loughlin, J. (1988). *Kids, drugs, and crime.* Lexington, MA: Lexington Books.

Chaiken, J., & Chaiken, M. (1990). Drugs and predatory crime. In M. Tonry & J. Q. Wilson (Eds.), *Drugs and crime* (Vol. 13; pp. 203–239). Chicago: University of Chicago Press.

Clayton, R. R., & Tuchfeld, B. S. (1982). The drug-crime debate: Obstacles to understanding the relationship. *Journal of Drug Issues, 12,* 153–166.

Cohen, M. A., Lipsey, M. W., Wilson, D. B., & Derzon, J. H. (1994). *The role of alcohol consumption in violent behavior: Preliminary findings.* Nashville, TN: Vanderbilt University.

Collins, J. J. (Ed.). (1981). *Drinking and crime.* New York: Guilford.

Collins, J. J. (1986). The relationship of problem drinking to individual offending sequences. In A. Blumstein, J. Cohen, J. Roth, & C. A. Visher (Eds.), *Criminal careers and "career criminals"* (Vol. 2; pp. 89–120). Washington, DC: National Academic Press.

Collins, J. J. (1993). Drinking and violence: An individual offender focus. In S. E. Martin (Ed.), *Alcohol and interpersonal violence: Fostering multidisciplinary perspectives* (NIAAA Research Monograph No. 24; pp. 221–235). Rockville, MD: National Institute of Health.

Collins, J. J., Hubbard, R. L., & Rachal, J. V. (1985). Expensive drug use and illegal income: A test of explanatory hypotheses. *Criminology, 23,* 743–764.

Collins, J. J., & Messerschmidt, P. M. (1993). Epidemiology of alcohol-related violence. *Alcohol Health & Research World, 17,* 93–100.

Collins, J. J., & Schlenger, W. E. (1988). Acute and chronic effects of alcohol use on violence. *Journal of Studies on Alcohol, 49,* 516–521.

Collins, J. J., Schlenger, W. E., & Jordan, B. K. (1988). Antisocial personality and substance abuse disorders. *Bulletin of the American Academy of Psychiatry Law, 16,* 187–198.

Cook, P. J., & Moore, M. J. (1993). Economic perspectives on reducing alcohol related violence. In S. E. Martin (Ed.), *Alcohol and interpersonal violence: Fostering multidisciplinary perspectives* (NIAAA Research Monograph No. 24; pp. 192–212). Rockville, MD: National Institute of Health.

Elliott, D. S., Huizinga, D., & Menard, S. (1989). *Multiple problem youth: Delinquency, substance abuse, and mental health problems.* New York: Springer-Verlag.

Fagan, J. (1989). The social organization of drug use and drug dealing among urban gangs. *Criminology, 27,* 633–667.

Fagan, J. (1990). Intoxication and aggression. In M. Tonry & J. Q. Wilson (Eds.), *Drugs and crime* (Vol. 13; pp. 241–320). Chicago: University of Chicago Press.

Fagan, J. (1993a). Interactions among drugs, alcohol, and violence. *Health Affairs, 12,* 65–79.

Fagan, J. (1993b). Set and setting revisited: Influences of alcohol and illicit drugs on the social context of violent events. In S. E. Martin (Ed.), *Alcohol and interpersonal violence: Fostering multidisciplinary perspectives* (NIAAA Research Monograph No. 24; pp. 161–191). Rockville, MD: National Institute of Health.

Fagan, J. (1994). Women and drugs revisited: Female participation in the cocaine economy. *The Journal of Drug Issues, 24,* 179–225.

Fagan, J., & Chin, K. (1990). Violence as regulation and social control in the distribution of crack. In M. de la Rosa, E. Lambert, & B. Gropper (Eds.), *Drugs and violence* (NIDA Research Monograph No. 103; pp. 8–43). Rockville, MD: National Institute on Drug Abuse.

Goldstein, P. J. (1981). Getting over: Economic alternatives to predatory crime among street drug users. In J. A. Inciardi (Ed.), *The drug-crime connection* (pp. 67–84). Beverly Hills, CA: Sage Publications.

Goldstein, P. J. (1985). The drugs/violence nexus: A tripartite conceptual framework. *Journal of Drug Issues, 15,* 493–506.

Goldstein, P. J. (1989). Drugs and violent crime. In N. A. Weiner & M. E. Wolfgang (Eds.), *Pathways to criminal violence* (pp. 16–48). Beverly Hills, CA: Sage Publications.

Goldstein, P. J., Brownstein, H. H., Ryan, P. J., & Bellucci, P. A. (1989). Crack and homicide in New York City, 1988: A conceptually based event analysis. *Contemporary Drug Problems, 16,* 651–687.

Gorman, D., & White, H. R. (1995). You can choose your friends, but do they choose your crime? Implications of differential association theories for crime prevention policy. In H. Barlow (Ed.), *Criminology and public policy: Putting theory to work* (pp. 131–155). Boulder, CO: Westview Press.

Graham, K., Schmidt, G., & Gillis, K. (1995, November). *Circumstances when drinking leads to aggression: An overview of research findings.* Paper presented at the International Conference on Social and Health Effects of Different Drinking Patterns, Toronto, Canada.

Gramckow, H., Stinson, F., Williams, G., Bertolucci, D., & Martin, S. (1995, November). *Alcohol and violent crime: Findings from the National Crime Victimization Survey, United States, 1991.* Paper presented at the International Conference on Social and Health Effects of Different Drinking Patterns, Toronto, Canada.

Gustafson, R. (1993). What do experimental paradigms tell us about alcohol-related aggressive responding? *Journal of Studies on Alcohol, Suppl. No. 11,* 20–29.

Hawkins, J. D., Catalano, R. F., & Miller, J. Y. (1992). Risk and protective factors for alcohol and other drug problems in adolescence and early adulthood: Implications for substance abuse prevention. *Psychological Bulletin, 112,* 64–105.

Hesselbrock, V. M., Hesselbrock, M. N., & Stabaenau, J. R. (1985). Alcoholism in men patients subtyped by family history and antisocial personality. *Journal of Studies on Alcohol, 46,* 59–64.

Inciardi, J. A., & Pottieger, A. E. (1991). Kids, crack, and crime. *Journal of Drug Issues, 21,* 257–270.

Ito, T. A., Miller, N., & Pollock, V. E. (1996). Alcohol and aggression: A meta-analysis on the moderating effects of inhibitory cues, triggering events, and self-focused attention. *Psychological Bulletin, 120,* 60–82.

Jessor, R., & Jessor, S. (1977). *Problem behavior and psychosocial development—A longitudinal study of youth.* New York: Academic Press.

Johnson, B. D., Wish, E., Schmeidler, J., & Huizinga, D. H. (1986). The concentration of delinquent offending: Serious drug involvement and high delinquency rates. In B. D. Johnson & E. Wish (Eds.), *Crime rates among drug abusing offenders* (pp. 106–143). New York: Interdisciplinary Research Center, Narcotic and Drug Research, Inc.

Kandel, D. B., Yamaguchi, K., & Chen, K. (1992). Stages of progression in drug involvement from adolescence to adulthood: Further evidence for the Gateway Theory. *Journal of Studies on Alcohol, 53,* 447–457.

Kaufman Kantor, G., & Straus, M. A. (1987). The "drunken bum" theory of wife beating. *Social Problems, 34,* 213–230.

Khantzian, E. J. (1985). The self-medication hypothesis of addictive disorders: Focus on heroin and cocaine dependence. *American Journal of Psychiatry, 142,* 1259–1264.

Lang, A. R. (1993). Alcohol-related violence: Psychological perspectives. In S. E. Martin (Ed.), *Alcohol and interpersonal violence: Fostering multidisciplinary perspectives* (NIAAA Research Monograph No. 24; pp. 121–147). Rockville, MD: National Institute of Health.

Leonard, K. E. (1993). Drinking patterns and intoxication in marital violence: Review, critique, and future directions for research. In S. E. Martin (Ed.), *Alcohol and interpersonal violence: Fostering multidisciplinary perspectives* (NIAAA Research Monograph No. 24; pp. 253–280). Rockville, MD: National Institute of Health.

Lindesmith, A. R. (1940). The drug addict as a psychopath. *American Sociological Review, 5*, 914–920.

Loeber, R. (1988). Natural histories of conduct problems, delinquency, and associated substance use. In B. B. Lahey & A. E. Kazdin (Eds.), *Advances in clinical child psychology* (Vol. 11; pp. 73–124). New York: Plenum.

MacAndrew, C. R., & Edgerton, R. B. (1969). *Drunken comportment: A social exploration.* Chicago: Aldine.

McBride, D. C. (1981). Drugs and violence. In J. A. Inciardi (Ed.), *The drugs-crime connection* (Vol. 5; pp. 105–123). Beverly Hills, CA: Sage Publications.

McBride, D. C., & Swartz, J. A. (1990). Drugs and violence in the age of crack cocaine. In R. Weisheit (Ed.), *Drugs, crime, and the criminal justice system* (pp. 141–169). Cincinnati, OH: ACJS/Anderson.

Miczek, K. A., DeBold, J. F., Haney, M., Tidey, J., Vivian, J., & Weerts, E. M. (1994). Alcohol, drugs of abuse, aggression, and violence. In A. J. Reiss & J. A. Roth (Eds.), *Understanding and preventing violence* (Vol. 3; pp. 377–468). Washington, DC: National Academy Press.

Miczek, K. A., Weerts, E. M., & DeBold, J. F. (1993). Alcohol use, aggression, and violence: Biobehavioral determinants. In S. E. Martin (Ed.), *Alcohol and interpersonal violence: Fostering multidisciplinary perspectives* (NIAAA Research Monograph No. 24; pp. 83–119). Rockville, MD: National Institute of Health.

Nadelmann, E. A. (1989). Drug prohibition in the United States: Costs, consequences, and alternatives. *Science, 245*, 939–947.

Nurco, D. C., Hanlon, T. E., Kinlock, T. W., & Duszynski, K. R. (1988). Differential patterns of narcotic addicts over an addiction career. *Criminology, 26*, 407–423.

Osgood, D. W. (1994, November). *Drugs, alcohol, and adolescent violence.* Paper presented at the American Society of Criminology Annual Meeting, Miami, FL.

Parker, R. N. (1993). The effects of context on alcohol and violence. *Alcohol Health & Research World, 17*, 117–122.

Pernanen, K. (1991). *Alcohol in human violence.* New York: Guilford.

Pernanen, K. (1993). Research approaches in the study of alcohol-related violence. *Alcohol Health & Research World, 17*, 101–107.

Pihl, R. O., & Peterson, J. (1993a). Alcohol and aggression: Three potential mechanisms of the drug effect. In S. E. Martin (Ed.), *Alcohol and interpersonal violence: Fostering multidisciplinary perspectives* (NIAAA Research Monograph No. 24; pp. 149–159). Rockville, MD: National Institute of Health.

Pihl, R. O., & Peterson, J. B. (1993b). Alcohol, serotonin, and aggression. *Alcohol Health & Research World, 17*, 113–116.

Pihl, R. O., Peterson, J. B., & Lau, M. A. (1993). A biosocial model of the alcohol-aggression relationship. *Journal of Studies on Alcohol, Supp. No. 11*, 128–139.

Regier, D. A., Farmer, M. E., Rae, D. S., Locke, B. Z., Keith, S. J., Judd, L. L., & Goodwin, F. K. (1990). Comorbidity of mental disorders with alcohol and other drug abuse: Results from the Epidemiologic Catchment Area (ECA) study. *Journal of the American Medical Association, 264*, 2511–2518.

Reiss, A. J., & Roth, J. A. (1993). *Understanding and preventing violence.* Washington, DC: National Academic Press.

Roizen, J. (1993). Issues in the epidemiology of alcohol and violence. In S. E. Martin (Ed.), *Alcohol and interpersonal violence: Fostering multidisciplinary perspectives* (NIAAA Research Monograph No. 24; pp. 3–36). Rockville, MD: National Institute of Health.

Roncek, D. W., & Maier, P. A. (1991). Bars, blocks, and crimes revisited: Linking the theory of routine activities to the empiricism of "hot spots." *Criminology, 29*, 725–753.

Scribner, R. A., MacKinnon, D. P., & Dwyer, J. H. (1995). The risk of assaultive violence and alcohol availability in Los Angeles county. *American Journal of Public Health, 85*, 335–340.

Shepherd, J. (1994). Violent crime: The role of alcohol and new approaches to the prevention of injury. *Alcohol & Alcoholism, 29*, 5–10.

Smith, S. S., & Newman, J. P. (1990). Alcohol and drug abuse-dependence disorders in psychopathic and nonpsychopathic criminal offenders. *Journal of Abnormal Psychology, 99*, 430–439.

Sommers, I., & Baskin, D. R. (1993). The situational context of violent female offending. *Journal of Research in Crime and Delinquency, 30*, 136–162.

Spunt, B. J., Goldstein, P. J., Bellucci, P. A., & Miller, T. (1990). Race/ethnicity and gender differences in the drugs-violence relationship. *Journal of Psychoactive Drugs, 22*, 293–303.

Streifel, C. (1993, November). *Gender, alcohol use, and crime.* Paper presented at the American Society of Criminology Annual Meeting, Phoenix, AZ.

Taylor, S. P. (1993). Experimental investigation of alcohol-induced aggression in humans. *Alcohol Health & Research World, 17*, 108–112.

Taylor, S. P., & Chermack, S. T. (1993). Alcohol, drugs, and human physical aggression. *Journal of Studies on Alcohol, Supp. No. 11*, 78–88.

Trebach, A. S. (1993). *Legalize it? Debating American drug policy.* Washington, DC: American University Press.

Van Kammen, W. B., & Loeber, R. (1994). Are fluctuations in delinquent activities related to the onset and offset in juvenile illegal drug use and drug dealing? *The Journal of Drug Issues, 24*, 9–24.

Virkkunen, M., & Linnoila, M. (1993). Brain serotonin, type II alcoholism, and impulsive violence. *Journal of Studies on Alcohol, Supp. No. 11*, 163–169.

White, H. R. (1990). The drug use-delinquency connection in adolescence. In R. Weisheit (Ed.), *Drugs, crime, and criminal justice* (pp. 215–256). Cincinnati, OH: Anderson Publishing Co.

White, H. R. (1992). Early problem behavior and later drug problems. *Journal of Research in Crime and Delinquency, 29*, 412–429.

White, H. R. (1997). Longitudinal perspective on alcohol use and aggression during adolescence. In M. Galanter (Ed.), *Recent developments in alcoholism: Alcohol and violence* (Vol. 13, pp. 81–103). New York: Plenum.

White, H. R., Brick, J., & Hansell, S. (1993). A longitudinal investigation of alcohol use and aggression in adolescence. *Journal of Studies on Alcohol, Suppl. No. 11*, 62–77.

White, H. R., & Hansell, S. (1996). The moderating effects of gender and hostility on the alcohol-aggression relationship. *Journal of Research in Crime and Delinquency, 33*, 451–472.

White, H. R., & Labouvie, E. W. (1994). Generality versus specificity of problem behavior: Psychological and functional differences. *The Journal of Drug Issues, 24,* 55–74.

Widom, C. S. (1993). Child abuse and alcohol use and abuse. In S. E. Martin (Ed.), *Alcohol and interpersonal violence: Fostering multidisciplinary perspectives* (NIAAA Research Monograph No. 24; pp. 291–314). Rockville, MD: National Institute of Health.

Woodiwiss, M. (1988). *Crime, crusades, and corruption: Prohibitions in the United States.* Totowa, NJ: Barnes and Noble.

Wright, K. N. (1993). Alcohol by prisoners. *Alcohol Health & Research World, 17,* 157–161.

Yates, W. R., Fulton, A. I., Gabel, J. M., & Brass, C. T. (1989). Personality risk factors for cocaine abuse. *American Journal of Public Health, 79,* 891–892.

Zucker, R. A. (1991). The concept of risk and the etiology of alcoholism: A probabilistic-developmental perspective. In D. J. Pittman & H. R. White (Eds.), *Society, culture, and drinking patterns reexamined* (pp. 513–532). New Brunswick, NJ: Rutgers Center of Alcohol Studies.

Zucker, R. A., & Gomberg, E. L. (1986). Etiology of alcoholism reconsidered: The case for a biopsychosocial process. *American Psychologist, 41,* 783–793.

CHAPTER 48

Sexual Aggression as Antisocial Behavior: A Developmental Model

MICHAEL C. SETO and HOWARD E. BARBAREE

Sexual aggression[1] is one of the major problems facing our society today. More than 160,000 rapes and 152,000 attempted rapes were reported in the United States in 1993, resulting in a combined incidence rate for rape and attempted rape of approximately 750 per 100,000 American women (Bastian, 1995). Estimates of the prevalence of sexual coercion experienced by females range from 14% to 25% in the majority of studies (see Koss, 1993, for a review). For methodological reasons such as sampling procedures and question format, Koss (1992, 1993) has argued cogently that the actual incidence and prevalence rates for sexual coercion are much higher. Moreover, the psychological sequelae of sexual victimization can be serious and are well documented, including severe anxiety, depression, substance abuse, and other symptoms of post-traumatic stress disorder (see Hanson, 1990, for a review).

Sexual aggression can be viewed as an expression of antisocial tendencies. Earlier clinical descriptions suggested that some individuals committed sexual offenses as part of a stable pattern of delinquency or criminality, indicated by their extensive antisocial histories (e.g., Amir, 1971; Cohen, Seghorn, & Calamus, 1969; Gebhard, Gagnon, Pomeroy, & Christenson, 1965). The sexual offenses of these men were viewed as opportunistic and impulsive and attributed to an indifference to the victim's distress. Recent studies also have shown that rapists often have a history of antisocial behavior, juvenile delinquency, and nonsexual crimes (e.g., Bard et al., 1987; Weinrott & Saylor, 1991).

Consistent with this view, psychopathy is increasingly important in theories of sexual aggression. Psychopathy, as measured using the Psychopathy Checklist (PCL-R; Hare, 1991), is a syn-drome of antisocial personality traits and indicators of an unstable, irresponsible lifestyle (see Hare & Hart, Chapter 3, this volume). Rice, Harris, and Quinsey (1990) found that scores on the PCL-R predicted both sexual and nonsexual recidivism in rapists, over and above variables such as age, offense history, and psychiatric history. This finding is consistent with a number of studies that find psychopathy predicts recidivism, especially violent recidivism, in general criminal samples (e.g., Hare, McPherson, & Forth, 1988; Harris, Rice, & Cormier, 1991; Serin, Peters, & Barbaree, 1990).

This chapter attempts to further our understanding of sexual aggression as an antisocial behavior. *Antisocial behavior* is defined here as behavior that causes harm, violates social norms, or contravenes criminal laws. We begin by briefly reviewing three general approaches to understanding sexual aggression. We then discuss some of the methodological issues in extant research, the current debate over the role of sexual arousal to rape, and several trends that we perceive in the research literature. We conclude by presenting a developmental model of sexual aggression that we believe integrates the existing findings and provides a heuristic framework for future research.

MODELS OF SEXUAL AGGRESSION

Reflecting the complexity of sexual aggression, many conceptual models can be found in the literature. A review of these models is beyond the scope of this chapter, but they can be broadly divided into three general approaches.

Psychopathological Models

Historically, models of sexual aggression have focused on the individual perpetrator, with the implicit or explicit view that they are different in some way from men who are not sexually aggressive and that this difference contributes directly to their offending. A great deal of research therefore has focused on factors such as social skills (e.g., Overholser & Beck, 1986), sexual adequacy (e.g., Karpman, 1954), attitudes about women (e.g., Scott & Tetreault, 1987), personality problems (see Levin & Stava, 1987, for a review), and impulsivity (e.g., Prentky & Knight, 1986). A

Preparation of this chapter was supported in part by a research contract cosponsored by the Ministry of the Solicitor-General and the Correctional Service of Canada. We would like to thank Martin Lalumière and the editors for their helpful comments on an earlier version of this manuscript.

[1]The terms *sexual coercion* and *sexual aggression* are used interchangeably. Rape, which is defined here as the attempted or completed oral, vaginal, or anal penetration of an unconsenting person, is an extreme form of sexual aggression.

number of authors have attempted to integrate the diverse research literature on the individual characteristics of sexually aggressive men (e.g., Hall & Hirschman, 1991; Malamuth, Heavey, & Linz, 1993; Marshall & Barbaree, 1984; Prentky & Knight, 1991).

Sociocultural Models

The view that sexual aggression depends on factors operating at the societal and cultural levels has been most clearly articulated by feminist authors (e.g., Brownmiller, 1975; Russell, 1984). In contrast to the psychopathological models, these models shift the emphasis from the deviant male as perpetrator to societal and cultural forces that promote and support sexual aggression toward women, in a continuum from subtle harassment and discrimination to violent assault (Darke, 1990; Herman, 1990). Also, in contrast to the evolutionary models discussed next, these models shift the emphasis from sexual to nonsexual motivations. According to these authors, sexual aggression is inherent in male-dominated societies and cultures in which sexual conquest is glorified and the use of coercive tactics to obtain sexual access is legitimized. Rape then can be viewed as an instrument of male dominance that keeps women in fear for their safety and thereby limits their ability to attain equality in terms of economic and political power (Brownmiller, 1975). Reflecting these influences, many current conceptualizations of sexual aggression ascribe an important role to sociocultural factors (see Baron, Straus, & Jaffee, 1988; Check & Malamuth, 1985; Stermac, Segal, & Gillis, 1990).

In support of the sociocultural view, cross-cultural studies find that rape is more prevalent in cultures judged to be more male dominated compared to those that are not (Sanday, 1981). Also, some studies by Malamuth and his colleagues have shown that men who endorse patriarchal attitudes and beliefs are more likely to admit a likelihood of engaging in rape if they could be assured that they would not be punished for it (e.g., Briere & Malamuth, 1983; Malamuth, 1986).

Like other sociocultural models of behavior, however, feminist-influenced explanations of sexual aggression do not address the question of ultimate cause, that is, *why* men would be interested in dominating women and controlling their sexuality, willing to use tactics such as sexual coercion, and motivated to pursue sexual intercourse with such persistence, although they can describe *how* these tendencies occur, that is, the proximate cause(s) of sexual aggression (see Buss, 1995; Smuts, 1995). Psychopathological models also do not address the question of ultimate cause. In contrast, evolutionary theory can and does address ultimate cause.

Evolutionary Models

Evolutionary theory has been successfully used to integrate diverse findings of sex differences and intrasex variability in mating behavior across demographic groups, cultures, and species (see Buss, 1994, for a review). In particular, evolutionary theory has been used to explain rape, based on observations of forced intercourse in nonhuman species (see Palmer, 1989, for a review). There are two major hypotheses about rape, both of which imply that all men are capable of sexual coercion under certain developmental or environmental conditions.

The mate deprivation hypothesis suggests that rape is an evolved facultative strategy used by unattractive, low social status, or poor men who are at a competitive disadvantage for attracting desirable mates (see Thornhill & Thornhill, 1992, for a review). Across demographic groups and cultures, women value wealth and social status more than youthfulness and physical attractiveness as desirable characteristics in a potential mate, whereas men show the opposite pattern of preferences (see Buss, 1994). For men, social status and wealth predict reproductive success in preindustrial societies and mating opportunities in industrial societies (Pérusse, 1993).

Consistent with the mate deprivation hypothesis, reproductive-aged women are overrepresented in samples of rape victims that are compared with the general population, whereas pre- and postreproductive-aged women are underrepresented (Shields & Shields, 1983). At the same time, men are most likely to commit rape during late adolescence and early adulthood, which is a period of intense mate competition because older men are wealthier and higher in status and therefore at a relative advantage in attracting women (Thornhill & Thornhill, 1983).

The second evolutionary hypothesis is that rape is a by-product of male mating and dominance efforts that persist despite female resistance (see Ellis, 1991). Consistent with the by-product hypothesis, and inconsistent with the mate deprivation hypothesis, sexual coercion is more likely to be reported by male college students with extensive sexual histories than those with less sexual experience (Kanin, 1985; Lalumière, Chalmers, Quinsey, & Seto, 1996). The high prevalence rates for sexual coercion in college-aged populations (Koss, Gidycz, & Wisniewski, 1987) and the tendency of men to perceive greater female sexual interest than women actually intend are also consistent with a by-product explanation (Craig Shea, 1993; Muehlenhard, 1988).

In addition, Smuts (1995) has applied evolutionary theory to understanding gender inequality in terms of conflicts of interest between males and females and the subsequent male motivation to control female sexuality. Interestingly, Smuts's arguments are compatible with the arguments of other feminist authors regarding the role of rape in patriarchal societies (Brownmiller, 1975; Russell, 1984).

AN INTEGRATED MODEL

Psychopathological, sociocultural, and evolutionary models are not necessarily incompatible because they differ in their level of analysis, with the first two focusing on the proximate psychological and sociocultural causes, respectively, and the third focusing on the ultimate causes. Marshall and Barbaree (1990) recently provided an example of an integrated model of sexual aggression that incorporated biological factors, childhood experiences, sociocultural influences, and situational events. Regarding biological factors, they referred to an evolutionary history that provides the human male with the capacity and motivation to use coercive tactics, including aggression, to further his mating efforts. The endocrine system, specifically the sex steroids, was assigned a primary proximate role in terms of regulating sexual drive and motivation. Marshall and Barbaree then described a socialization process in which males normally learn to inhibit sexually aggressive behavior, beginning with the development of secure attachment bonds. They argued that sex offenders fail to acquire effective inhibitory controls because their childhoods often are characterized by emotional, physical, and sexual abuse (Rada, 1978); ineffective parenting (Langevin et al., 1984); and a chaotic home environment (Knight, Prentky, Schneider, & Rosenberg, 1983). Marshall and Barbaree also discussed the potential influence of sociocultural factors on the development of inhibitory control and how situational factors might disinhibit this control under certain circumstances.

METHODOLOGICAL ISSUES

As in other areas of psychological study, much of the literature on sexual aggression has been descriptive, retrospective, and correlational in nature (e.g., Amir, 1971; Cohen et al., 1969; Gebhard et al., 1965). Four major methodological issues also stand out in a review of this literature.

Sampling Biases

Changes in legal definitions of sexual offenses and sentencing trends suggest differences across time in the composition of sex offenders who have been studied. For example, compared to now, acquaintance rapists were probably much less likely to have been charged or convicted in the first half of the century, particularly if the offenders were of high status and their victims were of low status. Comparing studies conducted in different time periods therefore can be problematic.

Selective sampling is a major problem in studies that use sex offenders who are incarcerated or otherwise identified by the criminal justice system. Only a small proportion of attempted or completed rapes are reported to authorities (Koss, 1992), and only some of the identified perpetrators are then convicted. Very few perpetrators voluntarily identify themselves. Rapists who are violent, repetitive, non-White, or of low socioeconomic status are probably overrepresented in incarcerated samples. The generalizability of findings based on criminal samples to the total population of sex offenders therefore is uncertain.

Appropriate Comparison Groups

Studies also vary in their choice of comparison groups, ranging from college students to men from the community to nonsex offenders. Although they are more difficult to recruit than students or men from the community, nonsex offenders matched on demographic variables such as age, education, marital status, and socioeconomic class are the preferred comparison group for making inferences about the causes and nature of sexual aggression. For example, Stermac and Quinsey (1986) found that their sample of 20 incarcerated rapists was less socially competent than a sample of 20 nonpsychiatric, noncriminal controls but did not differ from a sample of 20 incarcerated nonsex offenders.

At the same time, some volunteers from the community and some incarcerated offenders used as control subjects may have engaged in undetected sexual aggression in the past. Existing data

suggest that sexual coercion is not uncommon in college-aged samples (e.g., Koss et al., 1987). The undetected presence of sexually aggressive men in comparison groups presumably would reduce the reliability and power of statistical analyses.

Reliance on Self-Reports

Many studies depend exclusively on self-report data, either through interviews or the use of paper-and-pencil measures. Dissimulation can be a serious problem, especially because individuals may face legal or social sanctions for honest and full disclosure of their offense histories, sexual interests, and cognitions. For example, child molesters who were assured of their protection from potential legal consequences through a special federal certificate of confidentiality revealed that they had committed more sexual offenses than when they were interviewed without this assurance (Kaplan, Abel, Cunningham-Rathner, & Mittleman, 1990). Moreover, many sex offenders deny or minimize the nature of their sexual offenses (Barbaree, 1991). Dissimulation also is a potential problem in phallometric testing, a procedure that does not rely on self-report but may nonetheless be faked (Quinsey & Chaplin, 1988). Nonetheless, some data on delinquency suggest that confidential self-reports of criminal behavior can be reliable and valid (Hindelang, Hirschi, & Weiss, 1981).

Measurement Issues

Much of the published research has used different, single measures for constructs of interest. This raises concerns about measurement reliability, especially because there currently is no "gold standard" in the assessment instruments commonly used with sex offenders (see review by Hanson, Cox, & Woszczyna, 1991). Similarly, relatively little data are available on the reliability of phallometric testing of sexual arousal to rape (see the next section), despite the large body of experimental literature using this procedure (however, see Barbaree, Baxter, & Marshall, 1989; Davidson & Malcolm, 1985).

THE ROLE OF SEXUAL AROUSAL IN RAPE

Controversy exists regarding the specific role of sexual arousal to rape in sexual aggression. In the typical procedure, circumferential or volumetric changes in penile erection are measured while the subject is presented with different stimuli varying on dimensions of interest, such as descriptions of consenting sex, rape, and nonsexual violence (see Earls & Marshall, 1983; Laws & Osborn, 1983, for reviews of the methodology).

The measurement of changes in penile erection (phallometry) generally is considered to be a reliable and valid physiological measure of male sexual arousal and is more specific than general arousal measures such as heart rate, pupillary dilation, or skin responsivity (Barker & Howell, 1992; Zuckerman, 1971). Erectile responses often are quantified as the largest (peak) erectile response during a stimulus presentation. A deviance index, defined as the average erectile response to stimuli depicting inappropriate content (rape, nonsexual violence) relative to the average erectile response to stimuli depicting appropriate content (consensual sex), is used to summarize the individual's response pattern.

Two recent meta-analytic reviews provide convincing evidence for the ability of phallometric testing to discriminate rapists from nonrapists (Hall, Shondrick, & Hirschman, 1993; Lalumière & Quinsey, 1994). However, intragroup variability in sexual responding is large and there is substantial overlap in the distributions of rapists' and nonrapists' deviance indexes. One possible explanation for this overlap is voluntary control of sexual arousal by offenders who may face legal and social sanctions for exhibiting deviant sexual responses (Quinsey & Chaplin, 1988). Regardless of the correct explanation, phallometric testing has lower sensitivity than specificity, so the presence of arousal to inappropriate stimuli is more informative than its absence (Freund & Watson, 1991; Lalumière & Quinsey, 1993).

Phallometric testing also may have predictive validity because some data suggest rapists with higher deviance indexes are more likely to reoffend (Rice, Harris, & Quinsey, 1990). In this study, sexual arousal to nonsexual violence directed against a woman was a better predictor of recidivism than traditional criminological predictors such as age, education, and offense history. However, not all rapists have a sexual preference for rape or nonsexual violence. Some authors have gone so far as to suggest that sexual arousal specifically to rape is not important for many rapists (Blader & Marshall, 1989; Hall, 1989).

Even if sexual arousal to rape is acknowledged as important, there is disagreement about what it means. Some authors have suggested that sexual arousal to rape indicates a preference for such activity over consenting sex (Abel, Blanchard, Barlow, & Guild, 1977; Quinsey, 1984). Consistent with this view, some rapists report fantasizing and thinking about being sexually coercive, masturbating to these fantasies and thoughts, and preferentially purchasing pornography depicting sexual coercion. However, although rapists as a group can be discriminated from nonrapists by their response patterns, only some of them respond more to nonconsenting stimuli than to consenting stimuli (Lalumière & Quinsey, 1994). Other authors have suggested that rapists differ from other men in that they are not inhibited by cues of force and victim distress (Barbaree, 1990; Barbaree, Marshall, & Lanthier, 1979). In this view, men are excited by the sexual elements of stimuli depicting sexual coercion but are inhibited by the elements of force and victim distress. The inhibitory mechanism may involve vicarious emotional arousal due to an empathic response to victim distress or recognition of the social inappropriateness of showing sexual arousal to rape and is presumed to be absent or disrupted in some way in rapists.

DISINHIBITION

There may be both trait and state forms of disinhibition. Regarding trait disinhibition, Patterson and Newman (1993) suggested that syndromes of disinhibition such as impulsivity and psychopathy can be understood in terms of persistent information processing deficits. In particular, disinhibited individuals appear to have difficulty switching their attention to aversive contingencies that are not initially salient but become more conspicuous in approach-avoidance dilemmas. These hypothesized deficits result in response perseveration and a relative inability to delay gratification despite the risk of punishment (Newman, Kosson, & Patterson, 1992; Newman, Patterson, Howland, & Nichols, 1990).

Clinically, psychopaths are characterized by a callous disregard for the feelings of others, manipulativeness, and a chronic pattern of impulsive, antisocial behavior (Cleckley, 1976; Hare, 1991). Rather than having a preference for coercive sex over consenting sex, psychopaths and other persistently antisocial individuals may be more willing than nonpsychopaths to use coercion to obtain sex, indifferent to any subsequent victim distress, and inattentive to the potentially aversive consequences of their behavior. These trait-disinhibited men therefore would be expected to show indiscriminant responding rather than a preference for rape.

Regarding state disinhibition, a series of experimental studies has shown that situational factors such as alcohol or anger can temporarily disinhibit sexual arousal to rape (for reviews, see Barbaree, 1990; Seto & Barbaree, 1995). State-disinhibited men would be expected to show a normative pattern of arousal in the laboratory by responding more to consenting sex than nonconsenting sex, unless an effective disinhibiting situational factor also is present. The origins of individual differences in the type and strength of effective disinhibitors are unknown.

In terms of sexual deviance, Barbaree and Marshall (1991) reviewed the literature on the phallometric testing of rapists and identified six different models of sexual arousal to rape. These models can be broadly divided into those that focus on the sexual response (response control models) and those that focus on the way in which stimuli elicit sexual arousal (stimulus control models). These models also vary in complexity, ranging from Hall's (1989) suggestion that sex offenders differ from nonoffenders only in their ability to suppress sexual arousal across different kinds of stimuli, to Barbaree's (1990) suggestion that sexual arousal is augmented by compatible emotional states, so that responses to consenting sex are enhanced by positive feelings (e.g., affection) and responses to rape are enhanced by negative feelings (e.g., anger). The models also differ in whether they view deviant sexual arousal as a stable response pattern that distinguishes rapists from other men (trait models), or as a transient response that can potentially be elicited in any man (state models).

Extending this discussion, Barbaree and his colleagues have speculated that different models of sexual arousal to rape may apply to different rapist subtypes (Barbaree & Serin, 1993; Barbaree, Seto, Serin, Amos, & Preston, 1994). Three models of sexual arousal were proposed in this context. First, the paraphilic model suggests that some men show a stable response pattern of relatively strong sexual arousal to rape, consistent with the sexual preference hypothesis and, in the extreme cases, conceptualizations of sadism as a synergistic interaction of sexual and aggressive motivations. Second, the trait-inhibition model suggests that sexual arousal is excited by the sexual elements in a rape stimulus but is simultaneously inhibited by cues of force and victim distress in nonrapists. Men vary in their propensity to rape because of individual differences in the strength of inhibition, which in turn is related to individual differences in empathy, impression management, endorsement of rape-supportive attitudes and beliefs, and personality factors (Barbaree et al., 1979; Malamuth, 1986). Third, the state-disinhibition model suggests that men are normally inhibited by cues of force and victim distress but that this inhibition can be disrupted by situational factors such as anger, alcohol, and perceptions of victim provocativeness (for reviews, see Barbaree, 1990; Barbaree & Marshall, 1991; Seto & Barbaree, 1995).

Psychopathy and sexual deviance are not mutually exclusive factors. They may interact so that individuals scoring high in both dimensions are the most likely to have serious offense histories in terms of numbers of victims and degree of violence and the most likely to reoffend once identified (cf. Quinsey, 1984; Rice et al., 1990).

CURRENT TRENDS IN RESEARCH ON SEXUAL AGGRESSION

Typologies

Typologies attempt to address offender heterogeneity and inform decisions about treatment and disposition by identifying discrete groups of rapists who are similar in salient features, such as life history, attitudes, personality characteristics, or offense characteristics (Cohen et al., 1969; Gebhard et al., 1965; Groth & Birnbaum, 1979; Hall & Hirschman, 1991; Rada, 1978). Although some similarities can be found in the most salient types across these classification systems, there is a paucity of data on their reliability and validity.

However, Knight, Prentky, and their colleagues have written a series of empirical articles on the development of rapist and child molester typologies at the Massachusetts Treatment Center (MTC; see Knight & Prentky, 1990, for a review). These typologies were developed using an iterative strategy of rational and cluster-analytic procedures applied to variables thought to differentiate rapists, such as social competence, criminality, and impulsivity (see Prentky & Knight, 1991, for a review). The rapist typology requires a hierarchical series of decisions, resulting in nine subtypes that differ in their inferred motivations for rape, impulsivity, antisocial behavior, and social competence. These subtypes can be broadly divided into those in which the motivation for rape is primarily paraphilic (sexual subtypes) and those in which the motivation for rape is primarily antisocial, reflecting hostility toward women, opportunistic and impulsive offending, or a callous disregard for the victim (nonsexual subtypes).

Barbaree et al. (1994) provided independent evidence for the validity of the rapist typology. Rapists were classified according to the MTC typology and compared using a phallometric measure of sexual arousal, offense history, and the PCL-R. Subjects assigned to the sexual types exhibited a greater response to rape relative to consenting sex than subjects assigned to the nonsexual types. In contrast, subjects in the nonsexual types scored higher on the antisocial lifestyle factor of the Psychopathy Checklist.

Sexual Coercion in Nonincarcerated Samples

Malamuth and his colleagues have studied sexual aggression using a variety of research methodologies, including phallometric assessment, large sample surveys, and social psychological experiments using smaller samples (see Malamuth et al., 1993). This research includes a reanalysis by Malamuth, Sockloskie, Koss, and Tanaka (1991) of a large survey of American college men (N = 2,972) originally presented by Koss, Gidycz, and Wisniewski (1987) and a longitudinal study in which a sample of men were followed for 10 years (Malamuth, Linz, Heavey, Barnes, & Acker, 1995). Their research focused on a number of factors believed to contribute to male sexual aggression, including sexual arousal to rape, patriarchal attitudes and beliefs, hostility toward women, antisocial personality characteristics, and past sexual experience. Using a number of statistical techniques, including structural equation modeling, Malamuth et al. described two paths to sexual aggression, labeled *hostile masculinity* and *impersonal sex*. The hostile masculinity path includes sexual arousal in response to aggression, dominance motives, hostility toward women, and other attitudes that are presumed to facilitate the use of aggression against women. The impersonal sex path describes a man who approaches sex in an impersonal way, without emotional commitment to his partner. This path includes precocious sexual behavior in the man's history and sexual promiscuity, and it is consistent with the evolutionary by-product hypothesis of rape (cf. Lalumière et al., 1995). The convergence of these two paths greatly increases the likelihood that a man will be sexually aggressive.

The predominantly antisocial motivation of nonsexual subtypes in the MTC model, which focuses on *interindividual* differences, is conceptually similar to the hostile masculinity pathway described in Malamuth et al.'s (1993) model, which focuses on *intraindividual* differences. This similarity in findings with different populations (institutionalized sex offenders and sexually aggressive college students), different analytical strategies (interindividual and intraindividual), and different measures suggests the argument that antisocial tendencies are important in sexual aggression is robust.

Developmental Aspects

A developmental perspective appears to have a great deal of promise in the study of sexual aggression. Relationships between younger age of onset of aggressive behavior and greater chronicity, stability, and seriousness are well documented (see Farrington, Chapter 22, this volume). Some authors have argued for the existence of an antisocial syndrome characterized by an early onset, stability in the underlying trait despite changes in manifest behaviors as individuals grow older, and a chronic life course (Moffitt, 1993; Patterson, 1993).

Coercive sexual behavior may be one manifestation of an antisocial syndrome. For example, Elliott (1994) analyzed longitudinal self-report data from a national probability sample of 1,725 juveniles who were between the ages 11 and 17 when first interviewed in 1976. The offending reports obtained in this prospective research indicate that sexual aggression almost always emerged following a lengthy and increasingly serious history of offending. Aggravated assault preceded robbery in 85% of cases and rape in 92%, and robbery preceded rape in 72% of cases. These violent offenses were in most cases preceded by minor delinquency, as well as alcohol and marijuana use.

Relatively few data are available on the developmental course of sexual aggression (see Prentky & Knight, 1993, for a review).

Nonetheless, recent work on adolescent perpetrators suggests that sexual offending can begin quite early in adolescence, escalate in seriousness, and encompass a variety of acts and targets (for reviews, see Abel, Osborn, & Twigg, 1993; Barbaree, Hudson, & Seto, 1993). Abel and Rouleau (1990) found that approximately 30% of 126 rapists reported the onset of at least one deviant sexual interest before age 18. Identified juvenile sex offenders also report an early onset of deviant and nondeviant sexual behavior (Becker, Cunningham-Rathner, & Kaplan, 1986).

It has been suggested that for some men, sexual offending may be related to childhood experiences of sexual abuse, although Widom's (1989) review found no conclusive evidence for what has been called the *intergenerational transmission of abuse.* Nonetheless, the sexually coercive acts committed by some children may be a reaction to their own sexual abuse (e.g., Johnson & Berry, 1989). Some men abused as children exhibit a developmental progression in the severity of sexual offending, beginning with inappropriate sexual behavior as a child, leading to the use of sexual coercion as a young adolescent, and escalating to rape committed as an older adolescent or young adult. Consistent with this speculation, several studies of juvenile sex offenders have identified a relationship between a history of abuse and sexual responding to stimuli depicting girls (Becker, Hunter, Stein, & Kaplan, 1989; Becker, Kaplan, & Tenke, 1992). However, we are not aware of a published study of juvenile sex offenders using stimuli depicting nonconsenting sex with peer-age and adult women. Other factors obviously are involved because only some abused children become perpetrators, and only about a third of perpetrators report being abused (Becker et al., 1986). A prospective study of children who have been sexually abused and matched controls might be helpful in addressing this question.

Similarly, an early onset of sexual deviance may predict future severity of sexual offending in terms of its frequency, chronicity, and degree of violence. An important implication of this hypothesis is that chronic adult sex offenders can be identified early in life (Abel et al., 1993). Given that juvenile sex offenders are probably less well established in a chronic pattern of sexual offending than their adult counterparts (Hunter, Goodwin, & Becker, 1994), early interventions may be more promising than later attempts at rehabilitation.

A DEVELOPMENTAL MODEL OF SEXUAL AGGRESSION: RESEARCH FINDINGS AND FUTURE DIRECTIONS

Integrating aspects of the typological (interindividual differences) and structural modeling (intraindividual differences) findings and informed by evolutionary theory, we suggest there are at least two different kinds of developmental course for sexually aggressive men (cf. the dual pathways posited by Mealey, 1995, and Moffitt, 1993). In our model, rapists typically pursue a short-term sexual strategy that is characterized by early onset of sexual activity, having many sexual partners, and low levels of commitment (cf. Ellis, 1988, 1991). These males make many sexual advances; persist despite female resistance; and are willing to use a variety of tactics, including coercion, to obtain sex (Craig Shea, 1993;

Kanin, 1985; Lalumière et al., 1996). They are also more likely than nonoffenders to endorse rape-supportive attitudes and beliefs, be hostile and angry, be manipulative and aggressive in other aspects of their life, and exhibit other features of "hypermasculinity" (cf. Malamuth et al., 1993).

The first group of rapists is persistently antisocial and is characterized by an early onset of problem behavior and developmental stability in the extent and breadth of antisocial behavior, including substance abuse, property offenses, and nonsexual aggression. This group's developmental history is analogous to that of the "primary sociopathy" group described by Mealey (1995) and the "lifetime-course-persistent" group described by Moffitt (1993). Only a minority of the sexually coercive men identified in the research of Malamuth and his colleagues would be part of this group.

The second group of rapists is opportunistic and characterized by sexually coercive activity that mostly is confined to adolescence and young adulthood. Many, but not all, of these rapists are more likely to commit sexual assaults against acquaintances, including dates or girlfriends, rather than against strangers; some may also commit sexual assaults with co-offenders (i.e., group assaults). These individuals do not show the early onset, extent, and chronicity of other antisocial behavior that characterizes the persistently antisocial group. The developmental history of opportunistic rapists parallels what Mealey (1995) described as a "secondary sociopathy" group and what Moffitt (1993) described as an "adolescence-limited" group. Many of the sexually coercive men identified in the research of Malamuth and his colleagues would presumably be part of this group.

Rapists may share many features with other antisocial individuals but differ in the potential contribution of sexual deviance. Sexual deviance can be present in individuals of either group, indicated by a history of deviant sexual fantasies and thoughts, urges to engage in sexual aggression, and relatively high levels of sexual arousal to depictions of sexual aggression in pornography and other media. Men in the persistently antisocial group who also exhibit sexual deviance probably represent the most dangerous sex offenders in terms of the severity of their offenses and their risk for recidivism (Rice et al., 1990). Men in either group who exhibit sexual deviance will tend to have more extensive sexual offense histories and a greater risk for recidivism than those who do not.

Excluding sexually deviant individuals, we predict that men in the persistently antisocial group will tend to be indiscriminate in their sexual response to depictions of rape because they are much more likely to be trait-disinhibited than opportunistic men, whereas men in the opportunistic group will tend to be normal in their sexual response. At the same time, we predict that the relative responses to rape of men in both groups can be temporarily disinhibited by situational factors such as alcohol.

The strongest test of the model presented here would come from research on children who sexually act out and juvenile sex offenders. For example, it may be possible to identify paraphilic males at an early age by their early use of pornography, reinforcement of deviant sexual interests through masturbatory conditioning, and escalation in the variety and severity of inappropriate sexual behaviors (Abel et al., 1993; Becker et al., 1986; Longo, 1982). We could also directly test the hypothesis that different kinds of rapists differ in their relative response to rape. Unfortunately, little is known about the normative development of sexual preferences. This obviously constrains our understanding of sexual deviance. Research on the development of sexual preferences would be facilitated by the identification or construction of an ethical, valid, and unobtrusive measure of sexual interest for children (see Quinsey, Rice, Harris, & Reid, 1993).

The identification of antecedents to the two developmental courses to sexual aggression described here would require a study involving the long-term follow-up of a representative birth cohort. We expect that different antecedents are important in the two groups. Of particular interest are longitudinal studies of children at risk for entering a persistent antisocial life course (cf. Moffitt, 1993), such as children diagnosed with conduct disorder, demonstrating early behavior problems, and growing up in neglectful or abusive family environments (see Loeber & Farrington, Chapter 13, this volume). Potentially aiding such research, two recent studies have shown that a set of eight childhood and adolescent history items are good predictors of psychopathy as measured by the revised Psychopathy Checklist (Harris, Rice, & Quinsey, 1994; Seto, Khattar, Quinsey, & Lalumière, 1997): (a) arrest before the age of 16; (b) not living with both parents before age of 16 because of leaving home, divorce, abandonment, or institutionalization; (c) childhood aggressiveness, rated on a seven-point scale from 1 (no aggression) to 7 (occasional or frequent aggression); (d) childhood behavior problems (number of conduct disorder-related problem behaviors exhibited before the age of 15); (e) elementary school maladjustment, rated on a 4-point scale from 0 (none) to 3 (serious discipline or attendance problems); (f) school suspension or expulsion before the age of 16; (g) teenage alcohol abuse; and (h) parental alcohol abuse.

We hypothesize that a reliable and valid distinction can be made between persistently antisocial and opportunistic sex offenders in adolescence and young adulthood. The first group would be characterized by an early onset and an extensive antisocial history, whereas the other would have a later onset and relatively few indicators of an antisocial life course. Moffitt (1993) argued that a differential diagnosis would require information about the individual's childhood and early adolescence, because measures of frequency or seriousness of adolescent offending are not sufficiently discriminatory. We further predict that the two groups will differ in terms of offense characteristics such as the offender's relationship to victim, use of force, use of a weapon, substance use, and the participation of co-offenders. For example, we have already suggested that opportunistic rapists are more likely to offend against female acquaintances in dating situations or as participants in group assaults. We also predict that opportunistic men are more likely to use verbal coercion, physical restraint, or the administration of intoxicants than physical force or a weapon. Situational factors such as alcohol or anger may be more important in this opportunistic group. The opportunistic group is thought to be the larger of the two groups and responsible for the large majority of sexual assaults, many of which are not reported to authorities (Bureau of Justice Statistics, 1995; Koss et al., 1987). As a consequence, opportunistic rapists are less likely than persistently antisocial rapists to be incarcerated and will be underrepresented in prison samples.

We believe the developmental model proposed here connects a diversity of research findings in the literature, including early clinical distinctions made between "sexually deviant" and "amoral delinquent" offenders (Gebhard et al., 1965), current typological work on rapists (Barbaree et al., 1994; Knight & Prentky, 1990), individual differences in hostile masculinity and promiscuous sexuality (Malamuth et al., 1993), other developmental models of antisocial behavior (Moffitt, 1993; Patterson, 1993), surveys showing a high prevalence of sexual coerciveness in young adult populations (Koss et al., 1987), variability in the findings of studies using phallometric measures with rapists (Lalumière & Quinsey, 1993, 1994), and evolutionary explanations of rape (Ellis, 1991; Lalumière et al., 1994; Thornhill & Thornhill, 1992). It also is consistent with some of the findings regarding sociocultural influences on sexual aggression, because societies that Sanday (1981) described as "rape-supportive" presumably are more likely to tolerate opportunistic men who offend against friends or acquaintances.

Support for the validity of the developmental model proposed here has important implications for offender disposition, treatment planning, and public policy. For example, follow-up results with psychopaths suggest that persistently antisocial men will be resistant to treatment and likely to reoffend (Ogloff, Wong, & Greenwood, 1990; Rice, Harris, & Cormier, 1992). Disposition decisions regarding these individuals therefore should be conservative. For treatment planning, deviant fantasies and sexual arousal in the sexually deviant men may be most amenable to relapse prevention techniques, whereas more general forms of behavioral management may be more appropriate for the opportunistic group. Finally, in terms of public policy, early identification of and intervention with at-risk individuals would be warranted.

REFERENCES

Abel, G. G., Barlow, D. H., Blanchard, E. B., & Guild, D. (1977). The components of rapists' sexual arousal. *Archives of General Psychiatry, 34,* 895–908.

Abel, G. G., Osborn, C. A., & Twigg, D. A. (1993). Sexual assault through the life span: Adult offenders with juvenile histories. In H. E. Barbaree, W. L. Marshall, & S. M. Hudson (Eds.), *The juvenile sex offender* (pp. 104–117). New York: Guilford.

Abel, G. G., & Rouleau, J. (1990). The nature and extent of sexual assault. In W. L. Marshall, D. R. Laws, & H. E. Barbaree (Eds.), *Handbook of sexual assault: Issues, theories, and treatment of the offender* (pp. 9–21). New York: Plenum.

Amir, M. (1971). *Patterns of forcible rape.* Chicago: University of Chicago Press.

Barbaree, H. E. (1990). Stimulus control of sexual arousal: Its role in sexual assault. In W. L. Marshall, D. R. Laws, & H. E. Barbaree (Eds.), *Handbook of sexual assault: Issues, theories, and treatment of the offender* (pp. 115–142). New York: Plenum.

Barbaree, H. E. (1991). Denial and minimization among sex offenders: Assessment and treatment outcome. *Forum on Corrections Research, 3,* 30–33.

Barbaree, H. E., Baxter, D. J., & Marshall, W. L. (1989). The reliability of the rape index in a sample of rapists and nonrapists. *Violence and Victims, 4,* 299–306.

Barbaree, H. E., Hudson, S. M., & Seto, M. C. (1993). Sexual assault in society: The role of the juvenile offender. In W. L. Marshall, D. R. Laws, & H. E. Barbaree (Eds.), *Handbook of sexual assault: Issues, theories, and treatment of the offender* (pp. 1–24). New York: Plenum.

Barbaree, H. E., & Marshall, W. L. (1991). The role of male sexual arousal in rape: Six models. *Journal of Consulting and Clinical Psychology, 59,* 621–630.

Barbaree, H. E., Marshall, W. L., & Lanthier, R. D. (1979). Deviant sexual arousal in rapists. *Behaviour Research and Therapy, 24,* 513–520.

Barbaree, H. E., & Serin, R. C. (1993). Role of male sexual arousal during rape in various rapist subtypes. In G. C. N. Hall, R. Hirschman, J. R. Graham, & M. S. Zaragoza (Eds.), *Sexual aggression: Issues in etiology, assessment, and treatment* (pp. 99–114). Washington, DC: Taylor and Francis.

Barbaree, H. E., Seto, M. C., Serin, R. C., Amos, N. L., & Preston, D. L. (1994). Comparisons between sexual and non-sexual rapist subtypes: Sexual arousal to rape, offense precursors and offense characteristics. *Criminal Justice and Behavior, 21,* 95–114.

Bard, L. A., Carter, D. L., Cerce, D. D., Knight, R. A., Rosenberg, R., & Schneider, B. (1987). A descriptive study of rapists and child molesters: Developmental, clinical, and criminal characteristics. *Behavioural Sciences and the Law, 5,* 203–220.

Barker, J. G., & Howell, R. J. (1992). The plethysmograph: A review of recent literature. *Bulletin of the American Academy of Psychiatry and the Law, 20,* 13–25.

Baron, L., Straus, M. A., & Jaffee, D. (1988). Legitimate violence, violent attitudes, and rape: A test of the cultural spillover theory. *Annals of the New York Academy of Sciences, 528,* 79–110.

Bastian, L. (1995, May). National crime victimization survey: Criminal victimization 1993. *Bureau of Justice Statistics Bulletin.* Rockville, MD: Bureau of Justice Statistics Clearinghouse.

Becker, J. V., Cunningham-Rathner, J., & Kaplan, M. S. (1986). Adolescent sexual offenders: Demographics, criminal and sexual histories, and recommendations for reducing future offenses. *Journal of Interpersonal Violence, 1,* 431–445.

Becker, J. V., Hunter, J. A., Stein, R. M., & Kaplan, M. S. (1989). Factors associated with erection in adolescent sex offenders. *Journal of Psychopathology and Behavioral Assessment, 11,* 353–362.

Becker, J. V., Kaplan, M. S., & Tenke, C. E. (1992). The relationship of abuse history, denial and erectile response profiles of adolescent sexual perpetrators. *Behavior Therapy, 23,* 87–97.

Blader, J. C., & Marshall, W. L. (1989). Is assessment of sexual arousal in rapists worthwhile? A critique of current methods and the development of a response compatibility approach. *Clinical Psychology Review, 9,* 569–587.

Briere, J., & Malamuth, N. M. (1983). Self-reported likelihood of sexually aggressive behavior: Attitudinal versus sexual explanations. *Journal of Research in Personality, 17,* 315–323.

Brownmiller, S. (1975). *Against our will: Men, women, and rape.* New York: Simon & Schuster.

Bureau of Justice Statistics. (1995). *Violence against women: Estimates from the redesigned survey.* Washington, DC: U.S. Department of Justice.

Buss, D. M. (1994). *The evolution of desire.* New York: Basic Books.

Buss, D. M. (1995). Evolutionary psychology: A new paradigm for psychological science. *Psychological Inquiry, 6,* 1–30.

Check, J. V. P., & Malamuth, N. M. (1985). An empirical assessment of some feminist hypotheses about rape. *International Journal of Women's Studies, 8,* 414–423.

Cleckley, H. (1976). *The mask of sanity.* St. Louis: Mosby.

Cohen, M. L., Seghorn, T., & Calmas, W. (1969). Sociometric study of sex offenders. *Journal of Abnormal Psychology, 74,* 249–255.

Craig Shea, M. E. (1993). The effects of selective evaluation on the perception of female cues in sexually coercive and noncoercive males. *Archives of Sexual Behavior, 22,* 415–433.

Darke, J. L. (1990). Sexual aggression: Achieving power through humiliation. In W. L. Marshall, D. R. Laws, & H. E. Barbaree (Eds.), *Handbook of sexual assault: Issues, theories, and treatment of the offender* (pp. 55–72). New York: Plenum.

Davidson, P. R., & Malcolm, P. B. (1985). The reliability of the rape index: A rapist sample. *Behavioral Assessment, 7,* 283–292.

Earls, C. M., & Marshall, W. L. (1983). The current state of technology in the laboratory assessment of sexual arousal patterns. In J. G. Greer & I. R. Stuart (Eds.), *The sexual aggressor: Current perspectives on treatment* (pp. 336–362). New York: Van Nostrand Reinhold.

Elliott, D. S. (1994). Serious violent offenders: Onset, developmental course, and termination—the American Society of Criminology 1993 presidential address. *Criminology, 32,* 1–21.

Ellis, L. (1988). Criminal behavior and r/K selection: An extension of gene-based evolutionary theory. *Personality and Individual Differences, 9,* 697–708.

Ellis, L. (1991). A synthesized (biosocial) theory of rape. *Journal of Consulting and Clinical Psychology, 59,* 631–642.

Freund, K., & Watson, R. (1991). Assessment of the sensitivity and specificity of a phallometric test: An update of phallometric diagnosis of pedophilia. *Psychological Assessment, 3,* 254–260.

Gebhard, P. H., Gagnon, J. H., Pomeroy, W. B., & Christenson, C. V. (1965). *Sex offenders: An analysis of types.* New York: Harper and Row.

Groth, A. N., & Birnbaum, H. J. (1979). *Men who rape.* New York: Plenum.

Hall, G. C. N. (1989). Sexual arousal and arousability in a sexual offender population. *Journal of Consulting and Clinical Psychology, 98,* 145–149.

Hall, G. C. N., & Hirschman, R. (1991). Toward a theory of sexual aggression: A quadripartite model. *Journal of Consulting and Clinical Psychology, 59,* 662–669.

Hall, G. C. N., Shondrick, D. D., & Hirschman, R. (1993). The role of sexual arousal in sexually aggressive behavior: A meta-analysis. *Journal of Consulting and Clinical Psychology, 61,* 1091–1095.

Hanson, R. K. (1990). The psychological impact of sexual assault on women and children: A review. *Annals of Sex Research, 3,* 187–232.

Hanson, R. K., Cox, B., & Woszczyna, C. (1991). Assessing treatment outcome for sexual offenders. *Annals of Sex Research, 4,* 177–208.

Hare, R. D. (1991). *Manual for the revised Psychopathy Checklist.* Toronto: Multi-Health Systems.

Hare, R. D., McPherson, L. M., & Forth, A. E. (1988). Male psychopaths and their criminal careers. *Journal of Consulting and Clinical Psychology, 56,* 710–714.

Harris, G. T., Rice, M. E., & Cormier, C. A. (1991). Psychopathy and violent recidivism. *Law and Human Behavior, 15,* 625–637.

Harris, G. T., Rice, M. E., & Quinsey, V. L. (1994). Psychopathy as a taxon: Evidence that psychopaths are a discrete class. *Journal of Consulting and Clinical Psychology, 62,* 387–397.

Herman, J. L. (1990). Sex offenders: A feminist perspective. In W. L. Marshall, D. R. Laws, & H. E. Barbaree (Eds.), *Handbook of sexual assault: Issues, theories, and treatment of the offender* (pp. 177–199). New York: Plenum.

Hindelang, M. J., Hirschi, T., & Weiss, J. G. (1981). *Measuring delinquency.* Newbury Park, CA: Sage Publications.

Hunter, J. A., Jr., Goodwin, D. A., & Becker, J. V. (1994). The relationship between phallometrically measured deviant sexual arousal and clinical characteristics in juvenile sexual offenders. *Behaviour Research and Therapy, 32,* 533–538.

Johnson, T. C., & Berry, C. (1989). Children who molest: A treatment program. *Journal of Interpersonal Violence, 4,* 185–203.

Kanin, E. J. (1985). Date rapists: Differential sexual socialization and relative deprivation. *Archives of Sexual Behavior, 14,* 218–232.

Kaplan, M. S., Abel, G. G., Cunningham-Rathner, J., & Mittleman, M. S. (1990). The impact of parolees' perception of confidentiality of their self-reported crimes. *Annals of Sex Research, 3,* 293–303.

Karpman, B. (1954). *The sexual offender and his offenses: Etiology, pathology, psychodynamics and treatment.* New York: Julian Press.

Knight, R. A., & Prentky, R. A. (1990). Classifying sexual offenders. In W. L. Marshall, D. R. Laws, & H. E. Barbaree (Eds.), *Handbook of sexual assault: Issues, theories, and treatment of the offender* (pp. 23–52). New York: Plenum.

Knight, R., Prentky, R., Schneider, B., & Rosenberg, R. (1983). Linear causal modeling of adaptation and criminal history in sex offenders. In K. Van Dusen & S. Mednick (Eds.), *Prospective studies of crime and delinquency* (pp. 303–341). Boston: Kluwer-Nijhoff.

Koss, M. P. (1992). The underdetection of rape. *Journal of Social Issues, 48,* 63–75.

Koss, M. P. (1993). Detecting the scope of rape: A review of prevalence research methods. *Journal of Interpersonal Violence, 8,* 198–222.

Koss, M. P., Gidcyz, C. A., & Wisniewski, N. (1987). The scope of rape: Incidence and prevalence of sexual aggression and victimization in a national sample of higher education students. *Journal of Consulting and Clinical Psychology, 55,* 162–170.

Lalumière, M. L., & Quinsey, V. L. (1993). The sensitivity of phallometric measures with rapists. *Annals of Sex Research, 6,* 123–138.

Lalumière, M. L., & Quinsey, V. L. (1994). The discriminability of rapists from non-sex offenders using phallometric measures: A meta-analysis. *Criminal Justice and Behavior, 21,* 150–175.

Lalumière, M. L., Chalmers, L., Quinsey, V. L., & Seto, M. C. (1995). A test of the mate deprivation hypothesis of rape. *Ethology and Sociobiology, 17,* 299–318.

Langevin, R., Bain, J., Ben-Aron, M., Coulthard, R., Day, D., Handy, L., Jeasman, G., Hucker, S., Purdins, J., Roper, V., Russon, A., Webster, C., & Wortzman, G. (1984). Sexual aggression: Constructing a prediction equation. A controlled pilot study. In R. Langevin (Ed.), *Erotic preference, gender identity, and aggression in men: New research studies* (pp. 39–76). Hillsdale, NJ: Erlbaum.

Laws, D. R., & Osborn, C. A. (1983). How to build and operate a behavioral laboratory to evaluate and treat sexual deviance. In J. G. Greer & I. R. Stuart (Eds.), *The sexual aggressor: Current perspectives on treatment* (pp. 293–335). New York: Van Nostrand Reinhold.

Levin, S. M., & Stava, L. (1987). Personality characteristics of sex offenders: A review. *Archives of Sexual Behavior, 16,* 57–79.

Longo, R. E. (1982). Sexual learning and experience among adolescent sexual offenders. *International Journal of Offender Therapy and Comparative Criminology, 26,* 235–241.

Malamuth, N. M. (1986). Predictors of naturalistic sexual aggression. *Journal of Personality and Social Psychology, 50,* 953–962.

Malamuth, N. M., Heavey, C. L., & Linz, D. (1993). Predicting men's antisocial behavior against women: The interaction model of sexual aggression. In G. C. N. Hall, R. Hirschman, J. R. Graham, & M. S. Zaragoza (Eds.), *Sexual aggression: Issues in etiology, assessment, and treatment* (pp. 63–97). Washington, DC: Taylor and Francis.

Malamuth, N. M., Linz, D., Heavey, C. L., Barnes, G., & Acker, M. (1995). Using the confluence model of sexual aggression to predict men's conflict with women: A 10 year follow-up study. *Journal of Personality and Social Psychology, 69,* 353–369.

Malamuth, N. M., Sockloskie, R., Koss, M. P., & Tanaka, J. S. (1991). The characteristics of aggressors against women: Testing a model using a national sample of college students. *Journal of Consulting and Clinical Psychology, 59,* 670–681.

Marshall, W. L., & Barbaree, H. E. (1984). A behavioral view of rape. *International Journal of Law and Psychiatry, 7,* 51–77.

Marshall, W. L., & Barbaree, H. E. (1990). An integrated theory of the etiology of sexual offending. In W. L. Marshall, D. R. Laws, & H. E. Barbaree (Eds.), *Handbook of sexual assault: Issues, theories, and treatment of the offender* (pp. 257–275). New York: Plenum.

Mealey, L. (1995). The sociobiology of sociopathy: An integrated evolutionary model. *Behavioral and Brain Sciences, 18,* 523–599.

Moffitt, T. E. (1993). Adolescence-limited and life-course-persistent antisocial behavior: A developmental taxonomy. *Psychological Review, 100,* 674–701.

Muehlenhard, C. L. (1988). "Nice women" don't say yes and "real men" don't say no: How miscommunication and the double standard can cause sexual problems. *Women and Therapy, 7,* 95–108.

Newman, J. P., Kosson, D. S., & Patterson, C. M. (1992). Delay of gratification in psychopathic and nonpsychopathic offenders. *Journal of Abnormal Psychology, 101,* 630–636.

Newman, J. P., Patterson, C., Howland, E. W., & Nichols, S. L. (1990). Passive avoidance in psychopaths: The effects of reward. *Personality and Individual Differences, 11,* 1101–1114.

Ogloff, J. R., Wong, S., & Greenwood, A. (1990). Treating criminal psychopaths in a Therapeutic Community program. *Behavioral Sciences and the Law, 8,* 181–190.

Overholser, J. C., & Beck, S. (1986). Multimethod assessment of rapists, child molesters, and three control groups on behavioral and psychological measures. *Journal of Consulting and Clinical Psychology, 54,* 682–687.

Palmer, C. T. (1989). Rape in nonhuman animal species: Definitions, evidence, and implications. *Journal of Sex Research, 26,* 355–374.

Patterson, G. R. (1993). Orderly change in a stable world: The antisocial trait as a chimera. *Journal of Consulting and Clinical Psychology, 61,* 911–919.

Patterson, C. M., & Newman, J. P. (1993). Reflectivity and learning from aversive events: Toward a psychological mechanism for the syndromes of disinhibition. *Psychological Review, 100,* 716–736.

Pérusse, D. (1993). Cultural and reproductive success in industrial societies: Testing the relationship at the proximate and ultimate levels. *Behavioral and Brain Sciences, 16,* 267–283.

Prentky, R. A., & Knight, R. A. (1986). Impulsivity in the lifestyle and criminal behavior of sexual offenders. *Criminal Justice and Behavior, 13,* 141–164.

Prentky, R. A., & Knight, R. A. (1991). Identifying critical dimensions for discriminating among rapists. *Journal of Consulting and Clinical Psychology, 59,* 643–661.

Prentky, R. A., & Knight, R. A. (1993). Age of onset of sexual assault: Criminal and life history correlates. In G. C. N. Hall, R. Hirschman, J. R. Graham, & M. S. Zaragoza (Eds.), *Sexual aggression: Issues in etiology, assessment, and treatment* (pp. 43–62). Washington, DC: Taylor and Francis.

Quinsey, V. L. (1984). Sexual aggression: Studies of offenders against women. In D. Weisstub (Ed.), *Law and mental health: International perspectives* (vol. 1, pp. 84–121). Elmsford, NY: Pergamon.

Quinsey, V. L., & Chaplin, T. C. (1988). Preventing faking in phallometric assessments of sexual preference. *Annals of the New York Academy of Sciences, 528,* 49–58.

Quinsey, V. L., Rice, M. E., Harris, G. T., & Reid, K. S. (1993). The phylogenetic and ontogenetic development of sexual age preferences in males: Conceptual and measurement issues. In H. E. Barbaree, W. L. Marshall, & S. M. Hudson (Eds.), *The juvenile sex offender* (pp. 143–163). New York: Guilford.

Rada, R. T. (1978). *Clinical aspects of the rapist.* New York: Grune and Stratton.

Rice, M. E., Harris, G. T., & Cormier, C. A. (1992). An evaluation of a maximum security therapeutic community for psychopaths and other mentally disordered offenders. *Law and Human Behavior, 16,* 399–412.

Rice, M. E., Harris, G. T., & Quinsey, V. L. (1990). A follow-up of rapists assessed in a maximum-security psychiatric facility. *Journal of Interpersonal Violence, 5,* 435–448.

Russell, D. E. H. (1984). *Sexual exploitation: Rape, child sexual abuse and workplace harassment.* Beverly Hills, CA: Sage Publications.

Sanday, P. R. (1981). The socio-cultural aspect of rape. A cross-cultural study. *Journal of Social Issues, 37,* 5–27.

Scott, R. L., & Tetreault, L. A. (1987). Attitudes of rapists and other violent offenders toward women. *Journal of Social Psychology, 127,* 375–380.

Serin, R. C., Peters, R. D., & Barbaree, H. E. (1990). Predictors of psychopathy and release outcome in a criminal population. *Psychological Assessment, 2,* 419–422.

Seto, M. C., & Barbaree, H. E. (1995). The role of alcohol in sexual aggression. *Clinical Psychology Review, 15,* 545–566.

Seto, M. C., Khattar, N. A., Lalumière, M. L., & Quinsey, V. L. (1997). Deception and sexual strategy in psychopathy. *Personality and Individual Differences, 22,* 301–307.

Shields, W. M., & Shields, L. M. (1983). Forcible rape: An evolutionary perspective. *Ethology and Sociobiology, 4,* 115–136.

Smuts, B. B. (1995). The evolutionary origins of patriarchy. *Human Nature, 6,* 1–32.

Stermac, L. E., Segal, Z. V., & Gillis, R. (1990). Social and cultural factors in sexual assault. In W. L. Marshall, D. R. Laws, & H. E. Barbaree (Eds.), *Handbook of sexual assault: Issues, theories, and treatment of the offender* (pp. 143–159). New York: Plenum.

Stermac, L. E., & Quinsey, V. L. (1986). Social competence among rapists. *Behavioral Assessment, 8,* 171–185.

Thornhill, R., & Thornhill, N. W. (1983). Human rape: An evolutionary analysis. *Ethology and Sociobiology, 4,* 137–173.

Thornhill, R., & Thornhill, N. W. (1992). The evolutionary psychology of men's coercive sexuality. *Behavioral and Brain Sciences, 15,* 363–421.

Weinrott, M. R., & Saylor, M. (1991). Self-report of crimes committed by sex offenders. *Journal of Interpersonal Violence, 6,* 286–300.

Widom, C. S. (1989). Does violence beget violence? A critical examination of the literature. *Psychological Bulletin, 106,* 3–28.

Zuckerman, M. (1971). Physiological measures of sexual arousal in the human. *Psychological Bulletin, 75,* 297–329.

CHAPTER 49

Domestic Violence: Antisocial Behavior in the Family

JASLEAN J. LA TAILLADE and NEIL S. JACOBSON

About 13% of all murders in this country are husband-wife homicides (Ohrenstein, 1977). Indeed, domestic violence constitutes perhaps the single most common source of intentional injury among women (Stark & Flitcraft, 1991). Female victims of violence by male partners are more likely to be repeatedly attacked, raped, injured, or killed than women assaulted by other types of assailants with whom they have less frequent exposure (Browne & Williams, 1989, 1993; Finkelhor & Yllo, 1985; Langan & Innes, 1986; Lentzner & DeBerry, 1980; Russell, 1982). Estimates based on probability samples indicate that between 21% and 34% of all women will be physically assaulted by a man with whom they are intimate during adulthood (Frieze, Knoble, Washburn, & Zomnir, 1980; Russell, 1982). As many as one third to one half of married couples in this country are violent toward each other at least once (Straus, Gelles, & Steinmetz, 1980). Each year at least 1.6 million wives in the United States are severely assaulted by their husbands (Straus & Gelles, 1986).

The impact of marital violence on both the affected families and society is substantial. Domestic violence has been linked to chronic physical and stress-related disorders (Rosenbaum & O'Leary, 1986), suicide (Gayford, 1975), alcohol and drug abuse (Roy, 1977), child abuse (Walker, 1984), and child behavior disorders (McDonald & Jouriles, 1991). The psychological, social, and financial costs to society have led professionals in political, public, and mental health spheres to classify domestic violence as a serious social and public health problem.

HISTORICAL CONTEXT OF RESEARCH ON DOMESTIC VIOLENCE

Although domestic violence has a history as long as marriage itself (see Dobash & Dobash, 1979), only in the last two decades has it become recognized as a problem worthy of attention by researchers and clinicians. Domestic violence was initially seen as a rare occurrence, confined to the psychologically disturbed and economically disadvantaged. Clinicians first noted the occurrence of family violence through child abuse, stating that causal factors of violence to children resided in the personality or character disorders of the individual battering parents (Galdston, 1965; Kempe, Silverman, Steele, Droegemuller, & Silver, 1962; Steele & Pollock, 1974; Zalba, 1971). The few writings that focused primarily on husband to wife violence portrayed the battering husband and his wife as suffering from personality dysfunction (Schultz, 1960; Snell, Rosenwald, & Robey, 1964). The clinical nature of the subject population studied and the investigative procedures used contributed in large part to use of the psychopathological model to explain violent behavior (Gelles, 1987). The redefinition of child assault as a psychological illness in the parent prompted social work and medical professionals to focus their efforts on rehabilitating and treating the parents, rather than instituting legal reforms (Dutton, 1995).

In contrast, wife assault reform advocates mainly were lawyers and women's rights advocates, who viewed social inequality and legal ineffectiveness as the primary contributors to domestic violence (Dutton, 1995). Inspired by similar movements in Europe, women's groups began to organize safe houses and battered women's shelters in the United States as early as 1972. The women's movement identified wife assault as a social problem of great magnitude and incidence and brought to the attention of the criminal justice system its failure to effectively deal with batterers and their violent behavior. In addition, the movement sponsored legislation that made it easier for women to take legal action against domestic violence, including increasing criminal penalties, simplifying the process of filing criminal charges, and increasing accessibility to public assistance (Dutton, 1988). The political and legal efforts of the women's movement had a significant impact in highlighting the problems faced by battered women and making domestic violence a continuing national issue. The cumulation of these efforts was reflected in the inclusion of the Violence Against Women Act as part of the Violence Crime Control and Law Enforcement Act of 1994 (Title IV).

Fueled by the attention of women's groups to domestic violence, mental health professionals began to break away from conceptualizations of spousal abuse that focused on individual pathology (O'Leary, Vivian, & Malone, 1992). The results of research on wife abuse in the United States were first published in 1973 (Gelles & Cornell, 1990) and focused on estimating incidence rates and identifying factors associated with violence in the home. Information on the extent of the problem, patterns of violence, correlates with domestic violence, and other results were utilized by those who believed violence toward women deserved a high place on the public agenda (Gelles & Cornell, 1990).

In the 1980s research declined on the incidence of violence and violence among family members (Gelles, 1987) and increased in attention to individual characteristics associated with the batterer and his interaction with the social environment. Research in the 1990s not only has continued to develop and test the models and findings gathered from the previous decade but also expanded the scope of domestic violence research to other populations (ethnic minorities, same-sex relationships) and to factors specific to the dyadic relationship and has integrated interdisciplinary theoretical perspectives and methodologies.

THEORIES OF DOMESTIC VIOLENCE

Early theories of the causes of domestic violence were dominated by psychiatric explanations, which posited that husband to wife violence was a rare event committed only by men with diagnosable psychiatric disorders (see Dutton, 1988, for a review). Clinical syndrome explanations of husband to wife violence attributed it to psychological dependency (Faulk, 1974; Snell et al., 1964), brain lesions (Elliot, 1977), or sadistic character (Pizzey, 1974). Additionally, the women were labeled as *masochistic* and assumed to be seeking out abuse or having psychological needs met through the violence. Both partners were assumed to have long-standing disorders of personality, which resulted in the maladaptive behavior patterns. These explanations helped reinforce the view of husband to wife violence as a rare occurrence and the men who committed it as atypical and pathological (Dutton, 1995). Later empirical evidence that documented the prevalence of husband to wife violence prompted researchers and clinicians to formulate alternative theories to explain domestic violence (for a more extensive review, see Gelles & Straus, 1979).

Systemic Theories

Sociological theories examine the family as a social institution rather than focusing on individual intimate members to explain husband to wife violence. Sociologists contend that the family, with its emphasis on intimacy and privacy and use of ascribed roles for family members, contributes to the frequent and intense nature of intimate violence and its transmission across generations. Husband to wife violence is viewed as the result of a breakdown in family functioning, which arises from a combination of internal conflict and impinging external, social stressors. Sociological theorists assert that one can understand marital violence only by understanding the operation and function of the entire family system. Through this systemic perspective, the actions of each spouse are viewed largely as a function of the consequences of the actions provided by the partner (Margolin & Burman, 1993). As a result, responsibility for individual actions is dispersed among family members and the distinction between victim and batterer disappears (Bograd, 1988; Pressman & Rothery, 1989), although they are not equally at fault.

Both epidemiological and marital interaction studies have shown that violence is used as a tactic in conflict by both husbands and wives, and there is evidence that both batterers and their victims were abused as children (see Widom, Chapter 16, this volume, for a review of the effects of abuse on later offending). However, the majority of the claims of this model have not been supported. Although women do use aggression, rarely do they inflict the same amount or degree of injury and even more rarely do women instill fear in men; it is men who batter and use fear of threat of injury (as well as the violence itself) to subjugate and exploit. Additionally, in committing to the philosophy that most maladaptive behaviors are the result of faulty family functioning, other variables in the environment (e.g., sexism, racism, poverty) are missed that influence the behavior of individuals who also happen to be members of families.

Feminist Theory

The feminist perspective on husband to wife violence focuses on power and gender as the fundamental issues and bases its analyses on the patriarchal context, the culturally based patterns of male-female relations, and the unequal distribution of power in society (Bograd, 1988; Dobash & Dobash, 1979; Margolin & Burman, 1993). Rather than asking why this particular man beats his particular wife, feminist researchers try to comprehend why men in general use physical force against their partners and what function this behavior serves for a given society in a given historical context (Bograd, 1988; Dobash & Dobash, 1979; Martin, 1976; Pagelow, 1981; Russell, 1982; Schechter, 1982; Walker, 1984). Feminist theorists assert that the reality of domination at the social level is the most significant factor contributing to and maintaining husband to wife violence at the personal level. In response to their situation, women are encouraged to empower themselves as individuals, which frequently involves removing themselves from the abusive relationship (Margolin & Burman, 1993). Instituting structural changes aspects of the social context that implicitly supports violence against women and maintains a hierarchical power structure is seen as one solution to preventing husband to wife violence (Margolin & Burman, 1993).

Although applicable in heterosexual relationships, theorists have questioned whether a feminist analysis, which links violence toward women with gender and societal roles (Browne, 1993), is applicable to relationships with same-sex partners, specifically lesbian relationships. Additionally, feminist analyses are limited in their ability to explain why only a small proportion of men batter their wives. Although efforts are being made to explore the dynamics of violence in lesbian relationships (see Saakvitine & Pearlman, 1993), more research is required to determine the specific interactive effects of gender, power, and social systems and their impact on violent relationships.

Social Learning and Psychological Theories

Despite general agreement that one of the reasons husband to wife violence exists is societal norms that legitimize marital violence and permit men's domination over women, this still does not explain why some men are violent whereas others are not. In response, psychological and social learning theorists have attempted to identify characteristics that distinguish violent from nonviolent men, battered from nonbattered women, and violent from nonviolent couples (Margolin & Burman, 1993).

Psychological theories, which dominated the early literature on husband to wife violence (Faulk, 1974; Snell et al., 1964), view batterers as possessing aberrant or "abnormal" features that distinguish them from nonassaultive men. Research following this model has attempted to identify shared similarities within groups of assaultive men. In fact, batterers have been found to be a heterogeneous group, as evidenced by prior empirical studies of batterer typologies (e.g., Gondolf, 1987; Hamberger & Hastings, 1986; Saunders, 1992). Furthermore, many other studies examining batterer characteristics have failed to find differences between men who are violent with their wives versus men who do not batter their partners (see Holtzworth-Munroe & Stuart, 1994, for a review).

A social learning analysis attempts to differentiate assaultive from nonassaultive men on the basis of differences in the individual learning environment. Observational learning is the primary means by which individuals learn to perform aggressive behaviors and the rules and regulations of where, when, and against whom to enact these behaviors (Ganley, 1989). Utilization of these patterns of assault is contingent on "appropriate" instigators of aggression and the function of aggression in generating the rewards (or absence of punishment) that come with its usage (Bandura, 1979). What is considered an "appropriate" instigator by the batterer is shaped by his individual learning history. Use of violence is maintained by both internal (e.g., reduced tension) and external (e.g., subjugation and fear in the wife) reinforcers (Ganley, 1989) and justified by cognitive strategies (e.g., minimization or displacement of responsibility) that, as described by Bandura (1979), "neutralize" their ability for "self-punishment" of their violent behavior.

Social learning analyses have had the greatest influence in their contribution to an empirical and theoretical understanding of the origins of violent behavior and a foundation for the treatment of violent men (Ganley, 1981). Researchers have found evidence for many of the major tenets of this theory, including the presence of a history of violence in the batterer's family of origin (e.g., Browning & Dutton, 1986; Dutton, 1988, 1995).

Biological Theories

Researchers have examined physiological variables and their contribution to battering. Previous research linked physiology with aggressive and criminal behavior, demonstrating that low levels of physiological reactivity may lead to risk seeking and criminal behavior in the individual's attempt to seek increased stimulation (e.g., Schalling, Edman, & Asberg, 1983). Additionally, researchers have also found a link between lower levels of the major serotonin metabolite, 5-hydroxyindoleacetic acid, in the cerebrospinal fluid of individuals with extensive histories of aggressive behavior, poor impulse control, low self-esteem, and depression and individuals who repeatedly commit violent crimes (Berman, Kavoussi, & Coccaro, Chapter 27, this volume; Virkkunen & Linnoila, 1993). It is hypothesized that serotonin function modifies the learned association between punishment and the behavior that illicits punishment,

so that individuals with decreased serotonin functioning are more likely to respond aggressively to obtain rewards or deter punishment (Spoont, 1992).

Although no one has systematically studied links between serotonin function and battering, research among batterers found that men whose heart rates drop from baseline during arguments are more violent toward their partners than other wife assaulters, are generally violent, and are more psychologically abusive (Gottman et al., 1995; Jacobson, Gottman, & Shortt, 1995). Gottman et al. (1995) hypothesized that this pattern of physiological responding serves to focus their attention and maximize the impact of their attempts to control and subjugate their partners.

Evolutionary psychologists, in examining violent behavior, have attempted to integrate the influence of biology, environment, and evolutionary significance (e.g., Daly & Wilson, 1988; Daly, Wilson, & Weghorst, 1982). Evolutionary theories view aggression as based in human evolutionary history and existing as a function of both biology and environmental adaptation. Evolutionary psychologists hypothesize that violence functions to maintain or obtain social status, noting that in many situations, a man's reputation is contingent in part on maintaining a credible threat of violence; serotonin functioning may mediate the use of violence in these situations (Wright, 1995). It follows from the viewpoint of evolutionary psychology that violence will be reinforced if it enhances their status position relative to their wives. Men who feel threatened by their wives' rejection or moves toward independence may exhibit lower self-esteem, a marker for which may be reduced serotonin activity. They may both react physiologically and physically to maintain dominance over their wives. Batterers who are not as physiologically reactive (Gottman et al., 1995; Jacobson et al., 1995) still might be expected to exhibit high serotoninergic activity. These physiological states (physiological calming combined with high levels of serotenergic activity) may be the markers for psychological abuse and physical violence in a certain subtype of batterer. These types of batterers would not feel threatened by their wives but instead would respond to any perceived attempt to control them, wherever it came from. Further research is needed to determine the physiological underpinnings of battering.

Theoretical Integration

Advancements toward understanding the nature of men's violence against their partners will necessitate a multidisciplinary perspective that includes sociocultural, individual, psychological, physiological, marital, and familial factors (Dutton, 1995; Ganley, 1989). Attempts have been made to integrate these various perspectives (Ganley, 1989) or to draw similarities among them (Jacobson, 1994a, 1994b).

Jacobson (1994a, 1994b) has made the case for a contextualistic view of marital violence, which encompasses both feminist and social learning perspectives. Contextualism also provides a method, called a *functional analysis,* for uncovering variables in the environment that cause behavior. Behavior can be understood by examining its function in relation to the environment in which it occurs. The context relevant to domestic violence might include dyadic or family factors but might also include cultural practices and political systems that institutionalize the oppression of women.

CURRENT METHODOLOGICAL PROCEDURES FOR RESEARCHING DOMESTIC VIOLENCE

Although the knowledge base of domestic violence research has grown immensely over the last two decades, much about this phenomenon still is not understood. Next, we discuss pertinent methodological concerns and offer some suggestions for improvement in the study of marital violence.

Definitions of Husband to Wife Violence

Traditionally, domestic violence is the category of acts under which spouse abuse, family violence, and wife battering are generally classified. Definitions of violence vary across legal, research, and clinical settings (Stark & Flitcraft, 1991). Legal definitions include behaviors intended to cause physical harm or injury and threats or acts intended to control the individual. Legal parameters of what constitutes a "domestic" relationship also are variable and may focus on the age of the cohabitants, status of the cohabitants, and duration of the relationship (Stark & Flitcraft, 1991). Research definitions may include any act of force intended to control or harm and can extend to use of emotional or psychological aggression. Clinically, determination of violence is based on the therapists' notion of what it constitutes and may include in their judgment presence of psychological or social problems and fear in addition to physical injury.

Feminists argue that such terms obscure the dimensions of gender and power essential to understanding wife abuse (Margolin & Burman, 1993; Schechter, 1982; Yllo & Bograd, 1988). Yllo and Bograd (1988) explain that generic terms ignore the context of the violence, its origins and consequences, the role obligations of each family member, and the different mechanisms that lead to forms of abuse. This can result in biases in how the causes and solutions of spousal violence are conceptualized and treated (e.g., conjoint versus individual treatment; Yllo & Bograd, 1988). In fact, the various names given to the phenomenon of intimate violence reflect the schism in the way this problem is conceptualized and the methods of assessment strategies utilized (Margolin & Burman, 1993).

Data on the frequency of violence in marriage contribute to this confusion. Evidence exists for the mutuality of assault in violent couples (Straus & Gelles, 1986; Straus, Gelles, & Steinmetz, 1980), with some studies reporting instances of aggression in 90% of the couples sampled (Jacobson, Gottman, Waltz, Rushe, & Babcock, 1994). However, overreliance on survey methods for studying violence and questionnaires such as the Conflict Tactics Scale (CTS; Straus, 1979) obscures other important dimensions, including the function, context, and sequences of violence.

An important question in marital violence research is how to make distinctions between violent and nonviolent couples and between different types of aggression. As noted by Margolin (1987), such distinctions are crucial when examining factors correlated with and contributing to violence. Most researchers have used the CTS to classify violent and nonviolent couples. However, because the CTS measures the frequency of violent acts, it is unable to make the distinctions needed to make conclusions about the function of battering (Jacobson, 1994b). Although definitions of violence are sometimes clearly stated by researchers (such as intent to control or harm; Jacobson et al., 1994), parameters of those definitions are not readily measured by the CTS.

Additionally, feminist researchers contend that the gender-blind nature of the CTS ignores the influence of gender differences on the dynamics and outcomes of physically aggressive incidents. Physical menace is a powerful dynamic in male-female interactions. A recognition of the potential for severe bodily harm significantly affects women's but usually not men's response to actual assault. It is unlikely that many unarmed women, simply by physical menace, would put their male partners in fear of severe bodily harm or death (Browne, 1993). Furthermore, it is the husband's violence that elicits fear in his partner and gives him the ability to use violence as a means for control (Jacobson et al., 1994).

Others have objected to limiting the study of violence to discrete physical acts, because often these actions are only part of what is experienced in violent relationships (Dutton, 1988). Physical assault may be accompanied by verbal abuse and forms of psychological abuse, including destruction toward property, threats of violence, violence toward others (e.g., children, pets), actions taken to isolate the partner, and forms of degradation. Researchers have begun to integrate assessment of psychological abuse with measures of violence (e.g., Tolman, 1989) to understand the complexities of the battering dynamic.

Sample Selection

Comparisons across studies are often complicated by sample differences and lack of information about the criteria employed for selection (Rosenbaum, 1988). In their survey of the marital violence literature, Geffner, Rosenbaum, and Hughes (1988) found that only 16% of the studies described the criteria that defined the maritally violent sample. Even those that did exhibited significant variability, ranging from classification based on a subjective opinion of the participants to the number of physically aggressive incidents required (Rosenbaum, 1988).

Consistent use of a standardized, quantitative measure of marital violence, such as the CTS, in both group assignment and definition would help alleviate the inconsistencies across studies. Even among studies that use the CTS in classifying couples, however, there is variability in determination of the criterion that differentiates violent from nonviolent marriages. Burman, Margolin, and John (1993) used weighted scores on the CTS to classify couples, whereas Cordova, Jacobson, Gottman, Ruske, and Cox (1993), Babcock, Waltz, Jacobson, and Gottman (1993), and Jacobson et al. (1994) required either repeated acts of low-level violence or the occurrence of at least one moderate-to-serious violent episode, resulting in a more severely violent sample than the one studied by Margolin and her colleagues. Results from samples with only mild violence may not be generalizable to couples in which the women are battered and men are arrested (Cordova et al., 1993). Straus (1993) defined a "high-risk" subcategory of assaulters, who are distinguished by their use of chronic and severe violence and psychological abuse, as more representative of what we commonly think of as "batterers." Although the high-risk category may not be representative of community or survey populations of couples in which the violence is less frequent or severe, they do represent the level of clinical violence in offending populations (Straus, 1993).

Differences in where the samples were recruited introduce additional variance in interpretation of the findings. Samples of detected cases (batterers who have been identified through shelters or hospital visits) have been found to differ significantly in amount and severity of violence from random samples of the population. Shelter samples average more than one assault per week, as compared with abused women in the national survey who average six assaults per year (Straus, 1990). With detected cases, physical evidence, such as bruises, often is apparent, and at least one instance of violence is publicly known (Margolin, 1987). Such is not the case with couples recruited from the general population. Often evidence is less concrete, the retrospective accounts may not be as accurate, and the victims may have not reached the point of recognizing or acknowledging the presence of violence in the relationship (Margolin, 1987).

Specification in the nature of the intimate relationship (e.g., cohabitating, dating, legally married) as well as the duration of the relationship is not always made clear, contributing to further variability in findings. Even though the purpose is to examine "marital" or "spousal" violence, a true marital relationship often is not required (Rosenbaum, 1988). More frequently, an intimate, heterosexual, marriage-like relationship is required. Although researchers are making attempts to study dating, engaged, and newly married couples (e.g., Arias, Samios, & O'Leary, 1987; Follette & Alexander, 1992) as well as marital relationships of longer duration, future empirical efforts should examine the possible differences among these relationship categories and the development of violence over the course of the relationship.

Reporter Bias

Early research in domestic violence focused on the female victims, given their increased availability. With the proliferation of programs for batterers and couples, the availability of males as subjects increased. This is a significant methodological improvement, but researchers now are faced with the dilemma of whose report of violence to use for describing and classifying the couple. Spouses disagree often, about 50% of the time, on the occurrence of more innocuous behaviors, such as companionship activities, demonstrations of affection, and housekeeping (Jouriles & O'Leary, 1985). Studies that have examined the interspouse reliability of frequency and types of violent acts have reported only moderate levels of agreement (Browning & Dutton, 1986; Jouriles & O'Leary, 1985; Rosenbaum, 1988; Rosenbaum & O'Leary, 1981; Szinovacz, 1983).

The results on agreement between spouses in their reporting of violence vary considerably due to different samples and different agreement statistics (Margolin, 1987; Szinovacz, 1983). Edelson and Brugger (1984) examined agreement on men's use of violence as they began a counseling program for battering. There was low agreement at intake, particularly with respect to the threat of violence. The women generally reported higher instances of violence than did men. Men underreporting their own violence also was found by Jouriles and O'Leary (1985) in a sample of couples beginning marital therapy but not in a comparison community

sample. Overall agreement in both samples was low to moderate. In a sample of couples with the husband undergoing treatment for wife assault, assaultive men reported only about 50% as much violence as their wives reported them committing (Browning & Dutton, 1986). College undergraduates were significantly less likely to report physical aggression than other behaviors (Riggs, Murphy, & O'Leary, 1989). Additionally, they were more likely to report being the victims than the perpetrators of assault.

Although some of the discrepancies between reports can be accounted for by sample variability, more influential are the individual characteristics of spouses who may have different definitions and thresholds of violent behavior (Margolin, 1987). The more "low-level" forms of violence, such as pushing, grabbing, and throwing things at one another generally are not spontaneously labeled as abuse or violence by spouses, perhaps because this type of violence is seen as more "normative" (Straus et al., 1980) or because these types of behaviors generally do not result in visible injury (O'Leary & Murphy, 1991).

The socially undesirable nature of marital violence also contributes to differences in reporting violent behavior. Riggs et al. (1989), in a sample of undergraduates, investigated self-presentational strategies by asking respondents about their likelihood to report physical aggression. Participants would be much less likely to report physical aggression than other positive or negative relationship behaviors, especially if they were the perpetrators. Other researchers have used direct measures of socially desirable responding to determine its effects on reporting violent behavior (Arias & Beach, 1987; Dutton & Hemphill, 1992). Dutton and Hemphill (1992) assessed patterns of socially desirable responding among assaulters and victims of assault. They measured two dimensions of socially desirable responding: impression management and self-deception. Impression management involves purposeful manipulation of answers by respondents or lying; self-deception is conceptualized as a personality trait associated with high ego-resiliency, adjustment, and self-confidence. There were no significant relationships for victim reports between the social desirability measures and reports of violence. Among perpetrators, however, reports of their own verbal abuse ($r = -.38$, $p < .01$), emotional abuse ($r = -.50$, $p < .01$), and anger ($r = -.44$, $p < .01$) correlated negatively with their level of impression management. Although reports of their own violence were not significantly correlated with their level of impression management ($r = -.20$, n.s.), the magnitude of the association was twice that of their wives ($r = -.09$, n.s.).

Perhaps more influential than socially desirable responding in the lack of agreement between spouses is the effect of a man's denial on his underreporting of violence (Dutton, 1986, 1995; Ganley, 1981; Sonkin, Martin, & Walker, 1985). Dutton (1986), using a sample of self-referred and court-referred men, examined perpetrators' reports of physical aggression and the explanations given for their assault. Dutton found that men who minimized their use of violence were more likely to attribute the cause for the assault to their wives. Additionally, court-referred men were more likely to deny personal responsibility for their violence and attribute assaults to situational circumstances, such as alcohol use or uncontrollable arousal (Dutton, 1995).

Results across studies citing differences in spousal reports of violence generally indicate that the confidential report of the victim is less biased than the perpetrator reports, and it is a more valid indicator of the occurrence of physical aggression (Arias & Beach, 1987; Dutton & Hemphill, 1992; Riggs et al., 1989). These findings suggest that it is essential to obtain the wife's report when assessing husband to wife aggression (Dutton & Hemphill, 1992).

Control Groups

In previous research, the effects of violence have been difficult to separate from those due to marital distress (Margolin, John, & Gleberman, 1988; O'Leary et al., 1989; Rosenbaum & O'Leary, 1981). Early research often made use of "no violence" control groups. Group differences were impossible to interpret because control groups differed from the violent groups not only in their absence of violence but also in their level of marital satisfaction. Although there are exceptions, the majority of violent couples experience severe marital distress (Rosenbaum & O'Leary, 1981). The inclusion of a maritally distressed but nonviolent group can control for differences due to marital satisfaction.

However, given that violent groups often are more severely distressed than maritally distressed, nonviolent control groups (Rosenbaum, 1988), researchers are faced with the additional task of matching groups on levels of marital satisfaction. Among the studies that have included a distressed but nonviolent group, interpretation of group differences has remained ambiguous, because such control groups score higher on measures of marital satisfaction (Margolin et al., 1988; O'Leary et al., 1989). In their efforts to obtain adequate control subjects, some researchers have noted that it is difficult to obtain maritally distressed couples with absolutely no history of even low-level violence at any time in their relationship (Holtzworth-Munroe et al., 1992). A review of five marital violence studies found that over half of the samples of maritally distressed nonviolent couples reported husband violence over the course of their relationship and almost half reported it within the past year (Holtzworth-Munroe et al., 1992). Perhaps, assuming availability of adequate resources, researchers should attempt to recruit all available couples and include a "low-level" violence group, which can be matched with the other distressed groups on marital distress but distinct from the distressed violent group on frequency and severity of violence.

Previous observational research on violent couples has examined samples in which the frequency and severity of violence was mild (Margolin et al, 1988; O'Leary et al., 1989) compared to the types of severe violence facing the criminal justice system. It may be that many of the violent samples studied, in fact, were more similar to a "low-level" violence group than they were to a clinically violent one. Researchers should strive to incorporate a moderate-to-severe sample of violent couples to provide as strong a test as possible of the association between clinical levels of battering and variables related to marriage.

Observational Procedures and Marital Interaction

The majority of the investigations reported in the literature have employed retrospective, correlational, and cross-sectional designs and relied heavily on the use of paper-and-pencil measures, surveys, nonquantitative measures, and interview data. The limitations of retrospective and correlational designs suggest the need for more rigorous methods. To study the function, context, and sequence of violence, researchers have used observational methods developed in the marital interaction literature (Jacobson et al., 1994; Margolin et al., 1988).

Ethical considerations have placed considerable constraints on using observational methods. Presenting stimulus materials designed to induce conflict in the couple may raise the concern that this places the woman at increased risk for violent attacks. However, research employing marital interaction procedures found their subjects did not experience any adverse reactions as a result of the experimental procedures (Jacobson et al., 1994; Margolin et al., 1988). Unlike other violent crimes, when the victim and assailant are unrelated, domestic violence occurs in the context of an intimate relationship (Rosenbaum, 1988), making it reasonable to examine the spousal correlates of battering. If our ultimate goal is to understand the function and nature of domestic violence, then it is essential that we fully understand the nature and dynamics of this phenomenon in the context of the relationship. However, without clarifying the distinction between sequential dependency (e.g., antecedent behaviors increasing the probability of subsequent behavior) and causality, researchers risk "blaming the victim" (Jacobson, 1994a, 1994b). Although spousal correlates of battering can increase understanding of domestic violence, such empirical findings cannot exonerate the batterer of moral responsibility for his violent behavior.

Longitudinal Research

Collection of longitudinal data is essential for understanding the course of violence over time and the potential impact of these changes on marital stability and satisfaction. In conducting longitudinal research, investigators must determine the longitudinal variables to assess, the nature and sources of longitudinal data, and the appropriate follow-up intervals (Rosenbaum, 1988). At the very least, information on marital stability, marital satisfaction, and levels of aggression should be collected. Differential rates of compliance, however, may limit the interpretability of longitudinal data when it is obtained from only one spouse.

Often longitudinal research is complicated by selection of excessively lengthy follow-up intervals (Rosenbaum, 1988). Frequent follow-up intervals are essential not only for gathering multiple data points for changes in these relationships but also for tracking and locating subjects. Given the elevated divorce rates, transience, and mobility within these relationships (Rosenbaum, 1988), it is essential to regularly contact participants to maximize subject retention.

Ethical Considerations

Research involving violent couples introduces ethical considerations beyond those normally encountered by the investigator studying couple relationships. Selection of a community sample may place the wife at risk; for example, if the selection is based on her report, rather than a random occurrence. Even if the couple has agreed to participate in the research, experimenters should be aware of the possibility for coercion with regard to suppression of information, particularly in reports of severity of violence (Rosenbaum, 1988). To reduce the level of coercion, experimenters have attempted to obtain both consent and data separately for each spouse.

The issue of confidentiality is complicated when studying violent couples. For the victim's safety, it is crucial that her confidentiality be guaranteed and protected. Additionally, it is imperative that breeches to confidentiality, such as court subpoena, threats of homicide, or child abuse or neglect, be made clear to both parties and written in the consent form. Researchers can obtain a Federal Certificate of Confidentiality from the federal government to protect the confidentiality of research data from any court or government access.

Marital interaction experiments, which are designed to induce conflict in the couple, may place the wife at-risk for a violent attack. Researchers employing this procedure must take precautions to ensure the victim's safety, not only during the experiment but also for the time period immediately following. Adequate precautions should include assessment of both the victim's perception of her own safety, assessment of the potential for lethality and dangerousness of the batterer, and procedures for the development of a safety plan, if necessary. In our own research, we also called the wives in our study two weeks following their participation and asked if any violence may have been precipitated by our procedures. In cases of immediate risk, contact was made the day following participation or as determined by the safety plan. Additionally, we gave all women who participated referrals for shelters and individual and legal counseling after each assessment procedure. As stated by Margolin (1979), if in the course of the study the subject's safety is being compromised, the experimenter's ethical and moral responsibility is to attend to the needs of the subject and put aside research procedures.

RESEARCH ON MARITAL VIOLENCE

Characteristics of Batterers

In a comprehensive review of the literature, Hotaling and Sugarman (1986) evaluated the evidence for a variety of characteristics thought to be associated with marital violence. Eight variables were identified as possible risk markers for male batterers. To be a consistent risk marker, the variable had to have been directly examined in three studies and had to have a significant relationship in the predicted direction in at least 70% of the studies. Based on this criterion, men who assaulted their wives were more likely to be sexually aggressive toward their partners, to abuse their children, to have witnessed violence as a child, and to abuse alcohol. They were also found to have lower incomes and socioeconomic status, be less educated, and express less assertiveness when communicating with their wives. As previously discussed, however, studies that have compared maritally violent men to maritally distressed but nonviolent men in control groups have found that the significance of these risk markers has been inconsistent. As we noted previously, studies using this control group have often not found demographic differences between violent and distressed nonviolent men, and when there were differences, correlations

with the criterion variables were nonsignificant (e.g., Jacobson et al., 1994; Margolin et al. 1988). Research examining communication patterns in violent men have found that communication discrepancies between violent partners are due to a main effect for gender; wives in general are more communicative than their husbands, and violent and nonviolent husbands do not differ in communication styles (Babcock et al., 1993). However, some studies that have examined spouse-specific assertiveness have found that violent men report significantly greater assertion problems than distressed nonviolent men (O'Leary & Curley, 1986; Rosenbaum & O'Leary, 1981). Although violent men have been found to drink more, when compared with distressed nonviolent men, there was no significant difference in frequency of consumption (Barnett & Fagan, 1993; Van Hasselt, Morrison, & Bellack, 1985). Research examining family of origin variables has reported inconsistent findings, with history of child abuse victimization being an inconsistent predictor and witnessing parental violence a more consistent predictor across studies, varying only by the direction of violence witnessed (Dutton, 1988).

Researchers studying violent husbands often have treated batterers as a homogeneous group, averaging scores on measures of interest across all the violent men in their sample and then comparing that score to the control group (Holtzworth-Munroe & Stuart, 1994). Averaging has resulted in a lack of significant violent-nonviolent group differences or, alternatively, has lead to significant findings that are not replicable across samples. Men who physically assault their intimate partners vary in numerous ways: in the frequency and severity of their attacks, the degree of impairment in psychological functioning, personality characteristics, and in the function of their violent behavior. This heterogeneity has made it difficult to identify specific characteristics of men who assault their wives, and as a result, it has been difficult to develop models that explain violent behavior across the variability in men who batter.

Discrepancies in research findings may be reflective of the existence of different subtypes of batterers. Several researchers have noted the existence of possible subtypes and have attempted to create typologies of batterers (e.g., Caesar, 1988; Elbow, 1977; Gondolf, 1987; Hamberger & Hastings, 1986; Holtzworth-Munroe & Stuart, 1984; Saunders, 1992; Shields & Hanneke, 1983; Snyder & Fruchtman, 1981). Determination of subtypes has been based on (a) rational or deductive strategies, in which researchers delineated subtypes based on clinical observations (e.g., Elbow, 1977) or theoretical speculation, and (b) empirical or inductive strategies (e.g., Gondolf, 1988; Hamberger & Hastings, 1986; Saunders, 1992), which used factor analysis or cluster analysis to identify subgroups of batterers (Holtzworth-Munroe & Stuart, 1994).

Most researchers agree that a subgroup of batterers are violent outside the marriage (Dutton, 1988; Gondolf, 1988; La Taillade, Waltz, Jacobson, & Gottman, 1992; Widom, 1989). They also agree that another group of wife assaulters limit the use of their violence to the marital relationship. Researchers delineating batterers on their use of violence have found significant differences between these groups on risk markers thought to be characteristic of all batterers. Generally violent men have been found to engage in more severe violence and more violence with others; be more severely abused as children; have witnessed more parental violence; display antisocial behavior; have a history of criminal behavior and legal involvement; have their violence precipitated by general, nonrelationship specific events; and have high rates of substance abuse (Fagan, Stewart, & Hansen, 1983; La Taillade et al., 1992; Saunders, 1992; Shields, McCall, & Hanneke, 1988). In contrast, "family-only" assaultive men have been found to perceive more abandonment from female-initiated independence, see abandonment issues as relevant to their relationship and an instigator for aggression, use low-level forms of violence, have less violence in the family of origin, limit their use of violence to their partners, and have fewer legal problems than generally violent men (Dutton, 1988; Fagan et al., 1983; La Taillade et al., 1993; Saunders, 1992; Shields et al., 1988).

With few exceptions (e.g., Dutton, 1988; La Taillade et al., 1993), however, the majority of these studies have been descriptive in nature and have not systematically attempted to differentiate subtypes based on variables hypothesized to be related to the use of violence by each subtype (Holtzworth-Munroe & Stuart, 1994). Additionally, these studies have limited their samples to men who were seeking treatment for marital violence, were in treatment at the time of assessment (e.g., Hamberger & Hastings, 1986; Saunders, 1992), or relied on victim reports to categorize batterers (Gondolf, 1987). Men seeking or in treatment for marital violence have been found to be distinct from the larger population of batterers who are not court referred. Furthermore, the overreliance on self-report data in these studies places an additional caution in interpreting their findings.

In contrast to previous typology studies, Gottman et al. (1995) examined physiological responding in a community sample of moderate-to-severe violent couples as a basis for distinguishing these subtypes. Given that physiological responding has been related to criminality, antisocial behavior, and hostility, it was hypothesized that this class of variables would be relevant to maritally violent men and may be particularly characteristic of generally violent batterers. Additionally, Gottman et al. (1995) collected observational data on affect displayed during a marital interaction task with physiological responding, and self-report data. Collateral information was collected from the wives of the violent men. Theirs was the first study to combine observational, psychophysiological, and self-report perspectives.

Gottman et al. (1995) examined heart rate reactivity, a measure of physiological responding, as a basis for distinguishing these subtypes on their use of violence. Husbands who lowered their heart rates parasympathetically below baseline levels during the first 5 minutes of a marital interaction task were classified as Type 1 batterers, compared to the remaining husbands whose heart rates increased during marital conflict (classified as Type 2). Results showed that these two types differentiated themselves on measures thought to be characteristic of all batterers. Of the Type 1 husbands, 78% reported observing bidirectional or unilateral father to mother violence, compared to 22% in the Type 2 group (Jacobson et al., 1995). Interestingly, 23% of the Type 2 husbands reported witnessing unilateral father to mother violence, compared with 0% of Type 1 men. Type 1 husbands also were significantly more likely than Type 2 husbands to be violent toward friends, strangers, coworkers, and bosses; and they were more likely to use more severe violence (e.g., threatening or using a knife or a gun) against their wives. Additionally, Type 1 men had higher rates of

anger and verbal aggression, specifically belligerence and contempt, and were more likely to score high on personality profiles of antisocial, thought disordered, drug dependent, and aggressive sadistic types.

Thus, Gottman et al.'s results support the general conclusions of two types of batterers—those who are violent only with their wives, and those who are also violent outside the marriage (Holtzworth-Munroe & Stuart, 1994)—and that heart rate reactivity as a physiological marker is a potential index variable for building a typology. Gottman et al. believe the differences in exposure to parental violence in the histories of Type 1 and Type 2 men may indicate that the violence among Type 2 men has more to do with attitudes toward women than the battering exhibited by Type 1 men. The authors conclude that the parasympathetically driven heart rate deceleration in Type 1 men may be in the service of focused attention, and that the task of this attention may be the manipulation and control of their partners, such that her retaliation is minimized and her fear of her partner is increased. Gottman et al. state that Type 1 male batterers may not have impulse control problems at all but in fact may exercise too much control over their physiology. Future research to replicate these findings with a larger sample, with procedures to lengthen the baseline and more exactly determine the physiological mechanisms, are needed to determine the stability of these findings.

Characteristics of Battered Women

Early psychiatric studies adopted the stereotyped view that battered women were masculine, masochistic, frigid, or overly emotional, with a poor sense of reality or inappropriate sexual expression (Stark & Flitcraft, 1991). As researchers moved away from victim-blaming psychopathological explanations of violence, they found the women they interviewed who were subjected to frequent battering had developed significant psychological symptoms and that these symptoms were consistent across victims (Gelles, 1974; Straus, Gelles, & Steinmetz, 1980; Walker, 1979, 1984). Psychological sequelae found included anxiety, depression, substance abuse, low self-esteem, feelings of helplessness, sleep and appetite disturbances, fatigue, and disruption of interpersonal relationships (Astin, Lawrence, & Foy, 1993). Gelles and Harrop's (1989) random sampling of a cross-section of more than 3,000 women found that significant psychological distress (depression, stress, and somatic complaints) is associated with being a victim of marital violence, and that the distress increases with the severity of violence.

Noting that these sequelae were similar to those of individuals who survived a variety of traumatic events, some researchers and battered women's advocates have suggested that post-traumatic stress disorder (PTSD) is also the most accurate diagnosis for many victims of violence (Browne, 1993; Davidson & Foa, 1991; Goodman, Koss, & Russo, 1993; Koss, 1990). Studies that have attempted to directly assess rates of PTSD symptomatology have found estimates ranging from 45% in community samples (Houskamp & Foy, 1991) to 84% in shelters (Astin et al., 1993; Kemp, Rawlings, & Green, 1991).

Despite the popularity of the PTSD diagnosis to describe the symptoms of battered women, the diagnosis does not account for many of the symptoms manifested by victims of violence, thus failing to capture the depth and complexity of responses demonstrated by women in a violent relationship (Dutton, 1995). Most research that has focused on women's responses to assault by their male partners has been based on clinical interviews of the victim. Other studies have administered measures to women who have left their relationships, thus failing to account for differences in responses between women who have sought help through shelter services or community clinics and those who stayed in their relationship. Barely a handful of studies have examined rates of PTSD directly (Astin et al., 1993; Houskamp & Foy, 1991; Kemp et al., 1991), and their findings are limited by assessment variability, small sample size, and variability in sample selection.

Given the heterogeneity of the results, it may be that wives in violent relationships are as heterogeneous as their battering husbands. Sequelae that result from being in a violent relationship may vary by the type of batterer to whom one is married. Gottman et al. (1995) found that wives interacting with Type 1 husbands, who were more generally violent and verbally aggressive than Type 2 husbands, showed significantly less anger and more sadness and defensiveness than wives interacting with Type 2 husbands. The authors inferred that wives of Type 1 men may not feel safe expressing anger and may fear a heightened aggressive response if they did show anger. Gottman et al. concluded that this fear response may be why wives of Type 1 men are less likely to divorce than wives of Type 2 men (0% separation/divorce rate vs. 26.5%, respectively). Although this study did not attempt to directly examine psychological correlates of being married to a batterer, the findings are nonetheless provocative and indicative of the effect of relationship dynamics on battered women's responses to violence.

The traumatic nature of domestic violence must be taken into account to understand the behavior of battered women. Without a contextual interpretation of findings, researchers risk "pathologizing the victim." Characteristics of women in violent relationships should be viewed as risk factors or responses to abuse rather than etiological factors in the abuse. Consequently, characteristics associated with being a woman in a violent relationship can aid in our understanding of the phenomenon of husband to wife violence but do not change the responsibility of the batterer for his own behavior.

Characteristics of Violent Couples

Few researchers have studied the marital dynamics and patterns associated with violence in couples. Marital maladjustment and communication problems have been studied as factors contributing to marital violence (Hudson & McIntosh, 1981; Rosenbaum & O'Leary, 1981; Straus, Gelles, & Steinmetz, 1980; Telch & Lindquist, 1984) but have limited their methodology to administration of questionnaire data. Recently, researchers have utilized techniques developed in the marital interaction literature, specifically communication assessments. Interactional coding systems that examine marital communication (e.g., the Marital Interaction Coding System, MICS-III; Weiss & Summers, 1983) and expressions of affect during communication tasks (e.g., Specific Affect Coding System, SPAFF; Gottman, 1994) have been utilized to collect observational data during these marital interaction tasks.

Margolin and her associates (Burman, John, & Margolin, 1992; Burman, Margolin, & John, 1993; Margolin, John, & Gleberman,

1988) made the first attempt to use observational measures to study actual communication patterns in violent versus nonviolent couples and the affective responses displayed by both partners. Physically aggressive husbands were found to be more negative and evidenced more physiological arousal than their maritally distressed nonviolent counterparts; they tended to control the outcome of discussion by using coercive techniques more frequently than their wives. Wives in violent marriages, however, exhibited more negative behavior during the middle of the interaction than nonviolent wives; by the end of the interaction, they were indistinguishable. The investigators interpreted these findings as evidence that wives in violent marriages tend to back down to avoid further antagonization of their violent husbands. From sequential analyses, Margolin et al. (1988) found that wives in physically aggressive relationships were significantly more likely to reciprocate negative behavior than wives in the nonviolent control group. In contrast, violent husbands, although likely to become defensive after their partner's negative behavior, were no more likely to reciprocate negative behavior than husbands from other groups (Burman et al., 1992).

Although the results are provocative, the findings of Margolin et al. (1988) are to be interpreted with caution for several reasons. Couples in their physically aggressive group exhibited lower scores on marital satisfaction than couples in other groups, thus confounding the influence of physical aggression versus marital distress on the results. Additionally, almost half of the distressed nonviolent sample reported some physical abuse in the past year, and the majority reported a prior history of aggressive behavior. Finally, the couples in the physically aggressive group exhibited low levels of violence, thus creating ambiguity in the comparison between the control groups and the physically aggressive group.

Cordova, Jacobson, Gottman, Rushe, and Cox (1993) sought to test the findings from Margolin et al.'s studies, using a moderate-to-severe violent sample and a control group of distressed nonviolent couples matched on levels of marital distress. Couples' communication assessments were coded using the MICS-III, which delineated classes of aversive, facilitative, and neutral behaviors (Weiss & Summers, 1983). Interaction patterns were examined using lag sequential analyses to determine how the probability of an aversive behavior occurring changed over the course of the argument. Specifically, the authors tested for the presence of negative reciprocity, the tendency of spouses to continue negative behavior once it has begun. The sequential analyses provided no support for coercion theory hypothesis that husbands' aversiveness was reinforced by the cessation of wives' aversiveness. During the conflict discussions, wives gave no indications of using positive or neutral behavior to stop the husbands' aversiveness. Rather, wives of violent husbands were as likely as their husbands to reciprocate negative behavior. Thus, despite a history of being subjected to physical abuse, wives of violent husbands chose to stand up to rather than surrender to their husbands.

Despite the methodological improvements of Cordova et al.'s (1993) study, the generalizability of their findings are limited, because the laboratory interactions may not be representative of what transpires in the natural environment. In the most rigorous study to date, Jacobson et al. (1994) collected data on individual descriptions of home arguments, as well as laboratory interactions, to provide a more naturalistic index of the couples' interaction. From a community sample of couples, self-reported and observational data on affect, psychophysiology, and verbal content of violent arguments were collected over a series of two laboratory assessments.

During the nonviolent interactions and descriptions, both violent husbands and their wives displayed more anger than their distressed nonviolent counterparts. Examination of the more provocative expressions of anger, such as verbal aggression (e.g., belligerence and contempt), revealed that violent husbands were more belligerent and contemptuous than distressed nonviolent husbands. Jacobson et al. (1994) replicated the belligerence and contempt in violent husbands and found a surprisingly similar rate of belligerence and contempt in the wives. Violent wives also demonstrated higher levels of physiological arousal, tension, and fear than their distressed nonviolent counterparts. Contrary to popular conceptions of the violent relationship consisting of the volatile husband and the frightened wife, these authors found spouses who were equally angry and verbally aggressive.

Within the violent arguments, violence by the husband escalated in response to nonviolent as well as violent behaviors by the wife, including attempts by the wife to withdraw during the violent argument. Neither husbands nor wives reported any behavior that predicted cessation of violence by the husband. In contrast, violence by wives escalated only in response to violence or emotional abuse by their husbands. Thus, Jacobson et al.'s (1994) results confirm clinical descriptions that during violent arguments, once the violence starts, the wife can do nothing to stop it and husbands are the perpetrators of violence.

Jacobson et al.'s (1994) findings also bring to light important gender differences in the use of violence. Although the authors found a high level of bilateral violence in their sample, only violence by the husband produced fear in their partner. The authors conclude that this difference accounts for the unique ability of husbands to use violence as a means of psychological control over their partners. Additionally, wives in these violent relationships differentiated themselves from their husbands in their seemingly competing affects of tension, fear, and sadness, even though they matched their husbands on levels of verbal aggression. The authors interpret the violent wives' intense anger, combined with fear and sadness, to be a part of the experience of helplessness reported by battered women (Walker, 1984). The ambivalence associated with these competing affective responses may be an important component of an abusive relationship.

Longitudinal Research

Although one of the major questions in domestic violence research is how these relationships change over time, few studies have attempted to collect follow-up data on couples. Most longitudinal research on marital violence was conducted with women seeking aid at battered women's shelters. Very few studies have examined changes over time in violent relationships with a community sample or gathered data from both husband and wife. O'Leary and his associates (Murphy & O'Leary, 1989; O'Leary et al., 1989) collected longitudinal data on a community sample of engaged couples. O'Leary et al. (1989) found that partners who

used physical aggression before marriage were significantly likely to be violent 30 months later, giving evidence for the stability of physical aggression within relationships. O'Leary et al. (1989) found significant reductions in the physical aggression of women from before marriage to 18 and 30 months after marriage, but similar reductions were not found for men. Murphy and O'Leary (1989) found that individuals' own psychological aggression and aggression used by their partners predicted their first instances of violence in the marriage. Surprisingly, prior levels of marital distress were not predictive of first instances of aggression. Murphy and O'Leary concluded that the way couples resolve conflict, rather than distress in the relationship, is critical in understanding the development of marital violence.

Babcock, Jacobson, Gottman, and Cordova (1994) collected both observational and self-reported data at first assessment and 2 years later from a community sample of couples displaying moderate-to-severe levels of violence. In determining predictors of battered women leaving abusive relationships, they found that decision-making styles, sociological variables, and psychological symptoms were not adequate predictors for divorce in violent couples. Rather, they found the following variables in the wives to be pertinent to the relationship, specifically use of physical aggression, wives who feel isolated as a result of the relationship, physiological arousal in the wives, and use of defensiveness. Inclusion of these variables in a discriminant function analysis allowed the authors to correctly classify marital status 2 years later with 95% accuracy. Rather than being helpless, depressed, and dependent, it appears that women who are angry, defensive, aggressive, physiologically aroused, and even violent are the ones who will later divorce. Babcock et al. (1994) interpreted the constellation of these variables as a reflection of the wife who will divorce as one who will stand up for herself, using physical as well as verbal means. In their analysis, the bilaterally violent couples were particularly unstable and likely to divorce 2 years later.

LEGAL RESPONSES TO DOMESTIC VIOLENCE

Advocates of battered women have argued for the use of arrest as a means of halting domestic violence. Although it is not seen as a cure-all for marital violence, arrest is viewed by advocates as a means of empowerment for women, conveying both a message of societal intolerance for violence against women and availability of immediate protection to women in an abusive relationship (Holtzworth-Munroe, Beatty, & Anglin, 1995).

Sherman and Berk (1984) conducted one of the most influential studies on the effect of arrest on domestic assault. In this study, more than 300 cases of misdemeanor domestic assault in the Minneapolis area were assigned randomly to one of three conditions: (a) arrest of the suspect, (b) mediation and advice, or (c) separation of the couple. Over a 6-month period, the rate of recidivism of subjects who were arrested was approximately half the rate of subjects who had not been arrested, indicating that arrest was an effective deterrent against domestic violence (Holtzworth-Munroe et al., 1995). And most important, the reduced recidivism rate appeared to have been produced largely with repeat offenders, with only 19% of this group assaulting their wives after having been arrested

(Dutton, 1995). Impressed by the results of the Minneapolis study, the Attorney General of the United States recommended that arrest be made standard treatment in cases of misdemeanor domestic assault (U.S. Attorney General's Task Force on Domestic Violence, 1984) and police departments nationally decided to either allow or mandate arrest as the standard procedure for dealing with misdemeanor domestic assault (Dutton, 1995).

The National Institute of Justice funded replication studies in several major cities in response to increased interest in the effects of arrest on domestic violence. All replication studies examined cases of misdemeanor assault and improved on the initial Minneapolis study by separating determination of the eligibility of a case from random assignment to treatment (Holtzworth-Munroe et al., 1995). Police determined eligibility on arrival at the scene and then called a central number to obtain treatment assignment. In contrast to the initial study, rates of compliance with assigned treatment were high and outcome (at a minimum 6-month follow-up) was determined by both official records and victim interviews (Holtzworth-Munroe et al., 1995).

Results of the replication studies were mixed, however. In Omaha, Nebraska, Dunford, Huizinga, and Elliott (1990) found at a 6-month follow-up that arrest was no more effective in reducing recidivism than mediation or separation. In addition, cases assigned to the informal treatments, particularly mediation, tended to have lower rates of arrest recidivism at a 12-month follow-up than those assigned to arrest (Holtzworth-Munroe et al., 1995).

Hirschell, Hutchinson, Dean, Kelley, and Pesackis (1990) replicated the experiment in Charlotte, North Carolina, adding police-issued citations as a fourth treatment option and involving the entire police force 24 hours per day. At a 6-month follow-up, no significant group differences were found in the prevalence of recidivism, and arrest did not differ from the other conditions in incidence of recidivism (Holtzworth-Munroe et al., 1995).

In Milwaukee, Wisconsin, Sherman et al. (1992) examined whether arrest reduces recidivism for only certain types of offenders (Dutton, 1995). They found 7 to 9 months following the presenting incident that the arrest group had a higher rate of recidivism than the nonarrest group. Although the increase in rate of recidivism was small in magnitude, it was consistent across all measures of repeat violence (Dutton, 1995). Interestingly, arrest deterred violence among men who were employed or married but escalated violence among men who had a prior record of arrest, were unemployed, had less than a high school education, were not married, or were African American. The highest rates of recidivism occurred among unemployed men who received the short-arrest treatment. The authors described those men for whom arrest increased violence as "socially marginal," or those who had less stake in social conformity, and concluded that arrest works only for those who have something to lose by being arrested (Dutton, 1995). Therefore, in contrast with the original Minneapolis results, none of the replication studies to date supports an overall deterrent effect of arrest relative to other police interventions (Holtzworth-Munroe et al., 1995).

Court-mandated treatment can provide a means through which repeat wife abusers can learn alternative methods for conflict management, confront their attitudes toward women, improve their ability to identify and express anger, and have the negative conse-quences of their violence made salient to them (Dutton, 1995; for a review of treatment for domestic violence, see Holtzworth-Munroe et al., 1995). In combination with arrest, it can serve both didactic and deterrent functions in demonstrating to the assaulter that his behavior is socially unacceptable and will be met with legal sanctions. Furthermore, the combination of arrest with treatment emphasizes to the batterer personal responsibility for his use of violence (Dutton, 1995).

Rosenfeld (1992), in a review of 26 studies of treatment programs for marital violence, found that treatment seems to reduce police measures of recidivism by approximately 66%. However, the majority of the treatment studies reviewed were plagued with methodological problems, including small sample size and high subject attrition, lack of adequate control groups and random assignment to treatment, inconsistent use of outcome measures across studies, and follow-up periods too short to adequately assess the effects of treatment (Holtzworth-Munroe et al., 1995), making it difficult to assert the efficacy of treatment. Given that most treatment interventions are short term, we must question whether such interventions can effectively treat what is often a chronic and severe problem (Holtzworth-Munroe et al., 1995). Those men who enter the criminal justice system may be mostly Type 1 batterers, who, with a history of severe psychological and physical abuse, general violence, antisocial personality disorders, drug dependence, and low physiological reactivity, may be less likely to respond to treatment (Jacobson et al., 1995). Such interventions might be better matched with Type 2s. Other modes of treatment, such as conjoint therapy, would be contraindicated for Type 1 men and may be unethical. For wives who are not afraid of their partners, which is more the case for Type 2 men, conjoint therapy can be attempted, with appropriate controls to minimize the risk of violence during the course of treatment.

If psychotherapy is going to be successful in the treatment of domestic violence, it may need to be integrated with the larger community such that there is coordination between treatment providers, police officers, probation officers, prosecutors, judges, and advocates (Jacobson et al., 1995). The *Duluth model* (Pence & Paymar, 1993) is an example of such an intervention, as treatment includes attention to the entire social context of battering through such communitywide organizing. Although evaluations of such community interventions have shown reduced rates of recidivism compared to arrest alone (Pence & Shepard, 1988), these assessments suffer from the same methodological limitations noted in the treatment literature (Gelles, 1993). Nevertheless, the model's potential for reducing recidivism merits the attention of empirical scrutiny.

INTERVENTIONS IN MEDICAL SETTINGS

Whereas intervention for batterers is likely to occur through contacts with the legal system, wives are more likely to have contact in health care settings, where medical treatment is administered for injuries received from physical assault. Cantos, Neidig, and O'Leary (1994) found that significantly more women than their husbands sought medical assistance for injuries. Studies suggest that as many as 30% of women treated in emergency departments have injuries or symptoms related to physical abuse (McLeer &

Anwar, 1989), and injuries inflicted by a male partner result in 4.4 physician visits per year per 100 women (Schulman, 1979).

However, only 7.3% of severe assaults result in any medical attention (Stets & Straus, 1990). This low percentage is attributed to several factors, including poor assessment for domestic violence, failure to identify victims, physicians' fear of retaliation or desire to remain uninvolved, and punitive or neglectful responses by medical personnel that place the woman at greater risk for injury (Stark & Flitcraft, 1991). As hospital departments provide for many women the first opportunity to find support, assistance, or protection, the implementation of staff education, policies, and procedures for assessment of domestic violence can help increase the rate of identification of battered women and prevent further abuse.

In response to the serious health consequences spousal abuse poses to women, as well as the demand on hospital resources, the U.S. Department of Health and Human Services (Public Health Service, 1991) instituted as a national health objective for the year 2000 that at least 90% of hospital emergency departments have protocols for routinely identifying, treating, and referring victims of domestic violence. Stark and Flitcraft (1991), based on their review of health care settings, outline several interventions to increase identification of abused women. Use of direct questioning regarding both the nature of the current injuries and her history of traumatic injury is cited as a crucial step in patient identification. Routine intake of a trauma history allows for identification of women who are at-risk for future and more severe assaults. In addition to disclosure by the victim, identification of sexualized injuries on the victim (e.g., injury during pregnancy, central injuries to the chest area), gynecological and psychosomatic complaints often are indicators of abuse. As the greatest proportion of medical visits by battered women do not involve trauma but general medical, obstetric, behavioral, and psychiatric presentations, training in the assessment and intervention in spousal abuse should not be limited to emergency or trauma settings (Stark & Flitcraft, 1991). Once the woman's level of fear and capacity for self-protection is assessed, steps toward ensuring her safety and preventing future assaults can be implemented. Hospitals that have used these methods of identification and assessment have yielded consistent results, with some institutions increasing their rate of identification of battered women almost sixfold (McLeer & Anwar, 1989).

BEHAVIOR AND DETERRENCE BY WIVES

The potential for the impact of arrest and treatment is limited, because only 14.5% of wife assaulters come in contact with the police (Schulman, 1979; Straus & Gelles, 1985), with 21.2% of those cases resulting in arrest, and 0.5% receiving a conviction (Dutton, 1995). Therefore, only a small fraction of repeat assaulters are subjected to intervention by the criminal justice system. Medical personnel similarly are limited in their preventive efforts, with only 5% of domestic violence cases being detected by physicians (Goldberg & Tomlanovich, 1984). Examination of survey data reveals that the largest contributor to the prevention of recidivist wife assault is some combination of extralegal factors that prevents one third of men who have assaulted their wives from repeating the act within a year (Dutton, 1995).

Research has shown that one of the most influential of these factors include wives' reactions to their husbands' violence. Fagan (1989) and Bowker (1983) found that fear of divorce and fear of loss of the relationship were cited more often by wives than threat of legal sanction as factors that enabled batterers to desist and enter treatment (Dutton, 1995). Bowker (1983) found that battered women reported social disclosure of the assaults to be as effective as legal intervention in halting their husbands' abusive behavior. In addition, belief in the seriousness of their wives' threat of separation or divorce and disclosure of their violence to the police had as great an influence on their future violent behavior as their belief in the likelihood of future arrest (Bowker, 1983; Dutton, Hart, Kennedy, & Williams, 1992).

However, examination of the long-term effects of these interventions on reducing violence and facilitating wives' termination of the relationship has yielded mixed results. Sullivan, Campbell, Angelique, Eby, and Davidson (1994) examined the effects of an advocacy intervention program for women who left their abusive husbands. The intervention involved meeting with an advocate 4 to 6 hours per week for the first 10 weeks after leaving the shelter. Participants were randomly assigned to the intervention. At a 6-month follow-up, women in both groups reported increased social support, less depression, and increased sense of empowerment. However, although both groups reported some decrease in physical abuse over time, no statistically significant differences were found between those who had advocates and those who did not. Also, the intervention did not significantly increase the proportion of women who left their assailants. Use of temporary restraining orders, which forbid the assailant to come within a specified distance of the victim, have been found to have some deterrent value, but men who were unemployed, abused alcohol, or had a prior arrest record were more likely to violate the restraining order (Chaudhuri & Daly, 1992). Although these interventions may not have an effect on deterrence, they are influential in empowering battered women. Use of these strategies may not be as successful with husbands who do not perceive their wives' moves toward independence as a threat and when use of severe violence could successfully curtail the wife from leaving her husband (Gottman et al., 1995).

PREVENTION OF DOMESTIC VIOLENCE

Given that patterns of violent behavior may be learned early in life and that efforts made to treat domestic violence are limited in their efficacy, strategies aimed at preventing violence are warranted. The most well developed and researched of such programs are those aimed at preventing marital distress, which is associated with domestic violence (O'Leary et al., 1989; Rosenbaum & O'Leary, 1981). Markman's Prevention and Relationship and Enhancement Program (PREP), over the course of five sessions, instructs couples in constructive communication and conflict resolution skills, gender differences in communication styles, and other skills directed toward increasing intimacy in their relationships. Couples who participated in PREP, compared to couples who did not participate, reported fewer instances of spousal aggression 3 to 5 years after the intervention (Markman, Renick, Floyd, Stanley, & Clements, 1993).

As stated previously, research has demonstrated that use of physical aggression before marriage predicts use of violence after marriage and stability in the use of aggression over time. These violent patterns may be evident in dating relationships and as early as midadolescence (O'Leary, 1994). Approximately 35% of college students have reported at least one instance of violence in a dating relationship, as either the aggressor, victim, or both (Sugarman & Hotaling, 1989). Cascardi and O'Leary (1990) found that high school students may be at risk as well, with 26.6% of students reporting they had used aggression in their relationships and 34% having experienced violence. As a result, efforts are underway to target these student populations with programs designed to educate young persons about the prevalence, causes, and consequences of dating aggression; modify attitudes related to the use of violence; and teach skills for effective communication and conflict management that do not involve the use of violence (O'Leary, 1994). Jaffe, Sudermann, Reitzel, and Killip (1992) reported the results of such an intervention on high school students and found that significant, positive attitude, knowledge, and behavior changes were found at a posttest, 6 weeks later.

However, such preventitive efforts might be limited in their efficacy with Type 1s, whose patterns of violent behavior begin in childhood, are reinforced by the societal context, progress to antisocial behavior, and culminate in severe battering and general violence (Jacobson et al., 1995). Interventions directed at this population of batterers might do well to draw from programs directed at adult offenders (see Rice & Harris, Chapter 40, this volume, for a review) and juvenile delinquents (see Tolan & Gorman-Smith, Chapter 38, this volume, for a review), and target maintenance of control over women as a reinforcer and skills deficits that promote use of violence for conflict resolution. As conduct disorder is a precursor to juvenile delinquency and antisocial conduct, interventions that target acting-out behavior in children and parental practices that reinforce those behaviors (e.g., Greenberg, Coie, Dodge, & Bierman, 1989) may be crucial in preventing domestic violence with this population.

FUTURE DIRECTIONS

Research that has examined marital interactions of violent couples has provided substantial information about the conditions under which battering is most likely. Additionally, this research has yielded information about the characteristics of the partners of these marriages, Type 1s and Type 2s, and how their distinct use of psychological abuse and violence affects their partners. As Type 1s may constitute most of the battering population involved in the criminal justice system, being both psychologically abusive and physically violent, future studies should be directed toward this population, with prospective studies conducted to understand the relationship between childhood learning history, heart rate reactivity, and the developmental course of aggressive behavior in Type 1 batterers. Research that links current marital violence methodologies with studies of aggressive antisocial behavior is essential.

Development and research of primary prevention efforts are warranted, as current treatment approaches to domestic violence are ineffective against the population of batterers that produces enough severe and persistent violence to cause a social problem. In taking what is essentially a "Band-Aid" approach to domestic violence, these approaches attempt to instill change in individuals without addressing change in the social systems and culture of this subpopulation. Empirical investigations demonstrate that social and economic conditions that contribute to marginality and powerlessness in society are influential in maintaining domestic violence (e.g., Sherman et al., 1992); and until programs are developed that incorporate the criminal justice, therapeutic, advocacy, and community efforts, domestic violence will continue to be a growing national problem.

REFERENCES

Arias, I., & Beach, S. R. H. (1987). Validity of self-reports of marital violence. *Journal of Family Violence, 2*, 139–149.

Arias, I., Samios, M., & O'Leary, K. D. (1987). Prevalence and correlates of physical aggression during courtship. *Journal of Interpersonal Violence, 2*, 82–90.

Astin, M. C., Lawrence, K. J., & Foy, D. W. (1993). Posttraumatic stress disorder among battered women: Risk and resiliency factors. *Violence and Victims, 8*, 17–28.

Babcock, J. C., Jacobson, N. S., Gottman, J. M., & Cordova, J. C. (1994, November). Predictors of women leaving abusive relationships. In J. C. Babcock (Chair), *Longitudinal perspectives on domestic violence: Predicting changes in relationship status, satisfaction, and aggressive behavior.* Symposium conducted at the Association for the Advancement of Behavior Therapy, San Diego, CA.

Babcock, J. C., Waltz, J., Jacobson, N. S., & Gottman, J. M. (1993). Power and violence: The relation between communication patterns, power discrepancies, and domestic violence. *Journal of Consulting and Clinical Psychology, 61*, 40–50.

Bandura, A. (1979). The social learning perspective: Mechanisms of aggression. In H. Toch (Ed.), *Psychology of crime and criminal justice.* New York: Holt, Rinehart and Winston.

Barnett, O. W., & Fagan, R. W. (1993). Alcohol use in male spouse abusers and their female partners. *Journal of Family Violence, 8*, 1–25.

Bograd, M. (1988). Feminist perspectives on wife abuse: An introduction. In K. Yllo & M. Bograd (Eds.), *Feminist perspectives on wife abuse* (pp. 11–27). Newbury Park, CA: Sage Publications.

Bowker, L. H. (1983). *Beating wife beating.* Lexington, MA: Lexington Books.

Browne, A. (1993). Violence against women by male partners: Prevalence, outcomes, and policy implications. *American Psychologist, 48*, 1077–1087.

Browne, A., & Williams, K. R. (1989). Exploring the effect of resource availability and the likelihood of female-perpetrated homicides. *Law and Society Review, 23*, 75–94.

Browne, A., & Williams, K. R. (1993). Gender, intimacy, and lethal violence: Trends from 1976–1987. *Gender and Society, 7*, 78–98.

Browning, J., & Dutton, D. G. (1986). Assessment of wife assault with the Conflict Tactics Scale: Using couple data to quantify the differential reporting effect. *Journal of Marriage and the Family, 48*, 375–379.

Burman, B., John, R. S., & Margolin, G. (1992). Observed patterns of conflict in violent, nonviolent, and nondistressed couples. *Behavioral Assessment, 14*, pp. 15–37.

Burman, B., Margolin, G., & John, R. S. (1993). America's angriest home videos: Behavioral contingencies observed in home reenactments of marital conflict. *Journal of Consulting and Clinical Psychology, 61,* 28–39.

Caesar, P. L. (1986, August). Men who batter: A heterogeneous group. In L. K. Hamberger (Chair), *The male batterer: Characteristics of a heterogeneous population.* Symposium presented at the annual meeting of the American Psychological Association, Washington, DC.

Caesar, P. L. (1988). Exposure to violence in the families of origin among wife-abusers and maritally nonviolent men. *Violence and Victims, 3,* 49–63.

Cantos, A. L., Neidig, P. H., & O'Leary, K. D. (1994). Injuries of women and men in a treatment program for domestic violence. *Journal of Family Violence, 8,* 113–124.

Cascardi, M., & O'Leary, K. D. (1990). *Dating violence in high school: Prevalence and attributions.* Unpublished manuscript. State University of New York at Stony Brook.

Chaudhuri, M., & Daly, K. (1992). Do restraining orders help? Battered women's experience with male violence and the legal process. In E. S. Buzawa & C. G. Buzawa (Eds.), *Domestic violence: The changing criminal justice response.* Westport, CT: Auburn House.

Cordova, J. V., Jacobson, N. S., Gottman, J. M., Rushe, R., & Cox, G. (1993). Negative reciprocity and communication in couples with a violent husband. *Journal of Abnormal Psychology, 102,* 559–564.

Daly, M., & Wilson, M. (1988). *Homicide.* New York: Aldine.

Daly, M., Wilson, M., & Weghorst, S. J. (1982). Male sexual jealousy. *Ethology and Sociobiology, 3,* 11–27.

Davidson, J. R., & Foa, E. B. (1991). Diagnostic issues in posttraumatic stress disorder: Considerations for the *DSM-IV. Journal of Abnormal Psychology, 100,* 346–355.

Dobash, R. E., & Dobash, R. P. (1979). *Violence against wives: A case against patriarchy.* New York: Free Press.

Dunford, F. W., Huizinga, D., & Elliott, D. S. (1990). The role of arrest in domestic assault: The Omaha Police Experiment. *Criminology, 28,* 183–206.

Dutton, D. G. (1986). Wife assaulters' explanations for assault: The neutralization of self-punishment. *Canadian Journal of Behavioral Science, 18,* 381–390.

Dutton, D. G. (1988). *The domestic assault of women: Psychological and criminal justice perspectives.* Boston: Allyn & Bacon.

Dutton, D. G. (1995). *The domestic assault of women: Psychological and criminal justice perspectives* (2nd ed.). Vancouver, Canada: University of British Columbia Press.

Dutton, D. G., & Browning, J. J. (1988). Concern for power, fear of intimacy, and aversive stimuli for wife assault. In G. T. Hotaling, D. Finkelhor, J. T. Kirkpatrick, & M. A. Straus (Eds.), *Family abuse and its consequences: New directions in research* (pp. 163–175). Newbury Park, CA: Sage Publications.

Dutton, D. G., Hart, S. D., Kennedy, L. W., & Williams, K. R. (1992). Arrest and the reduction of repeat wife assault. In E. S. Buzawa & C. G. Buzawa (Eds.), *Domestic violence: The changing criminal justice response* (pp. 112–127). Westport, CT: Auburn House.

Dutton, D. G., & Hemphill, K. J. (1992). Patterns of socially desirable responding among perpetrators and victims of wife assault. *Violence and Victims, 7,* 29–39.

Dutton, D. G., & Painter, S. (1993a). Emotional attachments in abusive relationships: A test of traumatic bonding theory. *Violence and Victims, 8,* 105–120.

Dutton, D. G., & Painter, S. (1993b). The battered women syndrome: Effects of severity and intermittency of abuse. *American Journal of Orthopsychiatry, 63,* 614–622.

Edelson, J. L., & Brygger, M. P. (1984). *Gender differences in reporting of battering incidences.* Paper presented at the Second National Conference for Family Violence Researchers, Durham, NH.

Elbow, M. (1977). Theoretical considerations of violent marriages. *Social Casework, 58,* 515–526.

Elliot, F. (1977). The neurology of explosive rage: The episodic dyscontrol syndrome. In M. Roy (Ed.), *Battered women: A psychological study of domestic violence.* New York: Van Nostrand.

Fagan, J. A. (1989). Cessation of family violence: Deterrence and dissuasion. In L. Ohlin & M. Tonry (Eds.), *Family violence.* Chicago: University of Chicago Press.

Fagan, J. A., Stewart, D. K., & Hansen, K. V. (1983). Violent men or violent husbands? Background factors and situational correlates. In D. Finkelhor, R.J. Gelles, G.T. Hotaling, & M.A. Straus (Eds.), *The dark side of families: Current family violence research.* Beverly Hills, CA: Sage Publications.

Faulk, M. (1974, July). Men who assault their wives. *Medicine, Science, and the Law,* 180–183.

Finkelhor, D., & Yllo, K. (1985). *License to rape: Sexual abuse of wives.* New York: Holt, Rinehart and Winston.

Follette, V. M., & Alexander, P. C. (1992). Dating violence: Current and historical correlates. *Behavioral Assessment, 14,* 39–52.

Follingstad, D. R., Brennan, A. F., Hause, E. S., Polek, D. S., & Rutledge, L. L. (1991). Factors moderating physical and psychological symptoms of battered women. *Journal of Family Violence, 6,* 81–95.

Frieze, I. H., Knoble, J., Washburn, C., & Zomnir, G. (1980, March). Types of battered women. Paper presented at the meeting of the Annual Research Conference of the Association for Women in Psychology, Santa Monica, CA.

Galdston, R. (1965). Observations on children who have been physically abused and their parents. *American Journal of Psychiatry, 122,* 440–443.

Ganley, A. L. (1981). *Participant's manual: Court-mandated therapy for men who batter—A three day workshop for professionals.* Washington, DC: Center for Women Policy Studies.

Ganley, A. L. (1989). Integrating feminist and social learning analyses of aggression: Creating multiple models for intervention with men who batter. In P. L. Caesar & L. K. Hamberger (Eds.), *Treating men who batter: Theory, practice, and programs* (pp. 196–235). New York: Springer.

Gayford, J. J. (1975). Wife battering: A preliminary survey of 100 cases. *British Medical Journal, 1,* 195–197.

Geffner, R., Rosenbaum, A., & Hughes, H. (1988). Research issues concerning family violence. In V. B. Van Hasselt, R. L. Morrison, A. S. Bellack, & M. Hersen (Eds.), *Handbook of family violence* (pp. 457–481). New York: Plenum.

Gelles, R. J. (1974). *The violent home: A study of physical aggression between husbands and wives.* Newbury Park, CA: Sage Publications.

Gelles, R. J. (1987). The family and its role in the abuse of children. *Psychiatric Annals, 17,* 229–232.

Gelles, R. J. (1993). Constraints against family violence: How well do they work? *American Behavioral Scientist, 36,* pp. 575–586.

Gelles, R. J., & Cornell, C. P. (1990). *Intimate violence in families.* Newbury Park, CA: Sage Publications.

Gelles, R. J., & Harrop, J. W. (1989). Violence, battering, and psychological distress among women. *Journal of Interpersonal Violence, 4,* 400–420.

Gelles, R. J., & Straus, M. A. (1979). Determinants of violence in the family: Toward a theoretical integration. In W. Burr, R. Hill, I. I. Nye, & I. Reiss (Eds.), *Contemporary theories about the family* (Vol. 1) New York: Free Press.

Goldberg, W. G., & Tomlanovich, M. C. (1984). Domestic violence victims in the emergency department: New findings. *JAMA, 251,* 3259–3264.

Gondolf, E. W. (1987). Who are those guys? Toward a behavioral typology of batterers. *Violence and Victims, 3,* 187–203.

Goodman, L. A., Koss, M. P., & Russo, N. F. (1993). Violence against women: Physical and mental health effects: II. Research findings. *Applied and Preventitive Psychology, 2,* 79–89.

Gottman, J. M. (1994). *What predicts divorce? The relationship between marital processes and marital outcomes.* Hillsdale, NJ: Erlbaum.

Gottman, J. M., Jacobson, N. S., Rushe, R. H., Shortt, J. W., Babcock, J., La Taillade, J. J., & Waltz, J. (1995). The relationship between heart rate reactivity, emotionally aggressive behavior and general violence in batterers. *Journal of Family Psychology, 9,* 227–248.

Greenberg, M. T., Coie, J., Dodge, K., & Bierman, K. (1989). *F.A.A.S.T. Track: Families and Schools Together.* National Institute of Mental Health Grant, R18 MH50951.

Hamberger, L. K., & Hastings, J. E. (1986). Personality correlates of men who abuse their partners: A cross validation study. *Journal of Family Violence, 1,* 323–341.

Hirschel, J. D., Hutchinson, I. W., Dean, C. W., Kelley, J. J., & Pesackis, C. E. (1990). *Charlotte Spouse Assault Replication Project: Final report.* Unpublished manuscript.

Holtzworth-Munroe, A. (1992). Social skill deficits in maritally violent men: Interpreting the data using a social information processing model. *Clinical Psychology Review, 12,* 605–617.

Holtzworth-Munroe, A., Beatty, S. B., & Anglin, K. (1995). The assessment and treatment of marital violence. In N. S. Jacobson & A. S. Gurman (Eds.), *Clinical handbook of couple therapy* (2nd ed.; pp. 317–339). New York: Guilford.

Holtzworth-Munroe, A., & Stuart, G. L. (1994). Typologies of male batterers: Three subtypes and the differences among them. *Psychological Bulletin, 116,* 479–497.

Holtzworth-Munroe, A., Waltz, J., Jacobson, N. S., Monaco, V., Fehrenbach, P. A., & Gottman, J. M. (1992). Recruiting nonviolent men as control subjects for research on marital violence: How easily can it be done? *Violence and Victims, 7,* 79–88.

Hotaling, G. T., & Sugarman, D. B. (1986). An analysis of risk markers in husband to wife violence: The current state of knowledge. *Violence and Victims, 1,* 101–124.

Houskamp, B. M., & Foy, D. W. (1991). The assessment of posttraumatic stress disorder in battered women. *Journal of Interpersonal Violence, 6,* 367–375.

Hudson, W. W., & McIntosh, S. R. (1981). The assessment of spouse abuse: Two quantifiable dimensions. *Journal of Marriage and the Family, 43,* 873–885.

Jacobson, N. S. (1994a). Rewards and dangers in researching domestic violence. *Family Process, 33,* 81–85.

Jacobson, N. S. (1994b). Contextualism is dead: Long live contextualism. *Family Process, 33,* 97–100.

Jacobson, N. S., Gottman, J. M., & Shortt, J. W. (1995). The distinction between Type 1 and Type 2 batterers—Further considerations: Reply to Ornduff et al. (1995), Margolin et al. (1995), and Walker (1995). *Journal of Family Psychology, 9,* 272–279.

Jacobson, N. S., Gottman, J. M., Waltz, J., Rushe, R., Babcock, J. & Holtzworth-Munroe, A. (1994). Affect, verbal content, and psychophysiology in the arguments of couples with a violent husband. *Journal of Consulting and Clinical Psychology, 62,* 982–988.

Jaffe, P., Suderman, M., Reitzel, D., & Killip, S. M. (1992). An evaluation of a secondary school primary prevention program on violence and intimate relationships. *Violence and Victims, 7,* 129–154.

Jouriles, E. N., & O'Leary, K. D. (1985). Interspousal reliability of reports of marital violence. *Journal of Consulting and Clinical Psychology, 53,* 419–421.

Kemp, A., Rawlings, E. I., & Green, B. L. (1991). Post-traumatic stress disorder (PTSD) in battered women: A shelter sample. *Journal of Traumatic Stress, 4,* 137–148.

Kempe, C. H., Silverman, F. N., Steele, B. F., Droegemuller, W., & Silver, H. (1962). The battered child syndrome. *Journal of the American Medical Association, 181,* 107–112.

Koss, M. P. (1990). The women's mental health research agenda: Violence against women. *American Psychologist, 45,* 374–380.

Langan, P. A., & Innes, C. A. (1986). *Preventing domestic violence against women.* Washington, DC: U.S. Department of Justice, Bureau of Justice Statistics.

La Taillade, J. J., Waltz, J., Jacobson, N. S., & Gottman, J. M. (1992, November). *Marital versus other interpersonal violence: An examination of differences and correlates.* Poster presented at the meeting of the Association for the Advancement of Behavior Therapy, Boston, MA.

Lentzner, H. R., & DeBerry, M. M. (1980). *Intimate victims: A study of violence among friends and relatives.* Washington, DC: U.S. Department of Justice, Bureau of Justice Statistics.

Locke, H. J., & Wallace, K. M. (1959). Short-term marital adjustment and prediction tests: Their reliability and validity. *Journal of Marriage and Family Living, 21,* 251–255.

Maiuro, R. D., Cahn, T. S., Vitaliano, P., Wagner, P., & Zegree, J. B. (1988). Anger, hostility, and depression in domestically violent versus generally assaultive men and nonviolent control subjects. *Journal of Consulting and Clinical Psychology, 56,* 17–23.

Margolin, G. (1979). Conjoint marital therapy to enhance anger management and reduce spouse abuse. *American Journal of Family Therapy, 7,* 13–23.

Margolin, G. (1987). The multiple forms of aggressiveness between marital partners: How do we identify them? *Journal of Marital and Family Therapy, 13,* 77–84.

Margolin, G., & Burman, B. (1993). Wife abuse versus marital violence: Different terminologies, explanations, and solutions. *Clinical Psychology Review, 13,* 59–73.

Margolin, G., John, R. S., & Gleberman, L. (1988). Affective responses to conflictual discussion in violent and nonviolent couples. *Journal of Consulting and Clinical Psychology, 56,* 24–33.

Markman, H. J., Renick, M. J., Floyd, F. J., Stanley, S. M., & Clements, M. (1993). Preventing marital distress through communication and conflict management training: A 4- and 5- year follow-up. *Journal of Consulting and Clinical Psychology, 61,* 70–77.

Martin, D. (1976). *Battered wives.* San Francisco: Glide.

McDonald, R., & Jouriles, E. N. (1991, September). Marital aggression and child behavior problems: Research findings, mechanisms, and intervention strategies. *The Behavior Therapist,* 189–192.

McLeer, S. V., & Anwar, R. (1989). A study of battered women presenting in an emergency room department. *Journal of Public Health, 79,* 65–66.

Murphy, C. M., & O'Leary, K. D. (1989). Psychological aggression predicts physical aggression in early marriage. *Journal of Consulting and Clinical Psychology, 57,* 579–582.

Ohrenstein, M. (1977). *Battered women: Statewide task force study of battered women.* Senate publication, available from the office of New York State Senate Minority Leader, Albany, NY.

O'Leary, K. D. (1994). *Prevention of dating violence.* National Institute of Mental Health Grant, ROI MH47801.

O'Leary, K. D., & Arias, I. (1988). Assessing agreement of reports of spouse abuse. In G. T. Hotaling, D. Finkelhor, J. T. Kilpatrick, & M. A. Straus (Eds.), *New directions in family violence research.* Newbury Park, CA: Sage Publications.

O'Leary, K. D., Barling, J., Arias, I., Rosenbaum, A., Malone, J., & Tyree, A. (1989). Prevalence and stability of physical aggression between spouses: A longitudinal analysis. *Journal of Consulting and Clinical Psychology, 57,* 263–268.

O'Leary, K. D., & Curley, A. D. (1986). Assertion and spouse abuse: Correlates of spouse abuse. *Journal of Marital and Family Therapy, 12,* 284–289.

O'Leary, K. D., & Murphy, C. M. (1991). Clinical issues in the assessment of spouse abuse. In R. T. Hammerman & M. Hersen (Eds.), *Assessment of family violence: A clinical and legal sourcebook.* New York: Wiley.

O'Leary, K. D., Vivian, D., & Malone, J. (1992). Assessment of physical aggression against women in marriage: The need for multimodal assessment. *Behavior Assessment, 14,* 5–14.

Pagelow, M. D. (1981). *Woman-battering: Victims and their experiences.* Beverly Hills, CA: Sage Publications.

Pence, E. (1989). Batterer programs: Shifting from community collusion to community confrontation. In P. L. Caesar & L. K. Hamberger (Eds.), *Treating men who batter: Theory, practice, and programs* (pp. 24–50). New York: Springer.

Pence, E., & Paymar, M. (1993). *Education groups for men who batter: The Duluth model.* New York: Springer.

Pence, E., & Shepard, M. (1988). Integrating feminist theory and practice: The challenge of the battered woman's movement. In K. Yllo & M. Bograd (Eds.), *Feminist perspectives on wife abuse* (pp. 282–298). Newbury Park, CA: Sage Publications.

Pizzey, E. (1974). *Scream quietly or the neighbors will hear.* London: Penguin.

Pressman, B., & Rothery, M. (1989). Introduction: Implications of assault against women for professional helpers. In B. Pressman, G. Cameron, & M. Rothery (Eds.), *Intervening with assaulted women: Current theory, research, and practice* (pp. 21–46). Hillsdale, NJ: Erlbaum.

Public Health Service. (1991). *Healthy people 2000: National health promotion and disease prevention objectives—full report with commentary.* Washington, DC: U.S. Department of Health and Human Services, Public Health Service. DHHS publication no. (PHS) 91-50212.

Riggs, D. S., Murphy, C. M., & O'Leary, K. D. (1989). Intentional falsification in reports of interpartner aggression. *Journal of Interpersonal Violence, 4,* 220–232.

Rosenbaum, A. (1988). Methodological issues in marital violence research. *Journal of Family Violence, 3,* 91–104.

Rosenbaum, A., & O'Leary, K. D. (1981). Marital violence: Characteristics of abusive couples. *Journal of Consulting and Clinical Psychology, 41,* 63–71.

Rosenbaum, A., & O'Leary, K. D. (1986). The treatment of marital violence. In N. S. Jacobson & A. S. Gurman (Eds.), *Clinical handbook of marital therapy* (pp. 385–405). New York: Guilford.

Rosenfeld, B. D. (1992). Court-ordered treatment of spouse abuse. *Clinical Psychology Review, 12,* 205–226.

Rousanville, B. J. (1978). Battered wives: Barriers to identification and treatment. *American Journal of Orthopsychiatry, 48,* 487–494.

Roy, M. (Ed.). (1977). *Battered women: A psychosociological study of domestic violence.* New York: Van Nostrand Reinhold.

Russell, D. E. H. (1982). *Rape in marriage.* New York: Macmillan.

Saakvitne, K. W., & Pearlman, L. A. (1993). The impact of internalized misogyny and violence against women on feminine identity. In E. P. Cook (Ed.), *Women, relationships, and power.* Alexandria, VA: American Counseling Association.

Saunders, D. G. (1992). A typology of men who batter: Three types derived from cluster analysis. *American Journal of Orthopsychiatry, 62,* 264–275.

Schalling, D., Edman, G., & Asberg, M. (1983). Impulsive cognitive style and ability to tolerate boredom: Psychological studies of temperamental vulnerability. In M. Zuckerman (Ed.), *Biological bases of sensation seeking, impulsivity, and anxiety* (pp. 110–137). Hillsdale, NJ: Erlbaum.

Schechter, S. (1982). *Women and male violence: The visions and struggle of the battered women's movement.* Boston: South End Press.

Schulman, M. (1979). *A survey of spousal violence against women in Kentucky.* Washington, DC: U.S. Department of Justice, Law Enforcement.

Schultz, L. G. (1960). The wife assaulter. *Journal of Social Therapy, 6,* 103–112.

Sherman, L. W., & Berk, R. A. (1984). The specific deterrents effects of arrest for domestic assault. *American Sociological Review, 49,* 261.

Sherman, L. W., Schmidt, J. D., Rogan, D. P., Smith, D. A., Gartin, P. R., Cohn, E. G., Collins, D. J., & Bacich, A. R. (1992). The variable effects of arrest on criminal careers: The Milwaukee domestic violence experiment. *Journal of Criminal Law and Criminology, 83,* 137–169.

Shields, N., & Hanneke, C. (1983). Attribution processes in violent relationships: Perceptions with violent husbands and their wives. *Journal of Applied Social Psychology, 13,* 515–527.

Shields, N., McCall, G., & Hanneke, C. (1988). Patterns of family and nonfamily violence: Violent husbands and violent men. *Violence and Victims, 3,* 83–97.

Snell, J., Rosenwald, R., & Robey, A. (1964). The wife beater's wife: A study of family interaction. *Archives of General Psychiatry, 11,* 107–113.

Snyder, D. K., & Fruchtman, L. A. (1981). Differential patterns of wife abuse: A data based typology. *Journal of Consulting and Clinical Psychology, 49,* 878–885.

Sonkin, D. J., Martin, D., & Walker, L. E. A. (Eds.). (1985). *The male batterer: A treatment approach.* New York: Springer.

Spanier, G. B. (1976). Measuring dyadic adjustment: New scales for assessing the quality of marriage and similar dyads. *Journal of Marriage and the Family, 38,* 15–28.

Spoont, M. R. (1992). Modulatory role of serotonin in neural information processing: Implications for human psychopathology. *Psychological Bulletin, 112,* 330–350.

Stark, E. (1993). Mandatory arrest of batterers: A reply to its critics. *American Behavioral Scientist, 36,* 651–680.

Stark, E., & Flitcraft, A. H. (1991). Spouse abuse. In M. Rosenberg & M. A. Fenley (Eds.), *Violence in America: A public health approach* (pp. 123–157). New York: Oxford University Press.

Steele, B., & Pollock, C. (1974). A psychiatric study of parents who abuse infants and small children. In R. Helfer and C. Kempe (Eds.), *The battered child.* Chicago: University of Chicago Press.

Stets, J. E., & Straus, M. A. (1990). Gender differences in reporting violence and its medical and psychological consequences. In M. A. Straus & R. J. Gelles (Eds.), *Physical violence in American families: Risk factors and adaptations to violence in 8,145 families* (pp. 151–164). New Brunswick, NJ: Transaction Books.

Straus, M. A. (1979). Measuring intrafamily conflict and violence: The Conflict Tactics (CT) Scales. *Journal of Marriage and the Family, 41,* 75–86.

Straus, M. A. (1990). Injury and frequency of assault and the "Representative sample fallacy" in measuring wife beating and child abuse. In M. A. Straus & R. J. Gelles (Eds.), *Physical violence in American families: Risk factors and adaptations to violence in 8,145 families.* New Brunswick, NJ: Transaction Books.

Straus, M. A., & Gelles, R. J. (1985, November). *Is family violence increasing? A comparison of the 1975 and 1985 national survey rates.* Paper presented at the American Society of Criminology, San Diego, CA.

Straus, M. A., & Gelles, R. J. (1986). Societal change and change in family violence from 1975 to 1985 as revealed by two national surveys. *Journal of Marriage and the Family, 48,* 465–479.

Straus, M. A., & Gelles, R. J. (1990). *Physical violence in American families: Risk factors and adaption to violence in 8,145 families.* New Brunswick, NJ: Transaction Books.

Straus, M. A., Gelles, R. J., & Steinmetz, S. (1980). *Behind closed doors: Violence in the American family.* Garden City, NY: Anchor.

Sugarman, D. B., & Hotaling, G. T. (1989). Dating violence: Prevalence, context, and risk markers. In M. A. Pirog-Good & J. E. Stets (Eds.), *Violence in dating relationships: Emerging social issues.* New York: Praeger.

Sullivan, C. M., Campbell, R., Angelique, H., Eby, K. K., & Davidson, W. (1994). An advocacy intervention program for women with abusive partners. *American Journal of Community Psychology, 22,* 101–122.

Szinovak, M. E. (1983). Using couple data as a methodological tool: The case of marital violence. *Journal of Marriage and the Family, 45,* 633–644.

Telch, C. F., & Lundquist, C. U. (1984). Violent versus nonviolent couples: A comparison of patterns. *Psychotherapy, 21,* 242–248.

Tolman, R. M. (1989). The development of a measure of psychological maltreatment of women by their male partners. *Violence and Victims, 4,* 159–177.

U.S. Attorney General's Task Force on Domestic Violence. (1984). Report. (Rep. 17). *Final Report.* Washington, DC: Government Printing Office.

Van Hasselt, V. B., Morrison, R. L., & Bellack, A. S. (1985). Alcohol use in wife abusers and their spouses. *Addictive Behavior, 10,* 127–135.

Virkkunen, M., & Linnoila, M. (1993). Serotonin in personality disorders with habitual violence and impulsivity. In S. Hodgkins (Ed.), *Mental disorders and crime* (pp. 227–243). Newbury Park, CA: Sage Publications.

Walker, L. E. (1979). *The battered woman.* New York: Harper and Row.

Walker, L. E. (1984). *The battered women syndrome.* New York: Springer.

Weiss, R. L., & Summers, K. J. (1983). Marital interaction coding system–III. In E. Filsinger (Ed.), *Marriage and family assessment* (pp. 35–115). Beverly Hills, CA: Sage Publications.

Widom, C. (1989). Does violence beget violence? A critical examination of the literature. *Psychological Bulletin, 106,* 13–28.

Wright, R. (1995, March 13). The biology of violence. *The New Yorker,* pp. 68–77.

Yllo, K., & Bograd, M. (1988). *Feminist perspectives on wife abuse.* Newbury Park, CA: Sage Publications.

Zabba, S. (1971). Battered children. *Transaction, 8,* 58–61.

CHAPTER 50

Firearms and Youth Violence

JEFFREY FAGAN and DEANNA L. WILKINSON

Current trends in the use and deadly consequences of guns among adolescents reflect a crisis of social, health, and moral dimensions. The health dimensions are self-evident: At a time when national homicide rates are declining, the increasing rates of firearm deaths among teenagers signal a problem of epidemic proportions. The social dimensions also are readily apparent: Deaths of adolescents due to firearm injuries are disproportionately concentrated among non-Whites, and especially among African American teenagers and young adults. Only in times of civil war have there been higher within-group homicide rates in the United States. There appears to be a process of self-annihilation among male African American teens in inner cities that is unprecedented in American history. That we, as a society, tolerate this suggests the moral dimensions of the crisis. The moral crisis is compounded by the fact that homicides occur at a higher rate in the United States than in the other industrialized countries (Archer & Gartner, 1984; Gartner, 1990; Rose & McClain, 1990).

Unfortunately, few studies have examined these sharp increases in gun fatalities among young males. The literature on guns and adolescents is characterized by broad surveys that gauge how often students bring weapons to school, and how their outlooks have been affected by the presence of firearms (see, e.g., LH Research, 1993; but see Sheley, Wright, & Smith, 1993, for an exception). Most of these studies suffer from selection biases by excluding dropouts and institutionalized youths with higher rates of violence and weapons use (see, e.g., Fagan, Piper, & Moore, 1986). Research on inner-city adolescents often has confounded firearm use with other forms of adolescent violence (e.g., physical and sexual assault, robbery) or comorbid problem behaviors (e.g., substance use, school dropout, or teenage pregnancy). But there is no evidence that firearm use by adolescents is part of a generalized pattern of adolescent violence or a maladaptive developmental outcome. In fact, few studies have distinguished adolescents who are violent from those violent adolescents who carry or use firearms.

Perhaps most important, no studies have examined the specific role of firearms in violent events. The LH Research (1993) survey suggests that the number of events in which guns are used are a small fraction of the number of events in which guns are present. Although several studies attribute violence to the dynamics and contingencies in contexts such as gang conflicts, drug markets, domestic disputes, or robberies (Cook, 1976; Fagan, 1993), few studies have addressed the dynamics or antecedents of firearm use in inner cities among adolescents or young males, especially the mechanisms that escalate gun possession to gun use. The social and cultural landscape of inner-city neighborhoods described by Anderson (1990, 1994; see also Canada, 1995) provides further support for research focused on situational transactions. Social networks within neighborhoods in which these events are likely to occur are adaptive organizational responses to specific social and cultural contexts. The social exchanges within these networks provide specific motivations and social values that may limit the range of behavioral choices once conflicts arise. That is, research on adolescent firearm use has not yet analyzed the interactions of the characteristics of the individuals involved, the interpersonal transactions and interactions between the parties, or how the presence of guns affects the outcomes of these interactions. And no studies have focused on specific social or neighborhood contexts that also shape the outcomes of putative violent events. Such an approach seems necessary to explain the increase in firearm fatalities among young African Americans and to locate the problem in the specific contexts in which these events occur.

A TRANSACTIONAL FRAMEWORK ON FIREARMS AND YOUTH VIOLENCE

Violence research has increasingly adopted this type of situational or transactional approach to explain violent transactions, including the use of firearms (Cook, 1976, 1980, 1983; Cornish, 1993a, 1993b, 1994; Felson, 1993; Felson & Steadman, 1983; Luckenbill, 1977; Katz, 1988; Luckenbill & Doyle, 1989; Oliver, 1994; Sommers & Baskin, 1993). Situational approaches view violent events as interactions involving the confluence of motivations, perceptions, technology (in this case, weapons), the social control attributes of the immediate setting, and the ascribed meaning and status attached to the violent act.

One advantage of this view is that it addresses both the motivations that bring individuals to situations in which firearms are used and also the actual transactions and decisions that comprise the event. Individuals may employ "scripts" as part of a strategy of "impression management" to gain status and dominance in potentially violent transactions (Cornish, 1994). These perspectives make possible explanations that sort out the proximal effects of the presence of firearms and other situational elements from the distal influences of social psychological factors. Situational approaches are dynamic "theories of action" (Cornish, 1993a, 1993b, 1994) that take into account both motivations and decision making within events.

This seems to be an especially important perspective for understanding the dynamics of adolescent weapon use. Explanations of firearm use among adolescents require several levels of analysis: the motivations for carrying/using weapons, the nature of everyday life that gives rise to conflicts that turn lethal, the "scripts" of adolescent life that lead to escalation (and the factors that underlie those scripts), and the role of weapons in the decision-making processes of adolescents when they engage in disputes or even predatory violence. The presence of firearms is not an outcome of other processes, but part of a dynamic and interactive social process in which the anticipation or reality of firearms alters the decisions leading to violence and the outcomes of violent events.

This chapter examines the role of firearms in violent events among adolescent males. First, we review the patterns of firearm use among adolescents over time and in specific eras. Comparing historical periods allows us to identify factors that seem to have contributed to the recent escalation and the present-day crises. Second, using an event-based approach, the chapter suggests a framework for explaining interactions that involve adolescents and firearms. This approach does not deny the importance of the individual attributes that bring people to situations but recognizes that once there, other processes shape the outcomes of these events. Because violence generally is a highly contextualized event, the chapter also focuses on how specific contexts shape decisions by adolescents to carry or use weapons, and how scripts are developed and shaped through diffusion within closed social groups. We conclude with discussion of possible implications for intervention and prevention efforts.

FIREARMS AND ADOLESCENT VIOLENCE: HISTORICAL PERSPECTIVES

The Evolving Role of Firearms in Adolescent Violence

Gun use by adolescents has been part of recurring delinquency problems in the United States since the Colonial Era. Delinquent groups and street gangs have been involved in struggles to dominate urban areas beginning in the Revolutionary War period.[1] However, guns were rarely part of violence between these groups until the era following the Draft Riots of 1863, when gangs fought with every weapon then available including pistols, muskets, and

(rarely) cannons (Sante, 1991). With the advent of concealable handguns around 1850, homicide rates rose slightly but not enough to offset a long downward trend that had begun early in the 19th century (Gurr, 1981). Nevertheless, as smaller and more portable guns were developed, they became an important part of the milieu of gangs and street groups over the ensuring decades. Guns played a strategic role in settling conflicts and asserting dominance in matters of honor, territory, and business.

Firearms played a prominent role in the growth of organized crime groups beginning in the 1920s. Organized crime groups employed teenagers and street gangs in a variety of support roles, from running numbers to serving as lookouts for illegal gambling operations or liquor distribution points (Haller, 1989). Firearms were a prominent part of the security system used to protect liquor shipments, and Haller quotes documents from bootleggers and smugglers that claimed there was more danger from "rum pirates" than from other bootleggers or the police. However, despite the involvement of adolescents in street gangs and emerging organized crime groups, there is little evidence that this led to the use of guns by teenagers.

Even in this era when youth gangs were increasingly a part of the urban landscape, there was little mention of adolescent use of firearms in homicides or robberies. For example, the analysis by Bourdouris (1970) of homicides in Detroit from 1926 to 1968 does not mention adolescents. The data provide a composite picture of homicides as the product of quarrels between family members, lovers, or two males. Murders during robberies were rare. Neither Wolfgang (1958), Zahn (1980), nor Reidel & Zahn (1985) discussed adolescents in homicide research on early and mid-20th century trends. We many conclude by their silence that there were no noticeable differences between adolescents and adults or that the base rates among adolescents were so small that they were not worth mentioning.

Nor were there many mentions of firearms in field studies of gangs and group delinquency beginning in the 1920s. Although both common and makeshift weapons were used strategically in gang fights, firearms again were not mentioned as part of the everyday life of gang members or other delinquent youths, and firearms had a limited role in the social processes of delinquency (Cloward & Ohlin, 1960; Cohen, 1955; Miller, 1958; Spergel, 1990; Thrasher, 1927; Yablonsky, 1962).

By the 1960s, mentions of firearms in the literature on youth violence were more frequent but again not central in the delinquency literature. Although guns were prevalent in streetcorner life, there were distinct situations in which they were used and rules governing their use. They had a symbolic meaning in addition to their instrumental value and generally represented a threshold of commitment to "street life." Guns were rarely used by adolescents outside these contexts. Several studies of "streetcorner" life casually and very infrequently mentioned the presence of firearms and their use in settling interpersonal disputes (Anderson, 1978; Hannerz, 1969; Liebow, 1967; Suttles, 1968). Keiser's (1966) portrait of the Vice Lords also showed that weapons were not central to gang life but were used selectively and strategically in conflicts with other gangs and in gang "business." Among both gangs and "near groups," guns were valued as defensive weapons but sometimes also for offensives purposes. In most cases, guns were carried for show, with little intention to use them.

---

[1]Sante (1991) describes the struggles between late 18th-century street gangs of New York City, such as the Fly Boys, the Smith's Vly gang, and the Bowery Boys, to control territory and assert their authority. These gangs warred regularly over territory with weapons including stones, hobnail boots (good for kicking), and early versions of the blackjack. One or two members of each gang possessed pistols, but they were almost never used.

In the article "The Cherubs Are Rumbling," Bernstein (1958) describes how "Eddie" was the only one in a gang of about 35 Italian American teenagers to have a gun. His "zip gun" cost him $3.00 at the time. But according to Eddie's account, salesmen of secondhand weapons periodically visited the neighborhood offering guns at varying price. A "revolver" (presumably a .38) in good condition was reported to cost about $10, but handguns could be bought for considerably less if they were imperfect. Guns, however, were used more often for impression management—that is, to convey to others that someone with a gun "means business" and is a person to be taken seriously. In Bernstein's account, guns were carried by only a few members of the Cherubs and almost never used. Among the Cherub group; people carrying guns or even threatening to use them could be easily dissuaded from shooting if face-saving alternatives were presented (Bernstein, 1958).

Gun use was confined to specific situations and contingencies. Strodbeck and Short (1968) analyze a shooting by Duke, a gang leader, that captures several dimensions of the ecological dynamics of weapons use among adolescents in that era. Guns were a minor part of street scenes of delinquent youths, and usually the province of the "toughest" youths or the leadership of delinquent groups. Handguns were more often shown than used; their use was reserved for specific people in specific situations. Gun use was contingent and episodic, and gun episodes primarily were defensive or status conferring. Motivations for carrying and using guns often revolved around status concerns, and only after alternate outcomes had narrowed were guns actually fired. Although the neighborhoods where gangs lived were commonly viewed as "dangerous" places, the likelihood of young people carrying or using guns (and therefore being killed or injured) was quite low (see also Bernstein, 1958). This relatively low prevalence of gun possession was a factor in the decision about whether and how guns were used, and it seems that gun use occurred in very narrow circumstances.

Strodtbeck and Short characterized Duke's action as a complex decision reflecting elements of cognitive mediation of the risks and reward of alternative outcomes, a function of a utility-risk paradigm in which choices are contingent on in situ elevations of the risks and rewards of actions given specific contingencies. These decisions involved a "two-person game", the actor against the environment, where alternative courses of action became narrower as the risks increased. What motivated Duke in this incident was the threat to his leadership status. Guns were a last resort option because of the risks of arrest, primarily, but the risks of not using the gun to his status in the gang and in the neighborhood were quite high. The threat of retaliatory gun use was not evident in this incident. Duke never considered the possibility that bystanders had guns or were willing to use them. In fact,

> Once it was in his hands, it seems likely that Duke's perception of the norms of the group, along with the exigencies of the violence he faced, strongly determined that he use the gun. In this sense, his action rose "in the line of duty," as part of his leadership role. (Strodtbeck & Short, 1968, p. 279)

Nevertheless, the expectation of using guns was fairly high for specific types of conflicts. Beyond gangs and near groups, the fear of guns and community support for their use reflected what Strodtbeck and Short (1968) described as the widespread fear of sudden violence and the inability of police to stop it. Guns were status conferring, and a valuable asset in a context in which disputes were common and tended to be settled by violence and in which demonstrations of "toughness" were appropriate.

Current Trends in Guns and Violence Among Adolescents

The increase in homicides and other violent crimes in the United States beginning in the 1960s has been pronounced and well documented (Blumstein, 1995; Gurr, 1989). Because homicides are a bellwether crime for understanding violence, much of what we know about gun use among adolescents comes from the homicide literature. Both official records and ethnographic accounts confirm the increasing role of firearms in violent events beginning in this era (see, Potter & Mercy, Chapter 1, and Yung & Hammond, Chapter 45, both this volume).

Adolescent homicides, especially among young males ages 15 to 19, rose steadily from 1960 to 1992. Age-specific rates for 15- to 34-year-old males show that adolescents and young adults accounted for a steadily increasing share of homicide deaths and arrests throughout this period. The mortality rates for 15- to 19-year-old males increased by 154% from 1985 to 1991. The rate for 20- to 24-year-old males increased by 76% during this period. The ages 15 to 19 group moved from the lowest rates among the four age groups in 1985 to the second highest rate in 1991, surpassed by only 20- to 24-year-old males. Arrest rates showed parallel increases throughout the period: 127% increases for 15- to 19-year-old males and 43% for 20- to 24-year-old males. By 1991, males ages 15 to 19 were more likely to be arrested for murder than males in any other age group. Homicide arrest rates for older males (25–29, 30–34) declined during this period, indicating significant shifts in the composition of homicides. Overall, adolescent deaths by firearm injuries during this period were same gender-race-age homicides (Fingerhut, Ingram, & Feldman, 1992a).

The impact of the recent increases on adolescents has been dramatic. In 1990, firearm injuries accounted for one out of eight deaths of children ages 10 to 14, one of every four deaths among adolescents ages 15 to 19 and young adults 20 to 24 years of age, and one of every six deaths among adults 25 to 34 years of age (Fingerhut, 1993). From 1985 to 1991, firearm fatalities increased 127% among males 15 to 19 years of age, while declining by 1% for males 25 to 29 years of age and 13% for males 30 to 34 years of age (Centers for Disease Control and Prevention, 1994).

Most of the homicides committed by the two younger groups involved firearms. For example, among 15- to 19-year-old males, firearm homicides accounted for 88% of all the 1991 homicides within this age group, and 97% of the overall increase from 1985 to 1991 (Fingerhut, 1993). The increase in gun homicides among young males suggests not only behavioral changes but technological changes in the nature of guns and their availability (although this is an important issue, it is beyond the scope of this paper; see Koper, 1995).

Ethnographic studies confirm the growing use of guns among young males in urban areas since the 1960s. Mentions of guns beginning in the 1970s were more frequent and their influence on interpersonal violence was more widespread. For example, Moore (1978) and Vigil (1988) each describe how the use of guns changed behavioral codes and norms of when and in what situations violence was used. "Fair fights" (without guns) became unusual as gun use became normative. These patterns were accelerated by each successive generation of *klikas* (Chicano gangs or sets). Vigil's (1988) description of drive-by shootings was notable in its depiction of the number, variety, and firepower of the firearms commonly available to young Cholos. In addition to violence toward other gangs, Vigil describes other incidents in which gun violence was used to redress grievance against businesses and to resolve personal disputes over women or drugs.

The Disproportionate Effects of Gun Homicides on African American Adolescents

The increases in adolescent violence have been concentrated demographically and spatially among African American teenagers in urban areas (Fingerhut, Ingram, & Feldman, 1992b). Virtually all increases in homicide rates from 1985 to 1990 among people 10 to 34 years of age are attributable to deaths among African American males. Homicide death rates for African American males ages 15 to 19 rose from 28 per 100,000 persons in 1963 to 63 per 100,000 persons in 1970, declined slightly through 1985 to 50 per 100,000, and then increased to over 125 deaths per 100,000 by 1991 (Centers for Disease Control and Prevention, 1994). Among White males, the rates have increased more slowly over this time. Reiss and Roth (1993) used a broader age range of ages 15 to 24 and concluded much the same: Homicide rates rose throughout the late 1980s among African American males and by 1990 had surpassed the previous peak in 1970. Assuming that gun homicides remained a stable percentage of all homicides, it is safe to conclude that guns were more prevalent among young males, especially African Americans, and were used in a far wider range of circumstances beginning in the 1960s than in any previous era.

The disproportionate impact on African Americans is shocking. Among African American teenage males 15 to 19 years old, 60% of deaths resulted from a firearm injury, compared with 23% for White teenage males (Fingerhut 1993). Among females 15 to 19 years of age, 22% of African American female deaths resulted from firearm injury, compared with 10% of deaths among white females. From 1986 to 1990, firearm injuries were the leading cause of death among African American males from 10 to 34 years of age. Since 1988, the firearm death rate among African American male teenagers 15 to 19 years exceeded the death rate due to natural causes or any other cause. Young African American males were 4.7 times more likely to die from firearm injuries than from natural causes (Fingerhut, 1993). There were 30% more deaths among 10- to 14-year-old African American males from firearms than from motor vehicle injuries, the second leading cause. Moreover, these rates are rising.

The ecological clustering of adolescent firearms fatalities among African American adolescents in urban areas suggests that gun events are situated in the unique contexts of inner city life, and in the conditions of persistent (intergenerational) poverty and segregation that characterize urban life for many African Americans (Massey & Denton, 1993). If the recent upward trends in adolescent homicides with firearms began in inner cities and diffused through adolescent cultures to the suburbs, then our efforts to explain and address this crisis should look at it first as an inner-city phenomenon. Explanations of adolescent use of weapons requires an analysis of how these factors collide to produce firearm injuries and fatalities.

WHO CARRIES OR USES FIREARMS? CHARACTERISTICS AND RISK FACTORS FOR ADOLESCENT GUN VIOLENCE

Most of what we know about young people and guns comes either from newspaper and magazine features or a very small number of student surveys. The surveys typically measure student attitudes, behaviors, and opinions about guns in the school environment and attempt to locate characteristics and attitudes of youths who carry or use firearms.

The LH Survey

The most recent, by LH Research (1993), was a survey of 2,508 adolescents in 96 randomly selected elementary, middle, and senior high schools.[2] The results showed that handguns were a significant part of their everyday social ecology. About one in seven (15%) reported carrying a handgun in the past 30 days, and 4% reported taking a handgun to school during the year. Nine percent of the students reported shooting a gun at someone else, whereas 11% had been shot at by someone else during the past year. Thirty-nine percent of the youth reported that they personally knew someone who had been either killed or injured from gun fire. Twenty-two percent reported that carrying a handgun would make them feel safer if they were going to be in a physical fight. Fifty-nine percent of youths could get a handgun if they so desired, often within 24 hours (40%).

The presence of guns also affected their emotional well-being, including fear and shortened life expectancies. For example, 42% said they worry about "being wiped out from guns" before reaching adulthood. Not surprisingly, those who worry most and those who carry guns often are the same individuals. Guns also affected the routine activities of both gun-carrying and gun-avoiding students: Forty percent reported behavioral changes to cope with violence including decisions on where they go, where they stop on the street, nighttime activities, what neighborhoods they walk in, and their choice of friends.

There are several important limitations of the study, however, and in the end it fails to address the disproportionate rates of gun

---

[2]The survey was a simple random sample of classrooms in public, private, non-Catholic, and Catholic schools. The self-administered anonymous questionnaires included questions on gun ownership, carrying firearms, using guns, injury, and perceptions of safety. The sample was divided among central city schools (30%), suburban schools (46%), and schools in small towns or rural communities (24%). The sample was predominantly White (70%), with 16% African American students, 15% Latino students, and 4% Asian or Native American students. Most students (87%) attended public schools, with small samples from private non-Catholic schools (8%) and Catholic schools (5%).

fatalities among African American youths. The school-based sample underrepresents African American young males who are at the highest risk of mortality from guns and who have the highest concentration of risk factors. Dropouts, frequent absentees, and institutionalized youths also are excluded, a source of bias because these groups have higher rates of both violence and the risk factors for violence (Fagan et al., 1986). The analyses of gun possession and carrying by subgroups (area, gender, or ethnicity) were limited and selective, and the general population sample would likely yield cells too small for reliable comparisons if such controls were introduced. Nevertheless, the LH study suggests the pervasive influence of guns on the everyday decisions of young people in schools.

The Sheley, Wright, and Smith Survey

Some of the limitations in the LH survey were addressed in research by Sheley, Wright, and Smith (1993a, 1993b) and Sheley and Wright (1995). They interviewed 835 male inmates in three juveniles correctional institutions in four states and complemented this information with surveys of 758 male high school students from ten inner-city public schools in the largest cities in each state. Both student and inmate samples were voluntary, and nonincarcerated dropouts were not included. Most (84%) of the inmate sample reported that they had been threatened with a gun or shot at, and 83% owned a gun prior to incarceration. More than one in three inmates (38%) reported shooting a gun at someone. More than half owned three or more guns, and the age of first acquisition was 14 years. The preferred type of gun among respondents was a "well-made handgun" of large caliber (the 9 mm was the most popular).

Both the inmate and students sample described in more detail the ecology of guns within the social organization of their neighborhoods. They claimed that firearms were widely available at low costs in their neighborhoods. Distribution was informal, with guns bought and sold through family, friends, and street sources. Among incarcerated young males, 45% reported that they "had bought, sold, or traded 'lots' of guns." Stealing guns and using surrogate buyers in gun shops were common sources for obtaining guns. Motivation for owning and carrying guns was reported to be more for self-protection than for status. The drug business was a critical context for gun possession: 89% of inmate drug dealers and 75% of student dealers had carried guns. So too was gang membership: 68% of inmates and 22% of students were affiliated with a gang or quasi-gang, and 72% of inmates were involved in the instrumental use of guns.

Although the Sheley et al. (1993) study focused on inner cities, the voluntary samples raise concerns about selection bias and other measurement error. The study sampled disproportionately from states and cities with concentrations of gang activity, perhaps overstating the importance of gangs as a context for gun use. Like the LH Research survey, this study did not focus on events in which guns were used, only on individuals and their patterns of gun possession and gun use.

Other Adolescent Studies

Other studies have examined the prevalence of gun or weapon possession, but with little specificity. Inciardi, Horowitz, and Pot-

tieger (1993) interviewed 611 youths in inner-city neighborhoods in Miami as part of a study on crack cocaine and "street crime." They reported that 295 (48%) carried guns in the year preceding the interview. However, they do not report the percentage that used them or in what contexts (drug deals, robbery, or homicide). The National Youth Survey, a longitudinal study that tracked and interviewed 1,725 individuals from their adolescence in 1977 through 1990, is generally silent on the question of weapons (see, e.g., Elliott, Huizinga, & Menard, 1989). Based on 1,203 student surveys and interviews with dropouts in three cities with high gang concentrations, Fagan (1990) reported that 42.5% of gang males and 17.6% of non-gang males carried weapons. But the findings made no distinction between guns and other weapons (e.g., knives). In addition, Lizotte, Tesoriero, Thornberry, & Krohn (1994) examined the role of peers and social networks as well as lifestyles on firearm use and carrying using data from the Rochester Youth Survey. They found that individuals who possessed firearms for the purpose of "sport" were socialized into gun primarily within the family whereas youth who possessed guns for "self-protection" purposes were socialized into gun use within their peer networks.

These studies are not very helpful in explaining the use of firearms by young males. They typically confound firearm use with firearm possession and also with other forms of adolescent violence (such as physical and sexual assault, robbery) or poor developmental outcomes such as drug use, dropout, or adolescent pregnancy (e.g., Elliott et al., 1989). Few studies have distinguished adolescents who are violent from those violent adolescents who carry or use firearms. They often fail to distinguish firearms from other weapons, despite important strategic differences. There also is little information on nonlethal firearm use, virtually no information from gunshot victims, and little research on the situations and contexts in which adolescents carry or use guns. Only homicide research has examined the contexts surrounding firearm use, but most of these studies have focused on specific contexts such as spousal violence, gangs, or drug exchanges (see, e.g., Browne, 1987; Goldstein, Brownstein, Ryan, & Belluchi, 1989; Maxson, Gordon, & Klein, 1985).

Gender, Firearms, and Youth Violence

The growing presence and influence of firearms has had minimal influences on female adolescents. Historically, female offenders have not used weapons, but girls may carry weapons for males (Moore, 1978, 1991; Quicker, 1983; Valentine, 1978; Vigil, 1988). Homicide data also show the rate involvement of both gang and non-gang females in lethal violence (Maxson & Klein, 1989; Sommers & Baskin, 1993; Spergel, 1995). Bjerregaard and Lizotte (1995) omitted girls from their analysis of gun ownership among inner-city youths because "girls rarely own guns, whether for "sport or protection" (p. 43). *Uniform Crime Reports* data show that from 1976 to 1991 male homicide rates (involving both firearm and other weapons) among 17-year-olds were 11.5 times greater than female rates (Snyder & Sickmund, 1995). Female adolescents accounted for a lower percentage of homicides in 1991 (6.0%) than in 1976 (12.1%); the decline reflected stable numbers of female homicide perpetrators compared to sharply rising numbers of male offenders (Blumstein, 1995; Snyder &

Sickmund, 1995). Ethnographic studies offer somewhat contradictory evidence about women and guns. Campbell's (1984) study of girls in New York City gangs shows that by the 1980s, guns were a common feature of female gang life. But Taylor's (1993) study of female adolescents in Detroit offers a more qualified view. Although girls used guns less often than boys, young women often showed weapons to illustrate that they were not "soft" in relation to either predatory boys or girls.

Survey data also indicate low rates of gun or other weapon use by female adolescents. The Youth Risk Behavior Survey (U.S. Department of Health and Human Services, 1993) reported that 8% of female high school students carried a (nonspecified) weapon to school in 1990. When firearms are referred to specifically, the rates lower to about 1% (Callahan & Rivara, 1992; Sadowski, Cairns, & Earp, 1989). And Sheley et al. (1993) state that 9% of the female respondents reporting having owned a revolver at some time in their lives, 5% had owned an automatic or semi-automatic weapon, and fewer than 5% owned other types of firearms. Fewer than 3% carried weapons to school, and 8% carried them outside the home.

Finally, context is extremely important in determining comparative rates of weapons offenses by gender. For example, Fagan (1990) found that female gang members in three inner-city neighborhoods had significantly higher participation and offending rates for weapons offenses, including firearms, compared to non-gang males or females. The Sheley et al. survey also reported strong links between gun possession and drug and gang involvement in both female and male respondents. The importance of context for both males and females is discussed in greater detail in the sections that follow.

FIREARMS IN CONTEXT

Research to date has provided only a limited view of the contexts of and motivations for gun violence among adolescent males. There seems to be an increase in the number of situations and contexts in which conflicts arise that may escalate to lethal violence. The use of guns may reflect both an apparent lowering of the thresholds for using weapons to resolve conflicts and increasing motivations arising from "angry aggression" (Anderson, 1994; Bernard, 1990).

Recent survey research shows that offenders and high school students alike report "self-defense" as the most important reason for carrying firearms (LH Research, 1993; Sheley & Wright, 1995). As Wright and Rossi (1986) note "self-defense" has a number of different meanings, including defense against other youths in an increasingly hostile and unsafe environment as well as self-defense from law enforcement officials during the course of illegal activity. Defense of "self" seems to be recurrent theme is the stories of young inner-city males (Anderson, 1994; Black, 1993; Canada, 1995; Fagan & Wilkinson, 1995), and this defense lies at the heart of the quest for respect that motivates many violent confrontations. In this context, driven by fear, young people believe that life is dangerous, that anything (fatal) can happen at any time, and that having a gun is a necessary, if not attractive, option (LH Research, 1993). The more that guns are present within their social networks, the more they seem normative and the more inured kids become to the realities of guns. In a world in which they see themselves as having no power or control over the dangers and fears they evoke, guns provide a means to reduce fear and regain some defense against ever-present threats and enemies. Some young males may decide that the option of defense through gun use is too attractive to pass up, especially when weighed against the social and mortality costs of not carrying one.

The presence of weapons also may alter the scenarios that govern conflicts and the natural rules of their resolution. They also change strategic thinking in the unfolding of conflicts or fights. Fair fights traditionally have been defined as those without weapons, but they have declined in importance with the rise of weapons (see, e.g., Canada, 1995; Moore, 1991). Weapons, especially guns, represent a quick and oftentimes final resolution to conflicts. They also are the most efficient route to obtaining money or material possessions by illegal means. Following is a review of the contextual dynamics surrounding firearms use by adolescents.

Firearms in Situated Transactions

For many years, criminologists discounted the role of firearms in violent events. For example, Wolfgang (1958) thought firearms to be unimportant in the explanation of homicides. Recent analyses of the specific contexts of violence (e.g., homicides, gang violence, drug markets, robberies) do not discount guns in the explanation of violence, but place firearms as part of an ecology of violent events. These literatures suggest that gun use is infrequent and contingent, part of a context of a *situated transaction* noted by Luckenbill (1977) and Felson (1993). In fact, many of these studies are somewhat casual in reporting the presence of guns, noting that they are common features of these scenes. One consequence is that their influence has not been carefully examined, and gun events have not been accorded careful analysis.

For example, gangs have always been a venue in which weapons were prevalent, but the presence and types of weapons have changed the stakes and calculus of gang violence. Sanders (1994) reported that 38% of incidents of gang violence in San Diego in 1988 were drive-by shootings, up from 16% in 1981. Although drive-bys were favored by gangs more than 20 years ago (Miller, 1975), the increase in the use of manufactured (compared to homemade) guns has deemphasized the importance of fighting in resolving gang conflicts. If gangs are an important context of gun use, the growing number of gangs and gang youths may have increased market demand for guns. As gangs emerge in cities and new gangs form, and consequently more adolescents join gangs, the simple probability of a conflict between gangs and gang members grows (Fagan, 1992a). During periods of instability, both within and across gangs, the likelihood of disputes is especially high (Spergel, 1995). If guns proscribe the rules and nature of settling gang conflicts, the likelihood of disputes settled by guns increases together with the frequency of conflict.

Although drug markets are another context in which gun possession is common, the precise relationship between drugs and guns is uncertain. Guns have been characterized as necessary tools of the drug trade to protect the money, to protect dealers from assaults and robberies, to settle disputes over money or drugs, for instrumental displays of violence, to secure territory, and to preempt incursions in previous qualitative studies (Fagan & Chin, 1990; Goldstein et al., 1989; Sommers & Baskin, 1993). Young males may in fact be more vulnerable to gun use and victimization in drug markets than their older counterparts. They may lack experience or other affective skills to show the toughness necessary to survive. But homicides by and of young males continue to rise or remain stable even as drug markets contract (Reiss & Roth, 1993). Many homicides seem to be unrelated or tangential to drugs, involving material goods or personal slights. Although the increase in homicides may have at one time reflected the expansion of drug market, homicides now (nearly a decade after the emergence of crack markets) may reflect the residual effects of those markets. That is, guns that entered street networks during the expansion of drug markets remained part of the street ecology even as the drug economy subsided (Blumstein, 1995; Hamid, 1994).

Firearm use in robbery is the paradigm instrumental violent crime in the American consciousness. Because of its unpredictability and the threat of serious harm, it is one of the most feared crimes. Especially among adolescents, robberies often are unplanned or hastily planned events, the result of the instantaneous confluence of motivation and opportunity (Cook, 1986). Guns provide a tactical advantage in robberies, even beyond the advantage first created by the selection of time and circumstances that undermines the victim's expectations of safety. In an examination of patterns of force in robbery, Luckenbill (1980) found that choice of "coercive lethal resources" (weapon or no weapon) determined the offender's opening move and the subsequent patterns of behavior in the robbery event. Luckenbill concluded:

> Based on the observations of the interviewed offenders, offenders with lethal resources open the transformation process with a threat of force, whereas offenders with nonlethal resources open with incapacitating force. (p. 367)

Similarly, Skogan (1978) suggested that lethal weapons impact on the type, timing, and sequence of events that characterize robbery. In Skogan's hypothetical analysis of "life without lethal weapons" he suggests that offenders would face more resistance from victims (including fighting back or running away), use an increased amount of physical force to gain compliance, and select more vulnerable or easy targets in robberies. In reality, we may have experienced an increase in the availability and lethality of firearms; nevertheless, offenders may take on more "risky or harder" targets, anticipate little or no resistance when faced with a lethal weapon, and rely on threat of force that may or may not be followed up by use of force. As Skogan (1978) notes, offenders can do more with lethal weapons and be successful at it. Cook (1980) found that in robberies victims were more likely to be injured by unarmed (nongun) offenders than by offenders with a gun. He concluded that victims were sufficiently intimidated by the weapon to more readily comply with the offender's demands. However, Cook notes that the presence of a firearm opens the way for a robbery to become a homicide (Cook, 1982).

Whereas firearms may often be present during robberies, their use in the course of a robbery reflects other contingencies, or what

Zimring and Zuehl (1986) called "recreational violence." There are predictable stages for the robbery event, and when responses fail to meet the robber's expectations, threatened violence may become actual to gain compliance or to get the event back on its planned course (Feeney, 1986; Skogan, 1978). Force, including firing guns, often is not gratuitous in robberies, unless a robbery becomes a stage for acting out "toughness" or meanness. Difficulties are introduced in robbery situations when victims (or third parties for that matter) do not adhere to the robbery "script." At that point, the offender is faced with the decision to back up lethal threats imposed by the gun with action. This stage in the event may be complicated by the young offender's limited reasoning ability.

Adolescence is a developmental stage when abstract reasoning about the consequences of using guns and cognitive capacities to read social cues are incomplete (Kagan, 1989). The choices in these situations may be seen as "black and white" or "all or nothing" for the adolescent robber. During the course of a robbery, the teenager armed with a gun (presumably inexperienced) becomes an unstable actor in a scenario whose outcomes are dependent on a predictable set of interactions between the robber and the victim. It is when the initial definition of the situation strays from robbery to a threat, personal slight, or conflict (in the wake of resistance) that seemingly irrational violence occurs. When guns are present, the violence may become lethal.

The Symbolic Meanings and Intrinsic Rewards of Firearms

The symbolic and instrumental meanings of violent behavior have developed in a specific sociocultural context, a context that reflects the physical and social isolation that young people experience in inner cities. Historically, guns were an important part of the settling of North America by Europeans, and have remained an important part of the cultural landscape of the United States. To many Americans, guns were (and remain today) vital to the self-protection of American citizens (Gurr, 1981; Kleck, 1993). However, gun violence rates have varied across the country and until recently have been higher in the southern U.S. compared to other regions (see, for example, Butterfield, 1995). Some have interpreted this as evidence of a "southern subculture of violence" (Ayers, 1984; but see Cook, 1982), built on a "culture of honor" (Nisbet, 1993). The culture of honor has been extended and reinterpreted as part of the everyday social exchanges that often lead to lethal violence among youths in inner cities (Anderson, 1994).[3]

---

[3]This is a notion quite different from subcultural explanations of delinquency advanced in earlier eras (see, e.g., Cohen, 1955; Wolfgang, 1958; Wolfgang & Ferracuti, 1982). Subculture in these views involved a rejection of conventional (middle-class norms) in favor of norms and attitudes supportive of violence. No such rejection of middle-class norms is implied here. In fact, the culture that supports violence reflects many dimensions of mainstream culture, including the use of violence as social control, and the conflation of material wealth with status and identity. It reflects unique behavioral norms and social controls that develop in specific conditions of social isolation, and illustrates the importance of place in their development and communication (see also, Sampson & Wilson, 1995; Tienda, 1991; Wilson, 1987).

Guns have become a central part of that culture. Popular culture has served as a transmitter, amplifier, and interpreter of gun-related violence (LH Research, 1993; "Hard core rap lyrics," 1993). This context may shape how young males develop a range of behavioral styles and evaluate the contingencies of behavioral choices. The symbols and trappings of guns are widespread in music and film, and often irony or mockery of violence by these artists is confused with endorsement by the listeners and viewers. The celebration of gun possession (as symbol of safety and power) is commingled with the dress and speech codes that characterize the behaviors and contexts in which violence carries a positive value. This includes conceptions of manhood that place a high value on the willingness to "take a bullet" or otherwise engage in acts of extreme violence ("Kids know real deal," 1994).

The costs of violence, including death by gunfire, are rated very low in this context (Anderson, 1994; Kotlowitz, 1991; Sheley & Wright, 1995). Thus, what may appear as a problem of impulsive violence may in fact reflect a calculation of the benefits of restraint compared to the short-term payoffs from high-risk acts of violence. Guns offer one such payoff through their illustration of "toughness." Toughness has been central to adolescent masculine identity in many social contexts of American life. Physical prowess, emotional attachment, and the willingness to resort to violence to resolve interpersonal conflicts are hallmarks of adolescent masculinity (Anderson, 1994; Canada, 1994; Gibbs & Merighi, 1994; Katz, 1988; Toch, 1993).

Whereas these terms have been invoked recently to explain high rates of interpersonal violence among non-Whites in central cities, toughness has always been highly regarded and a source of considerable status among adolescents in a wide rang of adolescent subcultures, from streetcorner groups to gangs (Canada, 1995; Goffman, 1959, 1963, 1967; Toch, 1969, 1993; Whyte, 1943; Wolfgang & Ferracuti, 1982). In some cases, displays of toughness are aesthetic: Facial expression, symbols and clothing, physical posture and gestures, car styles, graffiti, and unique speech are all part of "street style" that may or may not be complemented by physical aggression. Although changing over time with tastes, these efforts at "impression management" to convey a "deviant aesthetic" and "alien sensibility" have been evident across ethnicities and cultures (Katz, 1988). Toughness requires young males to move beyond symbolic representation to physical violence. Firearms often are used to perpetuate and refine the aesthetic of toughness and to claim the identity of being among the toughest. Portrayals of gang members in the 1940s through the 1970s included descriptions of both common and outrageous firearms: navy flare guns, zip guns, sawed-off shotguns, revolvers, and a few automatic weapons (see, e.g., Keiser, 1969). These have become more common now because design changes have made them smaller, lighter, and more easily concealed.

Robbers and other fighters, seem to gain much pleasure from violence, including the use of guns and other weapons (see Katz, 1988, especially Chs. 3 and 6). There are several possible explanations, from the feelings of power and security that weapons may provide to the pleasures of dominance and unrestrained "ultimate" aggression that guns provide. The use of weapons may reflect a total identity that is geared to dominate if not humiliate adversaries. Some adversaries are created in order to express this dom-inance. Although this form of violence has a long history, its recent manifestation as "senseless" violence may in fact simply reflect the changes brought about by the availability of weapons and the meanings attached to them. The perpetuation of the sense of self and the image in the minds of others also are instrumental goals of much weapon use. There is a very low threshold for the use of violence for these ends. Some subcultures or networks also may reflect norms with which excessive violence, including weapons use, is valued, gains social rewards, and gives great personal pleasure. For example, this is true in some gang contexts in which "locura" acts of violence establish one's status in the gang. It is senseless only in the fact that the violence is an end unto itself. The use of weapons, especially guns, has elevated the level of domination. Guns can be used tactically to disable an opponent or to humiliate an opponent by evoking fear (begging, tears, soiling pants, etc.), even if there is little else to be gained from using the weapon.

Adolescent gathering locations are "hot spots" of violence where weapons are part of the scenario of fighting (see, e.g., Sanders, 1994). Weapons might include broken bottles, blades, swords, chains, pool cues, and firearms. What characterizes these locations is a combination of the composition or personality "set" of the individuals in that space, their expectancies about what might happen in that locale (at what time of the day), and the absence of social controls (restraints) in those spaces. These places are flashpoints for conflict, posturing, imaging, and impression management. Carrying weapons is an expressive part of this world, but their presence may alter the outcome of interactions whose intent is heavily weighted in specific developmental contexts.

A SITUATIONAL FRAMEWORK FOR VIOLENT EVENTS

The earlier discussion illustrates how dispute-related violent events can be viewed as social exchanges with identifiable rules and contingencies. Numerous studies have applied this framework with respect to violence, focusing on the interactional dynamics of situated transactions (Campbell, 1986; Felson, 1982; Felson & Steadman, 1983; Luckenbill, 1977; Luckenbill & Doyle, 1989; Oliver, 1994). It is through these processes and contingencies that individual characteristics such as "disputatiousness" are channeled into violent events. We argue that the presence of firearms presents a unique contingency that shapes decision-making patterns of individuals within disputes and also as they approach social interactions with the potential for becoming disputes (see Fagan & Wilkinson, 1995).

Luckenbill and Doyle (1989) argue that dispute-related violent events were the product of three successive events: "naming," "claiming," and "aggressing." At the naming stage, the first actor identifies a negative outcome as an injury that the second actor has caused (assigning blame). At the claiming stage, the injured party expresses a grievance and demands reparation from the adversary. The final stage determines whether the interaction is transformed into a dispute. The third event is the rejection of a claim (in whole or in part) by the harmdoer. According to Luckenbill and Doyle, *disputatiousness* is defined as the likelihood of naming and claiming, and *aggressiveness* is defined as the willingness to preserve and use force to settle the dispute. They claim that violence is triggered by norms of the code of personal honor and that differential disputatiousness and aggressiveness would depend on the situation.

Their study and others (Felson & Steadman, 1983; Oliver, 1994; Polk, 1994) have recognized the similarities the elements of situated transactions and what Goffman (1963) called the "Character Contest." Luckenbill (1977) used this concept to examine violent transactions resulting in homicide. According to Luckenbill and Doyle, a character contest goes something like this:

> One begins by attacking another's identity, challenging his or her claim to a valued position in the situation. The other defines the attack as offensive and retaliates, attempting to restore identity either by threatening to injure the challenger if he or she does not back down or by using force to make the challenger if he or she does not withdraw or by using limited force to make the challenger withdraw. Rather than back down and show weakness, the challenger maintains or intensifies the attack. Fearing a show of weakness and a loss of face, and recognizing that peaceful or mildly aggressive means have failed to settle the dispute, one or both mobilize available weapons and use massive force, leaving one dead or dying. (1989, p. 423)

This perspective emphasizes the role of social interaction over other "personality" explanations in aggressive behavior.[4] The social interactionist perspective interprets all aggressive behavior as goal-oriented or instrumental, that is, as an attempt to achieve what is valued. When applied to violence, it focuses on three central issues for understanding violence: the escalation of disputes, the role of social identities, and the role of third parties (Tedeschi & Felson, 1994). Felson (1993) describes the sequence of events in a social control process, similar to Black (1983). Katz (1988), Black (1983), and Felson (1993) identified three main goals of aggressive actions: (a) to compel and deter others, (b) to achieve a favorable social identity, and (c) to obtain justice. Violence is a function of events that occur during the incident and therefore is not predetermined by the initial goals of the actors (Felson & Steadman, 1983).

Tedeschi and Felson (1994) articulate three assumptions of the social interactionist perspective: (a) Harmdoing an the threat of harm are motivated by the desire to achieve personal goals; (b) situational factors should be emphasized including interpersonal relationships between actors, the social interchange between actors, and third parties; and (c) it is necessary to examine the perceptions, judgments, expectations, and values of the perpetrator. The actor makes a choice to engage in violent behavior because it seems to be the best alternative available in the situation. They explain that a decision maker is typically operating under one of two types of decision rules: the "minimax" principle (maximum benefits and minimize costs) and the "satisficing" principle (good

enough). A decision-making framework thus examines what goes on in the actor's mind during a violent event in terms of weighing the rewards and costs of an action while in pursuit of a desired outcome. If an actor determines that the benefits outweigh the costs of a violent action then he or she chooses to engage in the action. The presence of firearms is likely to alter both the selection of decision rules and the perceptions of the intentions and expectations of each of the parties.

Violence as Scripted Behavior

Cornish introduced the concept of *procedural scripts* to explain an offender's decision-making processes (see Cornish, 1993b, 1994). Cornish's conception of scripts and scripted behavior varies slightly from the type of script discussed by Tedeschi and Felson (1994). Cornish's script focuses in detail on the step-by-step procedures of committing crime that are learned, stored in memory, and enacted when situational cues are present. Tedeschi and Felson's use of the concept of scripts is a way of explaining behavior that is seemingly impulsive (nonrational) as habitual learned responses to situational cues that involve a limited number of decisions over which script is most cost effective in a given situation. Although different in emphasis, both usages should be explored in the future research in this area. Cornish states:

> The unfolding of a crime involves a variety of sequential dependencies within and between elements of the action: crimes are pushed along or impeded by situational contingencies—situated motives; opportunities in terms of settings; victims and targets; the presence of co-offenders; facilitators, such as guns and cars. (1994, p. 8)

The script framework is as an event schema to organize information about how to understand and enact commonplace behavioral processes or routines. The theory borrows heavily from cognitive psychology and was first articulated by Abelson (1976, 1981). A *script* is a cognitive structure or framework that, when activated, organizes a person's understanding of typical situations, allowing the person to have expectations and to make conclusions about the potential result of a set of events. Abelson explains:

> The script concept raises and sketchily addresses a number of fundamental psychological issues: within cognitive psychology, the nature of knowledge structures for representing ordinary experience; within social psychology, the way in which social reality is constructed and how constructions of reality translate into social behavior through action rules; in learning and developmental psychology, how and what knowledge structures are learned in the course of ordinary experience; in clinical psychology, how resonances between present situations and past schemata can preempt behavior maladaptively. (1981, p. 727)

Cornish uses the example of the "restaurant script" to explicate the theory. He argues that we all know how to "enter; wait to be seated; get the menu; order; eat; get the check; pay; and exit" (p. 8). He maintains that there are different levels of abstraction; for example, within the general script are related "tracks"—which organize knowledge about the various kinds of restaurants that require different procedures in specific contexts. The situation largely determines the props, casts, scenes, paths, actions, roles,

---

[4]See, for example, Fagan (1993), on the influence of set and setting on the outcomes of disputes in which the actors have been drinking. Felson, Baccaglini, and Gmelch (1986) also explains different outcomes of barroom disputes (brawls vs. crying in one's beer) as the interaction of the personality "set" of the actors and the social control mechanisms present in the "setting."

and locations. The script framework provides a useful way of understanding the decision-making process including calculation of risks, strategic decisions, and so forth.

Research on child and adolescent violence suggests several ways in which script theory can explain violent events: (a) Scripts are ways of organizing knowledge and behavioral choices (Abelson, 1976); (b) individuals learn behavioral repertoires for different situations (Abelson, 1981; Huesmann, 1988; Schank & Abelson, 1977; Tedeschi & Felson, 1994); (c) these repertoires are stored in memory as scripts and are elicited when cues are sensed in the environment (Abelson, 1981; Dodge & Crick, 1990; Huesmann, 1988; Tedeschi & Felson, 1994); (d) choice of scripts varies between individuals and some individuals will have limited choices (see Dodge & Crick, 1990); (e) individuals are more likely to repeat scripted behaviors when the previous experience was considered successful (Schank & Abelson, 1977); and (f) scripted behavior may become "automatic" without much thought or weighing of consequences (Abelson, 1981; Tedeschi & Felson, 1994).

Nisbet (1993) also uses the notion of script as a culturally specific cognitive structure to explain reactions to conflicts that arise when norms (in this case, codes of honor) are violated. Blumstein (1995) suggests that increased rates of incarceration of African American males, often for drug offenses, may contribute to violence scripts among inner-city youths. Young men returning to the community following periods of incarceration may reinforce the norms of toughness on the street with norms of toughness and violent scripts that were shaped and influenced by prison life (Toch, 1993).

The application of script theory to adolescent gun events as "situated transactions" may provide a level of understanding to a complex process that is not well understood. As described earlier in this chapter, there are a number of social interactional, developmental, contextual, cultural, and socio-economic factors that may impinge on the decision-making processes of young males in violent conflicts. Fagan and Wilkinson (1995) are currently engaged in research to reconstruct the stages and transactions within gun events among inner-city adolescent males.[5] Lengthy narrative interviews with young men who have been involved in gun violence are generating data on the dynamic exchanges within gun events, including those in which violence ensued and others in which violence was avoided. Respondents are asked to reconstruct three violent events: one in which guns were present and they were used, one in which guns were present and they were not used, and one in which guns were not present. Using subjects as their own controls allows us to assess person-event interactions (see Wilkinson & Fagan, 1996). The analysis of the interview narratives will focus on the presence of scripts, the various forms and types of scripts that are employed in specific contexts, how scripts are employed in different circumstances or contexts, and the roles of contexts and circumstances in shaping the outcomes of violent events.

---

[5]This research is supported by grants from the Centers for Disease Control and Prevention, the National Institute of Justice, and the National Science Foundation. Developmental and pilot research was supported by the Harry Frank Guggenheim Foundation.

IMPLICATIONS FOR PREVENTION AND INTERVENTION

For many adolescents in urban areas, violence has had a pervasive influence on their social and cognitive development (Richters & Martinez, 1993). Coupled with high adolescent mortality and firearm injury rates, the presence of firearms in their immediate social contexts objectifies and symbolizes their perceptions of risk and danger in the most common activities of everyday life. Even when not immediately present, the diffusion of violence and danger through popular culture and urban "legends" enhances the perceptions of personal risk. Rituals of mourning and burial, whether real or mythologized, have become cultural touchstones that are reinforced and internalized in normative beliefs and attitudes about the inevitability of violence.

Guns have become an important part of the discourse of social interactions, with both symbolic meaning (power and control) as well as strategic importance. Expressions of shortened life expectancies reflect processes of anticipatory socialization based on the perceived likelihood of victimization from lethal violence. Conversely and perversely, carrying firearms seems to enhance feelings of safety and personal efficacy among teenagers (LH Research, 1993; Sheley & Wright, 1995). The result is a developmental "ecology of violence," with which beliefs about guns and the dangers of everyday life may be internalized in early childhood and shape the cognitive frameworks for interpreting events and actions during adolescence. In turn, this context of danger, built in part around a dominating cognitive schema of violence and firearms, creates, shapes, and highly values scripts skewed toward violence and underscores the central role of guns in achieving the instrumental goals of aggressive actions or defensive violence in specific social contexts.

Interventions that adopt this perspective should naturally focus on the development of behavioral scripts, the contingencies within scripts that lead to violence, and the role of firearms in both scripts themselves and the contingencies that evoke them. Focusing on the role of guns within scripts assumes that guns may alter scripts in several ways. For example, guns may change the contingencies and reactions to provocations or threats and change strategic thinking about the intentions and actions of the other person in the dispute. The presence of guns in social interactions may also produce "moral" judgments that justify aggressive, proactive actions. Accordingly, the development of interventions should be specific to the contexts and contingencies of gun events, rather than simply interpersonal conflicts or disputes.

A variety of conflict resolution and violence prevention curricula have been developed that focus on social competence, problem-solving, and anger management skills. Many are school based, focusing on the development of knowledge of violence problems and attitudes about the desirability of violence to solve conflicts (see, e.g., Prothrow-Stith, 1987, 1991). These classroom-based preventive efforts also focus on self-esteem, comorbid problem behaviors such as substance use, and techniques for problem solving and conflict resolution. Evaluations suggest that these efforts often improve students' social skills as measured by verbal responses to hypothetical conflict situations about the self-reported likelihood of violent behavior (Brewer, Hawkins, Catalano, & Neckerman, 1995).

Despite their success, however, adolescent homicide rates among African American and other youths continue to rise. Accordingly, the limited success of these efforts may reflect the limited range of situational contexts and motivations implicit in the violent events they address. Few curricula directly address the context in which firearms are present and the potential effects of firearms in the unfolding of disputes. For example, scripts involving firearms often are effected under conditions of angry arousal and intensified emotional states (Fagan & Wilkinson, 1995; Wilkinson & Fagan, 1996). Decision-making behaviors modeled in classrooms may not anticipate the changes in cognition that occur under these conditions of emotional and physiological arousal. And the early reports from our research suggest that in many cases, firearms introduce complexity in decision making introduced by the actions of third parties or the longstanding nature of disputes that erupt periodically over many months. In other cases, firearms simply trump all other logic.

Preventive interventions must address the growing reality of firearms in the ecological contexts of development and the internalization of firearms in the development of scripts. Firearms present a level of danger—or strategic certainty—that is unequaled in events involving other weapons or in fair fights. Interventions should be specific to developmental stages. At early developmental stages, preventive efforts must recognize that for many youngsters with high exposure to lethal violence, the anticipation of lethal violence influences the formation of attitudes favorable to violence and scripts that explicitly incorporate lethal violence. At later developmental stages, the incorporation of strategic violence via firearms in the presentation of self can alter the course of disputes and narrow options for nonviolent behavioral choices or behavioral choices that do not include firearms or other lethal weapons.

Classroom methods rely on procedures that fail to approximate the conditions on the street where conflicts unfold, including those where guns are present (see, e.g., Bretherton, Collins, & Ferretti, 1993; Webster, 1993). They fail to address the role of bystanders and other contextual factors and do not incorporate the cognitive and emotional states of the disputants. They do not recognize the social embeddedness of disputants in peer networks in which the presentation of self carries enormous weight that is more important than other forms of self-perception and status (Anderson, in press). These curricula do not incorporate the strategic dimension that firearms introduce into the decision making of disputants. They do not recognize how violent discourse often can translate into violent action and where violence as symbol often is transformed into violence as substantive action designed to redress grievances or protect one's physical person.

These attributes of conflict, including the presence of guns and their effects on cognition and decision making, should inform the design of preventive efforts and interventions. Contingencies in a variety of contexts should be included: schools, parties, street-corner life, the workplace, and in dating situations. The within-event contingencies suggest that interventions should be built around stages and sequences of actions as well as around the scripts that individuals bring to events. Firearms can profoundly alter the event dynamics of disputes and should be explicitly incorporated into prevention activities. Interventions for adolescents should include theater and role play and employ methods in which facilitators "unpack" the stages of events in contexts where the provocative and steering behaviors of bystanders and other third parties are included. Efforts to increase the salience of the training events through provocation and arousal of participants to simulate the fear, anger, and complexity of disputes or situations where firearms are present are needed. Interventions also should teach noncombatants how their behaviors as bystanders can increase the risks of lethal violence for young men facing off on the street. Interventions for younger children should increase their recognition of their own (and others') scripts.

In addition, evaluations of these efforts should include a focus on events to determine the effects of interventions on decision making and event outcomes. Evaluations that address only attitudes about violence or self-reports of likely violent behaviors in potentially violent confrontations risk validity threats from social desirability in students' responses and short-term follow-ups that do not take into account intervening experiences. Incremental gains from interventions can be detected when interaction patterns are analyzed to assess how scripts may be altered, when events may be analyzed in a new or different framework, and when ultimately how the risks and likelihood of violence can be reduced.

CONCLUSIONS

We have attempted to examine the role of firearms in violent events among adolescent males in the inner city. By comparing the pattern of firearm use among adolescents across historical periods we were able to identify factors that seem to have contributed to the recent escalation and the present-day crises. Structural changes in communities and neighborhoods have preceded the rise in adolescent weapons use as have the nature and density of illegal markets as well as the availability and firepower of weapons themselves. These changes have reshaped both the social controls and street networks that in the past regulated violent transactions. There are a number of antecedents and factors contributing to the current crisis that we are only beginning to understand.

Explanations of firearms use among adolescents require several levels of analysis: the sources of weapons, the nature of everyday life that gives rise to conflicts that turn lethal, the scripts of adolescent life that lead to escalation (and the factors that underlie those scripts), the motivations for carrying/using weapons, and the role of weapons in the decision-making processes of adolescents when they engage in disputes or even predatory violence. The presence of firearms is not an outcome of other processes, but part of a dynamic and interactive social process in which the anticipation or reality of firearms alters the decisions leading to violence and the outcomes of violent events.

Using an event-based approach, the chapter suggests a conceptual framework for explaining interactions that involve adolescents and firearms. This approach does not deny the importance of the individual attributes that bring people to situations but recognizes that once there, other processes shape the outcomes of these events. Events are analyzed as "situated transactions," including rules that develop within specific contexts, the situations and contexts in which weapons are used, the motivations for carrying and using weapons, and the personality "sets" of groups that use weapons. There are "rules" that govern how disputes are settled, when and where firearms are used, and the significance of firearms within a broader adolescent culture. Violence scripts often are invoked. Such scripts may limit the behavioral and strategic options for resolving disputes. The presence of firearms may influence which scripts are invoked. Several theories from criminology, cognitive psychology, symbolic interactionism, and social psychology are brought to bear on the issue of the study of violent events. Because violence generally is a highly contextualized event, we have discussed the ways in which specific contexts shape decisions by adolescents to carry or use weapons and how scripts are developed and shaped through diffusion within closed social groups. Finally, to advance the study and prevention of violent events involving adolescents, interventions, research, and methodological innovation must reflect specificity about guns and their effects on cognition, moral development, and behavior.

REFERENCES

Abelson, R. P. (1976). Script processing in attitude formation and decision-making. In J. S. Carroll & J. W. Payne (Eds.), *Cognition and social behavior.* Hillsdale, NJ: Erlbaum.

Abelson, R. P. (1981). Psychological status of the script concept. *American Psychologist, 36*(7), 715–729.

Anderson, E. (1978). *A place on the corner.* Chicago: University of Chicago Press.

Anderson, E. (1990). *Streetwise.* Chicago: University of Chicago Press.

Anderson, E. (1994, May). The code of the streets. *The Atlantic Monthly,* pp. 81–94.

Anderson, E. (in press). *Violence and the inner city street code.* Chicago: University of Chicago Press.

Archer, D., & Gartner, R. (1984). *Violence and crime in cross-national perspective.* New Haven: Yale University Press.

Ayers, E. L. (1984). *Vengeance and justice: Crime and punishment in the nineteenth century American south.* New York: Oxford University Press.

Bernard, T. J. (1990). Angry aggression among the "Truly Disadvantaged." *Criminology, 28,* 73–96.

Bernstein, W. (1958). The cherubs are rumbling. In J. F. Short Jr. (Ed.), *Gang delinquency and delinquent subcultures* (pp. 22–52). New York: Harper & Row.

Bjerregard, B., & Lizotte, A. J. (1995). Gun ownership and gang membership. *Journal of Criminal Law and Criminology, 86*(1), 37–58.

Black, D. (1983). Crime as social control. *American Sociological Review, 48,* 34–45.

Block, R. (1977). *Violent crime: Environment, interaction, and death.* Lexington, MA: Lexington Books.

Blumstein, A. (1995). Youth violence, guns, and the illicit-drug industry. *Journal of Criminal Law and Criminology, 86*(1), 10–36.

Bogardus, E. (1943). Gangs of Mexican-American youth. *Sociology and Social Research, 28,* 55–66.

Bordua, D., & Lizotte, A. J. (1979). Patterns of legal firearms ownership: A cultural and situational analysis of Illinois counties. *Social Problems, 25,* 147–175.

Bourdouris, J. (1970). *Trends in homicide, Detroit, 1926–1968.* Ph.D. Dissertation, Wayne State University, Detroit, MI.

Bretherton, D., Collins, L., & Ferretti, C. (1993). Dealing with conflict: Assessment of a course for secondary school students. *Australian Psychologist, 28,* 105–111.

Brewer, D. D., Hawkins, J. D., Catalano, R. F., & Neckerman, H. J. (1995). Prevention of serious, violent and chronic juvenile offending: A review of evaluations of selected strategies in childhood, adolescence, and the community. In J. C. Howell, B. Krisberg, J. D. Hawkins, and J. J. Wilson (Eds.), *Serious, violent and chronic juvenile offenders: A sourcebook* (pp. 61–141). Thousand Oaks, CA: Sage Publications.

Browne, A. (1987). *When battered women kill.* New York: Free Press.

Butterfield, F. (1995). *All God's children.* New York: Knopf.

Callahan, C. M., & Rivara, R. P. (1992). Urban high school youth and handguns. *Journal of the American Medical Association, 267,* 3038–3042.

Campbell, A. (1984). *The girls in the gang.* New York: Basil Blackwell.

Campbell, A. (1986). The streets and violence. In A. Campbell & J. J. Gibbs (Eds.), *Violent transactions* (pp. 115–131). New York: Basil Blackwell.

Campbell, A., & Gibbs, J. (Eds.). (1986). *Violent transaction: The limits of personality.* New York: Basil Blackwell.

Canada, G. (1995). *Fist, knife, stick, gun.* Boston: Beacon Press.

Cheatwood, D., & Block, K. (1990). Youth and homicide: An investigation of the age factor in criminal homicide. *Justice Quarterly, 7,* 265–292.

Cloward, R. A., & Ohlin, L. E. (1960). *Delinquency and opportunity.* Glencoe, IL: Free Press.

Cohen, A. (1955). *Delinquent boys.* New York: Free Press.

Cook, P. J. (1976). A strategic choice analysis of robbery. In W. Skogan (Ed.), *Sample surveys of the victims of crime* (pp. 173–187). Cambridge, MA: Ballinger.

Cook, P. J. (1980). Reducing injury and death rates in robbery. *Policy Analysis, 6*(1), 21–45.

Cook, P. J. (1982). The role of firearms in violent crime: An interpretive view of the literature. In M. E. Wolfgang & N. A. Weiner, (Eds.), *Criminal violence* (pp. 236–291). Beverly Hills: Sage Publications.

Cook, P. J. (1983). The influence of gun availability on violent crime patterns. In M. Tonry & N. Morris (Eds.), *Crime and justice: An annual review of research* (Vol. 4, pp. 49–90). Chicago: University of Chicago Press.

Cook, P. J. (1986). The demand and supply of criminal opportunities. In M. Tonry & N. Morris (Eds.), *Crime and justice: An annual review of research* (Vol. 7, pp. 1–28). Chicago: University of Chicago Press.

Cook, P. J. (1991). The technology of personal violence. In M. Tonry & N. Morris (Eds.), *Crime and justice: An annual review of research* (Vol. 14, pp. 1–72). Chicago: University of Chicago Press.

Cook, P. J. (1993a, May). *Crimes as scripts.* Paper presented at the second annual seminar on Environmental Criminology and Crime Analysis, University of Miami, Coral Gables, FL.

Cook, P. J. (1993b). Theories of action in criminology: Learning theory and rational choice approaches. In R. V. Clarke & M. Felson (Eds.), *Routine activity and rational choice advances in criminological theory* (Vol. 5). New Brunswick, NJ: Transaction Books.

Cornish, D. (1994). The procedural analysis of offering. In R. V. Clarke (Ed.), *Crime prevention studies.* Monsey, NY: Criminal Justice Press.

Dodge, K. A., & Crick, N. R. (1990). Social information processing bases of aggressive behavior in children. *Personality and Social Psychology Bulletin, 16,* 8–22.

Elliott, D., Huizinga, D., & Menard, S. (1989). *Multiple problem youth: Delinquency, drugs, and mental health.* New York: Springer-Verlag.

Fagan, J. (1989). The social organization of drug use and drug dealing among urban gangs. *Criminology, 27,* 633–669.

Fagan, J. (1990). Social processes of delinquency and drug use among urban gangs. In C. R. Huff (Ed.), *Gangs in America* (pp. 183–219). Newbury Park, CA: Sage Publications.

Fagan, J. (1992a). Drug selling and licit income in distressed neighborhoods: The economic lives of drug users and dealers. In G. Peterson & A. Harrell (Eds.), *Drugs, crime and social isolation.* Washington, DC: Urban Institute Press.

Fagan, J. (1992b). The dynamics of crime and neighborhood change. In J. Fagan (Ed.), *The ecology of crime and drug use in inner cities.* New York: Social Science Research Council.

Fagan, J. (1994). Women and drug revisited: Female participation in the cocaine economy. *Journal of Drug Issues, 24*(2), 179–225.

Fagan, J. A. (1993). Set and setting revisited: Influences of alcohol and other drugs on the social context of violence. In S. E. Martin (Ed.), *Alcohol and violence: Approaches to interdisciplinary research* (pp. 161–192). NIAAA Research Monograph, National Institute on Alcohol Abuse and Alcoholism. Rockville, MD: Alcohol, Drug Abuse and Mental Health Administration.

Fagan, J., & Chin, C. (1990). Violence as regulation and social control in the distribution of crack. In M. de la Rosa, E. Lambert, & B. Gropper (Eds.), *Drugs and violence.* National Institute on Drug Abuse Research Monograph No. 103. DHHS Publication No. ADM 90-1721. Rockville, MD: U.S. Department of Health and Human Services.

Fagan, J., Piper, E., & Moore, M. (1986). Violent delinquents and urban youths. *Criminology, 24,* 439–471.

Fagan, J., & Wilkinson, D. L. (1995). *Situational contexts of gun use events among young males in the inner city.* A proposal submitted to the National Science Foundation, Arlington, VA.

Fagan, J., & Wilkinson, D. L. (1996). Interview transcription, case #G-66. New York: Center for Violence Research and Prevention, Columbia University.

Felson, R. B. (1982). Impression management and the escalation of aggression and violence. *Social Psychology Quarterly, 45,* 245–254.

Felson, R. B. (1984). Patterns of aggressive social interaction. In A. Mummendey (Ed.), *Social psychology of aggression: From individual behavior to social interaction.* New York: Springer-Verlag.

Felson, R. B. (1993). Predatory and dispute-related violence: A social interactionist approach. In R. V. Clarke & M. Felson (Eds.), *Routine activity and rational choice, Advances in criminological theory* (Vol. 5, pp. 103–126). New Brunswick, NJ: Transaction Books.

Felson, R. B., Baccaglini, W., & Gmelch, G. (1986). Bar-room brawls: Aggression and violence in Irish and American bars. In A. Campbell & J. J. Gibbs (Eds.), *Violent transactions* (pp. 153–166). New York: Basil Blackwell.

Felson, R. B., & Steadman, H. J. (1983). Situational factors in disputes leading to criminal violence. *Criminology, 21,* 59–74.

Fingerhut, L. A. (1993). Firearm mortality among children, youth and young adults 1–34 years of age, trends and current status: United States, 1985–1990. *Advance Data from Vital and Health Statistics, No. 231.* Hyattsville, MD: National Center for Health Statistics.

Fingerhut, L. A., Ingram, D. D., & Feldman, J. J. (1992a). Firearm and non-firearm homicide among persons 15 through 19 years of age: Differences by level of urbanization, United States, 1979 through 1989. *Journal of the American Medical Association, 267*(22), 3048–3053.

Fingerhut, L. A., Ingram, D. D., & Feldman, J. J. (1992b). Firearm homicide among black teenage males in metropolitan counties: Comparison of death rates in two periods, 1983 through 1985 and 1987 through 1989. *Journal of the American Medical Association, 267*(22), 3054–3058.

Fitzpatrick, K. (1993). Exposure to violence and presence of depression among low-income, African-American youth. *Journal of Consulting and Clinical Psychology, 61,* 528–531.

Gartner, R. (1990). The victims of homicide: A temporal and cross-national comparison. *American Sociological Review 55*(1), 92–106.

Gibbs, J. T., & Merighi, J. R. (1994). Young black males: Marginality, masculinity, and criminality. In T. Newburn & E. A. Stanko (Eds.), *Just boys doing business? Men, masculinities and crime* (pp. 64–80). New York: Routledge.

Goffman, E. (1959). *The presentation of self in everyday life.* Garden City, NY: Doubleday.

Goffman, E. (1963). *Stigma.* Englewood Cliffs, NJ: Prentice Hall.

Goffman, E. (1957). *Interaction ritual.* New York: Doubleday.

Goldstein, P. J., Brownstein, H. H., Ryan, P., & Belluci, P. A. (1989). Crack and homicide in New York City, 1989: A conceptually-based event analysis. *Contemporary Drug Problems, 16,* 651–687.

Gouze, K. R. (1987). Attention and social problem solving as correlates of aggression in preschool males. *Journal of Abnormal psychology, 15,* 181–197.

Gurr, T. R. (1981). Historical trends in violent crimes: A critical review of the evidence. In M. Tonry & N. Morris (Eds.), *Crime and justice: An annual review of research* (Vol. 3, pp. 295–353). Chicago: University of Chicago Press.

Gurr, T. R. (1989). Violence in America (introduction). In *Violence in America* (Part I, pp. 1–54). Newbury Park, CA: Sage Publications.

Haller, M. H. (1989). Bootlegging: The business and politics of violence. In T. R. Gurr (Ed.), *Violence in America* (Part I, pp. 146–162). Newbury Park, CA: Sage Publications.

Hamid, A. (1990). The political economy of crack-related violence. *Contemporary Drug Problems, 17,* 31–78.

Hamid, A. (1994). *Beaming up.* New York: Guilford.

Hannerz, U. (1969). *Soulside: Inquiries into ghetto culture and community.* New York: Columbia University Press.

Hard-core rap lyrics stir black backlash. (1993, August 15). *The New York Times.*

Huessman, L. R. (1988). An information processing model for the development of aggression. *Aggressive Behavior, 14,* 13–24.

Inciardi, J. A., Horowitz, R., & Pottieger, A. E. (1993). *Street kids, street drugs, street crime.* Belmont, CA: Wadsworth.

Kagan, J. (1989). *Unstable ideas: Temperament, cognition, and self.* Cambridge: Harvard University Press.

Katz, J. (1988). *Seductions of crime: Moral and sensual attractions of doing evil.* New York: Basic Books.

Keiser, R. L. (1969). *The Vice Lords: Warriors of the street.* New York: Holt, Rinehart and Winston.

Kids know the real deal. (1994, February 6). *The New York Times.*

Kleck, G. (1993). *Point blank.* New York: Free Press.

Koper, C. (1995). Just enough police presence: Reducing crime and disorderly behavior by optimizing patrol time in crime hot spots. *Justice Quarterly, 12*(4), 649–672.

Kotlowitz, A. (1991). *There are no children here.* New York: Anchor Books.

Lane, R. (1979). *Violent death in the city: Suicide, accident and murder in nineteenth-century Philadelphia.* Cambridge: Harvard University Press.

Lane, R. (1989). On the social meaning of homicide trends in America. In T. R. Gurr (Ed.), *Violence in America,* (Part I, pp. 55–79). Thousand Oaks, CA: Sage Publications.

LH Research. (1993). A survey of experiences, perceptions, and apprehensions about guns among young people in America. Cambridge: School of Public Health, Harvard University.

Liebow, E. (1967). *Talley's corner: A study of Negro streetcorner men.* Boston: Little, Brown.

Lizotte, A. J., Tesoriero, J. M., Thornberry, T., & Krohn, M. D. (1994). Patterns of adolescent firearms ownership and use. *Justice Quarterly, 11*(1), 51–73.

Luckenbill, D. F. (1977). Homicide as a situated transaction. *Social Problems, 25,* 176–186.

Luckenbill, D. F. (1980). Patterns of force in robbery. *Deviant Behavior, 1,* 361–378.

Luckenbill, D. F., & Doyle, D. P. (1989). Structural position and violence: Developing a cultural explanation. *Criminology, 27*(3), 419–436.

Massey, D. S., & Denton, N. A. (1993). *American apartheid: Segregation and the making of the underclass.* Cambridge: Harvard University Press.

Maxson, C. L., Gordon, M. A., & Klein, M. W. (1985). Differences between gang and nongang homicides. *Criminology, 23,* 209–222.

Maxson, C. L. & Klein, M. W. (1989). Street gang violence. In N. A. Weiner & M. E. Wolfgang (Eds.), *Pathways to criminal violence* (pp. 198–234). Newbury Park, CA: Sage Publications.

Mieczkowski, T. (1986). Geeking up and throwing down: Heroin street life in Detroit. *Criminology, 25,* 645–666.

Miller, W. B. (1958). Lower class culture as a generating milieu of gang delinquency. *Journal of Social Issues, 14,* 5–19.

Miller, W. B. (1975). *Violence by youth gangs and youth groups as a crime problem in major American cities.* Report to the National Institute for Juvenile Justice and Delinquency Prevention.

Moore, J. W. (1978). *Homeboys.* Philadelphia: Temple University Press.

Moore, J. W. (1991). *Going down to the barrio: Homeboys and homegirls in change.* Philadelphia: Temple University Press.

Nisbet, R. E. (1993). Violence and U.S. regional culture. *American Psychologist, 48,* 441–449.

O'Kane, J. (1992). *The crooked ladder: Gangsters, ethnicity, and the American dream.* New Brunswick, NJ: Transaction Publishers.

Oliver, W. (1994). *The violent social world of black men.* New York: Lexington Books.

Polk, K. (1994). *When men kill: Scenarios of masculine violence.* New York: Cambridge University Press.

Prothrow-Stith, D. (1987). *Violence prevention curriculum for adolescents.* Newton, MA: Education Development Center.

Prothrow-Stith, D. (1991). *Deadly consequences: How violence is destroying our teenage population.* New York: HarperCollins.

Quicker, J. (1983). *Homegirls: Characterizing Chicana gangs.* San Pedro, CA: International Universities Press.

Reidel, M., & Zahn, M. A. (1985). *The nature and patterns of American homicide.* Washington, DC: U.S. Department of Justice.

Reiss, A., & Roth, J. A. (Eds.). (1993). *Understanding and preventing violence.* Washington, DC: National Academy Press.

Rich, J. A., & Stone, D. A. (1996). The experience of violent injury for young African-American men: The meaning of being a "sucker." *Journal of General Internal Medicine, 11,* 77–82.

Richtes, J. E., & Martinez, P. (1993). The NIMH Community Violence Project: I. Children as victims of and witnesses to violence. *Psychiatry, 56,* 7–21.

Rose, H. M., & McClain, P. D. (1990). *Race, place, and risk: Black homicide in urban America.* Albany: SUNY Press.

Rule, B. G., Bisanz, G. L., & Kohn, M. (1985). Anatomy of a persuasion schema: Targets, goals, and strategies. *Journal of Personality and Social Psychology, 48,* 1127–1140.

Sadowski, L. S., Cairns, R. B., & Earp, J. A. (1989). Firearm ownership among nonurban adolescents. *American Journal of Diseases of Children, 143,* 1410–1413.

Sampson, R. J. (1987). Urban black violence: The effect of male joblessness and family disruption. *American Journal of Sociology, 93*(2), 348–382.

Sampson, R. J., & Lauritsen, J. (1994). Individual and community factors in violent offending and victimization. In A. J. Reiss & J. A. Roth (Eds.), *Understanding and preventing violence* (Vol. 3, pp. 1–110). Washington, DC: National Academy Press.

Sampson, R. J., & Wilson, W. J. (1995). Race, crime and urban inequality. In J. Hagan & R. Peterson (Eds.), *Crime and inequality* (pp. 37–54). Stanford, CA: Stanford University Press.

Sanders, W. (1994). *Gangbangs and drive-bys.* New York: Aldine de Gruyter.

Sante, Luc. (1991). *Low life.* New York: Farrar, Giroux and Straus.

Schank, R., & Abelson, R. (1977). *Scripts, plans, goals and understanding.* Hillsdale, NJ: Erlbaum.

Shaw, C. R., & McKay, H. D. (1942). *Juvenile delinquency and urban areas.* Chicago: University of Chicago Press.

Sheley, J., & Wright, J. (1995). *In the line of fire: Youth, guns, and violence in urban America.* New York: Aldine de Gruyter.

Sheley, J., Wright, J., & Smith, M. D. (1993a, Nov.–Dec.). Kids, guns and killing fields. *Society,* pp. 84–87.

Sheley, J., Wright, J., & Smith, M. D. (1993b). Firearms, violence and inner-city youth: A report of research findings. Final Report. Washington, DC: National Institute of Justice.

Skogan, W. (1978). Weapon use in robbery. In J. Inciardi & A. Pottieger (Eds.), *Violent crime: Historical and contemporary issues* (pp. 235–250). Beverly Hills, CA: Sage Publications.

Slaby, R. G., & Guerra, N. G. (1988). Cognitive mediators of aggression in adolescent offenders: I. Assessment. *Developmental Psychology, 24,* 580–588.

Snyder, H. N., & Sickmund, M. (1995). Juvenile offenders and victims: A national report. Washington, DC: Office of Juvenile Justice and Delinquency Prevention, U.S. Department of Justice.

Sommers, I., & Baskin, D. (1993). The situational context of violent female offending. *Journal of Research in Crime and Delinquency, 30,* 136–162.

Spergel, I. A. (1984). Violent gangs in Chicago: In search of social policy. *Social Service Review 58*(2), 199–225.

Spergel, I. (1989). Youth gangs: Continuity and change. In N. Morris & M. Tonry (Eds.), *Crime and justice: An annual review of research* (Vol. 12, pp. 171–276). Chicago: University of Chicago Press.

Spergel, I. A. (1990). Youth gangs: Problem and response. Unpublished. Chicago: University of Chicago.

Spergel, I. A. (1995). *The youth gang problem: A community approach.* New York: Oxford University Press.

Strodtbeck, F. L., & Short, J. F., Jr. (1968). Aleatory risks versus short-run hedonism in explanation of gang action. In J. F. Short Jr. (Ed.), *Gang delinquency and delinquent subcultures.* New York: Harper & Row.

Suttles, G. D. (1968). *The social order of the slum*. Chicago: University of Chicago Press.

Taylor, C. S. (1993). *Women, girls, gangs and crime*. East Lansing, MI: Michigan State University Press.

Tedeschi, J. T., & Felson, R. B. (1994). *Violence, aggression, and coercive actions*. Washington, DC: American Psychological Association.

Thrasher, F. M. (1927). *The gang: A study of 1,313 gangs in Chicago*. Chicago: University of Chicago Press.

Tienda, M. (1991). Poor people and poor places: Deciphering neighborhood effects on poverty outcomes. In J. Huber (Ed.), *Macro-micro linkages in sociology* (pp. 244–262). Newbury Park, CA: Sage Publications.

Toch, H. (1969). *Violent men: An inquiry into the psychology of violence*. Chicago: Aldine-Atherton.

Toch, H. (1993). Good violence and bad violence: Self-presentations of aggression through accounts and war stories. In R. B. Felson & J. Tedeschi (Eds.), *Aggression and violence: Social interactionist perspectives* (pp. 193–208). Washington, DC: American Psychological Association Press.

U.S. Department of Health and Human Services. (1993). Youth Risk Behavior Survey. *Journal of the U.S. Public Health Service, 108*, 60–66.

U.S. Department of Justice. (1992). *Uniform Crime Reports*. Washington, DC: Federal Bureau of Investigation.

Valentine, B. L. (1978). *Hustling and other hard work: Life styles in the ghetto*. New York: Free Press.

Vigil, J. D. (1988). *Barrio gangs*. Austin: University of Texas Press.

Vigil, J. D., & Yun, S. (1990). Vietnamese youth gangs in Southern California. In C. R. Huff (Ed.), *Gangs in America* (pp. 146–162). Newbury Park, CA: Sage Publications.

Webster, D. W. (1993). The unconvincing case for school-based conflict resolution programs for adolescents. *Health Affairs, 12*, 126–141.

Whyte, W. F. (1943). *Street corner society*. Chicago: University of Chicago Press.

Wilkinson, D. L., & Fagan, J. (1996). Understanding the role of firearms in violence "scripts": The dynamics of gun events among adolescent males. *Law and Contemporary Problems, 59*(1), 55–89.

Wilson, W. J. (1987). *The truly disadvantaged: The inner city, the underclass, and public policy*. Chicago: University of Chicago Press.

Wolfgang, M. (1958). *Patterns of criminal homicide*. Philadelphia: University of Pennsylvania Press.

Wolfgang, M., & Ferracuti, F. (1982). The *subculture of violence: Toward an interactionist theory in criminology* (2nd ed.). Beverly Hills, CA: Sage Publications.

Wright, J. D., Rossi, P. H., & Daly, K. (1983). *Under the gun*. Hawthorne, NY: Aldine de Gruyter.

Wright, J. D., & Rossi, P. H. (1986). *Armed and considered dangerous: A survey of felons and their firearms*. Hawthorne, NY: Aldine de Gruyter.

Wright, J. D. (1990). Guns and crime. In J. F. Sheley (Ed.), *Criminology: A contemporary handbook* (pp. 441–457). Belmont, CA: Wadsworth.

Yablonsky, K. (1962). *The violent gang*. New York: Macmillan.

Zahn, M. (1980). Homicide in the twentieth century United States. In J. Inciardi & C. Faupel (Eds.), *History and crime: Implications for criminal justice policy* (pp. 28–63). Beverly Hills, CA: Sage Publications.

Zimring, F. E., & Hawkins, G. (1997). *An American disease: Lethal violence and its control*. New York: Oxford University Press.

Zimring, F. E. (1991). Firearms, violence and public policy. *Scientific American, 265*, 48–54.

Zimring, A., & Zuehl, J. (1986). Victim injury and death in urban robbery: A Chicago study. *Journal of Legal Issues, 15*, 1–40.

Name Index

Aaron, P., 353
Abbar, L., 249
Abbott, D. H., 262
Abbott, M. A., 260
Abbott, R., 370
Abel, G. G., 428, 526, 527, 529
Abelson, R. P., 144, 559, 560
Aber, J. L., 161
Abikoff, H., 41, 44, 388
Abram, K., 97, 165
Abrams, N., 54
Achenbach, T. M., 36, 37, 39–41, 43, 128, 152, 161, 386, 390
Acker, M., 528
Adams, D. B., 256–258
Adams, M. S., 185
Adams, W. T., 496
Adan, A. M., 381
Adinoff, B., 306
Adler, F., 497, 500
Adler, R., 300
Adler, R. J., 52
Ageton, S. S., 43, 127, 220, 348, 407, 419, 420, 428, 497, 505
Agich, G. J., 465, 466, 471
Agnew, R. S., 223, 225, 228
Ågren, H., 310
Aiken, L. S., 456
Ainsworth, M. D. S., 153, 174, 194n
Akers, R. L., 208, 218, 219, 221, 223, 224, 226, 229
Akiskal, H. S., 75, 83
Akman, D., 162
Alarcon, R. D., 465, 466
Albers, H. E., 260–262
Albert, D. J., 257, 261
Alberts, J. R., 262
Alessi, N. E., 102, 282, 437
Alexander, C., 272
Alexander, P. C., 538
Alexander, W. F., 439, 449
Alfaro, J. D., 162

Allain, A. N., 282, 284
Allan, E., 497, 505
Allebeck, P., 446
Allen, D. L., 213
Allen, N., 54
Allen, R., 164
Allen, V., 129
Allison, P. D., 132
Allman, L., 68
Allport, G., 353
Allred, E. M., 274
Almeida, M. C., 417, 420
Almquist, J., 417
Alpern, L., 149
Alterman, A. I., 23–25, 61, 62, 280
Altman, H., 101
Ambrosini, P. J., 437
Amdur, R. L., 237
American Humane Society, 348
American Psychiatric Association (APA), 13, 16, 22, 24, 36–38, 60, 64, 70, 75–77, 79, 83, 94, 130, 140, 152, 160, 235, 388, 438, 439, 448, 463–465, 477, 491
Amir, M., 524, 526
Ammann, R., 95
Amos, N. L., 29, 30, 527
Amrung, S., 164
Amsterdam, E., 438–439
Anderson, C. A., 36, 38–40, 44, 45
Anderson, E. J., 188, 376, 551, 552, 556, 558, 561
Anderson, G. M., 308
Anderson, K. E., 44
Anderson, M., 474
Anderson, R. H., 298
Andison, F. S., 184
Andre, G., 272
Andrews, A., 95

Andrews, D. A., 22, 31, 426, 427, 429–431
Andrews, D. W., 206, 208, 212, 353, 419, 421
Andrews, K., 165, 223
Andrulonis, P. A., 84
Angelique, H., 545
Anglin, D., 479
Anglin, K., 543
Anglin, M. D., 429, 430
Angold, A., 42n
Anson, A. R., 381
Anthony, J. C., 348
Anwar, R., 545
Apfel, N. H., 377
Apospori, E., 477, 489
Appelbaum, P., 92, 93, 97n
Apter, A., 101, 103
Aranalde, M. A., 397
Arbisi, P., 327
Arbit, J., 488, 490
Arbona, C., 469
Archer, D., 551
Archer, J., 316, 317
Arias, I., 538, 539
Armao, B. B., 448
Arnett, P. A., 25, 284, 328, 330, 331
Arnold A., 321
Arnold, J., 98
Arora, R. C., 249
Arthur, M. W., 365–367, 371, 405
Ary, D. V., 370
Asberg, M., 249, 306, 536
Aseltine, R. H., 222, 228
Asenbaum, S., 298
Asghari, V., 248
Ashburn, L., 185
Asher, S. R., 45, 172–174, 195, 196, 504
Asnis, G. M., 307
Astill, J. L., 437
Astin, M. C., 541, 542

Asu, M. E., 282
Atkins, M. S., 44n, 176, 436
Attar, B., 376, 474, 481, 489, 491
Atwater, J. D., 390, 419
August, G. J., 53
Auld, P. A., 272
Austin, J., 409, 411
Austin, R. L., 499, 503
Austin, V., 83
Axelson, J. F., 260, 261
Aydin, O., 173
Ayers, C. D., 371
Ayers, E. L., 557
Azmitia, E. C., 262
Azrin, N. H., 142, 256

Babcock, J. C., 537, 540, 543
Babor, T. F., 339
Baccaglini, W., 559n
Bachorowski, J. A., 173, 326, 489
Bachman, J. G., 229, 357, 500
Bachrach, R. S., 189
Bach-Y-Rita, G., 102, 273, 274, 290
Badger, G. J., 369
Bahr, S. J., 223
Bailey, R., 25
Bain, J., 319
Baird, C., 458
Baker, L., 397, 475, 476
Baker, L. A., 244
Bakker, T. C. M., 257
Bale, R. N., 426, 430
Balis, E. U., 445, 447
Ball, J. C., 511, 518
Ball, S., 477
Balla, D. A., 272
Ballenger, J. C., 68, 306
Baltes, P. B., 132
Bamshad, M., 263
Bandler, R., 258

Subject Index